SOMME
1916

A BATTLEFIELD COMPANION

GERALD GLIDDON

The
History

Cover illustration: Men of 1/16th Londoners trudge across the Somme battlefield, October 1916 (IWM Q1561).

First published 1987
This updated edition published 2016

The History Press
The Mill, Brimscombe Port
Stroud, Gloucestershire, GL5 2QG
www.thehistorypress.co.uk

British Library Cataloguing in Publication Data.
A catalogue record for this book is available from the British Library.

ISBN 978 0 7509 6732 7

Typesetting and origination by The History Press
Printed and bound in Turkey

CONTENTS

BY THE SAME AUTHOR

When the Barrage Lifts: A Topographical History and Commentary on the Battle of the Somme 1916
Norfolk & Suffolk in the Great War (ed.)
VCs of the Somme: A Biographical Portrait
Legacy of the Somme 1916: The Battle in Fact, Film and Fiction
VCs of the First World War:
>   *1914*
>   *The Somme*
>   *Arras & Messines 1917*
>   *Cambrai 1917*
>   *Spring Offensive 1918*
>   *The Road to Victory 1918*
>   *The Final Days 1918*
>   *The Sideshows*
The Aristocracy & the Great War
VCs Handbook: The Western Front 1914–1918 (ed.)
Lutyens and the Great War (with Tim Skelton)
For Valour: Canadians and the Victoria Cross in the Great War (ed.)

PREFACE TO THIS EDITION

After *When the Barrage Lifts* was first published in July 1987, I received letters from numerous readers who seemed to welcome a fresh approach to the most remembered battle of the First World War. Several people suggested minor alterations and on re-reading and using the book myself I also found some errors that needed attention.

For the Leo Cooper edition, published in 1989, these changes were incorporated, together with an additional ten-page index of military formations and units. This edition went out of print in 1991 and for a third printing, issued by Alan Sutton Publishing Limited in 1994, I made a further fifty small changes. This latest version was reprinted twice more under the new title of *Battle of the Somme*, but went out of print in 2004.

The idea of a new and updated edition was first mooted in 2002, with the publisher commissioning it the following year. There appeared to be at least one very good reason as to why a new edition should be produced, as, like any work of reference, the book had simply become out of date. Another reason was that in the previous ten years, the field of research for study of the First World War had simply exploded. While in the 1980s one had to visit or write to public archives, museums or libraries in order to retrieve information, much of this same task could now be done from a computer in one's own home. Over the past decade I have combined these two methods, as have my colleagues who have assisted me. However, a note of caution should be sounded at this point, as information supplied via Internet sources should always be double-checked.

Other changes for the better have included the Commonwealth War Graves Commission having put their records of burials and commemorations online, which has been a huge boon for researchers. The release of Officers' Files at the Public Record Office, now renamed The National Archives, has been another bonus, as has the filming of files belonging to Other Ranks that had been damaged during the London Blitz and were known as the 'Burnt Files'. *Soldiers Died in the Great War* was issued by the Naval & Military Press in 1998, which was superceded by an improved version in 2003.

Official History Maps and Trench Maps are now available in compact disc form. The Dominion Archives held in Canberra, Ottawa and Wellington and so on have also become much more accessible. The reawakening of interest of regimental museums with the knowledge that more and more people are researching their ancestors, many of whom would have served in recent World Wars, has also been a great step forward. The start of work by the Imperial War Museum to put its holdings online is also work in progress. The list of research improvements is endless, but taken together, they have provided me with enough impetus to justify the need for a new version of this book, together with the approaching First World War centenary.

The reader familiar with earlier editions will find that not only has the number of entries increased from 200 to 322 (about 60 per cent) but many of the original entries have also been greatly expanded. The section on the Royal Flying Corps squadrons who served on the Somme in 1916 has been incorporated into the main structure of the book. In the entries for individual locations that follow, place names in capital letters indicate that there is an entry devoted to that location. Except in quoted material, modern spelling has been used for place names. Military units have been abbreviated throughout; full unit designations and a complete British, Empire and Dominion order of battle can be found in Appendix IV.

There has also been a major shift of focus with this new edition, in that the story of the involvement of troops of the British Expeditionary Force and their role in the back areas and front lines of the Somme has been taken back to the end of July 1915, when British troops first came to the area. More than 7,000 men were to lose their lives before the battle on 1 July 1916 had even begun.

This edition of *Somme 1916* has been updated to coincide with the centenary of the battle in 2016. During the period from July to November major commemorative events will be held, particularly in Albert, Newfoundland Park in Beaumont-Hamel, the Butte de Warlencourt, Contalmaison, Flers, Lochnagar Crater, Longueval, Mametz, Pozieres, Thiepval and Ulster Tower.

ACKNOWLEDGEMENTS

During the preparation of this new edition of what was originally called *When the Barrage Lifts*, I have received enormous support from four particular individuals, without whom the project would have been severely delayed. First and foremost they are Peter F. Batchelor and Graham Keech, who put in very long hours in The National Archives at Kew when gathering information from war diaries; Nick Reynolds of Sutton Publishing, who was not only very enthusiastic about the need for a new edition, but also kept my nose to the grindstone during a vital period of fatigue and computer failure and has been a tower of strength ever since. Lastly I would like to thank my wife Wynne, who must have been nearly driven mad by my continuous concentration on a long-ago battle, for her patience and total support.

During the preparation of the original version of this book and its successor, there have been many people who have been very helpful, and I would like to thank them again for their assistance and kindness. The staff of the Imperial War Museum in the Departments of Printed Books and Photographs; The National Archives; the Archivist at the Liddell Hart Centre, King's College, London; the Archivist at Churchill College, Cambridge; the Bodleian Library, Oxford; the Royal Artillery Institution, Woolwich; the National Army Museum; the Meteorological Office; the Commonwealth War Graves Commission; Correlli Barnett; the late Mrs Claire Blunden; John Bolton; Andrew England; Patrick Mahoney; Paul Reed; Col Philip Robinson RE of the Durand Mining Group; and Tony Spagnoly.

I would also like to thank the Naval & Military Press for their permission to use the CD-ROM produced by them together with the Imperial War Museum for permission to reproduce maps from the *Official History of the War: Military Operations in France and Belgium, 1916* (1932 and 1938), as well as their CD-ROM of trench maps of the Western Front; Her Majesty the Queen, for her gracious permission to use material from the Royal Archives; the Controller of HMSO for permission to use material from A.F. Becke, *The Order of Battle Divisions* (HMSO 1935–1945), 4 volumes; the Oxford University Press for lines from 'Crucifix Corner', 'Of Grandcourt' and 'Ballad of the Three Spectres', from the *Collected Poems of Ivor Gurney*, edited by P.J. Kavanagh (1982); A.P. Watt, on behalf of the Executors of the Estate of Robert Graves, for using lines from 'A Dead Boche', published in *Goliath and David* and 'A Letter to S.S. from Mametz Wood', published in *Fairies and Fusiliers* (1917); George Sassoon for the use of 8 lines from the poem 'At Carnoy', by Siegfried Sassoon, 3 July 1916; Mr Andrew Rawlinson and the Master, Fellows and Scholars of Churchill College, University of Cambridge, for permission to use material from General Lord Rawlinson's war diary; Bodley Head on behalf of the Estate of F. Scott Fitzgerald 1959; the Trustees of the Liddell Hart Centre for Military Archives, King's College, London; the Imperial War Museum for permission to use material from interviews with Cpl L.J. Ounsworth (332/12), Sgt C.R. Quinnel (554/18) and Capt R.C. Cooney (494/6) from the Department of Sound Records; also from Mr Christopher Skelton, for permission to quote from his father's papers deposited in the Department of Documents; Peter Liddle 1914–18, Personal Experience Archives at the University of Leeds; Peter Harris; Derek F. Heaney; Chris Baker, for information gleaned from his excellent website 'The Long, Long Trail'; and Jack Sheldon, for assistance from his book *The German Army on the Somme, 1914–1916* (Pen & Sword, 2004).

Lastly I would like to thank Peter F. Batchelor again, in his role as postcard collector, for his wisdom, encouragement and willingness to take on any task that I pushed in his direction.

Author's Introduction

Many readers will be aware of the significance of the date of 1 July 1916 and of it being the most disastrous day in terms of casualties ever in the history of the British Army. But for more than 7,000 men of the British Expeditionary Force serving in the Somme area, their lives were already over by that date. Indeed, the first casualties were among members of 48th and 4th Divisions as early as the end of July 1915. By the end of June 1916, 21 more divisions were to hand at least for a few weeks within the Somme area.

The first priority of these British divisions, who were initially part of Third Army, was the relief of French troops, whose line it had been since 1914. Secondly, troops were to be given battle training. Thirdly, they were to provide working parties for the very many tasks to be carried out before the planned big battle was due to begin. These tasks would have included the reinforcing of trench lines and communication trenches; the supplying of wiring parties; the building of camps, railways, first aid posts, casualty clearing stations and hospitals; the improvement of roads; the establishment of ammunition dumps and artillery battery positions; the digging of trenches to take signal cables, which had to be at least 6ft deep; the continuous revetting of trenches; camouflage; cemeteries; the cleaning up of villages, making them more sanitary; the establishment of a regular supply of clean water; and the arranging of accommodation and the feeding of horses. The list is endless, and although Royal Engineers carried out many of these tasks, they often needed the support of infantrymen as extra labour.

After a battalion had carried out a spell of several days in the front line, it then returned to its billets in a town or village or camp for a period of rest and training. It was often when expecting some 'rest' that men were called upon to provide working parties for the sort of duties just mentioned. Many divisions developed a close bond with a particular village, which in turn became 'home' for a short period. Civilians remained in these villages for as long as possible and not surprisingly they were elderly, women or children. War or no war, the harvest had to be attended to in the summer of 1915, and there are many instances of British troops helping out the civilians who had been robbed of their menfolk. Curiously, exactly the same situation occurred in villages on the other side of the front line, where German troops also assisted the local population to bring in the harvest. *Estaminets* too were often established, where the beer was cheap and wine in plentiful supply. There appears to have been often a genuine friendship between the French and the British, although of course there were problems when the military was accused of damaging French property or stealing the odd chicken, sheep or even cow. This friendship was particularly marked with men of the Newfoundland Regiment when they spent time in the village of Louvencourt prior to the battle.

On a recreational note, troops also became adept at providing their own entertainment and most divisions established concert parties, which performed regularly in village barns throughout the back areas. These concerts included variety acts and singing and gave a taste of home for officers and men, which was much appreciated. Films were often shown. Football matches, some between officers and men or between two battalions within the same brigade, were regularly organised and sports days too and even horseshows took place. Apart from home leave, troops were occasionally allowed to spend time in Amiens, providing they had an official pass and the inhabitants of that city carried on a relatively normal life. Troops could go shopping or more likely have a good meal and plenty to drink depending on their pockets. A visit to the red-light district would often add numbers to the casualty returns a short time later.

All this sounds like mixing hard work with play, a cushy existence and not particularly dangerous. However, a soldier could often be wounded or killed seemingly quite by chance, perhaps by one stray shell falling in the wrong place. Reading through war diaries, one comes across numerous instances of a billet or camp being shelled quite out of the blue. A parade of men formed up in a narrow village street could be hit, with extra injuries being caused by the blast and broken glass. There were instances of rogue shells exploding at an artillery or trench mortar battery. When men were having a demonstration of a bomb or grenade they were often closely packed, and when an accident occurred it could kill or maim a dozen men at a time. The human evidence of all these tragedies can be found in the cemeteries and where one comes across a group of men who died on the same day or even within a few days, this is often the reason.

This emphasis on what was happening behind the lines is not to detract from equal tragedies occurring nearer the front line and the worst day before the battle was 6 April, close to Beaumont-Hamel, when 112 casualties were suffered by 29th Division when the enemy put down a barrage which virtually destroyed the whole of the division's trench system in that section of the battlefield. Although the British carried out numerous raids in the early part of 1916, they were very often unsuccessful and in human terms very costly. On the other hand, when the Germans carried out a raid, they appeared to be more successful.

At the beginning of 1916, Gen J. Joffre, Commander-in-Chief of the French Army, and Gen Sir Douglas Haig agreed that the British and the French should carry out a joint offensive north of the Somme in July, but a week later Gen E. von Falkenhayn, Chief of the German General Staff, decided on an attack against the French at Verdun. Although Haig would have preferred a battle much further north, either towards Cambrai or in Flanders, he had agreed with Joffre's request, providing it was to be a joint offensive with the British playing the junior role. As the commitment of the French Army to the defence of Verdun continued with mounting casualties, Joffre had to inform Haig that in view of the situation the BEF would have to bear the brunt of the planned Somme offensive, with a much reduced presence of the French.

Prior to the end of February 1916, the Somme sector had been the responsibility of the British Third Army under Gen Sir Edmund Allenby. Two new armies were established; Fourth Army, under Lt Gen Sir Henry Rawlinson, was established at Querrieu, between Amiens and Albert, at the end of the month. They would take over much of the line from Third Army between the Somme and Serre. In addition, a Reserve Army was to be formed under Lt Gen Sir Hubert Gough, whose role at the start of the battle in July was to 'exploit the success achieved by the Fourth Army'.

Although there were many signs of a forthcoming offensive, both in the lines opposite the German front on the Somme and of an obvious build-up of men and armaments in Britain, it was not until the German High Command received aerial reconnaissance reports of pre-battle activity in early April that they began to take the matter seriously.

Nearly five months later, the French and British High Command finally agreed on a starting date for the Somme battle as being 29 June, but owing to poor weather, the time was put back by 48 hours to 1 July, which was also the 131st day of the Battle of Verdun. By this time, Fourth Army was responsible for half a million troops, broken down into five corps – VIII, X, III, XV and XIII – and fourteen divisions. The British part of the attack was to commence with 164 battalions, with a further 64 battalions in close reserve. The men were a mixture of Regulars and Territorials, now supplemented by volunteer troops of Kitchener's New Army. The role of the cavalry was to exploit the success of Fourth Army and push northwards and on to Bapaume.

A massive Allied bombardment began on 24 June, which, it was felt, would destroy the enemy front positions and allow their occupation by British and French troops. There would be no one left alive who would be able to repel the attacking divisions. Although this is not the place to go over the whys and wherefores, it does appear that this really was Haig's thinking and any evidence that differed from this optimism was seemingly fatally ignored or dismissed. One general even thought that only a dog would still be alive in the ruins of Thiepval and yet Capt Martin of 9th Devons had even made a plasticine model of the front at Mametz and forecast the position of the machine-gun post that would kill him. His forecast was correct in every detail and his body lies in Devonshire Cemetery as if to prove it.

To make matters worse, one of the biggest errors of the day was the premature explosion of mines at Hawthorn Redoubt, close to Beaumont-Hamel. Instead of the mine being blown at just before the start time of 0730 hours, it was blown at 0720 hours, thus giving the enemy a full 10-minute early warning of British intentions. One feels that one has to look for a culprit here and I would suggest that the corps commander, Lt Gen Sir A.G. Hunter-Weston, was guilty by seemingly caving in to the Royal Engineers' request for an early detonation without thinking of the dire consequences it would have on the battle.

What happened next at 0730 hours is now such a familiar and tragic story that it hardly needs retelling, but for the record, the only successes on the 25-mile front on this day were to the south of the battlefield, where the British captured the villages of Montauban-de-Picardie and Mametz, with the

French Army making progress further south in their attacks towards Péronne. The British Army suffered over 57,430 casualties, of whom 19,240 were killed. Further progress over the next 4 months was very slow and costly.

On 14 July, after a very hard struggle to capture Mametz Wood, which had been achieved two days before, the British attacked the German Second Line and captured the villages of Longueval and Bazentin-le-Petit. By 26 July, Pozières was taken and on 15 September, High Wood was finally captured on the same day as British-made tanks appeared for the first time on a battlefield. Two months later, in what was the fourth phase of the Battle of the Somme, the Battle of the Ancre began and Saint-Pierre Division and Beaumont-Hamel were captured, together with 4,000 prisoners. The battle finally spluttered out a few days later and the next real movement on the Somme front was when the enemy began to pull his troops back to a stronger defence line in early 1917.

The human cost of life as a result of the first Battle of the Somme will never be known exactly, but the majority of commentators have the British and German casualties down as being similar in the region of 419,000. The French cost was around 204,000 and in sheer numbers the Germans could be said to have therefore won the battle.

History has not been kind to Sir Douglas Haig, the Commander-in-Chief, but in recent years and led by the late John Terraine, a serious attempt has been made to rescue his reputation. The current scenario is now that the Battle of the Somme was necessary not only just to wear down the German Army, but it was also part of a learning curve that could only be sustained by a very large loss of life. Other points are that the battle broke the backbone of the German Army, i.e. their NCOs. In addition, the battle casualties were not so high when examined against the whole cost to the British Army throughout the war. The Allies won the last battle in 1918 and that was what really counted.

To some extent, much of this might well have been true, but I suspect the real truth is to be found, as so often, somewhere between the two extremes of Haig the Butcher and Haig the great Commander.

After the war, much of the Somme area was considered to be unusable, as the destruction had been so great. However, French farmers and other civilians were having none of that, and got back to work as soon as it was safe to do so. Obviously, roads and railways were the first priority, together with the clearing of the battlefield area of ammunition, the bodies of the fallen and the detritus of war.

The harvest was the next priority, and people were accommodated in temporary buildings and schools were also re-established. Many of the Somme villages were 'adopted' by British towns, whose populations contributed to the cost of reconstruction and vital equipment. Agricultural assistance was also given by the British including the supplying of farm animals and seed to assist with re-stocking of farms.

It was hardly surprising to learn that France and Belgium became places of pilgrimage, even as early as 1919 after the war had scarcely finished. The first people to travel were mostly members of families who had lost men during the war and were anxious to find out where they might have been buried or otherwise commemorated. Others were soldiers themselves who wished to return to the sites of their battlefield experiences. There was even a third group of travellers who were perhaps slightly voyeuristic and wanted to see for themselves where so much death and destruction had occurred.

Although many cemeteries had been set up during the war, hundreds more bodies were later brought into them during the next 20 years. The Thiepval Memorial to the Missing was dedicated in 1932 and that at Villers-Bretonneux as late as 1938. During the Second World War, this part of northern France was once more occupied until 1944, and the Imperial War Graves Commission now had the task of repairing 5 years of neglect to the Allied cemeteries.

The First World War as the Great War was now virtually out of fashion, as the concentration camps and the dropping of two atomic bombs, together with other recent memories of a second conflict that had brought death much closer to home, seemed to have eclipsed it for the time being. In 1971, Martin Middlebrook, a Lincolnshire farmer, published a book called *The First Day on the Somme*, which was to have a considerable effect on a whole new generation, who up to then might not have given this subject much thought. Slowly, battlefield visiting began to increase, and in 1980, the Western Front Association was launched, which has also contributed to a wider understanding of the subject.

New memorials have sprung up alongside new museums in Albert, Delville Wood and Péronne, and tourism is booming. A new Visitors' Centre was opened at Thiepval in the autumn of 2004, which is avowedly educational and will hopefully kindle interest in the young and maybe not so young, so that this area of northern France will continue to occupy a special place in the hearts and minds of the British and former Dominion nations.

LIST OF ABBREVIATIONS

2/Lt	Second Lieutenant
A/Capt	Acting Captain
A/Cpl	Acting Corporal
A/CSM	Acting Company Sergeant-Major
A/L/Cpl	Acting Lance-Corporal
A/Lt Col	Acting Lieutenant-Colonel
A/Maj	Acting Major
A/Sgt	Acting Sergeant
ASC	Army Service Corps
BEM	British Empire Medal
Bn	Battalion
Brig Gen	Brigadier-General
BSM	Battery Sergeant-Major
Bt	Baronet
BWM	British War Medal
Capt	Captain
CB	Companion of the Most Honourable Order of the Bath
CBE	Commander of the Most Excellent Order of the British Empire
Cdr	Commander (Royal Navy)
CMG	Companion of the Order of St Martin and St George
Col	Colonel
Coy	Company
CP	Collection Post
Cpl	Corporal
CPO	Chief Petty Officer (Royal Navy)
CQMS	Company Quartermaster Sergeant
CSM	Company Sergeant-Major
DCM	Distinguished Conduct Medal
DMS	Director of Medical Services
DOW	Died of Wounds
DSO	Distinguished Service Order
ED	Efficiency Decoration
Gdsmn	Guardsman
Gen	General
Gnr	Gunner
GOC	General Officer Commanding
Havildar	Sergeant (Indian infantry)
Hon.	Honourable
IOM	Indian Order of Merit
Jemadar	Lieutenant (Indian Army)
KBE	Knight of the British Empire

KIA	Killed in Action
L/Cpl	Lance-Corporal
L/Dafadar	Lance-Sergeant (Indian cavalry)
L/Naik	Lance-Corporal (Indian infantry)
L/Sgt	Lance-Sergeant
Lt	Lieutenant
Lt Col	Lieutenant-Colonel
Lt Gen	Lieutenant-General
Maj	Major
Maj Gen	Major-General
MBE	Member of the Most Excellent Order of the British Empire
MC	Military Cross
MID	Mentioned in Despatches
MM	Military Medal
MO	Medical Officer
MP	Member of Parliament
Naik	Corporal (Indian infantry)
NCO	Non-Commissioned Officer
Pte	Private
RA	Royal Artillery
RAMC	Royal Army Medical Corps
RCA	Royal Canadian Artillery
RE	Royal Engineers
RFA	Royal Field Artillery
RFC	Royal Flying Corps
Rfmn	Rifleman
RGA	Royal Garrison Artillery
RHA	Royal Horse Artillery
RMA	Royal Marine Artillery
Sepoy	Private (Indian infantry)
Sgt	Sergeant
Spr	Sapper
Sub Lt	Sub-Lieutenant (Royal Navy)
Subadar	Captain (Indian infantry)
T/2/Lt	Temporary Second Lieutenant
T/Capt	Temporary Captain
T/Cdr	Temporary Commander (Royal Navy)
T/Lt	Temporary Lieutenant
T/Lt Col	Temporary Lieutenant-Colonel
T/Maj	Temporary Major
TD	Territorial Decoration
VC	Victoria Cross
VM	Victory Medal

SOMME DIARY

This guide to the weather conditions during the eleven months prior to the start of the battle is based on war diary entries. The weather reports from the end of June 1916 are based on official records of the Meteorological Office covering the Albert district of Northern France. Daily rainfall is measured in millimetres, and the two degree measurements represent the highest and lowest Fahrenheit temperature each day. Trace means minimal rainfall.

A note too on the casualties mentioned prior to the Somme, as it should be stated that these are based on the records of the Commonwealth War Graves Commission and cover actual burials within the Department of the Somme. It naturally follows that casualties, in many cases, would have been higher than quoted, as men will often have died elsewhere.

The author has drawn upon the copy of Lt Gen Sir Henry Rawlinson's war diary kept in the archive of Churchill College, Cambridge, to form the basis for this chronology from February 1916. Reports on the weather prior to the end of June are taken from War Diaries kept at The National Archives and later weather reports are taken from official records kept at the Meteorological Office, Bracknell, Hertfordshire.

JULY 1915

19 July: Troops of 48th Division, part of British Third Army, arrive at Beauquesne and Authie to begin to take over front-line duties from the French.
20 July: Troops from 4th Division arrive in the Somme area, detraining at Doullens and Mondicourt.
26 July: Troops of 18th and 51st Divisions are transferred to the Somme area, the latter arriving to the east of Amiens.
26 and 31 July: Five men from 1st Royal Warwicks (10th Brigade, 4th Division) are killed on these dates and are among the very first men buried in Row A, Sucrerie Military Cemetery, Colincamps. The French had used the cemetery since the summer of 1915.

Thirty British soldiers are recorded by the Commonwealth War Graves Commission as having been buried in the last 13 days of July 1915 in the Department of the Somme.

AUGUST 1915

At the beginning of August, units from 5th Division begin to arrive on the Somme at Ribemont.
8 August: Three men of 1/5th Gordon Highlanders (153rd Brigade, 51st Division) are killed and are buried in I A 3–5 in Bécourt Military Cemetery.
16 August: Three men of 2nd Royal Dublin Fusiliers (10th Brigade, 4th Division) are killed and are buried next to each other in Row B in III B 3–4 of Sucrerie Military Cemetery, Colincamps.
19 August: Five men of 1/7th Black Watch (153rd Brigade, 51st Division) are killed. Four of them are buried in Row I A 13–16 of Bécourt Military Cemetery and one is commemorated on the Thiepval Memorial.
25 August: Four men of 7th Royal West Kents (55th Brigade, 18th Division) are killed, three of whom are buried in Point 110 Old Military Cemetery and one in Norfolk Cem Becordel I A 15.
27 August: Six men of 6th Royal Berkshires (53rd Brigade, 18th Division) are killed; five are buried in II Row C of Citadel New Military Cemetery and one in Corbie Communal Cemetery I A 24.
28 August: Two men of 6th Royal Berkshires (53rd Brigade, 18th Division) are killed and are buried in I A of Norfolk Cemetery.
29 August: After an explosion of a German camouflet, ten men of 7th Buffs (55th Brigade, 18th Division), attached to No. 178 Tunnelling Company, Royal Engineers, are killed; nine are commemorated on the Thiepval Memorial and one buried in Norfolk Cemetery I A 5. In addition, five men are wounded. Ten men of 7th Buffs (55th Brigade, 18th Division) are killed, of whom nine are commemorated on the Thiepval Memorial and one buried in Norfolk Cemetery I A 5. Two men of No. 174 Tunnelling Company, Royal Engineers, are killed and are also commemorated on the Thiepval Memorial.
30 August: Elements of 37th Division begin to arrive in the Somme area.
31 August: Six men from the 8th Leicester Bn are killed during a grenade practice demonstration and are buried together in a row in Montdicourt Communal Cemetery.

A total of 258 British soldiers died on the Somme in August.

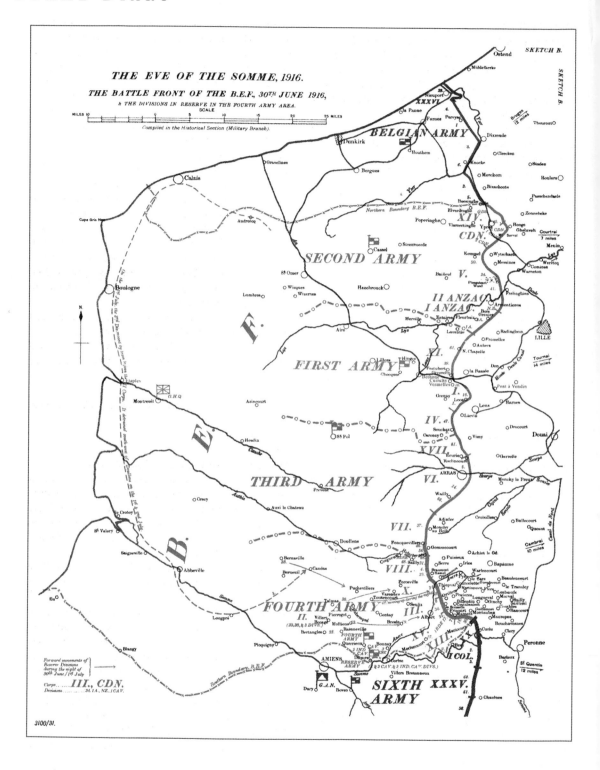

THE EVE OF THE SOMME, 1916.

THE BATTLE FRONT OF THE B.E.F., 30TH JUNE 1916,
& THE DIVISIONS IN RESERVE IN THE FOURTH ARMY AREA.

SEPTEMBER 1915

1 September: Four more men from 7th Buffs (55th Brigade, 18th Division) are killed and are buried in Point 110 Old Cemetery in Rows C & D. Six men from the 1st King's Own (Royal North Lancaster Regt.) (12th Brigade, 4th Division) arc killed and are buried in Row III C of Sucrerie Military Cemetery, Colincamps. They were in trenches between la Signy Farm and the Serre road when caught by enemy guns and trench mortars during the morning and afternoon.

6 September: Three men of No. 178 Tunnelling Company, Royal Engineers, die; they are commemorated on the Thiepval Memorial.

12 September: on a day of considerable activity, two mines are exploded and four men from 6th Northamptons (54th Brigade, 18th Division) are killed, of whom three are buried in Rows E & F of Point 110 Old Military Cemetery and one is commemorated on the Thiepval Memorial.

15 September: Five more men from 6th Northamptons die, of whom four are buried in Row F, Point 110 Old Military Cemetery and one in Saint-Pierre Cemetery I A 1, Amiens.

17 September: Three men of No. 178 Tunnelling Company are killed and are buried in I A & B in Norfolk Cemetery.

23 September: Three more men of 6th Royal Berkshires (53rd Brigade, 18th Division) are killed and are buried in I Row C of Bécourt Military Cemetery, followed by two more the following day.

25 September: Four members of 1/6th, 14th and 15th King's killed when on patrol at Curlu. Three are buried in Suzanne Communal Cemetery Extension in graves C 12, C 13 and C 14 respectively. The grave of the fourth man is in Assevillers New Brit Cemetery V B 6.

27 September: Four men of 1st Leinsters are killed and buried in Hangard Communal Cemetery Extension I G & K.

29 September: Five men of 10th Essex (53rd Brigade, 18th Division) are killed and are buried in I Row D of Albert Communal Cemetery Extension.

A total of 364 men died on the Somme in September.

OCTOBER 1915

4 October: Troops of 36th Division begin to arrive.

6 October: Nine men of 7th Oxford & Buckinghamshire Light Infantry are killed, of whom four are buried in Row C of Dartmoor Cemetery and five commemorated on the Thiepval Memorial.

8 October: Four men of 1/6th Argyll & Sutherland Highlanders (152nd Brigade, 51st Division) are killed and buried in Row B, Authuille Military Cemetery. Three men of No. 174 Company, Royal Engineers, die and are buried in Row G, Point 110 Old Military Cemetery.

15 October: Around this date, six men of 1/7th Gordon Highlanders (153rd Brigade, 51st Division) are killed near Authuille by enemy trench-mortar fire in reply to British shelling. One mortar hit a shelter, burying several men, and another landed close to a support trench. The six men are buried in Row B of Authuille Military Cemetery.

16 October: Three men of 8th Norfolks (53rd Brigade, 18th Division) are killed and are buried in Row C of Norfolk Cemetery, Graves 9 to 11.

20 October: As a result of the enemy exploding a mine near the Tambour at Fricourt, seven men of 7th Queen's (55th Brigade, 18th Division) are killed and are buried in I Rows B or C of Norfolk Cemetery. The men, attached to the mining section of 55th Brigade, had been caught east of the Tambour when cut off in a sap leading to a mine and were gassed. Six other men are sent to hospital. Four men of 8th East Surreys (55th Brigade, 18th Division) are also killed and are buried in I Row C of the same cemetery.

23 October: Gen Sir E. Allenby takes over command of Third Army from Gen Sir C. Monro. Four men of 1/5th Cheshires (14th Brigade, 5th Division) are killed and buried in Row C of Suzanne Communal Cemetery Extension.

A total of 383 men died on the Somme during October.

NOVEMBER 1915

1 November: Heavy snowfall.

2 November: Many trenches had fallen in.

3 November: Five men of 1st East Surreys (14th Brigade, 5th Division) are killed when a trench mortar falls into their trench while they are having a meal. Later the same day, a sixth man is killed in the South Péronne subsector. The six men are buried in II Row J of Cerisy-Gailly Military Cemetery.

5 November: Four men of No. 178 Tunnelling Company, Royal Engineers, are killed and are buried in Row B of Norfolk Cemetery.

7 November: When a sergeant and 11 grenadiers of 11th Royal Warwicks (112th Brigade, 37th Division) fail to return from a patrol, it is assumed that they have been taken prisoner. Eight men who are not found are commemorated on the Thiepval Memorial. Five men of 1st Royal Warwicks (10th Brigade, 4th Division) are killed and are buried in Plot II of Sucrerie Military Cemetery B, C, D and F.

9 November: Elements of 30th Division arrive in the Somme region, setting up their headquarters in Ailly-le-Haut-Clocher.

15 November: Heavy snowfall during the night. Further elements of 30th Division begin to arrive in the area.

16 November: Heavy snowfall during the night.

17 November: Snow and bitterly cold.

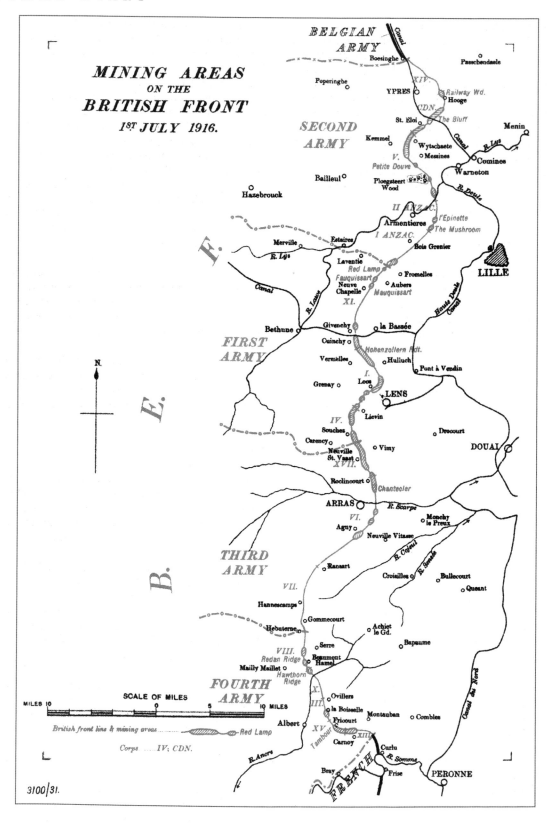

MINING AREAS
ON THE
BRITISH FRONT
1ST JULY 1916.

3100/31.

18 November: Bitterly cold.

19 November: A thaw set in. Around this date, 2nd Royal Inniskilling Fusiliers (14th Brigade, 5th Division) arrive in Suzanne, when an accident causes the death of three men and the wounding of four others. Two men are buried in Suzanne Communal Cemetery Extension B 9–10 and one man who dies the next day is buried in Chipilly Communal Cemetery D–1.

21/22 November: Six men of No. 179 Tunnelling Company, Royal Engineers, are killed; two are commemorated on the Thiepval Memorial and four are buried in I Row A of Albert Communal Cemetery Extension. They are killed by an enemy mine explosion, together with eight men of D Coy, 10th Bn Essex Regiment. They had been on duty at the Glory Hole in La Boisselle and were blown up by a German mine placed below where they were working.

24 November: A patrol of men of 2nd Manchesters (14th Brigade, 5th Division) is sent out, but finds no sign of the enemy. The group was later caught by enemy shelling. Six men died, of whom five are buried in II E of Cerisy-Gailly Military Cemetery and one in Row B of Suzanne Communal Cemetery Extension.

27 November: Elements of 32nd Division begin to arrive in the Somme area.

28 November: Very cold.

29 November: Very cold.

A total of 253 men died on the Somme during November.

DECEMBER 1915

1 December: Eight men from No. 183 Tunnelling Company, Royal Engineers, are killed near Fricourt after detonation of an enemy mine leads to the crushing of galleries; two men were gassed when escaping and one officer and two men were crushed in the collapse of a shaft lodgement. Four are commemorated on the Thiepval Memorial; four are buried in V–A of Citadel New Military Cemetery.

2 December: One man from No. 183 Tunnelling Company, Royal Engineers, is gassed when clearing up the above. Those killed are either buried in Citadel New Military Cemetery V A 13 or commemorated on the Thiepval Memorial.

3 December: Rain in the morning.

6 December: Rain all day.

7 December: 1st Cheshires (15th Brigade, 5th Division) carry out a successful raid south of Mametz, but lose one man; he is buried in Row D2 of Chipilly Communal Cemetery. Troops of 7th Division begin to arrive.

9 December: Rain all day.

11 December: Heavy frost.

12 December: Icy wind.

18 December: Cold and misty. No. 179 Tunnelling Company, Royal Engineers, lose two men, who are commemorated on the Thiepval Memorial.

19 December: No. 179 Tunnelling Company lose a further four men, who are also commemorated on the Thiepval Memorial.

20 December: Fine and clear day.

21 December: Rain all day. When the enemy explode two large mines in Tambour Diclos, Fricourt, 14 members of No. 178 Tunnelling Company, Royal Engineers, are killed. Seven of them are commemorated on the Thiepval Memorial and seven are buried in Row C, Plot I, Norfolk Cemetery.

22 December: Rain all day. Four men of 10th Royal Irish Rifles (25th Brigade, 8th Division) die and three are buried in Plots II and III of Sucrerie Military Cemetery. One is buried in C4 of Mailly-Maillet Communal Cemetery Extension.

23 December: Rain on and off all day.

25 December: Five men of 16th Royal Warwicks (15th Brigade, 5th Division) are killed; two men are buried in Row D of Chipilly Communal Cemetery and three in B and C of Plot III in Citadel New Military Cemetery.

31 December: Rain in the night and most of the day.

December was a particularly tragic month for tunnelling companies; at least 34 men were killed and more than half of the dead were never found. They were part of the 331 men who died from all British units that month.

JANUARY 1916

1 January: Rain all day.

2 January: Rain all day.

3 January: In trenches to the east of Hébuterne, seven men of 1/8th Worcesters (144th Brigade, 48th Division) are killed; they are commemorated on the Thiepval Memorial. Their French-built dugout did not protect them from heavy enemy shelling.

4 January: Rain all day. Six men of 1st East Lancashires (11th Brigade, 4th Division) are killed and are buried in Plot I, Row A, Hamel Military Cemetery. The enemy had been shelling Hamel for much of the day, including the use of aerial torpedoes, and also targeted the Jacob's Ladder positions behind the village with a shrapnel barrage. All communications are broken and Lancashire Post suffers badly.

6 January: Rain all day.

14 January: Fine all day. Four men from 17th King's (89th Brigade, 30th Division) die of wounds as a result of the premature explosion of a rifle grenade near Méricourt l'Abbé. Three men are buried in Cerisy-Gailly Military Cemetery I, A & H and one who dies later is buried in Corbie Communal Cemetery I C 22. Nine men, mainly from B Company, 2nd Royal Scots Fusiliers (90th Brigade, 30th Division), become casualties when the enemy systematically range buildings in the village of Suzanne, many of which are occupied by troops. Billets are hit and even the cellars are unsafe. The dead are later buried in Rows B and D, Suzanne Communal Cemetery Extension, and two who die of wounds are buried in Corbie Communal Cemetery. The remaining civilians in Suzanne are evacuated.

16 January: Rain all day.

18 January: Very wet day.

19 January: Fine day.

22 January: Wet.

24 January: Heavy German bombardment against Maricourt.

25 January: Fine.

26 January: Fine. Five men of 17th Northumberland Fusiliers (pioneers of 32nd Division) die and are buried in Row A, Authuille Military Cemetery.

27 January: Fine. Four men of the 15th Highland Light Infantry are killed and buried side by side in Row A of Authuille Military Cemetery.

28 January: Fine. The Kaiser's birthday. The village of Suzanne is heavily shelled. Three men from 17th King's and two men from 20th King's (both 89th Brigade, 30th Division) are killed during heavy shelling of Maricourt and are buried in Plot II, D, G & H of Cerisy-Gailly. Seven men of 17th, 18th (both 90th Brigade, 30th Division) and 19th Manchesters (21st Brigade, 30th Division) die and are buried in Corbie Communal Cemetery and Suzanne Communal Cemetery Extension. The Germans had taken Frise from the French on the other side of the River Somme, which explains all the shelling activity.

29 January: Fine. Three men of 18th Manchesters die; one is buried in Corbie Communal Cemetery Extension I-C-37 and two in Suzanne Communal Cemetery Extension Row D. A member of 19th Manchesters is buried next to the 18th man in Corbie in CCE.

30 January: Four men of 12th Middlesex (54th Brigade, 18th Division) are killed and are buried in Row B 24–27 of Méaulte Military Cemetery.

31 January: Fine and dull.

A total of 387 men died on the Somme during January.

FEBRUARY 1916

1 February: A fine spring day.

2 February: A fine but cold day. Elements of 49th Division begin to arrive on the Somme.

4 February: Rain all day. When the enemy blow a camouflet in Inch Street mine, 16 men and 2 officers of No. 185 Tunnelling Company, Royal Engineers, are killed. The men are buried in I-J-9 Bécourt Military Cemetery and the officers are buried in I–F 1 and 2 Albert Communal Cemetery Extension. In addition, six men of 18th Manchesters (90th Brigade, 30th Division), caught by shell-fire in Vaux, are buried

in Rows D and E of Suzanne Communal Cemetery Extension; a seventh man, who died of wounds, is buried in I-D-39 Corbie Communal Cemetery.

5 February: A fine day.

6 February: A dull day. Four men from 19th Manchesters (21st Brigade, 30th Division) die after being hit by a rifle grenade close to Carnoy; three of them are buried at Carnoy Military Cemetery H, J & K and one at Corbie Communal Cemetery I D 31. Six men from 24th Manchesters (pioneers of 7th Division) die and are buried in Point 110 Old Military Cemetery, Row J1 to J7, including a regimental sergeant-major next to a company sergeant-major. 2nd Royal Inniskilling Fusiliers (96th Brigade, 32nd Division) lose 8 men killed and 17 wounded when targeted in the line by enemy trench mortars. Two men from from the 20th Manchesters are in Plot V of Citadel New Military Cemetery, V D 18 & B 11.

7 February: Four men from 13th Royal Irish Rifles (108th Brigade, 36th Division) die, of whom three are buried in G4 to G6 of Mesnil Ridge Cemetery and one, who died of wounds, in Forceville Communal Cemetery and Extension. Four men from 1st South Staffords (91st Brigade, 7th Division) are killed when enemy blow a mine in front of their trenches, of whom three are buried in V A 2-A4 of Citadel New Military Cemetery and one is commemorated on the Thiepval Memorial. Ten men of 24th Manchesters (pioneers of 7th Division) die and are buried in Row B9–B19, Point 110 New Military Cemetery.

8 February: A fine day. Five members of the 12th New Heavy Battery Royal Garrison Artillery are killed and buried in Suzanne Communal Cemetery Extension Row E.

9 February: A fine day. Eight men from 2nd King's Own Yorkshire Light Infantry (97th Brigade, 32nd Division) die; seven are buried in Aveluy Communal Cemetery Extension Row C and one in the A.I.F Burial Ground, Flers IV H 20. Three men are killed in trenches in Authuille Wood when their dugout is blown in. Shelling of the wood was intense for several hours and it was later found that a whole gun team of 12th Heavy Battery, Royal Garrison Artillery, had been killed; five men are buried in Row E of Suzanne Communal Cemetery Extension. The French regain some trenches they had lost at Frise on 28 January. Elements of 46th Division begin to arrive in the Somme area.

10 February: A fine day.

11 February: Wet and cold.

12 February: Four men of 2nd Royal Inniskilling Fusiliers (96th Brigade, 32nd Division) die and are buried in A 31 to A 34 of Authuille Military Cemetery.

13 February: Four men of 2nd Gordon Highlanders (20th Brigade, 7th Division) die and are buried in I A or B Norfolk Cemetery.

15 February: Wet.

17 February: A fine day. Four men from 2nd Essex and six men from 2nd Lancashire Fusiliers (both 12th Brigade, 4th Division) die and are buried in Sucrerie Military Cemetery, Colincamps. Of the four men from the 2nd Essex, two are in III H of Sucrerie Military Cemetery, one in Euston Road Cemetery II C 2 and one on the Thiepval Memorial. Of the six 2nd Lancashire Fusiliers men, five are in the Sucrerie Military Cemetery side by side in III H 7–10 in the same row as the Essex men.

18 February: A fine day.

19 February: Prior to arriving at Querrieu to take over Fourth Army, Lt Gen Sir Henry Rawlinson attends a conference at Lt Gen Sir Charles Monro's First Army headquarters. Rawlinson is then allowed a week's leave before taking up his appointment. Maj Gen A.A. Montgomery is to be his Chief of Staff and Maj Gen J.F.N. Birch, formerly I Corps' Brigadier General Royal Artillery, is to be his artillery advisor; both men are to work with him at Querrieu. Eighteen men of 2nd Lancashire Fusiliers (12th Brigade, 4th Division) die, of whom 14 are buried in Plots I to III of Sucrerie Military Cemetery and 4 are commemorated on the Thiepval Memorial.

20 February: A fine day. Five men of 1/5th West Yorkshires (146th Brigade, 49th Division) die; three men are buried in Mill Road Cemetery and two are commemorated on the Thiepval Memorial.

21 February: Fine and cold. The Battle of Verdun begins after a heavy German attack.

22 February: Fine with snow. Thirteen men of 2nd Borders (20th Brigade, 7th Division) are killed, of whom all except one, commemorated on the Thiepval Memorial, are buried in Norfolk Cemetery in I Rows A and B. Back from leave, Rawlinson goes round XIII Corps' front and sees all over the French lines at Frise and Vaux Wood, as well as visiting Fricourt and Mametz. It is snowing for much of the tour and snow lies thickly at Méricourt l'Abbé.

23 February: Snows hard most of the day. Rawlinson visits VI Corps' front and gets a very good view of the ground and the enemy trenches at Thiepval, Ovillers and La Boisselle, before the snow blots out the view. He also visits some of the artillery batteries before returning to Querrieu in time for tea.

24 February: Heavy snow and frost. Fourth Army 'sets up shop' in the village of Querrieu and Rawlinson visits units of the Royal Flying Corps; writing of cooperation with artillery, he notes: 'it was far from what it should be . . .' Gen Sir E. Allenby, General Officer Commanding Third Army, visits Querrieu; he is to take over from the French XVII Corps. Rawlinson notes in his diary: 'I am not in favour of small pushes – they are expensive in casualties and

do no good . . .' A fourteenth man of 2nd Borders (20th Brigade, 7th Division) dies of wounds at Corbie and is buried in Corbie Communal Cemetery I D 11.

25 February: Heavy snow and hard frost. Rawlinson moves into the château at Querrieu.

26 February: Further snow before a thaw begins.

27 February: A dull day with the thaw quickly melting the snow. Rawlinson notes that the château is not very comfortable yet, as the electric light keeps going off and the fires smoke. In the afternoon he goes to Albert and later walks round the trenches opposite La Boisselle. Rawlinson's lines had now been extended to include Gommecourt as well as taking over the Tenth French Army front. Rawlinson is to keep Lt Gen Sir W.N. Congreve (XIII Corps) and Lt Gen Sir T.L.N. Morland (X Corps), but will lose Lt Gen J. Byng (XVII Corps): 'My line will be very thin.' He notes also that Haig is back from London, where he had seen Kitchener.

28 February: A fine but showery day. In the morning Rawlinson leaves for Beauquesne, where he holds talks with Gen Allenby and Lt Gen Byng. Back at Querrieu, he is ready to receive Haig at 1400hrs; before Haig leaves to see Gen Joffre at Chantilly, he tells Rawlinson that he can now also have VIII Corps, which is in the process of being raised. He can also have two Indian divisions as a reserve. Rawlinson notes that 'Uncle Harper [Maj Gen G.M. Harper, General Officer Commanding 51st Division] rode over and I rode back to tea with him' at 51st Division headquarters, which was at Flesselles.

29 February: A dull day with drizzle, although there still seems to be snow around, which continues to thaw. Lt Gen Congreve comes over to Querrieu after breakfast and Rawlinson rides over to Baizieux to see Lt Gen Morland, who is to move his headquarters to Toutencourt. VIII Corps is to begin to form at Marieux. Gen Allenby and Maj Gen H.M. Trenchard, Royal Flying Corps, come to lunch.

A total of 470 men died on the Somme in February 1916, a month that had also been particularly cold.

MARCH 1916

1 March: Fine but dull. At noon on this day, which is also Rawlinson's birthday, Fourth Army takes over the front-line section from the River Somme to the Somme–Mailly-Maillet line. At 1215hrs, Haig calls in from Chantilly and then rides out to have tea with Maj Gen F.I. Maxse, General Officer Commanding 18th Division, and Maj Gen H.E. Watts, General Officer Commanding 7th Division, but the former is out. Rawlinson notes that some roads are in a very bad state.

2 March: Rawlinson sees Gen Foch, soon to be commander of the French Northern Army Group, in the morning; after lunch he visits Mesnil and takes Maj Gen

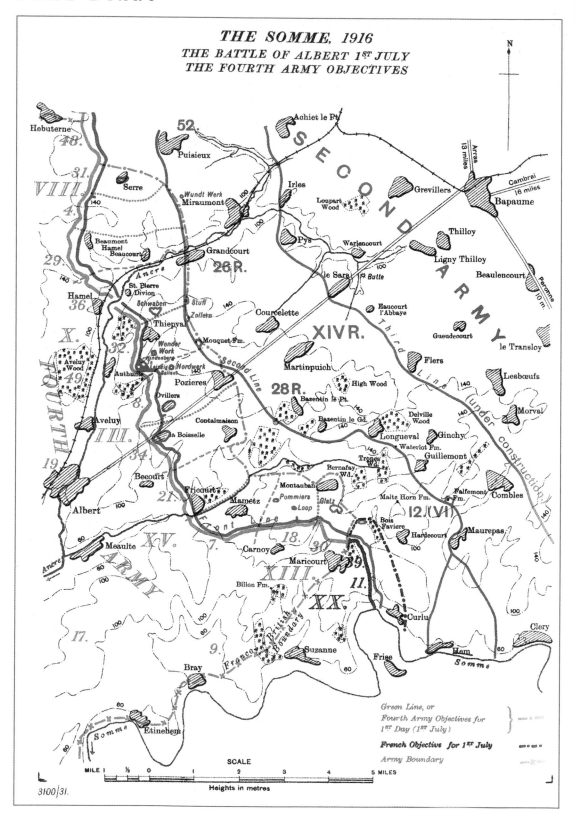

THE SOMME, 1916
THE BATTLE OF ALBERT 1ST JULY
THE FOURTH ARMY OBJECTIVES

O.S.W. Nugent, General Officer Commanding 36th Division, out to the observation station, where there is a very good view of Thiepval and the Ancre Valley. He later visits Maj Gen W.H. Rycroft, General Officer Commanding 32nd Division, at a 'splendid château' at Hénencourt, and gets home 'late' at 2000hrs.

3 March: A fine morning, followed by dull and wet weather. Rawlinson takes his first conference of Fourth Army's corps commanders, noting that Congreve and Morland are 'very intelligent and communicative'. Rawlinson then inspects III Army School at Flixecourt and after that drives on to Saint-Omer, where he is to stay with Haig. He is held up by bad roads and is half an hour late for dinner. Gen Allenby is also there.

4 March: A dull, damp and cold day. Rawlinson is still away and notes that the railway system will not now be ready until the end of April.

5 March: A bright cold day. Rawlinson visits Maj Gen R. Fanshawe, General Officer Commanding 48th Division, at Bus-lès-Artois, some 15 miles from Querrieu, so 'I had a good ride'. Maj Gen W. Lambton, General Officer Commanding 4th Division, comes to lunch.

6 March: A very cold but fine day with a little snow. Rawlinson visits Auchonvillers and the right bank of the Ancre. He mentions a good view that can be had from the hedge in a cemetery to the north of the village.

7 March: A fine cold day with some snow. Two enemy mines are exploded opposite Auchonvillers. Rawlinson has tea at Hébuterne.

8 March: A cold but fine day. Rawlinson leaves for Amiens, where he presents the Order of St John of Jerusalem to two nuns for their good work when the enemy briefly occupied Amiens in 1914. Back at Querrieu he entertains Ruthven of the staff of VII Corps before riding over to Maj Gen Maxse's 18th Division headquarters in the afternoon. Six men of 18th Manchesters (90th Brigade, 30th Division) are killed, of whom five are buried in Suzanne Communal Cemetery Extension Row F and one in Chipilly Communal Cemetery, A 19.

9 March: A dry fine day with slight snow. Gen Foch comes to lunch at Querrieu, after which Rawlinson takes to bed with flu.

10 March: A dry fine day with a little snow. The enemy raid 32nd Division positions near Thiepval and carry off one officer and eight other ranks, as well as inflicting 50 casualties. Twelve men, including one officer, of 16th Lancashire Fusiliers (96th Brigade, 32nd Division) are killed, of whom 10 are buried in Rows A, B or C of Authuille Military Cemetery and 2 in Aveluy Communal Cemetery Extension. A wiring party had been working in the lines when driven back into the trenches by a heavy bombardment and at one point the

enemy entered the British trenches. Five men are also killed when their dugout in a reserve line is crushed. In addition, seven men of 10th Royal Inniskilling Fusiliers (109th Brigade, 36th Division) are killed and are buried in Rows B and C, Authuille Military Cemetery.

11 March: A dull and cold morning. Rawlinson's doctor allows him to visit his office briefly, but he is still far from well. Lord Salisbury, who is staying with Maj Gen Maxse, comes to tea. Troops of 31st Division begin to arrive in the Somme area.

12 March: A fine day.

13 March: A fine day. One British aircraft is brought down near the Somme.

14 March: A fine day. Rawlinson is still far from well but Haig visits and informs him that he is to have Lt Gen H.S. Horne's XV Corps as well. Rawlinson plans a trip to the south of France in order to recuperate from his illness. Bray-sur-Somme and Sailly are bombed at night.

15 March: A fine day but cloudy. Haig decides to make Lt Gen Sir Hubert Gough commander of the Reserve Army. Four men of 17th Manchesters (90th Brigade, 30th Division) die, of whom three are buried in Suzanne Communal Cemetery F 18–20 and one in Chipilly Communal Cemetery, A–7.

17 March: Rawlinson leaves Amiens and journeys by train via Paris to Nice, where he stays in a convalescent home for officers run by the RAMC.

18 March: A fine day. Four men of 2nd Royal Inniskilling Fusiliers (96th Brigade, 32nd Division) are killed, three of whom are buried in Authuille Military Cemetery Row C and one, who died of wounds, in Millencourt Communal Cemetery Extension A 63.

19 March: During an enemy raid, 12 men of 1/6th Glosters (144th Brigade, 48th Division) are killed, of whom 10 are buried in I C, Sucrerie Cemetery, Colincamps, and 2 in Beauval Communal Cemetery, D 19 & 20. In addition, three men of 2nd Gordon Highlanders (20th Brigade, 7th Division) die, of whom two are buried in Méaulte Military Cemetery. In the south of France, Rawlinson receives a telegram from Haig's secretary, Philip Sassoon, telling him to stay put until he is completely fit.

20 March: Fine. Another Glosters man dies and is buried next to the two men from the above, 19 March, at Beauval CC.

21 March: Fine.

22 March: Wet.

23 March: A dull and very cold day.

24 March: Very cold.

25 March: Cold and showery. III Corps is established at Montigny. Four men of 20th Manchesters (22nd Brigade, 7th Division) die and are later buried in I E Dartmoor Cemetery, Bécordel-Bécourt. Three men of 2nd Royal Warwicks (also 22nd Brigade, 7th Division) are killed in the trenches and are buried in Rows D & E of Point 110 New Military Cemetery.

26 March: Cold and showery.

27 March: Cold and showery. Rawlinson finishes his period of recuperation at Nice and returns by train to Paris and Amiens, arriving back at Querrieu the following day. Sixteen men of 16th Highland Light Infantry (97th Brigade, 32nd Division) die, of whom 15 are buried in I Rows K & R of Bécourt Military Cemetery and 1 at I C – 8, Saint-Pierre Cemetery, Amiens. They were caught by the enemy while covering an 86-man-strong raiding party of 1st Dorsets (97th Brigade, 32nd Division). The raiders who worked under cover of a mine explosion at Y Sap soon after midnight achieved nothing but returned with 21 casualties, including four fatalities who had become tangled in enemy wire. Three men are buried in Millencourt Communal Extension Cemetery, B 62, C 44 and C 45, and a fourth, who died of wounds, at Saint-Pierre Cemetery, Amiens, I C 9. Lastly, three men of 6th Royal Berkshires (53rd Brigade, 18th Division) are killed in the shelling of Maricourt and are buried in Cerisy-Gailly Military Cemetery, II D 15, D 16 and D 22. Troops of 8th Division begin to arrive in the Somme area.

28 March: Cold with snow.

29 March: Cold with heavy snowfall in the afternoon. Lord Kitchener arrives in France and has talks with Haig. Elements of 29th Division begin to arrive in the Somme area.

30 March: Lord Kitchener arrives at Querrieu and Rawlinson notes in his diary that 'K is not in favour of a Big Push' but of smaller offensives which would kill Germans. This seems to be the way that Rawlinson had been thinking and forms the basis of the 'bite and hold' theory. Five men of 24th Manchesters (pioneers of 7th Division) are killed and are buried in Graves II B 11 – B 15 Citadel New Military Cemetery. Units of 30th Division begin to arrive in the Somme area.

31 March: A fine, spring-like day. After his discussion with Kitchener, Rawlinson is still thinking in terms of 'limited objectives'. He notes in his diary that his corps commanders are also of the same mind. He will take the matter up with Haig at a meeting of the Army Council at Saint-Pol the next day. In the afternoon he rides around the Méaulte–Albert sector. Three more men of 24th Manchesters (pioneers of 7th Division) die and are buried in Citadel New Military Cemetery.

The British forces suffered 485 fatal casualties in March.

APRIL 1916

1 April: A fine day. The enemy carry out hostile trench-mortar fire on the Fourth Army front, especially opposite La Boisselle.

2 April: A fine and very warm day. Lt Gen Congreve comes to lunch and the Prefect of the Somme to tea at Querrieu.

3 April: A fine day with a glorious morning, which later becomes a hot day. Rawlinson sends his battle plans to Haig, which had been drawn up by Maj Gen Montgomery when the Fourth Army commander was recuperating. Rawlinson visits Lt Gen A.G. Hunter-Weston, General Officer Commanding VIII Corps, commenting: 'Delightful galloping over these great rolling places.'

4 April: A cold but fine day. Rawlinson rides out from Morlancourt into the Maricourt salient as far as Bronfay Farm and sees Happy Valley. It is misty.

5 April: A fine day. A corps commanders' conference takes place at Querrieu Château. Together with Maj Gen Montgomery, Rawlinson then leaves for Haig's headquarters, where he arrives at tea time; later in the day, the two men hold discussions. In his diary entry of 5 April, Haig comments on studying Rawlinson's proposals. 'His intention is merely to take the Enemy's first and second system of trenches and "kill Germans". He looks upon the gaining of 3 or 4 kilometres more or less of ground immaterial. I think we can do better than this by getting as large a combined force of French and British [as possible] across the Somme and fighting the Enemy in the open.'

6 April: Fine and warm. There is a heavy enemy bombardment against the lines of 87th Brigade (29th Division) in the Beaumont-Hamel sector, which virtually destroys the British lines; this is followed by a very successful enemy raid. The whole operation results in 112 casualties, including those taken prisoner. 2nd South Wales Borderers and 1st Borders (both 87th Brigade, 29th Division) suffer in particular. Twenty-three men of 2nd South Wales Borderers are killed and are buried in Mesnil Ridge Cemetery, 2 being commemorated on the Thiepval Memorial; 3 more die of wounds on 7 April, of whom 2 are buried in Gézaincourt Communal Cemetery Extension and the third in Mesnil Ridge Cemetery. Fifteen men from 1st Borders die, of whom 13 are buried in Auchonvillers Communal Cemetery and one in Englebelmer Communal Cemetery and Englebelmer Communal Cemetery Extension; one is commemorated on the Thiepval Memorial. One more man died of wounds the next day at Corbie and was buried in Corbie Communal Cemetery. In addition, 21 men are missing; these men included some who were taken prisoner when the enemy entered their dugout. In addition to the above, five men of 14th Royal Irish Rifles (109th Brigade, 36th Division) are killed and are later buried in Hamel Military Cemetery. Four men of No. 178 Tunnelling Company, Royal Engineers, also die as a result of the enemy exploding a mine near the Tambour; their names are commemorated on the Thiepval Memorial.

7 April: A fine day. Rawlinson visits the Artillery and Trench Mortar School, as well as a large reserve aircraft depot at Candas near the airfield at Fienvillers, and expresses himself well pleased with its size and organisation. He then visits Lt Gen Morland at his headquarters at Toutencourt. Rawlinson is back at Querrieu in time for a meeting at 1730hrs with Gen Joffre, the French Commander-in-Chief. Three men of 7th Bedfords (54th Brigade, 18th Division) are killed and are buried in Plot I, Carnoy Military Cemetery. Three men of 2nd West Yorkshires (23rd Brigade, 8th Division) die in the front trenches and are buried in Bécourt Military Cemetery.

8 April: Fine and cold day. Army conference meeting, which Haig attends.

9 April: A very fine day. Rawlinson takes 'two chaps' up to Bronfay Farm to look at the ground towards Montauban. Bronfay Farm is shelled after he has left it. Notes that the Brickworks at Montauban is a permanent feature. Foch comes to tea. Thirteen men of 13th York and Lancasters (94th Brigade, 31st Division) die and are buried in Sucrerie Military Cemetery.

10 April: A fine and cold day. On the Fourth Army front, two camouflets explode at La Boisselle and the same area is also bombarded. Rawlinson travels to the Officers' School at Flixecourt, where he makes the opening address to a new course. Congreve calls in the morning and Lt Gens Morland and Hunter-Weston come to lunch. Five men of 2nd Royal Berkshires (25th Brigade, 8th Division) are killed and are buried in Bécourt Military Cemetery I H 5–9.

11 April: A day of heavy rain and hail storms. There is a heavy enemy bombardment during the night, which wounds 20 British and 25 French soldiers. After their trenches near Fricourt are very badly damaged by an enemy bombardment, 28 men of 1st Royal Irish Rifles (25th Brigade, 8th Division) are captured; 9 men die and are later buried in Plot I, Bécourt Military Cemetery, and 39 men are wounded. Three men of 10th Essex (53rd Brigade, 18th Division) die after their trenches are hit by enemy shelling and are buried in Cerisy-Gailly Military Cemetery. Three men of 1st East Yorkshires (64th Brigade, 21st Division) are killed in an enemy bombardment and are buried in Norfolk Cemetery. Six men of 9th King's Own Yorkshire Light Infantry (also 64th Brigade, 21st Division) also die, of whom four are buried in Dartmoor Cemetery, one in Corbie Communal Cemetery and one is commemorated on the Thiepval Memorial. Another man dies of wounds on 14 April and is buried in Corbie Communal Cemetery. The men had been caught by a heavy

bombardment when the enemy used a large number of rifle grenades and trench mortars. Lt Gen W.P. Pulteney, General Officer Commanding III Corps, lunches with Rawlinson at Querrieu. In the afternoon, Rawlinson visits 8th Division headquarters, which had only recently taken over the lines opposite La Boiselle. In his diary, he notes that his ride was spoilt by rain and that '8th Division did not come out well'. Back at Querrieu, Brig Gen H.R. Headlam, General Officer Commanding 64th Brigade (21st Division), calls in.

12 April: A wet and cold day. Rawlinson visits XIII Corps headquarters in the afternoon and talks to Lt Gen Congreve in the evening. He also visits Heilly and Méricourt l'Abbé railheads and has tea with Maj Gen C.W. Jacob, General Officer Commanding 21st Division. Philip Sassoon informs Rawlinson that Haig has left for a few days' rest in England. To the north of Carnoy, the enemy carry out a raid on 6th Northamptons (54th Brigade, 18th Division), who see them off, taking one prisoner; several German dead are left behind. However, in another raid, 13 men of 12th Middlesex (also 54th Brigade, 18th Division) are captured while carrying out a working party.

13 April: A cold day. Rawlinson travels to Valereux in order to attend a weapons demonstration, together with a large group of officers from divisions and brigades. Fourteen men of 6th Northamptons (54th Brigade, 18th Division) are killed in a heavy enemy bombardment and are buried in Rows R.S & T of Carnoy Military Cemetery; one man, who died of wounds the next day, is commemorated on the Thiepval Memorial.

14 April: A fine and cold day. In the afternoon, Rawlinson attends a lecture given by Gen Sir Henry Wilson, General Officer Commanding IV Corps, on the 'European situation'.

15 April: A fine and cold day. After lunch, Rawlinson and Maj Gen Montgomery travel to Montreuil to see Lt Gen L.E. Kiggell, Haig's Chief of the General Staff. Four men of 20th Manchesters (22nd Brigade, 7th Division) are killed, of whom two are buried in Citadel New Military Cemetery, Plot V Rows 16 & 17 and two in Point 110 New Military Cemetery, E 14 and E 12.

16 April: A fine day. Congreve lunches with Rawlinson. A corps commanders' conference is held between 1500hrs and 1630hrs. Maj Gen Montgomery is on leave. A captured Fokker machine is flown to 2nd Aircraft Depot at Candas.

17 April: Changeable weather. Rawlinson travels to Candas in order to inspect the Fokker and notes that Candas is full of machines of all types. The Allies intend to copy the system by which the Maxim machine gun fires through the propeller. On his way back he visits the railhead at Acheux, which he describes as 'getting on very slowly', then sees Maj Gen Nugent before riding to Englebelmer and has tea with Brig Gen J.B. Jardine of 32nd Division.

18 April: A wet and stormy day. Rawlinson gets a good ride over railway ground and visits Maj Gen Maxse at Etinehem.

19 April: Rain all day. Rawlinson works indoors most of the day. Haig returns from England. The enemy make a raid at Mansell Copse opposite Mametz and eight men are captured; a very bad day for 7th Division. Four men of 20th Manchesters (22nd Brigade, 7th Division) are killed and are buried in Plot V, Rows D & F of Citadel New Military Cemetery. Twenty men of 2nd Borders (20th Brigade, 7th Division) also die, of whom 13 are buried in Plot V of the same cemetery; in addition, the names of seven men are listed on the Thiepval Memorial. Five men of 6th Royal Berkshires (53rd Brigade, 18th Division) are killed in heavy shelling at Maricourt and are later buried in Cerisy-Gailly Military Cemetery Plot II, Rows F & G.

20 April: A fine day but very cold for the time of year. Five more men of 2nd Borders (20th Brigade, 7th Division) die of wounds; one is buried in Citadel New British Cemetery, V F 14, three in La Neuville British Cemetery Row A and one in Méricourt l'Abbé Communal Cemetery Extension I C 19. Rawlinson notes that 8th and 32nd Divisions are planning raids. After visiting the airfield at Bertangles, Rawlinson has tea with 48th Division and sees Maj Gen E.M. Perceval, General Officer Commanding 49th Division.

21 April: Fine morning followed by rain. Rawlinson visits 29th and 31st Divisions and VII Corps headquarters. Maricourt salient and Bray-sur-Somme are shelled. Four men of 4th Worcesters (88th Brigade, 29th Division) are killed, of whom three are buried in Mesnil Ridge Cemetery F 2 to F 4 and one is commemorated on the Thiepval Memorial.

22 April: Rawlinson describes the day as a 'poisonous wet day' and drives to the Officers' School at Flixecourt, at which he gives a short but complimentary speech before driving to GHQ to lunch with Lt Gen Kiggell. Haig is away in England. 97th Brigade (32nd Division) take part in a raid, taking 13 prisoners and accounting for 30 more. 8th Division carry out a raid opposite La Boisselle and manage to kill two Germans in their own trenches. Rawlinson notes that the raiders refused to follow their officers and is very displeased. Five men of 9th Royal Inniskilling Fusiliers (109th Brigade, 36th Division) are killed, of whom four are later buried in Authuille Military Cemetery, Rows C & D and one commemorated on the Thiepval Memorial.

Three men from 17th Highland Light Infantry (97th Brigade, 32nd Division) die, having been caught by enemy artillery fire after they had captured 13 of the enemy, and are buried in Aveluy Communal Cemetery Extension, Row E, as well as three men of 2nd Cameronians (23rd Brigade, 8th Division), D 30 to D 32.

23 April: Easter Sunday; fine. Rawlinson attends early communion and parade at 0930hrs. Five men of 2nd Royal Warwicks (22nd Brigade, 7th Division) are killed and are buried at Citadel New Military Cemetery, IV B 1 to 5.

24 April: A fine and warm spring day. Rawlinson rides over to see Lt Gen Pulteney and Lt Gen Horne comes in for tea.

25 April: Very fine for five days. Rawlinson rides over to Maricourt salient and visits brigade headquarters at Bray-sur-Somme, Suzanne and the valleys of Bronfay Farm, noting that there is ample room at Bronfay Wood and Maricourt for large guns. Lt Gen Pulteney visits Querrieu in the morning. Four men of 1st South Staffords (91st Brigade, 7th Division) are killed; one is buried in Bronfay Farm Military Cemetery I B 17, two in Citadel New Military Cemetery IV A 6 and A 8 and one at La Neuville Communal Cemetery A 10.

26 April: A very fine day. 18th Division carry out a successful raid north of Carnoy in which 10 of the enemy are either killed or taken prisoner. Rawlinson lunches with Gen Fayolle, General Officer Commanding French Sixth Army, at Boves, and later visits XIII and X Corps.

27 April: A very fine day. Rawlinson is given a flight over the Army area by a pilot from No. 4 Squadron, Royal Flying Corps, at Baizieux. Four men of 21st Manchesters (91st Brigade, 7th Division) are killed, of whom three are buried in Bronfay Farm Military Cemetery I Rows A and B, and one in Bray Military Cemetery I A 2. Four men of 12th Middlesex (54th Brigade, 18th Division) are killed and are buried in Carnoy Military Cemetery Row M 8 to 11. Five men of 13th Northumberland Fusiliers (62nd Brigade, 21st Division) are killed, four of whom are buried in Dartmoor Cemetery I Rows B, C & D and the fifth in Corbie Communal Cemetery I F 19. Four men of 9th Devons (20th Brigade, 7th Division) are killed; three of them are buried in Citadel New Military Cemetery V Row E and one in Méricourt l'Abbé Communal Cemetery Extension I B 13.

28 April: A very fine day. XV and VIII Corps hold a conference at Querrieu. Maj Gen R. Fanshawe, General Officer Commanding 48th Division, comes to lunch. Rawlinson spends the night at Roclincourt with IV Corps. An army conference is held at Cassel. Five more men of 13th Northumberland

Fusiliers (62nd Brigade, 21st Division) are killed, four of whom are buried in Dartmoor Cemetery and one commemorated on the Thiepval Memorial.

29 April: A very fine day. 29th Division carry out two raids at Beaumont-Hamel and six men from 2nd South Wales Borderers (87th Brigade, 29th Division) are killed, of whom five are buried in Plot II C 22-C 24, Auchonvillers Military Cemetery; the sixth man, Capt Byrne, was 'possible blown to pieces' and is commemorated on the Thiepval Memorial. Three more men die the next day and are buried at Miraumont Communal Cemetery A 8. Most of these casualties were the result of a raiding party that reached the wire five minutes too soon and was caught by 'friendly fire'. Five men of 11th Royal Fusiliers (54th Brigade, 18th Division) are killed, of whom four are buried in Carnoy Military Cemetery Row J 15 to J 18 and one in La Neuville Communal Cemetery A 1. Five men of 13th Northumberland Fusiliers (62nd Brigade, 21st Division) are killed, of whom three are buried in Dartmoor Cemetery I Rows B & C, one in Corbie Communal Cemetery I F 13 and one in Ville Sur Ancre Cemetery C 5.

30 April: A very fine day. Bécordel is very severely bombarded with gas shells and 35 officers and men are admitted to field ambulances as a result. Gens Foch and Fayolle appear at Querrieu at 0945hrs. Maj Gen Montgomery is back from leave. Carter, Aide-de-Camp to VIII Corps, comes over. Rawlinson notes that his landlady, a countess, comes over from Hénencourt to tea, accompanied by her Spanish niece; Madam la Comtesse 'was quite pleased with what she saw of the house'. Later, Rawlinson visits the cavalry. Five men of 8th King's Own Yorkshire Light Infantry (70th Brigade, 23rd Division) are killed and are buried in Bécourt Military Cemetery, I K 19. Four men of 12th Northumberland Fusiliers (62nd Brigade, 21st Division) are killed, of whom two are buried in Dartmoor Cemetery in Plot I B 23 and C 30, one in La Neuville Communal Cemetery A 14 and one in Serre Road Cemetery No. 2 A 11. Five men of 1st King's Own Scottish Borderers (87th Brigade, 29th Division) are killed and are buried in Auchonvillers Military Cemetery II D 14. Five men of 1st Royal Welsh Fusiliers (22nd Brigade, 7th Division) die and are buried in Citadel New Military Cemetery IV G 4 to G 8.

A total of 692 men of the British forces died on the Somme during April.

MAY 1916

1 May: A very fine day. The enemy bomb Allied trenches opposite La Boisselle. Rawlinson rides over to visit Lt Gen Horne in the afternoon. During the night, the enemy bombed British trenches at Hamel but were compelled to leave. Four men of 13th Northumberland Fusiliers (62nd Brigade, 21st Division) are killed, three of whom are buried in Corbie Communal Cemetery I F and one at La Neuville Communal Cemetery A 17.

2 May: A hot day with the odd thunderstorm. Rawlinson visits Lt Gen Hunter-Weston and notes that 'he is an intelligent man', but Rawlinson and Haig are never happy with VIII Corps, Hunter-Weston's command.

3 May: A fine but thundery day. Méaulte is bombed and one female civilian dies of wounds. Rawlinson notes that he is still in favour of limited objectives for the battle. When spending time south of the Péronne road near Maricourt, the enemy suddenly make an intense bombardment on the lines of 16th Manchesters (90th Brigade, 30th Division). A sap is blown in and four men are killed and are later buried in Cerisy-Gailly Military Cemetery II F 18–21; eight men are wounded.

4 May: A fine day. Rawlinson rides out to 32nd Division headquarters at Baizieux and visits Flixecourt to watch a smoke bomb demonstration, arranged for the benefit of about 50 French officers. Méaulte is heavily shelled again, resulting in 13 men wounded. Seven men of the 12th York and Lancaster Regiment die and are buried in Sucrerie NMC I Rows G & H. Troops of 34th and 56th Divisions begin to arrive in the Somme area.

5 May: A fine and warm day. Rawlinson is ill for part of the day but manages his daily ride before breakfast as usual. Still in the line near Maricourt, 16th Manchesters (90th Brigade, 30th Division) are targeted again by enemy artillery; A Company lose four men killed, buried at Cerisy-Gailly Military Cemetery II Row F, and six wounded. 15th Lancashire Fusiliers (96th Brigade, 32nd Division) carry out a successful raid north of Authuille Wood, losing four men killed and three wounded but capturing 5 Germans and killing 10. Three men are buried in Aveluy Communal Cemetery Extension Row E and one at Authuille Military Cemetery B 26. A fifth man of 15th Lancashire Fusiliers dies of wounds and is buried at Bouzincourt Communal Cemetery B 1; the burial date given by the Commonwealth War Graves Commission is 6 May. The enemy explode two mines at Mansell Copse but there are no casualties.

6 May: A fine day. Rawlinson attends an Army Council Conference at Aire and manages to have ¾ hour with Haig prior to the conference. Ten men of 14th Royal Irish Rifles (109th Brigade, 36th Division) die, of whom nine are buried in Authuille Military Cemetery Row D and one in Forceville Communal Cemetery and Extension I C 14.

7 May: Cloudy, cold with some rain. Gens Foch and Fayolle come to Querrieu in the afternoon to discuss the lines between the French and the British armies. Rawlinson visits Lt Gen Horne at teatime and then travels on to see Lt Gen Congreve.

8 May: A cloudy, cold day with some rain. Rawlinson spends a little time at the Officers' School at Flixecourt, where he addresses the latest class, and returns via Talmas, having a ride between Bouzincourt and Albert. Seven men of 19th Lancashire Fusiliers (14th Brigade, 32nd Division) die; six are buried in Row E, Authuille Military Cemetery and one in Warloy-Baillon Communal Cemetery B 14. Owing to the two sides conducting raids simultaneously on the night of 7/8 May, 1st Dorsets (14th Brigade, 32nd Division) suffer heavy casualties, of whom 12 are buried in Authuille Military Cemetery A 14 and one is commemorated on the Thiepval Memorial. Six men of 20th Manchesters (22nd Brigade, 7th Division) die, of whom five are buried in Citadel New Military Cemetery V Row C and one at La Neuville Communal Cemetery, Corbie A 22. Seventeen men of 9th Royal Inniskilling Fusiliers (109th Brigade, 36th Division) are killed; 15 are buried in Authuille Military Cemetery Rows A & D and two more at Forceville Communal Cemetery Extension I Row C 6. Elements of 19th Division begin to arrive in the Somme area.

9 May: Cold, windy and showery. Rawlinson rides out to see 21st Division near Contay and Lahoussoye but meets up with Haig at XIII Corps headquarters at Corbie on the way and accompanies him to 21st and 7th Divisions. Three more members of 9th Royal Inniskilling Fusiliers (109th Brigade, 36th Division) die of their wounds today. Two are in Beauval Communal Cemetery E 17 and E 18 and one in Gézaincourt CCE I B 17. Six men of 15th Durham Light Infantry (64th Brigade, 21st Division) are killed, five of whom are buried in Dartmoor Cemetery I E 20–24 and one in Corbie Communal Cemetery Extension I A 43. A seventh man of 20th Manchesters (22nd Brigade, 7th Division), wounded on 8 April, is buried in Corbie Communal Cemetery Extension I A 44.

10 May: A fine day. Rawlinson rides to VIII Corps and spends all day with Haig before returning at 1800hrs. Three mines explode in front of the Tambour at Fricourt.

11 May: A dull and cloudy day. Rawlinson and Haig spend the day inspecting I and III Corps with Lt Gen Pulteney. Fargny Mill near Maricourt is attacked by the enemy. Five men from 17th King's (89th Brigade, 30th Division) die as a result of the enemy shelling front-line defences at Maricourt; they are buried in II D 1 to 5, Cerisy-Gailly Military Cemetery. Seven men of 2nd Manchesters (14th Brigade, 32nd

Division) are killed and are later buried in Row C, Authuille Military Cemetery. Two men from 26th and three from 27th Northumberland Fusiliers (both 103rd Brigade, 34th Division) are killed and are buried in Row L, Bécourt Military Cemetery.

12 May: A fine and hot day. Rawlinson spends the day with Haig visiting 49th and 18th Divisions, returning to Querrieu at 1800hrs. Four men of 24th Manchesters (pioneers of 7th Division) are killed; three of them are buried at Citadel New Military Cemetery II A.15 and 16 and Lt J. Sutcliffe in Méaulte Military Cemetery C.30. Five men of 2nd Gordon Highlanders (20th Brigade, 7th Division) die and are later buried in Citadel New Military Cemetery V E & F. As 2nd Gordon Highlanders relieve 8th Devons (also 20th Brigade, 7th Division), the enemy kill 5 men and wounds 18 others. After being relieved, 8th Devons had chosen to walk across the open. Seven members of 18th Manchesters (90th Brigade, 30th Division) die, of whom six are remembered on the Thiepval Memorial and one is buried in Suzanne Communal Cemetery Extension G.12, where three men from 19th King's (89th Brigade, 30th Division) are also buried in Row G. These last-named were killed when a shell burst over their shelter near Etinehem. In his diary, Rawlinson notes that 30th Division had been involved in a sharp fight at Y Wood. The enemy used gas but two of their men were captured. Three members of 57th Battery, Royal Field Artillery (8th Division), die in a position in front of Aveluy after a round bursts at the base of one of their guns. They are buried in B 16 to B 18, Authuille Military Cemetery.

13 May: Heavy and continuous rain through the day. Rawlinson takes Haig up to the Grandstand near Dernancourt to get a better view of the enemy's preparations. It is very wet but the clouds lift for ½ hour and they manage to have a clear view of the Pozières Ridge. Nine more men of 18th Manchesters (90th Brigade, 30th Division) die, of whom two are commemorated on the Thiepval Memorial, one is buried in Bray Military Cemetery I A 11 and six at Suzanne Communal Cemetery Extension Row G. Three men from the 27th (Tyneside Irish) Battalion North Fusiliers are buried in Bécourt MC I L 8 to L 10.

14 May: Heavy rain. Rawlinson is visited by Lt Gen Pulteney, Freddy Maurice, Earl Percy and Lt Gen Morland. Another man from the 18th Mancheters dies and is buried in Corbie Communal Cemetery Extension I A 35.

15 May: A wet morning. Rawlinson has dinner with Brig Gen H.J. Elles from GHQ.

16 May: A fine day. Rawlinson visits 21st and 34th Divisions as they are engaged in training, and later walks up to Maxse's Redoubt to get a good look at Montauban. Heavy shelling on Hébuterne is followed by a raid that results in 15 men of 12th York and Lancasters (94th Brigade, 31st Division) being killed, 27 missing and 43 wounded. The fatalities are buried in Sucrerie Military Cemetery in I Rows F, G and H.

17 May: A fine and warm day. A corps conference is held at Querrieu Château at 1000hrs.

18 May: Fine and very warm.

19 May: Leaving Querrieu at 0700hrs, Rawlinson visits Haig's headquarters for a few minutes before catching the boat for England at Boulogne at 1115hrs, at the start of 10 days' leave. Lt Gen Morland is on board.

20 May: A very warm day.

21 May: A very hot day. Randall Davidson, the elderly Archbishop of Canterbury, is taken to the Grandstand to see the German lines. Five men of 2nd Lincolns (25th Brigade, 8th Division) are killed; four men are buried in Albert Communal Cemetery Extension I Row D and one in Warloy-Baillon Communal Cemetery A-4.

22 May: A fine day. During the evening there is a heavy bombardment of Colincamps, which caused heavy casualties. At one point the enemy raided a wiring party. Twelve men of 15th West Yorkshires (93rd Brigade, 31st Division) are killed; 11 men are buried in Sucrerie Military Cemetery I Rows L and J, and 1 man, who died of wounds, in Gézaincourt Communal Cemetery and Extension I C 8.

23 May: A showery day. Five men of 11th Suffolks (101st Brigade, 34th Division) die; one is buried at Albert Communal Cemetery Extension I D 24, two at Bécourt Military Cemetery I M 6 and M 8 and two at Méricourt l'Abbé Communal Cemetery Extension I Rows C & D.

24 May: A wet day. Five more men of 11th Suffolks (101st Brigade, 34th Division) die, of whom three are buried in Bécourt Military Cemetery and two at Méricourt l'Abbé Communal Cemetery Extension.

25 May: Heavy rain all night and all morning. Gen Sir William Robertson, Chief of the Imperial General Staff, visits Haig and the two men discuss the choice of a date for the Somme battle. Both men are keen on supporting the French, who by now have endured three months of fighting at Verdun. Two men of 12th East Yorkshires are killed and buried in Sucrerie Military Cemetery I Row H 81 and H 82. Four men of 13th East Yorkshires (both 92nd Brigade, 31st Division) are killed and also buried in Sucrerie Military Cemetery I H 55–H 58. Three men of No. 174 Tunnelling Company, Royal Engineers, are killed and are buried in the Citadel New Military Cemetery I F 1 to F 3.

26 May: A very wet day. Ten men of 12th East Yorkshires are killed and are buried in Sucrerie Military Cemetery I Rows D, F, H and L.

27 May: A fine day. Eight more men of 12th East Yorkshires are killed; seven are buried in Sucrerie Military Cemetery I G and one in Gézaincourt Communal Cemetery I C 1. Five men of 2nd Rifle Brigade (25th Brigade, 8th Division) are killed, of whom four are buried in Aveluy Communal Cemetery Extension E 7 to E 10 and one at Millencourt Communal Cemetery Extension B 2 who died of wounds.

28 May: A fine day. Two more men of 12th East Yorkshires die of wounds; one is buried in Gézaincourt Communal Cemetery Extension I E 9 and the other in Beauval Communal Cemetery E 29. Six men of 10th Yorkshires (62nd Brigade, 21st Division) are killed and are buried in Dartmoor Military Cemetery I Rows B & C. Four men of 1st Royal Welsh Fusiliers (22nd Brigade, 7th Division) die, three of whom are buried in Citadel New Military Cemetery III F 14 to F 16 and one in Corbie Communal Cemetery Extension I A 24. One, who died the next day, is buried in La Neuville Communal Cemetery A 44.

29 May: Rain all day. Rawlinson is back from leave. The French and Haig agree that the battle should start in the first week of July.

30 May: Heavy rain during the night and much colder. A corps commanders' conference is held at Querrieu at 1500hrs.

31 May: Rawlinson visits Maj Gen J.S.M. Shea, General Officer Commanding 30th Division, who had recently replaced Maj Gen W. Fry, returning via Bray-sur-Somme, Happy Valley and Mametz. Four men of 1st Essex (88th Brigade, 29th Division) are killed and are buried in Auchonvillers Military Cemetery I B and D.

A total of 836 men died on the Somme in May 1916.

JUNE 1916

1 June: A fine day. On a lovely morning, Rawlinson rode over to see 32nd and 8th Divisions before breakfast and watched them training. Nine members of No. 178 Tunnelling Company, Royal Engineers, are killed; their names are commemorated on the Thiepval Memorial.

2 June: A fine day. The Battle of Jutland begins, resulting in an inconclusive outcome. At 1000hrs, Rawlinson visits Gen Foch, who has recently been involved in a motor smash, leaving him badly shaken. Rawlinson drives to Saint-Riquier to observe training. Nine men of 22nd Manchesters (91st Brigade, 7th Division) are killed, of whom eight are commemorated on the Thiepval Memorial and one is buried at Bronfay Farm Military Cemetery I B 3. Four men of 11th Suffolks (101st Brigade, 34th Division) die and are buried in Bécourt Military Cemetery Row N of Plot I.

3 June: A fine day. Four men of 10th King's Own Yorkshire Light Infantry (64th Brigade, 21st Division) are killed, of whom two are buried in Norfolk Cemetery I C 59 and 60, one at Méaulte Military Cemetery B 15 and one at La Neuville Communal Cemetery A 51. Fifteen members of 34th Division are taken prisoner.

4 June: The worst day day for pre-Somme casualties with over 100 fatalities. A showery day with heavy rain at night.A church service is held in the grounds of the château. Two officers and 20 men from 10th East Yorkshires (92nd Brigade, 31st Division) are killed. The officers are buried at Bertrancourt Military Cemetery I C 1 and C 2 and the men in Sucrerie Military Cemetery I Row 1 apart from two in Beauval K C 1 and C 2. Two officers and 19 men of 1st East Yorkshires (64th Brigade, 21st Division) are killed and are buried in Norfolk Cemetery Row I A and Row B, apart from one man in Corbie Communal Cemetery Extension CCE I A 18. Six men of 14th York and Lancasters (94th Brigade, 31st Division) are killed; four men are buried in Sucrerie Military Cemetery I F 44, and I F 42, F 43 and F 46 and one at Beauval Communal Cemetery E 33, while a sixth is commemorated on the Thiepval Memorial. Ten men of 4th Worcesters (88th Brigade, 29th Division), engaged in a raiding party near the White City, are killed and are buried in Auchonvillers Military Cemetery II Rows C & D. Two officers and four men of 1st Lincolns (62nd Brigade, 21st Division) are killed when part of a raiding party of 7 officers and 100 men near the Tambour at Fricourt is caught by enemy artillery fire; they are buried in Dartmoor Cemetery I Rows B, C, D & E.

5 June: A showery day. Lt Gen Hunter-Weston calls in at Rawlinson's château at Querrieu. Rawlinson rides to Corbie. 11th Borders (97th Brigade, 32nd Division) carry out a raid on enemy trenches opposite Leipzig Salient but lose five men, including Lt W.S. Barnes, with two more men dying the following day; six are buried in Authuille Military Cemetery Row B, including Barnes. Six men of 21st (Tyneside Scottish) Battalion Northumberland Fusiliers (102nd Brigade, 34th Division) die, of whom five are buried in Bécourt Military Cemetery I, Rows N and O and one at Heilly Station Cemetery I C 2. Two more casualties from 4th Worcesters (88th Brigade, 29th Division) die at Gézaincourt and one is buried in Gézaincourt Communal Cemetery Extension I E 7, the other is buried in Mailly-Maillet Communal Cemetery Extension B 39. Three men of 10th East Yorkshires (92nd Brigade, 31st Division) die of wounds; two are buried in Abbeville Communal Cemetery and Extension Plots III and IV and one at Gézaincourt Communal Cemetery Extension I E 16. Three men from 2nd Devons in Aveluy Communal Cemetery Extension in Rows C & D.

6 June: Very wet all morning and dull. News is received of the death of Lord Kitchener, drowned when HMS *Hampshire* struck a mine off the Orkneys. After lunch, Rawlinson visits 34th Division. Six men of 9th Royal Irish Rifles (107th Brigade, 36th Division) are killed, of whom five are buried in Authuille Military Cemetery D 19 to D 23 and one at Forceville Communal Cemetery Extension I E 15.

7 June: A showery day. Rawlinson learns of Kitchener's death. During the afternoon, Rawlinson visits 31st Division and rides over to Bertrancourt and Colincamps where he sees Brig Gen C.B. Prowse. He visits the sugar refinery and has a 'good look round'.

8 June: Very wet all day. Rawlinson reports that a prisoner had mentioned that a large mine had been installed underneath Bois Français near Fricourt, but Rawlinson expressed doubts. Rawlinson visits 36th Division during training but is not satisfied. Gen Zelinsky of the French-Russian Mission comes to lunch and later walks around the lakes at Querrieu with Maj Gen Montgomery.

9 June: A showery day. Rawlinson visits Brig Gen F.C. Stanley, General Officer Commanding 89th Brigade (30th Division), near Ailly; Maj Gen Shea is there as well. Later, Rawlinson visits Maj Gen Maxse and the staff of 18th Division at their headquarters, and Maj Gen. T.J.M. Bridges, General Officer Commanding 19th Division. Three men from 15th West Yorkshires (93rd Brigade, 31st Division) die and are buried in Sucrerie Military Cemetery I G 3 to G 5, and two more who die the following day are buried in Plot I, graves I 87 and F 39. Troops of 17th Division begin to arrive in the Somme area.

10 June: Heavy rain. Rawlinson travels to Gézaincourt Officers' Hospital and then inspects a brigade of 31st Division, which he describes as the worst brigade he has seen. He then journeys to Bertangles and the squadrons there before going to the Grandstand. He then rides to Albert via Méaulte, where a car meets him and takes him to XIII Corps headquarters to see Lt Gen Congreve. Four men of 1st Lancashire Fusiliers (86th Brigade, 29th Division) are killed and are buried in Auchonvillers Military Cemetery II D 7 and A 19. Six men of 22nd (Tyneside Scottish) Northumberland Fusiliers (102nd Brigade, 34th Division) die and are buried in Bécourt Military Cemetery I Row O 17–24.

11 June: A wet day. After church, Rawlinson, accompanied by Maj Gen Montgomery, leaves for GHQ, where they lunch with Lt Gen Kiggell. Seventeen more men of 1st Lancashire Fusiliers (86th Brigade, 29th Division) die during a heavy enemy bombardment and are buried at Auchonvillers Military Cemetery Rows A & C and one in Beauval Communal Cemetery B 1. Nine men of 15th Royal

Irish Rifles (107th Brigade, 36th Division) die in the Hamel trenches after a violent bombardment, which was to cover an enemy trench raid and are buried in Hamel Military Cemetery I D & E. During the same period, seven men of 8th Royal Irish Rifles (107th Brigade, 36th Division) die and are buried in Authuille Military Cemetery Row D.

12 June: Whit Monday; wet and cold. A corps conference is held at 1000hrs at the château. Rawlinson rides out to Martinsart and meets Lt Gen Horne at Heilly during the afternoon. Six men of 1st Lancashire Fusiliers (86th Brigade, 29th Division) die, of whom three are buried in Auchonvillers Military Cemetery I B 21, one in Gézaincourt Communal Cemetery Extension I F 9, one in Louvencourt Military Cemetery I C 48 and the last in Beauval Communal Cemetery B 2.

13 June: A very wet day. A memorial service for Lord Kitchener is held in the recreation room of the château. Twelve men of 1st East Surreys (95th Brigade, 5th Division) die during the night as a result of enemy artillery fire as well as Allied shrapnel fire. The casualties are buried in Carnoy Military Cemetery Row E 10–20. A seventh member of 1st Lancashire Fusiliers (86th Brigade, 29th Division) dies of wounds received on 12 June and is buried in Louvencourt Military Cemetery I C 19. Elements of 9th and 25th Divisions begin to arrive in the Somme area.

14 June: A fine day. Clocks are changed at 2300hrs.

15 June: A fine cold day. Rawlinson attends an army council meeting at Saint-Pol. The roads are in poor condition. Rawlinson visits VIII Corps on his way back. Four men of 20th (Tyneside Scottish) Battalion Northumberland Fusiliers (102nd Brigade, 34th Division) are killed and are buried in Albert Communal Cemetery Extension I 18 to 21.

16 June: A fine day, with the roads drying out. Rawlinson visits X Corps and 36th and 32nd Divisions. After discussions with Gen Foch as to the starting time for the battle, he and Foch agree on 0730hrs, although Foch would have preferred 0900hrs and Rawlinson 0700hrs. Seven men of 7th Yorkshires (50th Brigade, 17th Division) are killed and are buried in Point 110 New Military Cemetery E 2 to E 8. Five men of 15th Highland Light Infantry (14th Brigade, 32nd Division) are killed, of whom four men are buried in Authuille Military Cemetery E 8 to 11 and the fifth in Saint-Ouen Communal Cemetery A 6.

17 June: Fine and warm. Four men of CLXIX Brigade, Royal Field Artillery (31st Division), are killed and are buried in Bertrancourt Military Cemetery I D 1 to 4. Four men of 8th North Staffords (57th Brigade, 19th Division) are killed and are buried in Albert Communal Cemetery Extension I E 3 to E 6.

18 June: Fine and warm. Rawlinson reaches GHQ by noon.

19 June: A dull day. Rawlinson visits XIII Corps and 30th Division. Four men of 2nd Gordon Highlanders (20th Brigade, 7th Division) are killed and are buried in Citadel New Military Cemetery V E 1 to E 5 and one other in B 2. Another man from the 8th North Staffords is buried in Albert Communal Cemetery Extension I E 7.

20 June: A fine day with showers at night. Foch arrives at the château at 1000hrs. Rawlinson visits flying squadrons at Abbeville and 17th Division headquarters.

21 June: A fine day. Rawlinson visits 32nd Division and the heavy artillery batteries in Albert. Three men of 1st Dorsets (14th Brigade, 32nd Division) are killed and are buried in Authuille Military Cemetery A and D.

22 June: A hot day. Lt Gen Sir Hubert Gough, General Officer Commanding Reserve (later Fifth) Army, comes to the château at 0930hrs and a corps conference is held at 1000hrs. Four men of 11th East Lancashires (94th Brigade, 31st Division) are killed and are buried in Bertrancourt Military Cemetery I Rows B or D. Six men of 12th Northumberland Fusiliers (62nd Brigade, 21st Division) die, of whom four are buried in Dartmoor Military Cemetery I, B, C, E & F and two are commemorated on the Thiepval Memorial. Sixteen men of (Tyneside Scottish) 22nd Northumberland Fusiliers (102nd Brigade, 34th Division) are killed, of whom six are buried at Heilly Station Cemetery I A, B, D and E and nine are buried in Albert Communal Cemetery Extension I Rows E and G and one is commemorated on the Thiepval Memorial.

23 June: A thunderstorm and heavy rain. Gen Foch visits Querrieu and requests a two-day postponement of the battle but Rawlinson does not have the responsibility to make such a decision. Later, Rawlinson visits Flixecourt to address the latest Officers' Course intake. He later observes 12th Division while training. Three more men of 11th East Lancashires (94th Brigade, 31st Division) are killed and are buried in Bertrancourt Military Cemetery I Rows A & D.

24 June: Rain 1mm. 72°–52°; overcast. The Allied bombardment begins and lasts for seven days.

25 June: Rain 1mm. 71°–54°; windy. Rawlinson visits Gen Foch in the morning. Ten men of 1st Royal Warwicks (10th Brigade, 4th Division) die; nine are buried in Auchonvillers Military Cemetery II Row B while the tenth is commemorated on the Thiepval Memorial. Thirteen men of 2nd Seaforth Highlanders (10th Brigade, 4th Division) are killed at Mailly-Maillet and buried in Mailly Wood Cemetery I A 1 to A 13. Four men of 7th Queens (Royal West Kents) (55th Brigade, 18th Division) are killed, three of whom are commemorated on the Thiepval Memorial and one is buried in Gézaincourt Communal Cemetery Extension I D 9. Eleven members of the Special

Brigade, Royal Engineers, die; of the 10 casualties of 1st Battalion, three are buried in Sucrerie Military Cemetery I Row F, two in one grave II B 18 in Auchonvillers Military Cemetery and two in Bertrancourt Military Cemetery I D 7 & 8, while three are commemorated on the Thiepval Memorial. The single casualty of 2nd Battalion is buried in Bécourt Military Cemetery I P 21.

26 June: Rain 6mm. 72°–52°; cloudy. Rawlinson visits the Grandstand at Dernancourt at 0900hrs and finds that officers from the 'Pool' – either his own staff or members of the senior command – are there. He lunches with XIII Corps. Four men of 1st Royal Warwicks (10th Brigade, 4th Division) are killed, of whom three are commemorated on the Thiepval Memorial and one is buried in Bertrancourt Military Cemetery I D 17. Twenty-one men of 1st Battalion and three of 2nd Battalion, Special Brigade, Royal Engineers, die, some of them from gas poisoning; they are buried in different cemeteries, although some are commemorated on the Thiepval Memorial. Fourteen men of 1/8th Middlesex (167th Brigade, 56th Division) are killed and are commemorated on the Thiepval Memorial. Eleven men of 20th King's (89th Brigade, 30th Division) die and are buried in Cerisy-Gailly Military Cemetery Row L. Seven men of 7th Bedfords (54th Brigade, 18th Division) are killed, of whom five are buried in Carnoy Military Cemetery Rows J & N and two commemorated on the Thiepval Memorial. Six men of 8th Suffolks (53rd Brigade, 18th Division) die; four are buried in Carnoy and two are commemorated on the Thiepval Memorial. Four men of 7th Borders (51st Brigade, 17th Division) are killed and are buried in Citadel New Military Cemetery IV Row F. Thirteen men of No. 97 Field Company, Royal Engineers (21st Division) die at Ville-sur-Ancre when their billets are shelled; ten are buried in Ville-sur-Ancre Communal Cemetery and Extension Rows A & B and three at Méricourt l'Abbé Communal Cemetery Extension I C & D. Six men of 2nd Rifle Brigade (25th Brigade, 8th Division) die, five of whom are buried in Aveluy Communal Cemetery Extension Rows E & F and one in Warloy-Baillon Communal Cemetery Extension V A 4. Ten men of 10th Lancashire Fusiliers (52nd Brigade, 17th Division) die, of whom six are buried at Citadel New Military Cemetery III E & F and four are commemorated on the Thiepval Memorial. Five men of 11th Royal Fusiliers (54th Brigade, 18th Division) die and are buried at Carnoy Military Cemetery L & N. Eight men of 12th Northumberland Fusiliers (62nd Brigade, 21st Division) are killed, of whom six are buried in Dartmoor Cemetery I F and one at Méricourt l'Abbé Communal Cemetery Extension I C 12, while one man is commemorated on the Thiepval Memorial.

Six from the 8th Suffolks die of whom four are buried in Carnoy Military Cemetery Row F.

27 June: Rain 8mm. 68°–54°; overcast and cloudy. Aeroplane work is interfered with. Rawlinson visits III and X Corps and Haig comes over for tea. Rawlinson takes him up to the Grandstand to have a look around. Twenty-two men of 10th Lancashire Fusiliers (52nd Brigade, 17th Division) are killed, of whom 17 are buried in Citadel New Military Cemetery III E & F and five are commemorated on the Thiepval Memorial. Eighteen men of 17th King's (89th Brigade, 30th Division) are killed and are buried in Cerisy-Gailly Military Cemetery II K. Four men of 1/1st Londons (167th Brigade, 56th Division) are killed and are commemorated on the Thiepval Memorial. Ten members of 1st Battalion, Special Brigade, Royal Engineers, die and are buried in seven different cemeteries, with one commemorated on the Thiepval Memorial. Nine men of 2nd Battalion, Special Brigade are also killed and are buried in seven different cemeteries, with one commemorated on the Thiepval Memorial. Four members of No. 5 Battery, Royal Field Artillery (XLV Brigade, 8th Division), are killed and are buried in Bertrancourt Communal Cemetery and Extension. Six men of 7th Borders (51st Brigade, 17th Division) are killed, of whom four are buried in Citadel New Military Cemetery, one in Morlancourt British Cemetery and one is commemorated on the Thiepval Memorial. Four men of 13th Royal Irish Rifles (108th Brigade, 36th Division) are killed and are buried in Authuille Military Cemetery. Six men of 8th Suffolks (53rd Brigade, 18th Division) die, of whom four are buried in Carnoy Military Cemetery F 26 to F 29 and two are commemorated on the Thiepval Memorial. Troops of 38th Division began to arrive in the Somme area. Four men from 92nd Coy MGC die and are listed on the Thiepval Memorial. Five men from the 2nd Kings Own Yorkshire Light Infantry are killed and buried in Bouzincourt Communal Cemetery Extension. Four men from the 5th Battery are in II C of Bertrancourt Communal Cemetery and Extension II Row C. Four men from the 13th Royal Irish Rifles are buried in Authuille Military Cemetery Rows B or G. Six men from the 7th Borders are in Citadel New Military Cemetery IV Row F.

28 June: Rain 2mm. 68°–50°; overcast with very heavy rain. The commencement of the battle is delayed until 0730hrs, 1 July, instead of 29 June. Haig and Gen Joffre come to tea with Rawlinson. Four men of 17th King's (89th Brigade, 30th Division) are killed and are buried in Cerisy-Gailly Military Cemetery, Plot II, Row K. Four men of 1/6th Royal Warwicks (143rd Brigade, 48th Division) die and are commemorated on the Thiepval Memorial. Four men of 2nd Borders (20th

Brigade, 7th Division) are killed, of whom three are buried in Citadel New Military Cemetery I E & F and one in Heilly Station Cemetery I G 6. Five men of 7th Borders (51st Brigade, 17th Division) die, of whom four are buried in Citadel New Military Cemetery IV Rows E & F and one is commemorated on the Thiepval Memorial. Six men from 'X' 12th Trench Mortar Battery, Royal Field Artillery (12th Division), are killed, of whom two are buried in Blighty Valley Cemetery II A 7 and A 8 and four are commemorated on the Thiepval Memorial. Fifteen members of 13th Royal Irish Rifles (108th Brigade, 36th Division) are killed by shelling in Martinsart village; fourteen are buried in Martinsart British Cemetery A 1 while one has a special memorial at Authuille Military Cemetery. Five men of 1st Lancashire Fusiliers (86th Brigade) die, of whom three men are buried at Auchonvillers Military Cemetery II B16–B17 and E 25 and one at C 60 of Redan Ridge Cemetery No. 2 at Beaumont-Hamel, while the last is commemorated on the Thiepval Memorial. Eight men of 1st Royal Dublin Fusiliers (86th Brigade, 29th Division) are killed, of whom three are buried in Auchonvillers Military Cemetery II B 7 and four at Row A of Hawthorn Ridge Cemetery No. 2, Auchonvillers, while one man is commemorated on the Thiepval Memorial. Four men from the 4th Middlesex die, of whom three are in Norfolk Cemetery I Row B and one in Méaulte MC C 16.

29 June: Some rain. 66°–52°; cloudy – low clouds and strong winds all day. If battle had begun on this day, then conditions underfoot would have been very slippery. Lt Gen Hunter-Weston visits Haig at Beauquesne and stays to lunch: 'He seemed quite satisfied and confident.' Rawlinson visits VIII Corps and Haig at Beauquesne on the way back and then 21st, 30th and 18th Divisions. Haig visits X Corps at Senlis and notes that Lt Gen Morland 'is quietly confident of success'. He then goes to see Lt Gen Pulteney at Montigny. Four men of 13th King's Royal Rifle Corps (111th Brigade, 37th Division) are killed and are commemorated on the Thiepval Memorial. Seven men of 13th Royal Irish Rifles (108th Brigade, 36th Division) die, of whom two are buried in Puchevillers British Cemetery I A 7 and A 8 and five, who died of wounds, are buried in Forceville Communal Cemetery II Row A. Four men of 6th Royal Berkshires (53rd Brigade, 18th Division) are killed, of whom three men are buried in Carnoy Military Cemetery Q 13 to Q 15 and one is commemorated on the Thiepval Memorial. Four men of 7th Queen's (55th Brigade, 18th Division) die, of whom two are buried in Carnoy Military Cemetery G 20 and G 21 and two in La Neuville Communal Cemetery B 4 and B 5. Seven men of 8th Somerset

Light Infantry (63rd Brigade, 21st Division) are killed and are buried in Norfolk Cemetery I A and I C. Five men of No. 126 Battery, Royal Field Artillery (XXIX Brigade, 4th Division), are killed and are buried in Sucrerie Military Cemetery I Row C 2 to C 6. Four men of 23rd (Tyneside Scottish) Northumberland Fusiliers (102nd Brigade, 34th Division) die, two of whom are buried in Albert Communal Cemetery Extension I E 33 and E 34 and two commemorated on the Thiepval Memorial.

30 June: 72°–48°; overcast with high wind, but conditions improve towards the evening. Rawlinson notes in his diary that the total number of men involved at the start of the battle is about 500,000; that there are 1,500 guns of which 450 are of a large calibre; and that 150,000 rounds were fired during the day and 50,000 during the night into the enemy front lines. Rawlinson visits 1st and 2nd Cavalry Divisions. Five men of 10th Essex (53rd Brigade, 18th Division) die and are commemorated on the Thiepval Memorial. Thirteen men of 12th Middlesex (54th Brigade, 18th Division) are killed, of whom nine are buried in Carnoy Military Cemetery Rows K, M & N and four are commemorated on the Thiepval Memorial. Twelve men of 18th West Yorkshires (93rd Brigade, 31st Division) die, of whom nine are commemorated on the Thiepval Memorial, two are buried in Bertrancourt Military Cemetery I E & F and one is buried in Mesnil Communal Cemetery Extension II A 6. Four men of 1st Royal Welsh Fusiliers (22nd Brigade, 7th Division) are killed, of whom three are commemorated on the Thiepval Memorial and one is buried in Citadel New Military Cemetery. Six men of 22nd (Tyneside Scottish) Northumberland Fusiliers (102nd Brigade, 34th Division) are killed, of whom four are commemorated on the Thiepval Memorial, one is buried in Bécourt Military Cemetery I Q 14 and one is buried in Warloy-Baillon Communal Cemetery and Extension I A 22.

In the month of June, the number of British and Dominion casualties reached 1,687. The total of casualties in the 11 months since British troops began to arrive on the Somme came to 6,177; of these, the figure of 21 should be deducted, as they served under an alias and therefore their names were included twice. Nine men who were known to have been burials from the Battle of Loos have also been deducted. It should be stressed that these figures are of men buried in the Department of the Somme. At the very least, there are at least a dozen cemeteries in the adjacent Pas de Calais that hold substantial numbers of men who died prior to the battle; these cemeteries are mainly to be found in the northern sector of the battlefield. For example, there are at least 900 pre-battle casualties buried in

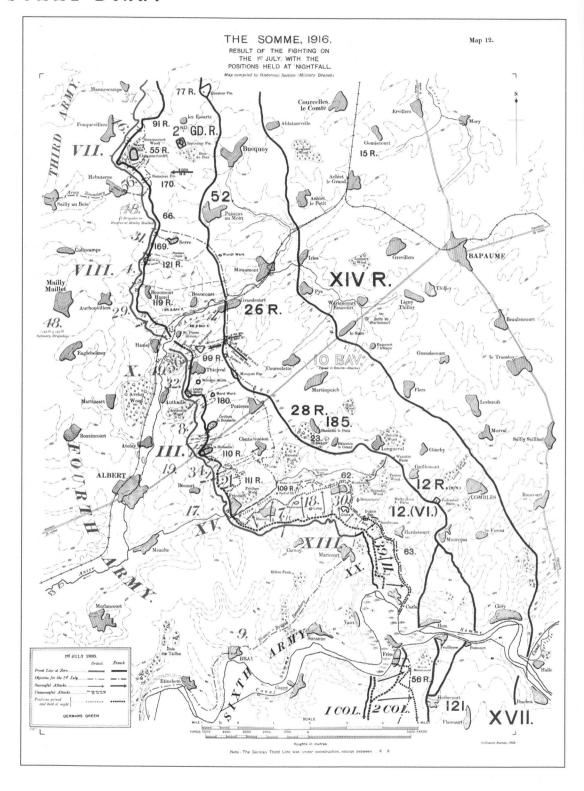

THE SOMME, 1916.
RESULT OF THE FIGHTING ON
THE 1ST JULY, WITH THE
POSITIONS HELD AT NIGHTFALL.
Map compiled by Historical Section (Military Branch)

Map 12.

the following: *Hébuterne Military Cemetery, Bienvillers Military Cemetery, Foncquevillers Military Cemetery, Berles-au-Bois Churchyard Extension, Humbercamps New Military Cemetery, Hannescamps New Military Cemetery and Warlincourt Halte British Cemetery.*

JULY 1916

1 July: 79°–52°; clear sky. Rawlinson visits his 'observation fort' at 0630hrs; it is very hazy but the mist lifts at 0730hrs, when the Allied attack begins. The combined Franco-British offensive opens on a 25-mile front both north and south of the Somme. The British capture Montauban and Mametz. The French attack towards Péronne and reach the outskirts of Hardecourt-au-Bois and Curlu. To the north-west of the Albert–Bapaume road, the British make little progress against the German defences, except for a small gain at the Leipzig Redoubt to the south of Thiepval. They fail at Gommecourt, Serre, Beaumont-Hamel, Thiepval and La Boisselle. Casualties are in the vicinity of 57,000, the highest casualty figure that the British Army ever suffered. Nine VC awards stemmed from the day's fighting: T/Capt E.N.F. Bell of 9th Royal Inniskilling Fusiliers (109th Brigade, 36th Division) at Thiepval; Lt G.S. Cather of 9th Royal Irish Fusiliers (108th Brigade, 36th Division) near Hamel; Capt J.L. Green RAMC, attached to 1/5th Sherwood Foresters (139th Brigade, 46th Division), at Foncquevillers; T/Maj S.W. Loudoun-Shand of 10th Yorkshires (62nd Brigade, 21st Division) near Fricourt; Pte W.F. McFadzean of 14th Royal Irish Rifles (109th Brigade, 36th Division) at Thiepval; Pte R. Quigg of 12th Royal Irish Rifles (108th Brigade, 36th Division) near Hamel; Drummer W.P. Ritchie of 2nd Seaforth Highlanders (10th Brigade, 4th Division) to the north of Beaumont-Hamel; Cpl G. Sanders of 1/7th West Yorkshires (146th Brigade, 49th Division) near Thiepval; and Sgt J.Y. Turnbull of 17th Highland Light Infantry (97th Brigade, 32nd Division) at the Leipzig Redoubt.

2 July: 75°–54°; clear sky, fine. Fricourt is surrendered by the Germans. Good deal of cloud in the morning. Rawlinson's estimate of casualties is 30,000. He is visited by Haig and Lt Gen Kiggell in the morning and later lunches with Gen Robertson.

3 July: Rain 2mm. 68°–55°; thunderstorms to the south-east. Fine day with some clouds. La Boisselle and part of Ovillers are captured. T/Lt Col A. Carton de Wiart, Commanding Officer 8th Glosters, and Pte T.G. Turrall of 10th Worcesters (both 57th Brigade, 19th Division) both win the VC at La Boisselle.

4 July: Rain 17mm. 70°–55°; overcast, thunderstorms, windy and cool air. La Boiselle is taken, as well as Bernafay Wood.

5 July: 72°–52°; low cloud until evening. Horseshoe Trench is taken; T/Lt D.S. Bell of 9th Yorkshires (69th Brigade, 23rd Division) gains the VC there. T/Lt T.O.L. Wilkinson of 7th Loyal North Lancashires (56th Brigade, 19th Division) gains the VC at La Boissele. Many Germans assemble in Mametz Wood.

6 July: Rain 2mm. 70°–54°; overcast and dull with showers at intervals. The attack on Trônes Wood is delayed for 24 hours. Lloyd George is appointed Secretary of State for War and Lord Derby Under-Secretary for War.

7 July: Rain 13mm. 70°–59°; overcast and showery. Contalmaison is captured as well as Leipzig Redoubt. Heavy rain in the evening and Contalmaison is lost. The British fail to get into Mametz Wood.

8 July: Rain 8mm. 73°–52°; overcast. British penetrate Trônes Wood. Haig visits Rawlinson.

9 July: 70°–53°; cloudy and fine. A large fire is reported at Martinpuich. Trônes Wood fighting continues. E.S. Montagu is appointed Minister of Munitions.

10 July: 82°–48°; overcast, very hot, no wind, thick cloud bank. Heavy fighting in Trônes Wood. 38th Division make progress in the fight for Mametz Wood.

11 July: 68°–52°; overcast. Contalmaison is held against counter-attacks. Fighting still in Trônes and Mametz Woods.

12 July: Rain–trace. 68°–??; fine but overcast. Mametz Wood is totally captured and Contalmaison counter-attacks are repulsed. Plans for dawn attacks on 14 July are finalised.

13 July: Rain–trace. 70°–54°; overcast, strong west wind and a little rain. The Battle of Albert, which began on 1 July, ends.

14 July: Fine but overcast. British attack the German Second Line, beginning at 0325hrs under very heavy bombardment. They capture Longueval and Bazentin-le-Petit and the whole of Trônes Wood, where Sgt W.E. Boulter of 6th Northamptons (54th Brigade, 18th Division) gains the VC. 2nd (Indian) Cavalry Division are sent in to the battle with High Wood as their objective. Haig and Gen Foch come to see Rawlinson to congratulate him on the success of the dawn advance.

15 July: 72°–47°; misty in the morning, which turns into a bright clear day. Beginning of the battle for Delville Wood. High Wood is not captured.

16 July: Rain 4mm. 73°–55°; dull and overcast. The British consolidate their positions and withdraw from High Wood.

17 July: 70°–59°; misty and overcast. Waterlôt Farm is taken to the east of Longueval. Ovillers is completely cleared of Germans. The Battle of Bazentin Ridge ends.

18 July: 72°–52°; overcast. The Germans make strong counter-attacks at Longueval and Delville Wood; Pte W.F. Faulds of 1st South African Infantry (South

THE SOMME. 1916 14ᵗʰ July.

Sketch II.

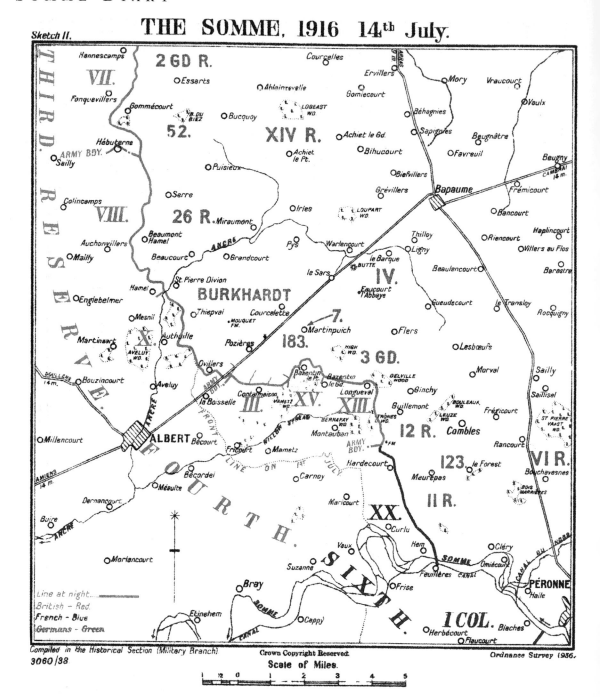

THIRD RESERVE

FOURTH.

SIXTH.

2 GD R.

VII.

52.

XIV R.

VIII.

26 R.

BURKHARDT

7.

183.

IV.

3 GD.

III.

XV.

XIII.

12 R.

123.

II R.

XX.

X.

VI R.

I COL.

Line at night..............
British – Red.
French – Blue.
Germans – Green.

Compiled in the Historical Section (Military Branch)
3060/38.

Crown Copyright Reserved.
Scale of Miles.

Ordnance Survey 1936.

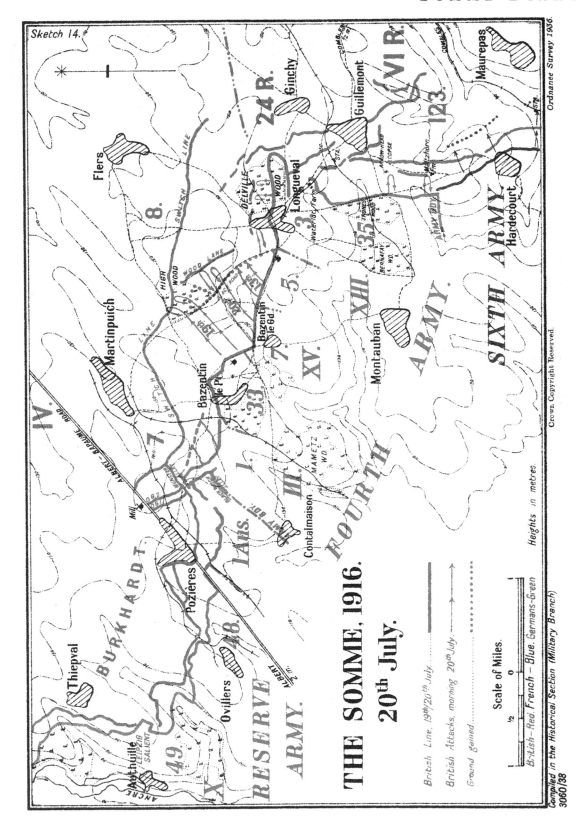

Sketch 14.

THE SOMME, 1916.
20th July.

British Line, 19th/20th July.
British Attacks, morning 20th July.
Ground gained.

Scale of Miles.

British – Red. French – Blue. Germans – Green.

Heights in metres.

Crown Copyright Reserved.

Ordnance Survey 1936.

Compiled in the Historical Section (Military Branch)
3060/38

African Brigade, 9th Division) gains the VC at the last-named. Drizzling rain after a dull morning.

19 July: 70°–50°; cloudy. The Allies attack Fromelles to the north of the Somme battlefield. The Germans attack Longueval and fighting in Delville Wood continues. 35th Division repulse enemy attacks on Waterlôt Farm and Trônes Wood.

20 July: 75°–52°; fine morning, clear skies. Fighting continues in Longueval and Delville Wood. Cpl J.J. Davies and Pte A. Hill, both of 10th Royal Welsh Fusiliers (76th Brigade, 3rd Division), are each awarded the VC for their role in the Delville Wood fighting and Pte T.W.H. Veale of 8th Devons (20th Brigade, 7th Division) gains the VC to the east of High Wood. B/Maj W. la Touche Congreve of 76th Brigade (3rd Division) is awarded the VC for actions between 6 and 20 July; he loses his life to a sniper's bullet.

21 July: 75°–52°; fine day with clear skies. Fighting at High Wood continues. Haig visits Rawlinson and impresses on him the need to capture the village of Guillemont.

22 July: Rain–trace. 77°–55°; clear sky, although dull early on. Violent fighting continues on the Pozières–Guillemont front. From the air a new German trench line is discovered in front of the Switch Line to the north-west of High Wood.

23 July: 68°–54°; overcast. The second phase of the Somme battle begins, which includes fierce fighting in and around the village of Pozières. The British recapture the whole of Longueval but the Germans retake the northern part of the village. The outskirts of Guillemont change hands twice. At Pozières, 2/Lt A.S. Blackburn of 10th Australian Battalion and Pte J. Leak of 9th Australian Battalion (both 3rd Australian Brigade, 1st Australian Division) each gain the VC. Rawlinson notes in his diary that the Germans had not relinquished their attacks in Verdun, although they had skimmed their line in order to release troops for the Somme battle.

24 July: 70°–55°; overcast and very hot. Fighting at Pozières continues and the Germans counter-attack at High Wood and Guillemont. Pte T. Cooke of 8th Australian Battalion (2nd Australian Brigade, 1st Australian Division) gains the VC at Pozières.

25 July: 66°–50°; overcast. The current series of attacks against High Wood ends. The Germans counter-attack in the Longueval and Bazentin areas. Pozières is almost entirely in Allied hands and the British push along the Albert–Bapaume road. Rawlinson visits Fricourt, which he describes as a series of craters.

26 July: 75°–55°; windy day. The whole of Pozières village is in Allied hands.

27 July: Rain 8mm. 81°–61°; a hazy day that became a clearer afternoon. The British make further attacks and gains in Delville Wood. Fighting continues near Pozières and at Longueval. Sgt A. Gill of 1st King's Royal Rifle Corps (99th Brigade, 2nd Division) wins the VC at Delville Wood.

28 July: 77°–59°; overcast and hot day. The British capture Longueval and Delville Wood and make further progress near Pozières. Sgt C.C. Castleton of No. 5 Company, Australian Machine Gun Corps (5th Australian Brigade, 2nd Australian Division) gains the VC near Pozières. Haig visits Rawlinson.

29 July: 81°–57°; overcast. German attempts to retake Delville Wood fail. Hand-to-hand fighting occurs to the north and north-east of Pozières. The Australians fail to take the windmill near Pozières and Munster Alley is still in contention.

30 July: 82°–57°; a clear day and very hot. The British make progress east of Waterlôt Farm and Trônes Wood. A large explosion occurs at Martinpuich. CSM G. Evans of 18th Manchesters (90th Brigade, 30th Division) wins the VC at Guillemont and Pte J. Miller of 7th King's Own (56th Brigade, 19th Division) at Bazentin-le-Petit. The attack against Guillemont does not succeed.

31 July: 82°–59°; a very hot day and hazy in the morning. Fighting for Guillemont continues. The Royal Flying Corps bombs Martinpuich.

AUGUST 1916

1 August: 86°–61°; a very hot day. North of Bazentin-le-Petit the German counter-attack is repulsed. Heavy fighting continues at Verdun.

2 August: 88°–57°. The German attack on Delville Wood is repulsed. There is more heavy fighting at Verdun. It is the hottest day so far in the Battle of the Somme.

3 August: 84°–57°; a hot and clear day. The British gain ground to the west of Pozières and the French make progress at Verdun. An explosion at Courcelette causes smoke to rise 2,000ft. In Britain, Sir Roger Casement is hanged.

4 August: 79°–52°. The Allies gain the German Second Line system on a front of 2,000yds to the north of Pozières. German counter-attacks at Verdun are repulsed.

5 August: 68°–48°; a clear day. The British advance their line near Pozières. Haig visits Rawlinson and is pleased at the Australian success near Pozières, which includes the taking of objectives and the capture of several hundred prisoners.

6 August: 75°–52°. Slight Allied progress to the east of Pozières towards Martinpuich. Pte W. Short of 8th Yorkshires (69th Brigade, 23rd Division) gains the VC at Munster Alley.

7 August: 73°–50°. The British attack the outskirts of Guillemont. German attacks to the north and north-east of Pozières are repulsed. The French make progress at Verdun. Lt Gen Kiggell writes to Rawlinson and indicates that reports of British casualties have been exaggerated at home.

8 August: 77°–52°. British fighting at Guillemont continues. The station is captured and the northern parts of the village, but not the southern end. 2/Lt G.G. Coury, attached to 1/4th South Lancashires (pioneers of 55th Division), gains the VC near Arrow Head Copse.

9 August: 84°–54°. Renewed Allied attacks against Guillemont fail. Although based at Saint-Pol, HM the King begins a 2-day visit to his armies on the Somme. Capt N.C. Chavasse RAMC, attached 1/10th King's (166th Brigade, 55th Division), wins the VC at Guillemont.

10 August: Rain 4mm. 70°–55°; heavy rain and low clouds throughout the day. HM the King visits the front and Rawlinson takes him to the craters at Bois Français. The King tells Rawlinson of a cabal at home that is out to oust Haig and curb the current offensive. The members of the cabal include Lord French, Winston Churchill and F.E. Smith. The British make progress to the north-west of Pozières.

11 August: 77°–59°; a stormy day and misty in the morning.

12 August: Rain 1mm. 82°–63°. The British advance on a 1-mile front north-west of Pozières. Pte M. O'Meara of 16th Australian Battalion (4th Australian Brigade, 4th Australian Division) wins the VC at Pozières for actions in the period 9–12 August.

13 August: 81°–59°; a windy day. 15th Division take Munster Alley.

14 August: Rain 2mm. 77°–59°; a showery day.

15 August: 75°–57°. HM the King returns to England after his visit to the Western Front. At night it rains hard.

16 August: Rain 2mm. 75°–55°. The British advance west and south-west of Guillemont. British pilot Lt Albert Ball takes on five hostile aeroplanes in his Nieuport Scout.

17 August: Rain 4mm. 72°–54°; a showery day with bright intervals.

18 August: Rain 1mm. 70°–55°; an overcast day. The British gain ground towards Ginchy and Guillemont. An enemy aircraft crashes near High Wood. 33rd Division fail to progress at High Wood.

19 August: Rain 2mm. 70°–50°; an overcast day. British gain ground in the Thiepval Ridge area.

20 August: 72°–54°; an overcast day. Germans counter-attack near Thiepval.

21 August: 72°–48°. The British make progress north-west of Pozières, Germans counter-attack near Thiepval.

22 August: 72°–52°. Two determined counter-attacks by the Germans south of Thiepval are beaten off. Haig

visits Rawlinson and chides him about Guillemont still not being in British hands.

23 August: 72°–54°. Fighting continues to the south of Thiepval. Strong German attacks at Guillemont repulsed. Rawlinson hears that 12 tanks have arrived.

24 August: 78°–55°. Further progress by the British towards Thiepval and the north-west part of Delville Wood. German attacks to the west of Ginchy are driven off.

25 August: Rain 8mm. 81°–61°; an overcast and cloudy day. The German attack south of Thiepval is repulsed and the enemy are driven out of Delville Wood and a line established along the north-east edge.

26 August: Rain 7mm. 75°–59°. The Germans counter-attack near Thiepval. Rawlinson sees the tanks in training and is impressed with them but thinks that their crews need much more training for battle conditions.

27 August: Rain 4mm. 73°–59°. 3rd Brigade (1st Division) attacks Grévillers. Italy declares war on Germany.

28 August: Rain slight. 73°–59°. Because of the considerable rainfall of the previous few days the conditions are getting worse and some trenches are ankle-deep in water. Lt Gen Kiggell visits Rawlinson and they discuss how best to use the tanks in battle. Rawlinson favours caution in their use.

29 August: Rain heavy, but no figures. 82°–59°. Since the battle began on 1 July, the British have captured 266 German officers, 15,203 other ranks, 86 guns and 160 machine guns. Von Hindenburg is appointed Chief of General Staff in place of von Falkenhayn, and Ludendorff becomes Chief Quartermaster General.

30 August: Rain 8mm. 63°–48°; an overcast and very wet day. The trenches at Guillemont are very wet and muddy.

31 August: 70°–52°; a fine day. Fierce German attacks between Ginchy and High Wood are repulsed. First sight of the German aircraft called the Albatros, which was to turn the air war in Germany's favour. This aircraft had twice the firepower of a British fighter and fired synchronised machine guns between its propeller blades. Albert Ball shoots down two enemy aircraft.

SEPTEMBER 1916

1 September: 72°–52°. German attacks at High Wood fail but they are back again in the eastern side of Delville Wood.

2 September: 75°–52°; a windy day. Rawlinson inspects the tanks again and is not pleased with their training and handling.

3 September: Rain 4mm. 72°–50°. The battle for Delville Wood ends and also that of Pozières Ridge. The battle for Guillemont is won by the British, but Ginchy is first taken and then lost. Four VCs are gained on

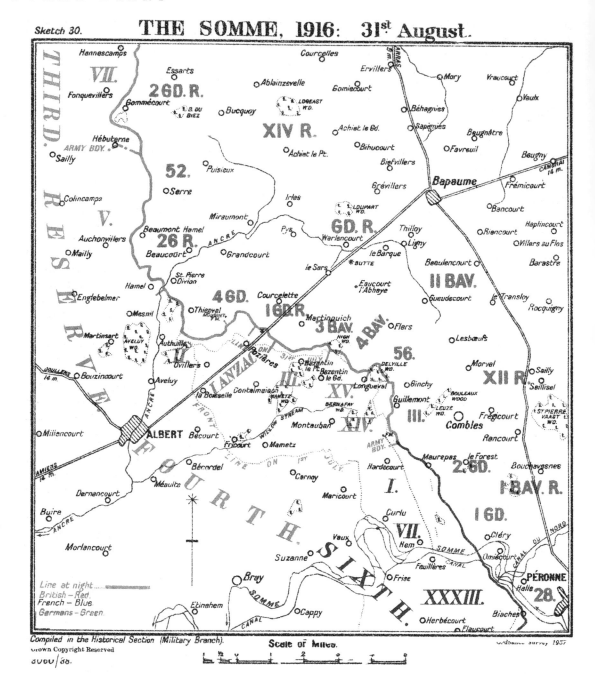

Sketch 30.

THE SOMME, 1916: 31ST August.

Compiled in the Historical Section (Military Branch).
Crown Copyright Reserved

Scale of Miles

Ordnance Survey, 1937

Line at night........
British – Red.
French – Blue.
Germans – Green.

this day; one by Capt W.B. Allen RAMC, attached 21st Field Ambulance (7th Division), near Mesnil and three at Guillemont; Lt J.V. Holland of 3rd Leinsters, attached 7th Leinsters (47th Brigade, 16th Division), Pte T. Hughes of 6th Connaughts (47th Brigade, 16th Division) and Sgt D. Jones of 12th King's (61st Brigade, 20th Division). Continuous fighting towards Faffemont Farm and High Wood.

4 September: Rain 25mm. 66°–52°; low clouds and showers all day. Another attack on Faffemont Farm fails. Haig has tea with Rawlinson and urges on him the necessity of pressing on and is pleased at the taking of Guillemont.

5 September: 63°–54°; an overcast and cloudy day. East of Guillemont the Allied line is carried forward 1,500yds and most of Leuze Wood is captured. The Allies now occupy the whole of the German Second Line. During the night, Faffemont Farm is taken.

6 September: 70°–52°; overcast. Guillemont is consolidated and the British advance to Ginchy completed. Leuze Wood is secured. The Prime Minister, H.H. Asquith, visits the front and inspects the ruins of Fricourt, accompanied by Maurice Hankey and Maurice Bonham-Carter, Principal Private Secretary. He lunches with Rawlinson.

7 September: 70°–54°; a fine clear day with much aerial activity.

8 September: 70°–55°; a fine warm day but overcast until 1300hrs. The Gloucestershire Regiment lose heavily in an attack to the west end of High Wood.

9 September: Rain 5mm. 75°–57°. Ginchy falls to the British. Trenches also taken to the north and east of Leuze Wood. Cpl L. Clarke of 2nd Canadian Battalion (1st Canadian Brigade, 1st Canadian Division) wins the VC near Pozières.

10 September: Rain 1mm. 68°–57°; an overcast day. The Germans counter-attack at Ginchy but are repulsed. The British line to the east of Guillemont is advanced. Rawlinson attends a conference featuring the role of the tanks in the forthcoming battle.

11 September: Rain–trace. 66°–54°; an overcast day. British artillery causes fires in German ammunition dump at Grandcourt. Rawlinson takes a break at Boulogne, to be ready for the 15 September attack.

12 September: 72°–55°; fine but dull. The French take the area to the south of Combles as far as the river. Intense British preparatory bombardment.

13 September: 72°–52°; a dull and overcast day. The French make progress south-east of Combles.

14 September: 61°–41°; a windy day and cold. The British storm trenches to the south-east of Thiepval and take the Wonderwork. Haig visits Rawlinson, who is now back from Boulogne. He urges that Martinpuich should be attacked in earnest and that the cavalry should be pushed out towards le Sars.

15 September: 59°–43°. This day is one of great progress for the Allies and the British begin the third phase of the Battle of the Somme by advancing on a 6-mile front to a depth of 2,000yds to 3,000yds. Flers, Martinpuich, Courcelette and High Wood are all captured and tanks make their first ever appearance in battle. The French Army progresses to the south of Rancourt and capture a system of trenches north of le Priez Farm. There are three VCs awarded on this day: Sgt D.F. Brown of 2nd Otagos (2nd New Zealand Brigade, New Zealand Division) east of High Wood, T/Lt Col J.V. Campbell of 3rd Coldstream Guards (1st Guards Brigade, Guards Division) at Ginchy and L/Sgt F. McNess of 1st Scots Guards (2nd Guards Brigade, Guards Division) close to Ginchy. Between 15 and 24 September, Manfred von Richthofen, the future German ace, shoots down his first aircraft, and Albert Ball shoots down four German aircraft in the same period. The day is cool with a morning mist and a slight ground haze. The main delay is that the Guards advancing towards Lesbœufs are held up by the Quadrilateral, a key German position near Ginchy. Rawlinson is very pleased with the part played by the tanks in the advance.

16 September: 66°–41°; a fine sunny day. The Germans counter-attack at Courcelette but the British gain some territory. Danube Trench and Mouquet Farm are taken by the Allies. Pte J.C. Kerr of 49th Canadian Battalion (7th Canadian Brigade, 3rd Canadian Division) gains the VC at Courcelette. The New Zealanders make progress to the north and west of Flers.

17 September: Rain 2mm. 63°–45°. A comparatively quiet day. 15th Division consolidate at Martinpuich. Haig visits Rawlinson and congratulates him on the progress of 15 and 16 September.

18 September: Rain 13mm. 63°–46°; continuous rain all day. 6th Division take the troublesome Quadrilateral between Ginchy and Bouleux Wood to a depth of 1,000yds.

19 September: Rain 3mm. 55°–43°; a wet and windy day, which hinders operations. Maj Gen Trenchard takes tea with Rawlinson and tells him that 400 aircraft have been got through since 1 July, from reserves now exhausted. Kiggell reports Haig's views as being that battle should continue until either a shortage of troops or a decline in the weather prevents further fighting.

20 September: Rain 1mm. 61°–48°; a showery and unpleasant day. The Germans suffer reversals at the hands of the French close to Combles. Rawlinson delays the next attack to 23 September. The wind and rain hamper the bringing up of munitions. Haig visits Rawlinson; it is agreed that the cavalry should be withdrawn.

21 September: Rain–trace. 59°–48°; a cloudy and showery day. The New Zealanders take Cough Drop Alley and a substantial part of the Flers Line, while 1st

THE TANKS AT FLERS
15th Sept., 1916.

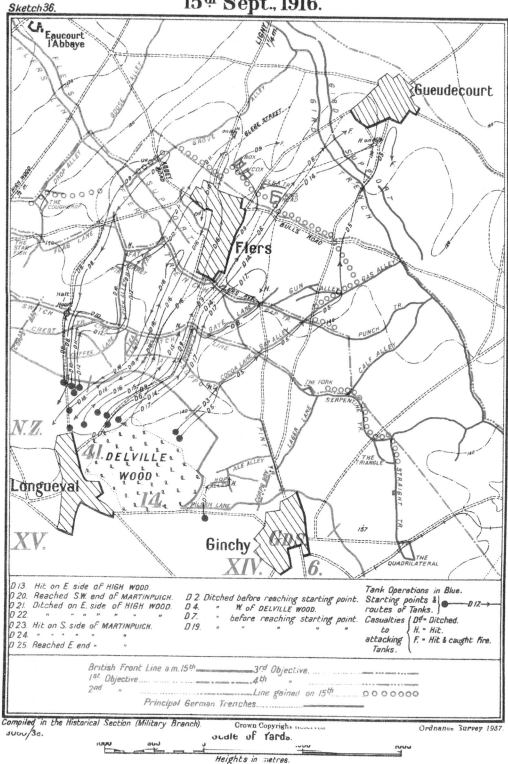

Sketch 36.

D 13. Hit on E. side of HIGH WOOD.
D 20. Reached S.W. end of MARTINPUICH.
D 21. Ditched on E. side of HIGH WOOD.
D 22.   "   "   "   "   "
D 23. Hit on S. side of MARTINPUICH.
D 24.   "   "   "   "   "
D 25. Reached E. end   "   "

D 2. Ditched before reaching starting point.
D 4.   "   "   W. of DELVILLE WOOD.
D 7.   "   "   before reaching starting point.
D 19.   "   "   "   "   "   "   "

Tank Operations in Blue.
Starting points &
routes of Tanks. ●━━ D 12 ━▶
Casualties ⎰ Dᵈ = Ditched.
    to   ⎱ H. = Hit.
attacking F. = Hit & caught fire.
  Tanks.

British Front Line a.m. 15th ————— 3rd Objective ....
1st Objective .... 4th   "
2nd   "   Line gained on 15th ○○○○○○○
Principal German Trenches ....

Compiled in the Historical Section (Military Branch).   Crown Copyright Reserved.   Ordnance Survey 1937.
3000/36.

Scale of Yards.

Heights in metres.

28

Division capture Starfish Trench. Albert Ball destroys two more enemy aircraft.

22 September: 64°–41°; a fine sunny day with a misty morning. The ground conditions are much improved as a result of a drying day. The British advance to the east of Courcelette. Gen Robertson has tea with Rawlinson and tells him that Lloyd George is concerned about the number of casualties and Haig's direction of the battle. The Battle of Flers-Courcelette ends.

23 September: 66°–43°; a fine warm day. The operations delayed until 23 September are put off until 25 September. A quiet day, with 23rd Division making some ground to the east of Martinpuich.

24 September: 72°–45°; a misty morning that turns into a very fine and warm autumn day. Enemy attack unsuccessfully to the west of Lesbœufs.

25 September: 73°–50°; a cloudless day. The Battle of Morval begins. A very successful day for the British; Lesbœufs and Morval are both captured. The village of Combles is hemmed in by the Allies and the French progress at Rancourt, le Priez Farm and Fregicourt. Pte T. Jones of 1st Cheshires (15th Brigade, 5th Division) gains the VC at Morval. Rawlinson is very pleased with Allied progress.

26 September: Rain–trace. 75°–54°. A fine day and another good one for the British advance. Combles falls to the Allies and Thiepval is at last captured. The Battle for Thiepval Ridge begins. The British also storm Gueudecourt. Ptes F.J. Edwards and R.E. Ryder, both of 12th Middlesex (54th Brigade, 18th Division), each gain the VC at Thiepval.

27 September: Rain–trace. 72°–52°; overcast with some showers in the afternoon. The British attack Stuff Redoubt and advance to the north of Flers, to the east of Eaucourt l'Abbaye.

28 September: Rain 1mm. 73°–54°; a fine warm day with some showers. The British attack the Schwaben Redoubt on the crest of the Thiepval Plateau, and capture most of it. They advance to the north and north-east of Courcelette, between Martinpuich and Gueudecourt. T/2/Lt T.E. Adlam of 7th Bedfords (54th Brigade, 18th Division) is awarded the VC for his gallantry during 27/28 September. The French make progress at Morval and the Battles of Morval Ridge end. Rawlinson inspects the ground conditions and describes them as appalling. The ground is so completely flattened that the extension of railways is made impossible. The whole ground is covered with troops, guns, lines and bivouacs. 'A German airman could not drop a brick without killing something,' he writes.

29 September: Rain 17mm. 61°–54°; a very wet and windy day. Very poor weather for flying observation and for the condition of the roads. The British capture Destremont Farm, a strongly defended group of buildings.

30 September: 63°–41°; a fine sunny day. The clocks are put back one hour at 0100hrs. The Battle of Transloy Ridge and Ancre Heights begins. The British attack on the line Eaucourt–le Sars (on the Albert–Bapaume road) and capture all their objectives on a front of 3,000yds. Eaucourt is occupied. T/Lt Col R.B. Bradford, Commanding Officer 1/9th Durham Light Infantry (151st Brigade, 50th Division), gains the VC at Eaucourt l'Abbaye and Albert Ball drives down two enemy aircraft near Gommecourt.

OCTOBER 1916

1 October: T/Capt A.C.T. White of 6th Yorkshires (32nd Brigade, 11th Division) is awarded the VC for his gallantry at Stuff Redoubt between 27 September and 1 October.

2 October: Rain 3mm. 57°–45°; a wet and misty day. The airmen cannot fly in the conditions. The Germans counter-attack in Eaucourt and the British fail to hold le Sars.

3 October: Rain–trace. 70°–50°; rainy and misty day. The British recover Eaucourt l'Abbaye. In the afternoon Rawlinson makes the first of two visits to local Royal Flying Corps fighter squadrons.

4 October: Rain 4mm. 66°–52°; overcast with a very wet morning, finer in the afternoon. The next operations are postponed for 48 hours by Rawlinson because of the poor weather. The roads and tracks are getting into a worse state each day because of the amount of recent rainfall. T/2/Lt H. Kelly of 10th Duke of Wellington's (69th Brigade, 23rd Division) wins the VC at le Sars. Albert Ball is posted back to the United Kingdom.

5 October: Rain 6mm. 66°–54°; overcast, windy with showers. The British advance north-west of Eaucourt and the French make progress east of Morval. The ground dries a little but in the evening it rains. Ground conditions are increasingly difficult for the collection of casualties and the bringing up of stores and munitions.

6 October: Rain 2mm. 70°–57°; sunny day that turns to rain at night. Rawlinson decides that the operations should go ahead on 7 October. The ground dries out a little owing to sun and wind. Pack horses are used in carrying ammunition and food for the infantry. Haig visits Rawlinson after lunch. Haig expresses the view that he wants the battle to go on until the winter, unless the weather makes it impossible.

7 October: Rain–trace. 66°–52°; fine day, windy and rain at night. The wind and low clouds interfere with flying, but the attack begins nevertheless, at 1345hrs. The British and French advance on the Albert–Bapaume road. The British advance 1,000yds

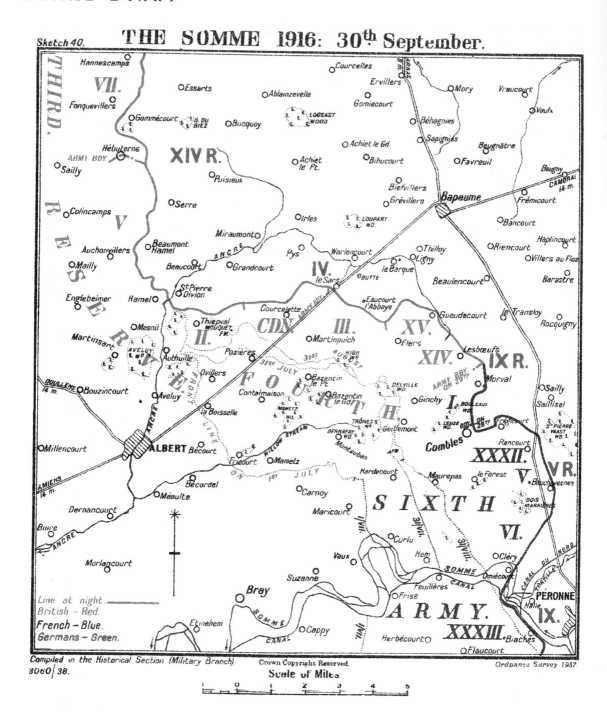

THE SOMME 1916: 30th September.

Sketch 40.

Scale of Miles

Compiled in the Historical Section (Military Branch).
3060/38.
Crown Copyright Reserved.
Ordnance Survey 1957.

Line at night.
British - Red.
French - Blue.
Germans - Green.

and capture le Sars. The French advance to the north-east of Morval and reach to within 200yds of Sailly. Rawlinson hears that Lord French is to visit the French.

8 October: 64°–54°; rain and then fine. North and east of Courcelette, the British line is advanced. The enemy attack and regain some trenches. The French have success at Sailly-Saillisel. The Canadians capture and then lose Regina Trench and the Quadrilateral (le Sars). Piper J.C.R. Richardson of 16th Canadian Battalion (3rd Canadian Brigade, 1st Canadian Division) gains the VC at Regina Trench.

9 October: 64°–50°; fine day. The British make progress to the east of le Sars towards the Butte de Warlencourt.

10 October: 68°–46°; fine sunny day. French success near Chaulnes. Rawlinson inspects both road and rail and sees roads that have 'simply disappeared'. The desolation, he writes, 'is appalling'.

11 October: 66°–50°; dull day with slight rain in the morning. The Battle of the Ancre Heights ends and the French repulse German attacks at Chaulnes Wood.

12 October: 61°–55°; dull day but dry. The British attack on a 4-mile front between Eaucourt and Bapaume. As a general undertaking the attack fails.

13 October: 61°–50°; dull day. Rawlinson holds a corps conference.

14 October: 61°–50°; overcast day. The French make progress. Rawlinson in his diary considers that the weather will bring the battle to a close soon. The glass is falling and the rain will shortly return. The roads will then become impassable and ammunition will not then be got to the guns. He writes that casualties so far since 1 July are 40,000.

15 October: Rain 3mm. 57°–41°; rain in the morning, fine later. The British make progress in the neighbourhood of the Schwaben Redoubt and Thiepval. Rawlinson's diary entry is mainly taken up with a 'plot' against Haig thought up by the cabal. Rawlinson inspects the ground at Longueval and Delville Wood, as well as High Wood. At this time it seems to Rawlinson that the Germans are reviving themselves in the battle and fighting with greater tenacity.

16 October: Rain–trace. 54°–36°. There is to be a white frost from 16 until 20 October. Bright sunny day, much colder. No operations.

17 October: Rain 3mm. 55°–43°; fine day, rain at night. Haig confers with Rawlinson about future battle plans.

18 October: Rain 4mm. 57°–48°; rain in the morning but clears up later. The Battle of the Transloy Ridge ends. The British make progress north of Gueudecourt and the French push the Germans out of Sailly. Rawlinson describes the progress during the day as partially successful.

19 October: Rain 4mm. 57°–37°; heavy rain during the day and especially in the morning. The Reserve Army operation is postponed for 48 hours. There was heavy rain the night before as well as in the morning of 19 October, and the roads and ground surface are in a dreadful state.

20 October: 48°–28°; fine day but very, very cold. The lowest temperature so far recorded during the Battle of the Somme. Heavy German attacks against the Schwaben and Stuff Redoubts on the Thiepval Plâteau are repulsed. An Albatros German aircraft is brought down close to High Wood. Much flying and many photographs taken from the air. Very clear day for observation.

21 October: 45°–28°; fine but very cold day. The British advance on a line between the Schwaben Redoubt and le Sars and take many prisoners. A.J. Balfour, First Lord of the Admiralty, visits Rawlinson and is anxious about the number of casualties and the supply of steel not being adequate.

22 October: Temperature not known; a fine, bright day but bitterly cold. The French carry ridge to the west of Sailly.

23 October: Rain 3mm. 55°–43°; a dull misty morning. The British advance towards le Transloy and capture 1,000yds of enemy trenches. Sgt R. Downie of 2nd Royal Dublin Fusiliers (10th Brigade, 4th Division) gains the VC to the east of Lesbœufs. Kiggell and Gough have tea with Rawlinson and they agree to postpone the planned attack from 25 to 26 October.

24 October: Rain 3mm. 54°–45°; a dull day with rain. The French have success at Verdun in that they retake Douaumont and capture 3,500 prisoners. Maj Gen Trenchard has tea with Rawlinson and tells him that the enemy are producing 1,000 aircraft a month, and that the Royal Flying Corps have lost 660 machines since 1 July.

25 October: Rain 2mm. 52°–45°; rain in the morning, which makes the condition of the roads very bad, and there are many supply lorries stuck, in particular in the area of Montauban. The shortage of supplies reduces the effectiveness of the artillery.

26 October: Rain 1mm. 55°–39°; a showery day, particularly in the morning. Rawlinson postpones the operations due to take place today until 30 October. He then goes away for a short break to Versailles. He notes that the weather is as bad as it can be.

27 October: Rain 1mm. 55°–43°; showery and cold day. The conditions are so bad that Rawlinson considers that it would be a physical impossibility for the infantry to advance. Even moving across a short distance would wear the troops out.

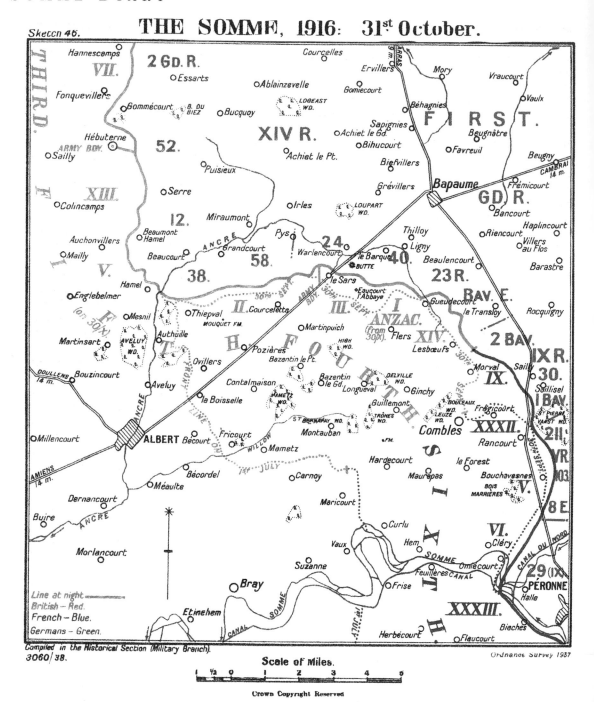

Sketch 46.

THE SOMME, 1916: 31st October.

Line at night ————
British – Red.
French – Blue.
Germans – Green.

Compiled in the Historical Section (Military Branch).
3060/38.

Ordnance Survey 1937

Scale of Miles.

Crown Copyright Reserved

28 October: Rain 8mm. 55°–41°; very wet and cold day. The German flying ace Oswald Boelcke is killed in a collision with one of his pilots. He was flying an Albatros D11 and had been credited with 40 'kills'.

29 October: Rain 7mm. 53°–45°; another very wet day. Allied forces take Dewdrop and Hazy Trenches in the morning.

30 October: Rain 7mm. 61°–48°; a wet and dull cold day. There are deluges of rain, which make the condition of the roads worse than ever. The French take trenches north-west of Sailly-Saillisel.

31 October: 63°–46°; The road and trench conditions are very bad indeed and the area around Gueudecourt is waterlogged. Rawlinson despairs of a further advance.

NOVEMBER 1916

1 November: Rain 2mm. 59°–46°. The German counter-attack against Sailly-Saillisel is repulsed. The Allies advance north-east of Lesbœufs. The Germans evacuate Fort Vaux at Verdun.

2 November: Rain 3mm. 57°–43°. The British capture trenches east of Gueudecourt.

3 November: Rain 1mm. 59°–48°. French advance to the outskirts of Vaux (Verdun).

4 November: Rain 2mm. 64°–52°; a wet and cloudy day. The French occupy Damlup (Verdun). Haig and Gen Foch have conference with Rawlinson.

5 November: 59°–48°; a clear day. The French occupy the whole of Vaux (Verdun). The British make some progress at the Butte de Warlencourt and towards le Transloy. I Anzac Corps gain and then lose Bayonet Trench. T/Lt E.P. Bennett of 2nd Worcesters (100th Brigade, 33rd Division) wins the VC at le Transloy.

6 November: 57°–45°; a cloudy day. French progress near Saint-Pierre-Vaast Wood.

7 November: Rain 12mm. 55°–45°. The British progress to the east of the Butte de Warlencourt.

8 November: Rain 2mm. 57°–43°. The Germans are repulsed at Saillisel.

9 November: 54°–30°; a bright and clear autumn day, frosty. Large aerial battle near Bapaume with 36 British and 40 Germans involved. Rawlinson notes that the British gunners are complaining that too many German aircraft are now over Allied territory.

10 November: 50°–30°. The British capture the east portion of Regina Trench to the north of Thiepval.

The French capture several German trenches to the north-east of Lesbœufs. Rawlinson tours part of the battlefield and visits Ginchy and Delville Wood. He wants to visit the orchard at the southernmost corner of Ginchy but is deterred by the German 5.9s dropping into it. He sees for himself how appalling the roads are beyond Ginchy.

11 November: Rain–trace. 55°–32°; misty day with low cloud, also frosty. The British bombard the Germans on the Ancre. German aircraft bomb at night and cause casualties.

12 November: Rain–trace. 50°–48°; a dull overcast day. Gen Wilson visits Rawlinson. It is hoped that the big attack will take place on the next day.

13 November: 54°–46°. The Battle of the Ancre begins on a foggy morning and Beaumont-Hamel is stormed by the British. They capture Saint-Pierre-Divion and Beaumont-Hamel and take over 3,000 prisoners. The beginning of the fourth phase of the Battle of the Somme. Pte J. Cunningham of 12th East Yorkshires (92nd Brigade, 31st Division) gains his VC opposite Hébuterne and T/Lt Col B.C. Freyberg, Commanding Officer Hood Battalion (189th Brigade, 63rd Division), his at Beaucourt-sur-l'Ancre. Rawlinson describes the operations as being a great day for Lt Gen Gough and Fifth Army.

14 November: 55°–36°; overcast day. The British capture Beaucourt-sur-l'Ancre and advance to the east of the Butte de Warlencourt. The number of prisoners taken in the 2 days reaches 5,200. The north-east winds are drying winds. Haig visits Rawlinson on his way to Paris for a conference and is delighted at Gough's success.

15 November: 46°–37°. German counter-attacks fail.

16 November: 41°–27°; clear but cold day. The British extend their line eastwards from Beaucourt-sur-l'Ancre and retreat from part of the ground to the east of the Butte de Warlencourt. Rawlinson takes Lord Milner, a key member of the British Cabinet, to Candas aerodrome and Maj Gen Trenchard shows them around. They also watch some flying arranged for them.

17 November: Rain 2mm. 37°–25°; clear day. Further advances on the Ancre.

18 November: Rain 8mm. 54°–36°. The British advance north and south of the Ancre and reach the outskirts of Grandcourt. The operations end and the Battle of the Somme is over.

Sketch 49.

THE SOMME, 1916: The end of the Battle.

THIRD.

VII. 49.

2 GD. R.

Hannescamps

Esserts

Courcelles

Ervillers

Mory

Vraucourt

Fonquevillers

Ablainzevelle

Gommécourt

Béhagnies

Vaulx

ARMY BDY.

Gommécourt

1. B. DU BIEZ

Bucquoy

LOGEAST WD.

XIV R.

Achiet le Gd.

Sapignies

Beugnâtre

FIRST.

Hébuterne

Achiet le Pt.

Bihucourt

Favreuil

Sailly

40.

52.

Puisieux

Biefvillers

Bapaume

Beugny

CAMBRAI 14 m.

XIII.

31.

Serre

Irles

Grévillers

GD. R.

Bancourt

Fremicourt

Colincamps

3.

208.

Miraumont

Pys

LOUPART WD.

Thilloy

Ligny

Riencourt

Haplincourt

Villers au Flos

Barastre

Beaumont Hamel

ANCRE

Grandcourt

Warlencourt

le Barque

BUTTE

4 GD.

Auchonvillers

Mailly

32. 37.

Beaucourt

223.

58.

I GD. R.

Beaulencourt

le Transloy

Rocquigny

St. Pierre Divion

18.

4 CDN.

le Sars

48.

23 R.

Gueudecourt

24 R.

Hamel

19.

Courcelette

Eaucourt

I.

L'Abbaye

2 AUS.

Englebelmer

Mesnil

II.

Thiepval

Martinpuich

III.

4 AUS.

GDS.

Lesbœufs

222.

XV.

Martinsart

AVELUY WD.

Authuille

Pozières

ANZAC.

Flers

29.

18.

17.

30.

Sailly

DOULLENS 14 m.

Bouzincourt

Ovillers

HIGH WD.

XIV.

DELVILLE WD.

Morval

IX.

39.

Saillisel

la Boisselle

Contalmaison

Bazentin le Pt.

Bazentin le Gd.

Longueval

Ginchy

BOULEAUX WD.

XX.

185.

ST. PIERRE VAAST WD.

MAMETZ WD.

Guillemont

LEUZE WD.

153.

16 R.

ALBERT

Bécourt

Fricourt

WILLOW STREAM

BERNAFAY WD.

Montauban

TRÔNES WD.

Combles

Rancourt

III.

AMIENS 14 m.

Bécordel

Mametz

Hardecourt

Maurepas

le Forest

Bouchavesnes

VR.

32.

Millencourt

ON 1ST JULY.

SIXTH.

VI.

Dernancourt

Méaulte

Carnoy

Maricourt

56.

Buire

ANCRE

Curlu

Cléry

12.

Morlancourt

Vaux

Hem

SOMME

Omiécourt

29.

PÉRONNE

Line at end of Battle.

British – Red.

Bray

Suzanne

Frise

Feuillères CANAL

Halle (SECOND)

French – Blue.

Germans – Green.

Etinehem

SOMME

Cappy

TENTH.

Herbécourt

Flaucourt

23.

XII.

Biaches

24.

Compiled in the Historical Section (Military Branch).
3060/38.

Ordnance Survey 1937.

Scale of Miles.

½ 0 1 2 3 4 5

Crown Copyright Reserved

A

ABBEVILLE is a town near the mouth of the River Somme on the main road between Boulogne and Paris. Although nowhere near the front line during the war, it nevertheless played a very important role as the headquarters of the British lines of communication, and supplies for the British sector arrived here via Saint-Valery. Three hospitals operated from there between 1915 and 1919, including No. 2 Stationary Hospital. Although the railway station was built 2 years before the war it is known as the Gare des Anglais because of its later links with the British Army.

On 24 August 1916, CXC Brigade, Royal Field Artillery (41st Division), arrived in the town and were billeted at l'Etoile. For the next 6 days they carried out various exercises and on 31 August took part in a divisional horse show. On the same day, Lt Col C.E. Stewart journeyed to the Somme battlefields, where he inspected battery positions. While doing so, he was killed and his orderly officer wounded. The news of this tragedy arrived at l'Etoile at midnight and Maj Wickham was sent to take over temporary command, as CXC Brigade were due to move up to the lines.

Abbeville Communal Cemetery is on high ground overlooking the town from the north: it contains six plots and includes burials from November 1914 to 1919. In July 1916, by agreement with the town authorities, it was decided to set up the Abbeville Communal Cemetery Extension. Lance Cpl. L.J. Keyworth who gained a VC at Givenchy on 25/26 May 1915 and who died of wounds in Abbeville is buried here III C 2. The cemetery therefore has casualties from this date and includes the graves of 12 members of Queen Mary's Army Auxiliary Corps, 9 of whom were killed during an air raid on 30 May 1918.

ACHEUX-EN-AMIÉNOIS is a village on the main road between ALBERT and DOULLENS, the D938, between FORCEVILLE and LOUVENCOURT. On 13 October 1915, Gen Sir Charles Monro, General Officer Commanding Third Army, inspected 1st Royal Dublin Fusiliers (86th Brigade, 29th Division), who were billeted here, in the grounds of the château. A week later, HM the King and M. Raymond Poincaré, the French President, inspected several units of VII Corps in the village. In January 1916, 1/6th and 1/5th Seaforth Highlanders (both of 152nd Brigade, 51st Division) were billeted in the village when they were carrying out work in the construction of a new railway cutting in the adjacent village of LÉALVILLERS. The pre-war light railway line took 'sitting cases' to GÉZAINCOURT.

In early February 1916, 36th Division established their headquarters in the village and VIII Corps Collecting Station arrived here in readiness for the start of the Battle of the Somme. The existing light railway from Acheux-en-Amiénois and its spur of a field 60cm system had been taken over from the French, in preparation for the dumping of vital materials. One line ran from MARTINSART through AVELUY WOOD to the north-east corner of Thiepval Wood and the other ran through the same wood to AUTHUILLE. Acheux-en-Amiénois became one of the principal railheads to be used by Fourth Army for supplies, engineering stores and for the collection of walking wounded, as well as a station for ambulance trains.

The 2nd Duke of Wellington's (12th Brigade, 4th Division) were engaged in fatigues on the new railway line here while it was snowing, conditions that 'kept all ranks fit'. For most of the same month, 89th Field Ambulance (29th Division) were carrying out work in the hospital here, which occupied the outbuildings of a convent in the rue de Bertrancourt. Their billeting accommodation was in farm buildings, which were 'very dirty'. The local school is close by and the large château and church are near neighbours at the end of the road. Much of this area, including the Hôtel de Ville, was relatively unscathed by the war. Also in February 1916, No. 121 Field Company, Royal Engineers (36th Division), were erecting baths in the village, in the large buildings of the sugar refinery on the VARENNES road, close to the railway station. This site, which was up for sale in October 2004, was considered for use as a hospital at the end of May 1916, but after the village was heavily shelled it was decided that this would not be prudent.

On 25 April 1916, Lt Gen Sir A.G. Hunter-Weston, General Officer Commanding VIII Corps, addressed the 2 officers and 89 men from 29th Division who had taken part in the Helles landings in the Dardanelles with him on 25 April 1915.

Acheux-en-Amiénois was the site of 29th Division's casualty clearing station, as well as divisional headquarters, at the beginning of the battle. South of the village was the site of No. 3 Casualty Clearing Station, close to the broad-gauge railway at VARENNES. It consisted of a large number of marquees close to the railway halt and was finished by 18 June, but was too far from the main Acheux-en-Amiénois railway station. On 27 June, when 110th Field Ambulance (36th Division) arrived from GÉZAINCOURT, 88 casualties were evacuated from here; at the end of June lying-down cases were evacuated to Nos. 29 and 49 Casualty Clearing Stations at GÉZAINCOURT. However, on 1 July the situation became chaotic; there was great congestion on the roads when the wounded were being brought in. The casualty clearing station became overwhelmed and 24 motor-buses were brought in to supplement the light railway which linked up with LOUVENCOURT and Vauchelles, and these were used for sitting cases only. By 2030hrs on 1 July, 124 lying and 997 sitting casualties had been evacuated. On 2 July, 1/3rd (South Midland) Field Ambulance (48th Division) were brought in to help out with the evacuation of the very large number of casualties being received. However, the situation gradually improved, and by 4 July the ambulance trains ceased to run from here, as they were no longer required.

After their disastrous involvement on the first day of the battle at BEAUMONT-HAMEL, 1st Lancashire Fusiliers (86th Brigade, 29th Division) returned to Acheux-en-Amiénois on 4 July. The village was also a rest camp for a battalion of the Border Regiment, and for 19th Northumberland Fusiliers (pioneers of 35th Division) who were in

huts in Acheux Wood on 5 July. On 8 July, 2nd King's Own Scottish Borderers (87th Brigade, 29th Division) also returned to Acheux-en-Amiénois.

In Acheux British Cemetery, designed by N.A. Rew, are the graves of men killed in July, August and September 1916. The field ambulance moved eastwards as the battle progressed and the cemetery was little used for the remainder of 1916. Towards the end of August, a battalion of the Duke of Wellington's Regiment were also here and 10th Essex (53rd Brigade, 18th Division) were in the wood, described as a 'pleasant beech wood', 7 miles west of THIEPVAL. However, towards the end of the month, the wood was described as having huts 'in a sea of mud connected by duckboard tracks together with abandoned railway platforms'. On 4 October, the Hood Battalion (63rd Division) arrived on their way to FORCEVILLE before being involved alongside 2nd Division in the ANCRE battle between 17 and 23 November.

In mid-November, Cpl Hellis of 1/22nd Londons (142nd Brigade, 47th Division) 'picked his way through the sombre wood in which stood the leaky, moss-grown, canvas-roofed shelters, through which ran a track of slippery narrow duckboards over a perfectly ink-like quagmire'.

Men of the Army Ordnance Corps play cards on a dump of trench mortar ammunition, known as 'Toffee Apples', Acheux-en-Amiénois, July 1916. *(IWM Q1375)*

Acheux British Cemetery, to the north-east of the former railway halt, contains the grave of 1 man who died prior to the battle and 42 from the battle itself; the remainder are of men who died in 1918. The 18-month gap between the burial dates reflects the period when the cemetery was not used. Pte W.B. Nelson (I.B.8) of 14th Durham Light Infantry (18th Brigade, 6th Division) was 'shot at dawn' on 11 August 1916.

In recent years a supermarket has been built close to the cemetery and the former railway line has been turned into a footpath. Unsurprisingly, there is no trace of the original Léalvillers Halt, but the fields between the cemetery and the halt would have been the ones containing the marquees of the casualty clearing station.

AILLY-SUR-SOMME, north-west of AMIENS on the south side of the River Somme, was a small manufacturing town prior to the First World War. 36th Division were billeted in this area and in RUBEMPRÉ and VIGNACOURT, between 5 and 8 October 1915 and 32nd Division had their headquarters here on 22 November. On 2 February 1916, 146th Brigade (49th Division) arrived here, having detrained at LONGUEAU near AMIENS. Already tired on arrival, when they reached the village they found their billets scattered over a wide area. 1/5th and 1/6th West Yorkshires (both of 146th Brigade, 49th Division) were billeted in the town itself and two other battalions stayed in FOURDRINOY, PICQUIGNY and BREILLY. There were good baths to be had in a factory on the Ailly-sur-Somme–Dreuil-lès-Amiens road (later the N235) as well as laundry facilities. In Ailly-sur-Somme itself there were at least 20 private houses, as well as several *estaminets* where 'egg and chips', together with coffee, could be obtained cheaply. The men of 1/6th West Yorkshires, according to the battalion history, appeared to have been 'favourably impressed' with their time in the area. On 10 February, 49th Division began to move up towards the line; travelling through heavy rain via MARTINSART and RUBEMPRÉ, by the time 146th Brigade reached MARTINSART on 11 February, everyone was soaked to the skin.

On 27 February, 169th Brigade (56th Division) arrived in Ailly-sur-Somme from HUPPY in bad weather, when the roads had been covered in snow. Three companies of 1/16th Londons (169th Brigade, 56th Division) were billeted in barns and one in school buildings until 12 March, when 169th Brigade left for the FIENVILLERS–GÉZAINCOURT area to the south-west of DOULLENS. In mid-April, two

companies from 2nd Wiltshires (21st Brigade, 30th Division) came here from PICQUIGNY to assist the Royal Engineers.

On 25 June, 1st Sherwood Foresters (24th Brigade, 23rd Division) arrived here, staying until 30 June, when they marched to RAINNEVILLE, north-east of AMIENS. Next day they marched 12 miles to Hénencourt Wood, where they remained for 3 days and heard the 'good news' of the Allied attacks.

Units of 21st Division, including 63rd Field Ambulance, were here on 10 July 1916, when the actual village was out of bounds. Men resting on the banks of the river stripped off and many swam in the River Somme: races were even organised. While this was going on, groups of French girls emerged from Ailly-sur-Somme and approached the naked men, offering to sell them chocolate and cake. It appeared the nakedness of the Tommies was forgotten by both parties. At 1630hrs, 63rd Field Ambulance packed up in motor ambulancies and left for CORBIE.

Ailly-sur-Somme Communal Cemetery includes the graves of three Allied soldiers, two of whom were buried in the children's plot.

ALBERT, known as 'Bert' to the Tommies, was the main town within the British sector of the battle area. Although it was mainly used as a billeting and supply town it was by no means automatically safe, as stray shells fell all the time, and there were many cases of newly settled troops being driven out by a sudden concentration of German shelling.

The town lies on the D929 main road, which leads straight in a north-easterly direction towards BAPAUME. It is north-east of AMIENS on the River Ancre and has a railway service on the main Paris, Lille, Arras and AMIENS line. During the war the main double line between AMIENS and Arras was available only as far as Albert, where it came under shell-fire.

In September 1914, Albert was held against the German advance by French troops and in January 1915 a bomb exploded at the foot of the dome of the famous Basilique Notre Dame de Brebières, whose 70m high tower was ornamented by a statue of the Virgin and the Infant Christ. The statue fell from its base and remained hanging at an angle of 45 degrees but was secured by French engineers. It was always said that its collapse would signal the end of the war. It became, along with the Angels of Mons, one of the most famous symbols of the First World War. It finally fell in April 1918 when targeted by British artillery, during a time when the enemy was using the building as an observation post. The town passed into British hands in the summer of 1915 and one of the first units to be billeted here, in the brewery, was No. 404 Field Company, Royal Engineers (51st Division).

On 21 August 1915, 1/6th Seaforth Highlanders (152nd Brigade, 51st Division), in reserve while the rest of 152nd Brigade was holding the trenches around LA BOISSELLE and BÉCOURT, moved up to billets in the town. Albert was not shelled much during this period and battalion headquarters was in a large château (Villers Rochers) with an excellent garden. The house was later used by Lt Gen The Hon. Sir Julian Byng when he was General Officer Commanding Third Army.

On 16 September 1915, 6th Royal Berkshires (53rd Brigade, 18th Division) came to Albert and took over trenches opposite LA BOISSELLE, with another battalion from 53rd Brigade to their left and one from 55th Brigade to their right. In October, 56th Field Ambulance (18th Division) ran an advanced dressing station in three large cellars in the town. When 90th Field Ambulance (32nd Division) were in an advanced dressing station in the town at the end of March 1916, a new collecting post was set up at 72 rue de la Fontaine, which replaced the one in the rue de Bapaume.

Long before the opening of the Somme battle, there was a great deal of mining activity in the LA BOISSELLE area, and many craters were from holes created by the explosion of mines. 6th Royal Berkshires were in and out of the line for the rest of the month, with rest periods at Albert.

There are very many references to Albert in memoirs and military histories and it would be appropriate to mention just a few. Firstly and appropriately, it featured in one of Henry Williamson's autobiographical novels, *The Golden Virgin*. The main character, Phillip Maddison, is an officer with 8th (Service) Battalion of the 'Prince Regent's Own Regiment'. Of the period around 11 June 1916, Williamson wrote: 'The British Front line lay upon a plateau one hundred metres above sea level. It faced the German lines on the slope, rising imperceptibly it passed through the two fortified villages of Ovillers and La Boisselle, to the horizon of one hundred and forty metres.' Maj Kingman's headquarters was in the support trenches, 600yds behind the firing line, at the crossroads known as Ovillers Post.

In late June 1916, 101st Brigade (34th Division) had its headquarters in Villers Rochers, which was described as 'a palatial billet'. At the same time, a battalion of 102nd Brigade (34th Division) occupied the 'cavernous garden'. A dressing station was set up in the Ecole Supérieur, and on 25 June two Royal

Army Medical Corps officers were killed by a shell and other men wounded. Both belonged to 104th Field Ambulance (34th Division) and were later buried in Albert Communal Cemetery Extension. At the end of June, a temporary casualty clearing station was set up by 2nd Field Ambulance (8th Division) at a place known as North Chimney.

III Corps established a main dressing station at Albert, which at the beginning of July also possessed a walking wounded post. A broad-gauge railway line was established between Albert and LONGUEAU (outside AMIENS), with a 12in howitzer in a cutting to the north of Albert railway station. When the Somme battle began, 19th Division were in reserve to the south-west of the town, while 34th Division were concentrating in the attacks towards LA BOISSELLE. The battle was a disaster for 34th Division, which attacked along the Albert–BAPAUME road. The village did not fall until 4 July, when it was captured by 19th Division.

In Albert's Moulin de Vivier hospital, the wounded began to come in at 1015hrs on 1 July; for some time motor ambulances were unable to reach the advanced dressing station because of British artillery fire across the road. Casualties had therefore to be carried over long distances. Many of the 21st Division casualties were picked up later by cars from 34th Division as the 21st Division cars did not travel close enough to the lines. Walking cases were sent to the divisional clearing station at DERNANCOURT and light cases sent there by horse transport. Tramways were also used for the collection of wounded; a tram truck held four stretcher cases. Casualties came down the trench known as Northumberland Avenue, although it was frequently blocked by troops going up the line to a field ambulance at Albert, which was choked by the number of wounded awaiting evacuation. The wounded arrived in far greater numbers than could be dealt with, which meant that two larger rooms in VIVIER MILL were also used and the courtyard was full of casualties, including wounded German prisoners of war. In addition, the number of cars was insufficient.

On 2 July the wounded were still coming in large numbers and the motor ambulances were now able to reach Bécourt Château, having used a different route from the previous day. Motor lorries were also used for transporting the wounded when the vehicles were well stocked with paliasses. Most of the wounded had been hit on 1 July and many

The ruined tower of Albert's Basilica, September 1916. *(IWM Q855)*

now came in suffering from gas gangrene. With the assistance of a German medical officer, the Germans awaiting treatment were housed in one room in the mill, where their own medical personnel treated them. On 4 July the flow of wounded at last began to slow, but sadly, cases of gas gangrene began to increase.

In his book *Three Years with the 9th Division*, W.D. Croft, formerly General Officer Commanding 27th Brigade (9th Division), mentioned that his brigade had arrived at Albert from MILLENCOURT on 4 July and then went on to Bécourt Wood, where they bivouacked. They later became involved in the fighting for the village of CONTALMAISON.

On 10 July, 57th Field Ambulance (34th Division) took over the civil hospital in the town when the 'commodious building' was occupied by the infantry; 6in howitzers were in the garden.

In *The 11th Royal Warwicks in France, 1915–16*, C.S. Collison wrote that on 16 July his battalion returned to Albert, where they were billeted near the wrecked railway station. Here they rested on 17 July, but at midnight were ordered to the trench system called Heligoland in the former German line south-east of LA BOISSELLE, as support to 68th Brigade, which was said to be about to attack POZIÈRES.

From 17–19 July, 1/5th Royal Warwicks (143rd Brigade, 48th Division) were at the Red House in bivouac at Albert. Charles Carrington, author of *Soldier from the Wars Returning* and a member of that battalion, was probably there at the time. On 19 July, Croft's 27th Brigade were relieved by an Australian brigade and returned to Albert, arriving there at 0400hrs on 20 July. On 23 July, 2nd King's Royal Rifle Corps (2nd Brigade, 1st Division) marched back to Albert from SCOTTS REDOUBT, where they remained for 2 or 3 days. In *And All For What?* D.W.J. Cuddeford of 12th Highland Light Infantry (46th Brigade, 15th Division) mentions detraining at Albert.

In August 1916, the back area around Albert presented a striking appearance; every hillside and hollow was marked by bivouacs and camps, bands played, bugles sounded, troops drilled, there were machine-gun and rifle ranges, bombing pitches, and bayonet courses, the roads were black with the endless lines of horses, motor lorries, cars, troops, railways and metre tracks, carrying loads of ammunition and materials among which gangs of prisoners worked, unceasingly, on road repairs, while overhead an endless procession of aeroplanes buzzed to and fro.

In the period 13/14 August, 6th Northamptons (54th Brigade, 18th Division) were at Maxse's

Convoy on a road near Albert, July 1916. *(IWM Q849)*

Redoubt, just east of Albert. On 20 September, 2nd King's Royal Rifle Corps moved to BLACK WOOD nearby from LOZENGE WOOD. Cuddeford wrote that at the end of September, after the capture of MARTINPUICH, 12th Highland Light Infantry spent one night in MAMETZ WOOD and then rejoined the transport at Albert before marching to FRANVILLERS. Brigade reserve were then in Albert, having been transferred from LAHOUSSOYE. They were back in Albert again in mid-October, probably after action at Prue Trench. In the history of 2/5th Glosters (184th Brigade, 61st Division), A.F. Barnes wrote that the battalion, to which the poet Ivor Gurney belonged, had arrived at Albert on 20 November from Robecq, where they had been since 27 October. They spent one night there; Barnes described the weather as being very wet and reported the battlefields as being in a deplorable state. On the following day they met their guides, who led them to the front line at GRANDCOURT at Tullock's Corner.

Albert was recaptured by the Germans in their great advance of March 1918, but the British took it back from them 5 months later.

Albert Communal Cemetery is on the south-east side of the town, at the junction of the roads to FRICOURT and MÉAULTE. Albert Communal Cemetery has the graves of 201 men who died prior to 1 July 1916. An Extension was used by fighting units and field ambulances from August 1915 to November 1916, more particularly in and after November 1916, when field ambulances were concentrated here. No. 2 Field Company, Australian Engineers (1st Australian Division), and 29th, 73rd and 102nd Canadian Battalions erected wooden memorials to their dead in the Extension.

Two officers of the Royal Army Medical Corps serving with 104th Field Ambulance (34th Division), both killed on 25 June 1916, are buried here. Capt K.H.A. Kellie (I.H.10) and Lt J.B. Haverson (I.H.11) were killed by enemy shelling while working in a dressing station in Albert. This cemetery has the graves of two men 'shot at dawn', Pioneer E. Beeby (I.R.43) of No. 212 Company, Royal Engineers (33rd Division), executed for desertion on 9 December 1916, and Pte H. Palmer (I.P.65) of 1/5th Northumberland Fusiliers (149th Brigade, 50th Division), executed for desertion on 27 October

1916. Other graves include those of Brig Gen H.F.H. Clifford DSO (I.L.1), General Officer Commanding 149th Brigade (50th Division), who was shot by a sniper in HIGH WOOD on 11 September 1916 when 'inspecting trenches near Mametz Wood' when in charge of his brigade, and Brig Gen R. Barnett-Barker, killed in action in March 1918.

Albert French National Cemetery is about ½ mile out of the town, on the north side of the FRICOURT road.

In the early 1930s Will R. Bird of 42nd Canadian Battalion (7th Canadian Brigade, 3rd Canadian Division), author of *Thirteen Years After*, wrote of Albert: 'It is all very modern . . . and Albert sees a multitude of tourists. Here and there we spot the old ruins, but the Grande Place and its Hôtel de Ville are most imposing . . .'. He saw most of the wreckage of war in the area close to the brand-new railway station.

Vera Brittain visited the town in 1921 and 1933. In her first visit she remembered it

as a humped ruin of stones and dust, with a few huts of reconstruction workers dotted here and there. Now a clean, bright, new town, though considerably smaller than the original, which was, our chauffeur said, the Coventry of France, and made bicycles and machinery. Now makes aeroplanes at the factory of Potez – one of the best in Northern France, which employs workers from all parts. . . .

During her 1933 visit Brittain lunched at the Hôtel de la Paix; the owner, an Italian, had fought on the Italian front and later became a waiter in France.

There is a Memorial to the Machine Gun Corps on the front of the Hôtel de Ville building in the centre of the town, which was set up by the Machine Gun Corps Old Comrades' Association and unveiled by Lt Col G.S. Hutchison at Easter 1939. The clock in the same building was presented to the town by the city of Birmingham, which adopted Albert after the war. The chimes are a replica of those of London's Big Ben.

Since the Second World War, a large and extensive museum called the Musée des Abris (*abris* means shelter) was set up in the mid-1980s below the main square in Albert, making use of the tunnels beneath it, some of which date back to medieval times, although they do not appear to have been used during 1916. The museum examines the Battle of the Somme through the use of life-size reconstructions of trenches, dugouts and positions; there are many maps and photographs as well as a large array of battefield relics on display. The basilica close by, which was only completed in 1900, had already been rebuilt by

1933; it can be climbed by arrangement with the local tourist office, and on a clear day the ascent is strongly recommended. In recent years, Albert has once more become a thriving town, benefitting in particular from the local tourist industry and the British obsession with the Battle of the Somme.

ALLONVILLE is a village to the north of the AMIENS–ALBERT road (the D929) and west of QUERRIEU. At the end of November 1915, 14th Royal Warwicks (at this time 95th Brigade, 32nd Division) were here briefly for billeting purposes, but the village was found to be unsuitable and so they moved on to PONT-NOYELLES. 14th Field Ambulance (5th Division) were here on 30 January 1916.

Although the walls of the former château are still clearly in place, there is little left of what was once used as a corps rest station. According to the book *Via Ypres*, in 1916 the hunting château was turned into a modern hospital, the work beginning 'with scrubbing of the floors'. The shooting box belonged to the Hennessey Three-Star Brandy family. The grounds and woods were turned into a convalescent camp and sick officers had rooms in the château. Units of 5th Division were billeted in the area 6–8 February; 14th Field Ambulance opened a dressing station in the château and one of their first cases was that of an officer of the Royal Flying Corps, who was brought here on 13 February and later taken to Wimille for burial. The château was possibly destroyed by German artillery fire in May 1940.

On 15 February 1916, 56th Field Ambulance (18th Division) took over the hospital from 14th Field Ambulance, only to be replaced in turn by 91st Field Ambulance (32nd Division) at the end of the month. On 4 March, 91st Field Ambulance left for BAIZIEUX, where they occupied a farmhouse. On 14 March, 56th Field Ambulance returned here, subsequently being replaced by 97th Field Ambulance (30th Division). On 18 March, 97th Field Ambulance took over the dressing station, and at the same time lent men to units of the Royal Engineers, who were carrying out work in the nearby forest. The Royal Flying Corps shared the village with the Army for a time; No. 9 Squadron, commanded by Maj A.B. Burdett, was based here from March to May 1916 and No. 34 Squadron, commanded by Maj J.A. Chamier, was based in the village from July 1916 until February 1917.

On 1 April 1916, 4th Middlesex and 8th Somerset Light Infantry (both of 63rd Brigade, 21st Division) detrained on the outskirts of AMIENS, at LONGPRÉ-LES-CORPS-SAINTS and LONGUEAU respectively, and marched the 7 miles to Allonville, which was then about 12 miles from the front line. They considered Allonville to be a clean and healthy little village with well-cultivated country around it, and spent a week in this 'delectable spot'.

On 2 April, 64th Field Ambulance (21st Division) were here, but they found their billets to be very bad, as well as small. The officers had the use of an old dairy house. At some point, 70th Field Ambulance (23rd Division) had their horse-lines in the château park.

On 30 April, 63rd Field Ambulance (21st Division) took over the corps rest station, having come from LA NEUVILLE; at the time of its arrival, the local church bells were ringing for Mass. As they left the village on 24 June, their new brass band caused a sensation as they passed through French villages on their way to BUIRE-SUR-L'ANCRE.

On 11 June, 17th Division's headquarters was in Allonville, together with its 51st Brigade. On 13 June, the division's 51st Field Ambulance were here and on 21 June, 22nd Field Ambulance (7th Division) left the village for MORLANCOURT. On 29 June, the divisional rest station was taken over by 69th Field Ambulance (23rd Division), when the village was home to 68th Brigade.

In mid-July, during the course of the battle, the cavalry had an advanced dressing station at Allonville. No. 39 Casualty Clearing Station was in the village from 31 July 1916 to 12 February 1917. At the end of the battle, a casualty clearing station was still in the village, and was used for cases of disease rather than battle wounds.

At the other end of the village from the château, Allonville Communal Cemetery has the graves of 78 men from the First World War and one airman from the Second World War. The First World War dead include 38 British and 40 Australians, the latter mainly from 14th Australian Battalion (4th Australian Brigade, 4th Australian Division), who died between August 1916 and January 1917 and from January 1918 to January 1919. Twenty-seven casualties date from the Battle of the Somme itself.

AMIENS was virtually the capital of the area behind the British and French lines. For a short period in August 1914 it served as a part of the British Advanced Base; captured by the Germans on 31 August, it was quickly retaken by the French 3 days later. In March 1918 the Germans failed to reach Amiens and in August that year the Allied counter-offensive then began.

German troops entering Amiens, August 1914.
(Peter F. Batchelor Collection)

Amiens is world famous for its Gothic cathedral, which has several memorials in it to the various Allied countries involved in the battle. There is also a memorial designed by Eric Gill to Lt Raymond Asquith, the prime minister's son, killed on 15 September 1916 when serving with 3rd Grenadier Guards (2nd Guards Brigade, Guards Division). The wording of the tablet (1922) was written by Raymond's widow Katherine with the assistance of Hilaire Belloc. A tablet (1921) to her brother, Edward Horner, also by Gill, is in Cambrai Cathedral close to one to Belloc's son, Louis.

Fourth Army headquarters was not far away, at QUERRIEU, on the D929 road; Basil Liddell Hart described the area between Amiens and Rouen as having about 3 miles of railway sidings, forming a huge distribution centre for Fourth Army.

On 5 August 1915, No. 1/1 (South Midland) Casualty Clearing Station transferred to a hospital here, and on 28 August began to prepare a hospital at the Lycée; they were here for much of the following year.

At the end of June 1916, Amiens was out of bounds to military personnel who did not have a special pass. At the time, the city appeared to be prosperous and carrying on quite normally. Several memoir-writers note that the ladies of fashion were much admired by British troops and that the city's restaurants and the red-light district did a very good trade.

At the beginning of the battle, the Assistant Directorate of Railway Transport was based at Amiens, and the Director of Medical Services of Fourth Army was in direct contact with him regarding the number of trains needed for transporting casualties. Unsurprisingly, these were initially too few, because the Director of Medical Services failed to estimate the demand accurately. As a backlog of wounded built up from 2 July, barges moored in the town were used in order to ease the situation.

Amiens was a favourite town of the Royal Flying Corps, who were able to visit its restaurants more frequently than the Army, although Siegfried Sassoon took some time off from the fighting and dined with friends at the Godbert Restaurant on 7 July; his companions included the prototype of Julian Durley, who appears in Sassoon's *Memoirs of an Infantry Officer*. They were often joined by members of the Press Corps, who were staying at the Hôtel du Rhin.

C.E. Montague, the journalist, who had enlisted in his forties and who, after a bomb mishap, had been awarded a commission and had left for France on 10 July, became an Intelligence Officer attached to GHQ. Montague was quartered in Amiens with Lt Col A.N. Lee, who was there to supervise the Press Corps. One of Lee's main duties was to conduct distinguished visitors around the front. The

visitors included J.M. Barrie, George Bernard Shaw, H.G. Wells, John Masefield, Muirhead Bone and Frances Dodd. Bone was the first official war artist at the front, and he met Montague in August 1916, possibly for the first time. Neville Lytton, a liaison officer who had formerly been a colleague of Edmund Blunden in 11th Royal Sussex, was summoned to an interview with Brig Gen J. Charteris, Haig's Brigadier General, General Staff (Intelligence), at Advanced Headquarters near DOULLENS. Lytton subsequently became a major and was sent to Amiens to learn press censorship, the main idea presumably being not to allow information to appear in the Allied press which would be of benefit to the German cause, and also, one imagines, to put the British Army in the best light. Although the war correspondent Philip Gibbs complained about restrictions, he didn't go into great detail as to what form this censorship took.

In mid-July 1916, 33rd Division were in the Amiens area. During the battle, patients at No. 1/1 (South Midland) Casualty Clearing Station had to be taken by ambulance car for entraining at LONGUEAU, to the south-east of Amiens, and from BEAUVAL and the CITADEL to GÉZAINCOURT. No. 1/1 Casualty Clearing Station then moved to VECQUEMONT, south-west of CORBIE. At one time, a motor ambulance convoy was parked on the Amiens–ALBERT road, but it was moved on to LAVIÉVILLE. At the end of the battle, a stationary hospital in Amiens had been taken over by the New Zealanders. Casualties transported by canal were often taken to ABBEVILLE.

On 8 September the Australian Official Historian, C.E.W. Bean, left Amiens for Calais, arriving in the United Kingdom on 10 September. When he returned to the Somme front, he escorted, among others, the Australian Prime Minister, William Hughes, and Keith Murdoch, the famous Australian journalist and father of the newspaper tycoon Rupert Murdoch.

In his autobiography, H.L.N. Dundas refers to being in a training area with 1st Scots Guards (2nd Guards Brigade, Guards Division) to the south-west of Amiens on 2 October. On 19 October, 10th King's Royal Rifle Corps (59th Brigade, 20th Division) were north of Amiens at CARDONNETTE. In *An Infant in Arms*, Graham Greenwell of 1/4th Oxfordshire & Buckinghamshire Light Infantry (145th Brigade, 48th Division) wrote that he was in a 'wretched village' full of Royal Flying Corps personnel, and that motor lorries were never silent. He was hoping to get a lift into Amiens if he stayed in the area long enough. He describes the roads as being ankle-deep in mud.

Although he did not take part in the 1916 fighting, the writer Dennis Wheatley did visit Amiens several times in 1917; in his autobiography he mentions the Salon Godbert as being the best restaurant, although there were others such as du Cathédral and the Hôtel du Rhin:

> In peacetime the latter had only a small restaurant but behind it a large Assembly Room where the richer citizens held wedding receptions, coming out and anniversary parties etc. During the war the whole big area was a restaurant with several scores of tables. I never saw a woman there but every night it was packed with British officers. The food was excellent and we had money to burn. All the main streets were crowded with figures in khaki and French girls plying a lucrative trade . . .

Wheatley returned to the Salon Godbert after the March 1918 retreat, only to find the place empty, the diners obviously having left in a hurry. The tables and kitchens had been left and food had become rotten. Just one man was there, who invited Wheatley in to have a look for himself.

In the 1920s, the *Ypres Times* ran a sort of tourist office-cum-battlefield guide arrangement, managed by a Capt Stuart Oswald. His file at The National Archives shows that he was a motor engineer and insurance broker. He served with transport during the war and was demobilised in France on 18 May 1920, when his address was 33 rue Charles Dubois, Amiens. Oswald was not alone in helping pilgrims to visit the battlefields, and his association with transport was probably very useful. Will R. Bird of 42nd Canadian Battalion (7th Canadian Brigade, 3rd Canadian Division), author of *Thirteen Years After*, said that Oswald's office was 'where you can hire cars with English drivers, and he sells a splendid map of all the Somme territory. In addition he is a most pleasant person, very eager to help whether there be profit or not . . .' Bird also talks of a hotel run by an Australian: 'It is a harum-scarum place in the evenings, with shouting and singing and much merriment and wild women . . .'

Just outside Amiens on the ALBERT road is a large civilian cemetery with 676 British graves dating from the 1915–18 fighting. In early September 1916 it was decided that the new cemetery at Saint-Pierre should be used solely for the burials of British casualties, including those patients who died at No. 1/1 (South Midland) Casualty Clearing Station, close to a railway line to the south-east of Amiens.

It may be just a good story, but rumour has it that during the First World War Amiens was saved from destruction by German artillery by the then Pope, Benedict XV, who had a word with the Kaiser, who had a word with his gunners. However, no similar conversation seems to have taken place in the early 1940s with either Göring or Hitler, when the Luftwaffe bombed the famous city. The German Army took the town on 18 May 1940, the main bombing targets being the station and marshalling yards at LONGUEAU and the area opposite the Gare du Nord, which was devastated first by the Germans and later by the RAF. According to a document in the Imperial War Museum (IWM 29/6 (442.6)), no fewer than 10,300 houses were destroyed in Amiens during the Second World War, many of them timber buildings. However, the cathedral and the famous belfry both survived.

Saint-Pierre Cemetery in the northern part of Amiens was probably once on the edge of the town, but is now surrounded by housing and showrooms. It shares grounds with Amiens Communal Cemetery; the layout of the graves at the back of the cemetery is mainly chronological, beginning in September 1915 and ending in October 1919, but shortly afterwards 33 more casualties from 1918 were brought in. The cemetery was designed by Sir Edwin Lutyens.

Saint-Acheul French National Cemetery is in the south-east quarter of Amiens, south of the main road to LONGUEAU. There is a British plot of 12 graves, of which 11 men were buried between August 1914 and August 1915 and one man from 1918. La Madeleine, a third town cemetery to the north-west of the city on the ARGŒUVES road, has one British war grave.

In the early 1920s, according to records held in the archive of the Commonwealth War Graves Commission, there was a scheme to erect a memorial in Amiens to 50,000 of the Missing from the German offensives in Picardy in early 1918, an idea which was later transferred to POZIÈRES. Another scheme was a joint Anglo-French memorial to be built at Amiens, which would honour the dead from both nations. It was to take the form of a sanctuary in the shape of a 'pantheon', which would have side chapels dedicated to particular divisions. The initial plan was to include the names of those men killed in the Somme battle on the walls, but with so many names to cope with, the plan was altered to include them in 'golden books' kept in the chapels. The design would be by a French architect. Although the British committee included Lord Derby, Earl Haig, Lord Balfour, Lord Milner, Herbert Asquith and others, the idea was later abandoned.

At a ceremony on 10 July 1921, the Croix de Guerre was awarded to representatives of 340 communes of the Somme, 'in recognition of the valour, self-sacrifice, and endurance displayed by their inhabitants during the war'. Guests at the ceremony included the French Marshal Foch and Lt Gen the Earl of Cavan, in 1916 General Officer Commanding XIV Corps, who represented the British government. The ceremonies began with a wreath-laying at the British and French cemeteries at Saint-Pierre. Later Lord Cavan had the honour of decorating the Somme communes, and expressed his joy at seeing children from the villages that the British Army had defended during the hostilities.

On 22 May 1923 a tour for 350 British schoolboys was organised, to allow them to pay a visit to the French battlefields. Half of the group were based in Amiens, where they occupied school buildings during the Whitsun holidays. The boys visited ALBERT; a party from Eastbourne had a special interest in visiting BRAY-SUR-SOMME because the town had been adopted by the Sussex town. BRAY-SUR-SOMME was decorated in their honour and the boys were made very welcome by the French children. After visiting some of the British cemeteries in the area, they were entertained to luncheon by the mayor and in the evening, when back in Amiens, were guests of honour of the town council. On 9 July 1923, HRH the Duke of Connaught unveiled a commemorative tablet in Amiens' famous Notre Dame Cathedral.

Following her visit to the cathedral on 4 August 1933, Vera Brittain implied in her journals, when she noticed some windows in one of the chapels boarded up, that the windows had been destroyed during the war. The windows were in fact removed at the very start of hostilities in 1914 by firemen from Paris, who took them to a place of safety. In addition, Brittain was puzzled by the relative lack of links with the role of British forces during the war, as opposed to those of the Dominion countries.

Since 1945 Amiens has once more become a thriving town; its cathedral, France's largest Gothic edifice, lovingly restored with much of the cost borne by the European Community, was added to the list of Unesco's World Heritage Sites in 1981. The West Façade in particular has received expert attention.

The famous floating water gardens known as the Hortillonnages 'cover 300 hectares of small islands and are criss-crossed by 55 km of canals . . .' It was during a boat trip in Amiens in the early 1990s that the novelist Sebastian Faulks was inspired to write *Birdsong*, his bestselling 1993 novel featuring the war and its later effects on survivors and their descendants between 1910 and 1979.

ANCRE VALLEY The River Ancre ran south-westwards from the direction of BAPAUME through the German lines and then divided the Allied line between HAMEL and THIEPVAL. During the war the river became choked with weeds, which if not dealt with threatened to lead to the river breaking its banks and the subsequent flooding of the valley. According to a document in The National Archives (WO 95/1695), found with the papers of 8th Division. By early May 1916 the water level in one place was already 'flushed with the top of the banks', while in other places the banks were leaking badly. The town major in ALBERT had discussed the possibility of the valley flooding with M. Julien, a councillor at Aveluy who had 22 years' experience of the river. He told the British that, prior to the war, several men were employed to cut the weeds and to repair the banks of the river. The valley was often visited by people going for carriage drives on a Sunday afternoon.

Accordingly, measures were put in hand to reduce the water level of the river, including the clearance of 'debris such as barbed wire booms, old boats, etc.' and repair the leaks in the river banks. A permanent squad of engineers, assisted by two Frenchmen who lived in the village of DERNAN-COURT and who had worked on the river prior to the war, were employed in order to prevent any further flooding if possible.

As a result of the neglect of the river much of the valley had become very marshy. The river had several crossing points, of which the Germans were well aware. These included BLACK HORSE BRIDGE, Authuille Bridge, Passerelle de Magenta, North and South Causeways and Hamel Bridge. Passerelle and Hamel Bridge were both subjected to severe machine-gun fire in the period 30 June/1 July. On the opening day of the battle, 9th Royal Irish Fusiliers and 12th Royal Irish Rifles (both 108th Brigade, 36th Division) were caught by machine-gun fire from an emplacement on top of a shaft, which the Germans had reached by tunnelling into the railway embankment on the edge of the river valley.

On 16 October the Hood Battalion (63rd Division) reached the Knightsbridge Sector, west of HAMEL, and on 18 October were relieved by the Howe Battalion (63rd Division). The Hood Battalion's right flank boundary was the road that wound along the flooded valley towards BEAUCOURT-SUR-L'ANCRE. On 20 October the Howe Battalion were relieved by the Hawke Battalion (63rd Division) and left for dry barns in ENGELBELMER.

ANGLE WOOD was in the centre of a three-pronged ravine near MALTZ HORN FARM and FAFFEMONT FARM, to the south-west of the village of COMBLES. In mid-August 1916, the Germans held these positions in strength, and the Allied plan was for the French to take the north end of the Wood. Capt O. Horsley of 2nd Gordon Highlanders (20th Brigade, 7th Division) was awarded the Military Cross for an incident on 18 August, when he led the first line of advance and consolidated his objective. Though wounded, Horsley directed operations from a shell-hole until the position was safe. On 22 August, 17th Lancashire Fusiliers (104th Brigade, 35th Division) took over from the French a section of the line that consisted of a chain of advance posts in front of Angle Wood and support reserve lines.

In early September, 1/5th Londons (169th Brigade, 56th Division) were in reserve in this small valley, living in shelters cut into the hillside or in trenches in DEATH VALLEY. In early to mid-September, Farm Line was the headquarters of 1/2nd Londons (169th Brigade, 56th Division). On the evening of 13 September, 1/16th Londons (169th Brigade, 56th Division) were relieved by 1/5th Londons and moved back to Angle Wood Valley to reorganise.

In *Four Years on the Western Front*, Aubrey Smith of 1/5th Londons mentions taking the water carts to Angle Wood over a mile beyond DEATH VALLEY. Up the MONTAUBAN-DE-PICARDIE road there was a large dressing station with several motor ambulances outside it. The far slope of DEATH VALLEY was very steep and muddy and at one moment it seemed as if they would come to a standstill. Smith took water there on alternate days. Having been relieved by 1/9th Londons (169th Brigade, 56th Division) on the evening of 23 September, 1/16th Londons moved back to FAFFEMONT FARM and on 24 September went into divisional reserve in Casement Trench, just north of MARICOURT. Smith was involved in the attack of 25 September, when 168th Brigade (56th Division) stormed BOULEUX WOOD after waiting a couple of minutes while the 15in railway gun at MARICOURT prepared to fire.

ARGŒUVES is north-west of AMIENS, close to the N235 road. 71st Field Ambulance (23rd Division) were in the village at the end of June 1916, at the same time as a section of 70th Field Ambulance (23rd Division). During the night of 1/2 July, 129th Field Ambulance (38th Division) moved here, and on 10 July, 101st Field Ambulance (33rd Division) were also in the village. On 30 September, elements of 165th Brigade (55th Division) were billeted in the village. During the war, three Allied casualties were buried in Argœuves Communal Cemetery.

ARQUÈVES is north-east of AMIENS, between RAINCHEVAL and LÉALVILLERS. On 12 October 1915, Nos. 121, 122 and 150 Field Companies, Royal Engineers (all 36th Division) arrived here, having marched from AILLY-SUR-SOMME; on the following day No. 121 Field Company laid out a camp and dug latrines in the village. The engineers returned to the Arquèves area on 7 November 1915, when two sections were at Vauchelles to the north. On 21 October, part of No. 121 Field Company left for Domart-en-Ponthieu. On 13 October, No. 150 Field Company cleaned up billets; the company were still in the village in the first half of November, when the men were billeted in barns. At the time the weather was very bad and clothes never dried out properly.

On 4 April 1916, 88th Field Ambulance (29th Division) arrived in Arquèves, taking over the hospital in the eighteenth-century church and the divisional rest station from 1/1st (South Midland) Field Ambulance (48th Division); 88th Field Ambulance stayed in the village until mid-June. On 23 September 1916, elements of 148th Brigade (49th Division) were billeted here.

ARROW HEAD COPSE, east of TRÔNES WOOD and south of the D64 road to GUILLEMONT, was captured by the Allies by mid-July 1916. In *Field Guns in France*, Lt Col Neil Fraser-Tytler of CL Brigade, Royal Field Artillery (30th Division), wrote that when his signals line broke down at this time, he went alone up the trench with the idea of reaching Arrow Head Copse, which was about 400yds beyond the front line. When within 25yds he sensed it was unoccupied. At the far side of the copse he found himself almost behind the German trenches at MALTZ HORN FARM and could see 16 Germans asleep in the trench. He returned for reinforcements and they reoccupied the copse, having given the Germans 60 rounds of rapid fire.

In early August 1916, the British used Arrow Head Copse as a strongpoint. During an advance on 8 August, 2/Lt G.G. Coury, attached to 1/4th King's Own (164th Brigade, 55th Division), was in command of two platoons ordered to dig a communication trench from the old firing line to the position won. By his fine example and utter contempt of danger, Coury kept up the spirits of his men and completed his task under intense fire. Later, after his battalion had suffered several casualties, he went out in front of the advanced position in broad daylight, and in full view of the enemy found his severely wounded commanding officer, Maj J.L. Swainson, and brought him back to the newly advanced trench over ground swept by machine-gun fire; he also assisted in rallying the attacking troops when they were shaken, and leading them forward. He was later awarded the Victoria Cross.

In *Stand To*, Capt F.C. Hitchcock of 2nd Leinsters (73rd Brigade, 24th Division) reported that on 18 August, Arrow Head Copse on his left flank had ceased to exist. In his novel *Peter Jackson, Cigar Merchant*, Gilbert Frankau mentioned that his battery had been in continuous action for 18 days and that some of the battery had been lost beyond Arrow Head Copse. On 28 August, a large projector, one of Lt W.H. Livens's unconventional weapons, was taken into the Copse and it was fired on 3 September; four others were fired in HIGH WOOD. In early September, 16th Division used Arrow Head Copse as a forward dump.

AUBIGNY is south-west of CORBIE. Aubigny British Cemetery has one casualty from April 1916 and the remainder are from the 1918 fighting. In *A Medico's Luck in the War*, Maj D. Rorie of the Royal Army Medical Corps, serving with 1/2nd (Highland) Field Ambulance (51st Division), wrote: 'we took over from the French four huts near the railway station and the hospice in the village, opening as a temporary CCS under XVII Corps. A few days later the CCS itself took over, with one section of ours to help; while the rest of the unit moved to Haute-Avesnes . . .'

AUCHONVILLERS is on the D73 road, 6 miles north of ALBERT; it lies halfway between MAILLY-MAILLET and BEAUMONT-HAMEL, with Hawthorn Ridge between it and BEAUMONT-HAMEL. In the summer of 1915 this part of the Ancre front was held by French troops, some of whom were later buried south-east of the village in Auchonvillers Communal Cemetery on the HAMEL road. During the war, the cemetery was badly shelled; it contains the graves with headstones made from red Corsehill Stone, of 15 men, including 13 men from 1st Borders (87th Brigade, 29th Division) who died on 6 April 1916. The two graves that now flank those of the men of 1st Borders are casualties from 1915 and 1918 respectively. Graves using similar red stone on the Somme can be found at

Martinsart British Cemetery and Méaulte Military Cemetery.

From the end of July to the end of October 1915, 1/5th South Lancashires (12th Brigade, 4th Division) were in the line here when not billeted at MAILLY-MAILLET. On 2 September 1915, 1st Royal Dublin Fusiliers (86th Brigade, 29th Division) arrived here from the trench lines opposite SERRE, and took over trenches to the east of it. The village had suffered greatly from shell-fire but even so there were a few habitable houses left among the shady orchards. Bricks from the village were used as foundations for a communication trench.

On 5 October 1915, 108th Field Ambulance (36th Division) opened a dressing and reception station here. At the beginning of July the village had a collecting post, and three pictures of it were published in the *Official Medical History*. By now the village possibly had three advanced dressing station or collecting posts. A walking wounded collecting post had been set up on the railway line a mile to the west of the village.

Having moved up from billets at ENGLE-BELMER on the evening of 3 April 1916, 2nd South Wales Borderers (87th Brigade, 29th Division) were in the Auchonvillers sector opposite BEAUMONT-HAMEL; their line included a sharp salient known as Mary Redan, which the enemy were keen on mining from time to time. It was the battalion's misfortune to be in this line at around 2100hrs on 5 April, when the enemy opened up a tremendous bombardment, causing very great damage and heavy casualties; 29 men were killed or died of wounds, 18 men missing and 36 officers and men wounded. The remaining men left for LOUVENCOURT on 8 April.

Auchonvillers, which was in 29th Division's sector at the beginning of the battle, was an important departure point for British troops; during the battle it was totally destroyed. During the early hours of 1 July, 16th Middlesex (86th Brigade, 29th Division) moved up from the AUCHONVILLERS–BEAUMONT-HAMEL road, opposite the famous Sunken Road. The German guns wrought terrible havoc and the Sunken Road, together with the ground opposite Hawthorn Ridge, became a death trap.

In November 1916, 180 bodies were found, victims of northerly fire on 1 July. Many of them were buried in Hawthorn Cemetery No. 1, south of the main road, on the north slope of the ridge and close to the 1 July front line. It was made by V Corps, who cleared the Ancre battlefields in the spring of 1917. The cemetery includes many unidentified soldiers from 29th Division, mainly those who fell on 1 July or on 13 November. In *The Fighting Newfoundlanders* it is mentioned that 1st Newfoundlanders had been reinforced by the arrival of 127 other ranks; on 14 July the battalion returned to trenches in the front line at a point over 450yds east of Auchonvillers, now numbering only a few officers and 260 rifles after their near annihilation on 1 July in what is now called NEWFOUNDLAND PARK.

In *Triple Challenge*, Hugh Wansey Bayly described his experiences in this sector during his time as a medical officer with 1st Scots Guards (2nd Guards Brigade, Guards Division). On 9 August 1916, 1st Scots Guards went into the line here; Bayly mentions being at the WHITE CITY, which was directly behind the Sunken Road. They alternated in the line with 3rd Grenadier Guards (2nd Guards Brigade, Guards Division) before leaving for BERTRANCOURT.

In *Undertones of War*, Edmund Blunden wrote of the time when, in early September 1916, his battalion, 11th Royal Sussex (116th Brigade, 39th Division), were reorganising the trenches in the Auchonvillers sector in front of BEAUMONT-HAMEL. As Field Works Officer, Blunden enjoyed his work, which took him up and down from the 'dreary and mutilated front line' where 'the little young poplars stood lightly at the extremity of Auchonvillers' orchards'. The long communication trenches had to be repaired daily, as it was a *minenwerfer* (mine-thrower) sector, the front line being stubbornly pounded by them.

On 17 October 1916, 51st Division took over the line from 63rd Division and spent their time mainly in preparation for the forthcoming Ancre Battle, which was destined to be postponed many times. Maj D. Rorie of the Royal Army Medical Corps, serving with 1/2nd (Highland) Field Ambulance (51st Division), wrote that one of the jobs his staff carried out was to make an extra entrance to a Relay Bearer Post at Tenderloin, and construct entirely new ones at Second Avenue and Uxbridge Road. They also had to pitprop a false roof at a collecting post in the stable of a farmyard at Auchonvillers, and to prop, sandbag and fit stretcher racks into the cellars of the brasserie at Mailly as an advanced dressing station. During the battle, a steady stream of motor transport slowly wound its way from Tenderloin along the much-battered AUCHONVILLERS–BEAUMONT-HAMEL road.

Rorie also mentioned that in November a '*chemin creux*' ran beside Auchonvillers, in which were several dugouts where the medical staff and the division on the left had regimental aid posts. On 16

November, Tenderloin Bearer Post in the WHITE CITY became headquarters for forward evacuation. On 17 November, J.A. Whitehead of CLXVIII Brigade, Royal Field Artillery (32nd Division), reported that his unit had moved to a position in front of Auchonvillers; the guns had been in MARTINSART and the wagon lines in SENLIS-LE-SEC.

Auchonvillers Military Cemetery is about 300yds from the church, at the end of a path leading north from the road to MAILLY-MAILLET; used by British field ambulances and fighting units, it was begun by French troops in June 1915. The graves are mainly from 1916 and 1918 but there are some from August 1915.

After the war the village was adopted by Winchester.

AUTHEUX is south-west of DOULLENS, north of the D925. On 20 December 1915, 2nd Wiltshires (21st Brigade, 30th Division) arrived here along with the rest of 21st Brigade. Although the buildings in the village appeared dilapidated they were found to be ideal for billets, and at Christmas each company chose the largest room or barn and set to work preparing it for a complete company to be seated for a Christmas dinner. According to the regimental history, Christmas

> was celebrated in right good old-fashioned style from morning to night. The cooks were very busy while the padre conducted church parade, during which the carols that were sung brought everyone a step nearer home. The men sat down to what was probably the biggest feast they had had in France, whilst their officers and non-commissioned officers worked hard seeing that all were served.
>
> The colonel visited each company, toasting their good health. In the evening a 'fine concert' took place in the billets of D Company.

While in the village, 2nd Wiltshires carried out short daily training for the next few days before 30th Division began moving up to the front on 6 January 1916, via BRAY-SUR-SOMME to the CARNOY front line, where they relieved troops from 56th Division.

AUTHIE, north-west of LOUVENCOURT, was 7 miles behind the lines. Records show it was used as a billeting village for British troops from as early as 19 July 1915. The first British troops to arrive in the area were men of No. 48 Divisional Signal Company, Royal Engineers (48th Division). Their divisional headquarters opened here on 1 August 1915 and 1/4th Glosters (144th Brigade, 48th Division) were here in August/September 1915, as well as 1/4th Royal Berkshires (145th Brigade, 48th Division). The village was never shelled and was one of the pleasantest in 48th Division's area. The regimental history notes of the village: 'It lay athwart a trout stream, in a deep beech-covered valley; the woods of which were speedily denuded to form hurdles and revetments for the Corps line . . .' On 17 September, 1/4th Royal Berkshires left for the front line.

Later the village had an advanced operative centre and a main dressing station, which was on a road leading northwards out of the village. In December 1915, 1/4th Royal Berkshires had an excellent Christmas dinner in the village, and they were back here in early May 1916. 1/2nd (South Midland) Field Ambulance (48th Division) were here for most of April 1916, when troops from their division were billeted in the area.

On 10 May 1916, 1/6th Royal Warwicks (143rd Brigade, 48th Division) withdrew to here from COURCELLES-AU-BOIS for a day's 'rest' after 2 days' exhausting digging work; the next day, 143rd Brigade marched to GÉZAINCOURT. At the end of May 1916, Authie Château was used as a corps operating centre for very severe cases. 1/2nd (South Midland) Field Ambulance were still here and the village had a divisional rest station as well.

On 1 June 1916, 1/8th Worcesters (144th Brigade, 48th Division) returned here from the line at HÉBUTERNE and stayed a night before marching the next day to join the rest of 144th Brigade in training at GÉZAINCOURT. At the end of June, 60th Field Ambulance (20th Division) were here and XIV Corps' operating station for early treatment as well as urgent abdominal cases was administered by 61st Field Ambulance (20th Division).

At the end of June, 11th East Yorks (92nd Brigade, 31st Division) left billets here for operations on 1 July.

During the battle the village of Auchonvillers was garrisoned by British troops and a heavy gun, set up on rails in order to avoid detection, was located in Authie. In September 1916, 2nd Division were resting and training here as well as in BUS-LÈS-ARTOIS and THIÈVRES. In the second half of November 1916, 31st Division's headquarters was here before moving to COUIN on 30 November. By the end of November the village was home to a motor ambulance convoy. There is still a sign 'Bus Street' in the south-eastern part of the village.

AUTHUILLE is on the D151 road and is on the eastern bank of the River Ancre. The village was on the edge of a marsh through which the River Ancre slowly flowed. Authuille Wood is on the south-east side of the village and THIEPVAL is to the north-west. To the west is AVELUY WOOD. In August 1915, Maj D. Rorie of the Royal Army Medical Corps, serving with 1/2nd (Highland) Field Ambulance (51st Division), wrote: 'This advanced dressing station was in the cowshed of a much battered farm, on the slope of a hill down towards the Ancre; but, pit-propped and with the roof and walls well sand-bagged, it was ultimately made fairly safe . . .'

In early August, 1/5th Seaforth Highlanders (152nd Brigade, 51st Division) took over the line here for the first time, in a period of the war which they much enjoyed when 'nicely ensconced in the beautiful valley of the Ancre . . .' Their regimental history described the scene:

Down this valley flows a nice little river where the water is clear and pure and the current can actually be seen, so different from the sluggish rivers of muddy, dirty water further north. In some places this river, owing to inattention to its banks since the war began, has overflowed and formed large shallows among the trees which surround its course.

Running parallel to the river is a railway, now disused, as it runs straight up the valley into the Boche lines, and has had to be barricaded by our men. On each side there rise fairly steep slopes, and on the eastern slope stands our village, pretty well shattered but with some houses habitable. The rest of the battalion is disposed of in shelters of wood, corrugated iron, and clay in the valley near the railway, and on the side of the slope, where they are quite sheltered, or nearly so, from shell-fire through the steepness of the hill-side. Above them are the trenches, looking in the distance like so many zig-zag, ugly white scars on the beautiful scene. These trenches were made by the French.

The dug-outs are marvellous. Fancy a small opening in the ground, and looking down you see a 12-foot ladder, on descending which you come to a large room cut out of the solid chalk, with generally primitive beds . . . In some of these dug-outs, there is, leading from the first floor, another opening and ladder going further down still, where you find a second chalk cavern underneath the first. . . .

The lines were quite near – sometimes less than 70yds apart – but the line was a very quiet one. The River Ancre itself was also a great attraction and every afternoon bathing parties took the opportunity of ridding themselves of some of the grime and dust of the campaign. On 14 August, 1/5th Seaforth Highlanders moved to BUIRE-SUR-L'ANCRE, where they stayed for a week. The battalion was back here on 30 September and for the rest of the year alternated between here and the Aveluy sector, resting in HÉNENCOURT or BOUZINCOURT.

During August 1915, 10th Essex (53rd Brigade, 18th Division) were here, when the village was not entirely ruined and several inhabitants were still living in it. In mid-January 1916, 15th Highland Light Infantry (14th Brigade, 32nd Division) returned to Authuille from the front line at THIEPVAL. Authuille was close to the front, but protected from observation by a crest of rising ground. Even so, German artillery fire could sweep the village at any time of the day or night. The billets in Authuille were good and had baths; more important, though, was the presence of a commodious cellarage in the village, where the troops lived by candlelight. In February, Authuille had few houses left which still had their roofs and most of the village was a shambles. On 19 March, 108th Field Ambulance (36th Division) set up a marquee to the north of the church and later attempted to disguise it by painting it. On 5/6 May, 15th Lancashire Fusiliers (96th Brigade, 32nd Division) carried out a successful raid, capturing several prisoners and killing or wounding more than 10 men at the cost of 3 men killed and 3 wounded.

In July 1916 the Allied line ran down roughly in a north–south direction to the east of Authuille, before turning in a more easterly direction that took it in front of the wood. The village was just behind the British trenches in 32nd Division's sector. BLIGHTY VALLEY or Nab Valley ran from the wood in a north-easterly direction and was also the border line between X Corps and III Corps. 32nd Division were assembled on the lower slopes of the Thiepval Spur from Authuille Wood to Thiepval Wood. At the beginning of the bombardment before the battle began the guns were standing wheel to wheel in the wood. The three battalions that were initially involved in the attack towards the Leipzig Salient were 1st Dorsets (14th Brigade, 32nd Division), 11th Borders (97th Brigade, 32nd Division) and 19th Lancashire Fusiliers (14th Brigade, 32nd Division).

In *The Weary Road*, Charles Douie of 1st Dorsets (14th Brigade, 32nd Division) vividly describes the part that his battalion played on 1 July. He wrote that on emerging from either of two trenches, including Hamilton Avenue, 1st Dorsets had the alternatives of going along the main road to Authuille North Barricade or following a safer track under the bank and on the edge of the stream to a ruined mill on the lower edge of the village. Here was a bridge just wide enough to take a trolley. Beyond the ruins of the village was another high bank, honeycombed by dugouts, and a long causeway across the marshes known as BLACK HORSE BRIDGE. From here the way to the south lay along the bank of the river towards Aveluy. Passing this way, Douie found a green meadow leading down to the Ancre. Across the river was a small château. CRUCIFIX CORNER lay ahead, 'girdled by tall trees', before he turned aside to enter Authuille Wood. It was thronged with fatigue parties busily engaged on completing bridges, gun positions, and ammunition dumps. On the western edge he came upon the Allied front line.

Concealed gun emplacements held guns, which were destined to fire over open sites at Leipzig Redoubt when the time came. He came to a bridge over a defile, which the plan of attack required 1st Dorsets to cross, and from a convenient machine-gun emplacement one could survey Leipzig Redoubt and the long valley up which the advance was planned to sweep. At its far end he could see MOUQUET FARM. The dugouts sheltering under the high bank of the Ancre at BLACK HORSE BRIDGE were the headquarters of the battalion resting at Brigade Reserve in the sector THIEPVAL to Authuille Wood. Douie had many memories of days and nights spent under this high bank.

Douie's description of the situation before the battle is included here because it tells us a great deal about the geography of the sector. Douie is also a useful source in describing the start of the battle. On 29 June, 1st Dorsets were in camp at SENLIS-LE-SEC; moving off to BLACK HORSE BRIDGE at 2030hrs on 30 June, the battalion arrived at dugouts at 0050hrs on 1 July. 1st Dorsets moved slowly through the wooded valley, 'lined on each side by little streets of faintly illuminated canvas huts' and passed through 'ghostly and barren country' into AVELUY WOOD and so to BLACK HORSE BRIDGE. They breakfasted at 0630hrs, a meal that was to be the last for so many of them. They then gathered under the high bank of the Ancre at BLACK HORSE BRIDGE. Under the bank they paraded at 0710hrs and began to leave the Black

Horse shelters, by platoons, at 150yd intervals; they went south-eastwards, heading through Authuille Wood, along Dumbarton Track. On the left, 17th and 16th Highland Light Infantry (both 97th Brigade, 32nd Division) were also to attack; 2nd King's Own Yorkshire Light Infantry (97th Brigade, 32nd Division) were to move in support and 11th Borders were in reserve. The last named had MOUQUET FARM as its special objective.

On the left 17th Highland Light Infantry passed over the enemy's front trenches and were soon engaged in heavy fighting in the maze of trenches forming the Leipzig Redoubt; the right of 16th Highland Light Infantry also gained the front line.

Meanwhile, 0730hrs having been planned as Zero Hour, 1st Dorsets waited about for a quarter of an hour in Authuille Wood, until receiving word that 11th Borders were advancing. Closely followed by 19th Lancashire Fusiliers, 1st Dorsets left the shelter of the wood and immediately came under concentrated machine-gun fire from the right. The distance from Dumbarton Trench at the edge of the wood to the front line was 100yds but the track was a marked exit point from the wood. The inevitable massacre occurred and they became involved with 11th Borders in front and 19th Lancashire Fusiliers behind. Indeed, many were killed by machine guns in the wood before the advance even began. The same bridge over a defile which the plan of attack had required them to cross was so heaped with dead and wounded as to be almost impassable.

On reaching the exit of the wood 1st Dorsets paused while a search was made for another way out. None was found; the wood was heavily wired. There was no alternative but to make a dash from the front line, and section by section the battalion crossed the bullet-swept area. The fire came from a strongpoint on the south side of the valley which flanked Thiepval Ridge. In the British Front Line, elements of 1st Dorsets became mixed up with 11th Borders. During the night it was reported that 15th Highland Light Infantry would relieve 1st Dorsets, who by 0200hrs on 2 July were well clear of the front trench. They did not go far, only to the dugouts and trenches that formed the northern defences of Authuille. Also held up by the congested trenches, 19th Lancashire Fusiliers stood fast. At 0100hrs on 2 July they too returned to dugouts at Authuille.

Vainly, 15th Highland Light Infantry sought to improve the position held in Leipzig Redoubt. During the night of 2/3 July, 1st Dorsets were ordered up to the old British Front Line between Thiepval Ridge and Chequerbent Street, and every man who could be spared was employed in

carrying bombs and ammunition to the Highland Light Infantry. On completion of relief 1st Dorsets marched back to SENLIS-LE-SEC.

At 2200hrs on 30 June, 11th Borders moved from dugouts at CRUCIFIX CORNER, north-east of Aveluy, to assembly trenches which had been dug for them in the thickest part of Authuille Wood. The battalion, which were mainly made up of men from the hills and dales of Cumberland and Westmorland who were under the patronage of the Earl of Lonsdale, were to move northwards out of the wood and then swing due east. On leaving their trenches in the wood, before even arriving at the British Front Line trench, the battalion came under terrific machine-gun fire. They were to the left of 1st Dorsets and were due to emerge from the front trench on a strip almost opposite Leipzig Redoubt. On leaving their trenches they were gunned down and suffered nearly 500 casualties out of 800 men, including 25 officers and 490 NCOs and other ranks. Very few got as far as the Highland Light Infantry had. Their commanding officer, Lt Col P.W. Machell, was one of those killed.

The idea of the Earl of Lonsdale in forming this special battalion was that if given the opportunity men would join up with their friends rather than be placed just anywhere in the ranks of the British Army. They were drawn from, among others, labourers, farm servants, shepherds, keepers, miners, industrial workers, clerks and small shopkeepers. They had carried out much of their basic training at a local racecourse at home. The casualties affected one small area of England, which subsequently took several generations to recover.

On 30 June, 19th Lancashire Fusiliers had moved forward to dugouts at BLACK HORSE BRIDGE, which they reached at about 0200hrs on 1 July. The right assaulting brigade of 32nd Division, 97th Brigade, had its headquarters in Authuille Wood; its task was to capture the front line system at Leipzig Redoubt. After 11th Borders were to pass through at 0830hrs and supposedly on to the German trenches, 14th Brigade, including 19th Lancashire Fusiliers, were to pass through and capture the German Intermediate Line. At 0710hrs, 19th Lancashire Fusiliers moved off behind 1st Dorsets and marched south along the bank of the River Ancre for 1,000yds, then turning eastwards into Authuille Wood, and moving slowly along one of the tracks leading through it. After 11th Borders and 1st Dorsets had been hit by the same fire from a German strongpoint, 19th Lancashire Fusiliers were held up by the congested trenches and stood fast.

A contributor to *Artillery and Trench Mortar Memories: 32nd Division* who was a witness to the above disaster wrote:

> the whole of the gun teams then went through the track in Blighty Wood to the main ammunition dump. Will any of us ever forget the journey that morning? Just to the right front of Rock Street gun pit the REs had cut a gap in the hedge on the edge of the wood, and through this gap marched our Infanteers – the 11th Borders and the 1st Dorsets – to be mown down like corn by Jerry's machine guns as fast as they marched through. The wood was being heavily shelled, and clambering on to the Artillery Bridge we found a slaughter-house.

On the morning of 1 July, the writer emerged from the gun pit at Rock Street. The Officer Commanding had just come down the ravine and under Artillery Bridge over Rock Street. The bridge was littered with dead and wounded. Through the gap in the hedge could be seen men falling all over the field. The gap had turned brown and formed a target for the German machine guns. The writer trekked to the dump in the wood. All down the track lay the dead and dying, 'for the Germans had found that track with their 5.9s'. He was never to forget 'that terrible scene of suffering and wounded that no one had time to attend to. These poor devils had crept together to die. Their eyes had a look that could not be described', which the writer knew that he would never forget. 2nd Manchesters (14th Brigade, 32nd Division) were passing this group under the command of 'Corky', so named on account of his cork leg. 2nd Manchesters went round Rock Street and attained their objective; by not going through the gap, they had escaped the fire from the Nord Werk.

South-east of the attack on Leipzig Redoubt on the north-east side of the wood, a similar tragedy had befallen 70th Brigade (8th Division), who were facing towards LA BOISSELLE. In front of the wood on 29/30 June, 8th York & Lancasters and 8th King's Own Yorkshire Light Infantry (both 70th Brigade, 23rd Division) were to lead the attack, with 9th York & Lancasters (70th Brigade, 23rd Division) and 11th Sherwood Foresters (70th Brigade, 8th Division) in support. After the disastrous attack, 8th King's Own Yorkshire Light Infantry and 8th York & Lancasters were withdrawn to Long Valley, along with the remnants of 9th York & Lancasters.

On 27 June, 11th Sherwood Foresters had come from BOUZINCOURT and had gone up to their assembly trenches in Glasgow Street. After the two attacking battalions went forward, two waves of 11th Sherwood Foresters advanced and were mown down. Their commanding officer, Lt Col H.F. Watson, was wounded in the chest when trying to rally his men. A third and futile attempt was carried out by means of a sunken road, but to no avail. They had reached the German Second Line but were completely held up by the Third. When they were relieved they went by train and marched to BRAY-SUR-SOMME via DERNANCOURT.

BLIGHTY VALLEY was the name given by the Army to the lower part of the deep valley running south-westwards through Authuille Wood to join the river between Authuille and Aveluy. After 1 July a railway was carried along it. The upper part was called Nab Valley. Blighty Valley Cemetery is almost at the mouth of the valley, a little way up its northern bank. It is partly in the communes of both Aveluy and Authuille. It was begun early in July 1916 and used until the following November by the troops taking part on that front.

In an unpublished manuscript at the Imperial War Museum, Gunner W.R. Price of CCXL Brigade, Royal Field Artillery (48th Division), wrote that his unit came from HÉBUTERNE on 20 July and set up their new position in Authuille Wood. On 21 and 22 July, 1/6th Glosters (144th Brigade, 48th Division) and the Anzacs attacked through them, encountering liquid fire. The Glosters reached and surmounted the LEIPZIG SALIENT. The battery then concentrated in shelling Pozières Ridge.

On 11 August, a battalion of the East Yorkshire Regiment were billeted in Authuille village. In mid-August, the headquarters of 7th Somerset Light Infantry (61st Brigade, 20th Division) was in the rectory in the village. On 25 September at Wood Post, a main communication trench, Brig Gen H.W. Higginson, General Officer Commanding 53rd Brigade (18th Division), wished 10th Essex (53rd Brigade, 18th Division) good luck. The accompanying tanks made the troops roar with laughter. On the same day, 17th King's Royal Rifle Corps (117th Brigade, 39th Division) went to Brigade Reserve and 8th Norfolks (53rd Brigade, 18th Division) proceeded to Wood Post in Authuille Wood in fighting order, in preparation for the attack against THIEPVAL, due to take place the next day. They were in Brigade Support and the attack went well. On 27 September they were in support to 7th Queen's (55th Brigade, 18th Division) and on 29 September were withdrawn to FORCEVILLE, except for B Company, who were left at CRUCIFIX CORNER for burial duties.

On 2 October, 8th Norfolks replaced 7th Queen's at North Bluff to the north of Authuille. Here indeed there were dugouts as there also were at South Bluff. On 10 October, 17th King's Royal Rifle Corps (117th Brigade, 39th Division) moved to North Bluff. On 16 October 63rd Division relieved Edmund Blunden's battalion, 11th Royal Sussex (116th Brigade, 39th Division); they immediately went into Authuille Wood in order to prepare for their attack against STUFF TRENCH. A motor ambulance convoy operated from the village. On 24 October, 75th Brigade of 25th Division were here. In *Undertones of War*, Blunden wrote that in November his battalion came away for a couple of nights and billeted in Authuille, built against the high bank called the Bluff, and there 'passed some pleasant hours'. They were not being shelled. In another section he describes this period in the following way: 'we rested in cabin like dugouts called Authuille Bluffs, on the steep rise from the Ancre inundations'.

As noted above, on 1 July 32nd Division had attacked the German line from Authuille and stormed the LEIPZIG SALIENT, but were fored to retire later in the day. The present Lonsdale Cemetery originally contained 96 graves of men from this action, the majority of them officers and men of 1st Dorsets, 11th Borders and the Highland Light Infantry. The cemetery was enlarged after the Armistice by the concentration of 1,425 casualties, mostly men who died in 1916 and whose remains were later found in the surrounding battlefields. A handsome memorial of Portland stone in memory of the Dorsetshire Regiment was set up and dedicated on 7 May 2011 and can be found close to Lonsdale Cemetery. The inscription 'Victory crowns the just' is taken from Thomas Hardy's poem 'Men Who March Away' (5 September 1914).

Quarry Post Cemetery was on the south-east side of the wood and was formerly 70th Brigade's aid post. It was used from July 1916 to February 1917, chiefly by units of 12th Division, but was later taken into Blighty Valley Cemetery.

Authuille Military Cemetery was used by field ambulances and fighting units from August 1915 to December 1916, and in 1917 and 1918 by Indian labour companies. This cemetery, with 305 graves of men who died prior to 1 July 1916 is the third highest of the department of the Somme. It stands on a steep slope falling from east to west, on the south side of the village between the ALBERT road and the Ancre. The graves of 13 men from the Dorsetshire Regiment, including Lt V.T. Bayly, who died on 6 May 1916, are in the front row nearest the river. There is also a memorial to five more men from the same regiment

'believed to be buried in the cemetery'; they died on 20/21 June 1916. Thirteen other men have special memorials.

After the war Blunden wrote a novel with Sylvia Norman called *We'll Shift Our Ground*, in which he describes the 'rambling' village of Authuille and notes that once more the river had been recalled to its proper channels. He had revisited the area and had passed the Bluffs, apprehensive still that once over the rise he would be treading on dead bodies on dead land.

The church door in Authuille displays a memorial to 15th, 16th and 17th Highland Light Infantry, who served with 32nd Division in this sector and 'who fought and died near the village of Authuille in the opening days of the Battle of the Somme . . .' To the left of the Church door is a black marble tablet to the battalions of the 15th, 16th and 17th Highland Light Infantry, members of the 32nd Division who served in the area in June/July 1916. The tablet was unveiled on 30 June 1996. Close to the Church is a small brick memorial to the memory of the 15th, 16th, and 19th Lancashire Fusiliers, best known as the Salford Pals. It was unveiled on 30 June 1995. Opposite is the City of Glasgow Memorial seat unveiled on 22 March 2003.

After the war, the village was adopted by the urban district of Leyton. Close to the village war memorial is a reminder of the men of the 15th, 16th (both 96th Brigade, 32nd Division) and 17th Lancashire Fusiliers (104th Brigade, 32nd Division) (the Salford 'Pals' battalions) who spent a night here before attacking the German-held stronghold village of THIEPVAL, only to be met by annihilating machine-gun fire. It was erected by members of the Western Front Association, who hold an annual wreathlaying ceremony here on 1 July.

AVELUY WOOD, being more than 1,600yds in width, is much larger than Authuille Wood and is on the west side of the River Ancre. It is north-west of Aveluy and is on the D50 road that runs north from ALBERT to HAMEL. In 1916, its 1,000 acres of fine timber sheltered the villages of BOUZINCOURT and MARTINSART from the enemy. Almost surrounded by marshes, the village lies between the Ancre and the ALBERT–Arras railway.

51st Division became associated with Aveluy Wood soon after they arrived in the Somme region. In *A Medico's Luck in the War*, Maj D. Rorie of the Royal Army Medical Corps, serving with 1/2nd (Highland) Field Ambulance (51st Division), mentioned a time in August 1915 when there 'were many good French shelters cut deep into

Aveluy Château. *(Peter F. Batchelor Collection)*

the solid chalk'. On 6 August 1915, 1/4th Loyal North Lancashires (at this time 154th Brigade, 51st Division) had their headquarters in the wood; after relief in the front line, they returned to billets in the village. 1/4th Loyal North Lancashires returned to the Wood in mid-October.

On 21 August, 1/5th Seaforth Highlanders (152nd Brigade, 51st Division) marched here from HÉNENCOURT and were often in this sector or at AUTHUILLE over the next few weeks. On 12 December the advanced dressing station in the north of the village had to be moved to a site to the south in order to avoid enemy shelling. It occupied several cellars. On 16 December, 1/6th Seaforth Highlanders (152nd Brigade, 51st Division) took over part of the line from 154th Brigade in the Wood sector. The trenches at that time were in a very bad way and were getting worse. While trying to improve the trenches, 1/6th Seaforth Highlanders were also having to help out with training and gave instructions to men from 11th Borders (97th Brigade, 32nd Division) whose first spell in the line this was. On 23 December, 16th Highland Light Infantry (97th Brigade, 32nd Division) relieved 1/6th Seaforth Highlanders, who 'plodded their way' to HÉNENCOURT.

Aveluy Wood was one of the centres of the attack against THIEPVAL and was to serve as a departure point for a new set of British trenches; prior to 1 July 1916, a whole division, together with scores of batteries, could easily be concealed in it. During the first 2 weeks of June, 1/7th West Yorkshires (146th Brigade, 49th Division) carried out tasks for 36th Division, when they worked on burying cables in trenches across the Wood. No. 130 Field Company, Royal Engineers (25th Division), also working for 36th Division, repaired the main railway line from the Wood to within 80yds of the front trenches, and made it fit for trolley traffic. Other tasks carried out included the preparation of gas emplacements as well as working on tracks above ground; these led from support trenches to front trenches and would be used for attacking troops. The footbridge over the River Ancre had also to be raised in order to allow for pontoons to pass underneath it. Construction work on landing stages and towpaths for pontoon traffic was also carried out.

In *Artillery and Trench Mortar Memories: 32nd Division*, Sgt Prince wrote that in April 1916, when in Aveluy, the following names all had their own little history: the Strawberry Bed, the Rose Garden, the Rat Hole, Jacob's Well, CRUCIFIX CORNER, Honeysuckle Cottage and the Chalk Pit. At the end of June he refers to the 'Flying Pig' as being at Rock Street gun position and to a heavy gun team at Rock Street in Oban Avenue.

At the beginning of the battle, Aveluy Wood was shared by 36th Division to the north and 32nd Division to the south; 36th Division's headquarters was in the Wood itself. Aveluy formed one of the three solid routes through the ANCRE VALLEY, which had been flooded following the destruction of the river embankments. Lancashire Dump, on the verge of the wood, is now the site of Aveluy Wood Cemetery and was originally called East Lancashire Dump. In preparation for the battle, a few days earlier, on 23 June, 108th Field Ambulance (36th Division) set up shelters for 45 lying-down cases.

On 27 June, 19th Lancashire Fusiliers (14th Brigade, 32nd Division) were at Shelter Trenches at the edge of the Wood, prior to their attack on the Leipzig Redoubt on 1 July. This action is referred to in the section on AUTHUILLE.

At about midnight on 30 June, 1/6th West Yorkshires (146th Brigade, 49th Division) went to assembly trenches in Aveluy Wood. During the march there they had followed lights, which were laid out at 500yd intervals. On 1 July they moved out of the Wood and across the river at Passerelle de Magenta to their trenches in Thiepval Wood. On the same date, 107th Brigade's (36th Division) assembly positions (less 15th Royal Irish Rifles) were in slit trenches in Aveluy Wood. The battalions marched up by cross-country tracks, marked by red lanterns; the 'down' track was marked by green lanterns. The night was a fine one. Other battalions from 49th Division moved into assembly trenches in the Wood after dark.

In *Artillery and Trench Mortar Memories: 32nd Division*, Sgt Prince mentions that at about 1930hrs on the night of 30 June at Oban Avenue the gun began firing one round every 15 minutes, until 0600hrs on 1 July, when gunfire was ordered and the strafe began in real earnest. At 0700hrs the gun ceased firing. At Rock Street 'nothing untoward' had happened and the French gun behaved 'remarkably well'. They cooked their food in a ravine.

On 1 July, 'an advanced dressing station was situated close to the Albert–Arras road in Aveluy Wood. Evacuation of wounded from the Regimental Aid Posts in Thiepval Wood and Authuille had to take place over Authuille Bridge, or by the tramway which crossed the Ancre to the north of it. The motors of the Field Ambulance were parked on the Martinsart–Albert road, south of the former village.'

In *A Brass Hat in No Man's Land*, Brig Gen F.P. Crozier (Commanding Officer 9th Royal Irish Rifles, 107th Brigade, 36th Division) provides a very detailed description of 36th Division's fighting on the front. On the evening of 30 June, when 107th Brigade were assembled in Aveluy Wood, Crozier and Col H.C. Bernard, Commanding Officer 10th Royal Irish Rifles (107th Brigade, 36th Division), were dubious about the possible success of 32nd Division's assault on THIEPVAL village on their right. 'If they fail?' 'Where are we on the flank?'

They decided that on marching through Thiepval Wood, if the village remained in German hands, they should meet in no man's land to alter their plans. If only one of them survived then it would be up to him to carry on for both battalions. If neither of them got that far, then the remaining senior officers would carry on. After a whistle had blown, the men fell in in fours in their companies on the HAMEL–ALBERT road. At 0730hrs they passed through Gordon Castle, in the centre of Thiepval Wood, and picked up coils of wire and iron posts. Crozier glanced to the right and through a gap in the trees saw 10th Royal Irish Rifles plodding on; it was 36th Division at its best. He later saw rows and rows of British soldiers lying dead, dying or wounded in no man's land, enough to convince him that the Germans still held THIEPVAL village. It was then 0800hrs; the village should have fallen 15 minutes earlier, to allow 36th Division's forward passage on its flank.

Also on 1 July, 15th Highland Light Infantry (14th Brigade, 32nd Division) paraded at 0640hrs on the Aveluy–AUTHUILLE road, which was packed with traffic, guns, limbers, carrying parties, troops and ambulance wagons. The day before they had sheltered at Brookers Pass, which was between CRUCIFIX CORNER and Aveluy Wood.

In *With a Machine Gun to Cambrai*, George Coppard mentions that on the afternoon of 1 July he was number two in a machine-gun team; climbing Coniston Steps, which were cut into a steep bank, he entered Aveluy Wood. It was being shelled heavily by lachrymatory or tear shells, which drenched the Wood. He said that the issued gas masks were of no use and that 'men staggered about like blind men'. A winding track led through the Wood, and many wounded and dying men lay on either side of it. When at nightfall they were at last clear of the Wood, Coppard's team mounted a Vickers gun near LA BOISSELLE. On 2 July, hundreds of dead, many from 37th Brigade (12th Division), were 'strung out like wreckage washed up to a high water mark. Quite as many dead on the enemy wire as on the ground. The wire was so dense that daylight could be barely seen through it.'

In early July, 104th Brigade (35th Division) bivouacked in Aveluy Wood; in the period 4/5 July, 75th Brigade (25th Division) withdrew here. In mid-July, companies of the Gloucestershire Regiment were in reserve in quarries just north of the village, near CRUCIFIX CORNER. Bernard Montgomery (104th Brigade, 35th Division), who was to command the British Eighth Army in the Second World War, was at this time on the staff of 104th Brigade; on 12 July he wrote home from BOUZINCOURT, saying that

104th Brigade had marched to Aveluy, about a mile west of LA BOISSELLE, then on to OVILLERS. Montgomery was not at all reticent about the use of place-names in his correspondence home.

In *Gunner on the Somme*, Gunner W.R. Price stated that CCXL Brigade, Royal Field Artillery (48th Division), took over from a unit of 12th Division at CRUCIFIX CORNER, on a steep chalk bank at a junction of the Arras–BAPAUME road near Aveluy. Price's unit was there until relieved by 25th Division's artillery on 28 August.

In early September – probably 4 September – 7th South Staffords (33rd Brigade, 11th Division) went via the ruined village of Aveluy and across the much-shelled bridge over the swollen River Ancre, past CRUCIFIX CORNER, and up the hill past the guns to Ovillers Post. On their right as they went forward were several rows of guns of all calibres lined up in Nab Valley. On 9 September, 6th East Yorkshires (11th Division pioneers) were based at the château at Aveluy. On 26 September, during the period when THIEPVAL fell finally to the British, the crossroads at the west end of the village was 'very unhealthy'. In early October, companies of 1/1st Cambridgeshires (118th Brigade, 39th Division) were in tents in Aveluy Wood.

In *Undertones of War*, Edmund Blunden describes Aveluy Wood having 'moss which is rimy' and that its red leaves 'made a carpet not a thread less fine than those in kings' houses'. He saw a signpost pointing between the trees 'Ride to Black Horse Bridge', and others, both French and English. But they 'turned along a road unmolested which led to a chasm of light between the trees', and then saw a downland cliff or quarry and a valley in the trees. But then they had to leave the road and file along the railway track, which despite all the 'incurable entanglements' of its telegraph wires 'might yet be doing its duty'. Below, 'among mighty trees of golden leaf', there was a track across the lagooned River Ancre. A trolley line crossed it as well, but disjointedly. Then Blunden's party passed the last muddy pool and derailed truck and came into a maze of trenches, formerly the old British system, which looked up towards 'lofty Thiepval'. Thiepval Wood was 200yds away, 'scowling, but at that moment dumb; disjointed, burnt, unchartable'. They were looking for Gordon House, a company headquarters; crawling along the wood edge, they 'entered the

British troops bathing near Aveluy Wood, August 1916. (IWM Q913)

earthy cave with its bunk beds and squatting figures'.

On 21 October, during the action at STUFF REDOUBT, 11th Royal Sussex (116th Brigade, 39th Division) were again holding the line at Thiepval Wood and stayed thereabouts, being shelled and carrying out digging and carrying duties. On or around 22 October at midnight, after they had taken or seized STUFF TRENCH, the 'portents of Aveluy Wood' seemed to Blunden 'remarkably comfortable'. On 25 October, 11th Royal Sussex again held the line at Thiepval Wood. Blunden mentions that they were still working in the Aveluy region around 7 November, when there was a severe winter storm. It seems that the enemy missed a golden opportunity in not shelling Lancashire Dump on the ALBERT–HAMEL road in Aveluy Wood.

In November there was an advanced dressing station or collection post close to the Wood. Marlborough Huts was the name of dugouts at CRUCIFIX CORNER close to Aveluy used by 8th North Staffords (57th Brigade, 19th Division), among other units, around 9 November.

On 26/27 March 1918 Aveluy and part of Aveluy Wood were captured by the Germans, who were in

turn driven out on 6 April. Minor fighting occurred in June 1918, and on 20 July a raid was carried out by the Germans, who were finally cleared out of the Wood area on 25 July 1918.

Aveluy Communal Cemetery is in the village and the Aveluy Communal Cemetery Extension is on the south side of it. The French began the Extension and it was continued by British units and field ambulances from August 1915 until March 1917. It slopes down to the north, away from the village, and a long stretch of the ANCRE VALLEY can be seen from it. Men buried in this cemetery include Lt Col F.C.B. West (J.46) of CCXLIII Brigade, Royal Field Artillery (48th Division), killed in action on 28 September 1916; Lt Col T.G.J. Torrie (M.50) of 2nd Life Guards, attached to 7th East Lancashires (56th Brigade, 19th Division), killed in action on 18 November 1916; Lt F.K. Bliss (J.19) of LIX Brigade, Royal Field Artillery (11th Division), brother of the composer Arthur Bliss, who died on 28 September 1916; and Capt The Hon. R.E. Philipps MC (H.32) of 9th Royal Fusiliers (36th Brigade, 12th Division), a son of Viscount St Davids, killed at OVILLERS on 7 July 1916.

In *Goodbye to the Battlefields*, Capt H.A. Taylor of the Royal Fusiliers noted that 'one looked in vain for some remnant of the old sawmills by the railway at Aveluy, where during the "rest periods"

The River Ancre at Aveluy.
(Peter F. Batchelor Collection)

tired battalions whiled away the time making duck boards for the trenches while shells screamed their way over the valley in an effort to find one or other of the many dumps about the railway.' Blunden revisited the area several times after the war and commented on one occasion that he 'never knew that Aveluy Wood was purple before – wild flowers were encouraged by great wars'.

In *The Wet Flanders Plain*, Henry Williamson wrote that after he made a visit to the area

> the rain drove across the undulating Somme country, and the Ulster Memorial Tower at Thiepval, on my left beyond the marsh was sometimes washed out by a grey mist. I walked on with head bowed to the remembered rain . . . now the wood is green, and the new growth was twelve feet high . . . The verdant waves rear against the black stumps of the trees which knew the lost generation that toiled along the road. The trees were sapless and stark; only crows perch on them; the graves of the lost generation near. In this pilgrimage there were loving thoughts for all things which suffered grievously.

Of a visit she made to the Wood in August 1933 Vera Brittain wrote:

> The original trees were all shattered but the undergrowth has now grown up sufficiently to create the distant impression of a wood. But between these new trees were sinister rust-red gaps of earth where trees grew sparsely or not at all – and these seemed to me perhaps the most significant thing that I saw, for the chauffeur told us that their redness & their barrenness was due to the explosion here of gas shells, which chemically changed the quality of the ground. Comparatively few gas shells were used in the Great War, but where they fell mark the only places where the inexhaustible capacity of Nature to repair its ravages has failed to operate. It reminded me that after the next War there will be no one left to put up memorials to the missing, for we shall all be missing. . . .

Brittain observed that Aveluy village was 'now rebuilt – new red-brick houses, white mortar, bright blue painted railings'.

The British trenches can still be easily traced in the Wood, as can many shell-holes.

B

BAILIFF WOOD is north-west of PEAKE WOODS, south-west from Contalmaison Wood and due west of the village of CONTALMAISON. Referring to the event of July 1916 in *Memoirs of a Camp Follower*, Philip Gosse of 69th Field Ambulance (23rd Division) noted that 'so great was the rush of wounded that kept pouring down from Peake Wood and Bailiff Wood that we soon had to give up our tents and attend to them on the open ground outside. Before long the whole place looked like a shambles, with wounded and bandaged men lying everywhere . . .'

Before July 1916 there were two stretches of railway line here, one which ran south towards PEAKE WOODS and the other which crossed from CONTALMAISON itself. They were both probably used by the Germans for bringing up ammunition and supplies.

Around 7 July, 12th Durham Light Infantry (68th Brigade, 23rd Division) had to attack the German line, which ran eastwards from the crossroads west of the wood to the outskirts of CONTALMAISON, and a platoon managed to reach PEAKE WOODS. The trench along the CONTALMAISON road was occupied as far as the remains of the German light railway and a block was made beyond. The eastern edge of Bailiff Wood was reached.

According to the *Official History of the War*, on 9 July 10th Duke of Wellington's (69th Brigade, 23rd Division), who at the time were attached to 24th Brigade, sent forward bombing parties and established a post south of CONTALMAISON from which machine-gun fire could sweep nearly the whole area. Patrols of 12th Durham Light Infantry entered Bailiff Wood, then a newly planted spinney of saplings only a few feet high, but could not remain there because of British artillery fire. The British plan was to seize the Wood by an advance of two companies from the west.

On 10 July, 11th West Yorkshires (69th Brigade, 23rd Division) were due to attack the Wood; they progressed and wheeled round northwards from the eastern exit of the Wood to capture a trench running east and west. It was during the 69th Brigade attack that 8th and 9th Yorkshires (both 69th Brigade, 23rd Division) attacked CONTALMAISON and lost very heavily, including five officers, six wounded and one missing. There were also 260 other rank casualties.

Close to the Wood is a memorial to the 27-year-old Capt F. Dodgson of 8th Yorkshires (69th

Brigade, 23rd Division), who was the officer missing on 10 July 1916 and whose body is now in Serre Road Cemetery No. 2 (XXXVIII.K.8); his name is also commemorated on the Thiepval Memorial. His next of kin lived in The Close in Salisbury and he had recently married. On 9 March 1917, the War Office told Dodgson's family that he was buried 150yds south of Bailiff Wood and a witness said that Dodgson was to the left of him in a trench at CONTALMAISON and was shot outright at the beginning of the charge. He had just taken over, as Capt Richards had been wounded a day or two before. Dodgson's body was brought in 6 weeks later by 9th South Staffords (pioneers of 23rd Division).

In the 1920s, French children used to play on the remains of the light railway, which had been improved by the British during the war. Beyond the Wood, in a sunken lane towards the chalk pit at POZIÈRES, is a British dugout which is in superb condition. In 2003 it was excavated, revealing that the bunker was very deep and had two chambers. One was brick lined and the second was concrete.

BAILLESCOURT FARM in BEAUCOURT-SUR-L'ANCRE once had a cemetery, made in 1917 in marshy ground between the Farm and the River Ancre. The graves of 64 soldiers and sailors who fell in the winter of 1916/17 were later transferred to Queen's Cemetery, Bucquoy. The Farm was occupied by 2/1st Honourable Artillery Company (22nd Brigade, 7th Division) in February 1917 after the enemy had left.

BAILLEULMONT is north-west of HUMBER-CAMPS and south of the N25 Arras–DOULLENS road. During the First World War it was mainly used for training and for recuperation of troops returning from the front line. It lies on the reverse slope of a crest.

In early July 1916, 1/6th Sherwood Foresters (139th Brigade, 46th Division) were in this area. The four Sherwood Forester battalions of 139th Brigade came to rest in the village every 18 days; each battalion in turn spent 6 days in the line, 6 days in support at Bellacourt and so on. Battalion headquarters was alternatively in the château or at a farmhouse by the church at Grosville.

In Bailleulmont Communal Cemetery to the south of the village there are 34 red sandstone graves of men; 4 are of men who died before 1 July 1916 and nine from the period of the 1916 Somme battle itself. There are also four graves here of men who deserted and were court-martialled and sentenced to death: Pte W.G. Hunt (A.7) of 18th Manchesters (90th Brigade, 30th Division), who died on 14 November 1916; Pte A. Longshaw (B.13) of 18th Manchesters, who died on 1 December 1916; Pte. A. Ingham (B.12) of 18th Manchesters, who died on 1 December 1916; and Pte B. O'Connell (C.7) of 1st Irish Guards (1st Guards Brigade, Guards Division), who died on 8 August 1918. Ingham's headstone carries the following inscription 'Shot at Dawn: one of the first to enlist. A worthy son of his father.' Ingham and Longshaw were friends and had been posted to 90th Company, Machine Gun Corps. They decided to desert and managed to get as far as a boat leaving Dieppe, where they were arrested.

BAIZIEUX is south of WARLOY-BAILLON and west of HÉNENCOURT. As early as 22 July 1915, the America Motor Volunteer Ambulance were established here. On 13 February 1916, 91st Field Ambulance (32nd Division) set up a divisional rest station here and a few days later 92nd Field Ambulance (32nd Division) were established in the château to the north-east of the village. On 21 February 1916 they were ordered to leave as X Corps required the building as a headquarters.

On 4 March 1916, 91st Field Ambulance took over the hospital in the village, occupying a farmhouse, and remained here until 5 April, when they left for SEPTENVILLE. On 4 May 1916, 34th Division had their headquarters here. From 27 March, Baizieux was also used as a base by No. 4 Squadron, Royal Flying Corps, commanded by Maj T.W.C. Carthew; their duties consisted mainly of artillery observation, reconnaissance and aerial photography. There seems to have been a conflict of interests here, as in early April the Army had allotted the château as an officers' hospital and as a divisional rest station for 8th Division, but on 7 April the building was found to be occupied by the Royal Flying Corps. In any case, use of the building as a hospital was later abandoned as the water supply was inadequate.

In the second half of June, 17th Highland Light Infantry (97th Brigade, 32nd Division) were involved in exercises when they were billeted at RUBEMPRÉ. On 30 June, 12th Division headquarters moved here and the infantry, marching after dark, reached HÉNENCOURT and MILLENCOURT by 1000hrs on 1 July. On the same day, 7th Royal Sussex and 8th Royal Fusiliers (both 36th Brigade, 12th Division) bivouacked at the divisional rest station established here.

On 1 and 4 July, elements of 23rd Division were in the area and 34th Division headquarters also returned here. Other divisions in the area from July to December 1916 included 1st, 19th, 50th, 15th, 47th and 9th. On 20 July, 11th Sherwood Foresters (at this time 70th Brigade, 23rd Division) bivouacked here, and in mid-August as well as being in tents they had shelters, mainly of brushwood, and had dug holes into the sides of the banks. The village had been 'much used' and by the end of August there had been a lot of rain. Billets in the village were used by 1/8th Durham Light Infantry (151st Brigade, 50th Division).

On or about 13 September, 2nd King's Royal Rifle Corps (2nd Brigade, 1st Division) trained here until 19 September, when they bivouacked in LOZENGE WOOD. On 19 September, 15th Division headquarters was at the château. On 4 October, 149th Brigade (50th Division) returned here from Eaucourt. In early November, Sir Douglas Haig inspected 10th Cameronians (46th Brigade, 15th Division) here. Battalions used the wood for bivouacs; it was about ¾ mile west of the village. The Communal Cemetery is north of the village.

BAPAUME is 12 miles north-east of ALBERT on the D929. As early as August 1914 it was in the battle line and, after the German push westwards, remained in their hands until March 1917, when it was occupied by 2nd Australian Division. On 1 July 1916, No. 27 Squadron, Royal Flying Corps, bombed the German headquarters here and on 3 July they bombed trains in the town. On 27 September, No. 27 Squadron clashed with Hauptmann Oswald Boelck's newly formed Jasta (Jagdstaffel or 'Hunting Squadron') 2 here.

By the end of 1916, most of the old buildings in the town had been destroyed, but a barn remained on the very outskirts of the town. Opposite is a water tower, which is on the site of one that fell in the 1917 battle and was later used as a warm and dry billet for troops. The Germans made use of underground bastions during their time there and left many buildings boobytrapped or mined. They came back during the March Offensive of 1918 and were driven out again on 29 August by the New Zealand Division.

Bapaume Communal Cemetery and Bapaume Australian Cemetery do not contain the graves of men killed in 1916. Capt Lord A.T.H. Lucas, while flying with No. 22 Squadron, Royal Flying Corps, was shot through the neck and as a result crashed at Mory Abbey north-west of the town and was buried at Honourable Artillery Company Cemetery, Ecoust-Saint-Mein.

Of her visit in August 1933, the writer Vera Brittain said the town had by now been completely rebuilt but was 'rather a messy mixture of old & new'. Bapaume was later 'adopted' by the city of Sheffield and the two communities were to form extremely close links in the following years. Sheffield assisted in both practical as well as financial terms. During the Second World War, a set of commemorative silver soldier figures, which had been presented by Sheffield to Bapaume, went missing after the Germans had ransacked the Hôtel de Ville. Anything they didn't like they flung down into the street and then made a bonfire of it. These items included a memorial casket, which a lady managed to save and hide for the rest of the war. As the original designs for the silver figures were available there was no problem of replacing them, which Sheffield duly did. In May 1946, a visit was also paid to the Mayor of Bapaume, who in turn visited Sheffield Park with the Mayor of PUISIEUX.

BAPAUME POST MILITARY CEMETERY is about 1 mile outside ALBERT on the main Bapaume road. It lies on the west side of Tara Hill and is south-west of Usna Hill. In early May 1916, 24th Field Ambulance (8th Division) set aside a small dugout here for the use of stretcher cases. In June 1916, the British Front Line crossed the road between the cemetery and LA BOISSELLE village and, as the attack on the village on 1 July was a failure, it was to be several days before it was captured.

At 0900hrs on 1 July, casualties, mainly the walking wounded, began to come in and motor ambulances from 104th Field Ambulance (34th Division) later came up to collect the very large number of wounded. The trenches were very muddy, which hampered rescue efforts. The cemetery was begun almost at once by the divisions involved in this sector. In October it was called Tara Bridge Cemetery. It was closed in January 1917 and fell into German hands in March 1918. After the Armistice, 257 graves were brought in from nearby, including a number from 34th Division which had attacked along the Bapaume road on 1 July and some of 38th Division who captured Usna Hill on 23 August 1918.

Those buried here include Lt Col W.T. Lyle (I.G.1) of 23rd Northumberland Fusiliers (102nd Brigade, 34th Division), killed in action on 1 July 1916. He was last seen alive 'with walking stick in hand, amongst his men, about 200 yards from German trenches'. On the same day, Lt Col C.C.A. Sillery (I.G.2), Commanding Officer 20th Northumberland Fusiliers (also 102nd Brigade, 34th Division), was also killed. Next to Sillery is the grave of Maj Sir F.H.E. Cunliffe (I.G.3), second-in-command of 13th Rifle Brigade (111th Brigade,

at this time attached to 34th Division). Born on 17 August 1879 and 6ft in height, he was 36 and ex-Indian Army. He died of wounds on 10 July. A note in his file (WO 339, 100236) dated 28 July 1916 refers to him as 'Missing' and his body had been lying out in the open for 2 to 3 days despite time spent on trying to locate it. It was found in front of CONTALMAISON and buried at the back of Torrey Hill. A note of 25 July 1916 by 'RBS', who attended his funeral, states: 'I saw him shot in the leg on the 10th [sic 11th] July 1916 about ¼ of a mile to the left of Contalmaison. I was about 50 yards off when this happened. He fell forward . . . we left him behind where he fell.' On 11/12 July, 13th Rifle Brigade advanced near LA BOISSELLE, but was forced to retire. When the major was found to be missing, a party of 10th Royal Fusiliers (111th Brigade, 37th Division) went out to look for him.

The cemetery was closed at the end of January 1917; on 26 March 1918 it fell into German hands, but was recovered during the Battle of Albert, 21–23 August 1918. After the Armistice, further graves of victims of the 1918 fighting from 34th and 38th Divisions were established. During the 1916 Somme battle, the site of the cemetery was close to a Collecting Post at the bottom of Northumberland Avenue.

BASIN WOOD was south-west of Matthew Copse near SERRE and adjacent to the communication trench named Sackville Street. It was also east of LA SIGNY FARM. In mid-May 1916 a battalion of the East Yorkshire Regiment established themselves in a dell here, sheltered by a few tree stumps. The Wood was established as a casualty clearing station and on the eve of the battle, 12th King's Own Yorkshire Light Infantry (pioneers of 31st Division) dug a large communal grave close to it. From 1 to 3 July, the casualty clearing station staff were very busy and stretcher cases were taken from there to Euston Dump, the ambulance collecting point.

BAVELINCOURT is on the D115 road, south of the D919 CONTAY–AMIENS road. On 31 August 1915, 1/2nd (Highland) Field Ambulance (51st Division) arrived here and set up at EBART FARM, a large complex of buildings close to the main road which could later accommodate 300 men and 6 officers. At the end of August and beginning of September 1915, 1/6th Royal Warwicks (143rd

A BE2c biplane flies over the mill at Baizieux, 25 August 1916. *(IWM Q4153)*

Brigade, 48th Division) spent 4 days here as part of Brigade Reserve and were back on 28 December when there was 'feasting and revelry'. They returned to the village a third time on 3 March 1916. On 8 July 1916, 1st Field Ambulance (1st Division) were stationed here.

Bavelincourt Communal Cemetery is on the east side of the village. It has the graves of 54 men, mainly from 58th and 47th Divisions, who died in 1918 and were brought by units and field ambulances, a quarter of them from the Royal Field Artillery.

BAVINCOURT is to the north-west of HUMBER-CAMPS on the north side of the N25 DOULLENS–Arras road. From 4 July 1916, 46th Division's headquarters was here; after being involved in the GOMMECOURT battle, 1/5th Lincolns (138th Brigade, 46th Division) marched back here by platoons to rest billets immediately to the north of the village. They rested on 12 July and the next day moved on to SAULTY to the south-west, where they were inspected by a new divisional commander, Maj Gen W. Thwaites. In 1925 there were five British graves in Bavincourt Communal Cemetery, which lies to the south of the village; at that time it was hopelessly neglected.

BAYENCOURT is due west of GOMMECOURT on the D23 road. During the summer of 1915 the village became the home to several of the battalions of 48th Division. In the latter part of July 1915, the regimental historian of 1/4th Royal Berkshires (145th Brigade, 48th Division) described Bayencourt as 'a stinking little village full of flies and harlots . . .'; 1/4th Royal Berkshires were due to relieve the French at HÉBUTERNE to the south-east. 1/5th Royal Warwicks (143rd Brigade, 48th Division) arrived here on 30 July and stayed until 6 August, before relieving 1/4th Glosters (144th Brigade, 48th Division) at COLINCAMPS for a week. Back in the village from 15 to 22 August, after staying a night in COLINCAMPS 1/5th Royal Warwicks left for BUS-LÈS-ARTOIS on 30 August before returning, 6–9 September. 1/6th Royal Warwicks (143rd Brigade, 48th Division) were also often billeted here. The pattern was 4 days in brigade reserve in the village, 8 days in the front line and 4 days in support. On 13 December, 2/Lt R.L. Johnston of 17th Manchesters (90th Brigade, 30th Division), in command of transport, became his battalion's first Somme officer casualty when he was killed by an anti-aircraft shell. He was buried at Foncquevillers Military Cemetery (I.K.28).

During their time working in the FONCQUE-VILLERS area to the north-east, 1/5th Royal Warwicks were able to celebrate Christmas here, which they did with 'due rejoicings'. Presents were received from the citizens of Birmingham and special food and drink were bought in DOULLENS, the nearest town. By then, 48th Division had established a Pierrot show, composed of soldiers who performed under the name of 'The Curios'. A cinema, presented by the Birmingham Small Arms Company, was installed in a barn in the village. Returning on 28 December, 1/6th Royal Warwicks had their Christmas late: 'There was feasting and revelry such as the startled inhabitants had never seen . . .' They were back in the village on 30 December.

By the spring of 1916 the village had been finally cleared of civilians. On 21 April, 1/7th Worcesters (144th Brigade, 48th Division) arrived here from the trenches and remained for 6 days before 144th Brigade took over trenches opposite Gommecourt Park.

By the end of May 1916 the village was home to 56th Division, who were preparing for the forthcoming battle. Their front-line positions were to be based in the village of HÉBUTERNE to the south-east, where they were to be involved in preparations for the battle over the next 4 weeks. The battle plan was for 56th and 46th Divisions to capture the strongly held village of GOMMECOURT.

On 28 May, after a week in the trenches, 1/5th Londons (169th Brigade, 56th Division) marched to Bayencourt and stayed until 3 June 1916, each night providing large working parties before leaving for HALLOY. It was decided to move the horse-lines and transport to safer areas and Aubrey Smith of 1/5th Londons drove his limber to a sheltered valley at COIGNEUX, about a mile away. His battalion were back from HALLOY on 13 June, where they remained for 3 days. As battle preparations intensified, the German shelling became heavier. The village was overrun by British artillery units, which made it even more of a target for German artillery.

Also on 28 May, 1/13th Londons (168th Brigade, 56th Division) took over the former billets of 1/4th Londons (168th Brigade, 56th Division), who had relieved them in the line. On 2 June, 1/4th Londons were back here 'where tea was served and valises picked up from the stores'. They had been relieved by 1/14th Londons (143rd Brigade, 48th Division) and later left for SOUASTRE.

From 3 to 5 June, 1/16th Londons (169th Brigade, 56th Division) were in Bayencourt. Their transport had gone to COIGNEUX and left for the front

2 days later after an interval of 4 months. On 16 June, they were relieved by 1/5th Londons and moved back to the village, where they remained until 21 June, when they were involved in 'exhausting work', providing materials for various dumps. On 21 June they returned to HALLOY.

In June a dressing station was being built for a heavy artillery brigade whose guns were hidden in orchards. On 13 June, 1/4th Londons returned here from HALLOY. 1/5th Londons also came to the village from HALLOY before moving to HÉBUTERNE on 16 June. Between 16 and 21 June, 1/16th Londons were back in the village, when they were also working in HÉBUTERNE. On 27 June, 1/14th Londons moved from PAS-EN-ARTOIS up to Bayencourt, which by that time was crowded with troops. So too did 1/12th Londons (143rd Brigade, 48th Division), who had also marched from HALLOY. Casualties began when some of the men from B Company were killed or wounded when enemy artillery was 'searching' for a particular gun position behind their billets. Meanwhile, a long-range battery of 9.2in howitzers continued to bombard Gommecourt Wood. On 30 June, 1/12th Londons marched to HÉBUTERNE along what was called the Blue Track. This track, on leaving Bayencourt, kept somewhat to the right of the Bayencourt–SAILLY-AU-BOIS road, dipped into the valley behind SAILLY-AU-BOIS, climbed the further side through an artillery and anti-aircraft encampment and, turning east, rounded the southern outskirts of the village into the plain between SAILLY-AU-BOIS and HÉBUTERNE, where many battery positions lay concealed. The road to SAILLY-AU-BOIS was 'screened' towards the end of June.

1/9th Londons (169th Brigade, 56th Division) left for HÉBUTERNE on 30 June, marching via SOUASTRE, where they left their packs, and then via Bayencourt to HÉBUTERNE, which they reached at 2000hrs. When 1/5th Londons left the mud and slush behind at HALLOY at the end of June, they thought they had left the bad weather and conditions behind, but it was just as bad when they returned to Bayencourt on the eve of the great battle. At the end of June, Aubrey Smith mentioned that the guns at the village as well as those at Bienvillers-au-Bois, SAINT-AMAND and SOUASTRE were all 'firing their hardest'. In Bayencourt a battery of 9.2in howitzers was firing towards German positions in Gommecourt Wood every 5 minutes.

Bayencourt was adopted by Bexhill-on-Sea after the war.

Bazentin-le-Petit, when in German hands.
(Peter F. Batchelor Collection)

BAZENTIN-LE-PETIT and **BAZENTIN-LE-GRAND** straddle the D20 road between CONTAL-MAISON and LONGUEVAL to the north-east of ALBERT. Bazentin-le-Petit is the larger of the two villages and north-east of MAMETZ WOOD. The village and its large wood are north of the D20 and a little further to the south-east across the road is the village of Bazentin-le-Grand with its much smaller wood.

In 1916 the two villages, together with their woods, were part of the German Second Line, which at this point guarded HIGH WOOD. Bazentin-le-Petit Communal Cemetery was to feature strongly in the fighting; due east of it was a windmill, which became equally important. Two communication trenches beyond the northern edge of the wood were called New Trench and Ait Alley. A walking wounded collecting post was here during the battle.

In *The War in the Air*, H.A. Jones noted that on 2 July, when the mist cleared north of Bazentin-le-Petit, a new trench was observed, which the Germans had thrown up several hundred yards in advance of the Switch Line, roughly parallel to the British forward positions between the village and HIGH WOOD. The German Intermediate Line, which was connected with the Switch Line by a communication trench along the MARTINPUICH– Bazentin road,

was also seen to be strongly manned by the enemy. No man's land in this area was over 1,000yds wide and where the German Second Line ran through the wood it was known as Circus Trench.

In an unpublished manuscript (LH7/1916/23), Basil Liddell Hart, serving with 9th King's Own Yorkshire Light Infantry (64th Brigade, 21st Division), wrote that the plan of attack was for Fourth Army to attack the German second system of defence from WATERLÔT FARM to the west end of Bazentin-le-Petit Wood. The first objective was the main second-line trenches and the second objective stretched from the north end of Bazentin-le-Petit Wood and village to the north of DELVILLE WOOD and LONGUEVAL. XIII Corps were to attack the right and XV Corps the left. Of XV Corps, 7th Division were to attack Bazentin-le-Petit Wood and village. The cavalry were to go through 'at all costs' and the way was to be made for them by the infantry.

The attack was to begin at 0325hrs on 14 July, shortly before dawn, from the north border of MAMETZ WOOD. 10th King's Own Yorkshire Light Infantry (64th Brigade, 21st Division) were in Quadrangle Trench, 9th King's Own Yorkshire Light

Infantry (64th Brigade, 21st Division) in BOTTOM WOOD and 15th Durham Light Infantry (64th Brigade, 21st Division) in Lonely Copse, while 1st East Yorkshires (64th Brigade, 21st Division) were to protect the flank from Pearl Wood along the west border of Bazentin-le-Petit Wood. Liddell Hart's battalion had come up from VILLE-SUR-ANCRE, drawing bombs and stores outside MÉAULTE; they then went up the FRICOURT road and stopped near the crossroads just east of BÉCORDEL for tea. At about 1800hrs on 13 July, they moved off in platoons towards the cemetery; Liddell Hart noticed that heavy guns were standing out in the open in rows along the line of the water-course, the field pieces being further forward along the line of the hedge from SHELTER WOOD to BOTTOM WOOD and in the valley behind. Here the guns were standing 'almost wheel to wheel' and the artillery of three divisions, some 200 guns, were in an area of about a square mile. They went through FRICOURT and passed Rose Cottage via the east

Refreshment caravans for the use of walking wounded during the Battle of Bazentin Ridge, 14 July 1916. On the left-hand one is the sign of 9th Division. (IWM Q164)

edge of Fricourt Wood and then down the hill across the railway and further up to BOTTOM WOOD.

The attack duly began at 0325hrs on 14 July and the first line of trenches known as Flat Iron Trenches and Villa Trenches was taken with little loss, as was Contalmaison Villa, which might have threatened their progress; the rations came as far as Railway Copse. 9th King's Own Yorkshire Light Infantry moved off alongside the railway at the base of the cliff and to the south-east of MAMETZ WOOD, while 10th King's Own Yorkshire Light Infantry were ordered up to Bazentin-le-Petit village and lost 200 men within an hour. 9th King's Own Yorkshire Light Infantry were dug in on the edge of MAMETZ WOOD; Liddell Hart recorded that 'in many places the dead were ten deep', and 50yds into the wood was 'a shambles'. He went up to visit 64th Brigade headquarters at the west corner of the wood, via the railway running through MAMETZ WOOD. On the night of 17/18 July they were relieved, but Liddell Hart was gassed close to MAMETZ WOOD.

After capturing Contalmaison and MAMETZ WOOD the British soon reached the Bazentin villages; on 14 July, after hard fighting, 3rd and 7th Divisions captured both villages and Bazentin Communal Cemetery and managed to hold out

against counter-attacks. To their left, 21st Division captured Bazentin-le-Petit Wood. The day began well with a successful dawn attack starting at 0325hrs with the assistance of a heavy bombardment. In its account of the day the *Official History of the War* noted that after the dawn assault of 14 July, and in spite of machine-gun fire from the houses at Bazentin-le-Grand, the British troops went forward after topping the ridge and captured the village. Large numbers of Germans could be seen moving up the slope towards HIGH WOOD. Bazentin-le-Grand Wood was taken on schedule. In Bazentin-le-Petit there was a counter-attack on a battalion of the Royal Irish Regiment but the cemetery on the eastern side was held. The village was consolidated.

The War in the Air by H.A. Jones noted that a desperate struggle began on 14 July before Bazentin-le-Petit, when the British attacked the German entrenchments, captured and lost the village several times, and finally remained masters of it. To consolidate the conquered line they immediately advanced beyond it. Penetrating into the German third line, they gained a footing in HIGH WOOD and on the slopes of Hill 155. In his papers Sir Douglas Haig noted that on 14 July the Germans had retaken Bazentin-le-Petit but lost it again to 7th Division in the evening. HIGH WOOD was entered and connected up with Bazentin-le-Petit.

In his account of the battle, 2/Lt H.J. Brooks of 21st Manchesters (91st Brigade, 7th Division) wrote that on 13 July he was bivouacked near Mametz Halt; on 14 July he passed MAMETZ WOOD towards Sabot Copse and was involved in an attempt to take Bazentin-le-Grand Wood to the north-east. In *The Battle of the Somme*, John Masefield noted that on the left, the British broke over the line into Bazentin-le-Petit Wood, which was defended much as MAMETZ WOOD had been. The British 'stormed its trenches, cleared out the machine guns and heavy guns hidden in it, and working right through it, emerged at the northern end with many prisoners and much material by 8 o'clock. In the centre the British got into le Grand Wood and also into le Grand village. They chased the enemy down the hill beyond and up the opposite slope and then got into le Petit and made it theirs.'

Casualties during the day's fighting included Lt Col A. St H. Gibbons, Commanding Officer 13th King's (9th Brigade, 3rd Division); mortally wounded, he died the next day and was buried at Daours Communal Cemetery Extension (I.B.2). Another senior officer, Lt Col J.G. Mignon of 8th Leicesters (110th Brigade, 37th Division) was killed at around 0500hrs on 14 July, together with 2/Lt

J.A. Alexander, during an attack on Bazentin-le-Petit Wood. Both men are commemorated on the Thiepval Memorial. Noel Compton-Burnett of 7th Leicesters (110th Brigade, 37th Division), a brother of the novelist Ivy Compton-Burnett, was killed in the initial attack in the small hours of 14 July.

1/4th Suffolks (98th Brigade, 33rd Division) moved up through BÉCORDEL to a position between FRICOURT and MAMETZ where they bivouacked during the night of 14/15 July. The battle of Bazentin Ridge was raging in all its fury and 1/4th Suffolks became involved at dawn. The battalion went into reserve in Shell (DEATH) VALLEY and dug itself into roadside trenches for the night. After a day of heavy shelling they returned to the front-line trenches, and a former enemy bomb store was found in the north-east corner of Bazentin-le-Petit Wood. The store was subsequently used as a battalion headquarters.

The two Bazentin villages and their woods, as well as other woods, such as Flat Iron Copse, witnessed several days of very fierce fighting before the Allies were to finally establish their new line securely. It should also be stressed that the Allied artillery played a particularly important role on this occasion and that the villages and woods had been virtually pulverised by the very considerable number of guns that were in action.

Capt Sir A.E. Dunbar of 12th West Yorkshires (9th Brigade, 3rd Division) was awarded the Military Cross for work at Bazentin-le-Grand on 14 July and at LONGUEVAL on 23 July. He led his company in an attack with great dash, and skilfully consolidated its position under heavy shell-fire.

A.A. Milne, who had been trained as a signals officer and was attached to 11th Royal Warwicks (112th Brigade, 37th Division) had a swift introduction to the battle. In order to gain experience, he went into action with Harrison, the recently appointed signals officer. The attack was timed for midnight and the objective was the Switch Line at Bazentin-le-Petit; the day before Harrison was wounded, with the result that Milne had to take his place. Headquarters was in a German dugout, which faced the wrong way. In an adjoining dugout was the headquarters of a battalion of the East Lancashire Regiment, who were sharing the attack. In the space between these two underground rooms were Milne's signallers.

2/Lt Ellenberger of 9th King's Own Yorkshire Light Infantry was up at Bazentin on 14 July. In *A Life of One's Own*, Gerald Brenan wrote that after mid-July the fighting in the direction of Bazentin-le-Grand had been very heavy. 'Both sides had dug themselves in and around one hastily scraped-up gun emplacement which commanded a drive through the trees, the khaki bodies lay in heaps, and all across the battlefield, corpses of men, dead horses and mules, hand grenades, gas masks, the German spiked parade helmets, water bottles, were scattered like debris on a beach.'

In his *Memoirs*, Basil Liddell Hart wrote that on 16 July he was sent up with his company to fill a gap that had arisen in the new front line on the front edge of Bazentin-le-Petit Wood. The German harassing fire was very unpleasant because their shells often hit the branches of trees and then exploded with a shower of falling splinters.

In *The Machine Gunner*, Arthur Russell of the Machine Gun Corps wrote that the rest of 33rd Division, including three sections of his company of machine-gunners, were to attack the German positions beyond the village of Bazentin-le-Petit and the approaches to HIGH WOOD, and had already moved ahead. Mametz Valley was behind them and because of the very heavy enemy shelling it was called the 'Valley of Death'. While his company was still in reserve, Russell had the job of section runner between section officer and company headquarters. On the morning of 17 July, the section had to take two guns to a forward position in the direction of Bazentin-le-Grand; to reach them they had to go round CATERPILLAR WOOD. This wood and the ground at the rear were often under heavy enemy shell-fire and were a maze of shell craters.

The War the Infantry Knew records that 2nd Royal Welsh Fusiliers (19th Brigade, 33rd Division) had become Brigade Support and French 75s had arrived in their rear. The Indian cavalry were placed behind these guns and were 'reached by German reply'. Batteries rolled all day into HAPPY VALLEY and onto the slight rise of Caterpillar Wood until the area was 'stiff with batteries'. On 17 July, 33rd Division were relieving 21st Division in the village cemetery. At midnight, 2nd Royal Welsh Fusiliers moved through a light barrage of explosives and bromine shells to relieve 4th King's (98th Brigade, 33rd Division) between the cemetery and the MARTINPUICH road. On 18 July, 33rd Division came under heavy bombardment.

On the same day, Robert Graves (2nd Royal Welsh Fusiliers) reported that 19th Brigade were in reserve and that they advanced to a position just north of Bazentin-le-Petit and relieved a badly shaken Tyneside company. Pte Frank Richards (2nd Royal Welsh Fusiliers) wrote that his company took over a shallow trench which ran into a cemetery to

the east of Bazentin-le-Petit; HIGH WOOD was about 700yds in front of them. In his part of the trench the shells fell in front and behind. In the evening he was relieved and returned to MAMETZ WOOD, where he received news of a proposed attack on HIGH WOOD.

Arthur Russell noted that on 18 July before midnight he set off with a guide at a slow pace between the woods of MAMETZ and Bazentin-le-Petit; the guide lost his way and had to return for further directions. They then entered a sunken road, a German target for their artillery, along the side of Bazentin-le-Petit Wood. The gun positions which Russell's party took were a little in front of Bazentin-le-Petit Wood; when dawn broke they saw that they were on slightly higher ground overlooking German positions some 300yds away.

In one of Basil Liddell Hart's letters to Robert Graves (LH1/327/35) he wrote that, presumably in the early hours of 18 July, Graves moved up to relieve an Irish battalion just north of Bazentin-le-Petit Wood. On the way Graves ran into the new phosgene gas shells. Liddell Hart, serving with 9th King's Own Yorkshire Light Infantry (64th Brigade, 21st Division), ran into them too, with worse results, on his way back through MAMETZ WOOD after being relieved. His company had been sent up there to fill a gap left by a battalion that had got lost. Liddell Hart had been slightly wounded on the way up. When the missing units turned up later in the day, Liddell Hart's company was kept as an immediate reserve just behind Bazentin-le-Petit Wood for a couple of days, and so got the 'benefit of the first heavy dose' of the new gas shell, which burst all along the light railway to MAMETZ WOOD while they were marching down it in the dark.

On 19 July, Pte Frank Richards of 2nd Royal Welsh Fusiliers noted that the enemy shelled his men heavily, but the other end of the company were not as lucky as they were; the shells burst on the parapet, blowing trenches and men to pieces. In the cemetery, the shells were throwing corpses and coffins out of graves, and some of the dead were lying alongside them.

Posted to D Company, Graves was gassed while going up through the ruins of Bazentin-le-Petit village. Having established contact with C Company behind them on the right and 1/4th Suffolks, 50yds to the left, Graves's men began to widen their trenches, which were scooped beside the road. They then built two strongpoints, which were to be held with Lewis guns. Graves visited one of the points and went along the Bazentin–HIGH WOOD road, where 20th Royal Fusiliers (19th Brigade,

33rd Division) were wandering about. They were a constant embarrassment to 19th Brigade. On 19 July, 2nd Royal Welsh Fusiliers were relieved and told that they were to attack HIGH WOOD. According to Graves, the French called it Raven Wood. Graves took command of B Company, who were to relieve 1st Cameronians (19th Brigade, 33rd Division) in Bazentin Churchyard on the reverse slope of a slight ridge, about ½ mile from the wood. They were to be in reserve to the commanding officer of 1/5th Cameronians (19th Brigade, 33rd Division) with 20th Royal Fusiliers in support.

However, Graves was wounded before the attack by a splinter of marble, perhaps from a headstone in Bazentin Cemetery, which lodged itself in his body; together with other wounds in his chest and thigh, he received a total of eight wounds. He was transported via HEILLY and Rouen to hospital in London. His death was announced in *The Times* in error, leading Siegfried Sassoon to believe that his friend had been killed on 20 July.

In *The War the Infantry Knew*, a contributor who must be Pte Frank Richards wrote that he was detailed with some signallers to use Bazentin-le-Petit windmill, 200yds east of the cemetery, as the forward post of a relay system. The windmill had been the target of first the British and then the German artillery before 2nd Royal Welsh Fusiliers captured it. The assembly positions for the attack on HIGH WOOD, north-east of the village, were on ground that rose fairly steeply and was covered with coarse grass or standing corn, which would give some cover in the first stage of the advance.

In mid-July, D.J. Price of 20th Royal Fusiliers was in front of Bazentin-le-Petit and was involved in the dawn attack on 20 July. He wrote of the terrible casualties and of being for a time separated from his comrades. His battalion later returned to the rear of MAMETZ WOOD. In *Old Soldiers Never Die*, Pte Frank Richards wrote that on 20 July, when he was a brigade signaller, he formed a transmitting station together with seven others between HIGH WOOD and brigade headquarters, which was situated on the fringe of MAMETZ WOOD. The signallers were to use the flag system and their position was the large mill in Bazentin-le-Petit, on rising ground about 600yds from HIGH WOOD. This position gave them a good view but exposed them to continuous shelling; five of the signalling team were sheltering in a hole nearby and were 'useless', according to Richards. On the right front of the mill, a battalion of the Manchester Regiment occupied some shallow trenches, and a dressing station was in the valley below.

Signalling was later abandoned and instead the signallers became runners between brigade head-quarters and HIGH WOOD, below which a company of the Argyll & Sutherland Highlanders were in some shell-holes and shallow trenches; 'fifteen minutes of concentrated fire . . . destroyed them'.

At 2200hrs, 19th Brigade was relieved, 20th Royal Fusiliers having been practically annihilated; 2nd Royal Welsh Fusiliers were not much better off. 20th Royal Fusiliers sent across their 'spare' parcels, and 2nd Royal Welsh Fusiliers went back to a village south of ALBERT to reorganise. 1/5th Cameronians and 20th Royal Fusiliers had pushed on to the other side of HIGH WOOD and three battalions had become mixed up in the wood, and the northern part was still in German hands. Advanced Brigade of 2nd Royal Welsh Fusiliers were in a quarry by the cemetery roadside.

In *The War The Infantry Knew*, J.C. Dunn noted that 2nd Royal Welsh Fusiliers were relieved 'amid confusion', and held in reserve among the shell-holes between the LONGUEVAL–CONTALMAISON road and Flat Iron Copse. The massed artillery were behind them and traffic was mostly through MONTAUBAN-DE-PICARDIE. The attacking troops of 19th Brigade were caught in a barrage. After their relief by 1st Queen's and a company of 16th King's Royal Rifle Corps (both 100th Brigade, 33rd Division), 2nd Royal Welsh Fusiliers bivou-acked on the south-east side of MAMETZ WOOD. At 1500hrs they marched back to BUIRE-SUR-L'ANCRE with the transport.

A battalion of the North Staffordshire Regiment took over the line from the cemetery to the windmill; their headquarters was in a chalk pit in German dugouts.

Arthur Russell reported that 1st Middlesex (98th Brigade, 33rd Division) were holding a section of the Bazentin front; during 4 days (17–21 July) they had suffered very heavy casualties in their advance from Mametz Valley. Early in the afternoon he had to take a message down to company headquarters, and was told to stay back and get his leg seen to instead of returning to the gun position. Moving as fast as he could down the shell-torn track down the side of Bazentin-le-Petit Wood, and across the more open ground into Mametz Valley after delivering his message, he now took the opportunity of going to 98th Brigade's advanced dressing station at the far side of the valley, about 500yds away, passing close to several batteries of field artillery on the way. He entered the advanced dressing station dugout, which was excavated into the bank of a stone quarry with 'a kind of covered verandah of corrugated iron and sandbags in front of it'. On the night of 21 July there were a lot of poison-gas shells and next morning 1st Middlesex went back to rest.

As previously mentioned, on 20 July Robert Graves had become a casualty when a third of 2nd Royal Welsh Fusiliers were knocked out before their attack had even begun. J.C. Dunn, the battalion medical officer, had been responsible for getting him down to the old German dressing station at the north end of MAMETZ WOOD. Graves was thought to have been mortally wounded but on 21 July was found to be still alive and was sent to HEILLY, the nearest field hospital. The pain of being jolted down HAPPY VALLEY made him 'wake up screaming'.

D.J. Price of 20th Royal Fusiliers, who had endured some of the horrors of HIGH WOOD, had enlisted under age; on 21 July he was told to report home, as his mother had managed to get him withdrawn from the line. Even so, Price rejoined the battalion in January 1917.

While trying to defeat a machine-gun post which had been causing havoc from a position known as the Barricade, Lt H.S.H. Wallace of 10th Worcesters (57th Brigade, 19th Division) was killed, close to the windmill at Bazentin-le-Petit. The site of the Barricade is to the north of the Wallace Memorial.

By 25 July, after 11 days of fighting, Bazentin-le-Petit Wood had become a carpet of corpses.

At Bazentin-le-Grand between 20 and 30 July the field artillery of four divisions were in action, but they were not coordinated.

In the Bazentin sector, telephone exchanges north of MAMETZ were established for infantry and one for artillery, with a cross-connection between them. At the end of July, Bazentin Military Cemetery was begun, outside the western wall in a German dugout.

In the last two days of July, James Miller of 7th King's Own (56th Brigade, 19th Division) won the Victoria Cross at Bazentin-le-Petit, when his battalion were consolidating a position after their capture by assault. Ordered to take an important message under heavy shell and rifle fire, and to bring back a reply at all costs, Miller was compelled to cross the open; on leaving the trench, he was shot almost immediately in the back, the bullet emerging from his abdomen. In spite of this, with heroic courage and self-sacrifice, he delivered his message, staggered back with the answer, and fell at the feet of the officer to whom the message was to be delivered. His grave is at Dartmoor Cemetery (I.C.64).

On 28 July, No. 82 Field Company, Royal Engineers, and 57th Brigade (both 19th Division) received orders to proceed to MAMETZ WOOD in order to take over dugouts from No. 94 Field

Company (also 19th Division). In the event, 57th Brigade orders were put off for 24 hours and No. 82 Field Company were attached to 58th Brigade instead. After dark on 29 July they were working at a dump to the north-east of Bazentin-le-Petit when enemy shelling caused 25 casualties within a few minutes, of whom 6 men were killed. Three men had been killed the previous night; these men were commemorated in the 'Nine Brave Men' in the village.

Maj Butterworth, Officer Commanding No. 82 Field Company, returned to the village in November 1917, and a granite block made in the divisional workshop was put up as a private memorial to those killed, using bricks from the ruins of the village. The memorial was restored in the 1980s and again most recently in 1998.

C.S. Collison of 11th Royal Warwicks (112th Brigade, 37th Division) wrote that on 3 August, 34th Division held the part of the front from the western edge of HIGH WOOD to a line of trenches running east and west, and about 300yds north of Bazentin-le-Petit. Two battalions of 111th Brigade (attached to 34th Division) and two of 101st Brigade (34th Division) were in the front line, their supports in the woods of MAMETZ and Bazentin-le-Petit. In reserve near BOTTOM WOOD were 6th Bedfords and 8th East Lancashires (both 112th Brigade, attached to 34th Division), with 10th Loyals (112th Brigade) in bivouacs about Bécourt Wood. On 5 August, Collison went forward via Quadrangle Trench and MAMETZ WOOD to arrange for the relief of 11th Suffolks (101st Brigade, 34th Division), who were entrenched on the southern outskirts of Bazentin-le-Petit Wood and the north-western part of MAMETZ WOOD.

On 13 August, 1/4th Suffolks (98th Brigade, 33rd Division) moved from Fricourt Wood to support trenches in Bazentin-le-Grand Wood. The former German Line ran south of Bazentin-le-Petit Wood. Edge Trench, on the northern edge of the wood, was still in German hands.

According to *The War The Infantry Knew*, on 18 August, 2nd Royal Welsh Fusiliers moved forward and arrived in the dark on the LONGUEVAL–Bazentin road below HIGH WOOD, where they waited.

Lt Col W.B. Lyons, Commanding Officer 2nd Royal Munster Fusiliers (3rd Brigade, 1st Division), was mortally wounded while making a personal reconnaissance. On 27 August, Edge Trench fell into British hands.

L/Cpl B.W. Whayman's unit was involved in fatigue-carrying parties and minelaying in HIGH

WOOD and in carrying trench mortar shells known as 'toffee apples'. The main communication trench at the time, known as High Alley, was in front of Bazentin-le-Grand; it was about 80yds long. Whayman's battalion relieved 1st Black Watch (1st Brigade, 1st Division) but were shelled by both sides. On relief they went to ALBERT. On 9 September, Whayman's battalion relieved 2nd Royal Munster Fusiliers, of whom only 20 men were left out of 60, and bivouacked at Bazentin for a week.

On 20 September, shelters and dugouts were built at Mill Road near Bazentin-le-Petit. The road ran east of a quarry where brigade headquarters was positioned. The two villages contained CPs for the wounded. Norman Gladden of 1/7th Northumberland Fusiliers (149th Brigade, 50th Division) later wrote that at 0630hrs on a morning in late September, they left for the reserve position and moved out of the wood and passed Bazentin-le-Petit, 'an immense rubbish heap of sheltered buildings which had been cordoned off and boldly signposted'. As they skirted the windward side the 'horrible stench of the unburied dead filled their nostrils'. The 'sickly smell of rotting humanity', which they were to come to know too well, so that it 'almost seeped into their dreams', overhung the pulverised village, 'like a pall above a communal tomb', as it indeed was.

The headquarters of 149th and 150th Brigades (both 50th Division) were here on 23/24 October and in November they entrained, 'a weak and weary collection of human wrecks', at the railhead, which had now been brought as far forward as Bazentin-le-Petit. Here, the landscape was acquiring a 'shipshape look', with new living quarters springing up like mushrooms in the form of neatly arranged hutments and other amenities.

In Bazentin Communal Cemetery, which in 1925 was 'simply a shambles', according to the Imperial War Graves Commission, are the graves of two men who died in August 1916. The Bazentin Communal Cemetery is east of the village next to the Bazentin Communal Cemetery Extension, which had been begun immediately after the capture of the village in mid-July and was used until December as a front-line cemetery. It was enlarged after the Armistice from battlefields of Bazentin and CONTALMAISON. The graves include 59 unidentified casualties, mainly of 1st Northamptons (2nd Brigade, 1st Division), whose graves had been destroyed and are now represented by special memorials. The ground rises to the north-west and east and falls to the south towards CATERPILLAR VALLEY. Begun in July 1916, Bazentin Military Cemetery is behind a group of cottages on the west side of the village and was used as a front-line cemetery until May 1917. On the west wall is the site of a German dugout. At the end of the battle the wood was almost impassable and the villages here were full of old trenches and the wreckage of strongpoints. The two villages were lost by the British in March 1918 and then retaken after the fall of THIEPVAL on 25 August 1918.

W.R. Bird of 42nd Canadian Battalion (7th Canadian Brigade, 3rd Canadian Division), author of *Thirteen Years After*, revisited the village in 1932 and wrote: 'There were many old cellars and ruins to be discovered, and the road twists as in other villages and winds uphill to Nissen huts placed side by side like a small camp. Wooden barns, concrete plain church, and a combined mairie and ecole, and you have the picture, but you need three inches of soft mud to squelch about your boots and the smell of middens in your nostrils to make you know where you are.'

In addition to the memorial to the Nine Brave Men from No. 3 Section of 82nd Field Company, who were killed between 29 and 31 July 1916, just outside Bazentin-le-Petit there is one to Capt H.S.H. Wallace of 10th Worcesters (57th Brigade, 19th Division) down a track in the direction of HIGH WOOD. He was killed on 22 July 1916 during an attempt by D Company to capture an enemy machine-gun post. As his body was never found his name is commemorated on the Thiepval Memorial. In 1925 his maiden aunt, a Miss Beatrice Heap, commissioned the erection of a memorial to her nephew, which was later looked after by the Imperial War Graves Commission on behalf of the commune until 1945. In 1991 it was in a bad state and so the Western Front Association, together with the Worcestershire Regiment and the commune itself, decided to have it repaired. The memorial was rededicated on 23 October 1994 in a service that took place in pouring rain.

BEAUCOURT-SUR-L'ANCRE is a village to the east of BEAUMONT-HAMEL and north-east of HAMEL on the D50 in the ANCRE VALLEY. In 1916 it was situated on the boundary of the German lines. At the beginning of the battle, it was a very strong defensive position that received relief and support from the enemy-held villages of GRAND-COURT and MIRAUMONT and from elsewhere behind the occupied area.

The battle for BEAUMONT-HAMEL and Beaucourt-sur-l'Ancre had been planned for October 1916 but had been postponed several times because of the unfavourable weather conditions. In the end it took place between 13 and 19 November.

The school at Bazentin after the war.
(*Peter F. Batchelor Collection*)

In brief, the first British objective was the strong line of German trenches; the second was Station Road, running from BEAUMONT-HAMEL to the ALBERT–Lille railway; the third was the trenches on the outskirts of Beaucourt-sur-l'Ancre and finally the village itself.

Beaucourt-sur-l'Ancre was to become most closely associated with 63rd Division; Douglas Jerrold, a member of that division, became the chief historian of the battle and it is from his books *The Hawke Battalion* and *The Royal Naval Division* that the author has drawn this short history of the battle. Assigned to V Corps for the planned attack to the north of the River Ancre, 63rd Division had a front 1,200yds wide, immediately north of the river and at right angles to the river valley, which at this point ran almost due east to Beaucourt-sur-l-Ancre. At the same time the German trenches ran roughly from north to south.

One of 63rd Division's objectives was the village of Beaucourt-sur-l'Ancre itself and the intervening positions opposite the British front. At a distance of between 150yds and 250yds from the British assembly trenches, on high ground, was the German front-line system; this consisted of three lines of trenches that formed the first objective, known for that purpose as the Dotted Green Line. Behind the front-line system and separated from it by a valley, through which Station Road ran, was a second ridge running from BEAUMONT-HAMEL to Beaucourt-sur-l'Ancre station. On this ridge was a strongly fortified position, called the Green Line. This was the second defined objective. The country immediately behind this line was featureless, except for the right front of the divisional sector, where it sloped up to the hill immediately, with the enemy forward system on this part of the line. On the western face of this hill was a trench, which continued parallel to the front across the more level ground on the left. This was known as the Yellow Line and formed 63rd Division's third objective. The final objective, known as the Red Line, was a roughly defined position to be taken up beyond Beaucourt-sur-l'Ancre, the capture of which would be a great success.

The first and third objectives were to be attacked by 1st Royal Marines and the Howe, Hawke and Hood Battalions, each advancing in four waves. The first four battalions would then rest on the first objective, the German Front Line trench, and reorganise. The second and fourth objectives were to be attacked by 2nd Royal Marines and the Anson, Nelson and Drake Battalions. The battalions were to pass through the lines and capture Station Road Valley, and the Green Line.

They would rest and reorganise, while the first four battalions passed through to the Yellow Line. The final assault on the village was then, after another pause, to be carried out by the battalions who reorganised on the Green Line. A subsection of the brigade machine-gun company was to accompany each battalion, and trench mortars were to follow as soon as possible.

In the early morning of 13 November the main problem initially was that the Hawke and the Hood Battalions, who were to lead the frontal attack with Hawke on the left and Hood on the right, were having to line up on the forward slope of the Allied position, since the reverse slope of the very steep crest of the ridge was needed to hide the supporting battalions. Further back still, in what were normally the reserve and support trenches, were packed two battalions of 190th Brigade. On 12 November, the day before, all surplus personnel had gone back to the transport lines at HÉDAUVILLE. Of the four Hawke Battalion companies, B were on the left, next to Cdr Fairfax's Howe Battalion.

The morning was very misty and abnormally dark. After a creeping barrage employing the full strength of the British artillery was opened on the narrow divisional front, the first wave of the Hawke Battalion moved off at 0545hrs into the mist; they were soon out of sight, when still only 70yds away. Soon the fourth wave, 50yds behind the others, was itself out of sight. Through the mist, and deafened by the explosions of guns, almost choked by lyddite, the Hawke Battalion simply disappeared. Less than 20 of the men and none of the officers were to come back unscathed. They had gone into action with over 400 officers and men.

The whole stretch of the front line could be seen to be in the possession of the enemy but it was the infamous Beaucourt-sur-l'Ancre Redoubt that had brought about the Hawke's downfall, directing heavy fire against the battalion, who had the misfortune to attack directly opposite it. On the left of the Redoubt, in touch with the right of the Howe Battalion, Sub Lt The Hon. V.S.T. Harmsworth RNVR, son of Lord Rothermere and nephew of Lord Northcliffe, was wounded in no man's land as he led the remains of his company to the German Second Line. Here the last of them were hit and Harmsworth himself was mortally wounded by machine-gun fire from the direction of the Redoubt. He was later buried in Ancre British Cemetery (V.E.19).

On the right of the line the Hood Battalion, perhaps because they kept closer to the barrage, reached the German Front Line and passed through it without a devastating number of casualties.

They proceeded to destroy the dugouts in the railway cutting to their right, part of a vast system of underground works running from the river to BEAUMONT-HAMEL. Lt Col B.C. Freyberg, Commanding Officer Hood Battalion, decided to throw the whole weight of his battalion into the next advance, instead of endeavouring to reorganise in the mist and darkness. The combined attack was brilliantly successful and the dugouts in Station Road yielded some 400 prisoners. The Hawke and Nelson Battalions, which had been so devastated by fire from the Redoubt, were put under Freyberg's command for the remainder of the battle. The Nelson Battalion had been attempting to assault the Station Road when they were enfiladed from the Redoubt.

Next to the Hawke and Nelson Battalions were the Howe and Anson Battalions; their flank was uncovered as a result of the failure of the attack against the Redoubt. On the extreme left of the attack, 1st and 2nd Marines met with disaster from enemy artillery at the very start; to their left, 51st Division engaged in a successful assault on BEAUMONT-HAMEL, the adjoining village.

There were now two parties on the Green Line and Freyberg's alone was secure in its communications, adequate in numbers and adequately officered. Together with Lt Cdr Gilliland he led two independent assaults on the Yellow Line. However, because of increasing communication problems, Freyberg was forbidden to carry on to the Red Line. The enemy still remained in the centre of their former front system.

One of the casualties of the Hood Battalion on 13 November was Lt Cdr F.S. Kelly. Born in 1881, he was an oarsman, composer and musician who had been educated at Eton and Balliol College, Oxford. He was a contemporary of Rupert Brooke and was one of Brooke's pallbearers when he was buried at Skyros. Kelly himself was later buried in Martinsart British Cemetery (I.H.25). Lt. H. Cecil (Royal Field Artillery) was awarded the Military Cross for laying and repairing a line while under fire on 13 November, and Cdr Sterndale-Bennett gained the Distinguished Service Order; assuming command of his battalion, he collected a party and bombed the enemy out of the Second Line, which had threatened to hold up the attack.

On 14 November, Allied artillery fire was opened on Munich Trench, which was opposite 51st and 2nd Divisions. 111th Brigade (37th Division) were sent to assist in the battle for Beaucourt-sur-l'Ancre. Guy Chapman's battalion, 13th Royal Fusiliers and 13th Rifle Brigade (both 111th Brigade, 37th Division), who had their right on Redoubt Valley, attacked from Station Road. A loss of direction at the beginning of the advance was partially corrected as a result of the sound of machine-gun fire from the village. Muck Trench then formed the second objective. About 480 men were collected at Beaucourt-sur-l'Ancre station and came under heavy machine-gun and rifle fire and then reached Freyberg's position. The latter led the mixed force into the village of Beaucourt-sur-l'Ancre while 13th King's Royal Rifle Corps, also of 111th Brigade, 37th Division pressed forward south-eastwards through the village.

Prisoners were captured from cellars and dugouts and a line was established around the eastern edge and the village fell by mid-morning. Jerrold asserted that Freyberg had arranged to assault the village with the help of 13th King's Royal Rifle Corps and 1/1st Honourable Artillery Company (190th Brigade, 63rd Division)) and had left the Hood and Drake Battalions in support. However, the unlooked-for arrival of 7th Royal Fusiliers (190th Brigade, 63rd Divison) behind the Yellow Line had caused considerable confusion. It was at this point that a separate battle was being fought by tanks against the enemy, who had still been occupying trenches around the Redoubt. The tanks, which had come from AUCHONVILLERS, got stuck. The whole German garrison (600 strong) were marched back to the British lines. The Redoubt and the village had been captured and it only remained to consolidate the hold on the village and clear up the situation on the flanks of the position. Freyberg was wounded for the third time and this time severely. He was awarded the Victoria Cross for his leadership on these 2 days.

The *Official History of the War* noted that, at 1300hrs on 14 November, German infantry were seen massing near BAILLESCOURT FARM, south-east of the village. The bridge over the river was held by 1/1st Honourable Artillery Company. The German counter-attack against Beaucourt-sur-l'Ancre did not materialise, however, and 63rd Division were relieved and the remains of the different battalions assembled and reorganised in the captured front-line system. They joined together at ENGLEBELMER from where they were taken in buses to ARQUÈVES, well behind the fighting zone. The story of the ill-fated Hawke Battalion, which had virtually ceased to exist on 13 November, has already been told. It played its part while the German machine-gunners, untouched by the Allied barrage, took toll of the eight lines of the Hawke and Nelson Battalions who were up against the Redoubt. There was a point of controversy about the immunity of the garrison of the Redoubt from the effects of the artillery barrage; the only possible explanation is that the exact position of the Redoubt was simply not known to the attackers and that no special artillery support had been requested.

The writer A.P. Herbert was not involved in the fighting on 13 November as he was with the cadre left behind in support and he reported to Maj Norris in the evening to join Freyberg's front force. Born in 1890, Herbert had joined the Hawke Battalion at a camp at ABBEVILLE that summer, after the Gallipoli campaign.

The position of 63rd Division as part of the British Army was an awkward one and the possibility of relegation from Naval to Army status was anathema to both Herbert and Jerrold. Herbert had been made Assistant Adjutant and was one of two officers from the battalion who had emerged unscathed. On the down side, during the fighting there occurred a failure of morale that resulted in the court-martial and execution of Sub Lt E. Dyett of the Nelson Battalion. Herbert may have known the circumstances, as well as knowing the individual concerned. Certainly he used aspects of the case in his book *The Secret Battle*, which he began to write in 1918.

After reorganisation, in 1916–17 the division ceased to be 'a semi-naval, semi-civilian force' and was integrated into the Army as 63rd Division. When it went into the line in February 1917, Herbert was on leave. On his return, according to Jerrold, as Adjutant he revitalised battalion headquarters. In September 1917, Herbert published a poem called 'Beaucourt-sur-l'Ancre Revisited', written seemingly as a result of a return visit to this part of the Somme battlefield. In it he refers to Suicide Corner, Kentish Caves and the place where Harmsworth was shot. He also mentions 'young James' and 'William'; these can be identified as two friends of Herbert's, James Cook and William Ker. Herbert died in 1971. Douglas Jerrold, whose writings have been much drawn upon for this section, was severely wounded on the Somme; after the war he became a writer and publisher, dying in 1964.

There is a memorial to 63rd Division in the village itself and another to a Pte D. Amos, who died near this spot on 21 November 1916. The memorial, located in d'Hollande Wood, takes the form of a wooden cross attached to a tree, which carries a brass plaque. The Naval Division Memorial was set up on the site that the 189th Infantry Brigade made its gallant stand (13/14 November) in an area of land owned by a Madame Maison and purchased for 250 francs. The memorial, mainly funded by Lord Rothermere and designed by the architect Alan G. Brace in 1921, was unveiled on 12 November 1922 by General Sir Hubert Gough together with Brig. Gen. Arthur Asquith in the presence of 200 survivors from the action. A small memorial plaque was also presented to the Mairie in Beaucourt.

Asquith, Freyberg and the Hon Lionel S. Montagu, a son of Baron Swaythling were chums, and 'Cardy' Montague oversaw the negotiations at Beaucourt with the owner of the proposed site for the memorial for the purchase of 250 francs. There is a link with the Hon Lionel Stuart Montague DSO (1883-1948) who travelled to France to select a suitable site in June 1921. Friend of Brigadier General A. Asquith. DSO for Beaucourt and awarded in 1917.

BEAUCOURT-SUR-L'HALLUE is on the D919 AMIENS–CONTAY road. In the First World War, the château was used for military purposes. Soon after British troops began to take over the lines from the French, 10th Essex (53rd Brigade, 18th Division) marched via the village and met up with two French battalions returning from the line after being relieved by the British. Mutual greetings were exchanged.

On 22 December 1915, 1/6th Black Watch (153rd Brigade, 51st Division) arrived here. On 6 January 1916, 1st East Surreys (95th Brigade, 5th Division) spent 5 weeks training here, before moving to POULAINVILLE on 13 February. No. 491 Field Company, Royal Engineers (5th Division), were also billeted here from 6 January, when they were involved in work at the sawmill and in improving billets at the château later in the month. No. 454 Field Company, Royal Engineers (49th Division), also carried out work at the sawmill. In March 1916, the headquarters of 146th Brigade (49th Division) was here.

BEAUMONT-HAMEL is a village on the D163 road between BEAUCOURT-SUR-L'ANCRE and AUCHONVILLERS, on the west bank of the River Ancre. There are three spurs, named AUCHON-VILLERS, BEAUCOURT-SUR-L'ANCRE and GRANDCOURT and between them there are shallow valleys separating the three villages. The village of Beaumont-Hamel connects with the road that runs eastwards from AUCHONVILLERS. A valley, called Y RAVINE in 1916, cuts into the south side of Hawthorn Ridge. The remaining valley was known as Beaucourt-sur-l'Ancre Valley; marked by the BEAUCOURT-SUR-L'ANCRE–PUISIEUX road, it passed south of SERRE. The COLINCAMPS–BEAUCOURT-SUR-L'ANCRE Spur was known as the REDAN RIDGE where it crossed the front line.

The German Front Line first ran along the eastern slope of the AUCHONVILLERS spur and then passed around the head of Y RAVINE to Hawthorn Ridge. It then crossed the shallow Beaumont-Hamel Valley and continued across to the Redan Bridge (Beaucourt-sur-l'Ancre Spur) and on to where SERRE stood. The German Intermediate Line, known as Munich Trench, began from Beaucourt-sur-l'Ancre Redoubt and went north and included the village of SERRE; the German Second Line ran from GRANDCOURT to PUISIEUX.

On 29 October 1915, 1st Royal Dublin Fusiliers (86th Brigade, 29th Division) arrived in this sector and were the first unit to occupy a position known as the WHITE CITY. In the months before the start of the battle, the Beaumont-Hamel sector was to become most associated with 29th Division, which had previously served in Gallipoli. Judging by the number of casualties 29th Division suffered during this period, it should have become clear to High Command just how strongly held the German defences in this sector were.

Before 1914 Beaumont-Hamel had about 162 houses and was the third largest village on the Somme. The village had a system of caves and underground passages, which had been excavated to obtain hard chalk for building. Later John Masefield described the village as being unrecognisable to its former occupants. The German position known as the Bergwerk was on the Beaucourt-sur-l'Ancre Ridge, immediately behind the northern end of Beaumont-Hamel.

On 1 July 1916, 29th Division (VIII Corps) was the main British formation to be involved in the battle for Beaumont-Hamel, with 36th Division (X Corps) on its right and 4th Division, facing towards REDAN RIDGE, on its left. In addition, there were 1/6th and 1/8th Royal Warwicks of 143rd Brigade (48th Division) on the extreme left. These two battalions were involved in the attack on the QUADRILATERAL towards Pendant Copse, to the south-east of SERRE, which was the objective of 31st Division. The ground the two battalions were to cover had a series of deep chalk pits that gave every advantage to the German defenders and the QUADRILATERAL, with a frontage of about 400yds, gave a flanking fire along the whole position. There were a great many machine guns. There was little cover between the German and the British trenches but there was a slight rise in the German direction.

At 0730hrs on 1 July, 1/8th Royal Warwicks moved off; by 0750hrs, the first four lines of enemy trench had been taken, and small groups penetrated SERRE and the outskirts of Beaumont-Hamel. Some troops even advanced as far as Pendant Copse, but were then driven back. The position was held tenaciously until 1330hrs, but as the neighbouring divisions, 29th and 31st, were making little or no progress, 4th Division were ordered to retire. Brig Gen C.B. Prowse, General Officer Commanding 11th Brigade (4th Division), was killed early in the action, when moving his headquarters forward from the former British line to the German trenches after their capture by 1/8th Royal Warwicks. The Germans counter-attacked later in the afternoon and large numbers of wounded men from 1/8th Royal Warwicks were left behind in the German lines.

The men of 1/6th Royal Warwicks were intended to capture the fifth and sixth lines but this was not to be, as they were decimated before they reached the higher ground in front of SERRE. In the evening the troops retired; 1/8th Royal Warwicks had suffered 573 casualties out of 600 men. The survivors withdrew to MAILLY-MAILLET and then rested in Couin Wood for 10 days.

Behind the two Royal Warwickshire battalions was 1st King's Own (12th Brigade, 4th Division), supporting 1st Rifle Brigade (11th Brigade, 4th Division) in the attack on the REDAN RIDGE. At 0720hrs the battalion moved off under artillery fire and were faced with uncut wire. Casualties were very considerable and by evening the men of 1st King's Own were back in their own lines. They too were withdrawn to MAILLY-MAILLET.

11th Brigade were to attack with 1st Rifle Brigade and 1st East Lancashires leading. 1st Rifle Brigade moved off at 0729hrs and 1st East Lancashires immediately came under fire from Ridge Redoubt and also from Beaumont-Hamel itself. The German wire was uncut and 1st Rifle Brigade were caught between the Quadrilateral and the Ridge Redoubt, from which murderous machine-gun fire came. The riflemen managed to bomb their way to their objective but were themselves bombed out in turn. The following morning, 1st Rifle Brigade were relieved by 1st Royal Irish Fusiliers (10th Brigade, 4th Division), having suffered 474 casualties.

Behind 1st Rifle Brigade, 1st Somerset Light Infantry (11th Brigade, 4th Division) moved off at 0730hrs and, along with other elements of 11th Brigade, quickly came under heavy rifle and machine-gun fire from both flanks. An eyewitness report of what happened can be read in A.H. Cook's account in *A Soldier's War*. At 0530hrs, the men of 1st Somerset Light Infantry breakfasted; at this time the German lines were one cloud of smoke from the Allied bombardment. Men from the battalion managed to get their scaling ladders into position in order to enable them to climb out of the trenches. There were also bridges for following troops to use. The guns then quietened and the Somersets thought that their part in the attack was going to be 'a cakewalk'.

At 0720hrs, the mine under Hawthorn Redoubt to the south exploded; the force of the explosion shook the Somersets' trenches. The Somersets were supposed to follow 1st Rifle Brigade at 0740hrs, but they were 'keen to be off', and followed up after only a few minutes. However, just before the forward troops reached the German lines, the enemy opened up with murderous machine-gun fire and the Somersets found themselves caught in no man's land. Men began to fall all around but the attackers were forced to go on, despite the whole front's being covered by strategically placed guns.

The Somersets then swung to the left, as to approach their objective directly meant that they would go over rising ground swept by machine-gun fire. The British guns had made a mess of the German trenches but there were few German dead to be seen, only the bodies of the British attackers. During the bombardment, the Germans had taken refuge in deep dugouts, some more than 30ft deep. Later the Somersets managed to obtain some support from 10th and 12th Brigades (4th Division), but their only hope was to consolidate their meagre gains. It was during this action that their commanding officer, Lt Col J.A. Thicknesse, was killed; he was later buried at Sucrerie Military Cemetery, COLINCAMPS (I.H.15).

At 0900hrs, 2nd Seaforth Highlanders (10th Brigade, 4th Division) came up with reinforcements. Small parties on the left had begun to bomb forward towards Munich Trench, but gradually Cook and his colleagues were driven back by the Germans through part of the QUADRILATERAL to the left of REDAN RIDGE. They used their own as well as German bombs and were finally relieved at 1100hrs. Men from various battalions ended up in the QUADRILATERAL and after dark the Somersets were relieved by 1st Royal Irish Fusiliers and withdrew to their own lines. At 1000hrs on 2 July, the Somersets found their brigade reserve at MAILLY-MAILLET. Cook noted that at the roll call, none of the 26 officers who had gone into action had returned and the casualties among the other ranks were 478. On 3 July they went into huts at BERTRANCOURT. It seemed to Cook that the previous day's battle had been a test of the respective merits of heavy artillery and machine guns and the machine guns had won. Strategically, the result of the attack had been absolutely nil.

To the right of 1st Rifle Brigade were 1st East Lancashires (11th Brigade, 4th Division), with 1st Hampshires (also 11th Brigade, 4th Division) behind them. Immediately after the British guns lifted from the German Front Line trenches, there came heavy machine-gun fire from that direction. One officer could see at least eight guns either from Ridge Redoubt or from Beaumont-Hamel itself. Simultaneously, the German artillery barrage came down in front of them. Many were killed on the uncut wire. The East Lancashires were relieved in the evening by 1st Royal Warwicks (10th Brigade, 4th Division), and went on to MAILLY-MAILLET before leaving for BERTRANCOURT on 3 July.

Moving off after 1st East Lancashires, 1st Hampshires found that the East Lancashires had been almost wiped out by machine-gun fire. Col Park fell before he could get halfway across, and the majority of the Hampshires were brought down before they reached the wire; 321 were killed and 265 wounded. The survivors went back to MAILLY-MAILLET on relief.

It was probably during this time that Drummer W.P. Ritchie of 2nd Seaforth Highlanders (10th Brigade, 4th Division) won the Victoria Cross. Ritchie, a headquarters orderly, left his shell-hole, jumped up onto the parapet of a German trench and sounded the advance on his bugle in order to encourage men of various regiments who were beginning to 'wander off'. This action was witnessed by Sir John Laurie, adjutant of 2nd Seaforth Highlanders, and Col Hopkinson. Ritchie, who later showed great bravery when delivering important messages over fire-swept ground, was probably close to Cook of 1st Somerset Light Infantry when the action took place.

To the right of 1st East Lancashires were 1st Lancashire Fusiliers (86th Brigade, 39th Division). Having trained in Mailly Wood, 1st Lancashire Fusiliers took up their positions the night before the attack in the famous Sunken Road, also known as Hunter's Lane, which ran in a northerly direction from the AUCHONVILLERS–Beaumont road, just outside the latter. The Sunken Road was between 10ft and 15ft deep; it was shallow at the northern end and overhung with trees at the southern end. The British had dug tunnels from the front line to this natural trench. At 0330hrs, one of the tunnels was opened; B and D Companies and the 12th Brigade bombing company, with eight Stokes mortars, occupied the Sunken Road, followed there by battalion headquarters at 0700hrs. They were to the east of The Bowery, WHITE CITY and JACOB'S LADDER.

A vivid description of the Sunken Road appears in John Masefield's book *The Old Front Line*. He described it as being 500yds long, and below the level of the fields on each side from its start in the valley road to a point about 200yds up the spur. It was the deep part, which was like a broad natural trench, which was known to the troops as the Sunken Road. The men had built up walls of sandbags in the road itself to reduce the effects of shell-fire. Defences cut into the chalk of the bank led to the field above, where machine-gun pits were positioned. The field in front of the Sunken Road was 'a fairly smooth slope' for about 50yds. Then there was a 'lynchet like a steep cliff' from 3ft to 12ft high, 'hardly to be noticed until almost upon it'.

From the Sunken Road the troops could not see the sudden dip down but 'rather a continuous grassy field, at first flat and then rising towards the enemy'. The Germans had a small salient thrusting out here and to reach it the British had to 'run across the field

from the Sunken Road, slide down the bank of the lynchet, and then run up the glacis to the parapet'. The Sunken Road was an advanced post or jumping-off point, the use of which would gain precious time when the attack commenced. However, mainly because of the unknown geographical hazards mentioned above, 1st Lancashire Fusiliers' attack was a disaster.

Before the battle began, the official War Office photographer, Geoffrey Malins, had as his destination the position known as the WHITE CITY. When the British arrived on this front in the summer of 1915, they had named this spur, slightly north of the AUCHONVILLERS–Beaumont-Hamel road, the WHITE CITY, due to the chalky texture of the ground with its trenches, dugouts, headquarters and aid posts. The steep western edge was virtually a reverse slope and gave protection from German shelling. Barricades of sandbags were erected here and the construction of communication trenches to the front line began. To this day the area that was formerly the WHITE CITY can still be easily traced in outline at the rear of the plâteau.

In *How I Filmed the War*, Malins wrote that on his way to the WHITE CITY he went down a trench called Tenderloin Street. About 100yds to his right, Malins' guide pointed out the brigade dugout, at the junction of King Street and St Helens Street. The two men then continued on by way of King Street to Lanwick Street, at the end of which they met up with an artillery observer officer, who was correcting the range of his guns. Malins then carried out some filming until the enemy began to use gas shells. He returned to the WHITE CITY; when it was dark, Malins and an officer retraced the earlier journey to King Street and followed it to JACOB'S LADDER.

JACOB'S LADDER was 'a sudden open space, as if the trench had been sliced off' and it left a clear view of the British front-line trenches, and also beyond them. Malins was on the bank of a small valley; leading down from the position were about 25 steps, hence the name of JACOB'S LADDER. This seemed to Malins to be a very good position from which to film, as the enemy lines could be seen some 70yds away.

The British plan was for the Stokes mortars to barrage the German Second Line from the Sunken Road. After returning to the WHITE CITY, Malins was invited to film 1st Lancashire Fusiliers in the Sunken Road. He found the battalion in position with bayonets fixed, crouching as close to the bank as possible. Knowing that the attack was timed for 0730hrs and wanting to obtain some footage of the intended mine explosion under Hawthorn Ridge,

White City near Beaumont-Hamel. *(IWM Q796)*

Malins set his camera going and planned to return at around 0630hrs. When he returned, however, most of JACOB'S LADDER had been blown down, so he found a new place for his camera on the side of a small bank, well protected by sandbags, which led off from the trench called the Moving Staircase. He began to film the explosion of the Hawthorn Ridge.

The Lancashire Fusiliers were cut down as soon as they left the Sunken Road, as were companies who had come up to join them in the attack. After noon, the attack was called off, by which time over 100 men lay wounded in the Sunken Road. At 1800hrs the road was evacuated, apart from a small holding party, snipers and shelling having caused havoc. On 4 July, the remaining men of 1st Lancashire Fusiliers marched back to Acheux Wood. In November 1916, 180 bodies of this battalion were found in the Sunken Road.

At this point it seems sensible to tell the story of the background of the mine explosion at Hawthorn Ridge; the main sources are the *History of the Corps of Royal Engineers* and the *Official History of the War*. The British plan of attack had always included provision to destroy Hawthorn Ridge with a mine. Just to the left of the road to

AUCHONVILLERS, the ridge or redoubt was part of the German Front Line defence of Beaumont-Hamel. Marked with a group of trees, the crater can be reached by a footpath that runs between two fields and is the highest point in the area. It can also be visited from the direction of Hawthorn Ridge Cemetery No. 1.

Work on the position, coded 'H3 Mine', began in the spring of 1916. It was 75ft deep and was directed towards Hawthorn Ridge, which was 1,050ft distant. By the end of May the mine gallery had been driven 900ft, despite considerable trouble caused by the hard chalk and the number of flints in the face. Silence was of course paramount and the face was softened by the application of water. The material had to be carefully dug out in order not to disclose what was going on. South of H3 Mine were two saps named First Avenue and Mary; both had emplacements for Stokes guns, and were well forward into no man's land. Russian saps usually were named after the communication trenches leading into them.

No. 252 Tunnelling Company, Royal Engineers, successfully laid the large mine under Hawthorn Redoubt, but a very great mistake was made at the last minute as a consequence of disagreement about when exactly it should be blown. The VIII Corps commander, the flamboyant Lt Gen A.G. Hunter-

Weston (late of the Royal Engineers) wanted to fire it at 0330hrs, 4 hours before Zero Hour. In his opinion this would result in the crater being occupied and possibly consolidated by the British before Zero Hour and by then the German alarm would have subsided. The views of General Headquarters were, however, against this plan, on the grounds that it was more likely that the enemy would occupy the crater first and therefore seize the advantage. In the end a compromise was made, which was probably the worst of the three choices. The mine was to be fired 10 minutes early, at 0720hrs, a decision which ignored the advice of the Engineers and resulted in the very situation occurring that was to be avoided at all costs. Already aware of the timing of the attack from captured Allied prisoners, together with other intelligence, the Germans were to make full use of this clear 10 minutes' warning.

The explosion of the mine was to begin the battle and also provide the first objective. 2nd Royal Fusiliers (86th Brigade, 29th Division) were to seize the Ridge, supported by 1st Royal Dublin Fusiliers and with 16th Middlesex (86th Brigade, 29th Division) to their left. At 0515hrs, as the bombardment was reaching a crescendo, 2nd Royal Fusiliers were in position between the AUCHONVILLERS road and just north of the River Ancre. Later a smoke barrage was put down. The artillery had to lift 10 minutes early because of the early blowing of the mine, alerting the Germans even more.

Malins has given us a graphic description of the explosion, and noted that the ground where he stood with his camera working 'gave a mighty convulsion and rocked and swayed. The earth rose in the air to the height of hundreds of feet and with a grinding roar fell back upon itself. All that was left was a mountain of smoke.' He was filming during all this period and produced what was to become possibly one of the most famous photographic images of the War, and one that is reproduced in countless books. The crater itself was 130 feet across and 40 feet deep; the Redoubt was completely destroyed, with three sections of the German garrison, and many neighbouring dugouts blocked. Despite this devastation, the Germans recovered, manning their remaining positions and even standing on their parapets in order to fire at their attackers.

First into action were D Company, 2nd Royal Fusiliers; rushing forward with machine guns towards the craters, they were met by a German barrage and machine-gun fire. Five minutes later, at Zero Hour, the whole line began to advance. When they reached the crater, D Company were only able to occupy the nearest lip, as the Germans had already occupied the other side. The attack was a complete fiasco, 2nd Royal Fusiliers and 16th Middlesex being cut down at the same time as 1st Lancashire Fusiliers attempted to advance from the Sunken Road; the Commanding Officer 2nd Royal Fusiliers, Lt Col A.V. Johnson, was wounded. On 4 July, 2nd Royal Fusiliers were relieved by two battalions of 4th Division.

After the battle Masefield visited the area and wrote: 'Right up on top, well behind our front line and close to one of our communication trenches, there is a good big hawthorn bush, in which a magpie had built her nest.'

Behind 2nd Royal Fusiliers, 16th Middlesex were to support 1st Lancashire Fusiliers and to cover 2nd Royal Fusiliers' left flank when they advanced against Hawthorn Ridge to take advantage of the mine explosion. From 23 to 30 June, 16th Middlesex had been in Acheux Wood; the battalion then marched to AUCHONVILLERS, arriving at 2230hrs. Mainly made up of men from public schools, 16th Middlesex moved up to assembly positions called Cripp's Cut and Cardiff Street in the early hours of 1 July. The four battalions of 86th Brigade were to assault the German trenches from a point about 100yds west of Hawthorn Redoubt to the northern edge of Beaumont-Hamel.

Like 2nd Royal Fusiliers, 16th Middlesex found their advance immediately stopped by German machine-gun fire. Terrible havoc ensued as 16th Middlesex were enfiladed by machine-gun fire from the north as well as from the crater, and very few men got beyond this point. Hawthorn Ridge was littered with the dead, many of whom were to remain there for a long time. Those men who did survive were relieved at noon on 3 July, moving back to 88 Trench and AUCHONVILLERS, and on 4 July returned to Englebelmer and Mailly Woods.

1st Royal Dublin Fusiliers were also in support to 2nd Royal Fusiliers in their attack against Hawthorn Ridge, but the Irish battalion's departure was held up by 2nd Royal Fusiliers' failure to progress and at noon the attack was abandoned. 1st Royal Fusiliers remained in the area for 3 weeks, however, before withdrawing to reserve near Mailly Wood, where they provided working parties and consolidation teams.

On the right of 1st Royal Dublin Fusiliers were 2nd South Wales Borderers (87th Brigade, 29th Division), who were to attack towards Y RAVINE; their story was the same as those of all the other battalions along this front and they lost over 400 men in casualties. They remained in the Somme line until nearly the end of July.

Mixed in with 2nd South Wales Borderers were elements of 1st Borders (87th Brigade, 29th Division), who were in support; they attacked through the same line, having formed up just beyond a sunken section of St John's Road, which ran from AUCHONVILLERS to HAMEL, with Thurles Dump to their left on the road itself. 1st Borders' objective, the Beaucourt-sur-l'Ancre Trenches, seems to have been wildly optimistic. Anyway they made little progress, and on 8 July were back in camp at ACHEUX-EN-AMIÉNOIS.

One of the battalions most written about since 1916 was 1st Newfoundlanders, who were serving with 88th Brigade of 29th Division. The battalion had been in France for 3 months and had made the village of LOUVENCOURT their home, having spent 34 days in billets there by the end of June. They therefore had a special relationship with the villagers. On 30 June, they left LOUVENCOURT heavily laden and marched via the east of ACHEUX-EN-AMIÉNOIS, bypassing Mailly; they struck out across open fields south of the village in single file for nearly half a mile. They were temporarily held up at Tipperary Avenue, a deep communication trench which they had helped to dig, and it was 0200hrs before they reached their destination, the deep dugouts in St John's Road support trench. 1st Newfoundlanders' 750yds section was directly opposite Y RAVINE, flanked by 4th Worcesters (88th Brigade, 29th Division) on the left and 1st Essex (88th Brigade, 29th Division) on the right. The last-named were supported by 2nd Hampshires (also 88th Brigade, 29th Division). Battle Headquarters was established in Fethard Trench, about 150yds in front of the Newfoundlanders and to their right. They had comparatively few casualties and spent their time in the Mary Redan sector of the front line, coming out of the line on 10 July.

Forming up in Hamel Road, which was renamed St John's Road, the Newfoundlanders were to simply follow in the steps of the attacking brigades at 0845hrs, using bridges placed for them by 87th Brigade, and proceed to Station Road where they would pause to re-form, and then continue. Instead, 1st Newfoundlanders' attack was a total disaster, and not helped by the artillery keeping to a pre-arranged timetable. Instead of bringing down fire on the German trenches, the gunners were keeping to their plan of lifting their fire every 2 minutes and were now shelling to the east of Station Road while British troops were pinned down in no man's land. The aid post was in St John's Road but the battalion were virtually annihilated, with 14 officers and 219

other ranks dead or died of wounds and 12 officers and 374 ranks wounded; 91 other ranks were also missing. 1st Newfoundlanders' casualties were the same as those of 10th West Yorkshires (50th Brigade, 17th Division) at FRICOURT on the same day. The officers had been dressed like the men, but each one went into action carrying a walking stick and pistol and was without a rifle.

On the right of 2nd South Wales Borderers were 1st King's Own Scottish Borderers, also of 87th Brigade, 29th Division who were to advance towards Station Road. They left their communication trenches on the north-east side of St John's Road, and were to the right of the Newfoundlanders; they reached trenches to the north of Mary Redan and faced towards BEAUCOURT-SUR-L'ANCRE station, in a parallel to Y RAVINE. The men of 1st King's Own Scottish Borderers were here until 1600hrs, when they withdrew to Fort Jackson, a defensive redoubt in the rear of their Support Line. Here they passed the night and many casualties had been avoided by falling back into the point of Mary Redan, where no man's land was at its narrowest. Fort Jackson was where the boundary between VIII and X Corps lay.

To the rear of 1st King's Own Scottish Borderers were the men of 1st Essex, who began their assault at 0845hrs and held the line Mary Redan–New Trench Regent Street. At 0500hrs on 2 July they were back at the Thurles Dump on St John's Road with Piccadilly on their right. The next day they were relieved by 1/5th Glosters (145th Brigade, 48th Division) and returned to ACHEUX-EN-AMIÉNOIS on 8 July.

1st Royal Inniskilling Fusiliers (87th Brigade, 29th Division) also advanced towards Station Road, but were largely gunned down by German machine-gunners firing from Y RAVINE; the battalion suffered 568 casualties in a few minutes, of whom 246 were killed.

After the totally disastrous results of the Allied attack at Beaumont-Hamel it is only natural to ask, 'What went wrong?' The answer to this question is probably 'several things'. All that was not lacking was the courage of the attacking troops.

Firstly, in the eyes of High Command, it seems that VIII Corps, coupled with the name of Lt Gen Hunter-Weston and 29th Division, simply could not do anything right. This animosity may well have been because the Division were 'tainted' as a result of having taken part in the failed Gallipoli campaign. The reality of the failed attacks on Beaumont-Hamel was that the enemy not only had the advantage of superior positions but were also able to man all key points with their machine guns. In addition, the guns used in the bombardment of the enemy positions did not carry the weight of the naval guns used at Gallipoli.

The second point is that High Command failed to grasp just how impregnable the defences of Beaumont-Hamel had become. Many British raids had been carried out in the months prior to the battle and most of them had ended disastrously. The raiders did gather experience from these failures, of course, but that was small comfort. The only really successful raid was that made by the enemy, when on 6 April they overwhelmed 2nd South Wales Borderers and 1st Borders, inflicting 100 casualties and capturing 12 men.

Thirdly, and probably most importantly, was the premature timing of the mine detonation at Hawthorn Ridge. It is difficult to uncover the persons responsible for the decision, which was disastrous not only for the Allied attack at Beaumont-Hamel but also for the opening day of the Battle of the Somme in general. Current thinking seems to point towards the decision's having been made by Hunter-Weston himself, although, according to research by Col Philip Robinson of the Durand Group and Andrew Green, Hunter-Weston had been persuaded by a request for the earlier time from one of the assaulting brigades. This request seems to have ignored the fact that debris from the explosion would only take about a minute to settle and the British track record of reaching a crater first had not been good in previous such operations. Although D Company, 2nd Royal Fusiliers, set off for the crater after the mine was detonated, closely followed by machine-gun and mortar teams, they were too late and the enemy reached the far side of the crater first.

In his papers Sir Douglas Haig commented that men of 29th Division who were 350yds from the enemy had hardly left their trench lines. It would be tempting to say that they were unable to, as so many of them became casualties in trying to do so. On 1 July, 29th Division had 15,000 casualties out of the British total of approximately 57,000.

In his history of 1/8th Worcesters (144th Brigade, 48th Division), Edward Corbett, also writing with hindsight, noted that at Beaumont-Hamel the caves and quarries should have been occupied and not the lines; the defeat caused a complete breakdown in morale and discipline, and the men had helped themselves to the emergency rations and rum.

Although during the summer months there was little Allied progress at Beaumont-Hamel, this is not to say that it was a quiet sector: over the next 4 months there was much military activity here.

High Command had not given up hope of launching a second attack and began to make preparations for one. Unfortunately, the weather conditions intervened; at the end of September, when 1st South Staffords (91st Brigade, 7th Division) took over part of the line here after being billeted at MAILLY-MAILLET, they found that in places the line was knee-deep in mud and water, and some men were even drowned. During the second week of November weather conditions slightly improved, however, and the Allies decided to make an attack on 13 November.

In preparation, Lt W.H. Livens had been experimenting with gas near the headquarters of Lt Gen Sir Hubert Gough, General Officer Commanding Reserve (later Fifth) Army, at TOUTENCOURT. On the night of 28 October, Livens supervised the letting go of 2,300lb of gas into the enemy's position near Beaumont-Hamel. The cylinders were makeshift things and were launched out of extemporised mortars which could only throw a short distance, but on bursting, the cylinders emitted a high concentration of gas, and thus caught the Germans before they had time to put on their masks.

Capt Dyson, a contributor to *Artillery and Trench Mortar Memories: 32nd Division*, noted that on 1 November he was at the headquarters at the windmill. One of the other contributors to this book recalled that on 7 November it seemed very hard to keep CLV Brigade, Royal Field Artillery (32nd Division), in such a horrible place as the WHITE CITY when they had nothing on earth to do except sit still and be shelled. At this time, the WHITE CITY was described as being a long row of dugouts in the chalk with open ground behind them. On 11 November, tanks moved up to the WHITE CITY ready for the 13 November battle. At this time the enemy were retaliating with gas and high explosive against MAILLY-MAILLET.

In his autobiography, A.A. Milne (11th Royal Warwicks, 112th Brigade, 37th Division) described his battalion's objective as being the Beauregard Dovecote. The attack was postponed, however, because of continuous rain. Milne was clearly unable to cope with the appalling conditions and was sent home in November with a 'mystery illness' and a very high temperature. It made him almost physically sick to think of 'the nightmare of mental and moral degradation'; it seemed impossible to him that 'any sensitive man could live through another war'. He was discharged in 1919.

Lt Gen Sir Hubert Gough, General Officer Commanding Reserve (later Fifth) Army, had been preparing attacks against Beaumont-Hamel,

BEAUCOURT-SUR-L'ANCRE and SERRE for some time now and the brief improvement in the weather allowed these to go forward. By this stage in the battle, the gains to the south of the River Ancre had put his attacking troops in a good position to take the German positions in enfilade. They were in the marshy ground around the river itself, though the attacking troops would have to concentrate at the few points where the marshes could be crossed, and the enemy could still cause havoc because they commanded the THIEPVAL heights. The line actually crossed the marshes and at SAINT-PIERRE-DIVION the marsh could be covered by enfilade fire from three sides.

The valley led up from the River Ancre to the ruins of Beaumont-Hamel, which formed a natural stronghold by the junction of several uplands, and as a result the area was broken and more difficult to fight over than most parts of the Western Front. The ruins of the village had provided the Germans with very good facilities for their defences and it was honeycombed with extensive caves. We hear a lot about these caves and one wonders if their importance has not been slightly exaggerated. Anyway, it is said that they were capable of sheltering several battalions from the effects of shell-fire and that they ran along the whole of the village of Beaumont-Hamel. There was also, of course, Y RAVINE, which ran along the southern edge of the village. It had precipitous banks, from which two arms emerged from the main stem in the direction of the British lines; it bristled with dugouts and was intersected by several trenches. It could contain a garrison and could easily be reinforced from the trenches or from Station Road behind it, and connected to the village with the Ancre. The sunken roads were ideal for troop shelter and these included Hunter's Lane and Waggon Road. There were cave entrances in both of these. Waggon Road ran in a north-westerly direction from the village across REDAN RIDGE and was deeply sunken and riddled with dugouts. On the north side of the village was a valley flanked by Beaumont-Hamel that ran parallel to Y RAVINE; the whole of the high ground between the ravine and the valley was heavily defended by thickly wired defences. As usual, the Germans had the best of the ground, and therefore had good reason with all these advantages to think that the place was impregnable.

The Battle of the Ancre, also known as the Second Battle for Beaumont-Hamel, was to last from 13 to 19 November. Those involved were: III Corps' 48th Division (Fourth Army); XI Corps, which contained 18th, 19th and 4th Canadian Divisions; V Corps, which included 2nd, 3rd, 32nd, 37th, 51st and 63rd Divisions; XIII Corps, from which 31st Division were represented; and finally 120th Brigade (40th Division), under the command of 31st Division. 32nd Division were involved during the period 17–19 November and the other divisions 13–19 November.

For reasons of space it has been decided only to cover in detail the actions of 2nd and 51st Divisions. The actions of 63rd Division are covered in the entry on BEAUCOURT-SUR-L'ANCRE.

6th Brigade (2nd Division) were on the line where the SERRE front line became the Beaumont-Hamel front line, and immediately to their front was the German stronghold called the Quadrilateral, the northern part of the REDAN RIDGE defences. To the north-east of 6th Brigade was Beaumont Trench and beyond that Waggon Road. 13th Essex (6th Brigade, 2nd Division) were to be on the right of the attack and 2nd South Staffords (6th Brigade, 2nd Division) on the left, with 17th Middlesex and 1st King's (both also 6th Brigade, 2nd Division) to their rear. On 11 November, 13th Essex entered their trenches immediately facing the Quadrilateral. Their attack 2 days later, however, became a stalemate, bogged down in the mud, and on 16 November 13th Essex were relieved by 1st Dorsets (14th Brigade, 32nd Division), returning to MAILLY-MAILLET before travelling by lorry to VAUCHELLES-LÈS-AUTHIE.

To the left of 13th Essex, 2nd South Staffords entered the assembly trenches south of SERRE on 12 November. After being involved in the initial fighting, 2nd South Staffords were relieved by 4th Royal Fusiliers (9th Brigade, 3rd Division) on 15 November and returned to Ellis Square and into rest billets at LOUVENCOURT before leaving by bus for MAILLY-MAILLET.

At 2316hrs on 12 November, 17th Middlesex left MAILLY-MAILLET; Pendant Copse, their objective on 13 November, was to the rear of the adjoining village of SERRE. There was confusion and muddle in the fog as much of the wire was uncut. Legend Trench was held and on 15 November they were relieved by 4th Royal Fusiliers and returned to the support trench in the Ellis Square area and then to MAILLY-MAILLET. On 16 November, 17th Middlesex bussed to billets at LOUVENCOURT.

On 15 November, 4th Royal Fusiliers had marched up to their assembly point, 1 mile south-east of ENGLEBELMER, to act as Brigade Reserve; they arrived at Station Road at about 0200hrs and remained there until 18 November. On 20 November they were relieved and went back to the German

Third Line and on 26 November went to billets at MAILLY-MAILLET.

On 13 November, 1st King's moved up to support 13th Essex, and on 15 November, parties of 1st King's were involved in cutting off the Quadrilateral position.

Down the line to the south, the four battalions of 5th Brigade (also 2nd Division) also faced REDAN RIDGE; 24th Royal Fusiliers and 2nd Highland Light Infantry were in front, with 17th Royal Fusiliers and 2nd Oxfordshire & Buckinghamshire Light Infantry in support. 17th Royal Fusiliers were the right support battalion. Coming up the night before the attack, 2nd Highland Light Infantry used tapes that had been laid out in no man's land, because over the months the trenches had become so deep. Within 6 minutes of their attack, 2nd Highland Light Infantry had captured the enemy line, in addition to many prisoners. Two companies of 23rd Royal Fusiliers (99th Brigade, 2nd Division) were then sent up to support 2nd Highland Light Infantry in an unsuccessful attack on Munich Trench. On 14 November, 2nd Highland Light Infantry were relieved and went back to MAILLY-MAILLET before embussing for BERTRANCOURT.

At 2215hrs on 12 November, 17th Royal Fusiliers left Mailly Wood; passing through the lines with 2nd Oxfordshire & Buckinghamshire Light Infantry, they attempted to advance from the German Third Line to Munich Trench and Frankfurt Trench. After 1030hrs the front was reorganised, with 17th Royal Fusiliers holding Crater Lane Trench. Small parties did manage to penetrate Munich Trench, part of the German Front Line, but in general their part of the attack failed. On 16/17 November, 17th Royal Fusiliers were relieved.

On 11 November, 2nd Oxfordshire & Buckinghamshire Light Infantry had taken over the Hôtel de Ville area of MAILLY-MAILLET; after dark on 12 November, the battalion moved forward to assembly trenches. Forming the first two waves of the attack, A Company were at Valade Trench, north of Sixth Avenue, and D Company thence southwards. C Company were in the north end of Mountjoy Trench and B Company thence towards the WHITE CITY. Battalion headquarters moved from the WHITE CITY to join 24th Royal Fusiliers in Buster Trench. Following 6th Brigade's lack of progress on the left, 2nd Oxfordshire & Buckinghamshire Light Infantry were withdrawn, going to MAILLY-MAILLET with 17th Royal Fusiliers on 17 November.

On 12 November, 22nd Royal Fusiliers (99th Brigade, 2nd Division) assembled at BERTRAN-COURT; at 0130hrs on 13 November, they began their march to the trenches near MAILLY-MAILLET. The battalion then moved up into Sixth Avenue and waited for 5th Brigade to move forward. At 0545hrs on 13 November, amid a terrible bombardment, 22nd Royal Fusiliers moved into a defensive position on the south side of the Quadrilateral, with battalion headquarters going to the WHITE CITY. On 14 November, two more companies joined in.

The enemy were still holding on to the Quadrilateral, which was composed of a cluster of trenches on high ground to the north. Following its capture on 15 November, 22nd Royal Fusiliers were relieved by 15th Highland Light Infantry (14th Brigade, 32nd Division) and went into billets at MAILLY-MAILLET. During this fighting the writer H.H. Munro, better known as Saki, had been killed by a sniper. He was a lance-sergeant with 22nd Royal Fusiliers, aged 45. His last words were said to have been 'Put that bloody cigarette out'. Munro had written many stories, including one called 'Birds of the Western Front'.

Overall 2nd Division, between Beaumont-Hamel and SERRE, were not able to enjoy the success of 51st Division's attacks further down the line to the south. It was true that in places German defences were broken into, but nowhere on a front sufficiently wide to make a serious gap, so that by nightfall those who got through had either to retire or be taken prisoner. The German line was restored intact.

Next to 5th Brigade were 152nd Brigade (51st Division), composed of 1/5th Seaforth Highlanders, 1/6th Seaforth Highlanders, 1/6th Gordon Highlanders and 1/8th Argyll & Sutherland Highlanders. The territory in front of them included Y RAVINE, with the southern section of Waggon Road to the left and the end of Station Trench and Station Road to the right. In the middle was the village of Beaumont-Hamel itself. An underground mine signalled the start of the battle and many machine-gun bullets were discharged into the mist, followed by the assaulting troops. At 0545hrs on 13 November, 1/5th Seaforth Highlanders led the attack, with their left flank on the AUCHONVILLERS–Beaumont-Hamel road, their final objective being a German trench 200yds east of the village. There was uncut wire and dense fog, and the British barrage was too far ahead; despite this, the German line was mainly carried. The second line was also carried but the third line was more stubborn. In the evening, 1/5th Seaforth Highlanders went through Beaumont-Hamel and consolidated the final objective; in so doing, they captured 600 prisoners out of 1,700. Sustaining 292 men missing, wounded or killed, 1/5th Seaforth Highlanders remained in the line until the night of 14/15 November, during which time they repelled several enemy counter-attacks. After a short rest they returned to the line on 19 November.

South of the Hawthorn Crater were 1/8th Argyll & Sutherland Highlanders, who suffered from machine-gun fire before the front was carried. Eventually the German line was taken and the advance continued into Beaumont-Hamel, where the enemy were slowly cleared from dugouts and cellars and a line was established on its eastern edge. Booty included machine guns, mortars, ammunition, bombs, grenades and an armourer's shop. Two tanks came up the road from AUCHONVILLERS to assist but became bogged down.

At 2130hrs on 12 November, 1/6th Seaforth Highlanders left their camp and marched towards the trenches. Having been successful in their attack, they returned to camp at MAILLY-MAILLET on 15 November and buried their dead at Mailly Wood Cemetery. On the night of 13/14 November, 1/6th Gordon Highlanders (152nd Brigade) and 1/4th Gordons (154th Brigade) took over the Green Line; New Munich Trench was held until 17 November, when it was handed over to 32nd Division.

With their headquarters at FORCEVILLE, 153rd Brigade (also 51st Division) had the hardest role to play; their objectives were the whole of Y RAVINE, together with Munich Trench and beyond it Frankfurt Trench. 1/6th Black Watch and 1/7th Gordon Highlanders led 153rd Brigade's attack, supported by 1/5th Gordon Highlanders and with 1/7th Black Watch (153rd Brigade) in reserve. On 11 November, 1/6th Black Watch were in Mailly Wood; they were to enter Y RAVINE from the north and bomb their way southwards instead of using the frontal attack method employed with such disastrous results on 1 July. On 12 November they left Mailly Wood and at 0545hrs on the following morning a mine explosion in front of them, accompanied by a tremendous barrage, was the signal for the beginning of the attack. By 2100hrs 1/6th Black Watch were established on the Green Line, handing over to 1/4th Gordon Highlanders on the morning of 14 November. After 2 days' fighting they marched back to camp behind Mailly Wood.

In appallingly muddy conditions and fog, 1/7th Gordon Highlanders took 4 hours to reach the line. However, the right of the battalion captured several lines and reached their objective, which was Station Road, known as the Green Line. The left side fared less well but many German prisoners were still captured. Although 1/7th Gordon Highlanders had to fall back on

Station Road, 1/6th Gordon Highlanders battled forward and the advance continued into Beaumont-Hamel. It was stubborn work clearing out the enemy from the underground positions, which included limestone caves as well as deep cellars and mined dugouts. The deep tunnels and catacombs had been places of refuge in the Wars of Religion and the Germans enlarged them and made an underground network of them, using strongpoints and redoubts like Redan Redoubt.

The enemy sent up rockets to signal to their artillery to open fire on the Allied positions but the mist hampered the defenders; 1/6th Black Watch and 1/7th Gordon Highlanders entered the German barrage area and the first signs to the enemy of the attackers' progress were a series of long continuous 'hurrahs' that came through the mist from the direction of Beaumont-Hamel. The enemy knew then that the British had broken through their defences. The bombing parties of 1/6th Black Watch had effected an entrance into the German trench from the western end of Y RAVINE. Although the right of 51st Division were held up, the left succeeded in pushing through into the village on a wide front. The capture of Frankfurt Trench was not in the end attempted. Assisting in the capture of the southern end of Beaumont-Hamel, 1/5th Gordon Highlanders then reached the second line.

By 0130hrs on 13 November, 1/7th Black Watch had come up from Mailly Wood and reached the reserve trenches in St John's Road; their objective was also Station Road (the Green Line) and Beaumont-Hamel. In Y RAVINE they mainly provided carrying parties. The attack succeeded and on 15 November, 153rd Brigade were relieved, returning to bivouacs at Mailly Wood until 18 November. It was frosty during this time, which would have greatly improved conditions in the battle, where it had been so muddy. A word of praise is appropriate for the artillery, who on 13 November had more guns firing in the rear around Beaumont-Hamel than there were on the whole 1 July front. Their bombardment of the enemy lines was a key factor in the struggle for Beaumont-Hamel, whose capture by the 51st Division must have surprised the Germans, because they had always thought it impregnable. In addition the number of prisoners captured came to over 7,000. However, to the north, SERRE had proved to be as difficult to capture as it had proved on 1 July.

The final line at the end of the battle took in the Quadrilateral, part of REDAN RIDGE across Lager Alley and Waggon Road and then downwards to Beaucourt Trench and BEAUCOURT-SUR-L'ANCRE itself.

After the battle was over, 20th Brigade (7th Division) arrived in the area and used a deep German dugout on the south-west spur as a battalion headquarters. 7th Division's left brigade were badly off as they were further back in the WHITE CITY, which was always wet and most unhealthy, but later on the dugout north of MAILLY-MAILLET known as Apple Trees was used. This, not being made from chalk, was much drier.

Ancre British Cemetery in Beaumont-Hamel is on the west side of the D50 road between Beaumont-Hamel and HAMEL and is close to the no man's land of 1916. The great majority of officers and men buried here are those who fell on 1 July, 3 September or 13 November; the cemetery has particular links with 63rd Division and their struggle for BEAUCOURT-SUR-L'ANCRE in November 1916. Those buried here include Lt Col R.C. Pierce of 1st Royal Inniskilling Fusiliers (VI.D.18), who was killed in action on 1 July 1916. According to the regimental history, 'the German defence system was very strong and the explosion at Hawthorn Mine on the left had not had the desired effect and even the reserves were brought up because of the exposed position. The 1st Bn. lost their CO, Lt Col Pierce.' Another casualty buried here was a son of the newspaper tycoon Lord Rothermere, Sub Lt The Hon. V.S.T. Harmsworth RNVR of the Hawke Battalion, who died on 13 November 1916.

Beaumont-Hamel Military Cemetery is about 500yds north-west of the village, close to the AUCHONVILLERS road; the cemetery rises from near the road in two rows. The graves are mainly those of Lancashire Fusiliers who died on 1 July and of other men killed in the November battles. A little west of this cemetery is the memorial to 1/8th Argyll & Sutherland Highlanders, almost on the site of their former battalion headquarters. They had played a prominent role in the capture of Y RAVINE.

Frankfurt Trench British Cemetery is named after a German trench 1 mile north-east of the village, which remained in German hands until the German retirement in early 1917. It contains graves of 161 soldiers from the United Kingdom who fell in November 1916 or in January 1917; made by V Corps, it was known as V Corps Cemetery No. 11. The cemetery is approached by a long path leading

Officers of the Queen's Royal (West Surrey) in a captured German dugout at Beaumont-Hamel in November 1916. Mr Basil Clarke, a war correspondent, is seated on the right. *(IWM Q1532)*

north from the road between Beaumont-Hamel and BEAUCOURT-SUR-L'ANCRE and commands wide views in all directions over the battlefields of 1916–18.

New Munich Trench British Cemetery, which, like Frankfurt Trench British Cemetery, is named after a former German trench, is about 150yds west of Waggon Road and stands on high ground. It is approached by the same path as that to Frankfurt Trench British Cemetery. Munich Trench was occupied by 51st Division on 15 November. New Munich Trench British Cemetery (or V Corps Cemetery No. 25) was dug on the previous night by No. 2/2 (Highland) Field Company, Royal Engineers, and a company of 1/8th Royal Scots (pioneers of 51st Division). It contains the graves of 146 soldiers who died in November 1916 or in January 1917, many of them members of the Highland Light Infantry.

Munich Trench Cemetery (V Corps Cemetery No. 8) contains the graves of 126 men from the United Kingdom and Waggon Road Cemetery (V Corps Cemetery No. 10) contains 195 graves, of which 49 belong to soldiers of 11th Borders (97th Brigade, 32nd Division) who attacked on the Ancre between July and November 1916. The 51st (Highland) Division flagstaff, erected in 1924 was later destroyed during a storm, but a replacement, which also includes a new plaque, was unveiled and rededicated on 13 November 2006.

BEAUQUESNE is to the north-west of PUCHE-VILLERS on the D23 road and is close to VERT GALAND. It was used for billeting as early as 19 July 1915, when units of 48th Division were here; at the same time, Third Army headquarters was also here. Towards the end of March 1916, 10th East Yorkshires (92nd Brigade, 31st Division) were billeted here for a short time 'in straw-filled barns' and the local civilians did their best to provide them with eggs and chips. Farm buildings were set out in a rectangular shape around a large manure pit in the centre into which some men accidentally stumbled. Troops were advised not to use a water pump near the heap to fill their water bottles.

The first Val Vion Château was originally built in 1784 and destroyed by fire 10 years later. On 19 July 1915, its replacement building became the head-quarters of Gen Sir Charles Monro, General Officer Commanding Third Army; Gen Sir Edmund Allenby, who succeeded Monro later that year, then took up residence there. In September 1915, Field Marshal Lord Kitchener and Gen Joffre visited the house.

Although Montreuil was his headquarters during the period of the Battle of the Somme, on 25 June Sir Douglas Haig moved to Val Vion Château, and used it as his advanced headquarters for the whole of the battle. The building was 10 miles from QUERRIEU, where Lt Gen Sir Henry Rawlinson, General Officer Commanding Fourth Army, had his headquarters and the headquarters of Lt Gen Sir Hubert Gough, General Officer Commanding Reserve (later Fifth) Army, at TOUTENCOURT, which was between the two. Haig shared the house with a mother and her young daughter, members of the Bouthors family who owned it. The young girl used to practice the piano while many of the important visitors or house guests were at meals or meetings. The majority of Haig's office staff carried out their duties in specially built huts in the grounds.

One member of Haig's staff was Sir Philip Sassoon. Born in 1888, he was a contemporary of Julian Grenfell at Oxford. During the war he became a member of Sir John French's staff; before French was dismissed, Sassoon worked with Rawlinson, then General Officer Commanding IV Corps, as his aide-de-camp. Sassoon became Haig's private secretary on 20 December 1915, soon after Haig became commander-in-chief of the British Expeditionary Force in France and Flanders. According to his file in the National Archives (WO374/60414), Sassoon had been a member of the East Kent Yeomanry from 7 November 1904 until 4 August 1914; he was then seconded as a second-lieutenant for service on the staff on 5 February 1915. He was to remain with Haig until 28 February 1919, and left the Army the following day, having earned various awards; he was Mentioned in Despatches on four occasions. He died in 1939.

On 1 July, the opening day of the battle, Haig attended a Scottish church service in one of the huts, taken by his personal chaplain, Revd G.S. Duncan, then drove to Fourth Army headquarters at QUERRIEU to confer with Rawlinson, General Officer Commanding Fourth Army. Revd Duncan mentions meeting John Buchan and Lord Crawford in the village; while he was with Haig at this time he also served as a chaplain to two casualty clearing stations at PUCHEVILLERS.

Haig had a stream of important visitors at this time, including Gens Joffre and Foch, HM King George V, Lord Northcliffe, David Lloyd George, Herbert Asquith, Reginald McKenna, Max Aitken, Col C. Repington (Military Correspondent of *The Times*), John Masefield, John Buchan, Lord Crawford, C.E. Montague and Sir John French. Maj Thompson was one of Haig's aides-de-camp; when the King made one of his visits to see his Army in August 1916, Thompson was seconded to him in order to arrange all the details of the trip. Thompson's photograph, as well as that of HRH the Prince of Wales, was often taken during the King's tour.

The King's London staff hoped that during his visit he would stay near Saint-Pol, a decision which did not go down well with GHQ, as they knew the royal party had no idea of how badly the roads were congested. The King made Haig's château his first port of call when he arrived in Beauquesne from Boulogne with HRH the Prince of Wales on 8 August. The King then had discussions with Haig before he left to travel via DOULLENS for Château Bryas near Saint-Pol. The King returned at 1300hrs on 12 August, when the famous picture was taken of him with Gens Foch and Joffre, Sir Douglas Haig and President Raymond Poincaré. After an alcohol-free lunch, the King had talks with Poincaré and Gen Joffre, accompanied by his son once more and arriving via Vauchelles. He visited the various offices of the Advanced General Headquarters and presented the Knight of the Grand Cross of the Royal Victorian Order to Haig and a Knight Commander of the Order of the Bath to Lt Gen L. Kiggell, Haig's Chief of General Staff. After leaving Beauquesne at 1535hrs the King drove to Cassel and stayed at Haig's house. It appears the King was very supportive of Haig and always used Haig's first name in their talks. The King was to prove a useful friend in the months to come.

It is staggering how much time Haig had to give not just to running the British Expeditionary Force as its Commander-in-Chief, but also in concerning himself with the needs of visitors. In addition, he was always required to be very diplomatic, and needed to maintain good relations with the Prime Minister, Herbert Asquith, the Secretary of State for War, David Lloyd George, and the Northcliffe press. There was no love lost between Haig and Lloyd George, but both men remained polite; indeed, Lloyd George was markedly more punctual in his dealings with Haig than he was with others. Nevertheless, Lloyd George did complain about Haig's military leadership behind his back.

In contrast, Haig got on well with Kitchener, and lost a valuable ally when the latter was drowned on his way to Russia in June 1916. Haig also liked Asquith and, according to his diaries, was quite amused in seeing just how much he drank, often knocking back brandies in large sherry glasses. However, when the British premier was 'in his cups', he was still able to understand the information which Haig imparted to him.

It appears that Haig never had much time for Sir John French; his dislike was heightened when at one point it appeared that Sir John had been sent over to France and Belgium by Lloyd George to assess the military situation and to find out how Haig was

perceived, even discussing Haig with the French High Command. Although Haig was appalled at this treachery, he was ever the considerate host, making sure his guests had everything they required, which with Sir John included taking the trouble to arrange a Guard of Honour for him when he disembarked, despite the suspicious circumstances of the visit.

In his diaries, Haig indicated that while he could accept criticism of his military leadership, he disliked people arguing about issues the real facts of which they had not grasped, and also when they refused to face him with their criticism, preferring to go behind his back.

The King made Haig a Field-Marshal at the end of 1916. After the war Haig was given an earldom, together with £100,000, and devoted himself to causes that assisted former soldiers and their families. He died in London of a heart attack in 1928 at the age of 66 and was buried in Scotland close to his home. His coffin had entered Scotland at midnight.

On 20 May 1940, Val Vion Château was destroyed by tank shelling and was rebuilt once more in 1951. The whole complex lies in a dip in the land close to a wood and close to the D11 and D31 roads to RAINCHEVAL.

During the war two Allied casualties were buried in Beauquesne Communal Cemetery to the north of the village close to the former railway line.

BEAUSSART is due west of MAILLY-MAILLET on the D176 BERTRANCOURT road. In March 1916, 18th Durham Light Infantry (93rd Brigade, 31st Division) arrived here and were welcomed to the village by 10th Royal Irish Rifles (107th Brigade, 36th Division). 18th Durham Light Infantry were back again briefly on 3 April. On 4 April, a section of 87th Field Ambulance (29th Division) arrived here and were allocated buildings unsuitable for use as a dressing station; all the houses and barns were infested with rats. Two days later, they were using two cottages, the church and a wooden hut, which provided accommodation for 100 lying-down cases. The accommodation for sitting-up cases was inadequate, however, and a suggestion was made for 87th Field Ambulance to move to MAILLY-MAILLET. Instead, they left for LOUVENCOURT on 13 April, where the accommodation was again filthy.

At the beginning of June, a section of No. 9 Field Company, Royal Engineers (4th Division), had been billeted in the village; returning on 23 June, they remained for a week. 1st Rifle Brigade (11th Brigade, 4th Division) were also here during June when carrying out further battle training. During the evening of 26 June, 2nd Royal Dublin Fusiliers (10th Brigade, 4th Division) arrived and bivouacked in orchards. The next day they were busy preparing for the coming battle.

On 1 July the enemy shelled to the north-west of BERTRANCOURT during the night and early morning but fortunately missed hitting the divisional clearing station at Beaussart, which dealt with 1,130 cases in 12 hours on the first day of the battle. An advanced dressing station was at Red House and the walking wounded were evacuated at once in case of enemy shelling.

BEAUVAL is on the main N25 road between DOULLENS and AMIENS. On 21 July 1915, No. 4 Casualty Clearing Station camped in a plot behind a jute factory and accommodation for 60 was organised in the reformatory which adjoined it. The officers' section was in the girls' school, which was ¾ mile away. Eleven days later, No. 1/1 (South Midland) Casualty Clearing Station arrived in the village and stayed for 4 days before transferring to a hospital in AMIENS.

Two months later, 109th Field Ambulance (36th Division) were billeted here around 20 October 1915, when a dressing station was established; soon a unit which would allow for 350 men to bathe was opened up, and by early November laundry facilities had also been organised.

In February 1916, 46th Division had a training school here. On 6 March, 1/6th Seaforth Highlanders (152nd Brigade, 51st Division) came here from RAINNEVILLE, prior to moving out of the Somme area. On 12 March, 1/7th Middlesex (167th Brigade, 56th Division) arrived here and stayed for 2 days before moving to Baudricourt. On 1 April, 89th Field Ambulance (29th Division) were here and at the end of April, 1st (South Midland) Field Ambulance (48th Division) were also billeted in the village, when they ran the hospital in the jute factory.

On 4 May, 144th Brigade (48th Division) marched here from COUIN, training and playing sport until 15 May, when they returned to COUIN and COIGNEUX to relieve 145th Brigade (also 48th Division). On 18 May, 145th Brigade marched here from COUIN and spent 2 weeks in excellent billets, carrying out route marches, range practices and platoon and company training. They left on 31 May for SAINT-RIQUIER.

On 9 June, 1/6th Royal Warwicks (143rd Brigade, 48th Division) arrived here from the HÉBUTERNE sector and carried out further battle training before leaving a fortnight later. On 14 June, 1st Somerset

Light Infantry (11th Brigade, 4th Division) arrived here; during their stay they were shown miniature models of the trenches that would concern them, and the brigadier lectured the officers and NCOs on the forthcoming attack. On the following day they left for BERTRANCOURT.

Between 11 and 18 September, 48th Division were resting in the Beauval area. On 30 September, 51st Division set up its headquarters here and the division's 153rd Brigade was also in the village.

Beauval was a medical centre, in that several casualty clearing stations were established here before and during the battle, including No. 4 Casualty Clearing Station (June 1915–October 1916) and No. 47 Casualty Clearing Station (October–December 1916). On 1 July, men from 29th Division at BEAUMONT-HAMEL were brought here, some by motor ambulance. As well as a motor ambulance convoy there was an advanced depot of medical stores in the village. Casualties were taken by motor to the railhead at GÉZAINCOURT, to the north-west, and the dead were taken to Beauval Communal Cemetery, on the north side of the village, where the Allied graves occupy a square of the brick-lined graveyard in the north-east corner. The last row appears to have been reserved for officers only and includes the graves of several Royal Flying Corps officers.

A few British burials were made as late as March 1918; after the war, 13 graves from Lucheux Military Cemetery, south of LUCHEUX, which had been made by French troops, were moved here to Rows A and G. The British plot was designed by G.H. Goldsmith; raised on terraces, it is part of a very impressive civilian cemetery which contains many strikingly designed memorials. Those buried here include Pte C. Depper of 1/4th Royal Berkshires, who was 'shot at dawn' for desertion on 13 September 1916 (G.1).

By 1916 the village had become a popular area for billeting and between February and October 1916, 6th, 20th, 25th, 29th, 31st, 32nd, 46th, 48th and 51st Divisions had brigades staying in the area. In addition, 6th, 29th, 32nd and 51st Divisions had their headquarters here from time to time.

BÉCORDEL-BÉCOURT is south of the ALBERT–PÉRONNE road, the D938. During the war the village became a well-used departure point, and supplies were brought up from the main railway line at DERNANCOURT via MÉAULTE. Battalions frequently bivouacked on the hill south of the village. The Allies also centred a huge artillery depot in this area of sunken woods. The troops used the sunken woods and were protected by deep shelters.

Villages were flattened and much of the ground was uprooted several times.

On 27 March 1916, Siegfried Sassoon of 2nd Royal Welsh Fusiliers (19th Brigade, 33rd Division) was in the district, noting that 'in the foreground Bécourt Church tower peeped above a shoulder of hill like a broken tooth'. On 30 April there was a very severe bombardment of the area, including gas shells, and 35 officers and men were admitted to the field ambulance.

At the beginning of the battle, 14th Field Ambulance (5th Division) were established in Bécordel-Bécourt; XV Corps had a walking wounded post here as well as an advanced dressing station. On 2 July, 7th York & Lancasters, pioneers of 17th Division, bivouacked in fields to the east of MÉAULTE, which may have been at the Sandpits Camp, and then moved via the adjoining village of Bécordel-Bécourt to a deep ravine. The valley was packed with guns and the battalion spent several days there in dugouts.

In early July, Sassoon recorded in his diary that 2nd Royal Welsh Fusiliers reached the hill above Bécordel-Bécourt at 0145hrs and slept for an hour in the long grass, with guns bombing and flashing all around in the valley below. Sassoon's battalion later reached HEILLY at about 0745hrs on 6 July. On the night of 14/15 July, 1/4th Suffolks (98th Brigade, 33rd Division) moved up through Bécordel-Bécourt to the position between FRICOURT and MAMETZ; at this time the Battle of Bazentin Ridge was raging in all its fury. 33rd Division's field ambulances were located between the village and FRICOURT.

On 17 July, 1st East Surreys (95th Brigade, 5th Division) bivouacked on the slopes of the hill just south of the village. Three days later, Brig Gen C.R. Ballard, General Officer Commanding 95th Brigade, was badly wounded here when a shell hit his headquarters. On 24 July, 15th Field Ambulance (5th Division) arrived here from MORLANCOURT.

On 6 August, 2nd Royal Welsh Fusiliers marched to the village and camped on the hillside behind Bécordel-Bécourt, where they remained for a week before moving to Fricourt Wood. During their stay it was very hot and on 30 August they marched in a downpour on busy roads to their former bivouac; the sun-baked slope had now become a slough up which two horses couldn't drag a mess cart. A camp had to be improvised. At this time it was rumoured that there were as many as 9,000 horses and mules in the vicinity and 17,000 at MÉAULTE. From 31 August, 21st Manchesters (91st Brigade, 7th Division) camped in Bécordel-Bécourt, before moving to ALBERT on 8 September.

In early September, XV Corps Main Dressing Station was established in the neighbourhood and the personnel of 63rd Field Ambulance (21st Division) were brought here on 9 September in motor wagons from HEILLY to run the station. They had been in the village in early July, and their unit history paints the picture: 'The familiar landmarks were hard to find. All the guns, except those of heaviest calibre (some of them French), had been moved forward; a Y.M.C.A. marquee had made its appearance. There were ammunition dumps, forage dumps, water points, cavalry, light railways – a general massing of strength. There was that pervading sense of liveliness, that atmosphere of expectation and tenseness which heralded a big attack.'

On 17 September, 9th King's Royal Rifle Corps (42nd Brigade, 14th Division) moved to their old camp at Bécordel-Bécourt, before going to BUIRE-SUR-L'ANCRE the next day.

In *Gallipoli to the Somme*, Alexander Aitken of 1st Otagos (1st New Zealand Brigade, New Zealand Division) notes that in either September or October the New Zealand infantry camped on a ridge near Bécordel-Bécourt overlooking FRICOURT in the zone of heavy artillery. Batteries were all around, a battery of 6-inchers, in cages of netting; two 6in naval guns, long-nosed monsters, contrasting with the stubby howitzers whose cough was heard from Bécourt Wood on the opposite slope. The French 75s were far away on the right camped on a crest commanding a view 6 miles in radius from THIEPVAL to LONGUEVAL. In front of the left-hand slope of the valley were the ruined bricks of FRICOURT. The valley rose suddenly on the right to a chalk spur named King George's Hill, with a great mine crater gouged in its side. On the lower slope of this spur was the old British Front Line and nearer Aitken's camp, the old Support Lines now tumbled in.

From FRICOURT a line of white road ran behind the hill to MAMETZ and MONTAUBAN-DE-PICARDIE, hidden from view. The stages of the battle were clearly and visibly marked by a rising series of woods: Fricourt Wood topping FRICOURT and, some distance beyond, the larger and infamous MAMETZ WOOD; and above again and much further away the straggling trees of HIGH WOOD on the left; the more extensive DELVILLE WOOD on the right, where the opposing lines faced each other. To the left across the valley between FRICOURT and ALBERT the ground rose to the THIEPVAL–POZIÈRES ridge, with the wood of BÉCOURT in the foreground.

Dartmoor Cemetery was begun by 5th Division as Bécordel-Bécourt Military Cemetery in August

1915. It is immediately north of the village, on the road to BÉCOURT, and is opposite Bécourt-Bécordel Communal Cemetery. In May 1916, its name was changed to Dartmoor Cemetery, at the request of 8th and 9th Devons (both 20th Brigade, 7th Division). It was designed by Sir Edwin Lutyens and had a dressing station next to it at the beginning of the battle. In 1917 Dartmoor Cemetery was hardly used. The New Zealand Division erected a memorial to their officers and men who fell near FLERS in September and October 1916. No. 100 Company, Machine Gun Corps (33rd Division), also erected a memorial to their losses in July 1916.

Buried here are Pte J. Miller VC (I.C.64) of 7th King's Own (56th Brigade, 19th Division), who died at BAZENTIN-LE-PETIT on 31 July 1916, as well as Lt Col H. Allardice (I.F.42) of 36th Jacob's Horse, attached 13th Northumberland Fusiliers (62nd Brigade, 21st Division), and Lt. H. Webber (I.E.54). When serving with 7th South Lancashires (56th Brigade, 19th Division) close to MAMETZ WOOD, the 68-year-old Webber was hit by a shell. Other graves are those of Sgt G. Lee (I.A.35) and Cpl R. Lee (I.A.36), a father and son both serving in CLVI Brigade, Royal Field Artillery (33rd Division), who were killed on the same day in September, and Pte J.J. Sweeney (I.B.1) of 1st Otagos (1st New Zealand Brigade, New Zealand Division) who was 'shot at dawn' for desertion. The Cemetery contains 768 graves.

Norfolk Cemetery is on the east side of the road to BÉCOURT, to the north of Dartmoor Cemetery. Units left for the front line from behind where Norfolk Cemetery is now; at the start of the battle, this was an ideal area for artillery batteries. The cemetery was begun by 1st Norfolks (15th Brigade, 5th Division) in August 1915, and was used by other units including 8th Norfolks (53rd Brigade, 18th Division) until August 1916. It lies in a long valley running north and south and on the road side has a long brick wall. After the Armistice, 268 graves from burials nearby were concentrated here.

Norfolk Cemetery includes graves of many men of 21st Division who had fallen during the successful capture of divisional objectives between Sausage Valley and FRICOURT at the start of the battle. T/Maj S.W. Loudoun-Shand VC (I.C.77) of 10th Yorkshires (62nd Brigade, 23rd Division) is buried here (see the FRICOURT entry), as is Lt Col C. Lynch (I.B.87) of 9th King's Own Yorkshire Light Infantry (64th Brigade, 21st Division), who was killed in action on 1 July. After his death in 1971, the ashes of Maj B.M. Cloutman VC were placed in the grave of his brother, Lt W.R. Cloutman (I.A.14) of No. 178 Tunnelling Company, Royal Engineers, who was killed on 22 August 1915

when trying to save the life of an injured sergeant. The Norfolk Cemetery contains the graves of about 20 members of No. 178 Tunnelling Company. It also has the graves of 228 men who died prior to 1 July 1916.

BÉCOURT, due east of ALBERT and south of LA BOISSELLE, was in a valley known as Sausage Valley in 1916, which ran from the village in a north-easterly direction, crossing no man's land and continuing through the German trench system in the direction of Contalmaison Wood. Bécourt is separated from BÉCORDEL-BÉCOURT to the south by Bécourt Wood. Bécourt Military Cemetery has 263 graves of men who died prior to 1 July 1916.

51st Division were one of the first British formations to arrive in the Somme area and 1/7th Gordon Highlanders (153rd Brigade, 51st Division) were in trenches here in August 1915 when relieved by 1/5th Seaforth Highlanders (152nd Brigade, 51st Division). The battalion headquarters was in Bécourt Château, 'once a splendid mansion-house embowered in lofty trees, and, although perched high above the trench line it has survived months of shelling wonderfully well and, although bearing a few honourable scars in roof and wall, it is still habitable in the military sense'. Attached to the château was a small chapel; swallows had nests above the altar. The Bécourt family vaults were beneath the chapel floor and the British troops, wrapped in blankets, had no qualms about making use of the recesses, where they slept peacefully until daylight called them back to duty. Although the château was generally in good condition, when the enemy had occupied the building earlier in the war they had smashed the place up inside – particularly any bedroom which had clearly belonged to the ladies of the house.

On 2 August, 1/5th Seaforth Highlanders left Bécourt for rest billets in HÉNENCOURT. On 21 August, 1/6th Seaforth Highlanders (also 152nd Brigade, 51st Division) sent up two platoons to assist and to act as support. The platoons spent their time building a redoubt to be used as a defence for the château. After 4 days they were relieved by two other platoons; the rest of the battalion were around LA BOISSELLE. Between 12 and 17 September, 152nd Brigade were here again in the front trenches, and 1/6th Seaforth Highlanders relieved 1/5th Seaforth Highlanders in front of the château.

On 8 April 1916, 24th Field Ambulance (8th Division) were preparing the château for the reception of walking and lying-down cases; by 12 May, 103rd Field Ambulance (34th Division) were running the advanced dressing station at the château. It was 34th Division which was allotted the task of capturing the village of LA BOISSELLE

Australian transport passing through Bécourt Wood near Albert, August 1916. *(IWM Q898)*

on the opening day of the battle. According to his papers held at the Imperial War Museum (77/3/1), Lt Col W.A. Vignoles, then a company commander with 10th Lincolns (101st Brigade, 34th Division), was back in the château, having been here at the end of May. At the end of June, 102nd Brigade (34th Division) included Bécourt Wood in their line and used the château, almost hidden by the Wood, as their headquarters. Brigade headquarters at the time was in a small two-roomed house, which was part of the farm called BELLEVUE situated about a mile to the rear of Bécourt. On 30 June, 11th Suffolks (101st Brigade, 34th Division) were in the Wood, part of which was used for battalion headquarters.

On the opening day of the battle, stretcher-bearers from 59th Field Ambulance (19th Division) were sent to help 103rd Field Ambulance (34th Division) with the very heavy casualties who were sent down to a hospital in ALBERT (see that entry). One of the wounded was Lt Col Vignoles, who was badly wounded in his left hand. He was unable to apply a tourniquet with the use of only his right hand, and his orderly bandaged up his wound as they sheltered in a shell-hole. Vignoles handed over his command and after reaching Bécourt Château joined the walking wounded as they made their way the 2 or

3 miles to ALBERT. He 'passed the little cemetery with its rows of graves of British soldiers, each with its small wooden cross. The wood was full of guns still firing rapidly.' He also noted that when near the church, he and other wounded men were given a glass of lemon by a man and a woman at a shop as they passed through the town to the hospital at VIVIER MILL.

On 22 September, Lt Col A.J.B. Addison, Commanding Officer 9th York & Lancasters (70th Brigade, 23rd Division), was buried in the Wood; aged 49, he was the son of Gen T. Addison, and had been killed in early July. The following account is based on Cathryn Corns' account (*Battlefields Review*, Issue 27). Addison had been in command of 9th York & Lancasters since they were formed in September 1914. At 2030hrs on 30 June, the battalion left Tyler's Redoubt, on high ground north of MILLENCOURT, to move towards positions in front of Authuille Wood. 70th Brigade were to advance towards the enemy Second Line on the right of MOUQUET FARM. 9th York & Lancasters was in support to 8th York & Lancasters (70th Brigade,

21st Division) and went into the attack at 0840hrs on 1 July, which resulted in very high casualties. At 1900hrs, the remnants of Addison's battalion returned to Long Valley, leaving for DERNAN-COURT and ARGŒUVES shortly afterwards.

Addison was wounded after leaving his head-quarters at Quarry Post and appears to have died of his injuries 2 or 3 days later; his body was not found until the now reconstituted battalion were at Bécourt Wood on 23 September. The battlefield was searched and Addison's body was found in no man's land near Aveluy and OVILLERS. Addison had written in his notebook, 'Tell the Regiment I hope they did well.'

The composer George Butterworth served with 13th Durham Light Infantry (68th Brigade, 23rd Division), which in the latter part of June had been sent south to AMIENS. After marching by easy stages, they bivouacked at MILLENCOURT, and moved up to ALBERT, where they lay in trenches one night. On 4 July, 13th Durham Light Infantry marched to Bécourt Wood; 23rd Division's objective included CONTALMAISON, BAILIFF WOOD and the area between them. From 7 to 10 July, 68th Brigade took part in the fighting on the CONTAL-MAISON front and later at POZIÈRES, where Butterworth was killed on 5 August.

2nd King's Royal Rifle Corps (2nd Brigade, 1st Division) bivouacked in the Wood before going to SCOTTS REDOUBT near CONTALMAISON on 17 July; 2 days later 10th Glosters (1st Brigade, 1st Division) bivouacked in the Wood and found it 'agreeable', due to the fine weather. The Australian historian C.E.W. Bean arrived at POZIÈRES on 31 July, when he camped on the edge of Bécourt Wood. On the same day, 11th Royal Warwicks (112nd Brigade, 37th Division) moved to a reserve position about Bécourt Wood. According to C.S. Collison, 11th Royal Warwicks occupied the Wood itself, together with their battalion headquarters. The traffic rolled continuously onward, past the château, and raised clouds of dust, which 'hung about in the hot, sultry air, and mantled everybody and everything with garments of white'. The château had become a hospital, and many of its rooms were in good condition, while the heavy shade of the wood surrounding protected it from the 'broiling sun and dusty thoroughfares'. Several trenches ran through the Wood, which the enemy shelled with resulting casualties. When not engaged, 11th Royal Warwicks spent time in examining the captured German defences, in particular those of the crushed and battered village of FRICOURT, the scene of especially heavy fighting. During the nights the artillery displayed great activity, and after dinner it was customary to mount the opposite rise, where a

wonderful view could be had of the line of bursting shells. Several howitzers 'added their voices to the clamour'.

On 13 August, 2nd King's Royal Rifle Corps were back again for one night in the Wood before joining divisional reserve at MAMETZ WOOD, returning again between 21 and 26 August; they returned to MAMETZ WOOD on 11 September and travelled back to Bécourt Wood once more on 12 September.

By September, the château was still hardly damaged and still used as a dressing station; graves had been made in the former gardens.

In mid-November, the cemetery next to the dressing station in the château had become very large, with padres busy burying the dead. There was also a wireless station at the château that possibly connected with brigade headquarters at MAMETZ WOOD. At the end of November, there was a main dressing station and walking wounded collecting station here.

Divisions involved here included 9th, 15th and 34th.

Pte J. Jackson of 1st Cameron Highlanders (1st Brigade, 1st Division) was here on 5 November, and wrote: 'The weather was very bad, each day being wetter than another, and it was extremely uncomfortable living in tents, especially when 14 men with all their kit were crowded into one tent.' On 9 November, Jackson's battalion, which was on fatigue duty, moved into newly built huts, which was a great improvement and even had a stove.

Bécourt Military Cemetery is on the west side of Bécourt Wood, on the south side of the road to ALBERT. It was begun in August 1915 by 51st Division and carried on by 18th Division and others in the line until the Battle of the Somme. It was to be continuously in use, chiefly by field ambulances, until April 1917. Bécourt village and its château were in the British lines, from which units continuously moved off to the front. One of the men buried in the cemetery was Lt Col Addison, mentioned above (I.W.23). Lt Col J.P.V. Hawksley of the Royal Field Artillery, killed on 8 August, is also buried here (I.V.28). One of the 'Nine Sappers' commemorated at BAZENTIN-LE-PETIT is also buried here, Sapper J. Higgins. The cemetery has the graves of 263 men who died prior to 1 July 1916.

BÉHENCOURT is north-west of AMIENS on the D78 road. On 21 August 1915, 2/1st (Highland) Field Ambulance (51st Division) arrived here. In March 1916, the village was home to 1/5th and 1/8th West Yorkshires (146th Brigade, 49th Division). While here, 1/5th West Yorkshires were one of the battalions working on the new railway line linking DAOURS to CONTAY. On 30 March, Field Marshal Lord Kitchener inspected the troops here when on short visit to France, during which time he attended an Allied Conference in Paris and had discussions with Haig. On 6 May, 104th Field Ambulance (34th Division) arrived here, and 200 members of the unit were billeted in a large loft. The patients and officers occupied tents. A divisional rest station was set up at the beginning of July and 46th Brigade (15th Division) were in the area on 19 September.

The village churchyard contains the graves of two men who died in 1916 prior to the battle and one man who died in 1918.

BELLE EGLISE FARM, on the south side of the D31 between ARQUÈVES and LÉALVILLERS, was a railhead for supplies and personnel; it was constructed by a pioneer battalion who had also worked on the railway.

BELLEVUE FARM is south-east of ALBERT, on the MÉAULTE road. Prior to the battle there was a nest of artillery batteries here and a brigade from 34th Division had its headquarters in the farm. At the beginning of July 1916, it was the home of the Royal Engineers and also of 102nd Brigade (34th Division). A 'reconnaissance for a decauville tramway, mule-drawn, will be made, and the line pegged out with numbered pegs. Starting point, near the cemetery, north-west of Bellevue Farm.' On 11 July, 9th Yorkshires (69th Brigade, 23rd Division) returned to the vicinity of the farm. In early August, 17th Division had their headquarters here and in divisional reserve close by were 50th Brigade, who left for POMMIERS REDOUBT on 4 August. Later in the battle, a cinema was established to entertain the troops.

BELLOY-SUR-SOMME is on the north bank of the River Somme, north-west of AMIENS; during the battle the village was divisional headquarters for 8th, 33rd, 7th and 20th Divisions. Elements of 7th Division rested here for 9 days after being in action in July fighting for the BAZENTIN villages and HIGH WOOD.

BERLES-AU-BOIS is north of FONCQUE-VILLERS. Berles Position Military Cemetery, Berles New Military Cemetery and Berles-au-Bois Churchyard Extension all have Allied casualties in them. Berles Position Military Cemetery was begun in July 1916; of the 50 graves, 49 are from the period of the battle. First used by the French, Berles-au-Bois Churchyard Extension was taken over by the

British in September 1915, after which time it was used by 46th Division in particular. The churchyard is between two farms and most of the 100-plus graves belong to men who died before the battle. There was an advanced dressing station here. At one point during the battle a shell fell during a divisional concert and killed Lt G. Dews of the Royal Army Medical Corps. The village contained some caves, which during the war were used for storage.

BERNAFAY WOOD is on the northern side of the D64 FRICOURT–GUILLEMONT road. It was very nearly captured by the British on 1 July 1916, the first day of the Somme battle, after MONTAUBAN-DE-PICARDIE had fallen. Beyond it is TRÔNES WOOD, which is some 330 yards distant. In following the battle, the two woods should really be considered as one rather than separately. The line reached on 1 July and maintained thereafter ran from the eastern outskirts of MONTAUBAN-DE-PICARDIE, south-west through the Brickworks, to FAVIÈRE WOOD. Patrols had been sent out and found the Wood to be empty except for a few Germans, who were made prisoners.

Much of the following account is based on material from 'The Other Side of the Hill', which first appeared in the *Army Quarterly* in 1927. On 1 July, close to the front of the new British line along the northern slope of Montauban Ridge and CATERPILLAR VALLEY, the bed of a small winding stream that rose in TRÔNES WOOD flowed westward to the River Ancre. On the far side of the stream the ground rose fairly steeply, 150ft in 1,000yds, and reached the German Second Line trench that was on top of the slope between BAZENTIN-LE-GRAND and LONGUEVAL. On the right, TRÔNES WOOD lay across the head of the valley; the German Second Line then swung round southwards from LONGUEVAL on the high ground beyond the wood through GUILLEMONT and then towards MAUREPAS. Its capture would threaten the rear of the Germans who were still holding on around OVILLERS and THIEPVAL. The capture of the CONTALMAISON and MAMETZ WOOD on the left flank was to be carried out simultaneously with the advance through TRÔNES WOOD and Bernafay Wood on the right.

In the afternoon of 1 July, the remaining German defenders of their front trenches on Montauban Ridge, the left of 28. Reserve Division and the right of 12. Infanterie Division, together with Bayerische-Reserve-Infanterie-Regiment Nr. 6 (10. Bayerische Infanterie Division) were back in the

German Second Line, BAZENTIN-LE-GRAND–LONGUEVAL–GUILLEMONT, having abandoned several of their battery positions along CATER-PILLAR VALLEY and in the two Woods. It was at this point that the British should have followed up their initial success as both Woods were almost completely devoid of enemy troops.

During the evening, 12. Reserve Division arrived in the area in great haste, and at 1845hrs came under the command of 28. Reserve Division. They were then ordered to advance eastwards and regain a footing on Montauban Ridge close to MONTAUBAN-DE-PICARDIE and FAVIÈRE WOOD. The last-named was held by the French. This advance was planned to be made with Reserve-Infanterie-Regiment Nr. 51, past the north of COMBLES and then north to GUILLEMONT and on towards the north-east corner of MONTAUBAN-DE-PICARDIE. Reserve-Infanterie-Regiment Nr. 38 were to attack FAVIÈRE WOOD in the centre, and to the left Reserve-Infanterie-Regiment Nr. 23 were to advance between MAUREPAS and CURLU, on the north bank of the River Somme.

It was the eastern front of the new MONTAUBAN-DE-PICARDIE salient which was the German target and on 2 July, north of Bernafay Wood, the leading companies of Bayerische Infanterie-Regiment Nr. 16 moved up from CATERPILLAR VALLEY and came across an advance post of 17th Manchesters (90th Brigade, 30th Division) in Triangle Point, to the north of MONTAUBAN-DE-PICARDIE on the road to BAZENTIN-LE-GRAND. The post was annihilated and about 100 German troops entered Montauban Alley at this point. British artillery fire helped to push the attackers back to the dead ground of CATERPILLAR VALLEY and at the Brickworks 20th King's (89th Brigade, 30th Division) repelled Reserve-Infanterie-Regiment Nr. 15, who then fell back into Bernafay Wood or back into the dead ground between the Wood and MALTZ HORN FARM.

On the same day, 2 July, 20th King's sent out patrols into Bernafay Wood and found it unoccupied. Orders were given to occupy it at 2100hrs on 3 July, and 9th Division captured a German dugout and set up a dressing station. According to 'The Other Side of the Hill', 9th Division's 27th Brigade, with 6th King's Own Scottish Borderers on the right and 12th Royal Scots on the left, advanced from the front of the Brickworks–MONTAUBAN-DE-PICARDIE front due south on the MARICOURT road. They captured isolated pockets of Germans and the Wood was claimed by 9th Division.

In *Field Guns in France*, Neil Fraser-Tytler noted that on the night of 2 July two battalions had captured the Wood and so the British held everything up to the skyline except TRÔNES WOOD. Troops on the right who had walked into Bernafay Wood almost without any opposition were restrained from advancing further. There had been a brief bombardment and the few Germans left in the Wood made no attempt to fight. 12th Royal Scots (27th Brigade, 9th Division) discovered four deserted field guns and one machine gun; although the Wood was in British hands, it proved to be a dismal prize, for the Germans continuously shelled it with considerable violence and caused numerous casualties. After a week the Wood presented a woeful spectacle. Before 3 July a man on the firing line could only see a few yards in front of him, but after 2 or 3 days of shelling he could see the far end with little difficulty, a formidable strongpoint was dug in the centre of the Wood. During their time here the two Scottish battalions only had six casualties.

In early July, Lt R.B. Talbot Kelly of LII Brigade, Royal Field Artillery (9th Division), wrote that as a forward observation officer of the Royal Field Artillery he was aware of a German field gun battery being captured in Bernafay Wood which had splendid dugouts for its personnel. In *We Band of Brothers*, G.W. Warwick wrote that on 8 July, 4th South African Infantry saw Bernafay Wood come under heavy German fire, huge explosions and columns of smoke, when he knew that 2nd South African Infantry were in the Wood. By 13 July, the British advance reached TRÔNES WOOD, due west of Bernafay, and it was taken in the second advance of 14 July. The line of this advance ran in part from the east of DELVILLE WOOD down to the south of TRÔNES WOOD; GUILLEMONT, GINCHY and the complete capture of DELVILLE WOOD were the next objectives. It was to be 2 months before they were all in Allied hands, however.

Warwick reported that 4th South African Infantry marched up to Bernafay Wood with a guide in the lead; at this time the Wood was under heavy shell-fire and the guide was killed. They were then ordered to about turn, and on reaching the road again, went forward to the front-line trench, held by 10th Argyll & Sutherland Highlanders (26th Brigade, 9th Division). Warwick's battalion then relieved 2nd South African Infantry in the Wood; Warwick's half of No. 14 Platoon occupied a large dugout whose entrances faced the Germans.

On 11 July, Warwick was posted with five others to a listening post on the edge of the Wood, facing towards DELVILLE WOOD. They came under heavy machine-gun fire, as well as violent shell-fire that brought down the trees in the Wood. On 12 July, the enemy concentrated their artillery on the Wood and every square yard was shelled. Six men of Warwick's half-platoon went to set a guard at the post. As they emerged from the entrance to the dugout, they raced through the shelling, to be met with rifle and machine-gun fire from the direction of DELVILLE WOOD. At 2100hrs, a shell burst over the six men; Warwick was hit by pieces of shrapnel, but was able to drag himself back to safety. His wounds were attended to and he was given plenty of rum. On 13 July he was carried from the regimental aid post in Bernafay Wood through a trench held by 10th Argyll & Sutherland Highlanders. On reaching the MARICOURT–MONTAUBAN-DE-PICARDIE–LONGUEVAL road his stretcher was placed on a two-wheeled limber which trundled him along. At a point sufficiently far enough behind the line, the stretcher was lifted into a small motor ambulance, which took him to a dressing station at MARICOURT. While in hospital, Warwick was told that 2nd South African Infantry had finally captured and held DELVILLE WOOD.

In *Field Guns in France*, Fraser-Tytler noted that on 23 July he was given orders to enfilade a hidden ravine strongly held by the Germans in the French sector opposite HARDECOURT-AU-BOIS. This consisted of moving howitzers right forward with their trails towards the Germans, and shooting back over the salient into the ravine. The site was not far from the north-west corner of Bernafay Wood. On 24 July he went to HARDECOURT-AU-BOIS, laying the communication lines as he went. From there, a distance of about 6,000yds from the gun, he measured and managed to register the ravine, which had proved to be a principal stumbling block in an abortive attack that the French had made a few days before and which they were thus very keen to shell heavily before the next attack. Fraser-Tytler's howitzer was close to the main road to LONGUEVAL and was continuously shelled. On 28 July, Fraser-Tytler went up to the advance gun again, and found nearby a French 75 team whose objective was the same ravine as his. They had found some wonderful dugouts in a deep quarry and he advised the British team to share it with them. He located the French battery; finding their line had been broken, he ran a line to his own battery. The French shelled the ravine vigorously all day.

On 22/23 August, 8th King's Royal Rifle Corps (41st Brigade, 14th Division) moved to the quarry from DELVILLE WOOD, before returning to DELVILLE WOOD. On 8 August, the battalion

headquarters of 2nd South Staffords (6th Brigade, 2nd Division) was here as part of the attack on GUILLEMONT; in his diary, Gen J.L. Jack wrote that when he was Commanding Officer 2nd West Yorkshires (146th Brigade, 49th Division) from 27 August, his battalion were in positions at the north-east of the 'skeleton' of Bernafay Wood. His bivouac was described as being Camp D; in reality, it consisted of nothing more than a few shell-holes and a few bits of derelict trenches which the men had covered with their waterproof sheets, a couple of tarpaulins and several sheets of corrugated iron. Battalion headquarters was in a small German trench, which was made more habitable by the discovery of an old door and a small piece of metal sheeting for a roof; a small disused shed and stove that had been found added to the amenities. Another battalion who had their headquarters in the quarry at the north end of Bernafay Wood were 21st Manchesters (91st Brigade, 7th Division). The battalion were gassed while there, before moving on to Pommiers Trench, with their headquarters moving to the top of TRÔNES WOOD.

After being in the limelight for the first part of July, Bernafay Wood hardly receives a mention in accounts during August, but became more important again in September. By 5 September, FAFFEMONT FARM and LEUZE WOOD, both near the village of COMBLES, had fallen to the Allies; the artillery of 35th and 56th Divisions, who had covered the front by their bombardment and barrage, had rendered this success possible. Their gun positions had been in Chimpanzee Valley and the area south-east of Bernafay Wood had been subjected to heavy bombardments and considerable gas shelling. During this time HRH the Prince of Wales, at the time on the staff of XIV Corps, was a frequent visitor to the division and brigade headquarters in the forward area, as well as to the rest bivouacs and transport lines.

On 3 September, 9th Devons (20th Brigade, 7th Division) drew detonated bombs at the quarry to the north of Bernafay Wood; 1st Welsh Guards (3rd Guards Brigade, Guards Division) were briefly at the Wood in the period 11–13 September. A forward depot had been established there for the 15 September battle, containing sufficient Royal Engineers stores for the purpose of the initial assault. During the days before the attack the sappers had laid out and marked several routes leading to the Wood for horse transport, and began the heavy task of clearing from the northern end of the Wood through TRÔNES WOOD to GINCHY.

In *The Turning Point*, H.P. Robinson, war correspondent of *The Times*, wrote that around the middle of September Bernafay Wood, which had been captured at the outset of the battle and where there was comparatively little resistance, was 'less utterly stripped of all semblances of a wood' than many others in the area. Of course there were no leaves on the trees, no signs of autumn foliage anywhere, but the Wood 'still stood reasonably compact, with a regular outline and enough bare poles standing to make it still a wood of moderate density'. On 16 September, 1st Lincolns (62nd Brigade, 21st Division) were part of brigade reserve in a valley bordering the edge of the Wood. Camp X was mentioned as being the Bernafay Wood camp.

In *Triple Challenge*, Hugh Wansey Bayly, at the time a medical officer with 1st Scots Guards (2nd Guards Brigade, Guards Division) wrote that having left HAPPY VALLEY and seen tanks for the first time, his unit had moved forward to Bernafay Wood on 12 September and relieved 1st Welsh Guards at GINCHY. 1st Scots Guards had previously rested at CARNOY, in a deep little valley where a howitzer was at work and the cavalry were collecting. Bayly refers to a Lt E. Holland, killed by a German sniper around 13 September, and on the night before the battle he attended a champagne supper in the headquarters dugout in Bernafay Wood. This would have been the night of 15 September; Bayly remarked that there were about 15 men there, including Sir Iain Colquohoun. Several were to be killed the following day. They moved off soon after midnight for the 0620hrs start. Their assembly area was the apex of a shallow salient immediately in front of GINCHY. About 750yds on the right flank was the German QUADRILATERAL. Bayly's party moved down the western edge of Bernafay Wood, turning right-handed along the northern margins of Bernafay Wood and TRÔNES WOOD and on into GUILLEMONT and so by the GINCHY–GUILLEMONT road to their assembly trenches on the right front of GINCHY.

In his novel *Other Ranks*, W.V. Tilsley of 1/4th Loyal North Lancashires (164th Brigade, 55th Division) wrote that a communication trench named Hop Alley ran down to a point of Bernafay Wood, ending by the roadside. Cookers came down the slope to Bernafay and soon 'they were munching ravenously at thick slices of bacon'. German observation balloons confined them to a trench and a battery of '5.9s barked away' in broad daylight from the starkness of Trônes. An ambulance crept into view behind the cookers and pulled up at the dressing station.

On 25 September, 9th Norfolks (71st Brigade, 6th Division) were billeted in the area. At the end

of September, 61st Brigade (20th Division) held the area on their own for a week; 60th Brigade (also 20th Division) were in support near TRÔNES WOOD, with 59th Brigade (also 20th Division) at CARNOY in the reserve; the division headquarters returned to Bernafay Wood. On 29 September, the divisional artillery headquarters was also established here, with the batteries in positions in a valley about 800yds to the north-east of DELVILLE WOOD, known from its map reference as 'Toc 7 Valley'. 20th Division had been one of the more successful divisions and had done good work in the battle to take GUILLEMONT.

In early October, Aubrey Smith of 1/5th Londons (169th Brigade, 56th Division), who was stationed at MÉAULTE, noted that his battalion was bivouacked near the Wood. The big guns had moved much further down the slope and a broad-gauge railway was being laid down close to GUILLEMONT. On one occasion he had to take a water cart beyond the Wood. From 2 to 8 October, 10th King's Royal Rifle Corps (59th Brigade, 20th Division) were in the Wood, having come up from CARNOY on their way to MÉAULTE.

During 1/2 October, 35th Brigade (12th Division) were in reserve in the Wood; on 2 October, 7th Norfolks (35th Brigade, 12th Division) marched up to the Wood. On 10 October, 7th Norfolks held the front line with other battalions. At around 1700hrs on 12 October, there was an attack on Bayonet Trench, which ran from the north-west of GUEUDE COURT across the Ligny-Thilloy road and then slightly south-west. The objectives were, firstly, Bayonet Trench and Scabbard Trench and secondly, to capture LUISENHOF FARM, which was adjacent to the FLERS road on the east side; the left of 7th Norfolks secured 100–200yds of Scabbard Trench. This was part of the battle for the Transloy Ridges.

On 20 October, 8th Division's headquarters opened at the Wood; on 22 October, at a short conference of battalion commanders on the march, Brig Gen Fagan announced to Gen Jack's horror that 8th Division were to attack 'presently'. On 23 October, 1st West Yorkshires (23rd Brigade, 8th Division) were to act in close support to the remainder of their brigade. So in the afternoon, accompanied by McLaren, his second in command, Hawley and some orderlies set off on foot to the valley beyond the GINCHY–Flers Ridge to select the best position for the battalion, which was to march at dusk.

On 30 October, 9th Northumberland Fusiliers (52nd Brigade, 17th Division) were at Camp D, near to Bernafay Wood, which they described as being 'a sea of mud without tents'. The roads en route had been full of mud and shell-holes. On the same day 2nd Royal Welsh Fusiliers (19th Brigade, 33rd Division) withdrew to reserve between TRÔNES and Bernafay Woods, when conditions were described as being wretched for all. 'Tents that leaked were issued and during heavy showers it looked as if the bellying tarpaulin roof of H.W.'s crazy shack would release a flood.' After a while they made a short move to the Brickworks, which was south-west of the Wood. Here the tents were in another sea of mud, but there were blankets for the men. At the beginning of November, rain fell in torrents and the wretched shelters between TRÔNES WOOD and Bernafay Wood were just mud holes. A divisional headquarters was here on 13/14 November.

Bernafay Wood North Cemetery was opposite the northern edge of the Wood, a little east of the LONGUEVAL–MARICOURT road. It was begun by the personnel of an advanced dressing station and used from July to October 1916. After the war, the graves from here were concentrated in Bernafay Wood British Cemetery, on the north-west side of the LONGUEVAL–MARICOURT road opposite the north-west corner of Bernafay Wood. It was begun by the men of a dressing station in August 1916 and was a front-line cemetery until April 1917. Lt Col C.S. Taylor of 28th Heavy Artillery Group, Royal Garrison Artillery, is buried here (H.33), having died of wounds on 6 November. The remains of many bodies from the battlefields to the east of the Wood were brought in after the Armistice.

In 1935, according to the *Ypres Times*, there were five giant, scarred old trees that stood out in the 'new' Bernafay Wood 'like so many grotesque aerial masts'; however, the Wood could still be seen through from one side to the other.

BERNAVILLE, south-west of DOULLENS, was part of the area where 36th Division billeted towards the end of October 1915; on 18 January 1916, 36th Division's headquarters was established here. From 10 February, the village was the home of 1/5th Sherwood Foresters (139th Brigade, 46th Division) before they left for MAILLY-MAILLET by lorry 5 days later. On 28 June, 129th Field Ambulance (38th Division) were stationed here. On 1 July, Bernaville was the home to 9th Brigade (3rd Division), together with the village of PROUVILLE. From 18 to 29 September, 48th Division rested here. Between January and November 1916, 17th, 19th, 31st, 51st and 55th Divisions were also in the vicinity.

BERNEUIL, south-west of DOULLENS, is on the D216 road. On 30 April 1916, 10th Field Ambulance (4th Division) were here. On the morning of 27 June, a tragic accident occurred involving 10th Cheshires (7th Brigade, 25th Division), caused by the explosion of a bomb. L/Cpl Rowlinson and Pte Nash were both killed; Pte Belsham died of wounds and four other men were wounded. Rowlinson and Nash were both buried in the Berneuil Communal Cemetery close to the centre of the village; their funeral was attended by officers and men of 10th Cheshires.

On 26 June, 77th Field Ambulance (25th Division) were here; 2 days later, 130th Field Ambulance (38th Division) arrived. Towards the end of June, 3rd Worcesters (7th Brigade, 25th Division) were billeted here for 3 days, before 25th Division moved towards the line on 27 June. On 1 July, Berneuil was one of three villages housing 8th Brigade (3rd Division).

BERTANGLES is to the north of AMIENS, west of the main N25 road. On 7 October 1915, 109th Field Ambulance (36th Division) established itself in the village alongside No. 150 Field Company, Royal Engineers (also 36th Division). On 19 October, 36th Divisional Train also moved here. Between 18 and 28 November, 17th Manchesters (90th Brigade, 30th Division) were billeted here.

In February 1916 the whole village was taken over by the Royal Flying Corps, and 15th Field Ambulance (5th Division) left the village at this time. No. 24 Squadron, Royal Flying Corps, commanded by Maj L.G. Hawker VC, was based in the village from February until December 1916. It appears that the Army did still send units here occasionally, however, as 98th Field Ambulance (30th Division) were in the village at the end of March.

In April, No. 22 Squadron, commanded by Maj R.B. Martyn, joined No. 24 Squadron at the airfield close to the village. No. 3 Squadron were here for a brief period in early April. In May, No. 24 Squadron moved their mess to a hut close to the aerodrome. On 23 May, 11th Brigade (4th Division) were here and on the same day 55th Field Ambulance (18th Division) also arrived. On 1 July, the village was partly the home to 69th Brigade (23rd Division), together with COISY.

In July, Fourteenth (Army) Wing (Fighting) and Third (Corps) Wing (Artillery) shared Bertangles Château as their headquarters; they also shared the mess in the building. On 25 August, No. 21 Squadron, commanded by Maj J.R. Campbell-Heathcote, moved here, and began flying operations the following day. Their 'inadequate' BE 12s were kept in a hangar next to the sheds housing No. 24 Squadron, until 3 days later a gale blew the hangar down and partly destroyed the aircraft inside.

Maj Gen H.M. Trenchard, General Officer Commanding First Wing, Royal Flying Corps, used the château as his headquarters throughout the whole Somme battle.

The Bertangles Communal Cemetery, to the west of the village, was the first burial place of the outstanding pilot of the war, Manfred von Richthofen, who was shot down in April 1918. His body was later taken to the German Cemetery at FRICOURT. In the mid-1920s a crumbling wooden propeller cross was still in the Bertangles Communal Cemetery, a reminder of the Royal Flying Corps' links with the village.

BERTEAUCOURT-LES-DAMES is a village north-west of AMIENS, between PERNOIS and SAINT-OUEN. From 21 November 1915, 10th Field Ambulance (4th Division) ran a divisional rest station here. From 28 November, 96th Field Ambulance (30th Division) established a hospital in three buildings here, as well as organising billets. On 19 January 1916, 109th Field Ambulance (36th Division) came here when No. 30 Casualty Clearing Station was also here. On 27 February 1916, 1/7th Middlesex (167th Brigade, 56th Division) arrived here, remaining until 12 March, when they left for BEAUVAL.

BERTRANCOURT is north-east of ACHEUX-EN-AMIÉNOIS on the D114 road. The British took over the sector from the French in July 1915 and the first burial in the Bertrancourt Military Cemetery to the south-west of the village dates from that month. On 25 July, 1st Royal Dublin Fusiliers (86th Brigade, 29th Division) arrived here, on the following day moving up to the front line and taking over trenches opposite SERRE from French troops of 3rd Battalion, 64th Infantry Regiment. The French had captured this section of the line from the enemy in early June 1915 and it contained a lot of very deep dugouts, some up to 20ft deep. At the time there were few signs of war although, significantly, the villages were only populated by women, children or the elderly. Bertrancourt, together with FORCEVILLE and MAILLY-MAILLET, was chosen as a site for a field ambulance in July 1915.

A unit from 36th Division were here in the second week of October. On 29 October, 1/5th South Lancashires (12th Brigade, 36th Division)

arrived here, where they were involved in intensive training, and they also provided working parties. In mid-November the field ambulance set up in the village was described as 'virtually a hospital'. 1/5th Seaforth Highlanders (152nd Brigade, 51st Division) spent Christmas in Bertrancourt.

In early January 1916, 1/5th South Lancashires left for HALLENCOURT, south-west of ABBEVILLE, before moving out of the area. In the third week of the same month, a field ambulance from 36th Division took over the cooperative stores here for use as a hospital, in addition to existing accommodation. On 4 February, 1/1st (South Midland) Field Ambulance (48th Division) took over the hospital here, remaining until 4 March. On 13 February, 2nd West Yorkshires (23rd Brigade, 8th Division) left the village to take over the front line at BEAUMONT-HAMEL the following day. On 5 March, 109th Field Ambulance (36th Division) were located in the centre of the village in an *estaminet* at the crossroads.

At this period, owing to bad weather and their constant use, the roads hereabouts were in a very poor state and at one point the road to MAILLY-MAILLET was blocked by snow. By now the local 'hospital' could cope with 150 patients. From 23 March, 95th Field Ambulance (31st Division) were here for about 5 weeks. Towards the end of April, 18th Durham Light Infantry (93rd Brigade, 31st Division) went into a hutment camp here, which was described as 'very fair'.

Bertrancourt now began a close relationship with 4th Division as they trained and made other preparations for the forthcoming offensive. On 12 May, 12th Field Ambulance (4th Division) arrived in the village, where 4th Division had set up their headquarters, and a barn near the main buildings housed the men who ran the motor ambulances here. They remained here for the rest of the month and throughout June. On 1 July, 4th Division were allocated the attacking line to the left of 29th Division at BEAUMONT-HAMEL and to the right of 31st Division in front of SERRE.

From 6 to 11 June, a detachment of 2nd Seaforth Highlanders (10th Brigade, 4th Division), working at WARNIMONT WOOD, were in tents here; they were picked up on 10 June and moved to BEAUSSART on the following day. On 13 June, 2nd Essex (12th Brigade, 4th Division) were here on brigade relief and were involved in cable-laying. Two days later, 1st Somerset Light Infantry (11th Brigade, 4th Division) arrived here from BEAUVAL and stayed a week, during which time they supplied working parties that operated by night and day.

Towards the end of June, the enemy began to target the 'behind the lines' villages, and shells fell on the village on 26 and 28 June, and on the cross-roads in particular. Part of 1/6th West Yorkshires (146th Brigade, 49th Division) were here at the end of June and 'had a lively time, champagne, games, and horseplay'. The men thought that if they were to die in the forthcoming battle they might as well spend their spare cash and have a good time before they did so.

At 2330hrs on 30 June, 2nd Lancashire Fusiliers (12th Brigade, 4th Division) left their orchard camp in the village for their assembly positions, north of MAILLY-MAILLET. By 0900hrs on 1 July they had reached the Roman road, which ran north-west from BEAUMONT-HAMEL; there was much crossfire coming from that village and also from SERRE. The enemy continued to shell the area north-west of Bertrancourt during the night and early morning of 1 July.

For the first half of July, 4th Division had their headquarters here, and in early July, No. 3 Section of No. 1/1 (Durham) Field Company, Royal Engineers, were repairing roads from the village as far as the railway crossing at BEAUSSART. From 11 until 16 July, 2nd Lancashire Fusiliers were back in the village, having suffered 368 casualties north of BEAUMONT-HAMEL, and settled down in what was described as a 'pleasant camp'. On 13 July, 650 men from 35th Brigade (4th Division), attached for work, were billeted here. When, on 20 July, 12th Division relieved 4th Division in the line close to BEAUMONT-HAMEL, their headquarters was also at Bertrancourt Camp. From 31 July, 25th Division had their headquarters here, as did 2nd Guards Brigade from 9 August. In *Triple Challenge*, Hugh Wansey Bayly, medical officer of 1st Scots Guards (2nd Guards Brigade, Guards Division) mentions that his unit camped at Bertrancourt before going into the line at HÉBUTERNE on 16 August.

At the end of August, 6th and 39th Divisions had brigades here. On 6 September, 132nd Field Ambulance (39th Division) moved here when the village was being shelled, and sometimes patients had to be moved to a field adjacent to the hospital. On 7 October, 3rd Division had its headquarters here.

In *The Middle Parts of Fortune*, Frederic Manning wrote that his battalion, 7th King's Shropshire Light Infantry (8th Brigade, 3rd Division), marched by the divisional artillery headquarters at Bertrancourt to COURCELLES-AU-BOIS; they had come from MAILLY-MAILLET.

Bertrancourt Military Cemetery, in the south of the village and close to the LOUVENCOURT road, was designed by Sir Reginald Blomfield. Burials were made there by field ambulances in 1916 and 1917. Plot I contains 218 British burials, many of men who either died of wounds or were killed in action before the start of the battle, and a total of 82 graves of men from Yorkshire or Lancashire regiments. On 31 July 1915, Pte Joseph Carr of 2nd Royal Dublin Fusiliers (10th Brigade, 4th Division) died of gunshot wounds to the abdomen, which were said to have been caused accidentally. He was buried by his colleagues in a plot of ground allocated by the mayor of the village about 300yds north-west of the junction of the LOUVENCOURT–Bertrancourt and ACHEUX–Bertrancourt roads, near a hawthorn tree. He was later reburied (I.3.A).

Plot II contains 198 British burials, including 117 of men of Lancashire territorial battalions, dating from 2 July 1916 to 23 August 1918. After the Battle of the Somme, the Bertrancourt Military Cemetery was used by corps or divisional parties in the critical period June to August 1918. Pte A.T. Ansted (I.J.12) of 4th Royal Fusiliers (9th Brigade, 3rd Division), 'shot at dawn' for desertion on 15 November 1916, is buried here. Another man buried here is Maj H. Smithers DSO (I.J.8) of No. 170 Siege Battery, Royal Garrison Artillery, who was killed by a dud shell when next to his second-in-command, Capt B.A. Carr. Carr took his place and was promoted to major on 9 December, later becoming a lieutenant-colonel.

BIENVILLERS-AU-BOIS is north-west of FONCQUEVILLERS, opposite GOMMECOURT on the D8 POMMIER–HANNESCAMPS road. During the war it was mainly a billeting village and there was also a dressing station here. On 13 February 1916, 1/8th Worcesters (144th Brigade, 48th Division) marched here from COURCELLES-AU-BOIS before going back into the line and billeting at HÉBUTERNE. On 17 March, 2nd Royal Dublin Fusiliers (10th Brigade, 4th Division) arrived here from SAINT-AMAND, and went into the line opposite the village. Reserve billets were about 2,000yds behind the line. On 10 May, 1/8th Sherwood Foresters (138th Brigade, 46th Division) arrived here from GAUDIEMPRÉ and spent 8 days improving the village defences and the approach trenches behind FONCQUEVILLERS, as well as working on cable trenches.

On 20 May, 1/5th Lincolns (138th Brigade, 46th Division) were here; at this time, the village was still occupied by many of its inhabitants and the land still cultivated, even quite close up to the trenches. The wooded nature of the terrain prevented direct enemy observation. From then until early June, 1/5th

Lincolns were occupied not in training but in building assembly trenches and communication trenches leading to FONCQUEVILLERS, which was directly in front of Bienvillers-au-Bois. They also worked on Midland Trench, an assembly trench to the rear of FONCQUEVILLERS, which was completed by early June. Half the battalion worked during the day and half during the night, where new trenches were set in the open. Progress with this work was rapid and 1/5th Lincolns were even given a day off by Maj Gen The Hon. E. Montagu-Stuart-Wortley, General Officer Commanding 46th Division. On 3 June the village was suddenly shelled heavily; several billets were hit, resulting in casualties.

From 3 to 6 June, 1/7th Sherwood Foresters (139th Brigade, 46th Division) were billeted here after being relieved by 1/8th Sherwood Foresters at FONCQUEVILLERS, and moved on to SUS-SAINT-LÉGER on 6 June. After another spell at FONCQUEVILLERS, 1/7th Sherwood Foresters were back here on 18 June, when they had to supply large working parties in muddy conditions, suffering continuous shelling and having to supply fighting and reconnoitring patrols each night. On 4 July, 1/7th Sherwood Foresters relieved 1/8th Sherwood Foresters in the line.

On 18 June, while men from the Sherwood Foresters occupied the village, there were guns everywhere, and in many of the orchards on the outskirts of the village they were wheel to wheel. A temporary field hospital had been erected near SAULTY station. In *Four Years on the Western Front*, Aubrey Smith mentions that 1/5th Londons (169th Brigade, 56th Division) reported that the guns here, as well as at BAYENCOURT, SAINT-AMAND and SOUASTRE, were firing their hardest at the end of June during the pre-battle bombardment. There was an advanced dressing station or collection point in the village. During the month, No. 1/1 (North Midland) Field Company, Royal Engineers (46th Division), carried out work on gun emplacements and deep dugouts.

In his manuscript *Saturday Afternoon Soldiers*, Signaller H.G.R. Williams of 1/5th Londons noted that at the beginning of the battle he was in C Company, and that they had trenches in the Bienvillers-au-Bois–FONCQUEVILLERS district. The signalmen were billeted at the village school in Bienvillers-au-Bois.

On 3 July, 11th Royal Warwicks (112nd Brigade, 37th Division), after 16 days in the trenches, passed a night at Bienvillers-au-Bois. After standing in the streets of HALLOY for 2½ hours waiting for motor lorries, their procession moved off at 0830hrs on 6 July and passed through AMIENS, reaching MILLENCOURT at 1600hrs.

On the evening of 22 July, 1/5th Lincolns were relieved by 1/4th Lincolns (also 138th Brigade, 46th Division) by 1915hrs and returned to Bienvillers-au-Bois, where they were billeted as brigade reserve; brigade headquarters was in the village. Having been out of the line for some time, 1/5th Lincolns returned to the trenches on 9 August. During this particular tour, gas cylinders were installed in a large number of front trenches, to the great disgust of the garrison; they were a constant source of annoyance, owing to possible leakage. They could also explode if hit by a German shell.

On 21 September, 2nd Royal Welsh Fusiliers (19th Brigade, 33rd Division) were billeted here.

Bienvillers-au-Bois Military Cemetery is south-west of Bienvillers-au-Bois, on the north side of the road to SOUASTRE. It was begun by 37th Division in September 1915 and carried on by other divisions in the line until March 1917 and reopened in 1918 when the village was again in the front line. Of the 1,605 burials, about 200 are of men who died before the battle. Between 1922 and 1924, 480 casualties, mainly from 1916, were brought in from the Ancre battlefield. One of these was Capt A.G. Lezard (IX.A.11) of 13th Rifle Brigade, a South African who had been killed at his artillery observation post on 31 January and buried in Bienvillers-au-Bois Communal Cemetery. He was a 'charming officer, bluff and hearty, and adored by his men. It was night when we buried him in the communal cemetery of Bienvillers. With slow, muffled tread we carried him up the village street, whilst someone swung a lantern in front and guns boomed and flared on our left.' Lezard was later transferred to Bienvillers-au-Bois Military Cemetery. Also buried here is Capt. W.L. Brodie VC who gained his award in Belgium on 12 December 1914, XVVIII F 15.

BILLON FARM, BILLON COPSE, BILLON WOOD and **BILLON WOOD VALLEY** can all be found close to the BRAY-SUR-SOMME–CARNOY Wood beyond BRONFAY FARM. The Copse is to the south-west, on the left side of the road, with the other three locations on the east side. The Farm comes first with the Wood further east and the Wood Valley running north to south from it.

In August 1915, 5th Division's artillery took up positions in the valley, north of SUZANNE, behind the crest of the ridge near Billon Farm and HAPPY VALLEY. The batteries were all screened. In early January 1916, three companies of 19th Manchesters (21st Brigade, 30th Division) were in Billon

Wood from 6 to 12 January, while a fourth were at BRONFAY FARM, about 600yds away to the south-west. On 12 January the four companies left for billets in BRAY-SUR-SOMME. Troops from 14th Royal Warwicks (13th Brigade, 5th Division) were here in mid-January; despite its being winter, they were living in dugouts or canvas tents. It was a support position from which they supplied working parties.

On 1 June, 18th Manchesters (90th Brigade, 30th Division) marched to camp here, where they remained until 12 June, when relieved by 20th King's (89th Brigade, 30th Division) and moving to reserve in billets in ETINEHEM. At the end of June, Billon Wood was the headquarters of No. 79 Field Company, Royal Engineers (18th Division); on 5 July they moved up to CARNOY.

Prior to the battle, a great deal of combat and medical preparation was carried out at Billon Farm, which became an advanced dressing station and was a receiving point for ambulance cars of the field ambulances, the cars returning via DIVE COPSE. In June, LXXXIV Brigade were one of the Royal Field Artillery brigades with batteries in the Wood; at this time their wagon lines were in TAILLES WOOD and their observation post was on the PÉRONNE road to the south. By 7/8 July their wagon lines had been moved forward to Billon Wood itself.

At the beginning of the battle, the whole area was linked with 18th and 30th Divisions, with 9th Division in reserve. To the west was the Franco-British Army boundary. Having been at BRAY-SUR-SOMME for a few days and at les Celestins, 9th Division were in corps reserve; they assembled in Billon Wood, 2 miles behind the front. Being close to the junction of the French lines, the Wood and the Valley were packed with French and British guns, mostly 4in and upwards. Some of them dated from 1872 and had been used in the Franco-Prussian War, but had been reduced in size. Trigger Wood at the bottom of Billon Wood Valley, and localities where they sheltered, were hidden from enemy view by the crest of Maricourt Wood. The enemy gassed the valley which advancing troops would have to cross.

On 1 July, No. 90 Field Company, Royal Engineers (9th Division), arrived here and were billeted in the village. 27th Field Ambulance (also 9th Division) dealt with walking wounded arriving at the farm on the same day. These were so numerous that many had to lie down in fields around the collecting station. Many more casualties arrived at night.

On 14 July a battalion of the Essex Regiment were in the Valley when the Indian cavalry thronged the road near their camp. On 20 July, 30th Division's headquarters moved from CORBIE to this area. On 18 August, 35th Division's advanced headquarters was established at the Farm, with the two brigade headquarters in Chimpanzee Trench. On 26 August, 5th Division's headquarters was in dugouts near the Farm, when 5th Division were on the Maltz Horn Ridge

On 6 September, 1st Norfolks (15th Brigade, 5th Division) were resting at the Farm after being at FAFFEMONT FARM, and 56th Division's headquarters opened in the Wood, which was then the limit for horse ambulances. There were dugouts and canvas trenches here. On 18 September, 14th Royal Warwicks were at the Farm, close to a 12in gun on the railway. The Farm building was really little more than an address in 1916, as it had been 'blown to the four winds'.

BIRCH TREE WOOD is north of FRICOURT and south-east of SCOTTS REDOUBT. The *Official History of the War* notes that on 1 July 1916 the German machine guns caused some loss before the leading lines of 1st Lincolns (62nd Brigade, 21st Division) reached the edge of SHELTER WOOD and the much smaller Birch Tree Wood just beyond it to the north-west. A large number of Germans emerged from dugouts and engaged 12th Northumberland Fusiliers (also 62nd Brigade). The Wood was captured, but a strong bombing counter-attack from the right delayed entry into SHELTER WOOD. On 8 July, Birch Tree Avenue, which ran towards PEAKE WOODS to the north-east, was occupied by 13th Durham Light Infantry (68th Brigade, 23rd Division) as far as a captured strongpoint.

BLACK HORSE BRIDGE led from the central track running through AVELUY WOOD from MARTINSART and over the D50 road to the marshes west of the wood, and continued over the River Ancre. The Black Horse shelters were 150yds south of AUTHUILLE and just over 1 mile from THIEPVAL. The whole position was one of safety, as it was protected by sloping ground under which troops could shelter. Work on the construction of dugouts was begun in early January 1916; on 4 March, 108th Field Ambulance (36th Division) took them over, but they were ordered out by 32nd Division, who wanted to use the shelters themselves. At some point 32nd Division had their own 90th Field Ambulance set up here.

To be fair to 32nd Division, both before and during the early part of the battle, the area was very much 'their patch'. Among other battalions, 15th Highland Light Infantry and 1st Dorsets (both 14th Brigade, 32nd Division) spent rest periods here before the battle; the adjoining sector was the pre-serve of 19th Lancashire Fusiliers and 2nd Man-chesters (both also 14th Brigade, 32nd Division). The battalion history of 15th Highland Light Infantry described the shelters in the following way:

> To understand these shelters, imagine a high bluff, crescent in shape, and on the face of it, built of sandbags, a large number of cave-like dwell-ings let into the hillside. There were three tiers of them, and at the foot lay a roadway. On the other side of the roadway was the Ancre, then a short stretch of grass, then a canal, then a marsh, then Aveluy Wood. It was a very quiet and pleasant place, although within about a 1,000 yards of the enemy's line. Nothing could touch it unless shells from Hamel on the flank, and even from there it was difficult. In warm days the troops bathed in the canal. At night they did fatigue and carrying work in and to the front line trenches.

It should be noted that the 15th Highland Light Infantry's historian described the River Ancre as a canal. These massive dugouts, together with the

Black Horse Shelters near Authuille on the Ancre, June 1917. (IWM Q6202)

north–south causeway, are still there as, of course, is the Ancre. As the spot has hardly altered topo-graphically, it is one of the most interesting places to visit on the whole Somme battlefield.

From 23 to 26 June, 16th Lancashire Fusiliers (96th Brigade, 32nd Division) were in the dugouts here. On the night of 30 June, 14th Brigade (32nd Division) moved into assembly positions at the shelters, as well as at CRUCIFIX CORNER to the south. On the opening morning of the battle, 1st Dorsets, on their way to Black Horse Bridge, found the roads thronged with transport, and passed through battery lines of massed artillery; behind ridges, the guns were almost wheel to wheel. The chalk pits were crowded with 'picketed gorses'. They came via AVELUY WOOD at 0630hrs and reached the Black Horse shelters before moving along the Dumbarton Track through Authuille Wood. The next day, 2nd South Lancashires (75th Brigade, 25th Division) reached their assembly positions east of the River Ancre, crossing by Black Horse Bridge.

Two months later, on 2/3 September, bombs and other battle equipment could be drawn at the bottom of Black Horse Road before the troops began crossing the Ancre. On 24 September, buses were able to reach this point, and one transported a section of 1/4th Duke of Wellington's (147th Brigade, 49th Division).

BLACK ROAD, the track running north-north-west to the southern corner of HIGH WOOD, was the first objective of 5th and 7th Divisions on 20 July 1916, according to the *Official History of the War*. The second objective, some 300yds beyond and parallel to the first, was a track called Wood Lane, which reached HIGH WOOD at its eastern corner. It was 33rd Division which were to cope with HIGH WOOD itself; later Wood Lane proved untenable but Black Road was consolidated.

BLACK WOOD was a small copse less than 1 mile from ALBERT, on the south side of the ALBERT–Bécourt Wood road, south of Tara Valley. Between 16 and 20 August 1916, 1st Glosters (3rd Brigade, 1st Division) bivouacked here; to the south, bivouacs, transport lines, supply depots and dumps of stores were spread over the country as far as the eye could see, and the strains of other people's bands and drums were heard all day and the greater part of the night. There was also much aerial activity, and batches of German prisoners passed the bivouac daily on the way to ALBERT.

On 5 September, 2nd King's Royal Rifle Corps (2nd Brigade, 1st Division) went via Black Wood to the west side of MAMETZ WOOD. On 20 September they returned to Black Wood and on 30 September marched to MILLENCOURT, where they rested.

BLIGHTY VALLEY is just south of AUTHUILLE village on the east side of the D151 road between Aveluy and Blighty Wood, where 'Bill Jackson', the notorious German machine-gunner, used to 'play the dickens'. Blighty Valley is most associated with the failed attacks towards OVILLERS by 8th Division on 1 July 1916. The following information is based on an unpublished diary of Brig Gen A.C. Johnstone, serving with 3rd Worcesters (7th Brigade, 25th Division). On the morning of 18 August, 3rd Worcesters went down to their old headquarters in Blighty Valley near Authuille Wood. An attack on their right had gone 'awfully well' as the objective was reached and 500 prisoners taken. On the next day Johnstone complained about the condition of the trenches that had been handed over to them and the following day the trenches were inspected by Maj Gen E.G.T. Bainbridge, General Officer Commanding 25th Division. Johnstone noted too that in the morning Allied artillery were causing a lot of harm by falling short. This was the heavy artillery, who 'as usual' were shooting off the map and had observers miles behind the line. He wrote that the field gunners were much more accurate.

On 3 September, Lt Col W.B. Gibbs, Commanding Officer 3rd Worcesters, was killed in action when involved in the LEIPZIG SALIENT action. Johnstone wrote the following in his diary:

September 3rd: The attack has apparently been a costly failure, and about 9am we received orders to march back once more to take over a part of the line held by the 75th Inf Brigade under whose orders we came once more. Reached Authuille about noon, things had quietened down pretty well by then. The Regiment has lost 3 of its best officers including Gibbs the C/O., and altogether the show seems to have been a most disastrous one. It was a task that should have been set to fresh troops – both the 1st Wilts and the Regiment (lent to the 75th Inf Brigade for the attack) have already done more than their share and are a bit tired.

On 6 September, Johnstone showed Lt Col C.G. Forsyth of 6th Yorkshires (32nd Brigade, 11th Division) around the trenches as his brigade were probably to relieve them the next day: 'They are absolutely fresh with battalions 1000 strong who have done nothing but train for about six months.'

In the regimental history, H.F. Stacke noted the following of the same events:

The battalion and the 1st Wilts were detached from the 7th Brigade. On the afternoon of the 2nd September the Worcesters marched forward from Bouzincourt to Black Horse Bridge near Authuille for another crack at the Leipzig Salient. The 3rd Worcs were to attack against the western side of a small salient from the original front line further down the slope. Further to the right the 1st Wilts would attack from the captured trenches of the eastern slope of Thiepval Spur. On the left of the Worcs the 2nd South Lancs would carry the front further to the north. At 5.10 am the British Bns advanced combined with a British bombardment. The Worcs reached the German line but although overwhelming them the German artillery bombed their own front line and the position became untenable. The C/O Col Gibbs was killed. The other two battalions suffered similar fates and the attack had failed.

At the end of September, Gunner W.R. Price of CCXL Brigade, Royal Field Artillery (48th Division), was positioned at POZIÈRES; he noted that he went to a spot near Blighty Wood and for the rest of the battle spent his time as part of a relieving battalion.

Blighty Valley Cemetery is almost at the head of the valley called Valle du Hem on modern maps, a short way up its northern bank. It was begun in early July and was used until the following November, at which time Plot 1 contained the graves of 212 soldiers. The cemetery was considerably expanded after the Armistice, with reburials of 789 more men. About half of the men in the cemetery died on 1 July in what was then very much the territory of 8th Division, and the headstones include the names of the men of several Yorkshire regiments who were killed on that day. The cemetery also contains the remains of 50 men who were first buried at Quarry Post Cemetery, on the south-east side of Authuille Wood.

The graves include those of four lieutenant-colonels. Lt Col B. Maddison (I.B.5) of 2nd Yorkshires (attached to 8th York & Lancasters, 70th Brigade, 23rd Division) was killed in action in the attack on OVILLERS on 1 July 1916 when 8th York & Lancasters suffered very heavy casualties, together with 9th York & Lancasters (also 70th Brigade, 23rd Division) and 8th King's Own Yorkshire Light Infantry (70th Brigade, 21st Division). Maddison was killed early in the attack, possibly in Nab Valley to the south of where the cemetery now is. Lt Col. E. Brown (III.B.7) Commanding Officer 1st Wiltshires (7th Brigade, 25th Division) was killed in action on 6 July. Lt Col W.B. Gibbs (I.D.36) of 3rd Worcesters (7th Brigade, 25th Division) was killed in action on 3 September. Lt Col C.G. Forsyth DSO (I.F.13), attached to 6th Yorkshires (32nd Brigade, 11th Division), died on 14 September during operations at Turk Street and WONDERWORK.

Blighty Valley Cemetery can be reached by travelling between Aveluy and THIEPVAL and is on the eastern side of the D151 road.

BOIS FRANÇAIS was the name given to the part of the front line that lay opposite the village of FRICOURT. To the east of it was a small quarry, and to the west it continued into what was known as Aeroplane Trench, which resembled the shape of an aeroplane with its branching saps. It had been an area for mining activity at least since the end of August 1915 if not earlier. To the north-west were Wing Corner and the village of FRICOURT.

Bois Français is most known in its connection with Bernard Adams and Siegfried Sassoon of 1st Royal Welsh Fusiliers (19th Brigade, 33rd Division). Adams wrote a book called *Nothing of Importance*, a record of 8 months at the front with his battalion, which was published by Methuen in 1917. The book contains maps that show considerable detail of this part of the Somme front and deals in part with the period of the build-up to the Somme battle. In the book the names of battalion members were changed and Sassoon was known as Scott. We know this from an annotated copy of the book in the Faculty Library at the University of Oxford; Sassoon made the annotations himself.

Adams wrote that 1st Royal Welsh Fusiliers held the trenches at Bois Français for over 4 months from February to June 1916. One could have an uninterrupted view not only of both front lines running down into Fricourt Valley but of both lines running up onto the high ground north of FRICOURT, with a very good view of FRICOURT itself as well as of Fricourt Wood. It was also clear that the Germans had a clear view of the British lines and communications in the valley. They could not see the Allied trenches to the east of Bois Français, however, nor had they an enfilade view, as the British communications were on the reverse slope of the shoulder of high ground. The British therefore had the advantage. The British could in addition get a degree of enfilade observation of the opposing trenches from a work called Bonté Redoubt or Point 87, which was also an artillery observation post about 1,000yds to the west of the Bois Français trenches. A battery of field artillery were at the same time stationed in the gully called Gibraltar, at the head of HAPPY VALLEY, which was immediately to the south, close to the village of BRAY-SUR-SOMME. Another battery were positioned just west of ALBERT and these were able to bring enfilade fire on the German trenches. Adams also mentions that howitzers were positioned in all sorts of places, some as far back as at MORLANCOURT. The woods also contained many batteries, especially TAILLES WOOD, and as the year progressed grew fuller and fuller.

When 1st Royal Welsh Fusiliers were out of the line, Adams explained, the battalion invariably supplied working parties, which could last as long as 9 hours. For a time they always went up the line via MÉAULTE, until the Germans took to shelling the road. They then began to use an alternative route, via TAILLES WOOD and Gibraltar. For either route, 1st Royal Welsh Fusiliers had to cross high ground south-west of Point 71 by way of the trench, but subsequently were unobserved once more. Adams mentioned that there was a series of dugouts along this road, and an array of units including companies in reserve, headquarters of the Royal Engineers, a dressing station, stores and field kitchens. The rations came up every evening from

BRAY-SUR-SOMME. Although the position could not be seen by the enemy, after a time the Germans did begin to shell it.

Adams wrote that he thought that the dugouts called Point 71 North were the best. His maps show these to have been just off the BRAY-SUR-SOMME–FRICOURT road, on the eastern side, and to the south-west of Bois Français. Here the bank sloped up very sharply from the road; this gave the dugouts security, except from shell-fire of high trajectory. However, it was dangerous to go along the road and turn the next corner, as one was then in full view of FRICOURT itself. Adams mentioned that his company, B Company, held part of Bois Français trenches, while C Company, which included Sassoon, held Point 71 North. MAPLE REDOUBT, which was 300yds to the south of Bois Français and battalion headquarters, contained bombers, medical staff and stretcher-bearers.

Adams's company headquarters was to the south of the Bois Français quarry, at a place named Trafalgar Square, but later moved to a position halfway up 76 Street. At Trafalgar Square there were also two signallers and a permanent wiring party, consisting of a corporal with five men; they worked by day on 'concertina' or 'gooseberry' wire and at night were out for 3 or 4 hours putting it up.

Several mine craters were within the Bois Français position; these were constantly being explored by either side. To this day the craters can be identified, with only cattle now to occupy them. The trench lines were in places only 60yds apart.

For the next section, the author has relied heavily on Sassoon's *Diaries*, edited by Rupert Hart-Davis, and Sassoon's autobiographical novels *Memoirs of a Fox-Hunting Man* and *Memoirs of an Infantry Officer*, in which he appears as 'George Sherston'. Sassoon states that Lewis guns and steel hats reached 1st Royal Welsh Fusiliers in February 1916; on 5 February he rode up from BRAY-SUR-SOMME and over the hill to the CITADEL, a camp further to the south on the BRAY-SUR-SOMME road. On 21 February, Maj Stockwell became the Commanding Officer 1st Royal Welsh Fusiliers; in his memoirs, Sassoon gives him the name 'Kinjack'. On 23 February, Sassoon went home on leave; in his memoirs, 'Sherston' brought back smoked salmon for his colleagues, returning to MORLANCOURT on 6 March. He described the village as being approached from five different roads, which converged 'in a friendly fashion with a little crop of houses'. There was a church with a slated tower and a giant vane, round which 'birds wheeled and cackled'. In the hollow ground in the middle, where

the five roads met, there was a congestion of farm buildings round an open space with a pond on one side of it. The long lines of high ground hid the rest of the world. At this period Sassoon was Transport Officer, and therefore slept in canvas huts close to the transport.

In Sassoon's memoirs, 'Sherston' went up to the front line using a communication trench called Canterbury Trench and then looked for Watling Street. There was a trench of this name and Canterbury Trench was in fact Canterbury Avenue. He passed the support company dugouts at MAPLE REDOUBT and then went down to the company headquarters dugouts. There were 20 steps down and on this occasion there had been snow. 'Kinjack' wanted the whole of their front rewired. The return journey was made down Canterbury Avenue to MORLANCOURT village. According to his *Diary*, Sassoon heard on 19 March that his and Robert Graves's great friend 2/Lt David Thomas had died of wounds. In Sassoon's memoirs he was buried near the ration dump; in reality Thomas was buried at Point 110 Cemetery. On that day Sassoon mentioned that he had escaped to the woods above SAILLY-LAURETTE to be alone with his grief for his dead friend.

Both Graves and Sassoon attended Thomas's burial and Sassoon described the event in his diary: 'In the half clouded moonlight the parson stood above the graves, and everything was dim but the striped flag laid across them. Robert Graves, beside me, with his white whimsical face twisted and grieving. Once we could not hear the solemn words for the noise of a machine gun along the line; when all was finished a canister fell a few hundred yards away to burst with a crash.'

On 27 March, Sassoon began 6 days in the trenches with C Company, which he had joined from the transport. In Sassoon's memoirs he was known as 'Kangaroo' and described a fine afternoon in the wood above MÉAULTE, where there were anemones and bluebells, and also some wild cherry in blossom. He noted that the rural spirit of the area had been affected by the presence of supply sheds and Royal Engineer stores and the sound of distant artillery. He described BÉCOURT church in the foreground, and his steel dugout as being very hot, with his colleagues Greave and Stockwell asleep on their beds and the servants singing and joking next door.

On 30 March, Sassoon explored no man's land with his friend Cpl R. O'Brien and disturbed the Germans by lobbying bombs at them in the mine crater area; each contained pools of water and nothing grew near them. Snags of iron jutted from their sides and there was trench refuse in the form of tin cans and coils of wire. On 31 March, he carried out more crater bombing and, on 2 April, went out of the line. On 10 April, he was at Point 71 North and mentioned further crater bombing. On 14 April, Sassoon rode near HEILLY through a strip of woodland on the hill above TREUX and MÉRICOURT-L'ABBÉ. On 22 April, he was back in trenches, which were waterlogged.

According to his memoirs, Sassoon left MORLANCOURT after Easter and went to the Fourth Army School for a month's refresher course. He left the village on 23 April and saw supply convoys, artillery horse-lines and the 'dirty white tents of a Red Cross camp'. Spring had arrived. Once at FLIXECOURT, which was between ABBEVILLE and AMIENS, he attended lectures and was trained for open warfare, dealing with gas and the use of the bayonet. He also got some reading done, which included *Mr Sponge's Sporting Tour*, Lamb's *Essays* and Hardy's *Far From the Madding Crowd*.

On 22 May Sassoon returned to MORLAN-COURT, at the end of a hot Saturday afternoon. The bus turned off the bumpy road from the town of CORBIE and crawled up the steep winding lane. He was then introduced to 'Fewnings', a newcomer to 1st Royal Welsh Fusiliers, and heard that a raid was being planned. In the evening of 23 May, he was on Crawley Ridge, south-west of Bois Français; looking across to FRICOURT, he saw trench mortars bursting in the village cemetery. FRICOURT at that time was a huddle of reddish roofs with an almost demolished church tower; the whiteness of the village was contrasted against the sombre green of Fricourt Wood, which was full of German batteries. White seams and heapings of trenches dug in the chalk stretched away up the hill. The sky was full of skylarks.

According to his memoirs, on 25 May Sassoon took a raiding party to 'Kinjack's headquarters at MAPLE REDOUBT; the raiding party then went up to the support trench. The raid's objective was to enter the enemy lip on the edge of the crater, to enter Kiel Trench at two points and to examine the section of trench thus isolated. Furthermore they were to capture prisoners, bomb dugouts and kill some Germans. They went across the craters and Kiel Trench was quiet. They found that they couldn't force their way through a second belt of wire and 14 men scrambled back. 'Mansfield' was hit and Sassoon carried in a wounded lance-corporal. Sassoon searched for a corporal who was down in one of the craters and found him in the second

crater, with a colleague at his side. A rope was sent for and they got the wounded man back to the parapet. Two men were killed on the raid and 10 were wounded.

According to Sassoon's diary, 27 men, including one officer and Cpl R. O'Brien, took part in the raid. Bombs were exchanged with the enemy and Sassoon, who was not officially on the raid, counted the men back; when they got to 16, he went in search of O'Brien, who was said to be wounded. He found him in the right-hand crater and, despite the Germans firing into the crater at point blank range, he prepared to get him out. O'Brien was seriously wounded and, being over 6ft tall, was difficult to move. Sassoon went back for help and eventually O'Brien was brought back, but was found to be dead. Sassoon returned to Point 71 North. For his action Sassoon was awarded the Military Cross, but the raid was not a success, and the commanding officer was 'pretty sick about the whole business'.

In his diary at the end of May, Sassoon described TAILLES WOOD as being full of men from the Border and Devonshire Regiments; when walking home he saw MORLANCOURT looking peaceful in a basin with smoke going up from it. On 31 May he was at the Bluff above SAILLY-LAURETTE and looked at the River Somme with its chain of lakes. On 1 June, a divisional concert was held in which Capt B. Hallam Radford took part. On 2 June, Sassoon was up at MAPLE REDOUBT and in the evening was in charge of a working party at BÉCORDEL-BÉCOURT. On 4 June, Sassoon was on duty at Point 71 North; on 9 June, his leave came through and he rode to MORLANCOURT with the quartermaster in a perfect sunset; the muddy road as they walked away from the CITADEL was red in front of them. He drove down to MÉRICOURT-L'ABBÉ station, probably on 10 June. On 19 June, he returned, when the battalion were at BUSSY-LÈS-DAOURS. Bullfrogs croaked continuously.

On 26 June, Sassoon noted in his *Diary* that MORLANCOURT was full of troops and supply columns and that he had passed a large new dressing station halfway between CORBIE and TAILLES WOOD. The tents were mostly camouflage colours. On 27 June, in a remark on the Allied bombardment, he said that the Germans had not retaliated much. As he went along Kingston Road Trench, FRICOURT was being shelled. Men of the Royal Irish Rifles were going along Point 71 North. The attack had been postponed and the men were at 'concert pitch'. They were due to enter the trenches in front of the cemetery by FRICOURT station. They marched up to TAILLES WOOD and were due to relieve 7th Borders (51st Brigade, 17th Division). In Sassoon's memoirs, he writes that New Trench, opposite Sunken Road Trench, had been 'a good deal knocked about'.

In his *Diary*, Sassoon mentioned on 28 June that he was reading Hardy's *Tess of the D'Urbervilles* in 85 Street dugouts. On 29 June, there was a steady bombardment; on 30 June, he went down Kingston Road, about 500yds behind the front trench where Sandown Avenue met Kingston Road. 20th Manchesters (22nd Brigade, 7th Division) were to the right on the edge of FRICOURT. In Sassoon's memoirs, he wrote that the gun at Wing Corner had been silent.

On 1 July, the first day of the battle, Sassoon watched 21st Division advancing about ¾ mile away on the left.

In early August 1916, when King George V was on a guided tour of the area, he was shown the grave of Pte A. Pennington of No. 145 Company, Machine Gun Corps (48th Division). A picture of the occasion was later published in the press, but the grave was lost later in the war, as Pennington's name is commemorated on the Thiepval Memorial. The Commonwealth War Graves Commission assert that Pennington died on 14 August, but this is wrong, as the King made his visit on 10 August; it is not known when the grave was first made.

Bernard Adams of 1st Royal Welsh Fusiliers (22nd Brigade, 7th Division), whose book contributed so much to this entry, died of wounds at SERRE on 27 February 1917 and was buried at Couin Military Cemetery (B.3).

BONNEVILLE is south-west of DOULLENS and at the end of March 1916, 88th Field Ambulance (29th Division) had been given instructions to choose a suitable building in the village in order to set up a hospital. When first coming to the Somme in early April 1916, 4th Worcesters (88th Brigade, 29th Division) were billeted here until their brigade left for LOUVENCOURT on 4 April. On 25 June 1916, 75th Field Ambulance were in the village.

Two men are buried in the Bonneville Communal Cemetery adjacent to the road to Motrelet: one Australian private who died in August 1916 and an officer who died in 1917.

BOTTOM WOOD is situated to the south-west of MAMETZ WOOD and 2,000yds south of CONTALMAISON, adjacent to the MAMETZ–CONTALMAISON road. It was captured by the British in the fighting between 2 and 13 July 1916.

In *The Old Front Line*, John Masefield described it as an oblong wood, and that just above it, running diagonally across the spur, was a linchet, once lined with trees. Beyond this was a half-sunken track running parallel with the linchet.

The *History of the 17th Northern Division* notes that on 3 July the leading company of 7th Borders (51st Brigade, 17th Division) passed on from Railway Alley into the western side of Bottom Wood, where they met with obstinate resistance. The Germans held the trench running north and south inside the margin of the Wood, where they had their machine guns, and crossfire of other guns came on the left from Quadrangle Trench, a little higher up the slope towards CONTALMAISON. An immense quantity of stores and material had been captured, particularly in a huge dugout a little south of SHELTER WOOD, an underground barrack, close to Bottom Wood.

Hedge lines ran from the Wood to both LOZENGE WOOD and SHELTER WOOD towards FRICOURT and from LOZENGE WOOD battalions formed up behind the hedge. SHELTER WOOD was a position where battalions changed over.

BOULEUX WOOD is just off to the right when coming from COMBLES on the D20 road to GINCHY and GUILLEMONT, and is long and narrow in shape. During the battle it was inevitably known as Bully Wood, and it cannot be studied without being related to LEUZE WOOD, which is across the road, and also to COMBLES itself. The period when it was prominent in the fighting was between 12 and 27 September 1916. GINCHY had fallen and the line from LESBŒUFS via MORVAL and COMBLES was the one that the Allies were attempting to achieve. The fighting was at its most intense in the approaches to COMBLES, which in part were guarded by the QUADRILATERAL, a German strongpoint about 1,000yds from GINCHY on the MORVAL road.

A German railway ran from the direction of COMBLES around the back of the Wood in the direction of TRÔNES WOOD. On 20 September a new trench was dug by 1/5th Cheshires (pioneers of 56th Division), which was named Gropi Trench after the unit's code name. A new trench on the eastern side of the Wood was named Ranger Trench. Gropi Trench stretched for about 1,000yds in front of the Wood. On 22 September the battalion headquarters of 1/7th Middlesex (167th Brigade, 56th Division) was in a little dell on the right of the line here. The German gun pits were north of the railway embankment to the east of the Wood. In *How I Filmed the*

War, the official War Office photographer, Geoffrey Malins, noted that on a date around 25 September he saw British troops pouring forward over open ground. He says that he raced towards them as fast as possible and filmed them going across first one section and then the other. German shells were falling near them, but missing most of them.

In *The Battle of the Somme*, Philip Gibbs noted there had been fierce hand-to-hand fighting in Bouleux Wood, and in the centre of it an unfortunate tank was crippled. He mentioned that instead of attacking the Wood itself, where the Germans were positioned in great force, the British were ordered to take two lines of trenches to the west of it, and then establish a flank. The Germans who massed at the Wood were therefore unable to put their machine guns to full use.

The line in the Wood was held by 56th Division, with 5th Division to their left, 6th Division beyond that and then the Guards Division, who were in front of LESBŒUFS.

BOUZINCOURT is situated on a ridge to the north-west of ALBERT and the Ancre and commands a wide view of the countryside. The road to Aveluy is the D104. On 29 July 1915, 1/6th Seaforth Highlanders (152nd Brigade, 51st Division) came here for the first time and the 'quaint and attractive village' was to become almost like home to them in the following months. Their regimental history notes that 'the village itself was a pleasant place, with its funny little church in the centre, flanked on either side by a pond, and with its numerous orchards and shady trees. The inhabitants were uniformly friendly.' At this time the village was immune from enemy shelling.

In August and September, 1/6th Seaforth Highlanders' main role was to provide working parties and carry out spells in the line, after which they were back in the village. On 26 September, when they were relieved in the line north-east of Aveluy by 2/5th Lancashire Fusiliers (154th Brigade, 51st Division), they returned to the village, where by now hot baths had been installed. After another session in the line they were back in the village at the beginning of November, and again later that month. While 1/8th Argyll & Sutherland Highlanders (152nd Brigade, 51st Division) were in the area, Pipe-Major W. Lawrie composed a tune as a gift to the French 116th Infantry Regiment, called 'Pipers of Bouzincourt'.

51st Division were not the only division with close links to the village, as 10th Essex (53rd Brigade, 18th Division) arrived here from

RUBEMPRÉ at 2200hrs on August Bank Holiday in 1915, using Bouzincourt as a base for working in the lines with units of 51st Division for instruction purposes. It was considered to be a better place than RUBEMPRÉ, as the barns were better and there was a greater supply of drinking water. It was not a clean village, however, and there were many 'offensive smells'.

At the same time, 6th Royal Berkshires (also 53rd Brigade, 18th Division) were here for a week when they were attached to 154th Brigade (51st Division) for instruction in trench warfare, before leaving for DAOURS on 13 August. Also in August, the French Army vacated trenches to the east of Aveluy, to be replaced by 1/8th King's (164th Brigade, 55th Division). Pte M. Burton of 1/4th King's Own (also 164th Brigade, 55th Division) was an early casualty, being killed on 14 August; he was the first man to be buried in Aveluy Communal Cemetery Extension (B.10).

In December, units of 32nd Division were in Bouzincourt, including 16th Highland Light Infantry (97th Brigade, 32nd Division). At this time, the village was sometimes the target of heavier calibre shells than just 'whizz bangs'. At Christmas, 1/5th Seaforth Highlanders (152nd Brigade, 51st Division) were here before returning to HÉNENCOURT for a short period. On 11 February 1916, 1/6th West Yorkshires (146th Brigade, 49th Division) arrived here from AILLY-SUR-SOMME in heavy rain and everyone was soaked to the skin. They left for their first turn in the line the next day. After two or three spells in the line at THIEPVAL, they were back in Bouzincourt at the end of the month.

From February 1916, the village was used by 1/1st (West Riding) Field Ambulance (49th Division). Their dressing station was in the school buildings (*Ecole du Commune*) and the *mairie*, with accommodation for about 30 patients; a few days later it was handed over to 36th Division. The school-house was also used as a headquarters for a field company, and in February sappers were helping to build a new road to MARTINSART to the north-east. At the time there were still many civilians living in the village, as there also were in MARTINSART and ENGLE-BELMER. Although there was always danger, both Bouzincourt and MARTINSART did have some protection, as they were sheltered from the enemy by the 1,000-acre AVELUY WOOD. The village was beyond the range of enemy guns, although the occasional 'whizz bang' (heavy calibre) did fall.

On 31 March, Bouzincourt was home to two companies of 1/6th West Yorkshires, who played several games of football and were watched by large crowds. In April, the school was inspected with a view to being used as an advanced dressing station; in the same month there is mention of an officers' hospital in the village. On 12 April, 17th Highland Light Infantry (97th Brigade, 32nd Division), who had been resting here for a week, moved to the line at AUTHUILLE. During May, the village was frequently shelled by the enemy, and on 1 June all horses were moved from ALBERT to horse-lines along the Bouzincourt–ALBERT road. By the end of June, a main dressing station had been established about 1 mile to the north-west of the village on the road to FORCEVILLE, now the D938. On 24 June, General Staff wagons were sent to the village by 110th Field Ambulance (36th Division) to collect lightly wounded casualties.

Both before and during the battle, the road from Bouzincourt to Black Horse Ridge near Authuille Wood was frequently used, and troop camps were set up in the open to the north-west and south-east of the village. On 24 June, 15th Highland Light Infantry (14th Brigade, 32nd Division) slept at Knights Redoubt, close to the village, in bivouacs. On 27 June, 9th Northumberland Fusiliers (52nd Brigade, 17th Division) were here, and on 1 July, 1/3rd Monmouths (pioneers of 49th Division) watched the progress of the battle from the high ground or ridge near the village. On the same day, 16th and 17th Highland Light Infantry (both 97th Brigade, 32nd Division) moved off from here on their way up to the line. After their mauling in the THIEPVAL sector on 1 July, 25th Division relieved them in the line during the night of 3/4 July, with 7th Brigade on the right and 75th Brigade on the left. At the same time 74th Brigade (also 25th Division) moved from WARLOY-BAILLON to Bouzincourt and 11th Lancashire Fusiliers (74th Brigade, 25th Division) bivouacked in huts.

On 7 July, 14th Brigade (32nd Division) were concentrated here in the camps in the open to the north-west and south-east of the village. At night on 9 July, 9th Essex (35th Brigade, 12th Division) were in hutments on the western edge of the village in a 'well used camp'. In a letter to his mother, Bernard Montgomery (104th Brigade, 35th Division) wrote that his unit were taken in buses to Bouzincourt and from there marched to Aveluy, about a mile west of LA BOISSELLE. 1st Dorsets (14th Brigade, 32nd Division) went back to Bouzincourt; on 14 July, they were back in the line, taking over from 96th Brigade (32nd Division). 1st Dorsets gained ground by digging a trench from their right and joining hands with the 75th Brigade east of the church – or where the church used to be.

On 17 July, 1/4th Oxfordshire & Buckinghamshire Light Infantry (145th Brigade, 48th Division) also used the huts on the west side of the village, with their transport in SENLIS-LE-SEC. They were brought to the village in 36 lorries. On 27 July, 12th Division's headquarters was established here, having previously been at BERTRANCOURT.

On 9 August, 1/4th Royal Berkshires (145th Brigade, 48th Division) bivouacked outside the village on the SENLIS-LE-SEC road; at this time the cellars of Bouzincourt were full of men, as there was constant long-range shelling going on. Over several weeks, many casualties had occurred in billets and camps outside Bouzincourt, especially those on the east side of the village. On 13 August, 1/7th Worcesters (144th Brigade, 48th Division) were in brigade reserve; divisional reserve were camped by the crossroads between the village and SENLIS-LE-SEC.

The Guards were also camped here in early August, and on 18 August the 'Brass Hats' watched the battle from the ridge here, including Lt Gen Sir Hubert Gough, General Officer Commanding Reserve (later Fifth) Army; Lt Gen C.W. Jacob, General Officer Commanding II Corps; and Lt Gen W. Birdwood, General Officer Commanding I Anzac Corps. They were watching a barrage on Leipzig Redoubt. In *Other Ranks*, W.V. Tilsley wrote that his battalion, 1/4th Loyal North Lancashires (164th Brigade, 55th Division), camped here for a week from 28 August before marching towards the front, the sound of guns getting stronger and stronger. They learned at this time that GUILLEMONT had at last fallen.

In his unpublished diary, Brig Gen A.C. Johnstone said that he had been given command of 10th Cheshires (7th Brigade, 25th Division), whom he joined when the brigade moved to Bouzincourt. On the next day, they moved out to billets about 1 mile outside. On 30 August – a 'perfectly vile' day, 'blowing and pouring with rain' – he managed to get 7th Brigade back to Bouzincourt, where the men could at least be under cover from the elements. On 31 August, at a little after 2200hrs, they suddenly received orders to relieve 8th Borders (75th Brigade, 25th Division) in the trenches in the LEIPZIG SALIENT.

On 2 September, 10th Cheshires moved back, except for one company, who were left in dugouts at CRUCIFIX CORNER. On 4 September it rained very hard in the afternoon and the trenches became a sea of mud. On the afternoon of 5 September, Johnstone went down to the reserve companies in AUTHUILLE. A day later, 10th Cheshires were relieved by 9th West

Yorkshires (32nd Brigade, 11th Division) during the morning and moved back to Bouzincourt.

In *Undertones of War*, Edmund Blunden mentioned a high-velocity gun firing at Bouzincourt; this is probably the same as that mentioned by Tilsley (see MAMETZ WOOD entry).

On 27 November, after the Battle of the Somme ended, 152nd Brigade (51st Division) arrived here and a motor ambulance convoy was stationed here. The field ambulance station ceased to be used in February 1917, when the British line went forward from the River Ancre.

Bouzincourt Communal Cemetery, designed by Sir Reginald Blomfield, is to the north-west of the village on the D104 road; it has 33 graves. Those dating from 1918 are in Rows C and D at the entrance and those from 1916 (Rows A and B) on the right of the central path. A chaplain to the forces 4th class, Revd D.V. O'Sullivan is buried close to the crucifix among the graves of French soldiers; he was killed on 5 July. The pre-1 July casualties mostly died in April and were members of 32nd Division. A number of men from the Highland Light Infantry are buried here, from the early July attacks. The register confirms that Bouzincourt was used as a field ambulance from early 1916 to February 1917 and for burials from March to July 1916, and again from April to June 1918.

The adjoining Bouzincourt Communal Cemetery Extension, designed by Sir Reginald Blomfield, was begun in May 1916 and used until February 1917. It was used not only for field ambulance burials but also for soldiers brought back from the battle area. It was reopened at the end of March 1918 until September of that year, and was mainly used by 38th Division. Twenty more graves were brought in during 1919 and in 1925 a further 108 from the Somme battlefields and from Framerville Churchyard. The graves include that of Pte A.G. Earp (I.C.25) of 1/5th Royal Warwicks (143rd Brigade, 48th Division) from Birmingham who was 'shot at dawn' on 22 July. Here also are the graves of two lieutenant-colonels, Lt Col R.L. Aspinall (II.B.9) of 11th Cheshires (75th Brigade, 25th Division), who died on 3 July when going forward with a reserve company, and Lt Col H. Brassey, attached to 8th South Lancashires (also 75th Brigade, 25th Division), who died on 15 July (II.F.1.).

There is a third cemetery at Bouzincourt, called Bouzincourt Ridge Cemetery, also designed by Blomfield, which rises north-west of ALBERT. The ridge was partly in German hands after March 1918 but their advance was stopped by 12th and 38th Divisions. The area was retaken by Allied forces at the end of August 1918. The Cemetery stands alongside a track that leads from ALBERT to Bouzincourt and contains 708 graves, including that of Lt Col J.S. Collings-Wells VC (III.E.12), Commanding Officer 4th Bedfords (190th Brigade, 63rd Division). The cemetery was begun in September 1918 with men being brought in and continued after the Armistice with the concentration of 568 graves from nearby. Almost 40 per cent of the graves are of unknown soldiers.

Between July 1915 and September 1916, 5th, 12th, 18th, 19th, 25th, 32nd, 36th, 48th and 51st Divisions were in the area. The tunnels under the church, used by troops as shelter during the war, are occasionally open to visitors.

BRAY-SUR-SOMME stands on the northern bank of a loop in the River Somme, 5 miles south-east of ALBERT. In August 1915, 56th Field Ambulance (18th Division) ran an advanced dressing station here. As the Franco-British Army boundary ran close to the town, troops from both nations made full use of Bray-sur-Somme for billeting and medical arrangements during the period 1915–16. In addition, a lake south-west of the town was used regularly as a bathing place for troops.

On 4 August, 1/9th Londons (13th Brigade, 5th Division) arrived here from RIBEMONT-SUR-ANCRE. The regimental history noted of the town that: 'we were to know and to it [*sic*] in the future as a home from home'. Guards were posted round the town and machine guns were set up for anti-aircraft work. During 1/9th Londons' first week here, a banquet was given by the sergeants of the French regiment that were about to leave, at which it was noticed that French NCOs seemed to be more important than their British counterparts and even had a batman each; red and white wine was issue to the French in the same way as rum was to British troops. 1/9th Londons stayed in Bray-sur-Somme for nearly a fortnight and took part in company training, which included swimming instruction. On 15 August, they left for BRONFAY FARM and 3 days later for CARNOY, having relieved 2nd King's Own Scottish Borderers (13th Brigade, 5th Division).

On 9 August, two battalions of 55th Brigade (18th Division) were in the town, while the other two were billeted in DERNANCOURT. In the third week of August, 10th Essex (53rd Brigade, 18th Division) were in the village at the same time as 8th Norfolks (also 53rd Brigade, 18th Division). Bray-sur-Somme was busy at the time; as well as the two battalions billeted in the village there were also the headquarters of two infantry brigades, several artillery units, headquarters troops and an abundance of transport lines. 6th Royal Berkshires (also 53rd Brigade, 18th Division) were here for a night before going up to the trenches opposite MAMETZ. On 19 August, the main dressing station in the town was moved to another position and taken over by 56th Field Ambulance (18th Division).

On 8 October, companies from 1/9th Londons were in the village again. On 11 November, an advanced dressing station moved into the hospice, which was behind the office of 13th Brigade (5th Division), close to the church; it could take 100 cases. Five days later, 2nd Royal Inniskilling Fusiliers (5th Brigade, 2nd Division) arrived in the town by bus before marching by companies to SUZANNE, where they joined 14th Brigade (5th Division). Around this period, the concert party which became the Whizz Bangs of 5th Division came into being at Bray-sur-Somme.

Between August 1915 and January 1916, sappers billeted to the south-west were sometimes working on the railway station. During the same period, Bray-sur-Somme was the centre of activities for 2nd Duke of Wellington's (13th Brigade, 5th Division), with much time spent not only in the town itself but also in CARNOY, BILLON WOOD and BRONFAY FARM, places nearer to the front line.

The enemy were well aware of how much the town was used for billeting purposes and shelled both the town and the area on a very regular basis. In daylight, roads to the front line became too dangerous, and the Bray-sur-Somme–FRICOURT road was out of bounds except at night. On 4 and 6 January 1916, a number of shells fell on the town and some buildings were demolished. On 6 January, 2nd Wiltshires (21st Brigade, 30th Division) arrived here for their first spell in the line at CARNOY. For the next few weeks they were in and out of the line and often billeted in the town. The norm was 6 days at the front and 3 days in Bray-sur-Somme. The severe winter took its toll on the troops, but Bray-sur-Somme supplied not only good billets but also hot baths. On 12 January, 19th Manchesters (21st Brigade, 30th Division) arrived in the town from BRONFAY FARM and BILLON WOOD, but were back in the front trenches 4 days later. For several weeks they were in and out of billets in Bray-sur-Somme and trenches at CARNOY. On 22 January, the road to CORBIE was heavily shelled; on 31 January, heavy shells fell in the valley to the north-east of the town, and again 2 days later.

From February to June 1916, Bray-sur-Somme was shelled regularly, almost every day. Advanced dressing stations were established in farms along the Bray-sur-Somme–FRICOURT road, as well as walking wounded CPs and an engineer dump. In addition, there was a straggler's post here. On 2 February, one shell fell in the middle of the main square, Place de la Liberté, demolishing all the windows of the *marie* and damaging the windows and façade of the church. After this, the remaining civilians in the town were evacuated. Two days later, more heavy shelling caused damage to an officers' mess and soldiers' billets. Two sappers were killed, and were buried in Chipilly on 5 and 6 February respectively. The shelling continued during the rest of the month, and on 14 February the church tower was the enemy target.

On 27 February, 2nd Wiltshires were relieved by 19th King's (89th Brigade, 30th Division) and returned to Bray-sur-Somme and FROISSY before moving on to BRONFAY FARM. In early March, after 2nd Wiltshires had been back in the line, they were relieved by 12th Middlesex (54th Brigade, 18th Division) and once more returned to billets in huts at Bray-sur-Somme and FROISSY. On 7 March, 19th Manchesters marched to TAILLES WOOD. On 14 March, 2nd Wiltshires marched out of Bray-sur-Somme to CORBIE, where they entrained for HANGEST-SUR-SOMME, with the exception of one company who were working on a new light railway at PONT-NOYELLES. On arrival at HANGEST-SUR-SOMME, they marched to FLIXE-COURT.

In March and April, the hospice was able to accommodate 100 casualties; its cellars were sandbagged for 50 casualties and staff. The wounded were then taken straight on to Nos. 5 or 21 Casualty Clearing Stations at CORBIE. South of the town on the CORBIE road was a rendezvous for vehicles conveying the walking wounded.

G.D. Fairley, a medical officer with 2nd Royal Scots (8th Brigade, 3rd Division), reported that his battalion were in billets in Bray-sur-Somme on 2 June, and that when the beginning of the battle was postponed on 28 June, Bray-sur-Somme was crowded with camps and horse-lines. During the battle, XIII Corps Main Dressing Station moved from DIVE COPSE to a site on the Bray-sur-Somme–MARICOURT road and No. 5 Casualty Clearing Station moved here from CORBIE via ALBERT. At Zero Hour on 1 July, the South African Brigade (9th Division) were here in reserve when 26th and 27th Brigades (both also 9th Division) were at MARICOURT and CHIPILLY respectively.

On 8 June, 17th Manchesters (90th Brigade, 30th Division) supplied working parties before moving to MARICOURT via BRONFAY FARM. The road was out of bounds in daylight hours. One company from 18th Manchesters 'was made responsible for the placing in position of ammunition, stores, &c., to be used by the 90th Brigade when the time came'.

At 1900hrs on 5 July, 1st Gordon Highlanders (76th Brigade, 3rd Division) reached the outskirts of Bray-sur-Somme. Cpl Robertson of 3rd Worcesters (7th Brigade, 25th Division) wrote that they were 'getting amongst it now', 'no more quietness'. There were batteries of French guns within 200yds of them that made a nerve-racking din. He talked with some of the French gunners, who showed him all the points of beauty about the famous 75s. He said that there was a terrific bombardment going on and that a wood near FRICOURT 'was getting pure hell from the Artillery'.

On 9 July, Robertson reported that the wood had not yet been taken and that there wasn't much of it left, just twisted stumps. He heard that they were not going in until it was taken. One of the gun crew told him that three of them flattened the whole village of FRICOURT. He said that he could believe it too, with the terrible concussion of them. At 1700hrs, their sister battalion arrived back from the line and there was great excitement in talking to them; the fighting was described as 'pure murder'. They were only 250 strong, having lost 650 men at FRICOURT.

The town continued to be used by Allied troops until it fell into enemy hands on 26 March 1918, only to be retaken by Australian troops on 24 August.

Bray Military Cemetery is north of Bray-sur-Somme, on the western side of the road to MARICOURT; it was begun by fighting units and field ambulances in April 1916. The narrow-gauge railway line from Bray-sur-Somme to FRICOURT ran along the western side of it via the Loop and Citadel New Military Cemetery. In September 1916, the front line having moved further east, it was used by XIV Corps Main Dressing Station. In the cemetery are the graves of 24 Egyptians and Indians, many of whom acted as labourers in the war. Also buried here is Cpl J. Wilton, who was 'shot at dawn' on 17 August 1916 and whose family lived in Doncaster (II.K.11). In 1917, Nos. 5, 38 and 48 Casualty Clearing Stations came forward and used it. The site of the Loop can be found 2 miles along the road to MARICOURT. It was specially built by British troops and became a very important unloading point for supplies; the first tanks were unloaded here in August 1916.

Bray Hill British Cemetery is on the west side of the D147 road from Bray-sur-Somme to FRICOURT

on the southern slope of a high plâteau, a little north of a chalk pit. It was made in August 1918 by 58th Division, who had been involved in the advance from CORBIE.

Bray Vale Cemetery, once known as Bray No. 2 British Cemetery, a concentration cemetery, is on the east side of the road to ALBERT, below the steepest part of the hill; it too was made in August 1918. The graves of men who died in 1916 are mainly those closest to the road and Plots III and IV were filled by the concentration of 165 graves originally around COURCELETTE and THIEPVAL. More than 60 per cent of the graves are of unknowns.

Bray-sur-Somme Communal Cemetery on the outskirts of the town has the graves of three British casualties; two on one side are those of Capt J.P. Longfield, an Irishman who served with 3rd Norfolks and who died on 30 September 1915, and Pte R.P. Morris of 1/4th Loyal North Lancashires (164th Brigade, 55th Division), who died on 29 July 1916. The third grave is of Pte G. Quinn of 2nd Leinsters, who died on 3 August 1915. The Bray-sur-Somme French National Cemetery adjoins this cemetery on the south side.

Bray-sur-Somme German Cemetery is on a hillside on the north-west side of the town and has 1,122 burials.

During the early part of the war, the church in the centre of the town, close to the hospice and other buildings used by the Army, had its bell stolen, and by the end of the war had been partially destroyed. The bell tower was restored in 1927. The former hospice may have been part of what is at present the *mairie* and town museum. The church contains a memorial to the French units who fought in the FARGNY MILL area during the war.

After the war, Bray-sur-Somme was adopted by Eastbourne.

BREILLY is south of the River Somme between AMIENS and PICQUIGNY on the N235 road. On 31 March 1916, 19th Manchesters (21st Brigade, 30th Division) arrived here from COISY and 'drill of various kinds was carried out'. On 6 April, they were inspected by Brig Gen The Hon. C.J. Sackville-West, General Officer Commanding 21st Brigade (30th Division); after indulging in battalion sports on 9 April, they returned to COISY the following day. On 15 June they were back here, but as there were not enough billets the men had to bivouac on the side of the Breilly–PICQUIGNY road. The next day they moved to Reincourt.

On 25 June and on 1 July, 70th Field Ambulance were here, less one section.

BRESLE is a village to the south-west of ALBERT between LAVIÉVILLE and FRANVILLERS. On 21 September 1915, Field Marshal Lord Kitchener inspected 8th East Surreys (55th Brigade, 18th Division) and 10th Essex (53rd Brigade, 18th Division) outside the village. Saint-Laurent Farm, which was to hold German prisoners, was to the south-west. When here on 2 June, Lt Col W.A. Vignoles, DSO & Bar, second in command of 10th Lincolns (101st Brigade, 34th Division) described the village as being 'very crowded'. He was billeted in a small farm. Two weeks later he was camped near ALBERT on the south side of the AMIENS road.

In the last few days of June, 58th Field Ambulance (19th Division) were in reserve here; 8th North Staffords (57th Brigade, 19th Division) were also in the village, where their time was spent in final preparations for the coming battle. They left on 30 June and marched to Tyler's Redoubt, where they were bivouacked for the night. They moved up in company order to a line of intermediate trenches close to the ALBERT–BOUZINCOURT road.

At Zero Hour on 1 July, a brigade of 12th Division were here, as well as elements of the British cavalry, who were awaiting orders to advance. At the end of July, 111th and 112nd Brigades (both 37th Division) were billeted in the village. During the battle there was a camp here on high ground just outside the village. At the end of August some of the German prisoners from Saint-Laurent Farm were at work cleaning and repairing roads, guarded by French sentries.

On 10 November, Gen Sir Douglas Haig inspected part of 15th Division here. Between July and November, units belonging to 1st, 15th, 23rd, 34th, 37th and 47th Divisions were here.

In 1925 there were still three Allied graves in the Bresle Communal Cemetery, which is to the north-west of the village.

BRIQUEMESNIL-FLOXICOURT is west of AMIENS; a small hospital was set up by mid-June 1916. During the battle, units of 30th Division rehearsed the 1 July attack with a full-scale facsimile battle landscape. Officers of 19th Manchesters (21st Brigade, 30th Division) 'went over the training ground, which had been arranged as a battlefield on a small scale; in the afternoons the Battalion went over in attack formation'. On 15 June, they moved on to BREILLY.

BRONFAY FARM is on the road from BRAY-SUR-SOMME to MARICOURT, with the buildings on the eastern side of the road. Across the road to the east is a small copse called Bronfay Wood. The area was shelled on 13 September 1915; towards the end of the year, 1st Royal West Kents (13th Brigade, 5th Division) were often billeted in this area and on one occasion a successful boxing competition was organised at Bronfay Farm. Later the ring was used for the boxing finals and for evening church services. On occasions, battalion hunts were organised, when everything that could move was chased, but the practice was stopped after French farmers complained of damage to their crops. Later a rat hunt was allowed, after which 530 dead rodents were laid out for inspection at the Farm.

Soon after, in early December, 14th Royal Warwicks (at this time 95th Brigade, 32nd Division) made their first tours to the front line trenches opposite CARNOY, which were then in an appalling state. Passing through the town of BRAY-SUR-SOMME on their way back to CARNOY, they saw support troops settled down in Bronfay Farm quite comfortably. The Royal Warwickshire Regiment's history noted that 'we could see braziers glowing and the lights of candles in the billets. This seemed to be quite a good position.' Some men of 14th Royal Warwicks (now 13th Brigade, 5th Division) were here in mid-January, when billeted in ruined farm outbuildings, while others were in dugouts and canvas tents in BILLON WOOD. Later in the month, when clothing was continuously 'soaked or plastered with mud', the troops made use of a deep pool of water in the courtyard of Bronfay Farm to wash their garments. The regimental history noted that in 1929 the farm 'appeared very much as we had left it in 1916, and there seemed little improvement in the road surface'.

On 6 January 1916, A Company, 19th Manchesters (21st Brigade, 30th Division), were billeted in Bronfay Farm with battalion headquarters, with the remaining companies in BILLON WOOD, about 600yds away. They provided working parties for the next 6 days before leaving for billets in BRAY-SUR-SOMME. On 8 January, units of 30th Division were driven out by the shelling. On 23 January, No. 202 Field Company, Royal Engineers (30th Division), had to reapir the road here, which had been heavily shelled.

At the end of February, 2nd Wiltshires (21st Brigade, 30th Division), who had been resting briefly in huts in BRAY-SUR-SOMME and FROISSY, arrived at the Farm, which was known as a halfway house on the BRAY-SUR-SOMME–CARNOY road. They provided working parties before returning to the CARNOY line on 5 March. This pattern continued for several weeks when they were in and out of the line. The Farm was often shelled but the men were frequently accommodated in huts and dugouts in BILLON WOOD in a small hollow to the east of the Farm. On 20 March, a collecting post for CARNOY ran from the Farm to the PÉRONNE road; one also ran to CARNOY.

In May, two dugouts at the Farm, which could take 20 casualties each, were set aside for casualties; during the day, cases were brought down by communication trench, but at night, wheeled stretchers could use the road. A tramway had been built, which ran via Bronfay Wood to the main PÉRONNE road.

Bronfay was where the actual trench line began; in this section the trenches were 8ft deep and cut from clay and chalk. By 18 June, a large underground dressing station, 30ft below ground, was nearing completion, of which 30th Division were 'very proud'. It was on a crest of a hill and made up of a corridor of dugouts covered by 12ft of sandbags, with room for 72 stretcher cases. The ruined farm buildings were used for billets.

G.D. Fairley, a medical officer with 2nd Royal Scots (8th Brigade, 3rd Division), noted that on 11 June his battalion passed Bronfay Farm on the way up to the trenches. B Copse was battalion headquarters, and U Works (Ludgate Hill) Aid Post was established in West Avenue Communication Trench with a collection point at Bronfay Farm. Fairley mentioned that on 27 June, hollows and banks were honeycombed with emplacements.

In early July, 8th Suffolks (53rd Brigade, 18th Division), who were in brigade reserve, did not take an active part as they were not called on to support the attack; instead they helped with carrying up ammunition and water. On 7 July, when they were passing the farm, they met 2nd Suffolks (76th Brigade, 3rd Division), who were going up the line. The latter played the Regimental March on their drums as each company went by. By the beginning of July, three advanced dressing stations were established.

On 6 July, Bronfay Wood accommodated 12th Middlesex (54th Brigade, 18th Division), who had marched here from Beetle and Maple Alleys. On the same day, trench bridges were being made at the Farm by a section from No. 63 Field Company, Royal Engineers (9th Division). From 6 July, No. 14 Casualty Clearing Station and Walking Wounded Post was established; at this time the Farm was a rest camp surrounded by bell tents, the home of 10th Essex (53rd Brigade, 18th Division) on 7 July.

By the second week of July the whole road up to Bronfay Farm was 1ft deep in mud and, of course, jammed with traffic. In mid-July, 35th Division's

headquarters was there during their involvement in the battle for Bazentin Ridge. On 8 August, 1st King's Royal Rifle Corps (99th Brigade, 2nd Division) were here in tents, about 300yds west of the Farm.

On 26 August, 1st Norfolks (15th Brigade, 5th Division), after training at le Quesnoy, bivouacked near the Farm, and at this time were employed in digging. Capt H.W. Crippen (II.A.2) , Royal Field Artillery (56th Division), may have been killed near here on 8 September, but 56th Division's war diary doesn't mention the fact. On 15 September, 10th King's Royal Rifle Corps (59th Brigade, 20th Division) bivouacked here.

In early October, the XIV Corps Main Dressing Station consisted of three marquees and bell tents, which were joined end to end with the least wounded at one end and the dying at the other.

Standing on high ground, Bronfay Farm Military Cemetery is opposite Bronfay Farm; it was begun by French troops in October 1914, but little used by them. It was used by British troops from August 1915 to February 1917, particularly in the Somme battle, when XIV Corps Main Dressing Station was at the Farm. After the Armistice, 42 graves from March, August and September 1918 were brought in from fields between Bronfay Farm and BRAY-SUR-SOMME. One of the graves here is of Lt Col H. Dalzell-Walton, aged 50, of 8th Royal Inniskilling Fusiliers (49th Brigade, 16th Division) (I.D.44), who was killed by a sniper on 9 September 1916 during an assault against GINCHY and trenches east of GUILLEMONT.

The area saw heavy fighting in 1918, particularly in March and August, and the cemetery burials reflect the human cost of these actions.

BUIRE-SUR-L'ANCRE is south-west of DER-NANCOURT on the D52 road. On 14 August 1915, 1/5th Seaforth Highlanders (152nd Brigade, 51st Division) arrived here from the line at AUTHUILLE before moving to BÉCOURT on 21 August. On 18 September 1915, 10th Essex (53rd Brigade, 18th Division) were in the village. In mid-October, 6th Royal Berkshires (also 53rd Brigade, 18th Division) arrived here, but by the last week of the month were back in the front line at ALBERT, opposite LA BOISSELLE. From 12 October, 8th Norfolks (also 53rd Brigade, 18th Division) were here.

From 23 April 1916, 8th Somerset Light Infantry (63rd Brigade, 21st Division) were billeted here after being relieved in the line, returning to the FRICOURT area on 12 May. On 24 June, 63rd Field Ambulance (21st Division) arrived here from

ALLONVILLE and they shared the village with many divisional troops. The village was always used for billeting purposes and especially so during the battle itself.

In early July, during the period when the British cavalry were awaiting orders to take part in the Allied advance, there were horse-lines here which extended in every direction; cavalry tracks wound round each end of the village, along which each morning an 'apparently unending stream' of cavalry, both British and Indian with mounted machine-gun attachments, horse gunners and signal sections moved up towards the battle. Each evening they returned 'to wait for what the next day would bring'.

In *Goodbye to All That*, Robert Graves wrote that 2nd Royal Welsh Fusiliers (19th Brigade, 33rd Division) 'came by easy stages' to Buire-sur-l'Ancre, reaching the village on 14 July. At the time they were close to the original front line where some of Graves's friends – Thomas, Richardson and Pritchard – had been killed earlier in the year.

On 21 July, the poet E. Alan Mackintosh was billeted here with 1/5th Seaforth Highlanders (152nd Brigade, 51st Division) prior to taking part in the HIGH WOOD fighting, in which he was wounded a few days later. No. 400 Field Company, Royal Engineers (51st Division), were also here in the second part of July. On 7 August, 5th Oxfordshire & Buckinghamshire Light Infantry (42nd Brigade, 14th Division) were camping in the village; their battalion headquarters was in a house close to the church. After their disastrous time in the fighting for the capture of MAMETZ WOOD, 38th Division came here and many of the men camped in tents in an old orchard.

On 18 September, 9th King's Royal Rifle Corps (42nd Brigade, 14th Division) moved to a camp south of ALBERT and about a mile to the north of Buire-sur-l'Ancre; on 22 September they moved off with the rest of 14th Division, using French buses as their transport. In early October 90th Brigade (30th Division) were billeted in the village, and on 24 October, 89th Brigade (also 30th Division) came here. On 11 November, 2nd Royal Welsh Fusiliers moved to Buire-sur-l'Ancre again before moving out of the Somme area altogether.

The village was often used as a divisional rest station; there used to be two Buire-sur-l'Ancre Communal Cemeteries but now there is only the one, north of the church. It has the graves of six soldiers, two who died prior to the battle and two during it.

Between April and October 1916, 5th, 12th, 17th, 21st, 24th, 29th, 30th, 33rd, 41st and 55th Divisions had their headquarters or brigades billeted here.

BUS-LÈS-ARTOIS is on the D176 road, with Bus Wood to the north of it. The château in the centre of the village, bearing the date of 1848, was often used as a military headquarters. The house survives but many of the adjacent buildings are in a dilapidated shape. In the second part of July 1915, 48th Division had an advanced headquarters here when they were taking over the lines from the French. On 31 July, No. 48 Divisional Signal Company, Royal Engineers (48th Division), were established in the harness room. On 3 August they camped at AUTHIE close to the château buildings and slept in a large barn.

On 1 January 1916, 8th Division's headquarters was at Bus-lès-Artois. At the end of January a battalion of 93rd Brigade (31st Division) were working on a coal dump in bitterly cold weather between here and BOUZINCOURT. This was the beginning of the village's close relationship with 31st Division, which was destined to take part in the battle opposite SERRE on 1 July. On 3 April, 18th Durham Light Infantry (also 93rd Brigade, 31st Division) moved 'into a cold and depressing hut camp in the wood . . . Our huts had no windows, no doors in the doorways, no floors and not furniture of any description.' They remained in this situation for a fortnight.

94th Field Ambulance (31st Division) were here for the whole of April. During May, 10th East Yorkshires (92nd Brigade, 31st Division) moved here from WARNIMONT WOOD and were camped here in an orchard among trees laden with apple and pear blossom. On 30 May, 12th York & Lancasters (94th Brigade, 31st Division) arrived here from COURCELLES-AU-BOIS; they spent 5 days here before moving to GÉZAINCOURT, south-west of DOULLENS, prior to moving back to the village for a day and then heading up to the line. On 3 June, 12th York & Lancasters were involved in an experiment to test communication between aircraft and infantry; on 5 June they marched north-westwards to GÉZAINCOURT.

As the beginning of the battle drew near, Bus-lès-Artois became a hotbed of working parties, and at the beginning of June, Bus Wood was alive with huts and bivouacs. On 6 June, 1/5th Sherwood Foresters (139th Brigade, 46th Division) had excellent billets here amid beautiful scenery, but the hard training affected their leisure. They spent several days felling trees in Lucheux Forest and were entertained by a concert party called the Whizz Bangs. At the sugar factory a water supply was set up and in mid-June a large ammunition dump was established. At the end of June rations dumped at the main dressing station, which had just been established, were taken up to the advanced dressing station at night.

After a tragedy in which their front-line trenches were blown in, with the loss of two officers and 20 men, 10th East Yorkshires arrived back in the village on 4 June, when friends and colleagues who had stayed behind in the village came out to meet them, enquiring anxiously about the fate of their chums who had not returned. One small compensation was that they were now in comfortable billets with 'a liberal supply of blankets and straw'. They spent the period organising for battle and supplying working parties. On a domestic note, 10th East Yorkshires listened to the band in the afternoon or early evening and 'as we lay in the long grass or strolled about listening to the music, the war seemed to fade far away and we felt ourselves transported back to Hull to imagine that the scene was one of the parks'. On 12 June (Whit Monday), 10th East Yorkshires left the village bound for a position to the south of John Copse opposite SERRE, where they relieved 16th West Yorkshires (93rd Brigade, 31st Division).

On 16 June 10th East Yorkshires were back in Bus-lès-Artois; by this time, the village had become a base for great ammunition parks and the civilian population talked of the forthcoming advance. This time they were billeted in barns which 'were cosy with soft warm straw. Like most farm buildings on the Somme, they consisted of a rough wooden framework filled in with mud and thatched with straw. A shell landing anywhere near would usually cause the walls to collapse outwards and the thatched roof to drop downwards.' During the following week, heavy guns drawn by caterpillar tractors rumbled their way through the village and batteries of French 75s cantered through the main street of the village. Huge reserve dumps of ammunition were 'springing up' all around. On 23 June, 10th East Yorkshires left the village and moved up towards the front line opposite SERRE.

On and around 1 July, a detachment of the Indian cavalry were resting their horses in the village. Transferred from VIII Corps, 12th Division's headquarters had moved to Bus-lès-Artois. In mid-July, 7th Royal Sussex (36th Brigade, 12th Division) were in huts and tents in Bus Wood. At the end of July, when the village was the headquarters of the Guards Division, W. Ewart of 2nd Scots Guards (3rd Guards Brigade, Guards Division) noted that they were in camp here, 'deeply hidden among young oak woods', on the top of a hill, and were visited by HM the King and HRH the Prince of Wales on 9 August. Driving here from the Saint-Pol area via Lucheux Forest, the royal party, escorted by Sir Douglas Haig and Maj Gen G. Feilding, General Officer Commanding Guards

Division, visited the Guards Division headquarters at 1135hrs and then the encampment of 3rd Guards Brigade, seeing 1st Grenadier Guards and 2nd Scots Guards. The King and the Prince then left to visit other Guards battalions at WARNIMONT WOOD and Vauchelles. On 13 August, Ewart's battalion went up to the front line; Ewart was ill at the time, however, and therefore missed the action at Ginchy station and LESBŒUFS.

On 19 August, 2nd Oxfordshire & Buckinghamshire Light Infantry (5th Brigade, 2nd Division) relieved 1st Coldstream Guards (2nd Guards Brigade) in new billets here, with headquarters under canvas just outside the village. On 21 August, 1st Scots Guards (also 2nd Guards Brigade) recuperated at Bus-lès-Artois.

In September, an advanced dressing station was here in the Red House. In early September, 1/4th Royal Berkshires (145th Brigade, 48th Division) were here while Maj Gen R. Fanshawe, General Officer Commanding 48th Division, was at the White Château with his headquarters. On 9 September, Lt Col A.H. Habgood of the Royal Army Medical Corps took over command of 142nd Field Ambulance (3rd Division) and wrote of his accommodation: 'Our billets in a large school building . . . The officers had a small house with lower rooms as a mess. The men were in elephant iron shelters. Accommodation for about 120 in these huts. Ground a sea of mud.'

On 1 October, 51st Division set up their headquarters here and their 152nd Brigade left for Warlencourt Wood the next day. In November, when the main dressing station was still in the village, the 'old huts' in Bus Wood were very muddy; the Ancre battle was continuously being postponed and camp conditions deteriorated.

Capt B. Hallam Radford (Gilbert the Filbert), who had fallen to his death from a balloon near Bus-lès-Artois and BERTRANCOURT, was buried at COUIN (II.C.15).

Bus-lès-Artois Communal Cemetery on the east side of the village has the graves of two soldiers who were buried here in August 1916 by 2nd Guards Brigade. Both Pte W. Green of 2nd Guards Company, Machine Gun Corps (Guards Division) and Cpl A.E. Worricker of 13th Essex (6th Brigade, 2nd Division) were killed on 21 August.

In 1928 the Leeds 'Pals' (15th West Yorkshires, 93rd Brigade, 31st Division) made a battlefield pilgrimage, which included a return to the village. Between April and November 1916, the Guards, 4th, 12th, 20th, 25th, 29th, 31st, 34th, 35th, 38th and 51st Divisions were linked with the village. A memorial dedicated to the Leeds 'Pals' was unveiled on 30 June 2006.

BUSSY-LÈS-DAOURS is due east of AMIENS and south of QUERRIEU. On 9 June, 1st Royal Welsh Fusiliers (22nd Brigade, 7th Division) were stationed here, with Siegfried Sassoon as one of their number, close to the River Hallue, a tributary of the River Ancre. On 11 June, 50th Brigade (17th Division) were here on the 'swampy banks of the river' before their headquarters moved forward to MORLANCOURT on 13 June. On 15 September, 6th Cavalry Brigade (3rd Cavalry Division) were here. Bussy-lès-Daours Communal Cemetery is to the south of the village.

BUTTE DE WARLENCOURT is just off the main ALBERT–BAPAUME road to the east after the village of LE SARS, when coming from the direction of ALBERT. It is bordered to the south by a narrow road towards GUEUDECOURT and is north of EAUCOURT L'ABBAYE.

In 1916 the Butte, of Roman origin, was a chalk-covered eminence some 50ft or 60ft high. It was on the slope of the spur overlooking the BAPAUME road where the Gird Line crossed it. At this time it was higher than it is today and stood out above the rest of the battlefield. It had played a prominent part in the war of 1871 and was honeycombed with many tunnels, even before the Germans fortified it so strongly that it became almost impossible to capture. It gave excellent observation of the low ground to the south-west and also in the opposite direction towards BAPAUME, in which there were many battery positions. Its possession was of equal importance to both sides.

In *Salute of Guns*, Donald Boyd wrote that in mid-September 1916, on the 'waste-torn earth where the front lines lay invisible' there was no recognisable landmark between the Butte, described as 'a chalk mound soaring over the fold of land from the left front', and the ruins of FLERS. In addition to having a warren of tunnels and strong machine-gun posts, it was surrounded by enormously thick belts of wire.

On 6 October, the Tangle trenches on the eastern side of LE SARS were occupied, but the attackers later withdrew. On 7 October, according to the *Official History of the War*, the remainder of LE SARS was captured when the attack was resumed against the Butte and Gird Lines as far west as the junction of the Gird and FLERS systems.

On 9 October, R. Derry was acting as a stretcher-bearer when he himself became wounded. There had been no artillery or tank support to the attack and many troops were killed even as they left their trenches. Boyd noted the infantry were to attack the Butte across 1,000yds of country under view through its whole length. The guns were in the open and the slope was 'dreary beyond description'. The attack 'was in broad daylight just before two o'clock'. The infantry moved forward in perfect formation and were mown down piecemeal as they advanced. Again the guns moved forward, to the crest, and were directed on to the German lines to support another futile attack on the Butte.

The *Official History of the War* notes that on 12 October, 9th Division were to capture firstly SNAG TRENCH and then the Butte and the Warlencourt Line. Included in these objectives was a trench named the Tail, located as running back from SNAG TRENCH towards the Butte, and a mound known as the Pimple at the western end of SNAG TRENCH. In a transcript in the Imperial War Museum, a Mr R.C. Cooney noted that on 12 October his unit had to attack up a reverse slope where they were quite protected from the Germans, and they were then to go over the hill towards the German lines with a very powerful machine-gun barrage rigged, which the preliminary bombardment did not disturb. They attacked in four lines, one after the other, and as each one went over the top it was caught by the machine guns and was 'pretty well wiped out'. In the last line, Cooney found himself the only one on his feet, so far as he could see, and so he got down into a hole and stayed there until it was dark. He had 'bullets through his hat', and he had a 'belt with a pistol'; 'a bullet had got inside the belt and out through the buckle', through his trousers and 'all over the place'. Even so, Cooney was unwounded.

Boyd continued that on the night of 13 October his unit pulled out the guns and brought them slowly down the crater field. W.D. Croft, historian of 9th Division and formerly General Officer Commanding 27th Brigade (9th Division), wrote that after taking SNAG TRENCH they pushed forward a bit on the high ground confronting the Butte, which he described as 'a great white cone' about 400yds away. That night they 'dug like beavers'.

The *Official History of the War* account of 5 November notes that the left of 1/6th Durham Light Infantry (151st Brigade, 50th Division) entered the German position with 1/9th Durham Light Infantry of the same brigade, and later broke through two lines of German trenches reaching the Butte, and established a post on the BAPAUME road, some parties even entering the Warlencourt Line. Men of 151st Brigade were seen on the Butte itself and the advanced posts were established in the afternoon. At 2200hrs the quarry west of the Butte was still held, and 500yds of the German line, but at about

The Butte de Warlencourt. *(Peter F. Batchelor Collection)*

midnight, German counter-attacks forced 1/6th and 1/9th Durham Light Infantry to withdraw.

In *The Machine Gunner*, Arthur Russell of the Machine Gun Corps notes that on 5 November, 'the Durham Brigade of the Territorials' (151st Brigade, 50th Division) attacked the Butte over ground not yet devastated by heavy shelling, as part of Fifth Army's preparation for the attack north of the River Ancre on 12 November. The Butte stood in the way of this offensive, a fortified hill that gave the Germans full observation of the entire Ancre sector. It was imperative that this hill fortress was captured before the main attack took place. The three infantry battalions were supported by No. 151 Company, Machine Gun Corps, and No. 151 Trench Mortar Battery. Zero Hour was 0910hrs and the weather was vile – wet, windy and foggy. A 10-minute bombardment was intended to soften up the enemy and destroy the barbed wire surrounding the Butte. An Australian brigade were to assist on the right flank of 1/8th Durham Light Infantry (also 151st Brigade, 50th Division), but became bogged down in no man's land. They found themselves knee-deep in thick gluey mud; many unable to move were shot down. 1/6th Durham Light Infantry fared little better, but 1/9th Durham Light Infantry captured the Butte and its garrison. Late that night the Germans counter-attacked and 151st Brigade, now decimated, had to retire to the original front line, where they were relieved by 150th Brigade (also 50th Division). For 1/8th and 1/9th Durham Light Infantry, this was the most disastrous day of the war.

In *Sir Douglas Haig's Great Push* the day is thus described: 'In the morning the Allies gained a footing on the western face of the Butte which the enemy had equipped with a bristling armoury of machine guns, many of which were in concrete emplacements; there was a sunken road leading back to the German support positions.'

Several times in October and November the British had attempted to achieve the impossible and each time their attacks failed against the formidable defences. In *Into Battle*, in an entry dated 25 October–13 November, John Glubb wrote: 'A week ago the 8th and 9th Durham Light Infantry attacked the Butte, and they took it, held it all day under heavy shelling and lost it again the next night.'

The period 13–18 November marked the limit of the attack on the Butte. Glubb also noted that after a brigade refit, 149th Brigade repeated the Durham Light Infantry's attack of the previous week, taking over 200yds of the enemy trenches, but not attempting the Butte itself.

After the war the Michelin battlefield guide noted of the Butte that the Warlencourt Ridge proper

consisted of two superimposed eminences; bare plâteau about two-thirds of a mile in width – now covered with graves – and a chalky torn hillock, which was the centre of the German position. Pierced with subterranean galleries, furrowed with successive lines of trenches, surrounded by a triple belt of entrenchments bristling with barbed wire entanglements and flanked at every angle by redoubts with innumerable mortars and machine guns, such was the ridge like an impregnable fortress which faced the British trenches throughout the winter of 1916–17. Although the Butte was overrun several times by British units the defenders from below ground counter-attacked and drove the attackers off, until 26 February 1917 when the Butte fell into British hands as the Germans withdrew to their new defence line.

For a time 1/6th, 1/8th and 1/9th Durham Light Infantry erected crosses on the Butte, with 1/9th Durham Light Infantry wanting top spot; 151st Brigade put up a brigade cross to prevent rivalry. All four crosses were returned to Durham in 1926.

In *Soldier from the Wars Returning*, Charles Carrington described the Butte as 'a dome of gleaming white chalk from which all vegetation had been blown away by shell-fire'; it was a 'most conspicuous object in the landscape'. It seemed to tower over the observer with its hidden machine-gun posts, which he now believed to be quite imaginary. He had observed the Durham Light Infantry in their unsuccessful attack from a reserve position far down the forward slope at Prue Trench.

In *An Onlooker in France*, the painter William Orpen noted that in the summer of 1917 the Butte 'stood out on the right, a heap of chalky mud, not a blade of grass round it, nothing but mud, with a white cross on top. On the left the Crown Prince's dugout and Gibraltar.' LE SARS and GRÉVILLERS were at that time the headquarters of Lt Gen W. Birdwood, General Officer Commanding I Anzac Corps. The Butte 'looked very beautiful in the afternoon light in the summer. Pale golden against the eastern sky, with the mangled remains of trees and houses, which was once le Sars, on the left. But what must it have looked like when the Somme

The Durham Light Infantry and the South African Memorials on the Butte de Warlencourt, 20 September 1917. *(IWM Q49393)*

was covered with snow, and the white-garmented Tommies used to raid it at night.'

In *The Challenge of the Dead*, Stephen Graham noted that one could walk up the Butte 'as one could walk upstairs', and that there were wooden monuments to the Durham Light Infantry and also 2nd South African Infantry. From the top there was a complete circle of view and one could see a light railway from it towards Eaucourt lined with 'desperate trees'.

In 1922 the Butte was chosen as a possible site for a memorial to the missing, but it was later realised that the scheme, to commemorate the 5,000 casualties from the Gommecourt Salient attack of 1 July together with subsequent fighting on the Ancre 1916–17, would not be feasible.

In the Warlencourt British Cemetery register it is noted that the cemetery bears witness to the very fierce fighting. The cemetery is on the south-east side of the ALBERT–BAPAUME road, to the north of the Butte; the gatehouse was designed by Sir Edwin Lutyens and King George V visited the cemetery on 12 May 1922. For greater detail see the WARLENCOURT-EAUCOURT entry.

In August 1982 a French First World War society, Le Souvenir Français, placed a commemorative plaque on the top of the Butte: 'To the memory of the British Troops who died on this hill during the Somme Battles, November 1916.'

In the late 1980s there was still a rather shaky wooden cross on the top of the Butte, together with the above French memorial, which took the form of a sword design. The wooden cross may have been a German one commemorating Infanterie-Regiment (14. Sächsische) Nr. 179, who captured the Butte during the war. In the late 1980s the Western Front Association were given the opportunity to purchase the hill, which they did, for £7,300. The Association then commissioned a brand new plaque and an orientation table, which were placed on the top of the hill and unveiled by the late John Terraine on 30 June 1990. However, the table soon had to be removed because of vandalism and is at present in ALBERT; additionally, the plaque was stolen. The upkeep of the Butte since 1990 has become an expensive operation and even clearing the ground in the first place was a somewhat hazardous business. However, during a recent visit by the author, it appeared to be very well cared for and visitors could use the small car park and the wooden staircase which leads to the top of the mound.

Having been continuously improved for visitor access, the Butte will be rededicated on 5 November 2016.

C

CABSTAND was the name of an advanced dressing station in the THIEPVAL sector under the control of No. 32 Main Dressing Station at BOUZINCOURT, whose field ambulances used it. Between 25 and 30 June 1916, 400 wounded passed through the station.

CAFTET WOOD is south-west of CARNOY on the left of the turn-off from the MARICOURT–FRICOURT road, the D938. Its northern edge faced onto the railway line between GUILLEMONT and MAMETZ. At the beginning of the 1916 battle, the Wood was just within the British XIII Corps lines and an advanced dressing station or CP was established there. On 1 July 1916, it was the assembly point of three companies of 6th Northamptons (54th Brigade, 18th Division). On 19 July, 35th Division had its headquarters in the Wood, which also contained its reserve battalions; it was to be 'home' for 106th Brigade (35th Division) for the rest of the month.

In mid-September, 2/Lt A.V. Burbery had been observing from a balloon, 3,000ft up, when the cable of the balloon was cut by a shell. He managed to destroy his papers, then ripped the balloon and reached the ground close to the Wood by parachute. He was awarded the Military Cross.

In November, 22nd Durham Light Infantry (pioneers of 8th Division) were camped in the Wood and were involved in making fascines as well as improving communication trenches.

CAMBRIDGE COPSE was west of MARICOURT and part of the assembly area of 90th Brigade (30th Division) in the small hours of 1 July 1916. Arriving here at 0045hrs, 16th Manchesters marched here from ETINEHEM and were inspected by Maj Gen J. Shea, General Officer Commanding 30th Division. An hour after Zero Hour, 16th and 17th Manchesters moved forward towards their objectives in MONTAUBAN-DE-PICARDIE. Oxford Copse nearby was a much longer copse and was also used as a point of assembly.

CANAPLES is north-west of AMIENS, close to the D933 road. On 28 November 1915, 18th Manchesters (90th Brigade, 30th Division) arrived in this village when they first came to the Somme area. While here they carried out training and wood-cutting fatigues; on 6 December they left for PUCHEVILLERS, but were back on 16 December, when they remained in the village over the Christmas period, until 6 January 1916. On 25 June, 25th Division headquarters was in the village.

CANDAS, south-west of DOULLENS, was an assembly area for 30th Division on 27 November 1915. At the end of December 1915, a new railway was being planned, which would use the new standard-gauge line; it would run 17 miles east from FIENVILLERS–Candas to ACHEUX-EN-AMIÉNOIS and provide five railheads to serve the battle.

On 3 January 1916, 18th King's left 89th Brigade (30th Division) here for 21st Brigade (30th Division). Most of No. 2/1 (North Midland) Field Company, Royal Engineers (46th Division), were based here from 9 February to 6 March. On 9 March 1916, 1/3rd (Highland) Field Ambulance (51st Division) were billeted here. On 30 September, 154th Brigade (51st Division) were in the village, as well as FIENVILLERS to the west. Although in 1916 Candas was mainly an important billeting village for the Royal Flying Corps, Army divisions were also stationed in the Candas area and used it for troop training purposes from January to November 1916, including 6th, 29th, 36th, 46th, 51st and 63rd Divisions.

Candas was the site of No. 2 Aircraft Depot, part of IV Brigade, and was conveniently near to the airfield at FIENVILLERS and the Royal Flying Corps headquarters. In April 1916, Lt Gen Sir Henry Rawlinson, General Officer Commanding Fourth Army, paid a visit to the depot, which was under the supervision of Maj R.C. Donaldson. He inspected the stores, which he described as being 'large and very important', for they furnished all the spare aircraft parts for the squadrons stationed in the Somme area. He commented that he thought the establishment was run very efficiently. At the beginning of July, the depot had a strength of 89 aircraft, a figure that included unserviceable machines. Candas also served as a landing ground but, according to Lt Insall, it could be blanketed off by a heavy type of thick fog, which could be expected in October.

The advanced headquarters of Hugh Dowding's Ninth Wing at the beginning of the battle was in the adjoining village of FIENVILLERS. Maj Gen H.M. Trenchard, General Officer Commanding First Wing, Royal Flying Corps, was billeted in the village with his aide-de-camp, Maurice Baring, who later wrote an excellent account called *Flying Corps Headquarters 1914–1918*. At the end of June, Baring mentions the village as not being far

from the No. 2 Aircraft Depot at Candas and that the headquarters was in a little square house which stood at the meeting of five crossroads, with three rooms and a kitchen downstairs and six bedrooms upstairs, four of which were turned into offices. Baring himself was billeted in a *notaire*'s house just opposite the headquarters.

CAPPY is on the D1 road to the south-east of BRAY-SUR-SOMME, on the south bank of the loop of the River Somme. At the beginning of the battle it was some way behind the Allied line and in fact lay just inside the French lines, the Franco-British Army boundary passing through BRAY-SUR-SOMME. In February 1916, No. 200 Field Company, Royal Engineers (30th Division), set up a very elaborate system of defence at an outpost position at Cappy Corner. In early 1916, when anticipating an enemy attack from the south-east, they established a series of defences in a group of buildings in the right-angled fork made by the D1 to BRAY-SUR-SOMME and the D197 to SUZANNE. Any invader would have to approach across the River Somme and its marshland, then move through wire entanglements set up on the left and right of the road and into machine-gun fire from the fortified buildings, as well as from several additional machine guns which were concealed.

The village suffered very little artillery damage during the war.

CARDONNETTE, north-west of AMIENS to the west of the D919 road, provided billets for 1/9th Londons (169th Brigade, 56th Division), who arrived here on 8 February 1916 and stayed for 4 days while they continued training. The villagers had set up a visitors' book and troops were invited to enter comments, sentiments or perhaps sketches as a souvenir of their stay in the village. The village, together with ALLONVILLE, was home to brigades from 17th Division in June and July 1916 and to 4th Division in mid-September.

CARNOY is between MAMETZ and MARI-COURT, north of the D938 road; during the First World War, the village contained a light railway that ran between PÉRONNE and ALBERT. After the lines were taken over from the French in August 1915, Royal Army Medical Corps dugouts and cellars and houses in the village were prepared for defence. On 5 August, 1st Royal West Kents (13th Brigade, 5th Division) were here when they relieved the French 293rd Infantry Regiment in the trenches. They spent several periods here in and out of the trenches when they were often at BRAY-SUR-SOMME, BILLON WOOD or BRONFAY FARM. Their battalion history noted that the enemy never shelled the road leading down into Carnoy at night when transport brought up the rations; perhaps there was an unwritten agreement not to shell each other's ration parties. On 18 August, 1/9th Londons (13th Brigade, 5th Division) arrived here from BRONFAY FARM for their first spell in Somme trenches and for a few weeks were either out of the line at BRAY-SUR-SOMME or at the front at Carnoy. In September, battalion headquarters was removed to BRONFAY FARM while companies were either at Carnoy or in BILLON WOOD.

On 30 September, 1/9th Londons left for billets in CHIPILLY when they were relieved at BRONFAY FARM. On 16 September, 8th Norfolks (53rd Brigade, 18th Division) held front-line trenches in this sector, which they had taken over from 10th Essex (also 53rd Brigade, 18th Division). This pattern continued for much of the rest of the year, although 8th Norfolks were sometimes in MAMETZ instead of Carnoy. In mid-October, members of 1/9th Londons were occupied in mining and carrying fatigues, including the construction of headquarters dugouts.

In mid-December, 14th Royal Warwicks (at this time 95th Brigade, 32nd Division) took over a sector at Carnoy from 2nd Duke of Wellington's (12th Brigade, 4th Division), when the battalion head-

The entrance to Carnoy, 1914–15.
(Peter F. Batchelor Collection)

quarters of both units were in the village at the same time. This was during a period when the trenches, owing to very bad weather, were in a very poor state. On 8 January, however, 14th Royal Warwicks (now 13th Brigade, 5th Division) were relieved and handed over their trenches, which by then were in much better condition, to 19th Manchesters (21st Brigade, 30th Division). Sadly, they left four of their comrades behind in the cemetery, side by side, near the ration dump. 14th Royal Warwicks then marched to BRAY-SUR-SOMME for the night before moving on to VAUX-SUR-SOMME.

On 10 January 1916, 2nd Wiltshires (21st Brigade, 30th Division) made their first visit to the front line here, where battalion headquarters was established. They relieved 1/9th Londons to the north-east of the village, where there was a small ravine known as TALUS BOISÉ. Battalion troops not in the line were either in reserve in Carnoy or back in BRAY-SUR-SOMME, resting. Though battalion headquarters remained in dugouts the whole time, the front-line troops made themselves as comfortable as possible, despite a heavy fall of snow towards the end of their first spell, which did not improve conditions. After a spell in the line, men returned to BRAY-SUR-SOMME for baths. Regimental transport came up to Carnoy every night, bringing food and other supplies. On 27 February, 2nd Wiltshires were relieved by 19th King's (89th Brigade, 30th Division) and left for BRAY-SUR-SOMME and FROISSY and then BRONFAY FARM on the BRAY-SUR-SOMME–Carnoy road.

On 12 April, the enemy raided the trenches of 6th Northamptons (54th Brigade, 18th Division); the defenders killed several of them and took another prisoner, and on 26 April they managed to take 10 of the enemy prisoner.

On 3 May, 2nd Wiltshires were back in the line here, this time to the right of their previous position, after relieving 11th Royal Fusiliers (54th Brigade, 18th Division). A week later, 2nd Wiltshires were themselves relieved, by 19th Manchesters, and moved to BRONFAY FARM and BILLON WOOD. On 15 May, 2nd Wiltshires returned to relieve 19th Manchesters; this interchanging system continued for several weeks. On 11 June, when relieved by 2nd Royal Scots Fusiliers (90th Brigade, 30th Division), 2nd Wiltshires marched to HEILLY, where they entrained for PICQUIGNY and then to billets at SAISSEVAL.

Between 24 May and 3 June, 6th Royal Berkshires (53rd Brigade, 18th Division) were in Carnoy; they spent a month in the back areas here, training for the battle. In mid-June, 7th Queen's (55th Brigade, 18th Division) arrived here and had two spells in the line before the offensive began. On 22 June, 2nd Wiltshires were back here after a night in tents at VAUX-SUR-SOMME, when they relieved 19th King's in the subsector facing MONTAUBAN-DE-PICARDIE. The preliminary Allied bombardment was about to begin.

On 1 July, the British objective on this part of the Somme front for 18th Division was the ground to the north of the MONTAUBAN-DE-PICARDIE–MAMETZ road, including POMMIERS REDOUBT and the Loop Redoubt. Also, if possible, patrols were to be pushed out towards Caterpillar Wood, which was south-east of MAMETZ WOOD. 18th Division's sector spread out in front of Carnoy with 55th Brigade to the right, 53rd Brigade in the centre and 54th Brigade on the left. The flanking formations were 30th Division, who were to capture MONTAUBAN-DE-PICARDIE on the right, and 7th Division, who were to take MAMETZ and reach a line overlooking MAMETZ WOOD. Advanced dressing stations and collection posts were in place at the beginning of July; during the battle, ambulance cars of the field ambulances arrived here at night, as well as at MARICOURT, and returned to DIVE COPSE before moving on to No. 21 Casualty Clearing Station at CORBIE or No. 45 Casualty Clearing Station at VECQUEMONT. On 1 July, however, the road to BRAY-SUR-SOMME was too full of shell-holes to be used. The village also had a waterpoint, in the form of 400-gallon water tanks, which were kept on trucks on the metre-gauge railway line here.

In July, 18th Division were part of XIII Corps and had a front of 2,500yds. The main objective of 55th Brigade was a trench line about 200yds to the north of the MONTAUBAN-DE-PICARDIE–MAMETZ road and also the western end of MONTAUBAN-DE-PICARDIE; 8th East Surreys (55th Brigade, 18th Division) were the battalion on the extreme right, with Breslau Trench as their first objective. It was during this action that one of the most famous Somme battle incidents took place. Capt W. Nevill, originally of the East Yorkshire Regiment, who was Officer Commanding B Company, 8th East Surreys, had sought permission from his Commanding Officer to bring back some footballs from leave for the attacking troops literally to 'kick-off' with. He had presented each platoon with a football and offered a prize to the first platoon to reach the German line, dribbling their football. At 0730hrs Nevill himself 'kicked off', having been the first to leave the company trench.

According to some reports, Nevill was shot before he had gone 20yds; another interpretation suggests that he reached the German wire before being killed, which meant that he would have covered about 400yds. T/2/Lt J.R. Ackerley of 8th East Surreys (55th Brigade, 18th Division), who after the war became a writer, was wounded in the same action, and his close colleague Bobby Soames who like Nevill began the advance with kicking a football was also killed. Ackerley described Nevill as a 'battalion buffoon', explaining that because he had loose dentures he could make terrifying grimaces. Ackerley is one of those who asserted that Nevill was killed immediately. Although wounded himself, Ackerley was more concerned over a bottle of 'Victory' whiskey that he had on him which had been smashed, and which might suggest to anyone who was to take him back to the British lines that he had been drinking. He therefore endeavoured to hide it from his rescuers. He wrote in his memoirs, *My Father and Myself*, that he had no taste for battle at all but he nevertheless became a company commander – simply because there was no one else left to carry out the job, he says. Everyone else had been killed.

Many of Nevill's letters have been deposited at the Imperial War Museum by his younger brother, as well as his identity disk. One of the footballs is an exhibit at the Queen's Regimental Museum. Nevill's body lies in Carnoy Military Cemetery (E.28). Having made little progress, 8th East Surreys were relieved at dawn on 2 July and returned to huts at Carnoy. Five of their officers had been killed.

On the left of 8th East Surreys, 7th Queen's were to attack northwards. In support were 7th Royal West

Kents and 7th Buffs (55th Brigade, 18th Division); the latter battalion's objective was a trench to the north of the MONTAUBAN-DE-PICARDIE–MAMETZ road, but first they had the special task of clearing Carnoy Craters, which took them 6 hours. They remained in front trenches until the night of 4/5 July and during this time were heavily shelled. Steadily the advance continued and by 1330hrs, 55th Brigade were at the final objective and, aided by three companies of 8th Suffolks (53rd Brigade, 18th Division), were working their way along Montauban Alley towards Loop Trench.

On 53rd Brigade's front, 8th Norfolks were on the right and 6th Royal Berkshires (also 53rd Brigade, 18th Division) on the left; 8th Norfolks were to bomb their way up Loop Trench. 6th Royal Berkshires reached a line in front of Mine Trench which was the most advanced of the German defences; at the west end of this trench was Casino Point, under which the British had exploded a mine with disastrous results for the enemy. (The crater was filled in some years ago.)

Mine Trench was captured by two advancing battalions and by 0750hrs, 6th Royal Berkshires had taken Bund Support Trench and had gone forward to Pommiers Trench. At 1515hrs, the right of 6th Royal Berkshires were held up, however, and they had to be assisted by the bombers of 10th Essex. It was not until 1830hrs that the final objective was reached, a line running east and west in front of Caterpillar Wood. Loop Trench had been handed over to 8th Norfolks when they came up.

The extreme left of 54th Brigade's attack was in the hands of 11th Royal Fusiliers, whose first involvement in battle this was. At 0700hrs, a thick mist had shrouded the foreground, but by 0730hrs this had cleared, and they began their advance towards POMMIERS REDOUBT, almost due north of their assembly position. Firstly, 11th Royal Fusiliers dealt with an attempt to check them at Austrian Support Trench, when a machine gun was taken between Bund Trench and Pommiers Trench. The battalion on their right, 6th Northamptons, had been held up by uncut wire, and the Germans in MAMETZ village used this time to strike against the battalion's left flank. A small party bombed up Black Alley, which ran parallel to 11th Royal Fusiliers' advance and led to Pommiers Trench. POMMIERS REDOUBT at this time was still to be taken. However, after hard fighting in the area of Black and Beetle Alleys, the advance continued, and by 0930hrs the obstacle had been gained. By the afternoon, 11th Royal Fusiliers were 1,000yds ahead of their flanking battalions, and reached

White Trench, which was below MAMETZ WOOD. A line of strongpoints was made later in the day. The enemy had been driven back from a depth of about 2,000yds. The night of 1 July was spent in Montauban Alley; 11th Royal Fusiliers had seen the German gunners rushing up with their teams immediately beyond CATERPILLAR WOOD in order to get them away. At 0300hrs on 2 July, 6th Royal Berkshires went back to Pommiers Trench and, after being relieved by 8th Suffolks, to Carnoy until 7 July.

Behind 6th Royal Berkshires, 10th Essex were to suffer from falling debris from the Casino Point explosion; they held and consolidated the Pommiers Line. 53rd Brigade had its main dumps on the Carnoy–MONTAUBAN-DE-PICARDIE road. 7th Bedfords (54th Brigade, 18th Division) were to the left of 6th Royal Berkshires; 12th Middlesex (the reserve battalion of 54th Brigade, 18th Division) went into action with 7th Bedfords on the right and 11th Royal Fusiliers on the left, with 6th Northamptons in support.

At Zero Hour on 1 July, 12th Middlesex were in deep dugouts; at 0830hrs, Lt Col F.A. Maxwell, Commanding Officer 12th Middlesex, moved to battalion headquarters at Piccadilly in the old British Front Line. At 1245hrs, 12th Middlesex moved up with men in Bund Trench and in Emden Trench, on the right of the Triangle; they also reached Austrian Support Trench. They remained in these positions for the rest of the day until, at 2030hrs on 2 July, they were relieved in the advance positions by 11th Royal Fusiliers. By this time, Maxwell's headquarters was in Black Alley. On 2/3 July, they relieved 11th Royal Fusiliers; at night on 6 July, 12th Middlesex were themselves relieved by 7th Bedfords and marched back to bivouacs west of Bronfay Wood.

As a postscript to 18th Division's role at Carnoy in early July, Lt W.H. Livens organised the use of gas projectors on the divisional front. He had been recruited from the Royal Engineers in order to combat the threat of German gas warfare. He was really an inventor and was to design several types of gas projector. On the same front was Maj A. Brooke, who was to become one of the top British military leaders in the Second World War. A member of the 18th Division artillery, he was an early supporter of the 'creeping barrage', and was more interested in destroying 'selected' enemy strongpoints, rather than just attempting to destroy the whole of the enemy line, and not succeeding.

Siegfried Sassoon of 1st Royal Welsh Fusiliers (22nd Brigade, 7th Division) wrote the following poem, dated 3 July 1916:

At Carnoy
Down in the hollow there's the whole Brigade
Camped in four groups: through twilight falling
     slow
I hear a sound of mouth-organs, ill-played,
And murmur of voices, gruff, confused, and low.
Crouched among thistle-tufts I've watched the
     glow
Of a blurred orange sunset flare and fade;
And I'm content. To-morrow we must go
To take some cursèd Wood . . . O world God
     made!

In early July, the official War Office photographer, Geoffrey Malins, took his car to the top of Carnoy Valley and left it at XV Corps Main Dressing Station, MINDEN POST, next to CAFTET WOOD at the head of the valley above Carnoy. It was just off the MAMETZ–MARICOURT road, and was to become probably the most famous dressing station on the Somme. All the XV Corps wounded passed through there after receiving attention at the advanced dressing station. Malins was advised to move his car as it was likely to be destroyed by German artillery, which despite a large red cross lying on the ground still treated the advanced dressing station as a legitimate target. Malins filmed

some scenes here before attempting to film in the Bernafay/MONTAUBAN-DE-PICARDIE direction but TRÔNES WOOD proved too 'hot' for him.

There was a military camp at Carnoy, which in early July consisted of dugouts, shacks and bivouacs; here too there was plenty of shelling. The valley of Carnoy had a military track and also a light railway and in addition was thickly populated with trench lines. Ammunition limbers made a continuous stream in both directions. Often men and horses were blown up, but the traffic never ceased. Carnoy had the name sometimes of DEATH VALLEY, as shells rained down on it so frequently. On 8/9 July, 2nd Suffolks (76th Brigade, 3rd Division) bivouacked here, as did 7th King's Shropshire Light Infantry (8th Brigade, 3rd Division) on 7 July and 18th King's (21st Brigade, 30th Division) on 9 July.

The artillery also massed here; at the end of July, one artillery brigade increased from 6 batteries to 20 in one night, and the heavier ordnance, 8in and 9.2in pieces, began firing at 2200hrs, according to Cpl L.J. Ounsworth (Imperial War Museum). Each battery was given about 50yds or 60yds of road and in ½ mile there could be found 80 guns. In *The Machine*

An 8-inch Mark V howitzer in a camouflaged emplacement near Carnoy, July 1916. *(IWM Q104)*

Gunner, Arthur Russell of the Machine Gun Corps also described the conditions at Carnoy. No. 166 Company found themselves in trench dugouts in Carnoy Valley during the Somme offensive. The trench, like the valley itself, was in enfilade (or end on) from the German line, about 1½ miles to 2 miles away. The dugouts were 'baby elephants', being half-loops of channelled steel bolted together to form an arched protection from the weather and also from the small shell-bursts; they were covered with earth about a couple of sandbags in depth. The 'baby elephants' were adjacent to each other, and were open-ended into the enfiladed trench. The men were in reserve in this position for a week or so, and some mornings they had to do physical exercises in the valley at 0700hrs in the full view of the German observation balloon. They were 'registered' and the company who relieved them were decimated.

At the end of July, 6th King's Shropshire Light Infantry (60th Brigade, 20th Division) were in craters close to the Carnoy–MONTAUBAN-DE-PICARDIE road. On 22 August, the headquarters of 20th Division was at MINDEN POST; 60th Brigade (20th Division) were in reserve at the craters, which were about 1,000yds from Carnoy itself.

In *Henry Dundas, Scots Guards*, H.L.N. Dundas noted that on 4 September, 2nd Guards Brigade moved to Carnoy from HAPPY VALLEY. He himself was with 1st Scots Guards, but was ill at CORBIE at the time.

Between 4 and 9 September Aubrey Smith of 1/5th Londons (169th Brigade, 56th Division) was with his transport at Carnoy; he described it as a ruined village which had harboured the battalion headquarters and aid posts of one or two units that had charged near this spot on 1 July. When moving down the hill he saw camps to the left, horse-lines to the right, British 9.2in howitzers on one side, water troughs on the other, and two lines of convoy splashing in the mud. The battalion had left by now, carrying on towards the front, while the transport plodded on to the prescribed area and the horse-lines on the far side of the village. Lewis gun limbers, cookers, water carts, mess carts, and medical carts were told not to unhook. They were 'shortly in an inferno, not of enemy fire but of Allied fire', in DEATH VALLEY, 'where guns of all calibres were massed'.

In early September, 3rd Guards Brigade (Guards Division) relieved 47th and 48th Brigades (both 16th Division); 4th Grenadier Guards (3rd Guards Brigade, Guards Division) were to relieve 47th Brigade on the right, while 1st Welsh Guards were to take over the front at the south-east of Ginchy

from 48th Brigade. A battalion of the Irish Guards were in support at BERNAFAY WOOD, while 2nd Scots Guards (also 3rd Guards Brigade, Guards Division) remained bivouacked in reserve, north of Carnoy. On 10 September, two companies of 2nd Scots Guards were sent up to BERNAFAY WOOD, followed in the afternoon by the rest of the battalion.

On 16 September, 1st Welsh Guards were resting on the slope of a hill near Carnoy. In the valley was a line of 9.2in howitzers and on the opposite slope were the cavalry lines, with their horses' knees in deep mud. All the transport for miles around watered their horses at a well in Carnoy Valley. On 17 September, 12th King's (61st Brigade, 20th Division) were based at Carnoy Craters. Following their involvement in the Battle of Guillemont on 7 September, 6th King's Shropshire Light Infantry were at CORBIE for a rest on 8 September. They moved to Carnoy next, returning to the trenches in front of WATERLÔT FARM on 16 September. The Germans counter-attacked on 17 and 18 September, but GUILLEMONT fell to the Allies and 20th Division left for a short rest. Later in the month, 6th King's Shropshire Light Infantry were back briefly at Carnoy.

On 19 September, 1st Scots Guards (2nd Guards Brigade, Guards Division) were ordered to move nearer the line and marched to Carnoy on 20 September. On 24 September, orders were received for them to move up next day, but they returned the same evening from TRÔNES WOOD. Meanwhile, 2nd Scots Guards (3rd Guards Brigade) had been resting and refitting at Carnoy. On 21 September, 3rd Guards Brigade was to relieve 59th Brigade (20th Division); 4th Grenadier Guards (3rd Guards Brigade), on the left, shared battalion headquarters with 2nd Scots Guards, on whose right were 3rd Coldstream Guards (1st Guards Brigade). The attack had been postponed until 25 September, owing to bad weather. After the battle, on the evening of 26 September, 2nd Guards Brigade relieved 1st and 3rd Guards Brigades and 2nd and 3rd Coldstream Guards (both 1st Guards Brigade) moved to bivouac at Carnoy.

On 27 September, 11th King's Royal Rifle Corps (59th Brigade, 20th Division) camped here and provided working parties; on 9 October, they left for the back areas. On 22 October, 2nd Royal Welsh Fusiliers (19th Brigade, 33rd Division) were here on their way to TRÔNES WOOD via GUILLEMONT and GINCHY. As the weeks went by the conditions at Carnoy grew worse, until towards the end of October the whole area was one expanse of mud;

horses had to be shot and lorries became stuck all over the place. Mention is made of a hutted camp in November and also of H Camp being situated in the village; in the same month, 24th Brigade (8th Division) were here. On 16 October, 88th Brigade (29th Division) moved here. In January 1917, Max Plowman of 10th West Yorkshires (50th Brigade, 17th Division) wrote that after being at FLERS, his unit just had time to clean up and look around the 'town of hutments that was Carnoy' before going back into the line, where he was wounded in the head. The village had been used as a collecting place for the wounded.

Work on Carnoy Military Cemetery, close to the former railway halt, was begun in August 1915 by 2nd King's Own Scottish Borderers (87th Brigade, 29th Division) and 2nd King's Own Yorkshire Light Infantry (at this time 13th Brigade, 5th Division) and used by field ambulances when the village was immediately south of the line. It 'continued in use by troops holding this sector until July 1916, when field ambulances came up and a camp was established on the higher ground north of the village'. It is on the south side of the village alongside the former railway halt, which closed in March 1917. Men buried here who died in the battle include a group of Army chaplains and four lieutenant-colonels. Carnoy Military Cemetery has the graves of 319 men who died prior to 1 July 1916 and is the second highest in the Department of the Somme.

Lt Col H. Budge (E.9) of 12th Royal Scots (27th Brigade, 9th Division) was killed on 13 July 1916 when 'caught by hostile shell-fire on the outskirts of Montauban'.

Lt Col R. Carden (S.22), 17th Lancers (attached 16th Royal Welsh Fusiliers, 115th Brigade, 38th Division), was killed during an attack against MAMETZ WOOD on 10 July 1916. Aged 38 and a South African War veteran, he was the son of Col F.W. Carden.

Brigadier-General Price-Davies met the officers of the 14th and 16th Battalions in Queen's Nullah and went through the orders with them, explaining any doubtful points. Colonel Carden, commanding the 16th Battalion, was told that although the time for starting was fixed for 4.15 a.m., he must not start before the 114th Brigade as he was nearest to the edge of the wood. Lieutenant-Colonel Carden was a gifted leader with a touch of fanaticism. He addressed his battalion before going into action: 'Make your peace with God. You are going to take that position, and some of us won't come back – but we are going to take it.' And tying a coloured handkerchief to his walking-stick he said, 'This will show you where I am.' In the end, those attacking

did not attack together and 16th Royal Welsh Fusiliers wavered before the German machine guns. Carden and other officers] steadied the men and led them forward. Carden, with his walking-stick aloft, was a conspicuous figure, in the soft light of early morning, calling on the men to advance. He was hit, and fell, but rose again. He led to the very edge of the wood, where he was killed.

Lt Col F. Curzon (R.34), Commanding Officer 6th Royal Irish (47th Brigade, 16th Division), a battalion he raised and trained, was killed in action at GINCHY on 9 September 1916, aged 57. He was the son of Lt Col E.G. Curzon.

Lt Col J. Lenox-Conyngham (R.33), Commanding Officer 6th Connaughts (also 47th Brigade, 16th Division), was killed in action on 3 September 1916. In *British Battalions on the Somme*, Ray Westlake notes of Lenox-Conyngham's leadership: 'When "springing forward at the head of his men [he] pointed with his cane to the enemy position – 'That, Connaught Rangers, is what you have to take' were his last words." This information was based on an NCO's report. Rowland Feilding was appointed to take over temporary command of 6th Connaughts and joined them in the afternoon of 6 July at Carnoy. He inherited his predecessor's fine mare.'

An Irishman, Lenox-Conyngham had been a career soldier who had served from 1881 to 1911 and awarded the KCB. He had commanded 6th Connaughts since the beginning of the war. Pte T. Hughes of the same battalion won his Victoria Cross in the same action in which Lenox-Conyngham was killed.

Capt H. Cubitt of 3rd Coldstream Guards (1st Guards Brigade, Guards Division), killed near GINCHY on 15 September, is also buried here (P.27). He was the eldest son of Lord Ashcombe and two of his younger brothers also died in the war.

At 0600hrs on 18 October, Pte H. Farr of 1st West Yorkshires (18th Brigade, 6th Division) was 'shot at dawn' here; his name is on the Thiepval Memorial.

Carnoy was 'adopted' by Swansea after the war.

CATERPILLAR VALLEY is between the village of MAMETZ and MAMETZ WOOD and lies south-east of CONTALMAISON and north-west of MONTAUBAN-DE-PICARDIE. The Valley extends from west to east in front of MAMETZ WOOD across the MONTAUBAN-DE-PICARDIE–LON-GUEVAL road and across the north or top of BERNAFAY WOOD towards TRÔNES WOOD and GUILLEMONT. Caterpillar Wood, which is in the eastern end of the Valley, is south of Flat Iron Copse and Sabot Copse. The name given to the Valley (which is deep and made of chalk) by the Army was presumably because it is caterpillar in shape and outline. The part of the Valley or low ground in front of MAMETZ WOOD is sometimes called HAPPY VALLEY, although the real HAPPY VALLEY is near BRAY-SUR-SOMME, to the south.

Caterpillar Wood was on a steep chalk bank and the Germans had made it into a strong redoubt to defend the flanks of the valley. Just to the north-east of it was a small fortified copse or dingle known as MARLBOROUGH WOOD. In early July 1916, forces advancing northwards from MONTAUBAN-DE-PICARDIE would have to seize the Wood before they could reach the Valley and proceed against the hill beyond. The Wood was the 'haunt' of German artillery.

Although on 1 July the troops of 18th and 7th Divisions did not reach all of their final first-day objectives, they had achieved much more success than most British divisions, having captured POMMIERS REDOUBT and MAMETZ village, which meant that they were in sight of, and in contact with, Caterpillar Wood and Valley. The Wood was in front of 18th Division and the western section of the Valley was in front of the 7th Division. The progress of the two British divisions was so rapid on the first day of the battle that across the Valley could be seen several hundreds of Germans streaming northwards along the BAZENTIN-LE-GRAND road. Many gunners of the German artillery were also forced to leave their guns behind.

On 4 July, 10th Essex (53rd Brigade, 18th Division) captured the Wood, together with MARL-BOROUGH WOOD; 54th Brigade (18th Division) took over later. Early on 11 July, 9th Devons (20th Brigade, 7th Division) reached Caterpillar Valley on the far bank of a depression, which was not deep enough for protection against howitzer fire. Caterpillar Trench, which ran south-eastwards towards the Allied lines, was in full view of the enemy at this time and could only be used at night. In *The Turning Point*, H.P. Robinson, war correspondent of *The Times*, noted that in early July the fighting in this area had been of the toughest kind and that the Germans had to be driven from Caterpillar Valley almost yard by yard and forced way up the slope to a line that was practically level with the middle of MAMETZ WOOD. Further to the east, BERNAFAY WOOD had been cleared without great loss, but then a desperate struggle ensued for the possession of TRÔNES WOOD.

Basil Liddell Hart of 9th King's Own Yorkshire Light Infantry (64th Brigade, 21st Division) noted that soon after midnight on 14 July, his battalion

assembled in the shelter of Caterpillar Valley, moving up in 'long wormlike lines of companies or platoons in single file'. At 0320hrs, the barrage fell on the German trenches; this was the night attack against BAZENTIN. Five minutes later the whole line moved forward and the whole of the German Second Line was rapidly overrun, and the attacking troops passed beyond; 21st Division passed through Bazentin-le-Petit Wood to the village, while 7th Division cleared Bazentin-le-Grand Wood and pushed up the slopes towards HIGH WOOD, 3rd Division captured BAZENTIN-LE-GRAND village and 9th Division fought their way with difficulty through LONGUEVAL to the outskirts of DELVILLE WOOD.

On 14 July, 2nd Suffolks (76th Brigade, 3rd Division) moved to the southern end of the Wood while the cavalry were concentrating in the Valley for an attack on HIGH WOOD. XV Brigade, Royal Field Artillery (5th Division), took up positions to support the infantry in the Valley, which lay between Pommiers Ridge and MAMETZ WOOD. After the cavalry had ridden through towards HIGH WOOD, 21st Manchesters (91st Brigade, 7th Division) were withdrawn 400yds to the rear of HIGH WOOD. Their headquarters was a former German battery and they were badly shelled. They had been involved with 1st South Staffords (also 91st Brigade, 7th Division) in fighting in HIGH WOOD itself, during which there had been a panic withdrawal. The battalion aid post was in Sabot Copse and 91st Brigade headquarters was at Caterpillar Wood. The situation was untenable and they withdrew to Mametz Halt.

On 18 July, the Germans counter-attacked and forced their way with fine courage but at great loss, and on 19 July, Caterpillar Valley was crammed with field artillery, because it was the only possible site for the more forward batteries. In addition to the Allied guns which presented easy targets, the German artillery caught dressing stations and field kitchens, which by necessity were also in the Valley. 15th Royal Warwicks (13th Brigade, 4th Division) were in trenches in front of the north section of the crossroads with the MONTAUBAN-DE-PICARDIE–BAZENTIN road. The present Quarry Cemetery was at that time used as a dressing station.

On 19 July, 1st Devons (95th Brigade, 3rd Division) left MONTAUBAN-DE-PICARDIE, when they took over part of the line 'in the hell called Caterpillar Valley' from 3rd Division and their Commanding Officer, Col L.H.M. Westrop, was wounded. When the 5th Division artillery came into the Valley to take up their positions, they thought it to be a most 'unhealthy' area. It was packed from end to end with guns of every sort: 9.2in, 8in, 6in, 4.5in howitzers, 60-pounders, anti-aircraft guns and literally hundreds of 18-pounder guns, which kept up an almost continuous roar by day and by night. They were overlooked by German positions at GINCHY to the east and had hardly any cover for detachments, which were maintained as small as possible in order to keep losses to the minimum. The troops dug holes in the ground and if possible covered them with corrugated iron and earth, which afforded scant protection against the 'Caterpillar Valley Barrage' that swept relentlessly down the Valley at intervals by day and night. In addition to the gun positions, a number of units had formed horse-lines towards the FRICOURT end of the Valley, and almost every square yard was occupied in some way or other. As the line for approaching reliefs or for ration and fatigue parties lay across Caterpillar Valley and over the slopes south and south-west of LONGUEVAL, the difficulties that had to be faced may be imagined. One artillery brigade with positions here was LXXXIV Brigade, Royal Field Artillery (18th Division), who on 22 July were withdrawn to their previous positions at BILLON WOOD near BRAY-SUR-SOMME and after breakfast moved back to TAILLES WOOD.

On the same day the danger of the Valley as a site for horse-lines was brought home to those who had used it as such. In the afternoon the Germans opened a sudden concentrated fire on them, and in order to prevent appalling losses, the horses were cut loose and they stampeded, terrified, down the Valley towards FRICOURT in a cloud of dust and shell smoke; it took several hours to collect them up again, and in the end not many were lost. The guns remained in Caterpillar Valley until 1 September, when they moved forward to BERNAFAY WOOD to support the attacks on GINCHY and GUILLEMONT and afterwards to positions around DELVILLE WOOD for the attack on the SWITCH TRENCH and GUEUDECOURT positions.

M.E.S. Laws, who was an artillery section commander, described the situation in the Valley after the initial attack and noted that the Valley had formerly been a German gun position where they had built excellent dugouts which later the British were to use. Unfortunately it was the very German familiarity with their former positions that led to considerable British casualties. In addition to continuous German shelling there were phosgene gas shells. Another hazard was that there was no water to be had and it had to be brought up by lorry in buckets, with each man only receiving a very small allowance.

H.E. Harvey of 22nd Royal Fusiliers (99th Brigade, 2nd Division) wrote in July that his battalion went on across the road that led to the Quarry and Caterpillar Valley, on past the uprooted orchard on the south side, down the broad road to BERNAFAY WOOD with 'its snapping batteries' of French 75mm pieces. The ground was captured only after very fierce fighting, in the latter part of July.

Between mid-August and 10 September, 47th Division's batteries were in position in BOTTOM WOOD with some further east near MONTAUBAN-DE-PICARDIE and in front of Caterpillar Valley. Further forward in the Valley, heavy howitzers stood in the open, lobbing their shells over a target miles away. Direct hits on either guns or dugouts were not unknown. In *Stand To*, Capt F.C. Hitchcock of 2nd Leinsters (73rd Brigade, 24th Division) noted that, prior to the attack on DELVILLE WOOD due west of MONTAUBAN-DE-PICARDIE, when they struck off for Caterpillar Valley, it was raining and the going was terribly heavy. The Valley was waterlogged and they all became caked in mud.

It was a miserable place, muddy, and all churned up by shell craters of all sizes that were now filled with water. The few trees there had been reduced to blackened stumps, and not a blade of grass was visible either in the valley or on the rising slopes. It was a valley of the dead and no one stayed in it longer than was necessary. The light railway which led up to Guillemont was completely torn up, lengths of it were standing up for ten feet in the air, with great shell craters under them. All along the valley were abandoned stores, boxes of SAA and the long shaped blue boxes which contained Mills Bombs. After a tiring tramp along the valley, they arrived at a dump called Green Dump; which was close to Longueval Trench and was always an unhealthy place.

Donald Boyd, author of *Salute of Guns*, had arrived on the Somme at the end of August and noted that the reconnoitring parties went up to Dead Man's Gulch to learn the position of the batteries that they were to relieve, but theirs was known, and they were told to go and search for it near Caterpillar Valley.

The lips of shell craters overlapped. Enormous speckled horse flies buzzed and darted about the sweat running off their faces. On the left of the track lay several small shattered woods from which rose a sickening hum, as though all the flies in France were meeting over the bodies whose decay pervaded the battlefield. The hill on the right was broken by a cleft, Caterpillar Valley. Its black walls were full of shell-holes and in places regularly grooved by the scraping of the infantry entrenching tool.

In *Gallipoli to the Somme*, Alexander Aitken of 1st Otagos (1st New Zealand Brigade, New Zealand Division) noted that in early September, road-mending and repairs were carried on in the Valley. The Valley road was so congested with traffic and limbers that troops were forced to walk along the sleepers of the railways, from which siding after siding led off to the wood on the left. Each siding had a howitzer among the trees, the largest being a 12in, which fired every few minutes. The road turned left at a corner and ran up to BAZENTIN. On this corner, a German high-velocity gun registered with accuracy at 5-minute intervals, and here they were amazed at the courage of the limber drivers who had to pass this point. Evidence of the July fighting lay all around. In addition to the ground being pitted with craters, there were dud shells all about, piles of anti-aircraft shells hurriedly abandoned, up on the wooded slope, sunk deep into the chalky earth, German dugouts, their entrances half-concealed by trees, many containing machine guns not yet cleared away, some facing so as to shoot over attackers in the back. Aitken mentioned that they filled in the craters and levelled and topped them off. The Germans all the time kept up their shelling of the corner. The New Zealand Division entered the Battle of the Somme on 11 September when they took over the line between DELVILLE WOOD and HIGH WOOD. They were due to take part in Fourth Army's attack of 15 September, which was to penetrate north and east towards BAPAUME. It was on 15 September that the tanks lumbered into action and came along Caterpillar Valley. On 1 October, 5th Division's guns again moved forward to positions in the vicinity of SWITCH TRENCH.

In *Field Guns in France*, Neil Fraser-Tytler noted that in early November, 'At night Caterpillar Valley is a wonderful sight. A perfect blaze of lights, extending 14 miles, as the valley contains the wagon lines of about three Corps.'

Because of the water shortage, scouts were detailed to report if water was running into any particular group of troughs, and when it did everyone hurried to it. The troughs could only water about 200 horses at a time. No one could approach them dismounted as the mud was almost waist deep. Towards the end of November, a broad-gauge line up the valley was nearing completion as were two hutted camps between HIGH WOOD and BAZENTIN-LE-PETIT and another just south of the latter. Having been taken by the Allies in July 1916, the area was lost to the Germans in March 1918.

On the south side of the road to LONGUEVAL is Caterpillar Valley Cemetery; which forms the eastern side of it is Caterpillar Valley (New Zealand) Memorial, Longueval, dedicated to those New Zealanders who fell in the Somme battles and whose graves are unknown. Ten years after the war there were problems about the land ownership in the area which, after much delay, were finally solved by 1935 when amendments to the ownership agreement were decided. There are also three memorials here to soldiers whose graves in McCormick's Post Cemetery near FLERS were destroyed by shell-fire.

Sir Herbert Baker was the architect of Caterpillar Valley Cemetery, which stands on a ridge from which LONGUEVAL and other villages, HIGH WOOD, DELVILLE WOOD and other woods are clearly visible. One of the men buried here is Lt Col W. Drysdale DSO (VI.E.11), Commanding Officer 7th Leicesters (110th Brigade, 21st Division), who died on 29 September 1916. During preliminary reconnaissance, he was killed by a sniper when his battalion was relieving 6th Leicesters (also 110th Brigade, 21st Division) to the north-north-east of GUEUDECOURT. Also here is Lt Col H. Knox (VIII.B.11) of 16th Manchesters (90th Brigade, 30th Division), killed on 13 October 1916 after his battalion had moved up to the front line and Gird Support with the headquarters in the trench. On 13 October, the position was heavily shelled and the headquarters section had to be moved, but Knox was mortally wounded.

In 1962/3, the walls around the cemetery were dismantled and replaced by a fence, excepting at the front of the cemetery, where the wall was rebuilt to a lower level as a retaining wall. In September 1991, a special 55th anniversary ceremony took place here at the New Zealand Memorial.

A picture of the cemetery by the war photographer Don McCullin appeared on a postage stamp in 1999. On 10 October 2004, the remains of an unknown New Zealand soldier were exhumed from Caterpillar Valley Cemetery and, in November, flown to New Zealand and reburied as part of a major ceremony on Armistice Day in the National War Memorial in Wellington. He was one of 9,000 New Zealand servicemen with no known graves and has been called an 'Unknown Warrior' rather than 'Unknown Soldier'. In addition, soil from two-time Victoria Cross winner Charles Upham's farm is buried with this anonymous man's remains.

CHÂTEAU DE LA HAIE was just off the FONCQUEVILLERS–BAYENCOURT road in the war years. In September 1915, 48th Division had their headquarters here, at which time No. 1/2 (South Midland) Field Company, Royal Engineers (48th Division), were working here; a track to the farm from the west was also improved. On 4 September, the headquarters of 143rd Brigade (also 48th Division) was here. 1/5th Royal Warwicks (143rd Brigade, 48th Division) spent time here in training or digging communication trenches at FONCQUEVILLERS. Sometimes they 'rested' at BAYENCOURT. Strangely, even by December the building, scarcely 1 mile from the line, was still virtually untouched by shell-fire and units continued to use the château and farm complex for billeting and training.

In early 1916, according to Lt Col V.F. Eberle, a Royal Engineer serving with 48th Division, the Divisional Report Centre was based here, 2,500yds behind the front line. No. 1/1 (South Midland) Field Company, Royal Engineers (48th Division), carried out various tasks, including setting up a cinema in a large barn that was also used for church services. It was packed out every night for performances by the Barn Owls or another troupe, the Orfhinds. On a more serious note, No. 1/1 (South Midland) Field Company carried out Bangalore Torpedo demonstrations near the château.

At one point 17th Manchesters (90th Brigade, 30th Division), when billeted here, used a communication known as la Haye Cut but found it in such a bad state that they preferred to use the road instead. On 11 February, the advanced dressing stations here and at FONCQUEVILLERS were handed over by 1/1st (South Midland) Field Ambulance to 1/3rd (South Midland) Field Ambulance (both 48th Division). In *History of the 17th Northern Division*, the château is mentioned as having been the headquarters of 56th Division, and was later the headquarters of 52nd Brigade (17th Division). In mid-May, 46th Division also used it. On 8 May, 137th Brigade (46th Division) had its headquarters here.

The building stood on an eminence, a large semi-castellated country house, having a courtyard on its eastern front with extensive stabling on both sides. Though it stood on the skyline at a range of not more than 4,000yds from the German batteries near Gommecourt Wood, it does not seem that they ever made it a target. Right and left of the château, the artillery of 56th Division were in position close by, a fact that made it all the more remarkable that the château had not attracted enemy fire. But around 18 August, the Germans changed their mind and the headquarters was subsequently moved to a larger house in the eastern outskirts of SOUASTRE. Today the complex is a working farm.

CHIMNEY TRENCH was south of BERNAFAY WOOD and the road to MONTAUBAN-DE-PICARDIE and north of a brickworks. In early August 1916, a battalion of the Prince of Wales's Volunteers (South Lancashire Regiment) was sheltering in the neighbourhood; on 19 August, two brigades of 35th Division were here, including 105th Brigade, who also occupied ARROW HEAD COPSE, which was to the north-east of GUILLE-MONT. An attack was planned for 17 September, but had to be cancelled owing to the muddy conditions. On 19 August, 14th Royal Warwicks (13th Brigade, 5th Division) were here until they were relieved by a brigade of the Guards Division.

CHIPILLY is a village on the north bank of the River Somme, south-east of MORLANCOURT, some 17 miles east of AMIENS. In August 1915, 5th Division took over the old château here; on 13 August, 15th Field Ambulance (5th Division) arrived here from ETINEHEM and a battalion from 5th Division were billeted here. 15th Field Ambulance ran a dressing station here and were responsible for it on many occasions in the following weeks. On occasions, barges were used to transport casualties, and on 9 October several barges arrived here from FROISSY for future use. Although six barges were attached to 15th Field Ambulance, only three of them had beds. There were 100 beds in all.

When bathing in rivers prior to the battle it was not uncommon for soldiers to get into difficulties while swimming. On 17 August, two men who were accidentally drowned near BRAY-SUR-SOMME were brought to Chipilly Communal Cemetery, becoming the first Army burials here.

On 30 September, 1/9th Londons (13th Brigade, 5th Division) arrived here from BRONFAY FARM; over the next few days they carried out company training, held concerts and had a series of football matches. Companies left on 8 October for BRAY-SUR-SOMME and ETINEHEM. Also in October, a field company from 5th Division were involved in cutting and crating timber in the village.

On 8 December, two companies of 14th Royal Warwicks (13th Brigade, 5th Division) arrived in the village after their first experience of the front line opposite CARNOY. At this time in December, the front-line trenches were in an appalling state caused by continuous heavy rain followed by a hard frost. This had made the soft earth crumble; in some places the mud was nearly waist-high and could cause men to sink up to their armpits.

On 4 January 1916, 16th Manchesters (90th Brigade, 30th Division) had marched 17 miles when they arrived here. In 1916, the village continued to be used by field ambulances, including 96th and 98th Field Ambulances (both 30th Division), and six barges under an officer from Fourth Army were still based here. From June to September 1916, No. 9 Squadron, Royal Flying Corps, commanded by Maj A.B. Burdett, was based in the village; they left for MORLANCOURT.

In March 1918, the village fell to the Germans during their great advance, and was only retaken by the Allies on 8 August. By then it had been badly knocked about and a quarry was used as a battalion headquarters.

Chipilly Communal Cemetery has a British plot, which was begun in August 1915 and used until March 1916 and then again between July and October 1916. There are 57 identified graves, of which 38 are from the pre-battle period in 1916. Chipilly Communal Cemetery Extension was made by the British in the period between March 1916 and February 1917 and has the graves of 31 identified casualties, including 25 from the pre-battle period in 1916. The two cemeteries are in the north-east of the village and overlook the village and the Somme Valley.

After the war, a memorial was erected in Chipilly to commemorate 58th Division as well as the Armies of Australia, Canada and France, who turned the tide of action on 8 August 1918. It was designed by Henri Desire, a sculptor known for his skill in representing animals, who built a memorial with a practical use as a water trough. The design is described as 'the British soldier comforting his wounded horse at Chipilly'. The water trough part of the memorial no longer functions. The original design was possibly influenced by the painting by J. Matania entitled *Goodbye Old Man*, in which a British artilleryman says his farewell to a dying horse, and also a poem depicting the same subject by Henry Chappell and called 'The Soldier's Kiss'.

THE CITADEL is just beyond the two points, 71 metres above sea level, known as 71 North and 71 South, and about 150yds north-east of the FRICOURT–BRAY-SUR-SOMME road. It first appears as a camp used by 5th Division, which had its headquarters here on 6 August 1915. The camp consisted of a collection of dugouts, to which several marquees were attached. As with BOIS FRANÇAIS, nearer to FRICOURT to the north, the whole area is steeped in literary associations through the memoirs of Siegfried Sassoon, Robert Graves and Bernard Adams, who were all members of the Royal Welsh Fusiliers and were in

this sector before the battle began. The 'sites' to seek out on a visit include Wellington Redoubt, which was at the junction of the MARICOURT road; MAPLE REDOUBT on the FRICOURT–MÉAULTE road; Reduit A, which is where the artillery had their guns; and of course the Citadel itself.

There are two roads that lead southwards from the FRICOURT–CARNOY road; the eastern one leads to Point 110 Old Military Cemetery and then, a little further on, to the Point 110 New Military Cemetery, FRICOURT. They are 1 kilometre south of FRICOURT on a track running between the roads from FRICOURT and MAMETZ to Bray. Both the new and old cemeteries are near the side of the track, the old being 230 metres north of the new. Access to the cemeteries is along a rough track which starts in tarmac and finishes with gravel, so it is possible to access the cemetery by car. A little further south and on the other road (the D147) to the west is the Citadel New Military Cemetery, formerly known as Citadel Camp. It is approximately 2.5 kilometres south of FRICOURT on the east side of the road to Bray-sur-Somme. Access is off a roundabout created as a result of the new airport nearby. Begun by French troops, Citadel Military Cemetery was used by the British from August 1915 until November 1916 and again in August 1918. It lies in the northern part of the valley from FRICOURT to the Somme known as 'Happy Valley'. The great majority of the burials were carried out from field ambulances before the Somme battle began. One of these pre-battle burials was that of Cpl R. O'Brien (III.F.17) of 1st Royal Welsh Fusiliers (22nd Brigade, 7th Division), who was rescued by Sassoon in a raid that went wrong at Bois Français Craters to the north on the front line. O'Brien had died even before he was rescued; the register at the cemetery gives his date of death as 26 May 1916.

On 16 April 1916, 21st Field Ambulance (7th Division) handed over the main dressing station hospital for stretcher cases to 23rd Field Ambulance (also 7th Division). Three days later, after a large enemy raid was carried out at Mansell Copse, motor ambulances were sent up from the Citadel and the walking wounded went to BRAY-SUR-SOMME.

In *Nothing of Importance*, Bernard Adams noted that after he had been wounded he had been attended to by a Royal Army Medical Corps doctor who had given him tea and a second 'label'. He had also been given an injection against tetanus. This was probably in June.

At the beginning of the battle, the Citadel sector was in 7th Division's area of XV Corps. A Company, 1st Royal Welsh Fusiliers, were at Point 71 South, B Company at Point 71 North and D Company at the BOIS FRANÇAIS quarry; 20th Manchesters (also 22nd Brigade, 7th Division) were to their right. The objectives were the villages of MAMETZ and FRICOURT. In early July, the battle moved slowly forward but the Citadel was in continuous use for medical and billeting purposes. In *Memoirs of an Infantry Officer*, Siegfried Sassoon wrote that his battalion, 1st Royal Welsh Fusiliers, arrived here from MORLANCOURT and bivouacked on the hill behind the Citadel. After going up the line, they returned and fell asleep to the sound of guns and rattling limbers on the Citadel road. At the same time, Frenchmen were at work on the railroad at the Citadel; there were also crowds of guns in the neighbourhood. On 7 July, 38th Division were here prior to the struggle for MAMETZ WOOD and on 11 July, 21st Manchesters (91st Brigade, 7th Division) arrived at the Citadel from BUIRE-SUR-L'ANCRE; 2 days later they bivouacked at MAMETZ WOOD.

On 21 July, the headquarters of 2nd Division and 30th Division were stationed here and on 27 July, 55th Division's headquarters was opened at the camp. On 1 and 2 August, 35th and 24th Divisions both had their headquarters here, and on 10 August, 2nd Division headquarters was back. Later relieved by 17th Division, the exhausted 5th Division were here in early August. During his visit to the area on 10 August, King George V motored past the billets of the 22nd Royal Fusiliers (99th Brigade, 2nd Division), 2nd Division headquarters and the headquarters of 105th Brigade (35th Division). On 25 August, 104th Brigade (also 35th Division) came here, and 10th King's Royal Rifle Corps (59th Brigade, 20th Division) were at the camp in brigade reserve on 22/23 August.

An observer described the camp at the end of August as follows: 'The camp was situated in a vast plain, devoid of landmarks and bare and desert-like. They sheltered in contraptions like chicken hutches, with rabbit wire walls. The ground was badly smashed up, and covered with horse-lines and transports of other units. A huge French gun mounted on railway lines would arrive and fire a shell, immediately pulling away to some place further back by a steam engine.'

By early September, the roads towards the Citadel were deep in mud. At this time the camp covered an enormous area on the rolling hillside and presented an astounding spectacle of units from every arm of the services, including 1/5th Cheshires (pioneers of 56th Division) on 5 September. During September, units of 5th and 20th Divisions were in the camp and on 9 September, 1st Welsh Guards (3rd Guards Brigade, Guards Division) dumped their packs here with the transport on their way to GUILLEMONT. On the afternoon of 9 September, Brig Gen L.M. Phillpotts CMG, DSO (II.A.1), Commander Royal Artillery

24th Division, was killed at Maltz Horn Valley, GUILLEMONT, together with his brigade-major, Capt H.W. Crippin (II.A.2), Royal Artillery (56th Division); the two men are buried side by side at Citadel New Military Cemetery. In *Bloody Red Tabs*, the authors wrote: 'This morning practically all officers of the Divisional Artillery rode over to the Citadel for the General's funeral. The two coffins were carried by sergeants of the various Brigades, and covered with Union Jacks. They were buried side by side.'

After being involved in the fighting for LEUZE WOOD near COMBLES, 1/16th Londons (169th Brigade, 56th Division) spent 11 and 12 September here in huts and tents, and after a short rest of some 30 hours, moved forward on 13 September to the old German trench system near the Crucifix to the north of HARDECOURT-AU-BOIS. In *The Irish Guards in the Great War*, Rudyard Kipling wrote that after their failure in the fighting of 15 September, no one seemed to recall accurately the order of events between the gathering in BERNAFAY WOOD and the arrival of the shadow of the battalion at Citadel Camp. In October, units of 4th and 17th Divisions were here, as well as 4th Division headquarters; in November, 1st Guards Brigade (Guards Division) and units of 29th Division were here.

Quite a number of the men who are buried at Citadel New Military Cemetery were famous, or had high rank, or came from aristocratic backgrounds, and part of the cemetery reads like a page of *Who's Who*. The main reason for this is the close association that the area had with the Guards brigades during their role in the September battles. On 18 September, Lt Col G.V. Baring (II.A.9), a Conservative MP and Commanding Officer 1st Coldstream Guards, was buried here in a service that took place in pouring rain; H.L.N. Dundas of 1st Scots Guards attended the burial. Baring is commemorated in Winchester Cathedral; in the 1960s his widow wrote to the Coldstream Guards offering them her late husband's sword, which was subsequently held in the Cathedral. Other links with the aristocracy include the graves of 2/Lt A. Wernher (II.A.5) of 1st Welsh Guards, who died on 10 September and 2/Lt E. Cazalet (II.A.4), also of 1st Welsh Guards, who died on the same day. Maj T.M.D. Bailie (II.A.13) of 1st Irish Guards (1st Guards Brigade, Guards Division) died on 15 September. On 25 September, Lt G.A. Arbuthnot (II.C.1), the son of a general, had been killed while serving with 2nd Grenadier Guards (1st Guards Brigade, Guards Division), as was Capt A.K.S. Cuninghame (II.C.3), also of 2nd Grenadier Guards, who was killed in action at LESBŒUFS. He had been the last survivor of the original battalion.

Kipling wrote that 1st Irish Guards (1st Guards Brigade) were relieved on the evening of 26 September by their sister battalion, 2nd Irish Guards (2nd Guards Brigade), who took over the whole of the LESBŒUFS ruins from 1st Guards Brigade; 1st Irish Guards went back with others through BERNAFAY WOOD, where they fed, and later returned to the Citadel.

Aubrey Smith of 1/5th Londons (168th Brigade, 56th Division) wrote that on 26 September, his transport section moved its lines to the neighbour-hood of the Citadel, the name given to several camps and huts used by the infantry. On this day, patrols of 1/5th Londons had worked their way into COMBLES, where they had joined up with the French. Troops of 5th Division arrived at the Citadel Camp at this time and 1st Bedfords (15th Brigade, 5th Division) lost some of their troops to German night bombers. After being involved in the battle for EAUCOURT L'ABBAYE, 1/16th Londons (169th Brigade, 56th Division) handed over to 1/13th Londons (168th Brigade, 56th Division) and the whole battalion were withdrawn to the Citadel.

One battalion, while at the Citadel, had been issued with spotlessly white new tents, which had to be smeared with 'cutch' to stain them brown. The pioneer battalions cleared away a lot of furze on the opposite slope, which allowed enlargement of the camp. On 21 October, 2nd Royal Welsh Fusiliers (19th Brigade, 33rd Division) were in tents at the camp, and on 2 November, the Prince of Wales visited 2nd Rifle Brigade (25th Brigade, 8th Division) here, in his capacity as their Colonel-in-Chief.

In *Twelve Days*, Sidney Rogerson of 2nd West Yorkshires (23rd Brigade, 8th Division) noted that on the evening of 7 November, when the offensive was spluttering out in a sea of mud, his battalion were at Citadel Camp. He described it as being 'a dreary collection of bell tents perched insecurely on the hillside near the one time village of Fricourt'. Although he was an officer, commanding B Company, he had less experience of France than his two officer colleagues, who both wore the 1914 Star. On 10 November, they were to leave the camp and move to a map reference in the 'particularly salubrious' locality near BERNAFAY WOOD, and on the morrow they were to move back again to the Citadel, whence they had set out a week before. On 15 November, the battalion fell in by companies outside their tents to drag themselves and their Lewis-gun carts across the 5½ miles that separated the Brickworks from the Citadel. The carts were described as 'lunatic vehicles' that resembled a

species of shortened coffin; they were mounted on two wheels and provided with handles which were so near to the ground that the wretched pusher had almost to double up to grip them. At long last they came into sight of the familiar dirty bell tents and the high bank.

CLAIRFAYE FARM is between LÉALVILLERS and VARENNES on high ground slightly protected by a copse. During the war it had particular links with 36th Division, whose 108th Brigade were billeted in VARENNES and the neighbouring villages of LÉALVILLERS and HARPONVILLE. Prior to the battle, 36th Division carried out elaborate training exercises using a system of dummy trenches marked out with plough and spade representing the German SCHWABEN REDOUBT system to be attacked. This large training ground was known as Clairfaye Trenches. Although Clairfaye Farm was ideal for this sort of training, it is most famous for its use as a hospital. Its links with 109th and 110th Field Ambulances (both 36th Division) began 9 months before the planned battle. The Farm was connected to VARENNES by rail.

As early as 16 October 1915, the Farm was being run for the lightly wounded by 110th Field Ambulance, who were superintending patients in tents and bivouacs. On 5 November, the divisional rest station was taken over by 110th Field Ambulance and on 11 November, three new huts arrived, which were then put up.

On 28 April 1916, it was decided to build more huts here for the use of the evacuated and on 30 April the accommodation was further increased by the erection of several marquees. At the end of May, when 109th Field Ambulance moved back to the Farm, they brought with them lots of stores and their move took up most of the day. They took over the hospital the next day.

In *History of the 36th (Ulster) Division*, Cyril Falls described the medical arrangements for the southern part of the front as being peculiarly difficult:

The two Main Dressing Stations, for stretcher cases and 'walking wounded' respectively were at Forceville, manned by 108 Field Ambulance, and Clairfaye Farm, further west manned by 110 Field Ambulance. . . The motors of the Field Ambulance were parked on the Martinsart–Albert road south of the former village. For 'walking wounded' there was a collecting station west of Martinsart, whence horsed wagons carried them by a cross-country track through Hédauville to Clairfaye . . .

By 24 June, nine huts and one shelter were com-pleted; 600 patients could now be accom-modated, together with cooking arrangements for 1,000. Two horse ambulances arrived to assist with bringing the lightly wounded to the Farm. By 27 June, the Farm, in the hands of 110th Field Ambulance again, was beginning to get busy when 50 slightly wounded casualties arrived. By 0800hrs on 1 July, casualties from the attack at THIEPVAL began to arrive at FORCEVILLE, where they were fed and then sent on to Clairfaye. During the first 12 hours, the field ambulances admitted 500 stretcher cases.

At the Farm itself, a large number of wounded began to arrive; by 1100hrs, all forms of transport were being used to cope with the sheer number of casualties. They came by bus and motor ambulance and by any kind of conveyance, arriving all day, and were then evacuated by train. At 1300hrs, one officer, together with 18 other ranks, proceeded to THIEPVAL and a similar group to HAMEL, in order to reinforce the bearer subdivision. In response to a wire on 2 July, 110th Field Ambulance despatched 100 stretchers and blankets to Paisley Avenue at THIEPVAL, which were sent immediately. It should be noted that only 32 stretcher-bearers were allocated to each battalion.

On 5 July, after their abortive struggles to capture and hold the SCHWABEN REDOUBT at THIEPVAL, 36th Division were relieved by 49th Division, and 1/3rd (West Riding) Field Ambulance took over the divisional rest station here. At the end of November, there were two casualty clearing stations at the Farm, which housed a motor ambu-lance convoy attached to Fifth Army during the later stages of the battle.

COIGNEUX is a village between COUIN and SAILLY-AU-BOIS on the D152 road. Prior to the battle it was mostly used by units of 48th and 56th Divisions. On 27 July 1915, 1/3rd (South Midland) Field Ambulance (48th Division) arrived in the village and bivouacked in a field and also in the wood. In February 1916, one of the field companies of 48th Division worked at a quarry between COUIN and BAYENCOURT, and also at another quarry at BUS-LÈS-ARTOIS to the south. On 1 February, hurdles were being made by No. 1/1 (South Midland) Field Company, Royal Engineers (48th Division), in the wood here and a store for the Royal Engineers was begun.

On 15 May, after a period of training at BEAUVAL, 144th Brigade (48th Division) marched back to Coigneux and COUIN where they relieved 145th Brigade (also 48th Division). On 13 June,

1/8th Worcesters (144th Brigade, 48th Division) arrived here from Hem near DOULLENS for the night before moving to LOUVENCOURT and ACHEUX-EN-AMIÉNOIS. On 15 June, 1/7th Worcesters (also 144th Brigade, 48th Division) arrived here from Mezerolles, where they camped. Five days later, 1/8th Worcesters moved into billets close to here.

In *Four Years on the Western Front*, Aubrey Smith noted that at the end of May, 1/5th Londons (169th Brigade, 56th Division) had moved their horse-lines from BAYENCOURT to a sheltered valley near Coigneux, about 1 mile away; this would be on the western side of the road north-west to SOUASTRE. While there, companies who were close at hand went up to the line each night to carry out digging and other fatigues. On 3 June, 1/16th Londons (also 169th Brigade, 56th Division) moved here. In *Cannon Fodder*, A.S. Dolden of 1/14th Londons (168th Brigade, 56th Division) noted that at 2100hrs on 30 June, his battalion went to take up positions at HÉBUTERNE ready for 1 July; the cookers were taken by horse transport to the transport line at HAPPY VALLEY, which lay between Coigneux and SOUASTRE. This would be the same valley as that mentioned above by Aubrey Smith. On 1 July, 145th Brigade (48th Division) were here as part of the reserve to 143rd Brigade (also 48th Division) who were in the front line between HÉBUTERNE and SERRE.

On 11 July, 38th Division, after being relieved at MAMETZ WOOD, came to Coigneux and relieved 48th Division, who were taking over the line south of HÉBUTERNE. On 7 August, 61st Brigade (20th Division) were relieved by 71st Brigade (25th Division). In early September, 2nd Oxfordshire & Buckinghamshire Light Infantry (5th Brigade, 2nd Division) were in huts in the wood in divisional reserve and 1/4th Oxfordshire & Buckinghamshire Light Infantry (145th Brigade, 48th Division) moved via Jena Track and Valley Road to bivouac between the Dell and Coigneux. In November, there was a main dressing station in the village, as well as an advanced dressing station.

An article was published in *The Times* dated 31 May 1954, called 'The Somme Front Revisited, Thirty-Nine Years After', clearly written by a former member of the Royal Artillery. Like most ex-soldiers when visiting battlefields, he sought out positions which he formerly occupied, and was impressed as to just how much of the area had returned to normal. However, in his quest he had more success when visiting Coigneux:

Finally we came by a rough track to little Coigneux where the battery had its horse-lines. Here was no change except for a number of cars and an air of prosperity. Farm L'Hirondelle had not altered and the cows in their sheds seemed as comfortable and warm there as (on the whole) we had been. The winter horse-lines had become a thick orchard of old trees. The meadows were dry and hard, where at one time the horses had stood in liquid freezing mud. A recollection came of tall grey poplars in a meadow by a stream, and wild daffodils. The daffodils were still there and there were many more.

COISY is north-east of Amiens on the D11 road. On 29 July 1915, LXXXIV Brigade, Royal Field Artillery (18th Division), arrived here before moving to HEILLY and up to the lines 4 days later. It was also where much of 36th Division carried out its training exercises in October.

In the second week of February 1916, 15th Royal Warwicks (13th Brigade, 5th Division) were here. On 29 March, 19th Manchesters (21st Brigade, 30th Division) passed through the village for a night but were back again on 10 April for 2 days before moving on to FRÉCHENCOURT. On 11 June, together with the village of POULAINVILLE, the village was used for billeting purposes by 52nd Brigade (17th Division). On 1 July, the village, together with BERTANGLES to the west, was the base for 69th Brigade (23rd Division), while 68th Brigade (also 23rd Division) were at POULAINVILLE and ALLONVILLE.

COLINCAMPS, a village due west of SERRE, became very important as it was the nearest village of any size to the front in the SERRE sector. In the words of one commentator, it became a network of Allied defences; 'an intermediate city with streets, lanes, alleys, woods, copses, avenues and the like' was built up here.

On 5 February 1916, No. 9 Field Company, Royal Engineers (4th Division), arrived here while their horse-lines were still in Mailly to the south. On 4 March, other units of 48th Division were billeted here and sappers were making use of a water supply from the Sucrerie (sugar refinery), 1 mile to the east. Occasionally the village was shelled and at the end of the month two billets received direct hits. A few days later on 2 April, 1/7th Worcesters (144th Brigade, 48th Division) marched here to relieve 1/5th Glosters (145th Brigade, 48th Division). The following night, 1/7th Worcesters were relieved by 1/8th Worcesters (also 144th Brigade, 48th Division).

From April, the village became the home of 31st Division, who were training to take part in the opening offensive on the SERRE front, to the east. A main dressing station was set up in the village on 21 April. At the beginning of June, sappers erected a screen across the COURCELLES-AU-BOIS road to the west. On 3 and 4 June, 11th East Lancashires (94th Brigade, 31st Division) took part in a raid made from Colincamps; soon after, the enemy replied with a very heavy bombardment, which blew in the front-line trenches of their sister battalion, 10th East Yorkshires (92nd Brigade, 31st Division), who lost 2 officers and 20 men as well as 47 men wounded. The 22 dead 'were lying at Sackville Street Dump on the light railway and awaiting stretcher parties at nightfall, when bodies were to be conveyed to the ever-growing cemetery near the Sucrerie'. The Sucrerie, close to the Mailly–SERRE road, was also where shallow communication trenches were made to the front line at SERRE.

At this time, 18th Durham Light Infantry (93rd Brigade, 31st Division) were also in the village and were receiving increasing attention from German gunners. The battalion were engaged 'in digging assembly trenches, making dugouts and aid posts, burying cable and in other preparations for the great offensive'. The last civilians left the village on 14 June.

The HÉBUTERNE and Colincamps sectors were of great importance, for in large measure they commanded the valleys and spurs which ran from HÉBUTERNE in the south and south-easterly directions, along which both sides made their lines of defence and placed their artillery. The plain became full of battery positions, both heavy and field. Similarly, the Germans had large numbers of guns defending the Gommecourt Salient to the north and were active towards the British lines and also HÉBUTERNE and Colincamps. Except on the Hébuterne–Gommecourt ridge, where the two sides were on equal terms, the ground sloped down towards the German lines.

The Sucrerie facing the SERRE–Mailly road was already a heap of ruins; it lay just south of the famous Euston Dump, which was an entrance and exit point from the front using shallow communication trenches, except when German observation balloons hovered overhead. From this corner the road leads directly to SERRE and the road south-eastwards to AUCHONVILLERS is sunken.

Euston Dump was the main dump for, among other battalions, 10th East Yorkshires; towards the end of June, a party unloaded a fleet of lorries at the dump while wearing gas masks and took up heavy cylinders slung on a long pole towards emplacements which had been prepared under the front-line fire-steps.

As has been noted the village was the territory of 31st Division; on 1 July, 93rd and 94th Brigades (both 31st Division) were to attempt to take SERRE with the support of 92nd Brigade. On the eve of the battle, 16th and 18th West Yorkshires (both 93rd Brigade, 31st Division) were camped in an orchard to the north-west of the village, where they ate bully beef for supper.

The headquarters of 12th York & Lancasters (94th Brigade, 31st Division) was in an oblong schoolroom built of chalk with a slate roof in the village itself. Later, many men marched past the sugar factory on their way up to the line, passing rows of massed graves that had been made ready for the battle.

After the tragic events in front of the German-held villages of SERRE and PUISIEUX on 1 July, Gerald Brenan mentions these same graves in a harrowing extract in his autobiography, *A Life of One's Own*, which concerns events around early July. He had received orders to take his platoon to Colincamps, 1 or 2 miles along the ridge from HÉBUTERNE, for a burial party. The bodies, hundreds of them, were brought up on a trench railway from the front line, and bundled out onto the ground. Legs had broken off from trunks, heads rolled off at a touch and horrible liquids oozed out of the cavities. A sickening stench filled the air and obscene flies crept and buzzed, not to speak of the worms that wriggled in the putrefaction. Brenan's platoon were to cut the identity numbers from the corpses and then shovel them into shallow trenches which they had dug nearby. After 3 days of this he took a shovel and worked himself, and found that his morale completely vanished; he knew that if they were asked to go over the top the next morning that he would be unable to do so. The stench had brought the fear of death 'to his very bones'.

In his autobiographical novel, Frederic Manning of 7th King's Shropshire Light Infantry (8th Brigade, 3rd Division) mentioned that after his battalion had left COURCELLES-AU-BOIS for Colincamps, as they mounted the hill they came under direct enemy observation for about 300yds, so the road had been camouflaged with netting. At the top of the hill was a bend, and commanding the road, as well as another lesser road, was a more than usually substantial barn, a kind of bastion to the outskirts of Colincamps itself. The street at Colincamps ended, and the houses with it, on meeting a road with MAILLY-MAILLET to the right, and on the left continuing to the sugar factory, where it joined the main road from Mailly

to SERRE. They turned left down the hill road curving into the valley, and there was another military control. Leaving the road and picking their way between the gun pits and dugouts, they came again to Southern Avenue. When 'Bourne' returned to Colincamps, he met up with some Gordon Highlanders in order to obtain some brigade messages. He thought that it would be better to use Railway Avenue, as the Germans seemed to have got the Southern Avenue 'pretty taped'. He wrote that the shelling was worse in the corner in the direction of COURCELLES-AU-BOIS, and to have extended on this side further along the Mailly road. He made for the corner of Colincamps, doubling up the short rise with difficulty, and arrived at a relay post in a cellar. Only a few shells came into COURCELLES-AU-BOIS, said the runner, but they knew that the village and the dump were 'getting it'. After 3 days in the trenches the battalion were relieved and moved to COURCELLES-AU-BOIS. Unfortunately there is no date for this extract but as an account of the area it appears to be completely accurate.

On 2 July, 94th Field Ambulance (31st Division) were overwhelmed by having to cope with so many casualties, which only began to fall in number after a few days. The enemy continued to shell the village, and in mid-August it was described as having a variety of rest huts, ruins and trenches. It still had an advanced dressing station here in November.

Sucrerie Military Cemetery is 1 mile east of the village and 300yds north of the road to SERRE from Mailly. It stands on the south side of a private avenue leading from Colincamps to the site of the former sugar factory, but is approached from the other side of the path. The cemetery was begun by French troops when they occupied the sector in early summer 1915 and buried 285 of the men whose remains were later removed. It was extended by the British from 26 July 1915, when the first British casualties were buried. The cemetery stands on a wide plateau among cornfields, and there may be more pre-1 July 1916 casualties buried here than in any other cemetery on the Somme; the number of listed graves is now 894. There are more men (439) buried here who died in the 11 months prior to 1 July 1916 than in any other cemetery in the Department of the Somme. Two Lieutenant Colonels are buried here, J.A. Thicknesse (I.H.15) of 1st Somerset Light Infantry (11th Brigade, 4th Division) and The Hon. L.C.W. Palk (I.H.14), Commanding Officer 1st Hampshires (11th Brigade, 4th Division). They were said to have been killed with two other senior officers, D. Wood of 1st Rifle Brigade (11th Brigade, 4th Division) and E.A. Innes of 1/8th

Royal Warwicks (143rd Brigade, 48th Division), but these two men have their names on the Thiepval Memorial.

Lt Col Thicknesse is commemorated in St Mary Magdalene Church in Taunton, Somerset, in the same church as Brig Gen C.B. Prowse, General Officer Commanding 11th Brigade (4th Division). For many years the wooden cross from Prowse's grave in France hung in the church, but was later used as a cross strut of a table close to the Book of Remembrance.

As for Palk, he had insisted that 1 July 'was the greatest day the British Army had ever had'; starting at 0740hrs, he calmly led his men forward with his walking stick, having 'dressed himself up in his best clothes, [having] put on white gloves, and led the whole of his battalion forward across No Man's Land', where he himself and most of those with him became casualties. While lying mortally wounded in a shell-hole, he turned to another man lying next to him and said, 'If you know of a better 'ole, go to it.'

After 1st East Lancashires (11th Brigade, 4th Division) had been almost wiped out by fire from Ridge Redoubt, 1st Hampshires (11th Brigade, 4th Division) had followed; before they could get halfway across, or even reached the wire, the battalion were destroyed, losing 500 casualties. Thicknesse was killed in similar circumstances. Later, men from various battalions ended up in the Quadrilateral position near the Serre–Mailly road. After dark they were relieved and withdrew into their own divisional lines in Mailly. Also buried here is Capt G. Alison of the Seaforth Highlanders (I.H.36), a brother of Sir Archibald, 4th Baronet, who was also killed on 1 July 1916.

Euston Road Cemetery is close to the former dump of the same name and road junction. There are only five graves from the period prior to the Somme battle; Plot I, apart from several German graves in the back row, are from the main battle period and many are packed close together, showing the haste with which men were buried. The cemetery is particularly associated with the unsuccessful SERRE attack of 1 July, the capture of BEAUMONT-HAMEL on 13 November, and the attack on 5 April 1918 on 3rd New Zealand Rifle Brigade trenches in front of the village. After the German retreat in March 1917 it was little used until April and May 1918. The cemetery was designed by Sir Reginald Blomfield; after the Armistice, 758 graves were brought in from the local communes. The total number of identified casualties is 1,123.

Colincamps Communal Cemetery, on the east side of the road to MAILLY-MAILLET, contains the graves of nine New Zealand men who died when defending the village against the German advance in April and May 1918.

COMBLES is 10 miles east of ALBERT on the D20 RANCOURT–GUILLEMONT road and north-east of FAFFEMONT FARM. By the summer of 1916, the Germans had been in occupation for 2½ years and had built formidable entrenchments and extensive subterranean defences both in and around the town. The enemy had turned the town into a redoubt or fortified stronghold and opposite their position was the junction between the British and French lines. The town did not suffer to the same degree as neighbouring villages, as it was protected by the surrounding hills. It was an exceedingly strong position, as in addition to the hills giving it protection it was enclosed at the bottom of a valley, and was out of reach of the Allied artillery. The town was so well fortified and immune to artillery that it would be better to enter it 'by the back door rather than by the front'. The enemy were determined to hold on to the town, which they managed until mid-September.

The battle for the central ridge raged all through August 1916 and LONGUEVAL and DELVILLE WOOD were still in German hands at this time and most of GUILLEMONT as well. Combles Trench was a German trench running along the south-west face of Combles; it was not appreciated by the attackers that it was protected by strong uncut wire entanglements, which in turn were hidden by standing corn and weeds. It was also under heavy machine-gun protection from BOULEUX WOOD to the north. 7th Royal Irish Fusiliers (49th Brigade, 16th Division) were one of the battalions who had to wade through the corn with the belts of wire 'sown' in it.

The capture of Combles was planned to be part of the Battle of Morval, which also included the taking of LESBŒUFS and GUEUDECOURT. The Allies made progress in the first half of September in the whole region and the villages of Forest, MAUREPAS, GUILLEMONT and GINCHY fell during this period.

An article on their defence of Combles called 'Im Felde Unbesiegt' by the German Generalleutnant Balck appeared in volume LXX of the *RUSI Journal*; the relevant passage noted that

from 12 to 16 September the Allies, although they had worked well forward on both sides of Combles had still failed to compel its evacuation. They therefore determined to devote their next operations to the capture of the town and its garrison, in the same way that they had invested and secured Guillemont a few days previously, despite all efforts to relieve it. Each Regiment of the German Division had one battalion in the line, one in reserve, and one resting. On the right in touch with the left of the 52nd Res. Division, the 236 Res. Reg. held Morval, then came the 235th and 234th Res. Reg; the latter in Combles. There were very few machine guns available and there were about 1,200 rifles in line. Opposed to this thin line were five French and British Divs. all good troops; among the latter were Guards, Canadians and Scotch, with others in reserve, and Cavalry behind.

Generalleutnant Balck was at the time commander of 51. Reserve Division, which had been in a quiet part of Flanders since August 1914 and came to the Somme region in September 1916. The ground around Combles at this time was nothing but a 'field of craters', though shelters might be found in the deep catacombs beneath the houses of the town. In this sector, trenches, dugouts, wire, communications, had been blown out of existence; the infantry, in order to conceal their positions from hostile aircraft and artillery observation, had to establish themselves as best they could in lines of shell-holes. Rear lines of defence did not exist, supplies and ammunition, owing to the constant hostile barrage, could be brought up only by night. Balck recommended that they pay close attention to cooperation with their neighbours and also with the artillery; and immediate counter-strokes should be carried out in order to recover any lost position. He also asked for reports to be sent back as frequently as possible by all available means. On 3 September, 51. Reserve Division took over the reserve line and the front line on the fourth night after the issue of the first orders for their move.

Balck wrote that they were outnumbered by six men to one at least. All day long the hostile fire, skilfully directed from the air, continued against the German positions; the artillery at the latter's disposal (18 field batteries and 56 heavy guns) was insufficient to counter it effectively. The infantry of the defence, therefore, could only work at night, and were exposed throughout the daylight hours to the destructive effect of hostile bombardment. The British and French, who were kept far back and only brought up shortly before the opening of their attacks, thus had both morally and materially a great advantage. The ridge of high ground which had been the object of the Allied attack was cleft towards its southern end by a broad and deep valley known as Combles Valley. Immediately to the north of the town the valley widened out into a basin and then forked, running north-east and skirting the spur on which MORVAL stood.

In *The Irish Guards in the Great War*, Rudyard Kipling noted that the Allied advance held the main ridge of land in the Combles sector (in mid-September) but had not gone beyond it. The French left was almost equally restricted by the valley where Combles, among its quarries and hidden shelters, squatted and dealt death, with all the heights to the north, MORVAL, LESBŒUFS and LE TRANSLOY joined, with SAILLY-SAILLISEL and Saint-Pierre-Vaast in the east, to make sure. It was necessary, then, to free the ground at the junction of the two armies in the direction of MORVAL, which commanded far too complete a fire; also beyond GINCHY towards LESBŒUFS where the outlying spurs of high land raked LEUZE WOOD, a wood which was north-west of Combles and opposite BOULEUX WOOD.

By mid-September, Combles had finally become untenable to the Germans because it was dominated by the British right at LEUZE WOOD and by the French on the opposite heights. Balck noted that on 20 September the British captured and consolidated a portion of the line held by 52. Reserve Division and on 22 September the French drove 213. Infanterie Division, on the left of 51. Reserve Division, from the sugar factory south of Combles. Early on 25 September, it became clear to the Germans that the expected large-scale attack was about to take place. The advance was accomplished, assisted by swarms of low flying aeroplanes. South of Combles the French stormed Le Priez Farm, driving back 213. Infanterie Division, continued their advance and occupied RANCOURT. The *Official History of the War* notes that it was reported that the Germans were going to evacuate Combles on the night of 25 September. Subsequently, a detachment of the 1/14th Londons (168th Brigade, 56th Division) worked through the northern half of BOULEUX WOOD, finding no Germans, while 1/1st Londons (167th Brigade, 56th Division) did likewise through the southern half. Patrols of the last named reached as far as the orchard and one had entered Combles and joined up with the French. Further south, 1/5th Londons (169th Brigade, 56th Division) were working steadily forward down Combles Trench and joined hands with the French at the light railway track. 1/1st Londons then pushed into the village on the GINCHY road and it became clear that most of the enemy had indeed already left the town.

In the Michelin battlefield guide is the following account:

A fresh Anglo/French attack was launched on 25 September, after a terrific bombardment, with the object of encircling the fortress by the capture of the strongpoints which still protected it on the east and north. On the south-east the French started from their trenches in the old German positions at le Priez Farm – a powerful redoubt protected by six lines of defences which they had carried by assault on 14 September and captured the hamlet of Fregicourt. On the east they carried Rancourt village, and all intermediary positions between these two points, advancing as far as the north-west corner of St Pierre Vaast Wood. On the north the British took the fortified villages of Morval and Lesbœufs and nearly joined hands with the French – traces of German occupation include concrete shelters, strong-points for machine guns, underground passages, chambers etc. The tunnels excavated out of solid rock under Lamotte Castle, which had already existed before the war, were the most important of the subterranean organisations. The Germans utilised them as posts of commandment, dressing stations, mustering places etc. They were large enough to shelter several companies a time and were sufficiently proof against the heaviest projectiles. Opposite the 'ruined' church was the entrance to the underground passages and chambers to Lamotte Castle.

In an account of the day's events in *Sir Douglas Haig's Great Push*, it is noted that for the Allies Tuesday, 26 September was perhaps the greatest day in the whole of the Battle of the Somme. In the early dawn the French forced their way into the cemetery and south-east part of Combles, while simultaneously the British broke the last of the trenches into the village from the west. The German garrison though, by this time reduced to about two battalions, offered stout resistance, but by 1030hrs the British and French advance parties had come in touch near the railway station, where they saluted one another and shook hands over '*la Belle Alliance*'. A concerted assault was then delivered, and by noon the whole of the town was in Allied hands.

In *Johnny Get Your Gun*, J.F. Tucker of 1/13th Londons (168th Brigade, 56th Division) noted that after being unsuccessful in the joint Allied operation it was decided to attack the town of Combles on each flank. 1/14th Londons led the fighting around BOULEUX WOOD, the French attacking the other side of Combles. The QUADRILATERAL strongpoint had been captured by the Guards, thus protecting the British left flank from enfilading fire, which had held up previous assaults. Four tanks were also due to take part, but three of them broke down at the start and the fourth was soon hit by a shell; 1/13th Londons were in support. This time everything went well; the British and the French broke through on each side, forcing the Germans to withdraw from the town, 1/14th Londons joining up with the French in Combles. Tucker himself was detailed with one other man to go to LEUZE WOOD, where they 'chanced it' and scampered forward to the low parapet and into a clearing some 50yds square, which had been dug out about 6ft below the surrounding ground inside the corner of the remains of LEUZE WOOD.

Aubrey Smith, serving with the transport of 1/5th Londons (169th Brigade, 56th Division), noted that patrols worked their way into Combles, where they met the French from the other side. This 'pinching out' process had been successful, for the attack of the preceding day had forced the Germans to evacuate the town – some hundreds of prisoners trooping along past the CITADEL in the evening as a result of the fighting. They set to work to build a bivouac near the Sandpits on the ALBERT–BRAY-SUR-SOMME road. He presumably meant near MÉAULTE.

Generalleutnant Balck noted his view of the day that the town itself had been heavily shelled throughout the night of 24/25 September, and only with great difficulty could food and water be got up to the German garrison. A wide gap had opened up between the flanks of 52. and 51. Reserve Divisions and the garrison at Combles. Therefore the withdrawal of troops from the town began at about 2030hrs and the front lines were evacuated at about 2200hrs. The Germans re-established a fighting front west of SAILLY-SAILLISEL which, however, had no great power of resistance; fortunately, the Allies occupied Combles at midday on 26 September. On 27 September, part of the front of 213. Infanterie Division in front of RANCOURT was carried by the French; SAILLY-SAILLISEL, which at one time seemed endangered, held firm, despite continued Allied efforts to capture it both on 27 and 28 September. On the evening of the latter day, 51. Reserve Division were relieved and sent back to rest behind the lines.

In his memoirs, Gen Ludendorff wrote of the period: 'Great were our losses . . . the enemy took Rancourt, Morval, Gueudecourt, and the hotly contested Combles.'

As a result of this important advance, 1,200 prisoners were taken by the Allies, together with enormous quantities of war material. The sunken road to SAILLY-SAILLISEL was the only line of communication left to the Germans and it was shelled by both sides, which resulted in very heavy losses for the enemy. During September, Capt E.P. Dark, a medical officer with 9th Field Ambulance (Guards Division), was instructed to take over an advanced dressing station which turned out to be 'a sort of little hut, pretty well sand-bagged, with a couple of bunks and a good brazier. We were lucky in that we found a large dump of coal briquettes in Combles, so had as much fuel as we wanted. The dressing station wasa Nissen hut close by, also well sand-bagged.'

In *Have You Forgotten Yet?* C.P. Blacker of 4th Coldstream Guards (pioneers of the Guards Division) noted that at the end of December 1916, his division took over some of the lines here which had been captured by the French on 26 September. Largely demolished, but not yet reduced to rubble, the town had been left by the French in a mess as usual. The town boasted deep cellars, which had initially been used by the Germans, then by the French and finally by the British.

During the German advance in March 1918, Combles was once again the scene of fierce fighting; South Africans and New Zealanders, along with the British, attempted a stand here but were driven out on 24 March. Five months later the Allies regained the town on 29 August, with the Germans this time being routed by 18th Division. By now Combles had become simply a pile of bricks and the narrow-gauge railway in the valley was reduced to a mass of twisted metal.

The Combles Guards' Cemetery is on the south-west outskirts of the town, 74yds from a byroad towards MAUREPAS. It was begun by the Guards Division in September 1916 and carried on by other units until March 1917 and to a small extent in August and September 1918. After the Armistice, 56 graves were brought into Plot II from Priez Farm Cemetery, which stood at the south-east corner of le Priez Farm on the north side of the RANCOURT road; the farm was captured by 18th Division on 1 September 1918.

Combles Communal Cemetery is a triangular piece of ground on the north-east side of the town, at the parting of the roads to Fregicourt and LE TRANSLOY, and once had the grave of a wounded signaller, captured and subsequently buried by a Bavarian field ambulance in 1915. His remains were later transferred to Combles Communal Cemetery Extension, which is at the back, or north-east, of the Combles Communal Cemetery and was begun in October 1916 by French troops; the 94

French graves made in that year have since been moved to another cemetery and the first British burials were made in December. However, they had been preceded by the graves of 194 Germans buried in June–August 1916, which were later removed from Plot I. The following were among those brought into the Combles Communal Cemetery Extension: Fregicourt Communal Cemetery, situated in a hamlet between Combles and Saillisel; Leuze Wood Cemetery, at the north-east corner of LEUZE WOOD; Longtree Dump Military Cemetery, SAILLY-SAILLISEL, a little south of the MORVAL–SAILLY-SAILLISEL road; and Maurepas Military Cemetery on the south-west side of MAUREPAS village.

The cemetery register, published in 1929, recorded the names of 1,050 men, actual or commemorated. The Imperial War Graves Commission made use of some spare land for more burials here in the early 1930s and 448 bodies were reburied in the period from 10 December 1932 to 24 May 1953.

In 1923, Boyd Cable wrote several articles for *The Times* under the heading of 'The Vanishing Front'; in October, he wrote of Combles after the war: 'Being rebuilt on the two sides of a steep valley, it arrests the eye as a surprising spectacle of reconstruction work. As one looks down on the red houses and across the valley at the climbing street and roofs piled one above another like oranges on a barrow, Combles seems a wholly rebuilt village.'

CONTALMAISON is 4 miles north-east of ALBERT on the D104 road between LA BOISSELLE and LONGUEVAL. North-west of MAMETZ WOOD, it had a dominating position at the junction of several roads and was surrounded with redoubts, and defended by the Prussian Guards. John Masefield described it as lying on the top of a spur some 500yds to the north-east of HORSESHOE TRENCH. It had a perfect field of fire in all directions and was trenched with a wired line, which was strongly held. The château was just to the north of the church and slightly above the rest of the village. Up and until the village was captured an observation post, known as the Contalmaison Tower, had direct communication links with German HQ in the cellars of the Chateau. There was a chalk pit near the village, which at the beginning of the war possessed 72 houses, making it the seventh largest village on the Somme. The cutting called Contalmaison Villa was situated at the northern point of a fault to the ridge whose crest sloped greatly downwards for a distance of 800yds, when it descended more steeply towards FRICOURT.

The original Allied plan was for 34th Division to capture the village and establish a line in front of the German Second Line during the evening of 1 July. Although this was not to be, several small parties from this division did manage to reach the village that day.

Masefield wrote that rain hindered the advance throughout the next 3 days, and attacks on the approaches to the village and MAMETZ WOOD proceeded. On the west side of the Contalmaison spur the British carried the fortified copses and HORSESHOE TRENCH after 3 days of most bloody and determined fighting. On the east side of the spur, the British attacked the QUADRANGLE, and on gaining three sides of it, attacked the fourth side. This fourth side, known as Quadrangle Support, could be reinforced from the village and from MAMETZ WOOD, and could be observed and fired into from both places; the British got into it and took it in a night attack, but could not hold it.

When the Horseshoe fell early on 7 July, a big attack was put in against the whole of the two spurs, beginning with a very heavy bombardment upon the ruins of the village and the wood. The British reached the village, took part of it, and found and released in one of the dugouts there, a party of Northumberland Fusiliers who had been captured by the Germans on 2 July.

The only 'easy approach' to the village was from the west, near to the Horseshoe, where the slope is gentler than it is to the south or south-west. The eastern approach was still blocked by Quadrangle Support. The 'easy approach' was not without its difficulties; troops using it had to go down a slope into Shelter Valley, which was open and in fact without shelter, and was in full view of the enemy entrenched above them.

The British line 'bulged out' towards Contalmaison village, but a wood called BAILIFF WOOD stood between the British and the mainly German-held village. A battalion of the Durham Light Infantry belonging to 68th Brigade (23rd Division) sent out patrols and found that the wood was occupied on its southern face when they came under heavy machine-gun fire from it as well as from Contalmaison and Quadrangle Support. However, later they did in fact capture the wood, consolidated its eastern face, and reached a point 50yds to the north-west of the village, where they came under heavy machine-gun fire. The Germans counter-attacked and pushed back the British, who then retaliated. A German gun position and four guns were abandoned by the Germans and the British pushed northwards until they overlooked POZIÈRES. Machine guns had been established in the north end of BAILIFF WOOD. Contalmaison on the right still had not been taken, and it was decided, because of the exposure, to try again from the east when the troops could reach their positions without being observed.

At midnight (7/8 July), companies of 11th Royal Warwicks (112nd Brigade, 37th Division) were to occupy the work in the German line known as Heligoland. The remainder of the battalion passed the night on the Tara-Usna Ridge. 11th Royal Warwicks had received orders to relieve 58th Brigade (19th Division) in the positions between LA BOISSELLE and Contalmaison, which had been taken on 7 July. At 2045hrs on a fine evening, the battalion passed the south end of the ridge, crossed the old front line, and thence went up Sausage Valley into the battle zone. Headquarters was established about 300yds south-west of the lines in an extensive dugout. The previous day it had been the battle centre of the German regimental commander; it was two storeys deep and fitted up in the most complete and elaborate way with all modern conveniences. Here 11th Royal Warwicks installed the first aid post, the headquarters signallers and orderlies and a section of No. 112 Company, Machine Gun Corps.

W.D. Croft wrote that on 7 July, his 68th Brigade (23rd Division), which had been at Bécourt Wood in bivouacs, set off to try and capture part of Contalmaison village. Their advance was heavily enfiladed from Quadrangle Trench and also by fire from BAILIFF WOOD. Because of their exposed positions, they were not assisted by reinforcements being sent up. A battalion of the Durham Light Infantry were in the vacated assembly trenches. Croft decided to concentrate on the left, which was less exposed, and after dark the German redoubt at Point 81 was captured and posts established. On the west side there was open ground, swept by the German guns, across which there were only two lines of approach: one, by inadequate communication trenches, from which it was impossible to debauch; the other, by the direct approach from the south which was completely at the mercy of German artillery in the POZIÈRES direction.

Philip Gibbs wrote that 'Our guns were concentrating their fire along a line north of Birch Tree Wood from Horseshoe Trench, now in our hands, across Peake Woods and Quadrangle Trench away to Mametz Wood on the right. We were also putting a terrific barrage around the village of Contalmaison and Acid Drop Copse.' In his *The War Dispatches*, he wrote of Contalmaison: 'There were moments when its old French château, set in a little wood, was lit up by a splash of golden light as the white clouds drifted by, so that I could almost count its bricks, and could see how the shells which I watched yesterday had opened its roofs. But the left-hand tower was knocked off this morning by a direct hit from the same battery which took the whole tower *en passant.*'

On the left of Contalmaison was BAILIFF WOOD, north-eastwards of the Horseshoe Redoubt; away to the right of Contalmaison was MAMETZ WOOD, even more important both in size and position, with BERNAFAY WOOD still further eastwards and TRÔNES WOOD on the right again. Other small woods or copses south of Contalmaison were strong fighting points, from SHELTER WOOD to Round Wood and Birch Wood at the top of the sunken road and PEAKE WOODS to the left of Quadrangle Trench. Some of these places were but a few shell-slashed trees serving as landmarks, but BAILIFF WOOD, MAMETZ WOOD, BERNAFAY WOOD and TRÔNES WOOD were still dense thickets under heavy foliage, hiding both Allied and German troops but giving no protection from shell-fire.

The main trench leading up to Contalmaison was the sunken road that went up between Round Wood and Birch Wood, and was being heavily barraged by the enemy's guns, sweeping down from POZIÈRES. Further up and slanting right to Pearl Alley was a shallow trench. A curious affair was happening in a trench called Old Jaeger Trench, running out of Horseshoe towards a German redoubt to the west of PEAKE WOODS. Part of this trench was held by the troops on the left and part by the troops on the right, and both reported and believed that they held all of it. The truth was that a gap in the middle was still held by a party of Germans, who had machine guns and bombs with which, soon, they made themselves unpleasant. Orders were sent to clear the trench of these 'ugly customers' and it was done by the troops on the left. Then orders were given to clear forward to a triangle to the right of the Old Jaeger. It was a strong redoubt – it yielded finally when the troops on the right fought their way up to PEAKE WOODS, captured it, and enfiladed the enemy with machine-gun fire.

According to their war diary entry of 8 July (WO95/1722), 2nd Northamptons (24th Brigade, 23rd Division) found that the enemy had evacuated the village and therefore they and 1st Worcesters (also 23rd Brigade, 24th Division) were to occupy the village. However, as the four companies moved forward, they were severely hampered by heavy machine-gun and artillery fire, and although one

Contalmaison Château when in German hands, 1915–16. *(Peter F. Batchelor Collection)*

company commander reached a line a little beyond PEAKE WOODS, hardly any men accompanied him. Most of the company commanders were either killed or severely wounded in this advance; one of them, Maj F.T. Williams, was taken to hospital at Rouen, where he died after 4 days. His grave is in Saint-Sever Cemetery (A.3.3) and his rank after his death was given as lieutenant-colonel.

On 9 July, 23rd Division attacked Contalmaison with 24th and 68th Brigades from the south and west of the village; 69th Brigade was to pass through the lines of the other brigades on the following day. The enemy bombarded 68th Brigade's shallow trenches, which were full of men. 12th Durham Light Infantry (68th Brigade, 23rd Division) consolidated ground from which 69th Brigade attacked. 8th Royal Berkshires (1st Brigade, 1st Division) marched to ALBERT and took over two trenches from 10th Glosters (also 1st Brigade, 1st Division), who had relieved 24th Brigade (23rd Division) in the afternoon.

On 11 July, 13th Durham Light Infantry (68th Brigade, 23rd Division) were relieved. At 2115hrs, 8th Yorkshires (69th Brigade, 23rd Division), who had taken Contalmaison the previous night, were relieved. 8th Royal Berkshires established themselves in the château grounds, with 1st Black Watch (also 1st Brigade, 1st Division) on the left. In the château were cellars, which were occupied by a German medical officer in charge of the 110 wounded Germans. Before morning, 8th Royal Berkshires were to take the cutting north-east of the château. Since 3 July, 7th, 17th and 23rd Divisions had all attempted to capture the village; in the end it was captured by 17th and 38th Divisions. Geoffrey Malins, the official War Office photographer, filmed in the village on 9 and 10 July, soon after its capture.

In *The Turning Point*, H.P. Robinson, war correspondent of *The Times*, noted that by 10 July the British had worked their way up on the left, or west, side into BAILIFF WOOD, which, while the British had penetrated it before, was higher than at any point that they had formerly occupied. At 1630hrs on 10 July, 11th Royal Warwicks assembled in outer trenches and launched an attack against the village from the west. An attempt by the Prussian Guard to counter-attack was bloodily repulsed, and Lewis guns caught the disordered elements of that force as they emerged from the outskirts of the village. At 1935hrs, more orders arrived; this time to seize BAILIFF WOOD in conjunction with a battalion of 11th Brigade (4th Division). The Germans were shelled out of Quadrangle Trench and the village was heavily bombarded as well. HORSESHOE TRENCH was captured and 2/Lt D. Bell of 9th Yorkshires (69th Brigade, 23rd Division), shortly to be awarded a posthumous Victoria Cross, was killed in repelling Germans trying to enter the village.

Sir Douglas Haig's Great Push states that BAILIFF WOOD had been carried by a 'dashing assault'; the prospects on the western side were so good that it was decided to make the effort there, instead of from the south, in spite of the distance to be covered. The Germans had expected the attack from the south, and most of the machine guns were trained that way when, towards 0500hrs on 11 July, the British advanced upon them from the east. They had to traverse some 1,100yds to open ground, and the infantry advanced to push forward more rapidly; by 0700hrs the whole of the village was in their possession. The artillery had materially contributed to the success.

Relieved by 10th Loyal North Lancashires (112th Brigade, attached 34th Division), 11th Royal Warwicks returned to the Tara-Usna Ridge and became brigade reserve, bivouacking on the reverse slope of the Tara-Usna Ridge; the enemy shelled the position with 5.9in pieces. On 13 July, 11th Royal Warwicks were relieved and went into close support; on 16 July, they were ordered to support 111th Brigade (attached 34th Division) and moved to the chalk pit, carrying spare ammunition and bombs to form a dump there.

At midnight on 12/13 July, Pearl Wood was taken by a patrol; at the same time, a battalion of the Black Watch captured Contalmaison Wood to the left of the château. At 1500hrs on 13 July, the battalion were moved from the château so that their left was now at the Stanley's Hole, and their centre in the sunken road to the right of 1st Division; 8th Royal Berkshires were ordered to move up to get into the German Second Line. In the late afternoon of 14 July, 1st Glosters (3rd Brigade, 1st Division) were given instructions to take over the line near Contalmaison, which lay just north of the village, along the road to LONGUEVAL, and continued westward of the junction of the latter with the road leading to MARTINPUICH. On either side of their point of union the roads had high banks, and this was the area known as the Stanley's Hole. D Company held the trenches on the right and B Company held the Stanley's Hole and its continuation westward; A and C Companies were in support in lengths of trench among the ruins of the village, at the western edge of which headquarters was lodged in a cellar. The site of the former church was marked by a great white stone; all that remained of the château was its vast cellars, now used as a dressing station; the other house, flimsily built, had vanished. In *Memoirs of a Camp Follower*, Philip Gosse of 69th Field Ambulance (23rd Division) wrote of his time here during the battle:

> Our advanced dressing station was in some wonderful German dugouts beneath a great heap of bricks and rubble which once had been the Château of Contalmaison. Marvelous and elaborate dugouts these were, far better that any we ever had to show. You went down a flight of steps, deeper and deeper, some quite large ones, dug out of the solid earth. . . . These dugouts, when we first occupied them, were in a state of great disorder, with every evidence of the hurried departure of the previous tenants.

It was also clear to Gosse that at one point women used to occupy part of these cellars. 'There was plenty of work to do at Contalmaison, for the wounded kept pouring down in a steady stream which grew to a flood wherever a battle was being fought on the ridge above.'

There were dugouts in the Stanley's Hole, and there was a cemetery south of the village, on the road that led to MAMETZ WOOD. Close to it was a very large dugout, which had a wonderful view of the ground over which the attackers were to advance. Close to the entrance lay a machine gun, with its German crew dead around it. On 15 July, a long sap called Pearl Alley, which ran forward from near the right of 1st Glosters' line, was found to be unoccupied and steps were taken to prevent the Germans from getting hold of it. In addition, Contalmaison Villa, nearly half a mile forward on the MARTINPUICH road, was found to be empty and was occupied. The small copse called Pearl Wood was secured as well. During the night of 15/16 July, 3rd Brigade were involved in a successful night attack, in which 1st Glosters had 450yds of enemy line to capture; on the left, 2nd Royal Munster Fusiliers (3rd Brigade, 1st Division) were equally successful. 1st Glosters attacked and took the German positions, which appeared to be more or less parallel with a line drawn from Contalmaison to Pearl Wood, south-south-east of the Villa. A signalling lamp was placed in Pearl Wood so that it could be seen from the Villa. 1st Glosters also took part in evicting the enemy from Bazentin Wood. Late in the evening of 17 July, 1st Glosters were relieved and went out to SCOTTS REDOUBT to rest. In the main, A.W. Pagan's book *Infantry* has provided this account of 1st Glosters' doings.

At 2000hrs on 17 July, 12th Durham Light Infantry attacked and were heavily caught by machine-gun fire; subsequently, the attack planned for 18 July was cancelled. Over the next 2 days, 12th Durham Light Infantry dug trenches and consolidated. Croft's 68th Brigade headquarters was in Sausage Valley in a deep German dugout. On 19 July, there was a heavy gas bombardment. His brigade were relieved by an Australian brigade and returned to ALBERT. A few days later, they joined the right of an Australian division; the dividing line was MUNSTER ALLEY. It had been the scene of heavy fighting by both the British and the Australians. On 26/27 July, they relieved the Australians in turn. The château had an advanced dressing station and another post was at the edge of MAMETZ WOOD. On 27 July, after a heavy bomb fight, 12th Durham Light Infantry first gained 70yds and 'locked' the trench; that night they deepened a ditch called Lancashire Trench. On 28 July, no progress was made in MUNSTER ALLEY and that night they were relieved.

Pte W. Short of 8th Yorkshires (69th Brigade, 23rd Division) was to be awarded the Victoria Cross for an action on 6 August at MUNSTER ALLEY, near which the composer George Butterworth of 13th Durham Light Infantry (68th Brigade, 23rd Division) had been killed previously. Born in Middlesbrough, Short was foremost in the attack, bombing the Germans with great gallantry, when he was severely wounded in the foot. He was urged to go back, but refused and lay in the trench adjusting detonators and straightening the pins of bombs for his comrades. He died before he could be carried out of the trench. For the previous 11 months he had always volunteered for dangerous enterprises, and had always set a magnificent example of bravery and devotion to duty. His grave (II.B.16) is in Contalmaison Château Cemetery.

D.W.J. Cuddeford of C Company, 12th Highland Light Infantry (46th Brigade, 15th Division), arrived from the 15th Division detail near CORBIE with another officer of his battalion and occupied a recently captured German trench near Villa Wood, Contalmaison. On 12 August, 12th Highland Light Infantry had gone over the top for the first time in that sector against a strong system of trenches known as the Switch Line, in front of BAZENTIN-LE-PETIT and a little to the left of HIGH WOOD. The attack was unsuccessful, but a second attack on 25 August succeeded. The battalion then withdrew into reserve, but went into the line again in early September. Having been in the line again, on 13 September they were withdrawn to reserve trenches in the neighbourhood of Villa Wood. 12th Highland Light Infantry were to act as brigade reserve and also supply ammunition carrying parties; Cuddeford was in charge of one of these. Relieved by 8th/10th Gordon Highlanders (44th Brigade, 15th Division), the battalion went back to the dugouts near Villa Wood, between Contalmaison and BAZENTIN-LE-PETIT and close to MAMETZ WOOD.

On 14 September, battalions supplied working parties for road-mending based at the Stanley's Hole. Nissen huts were built on either side of the FRICOURT–Contalmaison road.

The château was headquarters of a field ambulance towards the end of September; in his memoir, Philip Gosse wrote: 'on September 24th the Colonel and I were standing outside a former German dugout in Martinpuich when the Colonel was suddenly killed by a bullet to the brain. He was buried that night in the garden of the Château . . . The chaplain who conducted the hurried service wore his surplice over his uniform, and like the mourners, kept his steel hat on, for there was a lot of shelling going on all round.'

In *The Great War As I Saw It*, F.G. Scott, a member of the Canadian forces, noted that in September, at the corner of a branch road just above the ruins of Contalmaison, their engineers had put up a little shack which was used by Army chaplains and where coffee and biscuits were distributed. It was called Casualty Corner and had been started by the Australians. The once fine château was now a heap of bricks, and as already mentioned the Germans had used the cellars as a dressing station, which was very large and had dugouts branching off from it. The road turning to the left led down to a waste of weary ground in a wide valley where many different units were stationed in dugouts and holes in the ground. Towards POZIÈRES road was the famous Chalk Pit. In the hillside were large dugouts, used when the battalions were out of the line. There was also a light railway.

On one of his 'tours', C.E. Montague took Muirhead Bone to Contalmaison and showed him the dressing station there; the château itself at this time had been destroyed. Later they went back down the slope to eat their lunch and below them was the battle. Despite Montague's calm elation at the scene, Bone wrote that the sandwiches and his teeth didn't seem to keep proper time together.

In October, there were many camps established in the area around the village, which were regularly

Contalmaison Château after July 1916.
(Peter F. Batchelor Collection)

shelled by the enemy. One camp was at Acid Drop Copse, which caught the German barrage. On 2 November, 1/4th Oxfordshire & Buckinghamshire Light Infantry (145th Brigade, 48th Division) were in support between LE SARS and MARTINPUICH. They moved forward via Tramway and the Corduroy Track. In a letter dated that day, Graham Greenwell, who was in this battalion, wrote 'a hurried line amidst filthiest surrounds to let you know that we are just off to the trenches. Last night we camped on what was German ground before 1 July, in a filthy, muddy camp of tents and bivouacs; outside the remains of what had been a famous village during the "Push". The mud is perfectly ghastly, never have I seen anything like it: men and horses are caked in it from head to foot. It takes ten horses to get the smallest guns out.'

Charles Carrington of 1/5th Royal Warwicks (143rd Brigade, 48th Division) noted that in November he went to a new raw camp made of 'Elephant Huts' at SCOTTS REDOUBT near Contalmaison in the devastated area, a commanding height from which one could obtain a view for about 4 or 5 miles in any direction over a landscape entirely composed of mud. The Germans were 7 miles away and they were safe, except from very long-range shell-fire. One camp was known as Contalmaison Villa Camp and another near the village was called Pioneer Camp. At the end of November, the village was 'flatter' than ever, but the deep machine-gun dugouts were still there, intact.

After the war, Marshal Foch unveiled a memorial to the 102nd (Tyneside Scottish) and 103rd (Tyneside Irish) Brigades. It was designed as a semicircular seat and is on the ALBERT road at a point where it branches off to Contalmaison.

Contalmaison Château Cemetery is within the château grounds on the north side of the main street, and the pathway to it passes the ruins of the château; begun by fighting units on the evening of 14 July, it was used by field ambulances from September 1916 to March 1917. Pte W. Short VC, who died on 6 August, is buried here (II.B.16), as is Lt Col A.N. Walker RAMC (I.A.22), who was killed on 24 September by a shot which penetrated his helmet and brain. He was buried during shelling in the 'garden' of the château that same evening. Further burials were made in Plot I in August and September 1918 and 47 graves were added after the Armistice.

The Sunken Road Cemeteries are in fields a little east of the Contalmaison–POZIÈRES road, 135 yards apart. The site was formerly wooded; the Sunken Road Cemetery is in Défrichés Wood while the 2nd Canadian Cemetery, Sunken Road, is in Derrieux Wood valley. They were made in July–October 1916, during the middle fighting in the Somme offensive. Sunken Road Cemetery contains the graves of 148 Canadians and 61 Australian soldiers and 5 men of the Royal Artillery. The 2nd Canadian Cemetery, Sunken Road, contains the graves of 44 soldiers of 2nd Canadian Battalion (1st Canadian Brigade, 1st Canadian Division) who died in September and October 1916.

In March 1918, the Germans recaptured Contalmaison; it was recaptured by 38th Division on 24 August. In the early 1920s, the village was chosen to be a possible site for a memorial to 55,000 missing from the Somme battle of 1916 but the scheme was later abandoned. On 7 November 2004, at a site close to the church, a memorial costing £50,000 was dedicated to the memory of 16th (S) Battalion, Royal Scots (Lothian Regiment, 101st Brigade, 34th Division), who had strong associations with the Somme and also with Heart of Midlothian Football Club. The memorial takes the form of a cairn.

At the rear of Contalmaison Communal Cemetery is a memorial to the 12th Manchesters, first erected in 1927 and revamped and rededicated on 7 July 2008. On the morning of 7 July 1916, the battalion suffered 555 casualties including 16 officers during an attach on Quadrangle Support close to Mametz Wood.

CONTAY, a village about 11 miles north-east of AMIENS on the Arras road (the D919), was one of the principal railheads for ammunition in 1916, and there was a huge dump established here by the start of the battle. Because of this ammunition dump, no casualty clearing station was ever set up here. According to the *Royal Engineers History*, the roads in the area behind the front where the troops would have to be concentrated were few and indifferent and, owing to enemy observation, there was only one road near the front (the CONTAY–HÉDAUVILLE–ENGLEBELMER–MARTINSART–Aveluy road) that could be used by day and night. A large sign directing transport lorries to HÉRISSART was painted by the Army on a wall in the centre of the village, but no longer exists.

On 5 February 1916, 31st Field Ambulance (32nd Division) were here. By 26 March, the new DAOURS–Contay broad-gauge rail line was completed, but for the immediate future it was not used by ambulance trains. Another village on the new line was FRÉCHENCOURT, to the south. Work was also being carried out at sawmills in Contay Wood, where troops were billeted; there was also an isolation camp in the Wood, where 11th Borders (97th Brigade, 32nd Division) spent the month of April. After a church parade on 18 June, 97th Brigade were addressed by Maj Gen W.H. Rycroft, General Officer Commanding 32nd Division, who spoke of the coming offensive.

Units of 32nd Division returned to Contay after their failed attempts to capture the fortress village of THIEPVAL and the LEIPZIG SALIENT to the south. On 3 July, 2nd King's Own Yorkshire Light Infantry (97th Brigade, 32nd Division) were in huts in the Wood, and on the same night the surviving members of 11th Borders marched back here; 16th Highland Light Infantry (also 97th Brigade, 32nd Division) were also here in hutments, having come from dugouts at CRUCIFIX CORNER near AUTHUILLE. On 9 July, 32nd Division headquarters moved to Contay.

During one of his visits to the Western Front, King George V left QUERRIEU (Fourth Army headquarters) on 10 August for Contay where Lt Gen Sir Hubert Gough, General Officer Commanding Reserve (later Fifth) Army, and Lt Gen W. Birdwood, General Officer Commanding I Anzac Corps, were waiting to greet him. The King motored through the Australian lines and was 'cheered tremendously', according to his diary. The King's party went on to WARLOY-BAILLON.

In early September, 4th Cheshires (pioneers of 56th Division) were in bivouacs in the Wood. The casualty clearing station that had been established in Contay was still here in November, and was used by ambulance trains that ran on the Contay–VECQUEMONT line. The latter-named station was due south of Contay and close to the Somme river valley. At VADENCOURT, to the north-east of Contay, XV Corps had a CP for wounded.

Throughout the battle, Contay was in constant use for all military purposes as well as for field ambulances; although 32nd Division were most strongly associated with the village, particularly prior to the battle, at various times 5th, 11th, 12th, 25th, 35th, 49th and 50th Divisions used it for short periods.

Contay British Cemetery lies on the left or north-east side of the road to FRANVILLERS, beside a quarry. The site was chosen in August 1916 for No. 49 Casualty Clearing Station, which was joined by No. 9 Casualty Clearing Station in September; apart from two burials from November 1915, there are no pre-battle casualties buried here. The burials in Plots I to IV and the majority in Plots VII and VIII cover the period from August 1916 to March 1917. The German withdrawal on the Somme front in early 1917 took the medical units further east. The cemetery was used again in April 1918, during the German advance, when 38th Division and others used it for burials, the last of which took place in August. With more than 1,000 graves, the cemetery is one of the most beautifully designed in the Somme battlefield, and sited on the side of a hill; designed by Sir Reginald Blomfield, it was built in a stepped style that takes full advantage of the sloping nature of the ground. It has become very much an 'English garden'.

COPSE VALLEY was to the south of the PÉRONNE road, the D938, between CARNOY and MARICOURT. At the beginning of the battle, the Franco-British Army boundary ran across it from north to south, and a canvas camp which had been assembled by 8th Royal Sussex (pioneers of 18th Division) was in the valley. In mid-July, 2nd Wiltshires (21st Brigade, 30th Division) were billeted here for one night during their involvement in the TRÔNES WOOD fighting.

CORBIE is a small town at the junction of the Rivers Somme and Ancre, 9 miles east of AMIENS and south-west of ALBERT, on the north bank of the Somme. There were caves in Corbie similar to those at BEAUMONT-HAMEL and NAOURS; presumably they were associated with the famous abbey, part of which still stands and is used today. When the British took over the area from BERLES-AU-BOIS southward to the Somme in July 1915, the town was about 13 miles behind the front trenches. It was part of the Third Army Sector, and at once became an important medical centre as well as major billeting area for the British Army. Two

casualty clearing stations were based in the town; No. 5 arrived first and No. 21 later, setting up in a building at LA NEUVILLE, close to the Ancre. On 22 July, No. 5 Casualty Clearing Station first took over the hospital in *Ecole des Garçons*, which was close to the Hôtel de Ville. The hospital would take 100 lying cases and the *Salle de Théâtre* would accommodate the same number; a marquee was pitched in the yard. On 1 August, the local hospice was taken over as an officers' hospital.

From 26 to 29 July, 51st Division were concentrated here, succeeded by 5th Division until 2 August. On 17 August, 13th Field Ambulance (5th Division) evacuated a divisional rest station to Corbie from ETINEHEM, where their location was in two schools, the *Ensignment Primaire* and *Ecole Superieur*, and also under canvas in an orchard. On 24 September, 13th Field Ambulance were again in the town, when the *Ecole Maternelle* and *Ecole Primaire* were evacuated to Château Corbie, which had been vacated by the French. It had small rooms, but at least the whole station was established in one complex, including the stables; the previous accommodation had only been in four buildings. However, the château could be very cold, and had to be warmed by braziers.

In early January 1916, 13th Field Ambulance were in Corbie. At the end of the month, 22nd Field Ambulance (7th Division) took over their billets and, on 5 February, Château Corbie and the officers' rest station. 1st Royal West Kents (13th Brigade, 5th Division) were billeted here for a month until leaving for RAINNEVILLE on 6 February. 1/5th Seaforth Highlanders (152nd Brigade, 51st Division) arrived here from ACHEUX-EN-AMIÉNOIS, where they spent 12 days in billets; on 20 February, they moved to TAILLES WOOD, between Corbie and BRAY-SUR-SOMME. In early February, as a result of so many troops being billeted in Corbie, the town's sewage system was unable to cope. On 8 February, 1/6th Seaforth Highlanders (also 152nd Brigade, 51st Division) came here from PIERRE-GOT, having marched along the Somme Valley; they were here for about 10 days before moving up to ETINEHEM on 18 February. For some reason, they were back here after only 1 day at ETINEHEM. During the next 9 days they spent their time working at the railway station at DAOURS under the guidance of the Royal Engineers; on 29 February, they returned to PIERREGOT.

From 13 March, 6th Royal Berkshires (53rd Brigade, 18th Division) were billeted in the town, and were back again on 22 May for 2 days before moving to CARNOY. For much of March, 55th

The hospice at Corbie before the war.
(Peter F. Batchelor Collection)

Field Ambulance (18th Division) ran the divisional rest station at the château, together with 96th Field Ambulance (30th Division). In April, No. 21 Casualty Clearing Station was in the town. On 3 May, 2nd Wiltshires (21st Brigade, 30th Division) were here for 2 days before returning to the front near CARNOY. On 13 June, a memorial service for Field Marshal Lord Kitchener, who had recently drowned at sea, was held in the casualty clearing station. On 18 June, 27th Field Ambulance (9th Division) took over from a field ambulance of 30th Division at the château, at a time when 9th Division's headquarters was in the town.

In *Gas*, C.H. Foulkes notes that four large flame projectors and 16 portable machines were unloaded in Corbie on 26 June; three of the larger machines were set up on 18th Division's front, at the head of existing mine galleries. They were discharged at separate times during the early hours of 30 June, 24 hours before the battle began. By the beginning of the battle, Corbie had become one of the principal railheads for ammunition. Of 5th Division's three field ambulances, 15th Field Ambulance had charge of the arrangements for evacuating casualties from the forward area, the advanced dressing station being on the MAMETZ–MONTAUBAN-DE-PICARDIE road; 14th Field Ambulance was at Bécordel and the 13th Field Ambulance at Corbie.

On 1 July, No. 36 Casualty Clearing Station at HEILLY became overwhelmed by the number of casualties and the 'overflow' were sent on to Corbie. On 2 July, 68 officers and 489 other ranks arrived; on 3 July the figure was 53 officers and 1,058 other ranks, but the number arriving was much fewer on the following day.

In *Now it Can be Told*, Philip Gibbs wrote the following of a visit to a hospital in Corbie:

We called the hospital at Corbie the 'Butcher's Shop'. It was in a pretty spot in that little town with a big church whose tall white towers looked down a broad sweep of the Somme, so for miles they were a landmark behind the battlefields. Behind the lines during these first battles, but later, in 1918, when the enemy came nearly to the gates of Amiens, a stronghold of the Australians, who garrisoned it and sniped pigeons for their pots off the top of the towers, and took no notice of 'whizz bangs' which broke through the roofs of cottages and barns. It was a safe, snug place on July of 16, but the Butcher's Shop at a corner of the square was not a pretty spot.

The colonel in charge greeted Gibbs cheerily: "'Come and have a look at my cases. They're the worst possible; stomach wounds, compound fractures, and all that. We lop off limbs here all day long, and all night. You've no idea!'" Gibbs was very reluctant to visit the wards, but wrote:

These were the victims of 'Victory' and the red fruit of war's harvest-fields. A new batch of 'cases' had just arrived. More were being brought in on stretchers. They were laid down in rows on the floorboards. The colonel bent down to some of them and drew their blankets back, and now and then felt a man's pulse. Most of them were unconscious, breathing with the hard snuffle of dying men. Their skin was already darkening to the death-tint, which is not white. They were all plastered with a grey clay and this mud on their faces was, in some cases, mixed with thick clots of blood, making hard incrustation from scalp to skin. In one long, narrow room there were about thirty beds, and in each bed lay a young British soldier, or part of a young British soldier. There was not much left of one of them. Both his legs had been amputated to the thigh, and both his arms to the shoulder-blades.

In his memoirs, Siegfried Sassoon said that on 9 July he rode over to Corbie and visited 'Norman Loder' (Denis Milden) 'in a garden in a splendid billet'. Riding back home he let his mare 'gaze in the still pools'.

G.W. Warwick of 4th South African Infantry (South African Brigade, 9th Division) had briefly stayed in a lemonade factory before moving up to WELCOME WOODS; 3 weeks later, in mid-July, he was wounded and a motor ambulance took him and other casualties to the dressing station at Corbie, which he says was a school. On 14 July, Warwick was operated on and on 15 July he was taken by motor ambulance to a railway station a few miles away. The stretchers were placed on the platform, with the faces of the casualties towards the sun. The hospital train arrived at 1300hrs and they travelled via AMIENS to ETAPLES and on to 'Blighty'.

Basil Liddell Hart of 9th King's Own Light Infantry (64th Brigade, 21st Division) noted that he had been carted off on a stretcher to the nearest field ambulance and then to a casualty clearing station at Corbie. He felt quite well but was sent to a hospital in Rouen for a fortnight, during which time the King visited the wards.

On 10 August, 35th Division headquarters was at Corbie, having moved there from Cavillon; later,

15th Division had a detail camp in the area, midway on the road between MÉRICOURT-L'ABBÉ and RIBEMONT-SUR-ANCRE.

On 3 September, the town was full of British wounded and also of German prisoners. In *Triple Challenge*, Hugh Wansey Bayly, a medical officer with 1st Scots Guards, noted that while at MORLANCOURT their bombing officer, a man called Leach, was killed in a bombing accident on 3 September and that he had been recommended for a posthumous Albert Medal for the way that he sacrificed his own life and saved those of others.

Aubrey Smith of 1/5th Londons (169th Brigade, 56th Division) wrote that in early September, Corbie was crowded out with the four battalions of his brigade, who settled down in billets with a feeling that their training would be continued for a few days. All the familiar signs of a battle area were there: endless lorry convoys passing in both directions, French transport followed by British, French lorries, French artillery, British ambulances, British heavy guns drawn by tractors. There were also, he says, colossal dumps and 'myriads of horses'. 169th Brigade lined up in the street and moved off; Smith squeezed into his allotted position in the convoy with the transport and they headed off up the road towards BRAY-SUR-SOMME and MORLAN-COURT.

In early September, H.L.N. Dundas of 1st Scots Guards (2nd Guards Brigade, Guards Division) was at Corbie at a corps rest station with stomach trouble, while 1st Scots Guards were at CARNOY. He described the rest station as being 'a sort of château place' in the middle of the town. On 13 September, Dundas left the town to rejoin his battalion but did not take part in 2nd Guards Brigade's attack of 15 September.

In *A Soldier's Diary*, Capt G.A. Prideaux of 1st Somerset Light Infantry (11th Brigade, 4th Division) noted that 11th Brigade headquarters was at Corbie, which he described as being a nice clean town with fine houses. The town was also the headquarters of the Army Graves Registration Service and later of International War Graves. The Commission was responsible for the work on the cemeteries which, even during the war, were in many cases flower gardens, where the troops used to go for a peaceful hour or two. During the battle the town, together with the village of ETINEHEM, became the main base for Fourth Army's pigeon lofts.

In early October, 1st Newfoundlanders (88th Brigade, 29th Division) were billeted in the town, only to hear that they were to go into the line on the night of 10 October. It had been decided that for the

Fourth Army attack, 88th Brigade (29th Division) should be temporarily attached to 12th Division, who were in position at GUEUDECOURT. On 19 October, 16th King's Royal Rifle Corps (100th Brigade, 33rd Division) were billeted here before going on to MÉAULTE and Mansel Camp. No. 5 Casualty Clearing Station remained at Corbie until October, but No. 21 Casualty Clearing Station stayed throughout the battle and until the spring of 1917.

The divisions billeted in Corbie from time to time included 3rd, 4th, 5th, 7th, 9th, 16th, 18th, 21st, 20th, 30th, 24th, 29th, 51st and 56th Divisions, many of whom had their headquarters in the town.

Corbie Communal Cemetery lies to the north-east of the town, between the roads to BRAY-SUR-SOMME and VAUX-SUR-SOMME; Corbie Communal Cemetery Extension is to the east of it. The graves are mainly of casualties who came from Nos. 5 and 21 Casualty Clearing Stations and some of the burials may be among the very earliest British graves in the Somme area. The Cemetery Extension was begun in May when the British plot was full. Plot I and most of Plot II of the Extension contain the remains of men who died of wounds in the first Battle of the Somme. In 1918, with the Germans only 5½ miles away, the Corbie Communal Cemetery was used again, this time by the field ambulances of 47th Division and later by 12th Australian Field Ambulance (4th Australian Division). There are 249 graves here.

The Corbie Communal Cemetery Extension, designed by Charles Holden, was begun after May 1916. The majority of the graves are of officers and men who died of wounds during the Battle of the Somme; the remainder are of men who died in 1918. All told, there are 916 graves here. Those buried here include B/Maj W. la Touche Congreve VC, DSO, MC (I.F.25) of the Rifle Brigade. He died on 20 July 1916 and was awarded a posthumous Victoria Cross; only 7 weeks earlier, he had married Pamela Maude and the inscription on his grave probably refers to her expecting the birth of a child. Indeed, a daughter was born a few months later. When on leave, Congreve visited Edward Hudson, editor of *Country Life*, for which he wrote the occasional article; Hudson planned to leave Lindisfarne for him and Pamela to live in. Congreve's grave is next to that of Lt Col H. Bircham (I.F.34), formerly Commanding Officer 2nd King's Royal Rifle Corps (2nd Brigade, 1st Division), who was mortally wounded by a shell on 23 July at the Switch Line Trench, POZIÈRES. Educated at Eton and Sandhurst, Bircham was a veteran of the South African War and had gained a DSO at Hooge Château near Ypres in March 1915.

He had previously been badly wounded and was twice mentioned in despatches. Other senior officers buried here include Lt Col W.A. Smith (I.C.59) of 18th Manchesters (90th Brigade, 30th Division), who died of wounds sustained in TRÔNES WOOD on 7 July; his inscription reads: 'As dying and behold we live as chastened and not killed.' Lt Col J.L. Swainson (II.A.72) of 6th Duke of Cornwall's Light Infantry (43rd Brigade, 14th Division) died of wounds on 9 August.

Other graves include Pte J. Cary (II.C.86) of 7th Royal Irish Fusiliers (49th Brigade, 16th Division), 'shot at dawn' on 15 September 1916, and 2/Lt S.L.M. Mansel-Carey (I.D.9), attached to 9th Devons (20th Brigade, 7th Division), who died of wounds on 24 February 1916. He was mortally wounded just off the main road near what was later called Devonshire Cemetery. It is possible that Mansel Copse was named after him, but if so, it was before he was killed, as trench maps show Mansel Copse or Mansell Copse marked as such in 1915.

In Corbie Abbey, there is a memorial tablet to Congreve, designed by Sir Edwin Lutyens. The abbey church was a prominent landmark in the middle of the war.

Much of the destruction of the town occurred in 1918, when it lay under siege to the advancing enemy. It was saved by the river crossings and an extremely thin line of British troops to the north and south of the Somme at SAILLY-LE-SEC and HAMEL. It now boasts many 'reproduction buildings'.

COUGH DROP, to the north of HIGH WOOD, was formerly a key position for the enemy in their defence of HIGH WOOD in the weeks of the battle prior to mid-September, when the whole of the Wood was finally taken. According to 47th Division's divisional history, on 1 October 1916, the Cough Drop was accessible by day and provided excellent shelter, and was selected as a site for an advanced dressing station. The enemy had left behind a wonderful dugout, which they themselves had used as an aid post, with three entrances in the side of the bank. This aid post provided accommodation for some 70 stretcher cases, but was destroyed owing to a chapter of accidents on 2 October when someone was 'mucking about' with a primus stove. Although the well-timbered dugout caught fire, everyone escaped. In addition, an immense quantity of stores was destroyed, but far worse was that this precious haven, where, in emergency, so many wounded could have been housed out of harm's way, had 'gone west' for good.

In *The Somme, 1916*, Norman Gladden of 1/7th Northumberland Fusiliers (149th Brigade, 50th Division) noted that his company found their position in reserve in a trench known as Cough Drop Alley. In front of them was a low rise, behind which lay the shattered village of FLERS, which had been captured when tanks were used for the first time. Their trench cut across towards the ridge while others zigzagged to left and right. Towards the horizon, further to the right there was a fringe of trees, with rolling country just discernible beyond. Somewhere on this side of the trees the Germans were entrenched and in that direction shells were continuously bursting.

COUIN is a village and commune 9 miles east of DOULLENS, on the D2 road between SOUASTRE and AUTHIE. Couin Château was occupied by the French Army in the early part of the war, and used as a British Army divisional headquarters from 1915 until 1918. In September 1915, 48th Division began its links with the village, when sappers who were bivouacked in the wood moved to ROSSIGNOL FARM, which was to the east, close to the road to BAYENCOURT, where they were completing work on hutting and other camp arrangements. During the coming months, 48th Division were to be in and out of the lines at HÉBUTERNE, to the south of GOMMECOURT, in preparation for the forthcoming offensive. On 7 December, 17th Manchesters (90th Brigade, 30th Division) were here for a week when their officers were given lessons in trench warfare by members of 143rd Brigade (48th Division) under the most 'realistic conditions', their camp being deep in mud; they were back here for a night under canvas on 14 December.

In January 1916, 1/1st Buckinghamshires (145th Brigade, 48th Division) were stationed here; their battalion history notes of Couin: 'There was nothing particularly attractive about this village on the hill, but owing to the regularity of our visits and the duration of our stays there, we became almost part of the place, with the result that we became fond of it.' Another field ambulance, from 4th Division, were billeted here in February.

At the bottom of the hill before the village, one of the few original military water direction notices can still be seen, on a brick barn wall. This direction sign was there in 1916, when 63rd Division were assembling:

Water Carts
Bottle Fillers
100 Yards (with left arrow)

It is thought that it might have been placed there by 94th Brigade (31st Division). In 2004, it was incorporated into changes made to the building of which it was part. It has been joined by a memorial to animals and pigeons killed in the war, which was unveiled in 2004.

On 14 April, 1/8th Worcesters (144th Brigade, 48th Division) went into divisional reserve here, where they rested and trained for a fortnight. On 4 May, 144th Brigade marched westwards from Couin for rest and training at BEAUVAL. On 15 May they were back in COIGNEUX and Couin when they relieved 145th Brigade (also 48th Division). On 24 May, 1/6th Royal Warwicks (143rd Brigade, 48th Division) marched here from GÉZAINCOURT with the rest of 143rd Brigade; the troops used the woods and the hills between Couin and AUTHIE for battle training. On 28 May, 143rd Brigade returned to GÉZAINCOURT but 3 days later were back in Couin Wood before leaving for SAILLY-AU-BOIS the next day. Men from 1/1st Buckinghamshires were often in the Couin area; some of them occupied rest billets next to the church in rue Principale.

On 29 May, one of 56th Division's field ambulances moved to a permanent camp of hutments in the village and cases for the main dressing station were sent here from HÉBUTERNE. At the end of the month, 2/3rd (London) Field Ambulance (56th Division) reported: 'We arrived at night in the rain at a place about 1 mile from Hébuterne and camped in tents on a hill, no room for us all, so I lay down under a wagon for the night, watching and listening to the flashes and noises of the barrage. Next day we took over huts down below the hill and prepared to make ready the dressing station for the offensive on July 1st.'

On 1 June, 1/7th Royal Warwicks (144th Brigade, 48th Division) returned to Couin from trenches at HÉBUTERNE and next day marched to GÉZAIN-COURT, where they joined the rest of 144th Brigade for training. From 13 to 21 June, 1/5th Royal Warwicks (143rd Brigade, 48th Division) camped in the park here; the author Charles Carrington may have been with them. They were camped for much of the time in 'beautiful park'. The pre-battle artillery bombardment, which lasted from 24 June to 1 July, was watched from the hill at the top of the village. In the last week of June, 1/4th Royal Berkshires (145th Brigade, 48th Division) were in huts in the village while 1/1st Buckinghamshires were in the woods, both battalions being in divisional reserve; the huts were described as being 'damp, ill-ventilated and crowded'.

On 1 July, a main dressing station was set up in 'fields of standing corn'. On 3 July, 48th Division returned to the village and in mid-July, 1/6th Glosters (143rd Brigade, 48th Division) were relieved and marched back to billets on the south side of the Couin–SAINT-LÉGER-LÈS-AUTHIE road. At the same time, 1/4th Oxfordshire & Buckinghamshire Light Infantry (145th Brigade, 48th Division) were bivouacked between Couin and SAINT-LÉGER-LÈS-AUTHIE. On 26 July, 11th Durham Light Infantry (pioneers of 20th Division) arrived in the village and discovered 'filthy billets'. Two days later they left for the nearby Dell. At this time, the headquarters of 20th Division was at Couin Château. On 7 August, 7th Somerset Light Infantry (61st Brigade, 20th Division), in divisional reserve, were camped in tents in a field along the side of the wood.

Capt B.H. Radford, better known as 'Gilbert the Filbert', was a member of the Kite Balloon Section of the Royal Flying Corps. On 20 August, he took Lts P.B. Moxon and G. McCall up in his balloon from which they looked across the hills and railway stations of the ANCRE VALLEY into THIEPVAL. Unfortunately the balloon ran into difficulties and the two passengers were forced to jump out with parachutes. Radford, remaining on the edge of the basket, fell to his death on the ACHEUX-EN-AMIÉNOIS road. He was found without a parachute, possibly as there had not been enough to go round. Lt Raymond Asquith, who could be called a rival of Radford's for Lady Diana Cooper's affections, said rather brutally in a letter to her that Radford 'was dreadfully forshortened' and that he was 'only recognised by his cigarette case'. Radford is buried in Couin British Cemetery (II.C.15).

In September, 2nd Oxfordshire & Buckinghamshire Light Infantry (5th Brigade, 2nd Division) practised cooperation in the area with the Royal Flying Corps. On 1 October, 2nd Division opened their headquarters here; 31st Division headquarters was here at the end of November. Also in November, the motor ambulance convoy was transferred from Fourth Army to Couin.

Couin Communal Cemetery, which in the mid-1920s was 'hopelessly overgrown', has the grave of one Australian soldier.

Designed by Sir Reginald Blomfield, Couin British Cemetery and Couin New British Cemetery are a little to the north of the village, and face each other on high ground across the road to SOUASTRE, at its junction with the road to HÉNU. Originally sited in a beautiful apple orchard, Couin British Cemetery was begun in May 1916 by the field ambulances of 48th Division; there are about 26 pre-battle casualties here. It was later used by units and field ambulances during the battles and became full, with over 400 graves by the end of January 1917, and further extension was not possible. Approximately one in eight of the graves here are members of the Royal Field Artillery. The burials here include Brig Gen W. Long CMG, DSO (VI.C.19) of 2nd Dragoons (Royal Scots Greys), who commanded 56th Brigade (19th Division) and died on 28 January 1917 and Lt Col W.R. Stewart DSO, MC (VI.C.3) of 13th Rifle Brigade, who died on 8 April 1918.

Couin New British Cemetery, designed by Sir Reginal Blomfield, is across the road from Couin British Cemetery; it was used by field ambulances from January 1917. The writer Bernard Adams (I.7.B) of 1st Royal Welsh Fusiliers (22nd Brigade, 7th Division), who died of wounds on 27 February 1917, is buried here, as is Sgt R.C. Travis (G.5) of 2nd Otagos (2nd New Zealand Brigade, New Zealand Division), who gained the Victoria Cross at ROSSIGNOL WOOD close to GOMMECOURT and was killed on 25 July 1918. The cemetery register lists 360 burials. In 1964, the 50th anniversary of the start of the First World War, the New Zealand Ambassador attended special ceremonies at Sgt Travis's grave, as well as at the New Zealand memorials at LONGUEVAL.

Couin Château may well have been used by the German Army as a headquarters during the Second World War. At the time of writing it is open to visitors in the period March/October.

COURCELETTE is just off the main ALBERT–BAPAUME road (the D929), 7 miles north-east of ALBERT, and south-west of LE SARS. Historically it is a village mainly associated with the Canadian Army. In September 1916, the Fourth Army plan in what was to become known as the Battle of Flers-Courcelette would include the capture of MARTIN-PUICH to the south-east and, more importantly, HIGH WOOD, with its observation over the enemy back areas. The date of this planned attack was 15 September and the Canadian units due to take part were 27th, 28th and 31st Battalions, with 29th Battalion in brigade reserve (all 6th Canadian Brigade, 1st Canadian Division). It was understood that 27th Battalion were to attack the right sector and 28th Battalion the left sector, while 31st Battalion were to act as moppers up, though on the day 31st Battalion went ahead on their own and made greater progress than their sister battalions. With a frontage of about 1,800yds, 6th Canadian Brigade's objectives were up to 1 mile away and included Sugar Trench, Sugar Refinery and Sugar Ridge. On the right, 4th Canadian Brigade, with 18th, 20th and 21st Battalions, were to advance straight through to their objective. Three tanks began behind 6th Canadian Brigade at Pozières Mill and made their way slowly towards the Sugar Factory. Three other tanks left a point to the north-west in order to go round the back of POZIÈRES to get to a point to the north-west of MARTINPUICH.

In *The Fifth Army*, Lt Gen Sir Hubert Gough, General Officer Commanding Reserve (later Fifth) Army, wrote that on this occasion the direction of the Allied advance had been altered and instead of being generally northwards against MOUQUET FARM and THIEPVAL, his command was to attack eastwards and north-eastwards towards Courcelette, with the right on the ALBERT–BAPAUME road. Fourth Army extended the attack south of this road, thus including MARTINPUICH in the sphere of its operations. As far as the Reserve Army was concerned, the attack on Courcelette on 15 September was the first occasion in which tanks had been employed, with six tanks cooperating with the Canadians. About 50 tanks were available at this time, and the majority of these were under Fourth Army, 7 only being allotted to the Reserve Army. Of this number, a total of 17 were destined not to even reach their starting points, and the ones which were working with the Canadians began half an hour after the infantry. Some of the attacking tanks were either ditched or knocked down and were unable to reach the German points of resistance such as the Sugar Refinery in front of the village.

However, the remaining tanks had an immediate and decisive effect on the enemy, who in many cases simply ran away. Although it was to be the tanks that carried the day, it should not be overlooked that the Canadian infantry still had a very tough day of fighting despite their success. The fighting had become desperate and the assaulting troops broke against the double line of German trenches, flanked by redoubts and salients armed with mortars and machine guns. Further artillery preparation was necessary. The assault was hard and costly and the German fire from rifles and machine guns was withering. The enemy had dug new trenches in preparation, called Fabeck Trench, which were north-west of MOUQUET FARM, as well as the Zollern Trench, which was to the north of the Fabeck. These trenches had not been destroyed by the Allied artillery and it was not until 1800hrs, after fighting had been going on for 12 hours, that Courcelette was finally taken by the Canadians,

when one tank immediately set about clearing the streets. At the Sugar Factory, a tank named *Crème de Menthe* knocked down the walls and crushed machine guns that were hidden behind them, and then destroyed all the defence works and quickly overcame the German resistance. According to *The War in the Air* by H.A. Jones, after the village had been captured, flares had been lit in semicircles around the village to indicate that it was wholly in Allied hands. Observers from No. 7 Squadron, Royal Flying Corps, watched the Canadians move down the slope on the western face of the village; the flares were seen at 1930hrs and were reported to be burning in a line as far as MARTINPUICH, the latter village having been virtually battered to pulp before being captured. The success against Courcelette and MARTINPUICH followed on the success earlier in the day against FLERS, where the first tank had gone into action.

The Canadian wounded were carried on trolleys down to POZIÈRES and then transported by lorry to hospital. On the following day, Pte J.C. Kerr of 49th Canadian Battalion (7th Canadian Brigade, 3rd Canadian Division) gained the Victoria Cross. His battalion were to advance on the left of the Canadian attack and then occupy a forward line within assaulting distance of the Zollern Trench. This the battalion failed to accomplish, being handicapped by ground difficulties and exposure to accurate machine-gun fire; but the two companies took and held the Chalk Pit in advance of the Fabeck Trench, to which communication was then dug. Kerr's Victoria Cross citation reads in part:

> During a bombing attack he was acting bayonet man, and, knowing that bombs were running short, he ran along the parados under heavy fire until he was in close contact with the enemy, when he opened fire on them at point blank range, and inflicted heavy loss. The enemy, thinking that they were surrounded, surrendered. Sixty-two prisoners were taken, and 250 yards of enemy trench captured. Before carrying out this very plucky act Kerr's fingers had been blown off by a bomb. Later with two other men, he escorted back prisoners under fire, then returned to report himself for duty before having his wounds dressed.

49th Battalion took up battle positions at a point near the sunken road, before and to the left of Courcelette, with other battalions of 7th Canadian Brigade; 49th Battalion supported Princess Patricia's Canadian Light Infantry, and 42nd Battalion was on the extreme left of the frontage of operations.

The writer C.E. Montague, who later showed important visitors round the Western Front, came to Courcelette Sugar Factory ruins with a party on 1 October. They were shelled there for some time with high explosive and were showered with earth and shrapnel. The group then went back to the artillery lines, where they waited during an attack on the front. They set out homewards at 1630hrs across the shelled area; none came very close but Montague's 'flock' were very nervous and apt to scatter. They went 'home' by dark roads, arriving at AMIENS at 2015hrs.

In *The Great War as I Saw It*, F.G. Scott noted that after Courcelette was taken, the Canadian front line lay beyond it past DEATH VALLEY on the slope leading down to REGINA TRENCH, which ran across the ridge. Their various fighting units were scattered over all this stretch of country as it got 'waste and dreary' towards the end of September. He referred to a piper who won the Victoria Cross in the attack on REGINA TRENCH and says that several tanks were knocked out near Courcelette; one lay partly in the ditch by the road. On 26 September, having walked up from POZIÈRES using a railway track, Scott spent some time in the dressing station in the sunken road close to Courcelette. The station had once been the dugout of an enemy battery and its openings were on the side of the road facing the Germans, who knew its location perfectly. There

was a large dressing station in the cellars of the Red Château in the village. The wounded waiting for the ambulance were in a dugout and shelter by the road called Dead Man's Trench, which contained many German bodies.

Courcelette remained very close to the front line until the German retreat in February 1917. It was again captured on 25 March 1918 and recaptured on 24 August. After the war it was 'adopted' by Brighouse.

Courcelette British Cemetery is half a mile south-west of the village and was begun in the November 1916 as Mouquet Road Cemetery or Sunken Road Cemetery. It was greatly enlarged after the Armistice by the concentration of 1,882 graves of men who had mostly fallen in 1916 around Courcelette and POZIÈRES. It stands in a hollow surrounded by cultivated land. The cemetery register lists the details of 1,956 burials. In 1958, a large circular feature of lavender had grown up and become unkempt. The Commonwealth War Graves Commission decided that it should be grubbed up and replaced with grass.

The remains of an Australian soldier in full kit, with his aluminium dog tag, were discovered by a farmer in the winter of 1997/98. He was later

La rue de Pozières, Courcelette, after the war.
(Peter F. Batchelor Collection)

identified at Pte R.G. Bosisto of 27th Australian Battalion (7th Australian Brigade, 2nd Australian Division), who died near POZIÈRES windmill on 4 August 1916. On 5 July 1998, his remains were reburied among the graves of his comrades at a very moving service arranged by the Australian government. Bosisto, born in 1893, had been declared missing and killed in action; after he was officially identified, he was laid to rest within sight of the spot where he died by members of the current 27th Australian Battalion. The Australian Minister of Veterans' Affairs attended the service, alongside members of Bosisto's family and surviving veterans.

In *Goodbye to the Battlefields*, Capt H.A. Taylor of the Royal Fusiliers noted that after the war a black fragment of the old sugar factory was built into the long wall of a new farmhouse. One of the cellars in the main street was known to the soldiers as Number Ten Dugout and one used to pass this spot on the way to REGINA TRENCH and Dyke Valley. Nearby were Manchester Dump and two ground features known as the Pope's Nose and Lady's Leg. In winter the line ran from Courcelette to GRANDCOURT and MIRAUMONT. Many dead Germans had been found in the village, presumably killed in the bombardment preceding its capture on

Courcelette British Cemetery.
(Peter F. Batchelor Collection)

15 September. When being cleared and widened, the sunken road yielded up 100 bodies. The old sugar refinery was between a great barn and a water tower and by 1931 had been replaced by a new building, which was owned by the mayor.

In *Thirteen Years After*, Will R. Bird of 42nd Canadian Battalion (7th Canadian Brigade, 3rd Canadian Division) noted during his visit in 1931: 'The church is very new, and the memorial of the French is nearby. The houses also look quite new, and here and there you see old cellars and low ruins.' A lady who ran a café and who lived in the village under the 18-month German occupation told Bird that in 1916 the British shells came very near and the Germans were remarkably adept at taking cover. After the people returned to the ruins of Courcelette and started rebuilding, they found many German dead in the cellars, where they had been crushed by the barrage preceding the village's capture.

COURCELLES-AU-BOIS is a village 8 miles north of ALBERT, in the hilly country north-west of that town. The British first came to the village in July 1915; on 25 July, 1/6th Royal Warwicks (143rd Brigade, 48th Division) spent several days here when they provided working parties. During this period the ground was very wet and the French trench system began to break up, owing to a lack of

revetting. Conditions became very poor and stores for the front had to be taken along a 'quagmire' of 1½ miles. After 8 days the troops were able to paddle out and dry themselves off. After a short but wet visit to the front line, they moved back 10 miles to WARNIMONT WOOD.

In September, 1/7th Worcesters (144th Brigade, 48th Division) were here. Other units of 48th Division used the village in early 1916, 144th Brigade coming here from HÉBUTERNE in early February before moving on after 5 days. In January, a Royal Engineers' park was built here; in March, a section of No. 210 Field Company, Royal Engineers (31st Division), took over the park and sawmill and remained here for several weeks. In April, a field company of 31st Division were here, working at the same sawmill.

According to the regimental history, on 11 April, 10th East Yorkshires (92nd Brigade, 31st Division) were in 'cosy barns' and provided working parties, on occasions involved in having to push trolleys loaded with barbed wire, 'Corkscrews', 'concertinas' and 'gooseberries', as well as sump boards, down the light railway from Euston Dump to the Support Line. Transport and stores remained in the village in early May; by then the village had been wrecked by enemy artillery and

> would be best remembered by its church, whose tall spire was neatly pierced by a shell-hole in the exact position where one would expect to see a clock. Quite a number of French peasants clung tenaciously to their ruined farms in the surrounding district, working their land in spite of the constant danger, and there was some difficulty in getting them to evacuate when the sector livened up a few weeks later. The straw-thatched barns, whose walls were of brushwood and mud, looked like making cosy billets, especially as they had been fitted with tiers of beds made of wire netting, so that some of them could accommodate fully 100 men. These beds were however of little use, for neither officers nor men were allowed to undress while the Battalion was in close support . . .

On one occasion around Easter, when 10th East Yorkshires were on their way to BUS-LÈS-ARTOIS, their kindly chaplain, Revd R.M. Kedward, set out buns and hot drinks in a barn here to help them on their way to their rest billets.

On 8 May, 1/6th Royal Warwicks moved here from Couin Wood, where for 2 nights they dug 'new-fangled works and cable trenches'. Exhausted,

they then left for Authie. On 20 May, 12th York & Lancasters (94th Brigade, 31st Division) arrived here after a 5-day spell in the line opposite SERRE; moving to Bus Wood on 30 May. On 4 June, 18th Durham Light Infantry (93rd Brigade, 31st Division) moved here, where enemy shelling had meant 'trenches for bombardment cover had to be dug outside the village'; for safety, they lived in these trenches around the clock. At the time French civilians were still in the village and the task of evacuating them, and especially the farmers who wished to remain at work, was begun. During their time here, 18th Durham Light Infantry practised making and using Bangalore torpedoes. At the end of June, 11th East Lancashires (also 94th Brigade, 31st Division) were resting just outside the village, having tea and biscuits in the sunshine before leaving at dusk for COLINCAMPS along the ½ mile paved road. Progress was slow because so many other troops and transport were on the move.

While staying at BERTRANCOURT, Geoffrey Malins, the official War Office photographer, described Courcelles-au-Bois as being mostly derelict. On 1 September, one company of 2nd Oxfordshire & Buckinghamshire Light Infantry (5th Brigade, 2nd Division) were in huts and tents here, another being at COLINCAMPS. Around 17 October, 2nd Suffolks (76th Brigade, 3rd Division) marched through BUS-LÈS-ARTOIS to Courcelles-au-Bois and reported that there was considerable shelling there and that a pair of 9.2in pieces were behind their mess. All around the village, guns were being hauled into position and aeroplanes overhead were heavily shelled. On 23 October, a party from headquarters went up to Dunmow Trench in preparation for a battalion against SERRE, which was due to take place on 25 October. That day, 2nd Suffolks' positions were taken over by 8th King's Own (also 76th Brigade, 3rd Division) and they returned to Courcelles-au-Bois, as the attack had been indefinitely postponed. This time 2nd Suffolks' mess was in a château. After 3 more days they left for BUS-LÈS-ARTOIS.

In *The Middle Parts of Fortune*, Frederic Manning of 7th King's Shropshire Light Infantry (8th Brigade, 3rd Division) wrote:

> After three days in the trenches, the battalion was relieved, and moved to Courcelles, where they were to remain for one night on their way to rest-billets at Bus. The village had been shelled from time to time, but had not been damaged to quite the same extent as Colincamps, which offered, on the crest of the hill, a more

conspicuous target. Courcelles was uncovered at one end, but screened partially by rising ground on two sides. As Corporal Williams had said of Mailly-Maillet, it was simply lousy with guns . . . Monster guns, too, were secreted somehow in the courtyards of houses in the village itself . . . Battalion headquarters in Courcelles was a small château, which stood, with its farm buildings, on a little hill practically encircled by a road . . . The rain continued, broken only by intervals of mist or fog, and spells of cold, which became more intense as the weeks drew on into November. The relay-post at Colincamps was abandoned; and they took their messages direct from the trenches to Courcelles.

While this extract may well be from a novel, it nevertheless sounds very authentic and it is clear that the area was full of considerable artillery activity which encouraged German retaliation.

Courcelles-au-Bois Communal Cemetery and Courcelles-au-Bois Communal Cemetery Extension are located to the north of the village, at the junction of the roads to COIGNEUX and SAILLY-AU-BOIS. The Communal Cemetery contained the graves of three British soldiers who were buried on the north side in September 1916; and in the following month the Communal Cemetery Extension, designed by F. Higginson, was opened. Many of the graves are of soldiers from the King's Shropshire Light Infantry (Manning's regiment) who were killed between October and December 1916. As with several other cemeteries on the Somme, the headstones are made from red sandstone. The cemetery was used by field ambulances and fighting units until March 1917, when the German Army retreated from the Somme, and again from April 1918 during the defence of AMIENS, when the village was in German hands for 4 months. The three graves in the Communal Cemetery were moved into the Communal Cemetery Extension in 1934, and where there are 115 graves.

CRUCIFIX CORNER was on the crossroads close to Authuille Wood on the D50 road out of Aveluy. Across the road was a quarry; just beyond it, on the beginning of the road to OVILLERS, was the site of Crucifix Corner, one of many places on the Western Front with this name. This one was also known as Quarry Dugouts, as it consisted of a series of shelters in the chalk cliff. During the war it was a strongly fortified position and in early January 1916, members of 32nd Division constructed dugouts here which eventually would accommodate 60 wounded at a time. The sector became closely

associated with 32nd Division; on 24 June, 2nd King's Own Yorkshire Light Infantry (97th Brigade, 32nd Division) were here in positions of readiness for front-line duty. On 1 July, units from 14th Brigade (32nd Division) were here, including 2nd Manchesters, when the position became overwhelmed with the numbers of wounded collected here. In addition, many dead were brought down from 8th Division's front opposite OVILLERS for burial in the nearest Communal Cemetery. It had become a place of horror, which cannot now be imagined. Later in the day, two battalions from 147th Brigade (49th Division) replaced the units from 32nd Division.

After the casualties of early July had tailed off, No. 30 Field Company, Royal Engineers (25th Division) came here; on 4 July, they began work on a shed in the quarry for the storage of small-arms ammunition. The dugouts here were reserve ones and while staying here on 25 September, 10th Essex (53rd Brigade, 18th Division) saw their first tanks, when the tanks were on their way up to concealed positions in BLIGHTY VALLEY.

Ivor Gurney of 2/5th Glosters (184th Brigade, 61st Division) has left a poem called 'Crucifix Corner'; he was probably there in November or after.

Crucifix Corner
There was a water dump there and regimental
Carts came every day to line up and fill full
These rolling tanks with chlorinated clay mixture
And curse the mud with vain terrible vexture
Aveluy across the valley, billets, shacks, ruins.

The Ancre marshes reminded Gurney of the River Severn near his home in Gloucestershire.

CURLU is a village between FARGNY MILL and Hem on the north side of the Somme marshes, south of the D938 road. At the start of the battle, it was in enemy hands and was close to where the British and French Armies joined. A steep hill on the east side of Hardecourt Valley, known as le Chapeau de Gendarme, gave the enemy some protection from enemy observation. On one occasion the French 11th Division did very well here, when they surprised the enemy as they climbed this hill and overwhelmed the German defenders.

During the early part of the war, Curlu village church was used by the enemy as an emergency hospital, and it did not see any real action until after the first Somme battle. The Germans had a flagstaff on top of the hill above the village but during the

A dugout in a trench being used as a canteen at Crucifix Corner, near Aveluy, September 1916. *(IWM Q1096)*

Battle of Loos in 1915, the flag was down for several days.

In the early 1930s, the mayor of Curlu wrote to the Imperial War Graves Commission and suggested that it might be a good idea if the British were to erect a memorial to the role of the British Army in the commune of Curlu-Fargny, to be placed in the church at Curlu, which was about to be reopened after being restored. The village had been razed to the ground during the war and was rebuilt in the very short time of 12 years. The mayor's reasoning was that unless a memorial were erected, future generations would not be aware of the British Army's role during the war years. The Imperial War Graves Commission were immediately enthusiastic about the mayor's idea, and put in hand the design of a memorial, to be based on those set up in French cathedrals in Northern France in the 1920s. The inscription was to be:

To the memory
Of the British Soldiers
Who fell at Curlu 1917–1918
In defence of right and liberty
Lord have mercy upon them.

D

DANTZIG ALLEY was a German trench running from the south-west of MAMETZ through the north of the village and then in an easterly direction parallel to the present D64 road to MONTAUBAN-DE-PICARDIE; the Dantzig Alley British Cemetery, named after it, is on the north side of the same section of road. Further eastwards, Dantzig Alley became a German strongpoint known as POMMIERS REDOUBT. MAMETZ WOOD was to the north and CONTALMAISON to the north-west.

On 1 July 1916, Dantzig Alley, together with the village of MAMETZ, formed 7th Division's major objectives. An account in *Sir Douglas Haig's Great Push* spells out some of the problems any attacker would have to face against a determined foe: 'on the ridge by Mametz, their machine-guns had been so effectively hidden as to escape our bombardment, for no artillery can destroy every cache; and here the Germans offered a desperate resistance, emerging from the enormously deep dug-outs, such as are easily excavated in this hilly and chalky country, in which they had remained secure, and working their machine-guns with the utmost skill and determination.'

22nd Manchesters (91st Brigade, 7th Division) began their advance from the valley between the MAMETZ–CARNOY road to the east and Mansell Copse to the west, and successfully reached the eastern section of Dantzig Alley soon after 0800hrs on 1 July, but were then pushed out again for a short period by German troops in Fritz Trench just beyond.

Capt Hawkins, in charge of No. 3 Kite Balloon Section, was observing infantry progress on this front and was able to direct a siege battery on Fritz Trench so effectively that 2nd Queen's (also 91st Brigade, 7th Division) were able to take Dantzig Alley in the afternoon with only small losses.

According to war correspondent Philip Gibbs, in the part of the Dantzig Alley to the south-west of MAMETZ, 2nd Gordon Highlanders (20th Brigade, 7th Division) rushed forward with great enthusiasm until they reached the fringe of the village, when quite suddenly they faced rapid machine-gun fire

British troops at an entrance to a German dugout in Dantzig Alley, Fricourt, July 1916. *(IWM Q814)*

and a storm of bombs. They flung themselves on the Dantzig Alley position and had some difficulty in clearing it of the enemy. Between 2nd Gordons, 22nd Manchesters and 2nd Queen's were 1st South Staffords (91st Brigade, 7th Division), who quickly reached Bunny Alley, which was north-west of the village and connected with Fritz Trench. By the end of the day, after very hard fighting, 7th Division were able to boast that they had not only taken Dantzig Alley and MAMETZ village, but that they had almost reached their original planned objective in front of MAMETZ WOOD.

Dantzig Alley British Cemetery was begun later in July and used by fighting units and field ambulances until November. The village was lost in March 1918 and recaptured in August. At the end of the war there were 183 graves in Plot I, but later nearly 1,800 more burials were made from the battlefields to the east and north of the village. In Plot I are graves belonging to 7th Division men killed on 1 July and also troops from 18th and 30th Divisions who were fighting successfully to the east of them. The graves of 24 men from 20th Manchesters (22nd Brigade, 7th Division) were brought in from Aeroplane Cemetery at FRICOURT, which was part of the old German Front Line. The graves here also

include the remains of three lieutenant-colonels who died in 1916. Lt Col H. Burnaby (I.D.31) of 11th Queen's (123rd Brigade, 41st Division) was killed on 8 September 'when reconnoitering front-line trenches near Delville Wood'; Lt Col F.L. Sharp (I.C.21) of XXXIX Brigade, Royal Field Artillery (1st Division), died on 13 August; and Lt Col C.E. Stewart (I.B.33) of CXC Brigade, Royal Field Artillery (41st Division), died on 31 August.

Dantzig Alley British Cemetery stands on high ground, among cultivated fields; from it one has a panoramic view of the battlefield, with MAMETZ WOOD in its centre. Just inside the cemetery is a stone dedicated to men of the Royal Welsh Fusiliers killed on the Somme between 1914 and 1918 and at the back of the cemetery is a memorial seat dedicated to 14th Royal Welsh Fusiliers (113th Brigade, 38th Division), who lost so many men in the fighting for the possession of MAMETZ WOOD in early July 1916.

DAOURS is a large village to the west of the confluence of the Rivers Somme and Ancre, between AMIENS and CORBIE on the east side of the River Hallue. To the east of the village, the River Somme and the Somme Canal run parallel in a north–south direction. The village's links with the British Army began on 3 August 1915, when 13th Field Ambulance (5th Division) arrived here and were billeted in a former factory, just to the north of the D1 road to CORBIE and west of the Somme Canal, between it and the river. All their tents and marquees were erected in a wood, and a field next to the bridge over the canal was chosen for use as a tent station.

During the next few months, the village was to become familiar to many troops when out of the line, and in particular to men from 18th Division, who were often billeted here between August 1915 and February 1916. On 15 August, 54th Field Ambulance (18th Division) ran their divisional rest station here. 18th Division's 53rd Brigade rendezvoused here for training, prior to taking over a sector of their own. The battalion history of 10th Essex (53rd Brigade, 18th Division) noted that 'Daours was quite the best French village we had been in up-to-date'. On 29 September, XV Corps moved their headquarters here from HEILLY, where they had been for 10 days.

In January 1916, 18th Divisional Rest Station ocupied buildings still to the west of the Somme Canal; these were probably the same as those used by 2/1st (Highland) Field Ambulance (51st Division) in February, when they took over buildings of

a 'disused mill' from 56th Division, positioned immediately west of the canal running north to south on the eastern side of the town. Many of the casualties here suffered from scabies or venereal disease contracted in AMIENS. The adjacent building to the mill was a *belle maison*, which was acquired for use as an officers' hospital.

During the last part of February, 1/6th Seaforth Highlanders (152nd Brigade, 51st Division), billeted at CORBIE, spent their time working at Daours railway station under the direction of the Royal Engineers. A new broad-gauge line from Daours and VECQUEMONT, an adjoining village to the south, was being prepared as far as QUERRIEU and CONTAY, which would allow ambulance trains to evacuate casualties, and thus take pressure off the roads. This line was finished on 26 March.

From early August 1915 to April 1916, units from 5th, 18th, 30th, 49th, 51st and 56th Divisions passed through Daours for either training, rest, work on the new branch line or medical purposes.

The village became the headquarters for Lt Gen Sir Hubert Gough, General Officer Commanding Reserve (later Fifth) Army, and at Zero Hour on 1 July, the cavalry were waiting here in reserve for the orders which never came.

During the battle itself, 6th, 29th, 30th and 33rd Divisions either rested or trained here, as well as in VECQUEMONT.

Daours Communal Cemetery was a mile from Daours Halt, to the left of the D115 road to PONT-NOYELLES; the first British burial took place in February 1916 and a second in May. The preparations for the offensive involved a grouping of casualty clearing stations, including 1/1st (South Midland) Field Ambulance (48th Division), 21st Field Ambulance (7th Division), 34th Field Ambulance (11th Division), 45th Field Ambulance (15th Division) and Lucknow Cavalry Field Ambulance (2nd (Indian) Cavalry Division). Section B and later the Daours Communal Cemetery Extension, designed by Sir Edwin Lutyens, were begun on the south side of the Communal Cemetery. The burials of June to November 1916 are in Plots I and II, as well as Row A of Plot III, and the Indian Plot. As the Allied advance progressed, the hospitals went forward with it. However, after the German advance in the spring of 1918, burials recommenced in April in what for a time was almost a front-line cemetery. In August Nos. 5, 37, 41, 53, 55 and 61 Casualty Clearing Stations came forward again. The identified casualties here number 1,225.

The east of the cemetery offers a commanding view of the Somme Valley. There are 1,227 burials recorded in the two cemeteries combined. These include the graves of two lieutenant-colonels buried close to the entrance. Lt Col A. St H. Gibbons (I.B.2) of 13th King's (9th Brigade, 3rd Division) died on 15 July of wounds received the day before during the fighting near LONGUEVAL, and Lt Col M.B. Stow (II.A.7) of 1st East Yorkshires (64th Brigade, 21st Division) died of wounds on 2 July, after his battalion were involved in the fighting at SHELTER WOOD and BIRCH TREE WOOD. His grave inscription reads: 'Splendid he passed into the light that nevermore shall fade.'

According to the *Ypres Times*, in 1935, every house in the village of Daours still carried its original billeting notice; so many men, so many horses.

DEATH VALLEY (1) ran between MONTAUBAN-DE-PICARDIE and LONGUEVAL to the north-east and just in front of DELVILLE WOOD, and was often deluged with German shells. The communication trench was called Y & L Alley and was littered with remains from the trenches of both sides, as well as the dead bodies of mules and horses. In an issue of *Boy David*, the journal of the Machine Gun Corps, it was noted that in the early days of the Somme battle the losses in Death Valley were truly terrible until the British pioneers made a communication trench over 1,000yds long in a single night. It was so narrow that they could only just pass each other in it; much more importantly, it was very deep, and saved many lives.

In early September, Aubrey Smith of 1/5th Londons (169th Brigade, 56th Division) noted that beyond CARNOY they were shortly in an inferno, not of enemy but of British fire: here in Death Valley, guns of all calibres were massed in such numbers that one fired almost every second. After delivering his cookers, Smith returned home, to be held up by a traffic jam. In the evening, some of the battalions moved up from Death Valley to the neighbourhood of FAFFEMONT FARM, which meant that they were going to take part in an attack.

On 8 September, there was an exceptionally heavy bombardment; the Allied guns stood out boldly in the open, providing clear proof of British aerial supremacy. Smith's unit were transferred to HAPPY VALLEY at daylight:

> Now I could see all those batteries which had startled me so much upon the first nightly trip, 9.2s, six inch howitzers, 8 inch guns and French artillery. However I had to stop at Death Valley, for from that point water would have to be taken up in petrol cans on pack ponies. The sun was

low in the heavens as I stood in Death Valley and looked around at the scene of desolation. Dead horses, smashed limbers, and numerous stray shell cases lay about, the whole place hopeless. The reek from the guns, the dead horses, the foul soil and the lachrymatory shells made the place repulsive and horrible.

In his novel *The Somme*, A.D. Gristwood noted that at some point in September, the cookers lay in a deep hollow a mile to the rear of the line (outside COMBLES). The place was known as Death Valley, by no means without reason. There, the foremost batteries and fatigue parties waited until dark in a whirlpool of hurry. Always new guns were arriving; ration wagons, water carts, field kitchen mules, Royal Engineers, camouflage materials, corrugated iron, timber, barbed wire, sandbags in thousands. No lorries or ambulances could reach Death Valley, however, which lay far from paved roads among the uplands of the Somme. The 'Loamshires' first sight of the Somme battlefield was gained from the Crucifix above Death Valley. This ancient iron cross, rusty, bent and ominous, yet remained as a notorious landmark on the hillside; from the shattered trenches nearby they looked forward across the valley to a hideous welter of dust and smoke and intolerable noise. From Death Valley the 'Loamshires' marched over the hills to MÉAULTE.

When resting in ANGLE WOOD, A.S. Dolden of 1/14th Londons (168th Brigade, 56th Division) noted that there were many French and German bodies covered in bluebottle flies. He took up his position in Death Valley slightly behind the line. Later relieved by 1/13th Londons (also 168th Brigade, 56th Division), 1/14th Londons then took up positions on the top of the ridge just above their cooker in Death Valley.

DEATH VALLEY (2), also known as Valley of Death of Mametz Wood, ran from the west of MAMETZ WOOD in an easterly direction towards CATERPILLAR VALLEY. In the same way that there was more than one position known as HAPPY VALLEY, there was certainly more than one Death Valley in the Somme area. There is a description of it at the end of July as being a perfect inferno of bursting shells that concentrated on a narrow valley and road; the gun limbers went steadily up and down carrying their precious and necessary loads of shells to the guns which were banked almost wheel to wheel on the slope behind Bazentin Wood and were firing at this time all afternoon and evening, in the attack on HIGH WOOD.

In *The Machine Gunner*, Arthur Russell of No. 98 Company, Machine Gun Corps (33rd Division), notes that having gone up the line again, his unit eventually came to a halt in the reserve lines halfway down 'that all too familiar Valley of Death'. They were in reserve for 5 days and on 10 August moved up to the front line in front of HIGH WOOD; 33rd Division were holding the southern half of the partly captured wood, which was a German stronghold. There was a well-dug communication trench up the gentle slope beyond BAZENTIN-LE-GRAND and then on to HIGH WOOD itself. However, they were given orders to return, as they had gone too far forward and one section had been hit.

In his diary, kept at the Suffolk Regimental Museum, C.C.S. Gibbs MC noted that in mid-August, Death Valley had in it decaying dumps of barbed wire, boots, tin hats and shell-holes, alongside the farm track that ran along its southern side – 300yds to the borders of MAMETZ WOOD. On the south side of the track was a hill rising in a series of terraces of some 30ft, and in these terraces were old German dugouts and disused aid posts.

DELVILLE WOOD, adjacent to the village of LONGUEVAL, is north of the D20 road to the west of GINCHY; its north-west edge is bordered by the D197 road to FLERS. Prior to the start of the Somme battle, the German Front Line ran from the south of Bazentin-le-Grand to the southern edge of LONGUEVAL village and then bent south-eastwards past WATERLÔT FARM and then in front of GUILLEMONT and FAFFEMONT FARM. The German Intermediate Line ran correspondingly behind the Wood. The whole area originally formed part of the German Second Line defences.

By 13 July 1916, the British front to the south-west ran from the north of MONTAUBAN-DE-PICARDIE, skirting the north of BERNAFAY WOOD to TRÔNES WOOD, where it turned south alongside the eastern edge of TRÔNES WOOD and on reaching the southern edge turned in a south-easterly direction towards HARDECOURT-AU-BOIS. On the following day, most of the village of LONGUEVAL was captured by 9th Division; the South African Brigade (9th Division) captured Delville Wood, with the exception of its north-west corner. In *We Band of Brothers*, G.W. Warwick of 4th South African Infantry (South African Brigade, 9th Division) noted that the South African Brigade consisted of four battalions, 1st, 2nd and 3rd South African Infantry from Cape Province, Natal & Orange Free State and Transvaal & Rhodesia

respectively, and 4th South African Infantry (Scottish), referred to by other members of the brigade as 'Our Jocks'. Among the older men were some who had fought in the South African War, some on the Boer side and others on the side of the British. The South Africans had moved forward from MARICOURT to MONTAUBAN-DE-PICARDIE and during a fury of action held part of TRÔNES WOOD and BERNAFAY WOOD. The South African Brigade had a strength of 121 officers and 3,032 NCOs and men. On 14 July, they had been in reserve at MONTAUBAN-DE-PICARDIE, less one battalion sent to assist the clearing of LONGUE-VAL; the brigade went into action on the morning of 15 July.

In *The Turning Point*, H.P. Robinson, war correspondent of *The Times*, noted that one speaks of LONGUEVAL and Delville Wood as if they were two separate positions; but, as a matter of fact, the Wood engulfs the village, or the village is so embowed in trees that it is part of the Wood. At the place where the two meet together, or where the building of the village ceases and the Wood proper begins, the Germans had made some particularly strong fortified positions, with machine guns and two field guns, which fired at point blank range from about 150yds as British troops reached the edge of the ruins.

In Delville Wood there was a series of rides: running in a north-westerly direction were Buchanan Street, which ran into the Strand; Campbell Street, which ran into Regent Street; and King Street, which became Bond Street. Going from west to east, the rides were Princes Street, Rotten Row and Haymarket. Other names, mainly associated with London, were given to other trenches and tracks, such as High Holborn, which led south-eastwards; Sloane Street, which was to the south-west of LONGUEVAL; Dover Street, which was south of the village; South Street, which was the road from the village to GINCHY; Duke Street, and so on. Flers Road led out of the north of the Wood and North Street, on its west side, led to the SWITCH TRENCH after crossing Orchard Trench, which connected the track to HIGH WOOD. In addition to the above, there were many trench names chosen mostly with beer as a theme, including Hop, Beer, Vat, Stout, Pilsen, Bitter, Ale, Pint and several others.

The horrendous battle for the complete capture of the Wood was to rage for 7 weeks, from 15 July until 3 September, with the advantage continually changing from one side to the other and then back again. Over this period, 2nd, 3rd, 7th, 9th, 14th, 20th and 24th Divisions took part in the fighting, as did 53rd Brigade (18th Division). After Delville Wood had nearly been completely captured by the Allies, the Germans counter-attacked with lachrymatory and asphyxiating gas shells, forcing the attackers to fall back a few days later. However, the Allies soon returned to the attack, and a terrible struggle began, which was to last for 5 days and nights without intermission. Owing to the height of the trees, no close artillery support was possible.

In his diary, published in *The Springbok* of March 1936, John Hay of 4th South African Infantry noted that on going up the line, in a shed in FRICOURT, they had picked up 45lb mortar bombs, which were 3ft long with 'footballs' on them. They were already carrying full packs and subsequently had numerous stops, and finally they left their packs behind at MONTAUBAN-DE-PICARDIE on 14 July. They left TRÔNES WOOD on their right flank, having previously fought over this ground on 10 July and defended the wood and entered the German Second Line Position. The bombs were left at the rear of LONGUEVAL. They went back to MONTAUBAN-DE-PICARDIE and had breakfast, and then returned towards the line and came across the captured German trenches just where the road led up to HIGH WOOD. Following the road up, they came across, on the right of the road, a German sniper's post made of concrete. From the slits almost the whole of the Somme Valley could be seen, and Hay saw the British cavalry return from HIGH WOOD. By 0700hrs on 16 July, all of the Wood south of Princes Street had been captured, but after this initial success the advance was halted by a bombardment; this continued with only short lulls until the evening of 17 July, when LONGUEVAL village burst into flames; the whole Wood was enveloped in smoke, and the name Devil's Wood was felt by many to be more appropriate. All except the south-west corner was retaken by the Germans, and attacks were made on Princes Street and Buchanan Street. Men of 3rd South African Infantry on the eastern side of the Wood were practically cut off; after a night of hand-to-hand fighting under appalling conditions, they were forced at dawn on 18 July to surrender for lack of ammunition. Under heavy bombardment, between 15 and 17 July, the South Africans fought their way into the Wood, and despite heavy losses had taken all the Wood except the south-west corner by 17 July. Cut off, 3rd South African Infantry had to surrender – 3 officers and 150 men. The Commanding Officer of 2nd South African Infantry gathered together 140 men of all ranks from the four battalions and fought his way through to rejoin the brigade. At 1800hrs on 20 July, the South African Brigade was behind the Voortrekkers doublecross; the tree here is the only surviving original tree, and full of shrapnel.

On 18 July, the survivors of the three battalions were forced back to Buchanan Street. The German artillery had begun a barrage for their great counter-attack and many huge trees fell as a result. The Germans counter-attacked successfully, but at a great cost in men. Despite the Allies losing the greater part of the Wood, their line held fairly well and it was possible to keep Group informed (according to Neil Fraser-Tytler) and to shoot five or six batteries on various good targets around GUILLEMONT. Fraser-Tytler returned to Group Headquarters at MARICOURT and maintained the communication line with TRÔNES WOOD. This was the only means of divisional communication with the front line, but it was an expensive luxury and needed continuous repair by 8 to 10 men, and Fraser-Tytler's signallers were naturally becoming tired.

Pte W.F. Faulds of 1st South African Infantry was awarded the Victoria Cross for his actions on 18 July. His VC citation in brief was:

A bombing party under Lieut. Craig attempted to rush over 40 yards of ground which lay between the British and enemy trenches. Coming under very heavy fire and machine-gun fire the officer and the majority of the party were killed or wounded. Unable to move, Lieut. Craig lay midway between the two lines of trench, the ground being quite open. In full daylight Private Faulds, accompanied by two other men, climbed over the parapet, ran out, picked up the officer, and carried him back, one man being severely wounded in so doing. Two days later Private Faulds again showed most conspicuous bravery in going out alone to bring in a wounded man and carrying him nearly half a mile to a dressing station, subsequently rejoining his platoon. The artillery fire was at the time so intense that stretcher-bearers and others considered that any attempt to bring in the wounded men meant certain death. This risk Private Faulds faced unflinchingly and his bravery was crowned with success.

The South African Brigade retired on 19/20 July, and on their return to MONTAUBAN-DE-PICARDIE only one-third of the brigade were left to answer the roll call. For 3 days the fight had gone on when the brigade had stood its ground. Tired, hungry and exhausted, the men held on and went forward, clearing the Wood bit by bit. When the South Africans assembled at HAPPY VALLEY after TALUS BOISÉ, they had lost 2,400 of their number. The battle had begun on 15 July and already the brigade had fought through a fortnight's continuous action. When they were relieved, Col Thackeray marched out with two officers, both of whom were wounded, and 140 other ranks, made up of details from all battalions of the brigade. On the morning of 18 July, Thackeray had been holding the Wood with nine and a half companies, about 1,500 men; 2 days later he had 140.

The *History of the Royal Fusiliers* notes that on 19 July the Allies were occupied by the struggle to clear the Wood once again; it was in the lull after the fighting had temporarily died down that 4th Royal Fusiliers (9th Brigade, 3rd Division) took over from battalions of the Essex Regiment, the Suffolk Regiment and the Royal Welsh Fusiliers in the south-east of Delville Wood. There were many casualties in 4th Royal Fusiliers, including men who had not taken a direct part in the attack.

The *History of the Norfolk Regiment* notes that 8th Norfolks (53rd Brigade, 18th Division) were ordered up the valley north-east of CARNOY to relieve the South African Brigade, in order to prepare for a counter-attack on Delville Wood. Reaching the valley at 0430hrs, they were then ordered to be in position by 0615hrs. 53rd Brigade's orders required the battalion to capture the whole of the southern portion of the Wood, but 8th Norfolks found it impossible to make progress. The attacks of the other battalions in LONGUEVAL and the northern parts of Delville Wood could make but little progress, and they had to dig themselves in, as had 8th Norfolks in the southern positions. Here from the afternoon of 19 July until the early morning of 22 July, when it was relieved, 53rd Brigade had to hold on to the captured portion of the Wood against a tremendous bombardment, perpetual fire from snipers and innumerable attacks by small parties of Germans in the tangled undergrowth and among ruined trees.

Two men gained the Victoria Cross on 20 July, firstly Cpl J.J. Davies of 10th Royal Welsh Fusiliers (76th Brigade, 3rd Division), whose citation was as follows:

Prior to an attack on the enemy in a wood he became separated with eight men from the rest of the company. When the enemy delivered their second counter-attack his party was completely surrounded, but he got them into a shell-hole, and by throwing bombs and opening rapid fire succeeded in routing them. Not content with this,

he followed them up in their retreat, and bayoneted several of them.

The other Victoria Cross winner on this day was Pte A. Hill, also of 10th Royal Welsh Fusiliers at Delville Wood. His citation tells the story:

When his battalion had deployed under very heavy fire for an attack on the enemy in a wood he dashed forward when the order to charge was given, and meeting two of the enemy suddenly, bayoneted them both. He was sent later by his platoon sergeant to get in touch with the company, and, finding himself cut off and almost surrounded by some twenty of the enemy, attacked them with bombs, killing and wounding many and scattering the remainder. Then he joined the sergeant of his company, and helped him to fight the way back to the lines. When he got back, hearing that his company officer and scout were lying out wounded, he went out and assisted to bring in the wounded officer, two other men bringing in the scout. Finally he himself captured and brought in two of the enemy.

Cpl Robertson of 3rd Worcesters (7th Brigade, 25th Division) wrote that on 21 July they were off again to Delville Wood: 'Gee that wood will drive me mad – had enough of it on the 18th. We go through the remains of Longueval. Take up our positions in the remains of a trench running along the edge of Delville Wood, this is the bit we suffered for three days ago. Imagine sacrificing 800 men for about 200 yards of ground.'

War correspondent Philip Gibbs wrote:

The German soldiers (21 July) have the advantage in defence. They have placed their machine-guns behind barricades of great tree-trunks, hidden their sharpshooters up in the foliage of trees still standing above all the litter of branches smashed down by shrapnel and high explosives, and send a patter of bullets across to our men, who have dug holes for themselves below the tough roots.

There is no need for either side to do any wood-chopping for the building of their barricades. Great numbers of trees have fallen, cut clean in half by heavy shells, and lie across each other in the tangle of brushwood. Branches have been lopped off or torn off, and are piled up as though for a bonfire. The broken trunks stick up in a ghastly way, stripped of their bark, and enormous roots to which the earth still clings have been torn out of the ground as though by a hurricane, and stretch their tentacles out above deep pits.

The wood is strewn with dead, and wounded men are so caught in the jungle of fallen branches that they can hardly crawl through it. Even the unwounded have to crawl on their way forward to fight over, or underneath, the great trunks which lie across the tracks.

On 22 July, Gibbs could see about 5 miles back into German territory; the enemy were established on the ridge, which accounts for the efforts the Allies made to dislodge them. On 23 July, the remaining men of the South African Brigade, who had been recovering at HAPPY VALLEY, moved from there via MÉAULTE to MARICOURT; there, they were set upon by a 'plague' of war correspondents.

In *Battle-line Narratives, 1915–1918*, H.E. Harvey of 22nd Royal Fusiliers (99th Brigade, 2nd Division) noted that after passing through FRICOURT, his battalion were told to draw extra rounds and bombs; they advanced, eventually arriving in the 'odious destruction' of Delville Wood. A little after 0700hrs on 27 July, 99th Brigade made the final assault to clear the enemy from the Wood; 1st Royal Berkshires, 1st King's Royal Rifle Corps and 23rd Royal Fusiliers (all 99th Brigade, 2nd Division) led the attack, driving the enemy to the further fringe of the deadly area. Every man of 22nd Royal Fusiliers and 17th Middlesex (6th Brigade, 2nd Division) and other men of various units were rounded up by Lt Col A. Grenfell, in charge of cavalry reserves at MONTAUBAN-DE-PICARDIE, and Delville Wood was captured and held.

On 27 July, Sgt A. Gill of 1st King's Royal Rifle Corps gained a Victoria Cross. His citation was as follows:

For most conspicuous bravery. The enemy made a very strong counter-attack on the right flank of the battalion, and rushed the bombing post, after killing all the company bombers. Sergt. Gill rallied the remnants of his platoon, none of whom were skilled bombers, and reorganised his defences, a most difficult and dangerous task, the trenches being very shallow and much damaged. Soon afterwards the enemy nearly surrounded his platoon by creeping up through the thick undergrowth, and commenced sniping at about 20 yards range. Although it was almost certain death, Sergt. Gill stood boldly up in order to direct the fire of his men. He was killed almost at once, but not before he had shown his men where

the enemy were, and thus enabled them to hold up their advance. By his supreme devotion and self-sacrifice he saved a very dangerous situation.

Gill was buried in Delville Wood Cemetery (IV.C.3). Later in the day, 2nd Division retook Delville Wood and held it until 4 August, when 17th Division took it over.

In *History of the Royal Fusiliers*, it is stated that on 27 July the Wood was once again overrun. Four battalions of the Royal Fusiliers claimed a share in the exploit, and the place of honour was given to 23rd Royal Fusiliers. They had had a comfortable time at BERNAFAY WOOD prior to the attack and had formed up in a trench at the edge of the Wood, with 1st King's Royal Rifle Corps on the right and 1st Royal Berkshires in support; 17th Royal Fusiliers (5th Brigade, 2nd Division) lay south of the Wood with 22nd Royal Fusiliers forward on the left. In the afternoon, two companies of 17th Royal Fusiliers moved up to the Wood; before the end of the day, every available man of 22nd Royal Fusiliers had been thrown into the struggle on the right. On 28 July, Delville Wood was temporarily cleared of its last German occupants, when on both sides the losses had been very heavy. Three German regiments were completely annihilated.

On 30 July, C Company, 24th Royal Fusiliers (5th Brigade, 2nd Division), were engaged; they had taken over the front line from the southern edge of the Wood as far as WATERLÔT FARM on the previous day. On 30 July, they advanced against a German trench some 600yds east of WATERLÔT FARM. Fighting was still continuing around Delville Wood. In *The Fifth Army*, Lt Gen Sir Hubert Gough, General Officer Commanding Reserve (later Fifth) Army, noted that although the Germans had counter-attacked with the assistance of flame-throwers, the British never made a general practice of this form of warfare, though it was used once in Delville Wood by Fourth Army.

By 1/2 August, Delville Wood was a vast tangle of trees that had fallen, full of fragments of crumpled trenches and 'scrapes', which were full of dead soldiers; the enemy still held the front edge of the Wood. Cpl J. Delaney, a noted boxer, had been killed in the attack by 23rd Royal Fusiliers. From 11 August, 7th, 8th and 9th Rifle Brigade (41st Brigade, 14th Division) were in reserve in the Delville Wood area; 14th Division were to clear the Wood of enemy resistance.

On 22 August, 9th Rifle Brigade who were in the Delville Wood locality and were to assist the advance of 9th King's Royal Rifle Corps (42nd

Brigade, 14th Division), while 61st Brigade (20th Division) had a battalion and a half in front trenches, continuing the line to a point south of the south-east corner of the Wood; brigade headquarters was north-east of BERNAFAY WOOD. By 24 August, the situation had much improved because of an attack in which 20th Royal Fusiliers (19th Brigade, 33rd Division) took part. The *Stafford Knot* noted that 1st North Staffords (72nd Brigade, 24th Division) had come out of the line on 25 August after spending just over a fortnight in the GUILLEMONT sector, where they had had an unpleasant time and suffered some 150 casualties, but had not actually been committed to an assault.

On 26 August, 22nd Brigade (7th Division) relieved elements of 14th Division on the eastern edge of Delville Wood and parts of 20th Division facing GINCHY. At the time, although the enemy had been dislodged from all but a small corner of the Wood, they were holding several trenches that ran into it, which prevented the British from establishing more than a slight hold on them. These trenches ran across the top of the ridge leading from the Wood eastward and flanked the approaches to GINCHY from the west; their capture was therefore essential, and early on the morning of 27 August, bombers of 1st Royal Welsh Fusiliers (22nd Brigade, 7th Division) began fighting for the possession of Ale Alley, which entered the Wood from the north-east corner. The attack went on for several days and involved 1st South Staffords, 2nd Queen's and 21st Manchesters (all 91st Brigade, 7th Division).

Conditions within what remained of the Wood were quite ghastly; no foliage was left and the stumps of trees were twisted in all directions. One particular difficulty was that the trees tended to change their shape after each bombardment and guides who had been in the area for some days would become lost as they tried to locate landmarks. Heavy rain and shell-fire had reduced the ground to a quagmire, and the so-called trenches, often mere ditches connecting shell-holes, were sometimes in liquid mud. The most horrible thing, though, was the presence of hundreds of unburied corpses belonging to both sides, some of which had been there for several weeks. The sight of these decaying bodies was bad enough, but worse still was the stench, for the sickly smell of death pervaded everything.

It was in these conditions that 1st South Staffords moved into Delville Wood on 29 August, as the left forward battalion of 7th Division, to occupy the trenches facing the direction of GINCHY. Two companies were forward in Beer Trench, between Hop Alley and Pilsen Lane, with a detached

strongpoint in Ale Alley; another company were in support in Diagonal Trench, and another in reserve, just south-west of the Wood. 1st South Staffords had been out of the line for 5 weeks, recovering from their July experiences when they had suffered over 300 casualties in the attacks on MAMETZ WOOD. On 30 August, 1st North Staffords took over the sector on their left as the right forward battalion of the division. Two companies held Edge and Inner Trenches, while another company were in support in Devil's Trench and another in reserve (according to the *Stafford Knot*).

On 30/31 August, Capt F.C. Hitchcock of 2nd Leinsters (73rd Brigade, 24th Division) was detailed to bring up his platoon in support of 9th Royal Sussex (also 73rd Brigade, 24th Division). Hitchcock's way lay up a slope, on top of which they scrambled into a shallow communication trench as they were quite visible to the enemy, who were then sniping at them. They made their way to due west of Delville Wood; the exact position was at the junction of Plum Street with Chesney Walk. Hitchcock's platoon were ordered up Plum Street and were to bomb the enemy, who had a position at the T-junction formed by Orchard Trench, which they knew to be held by the enemy in strength. To quote Hitchcock: 'In broad daylight I was ordered to advance up an exposed communication trench with my platoon in file', the objective being to capture the enemy post at Orchard Trench,

> and with bent heads we turned into Plum Street, which was at right angles to Chesney Walk. We advanced very cautiously, as 150 yards ahead of us, on commanding ground, was the Boche post. Along the left-hand side of Plum Street were the shattered stumps of trees, and when we had advanced some 20 yards only . . . bombs rained down all around us. My bombers retaliated, and after a short exchange, the Boches whom we could see quite distinctly wearing their coal-scuttle shaped helmets, retired. We again advanced, but crawling on hands and knees, as the trench was completely obliterated. Enemy snipers now started to worry us, as our screen of smoke from the bombs cleared off. Some men were hit behind me.

The *Stafford Knot* noted that at the end of August, the fighting having swayed to and fro, the Germans were finally expelled. Among the units involved had been 2nd South Staffords (6th Brigade, 2nd Division), who had positions against the German attacks for 4 days at the end of July, incurring over 300 casualties. Having come up via MONTAUBAN-DE-PICARDIE, 1st Rifle Brigade (11th Brigade, 4th Division) had gone to trenches east of Delville Wood. The *Stafford Knot* mentioned that the next morning the whole Wood was heavily shelled; at about 1100hrs, the bombardment became intensive. At about 1230hrs, the assault came in. The Germans in 2nd South Staffords' sector tried to bomb their way forward along Ale Alley and from the right, into Bitter Trench, but were held up and no ground was lost; 1st North Staffords lost a little ground, however. In the afternoon a company of 2nd South Staffords were led forward from the almost obliterated Diagonal Trench, then in a second enemy counter-attack were reduced to less than half-strength and ran out of grenades. In the early evening the Germans broke through near the junction of Hop Alley and Bitter Trench. Meanwhile, the pressure on 1st North Staffords' other flank had been successfully held. Had they not held their ground there was real danger of the whole defence of Delville Wood crumbling; however, 2nd South Staffords were relieved during the night by 2nd Queen's and reserves were brought up for 1st North Staffords. The next night, 1st North Staffords were relieved by 9th East Surreys (72nd Brigade, 24th Division); Maj Dugmore of the Prince of Wales's (North Staffordshire Regiment) was to take over command of 9th East Surreys, whose commanding officer and second in command had both been killed.

On 1 September, 12th Royal Fusiliers (17th Brigade, 24th Division) were suddenly ordered up to the front; on the way up they were delayed for 2 hours in CATERPILLAR VALLEY, owing to a very heavy gas barrage. The guides had gone astray, and it was not until 0330hrs that the battalion were in Carlton Trench, which lay between Delville Wood and HIGH WOOD. At midday the whole line advanced; the sector between HIGH WOOD and Delville Wood was obstinately defended. The main objective for 8th Buffs (17th Brigade, 24th Division) was the strongpoint at the junction of the Wood Lane Trench and Tea Trench, in the north-west corner of Delville Wood. On 4 September, it was fairly quiet, and on the night of 5/6 September, 1st North Staffords and 9th East Surreys were both relieved. After 7 weeks, the battle of Delville Wood officially ended on 3 September.

The two battalions of the Staffordshire regiments could claim that they had met and blunted the last German effort to regain this vital feature. The 38th Division suffered 270 casualties and the 64th Division 214. GINCHY fell a week later and the German Second Line in this part of the front was finally broken. On 7 September, Lt Col H.B. Burnaby of 11th Queen's (123rd Brigade, 41st Division) was killed while reconnoitring Delville Wood, and buried at Dantzig Alley British Cemetery (I.D.31).

In *Other Ranks*, W.V. Tilsley of 1/4th Loyal North Lancashires (164th Brigade, 55th Division) noted that on his way to the front on 7 September, the path wheeled at the edge of the gutted Delville Wood. The black mass of the Wood receded on the left rear, but still they 'lunged on' behind some 'wonderful brave' men in front. Having recently treated Lt Raymond Asquith of 3rd Grenadier Guards (2nd Guards Brigade, Guards Division) and Capt 'Sloper' Mackenzie of the Grenadier Guards, H.W. Bayly, a medical officer with 1st Scots Guards (2nd Guards Brigade, Guards Division), was himself wounded in the leg and on 16 September was taken from the field ambulance near Delville Wood to the casualty clearing station.

According to the *History of the Royal Fusiliers*, in mid-September the Londoners left; sharing in the honour of the capture of FLERS, was 14th Division, which had recently come to the Somme after spending 9 months in the Ypres Salient. They had to make an advance from positions at the eastern end of Delville Wood of some 2,500yds, carrying four successive German lines, the Switch Line, Brown, Tea, Support and Gap Trenches. On 21 September, a salvage party was requisitioned to aid in widening and deepening an old track through Delville Wood.

In *Field Guns in France*, Neil Fraser-Tytler of CL Brigade, Royal Field Artillery (30th Division), noted that in early November his unit were taking over an empty gun position in Delville Wood; as soon as they collected some new guns they were to 'open shop'. All along the road to the Wood there were 'Archies' mounted on motor lorries. In making his position and planning dugouts, Fraser-Tytler noted that they always appeared to be sited on top of several buried Germans.

At the end of April 1918, Delville Wood was lost to the enemy; during the Allied advance there was more heavy fighting in the area.

Delville Wood Cemetery is immediately south of the Wood, on the south side of the LONGUEVAL–GINCHY road. It was made after the Armistice, by the concentration of a few small cemeteries and of isolated graves, almost all from July, August and September 1916. It covers an area of 17,900sq yds and contains 5,206 graves, of which nearly two-thirds are of unknowns. At least 10 cemeteries were concentrated here after the Armistice, including Angle Wood Cemetery at GINCHY, north-west of

Delville Wood in September 1916. *(IWM Q1259)*

MAUREPAS, where 27 men who died in August/September 1916, mainly from the London Regiment, were buried in a shell-hole; Battery Copse Cemetery, between CURLU and MAUREPAS, which once contained 17 British graves from 1916–18; and Courcelette Communal Cemetery German Extension, which had four Allied graves in it.

During the Battle of the Somme, many individual unit memorials were erected across the battlefield, and those which were not returned to regimental depots in the UK were allowed to disintegrate. Even in the mid-1920s, memorials to 1st North Staffords and No. 64 Field Company, Royal Engineers (9th Division) were still in the Wood.

The South African Memorial stands opposite Delville Wood Cemetery; together they form a single architectural design. The central avenue of the cemetery is continued across the LONGUEVAL–GINCHY road by a grass road, in a wide clearing, running northward into Delville Wood; across the clearing, at the top of a low rise, is the memorial to those South Africans who died in the First World War. It is a flint and stone screen, with a shelter at each end and in the middle an arch surmounted by figures of a horse and two men (representing the two races of the Union) in bronze. It was unveiled by the widow of Gen Louis Botha on 10 October 1926, a significant day in South African history. Marshal Joffre had been invited to the ceremonies but his age prevented him from making the journey and his place was taken by Gen Barbier. The memorial, designed by Sir Herbert Baker, does not bear the names of any of the dead; those of the South African dead are recorded in the same cemeteries, or on the same memorials as those of the corps and regiments of the British Army. Baker, one of the three principal architects employed by the Imperial War Graves Commission, worked with the Commission from 13 August 1919 to 31 March 1928. He had lived in South Africa for 25 years and at one time served with Lord Milner, in 1916 a member of the War Cabinet. In addition to the South African Memorial, he also designed 112 cemeteries in France and Belgium.

Some of the original tree trunks had been preserved. There is a postwar description of the Wood taken from the *Ypres Times* (in the 1930s):

The old drives that intersected 'Devils' are back, too, and little cairns perpetuating the war-time nomenclature bestowed upon them. Thus you come upon Campbell Street and your Rotton Row, your Princes Street and Regent Street. At the foot of these bournes are rusted machine-gun tripods . . . scores of South African oaks, dressed in regular 'parade ground' lines, have been planted, in that magnificent expanse of turf lining the Longueval-Ginchy road with the Union's memorial . . . From the summit of the twin turrets, approached by short winding stairways, a wonderful panorama of the new Somme is gained, with the lone New Zealanders' Memorial chiselled out in the centre of the canvas . . . as many as 42 villages can be seen from this monument.

At this time, there were arrowhead signs pointing to famous 'warm corners' and a house built in the English style, standing on the LONGUEVAL side of the Wood and bordering the wide drive, which contained a rest room for pilgrims or tourists. In June 1934, in a year when there were many 'official visits' to the Western Front commemorating the 20 years since 1914, a group of South African ex-servicemen and their wives were visiting Belgium and France, accompanied by Lady Haig and the South African Minister at The Hague. On 12 June the group arrived at Delville Wood and took part in a 'very moving service'.

On 16 July 1956, a special 40th anniversary service was held here, attended by the Prefect of the Somme, the South African and New Zealand ambassadors and 25 veterans of the battle; the director-general of the Commonwealth War Graves Commission was also present. The two members of the Royal Welsh Fusiliers who won the Victoria Cross here, Cpl Davies and Pte Hill, now have a special memorial in the Wood.

In February 1971, the South African government began thinning out the trees in Delville Wood and only one surviving still existed. In the same year the caretaker's cottage was renovated.

In 1974, the South African Legion held a special anniversary service here commemorating the 60th anniversary of the start of the war. In 1979, according to the Commonwealth War Graves Commission's Annual Report, deer, after a very good breeding season, were becoming a problem and needed to be culled. Fortunately for the deer, the French authorities offered to take 50 animals to a national park, which left 17 beasts.

In 1984, the foundation stone was laid for the building of a new museum at Delville Wood, which was opened on 11 November 1986; it would complement the memorial to the South African forces and set out to tell the story of South Africa's role in both world wars. At the same time, a visitors' centre was built close to the LONGUEVAL–GINCHY road, complete with generous parking facilities, a shop and toilets. During the season, it is open every day of the week except Mondays, closing from mid-November until mid-February. Underlining the growing interest in the Battle of the Somme, no fewer than 40 coaches have been known to turn up at Delville Wood in early July.

Special services continue to be held here; on 1 July 1986, HRH the Duke of Kent attended one, and 5 years later, another took place at which the average age of the South African veterans was 95.

DERNANCOURT is a village north of the D120 road between VILLE-SUR-ANCRE and MÉAULTE in the Ancre valley; the main rail route runs through it. A spur line was constructed in November 1915, which left the main line at Dernancourt, and at the request of Fourth Army extended eastwards in order to serve gun positions on the high ground to the south-east of ALBERT. The Dernancourt line was further extended to the Loop, east of the BRAY-SUR-SOMME–FRICOURT line. Dumps were fed by this line; even so, the greater part of the ammunition supply was still carried forward by lorry or wagon.

The whole area was in constant use for training, camping or bivouacking, medical services and for storage dumps. On 8 August 1915, 7th Queen's and 8th East Surreys (55th Brigade, 18th Division) marched the 7 miles from LAHOUSSOYE and remained in the village for a fortnight. At this time some of their companies were attached to 5th Division for instruction in trench duty. It was a quiet period when few casualties were sustained.

On 7 February 1916, 2/1st (Highland) Field Ambulance (51st Division) took over from 56th Field Ambulance (18th Division) at Dernancourt. On 29 February, 17th Highland Light Infantry (97th Brigade, 32nd Division) arrived here, having endured muddy conditions at Hénencourt Wood, and were housed in good and comfortable billets; they then left for the front after a short period. On 29 May, 103rd Field Ambulance (34th Division) were stationed in barns here. There was a large Royal Engineers' dump in the village, which in June was beginning to attract the attention of the German gunners.

On 13 June, when 8th North Staffords (57th Brigade, 19th Division) were here, they camped in tents in a hollow close to the railway line between

Dernancourt and ALBERT. Arriving the day before, 57th Brigade supplied working parties for work behind the line for the next fortnight. At the same time, groups of officers and NCOs made visits to the trenches in front of FRICOURT and MAMETZ. Other battalions camped on the hillside here, and units of 21st Division were here on 4 July. Around 20 July, 2nd Gordon Highlanders (20th Brigade, 7th Division) rested here after being in action at HIGH WOOD; their Commanding Officer, Lt Col B.G.R. Gordon, had been killed during the relief.

The Dernancourt branch railway line mentioned above was carried to the terminus called the Loop, just east of the BRAY-SUR-SOMME–FRICOURT road, with sidings at Ford Spur, GROVE TOWN and HAPPY VALLEY. This line led towards the junction point of the British and French Armies; a short branch off it from Pilla Junction led southwards to a 'breezy' railhead, aptly named Bel Air. Ambulance trains used the Dernancourt–the Loop branch line and the village was a walking wounded and collecting station. X Corps used the Dernancourt–MARICOURT line for the clearing of lightly wounded cases from corps collecting posts in the neighbourhood of CARNOY and MARICOURT.

Siegfried Sassoon of 1st Royal Welsh Fusiliers (22nd Brigade, 7th Division) noted in his *Diary* on 21 July that his battalion transport moved to a hill south-west of Dernancourt on the evening of 20 July. The battalion were expected to return from the trenches at about midnight, and finally arrived at 0545hrs. Sassoon and the transport waited for 6 hours at the crossroads.

In *A Subaltern on the Somme*, Max Plowman of 10th West Yorkshires (50th Brigade, 17th Division) noted that they were at Dernancourt in August and the field where they slept by the crossroads in the open was called BELLEVUE FARM, although Plowman saw no farm. ALBERT lay below them to the north. Hardy, a fellow lieutenant, went on one occasion with Plowman on an expedition to POMMIERS REDOUBT, close to MAMETZ village.

On 8 August, 8th King's Royal Rifle Corps (41st Brigade, 14th Division) moved to Dernancourt, leaving for POMMIERS REDOUBT a week later. On the same day, 7th King's Royal Rifle Corps (also 41st Brigade, 14th Division) also arrived, by train; they left for POMMIERS REDOUBT on 11 August and returned on 27 August. At the end of August, XV Corps Main Dressing Station was formed in the village, on the right bank of the Ancre between Dernancourt and BUIRE-SUR-L'ANCRE, and the Extension to Dernancourt Communal Cemetery was

opened. On 24th August, 2nd King's Own Scottish Borderers (13th Brigade, 5th Division), having first marched and then spent a lot of time in a train that 'crawled', arrived finally at Dernancourt camp from MÉRICOURT-L'ABBÉ station to the south-west. Also on that day, 5th Division, after a rest, moved by rail to the Dernancourt area and joined Lt Gen the Earl of Cavan's XIV Corps. On the next day, 2nd King's Own Scottish Borderers marched to HAPPY VALLEY, west of BRONFAY FARM, where, in quieter times, battalion headquarters used to be.

In September, Nos. 45 and 1/1 (South Midland) Casualty Clearing Stations arrived in Dernancourt and remained here for 6 months. Around 6 September, 18th King's Royal Rifle Corps (122nd Brigade, 41st Division) moved to the village, and carried out training in the area before moving to FRICOURT on 12 September. During this period, 7th Division had two of their brigades, 22nd and 91st, in the area; at the time, the billets were thought to be most unsatisfactory and absolutely filthy. 22nd Brigade cleaned them up, and the village too, and burnt mountains of refuse; they also transformed the sanitary arrangements.

Between 9 and 11 September, 1/9th King's (165th Brigade, 55th Division) bivouacked outside the village, but they had to move after a while, as a long-range gun 'shelled them out of it'. On 11 September, 9th King's Royal Rifle Corps (42nd Brigade, 14th Division) arrived here, and camped in a field north of the railway. Another battalion of the King's Royal Rifle Corps was back in the area on 10 September, having been out of the battle area for 10 days; they left the village for FRICOURT the following day. On 17 September, 7th King's Royal Rifle Corps arrived here for a stay that lasted until 22 September; 8th King's Royal Rifle Corps arrived on 17 September. On 19 September, 18th King's Royal Rifle Corps arrived and were in the village until 2 October, when they left for MAMETZ WOOD for one night. Nos. 47, 48 and 55 Casualty Clearing Stations used an area to the north-west of Dernancourt under the name of EDGEHILL, which took its name from its situation on rising ground.

In the second half of September, 11th King's (pioneers of 14th Division) were billeted in huts here at No. 1 Camp. It was a curious sight to see from this hill at night the campfires burning all around the countryside; it gave very much the appearance of a victorious army. This was before night bombing began. On 24 October, the Germans were still firing long-range shells into the village.

Divisions who had units here included 18th and 33rd Divisions in July 1916; 5th, 17th, 33rd and 55th

Divisions in August; 17th, 24th and 30th Divisions in September; and 12th, 29th and 30th Divisions in October.

Dernancourt Communal Cemetery is a little west of the village, across the railway line; Dernancourt Communal Cemetery Extension is on the north-west side. The Communal Cemetery was used for British burials from field ambulances from September 1915 to August 1916, and again in the March 1918 retreat. There are 127 burials here, of soldiers who were buried from field ambulances at Dernancourt, including Lt Col B.G.R. Gordon (K.4) of 2nd Gordon Highlanders (20th Brigade, 7th Division), who died on 20 July in the battle for HIGH WOOD. Although 33rd Division were to take HIGH WOOD, 20th Brigade were first asked to clear the eastern edge of the wood with roads running southwards. At 0345hrs on 20 July, 2nd Gordon Highlanders advanced on a four-platoon frontage; the first road was reached but machine guns, some of them hidden in the corn, cut the kilted attackers down. Gordon was killed during the relief and the remaining men moved back to Dernancourt.

Designed by Lutyens and finished in 1925, the Dernancourt Communal Cemetery Extension contains the graves of 2,166 men and includes those brought in after the war from 1918 cemeteries at Moor Cemetery, Edgehill and the Albert Road Cemetery at BUIRE-SUR-L'ANCRE. Sgt T.J. Harris, who won his Victoria Cross at MORLANCOURT in August 1918, is buried here (VIII.J.20).

DESTREMONT FARM is now no more, but was on the site of today's le Château Ferme, which is on the left of the D929 ALBERT–BAPAUME road, south of LE SARS; EAUCOURT L'ABBAYE is due east. Eventually captured early in the morning of 29 September 1916, the Farm had been a strongly defended group of buildings; the taking of it assisted the attack on the Flers Line on the left flank. It was captured at 0530hrs by a company of 8th York & Lancasters (70th Brigade, 23rd Division) who, having stormed the farm buildings, made contact with Canadian troops on the left later in the day.

There were assembly trenches behind the farm buildings in October. The farmhouse building itself had two large cellars impervious to artillery fire, and men were able to shelter here.

DEWDROP TRENCH crossed the LESBŒUFS–LE TRANSLOY road, just beyond Rainy Trench on the east side of the road. At the end of October 1916, Dewdrop Trench was captured by 33rd Division. During the night of 5 November, C Company, 2nd

Royal Welsh Fusiliers (19th Brigade, 33rd Division), were ordered up into Dewdrop; the condition of the ground was very bad.

In *Twelve Days*, Sidney Rogerson of 2nd West Yorkshires (23rd Brigade, 8th Division) noted that he crossed a low valley where the shell-ploughed ground was carpeted with dead, the khaki out-numbering the field-grey by three to one. There must have been 200 or 300 bodies lying in an area of a few hundred yards around Dewdrop Trench, once a substantial German reserve line, but now a shambles of corpses, smashed dugouts, twisted iron and wire. The two companies were both posted on the newly captured ridge, and though their fronts were touch-ing, their flanks were both entirely in the air. The only approximation to a trench was the one in which they were sitting, already christened Autumn Trench, which was merely a narrow, unrevetted channel, without shelters or fire-steps, and in which A Company had its headquarters, some 150yds to the left. Fall Trench was the communication trench, but the German position was unclear. The day passed slowly, with the sun doing its best to cheer the bruised landscape, won at the cost of so many thousands of lives, which could be seen stretching away for miles behind. Below in the valley ran Dewdrop Trench with its piles of dead. Beyond it the ground climbed slightly to where the remains of Lesbœufs Wood poked jagged, splintered fingers at the sky. Somewhere to the left was SAILLY-SAILLISEL, and to the right were GINCHY and MORVAL. The middle distance was as featureless as the ground to the rear, save where, on a slope, a tumbled outline of masonry was recognisable as Cemetery Circle, supposed to be an enemy strongpoint. This fragment was all that remained of Zenith Trench which, with the help of the mud, had resisted the 'Full Dress' attack which had cost the British so heavily last time they had been in the line.

DIVE COPSE was the site of XIV Corps Main Dressing Station at the beginning of July 1916. The ground to the north of the cemetery close to the BRAY-SUR-SOMME–CORBIE road was used by a group of field ambulances and was established at Dive Copse. The Copse was named after a Capt Dive of 96th Field Ambulance (30th Division), the first officer to be in command of the main dressing station. There was also a motor ambulance convoy based here, as well as a divisional rest station. It was used for the greater part of the battle, and in November, a divisional rest station was still in the area.

To the south of the Copse, on the east side of the road to SAILLY-LE-SEC, is Dive Copse Cemetery, designed by Sir Edwin Lutyens, which contains 597 graves. Plots I and II were used during the first 3 months of the battle and Plot III has the graves of 77 men who died during the fighting in August 1918. Later, 115 bodies were brought in from the adjacent battlefields.

Lt Col D.G. Blois DSO (II.A.22), commander of LXXXIV Brigade, Royal Field Artillery (18th Division), who died of wounds on 14 July, is buried here. According to Lt (later Col) F.J. Rice of the same brigade, Blois, son of Sir John Blois, 'rode forward with his orderly and trumpeter to reconnoitre when anyone less gallant would have gone on foot. A 15cm H.E. shell burst almost under his horse and he was mortally wounded, and died at Corbie.' Lt Col H. Cornes then took over the brigade. The grave of Lt. Col. W.D. Oswald who died on admission to Dive Copse is buried in II B 15.

DOULLENS, once a major railhead for the Somme battlefield, is a town between Saint-Pol and AMIENS. In the early part of the First World War, it was Gen Foch's headquarters; from the summer of 1915 until March 1916, it was at a junction between the French Tenth Army (on the Arras front) and the British Third Army on the Somme. The Citadelle, to the south-west of the town, was a French military hospital used by both armies, who also shared the railhead.

On 6 September 1915, No. 19 Casualty Clearing Station took over the *Ecole Moderne* and Château Degore and, after a clean-up operation, opened the buildings as a hospital; within a few days, both buildings were equipped with 95 beds. A few weeks later, 36th Division arrived in the Doullens area and moved into new billets. At the end of February 1916, 13th Field Ambulance (5th Division) opened in school buildings in the main street; on 27 February, a very large number of French troops went through the town on their way to try to help stem the German advance at Verdun.

During March, the British no longer shared this front with the French, as their Third Army took over responsibility. On 3 March, No. 41 Casualty Clearing Station arrived in the town and took over a 'jute shed' close to the r ailway station, which had previously been used by the French as a hospital.

Doullens when occupied by German troops, September 1914. *(Peter F. Batchelor Collection)*

Three days later, they took over the *Ecoles Communales*, 150yds from these sheds, which had been previously occupied by the French ambulance; the casualty clearing station's officers' mess was at 87 rue du Bourg. Also on 6 March, 2/1st (Highland) Field Ambulance (51st Division) opened a hospital in school buildings in the town for the sick.

On 11 June, No. 11 Casualty Clearing Station took over the French hospital at the Citadelle; as the build-up to the battle grew, they received 154 patients on 29 June and 108 on 1 July, most of whom were stretcher cases. On 25 June, No. 35 Casualty Clearing Station opened a hospital and received 220 casualties, including 28 men who had been gassed. The next day, they received another 220 patients, then 130 the following day, 400 on 2 July and more than 500 on 5 July. From 7 July, the number of casualties began to decrease.

The largest military hospital in Doullens was run by No. 41 Casualty Clearing Station, who on 2 July alone admitted 1,024 wounded and evacuated 761, most of the cases being from the Fourth Army sector. The next day they admitted 150 wounded, including two Germans, and evacuated 317; on 4 July, they received 207 cases, including one German, and evacuated 202.

After the first day of the battle, many of the casualties from the GOMMECOURT battlefield were taken to the railway halt at Doullens, as well as to WARLINCOURT-LÈS-PAS. A metre-gauge railway line had been built from CANDAS to ACHEUX-EN-AMIÉNOIS. Another medical link, 3 miles west of the town, is Recmenil Farm, which in 1916 was used as a casualty clearing station for the sick and infectious. Later in the battle, No. 19 Casualty Clearing Station was placed at the disposal of the Reserve Army for the Ancre attack.

Doullens was a major component of the medical chain assisting casualties on their way from the battlefield to hospital and eventual recovery. By the end of 1916, Nos. 11 and 35 Casualty Clearing Stations were replaced by No. 3 Canadian Stationary Hospital, and No. 2/1 (Northumbrian) Casualty Clearing Station and the Canadian Casualty Clearing Station remained in the town until June 1918. In May 1918, the hospital at the Citadelle was bombed, resulting in many casualties.

Doullens was much used by the British Army for billeting purposes, and men based outside the town were able to visit it in the evening; certainly members of 12th York & Lancasters (94th Brigade, 31st Division) did so when they were billeted at GÉZAINCOURT to the south-west, 5–13 June.

Between October 1915 and November 1916, several divisions used Doullens as a headquarters, firstly 36th Division and, from February to the end of June, 19th, 37th and 46th Divisions. Between July and November 1916, at least 15 British divisions had links or headquarters in the area: 7th, 11th, 12th, 17th, 18th, 19th, 20th, 29th, 32nd, 35th, 39th, 48th, 51st, 56th and 63rd Divisions.

In February 1916, British medical units began to use Doullens Communal Cemetery French Extension (No. 1) to the west of the town; by the spring of 1918, after the German advance, it was full. It contains the graves of 1,335 Commonwealth troops, as well as French and German troops from the same period. In May 1940, Doullens was bombed and 35 British troops who died on 20/21 May when helping to defend the town are buried here.

Designed by Charles Holden, the Doullens Communal Cemetery Extension (No. 2) was set up opposite the Doullens Communal Cemetery. There are many graves, including those of German casualties, which have the date of death of February 1919; this may mean that they died of influenza. All told, there are the graves of 374 Commonwealth soldiers here. The Communal Cemetery itself has the graves of 10 British troops killed in the Second World War.

DURY, a south-western suburb of AMIENS, had a cemetery in the grounds of a local lunatic asylum. After the war, the Imperial War Graves Commission decided that it would have to be moved, as one could not run the risk of having visitors to the graveyard being confronted by the inmates of the hospital.

E

EAUCOURT L'ABBAYE is north-west of MARTINPUICH and south-east of LE SARS. In 1916, an enemy line ran in front of the Abbaye and LE SARS. DESTREMONT FARM, which was south-west of LE SARS, had been converted by the Germans into a fortress, as had an old quarry just south of Eaucourt l'Abbaye. These formed a series of extremely strong positions until the Allies made progress in early October. Further to the east, where a shallow sunken road running north from HIGH WOOD crossed the German Third Line, was a group of fortified positions that was intersected by two trenches known as Drop Trench and Goose Alley, which formed a quadrilateral. Further to the north-east was another series of formidable positions that were known as Factory Corner.

On 25 September, 2nd King's Royal Rifle Corps (2nd Brigade, 1st Division) went into trenches here when they relieved 1st Black Watch (1st Brigade, 1st Division) and were involved in an attack on the Flers Line in the next 24 hours. Progress was made in the advance towards the line between Eaucourt l'Abbaye and LE SARS, on which the Germans had fallen back after a successful attack on part of the line north-west of GUEUDECOURT on 27 September. By dawn on 29 September, 47th Division – who were eventually to capture Eaucourt l'Abbaye – sent up 141st Brigade to take over the line from 1st Division. A further advance was intended, in which the objective was the Abbaye itself; it was made up of a group of houses round the old Abbaye buildings, which were reputed to possess extensive cellars. Lying low at the point where a short valley from the HIGH WOOD direction turns at a right angle north-west of the main ALBERT–BAPAUME road, Eaucourt l'Abbaye is therefore commanded by higher ground on each side, except from the north-west.

It was important before the attack began to push forward along the Flers Line on the high ground to the south-west of the buildings. 1/18th Londons (141st Brigade, 47th Division) were given this task; the first attempt on 29 September was unsuccessful, but on 30 September they gained the ground required. 2/Lt E.G. Steel of 1/20th Londons (also 141st Brigade, 47th Division) was awarded the Military Cross for leading his platoon to their final objective and for maintaining the position for 4 days, 1–4 October. After their involvement at HIGH WOOD, 1/15th Londons (140th Brigade, 47th Division) had occupied some disused trenches that were entirely devoid of dugouts in the QUADRANGLE, close to MAMETZ WOOD. Here they spent several days waiting for news of 141st Brigade's attack on Eaucourt l'Abbaye, before the relief took place on the night of 4 October. On 1 October, 1/18th Londons had been held up by continuous machine-gun fire from the west corner of the Abbaye complex; later, the tanks were to silence these particular guns, whereupon 1/19th and 1/20th Londons (both 141st Brigade, 47th Division) rushed through the village and established a line to the north of it.

To the left of 47th Division, 50th Division were also involved in the fighting on 1 October. Lt Col R.B.T. Bradford of 1/9th Durham Light Infantry (151st Brigade, 50th Division) was awarded the Victoria Cross for his fine leadership at Eaucourt l'Abbaye. In brief, the citation for the award reads:

> For most conspicuous bravery and good leadership in attack, whereby he saved the situation on the right flank of his Brigade and of the Division. Lieut.-Colonel Bradford's battalion was in support. A leading battalion having suffered very severe casualties and the Commander wounded, its flank became dangerously exposed at close quarters to the enemy. Raked by machine-gun fire, the situation of the battalion was critical. At the request of the wounded Commander, Lieut.-Colonel Bradford asked permission to command the exposed battalion in addition to his own. Permission granted, he at once proceeded to the foremost lines. By his fearless energy under fire of all descriptions, and his skilful leadership of the two battalions, regardless of all danger, he succeeded in rallying the attack, captured and defended the objective, and so secured the flank.

In *Sir Douglas Haig's Great Push*, it is noted that the second trench in front of Eaucourt l'Abbaye was easily carried, as were the double line of trenches away on the left of the attack outside LE SARS. There was, however, a piece of ground on the right of the advance to Eaucourt l'Abbaye, where machine guns, skilfully placed and protected by a stretch of barbed wire which the British artillery had failed to destroy, caused the British not a few casualties, until the tanks came up and flattened the entanglements, rolled down the sandbag defences, and wiped out machine guns and gunners. This was the group of entanglements named the Circus.

On 1 October, four divisions had been involved in the attack, with the tanks advancing on either side of the Eaucourt l'Abbaye–Flers Line. The British attack on this day achieved the capture of a front that was 3,000yds long, although it was reported that 47th Division did not keep up close enough to the artillery barrage. Despite the success of the British on this day, they were to lose ground over the next few days before securing the Abbaye and LE SARS permanently.

On 2 October, the Germans regained a footing in Eaucourt l'Abbaye and LE SARS which was not held. In the history of 47th Division it is noted that two companies of 1/18th Londons attacked up the Flers Line successfully, got through Eaucourt l'Abbaye and completed the circuit of British troops around the village. The capture of the village brought several of the batteries over from HIGH WOOD into a little valley beyond the Starfish, where they maintained a precarious existence for the remainder of their stay on the Somme, and helped to cover the gallant but unsuccessful attacks of 47th Division, and later of 9th Division on the BUTTE DE WARLENCOURT.

On 3 October, 47th Division regained Eaucourt l'Abbaye, and on 4 October, the Germans were driven out. That night, 1/17th Londons (141st Brigade, 47th Division) were relieved by 1/15th Londons in the Flers Line at Eaucourt l'Abbaye. This relief was an ordeal almost as trying as a battle, as troops had to struggle through the mud and through HIGH WOOD in the pitch dark; when they eventually reached the Flers Line, they were exhausted.

On 5 October, 1/6th Londons (also 140th Brigade, 47th Division) gained an important point by occupying the old mill 500yds west of Eaucourt l'Abbaye. War correspondent Philip Gibbs wrote of this incident: 'Yesterday the sky cleared and the men who had taken l'Abbaye by such gallant struggle pushed out and seized the mill house to the west of those ruins between it and the tanks, from which the Germans had been maintaining heavy machine-gun fire!' In *Sir Douglas Haig's Great Push*, it is noted of the same incident that on the night of 5 October, the British advanced their position north-east of Eaucourt l'Abbaye. On the northern part of their front they discharged gas at two points against the enemy's trenches, and carried out several successful raids.

According to 47th Division's divisional history, on 7 October

the main German line of defence opposite was the Gird Line, running north-west from Gueudecourt to Warlencourt, and including the Butte de Warlencourt. Anticipating an attack on this important line, the Germans had dug a new trench across the Allied front over the high ground north of Eaucourt l'Abbaye, westward in the valley. This trench named Diagonal was the first objective of the 14th Brigade of the 32nd Division; their final objective was the Gird Line, including the Butte itself.

On the right some progress was made, and a line was established along the sunken road leading north-west from the Abbaye to le Barque. On the left, companies of 1/8th Londons (140th Brigade, 47th Division), followed by 1/7th Londons (also 140th Brigade, 47th Division), tried to advance down the slope, forward of the mill; they met, in addition to fire from Diagonal Trench, the full force of the

enemy artillery and machine-gun fire, cleverly sited in depth so as to bring a withering fire to bear along the western slopes leading up to the Butte and the high ground to the south of it. From across the valley the enemy had magnificent observation of the ground leading to the British objective, and made full use of it. Although attacked by four divisions, the Butte was not captured until the enemy left it in their general retirement at the end of February 1917.

The *History of the Civil Service Rifles* (1/15th Londons, 140th Brigade, 47th Division) takes up the story. On 7 October, they learnt that they were to attack the BUTTE DE WARLENCOURT line, an objective some 2,800yds distant. Zero Hour was 1400hrs, and other companies occupied the same relative positions as they had at HIGH WOOD, A Company again being on the right. The three companies on the left were unfortunate once more, for they had to file through the village of Eaucourt l'Abbaye soon after leaving their assembly trenches and had to extend their right into waves again after negotiating the village. They were caught by the full fury of the German artillery barrage and those men who got through the village were swept down by a most intense machine-gun fire. On the right, A Company made some little progress, and crossing the Eaucourt l'Abbaye–le Barque road dug a new line alongside the remnant of other divisions, all of whom had met a similar fate. There was an artillery creeping barrage on this occasion, it is true, but as it moved at the rate of 100yds per minute and there were 2,800yds between the jumping-off trenches and the objective, the advancing waves of infantry soon got badly left behind. The losses of 7 October amounted to 5 officers and 344 other ranks; it should be remembered that on this occasion, 1/15th Londons were not more than 500 strong at the outset. The relief by 7th Seaforth Highlanders (26th Brigade, 9th Division) took place on 9 October, and was a welcome contrast to the previous one in this section; the men quickly found their way out and reached the transport lines in BOTTOM WOOD before midnight.

There is another description, from C.P. Clayton of 2nd Welsh (3rd Brigade, 1st Division), who described the October–November period. His battalion were in support and they had had long nights of digging and carrying, under wretched conditions. Just ½ mile to their left was the ruined monastery of Eaucourt l'Abbaye. They were told that 1st Glosters (3rd Brigade, 1st Division) were mostly living in the cellars under the ruins. Clayton received his brigade orders to send a company to clear trenches which led from the Abbaye to the rear. The trench was shown on the map and had been roofed in places with sheet iron, lightly covered with earth to conceal it from aerial observation. Suddenly, right at his feet he saw a ray of light, and found that the trench entered Eaucourt l'Abbaye by a flight of steep steps. At the foot of the steps were a section of 1st Glosters taking their rest, and from one room to another his party were directed until they came to the company commander, in a tiny office of his own.

In Gird Trench, by the main road to Eaucourt l'Abbaye, there still exists some elephant hutting on the north bend used by the New Zealanders and British when attacking the Gird System.

In *The Somme*, Norman Gladden of 1/7th Northumberland Fusiliers (149th Brigade, 50th Division) described the conditions his battalion encountered. The morning of 6 November was cold and wet, and drizzle continued as they filed along the light railway track towards the line. Heavy clouds hung low in the sky. They approached a low ridge and a line of trees where, the guide told them, the dressing station was situated. Heavy shells were falling away to the right and these made them hurry as the path turned into a sort of cutting. They came across a pile of shattered brickwork, which marked the former hamlet of Eaucourt, as shown by a noticeboard. A little further on they came upon the cabin and shelters that formed the dressing station in what seemed to them to be a very exposed position and under a row of tall trees, which had suggested its name of Seven Elms; stretchers bearing those who had received medical attention were loaded onto the light railway which was to convey them to the rear. As they loitered under cover of the cutting beneath the broken elms, Gladden found it difficult to understand why this forward dressing station hadn't been discovered by the enemy gunners and destroyed. It was in a very exposed position for such an activity.

Pte J. Jackson of 1st Cameron Highlanders (1st Brigade, 1st Division) noted in his diary: 'D Company went into reserve in Eaucourt l'Abbaye, an old mansion [*sic*] which had been levelled to the ground, and of which, only the cellars remained, but these formed a safe shelter, being practically shell proof.'

EBART FARM's main buildings are at the junction of the CONTAY–BEAUCOURT-SUR-L'HALLUE road (the D919). At the end of August 1915, the field ambulances of 51st Division arrived here and remained for at least 4 months. Casualties from the advanced dressing station at AUTHUILLE were sent here regularly.

On 24 December, 91st Field Ambulance (32nd Division) arrived and were here until 12 February 1916, when 1/3rd (West Riding) Field Ambulance (49th Division) took over the divisional rest station. Their war diary (WO95/2790) described the location as

a large empty farm. One wing is set apart for patients, another wing for Field Ambulance personnel and the two other wings for officers, stores, bath houses etc. On another farm on the opposite side of the road horses are stabled and wagons parked. At a neighbouring château Motor Transport, drivers and motor ambulances are billeted, and the officers. Accommodation for patients is very limited but the place can be expanded by installing bunks on the tier system. We are supposed to be running a rest station but at present only have accommodation for about 80 cases. At 3pm 119 'unfits' arrived transferred from 1/2 WR FA. These are mostly chronic cases, permanently unfit for trench duty.

After only 2 days, 1/3rd (West Riding) Field Ambulance left for BREILLY and were replaced by Maj Dobson and 20 men from 1/2nd (West Riding) Field Ambulance (also 49th Division), who remained here until 17 February, when they were replaced by 1/1st (West Riding) Field Ambulance (also 49th Division).

On 1 March, 1/3rd (West Riding) Field Ambulance arrived back at the farm, where they remained until 28 March, when they left for PIERREGOT. In mid-March, the billiard room in the château had been opened as a nine-bed hospital for officers. At the end of March, 12 bell tents and 2 operating tents were erected. In early June, patients with scabies were dealt with here. On modern maps, the farm is called Esbart.

ECLUSIER-VAUX, 3 miles from BRAY-SUR-SOMME, is a village on the Somme Canal between FRISE and CAPPY. In 1915–16, it was at a point very close to the French lines. If the enemy managed to cross they would be able to get behind the British lines at Royal Dragon's Wood and put the guns in that part of the line out of action.

On 17 August 1915, 15th Field Ambulance (5th Division) moved to an advance collecting point here. In the early part of 1916, the area became the responsibility of 30th Division; in February, 17th Manchesters (90th Brigade, 30th Division) had a small detachment here, guarding the crossing after an enemy raid on French lines at FRISE on 28 January. The trench was too shallow to use safely, and part of the detachment was 'lying hidden in the buildings and garden of a small farm by Eclusier bridge – the only building in the village which had not yet been destroyed'. At the same time their colleagues went across the canal to Royal Dragon's Wood for picks and shovels, but within a short period the detachment returned to SUZANNE. It was replaced by a French company who guarded the bridge here.

Eclusier Communal Cemetery, to the north-west of the village, has the graves of 23 British soldiers who died in 1917.

EDGEHILL was a railway siding for supplies, to the north-east of the village of DERNANCOURT; it took its name from its position on rising ground. By the beginning of the battle it was one of the principal railheads used for supplies and the siding had been built in a field between Dernancourt Junction and Buire Halt.

On 7 August 1916, 1/5th Seaforth Highlanders (152nd Brigade, 51st Division) bivouacked here. From 18 September to 15 April 1917, No. 45 Casualty Clearing Station was here; arriving on the same day, No. 56 Casualty Clearing Station left for GROVE TOWN on 15 October and returned on 23 October, remaining until 25 February 1917.

On 15 November, 12th Manchesters (52nd Brigade. 17th Division) entrained here for the village of HANGEST-SUR-SOMME.

ENGLEBELMER is on the D129 road south-east of MAILLY-MAILLET, 4½ miles north-west of ALBERT. On 31 July 1915, 11th Brigade (4th Division) arrived here. On 17 November, units from 89th and 90th Brigades (both 30th Division) arrived in the village for their introduction to trench warfare and to mud. In particular, 18th Manchesters (90th Brigade, 30th Division) learnt about the latter, 'which was as glutinous and abundant as anything that we had to cope with afterwards'. On 16 November, they returned to CANAPLES, where they were to spend Christmas.

Englebelmer was behind the lines during the whole of the war. Until the end of 1916, it was used as a field ambulance station; a divisional rest station for casualties was also set up here, and an advanced dressing station was at Mesnil. There were still many civilians living in the village in February 1916. 87th Brigade (29th Division) had their headquarters in the village, which the regimental history of The King's Own Scottish Borderers described as being a 'smelly, flea-bitten but picturesquely straggling village with a good church'.

On 3 April, 2nd South Wales Borderers (also 87th Brigade, 29th Division) left their billets here to march to the AUCHONVILLERS sector.

Prior to the start of the battle, 29th, 30th, 31st and 36th Divisions were most closely associated with the village. On 24 June, General Staff wagons were sent up from CLAIRFAYE FARM in order to collect lightly wounded. On the eve of the battle, 30 June, 1st King's Own Scottish Borderers (87th Brigade, 29th Division) marched up from Acheux Wood on their way to the front, which lay along a communication trench called Gabion Avenue, which began almost as soon as Englebelmer ended.

In the period 30 June/1 July, 1st Newfoundlanders (88th Brigade, 29th Division) had their cookers assembled in a wood near the village; in the early hours of 1 July, their 'ten per cent cadre', who had moved up to the wood, supplied carrying parties to bring the troops in the dugouts their hot breakfast. On 6 July, after their crippling losses at BEAUMONT-HAMEL on 1 July, 1st Newfoundlanders arrived back in the village and stayed there, amid continuous shelling. Early on 8 July, they withdrew to tents at Mailly Wood to the north-west.

In *Somme Overflows* and *The Mind's Eye*, the poet Edmund Blunden of 11th Royal Sussex (116th Brigade, 39th Division) mentions being billeted at Englebelmer:

> After several postponements we made our first appearance in the fighting. In the cold early mist of 2 September (5.10 a.m.) our Division went over and later the shattered battalions withdrew from the valleys and ridges still echoing with bombardment and the pounding of machine guns. The Somme pulled us under once, and we emerged gasping . . . and once in, appeared unlikely ever to get out . . . In these trenches we worked hard and were gas shelled and trench mortared not too violently most days; but the minewerfers caused casualties. The battalion relieved by the Cheshires assembled in a trench along Hamel village street and in the setting sun arrived in Englebelmer, three hundred fewer in number than when it passed through earlier.

On 4 October, Blunden noted that under a burst of gas shelling they were relieved, but only that they might make a circuit through Englebelmer Wood and Martinsart Wood, on their way up to the HAMEL trenches. Neville Lytton, author of *The Press and the General Staff*, had been with Blunden while in training in England with 11th Royal Sussex; he seems to have been in the same area around

3 September, but not as a fellow participant in trench duties, as he was probably based at Englebelmer in brigade headquarters.

Having been relieved, the Hood Battalion (189th Brigade, 63rd Division) were billeted in barns in the village until 23 October, when they went to Mesnil, to the south-east. On 4 November, they were back there again for the final Somme battles, having been to PUCHEVILLERS. The Hawke Battalion (also 189th Brigade, 63rd Division) 'derived some comfort from the village' in the period before the final battles began on 13 November, although very little safety. Here, by day men could walk about or sit above ground with at least a roof over their heads. When the battalion were here they were required to supply working parties and digging parties to their total strength, and a good deal beyond it, every night. These parties began with a march of 3 miles or more to the HAMEL trenches, which were due east of the village, and due west of THIEPVAL; this led to the battalion losing 150 men even before going into action. During this period, Lt E. Dyett of the Nelson Battalion (also 189th Brigade, 63rd Division) was arrested in a farmhouse here for being absent from his battalion; he was later tried in a farmhouse at Champneuf on 26 December and executed. He was buried at Le Crotoy Communal Cemetery on the coast.

When fighting returned to the area in 1918, the field ambulance station at Englebelmer was used once more, when it was liable to occasional shelling.

Englebelmer Communal Cemetery to the south-west of the village was used for British burials from June to September 1916 and again in May 1918. There are graves here of 52 soldiers and sailors from 63rd Division. In Row B of Plot II are five graves of men from the York and Lancashire Regiment, who all died on 13 August 1916. Four graves are of men from 89th Brigade's (30th Division) raid on 28 June 1916, graves A.6 to A.8. There are also four graves of men from the Bedfordshire Regiment. Englebelmer Communal Cemetery Extension is at the south-west corner of the Communal Cemetery, away from the road; it was begun in October 1916, closed in March 1917, and used again in 1918. After the Armistice, 49 graves were brought into it from Beaussart Communal Cemetery Extension, MAILLY-MAILLET, and from the battlefields immediately north and east of the village. There is a special memorial to two men from here whose graves were later destroyed. The cemetery commands extensive views to the west and south and has the graves of 148 identified casualties.

After the war, Englebelmer was 'adopted' by Winchester, Hampshire.

ETAPLES was the site of an immense camp and a number of hospitals during the First World War. The area was remote from attack except from the air and was accessible by rail from the northern and southern battlefields. During 1917 alone, 100,000 troops were stationed here among the sand-dunes. The writers Vera Brittain and Winifred Holtby were two of the nurses who worked in the military hospitals here. In fact Brittain had been a VAD at No. 24 General Hospital in 1917–18 and Holtby, a member of the Queen Mary's Army Auxiliary Corps, was at Camiers in 1918. During the war, thousands of casualties were brought to the hospitals here from the battlefields, many of whom were to die here. In turn a huge cemetery was required, which was designed by Sir Edwin Lutyens in partnership with Gertrude Jekyll. Architecturally it became a perfect example of Lutyens' skills when working with landscape, together with the need to accommodate more than 11,000 graves. As a design it is brilliant, and also a most moving place to visit. The soil here is 'sticky clay over chalk and covered by sand'.

Casualties buried here include at least three lieutenant-colonels who were wounded in the Somme battle. Lt Col A. Holdsworth (I.A.33) of 2nd Royal Berkshires (25th Brigade, 8th Division) died of wounds on 7 July after his battalion had made a successful attack against OVILLERS-LA-BOISSELLE on 1 July; Lt Col E. Scott (I.A.40) of 1/6th West Yorkshires (146th Brigade, 49th Division) died of wounds on 9 August; and Lt Col W. Ash (I.A.53) of 2nd Middlesex (23rd Brigade, 8th Division) died of wounds on 20 September.

In 1933, when Brittain and Holtby made a return visit to Etaples, the site of the huts which had been No. 24 General Hospital was 'now humped and covered in ragwort'.

ETINEHEM is on the north bank of the Somme between BRAY-SUR-SOMME and CHIPILLY, 6 miles south of ALBERT. With CORBIE, it was to provide the main pigeon lofts for Fourth Army's pigeon baskets. There was also an ammunition refilling point in the village, where material came up by barge before being unloaded and taken on to battery dumps by lorry; if a barge broke down, lorries were used instead.

Arthur Taylor noted that, like BRAY-SUR-SOMME, Etinehem had a port in the old river and one could still reach the village if using a small boat. The area is associated with the writer Georges Duhamel, who wrote a book that was translated with the title *Civilization*. During the 1916 Somme battle, Duhamel worked with a French medical team

Entreé de la rue de Chipilly, Etinehem.
(Peter F. Batchelor Collection)

here in a tented hospital, and strove 'to deal with the appalling stream of casualties flowing endlessly back and from the front line only a few kms away'. The landscape was described as

> a scorched, ruined, fly-infested dustbowl, turned instantly to mud in the rain; a town of Red-Cross tents, a makeshift cemetery, constantly in use for burial; British and French artillery pieces pounding the far enemy positions. Every day, twenty thousand horses were brought down to the pasture lands by the river to drink; every day barges arrived and departed from the quay, bringing ammunition and supplies, carrying the patched-up wounded back to Amiens.

On 7 August 1915, elements of 55th Brigade (18th Division) were here under instruction from 5th Division. On the next day, 15th Field Ambulance (5th Division) left the bigger of two châteaux for a smaller one, as it was required as a forward rest station and taken over by 13th Field Ambulance (also 5th Division), with accommodation for 200 men in the château or grounds. A dining hall was set up in the garage and men took baths in old wine casks; other men bathed in a pond specially dug for non-swimmers in the sides of the lake. This situation did not last long, as 5th Division headquarters had designs on the building and moved into it on 17 August, where it was to remain for the whole time the Division were in this sector. On the same day, 13th Field Ambulance moved to CORBIE. Later in the war, the château was destroyed

On 13 August, two men died of chest wounds. There were six other British burials from August and September 1915 in Etinehem Communal Cemetery, to the south-east of the village, which were later transferred; one grave had already been destroyed by shell-fire.

South of the BRAY-SUR-SOMME–CORBIE road, at a road crossing known as Côte (ACC) 80, is the Côte 80 French National Cemetery, which was formed by French field ambulances in June–October 1916; Australian troops added burials to it in August 1918. Nineteen of the 49 British graves are of men from the United Kingdom, one of whom, a Royal Field Artillery driver, died in September 1915.

On 18 February 1916, 1/6th Seaforth Highlanders (152nd Brigade, 51st Division) moved here from CORBIE, after an exhausting march. This was due to the roads having been turned into swamps by recent rains and heavy traffic. After one day's rest they were ordered back to CORBIE on 20 February.

Apart from 5th, 18th and 9th Divisions, the other formation which had most links with the village from January to July 1916 was 30th Division. On the night of 1/2 June, 16th Manchesters (90th Brigade, 30th Division) moved into a camp here; 4 weeks later, at 1900hrs on 30 June, they marched off from here, reaching their assembly trenches close to CAMBRIDGE COPSE in the MARICOURT area at 0045hrs. Their sister battalion, 17th Manchesters, did likewise; both battalions had been inspected by their divisional commander, Maj Gen Shea, as well as their brigade commander. On 12 June, 18th Manchesters (also 90th Brigade, 30th Division) moved to billets here in reserve to 30th Division, and supplied working parties; they left for SAISSEVAL (by train from HEILLY to AILLY-SUR-SOMME) on 18 June, but returned to Etinehem on 26 June. On 22 June, 19th Manchesters (21st Brigade, 30th Division) were here before moving to BRAY-SUR-SOMME the next day. During the night of 30 June, they took up battle positions, with 20th King's (89th Brigade, 30th Division) to their right and 18th King's (21st Brigade, 30th Division) on their left.

After the 1916 battles and the enemy withdrawal in 1917, the enemy returned when the Germans took over Etinehem in March 1918; it was recaptured by 50th Australian Battalion (13th Australian Brigade, 4th Australian Division) on 10 August.

F

FAFFEMONT FARM, also known as Falfemont, is today south-west of COMBLES. It should not be confused with the site of the original, which during the first weeks of the Battle of the Somme was a German fortified strongpoint, south-east of WEDGE WOOD and GUILLEMONT and south-west of LEUZE WOOD. It was situated on high ground overlooking the Allied positions and was rectangular in shape.

The ground between MALTZ HORN FARM (north of HARDECOURT-AU-BOIS) and Faffemont Farm was broken by a three-pronged ravine with ANGLE WOOD in its centre. On 24 August 1916, 17th Lancashire Fusiliers (104th Brigade, 35th Division) were to be involved in an attack to be carried out against Faffemont Ridge, while the French were to attack Oakhanger Wood to the south-east of the Farm. However, the attack was later postponed; the French were under the

impression that the Farm was deserted during this period, which it was not.

On 3 September, the British planned to make an attack on the Farm, together with WEDGE WOOD, in tandem with a barrage from French artillery; the French Army on the British right would then be able to move forward. The division chosen was 5th Division; 2nd King's Own Scottish Borderers, 14th Royal Warwicks and 15th Royal Warwicks (all 13th Brigade, 5th Division) were the units involved. On 2 September, 2nd King's Own Scottish Borderers moved up to ANGLE WOOD, from where they would launch an attack. The Farm was bombarded on the same day, but German reinforcements could be seen emerging from LEUZE WOOD on their way to it. At 0900hrs on 3 September, the attack began; despite the assurances from the French, for some reason there was no bombardment, and thus no protective barrage, and the whole attack was annihilated in the 500yds in front of the Farm as German machine guns cut the attackers down from their strongly held positions. The war diary (WO95/1552) stated that 2nd King's Own Scottish Borderers lost some of their best officers; at least eight were killed and two wounded. Of the other ranks, 91 were killed, 137 wounded and 55 missing, making a total of 283. The men who had survived were relieved at midnight; on 6 September, Maj Gen R.Stephens, General Officer Commanding 5th Division, addressed 13th Brigade and apologised for the disaster, but did not explain how it happened or why the attack was not called off.

Faffemont Farm was finally taken in the early hours of 5 September by 1st Cheshires and 1st Bedfords (both 15th Brigade, 5th Division) after 1st Norfolks (also 15th Brigade, 5th Division) had been held up in the front. No part of the Farm was left standing by this time, nor were there any dugouts or trenches. The battalions therefore had to spend the night in the open, as a few bricks were all that was left of what had been a vital part of the German defence system. Later, 16th Royal Warwicks (also 15th Brigade, 5th Division) established a line down the slope of the ravine, linking 95th Brigade (5th Division) in LEUZE WOOD with the French left, which was now in Savernake Wood.

The Fifth Division in the Great War pays a special tribute to the artillery of 35th and 56th Divisions who covered the divisional front, as their bombardment and barrage fire had rendered possible the success of taking the Farm. The gun positions in Chimpanzee Valley and the area south-east of BERNAFAY WOOD were subjected to heavy bombardments, with much gas shelling. On

10 September, 1st East Surreys (95th Brigade, 5th Division) had two companies in trenches halfway up the slope to the Farm in Faffemont Wood.

Amid the farm crops is a three-man grave containing the bodies of Capt Heumann of 1/2nd Londons (169th Brigade, 56th Division), Sgt Maj Mills (known, of course, as Bertram) and Sgt Torrance. The author thanks the late Mr A. Spagnoly for the account of how the men came to be in this small grave, which is quite separate from any cemetery. Heumann was killed in an abortive attack by A and B Companies of 1/2nd Londons, as 169th Brigade endeavoured to get into the sunken road behind COMBLES and Loop Trench, and thus loosen the grip on COMBLES. A Company bombed across the Wood to Loop Trench and the Germans massed for a counter-attack. B Company under Heumann were at a spot south-east of the Wood called Lone Tree. Heumann was ordered to attack Q Trench, or Leuzenake Trench, running from the Wood, and divert or dissipate the counter-attack; he was sitting in a shell-hole at Lone Tree, briefing his officers, when a shell burst overhead, killing both him and Mills. Both men were quickly buried where they fell. Just how Sgt Torrance, who was killed on the same day at the Wood, came to be with them, only stretcher-bearers clearing up that night could say. The attack went in under another officer, and was partially successful, managing to get into Q Trench; 4 officers and 23 other ranks died in the action. The ground gained was 55 yards. There were also 98 wounded.

J.F. Tucker, author of *Johnny Get Your Gun*, served in 1/13th Londons (168th Brigade, 56th Division); he wrote vividly of the action at Faffemont Wood, which actually contained farm buildings in 1916. In particular, he mentions coming across a trench full of dead Prussian Guards wearing white vests. There were also many dead of the Royal Irish Rifles. Tucker also mentions the death, in September, of Maj C.C. Dickens of 1/13th Londons, grandson of the famous novelist.

According to papers at the Liddle Collection at Leeds University, L/Cpl H.G.R. Williams of 1/5th Londons (169th Brigade, 56th Division), when going up the line, came across the bodies of men of 1/13th Londons who had been killed in a recent attack on Faffemont Farm. He too noted the lack of actual dugouts or shelters in the area of the Farm, and also that his battalion were shelled by a French battery.

FARGNY MILL, north of VAUX-SUR-SOMME on the north bank of the Somme Canal and marshes, was a small redoubt which saw fierce fighting in

the Franco-Prussian war of 1870. Prior to the Battle of the Somme, it was part of the VAUX sector, the most southern point of the British line, the front line at this point having turned almost due south from MARICOURT. It was a natural cut-off point, as the next section of territory was made up of a series of marshes; much of the time, a 'live and let live' system was adopted by both British and German troops, as well as by French troops, whose territory this really was.

On 8 August 1915, Lt Col S.J. Ormsby of 15th Field Ambulance (5th Division) took over a regimental aid post at MARICOURT. Ormsby met up with a French medical officer, who took him via a communication trench about 2 miles to the regimental aid post at Fargny Mill, which was 65yds from the German trenches. The regimental aid post was located in the cellar of the mill house, which had been completely wrecked by shell-fire. Stretcher-bearers could only collect casualties from it at night.

It will come as no surprise that the compilers of battalion histories of 16th, 17th and 18th Manchesters (all 90th Brigade, 30th Division) have left detailed accounts of their time, both here and at MARICOURT to the north, as they spent several months here in and out of the line. 18th Manchesters' battalion history stated: 'In many ways the Vaux sector was unique. It was the right flank of the British front, and besides the pleasant intimacy with our Allies, which the work of liaison afforded to officers and men, the sector was attractive. It was extensive – covering nearly two miles of front – and its defence gave an interest – which strongly contrasted with the monotony of trench warfare.'

Fargny Mill was a redoubt where a composite company lived in trenches. The position consisted of the actual mill buildings, which sheltered headquarters 'from which a series of communication trenches in star formation' projected. In addition to sap-heads, there was a listening post or 'crow's nest' within 35yds of the enemy, cut into the side of a cliff known as le Chapeau de Gendarme. The mill was almost isolated by day, as it would be foolish to use the road from VAUX-SUR-SOMME during the hours of daylight when it would be under obser-vation from the enemy at CURLU. The road was therefore in constant use at night and a trench running from Vaux Wood was in full view of the enemy for half its length. It was hardly surprising that visits by the staff were rare.

An enemy raid against the redoubt on 28 January 1916 (the Kaiser's birthday) and attempt to cut the wire was beaten off, but for most of the time the small British garrison was little troubled. However, the French did lose possession of the neighbouring village of FRISE across the marshes, together with 600 troops, and during the next few weeks the enemy attempted to establish posts in the small copse known as Lodge Wood at the head of Trafford Park, which gave them a clear view of Fargny Mill and in effect control of the marshes.

On 11 March, artillery support was called for, which Maj N. Fraser-Tytler of CL Brigade, Royal Field Artillery (30th Division), provided: 'so excellent was the shooting that every shot fell about the enemy's position in Lodge Wood'. Plans for a 'long stay' by enemy troops were in tatters.

18th Manchesters (90th Brigade, 30th Division) held posts on the Somme marshes and at Fargny Mill:

Thence the trenches rose steeply in front of Fargny Wood, and on past the enigmatic sunken 'Y' Wood, the crest of which was held by the Germans across the Péronne Road. From this point it followed a line about 100 yards in front of the perimeter of Maricourt Wood, at a northern extremity of which it bent at right angles at Machine Gun Wood. This portion was held by battalions of the King's Liverpool Regt. (89th Brigade). They were miserable trenches – with a wretched and inadequate system of communication that caused irritating blocks during relief, with wire that was thin, dugouts there were none – only a few splinter-proof shelters. Some of the platoons in the front line – and a number of posts – were completely isolated.

FAVIÈRE WOOD, north-east of MARICOURT and south of BERNAFAY and TRÔNES WOODS, had formerly been a German dressing station. On 1 July 1916, the British reached the edge of the Wood running north–south and captured it between 2 and 13 July. On 1 July, several German trench lines were taken.

In *The Battle of the Somme*, John Masefield noted that one of the thrusts of the attack had been towards the 'romantic dingle' of Favière Wood. At the end of July, there was a French brigade headquarters at the Wood; battalions bivouacked in the trenches there, and in mid-September there were some French 75mm artillery pieces in front of Favière Wood, as well as a French howitzer. A new fire trench was dug, which was called Cheshire Trench.

FIENVILLERS is south-west of DOULLENS on the D31 and D925. Units of 30th Division were here at the end of November 1915, when 97th Field

Ambulance (30th Division) established a hospital here in a barn. A large depository opposite was used for other purposes and the village was used by 30th Division as a divisional headquarters.

From 29 February, No. 1/2 (North Midland) Field Company, Royal Engineers (46th Division), stayed for a week in Fienvillers. From 12 to 14 March, 169th Brigade (56th Division) were here. From 18 August, 60th Brigade (20th Division) were in the Fienvillers–CANDAS area for a time.

In June 1916, No. 21 Squadron, Royal Flying Corps, commanded by Maj J.R. Campbell-Heathcote, was here before moving to Boisdinghem. No. 27 Squadron also came in June, commanded firstly by Maj A.E. Borton and then by Maj E. Smith; they stayed until May 1917. In August, Maj R.M. Rodwell's No. 19 Squadron came here from Saint-Omer, staying until April 1917, and Maj W.R. Read's No. 45 Squadron was here from August to November. In September, No. 23 Squadron, commanded by Maj A. Ross-Hume, was here briefly and No. 70 Squadron was here from July to December.

Fienvillers British Cemetery, south-west of the village, has the grave of one man who died in 1916; the other burials were from Nos. 34 and 38 Casualty Clearing Stations during the fighting for the defence of AMIENS in 1918.

FLERS is 9 miles north-east of ALBERT and 4 miles south of BAPAUME on the D197 road between LONGUEVAL and Ligny-Thilloy. On 15 September 1916, the village was the objective of Fourth Army's XV Corps, comprising 14th, 21st, 41st, 55th and the New Zealand Divisions. This action was to be the first occasion on which tanks were used on a battlefield. The tanks, which had recently arrived from England and had been transported to the Loop, a railway 'station' north of BRAY-SUR-SOMME, were moved on 14 September to the Green Dump Valley in readiness. The British Front Line was in front of the north and north-east of DELVILLE WOOD.

The first objective was the Switch Line, the second was Flers Trench, which was just before the village, and the third Bulls Road, which was at the end of the village. Beyond Flers were German positions called Flea Trench and Box and Cox; beyond all these lines and objectives were the Gird Lines (which was actually the fourth objective) and the village of GUEUDECOURT. The brunt of the attack was to be carried out by 14th Division, 41st Division and the New Zealand Division. Before Zero Hour, 14th Division were to deal with the Germans who were in a 'pocket' east of DELVILLE WOOD. Of the four tanks assigned to 14th Division, two were ditched at the start of the battle. Switch Line was captured at about 0700hrs; at about 0900hrs, Gap Trench was passed over when the third objective was within sight. In particular, 9th Rifle Brigade (42nd Brigade, 14th Division) were hit by enfilade machine-gun fire as they approached Bulls Road.

In the centre of XV Corps' front, 41st Division's task was to capture the village in the course of its advance to the third objective, Bulls Road. Most of the tanks were kept for this part of the attack, with four beginning from the LONGUEVAL–Flers road, and six from the northern end of LONGUEVAL village; others were to be part of the New Zealanders' attack towards GUEUDECOURT. Seven got to the start line but probably none of them actually began in front of the infantry. 41st Division began with 124th Brigade on the right, 10th Queen's and 21st King's Royal Rifle Corps in front and 26th and 32nd Royal Fusiliers in the second line. As already mentioned, the Switch Line was reached by 0700hrs, and the advance to the second line was successful half an hour later. 21st King's Royal Rifle Corps, predominantly made up of men from Northumberland and Durham, took part in the attack to the east of the village, in which they carried three lines of trenches. The battalion casualties were very heavy, though, including Lord Feversham, its commanding officer. The senior officer of 10th Queen's, Lt Col A.F. Townsend, was also a casualty, being mortally wounded by shrapnel during the attack on Flers Trench.

When 122nd Brigade (41st Division) attacked Flers village, one tank went forward into the village, arriving by 0820hrs. Three more were on the east side of the village, breaking into houses and German strongpoints and forcing the enemy to flee towards GUEUDECOURT. The first battalion actually into Flers were 12th East Surreys (122nd Brigade, 41st Division); the main opposition at the time was a German machine gun at the crossroads in the centre of the village, which was eventually dealt with by a tank.

18th King's Royal Rifle Corps and 15th Hampshires (both 122nd Brigade, 41st Division) were in the leading line, their objective being Flers Trench; the supporting battalions, including 11th Royal West Kents (also 122nd Brigade, 41st Division), went through their lines. 15th Hampshires were quickly into Tea Support, which was also the German Front Line; they mastered the Switch Line and also reached Flers. After dark, having suffered very heavy casualties, they returned to York Trench in reserve. During their part of the fighting, 18th King's Royal Rifle Corps had 7 officers killed, including Lt Col C.P. Marten, as well as 57 other ranks. Marten was later buried in Serre Road Cemetery No. 2 (XXXIV.J.1).

The whole of the forward crest of the main ridge on a section of 5 miles from DELVILLE WOOD to MOUQUET FARM was now in Allied hands, which provided very valuable observation. As has already been stated, 26th and 32nd Royal Fusiliers were both in support, 32nd on the right and 26th on the left, following 10th Queen's and 21st King's Royal Rifle Corps. Three tanks had been allotted to 124th Brigade.

32nd Royal Fusiliers met with little resistance in Tea Support and the SWITCH TRENCH. Box and Cox were a sort of double or twin German redoubt; when the Londoners came to clear them out, they found them full of German dead, and six machine guns were captured.

On 15 September, 49 tanks were employed, of which 32 reached the starting point. Of these, nine pushed ahead with the infantry; nine failed to catch the infantry but nevertheless helped in clearing captured ground; nine broke down; and five were ditched in the centre of the battlefield. The first nine were especially useful in capturing Flers. The first tank into Flers was Lt S.H. Hastie's D17, while Lt A.E. Arnold's D16 moved up on the western edge of the village.

The War in the Air by H.A. Jones contains a report by a Royal Flying Corps observer who watched the infantry move over the open ground behind the creeping barrage. The objectives were taken fairly quickly and air reports showed that north of Flers, the Allies were holding Box and Cox and the Flame, and to the north-east were strongly established in groups of trenches known as Flea Trench and Hogs Head, the latter being a strongpoint in Flers Wood. Elsewhere, XV Corps were holding their objectives. Three tanks nearly reached GUEUDECOURT but were hit and caught fire. Of the others, two returned and six were ditched; the rest were hit, with two others catching fire. They moved forward in 'lanes' left clear by the barrages, and tank tapers were laid out for them. The trenches had to be filled in to enable them to proceed.

Flers was captured by 41st Division and the New Zealand Division, and further progress was made over the next few days. It was the first involvement in a Western Front attack for the New Zealanders, who had been refitted and been reinforced after their 'blooding' on the Gallipoli peninsula. There are graves of 120 New Zealanders in Bulls Road Cemetery, east of Flers.

A Mark I tank (C19 *Clan Leslie*) of C Company in Chimpanzee Valley, 15 September 1916. *(IWM Q5574)*

Anthony Eden served as a temporary officer with 21st King's Royal Rifle Corps (124th Brigade, 41st Division) on the Somme. He was under the command of Lord Feversham, who was not a regular soldier. Eden's early training had been at Duncombe Park; after service at Plug Street Wood, his battalion was transferred to the Somme. On 14 September, it was decided that Eden should form part of the cadre of men and officers who were to stay behind while the attack planned for 15 September took place. Eden was upset by this decision, but was told that there would be plenty of time for fighting later on. The battalion headquarters was at the back of DELVILLE WOOD in an assembly trench. On 15 September, Lord Feversham was killed leading his men in an attack on the ridge east of Flers and facing Gird Ridge. On 16 September, a roll-call took place and many able men were found to be missing, killed or wounded. The position of commanding officer was taken over by Maj G. Foljambe, a regular soldier who immediately made Eden his adjutant. Eden protested about being thrown in at the deep end, but to no avail. The two used to go riding together and Feversham's horse was used on these occasions.

A Lancashire battalion left MÉAULTE on 16 September, and bivouacked under groundsheets leading up Flers way. On the same road, 'dusky sons of India', facetiously known as Bengal Lights (they exchanged bully for chapatti, a sort of tasty pancake made from 'dog' biscuits), moved up to a slippery reserve line behind Flers. In *Gallipoli to the Somme*, Alexander Aitken of 1st Otagos (1st New Zealand Brigade, New Zealand Division) noted that he was in Fat Trench in front of Flers, having been misled by the guides. It was a trench south-west of the village.

The next main attack after 15 September was to take place on 25 September. The weather had been poor; 18 and 19 September were very wet days, and 20 September was a day of rainstorms. On 18 September, Capt W.G. Newton of 1/23rd Londons (142nd Brigade, 47th Division) was awarded the Military Cross for placing a lamp in the open to guide the night assault. Later, although wounded, he rallied his men and bombed the enemy with courage and determination. In the battle of 25 September, which was known as the Battle of Morval, the New Zealand Division captured Factory Corner, which was on the road between GUEUDECOURT and

EAUCOURT L'ABBAYE. They were to be between Flers and MARTINPUICH during the next 3 days.

In *39 Months*, D.V. Kelly of the Leicestershire Regiment mentions that he had walked to Flers looking for a brigade headquarters to occupy after the imminent attack on the village of GUEUDE-COURT. He found a bank running roughly north to south, close to the MONTAUBAN-DE-PICARDIE–LONGUEVAL road and a few hundred yards from Flers. Nearby lay a tank; the site was marked S.6d 8.2 on the map. It was close to the existing front line and a working party were soon digging a hole in the bank for accommodation. The headquarters was at one corner of the ridge, while on the left, GUEUDECOURT village lay right in front, and LESBŒUFS and MORVAL were on the right. The attack was fixed for 1235hrs on 25 September. Kelly was sitting in the Switch Line, waiting for the attack to begin. 8th and 9th Leicesters (110th Brigade, 37th Division) rose out of their assembly trenches just below the crest of the ridge, while away to the right for miles it was possible to see the irregular waves of the Allied infantry, which included the Guards Division. That night, 6th Leicesters (also 110th Brigade, 37th Division) moved along the partly German trench that had given so much trouble the day before, and enabled Kelly's men to clean it up. 110th Brigade had now taken all of their objectives as they had also done at BAZENTIN in July. The casualties were believed to be about 1,400.

In *Field Guns in France*, Neil Fraser-Tytler of CL Brigade, Royal Field Artillery (30th Division), mentions that a big gain had been achieved beyond Flers. On 30 September, Fraser-Tytler's unit began preparing the position that they were then occupying, which was a sunken road running into the south-western corner of Flers. He was allotted a position in DELVILLE WOOD, wedged in among a host of other batteries. He looked for and found a more forward position, which was close up to the Germans and well away from the other batteries. This was the LONGUEVAL position.

Lt Col W.C.C. Ash, Commanding Officer 23rd Middlesex (123rd Brigade, 41st Division), was wounded in the same attack as Lord Feversham. He died a fortnight later, on 29 September.

By 1 October, the New Zealand Division had taken the Gird Trench, Circus Trench and Gird Support, to the north of the GUEUDECOURT–EAUCOURT L'ABBAYE road. On 2 October, Fraser-Tytler had moved his guns forward from in front of DELVILLE WOOD, trudging up the 'much barraged' road from the Wood to Flers. They were on a forward slope, which was so close to the Germans that all the shelling went over their heads into the crowded Delville Valley.

From October, Flers itself became a deathtrap and the l'Abbaye road going out of the village was the scene of frequent shelling. Early in the month, when reconnoitring the ground, Foljambe and Eden of 21st King's Royal Rifle Corps went close to Gird Ridge. A planned attack was postponed because of the very poor weather and was now due to take place on 7 October. A day later, battalion headquarters was moved to Factory Corner, which was now a battered building with only cellars left intact. On 10 October, they were about to be relieved when they received news that Feversham's body had been found. Eden was put in charge of the party detailed to recover the body and give it a suitable burial; it was found on a forward slope of a lip in the ground. Feversham had been of middle height, thickset with a bristling moustache. He was, in Eden's words, essentially a commander and was at his best and happiest on a horse. Eden was in charge of the burial, which took place in a meadow close to Factory Corner.

After 22 October, 2nd Royal Welsh Fusiliers (19th Brigade, 33rd Divison) arrived at Serpentine Trench, which was part of the Flers Line between GINCHY and MORVAL. The New Zealand Division went north on 10 and 11 October, but their artillery remained on the Somme for the rest of the month. During the Battle of the Somme, the New Zealanders had fought for 23 consecutive days, had advanced more than 2 miles and had captured 5 miles of enemy front line. They took nearly 1,000 prisoners and many machine guns; but they brought back all their machine guns and Lewis guns, and lost fewer than 20 prisoners themselves. Their casualties were 7,000; of these, 1,560 were killed in action or died of wounds.

On 29 October, 1/4th Suffolks (98th Brigade, 33rd Division) moved back to the Flers Line after DEWDROP TRENCH.

In *The Somme, 1916*, Norman Gladden of 1/7th Northumberland Fusiliers (149th Brigade, 50th Division) noted that at the end of October he was sent to Flers village to bring back duckboards that had been dumped there. It was a weird, deserted place, especially at that time of the day, dominated by the abandoned tank, looking ridiculous in its early demise. On 31 October, they moved forward to the Flers Line support trench and the mud in places was so deep as to make movement almost impossible. Gladden noted that in mid-November, Flers Switch was to be their billet for the night; later in the day, however, they were withdrawn to reserve in Prue Trench, which had been altered out of all recognition since their earlier occupancy. It had been converted by the Royal Engineers into winter quarters, with a row of neatly sandbagged dugouts under semicircular iron roofs which, if not exactly shell-proof, provided 'the acme of comfort' after their recent exposure.

In *A Subaltern on the Somme*, Max Plowman noted that in January 1917, 10th West Yorkshires (50th Brigade, 17th Division) were occupying a large dugout, with officers at one end and the men at the other, at a spot near Flers called Bull Dump; presumably this was near or in Bulls Road, to the north of Flers. They came out in the rain and just had time to get clean and look round the town of hutments that was once CARNOY.

On 15 May 1932, the memorial to 41st Division in Flers was unveiled at the end of the village and then handed over to the mayor for safe-keeping. A New Army formation, 41st Division included units from many parts of England, and regimental badges decorated the enclosing pillars. The rifle of the bronze infantryman points in the direction of tanks coming from POZIÈRES; the design of the memorial is a copy or duplicate of the one that stands in High Holborn.

We have seen that Lord Feversham had been buried in an isolated grave; in 1935, the *Ypres Times* records that there was a notice by the roadside saying 'This way to Lord Feversham's Grave'. A quarter of a mile through thigh-high crops brought one to a little lychgate built over a flagstone that was inscribed 'Charles William Reginald, 2nd Earl of Feversham, Lt. Col. Commanding 21st King's Royal Rifle Corps, killed in action on this spot, September 15th 1916'. The same writer mentioned that recently (mid-1930s), 40 bodies had been discovered in this area, all in a cluster where they had fallen. Flers had built itself a brewery since the First World War and had been 'adopted' by Portsmouth.

There are two main cemeteries in Flers; the first is the A.I.F Burial Ground, Grass Lane, Flers almost in the centre of the battlefield and about 4 miles south-west of BAPAUME. It is a mile north-east of the village of Flers, on the side of a track known to the Army in 1916 as Grass Lane. Australian medical units stationed in caves in the neighbourhood began the cemetery to receive the graves of soldiers killed in the fighting during the autumn of 1916. The local name of the site is Aux Caves. Designed by Sir Herbert Baker, the cemetery was begun in the period November 1916–February 1917. It was greatly enlarged after the Armistice by the concentration of 3,842 British and French graves, and afterwards from a wider area; the great majority of the graves date from the autumn of 1916. Sgt H. Jackson

(XV.A.21/30), who won a Victoria Cross at Hermies on 22 March 1918, is buried here. Two burial grounds were concentrated here, Factory Corner, west of the crossing of the roads from EAUCOURT L'ABBAYE to GUEUDECOURT, and North Road Cemetery. Capt H.W. Trefusis (III.B.20) of 1st Northamptons (2nd Brigade, 1st Division), a son of the Bishop of Crediton, was killed in action on 7 November and buried here. The AIF Cemetery stands in open undulating farmland; GUEUDECOURT is over the hill to the east, and beyond it is the Newfoundland Memorial, recalling a successful attack on 12 October. In 1937, the New Zealand wooden memorial cross, which had stood at Factory Corner, was destroyed by orders of the New Zealand government, and the ashes were scattered over New Zealand graves in the cemetery. After the Second World War, Lord Feversham's body was transferred here (III.L.29).

In April 2003, the remains of an unknown Royal Fusilier were buried next to the reinterred Lord Feversham. The Fusilier had been found the previous year near GUEUDECOURT, where he had fallen in October 1916.

The other cemetery is Bulls Road Cemetery, which was begun on 19 September and was used by fighting units, mainly Australian, until March 1917. More graves were brought in after the Armistice from the fields between Flers and LONGUEVAL. It stands on sloping ground, and LONGUEVAL and Ligny-Thilloy can be seen from it. Its name was possibly derived from an allusion to LESBŒUFS road. On 10 July 2011 a memorial to the players of Clapton Orient, who served in the 1st Football Battalion of the 17th Middlesex, who died in the Battle of the Somme in 1916, was unveiled.

FLESSELLES, north of AMIENS, is due west of VILLERS-BOCAGE on the D113 road to VIGNACOURT. Prior to the 1916 battle, an ammunition dump had been established; from July 1915 to the end of September 1916, 3rd, 8th, 18th, 19th, 30th, 32nd, 36th and 51st Divisions carried out training here.

18th Division were one of the first to arrive, concentrating here 26–28 July 1915; and nearly 5 months later, on 21 December, they returned to the village. In early October 1915, 36th Division's headquarters was here, and in mid-November, No. 202 Field Company, Royal Engineers (30th Division), were billeted in barns here. At the beginning of December, and again a month later, 32nd Division's headquarters was here, followed by 51st Division's headquarters on 2 January 1916 and again 6–31 January. They were back here on 1 March, having moved from DAOURS.

From 8 March, 8th Division were in the area; on 28 March, 25th Brigade (8th Division) were at Flesselles, while 23rd Brigade (also 8th Division) were at Bourdon and 70th Brigade (also 8th Division) were at VIGNACOURT. 2nd West Yorkshires (23rd Brigade, 8th Division) were at SAINT-VAAST-EN-CHAUSSÉE and 24th Field Ambulance (8th Division) marched here from LONGUEAU. The hospital was set up in a former concert hall and had a capacity for 30 patients. Billets were set up in farm sheds and the beds were in tiers. In April, 8th Division went into the line north of the ALBERT–BAPAUME road.

On 25 March, 92nd Brigade (32nd Division) were here with field ambulances. From 10 to 28 May, 19th Division were in the area, with their divisional headquarters in Flesselles; 58th Brigade (19th Divison) were with them. At the beginning of June, 7th South Lancashires (56th Brigade, 19th Division) were billeted here and carried out intensive training until the end of the month, when they moved to Hénencourt Wood prior to the battle.

In June, Flesselles and the surrounding villages 'were really nothing more than mud and plaster hovels, and billets were accordingly far from appreciated', according to Lt Col E.H.E. Collen CMG, DSO (IWM 79/21/1). Further, there were no bath or laundry facilities.

On 3 July, 3rd Division had their divisional headquarters here; on 29 July, 1/3rd (Highland) Field Ambulance (51st Division) were here, followed by 90th Brigade (30th Division) on 29 September.

FLIXECOURT, on the N1 road, is north-west of AMIENS on the north side of the River Somme. It was a well-built village and hardly touched by the war in early 1916 when 2nd Wiltshires (21st Brigade, 30th Division) arrived here from the CARNOY front for a few days' rest.

Possibly the largest employer in the village was the Saint-Frères canvas-weaving works, which was busy producing thousands of sandbags and other materials for the French Army. The building also housed Fourth Army's School for officers and non-commissioned officers; they had just taken over the school from Third Army, and 2nd Wiltshires helped them to set it up. The officer training courses were to become a regular feature and Lt Gen Sir Henry Rawlinson, General Officer Commanding Fourth Army, regularly addressed each intake of students during the following weeks, driving over from his headquarters at QUERRIEU. 2nd Wiltshires were here for nearly a fortnight before moving to PICQUIGNY, closer to AMIENS on the south side of the River Somme.

FONCQUEVILLERS, known as Funkyvillas to the Tommies, is a village on the D3 road, south-west of HANNESCAMPS and north-west of GOMMECOURT. It was in Allied hands in 1915 and 1916, and when the British arrived to take over they found that the French and Germans had followed a 'live and let live system'; on his arrival, to his dismay, a British officer discovered a Frenchman resting on top of a wagon reading a newspaper.

The Allied front line ran between this village and the German-held village of GOMMECOURT, which had been turned into a defensive fortress by the Germans and which protruded into a gap between the Allied-held Foncquevillers to the north and HÉBUTERNE to the south.

Prior to their involvement in the abortive attack against Gommecourt on 1 July 1916, 46th Division made Foncquevillers their 'home' for several months; the division, part of VII Corps, was made up of regiments from Staffordshire, Leicestershire, Nottinghamshire, Lincolnshire and Derbyshire, and many of the communication trenches bore names of famous Midland towns.

However, 46th Division were not the only British formation to be associated with the area, as 48th and 49th Divisions also had units here from time to time. In mid-September 1915, 1/5th Royal Warwicks (143rd Brigade, 48th Division) were here and brigade headquarters was at CHÂTEAU DE LA HAIE, and the battalion were here again at the end of the month. For several weeks, they were either at the Château, Foncquevillers or BAYENCOURT.

Before the battle began, Bruce Bairnsfather of 1/4th Duke of Wellington's (147th Brigade, 49th Division), the creator of 'Old Bill', was in shelters and dugouts on the road between Foncquevillers and HÉBUTERNE. It was known as Thorpe Street and was a 'straight line' between the two villages, just behind the Allied front line. The most dangerous spot at this time was the western end of the village. To the north-west of Foncquevillers were BIENVILLERS-AU-BOIS and a long communication trench named Berlin Street, about 800yds from the German line and facing the village from the south-east along the side of Gommecourt Wood.

In May 1916, two important communication trenches in use were Crawl Boys Lane to the north of the sector and Roberts Avenue to the south of it. There was an artillery observation post in the village, which took the form of a brick square tower, built within the walls of an old house knocked about by shell-fire.

On 5 May, 1/6th Royal Warwicks (143rd Brigade, 48th Division) were here; a few days later, they were relieved in the trenches by 1/5th South Staffords (137th Brigade, 46th Division) and returned to Couin Wood. One of the tasks put in hand was the sapping of a new entrance to the crypt of the village church, which was an ongoing job for field companies of 46th Division. On 8 May, 1/1st (North Midland) Field Ambulance (46th Division) took over the hospital or dressing station in the village.

On 19 May, when 139th Brigade (46th Division) relieved 137th Brigade in trenches west of Foncquevillers, 1/7th Sherwood Foresters (139th Brigade, 46th Division) moved here from HUMBERCAMPS via POMMIER and BIENVILLERS-AU-BOIS and entered Berlin Street. The battalion spent their time in improving and maintaining trenches. It was possible to walk down the village street screened from German observation by the houses, which were in a fair state of repair. Several civilian inhabitants were still in the village and one French farmer continued to plough his land in daylight, 1,000yds from the German lines.

Also on 19 May, 1/5th Sherwood Foresters (139th Brigade, 46th Division) relieved 1/5th South Staffords in the right sector in front of the village; 1/5th Sherwood Foresters were relieved in turn by 1/5th Leicesters (138th Brigade, 46th Division) on 4 June. On the same day, 1/8th Sherwood Foresters (139th Brigade, 46th Division) relieved 1/5th North Staffords (137th Brigade, 46th Division). According to the regimental history, battalion officers lived in some comfort in reserve when the battalion were holding the front line; although battalion headquarters was only about 100yds from the enemy, their dugouts were made for comfort rather than safety and were decorated with pictures, probably from houses in the village. The surrounds of the dugouts had been turned into elegant garden plots. Their main work at this period was in digging out old communication trenches from the village to the front, a distance of about 700yds.

On 3/4 June, 1/5th Lincolns (138th Brigade, 46th Division) were in Foncquevillers; they began to dig a new advance trench about 400yds long, which was completed by 10 June. They were later in huts in HUMBERCAMPS, where there was a 15in gun close to their billets. Also in early June, 1/6th South Staffords (137th Brigade, 46th Division) were providing working parties while billeted in HUMBERCAMPS. This work was on top of a tiring march at night and in the early morning.

On 18 June, 1/8th Sherwood Foresters were back in the village, when they took over the left subsector of 1/5th Lincolns; on 1 July, they took up their battle positions. The village was heavily shelled on 22 June.

Brushwood from Lucheux Forest had been used for the construction of the many communication trenches, in particular Roberts Avenue and Stratford Avenue. Other trench names included Cape Avenue, Raymond Avenue, Lincoln Lane, Leicester Street, Derby Dyke, Nottingham Street, Brasserie Trench and St Martin's Lane. In front of 138th Brigade's section was the strong German position called the Z and Little Z, which protruded into the line at the extreme left of the attack and lay in front of Schwalben Nest. Prior to the battle, the enemy had been putting down heavy bombardments every night; it was especially hazardous to be using roads or communication trenches.

On 30 June, 1/7th Sherwood Foresters marched here from BIENVILLERS-AU-BOIS and drew supplies of bombs, grenades, barbed wire and others. Afterwards, the troops were allowed a short rest in the orchards on the outskirts of the village; sitting on sandbags, they ate enormous bacon sandwiches, and the Padre said a few prayers. After 2100hrs, 1/7th Sherwood Foresters began to move off up the line; conditions were very muddy, and on reaching the front position, the troops were already very exhausted. Their sister battalion, 1/5th Sherwood Foresters, reached the village to relieve 1/6th Sherwood Foresters, and also drew supplies and rested in the orchards.

Regent Street, in 1/5th Sherwood Foresters' sector, commenced at the brewery north of the village, and then ran due east before crossing the La Brayelle road in a south-easterly direction, meeting the Allied front line 150yds from the road. Nearby, Roberts Avenue ran practically parallel with the La Brayelle road, crossed Support Trench and met with the Russian Sap, which was a tunnel as close to the start line as possible. 1/5th Sherwood Foresters' battalion headquarters was at the end of Rotten Row.

On the first day of the battle, 1 July, the battalions of 46th Division who were involved mostly in this sector were Territorial units of the Sherwood Foresters (Nottinghamshire and Derbyshire Regiment), the South Staffordshire Regiment, the Prince of Wales's (North Staffordshire) Regiment and the Lincolnshire Regiment. For a description of what happened to them, the reader is referred to the entry for GOMMECOURT. Prior to the battle, an advanced dressing station had been established here in Foncquevillers; on 1 July, motor ambulances were able to get right up to the dressing station.

At 1300hrs, there was congestion in dealing with the large number of casualties; after 1500hrs, many casualties were sent straight to ambulance trains, and some to a casualty clearing station. Within the first 36 hours, 1,530 cases had been dealt with, of whom 7 men died. By noon on 2 July, the hospital was almost empty. A second dressing station was opened on 1 July, but casualty evacuation was very difficult, as many communication trenches were waist-deep in water and were heavily shelled.

On 19 September, 16th King's Royal Rifle Corps (100th Brigade, 33rd Division) took over the right sector; a month later, they were billeted at CORBIE.

Foncquevillers Military Cemetery, on the western outskirts of the village, had been made by French troops before being taken over by the British in the summer of 1915; it was used by units and field ambulances until March 1917. It was used again in March and April 1918, and after the war 74 graves were brought in from the battlefields to the east of the village. The burials of men from Midlands regiments who died in early July 1916 are especially numerous and are in a mass grave in Plot I. Of the 648 burials, about 170 are of men who died prior to the battle.

La rue Basse, Foncquevillers.
(Peter F. Batchelor Collection)

Capt J.L. Green VC (III.D.15) of the Royal Army Medical Corps (attached 1/5th Sherwood Foresters) is buried here. He was posthumously awarded the Victoria Cross, having been killed on 1 July in the GOMMECOURT area.

Probably owing to its close association with Midlands regiments after the war, Foncquevillers was 'adopted' by the Midlands town of Derby.

FORCEVILLE is 6 miles from ALBERT on the D938 main road between ALBERT and DOULLENS. The French were in the village in 1915, followed by the British Third Army; Fourth Army were in occupation until 20 July 1916, when Forceville was included in the area of the Reserve Army (later Fifth Army).

The second British formation to arrive in the Somme sector was 4th Divison. On 23 July 1915, 12th Field Ambulance (4th Division) marched here to search for a suitable site; on the next day, they took over a house and farm from 12th Brigade (4th Division) for use as a dressing station. Eventually the dressing station on the south side of the main road and close to the church was greatly expanded and included a receiving shed, three wards, a marquee, an officers' hospital and all the necessary stores and buildings required for the running of a main dressing station. The church itself was used for the lightly wounded.

On 27 July, 1/5th South Lancashires (12th Brigade, 4th Division) came to Forceville, remaining for 6 days before moving up to trenches in front of AUCHONVILLERS, opposite BEAUMONT-HAMEL. In mid-October, 108th Field Ambulance (36th Division) were here; in early November, Royal Engineers of 4th Division worked on ablutions sheds both in the village and at ACHEUX-EN-AMIÉNOIS, to the north-west. During one of his periodic visits to the Western Front, HM the King visited Forceville on 25 October.

For about 5 months prior to the battle, 108th Field Ambulance (36th Division) were in charge of the main dressing station here; battalions of 36th Division were often billeted here, including 13th Royal Irish Rifles (108th Brigade, 36th Division), who arrived here on 27 March 1916. On 13 June, No. 130 Field Company, Royal Engineers (25th Division), marched here; three lorries came to meet them 10 miles out and helped them with carrying stores and equipment.

On 19 June, preliminary orders for 14th Royal Irish Rifles (109th Brigade, 36th Division), who were to take part in the attempt to capture THIEP-VAL on the first day of the battle, came through; the officers of 9th Royal Irish Rifles (107th Brigade, 36th Division) received their orders in June when they were in Forceville. According to Philip Orr's *The Road to the Somme*, Brig Gen F.P. Crozier 'lectured them all for hours in a big barn, aided by a cloth map twenty foot square'. 14th Royal Irish Rifles had their headquarters in the village and were to move off to Thiepval Wood on the eve of the battle. Orr wrote: 'The YCVs packed and sent off their rucksacks, and left Forceville at 9.30 p.m. They marched in platoons past the village of Englebelmer where German shells were dropping, then there was a halt just short of Martinsart, where mounted officers left their horses and proceeded on foot.'

On 22 June, No. 121 Field Company, Royal Engineers (36th Division), brought pontoons up from here to place in the River Ancre; 4 days later, 110th Field Ambulance (36th Division) sent three horse ambulances from CLAIRFAYE FARM to join up with 108th Field Ambulance to help with the transporting of lightly wounded casualties.

In *History of the 36th (Ulster) Division*, Cyril Falls wrote of the problems of making adequate medical provision:

The two Main Dressing Stations, for stretcher cases and 'walking wounded' respectively, were at Forceville, manned by the 108th Field Ambulance, and Clairfaye Farm, further west, manned by 110th Field Ambulance. The Advanced Dressing Station was situated close to the Albert–Arras Road in Aveluy Wood. Evacuation of wounded from the Regimental Aid Posts in Thiepval Wood and Authuille had to take place over Authuille Bridge, or by the trench tramway which crossed the Ancre to the north of it. The motors of the Field Ambulance were parked on the Martinsart–Albert Road, south of the former village. For 'walking wounded' there was a collecting station west of Martinsart whence horsed wagons carried them by a cross-country track through Hédauville to Clairfaye.

At 0800hrs on 1 July, the wounded from THIEP-VAL began to arrive, and after a short time the main dressing station was 'very soon clogged with wounded'. Casualties were fed and then sent on; during the first 12 hours, 500 stretcher cases were admitted. Cyril Falls noted that 'at one point the overcrowding of the Main Dressing Station at Forceville, due to the strain upon the Motor Ambulance Convoy which evacuated the wounded to the Casualty Clearing Stations, gave rise to much anxiety'.

At 0830hrs, 108th Field Ambulance received a message from a runner stating that there were 300 or 400 dead or wounded lying out in no man's land. At first, the message was not believed, but after confirmation a group of orderlies and lightly wounded were sent up to Thiepval Wood in order to set up a new first-aid station.

On 5 July, when the number of casualties had greatly diminished, 1/2nd (West Riding) Field Ambulance (49th Division) took over the main dressing station at Forceville; their war diary (WO95/2789) described it as 'the best site for a Field Ambulance which has yet been occupied by this unit. The place was taken over from the 108th Field Ambulance (36th Division) on July 5th. The 108th Field Ambulance had been in occupation for 5 months and made great improvements and erected several sheds in view of the present heavy fighting.'

The huts and a large room over the main building could take 350 lying patients and the lightly wounded would be sent on by transport to CLAIR-FAYE FARM. When large numbers of casualties came through, they were sent straight on in the vehicle that brought them, after a quick check on their condition by a medical officer. If a seriously wounded casualty was suffering from chest or abdomen wounds, he would normally be sent on to WARLOY-BAILLON, where special arrangements to treat such cases were in place.

From 5 July to early September, Forceville was used mostly by 49th Division; on 8 September, the hospital received a direct hit from German shells and, although the building was much damaged, there were no casualties. It was then decided to fall back on a camp hospital at VARENNES to provide for convoys of the wounded. For the next 2 months, the village was used by 18th, 25th, 51st and 63rd Divisions; the latter had its divisional headquarters here on 13 November.

In *The Hawke Battalion: Somme Personal Records*, it is noted that the Hawke Battalion (189th Brigade, 63rd Division) left the training area on 7 October, and arrived that same evening at Forceville, a small town some 4 miles east of Thiepval Ridge, and one of the recognised centres for units arriving to take part in the Somme battles.

In *Call To Arms*, J. Murray of the Hood Battalion (also 189th Brigade, 63rd Division) wrote that he arrived at ACHEUX-EN-AMIÉNOIS and on 4 October moved to Forceville. Murray's battalion were working up the line in the period 6 to 16 October. During this time they stayed in barns in the village before leaving for the Knightsbridge sector in the ANCRE VALLEY.

Forceville Communal Cemetery and Forceville Communal Cemetery Extension, designed by Charles Holden, lie to the west of the village off the main road. During the Somme battle the cemetery Extension was about 200yds from the hospital complex; it has over 305 burials, of which 86 men who mostly died of wounds prior to 1 July 1916 were buried in Plot I. One of the earliest burials was that of Pte G. Webber of 1st Somerset Light Infantry (11th Brigade, 4th Division), who died on 5 August 1915. There was a long gap between burials in the autumn of 1916 and the British move eastwards in April 1917. Three men are buried in the Communal Cemetery, which adjoins the Extension.

If one walks down the rue d'Eglise, one comes to the church and former hospital complex, the latter forming an arc of buildings including the church; all would probably have been used for some medical use or other. Adjacent to the Communal Cemetery, this Cemetery was one of the first three designed after the war, each by Sir Reginald Blomfield. According to Philip Longworth's *The Unending Vigil*, the other two cemeteries were le Treport and Louvencourt. By 21 January 1920, the walls and paths were

nearly completed together with the Record House and the foundations of the Cross and Great War Stone . . . But the most successful of the three

was Forceville. Perhaps the contrast helped, for you approached it down the side of a village cemetery crowded with ornate tombs, dilapidated ironwork and artificial flowers. The military cemetery, enclosed in breast high walls crowned with flowers and backed with yew hedges, was a neat enclosure of shorn grass and white Portland stone walks. The place was given a vertical proportion by some old poplars which had been left in place and new lindens had been planned to give shade.

The Times reviewed the new design, calling it a 'strangely stirring place'. Sir Frederic Kenyon, director of the British Museum, wrote of the cemetery that 'the wall fades away into nothing in part of the surroundings', giving a pleasant effect of an English country churchyard. Not only was it one of the first cemeteries to be ready, but the register was also one of the first two published, in 1920 (le Treport being the other).

HM the King, probably in 1922, visited the cemetery with Field Marshal Haig and Maj Gen Sir F. Ware of the Imperial War Graves Commission.

FOUILLOY is a suburb of CORBIE on the D1 road. On 18 September 1915, No. 28 Casualty Clearing Station opened in the village. Fouilloy Communal Cemetery is north of the road between the village and AUBIGNY.

FOURDRINOY is west of AMIENS and to the south of the River Somme. On 2 February 1916, 1/7th and 1/8th West Yorkshires (146th Brigade, 49th Division) were billeted here for just over a week when the other two battalions of 146th Brigade, 1/5th and 1/6th West Yorkshires, were billeted in AILLY-SUR-SOMME, to the north-east.

FRANVILLERS is 7 miles south-west of ALBERT, just north of the main road to AMIENS and 2 miles from HEILLY; it is the former site of No. 36 Casualty Clearing Station, a large hospital adjacent to the railway. One of the earliest units to make use of the village was 1/7th Gordon Highlanders (153rd Brigade, 51st Division), who were billeted in barns here in July 1915; their war diary described Franvillers as 'not an elegant village'. On 6 February 1916, 54th Field Ambulance (18th Division) were at the commune school here and on 11 March, 98th Field Ambulance (30th Division) ran the divisional rest station here. On 14 March, 53rd Brigade (18th Division) left this area for ETINEHEM; on the same day, 54th Field Ambulance returned here.

On 27 May, the first of what became a series of concerts was given in the yard behind the school, and 3 days later an officers' ward with four patients was opened.

The main role of Franvillers in the war was to be a medical one, dealing with casualties from the battle, especially in early July 1916. Prior to the battle, units from 18th, 32nd and 34th Divisions were here; on 10 May, the divisional rest station at the school was taken over by 102nd Field Ambulance (34th Division). Having journeyed from LAHOUSSOYE, their personnel, horses and transport were camped in an orchard about 100yds from the main road leading into the village. The plan was to increase the capacity from 80 patients to 132 and 'Orchard Camp' was laid out in such a way that marquees and huts could be erected for 500 patients if necessary. On the following day, the front of the school was white-washed and red crosses were painted on the gate posts; eight marquees were then put up. Patients were evacuated from here to No. 36 Casualty Clearing Station at HEILLY, infectious cases were sent to SAINT-OUEN and scabies cases to EBART FARM. Owing to the foresight of the field ambulances, this hospital dealt with the casualties of 1 July as well as possible in the unique circumstances.

On the very wet morning of 10 August, HM the King, paying a visit to his troops on the Western Front, left Château Bryas near Saint-Pol for Franvillers, where he was to be received by Lt Gen Sir Henry Rawlinson, General Officer Commanding Fourth Army. The weather caused some concern to Geoffrey Malins, the official War Office photographer, as on that day he especially wanted to obtain good film, although it had stopped raining by 1030hrs. Rawlinson's official cars pulled up on the main road in the village; as they had about 15 minutes to wait, Malins set up his camera ready to film HM the King's meeting with Rawlinson. While waiting, Rawlinson talked to Malins about his work, and in particular his filming of 29th Division at BEAUMONT-HAMEL on 1 July. Shortly after the royal party arrived, HM the King alighted and greeted the general. Rawlinson then joined HM the King in his car, and they travelled along the main AMIENS–ALBERT road before turning off through DERNANCOURT and going across the river to MÉAULTE, on their way to the battlefield at FRICOURT, when they were escorted by Lt Gen Sir Walter Congreve VC, General Officer Commanding XIII Corps.

The Prime Minister, Mr H. Asquith (in black hat), watches the return of a squadron of aeroplanes at Royal Flying Corps headquarters, Fienvillers, 7 August 1916. Maj Gen Trenchard is in the centre and to his right is Maurice Baring. See FIENVILLERS, p. 183. *(IWM Q4192)*

From 1 July, units of 5th, 9th, 12th, 15th, 19th, 23rd, 34th and 47th Divisions were in the area; 9th, 15th, 19th, 34th and 47th Divisions had men billeted here after 1 July.

Franvillers Communal Cemetery, south-east of the village and close to the AMIENS–ALBERT road, was occasionally used between May 1916 and May 1918, and includes the graves of four men from the United Kingdom who died in 1916. Franvillers Communal Cemetery Extension, which was designed by W.C. von Berg, was used between April and August 1918 and has the graves of 248 Commonwealth soldiers and 5 Germans.

FRÉCHENCOURT is north-east of AMIENS on the D115E road, to the north of the former Fourth Army headquarters at QUERRIEU. 14th Field Ambulance (5th Division) remained in the village until 6 February. On 11 February, 91st Field Ambulance (32nd Division) took over the *curé*'s empty house as a temporary hospital and their personnel were billeted in barns. Three days later, a party of men were engaged in cleaning up the château for use as a hospital.

In March, 1/7th West Yorkshires (146th Brigade, 49th Division) were billeted in the village when construction work was being carried out on the new railway which was to link up the principal villages between DAOURS and CONTAY via Fréchencourt. The line linked PONT-NOYELLES with BÉHENCOURT, running roughly in a north-easterly direction; sidings were set up at Fréchencourt, close to the crossroads east of the village. On 15 March, 19th Manchesters (21st Brigade, 30th Division) came to the village from TAILLES WOOD via CORBIE and remained here until 29 March, when they too provided fatigue parties for work on the new railway line. They then left for a night at COISY before moving to BREILLY. On 29 March, 18th Manchesters (90th Brigade, 30th Division) arrived here from TAILLES WOOD and stayed for 11 days. During this time they were under the instructions of the Royal Engineers in building the new railway line. They left for POULAINVILLE on 10 April.

On 12 April, 19th Manchesters were here again, and remained until 2 May. For most of May, the battalion alternated between CORBIE, BRAY-SUR-SOMME, BILLON WOOD, BRONFAY FARM and the trenches at CARNOY. On 12 May, Royal Engineers from 19th Division were felling trees in the local wood and dumping them outside the wood, from where they were collected up and taken to MONTIGNY; the timber was then turned into 9ft × 6ft props. On 14 June, 59th Field Ambulance (19th

Division) were running a medical rest camp here; at the end of the month, 12th Middlesex (54th Brigade, 18th Division) arrived in Fréchencourt at midnight.

Fréchencourt became a principal railhead village for supplies; initially, the broad-gauge line was not intended for use for medical purposes, but this rule was later altered. At the beginning of the battle there was a III Corps walking wounded collecting station here, and the lightly wounded were entrained here for the casualty clearing station at VECQUEMONT, to the south. By 2 July, the medical rest camp had become choked with the vast number of casualties; at 1300hrs, 15 lorries were instructed to clear the backlog, leaving 120 stretcher cases only.

One of the buildings in the centre of the village still carries the village name, painted on it by the military. Fréchencourt Communal Cemetery, in the valley of the River Hallue, was used in between April and August 1918, and 50 of the 57 casualties buried there are artillerymen.

FRÉVENT is on the Saint-Pol–DOULLENS road, the D916; between 9 and 11 March 1916, 51st Division had their divisional headquarters in the village. On 17 March, No. 43 Casualty Clearing Station arrived here and remained until June, when it became part of the Lucknow Casualty Clearing Station. From the latter part of March 1916 until early May, 56th Division were in training in the area; afterwards, they moved to VII Corps' area and took over from 46th Division in front of HÉBUTERNE, opposite GOMMECOURT; 20th and 32nd Divisions also had links with the village.

Frévent was an important line of communication village during the war. After No. 43 Casualty Clearing Station left, No. 6 Stationary Hospital was set up here from June 1916 to August 1918. Also here in 1918 were No. 3 Canadian, No. 19 and No. 43 Casualty Clearing Stations.

Most of the burials from these hospitals would have been carried out in the two cemeteries, the Saint-Hilaire Cemetery and the Saint-Hilaire Cemetery Extension on the eastern side of the town, on the south side of the D54 road to Sericourt. The former, which was used until March 1918, has the graves of 210 Commonwealth troops from the First World War and 12 from May and June 1940, when British troops were withdrawing.

The majority of the 304 Commonwealth graves in the latter cemetery are from the March to August 1918 fighting.

FRICOURT is a village on the D147 road between CONTALMAISON and BRAY-SUR-SOMME. In

1916, it had a station on a light railway running from ALBERT to Montdidier and PÉRONNE.

One of the most important historical links with the First World War was the Tambour, a series of craters on the west side of the village that were to be the scene of very considerable mining and counter-mining activity. According to papers held at The National Archives (WO95/405), members of No. 178 Tunnelling Company, Royal Engineers (X Corps), began work on the Tambour as early as 4 August 1915, after the French had already carried out mining activity here; at one point, a trench tramway was set up here. No. 178 Tunnelling Company took over responsibility for the position, which seems to have been a deadly spot for both sides alike. One sapper was asphyxiated at some point, and on 21 August, Lt W.R. Cloutman was killed undergound when trying to rescue 22 men. He was later interred in Norfolk Cemetery at BÉCORDEL-BÉCOURT (I.A.14). A week later, three men were buried, four men killed when gassed and eight others gassed and wounded as a result of an enemy camouflet. (A camouflet is a mine used underground to destroy an enemy gun emplacement.) The death toll continued, with 11 deaths in September and 14 more in October.

The biggest disaster to befall No. 178 Tunnelling Company was the death of 18 men 4 days before Christmas Day, due to a mine explosion. No. 178 were not alone in having casualties; at 2000hrs on 1 December, when No. 183 Tunnelling Company were in residence, the enemy exploded a mine and smashed two galleries. Lt H.L. Twite of the Royal Field Artillery was killed and nine men were caught in the crush in the broken galleries. Two men were gassed when trying to escape and an officer and two men were crushed in the collapse of the shaft lodgement. Next day, another man was gassed while involved in the clearing-up operations. Lt Twite was taken to Citadel New Military Cemetery for burial (V.A.16).

On 29 December, a disaster befell 6th Northamptons (54th Brigade, 18th Division) when 19 men were captured as they sheltered in a cellar. On 6 April 1916, four more men were killed during a mine explosion; 5 weeks later, three large mines were exploded in the area. On 1 June, seven more sappers died in the craters.

Although the Tambour had been in hot dispute since at least 1915, the village of Fricourt itself had been in German hands and was scheduled to be one of the main objectives for capture on 1 July. In addition to the Tambour, there were several features that were to become well known, including

Fricourt Wood to the north-east and the château which bordered the village and wood; there was also Rose Cottage, which later became a familiar landmark on the eastern side of the village. Then there was Lozenge Trench, which in most accounts of the fighting became known as the Sunken Road.

Fricourt was the 'second' village of the Somme before the battle, and had 176 houses. Rose Cottage was built of red brick; when its name appeared on trench maps in 1915, it was covered in creepers, with 'a fine rose garden'. On 2 August 1915, 1st Norfolks (15th Brigade, 5th Division) began their first spell in Somme trenches here when they relieved the French 19th Infantry Regiment; 1st Norfolks then moved to billets in MORLANCOURT. In early February, 7th Division took over the lines opposite Fricourt, including the Tambour. One of the division's battalions was 1st Royal Welsh Fusiliers (22nd Brigade) and the area to the south towards BRAY-SUR-SOMME became closely associated with the writers Siegfried Sassoon, Robert Graves and Bernard Adams.

In *Nothing of Importance*, Adams wrote a very detailed account of the area. In the period February/March 1916 he noted that

> Fricourt lay in full view before me . . . In the centre stood the white ruins of the church, still higher than the houses around it . . . All around were houses; roof-less, wall-less skeletons all of them . . . On the extreme right was Rose Cottage, a well-known artillery mark; just to its left were some large park gates, with stone pillars, leading into Fricourt Wood . . . the extreme northern part of the village was invisible, as the ground fell away north of the church. I could see where the road disappeared from view; then beyond, clear of houses, the road reappeared and ran straight up to the skyline, a mile further on. A communication trench crossed this road . . . With my glasses I could see every detail; beyond the communication trench were various small copses, and tracks running over the field; on the skyline, about three thousand yards away, was a long row of bushes . . . And just to the left of it all ran, the two white lace borders of chalk trenches, winding and wobbling along, up, up, up until they disappeared over the hill to Boiselle . . . Due west of Fricourt Church they touched in a small crater chain.

Robert Graves rejoined 1st Royal Welsh Fusiliers in March, when they were in and out of the trenches facing Fricourt, with billets at MORLANCOURT. The trenches were cut in chalk, better than clay in wet weather. The opposing lines came close together in this sector. The greatest trial, he wrote, was the German canister ammunition, a 2-gallon drum with ammonal and a smell like marzipan. It was full of scrap metal and rubbish and had a demoralising effect, even on those in the deepest dugouts.

In *The Old Front Line*, John Masefield noted that the ravine in front of the village was the gully between two spurs; it sheltered the sunken road to CONTALMAISON; a glance was enough to show that it was a strong position, that Fricourt was one of the boasts of the enemy on this front. Fricourt was strong in itself, like GOMMECOURT, and was perhaps the only place in the field that was as strong. It had, as at GOMMECOURT, a natural glacis up to the front line, which was deep, strong and well wired. Behind the front line was a wired second line, and behind that the rising spur on which the village stood, commanding both with machine-gun emplacements. The Germans did indeed turn the village into a fortress during their stay, which had begun in 1915, and in time the village became completely ruined. It consisted of a series of blockhouses and redoubts, with numerous machine guns. Underneath the houses were deep, comfortable shelters, some as much as 45ft deep.

Buried in Point 110 New Military Cemetery, south of Fricourt, is 2/Lt David Thomas (D.3), a friend of both Graves and Sassoon, who died of wounds in March before the battle began. Both men were distraught at the loss of this very dear friend and Graves wrote a poem called 'Goliath and David', dedicated to 'D.C.T. killed at Fricourt, March 1916'. In his *Diary*, Sassoon described the moving night-time burial: 'Everything was dim but the striped flag laid across the body. Robert Graves, beside me, with his white whimsical face twisted and grieving. Once we could not hear the solemn words for the noise of a machine gun along the line; when all was finished a canister fell a few hundred yards away to burst with a crash.' Also buried close to Thomas are 2/Lt D. Pritchard (D.5) and Capt M.S. Richardson (D.4), both of 1st Royal Welsh Fusiliers.

In his diary entry of 23 May, Sassoon noted that trench mortars were bursting in the cemetery on Crawley Ridge, site of a regimental aid post, as he went across to Fricourt in the evening. Fricourt was a huddle of reddish roofs, skeleton village, church tower – white, almost demolished, a patch of white against the sombre green of Fricourt Wood, which was full of German batteries. Away up the hillside, the white seams and heapings of trenches dug in the chalk. The sky was full of lark song. On 23 June, Sassoon wrote that after a bombardment by

the Allies the Germans had not retaliated much, although Fricourt was being shelled as he went along Kingston Road Trench, where his company were to go the next day. Men of the Royal Irish Rifles were scuffling along Point 71 North, the attack had been postponed, and the men, according to Sassoon, were at 'concert pitch'. They marched up to TAILLES WOOD and relieved 7th Borders (51st Brigade, 17th Division); conditions were muddy. On 28 June, Sassoon recorded that he was reading *Tess of the D'Urbervilles* in 85 Street dugouts. On 29 June, there was a continuous bombardment.

A famous incident took place at this time concerning 9th King's Own Yorkshire Light Infantry (64th Brigade, 21st Division). The Commanding Officer, Lt Col C.W.D. Lynch DSO, was very unpopular with his brother officers because of what had happened at the Battle of Loos, and the way that he had subsequently treated them. As a result, six of them put in for a transfer, including some to the kite balloon section. Two days before the battle began, in the officers' mess in a farmhouse/château in LA NEUVILLE, CORBIE, it was suggested that the health of the regiment should be toasted, coupled with the name of the commanding officer. There was some demur at this and several of the officers refused to take part in the toast, but Capt G. Haswell, the senior officer present, stepped in and saved the situation; he proposed the following toast: 'Gentlemen, I give you the toast of the King's Own Yorkshire Light Infantry, and in particular the 9th Battalion of the Regiment' – a slight pause – 'Gentlemen, when the barrage lifts . . .' This toast appeared subsequently in the Memoriam column of *The Times* for many years following the war.

On 1 July, however, 24 officers of the King's Own Yorkshire Light Infantry became casualties, 12 of whom died, including Lt Col Lynch (I.B.87), who was probably killed by a shell while leading his battalion. He was buried in Norfolk Cemetery, BÉCORDEL-BÉCOURT, as was Capt Haswell (I.B.92) and several other officers from the battalion.

To set the scene of the battle, which was due to begin on 1 July, after a 2-day postponement, it is best to rely on the account given in the *Official History of the War*. On 1 July, XV Corps, on the left of XIII Corps, faced the head of the Fricourt salient, the cornerstone of the German line between the Rivers Ancre and Somme. The slopes of the BAZENTIN–POZIÈRES ridge were broken through by the Willow Stream and its feeders. The centre valley ran up the western side of MAMETZ WOOD, with Caterpillar Way to the east and CONTAL-MAISON to the north-west. The Willow Stream made the boundary between the two divisions of XV Corps in the front line, 7th Division on the right, facing north opposite MAMETZ village on the lower slopes of the Mametz Spur, and 21st Division on the east, along the western slopes of the Fricourt Spur. The German defences about Fricourt were of exceptional strength and 1,200yds deep, and in the front line there were many salients and flanks. The front system was backed up by two intermediate lines; Fritz Trench–Railway Alley–Crucifix Trench and White Trench–Wood Trench–Quadrangle Trench.

The two battalions that were to be involved on 7th Division's front closest to Fricourt were 20th Manchesters and 1st Royal Welsh Fusiliers (both 22nd Brigade); the other elements of the division were more involved in the fighting on the MAMETZ side. Sassoon observed the progress of the battle on this section and wrote in his diary that 20th Manchesters were in front of 1st Royal Welsh Fusiliers, who were about 500yds from the front trench where Sandown Road met Kingston Road. He stated the barrage was working to the right of Fricourt and beyond. He could see the Division advancing about ¾ mile away on the left; he could also see some Yorkshiremen of 50th Brigade (17th Division) on the left, watching the advance and cheering as if it was a football match.

By 0930hrs, 21st Division were still going across on the left, apparently with no casualties. Trench mortars were 'knocking hell' out of Sunken Road Trench, close to Aeroplane Trench on the track at Fricourt. At 0950hrs, Fricourt was half hidden by clouds of smoke and the British were still advancing on the left in small parties. Sassoon mentions another huge explosion. At 1015hrs, he said, he could see 20th Manchesters in the front trench, getting ready to go over. Two hundred shells burst close to German prisoners at 84 Street. On the left of the Allied attack, 21st Division were still trotting along the skyline towards LA BOISSELLE. The barrage was going strong to the right of Contalmaison Ridge, and the Allies were shelling the MAMETZ area particularly heavily.

At 1330hrs, 20th Manchesters emerged from New Trench and took the Sunken Road Trench; Sassoon could see about 400 of them, and about 25 casualties on the left, caused by a machine gun at Fricourt. Then, he says, the 'swarm of ants' disappeared over the hill. At 1450hrs no man's land was empty except for casualties. Later, he said, 20th Manchesters had been held up behind the Sunken Road and were holding Bois Français Support.

By the end of 1 July in this sector, 20th Manchesters had got just beyond the Bois Français

Craters to the Support Line and 1st Royal Welsh Fusiliers, attacking in a north-easterly direction, had taken the Sunken Road Trench. They were poised to move beyond Fricourt, which was due to be 'pinched out' by attacks on both sides.

Further to the north-west of 1st Royal Welsh Fusiliers, between the battalion and the Tambour, were some battalions of 50th Brigade (17th Division, attached 21st Division); 7th Yorkshires held the line from the cemetery to the Tambour and 10th West Yorkshires held the line from the Tambour to the apex at Purfleet. 7th East Yorkshires were in BÉCORDEL-BÉCOURT and Bonté Redoubt in support, with 6th Dorsets to their left.

The regimental history of the Princess of Wales's Own (Yorkshire) Regiment noted that the key to capturing Fricourt was Wing Corner, which was just to the north of 1st Royal Welsh Fusiliers' position, where the Germans would be able to see on both sides of the attack coming towards them; the other strongpoint was thought to be Wicket Corner. On 27 June, 7th Yorkshires had been billeted in houses and barns in Ville and at night had gone to trenches in front of Fricourt. The German trenches were full of men who were pouring out of the left section, the Tambour; the companies of 7th Yorkshires had no chance, and were literally mown down. At 1815hrs, having suffered 352 casualties, 7th Yorkshires were relieved by 6th Dorsets; the dead were thick on the ground. 50th Brigade's attack had failed and was not renewed that day. 6th Dorsets spent the night near Fricourt Cemetery and recovered many of the wounded; at dawn on 2 July, they moved back to MÉAULTE.

On the left of 7th Yorkshires and 6th Dorsets were 10th West Yorkshires. In the attack, two of their leading companies made rapid progress in reaching König Trench and pressed on for the northern edge of the village. However, it was the third and fourth companies that caught the full brunt of the German machine-gun fire, which came mainly from the left flank. The companies were cut down and virtually annihilated, as they hadn't the advantage of the Tambour mines. Casualties included Lt Col A. Dickson (C.12), who lies with his men in the part of no man's land where they fell, in what is now Fricourt New Military Cemetery. His second in command, Maj J.L. Knott DSO, together with his adjutant, were also killed.

The poet A. Victor Ratcliffe, born in 1887, was a lieutenant with 10th West Yorkshires; he, too, became a casualty, from shell-fire. His work had been published in a volume entitled *Soldier Poets*. A witness, one Pte W. Cheesborough, wrote a note which is in Ratcliffe's army file at The National Archives: 'I saw him struck by a shell and killed instantaneously within 2 or 3 yards of me. I was wounded about half an hour afterwards and on returning over the old ground I came across Lt Ratcliffe's body. I noticed the identification disc on his wrist.' Ratcliffe was buried in Fricourt New Military Cemetery (Row 3, Grave 9). In his will he left all his manuscripts to his fiancée, Pauline Benson Clough. On 11 October, his identification tag, which had been found at Fricourt at the beginning of July, was sent from the British Red Cross Society to the War Office, who later sent it on to his mother.

It was calculated that 10th West Yorkshires' casualties were higher than those of any other British battalion on 1 July. In *The History of the West Yorkshire Regiment*, E. Wyrall wrote of the battalion:

> They had orders to advance against Fricourt village on 1 July at 7.30 am. They were to converge near the north east end of Fricourt Wood. The battalion was on the left of the attack from the German Tambour as far as the apex of 'Purfleet'. They were to co-operate with the 7th Yorks from the Wing Corner to south of the German Tambour. The boundary between the two villages was in the village a line running through the wood. The two leading companies made rapid progress as the enemy was not quick enough. They got into Konig Trench and pressed on for the northern edge of Fricourt village. The third and fourth companies were not so lucky, the enemy had more time to come out and man his guns and there was less protection from the artillery. Lt Col Dickson and his 2nd in command Major Knott were both killed. The two leading companies lacked support and were practically surrounded and wiped out. The 7th Yorks tried to reach them but were also cut down. The MG fire was mainly from the left flank. 750 other ranks were casualties. The battalion withdrew to Ville and then to Méaulte and on the 2nd. Fricourt was evacuated that night.

At 0900hrs, two companies of 7th East Yorkshires moved up to Kingston Road from Bonté Redoubt; another company were in Surrey Street and further elements advanced towards the edge of the village. They had attacked in the afternoon but, like 10th West Yorkshires, were met by murderous machine-gun fire. During the night, 7th East Yorkshires were relieved and marched back to HEILLY and MÉAULTE to reorganise.

There have been several references to mines at the Tambour. Their purpose was to distract the enemy's attention and to form craters which would block enfilade fire against 21st Division and the 50th Brigade (17th Division) from the northern face of the German position. Three large mines against the Germans had been driven, prepared by No. 178 Tunnelling Company; these were fired at about 0727hrs on 1 July. Two mines were exploded, but not the third; the Germans established themselves rapidly, before the British infantry could reach them. This story is similar to that at Hawthorn Redoubt at BEAUMONT-HAMEL, a little earlier in the day.

In addition to this activity, three Russian saps had been driven out in this sector, for the purpose of having emplacements at their mouths, or terminals, which could accommodate flame-throwers. Of these, only Dinner Street was used, as the German line opposite the other two (Purfleet and Balmoral Street) was not captured. Lt A.J. Willis of 10th York & Lancasters (63rd Brigade, 21st Division), who was wounded on 1 July, mentions the Matterhorn Crater as being in front of the Tambour; it was about 50ft deep. Today, the bumpy ground caused by all these operations is quite noticeable and only cattle are now in occupation. Willis was sniped when going forward, from the direction of Fricourt Wood.

The next battalion to be briefly dealt with is 10th Yorkshires (62nd Brigade, 21st Division), who were in reserve behind 10th West Yorkshires. On 29 June, they had been in billets in BUIRE-SUR-L'ANCRE, and on the night of 30 June they were in Queen's Redoubt, which was in front of the wood south of Bécourt Château. Part of 10th Yorkshires assisted 15th Durham Light Infantry (64th Brigade, 21st Division), pushing on to the sunken road that ran north and south through Fricourt and in support at Lozenge Alley, where they consolidated. This was part of the capture of Fricourt by an encircling movement. One of the heroes of 10th Yorkshires was T/Maj S.W. Loudoun-Shand VC, who died in his front trenches and was buried in Norfolk Cemetery (I.C.77). The citation for his Victoria Cross says that it was awarded

> For most conspicuous bravery. When his company attempted to climb over the parapet to attack the enemy's trenches, they were met by very fierce machine-gun fire, which temporarily stopped their progress. Major Loudoun-Shand immediately leapt on to the parapet, helped the men over it, and encouraged them in every way until he fell mortally wounded. Even then he insisted on being propped up in the trench, and

went on encouraging the non-commissioned officers and men until he died.

Loudoun-Shand previously fought in the Boer War.

To the left of 10th West Yorkshires were 4th Middlesex (63rd Brigade, 21st Division) who had moved up on 30 June; on their left were 8th Somerset Light Infantry (also 63rd Brigade, 21st Division). The supporting battalions were 10th York & Lancasters and 8th Lincolns (also 63rd Brigade, 21st Division). At 0730hrs, after two mines had been exploded to the right of the Tambour, they attempted to leave their trenches, but were met by violent machine-gun fire. It was decided to hold on to Empress Trench and consolidate. 4th Middlesex's right flank was exposed and their left was held by scattered parties of 8th Somerset Light Infantry. By 0915hrs, supporting battalions had begun to arrive.

In support, 8th Lincolns had one company in the rear of 8th Somerset Light Infantry and cleared the front line. The battalions worked their way down German communication trenches by bombing Dart Lane and Brandy Trench when Lozenge Alley was reached. This position was held at night. Their right flank was attacked from Fricourt up Lonely Trench, but later that night the enemy retired.

The last two battalions of 64th Brigade (21st Division) in this sector were 9th and 10th King's Own Yorkshire Light Infantry, supported by 15th Durham Light Infantry and 1st East Yorkshires (also 64th Brigade, 21st Division). They were to lose Lt Col H.J. King of 10th King's Own Yorkshire Light Infantry, who was wounded, and Lt Col M.B. Stow of 1st East Yorkshires, mortally wounded. On 26 June, 9th and 10th King's Own Yorkshire Light Infantry moved up to BUIRE-SUR-L'ANCRE.

On 1 July, 9th King's Own Yorkshire Light Infantry left from a Russian sap; only five officers, including 2/Lt Ellenberger, managed to get past even the first German trench. They reached CRUCIFIX CORNER and Brig Gen Headlam, Officer Commanding 64th Brigade, had his headquarters in the Sunken Road. At 0845hrs, Capt L.D. Spicer reached the Sunken Road from reserve at BUIRE-SUR-L'ANCRE; his instructions were to reorganise the battalion and to take charge. As 9th King's Own Yorkshire Light Infantry were relieved by 62nd Brigade, in reserve, they were to go back to South Sausage Support. On his way, Spicer had come across a lot of men of 1st Lincolns and 10th Yorkshires, who were obviously resting on the way to the Sunken Road. They were part of 62nd Brigade, which had been told to relieve 9th King's Own Yorkshire Light Infantry. Spicer was directed by

them to the Sunken Road, but thought he was in Lozenge Alley, which was too far over to the right.

Spicer hurried on and finally arrived at the end of the trench, where they were digging a small sap onto the road. He was warned of sniper activity in Fricourt Farm, because the enemy could see anyone getting out. Spicer dived across the road to safety under an embankment on the far side. The others joined him and they then proceeded up the Sunken Road, which was full of men. Once they got to the German lines, the place had seemed full of English troops. He found CSM Warren and told him about the relief and that he was therefore to return the men to South Sausage Support. He found that battalion headquarters had been established at a large German dugout, which was approached by a covered entrance; it had been converted into a temporary dressing station. When they were ready to move off, the commanding officer of 1st Lincolns gave orders that none of Spicer's brigade were to leave the Sunken Road until the whole of 62nd Brigade were in.

During the night, the enemy were quiet, except for a certain amount of shelling. The dugout was a fine example of trench architecture. It was about 25ft deep, with several rooms, both sleeping and living, and it possessed a large oven. Forty German prisoners were taken at the dugout and it also accommodated wounded from both sides. There was a quantity of stores there, which included cigars, cigarettes, chocolate and soda water; the latter was drunk by the British.

R.C. Money of 15th Durham Light Infantry noted that on 1 July, his unit followed 9th King's Own Yorkshire Light Infantry, incurring severe casualties; they went down Lozenge Alley and found the remains of the battalion at the Sunken Road. He noted that the men seemed to be sitting around waiting for orders, as their commanding officer had become a casualty. 64th Brigade were left 'in the air' and they went back. Money himself was wounded and returned home on 3/4 July.

According to the historian of 17th Division, the afternoon of 1 July saw 21st Division's advance brought to a standstill in front of the German trenches in LOZENGE WOOD on the Fricourt–CONTALMAISON road. On the other side of the salient, 7th Division were held up in the southern outskirts of MAMETZ. The plan to cut off Fricourt by using two divisions to join hands on the higher ground to the north of the village had failed; there was a gap of nearly 2 miles between them. During the afternoon, 7th Yorkshires were ordered to attack the west front of the village, with 7th East Yorkshires in close support. They were caught in a barrage fire, and machine guns opened on them along the margin of the village. The attack had failed, and the remnants of 7th Yorkshires struggled back to their trenches.

In *Sir Douglas Haig's Great Push*, it is noted that beyond the third line to the left of Fricourt lay a work called Crucifix Trench, the possession of which could greatly facilitate the capture of the village. It was against this that the 50th Brigade troops advanced, but they were heavily shelled and machine-gunned. Further progress was impossible, since just beyond the captured trench was a wood called SHELTER WOOD, at the south-east corner of which the enemy had erected a redoubt that bristled with machine guns.

Fricourt had turned out to be a particularly difficult village to take because of its location in a valley, west of MAMETZ WOOD; because Fricourt Wood sloped up towards MAMETZ, the enemy who were entrenched could bring flanking fire to bear on Fricourt Wood. On the other side, the British artillery were not able to inflict as much damage as they would have liked, again because of the sheltered position of the village.

An article on the Battle of the Somme in *The Territorial* (July 1937) states that 'when the village was eventually entered they were swept by machine-gun fire along the streets. The advance beyond Fricourt was even more difficult. Strongly defended woods and plantations up the slopes were honeycombed with enemy machine guns and sniper's posts, each of which had to be cleared by hand to hand fighting at bayonet point.'

Despite the very considerable damage they had inflicted upon the Allied attack on the village on 1 July, the enemy decided that the position was no longer tenable and therefore planned to fall back on the village of CONTALMAISON to the north-east, where they would make a stand. This is not to say that they just presented Fricourt and Fricourt Wood to the British on a plate, but rather that they made the Allies fight for every foot of the way.

In his *Diary*, Sassoon noted that on 2 July, Fricourt and Rose Trench were to be attacked again, although he was not himself involved in the fighting. At 1430hrs, the adjutant reported that these two had been taken without resistance and that there had not been a bombardment. 7th Division were reported as having taken many prisoners, including 200 taken by 1st Royal Welsh Fusiliers. Fricourt had become full of British troops and 7th Division had reached a line just short of MAMETZ WOOD. Sassoon also adds that 2nd Queen's (91st Brigade, 7th Division) had 'legged it as usual'.

17th Division first had an inkling that the Germans were pulling out of the village when prisoners began to be brought back to the Allied line, for it was prisoners who gave the British the information about the German evacuation. The order was subsequently given for a brigade to push forward to occupy the village, with Fricourt Farm and Wood for their second objective. Shortly after noon on 2 July, it was reported that the brigade had pushed out northwards towards Fricourt Farm; the latter was to the north-east of Fricourt Wood and close to the Poodles and LOZENGE WOOD.

At the farm, 7th Lincolns (51st Brigade, 17th Division) were preparing to make an attack on the wood; they had already come under heavy machine-gun fire from Fricourt Wood when they reached the north-east line of the village. According to 17th Division's history, what was described on the maps as Fricourt Wood was at the time the park of the Fricourt Château, a building that was just outside the village. The enemy had abandoned it, and 7th Lincolns used it as their headquarters. But the Germans still held on to the park. From the park in front of the château was a wide clearing that stretched for about ¼ mile, to a ride that traversed the wood from east to west. The clearing had been a grassy lawn; because of the bombardment and obstacles, movement through it would be very slow. The Germans had machine guns among the trees, and more were hidden near the cross-ride in order for the machine-gunners to sweep the park's central clearing.

During the middle of the afternoon, 7th Lincolns advanced into the wood and pushed right through it. On their left were 8th South Staffords and 10th Sherwood Foresters (both also 51st Brigade, 17th Division); these two battalions went forward along the northern edge of the wood. The advance had reached Fricourt Farm by now, but the Germans still held not only a trench that ran from it nearly as far as the railway, but also a trench strongly wired and running parallel to the margin of the wood about 150yds from it. This was known as Crucifix Trench, and was just to the north of the Poodles. It took its name from a roadside cross on the slope near its northern end. Here a heavy fire of machine guns and rifles was directed from the wood. At dusk there was still a lot of firing in front of Crucifix Trench and British 'bombers' were fighting their way at the end of Railway Alley Trench, which was near the farm.

The cellars of the château were used as a brigade headquarters; above ground, the building was a ruin of fallen brick and rubble, and only its southern wall was still standing. The strongly vaulted cellars had withstood the bombardments.

On 21st Division's front, on the left of 17th Division, we know that 10th York & Lancasters went up to join 62nd Brigade via the famous Sunken Road, which ran virtually from north to south through the whole of the village. They occupied part of Dingle Trench, which was to the north-west of Crucifix Alley, and their headquarters was part of the Sunken Road to the south of Round Wood.

At 0700hrs on 2 July, 9th King's Own Yorkshire Light Infantry, who were actively involved on 1 July, were allowed to go at last, having been relieved and then been held up by the non-arrival of two and half companies of 12th Northumberland Fusiliers (62nd Brigade, 21st Division). They filed down Patch Alley and then, according to Spicer, to positions in South Sausage Support. After establishing a battalion headquarters in a dugout at the junction of the Support and the front line, 9th King's Own Yorkshire Light Infantry spent the day consolidating and 'reversing' the trench. Their men had had no sleep for two nights, having been in the trenches for four nights before that. They did manage to get some food and tea from Queen's Redoubt, though; bearers from 53rd Field Ambulance (17th Division) came to the Redoubt to collect casualties lying there.

Having been badly cut up, 63rd Brigade (21st Division) took over a great German dugout containing hundreds of beds; it had been fitted with electric light. In *War Letters to a Wife*, R. Feilding described a dugout that was possibly the same one, although he is by no means the only commentator to remark on the dugouts of Fricourt; indeed, they became a centre of attraction, even to HM the King, as will be seen later. Feilding reported:

This dugout beats all the ones that I had previously seen. It might also be described as an underground house, where instead of going upstairs you went down, by one flight after another, to the different storeys. There were three floors, the deepest being 60 feet or more from the door by which one entered. The entrance hall, so to speak was the brick cellar of a former house. There were two entrances, only one of which, however, could be recognised from the inside, since the doorway had been blown in. The other door, by which we entered, had been partly closed by a shell, a hole being left behind revealing heavy trench bombs, grenades, steel helmets, underclothing etc. Many rifles hung from the wooden walls of the first flight of stairs. Nooks and corners were occupied by sleeping bunks.

Beyond Railway Alley on the left was a small crescent-shaped spinney called SHELTER WOOD, which had been full of Germans and which was captured by an attack from the west. The possession of the wood subsequently isolated the Germans who were in Railway Alley from support on that side. From the Alley, though, and from the Poodles and Railway Copse, there was a withering fire from German machine guns and rifles as the British infantry advanced. The capture of these positions virtually finished off the German salient position between the two sections of the British advance, so that a line from LA BOISSELLE on the left to MONTAUBAN-DE-PICARDIE on the right was held. On the right, northwards from MONTAUBAN-DE-PICARDIE the British artillery bombarded the lines of Caterpillar Wood, which reduced its resistance to 18th Division on the MONTAUBAN-DE-PICARDIE front.

Sir Douglas Haig's Great Push notes that the capture of Fricourt was the supreme achievement of the day. The ground that had been won the previous day had been heavily shelled during the night, but the British had held on to it with splendid determination, and slowly the salient became contracted. The villages like MAMETZ and MONTAUBAN-DE-PICARDIE had been pounded to bits and were simply ruins.

In *The Battle of the Somme*, John Masefield noted that Fricourt Wood was now (2 July) outflanked on the east by British troops in MAMETZ, but it was still a strong enemy fortress – like all other parts of the salient, the wood was edged and crossed with deep and strong trenches of the usual enemy pattern. Above the highest, northern part of the wood the ground rose to a chalk tableland, about as big as the wood and shaped rather like a boot raised to squash Fricourt flat. On this small boot-shaped plateau were more defences; at the heel was the deep valley of the CONTALMAISON road, the sole was the valley of MAMETZ, and the instep was a deep romantic curving valley, with the abrupt, sharply cut sides so often seen in chalk country. This last valley, from its depth, steepness and isolation, was known by the British as Shelter Valley.

The defences of the boot-shaped tableland were as follows: a line of trench known as Railway Alley, which ran north-east from Fricourt Wood towards the toe; odds and ends about a farm, a copse called the Poodles, and a crucifix along the leg of the boot; a strong field fortress in the biggish copse called SHELTER WOOD which hung like a curtain of shrubs and trees on the steep wall of the valley, at the top of the leg; the trenched copses LOZENGE WOOD and the Dingle, on the heel and the back.

Royal Field Artillery horses watering on the Fricourt–Mametz road, July 1916. *(IWM Q882)*

At dawn on 2 July, British troops advanced to storm Fricourt Wood, the CONTALMAISON road, SHELTER WOOD and as much of the boot-shaped plateau as they could take.

As the British advanced, the massed guns in all the trenches and strongholds opened up on them. They got across the field of fire into Fricourt Wood. They climbed over fallen trees and were caught in branches, and were shot when caught. It took them all day to clear that jungle – and by dark they were almost out of the northern end, where Railway Alley lay in front of them on the roll of the hill. Further to the north, on the top of the leg of the boot, the British stormed SHELTER WOOD – till the wood was heaped with corpses, but in Allied hands. The dugouts, which had once been the headquarters of a hidden battery in the gully, were taken over as dressing stations.

In his diary entry for 3 July, Sassoon wrote that 1st Royal Welsh Fusiliers assembled at Point 71 North and marched to a point north-west of CARNOY where 22nd Brigade (7th Division) had concentrated. The four battalions piled arms and lay down in an open grassy hollow south of the CARNOY–MAMETZ road, with a fine view of where 91st Brigade (7th Division) had attacked on 1 July, about 600yds away. After lunch, Brig Gen J.R. Minshull-Ford, Officer Commanding 22nd Brigade, rode round to congratulate his men on what they had achieved in the previous few days. 1st Royal Welsh Fusiliers were about 420 strong and 20th Manchesters had been reduced to about 250 men; 2nd Royal Warwicks (22nd Brigade, 7th Division) and 2nd Royal Irish had not yet been in action. The four battalions were in four groups. A little smoke drifted from tiny bivouac fires. At the end of the hollow was the road to MAMETZ, where some captured guns had been recently brought along. Beyond that, the ground rose towards the Bazentin Ridge. Sassoon wrote a poem called 'At Carnoy'; the first line reads 'Down in the hollow there's the whole Brigade' (See CARNOY entry).

Meanwhile, on the left of Sassoon's 7th Division, 21st Division were clearing Railway Alley and had secured the rest of the village of Fricourt by capturing the other fortresses, the Poodles and the Crucifix.

In *Letters from France 1915–1918*, Capt L.D. Spicer of 9th King's Own Yorkshire Light Infantry wrote that 62nd Brigade had attacked SHELTER WOOD and had captured over 1,000 prisoners, who had passed through 9th King's Own Yorkshire Light Infantry's trenches. At noon, the battalion had received orders that 21st Division were going to take up a new line in support, and occupied a small piece of line from the junction of Patch Alley and South Sausage Support to the left. The trenches were obliterated; despite shelling, they carried out this work in order to be ready to hand over. Because there were so many men in this part of the line, there was a lot of shelling, and away above CONTAL-MAISON was a German kite balloon. On 4 July, 9th King's Own Yorkshire Light Infantry were relieved and marched out straight to DERNANCOURT; from there, they entrained for PICQUIGNY.

The *Official History of the War* recorded that on 3 July, Fricourt Wood was taken in an enveloping attack by 13th Northumberland Fusiliers (62nd Brigade, 21st Division), covered by Stokes mortar fire. Many prisoners were taken and a German counter-attack against BOTTOM and SHELTER WOODS was repulsed.

In *The Turning Point*, H.P. Robinson, war correspondent of *The Times*, noted that on 5 July the British had forced their way for about 1,000yds beyond MONTAUBAN-DE-PICARDIE, which was to the right of fierce fighting. This brought the British to almost abreast of MAMETZ WOOD. On the further left, there was prolonged fighting for the possession of a wood called BIRCH TREE WOOD and also for PEAKE WOODS, and a formidable group of trenches close to PEAKE WOODS known as the Horseshoes. The British attacked from two sides simultaneously; it was not until they took the Horseshoes on the night of 6/7 July that the situation was cleared.

On 7 July, 110th Brigade (37th Division) were attached to 21st Division, replacing 63rd Brigade. In *39 Months*, D.V. Kelly wrote about 110th Brigade, which was made up of four service battalions of the Leicestershire Regiment (6th, 7th, 8th and 9th Leicesters). On 10 July, Kelly went round the lines with the brigade bombing officer and saw trenches that had been heaped with dead, mostly Yorkshiremen, he thought. When CONTALMAISON was attacked, the wounded came via SCOTTS RE-DOUBT to the advanced dressing station at Fricourt and were evacuated in ambulance cars. Kelly also remembers that 9th Leicesters' battalion head-quarters was in a deep dugout in a copse. By now, Fricourt village was full of field guns and howitzers.

53rd Field Ambulance (17th Division) used a dugout called the Subway, which was close to the BÉCORDEL-BÉCOURT end of the road to Fricourt; they pitched a small camp here on 5/6 July. On 6 July, 53rd Field Ambulance cleared 500 casualties from here to the main dressing station at MÉRICOURT-L'ABBÉ and the 17th Division collecting station at MÉAULTE; ambulance cars could get to the Subway. From MÉAULTE, the wounded were cleared to either MARICOURT or VECQUEMONT. On 7 July, six of the wounded died here and were buried in Subway Cemetery. On 8 July, 375 other ranks passed through the dugout.

In *Memoirs of a Camp Follower*, Philip Gosse of 69th Field Ambulance (23rd Division) noted there was nothing left of the village by 9 July; part of the advanced dressing station was in tents, so hundreds of wounded were lying out in the open awaiting attention.

A note in the *History of the Royal Engineers* states that an elaborate plan for carrying water forward had been worked out by Maj H.S. Rogers for Fourth Army. The careful arrangements proved of great value in subsequent operations. 'The most successful pipe-line in point of time was the extension of the Fricourt System, one water point had actually been established in Fricourt within 12 hours of the village being taken. The entire system had been completed in about ten days from then.'

In *Sagittarius Rising*, Cecil Lewis mentioned that on one occasion when the weather was bad for flying, a small party from his Royal Flying Corps squadron set out in a tender for a visit to the front. Because of the state of the roads, Lewis's party were forced to leave their vehicle near the former front line at Fricourt. They then set out on foot towards Caterpillar Wood to visit a 9in howitzer battery. The party passed through the formidable Fricourt defences and dugouts and noted its commanding position. They walked on past MAMETZ and up the valley, observing and taking in everything. There was little troop movement at the time. Batteries were perched below the crest of the rise. They discovered the battery that they had set out to visit, who were snug in a little valley and living in 'large tubular steel caissons, corrugated and shell proof'.

Gosse wrote of a time when there was a lull between battles and an invitation to a dinner party, to be given by 9th Yorkshires. Looking forward to a convivial evening, the guests sat down at the table, when the sound of a gong was heard. 'This was not a dinner gong but a warning that gas shells were coming over . . . Thus what was to have been a unique and wonderful dinner-party became a complete fiasco.'

On 13 July, Lt Col E.H.E. Collen visited Fricourt and medical shelters in the dugouts: 'Most of them are about 30 ft deep with little offices, operating

Troops moving up through the ruins of Fricourt for the attack on Contalmaison, 10 July 1916. *(IWM Q4087)*

rooms etc and then down another 8–10 steps there were lots of bunks. The smell etc made one nearly sick' (IWM 79/21/1).

In *The War the Infantry Knew*, a history of 2nd Royal Welsh Fusiliers (58th Brigade, 33rd Division) compiled by Capt J.C. Dunn, one of its contributors wrote that on 15 July the battalion moved on down the Fricourt road in heavy mist; they went via BÉCORDEL and then detoured to the right beyond Fricourt because of German shelling. At 0800hrs the mist cleared, and they found themselves among the dead of 38th Division; many friends were recognised and quickly buried. The objective of the division was the Switch Line and HIGH WOOD.

On and around 19 July, 5th Division were at Rose Cottage in Fricourt. The peaceful beauty suggested by the name was not borne out in actuality, as the area was pitted with shell-holes and covered with debris, the only cover consisting of a few tarpaulins stretched over poles, and a Nissen hut. The ruins of a red-brick cottage in one corner provided the origin of the name.

In *Old Soldiers Never Die*, Pte Frank Richards of 2nd Royal Welsh Fusiliers wrote that his battalion left ALBERT on 20 July and moved in stages up to Fricourt Wood. He records that he camped in shacks in the wood and was shelled by the enemy.

On 21 July, 1/5th Seaforth Highlanders (152nd Brigade, 51st Division) bivouacked on the edge of Fricourt Wood for the night. Across the valley lay MAMETZ village and in front of them was the dark mass of MAMETZ WOOD. The whole of 152nd Brigade were bivouacked in an open field on the south side of Fricourt Wood in BÉCORDEL. In the valley ran the chief road, which wound its way through MAMETZ past MAMETZ WOOD to BAZENTIN-LE-GRAND. All along the side of the road were gun emplacements. Because of enemy shelling, they had moved back to MÉAULTE. In *Flying Corps Headquarters 1914–1918*, Maurice Baring noted that on 24 July, he went with Maj Gen H.M. Trenchard, General Officer Commanding First Wing, Royal Flying Corps, to Fricourt to see the ground wireless stations and mechanics.

In an entry in *Stand To*, dated 4 August, Capt F.C. Hitchcock of 2nd Leinsters (73rd Brigade, 24th Division) wrote that he and some companions toured the old German Front Line at Fricourt and were surprised and amazed when they saw the stronghold on the commanding ground north of the village. It looked to them as if it was impregnable, but the several mine craters told the tale of its capture. Masses of *chevaux de fries* and barbed wire were heaped up all over the area. There was an Indian encampment close by; a Punjabi regiment, employed on the lines of communication.

On 6 August, 1/4th Suffolks (98th Brigade, 33rd Division) took over trenches in Fricourt Wood, and during the next few days furnished working parties for the construction of Thistle Alley communication trench. In *A Subaltern on the Somme*, Max Plowman of 10th West Yorkshires (50th Brigade, 17th Division) wrote that in early August he left DERNAN-COURT with his battalion:

We descended the long hill leading to Fricourt, dodging about the stream of traffic that stirs the dust of the road to a thick haze. Near the bottom of the hill we come upon the old front line of the 1 July. The country here is stricken waste . . . On the far side, in the face of a steep rise, we see the remains of what were deep, German dug-outs, but everything needs pointing out, for the general impression is a wilderness without verdure or growth of any kind. To our right, we noticed a ruined cemetery.

Perhaps the high spot of Fricourt's history, from the British Army's point of view, was of the visit of HM King George V on 10 August. There are several accounts of this visit, including the King's own in his diary:

We walked across no man's land and the German first line trenches and support trenches to an observation post just south and between the villages of Fricourt and Mametz. From there we got a fairly good view of the ground in front, but unfortunately the visibility was low, it was possible to make out Pozières, Contalmaison, the Bois de Mametz, where all the fighting is going on now and there was plenty of shelling going on all the time, we were about three and a half miles from our front line. It was interesting seeing the trenches and every kind of thing lying about from shells to clothes and empty bottles. The masses of shell-holes and lines of craters caused by mines are extraordinary. I went down into one German dugout about 30 feet deep, but I didn't stop long as I think a dead German was in it. I saw the grave of a French officer killed at the beginning of this year, before we took over the line, another of an unknown British soldier and a third of an English soldier with his steel helmet lying on the grave with a hole right through it which killed him and lastly a grave of a German with his boots sticking out of the ground. All very pathetic, which is war.

After filming at FRANVILLERS, the official War Office photographer, Geoffrey Malins, noted that the news of HM the King's arrival and journey to Fricourt had spread, for everywhere numbers of troops were scattered along the roadside. The spot where the King alighted in Fricourt was arranged in the form of a circle, with underground tunnels and dugouts of great depth. In various sections of the wall were machine-gun emplacements, the whole being on top of a hill which had formed a formidable obstacle to the British troops. The hill was now known as King George's Hill. At a second stop, the King was on a hilltop and a general described the various movements of the attack and the fall of Fricourt. The guide for the party was a lieutenant of the Royal Engineers, who suddenly called attention to an old German trench. The Prince of Wales first entered it and examined from above the depths of an old dugout. The party then halted at another dugout, the guide entered and for some moments did not reappear, while the King and the general stood gazing. The King walked over former mine craters and stood using his deer-stalking glasses and watching the bombardment of POZIÈRES; at one point he picked up a piece of shrapnel as a souvenir. Malins's car had a flat tyre after the King's party had moved on, and he made hurried tracks for a casualty clearing station, which the King was due to visit.

The war correspondent Philip Gibbs was another witness to the royal visit. Gibbs wrote that when he was on what was named King George's Hill, to the south of Fricourt, the King looked down on the white ghastliness of its ruins. Half a mile away lay MAMETZ and in front was CONTALMAISON, with the ruins of its château standing among charred tree trunks. Although the day was misty, the King could see MONTAUBAN-DE-PICARDIE and TRÔNES WOOD and a little way over to LA BOISSELLE, and massed smoke clouds over POZIÈRES. Gibbs says that the King found the inscription on a cross that marked the bodies of two soldiers of the Border Regiment, and that he went into a German dugout, but did not go into the very depths of it.

In *At GHQ*, Brig Gen J. Charteris, Brigadier General, General Staff (Intelligence), wrote that 'His Majesty's visit had been a great success. We took him to Fricourt and even a bit farther forward than that, so that he was very close to the fighting line.

The King had been followed by cameras everywhere, and the whole visit is being well written up in a series of articles which will appear as soon as he is safely back in England.'

On 12 August, 9th King's Royal Rifle Corps (42nd Brigade, 14th Division) marched to billets at Fricourt from MÉRICOURT-L'ABBÉ, and on 19 August they moved to MONTAUBAN-DE-PICARDIE. On 13 August, 2nd Royal Welsh Fusiliers moved from Bécordel to Fricourt Wood. They occupied a three-storey dugout, which was completely underground. They supplied working parties for digging a communication trench to HIGH WOOD and to carry materials from the BAZENTIN dumps. Also on 13 August, 1/4th Suffolks (98th Brigade, 33rd Division) moved from Fricourt Wood to support trenches in BAZENTIN-LE-GRAND. On 19 August, they moved from a corner of HIGH WOOD back to Fricourt Wood, and at sundown moved to a camp near MÉAULTE, near the ALBERT road.

On 27 August, 2nd Royal Welsh Fusiliers relieved 1st Black Watch (1st Brigade, 1st Division) and

Mr Lloyd George (second from right) with Lord Reading (right) on King George's Hill, near Fricourt, 12 September 1916. *(IWM Q1196)*

arrived at Fricourt Wood, which was very muddy. On 6 September, Fricourt was to receive further distinguished visitors; in fact, once it had fallen to the Allies, and provided it was safe to take visitors, the village had become a 'prime attraction'. The main reason was to see the elaborate defences and dugouts that the always practical Germans had constructed. On 6 September, the Prime Minister, Herbert Asquith, together with Maurice Hankey, who was Secretary to the War Cabinet, came to see the village. Asquith had requested that his son Raymond, who was with 3rd Grenadier Guards (2nd Guards Brigade, Guards Division) in the vicinity, should meet the party at the crossroads close to the village.

Once the party had arrived, they had to seek shelter, as the Germans were bombarding the village. They sheltered in the famous German dugout, which at this time was the headquarters of 7th Division. Lt Raymond Asquith wrote that he received a telegram while he was training, which asked him to meet his father at the village, on the crossroads K6d, at 1045hrs. Raymond rode over on horseback and reached the rendezvous exactly on time, and waited for an hour on a very muddy road that was congested with lorries and troops and which was surrounded by barking guns. Then two handsome motors arrived

Fricourt Château before the war.
(Peter F. Batchelor Collection)

from General Headquarters. His father was in one with two staff officers, and in the other was Hankey, together with Maurice Bonham-Carter and 'one of those nondescripts who hang about the corridors of Downing Street in the twilight region between the civil and the domestic service'. They went up to see some of the captured German dugouts, and just as they were arriving the Germans began to send over a few shells from a 4.2in field howitzer. The shells fell about 200yds behind the party and they quickly sheltered in a large and commodious dugout for ½ hour. The Prime Minister then drove off to lunch with Lt Gen Sir Henry Rawlinson, General Officer Commanding Fourth Army, and Raymond rode back to rejoin his unit. It was to be the last time that the two men met, for shortly afterwards Raymond was mortally wounded. A few days after Asquith's visit, Lloyd George, who was Secretary of War, also visited Fricourt and 38th Division. He was to become Prime Minister 3 months later, in December 1916.

In the period 10–12 September, 47th Division were occupying a large area before going up to the line and the slopes were covered with transport of all kinds; the cavalry also waited once more for its opportunity to 'break through'. On 11 September,

7th King's Royal Rifle Corps (41st Brigade, 14th Division) were in tents in Fricourt, having come from DERNANCOURT; on 16 September they were back at the transport camp at Fricourt.

On 12 September, 18th King's Royal Rifle Corps (122nd Brigade, 41st Division) moved to Fricourt from DERNANCOURT, and on the night of 14 September took up positions at Tea Trench, prior to the FLERS battle.

On 25 September, Aubrey Smith of 1/5th Londons (169th Brigade, 56th Division) set off from MARICOURT for Fricourt, where the next water supply was situated. While looking for signs of drinking water at Fricourt, Smith's transport section moved its line to the neighbourhood of the CITADEL, south of Fricourt on the road to BRAY-SUR-SOMME.

In early October, conditions at the CITADEL were very muddy. The state of the countryside at this time was deplorable and the continuous rain of October in fact caused great hardship. According to the *History of the 12th Division*, on the road from Fricourt to MONTAUBAN-DE-PICARDIE, which was no wider than an ordinary country road and which at times had to take a double line of traffic, there was an instruction to users that it was forbidden to proceed against the traffic. Also, artillery limbers were unable to get across country. Shells were carried by pack horses, which often sank over their hocks in the mud. The conditions were of the worst and 12th Division made little progress at this time.

At Fricourt there was a camp named Mansell; towards the end of October, 25th Division's headquarters was at Fricourt Farm. From August, 7th, 9th, 14th, 21st, 29th, 30th, 41st, 47th and 50th Divisions had units in the Fricourt area; some of them had their divisional headquarters here, usually at the château.

On 8 November, 2nd Royal Welsh Fusiliers were relieved and moved via MONTAUBAN-DE-PICARDIE and Fricourt to billets at MÉAULTE.

During the battle, No. 25 Casualty Clearing Station (Fourth Army) was at Fricourt with XIV Corps and the village was also a collecting station for walking wounded. In November, there was a motor ambulance convoy in the village. There was also a railway line towards BAZENTIN and LONGUEVAL, which at the time was not in use, built to the British standard gauge.

Fricourt British Cemetery (Bray Road) is out in the fields, close to the Tambour mine craters in the former no man's land; it was made by 7th East Yorkshires between 5 and 11 July. Associated especially with the men of 7th Yorkshires, many of whom were killed on the morning of 1 July, the cemetery was used until the end of October and then again in 1918. Eighty-nine of the graves out of 132 belong to men of the Princess of Wales's Own (Yorkshire) Regiment and 59 of the burials are in two large graves in the centre of Row A. After the war, 7th Yorkshires erected a granite monument to their dead of the first part of July 1916. The original cemetery register of 132 Commonwealth burials used to include the name of Maj R.G. Raper (B.24.A) of 8th South Staffords (51st Brigade, 17th Division) when his body lay close to the road opposite the cemetery. His remains were taken into the cemetery in the 1960s. The road was named after him.

Fricourt New Military Cemetery lies to the west, off the north end of Fricourt on the former German Front Line; it is, in fact, four large graves made by 10th Yorkshires after the occupation of Fricourt, and contains the graves of a few men who were killed in September 1916; 159 graves are of 10th West Yorkshires and 38 of 7th East Yorkshires.

One of the few German cemeteries in the area is here, on the north-west side of Fricourt Wood. Fricourt German Cemetery contains the resting places for 17, 027 German soldiers, of whom less than a third are in individual graves. After 1918, the Germans had no organisation equivalent to the Allied Imperial War Graves Commission, and subsequently the German dead were buried in one large utilitarian

cemetery, a harsh contrast to the British cemeteries of which there are about 100 in the area. Each metal cross on a grave carries at least two names. A high proportion of German dead were not recovered from the Somme. One assumes that the British have the monopoly of battlefield visiting, but during the 1930s a party of Germans visited Fricourt every July and gathered in a spot close to the village. Maybe they came here to visit fallen comrades in the local German cemetery. In 1919, the body of German air ace Manfred von Richthofen was moved from BERTANGLES, where his grave was being vandalised, to Fricourt German Cemetery, before being taken back to Germany 6 years later. Over the years, one feels that the locals were not too keen on having a German cemetery in their village, but perhaps in recent years this attitude has mellowed. Although probably not visited by many British visitors, a service did take place here on 1 July 2000, when the 5,000 German dead were honoured by the French, British and German nations at a ceremony at which wreaths were laid by the mayors of ALBERT and Fricourt.

Peake Wood Cemetery is on the north-west side of the road, almost opposite the former copse of that name, about ½ mile from CONTALMAISON. It stands on the side of a hill and CONTALMAISON and POZIÈRES can be seen from it; the cemetery register lists 101 Commonwealth burials. The wood fell into British hands on 5 July and the cemetery was not begun until the later part of that month; it was used as a front-line cemetery until February 1917. It fell into enemy hands in March 1918, but was recaptured in August.

As already referred to above, about 1 mile south of Fricourt, on a track running between the roads from Fricourt and MAMETZ to BRAY-SUR-SOMME, are two cemeteries, both on or near the side of the track. Point 110 Old Military Cemetery was begun by French troops in February 1915 and continued by 1st Dorsets (14th Brigade, 32nd Division) and other British units from August 1915 until September 1916. It holds the graves of 92 Commonwealth troops.

Point 110 New Military Cemetery was begun by the French 403rd Infantry Regiment in May and June 1915 and continued by British units between February and July 1916. The name is taken from the map contour. It contains the graves of 64 Commonwealth soldiers.

After the war, the commune of Fricourt was 'adopted' by the county borough of Ipswich.

When the writer Boyd Cable visited the village in 1923 and wrote about it in *The Times*, he reported of Fricourt:

I reckoned that Fricourt I knew as a huddle of trenches and ruins just inside the point of the German lines . . . would be changed; but I had not allowed for the greatness of the change, for the completely different aspect of the cultivated fields and rebuilt village and farms . . . When you climb the road over the hill on 'our side' of Fricourt and look back on it you can see one clump of broken mounds and tall weeds which is all that remains to show where the miles upon miles of German trenches once seemed every yard of hillside we could see from our lines.

FRISE, south-east of SUZANNE across the Somme Canal and marshes, was the southernmost part of the British sector of the Allied lines when 14th Brigade (5th Division) took over a sector from French troops to the west of the village on 3 August 1915.

On 28 January 1916, the German Army made a successful raid on the French positions at Frise, when they advanced as close as 1 mile distant from the French brigade headquarters and captured the outlying posts here. Realising that the whole MARICOURT salient might be lost, the French rushed up reinforcements and drove the enemy back within safety limits. The French artillery fired all day and British guns across the river gave effective support. The enemy used lachrymatory or tear shells during the attack and the canal bridge was destroyed.

Until the start of the Somme battle, the front line ran across the river, with the Germans occupying Feuillières while the French held a line running from Frise to the heights of CURLU. Blaise Cendrars, the Swiss-born writer, served in the area with the French Army, and a road behind the green was later named after him. The trenches ran from the church, across the green, through the then ruined and empty canal and into a farm called la Grenouillère, which is directly opposite la Fermen de l'Ecluse. Cendrars was a corporal in charge of a small detachment whose duties were to patrol the river at night in a punt in order to check on their advance posts and to make sure the enemy had not made any changes in their positions. He wrote: 'I enjoyed the little war my section was carryng on within the big war. From this point of view, Frise was a marvellous sector. We were at the end of the world, at the terminus of the trenches, at the only point in the whole front where they were interrupted for a width of some ten miles by the swamps and the meanderings of the Somme.'

It could be a highly dangerous place, as one never knew if one was being observed by the other side, and special care needed to be taken. Not long after Cendrars left the village, the enemy levelled it to the ground. From the reconstructed church belfry, a sniper colleague of Cendrars called Bikoff spent hours picking off Germans when they dared to cross a narrow gap in their sandbagged defences, with a black curtain behind him to prevent him from being silhouetted against the sky. Bikoff's gun was permanently set up on a stand and he swore 'he couldn't miss'. Before he left, Cendrars boobytrapped a gramo-phone playing the 'Marseillaise', placing it close to the enemy lines as he knew their curiosity would be aroused. Cendrars served in the French Foreign Legion until losing a right arm and being discharged.

In the communal churchyard is the grave of Maj G.E.B. Watson DSO, MC, who was killed in 1918.

FROISSY is a small village south of BRAY-SUR-SOMME on the Somme Canal. On 6 September 1915, the idea was mooted of setting up a mooring here for ambulance barges to be used on the canal. The Royal Engineers were to arrange the moorings and landing stages. However, the idea appears to have been abandoned, and the barges had returned to CHIPILLY by 9 October.

On 31 January 1916, No. 202 Field Company, Royal Engineers (30th Division), destroyed a chimney here when they 'blew it down', as it had been used by the enemy for ranging purposes.

After being relieved in the line at CARNOY, 2nd Wiltshires (21st Brigade, 30th Division) rested in huts at BRAY-SUR-SOMME and Froissy before moving to BRONFAY FARM on the BRAY-SUR-SOMME–CARNOY road. They were back here in early March, after another spell in the line.

G

GAUDIEMPRÉ is south of the Arras–DOULLENS road, on the D1. Although it was used by British troops in the autumn of 1915, it was not thought to be a good village for billeting purposes; until conditions improved troops sometimes stayed at HUMBERCAMPS, a village to the east, instead. The nearest railway link was at Warlincourt Halt to the north-west.

The village became mostly associated with 46th Division, whose first role in the forthcoming battle was to share with 56th Division the task of capturing the fortress village of GOMMECOURT.

On 7 May 1916, 1/8th Sherwood Foresters (139th Brigade, 46th Division) arrived in the village, where they remained for 3 days before leaving for BIENVILLERS-AU-BOIS, closer to the lines. They left their transport behind in the village and moved to LA BAZÈQUE FARM, north-west of HUMBER-CAMPS, on 11 May. On 7 May, No. 1/2 (North Midland) Field Company, Royal Engineers (46th Division), also came to Gaudiempré.

Three weeks later, No. 1/1 (North Midland) Field Company, Royal Engineers (46th Division), were working on setting up a dressing station here; this hut hospital was on the Gaudiempré–SAINT-AMAND road, which is now numbered the D23. On 25 May, five bombs fell 200yds from the hospital buildings but did not cause any damage. On 26 June, 1/2nd (North Midland) Field Ambulance (46th Division) arrived in the village on a very hot day, only to find the huts they were allocated for billeting purposes were very wet and unfit for occupation; they put up in barns in the village instead. By the evening of the battle, the hut hospital was almost completed. It consisted of 16 canvas or tarpaulin huts, with a larger one to which patients were to be first admitted.

On 1 July, the first day of the battle, it was found that General Service wagons were especially good for transporting large numbers of slightly wounded casualties. After the early failure of the attempts to capture GOMMECOURT, many of 46th Division casualties were brought back to Gaudiempré, but considerable congestion in their handling occurred, and after 1500hrs many cases went straight to ambulance trains. Within 36 hours of the start of the battle, the hospital handled over 1,530 casualties, of whom 7 died and were buried in the village. By 6 July, the casualties from the GOMMECOURT battlefield had slowed down to a trickle.

In mid-July, a field ambulance of 56th Division ran a sick station here for a month; the war diary noted of the countryside that there were 'ripe fields of corn and scenes of harvesting'.

GERMAN ROAD was to run from FRICOURT through DEATH VALLEY, south of MAMETZ WOOD and on to the BAZENTIN villages. At the end of August 1916, work on this road was being carried out. It became the main track used by 47th Division in their actions against HIGH WOOD, and on 14 September it was packed with 6in naval guns and 9.2in howitzers; 12in and 15in guns were mounted on railway mountings. On the following day HIGH WOOD fell, after tanks also used German Road.

GÉZAINCOURT is south-west of DOULLENS, on the D126 road between Bretel and Bagneux, in a wooded valley south of the River Authie. Its

association with the First World War was mainly through the handling of thousands of wounded from the Somme battlefields. It also had a station on the railway line between AMIENS and DOULLENS and a branch line to the south-west of the village, running in a westerly direction.

On 24 September 1915, No. 29 Casualty Clearing Station arrived in the village and took over 12 small marquees in a field south of the railway station and adjoining it. These marquees were to be occupied temporarily. No. 29 Casualty Clearing Station was under the control of Third Army; its orders were to take in the slightly wounded cases, which would be brought in from the light railway here linked to ALBERT. More serious cases were to be taken by motor ambulance wagons to other clearing stations. The plan at the time was to arrange a system that would allow for the regular evacuation of casualties by train to base hospitals in Rouen.

On 3 October, conditions were finalised with the owner of the field in which No. 29 Casualty Clearing Station was encamped, with the British government paying him a small rental. The local council was also approached regarding the appropiation of a piece of land in which to bury English dead. This would have been adjacent to Gézaincourt Communal Cemetery, which is on the east side of the village. There was also a French hospital in the town, and a small group of nursing sisters were billeted there soon after their arrival for work at the casualty clearing station.

On 22 October, Gézaincourt was one of three villages used for billeting purposes by 36th Division. On 17 November, Gen Sir Edmund Allenby, General Officer Commanding Third Army, inspected the camp and recommended improved drainage. On 6 December, an elderly Frenchman who lived in a hospice was accidentally knocked down by an ambu-lance in the main street and was operated on in the casualty clearing station, but sadly he died soon after.

In mid-January 1916, there was a problem with ambulance trains stopping at the Halt instead of the station, which would have been much more con-venient for the loading of casualties. Casualties had to be taken from the casualty clearing station to the Halt in trucks on the narrow-gauge railway. On 31 January, No. 21 Ambulance Train 229 Rouen stopped here to load up 74 patients; 84 left on 8 February.

On 20 February, No. 1/1 (North Midland) Field Company, Royal Engineers (46th Division), were in the village. From 25 to 29 February, 14th Field Ambulance (5th Division) were here. On 12 March, 169th Brigade (56th Division) arrived in the area from AILLY-SUR-SOMME; 1/16th Londons (169th Brigade, 56th Division) were in the village for 4 days before leaving for Monchaux, outside the Somme area.

Towards the end of March, negotiations opened concerning the use of the local château as an officers' hospital, but the owner was holding out for a rent of 900 francs a month and the negotiations took 3 or 4 weeks; it finally opened at the beginning of May. The band of 48th Division used to play in the grounds. At the same time as the château negotiations, a field was acquired adjoining Gézaincourt Communal Cemetery for use for further British burials.

On 4 May, baths opened in the village and a week later 143rd Brigade (48th Division) arrived here and serious training for the coming battle began: 'It was a pretty village, with apple orchards growing over chalk downs.' For light relief, boxing competitions were organised. Tragically, 12 men were wounded and at least 6 men were killed at a camp close to the casualty clearing station as the result of a trench mortar accident on 22 May; the dead were buried with full military honours in Gézaincourt Communal Cemetery Extension. 143rd Brigade left the village for COUIN for further training, but were back in Gézaincourt on 28 May for a bathe in the pool before returning to Couin Wood on 31 May. The following day, 1/5th Royal Warwicks (143rd Brigade, 48th Division) relieved 1/4th Glosters (144th Brigade, 48th Division) at HÉBUTERNE. After a few days of moderate quiet, the battalion left for SAILLY-AU-BOIS on 8 June.

On 2 June, 144th Brigade (48th Division) gathered here for a day before marching westwards to SAINT-RIQUIER for brigade training. On 5 June, 12th York & Lancasters (94th Brigade, 31st Division) marched to here from Bus Wood, where they were to practise for the battle with the other battalions in their brigade. While staying in this 'lovely valley' for 8 days, the men were able to make frequent visits to DOULLENS.

On 1 July, 3,309 casualties from the battlefield were brought to the casualty clearing station by train or road; in the first 24 hours of the battle, no fewer than five trains were waiting for casualties to arrive from the front. By 1500hrs, 323 men had been evacuated, but on 2 July it was much worse, with the admission of 4,573 casualties; the casualty clearing station sent out 422 lying, 3,102 by train and 490 by bus. At one point, 2,000 men were sleeping in an adjacent field to the camp prior to going through the reception process. The total dealt with on 3 July was 3,304.

On 4 July, No. 49 Casualty Clearing Station was hastily sent up from Rouen to assist in coping with the flood of wounded from the beginning of the battle, and many of the casualties were brought here on the narrow-gauge railway. The casualty clearing station was later replaced by No. 11 Casualty Clearing Station from the Citadelle, close to DOULLENS.

On 18 August, 61st Brigade (20th Division) were in the area; 4 days later, 3rd Guards Brigade (Guards Division) were in the vicinity, as well as at Hem. On 10 September, elements of 7th Brigade (25th Division) were at Gézaincourt; towards the end of the month, the whole of the brigade were here. On 30 September, 152nd Brigade (51st Division) moved here; on 24 October, 7th Brigade (25th Division) were here again. On 25 November, half of 97th Brigade (32nd Division) were here and at BEAUVAL, and on 27 November, part of 57th Brigade (19th Division) were here.

Gézaincourt Communal Cemetery is just outside the village, on the DOULLENS road; the Gézaincourt Communal Cemetery Extension joins it. The former was used for the burial of nine soldiers who died of wounds between October 1915 and March 1916. The latter, designed by Sir Edwin Lutyens, was begun in March 1916. It was used for a year and then again in March–October 1918, primarily taking casualties from No. 3 Canadian Stationary Hospital. Most of the Somme battle casualties would have been from the local casualty clearing stations. The graves include those of 14 men who died as a result of an accident involving their leave train at Gézaincourt station in November 1916. There are 40 New Zealand troops buried here and 25 of the Manchester Regiment. A man shot for desertion is also here, Pte W.E. Anderson (I.P.1) of 5th Dorsets (34th Brigade, 11th Division). In all, there are 596 Commonwealth casualties in the cemetery.

GINCHY is north-east of GUILLEMONT, situated at the crossing of six roads. It stood on a high plain that defended COMBLES, 1½ miles to the south-east, and was an important forward position in the German defence line. On 3 September, 7th Division initially captured the village; this was also the day that GUILLEMONT fell to the Allies. The final objective of 7th Division had been the high ground to the east of the village, on a line that was approximately north and south through Ginchy Telegraph, which was the site of a former semaphore station at Point 157.

Ginchy was protected by a crescent-shaped defence line that ran from north to south and 'wrapped' itself around the village. The trenches that were immediately in front of the village were named Porter Trench and Stout Trench. To the north of them was Beer Trench, and to the south, towards GUILLEMONT, was ZZ Trench.

Bombers of 91st Brigade (7th Division) and elements of 22nd Brigade (also 7th Division), including 1st Royal Welsh Fusiliers and 20th Manchesters, were involved in the fighting. A German counter-attack pushed 20th Manchesters, who had reached the village, back as far as Porter Trench. Later in the day, 20th Manchesters retired, as 2nd Royal Irish (22nd Brigade, 7th Division) were to reoccupy Ginchy. However, German artillery was very heavy and by mid-evening the enemy had reoccupied the village.

On 3 September, 2/Lt F.E.S. Phillips of the Royal Flying Corps received the Military Cross for 'excellent work' when he carried out fine contact patrol work. On one occasion, he came down so low that his aircraft was hit by machine guns and rifle fire. Despite this, he carried on and successfully signalled to the British artillery when the enemy was massing for a counter-attack.

On 4 September, 9th Devons and a company of 2nd Borders (both 20th Brigade, 7th Division) made another attack on Ginchy; they entered the village, but later withdrew. Several more attacks had to be made on the village before it was finally captured.

On 5 September, 16th (Irish) Division assaulted the village but failed to capture it, as well as the German strongpoint named THE QUADRILATERAL, which was to the south of the MORVAL road. 1st Royal Munster Fusiliers (48th Brigade, 16th Division) then relieved 8th King's Royal Rifle Corps (41st Brigade, 14th Division) in trenches facing the village astride the railway to the south. On 6 September, 2nd Gordons (20th Brigade, 7th Division) tried three times to capture Ginchy but their casualties were very high, including three company commanders.

On 7 September, the sunken road was reported as being full of German dead, who had been caught by British artillery on 3 September. On 8 September, the battalion headquarters of 7th Royal Inniskilling Fusiliers (49th Brigade, 16th Division) was in a position known as Mount Street. At this time, Maj W. Redmond MP was a member of 6th Royal Irish Rifles (47th Brigade, 16th Division). On 9 September, the left of the attack was to be delivered by 16th Division; already weakened by the previous fighting, 48th Brigade (16th Division) moved off at 1645hrs. On their right, 47th Brigade (also 16th Division) were stopped by machine-gun fire, and 7th Royal Inniskilling Fusiliers were brought up as reinforcements.

A wheel to the flank routed the nearest Germans, and 8th Royal Munster Fusiliers (48th Brigade, 16th Division) pressed on beyond the GUILLEMONT road. Having met with slight opposition, 7th Royal Irish Rifles (48th Brigade, 16th Division) began to clear the western part of the village with men of 8th Royal Dublin Fusiliers (also 48th Brigade, 16th Division) who had followed 1st Royal Munster Fusiliers and carried on the attack through the village, as 8th Royal Inniskilling Fusiliers (49th Brigade, 16th Division) came in on the right. 9th Royal Dublin Fusiliers (48th Brigade, 16th Division) and 7th Royal Irish Rifles and some of 7th Royal Irish Fusiliers (49th Brigade, 16th Division) also helped to clear the western part of the village. A few Germans surrendered and some fled towards FLERS and LESBŒUFS. 47th Brigade were checked in front of the QUADRILATERAL, to the east of the village; on their right 56th Division succeeded in forcing their way to BOULEUX WOOD to the south-east, but could make no further progress, owing to their left flank being uncovered as a result of 47th Brigade's failure to reach their objective.

At 0400hrs, a heavy enemy barrage was put down on the assembly trenches of 1/4th Londons (168th Brigade, 56th Division) in LEUZE WOOD. Moving forward in six waves, in little over 1 hour 1/4th Londons had captured their objectives and pushed out advance posts in positions overlooking the MORVAL–LESBŒUFS road.

During the clearing of houses in Ginchy, Irish nationalist and poet T.M. Kettle was killed while fighting with 9th Royal Dublin Fusiliers. He has no grave but his name appears on the Thiepval Memorial panels. Born in 1880, Kettle was a writer of prose and poetry, barrister and professor at Dublin University. He had been an MP at Westminster but had resigned to give more time to his work as Professor of Economics. Kettle, whose health was broken by the war, had been on leave in Dublin a few weeks before during the Easter Rising. He had been much distressed by the turn of events, and the conflict of his role as an officer in the British Army while his friends were executed by the British authorities must have been quite a conundrum for him. He died for the Allied cause, although he believed in a free and united Ireland.

The honour of capturing the village of Ginchy fell to 48th Brigade, together with two battalions of 49th Brigade (both 16th Division), after several days of very heavy fighting. However, the enemy did not give up and entered the village once again during the next 24 hours, but they were never to regain it in the 1916 battles. For the British, the new position formed an awkward salient that invited counter-attacks. In John Buchan's words, 'the British made good the old German second position, and had won the crest of the uplands, while the French section had advanced almost to the gates of Péronne. The moment was in a very real sense the end of a phase, the first and perhaps the most critical phase of the Somme battle.'

On the outskirts of Ginchy, a road made of planks had been constructed over the original road, which had been totally destroyed; it ran from Ginchy to the top of the Hogsback and extended for several miles.

Apart, of course, from preventing the enemy from retaking the village, the next task for the Allies was to capture the QUADRILATERAL on the south side of the road to MORVAL. It was at the top of the Ginchy–LEUZE WOOD spur, just south of the railway; communication with the sunken road was provided by a four-sided trench, 300 × 150yds, sited where the roads to MORVAL from Ginchy and GUILLEMONT respectively met. The Ginchy–MORVAL road, as it approached the latter, was a sunken road and concealed anything in it, and just about halfway between the two villages a railway to the south almost touched the road. Where the road and railway most closely approached, the Germans had constructed a very 'strong work', which was in turn close to BOULEUX WOOD, which guarded COMBLES.

In the *Official History of the War*, it was noted that in the period 9/10 September, 3rd Guards Brigade (Guards Division) took over Ginchy from 48th Brigade (16th Division); later, 4th Grenadier Guards (3rd Guards Brigade, Guards Division) relieved 47th Brigade (also 16th Division). Their positions south of Ginchy were in the angle formed by the WEDGE WOOD–Ginchy road and the LEUZE WOOD–GUILLEMONT road. Contact with 1st Welsh Guards (3rd Guards Brigade, Guards Division) was lost until 10 September, when 1st Grenadier Guards (also 3rd Guards Brigade, Guards Division) were sent up to fill the gap between 1st Welsh Guards and 4th Grenadier Guards. Fighting continued, as the Allies were chiefly concerned to push forward the centre so as to include the QUADRILATERAL and Ginchy Telegraph in the line on their left before a further big offensive.

2/Lt A.P. Wernher of 1st Welsh Guards, son of Sir Julius Wernher, was wounded at this time and then killed by a sniper when being carried to safety.

A bombardment during the Battle of Ginchy seen from Trônes Wood, 9 September 1916. *(IWM Q4226)*

213

He was later buried in Citadel New Military Cemetery (II.A.5), where so many of his colleagues also lie. On the night of 11/12 September, 3rd Guards Brigade's sector was taken over by 1st Grenadier Guards and 2nd Scots Guards (both 3rd Guards Brigade, Guards Division), with orders to round up any of the enemy who still occupied the re-entrance in the brigade's front. Many Germans were captured; at 0600hrs on 12 September, 1st Grenadier Guards made slight progress towards Ginchy Telegraph, while 1/8th Middlesex (167th Brigade, 56th Division) did likewise southeast of the QUADRILATERAL. As a converging movement, however, it failed.

By this time, 6th Division had taken over from 56th Division and the right of the Guards Division, the centre of XIV Corps front, from the LEUZE WOOD–MORVAL road to the outskirts of Ginchy. The line of the LEUZE WOOD–Ginchy road was gained and held, but further advance was prevented by enemy machine guns; 9th Suffolks and 2nd Sherwood Foresters (both 71st Brigade, 6th Division) lost heavily.

The QUADRILATERAL, brilliantly sited and bristling with machine guns, had been one of the pre-15 September objectives; it stubbornly remained in German hands. An officer of the Sherwood Foresters (Nottinghamshire and Derbyshire Regiment), Capt J.F. Gibbons, received the Military Cross for bravery on 13 September; he reconnoitred the position under heavy fire and later organised and led his company in attack, but was then severely wounded.

A day of excellent progress for the Allies, 15 September saw the successful capture of COURCELETTE, HIGH WOOD, MARTINPUICH and, to the east, the village of FLERS. However, it is the advance from Ginchy towards LESBŒUFS which concerns us here. Accounts of the Guards Division's involvement on this day include the various regimental histories and excellent accounts by or about Harold Macmillan and Oliver Lyttelton.

The plan was that the three Guards brigades should take four lines of objectives, which all had a different colour code: Green, Brown, Blue and Red. These would then give them possession of Flers Ridge, which covered the approaches to BAPAUME and LESBŒUFS, to the east of FLERS. The Guards brigades were to be supported by 10 tanks and the cavalry were to be brought up for the breakthrough. At this time, the Guards Division were in XIV Corps; the boundary line with XV Corps on the left ran from the junction of the Ginchy–FLERS and Ginchy–GUEUDECOURT roads, a little to the north of Ginchy and along the latter road for about 800yds.

In his memoirs, Harold Macmillan of 3rd Grenadier Guards (2nd Guards Brigade, Guards Division) wrote that on the night of 12 September, his battalion took over part of the line previously occupied by 3rd Guards Brigade. He was told that it was likely that his brigade and 1st Guards Brigade would be leading the advance on 15 September, leaving 3rd Guards Brigade in reserve. In order to have a good jumping-off place, it was essential to gain certain ground, small in area but strongly held. They had to deal with enemy machine-gun posts set up in an orchard on the northern edge of Ginchy. Two platoons were detailed for this work and they were very successful; the orchard was cleared of all Germans, despite heavy resistance and the bright moonlight. All the next day, 13 September, Macmillan's battalion remained in the front line, where it was heavily shelled.

The night before, the Guards Division came up the line from bivouacs at CARNOY via MONTAUBAN-DE-PICARDIE, and saw many artillery batteries firing on the German positions. In fact, this barrage lasted for 3 days and became a 'creeping barrage' after the attack began.

Oliver Lyttelton, who, like Harold Macmillan, was with 3rd Grenadier Guards, was adjutant to its commanding officer, Lt Col B.N. Sergison-Brooke; he noted in his memoir that they set off in the dark along the road through MONTAUBAN-DE-PICARDIE, then crossed a wood and came to an area of ground which was like a 'rough sea', grass-less and featureless. They made their way up a slope and there were a few salvoes of gas shells.

Rudyard Kipling noted that on 14 September, 1st Guards Brigade moved to shell-holes and fragments of trench that were to form their assembly positions, which were on a front of about 500yds between DELVILLE WOOD and the western side of Ginchy. The Guards brigades formed up amid shell craters clear of Ginchy, because the ruins were frequently bombarded by the enemy. On the right were 3rd Grenadier Guards and 1st Coldstream Guards (both 2nd Guards Brigade) under Brig Gen J. (later General Sir John) Ponsonby; 3rd Grenadier Guards and 2nd Irish Guards were behind them. To the left, 2nd and 3rd Coldstream Guards (both 1st Guards Brigade) were in the front, with 1st Irish Guards (also 1st Guards Brigade) in the second line and 1st Grenadier Guards in the rear. 2nd and 3rd Coldstream Guards were to carry the advance as far as the third, or Blue, line, in front of LESBŒUFS. Of the 10 tanks that were to take part, only 3 turned up, and these were not successful; they had moved up from the Loop. 2nd Guards Brigade had their headquarters in Dummy Trench, west of TRÔNES WOOD, and 1st Guards Brigade had theirs in BERNAFAY WOOD.

The early morning was misty, and the ground was still wet and slippery as there had been a lot of rain prior to 15 September. The battalion headquarters of 3rd Grenadier Guards, with Lt Col Sergison-Brooke, the adjutant Oliver Lyttelton, the signals officer, the sergeant-major, drill sergeant and headquarters signallers, was established in a few shell-holes between the first and second waves of the attack. The attackers formed themselves up in the open, and at 0600hrs the heavy guns barraged the enemy lines, and in turn the enemy shelled Ginchy.

At 0620hrs, the attackers set off under a creeping barrage, but were immediately met by withering fire from the direction of the QUADRILATERAL to the north-east, which had not yet been silenced by the flanking brigades of 6th Division. The three battalions of the Coldstream Guards in the front lines advanced too far over to the left, and 3rd Grenadier Guards, the other front battalion, carried straight on towards their objectives; this resulted in a gap between them and the Coldstream battalions. 2nd Grenadier Guards, a supporting battalion of 1st Guards Brigade (Guards Division), lost sight of the three Coldstream battalions; advancing with their right on the Ginchy–LESBŒUFS road, they came across a trench full of Germans instead of the expected Guardsmen. In the muddle, the Coldstreams assumed quite wrongly that they had reached at least their third objective, when in fact they had only reached their first, which was beyond a German strongpoint named the Triangle. 1st Guards Brigade had been under fire from the junction of Pint Trench and the sunken part of the FLERS road. 1st Irish Guards, who were in the second line of 1st Guards Brigade, were close up in the attack and suffered many casualties, together with the Coldstream battalions.

During the fighting, Lt Col Sergison-Brooke was wounded and Lt Col G. Baring, Commanding Officer 1st Coldstream Guards, son of 5th Baron Ashburton, was killed; he was later buried at Citadel New Military Cemetery (II.A.9.). Oliver Lyttelton organised a party of men from various Guards battalions, which came to about 100 men, and put himself in command. At one point, Lyttelton recalls seeing Lt Col J. Campbell, Commanding Officer 3rd Coldstream Guards, in a nearby shell-hole, together with his famous hunting horn; Campbell was to receive the Victoria Cross for his leadership during the battle. The outskirts of LESBŒUFS were just in front of Lyttelton's party and he joined up with

Maj Rocke down the hill towards the village. A large party of Germans attacked them; the two sides fought and the situation became very confused. At one point, Lyttelton threw down a pistol empty of ammunition, and the German party mistakenly took it to be a bomb and retreated in good order. Casualties were very heavy. The rapid fire of Lyttelton's party put paid to another counter-attack and Lyttelton was ordered to report to Brig Gen J. Ponsonby, whose headquarters was in a trench covered by galvanised sheets and camouflage. Later, Lyttelton met up with Cecil Boyd Rochfort of the Scots Guards, who was marching with some details. They tramped across the Ginchy Valley, using duckboards, during heavy shelling.

To the right of the above two Guards brigades were 56th Division, and on their left, 6th Division. 56th Division were to establish themselves in Combles Ravine and move towards BOULEUX WOOD; 6th Division and the Guards brigades were to advance in a north-easterly direction and to cover the highest part of the ridge to MORVAL and LESBŒUFS. Three tanks were to take the QUAD-RILATERAL, east of Ginchy. To the right of the line, 169th Brigade (56th Division) almost reached their objectives for the day. At 0620hrs, Zero Hour, 6th Division attacked the QUADRILATERAL, which lay behind a crest of high ground and was protected by wire lying in a depression. On this front 16th Brigade (6th Division) met deadly machine-gun fire.

There are many accounts of the action of the Guards brigades at Ginchy; for this account, the author has mainly used the *History of the Guards Division*, together with Harold Macmillan's memoirs, *The Winds of Change*. In the former, it is noted that during the night of 13/14 September the Grenadier Guards advanced along the Ginchy–FLERS road; driving the enemy out of the orchard, which was about 400yds north of Ginchy, they dug themselves in. On 14 September, the Guards Division's headquarters moved forward to BERNAFAY WOOD; on the same day, 2nd Grenadier Guards' trenches received a direct hit from a large bomb and a company commander was led away, suffering from shellshock.

H-Day was set for 15 September; during the night, which was a very cold one, the men of the Guards Division went to their various assembly positions. The first sign of dawn was at around 0530hrs. The front that the Guards had to cover was 1,200yds in length and the reading of maps was to prove very difficult in this moonscape; it cannot be mentioned too often that the landscape was by now almost completely featureless, with even the roads gone. Great emphasis was placed on driving the enemy out of any territory that they were occupying on the north-eastern outskirts of Ginchy, and it was pointed out that any opposition from this quarter could jeopardise the planned advance of 15 September and would assuredly cause high casualties. Two particular places just north-east of Ginchy had been cleared of the enemy before 2nd Irish Guards and 2nd Grenadier Guards took over the line. In order to gain more ground for the launch of the attack on the right of the Guards, it was thought advisable to take possession of a trench east of Ginchy, which actually formed part of the QUADRILATERAL. Although artillery was brought in to achieve this, it was inadequately organised and used hurriedly, and the action ended in failure.

In his version of events, Harold Macmillan noted that on 15 September, in accordance with their orders, 3rd Grenadier Guards moved off just after dawn, advancing in platoons in artillery formation about 300 to 400yds behind 1st Coldstream Guards. When they reached Ginchy, there was a very heavy barrage raining down, and they were almost blinded by the noise and confusion. Much of the bombardment was directed on the area a little to the south of the village. They were also harassed by heavy fire coming from the right; some even appeared to be coming from the rear. This was the most dangerous part of the line, where there was a junction between the Guards Division and the neighbouring 6th Division.

As Macmillan was moving forward with his platoon he was wounded in the knee, just below the kneecap, by a piece of shell. However, he managed to continue and did not feel much discomfort until later. They were going forward in accordance with their orders, with their right on the Ginchy–LESBŒUFS road, but 2nd and 3rd Coldstream Guards were nowhere to be seen. What actually happened was that the whole of the leading attack had swerved to the left, and therefore the Coldstream battalions were no longer in front of the Grenadier Guards battalions whom they were meant to be supporting.

Macmillan remembered that they halted for what seemed a long time, which in fact was about 20 minutes, and then the order was given to move on again to what they believed to be the first objective, which they confidently expected to be in the hands of their friends the Coldstreams. But the objective was still held by the enemy. The creeping barrage had ceased and therefore they had no artillery support of any kind. The British artillery had opened up at 0600hrs, but to add to the confusion the enemy

response was very swift and British shells fell on the former Guards' positions anyway. All the Guards could do, therefore, was to deploy and attack.

The advance was chaotic and the front very narrow. The fact that the three Coldstream battalions had moved too far to the left meant that 2nd and 3rd Grenadier Guards lost their sense of direction; in addition, 2nd Grenadier Guards were caught up in an enemy barrage of huge shells. Macmillan's group went forward in artillery formation and lost heavily. Machine-gun fire was coming from their left flank and Macmillan took a party in that direction in order to silence it. Although the enemy gunners were dealt with, Macmillan was wounded again, being shot at close range while half crawling, half crouching. This time he was hit in the left thigh or buttock by machine-gun bullets.

Macmillan rolled down into a large shell-hole, where he lay, dazed but not unconscious, and dosed himself with morphine. While there in his dazed state, he read from a pocket edition of Aeschylus's *Prometheus* (in the original); at one point, German soldiers ran around the lip of the shell-hole, but he lay 'doggo'. When it was dark, he was brought back to the Guards' trenches and was taken to where the commanding officer had made his headquarters. He was then carried by stretcher to Ginchy; leaving his bearers, he hobbled on. He felt safer once he had left Ginchy, as it was being continuously shelled, and he was later picked up by a transport of the Sherwood Foresters (Nottinghamshire and Derbyshire Regiment). The casualties suffered by 2nd Grenadier Guards in the operations of 13–15 September had been very severe.

From the *History of the Guards Division*, we have the following account. On the right of 2nd Guards Brigade, 3rd Grenadier Guards and 1st Coldstream Guards took over the line from 1st Scots Guards. The trenches then occupied by 3rd Grenadier Guards ran about 300yds east of Ginchy; those of 1st Coldstream Guards on their left were astride the Ginchy–LESBŒUFS road. 1st Scots Guards remained in the rear of 3rd Grenadier Guards and 2nd Irish Guards in the rear of 1st Coldstream Guards. The front of 6th Division, on the right of 2nd Guards Brigade, ran in a south-easterly direction along the Ginchy–COMBLES road, about 300yds behind the right flank of 1st Scots Guards.

H.L.N. Dundas of 1st Scots Guards missed the 15 September fighting, as he was ill at the time, but he knew that the whole of his brigade were bivouacked on a hillside, and six divisions of the cavalry were close by. He described reports of the Ginchy fighting as being very severe and the casualties as being very high. His battalion's strength was reduced from 750 to 142 and he mentions in particular the deaths of 2/Lt A.P. Wernher, a contemporary at Eton, and Lt E. Cazalet, both of 1st Welsh Guards (3rd Guards Brigade, Guards Division). We also know that Capt 'Sloper' Mackenzie of the Grenadier Guards was mortally wounded in the same attack, as was the most famous of that generation, Lt Raymond Asquith, when leading his company. Asquith had joined 1/16th Londons (169th Brigade, 56th Division) in the early days of the war, but was later transferred to 3rd Grenadier Guards (2nd Guards Brigade, Guards Division). Only a short time before, he had met his father, the Prime Minister (see entry for FRICOURT), in what was to be their last meeting.

Hugh Wansey Bayly MC, medical officer of 1st Scots Guards, mentioned that the assembly trenches were on the right front of Ginchy, north of Ginchy Telegraph; his aid post was in front of the Ginchy–MORVAL road and about 200yds east of the Ginchy–LESBŒUFS road. He saw three tanks advancing, which drew German fire, and he heard Col Campbell's hunting horn when he was leading 3rd Coldstream Guards on the extreme left of the Guards front. It seems that, owing to the confusion and with the Guards Division in deep trouble, Campbell was unaware of just which objective had been reached. He blew his horn in order to stop his men from going forward in case they were caught by their own artillery. They had reached what was known as the Green Line and not the Brown.

Despite it all, a small group of men drawn from various battalions pressed on towards LESBŒUFS, led by Harold Alexander of the Irish Guards, later a field marshal and cabinet minister. Finding themselves alone, they sent back to brigade for instructions and support, but met with no response; as the hours went by, the men, in standing crops, became aware that the enemy knew exactly where they were and were beginning to surround them. By sheer adrenalin and determination, the Guards took on the enemy, who outnumbered them heavily, and lost a third of their group in the process. It was during this incident that Oliver Lyttelton, having used up six rounds of his pistol, threw the empty gun at the enemy, who thought it was a bomb. The group took advantage of the slight pause and raced from the scene; when other Guardsmen saw what was going on, they fired into the ranks of the German pursuers.

Bayly administered morphine to Raymond Asquith and Mackenzie of the Grenadier Guards, both of whom had penetrating chest wounds, and sent them down the line. Lt M. Tennant of the Scots Guards was also killed by a shell on 16 September; he was a cousin of Lt The Hon. E.W. Tennant of 4th Grenadier Guards (3rd Guards Brigade, Guards Division), who was to be killed at Gas Alley 6 days later.

B/Lt Col J.V. Campbell, Commanding Officer 3rd Coldstream Guards (1st Guards Brigade, Guards Division), was awarded the Victoria Cross on 15 September. According to his citation,

> Seeing that the first two waves of his battalion had been decimated by machine-gun and rifle fire, he took personal command of the third line, rallied his men with the utmost gallantry and led them against the enemy machine guns, capturing the guns and killing the personnel. Later in the day, after consultation with other unit commanders, he again rallied the survivors of his battalion, and led them through a very hostile fire barrage against the objective. He was one of the first to enter the enemy trench.

Another Victoria Cross winner on the same day was L/Sgt F. McNess of 1st Scots Guards:

> During a severe engagement he led his men on with the greatest dash in face of heavy shell and machine-gun fire. When the first line of enemy trenches was reached it was found that the left flank was exposed, and that the enemy was bombing down the trench. Sergt. McNess thereupon organised a counter-attack and led it in person. He was severely wounded in the neck and jaw, but went on, passing through the barrage of hostile bombs, in order to bring up fresh supplies of bombs to his men. Finally he established a 'block' and continued encouraging his men and throwing bombs until he was utterly exhausted by loss of blood.

On 16 September, Lt Gen the Earl of Cavan, General Officer Commanding XIV Corps, informed Lyttelton that he was to be awarded the Distinguished Service Order for his achievements on the previous day. His battalion were back at camp at the CITADEL, south of FRICOURT. Orders for 16 September were that the third objective and then LESBŒUFS should be taken, which would then form a defensive flank towards MORVAL and link up on the left; the attackers were 61st Brigade (20th Division) and 3rd Guards Brigade. Zero Hour was 0925hrs. Advancing behind a creeping barrage, 61st Brigade were able to reach the original third objective, in front of LESBŒUFS; on their left, however, 3rd Guards Brigade began late and made little headway. 1st Grenadier Guards and 1st Welsh Guards had to dig in where they were facing, north instead of north-east; during the fighting, Capt Lord Clive of 1st Welsh Guards was seriously wounded and sent home, where he died a few weeks later. Lt M. Tennant of the Scots Guards, killed on 16 September, was buried in the Ginchy Guards' Cemetery in the village.

The Guards Division were relieved altogether on this front by battalions belonging to 59th and 60th Brigades (both 20th Division). Two battalions of 59th Brigade were successful in an attack and on 17 September, 60th Brigade, in the right sector of 20th Division, attacked south of the Ginchy–LESBŒUFS road.

On 19 September, elements of the Guards Division attended a church service and were later thanked for their achievement by Brig Gen J. Ponsonby. During this time there was more rain, making conditions even more difficult for the men and for transport; roads and tracks became very slimy and increasingly difficult to negotiate. After 2 or 3 days' rest, the Guards Division were to relieve 20th Division in the line, and went up via reserve trenches at WATERLÔT FARM, close to LONGUEVAL.

The ruins of Ginchy in September 1916. *(IWM Q4295)*

On 18 September, according to the *Official History of the War*, 6th Division's attack on the QUADRILATERAL and Straight Trench resulted in complete success and the establishment of a new line 500yds beyond, overlooking the valley in front of MORVAL. After an accurate barrage, 1st King's Shropshire Light Infantry (16th Brigade, 6th Division) advanced from the Ginchy–COMBLES road at 0550hrs, with their left on the railway track; keeping close behind the barrage, they swept into the QUADRILATERAL. Its capture allowed the advance to go forward 1,000yds to within ½ mile of MORVAL and LESBŒUFS. 5th Division's front now extended some 2,000yds from the north edge of BOULEUX WOOD, and lay on the slope of Ginchy Telegraph.

On 22 September, Lt The Hon. E.W. Tennant of 4th Grenadier Guards (3rd Guards Brigade, Guards Division), son of Baron Glenconner, was killed. Born in 1897, he served with Osbert Sitwell. Tennant was hit in Gas Alley, a trench that ran north-east of Ginchy towards LESBŒUFS, and close to the present-day Guards Memorial on the Ginchy–LESBŒUFS road. He was buried near to his friend Lt Raymond Asquith at Guillemont Road Cemetery (I.B.48). In October, a memorial service for his life was arranged in London.

As for Harold Macmillan, his short army career was now over. He had been shot in the head, face, hand, knee and most recently in the back. His right arm and left leg never worked properly again and eventually he had to wear a corset for the rest of his life, which went some way to keeping the shrapnel still in his body from moving around too much. He had been very fortunate to escape death and was still in a London hospital at Christmas, by which time his wounds had become infected. His life was by no means out of danger, but with nursing care and devotion on the part of his mother, he eventually made a recovery.

In the period 26–30 September, 2nd King's Own Scottish Borderers (13th Brigade, 5th Division) remained in trenches north-east of Ginchy and returned to CARNOY on 1 October. On 7 October, 1/16th Londons (169th Brigade, 56th Division) occupied a forward position south of Ginchy when they were 'on loan' to 167th Brigade, carrying stores and ammunition to the forward trenches. In early October, Carnoy Dressing Station was situated between Ginchy and LESBŒUFS.

In *A Subaltern on the Somme*, Max Plowman of 10th West Yorkshires (50th Brigade, 17th Division) was on the eastern side of Ginchy; he describes being confronted with a wide rolling plain, over which there was no road except for a single 'duck walk' track. Slowly, Plowman's battalion stretched itself out in single file along this track; one by one the men followed each other, till the trail extended like the vertebrae of an endless snake. On either side lay the open plain, and shell-holes filled with water appeared in endless succession. In a letter, Plowman referred to being at LESBŒUFS in October and November, and having nearly starved because communication lines across the morass between Ginchy and LESBŒUFS were almost impassable. During November, there was an advance dressing station or collecting post in the village.

Ernest Shepard, serving with the Royal Artillery, was in Ginchy in November and noted that there were tea rooms in the village: 'A bowl of hot tea, some biscuits and a cigarette is given to each man. The shed is constructed of stout timber, corrugated iron and sand-bagged and has an entrance one end and an exit at the other. It is open day and night and the staff is kept busy practically all the time. The tea is excellent, the place well up to the front so the Infantry can get a hot drink very soon after being relieved from the trenches.'

After the war, memorial plaques to the memory of Lt C.P.M. Irwin, attached 7th Royal Irish Fusiliers, killed on 9 September 1916 and buried in Delville Wood Cemetery, and Maj C.C. Dickens of 1/13th Londons, killed the next day, were placed in the local church and in 1995 Dickens' original cross was presented to the church for safekeeping. In October 1928, Gen Sir G. Feilding, formerly General Officer Commanding Guards Division, unveiled the Guards Division Memorial on the left of the Ginchy–LESBŒUFS road in about the location where it had been crossed by the Green Line.

GOMMECOURT, 9 miles north of ALBERT, is south-east of FONCQUEVILLERS and north-east of HÉBUTERNE on the D6 road to PUISIEUX. In 1915 and early 1916, the front line here made a sharp change of direction to the north-east, running up around Arras and northward to la Bassée. The resultant bend became known as the Gommecourt Salient.

The plan to take Gommecourt was a subsidiary one, a sort of distraction that VII Corps of Third Army were to provide, to the left of the main thrust of Fourth Army to the south of the Somme battlefield. The attack of 46th Division was to be carried out from FONCQUEVILLERS; 139th Brigade, on the left, were to attack between the northern edge of Gommecourt Wood and The Little Z. The first three German lines were to be captured, and in conjunction with 56th Division's attack on the right, the Allied lines were to be carried to a point just east of Gommecourt village; 46th and 56th Divisions were to 'join hands', having cut off the enemy. The aim of the two divisions was not so much to capture Gommecourt as to prevent its defenders from being of use to their colleagues further south.

In *The Old Front Line*, John Masefield noted that it was doubtful whether any point on the Western Front in France was stronger than Gommecourt. Seen from the British Front Line at HÉBUTERNE, it was little more than a few red buildings, standing in woodland in a rise of ground which hid the village to the north, the west and the south-west. A big spur of woodlands known as Gommecourt Park thrust boldly out from the village towards the plateau on which the English lines stood. This spur, which was strongly fortified by the enemy, made the greater part of the salient in the enemy lines. Apart from the Wood and Park, the other very significant locations were: the Z; Little Z; Kern Redoubt, which was close to the cemetery; the Quadrilateral; Nameless Farm; and Sixteen Poplars. Gommecourt cemetery, located in the village itself, had been made into a formidable strongpoint, but the Quadrilateral, 250yds east of the village, had been designed to be strong enough to drive the attackers back should they break through into Gommecourt

Gommecourt Park. *(IWM Q51314)*

Park and village; there were many dugouts close to it, providing artillery protection. The outline of the Quadrilateral can still be traced.

Masefield described the Gommecourt position as being immensely strong in itself, with a perfect field of fire for the defenders. In front of it was the usual system of barbed wire over a depth of 50yds and behind it, the first enemy line, from which many communication trenches ran to the central fortress of the salient, which was known as Kern Redoubt, and to the Support Line. The enemy had 12 machine guns, both in and in front of this redoubt, the sites of which were continually being changed to confuse the attackers.

Between HÉBUTERNE and Gommecourt there were two systems of trenches, which were about 400yds apart. The front one was about 400yds from the British line and ran in a south-easterly direction from the village; it consisted of three lines of trenches which were parallel with each other. The distance between the first and second lines was about 100yds and between the second and third about 170yds.

To the right of 56th Division's front, to be attacked by 169th Brigade, were the remains of the farm known as Nameless Farm; the road running parallel to the third German trench was known as Nameless Farm Road. The task of 169th Brigade was to be carried out in four successive phases. First, they were to capture the first three lines of the first German trench system and link up with 168th Brigade (also 56th Division) at a point in Fall Trench, 50yds north-west of its junction with Epte Communication Trench; second, they were to capture Ems and Etch communication trenches and the Quadrilateral; third, they were to join up with 46th Division on the ridge to the east of Gommecourt village; and fourth, they were to clear the village and Gommecourt Park. Thus the line would be straightened out by 46th Division from the point known as Sixteen Poplars in the south to the Z in the north. If the plan were successful, then the village would be surrounded, and the final capture of the garrison was thought to be a relatively simple matter.

The *Official History of the War* notes that the subsidiary offensive against Gommecourt was given to VII Corps. Between it and the left of the main attack against BEAUMONT-HAMEL and SERRE, carried out by VIII Corps, there would be left a 2-mile gap from which no attack would be made, owing to the lack of troops. Gommecourt stood at the junction of four low ridges, with one arm stretching towards Essarts, ROSSIGNOL WOOD, the western edge of HÉBUTERNE and the eastern edge to FONCQUEVILLERS. On the south-west face of the salient, almost as far south as Nameless Farm, the British and German trenches were nearly on the same level, with a dip that had a hedge between them beyond this point. Both were on the west side of the wide valley between ROSSIGNOL WOOD and HÉBUTERNE, the British line thus being on a forward and the German on a reverse slope.

The enemy artillery posts were on the eastern side of the valley. When the new line nearer to the enemy was being dug, carts full of empty biscuit tins were driven up and down in HÉBUTERNE in order to disguise the noise of the preparations.

In *Pilgrimage*, Lt Col G.S. Hutchison noted that the terrain favoured the defenders, who had done so much to improve on it, but despite the German strength and the German artillery the London battalions were confident that they could get into the German positions and secure them.

At the beginning of 1916, 56th Division had been moved to hold the line opposite the Gommecourt positions. From the reserve at SAINT-AMAND, on 20 May, 1/14th Londons (168th Brigade, 56th Division) moved to HALLOY for intensive divisional training, where they were accommodated in huts. For training purposes they had a 'layout' of the position at Gommecourt, which had been marked out, complete with dugouts; it was set out on undulating ground near Hurtebise Farm. After 'rehearsing the battle', they left for SOUASTRE on 1 June. On the following day they moved towards the front to the east of HÉBUTERNE, and were involved in the divisional task of digging new trenches 300yds closer to the enemy than before, which drew enemy fire. On 8 June, they were relieved by 1/12th Londons (168th Brigade, 56th Division); the battalion remained at HÉBUTERNE and supplied working parties.

On 21 June, 1/14th Londons marched back to PAS-EN-ARTOIS, where they remained in huts. On 27 June, they moved to BAYENCOURT; in the village there was a battery of 9.2in howitzers bombarding Gommecourt Wood, and firing every 5 minutes. By 2200hrs on 30 June, they were in their assembly positions, but the new and hastily dug assembly trenches were of little use, as they did not afford proper protection. The battalion were on the extreme right of the attack, with their right company

almost on the line of the HÉBUTERNE–PUISIEUX road. They left their trenches at 0730hrs with the protection of a smoke screen, but were immediately caught by an enemy barrage, but pressed on despite this. They held the line in front of Fame Trench and the west end of Fable Trench.

At around 0900hrs, 1/12th Londons, on the left of 1/14th Londons, were driven back by the enemy; this in turn exposed the left flank of 1/14th Londons. In the afternoon, the situation deteriorated, and they were joined by 1/13th Londons (168th Brigade, 56th Division) and 1/9th Londons (169th Brigade, 56th Division); howitzer fire poured down on them, and they could see audacious German batteries boldly galloping up and opening fire from a slope close to ROSSIGNOL WOOD, north-east of their position. A withdrawal was inevitable and they went back to the old British Front Line near HÉBUTERNE, just north of the road to PUISIEUX. The position was simply not tenable; it was exposed and enemy observation was complete. Also, British counter-battery work was sadly lacking.

The battalion cookers were taken by horses to the transport line at HAPPY VALLEY, between COIGNEUX and SOUASTRE. In the evening, the remnants of 1/14th Londons moved to SAILLY-AU-BOIS, the wounded having been taken to HÉBUTERNE where stretcher-bearers of the Royal Army Medical Corps took them over. On 2 July, they were joined by battalion reserves and then marched to SOUASTRE, where they stayed for a few hours. On the night of 2/3 July, they marched to FONCQUEVILLERS and were then sent into trenches that faced Gommecourt Park. They were there for 4 days and were then relieved by 1/9th Londons and returned to SOUASTRE. For the next few weeks they were in and out of HÉBUTERNE trenches; when not in the front line, they were billeted at BAYENCOURT and SAILLY-AU-BOIS.

On the left of 1/14th Londons were 1/12th Londons. In *Attack: an Infantry Subaltern's Impressions of July 1, 1916*, former platoon commander Edward Liveing of 1/12th Londons provides an excellent and often-quoted published account of his battalion's involvement in the battle. The night before, Liveing noted, in a little courtyard, he called his old platoon to attention for the last time, shook hands with officers who were left in reserve, marched off up the road and made a turning on to Blue Track. They had gone along about a quarter of the distance between BAYENCOURT and SAILLY-AU-BOIS when a messenger caught up with them and they had to halt. On the left nearby was the spire of BAYENCOURT church. On the right was

SAILLY-AU-BOIS in a girdle of trees. Along the side of the valley running out from behind SAILLY-AU-BOIS arose numerous pillars of smoke from the wood fires and kitchens of artillery encampments.

Going round SAILLY-AU-BOIS, Liveing arrived in the middle of more battery positions in the level plain behind HÉBUTERNE; his unit's destination was a dump close to the ruined church there, where they picked up materials. They entered a communication trench called Wood Street, and then turned sharp right into Boulevard Street and clattered along the brick-floored trench. They arrived at a belt of trees marking the orchard and turned right into Cross Street, which was behind the trees, and came to Woman Street. They were then directly in line with their front line and objective, which was in the area of Nameless Farm. Liveing mentions that at one point a German searchlight from the direction of Serre Wood seemingly turned itself almost dead on him. They were to move off at 0730hrs plus 45 seconds on 1 July; Liveing was in charge of No. 5 Platoon, part of the third wave. His life was to be saved by Rfmn C.S. Dennison, his platoon observer; despite this, Liveing was still wounded badly in the thigh, while 1/12th Londons had reached as far as the German wire.

Liveing's account then details his return and his treatment as a casualty. From a first-aid post at Cross Street he was taken to an advanced dressing station, which was a well-sandbagged house reached through an archway and courtyard; this would have been at HÉBUTERNE. A dugout had been tunnelled out beneath the courtyard, and surgical operations were performed here. Liveing was taken by ambulance through the village of SAILLY-AU-BOIS. At about 1130hrs it arrived at COUIN, which was the headquarters of 2/1st (London) Field Ambulance (56th Division). From there they went to the casualty clearing station via SOUASTRE where previously they had 'spent some pleasant evenings at the Divisional theatre'. The casualty clearing station was situated in the grounds of a château in the area of the Arras–DOULLENS road.

Back at Gommecourt, to the left of 1/12th Londons were 1/9th Londons; their objective was enemy ground to the left of Nameless Farm. On 30 June, they assembled for the march up the line and left their packs stored in old barns at SOUASTRE. They then made their way up to the front via communication trenches. In *From Ypres to Cambrai*, Frank Hawkins wrote about his experience with 1/9th Londons; like Liveing, Hawkins was quickly wounded, and his account is less detailed than Liveing's.

On 1 July, 1/9th Londons had about 500yds of no man's land to cross as one of the leading battalions of 56th Division, and smoke was discharged to assist them in their advance. They had erected ladders in the trenches, which they used to climb out into the open. The enemy barrage was very heavy and as they moved forward they could see, through the drifting smoke, the first line of the German infantry waiting for them. Parties of 1/9th Londons reached as far as Nameless Farm Road, where they became muddled up with 1/16th Londons (169th Brigade, 56th Division), who were on their left flank. They lined a steep bank, about 4½ft high, on the side that was close to the enemy; the range of this bank was well known to the opposing machine-gunners and it was also under point-blank rifle fire from Fellow Street, a German line leading from Nameless Farm.

1/16th Londons, on the left flank of 1/9th Londons, have left possibly the most detailed account of 56th Division's fighting on this day. Their history also contains some useful photographs and a panoramic photograph of the ground that 56th Division were to cover in their hopeless task of capturing this southern part of Gommecourt facing Gommecourt Park.

It has already been noted that 56th Division came to this sector on 5 May; during the nights of 25 to 27 May, several battalions – nearly 3,000 men – were involved in digging a new trench closer to the enemy line. They also dug new communication trenches as well. During this time 8 men were killed and 55 wounded. On 6 June a new trench was dug in Y Sector, opposite the south-west corner of Gommecourt Park. The Park was honeycombed with deep dugouts and the ground in front of it was known as the Mousetrap. The German Front Line ran along the edge of it and remains of the trench line can still be easily seen.

During the early hours of the night of 30 June/1 July, 1/16th Londons moved forward from their billets at SAINT-AMAND, reaching their assembly trenches at 0200hrs on 1 July. At Zero Hour, they moved off and went steadily forward and found that the enemy lines to the left of Nameless Farm, the German Second Line, had been 'imperfectly destroyed' by the Allied artillery, and both were still strongly held. Both 1/16th Londons and 1/9th Londons had to wait under galling machine-gun fire from the right, close to Nameless Farm, and also from Etch Trench, close to the enemy front line. As noted above, the two battalions became mixed up when Nameless Farm Road was reached; German machine-gunners even emerged from their dugouts and fired into the rear of the advancing battalions.

An attempt was made by 1/16th Londons to reach the German strongpoint called the Quadrilateral using bombers, but it was repelled.

From the moment that the attack of 46th Division on the northern face of the salient failed, the fate of 56th Division's assault battalions was sealed, for it meant that the Germans could concentrate the fire from a large number of guns behind the village of Gommecourt onto the area of the southern attack. By the end of 1 July, 1/16th Londons were bereft of officers; like the other London Territorial battalions, they had been brought to a standstill by the concentration of enemy guns and the fact that they were cut off from reinforcements. The 198 survivors marched from support trenches, where they assembled after the day's fighting, and then to BAYENCOURT, where they billeted for the night. On 3 July, they moved to SAINT-AMAND and on 4 July were reinforced by a draft of 268 men. On 6 July, they went back to the trenches to relieve the 1/4th Londons (168th Brigade, 56th Division) in the late afternoon. The portion of the line that they took over lay to the north of the Gommecourt Salient, between FONCQUEVILLERS and BIENVILLERS-AU-BOIS, and was known as Z Sector.

Since 1 July, there had been a lot of rain, and in the communication trenches men stood waist-deep in water; as a large portion of the new draft were 'Bantams', recruits of small stature, they had particular problems with these trench conditions. Very heavy rain fell on 7 July, and on 22 July, 1/16th Londons were relieved by 1/9th Londons and moved back to SAINT-AMAND for a week. On 30 July, they relieved 1/9th Londons in the old trenches at FONCQUEVILLERS, and remained there until 7 August.

On the left of 1/16th Londons were 1/5th Londons (169th Brigade, 56th Division). On 27 June, 1/5th Londons left HALLOY and went into huts at SOUASTRE, which was where the divisional concert party used to perform, in particular the Bow Bells Concert Party. Aubrey Smith, with the transport of 1/5th Londons (169th Brigade, 56th Division), wrote *Four Years on the Western Front*; he was one of those who waited all day for news of the attack. So much had been expected in the way of success that they were not just extremely saddened by the appalling casualties and the destruction of a battalion, but also surprised at the complete failure of the operation. In brief, he reported on what happened.

The Allied bombardment had seemed to be successful and 1/5th Londons, who were to take part in the attack against Gommecourt Park, stood up and watched the Wood being pulverised. As the enemy put down a protective barrage, 1/5th Londons began their attack, under cover of numerous smoke bombs; they were to cover about 300yds, and the German machine-gunners had a good view of them as they advanced towards them. They reached the first, second and even third lines, but there were no reinforcements to take the place of the men who had already been killed or wounded. However, Germans appeared from deep dugouts, which the artillery had not penetrated, and bombers appeared from them by the hundred; as a result, the advancing Londoners were surrounded and cut off. Further, the enemy barrage increased in intensity and reinforcements could not get through. The failure of the attack to the north brought German reinforcements to the southern part of the salient. The British were simply cut down; Smith lists casualties as being 588, a figure which included 19 officers.

In the early afternoon of 2 July, a German medical officer came towards the British lines and an armistice was arranged, allowing wounded to be taken from the battlefield. Some men, however, were still lying out in the field as late as 6 July. 1/5th Londons had got as far as the trenches near the Gommecourt–HÉBUTERNE road. Signalman H.G.R. Williams of 1/5th Londons noted that on 1 July, because of the complete chaos, no signals were actually received after the attack began. If this were so, then it would explain the lack of reinforcements.

The last battalion of 56th Division involved on this side of the Gommecourt battle were 1/2nd Londons (169th Brigade, 56th Division), to the left of 1/5th Londons in the Z Hedge area. On 1 July, 1/2nd Londons lay in the front line until 1430hrs, when D Company were ordered up to the German first-line Ferret Trench; three unsuccessful attempts to cross the open ground in the face of artillery and machine-gun fire had been made with the additional help of A and C Companies. Soon after noon, the Germans showed a white flag in Ferret Trench and a formal truce took place, which lasted for about 1 hour while the wounded were collected. The role of 1/3rd Londons (167th Brigade, 56th Division) was to dig a communication trench from Z Hedge to the junction of Fir and Firm Trenches on the left of the point which C Company attacked, but when this began at 1010hrs, the German barrage was so heavy that the attacks had to be abandoned. Z Hedge was very heavily shelled.

The line on 46th Division's front was ½ mile to the north of HÉBUTERNE, just east of FONCQUEVILLERS, and was held by the enemy northwards towards Monchy-au-Bois; FONCQUEVILLERS was the centre of the position. The chief work carried out prior to the battle was the digging out of former communication trenches from FONCQUE-VILLERS to the front line, a distance of about 700yds. There were about a dozen of these, several of which were named after Midlands regiments and locations: the main one was Stafford Avenue, in the centre, and others were Lincoln Lane, Leicester Street, Nottingham Street, Derby Dyke, Roberts Avenue, Rotten Row and so on. All of them had to be dug about 2ft below their existing level, which made them about 7ft deep. In addition, trenches for the support and reserve troops had to be prepared. There were also some Russian saps made, which were to allow troops to enter the line close to the front, having been hidden with only a thin covering of earth to shield them. Dugouts had to be made for forward battalion headquarters and many miles of narrow cable trenches dug, which had to be about 6ft down for the protection of the wires running from forward headquarters to brigade, division or artillery headquarters. In addition to this, large quantities of stores and supplies had to be carried to dumps in the forward positions, including bombs and ammunition.

The enemy's position was very strongly fortified and indeed was, along with FRICOURT, one of the best defended of the German fortified villages. The trenches were very well constructed and also deep. The wire in front of them was almost impossible to get through and the dugouts were so deep that they were proof against any except the heaviest of Allied barrages. There was also a long subterranean passage, built behind Gommecourt Wood, which connected up with the German Second Line. Reinforcements could therefore be brought up quickly in case of a counter-attack. Some of the German wire protecting the trenches and lines was 40yds broad and built on iron stakes interlaced with barbed wire. In addition, machine-gun redoubts were built to protect specific points; behind all this were the artillery, who knew to a foot their own and also the British trenches.

To the north of the line was Pigeon Wood, and opposite the left of 46th Division front was a small salient of trenches called the Z. In the middle of no man's land, which averaged about 400yds in width, were the ruins of Gommecourt sugar refinery, which was 20yds from the main FONCQUEVILLERS–Gommecourt road. Before the battle it was in reasonable condition, providing accommodation for the battalion headquarters, support companies, baths and canteens.

A full-size model of the German lines was dug near Lucheux Forest, where the attacking brigades

trained and practised. Here the trenches were dug to the depth of 2ft and tape-lines were laid down for the troops to form up on, and the whole attack was rehearsed as a 'drill'. It was this sort of tactic that contributed to the lack of progress on the day. It was against this background, with the odds over-whelmingly in favour of the defenders, that the British were to make one of their most disastrous attacks of the first day of the Somme battle.

On the right of 46th Division's attack at Gomme-court on 1 July were 137th Brigade, with 1/6th South Staffords and 1/6th North Staffords in the front and 1/5th South Staffords and 1/5th North Staffords in support. In reserve were 1/5th Lincolns, attached from 138th Brigade (46th Division); they supplied carrying parties.

Having been in the line in mid-June, 1/6th South Staffords were at Bus Saint-Léger for training, 18–21 June; on 23 June they returned to SOUASTRE. When they were in the line, their front was 250yds from the Germans on the flank close to the FONCQUEVILLERS–Gommecourt road. A new assembly trench had been built by them and 1/6th North Staffords; the Germans were aware of this new work, and there were casualties as a result.

On the evening of 30 June, 1/6th South Staffords moved up to their assembly positions. They set off at 0730hrs on 1 July, but it was a hopeless task, and they were severely affected by flanking fire from saps and shell-holes to the south. Some of them reached the enemy wire, but here they were mostly shot down or hit by hand grenades; a few men entered the front trenches but were driven out. Casualties were about 220 to 240. In the evening, after they had been withdrawn, 1/6th South Staffords assembled and proceeded to SAINT-AMAND, where they spent the night.

Being in the same frontal attack, 1/6th North Staffords suffered in a similar fashion and sustained 305 casualties. By 0900hrs, the general officer commanding 137th Brigade knew that the assault had failed; he endeavoured to organise a second attack using 1/5th South Staffords and 1/5th North Staffords, but they were already very short of men and their officers had mostly become casualties, and the general conditions up and down the trenches were chaotic. The troops had been trained to follow a certain plan of action, of which this new attack was not a part.

On 1 July, 1/5th South Staffords suffered 219 casualties, including 14 officers; they had taken up position behind their sister battalion, 1/6th South Staffords, in lines of attack. When the attack began, they were overwhelmed by the German barrage, which especially caught parties of men who were in communication trenches; as a result, they could not be of assistance to 1/6th North Staffords, who were being shot down by machine guns and rifles.

On the left of 137th Brigade, who had such a disastrous time, were 139th Brigade, who managed better. 1/5th and 1/7th Sherwood Foresters were in the front line, with one company of 1/8th Sherwood Foresters (138th Brigade, 46th Division) on their left; in support were 1/6th Sherwood Foresters and in reserve, more companies of 1/8th Sherwood Foresters. The brigade line was roughly from La Brayelle road on the north to the northern end of Gommecourt Wood on the south, where 139th Brigade joined up with 1/6th North Staffords. The communication trenches allocated to them included Regent Street, Roberts Avenue, Rotten Row and Stafford Avenue. Regent Street began at the brewery in FONCQUEVILLERS, then running due east and crossing the La Brayelle road in a south-easterly direction and meeting the front line 150yds to the south of the road. Roberts Avenue ran practically parallel with the La Brayelle road, crossed Support Trench and met the front line at Russian Sap, which was a tunnel as close to the start line as possible. 1/5th Sherwood Foresters' battalion headquarters was at the western end of Rotten Row and joined the front line about 100yds south of Roberts Avenue. Stafford Avenue joined the front line 100yds south of Rotten Row. The Z and Little Z were jumping-off trenches.

On the evening of 30 June, 1/5th Sherwood Foresters arrived at FONCQUEVILLERS from POMMIER; battalion headquarters was then in Crawl Boys Lane on the FONCQUEVILLERS–Gommecourt road at the junction of Colonels Walk. Companies moved up at about midnight into the muddy trenches.

When, on the night before the battle, the battalions of 139th Brigade reached FONCQUEVILLERS, their cookers were taken down the western edge of the wood behind the village, where the troops were issued with supper and rum at about 2200hrs. In addition to the following day's ration, each man carried a bacon and bread sandwich.

The *Official History of the War* noted that the first three waves of 139th Brigade suffered considerable casualties, but reached and broke into the German front trench; some parties advanced to the second, but there was some loss of direction on the left, as air observers reported British soldiers in the Z and Little Z. Succeeding waves were met by heavy fire, and contact with the leading line was lost. The Sherwood Foresters were also attacked from the rear, by Germans who had been in deep dugouts which had not been dealt with; the enemy also bombed men who were sheltering in the shell-holes. Even though a lodgement was made in the German line, this could not be supported, although several attempts were made in the afternoon.

The battalions of 139th Brigade had reached their assembly positions early on 1 July. The British bombardment opened at 0625hrs and the discharge of smoke from their front line began 1 hour later. Under cover of this, the assaulting battalions moved from the advance trenches. A heavy and accurate barrage was immediately put down on the front line and Support Lines by the enemy, who were obviously aware in advance of the extent of the attack. At about 0800hrs, the forward trenches were cleared of troops. The trenches were in many parts deep in mud and water. Communication lines were often blocked by dead bodies or by wounded men, or were blown in. Little progress was possible. Scraps of news came through but it soon became evident that the attack on their front had not succeeded. They later learned that, owing to the difficulty experienced by the supporting waves in getting across their own waterlogged trenches, they lost the advantage of the barrage, and that smoke had cleared long before the assaulting troops had got across no man's land. The long Allied bombardment had had little effect on the German trenches, dugouts and wire, and the attackers were met by rifle and machine-gun fire, shell-fire and uncut wire.

The War in the Air by H.A. Jones notes that British observers had watched the leading waves of 139th Brigade pass over the front line and make their way gradually towards the northern corner of what was left of Gommecourt Wood. As the waves passed on their way, the observers then saw the German infantry come scrambling from the shelter of their dugouts and reoccupy their front line trenches. The rear waves, which had been given the task of clearing the dugouts, never got across no man's land, owing to the heavy artillery and machine-gun barrage.

The men who had been cut off behind the German lines fought desperately all day. It proved impossible to develop fresh attacks to help them. It was hoped to renew the attack, but lack of smoke bomb protection, chaos in the communication trenches and the continued alertness of the enemy led to the eventual abandonment of the plan of attack again. A few men even returned as late as 2130hrs.

In the evening, 1/8th Sherwood Foresters took over from the remnants of 1/5th and 1/7th Sherwood Foresters, and were later relieved by 1/5th Lincolns; 1/5th Sherwood Foresters marched back to BIENVILLERS-AU-BOIS, having suffered 491 casualties out of a total of 734 men. Lt Cols L.A. Hind and D.D. Winch were both among them. After 1 July, the battalion spent that night and the following day in collecting up the wounded and tidying up the position, and were relieved on 3 July.

In the *History of the Sherwood Foresters*, it is noted that 'It must have been quite obvious to the enemy that their attack was to be the flank of the Somme attack, although some demonstration was made by the 37th Division to their left. The enemy therefore were able to bring all their guns from the direction of Adinfer Wood to bear on no man's land on the Sherwood For. Front.'

On the extreme left of 46th Division's attack against Gommecourt Wood was a part of 11th Royal Warwicks (112th Brigade, 37th Division). In the battalion history of 11th Royal Warwicks, it is noted that the slopes around Pigeon Wood, opposite the Z and Little Z, and all the ground from Z Trench up to Gommecourt, ground which had recently been more or less green, was now 'so thrown about and shattered that it appeared like waves and hillocks of brown earth, and every vestige of grass soon disappeared'. 11th Royal Warwicks were involved in the trenches for 16 days; on 3 July, they were relieved by 1/5th Lincolns.

On the right, behind 137th Brigade's attacking battalions, were 1/5th Leicesters (138th Brigade, 46th Division). In June they had moved up to FONCQUEVILLERS and had relieved 1/5th Sherwood Foresters in the right sector, opposite Gommecourt Park. A road and bank parallel with the front line, and about 300yds behind it, provided the battalion headquarters. Behind this again, the Bluff, a steep bank, gave the support company a good home. 137th Brigade had so much work in the way of new trench digging and other duties that they were lent 1/5th Leicesters to help out. The latter were to advance as the ninth wave behind the attackers, while one company were to dig a trench joining the sugar refinery to the German Front Line, a communication trench for use after the battle. The new assembly trenches that had been so recently dug had become full of water because June was such a wet month.

Soon after midnight on 30 June, they moved up to Midland Trench, an assembly trench running north to south about 700yds west of FONCQUEVILLERS church. A and D Companies were in cellars and dugouts in the village, since they would be needed first. There were many communication trenches up which they could advance, and at the last minute, all of them were made 'up' trenches until after the

attack. After the attack had begun and the fourth wave was advancing, the smoke blew away and the whole of the attack was revealed. On the right, 137th Brigade, passing the sugar refinery, found the German wire still too strong. The rear waves had no protection and the fifth wave was enfiladed by machine-gun fire from the north, from the Z and from the front line. Two leading battalions of 139th Brigade were seen crossing no man's land unscattered, and had then entered the German lines complete; they were never seen again. Other battalions lost their leading waves and sent back messages for smoke and reinforcements.

Gallant efforts were made to take the Wood. The situation became critical and they were still due to join hands with 56th Division's attackers. The lines became congested and the divisional artillery did nothing in the way of counter-battery work. A further attack planned for mid-afternoon was abandoned; later, 1/5th Leicesters took over the front line from 137th Brigade, while 1/5th Lincolns came in on the left and relieved 139th Brigade.

On 18 June, 1/5th Lincolns had been at FONCQUEVILLERS; they were later billeted at SAINT-AMAND, HUMBERCAMPS, WARLINCOURT-LÈS-PAS and SOUASTRE. On the morning of 1 July, the battalion advanced by platoons in artillery formation across the open ground between SOUASTRE and FONCQUEVILLERS, and reached Midland Trench in the rear of the village, where they spent the rest of the day. Some officers were instructed to reconnoitre the enemy front-line trenches in front of Gommecourt Wood. There was the possibility that the battalions might be called upon to capture an enemy trench with uncut wire which had not been taken during the day, and the Germans would be on the alert; the plan was scrapped, however.

The following day was mostly spent in getting in the wounded, and on 3 July, 1/4th Londons began to relieve them. 1/5th Lincolns proceeded to FONCQUEVILLERS, but instead of returning to billets they were instructed to relieve 11th Royal Warwicks in a sector of the trenches immediately to the north of those previously occupied. Their right was on the La Brayelle road. Rain fell heavily during the next few days and the trenches were, in places, in 4ft of water.

On 9 July, two companies were relieved by 1/16th Londons and on 11 July, 8th Lincolns (110th Brigade, 37th Division) were relieved by a company of 8th Somerset Light Infantry (also 110th Brigade, 37th Division). On the nights of 9 and 10 July, a strong carrying party was assisted by the support company to carry gas cylinders under supervision of the Royal Engineers from HANNESCAMPS to the front trenches held by 1/4th Leicesters before Monchy, in preparation for the gas cloud attack on the German trenches.

In *Pilgrimage*, Lt Col G.S. Hutchison has some pertinent things to say about the battle of Gommecourt on 1 July; he wrote that leading companies of 1/6th North Staffords and 1/6th South Staffords, Territorial battalions from Wolverhampton and Hanley, were caught by fire opposite uncut wire, on which most who arrived there were either shot or bombed by the defenders. 46th Division's attack failed completely and one of the brigade commanders who had seen these two battalions massacred, Brig Gen H.B. Williams, declined to send forward their sister battalions later in the afternoon.

Hutchison also wrote that the first phase of the battle can best be studied by going to FONCQUE-VILLERS; it was a village which, although 1 mile behind the front line, had been immune from shell-fire. He noted that the attack was to emerge on 1 July from the lines in front of HÉBUTERNE and then wrest the Park from the Germans, squeeze out the high ground at BEAUMONT-HAMEL and then force the Germans to retreat beyond the valley of the River Ancre. The attack completely failed, although a single German infantry regiment faced an assault of 10,000 men. Comparatively few men reached the German lines; finding themselves unsupported and heavily bombed from both flanks, they were finally overwhelmed by counter-attack and were killed or captured. The ravine lying between the lines was heaped with dead, who lay there for weeks, the prey of rats and of myriads of swollen flies. The extent of the failure appeared to Hutchison to be unbelievable. Superb battalions were reduced within a few minutes to but skeletons of their original strength.

In *Sir Douglas Haig's Command*, G.A.B. Dewar and J.H. Boraston make a different point: 'The failure of the subsidiary attack must be ascribed, in part at least, to the faulty handling of the supporting troops of the Division.' With the idea of securing protection and avoiding casualties, an attempt was made to bring these troops forward through communication trenches instead of across the open, with the results that the trenches became hopelessly blocked, the assault troops were left unsupported, and such of the support troops as succeeded at last in getting forward were met by withering fire from trenches and strongpoints that their slow advance had given the enemy time to reoccupy. So far as

this Division were concerned, the want of success was clearly due to a lack of knowledge of, and training in, the offensive tactics suited to the new type of fighting.

On the other hand, Lt Gen T. Snow, General Officer Commanding VII Corps, passed on this message to the troops. He said that he wished all ranks to understand that the attack on the Gommecourt salient in cooperation with 56th Division embraced two purposes: the capture of the position and the retaining of considerable numbers of German troops in the immediate front in order to prevent them taking part in resisting the advance of the Allied troops to the south. Although the first purpose was not achieved, the second was fulfilled, and there was no doubt that the action assisted the men of Fourth Army, to the right, and contributed to their success.

Despite Snow's comforting words, it was considered, at least by the Sherwood Foresters, that the action was undeniably a failure. The retention of enemy troops on the British front was achieved by the artillery and other preparations, and the extra German Division were lured in to the line opposite the Midlanders at least 3 days before the battle. The actual assault made no difference to this. The object was to capture Gommecourt and this they failed to do. Obvious reasons were apparent to all: the rapid dispersal of the smoke barrage; the terrible enfilade bombardment from the left, consequent on the inactivity on the left; the failure of the artillery to smash up German posts, and in some cases German wire; and perhaps the fact that the pre-battle preparations were observed and known by the Germans, who were therefore fully prepared for the attack when it came.

A document published by German sources, entitled the 'Defence of Gommecourt' is worth quoting from, as it tells of the experiences of the German defenders at Gommecourt, both on 1 July and during the period immediately before. The document is based on the war diary of Reserve-Infanterie-Regiment Nr. 55 of 2. Garde Reserve Division. The abbreviated extract tells of the severe effects of the Allied bombardment, especially on Kern Redoubt. On one occasion it was partly blown in. Splinter shells destroyed emplacements of several trench mortars and a battery in Biez Wood received several direct hits. Despite the bombardment, the telephone linesman succeeded in maintaining communication most of the time during the build-up to 1 July.

On 1 July, the bombardment shortly before the attack succeeded in rendering the front sectors of G1, which was the ground in front of 139th Brigade on the Wood section, and G5, the section that contained the cemetery, ripe for assault. On the G1 sector, the plan was presumably to help to cut off the garrison at Gommecourt. Strong British skirmishes were made from Pilier Farm and bombers and flame projectors were used. The British were repulsed and did not gain a footing in the sector. An energetic British attack was delivered against G5. The other sectors were kept under a heavy bombardment, which was not followed by an infantry attack.

On the G5 sector, many dugout entrances were blown in, trenches flattened and much wire destroyed. The front trench was enfiladed from the direction of FONCQUEVILLERS; Gommecourt Cemetery was overrun and Kern Redoubt was reached. Successive attacks advanced from Patrol Wood. The British were driven back to the cemetery with help from their colleagues holding Kern Redoubt, and by 1600hrs, portions of the G5 sector had been won back. An Allied prisoner stated that it was intended to cut off Gommecourt village. The greatest danger, therefore, lay in G1 and G5 sectors and on the left flank of Kern Redoubt. Communication was cut and not re-established until the evening. The battalion command post was at Point 147, from where the situation could be observed. It is acknowledged that the equipment and preparation of the British attack were magnificent. The troops had been amply provided with machine guns, Lewis guns, trench mortars and storming ladders, and the officers were provided with excellent maps giving the fullest details of the German positions and trench systems. German losses on 1 July in this section were 708 men, including those killed, missing or wounded. They had been able to live in their dugouts throughout the 7-day bombardment. Prisoners agreed that the German machine-gun fire had been very effective.

Many of the British casualties on 1 July were taken to the rail halts at DOULLENS and WARLINCOURT-LÈS-PAS. Senior officer casualties included Lt Col L.A. Hind of 1/7th Sherwood Foresters, Lt Col C.E. Boote of 1/5th North Staffords and Lt Col D.D. Wilson of 1/5th Sherwood Foresters, all of whom were killed. After 1 July, Gommecourt is rarely mentioned in the history books; the British were never to capture it. It was relinquished by the Germans on 27 February 1917, when they retreated to the Hindenburg Line.

Gommecourt Wood New Cemetery is on the south side of the road to FONCQUEVILLERS, west of the Wood. It was made after the Armistice

by the concentration of graves from certain smaller burial grounds and from the battlefields of July 1916, including 55 from Bastion Cemetery in the former enemy lines north of the Wood. Two-thirds of the graves are unnamed. Buried there is Lt Col C.E. Boote (II.B.12); aged 41, he was a member of 1/5th North Staffords. The regimental historian wrote the following of an incident on 23 June 1916: 'It was a vile night, raining and cold, Major Charles Boote (who had been with the 5th until the end of 1915, and was now in command of the 6th North Staffs) came along and chaffed us. "What the 5th North working again! Well, well, well!" Everyone grinned, and felt better. We pushed off, past Church Corner.' Boote was one of nine officers of 1/6th North Staffords who fell on 1 July. Hind's name is commemorated on the Thiepval Memorial and Wilson's on Neuve-Chapelle Indian Memorial.

On one of the cemetery walls is a plaque to the memory of 46th Division. In the 1920s a memorial cross was moved to this cemetery for safety, from a spot with the map reference 57d E28.c.5.4. The cemetery register lists 739 casualties.

Gommecourt British Cemetery No. 2 is in open cultivated farmland, ¾ mile south of Gommecourt village, 60yds north of a road running from HÉBUTERNE to Bucquoy. Four cemeteries had been made in 1917 when the battlefields were cleared, and Gommecourt British Cemeteries Nos. 1, 3 and 4 were concentrated into Gommecourt British Cemetery No. 2 after the Armistice. These cemeteries mostly contained men from 56th Division who died in July 1916, especially Plot I; 1,365 graves are recorded.

Gommecourt British Cemetery No. 1, 100yds north-west of No. 2, contained the graves of 107 soldiers, mainly of 56th Division, who fell on 1 July; it was concentrated into Gommecourt British Cemetery No. 2 after the Armistice. On 12 November, Gommecourt British Cemetery No. 3, at the south-west corner of the village and also containing 56th Division graves from 1 July, was also concentrated with No. 2. Gommecourt British Cemetery No. 4, south of Gommecourt British Cemetery No. 1, also contained the graves of men from 56th Division, 70 of them from 1 July and 12 November as well as actions at the end of February 1917.

One would asume that if 56th Division were to be commemorated, then the plaque might have been erected in this cemetery, which was designed by Sir Reginald Blomfield. However, such a plaque was instead affixed to the wall of the Convent of St Augustine in Arras.

GORENFLOS, to the east of ABBEVILLE, was where companies of 1/5th Sherwood Foresters (139th Brigade, 46th Division) rejoined their parent unit, having arrived on 27 January 1916; they spent much of the next 2 weeks carrying out light training. The evenings were enlivened by the bugle band playing 'Beating Retreat', which was much enjoyed by civilians and military alike. On 10 February, 1/5th Sherwood Foresters left for BERNAVILLE to the north-east.

GRANDCOURT is on the south bank of the River Ancre, between SAINT-PIERRE-DIVION and MIRAUMONT on the D151 road. In 1916 it was part of the German entrenchment of the Ancre to SAINT-PIERRE-DIVION; the enemy were very well dug in here.

On 1 July, elements of 36th Division, advancing from the direction of Thiepval Wood, actually reached as far as Grandcourt village, having taken the immensely strong SCHWABEN REDOUBT. This was a tremendous achievement, but it could not be sustained, owing to lack of reinforcements and support. It was the German Infanterie-Regiment (8. Württembergisches) Nr. 180 (26. Reserve Infanterie Division) who faced the Irish battalions advancing from the eastern face of the SCHWABEN REDOUBT. Some of the Irishmen even reached a German field artillery battery, which was in a field in Battery Valley running from the south-west of Grandcourt in the direction of the Schwaben. Other members of 36th Division reached as far as the south of the Grandcourt/THIEPVAL road crossing. Previously the enemy enfiladed the ANCRE VALLEY with a high-velocity gun, which had been brought up at night on the Grandcourt–BEAUCOURT-SUR-L'ANCRE railway, just far enough to fire southwards.

Between Grandcourt and COURCELETTE (to have been taken by 2nd Canadian Division on 15 September), but closer to the latter, is the Regina Trench Cemetery. It is named after a German work that was captured for a time on 1 October by 5th Canadian Brigade (2nd Canadian Division), and again by 1st and 3rd Canadian Divisions on 8 October; it was finally cleared on 11 November by 4th Canadian Division. The cemetery is on a side road called Twenty-three Road, leading from Grandcourt Road to West Miraumont Road; the trench ran, roughly east and west, about 500yds north of it. In early November the Allied line still ran south of the River Ancre and then in front of Grandcourt. After the whole of REGINA TRENCH was at last in the hands of the Allies, it was planned to bring up the line north of the river, level with

these positions, and to prepare for another attack on the village of BEAUMONT-HAMEL.

On 13 November, the line ran down from a north-easterly direction and then took up the majority of Battery Valley, which ran almost north to south. The Battle of the Ancre lasted from 13 to 19 November. To the south-east was Grandcourt Trench; to its south were Desire Trench and Support Trench, where the British line was consolidated at the end of the fighting. Behind Desire Trench and in front of COURCELETTE was REGINA TRENCH, and the famous BAILLESCOURT FARM was just across the River Ancre. 19th Division were to attack from the south-west, with 11th Canadian Brigade (4th Canadian Division) to the south-east.

On 17 November, 8th North Staffords (57th Brigade, 19th Division) were cut off at Grandcourt, and their attack subsequently failed. On the same date, 8th East Lancashires (112th Brigade, 37th Division) had been given the task of taking BAILLESCOURT FARM, which stood on a sheer bank at least 30ft high. The whole valley was commanded by the Germans on the hills beyond; owing to the nature of the boggy ground, the Allies did not reach the outskirts of Grandcourt until 18 November 1916.

Heavy fighting took place during the following months but the village was never captured. On 5/6 February 1917, when patrols of the Howe Battalion (63rd Division) entered the village, they found it empty.

By 21 November, BAILLESCOURT FARM had been captured by 63rd Division. At one time, Henry Williamson was at the farm; he used the ammunition boxes made of deal for heating, as they provided excellent fuel. Ever after, he associated the smell of burning deal wood with the farm. It became one of the largest farms on the Somme and was run as a cooperative.

On 21 November, the poet Ivor Gurney arrived in the area with his battalion, 2/5th Glosters (184th Brigade, 61st Division). They met their guides at Tullock's Corner and the battalion were for 3 or 4 days behind the Grandcourt Trenches, which stretched about 3,000yds from Irving Post to Towse Burrows. The conditions were very primitive, with men clinging to shell-holes, and the mud was deep enough to completely submerge a gun team and limber. Masses of unburied dead were strewn over the surrounding battlefields and there was no sign of organised trenches, merely shell-holes that joined up to one another, and there were no landmarks anywhere. Gurney wrote a poem about the living conditions of the Canadians.

Of Grandcourt
Through miles of mud we travelled, and by sick
    valleys –
The Valley of Death at last – most evil alleys,
To Grandcourt trenches reserve – and the hell's
    name it did deserve.
Rain there was – tired and weak I was, glad for
    an end.

On 26 November, Gurney's battalion marched back to Wellington Huts.

The original part of Regina Trench Cemetery (later Plot II, Rows A to D) was made in 1916–17 and contains 179 graves, of which more than half are Canadian. After the war, the cemetery was completed by the concentration of 2,086 graves from Grandcourt, COURCELETTE and MIRAUMONT; most of these men would have died between October 1916 and February 1917. The cemetery is between Grandcourt and COURCELETTE and commemorates the Canadian actions in October and November 1916, when Canadian troops took, among other positions, the longest trench built by the Germans on the Western Front, namely REGINA TRENCH. The cemetery stands in bleak open country in an area known as Plaine de Courcelette, with extensive views to the north and east.

W.R. Bird of 42nd Canadian Battalion (7th Canadian Brigade, 3rd Canadian Division), author of *Thirteen Years After*, came to Grandcourt in 1931; in the sunken road near the cemetery, he came across a road gang who, during their digging, had uncovered the remains of German equipment. Even then, Bird could find no trace of the original REGINA TRENCH.

Grandcourt Road Cemetery is about 1 mile south-east of the village, on a sunken road known as Stump Road or Grandcourt Road, and has wide views to the north. It was made in the spring of 1917, when the battlefield around was cleared, and contains the graves of 390 Commonwealth troops. On the crest of the hill is part of the German STUFF REDOUBT, part of their second line.

Stump Road Cemetery is 40yds from the road, across some fields, and stands below the ridge between Grandcourt and POZIÈRES. Stump Road was a sunken road running south from the village up the hill towards POZIÈRES. After local attacks were made in November 1916, 7th Buffs (55th Brigade, 18th Division) made the first burials in the following month; the cemetery register lists the names of 263 men; many of the 50 unknowns are also from 18th Division.

Opposite BAILLESCOURT FARM is Boom Ravine, which presumably got its name from its association with the German artillery. Early in 1917 it was 'found out' by the British artillery and both war correspondent Philip Gibbs and author John Masefield have commented on the utter destruction in the ravine and the number of German dead lying in the valley.

After the war, Grandcourt was adopted by Stourbridge. In recent years, BAILLESCOURT FARM has become one of the largest farms on the Somme and at present is a riding and activity centre, with student accommodation for school groups.

THE GRANDSTAND is past the DERNANCOURT cemeteries in a northerly direction, along a farm track; it offers an excellent view of the 1915/16 battlefield, with AUCHONVILLERS to the left and MÉAULTE to the right. The BAPAUME road can be traced easily by a line of large factory buildings.

One of the earliest written mentions of the Grandstand appears in the papers of Col F.J. Rice when he was a lieutenant and serving with LXXXIV Brigade, Royal Field Artillery (18th Division), at the end of June 1915. His unit had come to the area to take over from French artillery units 1 mile east of MÉAULTE, close to a factory. Rice, who was on horseback, accompanied the French to their observation post near DERNANCOURT, which even then was already named the Grandstand. Rice was amazed by the sight of troops walking about without concern for their safety, but at the time things were very quiet.

In the following months, many senior British figures came here to survey the battlefield; the position became even more significant at the time of the Allied pre-battle bombardment at the end of June 1916 and during the attack on the misty morning of 1 July. Lt Gen Sir Henry Rawlinson, General Officer Commanding Fourth Army, studied the battlefield from this point, and used to bring guests here; he even had a hut erected for his personal use. From his diary, we know that he came here at 0900hrs on 26 June to see the concentration of artillery fire; the next day, 'Haig came over and I took him up to the Grandstand to have a look round'.

The war correspondent Philip Gibbs also appears to have visited the Grandstand, and in his *The War Dispatches* wrote of viewing an arc of landscape stretching from AUCHONVILLERS to BRAY-SUR-SOMME: 'I stood with a few officers in the centre of a crescent sweeping round from Auchonvillers, Thiepval, La Boisselle and Fricourt, to Bray, on the Somme at the southern end of the curve. Here in this beetroot field on high ground, we stood watching one of the greatest artillery battles in which British gunners have been engaged.' Gibbs was told at midnight that the attack was to take place at 0730hrs on the following day.

On 1 July, Rawlinson watched the initial assault from 0630hrs until 0800hrs from a 'specially constructed platform near Albert'; it was very hazy, but the visibility improved at 0730hrs. This platform was at PONT-NOYELLES, near Fourth Army headquarters. Later, Rawlinson returned to Querrieu Château, in order to await reports from his five corps commanders. After lunch, Haig drove over from BEAUQUESNE to confer; at 2100hrs, Marshal Foch arrived to report on the French successes of the day.

GRENAS is a hamlet near HALLOY and south of the DOULLENS–Arras road, the N25. Towards the end of May 1916, it was home to a brigade of 56th Division when in divisional reserve; brigade headquarters opened here on 21 May.

GRÉVILLERS is a village 2 miles west of BAPAUME. By 7 August 1916, the village had been reduced to a ruin by Allied artillery and bombing. On the north side of the BAPAUME road is Grévillers British Cemetery, designed by Sir Edwin Lutyens; Bayonet Trench Cemetery in GUEUDECOURT was concentrated here, with the graves of 19 men of the Australian Imperial Force killed on 5 November 1916. On the rear wall of this cemetery is a memorial to the New Zealand Missing from their actions during the 1918 Battle of the Somme and Advance to Victory.

GROVE TOWN, a railway station on the DERNANCOURT–MÉAULTE–the Loop–Plateau line, lay south-east of MÉAULTE. Apart from sidings, there was not much by way of geographical features, and the area's main use was for camps or the entraining or detraining of troops and equipment. By the end of June 1916, Grove Town was known as 'a city of dumps'.

It is well known that Capt D.L. Martin of 9th Devons (20th Brigade, 7th Division) forecast how he and others would be killed on 1 July by machine-gun fire from the Shrine during an attack against the village of MAMETZ. Not so well known, perhaps, is that the model of the FRICOURT–MAMETZ area that he made when at home on leave prior to the battle was on display at 20th Brigade headquarters at Grove Town, and all officers were invited to inspect it. Martin was almost the first man to die in the attack, exactly as he had predicted. The model survived the war, but the author has yet to track it down.

On 30 June, 9th Division moved here and established the divisional headquarters. In *We Band of Brothers*, G.W. Warwick of 4th South African Infantry (South African Brigade, 9th Division) noted that after SUZANNE they arrived at Grove Town camp, which was fairly close to the station and is the site of the present-day military cemetery. Warwick noted that the camp had a high-sounding name and consisted of a wide-open space with tents and barbed wire enclosures for German prisoners; there was no town. On 2 July, 4th South African Infantry left the camp by companies and marched up to the front trenches; the next day, they found themselves in proper dugouts in a narrow valley (BILLON WOOD VALLEY), which was full of French 75mm and other guns. The boundary of the two Allied armies was close by. At 0730hrs on 4 July, they marched to a Royal Engineers dump and filled up trucks on a small tramline with barbed wire and timber. They pushed the trucks along by hand and arrived eventually at a valley where the materials were unloaded. On the return journey, they had joyrides on the trucks and a group of Argyll & Sutherland Highlanders passed them. On 5 July, they cleaned their rifles, packed up and marched to the old German trenches opposite MARICOURT.

As the battle advanced in September and October, Grove Town was chosen as the site of a new casualty clearing station. Accordingly, No. 3 Casualty Clearing Station, from HEILLY, was established by the side of the railway. Nos. 3 and 4 came from VECQUEMONT and No. 48 was also established here, in the period 10 to 12 September; No. 34 between 11 and 18 September and No. 56 from 18 to 22 October. In November, there were still six casualty clearing stations in the vicinity.

In *Twelve Days*, Sidney Rogerson of 2nd West Yorkshires (23rd Brigade, 8th Division) noted that Grove Town was a station only in the sense that special trains stopped there; it was not even worth the description of a siding, and possessed no more shelter than it did platform. Rogerson was involved in a long wait for a 'missing' train; the troops began to wander further afield, and towards the dripping tents of the casualty clearing station. One of his NCOs hurried back to Rogerson and informed him that behind one of the big marquees, a dump of equipment from the wounded or dead had been made. Later on, the station also became a railhead for tanks.

As well as 7th and 9th Divisions, 17th, 18th, 38th and 51st Divisions had links with Grove Town.

Grove Town Cemetery, designed by Sir Edwin Lutyens, is all that remains of the Grove Town connection. It is to be found about halfway along a secondary road leading from the main road to

BRAY-SUR-SOMME. In September 1916, Nos. 34 and 2/2 (London) Casualty Clearing Stations were established at this point, which was called locally 'la Demie-Lieue'. The cemetery stands on high ground overlooking BRAY-SUR-SOMME and the Somme Valley. One of the graves is of Lt Col (B/ Maj) T.H.P. Morris (I.C.42) of 9th Rifle Brigade (41st Brigade, 14th Division); in August, he had taken part in the DELVILLE WOOD fighting, and was mortally wounded in an attack towards Bulls Road at FLERS and died 3 days later. Another grave is that of the journalist and poet Sgt L. Coulson (I.J.24) of 1/12th Londons (168th Brigade, 56th Division). He became postumously famous for his poem 'Who Made the Law?' Often appearing in anthologies, it was originally published in a collection called *From an Outpost*. Coulson was mortally wounded at LESBŒUFS on 7 October and died a few hours later at a casualty clearing station at Grove Town.

GUEUDECOURT is a village on the D74 road between LE SARS and LESBŒUFS, north-east of FLERS. The centre of many actions to capture it between 18 and 27 September 1916, the village was protected to the south-west, towards FLERS, by Gird Trench and beyond that by Gird Support. To the west, along the road to Eaucourt, were Seven Dials and Factory Corner; to the north-west, on the road to Ligny-Thilloy, was LUISENHOF FARM. The road is now the D10 and the farm was on the east side. When the Gird Trenches were in enemy hands, the lines were 500yds apart, running from the north-west to the south-east across the divisional front, in the rear of the BUTTE DE WARLENCOURT. Beyond the Gird Trenches lay a stretch of unspoilt open country, with BAPAUME clearly visible; midway, almost hidden in a small valley, was le Barque.

On 15 September, the day that FLERS fell, a Mark I tank had actually reached as far as Gueude-court, where its very novelty struck horror into the enemy. It waddled into the village and engaged a whole battery of German guns, before being hit and catching fire. At least one enemy gun had been destroyed, if not two.

In *Another World 1787–1917*, Anthony Eden of 21st King's Royal Rifle Corps (124th Brigade, 41st Division) tells briefly the story of what happened in the direction of Gueudecourt on 15 September, the day that FLERS fell. Two battalions of 124th Brigade, 21st King's Royal Rifle Corps and 10th Queen's, were, by the afternoon, in a line on a position that was to the east of FLERS facing Gird Ridge. They appeared to be well in advance of the troops on either flank, but still capable of holding on to the ground that they had taken. Their next objective was the Gird Ridge, a formidable obstacle that the Germans had strongly entrenched with wire that remained uncut.

Despite this obstacle, the brigadier-general wanted to proceed, as a further advance might help the divisions on the right who were held up around LESBŒUFS and MORVAL and had suffered heavy casualties. The attack took place without any further preparation and failed, with heavy losses. Eden thought that maybe it was the success of the advance of the 41st Division that had encouraged the Brigade to try and take the ridge when the defences were far too strong to be captured without effective artillery bombardment.

From Bulls Road, which ran along the north-east front of FLERS, a clear view of German movements could be had, and parties of them could be seen coming from the direction of LE TRANSLOY. The communication between the two lines was very shallow. The main approach to the front was down an open valley, into which shells dropped contin-uously, against the side of a sunken road to the east of FLERS. Part of the attack was coming from Gas Alley to the south-east of Gueudecourt. It was previously a German communication trench, which 1st Lincolns (62nd Brigade, 21st Division) began consolidating. They were, however, subjected to continuous fire, and decimated.

On 16 September, 2/Lt Ellenberger of 9th King's Own Yorkshire Light Infantry (64th Brigade, 21st Division) noted that they advanced nearly ½ mile over no man's land, preceded by a tank which had straddled the German front trench and subsequently burst into flames. None of them got nearer than 100yds or so. In *The Turning Point*, H.P. Robinson, war correspondent of *The Times*, noted that the German artillery barraged the support trenches heavily and that Gueudecourt was very strongly defended. He meant that the Gird System was under bombardment.

The road from GINCHY, running due north, crossed the Gird System at a point just below the village in a deep ravine. The ravine itself, forked at this point, ran into two legs on the eastern and western sides of Gueudecourt; across these, a little higher up, the road from LE TRANSLOY to Eaucourt cut across through a deep gulley on both sides of the village. In the village itself were machine-gun posts, and in between these trenches and ravines lurked minor defended holes and hidden strongholds. By 25 September, the British Front Line ran along the southern edge of Gueudecourt.

In *Gallipoli to the Somme*, Alexander Aitken of 1st Otagos (1st New Zealand Brigade, New Zealand Division) noted that on 25 September they assembled in Grove Alley, which ran in a south-westerly direction between the front of Gueudecourt and the front of FLERS. Grove Alley faced in a north-westerly direction, and in a very carefully planned advance, the New Zealanders entered the German trenches in Goose Alley, a trench running towards the Gird System. The plan was that they should advance to the north-east and capture Gird Trench.

To paraphrase the *Official History of the War*, a tank from FLERS that was to assist in capturing Gird Trench in the plan for 26 September came up and was followed by bombers of 7th Leicesters (110th Brigade, 37th Division), with two companies in support. The enemy was driven steadily south-eastwards towards the Guards Division; 370 Germans surrendered at this time and British losses were minimal. The Gird Trenches were then occupied by 15th Durham Light Infantry (64th Brigade, 21st Division); infantry patrols were instructed to enter the village and the cavalry were called upon. A squadron of 19th Lancers (Fane's Horse) (Sialkot Cavalry Brigade, 1st Indian Cavalry Division), left MAMETZ and proceeded mostly at a trot up by a track east of FLERS and then turned towards Gueudecourt, in the process crossing two trenches full of British infantry. They were under artillery and machine-gun fire from the right front and had to withdraw because of heavy shelling. Later they had another try at entering the village from the south-west, at about 1415hrs, but this time they were dismounted. A troop of the South Irish Horse also had to resort to going by foot, and they too came under fire. The cavalry withdrew at about 1800hrs, by which time 110th Brigade (37th Division) had entered the village. Three battalions of the enemy had advanced from the direction of Thilloy and took cover in the long grass and standing crops 1 mile to the north of the village, but the Allied artillery 'searched them out'; British troops dug in on the far edge of the village.

In his book, Aitken has this to say about what was a disastrous time for the New Zealanders, in their attack on Gird Trench. There was little cover for their advance as the ground sloped slightly down; they could be clearly seen by the Germans and would be machine-gunned. Unlike the attack on 25 September, when they had 23 minutes to cross 700yds, they were only to be allowed a bare 8 minutes for the crossing of 1,000yds, over land which was far more exposed to fire; also there was

little artillery protection. Aitken's platoon followed quickly up Goose Alley and climbed out on the right at the point where the sunken road from FLERS to EAUCOURT L'ABBAYE crossed it. As they reached the road that ran due west to east, from the Abbaye to Factory Corner, they came under fire from machine guns and from their own artillery. The New Zealanders were virtually annihilated and Aitken himself was wounded. Nevertheless, the trenches were reached by the next day, 28 September, when the village fell.

On the night of 1/2 October, 12th Division relieved 21st Division, with 37th Brigade taking over the right, including the northern and eastern extremities of Gueudecourt, and the 36th Brigade on the left, occupying Gird and Gird Support Trenches.

The next battle in this area was the Battle of the Transloy Ridges, lasting from 7 to 20 October; as has been mentioned, Gueudecourt was in the hands of 37th Brigade at the time. To the north-east of the village there were many trenches with unusual names, including Bayonet, Hilt, Rainbow and beyond them Bacon, Grease, Mild and beyond them Barley, Bread, Stormy and Cloudy Trenches; all these were in the direction of the village of Beaulencourt to the north-east.

At this time Fourth Army were occupying the whole front from LESBŒUFS to DESTREMONT FARM in support of the French advance at SAILLY-SAILLISEL. On a front stretching roughly between the road from HIGH WOOD to le Barque and the road that ran north from Gueudecourt, 9th Royal Fusiliers (36th Brigade, 12th Division) were on the extreme right and 26th Royal Fusiliers (124th Brigade, 41st Division) on the extreme left. Before these battalions lay the trenches and strongpoints that formed the outer defences of Ligny-Thilloy. On 7 October, 8th and 9th Royal Fusiliers (both 36th Brigade, 12th Division) were involved in an unsuccessful attack on the very strongly held positions towards Bayonet Trench.

Anthony Eden of 21st King's Royal Rifle Corps, which at the beginning of the Transloy Ridges action was to the left of 12th Division, wrote: 'The incline at Gird Ridge towards the front line was a gentle one into a valley of dead ground which extended for at least a hundred yards. It ended against a bank topped with some scruffy and shell torn bushes.' Eden's commanding officer, Maj G. Foljambe, decided that the foot of the bank should be their headquarters from before Zero Hour. The attack was postponed for 2 days until 7 October, when the weather grew rapidly worse; Turk Lane, which was waterlogged in several places, was the only communication trench.

At 1400hrs, the British barrage came down; this brought an immediate response from the Germans, who fired on the Gird Ridge and elsewhere. Ordered to provide close support, 21st King's Royal Rifle Corps could also hear the machine-gun fire that the Royal Fusiliers were enduring. The British preliminary bombardment had not silenced the machine guns and very soon 21st King's Royal Rifle Corps came over the slope and down the ridge towards the battalion headquarters. Nothing went right; the machine-gunners took heavy toll of the Riflemen in addition to the Fusiliers.

On the evening of 8 October, 21st King's Royal Rifle Corps moved their headquarters to Factory Corner, at a crossroads on the Gueudecourt–Eaucourt road. Under this battered building, of which nothing but rubble remained, were some quite strong cellars; these could just accommodate two battalion headquarters with their staffs and signallers. Unfortunately, the site was also well known to the enemy, who had previously used the factory cellars themselves, and as a result kept up an almost continuous bombardment. Eden preferred the bank. They remained there through 9 October, and were relieved the next night by 17th Manchesters and 2nd Royal Scots Fusiliers (both 90th Brigade, 30th Division).

On 9 October, 1st Newfoundlanders (88th Brigade, 29th Division) came to relieve the Royal Fusiliers battalions via CORBIE and BERNAFAY WOOD and then DELVILLE WOOD. By 0930hrs, 1st Newfoundlanders were manning a 500yd section on the northern outskirts of Gueudecourt, immediately to the left of the road running north-eastwards to Beaulencourt; 1st Essex (also 88th Brigade, 29th Division) were in positions of support to the rear. 88th Brigade's first objective was Green Line, about 400yds from the British Front Line; this would necessitate the capture of a part of Hilt Trench, while its extensions of Rainbow Trench to the south-east and Bayonet Trench to the north-west formed the main German position opposite Fourth Army. Brown Line, about 400yds beyond Green Line, was the second objective. Zero Hour was set at 1405hrs; during the night, 1st Essex had moved up to the left of 1st Newfoundlanders and 2nd Hampshires (also 88th Brigade, 29th Division) took over from 1st Essex in support, and 4th Worcesters (also 88th Brigade, 29th Division) had arived from CORBIE.

Due to an excellent creeping barrage, the two attacking battalions kept pace with the first part of the attack, which was successful; the enemy machine-gunners were kept at bay and Hilt Trench was captured. However, 1st Essex got into trouble as 35th Brigade (12th Division) left an open flank next to them. This in turn depleted the flank of 1st Newfoundlanders, and bombing parties had to be quickly organised. Their trench lay in a small depression overlooking the German-held ridge to the north-east.

On 13 October, 1st Newfoundlanders handed over responsibility for Hilt Trench and returned to a position close to Bull Trench at FLERS. Between 10 October and their relief, they suffered 239 casualties.

In *Field Guns in France*, Lt N. Fraser-Tytler of CL Brigade, Royal Field Artillery (30th Division), noted that on 15 October, the area to the north of Gueudecourt was a collection of German saps and strongpoints based on an old gun position, the whole lying in a curious salient, surrounded on three sides by Allied trenches. As a consequence, the Germans were immune from routine harassing fire. He noted that his unit continued laying their communication cables and reported to brigade whenever they spotted 'a host of German helmets'.

On 16 October, 9th Norfolks (71st Brigade, 6th Division) were in front of trenches towards the enemy ridge east of Gueudecourt facing LE TRANSLOY, with their battalion headquarters on a reverse slope. On 18 October, 12th Division's objective was Mild Trench, approximately 1,000yds out of Gueudecourt on the road to Beaulencourt. Part of Mild Trench was captured before their relief on 19 October, but the fighting was very costly in terms of casualties.

In the fighting between 23 October and 5 November, 1st Australian Division and 2nd Division held the village; 8th Division, followed by 17th Division, were to their right.

On 17 November, the front line ran in front of the village south of Ligny-Thilloy and west of LE TRANSLOY. On the outskirts of the village on the Beaulencourt road stands the Newfoundland Memorial above a former strongpoint with a curve of trenches and machine-gun posts that had been the site of the regimental position. It is close to the final line reached by the British Army by the end of Fourth Army's operations in this sector on 5 November.

GUILLEMONT is on the D20 going eastwards to COMBLES and on the D64 road going south-west to MONTAUBAN-DE-PICARDIE; LONGUEVAL and DELVILLE WOOD lie to the north-west and GINCHY is to the north-east.

In the second half of July 1916, there was continuous fighting for possession of the village; it was briefly captured by 2nd Royal Scots Fusiliers (90th Brigade, 30th Division) on 30 July, but they were obliged to retire. On 8 August, 55th Division also entered the village briefly, and 10 days later it was reached by 2nd Division. Guillemont was finally captured by 20th Division and part of the 16th Division on 3 September; it remained in Allied hands until March 1918, when it was retaken by the Germans, only to be liberated at the end of August by 18th and 38th Divisions.

A main German line ran in a south-easterly direction from LONGUEVAL in front of the village, which took in the railway station and quarry. It continued around the back of ARROW HEAD COPSE and went behind WEDGE WOOD towards the French lines beyond MAUREPAS.

The problem with attacking the village was that the way lay over perfectly bare country; the enemy had excellent observation from LEUZE WOOD and beyond, to the east of Guillemont. The quarry to the west of the village had been made into a strong redoubt and the ground to the south of it between MALTZ HORN FARM and FAFFEMONT FARM, with ANGLE WOOD in the centre, was held by the enemy in considerable strength. A trench known as Brighton Road Trench was north of Guillemont station.

According to Basil Liddell Hart in his *History of the First World War*, the village became a shambles of horror. The way to it from TRÔNES WOOD was down a slope, up another slope – now only a few hundred yards of farm road, yet in July and August 1916 it seemed to be an infinite distance. On 23 July, 21st Brigade (30th Division) tried to enter Guillemont but were let down by a lack of artillery support; 19th Manchesters advanced from TRÔNES WOOD, aided by 2nd Yorkshires (both 21st Brigade, 30th Division), but both had to withdraw, with 19th Manchesters suffering many casualties.

The date for the next attempt to take the village was 30 July; this time, it was planned that 30th Division would attack through 35th Division's lines. 89th Brigade (30th Division) were to advance as far as the southern edge of the village, while 5th Brigade (2nd Division) were to take Guillemont station, as well as the German trenches to the north of it. During the night of 29/30 July, the German artillery bombarded the TRÔNES WOOD area very heavily, and in the morning there was a thick mist, with visibility down to about 40yds in places. Zero Hour was 0445hrs; MALTZ HORN FARM was quickly taken and the advance carried on downhill in an easterly direction. 2nd Royal Scots Fusiliers advanced from TRÔNES WOOD and

entered the village from the south-west, and after waiting for the barrage to catch up, proceeded to the north-west of the village and joined up with 18th Manchesters (90th Brigade, 30th Division). The latter were severely hampered by crossfire of machine guns from both the Quarries and Guillemont station. Uncut wire at the station held up companies of 16th Manchesters (also 90th Brigade, 30th Division). During the afternoon the Germans counter-attacked and the Allied barrage was hampered by the fact that three companies of 2nd Royal Scots Fusiliers were holding out in the village. They virtually disappeared as the enemy managed to appear behind them from WEDGE WOOD to the south and cut them off.

Throughout the day, communication was very difficult. CSM G. Evans of 18th Manchesters was awarded the Victoria Cross for his gallant service as a runner:

> when under heavy rifle and machine-gun fire he volunteered to take back an important message after five runners had been killed in attempting to do so. He had to cover about 700 yards, the whole of which was under observation from the enemy. Company Sergt.-Major Evans, however, succeeded in delivering the message, and although wounded, rejoined his company, although advised to go to the dressing station. The return journey to the company again meant a journey of 700 yards under severe rifle and machine-gun fire, but by dodging from shell-hole to shell-hole he was able to do so, and was taken prisoner some hours later.

2nd Division also made an attempt on the village, using 2nd Oxfordshire & Buckinghamshire Light Infantry and 24th Royal Fusiliers (both 5th Brigade). The *Official History of the War* noted that it was hardly surprising that the attack failed, as did that of 23 July, for the tactics were the same. An attack from the west up the exposed shallow trough marking the termination of CATERPILLAR VALLEY, and from the south-west over ground that was sloping and devoid of cover, had little chance of success.

As a consequence of these failures, another plan of attack was made; this time it would be carried out on 8 August. 55th Division were to capture the village, except for the northern edge and the railway station, which were both to be objectives of 2nd Division. Zero Hour was 0420hrs, and once again it was a misty morning. Those involved included 1/5th King's (165th Brigade, 55th Division) and 1/4th King's Own (164th Brigade, 55th Division); both battalions were to be checked opposite the south-west part of the village. 1/8th King's (also 164th Brigade, 55th Division) got as far as the Quarries and fought their way into Guillemont, but were never seen again. 2/Lt G.G. Coury of 3rd South Lancashires (attached 1/4th South Lancashires, pioneers of 55th Division) was awarded the Victoria Cross for helping to bring in Maj J.L. Swainson, who died within minutes of being rescued. This action took place close to ARROW HEAD COPSE.

2nd Division duly attacked, using two battalions of 6th Brigade, 1st King's and 17th Middlesex, but made little progress. 166th Brigade relieved 164th Brigade (both 55th Division); 1/10th King's (166th Brigade, 55th Division) lost heavily, and 1/5th Loyal North Lancashires (also 166th Brigade, 55th Division) and 1/7th King's (165th Brigade, 55th Division) made little headway. 2nd Division put in 13th Essex and 17th Middlesex (both 6th Brigade, 2nd Division), but they too failed. During the day's fighting, 1/8th King's and 1st King's had been virtually cut off in the fight for the village.

Summing up the problem the attackers had, H.P. Robinson, war correspondent of *The Times*, noted in *The Turning Point* that the difficulty with Guillemont lay chiefly to the south of the village, in the region of ARROW HEAD COPSE, by MALTZ HORN FARM to the junction with the French Army near ANGLE WOOD; the lie of the ground there, with the low wooded ravine running out north-eastward from ANGLE WOOD, was particularly adapted to defence. The Machine Gun House also played a vital role in the German defences.

The *History of the Royal Fusiliers* notes that three battalions of the regiment played a part in these operations; 1st Royal Fusiliers (17th Brigade, 24th Division) were in the area from 8 August, when they took over trenches from DELVILLE WOOD to TRÔNES WOOD.

Capt N.G. Chavasse of the Royal Army Medical Corps, attached to 1/10th King's, received the Victoria Cross for his bravery on 9 August.

Though severely wounded early in the attack whilst carrying a wounded soldier to the dressing station he refused to leave his post, and for 2 days not only continued to perform his duties but in addition went out repeatedly under heavy fire to search for and attend to the wounded who were lying out. During these searches, although practically without food, worn with fatigue and faint with his wound, he assisted to carry in a number of badly wounded men over heavy and difficult ground. By his extraordinary energy and inspiring

example he was instrumental in rescuing many wounded who would have otherwise undoubtedly succumbed under the bad weather conditions.

Chavasse was to be awarded a bar to his VC in February 1917 for bravery at Wieltje, Ypres.

On 12 August, the British were involved in a joint attack with the French in which their role was to capture a spur to the south of Guillemont. The attack again failed.

From 12 to 14 August, 3rd Rifle Brigade (17th Brigade, 24th Division) were in reserve just to the west of Guillemont. Andrew Buxton was a member of this battalion; one of his fellow officers was 2/Lt R.E. Vernéde, the French writer and poet. On 8 August, Buxton reported seeing masses of guns in the area as he went up the west side of BERNAFAY WOOD and Longueval Alley towards the top of TRÔNES WOOD. On 12 August, he was involved in working on trenches at LONGUEVAL. On 15 August, there had been heavy rain, and Buxton observed Guillemont from ARROW HEAD COPSE.

In the Imperial War Museum's oral history collection is a recording of Lt E.K. Page, an artillery section commander. He had been posted to No. 6 Battery, XL Brigade, Royal Field Artillery (3rd Division), joining them in action on or about 15–16 August near MARICOURT. His Division were next to the French, on the front FAFFEMONT FARM–Guillemont. He was sent to man the night observation post, which was 'a very alarming experience' for a young officer. Observation post work was very unpleasant, especially in hot August weather with many corpses remaining unburied.

On 17 August, the headquarters of 1st Royal Fusiliers was at WATERLÔT FARM. The next attack was to begin at 1445hrs on 18 August on a broad front, with three other divisions cooperating; 3rd Rifle Brigade's objective was Guillemont station, while 8th Buffs (17th Brigade, 24th Division) were directed against a trench some 200yds from the front line in the direction of GINCHY. The station, lying on a light railway just to the north of the village, had become a tactical feature of some importance, and later in the month was to be the scene of a vigorous counter-attack. 12th Royal Fusiliers (also 17th Brigade, 24th Division) were in reserve during the battle.

The latest plan was to capture Guillemont with the assistance of the French; this time, the attack would be spread over 2 days. XIV Corps' objective on 18 August was a line from ANGLE WOOD to the spur south of Guillemont, and then through the west side of the village to the railway station and the German

Front Line further to the north. On the right of the village, 76th Brigade (3rd Division) attacked in the area of Lonely Trench, but the attack failed. On the right section of 24th Division, 73rd Brigade attacked, but were also checked. A section of 7th Northamptons (73rd Brigade, 24th Division) made a lodgement in the Quarries, south of the station, and were reinforced by 9th Royal Sussex (also 73rd Brigade, 24th Division). It was during these actions that Lt Col E.R. Mobbs DSO, Officer Commanding 7th Northamptons, was severely wounded.

On the left, 3rd Rifle Brigade had some success and, together with 8th Buffs, were involved in a successful bombing attack on ZZ Trench; the two battalions then 'joined hands' and moved north-eastwards. However, later in the day the German counter-attacks, supported by artillery, regained the ground. During the night of 19/20 August, 3rd Division were relieved by 35th Division.

One of 5 officers and 20 men of his battalion killed on 18 August 1916, 2/Lt G.F. Marsden-Smedley of 5th Rifle Brigade (attached 3rd Rifle Brigade, 17th Brigade, 24th Division) has a small memorial, erected close to the Guillemont–LONGUEVAL road (High Holborn) in the 1920s. This is probably on the site of the German Front Line trench dug in defence of the ruins of the station that was such a bone of contention between the opposing sides. Marsden-Smedley is also commemorated on the Thiepval Memorial. The War Office wrote to his family giving them details of his burial at a point between TRÔNES WOOD and Guillemont with a 'durable wooden cross'. No effects were found on his body. By the mid-1990s, the memorial was in a sorry state; a major refurbishment was organised and a service of rededication took place on 19 July 1997, attended by his family as well as by local dignitaries.

We have a detailed account of the fighting here at this time in *Stand To*, written by Capt F.C. Hitchcock of 2nd Leinsters (73rd Brigade, 24th Division). The ruins of Guillemont stood on the highest point of the ridge and dominated the surrounding countryside. The Germans were only too well aware of its importance and had already 'seen off' the Allied attacks on three occasions. Hitchcock viewed the attack from battalion headquarters at the Brickworks, which was about 1,000yds as the crow flies from the jumping-off trenches before Guillemont. The attack had got to within 30yds of the objectives, but when the barrage lifted, the Germans rushed up from deep dugouts and directed withering fire on the troops; machine guns concealed in a sunken road running between the advancing battalions also enfiladed the two units. The attack failed.

On the left, 17th Brigade captured some small posts near WATERLÔT FARM and a party of 7th Northamptons captured a small post at the Quarries, close to the station (see above); they were relieved by 1st North Staffords (72nd Brigade, 24th Division) during the night, and went to sleep in funk-holes. On waking, they found themselves surrounded by dead of 1st North Staffords, who had been caught by the enemy when involved in the relief during the night.

Also on 20 August, Buxton of 3rd Rifle Brigade remarks that there was a dugout with two entrances at Guillemont. On 21 August, he mentions Brompton Road and Hill Street, which was a continuation of High Holborn, and noted that a new line was being established from the east end of the station to Brompton Road.

The *Official History of the War* noted that on 21 August, 3rd Rifle Brigade and 8th Buffs were occupying without fighting most of the portion of ZZ Trench in their sector, but that further fighting later in the day was unsuccessful. Between 18 and 22 August, 3rd Rifle Brigade maintained hold of the station, taking some prisoners on 18 August. On 21 August, battalions of the Royal Fusiliers attacked in the rear of the enemy's position in the Quarries to the west of the village. One of the reasons the village was held so doggedly was that the enemy had strong supports in tunnel dugouts.

One of the minor excitements of the battle occurred on 21 August, when continuous explosions came from the Stokes mortar ammunition dump. 1st Royal Fusiliers advanced at 1530hrs, their objectives being Hill Street and Brompton Road. On relief, they went to HAPPY VALLEY near BRAY-SUR-SOMME, as did Buxton with 3rd Rifle Brigade on 22 August. Also on 22 August, 20th Division relieved 24th Division in the sector north of the Guillemont–MONTAUBAN-DE-PICARDIE road; 6th Division's artillery, which had been attached to 20th Division since 17 August, when they had replaced that of the Guards, also moved into the new area. On 22 August, 11th King's Royal Rifle Corps (59th Brigade, 20th Division) were in the area; they were attacked by the enemy on the following day and relieved by 11th Rifle Brigade (59th Brigade, 20th Division) on 24 August.

By a coincidence, Ernst Jünger of Füsilier-Regiment *Generalfeldmarschall Prinz Albrecht von Preußen* (Hannoverschen) Nr. 73 (111. Infanterie Division), the author of *The Storm of Steel*, and Hitchcock faced one another at the front line near the station in the period 24–26 August. Jünger arrived in the Somme area at SAILLY-SAILLISEL on 23 August before staying a night in the almost totally destroyed village of COMBLES. It is clear from his writings that his 48-hour stay in the German lines at Guillemont was extremely unpleasant and that he was glad to be relieved. Both sides suffered equally, although the British artillery were particularly effective, as was aerial observation from balloons and aircraft. Jünger was soon wounded on his return to COMBLES, and was then taken off to hospital at Fins and later SAINT-QUENTIN.

On 25 August, the trenches were on low foreground in the valley south of Guillemont; at this time, 20th Division's positions were 600yds to 800yds south-west of FAFFEMONT FARM. At night, a trench was being dug 400yds nearer the enemy lines, which was to be used as a new jumping-off position. German troops were spotted in an old concrete gun pit some 300yds beyond the Allied front line. A further attack was planned for 27 August, but at this time bad weather set in and this, together with heavy hostile shelling in which gas shells were largely used, made the work extremely difficult. The trenches became waterlogged and deep in mud. The state of the CARNOY–MONTAUBAN-DE-PICARDIE road was such that at one time on 29 August, 37 vehicles were either broken down there or stuck in the mud.

At the end of August, the enemy line continued to run a little to the west and north-west of Guillemont, which, being part of the German original line of defence, was still strongly fortified. To the north, high ground extended for about 3,000yds, with the village of GINCHY at the highest point. Running more or less south from the south-west corner of the village were two sunken roads, which gave more trouble than any other obstacle encountered both in this battle and in earlier attempts to capture Guillemont.

The plan on this occasion was to attack the village from the north side, as well as from the west and south. To carry out this plan it was necessary to dig assembly trenches to the north of Guillemont station. 59th Brigade (20th Division) were to cover the right of the attack with their headquarters at the Brickworks, while 47th Brigade (16th Division) were to cover the left flank, their headquarters being near the north-east corner of BERNAFAY WOOD. Two supporting battalions also came from 61st Brigade (20th Division).

On 3 September, 59th Brigade had the southern part of Guillemont as their objective; 6th Oxfordshire & Buckinghamshire Light Infantry (60th Brigade, 20th Division) and 7th Somerset Light Infantry (61st Brigade, 20th Division) came up to help with the assault. Between 3 and 5 September,

10th and 11th Rifle Brigade were very successful in the attacks on Guillemont, and 150 prisoners were captured.

47th Brigade (16th Division) were brought up to replace 60th Brigade in the attack on the northern part of the village. On the left of 59th Brigade, 10th King's Royal Rifle Corps pressed forward; 6th Connaughts (47th Brigade, 16th Division) followed suit on the northern side of Mount Street. To confuse matters, an observer of 6th Connaughts' role wrote that a part of the battalion 'ran away like a rabble' despite the pleas of their officers. This same man, 2nd Lt H.D. Paviere of No. 61 Company, Machine Gun Corps (Liddle Collection at Leeds), also reports that on one occasion he sheltered in the tomb of the Waterlôt family in Guillemont churchyard.

At this time, Pte T. Hughes of 6th Connaughts won the Victoria Cross. Part of his citation reads: 'he was wounded in an attack, but returned at once to the firing line after his wounds were dressed. Later, seeing a hostile machine-gun, he dashed out in front of his company, shot the gunner, and single-handed captured the gun. Though again wounded he brought back three or four prisoners.'

At midday, the rest of the line advanced and from right to left, 10th and 11th Rifle Brigade and 10th King's Royal Rifle Corps reached their objectives. 10th King's Royal Rifle Corps had to mop up at the Quarries after 6th Connaughts had rushed forward without consolidating the position; on the left of the division, 7th Leinsters (47th Brigade, 16th Division) captured the trenches beyond Guillemont station.

Lt J.V. Holland of 3rd Leinsters (attached 7th Leinsters) gained the Victoria Cross for his bravery at this time. In part his citation reads:

> during a heavy engagement when, not content with bombing hostile dug-outs within the objective, he fearlessly led his bombers through our own artillery barrage and cleared a great part of the village in front. He started out with 26 bombers and finished up with only five, after capturing some 50 prisoners. By this very gallant action he undoubtedly broke the spirit of the enemy, and thus saved us many casualties when the battalion made a further advance. He was far from well at the time, and later had to go to hospital.

Advance to the second objective began at 1250hrs. In 59th Brigade, the leading battalions were reinforced by 6th Oxfordshire & Buckinghamshire Light Infantry and 7th Somerset Light Infantry. 8th Royal Munster Fusiliers (47th Brigade, 16th

Division) passed through 6th Connaughts' lines. During this fighting, Capt C.S. Chandler of 8th Royal Munster Fusiliers won the Military Cross when 'although wounded [he] led his men and beat off repeated German attacks'. By 1315hrs, North and South Street were being consolidated.

In 47th Brigade, 6th Royal Irish took up the attack and had reached a position to the north of 59th Brigade's line; the Irish had held the sunken road and had suffered losses through shell-fire before reaching the road. Earlier in the day, a 'push pipe' mine had been exploded, with the object of destroying a German machine-gun emplacement in the line of the sunken road opposite ARROW HEAD COPSE; in the event, it didn't reach that far – and gunfire destroyed it anyway.

59th Brigade ordered forward 7th Duke of Cornwall's Light Infantry (61st Brigade, 20th Division) into Guillemont and contact was made with 95th Brigade (5th Division). At this time, Capt A.K. Totton of 1st Duke of Cornwall's Light Infantry (95th Brigade, 5th Division) was awarded the Military Cross for his bravery. Although wounded, he led his men on to the first objective, where he bombed the enemy dugouts and was again hit by a bomb. He then went on to the second objective, being wounded a third time on the way. Meanwhile 7th Division had entered GINCHY, but were soon forced out. At Guillemont the flanks were secured and the village was at last taken by the Allies.

Sgt D. Jones of 12th King's (61st Brigade, 20th Division) was awarded the Victoria Cross when in charge of a platoon well forward of the village, towards GINCHY.

> The platoon to which he belonged was ordered to a forward position, and during the advance came under heavy machine-gun fire, the officer being killed and the platoon suffering heavy losses. Sergt. Jones led forward the remainder, occupied the position, and held it for 2 days and 2 nights without food or water, until relieved. On the second day he drove back three counter-attacks inflicting heavy losses.

Jones was later killed, on 7 October, and is buried at Bancourt British Cemetery near BAPAUME (V.F.20).

The writer Gilbert Frankau was possibly also involved in the battle. He had formerly been in 9th East Surreys and in 1915 was transferred to the Royal Artillery. He later wrote a novel entitled *Peter Jackson, Cigar Merchant*, in which he fictionalised

his war service experience; for example, he uses the name of 'The Chalkshires' or 'The Fourthdowns'. In the book, the hero's battery sets off for the Somme with four guns, eight wagons, a water cart, 125 horses and 138 helmeted men, heavy transport bringing up the rear. At Guillemont, 'Peter Jackson' was wounded and was taken back to London. He writes of the experiences of being a liaison officer; it seems likely that Frankau himself was such an officer.

Still with the Royal Artillery, we have the following from *The War Diary of the Master of Belhaven*. The Master's name was Lt Col The Hon. R.G.A. Hamilton, in charge of an artillery brigade of 24th Division; in 1917, he returned to the area and saw hundreds of white crosses in the long grass. In many cases, rifles were stuck in the ground with a steel helmet on top. From GINCHY, he made his way down the famous sunken road, which was the final objective for 3 September 1916 in what was left of Guillemont. He found the sunken road where his guns were formerly and went along it to the Quarries. The hundreds of dead had gone. There was rank vegetation and a famous concrete machine-gun emplacement that had defied the British artillery. Hamilton left his horse and walked to ARROW HEAD COPSE. There was at the time a large railway junction at the corner of TRÔNES WOOD.

In the end, Guillemont, the village that had been converted into a fortress with a chain of dugouts and tunnels that defied the heaviest artillery barrages, fell to 20th Division and part of 16th Division. John Buchan wrote as follows:

> The British right, attacking in the afternoon, swept through Guillemont to the sunken road – 500 yards to the east. They captured Ginchy also but were forced later in the day to relinquish the eastern part of that village. Further south they fought to the east of Faffemont Farm, where they joined hands with the triumphant French . . . So Guillemont was a triumph for the troops of Southern and Western Ireland. The men of Munster, Leinster, and Connaught broke through the intricate defences of the enemy as a torrent sweeps down rubble. The place was one of the strongest of all the many fortified villages in the German line, and its capture was the most important since the taking of Pozières.

In *The Turning Point*, H.P. Robinson, war correspondent of *The Times*, noted that the result of the capture of Guillemont was that the lower corner of

DELVILLE WOOD down to Angle Wood Ravine allowed the whole of the British line to be pushed forward. What had been the German second main line was now British as far as the junction with the French. It was the labyrinth of tunnels in the village which explained the fates of the disappearing battalions, 1st and 8th King's, as well as 2nd Royal Scots Fusiliers.

Basil Liddell Hart of 9th King's Own Yorkshire Light Infantry (64th Brigade, 21st Division) commented that at last, on 3 September, Guillemont was secured. GINCHY, a few hundred yards further up the slope, was a similar obstruction for another 6 days.

On 4 and 5 September, divisional orders instructed 48th and 59th Brigades (both 16th Division) to relieve 47th Brigade (also 16th Division) and 60th Brigade (20th Division). On 9 September, 1st Welsh Guards (3rd Guards Brigade, Guards Division) left Citadel Camp, south of FRICOURT, for Guillemont; their headquarters was on the outskirts of the village. 4th Grenadier Guards (also 3rd Guards Brigade, Guards Division) were led to the incorrect line, somewhere to

The road leading to Guillemont, 11 September 1916. (IWM Q1163)

the east of the village. 2/Lt E. Cazalet of 1st Welsh Guards was killed by a shell on 10 September and is buried at Citadel Cemetery (II.A.4).

According to a file in the Imperial War Museum (IWM 81/19/1 & 1A), Lt Col P.F. Story DSO & Bar was Officer Commanding No. 96 Field Company, Royal Engineers (20th Division), at Guillemont on 10 September. In a letter sent home, Story mentioned that his division had taken the village on or about 3 September, when his brigade were on the right; 2 of his officers and 41 sappers were wounded, 600 Germans were taken prisoner and many others were killed or wounded who belonged to Jünger's regiment, Füsilier-Regiment Nr. 73. 'Guillemont was blotted right out, not one brick standing on another – nothing but a sea of crump holes of all sorts and sizes.'

In *Victorian Son*, Stuart Cloete of 9th King's Own Yorkshire Light Infantry wrote of this same period: 'One day I was sent to reconnoitre a position at Guillemont. I saw white-painted noticeboards with the name Guillemont on them, but no village. It was behind the lines. Even the glasses showed nothing. Then I watched the shells bursting and noticed that in one place they were sending up clouds of red brick dust. I had found my village.'

On 24 September, Geoffrey Malins, the official War Office photographer had this to say about the scene at Guillemont: 'Before the 25 September attack the village of Guillemont did not exist, in fact, it was an absolute impossibility to tell where the fields ended and the village began.'

Guillemont was one of the most awful specimens of the devastating trail of war that existed on the Western Front. The Germans had turned the village into a veritable fortress; trenches and strongpoints, bristling with machine guns, commanded every point that gave vantage to the enemy. Between 26 and 27 September, 10th and 11th Rifle Brigade (both 59th Brigade, 20th Division) were in reserve and handed over to the French on 27 September. In early October, Lt N. Fraser-Tytler of CL Brigade, Royal Field Artillery (30th Division), wrote that the station in the village, a mass of craters, was then headquarters of a brigade of the Guards Division.

In *2/3rd City of London Field Ambulance* is the following entry for around 9 October: 'The area round Leuze Wood, Guillemont and Ginchy was a nightmare. There had been little time to devote to the burial of the dead and the corpses lay literally in heaps where the fighting had been severe.'

In *Twelve Days*, Sidney Rogerson of 2nd West Yorkshires (23rd Brigade, 8th Division) wrote that on 16 November, orders were brutally short. One item was enough. The battalion was to find a working party of 6 officers and 300 men. The party was set to work till 1600hrs and was required to supply labour for a Decauville railway track, which the sappers were laying at Guillemont, 'of all unhealthy places'. In November the village was a walking wounded station.

In his book *A Subaltern on the Somme*, Max Plowman of 10th West Yorkshires (50th Brigade, 17th Division) noted that in January 1917, after taking part in training courses, 'this afternoon we marched to Guillemont, where we spent the night in shelters that were half dugouts. Shells dropped in Trones Wood as we came by, but otherwise the march was uneventful. As a battalion we tramped the old duck boards again yesterday, and now we have two companies in the front line (this time to the right of Lesbœufs).'

Guillemont Road Cemetery is between the village and TRÔNES WOOD, on the north side of the D64 road to MONTAUBAN-DE-PICARDIE. Just inside the entrance is the grave of Lt Raymond Asquith of 3rd Grenadier Guards (2nd Guards Brigade, Guards Division), a son of the former prime minister. The cemetery was begun by fighting units of the Guards Division and field ambulances after the battle for Guillemont and was closed in March 1917, when it contained 121 graves. It was greatly increased after

the Armistice by the concentration of 2,139 graves, almost all from the period July–September 1916 and from the battlefield surrounding the village.

Asquith had been mortally wounded while leading a half-company of 3rd Grenadier Guards (2nd Guards Brigade, Guards Division) in the attack towards LESBŒUFS. He was later given morphine by the medical officer of 1st Scots Guards (also 2nd Guards Brigade, Guards Division) but died at the dressing station. Asquith is buried in Grave I.B.3 and his grave inscription was taken from the Epilogue of Shakespeare's *King Henry V*: 'Small time, but in that small most greatly lived this star of England.' A friend of Asquith's, Lt The Hon. E.W. Tennant of 4th Grenadier Guards (3rd Guards Brigade, Guards Division), is also buried in the cemetery close by; a son of Baron Glenconner, he was killed on 22 September.

Behind the grave of Raymond Asquith is that of Lt Col J.C. Stormonth Darling (I.C.1) of 1st Cameronians, Commanding Officer 1/9th Highland Light Infantry (100th Brigade, 33rd Division), who was killed by a sniper in the front line beyond LES-BŒUFS on 1 November while touring the trenches and brought back to this cemetery for burial by his men. 1/9th Highland Light Infantry had been previously ordered to attack the low ridge in front of LE TRANSLOY, but the attack 'petered out in mud'.

Also buried here is Lt Col A. Mack (IX.A.2) of 9th Suffolks (71st Brigade, 6th Division), killed in action on 15 September. At the end of June 1915, 9th Suffolks left England without Capt Mack, who had broken a small bone in his foot and followed later; in mid-May 1916, he took over when the commanding officer was wounded. Reaching ALBERT on 4 August, 9th Suffolks took over trenches in front of Mailly-Maillet Wood. Until 28 August, with an intermission at LOUVENCOURT, they were involved in clearing the 36th Division battlefield. On 13 September, they took part in a 6th Division attack on the Quadrilateral near GINCHY. Two days later the fighting continued; Zero Hour was 0620hrs, with 9th Suffolks supporting 9th Norfolks (71st Brigade, 6th Division). At 0830hrs, Mack, who had moved his headquarters into the front-line trenches at Zero Hour, was killed by machine-gun fire while watching the battalion. All the senior officers were either killed or wounded. No medals were awarded as Mack was no longer there to recommend them.

Deeply involved in attempts to capture Guillemont, 3rd Rifle Brigade were commemorated by a memorial cross retained in Guillemont Road Cemetery. It was dedicated to the memory of 74 officers and men who were killed or missing in the August–September 1916 period. The cross was offered

La rue d'En-Bas, Guillemont, after the war.
(Peter F. Batchelor Collection)

to the Rifle Brigade for their museum in Winchester and was returned to England in 1932.

In the Imperial War Graves Commission Archive it is noted that in the early 1930s Guillemont Road Cemetery was considered for use for further burials, but the owner of the proposed land placed 'unreasonable demands' and the work was transferred elsewhere.

During the war a battlefield memorial had been erected to commemorate 2 officers and 53 men of 11th King's Royal Rifle Corps killed or missing during the fighting at Guillemont in August and September 1916. Two copper plates bearing the 55 names were found in the Guillemont Communal Cemetery in 1931 and returned to the King's Royal Rifle Corps Depot for the regimental museum.

After the war Guillemont was 'adopted' by Hornsey and in 1917 a wooden memorial was erected to the 16th (Irish) Division close to the church. The 20th Division erected a wooden memorial of their own at the crossroads 500yds east of the village. It was later replaced by a more permanent one close to the same spot. In 1926 the 16th (Irish) memorial was replaced by a granite one. The wooden memorial was taken back to Ireland, where it became part of the Dublin Irish National Memorial.

H

HALLENCOURT is north-west of Amiens on the D173 road. Between August and November 1916, 4th, 5th, 6th, 7th, 16th, 33rd, 34th, 37th and 56th Divisions had links with the area and several of them had their divisional headquarters here.

Hallencourt Communal Cemetery can be found on the west side of the road to Sorel. Pte F. Hughes of 2nd Canterburys (2nd New Zealand Brigade, New Zealand Division), executed on 25 August 1916, is buried here.

HALLOY is on the D24, just south of the DOULLENS–Arras road, in 1916 due west of the GOMMECOURT lines. On 5 November 1915, elements of 109th Brigade (36th Division) were billeted here. In mid-February 1916, 19th Manchesters (attached 110th Brigade, 37th Division) were here.

In May and June, 56th Division virtually took over the village for training purposes and on 7 May, 1/5th and 1/16th Londons (both 169th Brigade, 56th Division) arrived here and went into hutments. Now part of VII Corps, 56th Division were concerned with preparation for the approaching battle. 1/16th Londons spent some time felling trees for the construction of gun emplacements and were required to be 'hewers of stone from quarries for the same purpose, and to unload trains at Mondicourt Station'; the station was to the north-west, close to the DOULLENS–Arras road. On 3 June, 1/16th Londons left Halloy for BAYENCOURT, with their transport going to COIGNEUX. On 20 June, 1/5th Londons marched to SAINT-AMAND.

On the same day, 1/14th Londons (168th Brigade, 56th Division) moved into huts at Halloy for intensive training. 'A system of trenches based on aeroplane photographs of the enemy's position between Gommecourt Wood and the Hebuterne–Puisieux Road had been marked out and dug out on the undulating ground near Hurtebise Farm.' South-east of the village, a track connected Halloy with Hurtebise Farm, north-west of the village of Famechon. The full-sized training model was used first by companies and battalions and then by the whole brigade; occasionally, training was carried out under a cover of smoke-screen.

In *Cannon Fodder*, A.S. Dolden wrote of his time with 1/14th Londons. On 20 May, when 1/12th Londons (168th Brigade, 56th Division) were also in the village, Dolden arrived here with his cookers, dispensed tea in an orchard and slept in a local barn. He wrote that the supply of water to the village was very bad and that he had to travel 3 miles to collect it. Aubrey Smith of 1/5th Londons (169th Brigade, 56th Division) wrote that in early June they were at Halloy again, and that his battalion were involved in battle rehearsals in the neighbouring wheatfields. Later, Smith's brigade moved up to the firing line again while the transport, which Smith was with, made their quarters at SOUASTRE. Although it was June, the weather was appalling; training was carried out in a morass and the GOMMECOURT rehearsals had to take place in slush and mud. In addition, roads were deep in mud and the back areas were also very bad.

On 2 June, 1/4th Londons (168th Brigade, 56th Division) arrived here from SOUASTRE and also spent their time in training; although retaining their billets, they were attached for duty with 169th Brigade. Among other tasks, the troops dug road materials in the Halloy quarries and carried logs for gun emplacements at PAS-EN-ARTOIS. They left Halloy for HÉBUTERNE on 13 June. On 3 June, 1/5th Londons returned here for training, also leaving on 13 June, for BAYENCOURT. They were back here on 22 June and continued to practise for the attack until 26 June, when a full-blown rehearsal took place.

On 8 June, 1/9th Londons (169th Brigade, 56th Division) were here for practice training until 13 June, when companies left for SAILLY-AU-BOIS and HÉBUTERNE; 169th Brigade were back here from 22 to 27 June, when they repeated the battle training over and over again. During this period, a 'memorable dinner' was held in a big hut on 22 June, when about 40 officers gathered as a sort of 'send off' for the 'Great Push'. Menu cards were passed round for autographing and 'a very pleasant evening was spent'. Eight days later, the names of 16 of the officers featured in the casualty lists for 1 July.

From 13 to 16 June, 1/7th Middlesex (167th Brigade, 56th Division) were here, afterwards moving to SAINT-AMAND. On 21 June, 1/16th Londons left BAYENCOURT for Halloy to complete their final training and to rehearse their part in the forthcoming attack; 1/12th Londons too were in huts in the village. Battalions from 56th Division were in and out all the time, having marched

> down the long tree-bordered hill into Pas and up again to Halloy . . . That peaceful little village seemed miles away from the warfare. An Army canteen had been installed, and there were several 'estaminets' where 'Veuve Clicquot' could be bought at 9 francs the bottle and 'vin ordinaire' and beer were wonderfully cheap, so that altogether Halloy was the ideal spot after Hebuterne. The only drawback to our comfort was the rain, which poured through the canvas huts in which the two brigades were billeted.

They spent their time, as did all other units, in practising the battle over replica trenches. On 27 June, the two brigades moved up to billets and bivouacs behind the front and 1/12th Londons moved to BAYENCOURT.

Aubrey Smith mentioned the new horse gasmasks that had been issued, and described attempts to fit the 'absurd respirators'. Smith's unit left Halloy on 27 June, when the companies went into huts at SOUASTRE, in the neighbourhood of a 12in gun. Transport made for SAINT-AMAND. During this time the divisional concert party, aptly called the Bow Bells, gave concerts in barns in SOUASTRE and Halloy.

This is not the place to discuss the GOMME-COURT debacle of 1 July, which occurred despite the intensive training. There is little doubt that 56th Division blamed 46th Division for the failure, but it wasn't as simple as that. Lt Gen T. Snow, General Officer Commanding VII Corps, came to Halloy and gave what in the circumstances was a very tactless speech to the survivors (Cab 45/1321 Letter A); 'when I heard that you had been driven back, I didn't care a damn. It did not matter whether you took your objectives or not. Our attack was only a feint to keep the German Guards Division occupied whilst the main attack was being made down south.' In July, units of 20th and 32nd Divisions were here, followed by elements of 32nd and 49th Divisions in September. At the end of October, 89th Brigade (30th Division) were here.

HAMEL is a village adjacent to the main railway line on the D50 road in the valley of the River Ancre; it is south of BEAUMONT-HAMEL and west of THIEPVAL. In 1915, the enemy lines crossed the valley in a solid wave to the north-east of the village and had the advantage of being partly protected by the river and marshes. The Allied lines were north of Hamel across the marshes and in front of Thiepval Wood.

During the summer of 1915, British 51st Division took over the Allied lines here from the French 22nd Division. In the following months, owing to its close proximity to the German Front Line, Hamel was often badly shelled, especially as the countdown to the end of June began.

By the end of March 1916, the north section of the front line had been shortened and 36th Division were now responsible for a sector known as 'astride the Ancre', with Hamel and Thiepval Wood as subsectors. The Wood was a dangerous place to loiter and the battalion in the Hamel sector had the additional task of being responsible for defending the swampy ANCRE VALLEY. Obviously, any attempt at making a trench line across swampy marsh was impossible; instead, a series of posts took its place. Hamel was to become very much a 'home' to 36th Division, and trenches were given names originating from Ulster.

May was mainly taken up with divisional training, much of it carried out near CLAIRFAYE FARM. Occasionally, raids on the enemy lines were organised; unfortunately, on 7 May, the night chosen was the same as that selected by the enemy, who carried out a raid on the lines of the adjacent 32nd Division. Many Ulstermen became casualties when they were trapped and pinned down in the Sunken Road.

In *The Old Front Line*, John Masefield noted that the church and the churchyard at Hamel made good posts from which British snipers could shoot across the river at the enemy, who were in SCHWABEN REDOUBT, the German stronghold almost due east of the village. One of the most frequently used causeways on the Ancre was directly in front of Hamel on the line of the road to the old mill, which lay to the left of the causeway on a sort of green island. The mill, which had not been destroyed at this time, could still be seen among the ruins. The Germans had a dressing station there at some time; its foundations are still there.

On 26 June, two heavy bridges were put across trenches between Mesnil and Hamel.

In preparation for dealing with the expected casualties on 1 July, there was a walking wounded collecting station for 36th Division here. The evacuation plan was simple, with a special route to be followed, described as 'a specially dug trench from the village to a point where the Hamel–Albert road was screened from observation'. Casualties would then be taken to dressing stations manned by 110th Field Ambulance (36th Division) at CLAIR-FAYE FARM, where the walking wounded would be dealt with, or to FORCEVILLE, manned by 108th Field Ambulance (also 36th Division) for lying cases.

36th Division had the task north of the River Ancre of moving across a valley north of the village, through the enemy lines, to the railway station at BEAUCOURT-SUR-L'ANCRE. By 0730hrs on 1 July, the trenches in front of the subsectors at Hamel and Thiepval Wood were packed with troops.

In *The Road to the Somme*, Philip Orr writes of an important command post in Hamel village in a 'stone-walled cottage with sandbagged windows and the only ventilation through the fireplace. On one wall was a large map of the entire British front and another of the 36th's area of attack. There were numerous telephones, and lighting was by paraffin lamps, some of them suspended from the beams. Near the cottage was a hastily built latrine . . .'

On 1 July, the main attacking troops in the Hamel sector on the west side of the River Ancre were 9th Royal Irish Fusiliers and 12th Royal Irish Rifles (both 108th Brigade, 36th Division); by the end of the day, they had made little progress. They had been attacking in a north-easterly direction, to the left of the Ancre marshland. One member of each battalion was to gain the Victoria Cross this day. T/ Lt G. St G.S. Cather, battalion adjutant of 9th Royal Irish Rifles (107th Brigade, 36th Division), won his posthumous VC for his courage near Hamel. The citation reads:

From 7 p.m. until midnight he searched No Man's Land and brought in three wounded men. Next morning at 8 a.m. he continued his search, brought in another wounded man, and gave water to others, arranging for their rescue later. Finally at 10.30 a.m he took water to another man, and was proceeding further when he himself was killed. All this was carried out in full view of the enemy, and under their direct machine-gun fire and intermittent artillery fire.

His name is commemorated on the Thiepval Memorial.

The second VC was Pte P. Quigg of 12th Royal Irish Rifles. His citation says:

He advanced to the assault with his platoon three times. Early next morning, hearing a rumour that his platoon officer was lying out wounded, he went out seven times to look for him under very heavy shell-fire and machine-gun fire, each time bringing back a wounded man. The last man he dragged in on a waterproof sheet from within a few yards of the enemy's wire. He was seven hours engaged in this most gallant work, and finally was so exhausted that he had to give it up . . .'

By mid-morning, according to Philip Orr, the atmosphere at the Hamel command post had grown grim: 'the air inside the sandbagged cottage grew stickier and more unpleasant in the July heat . . . Everyone felt cut off from the battle but they knew, despite all the confusion of reports coming in, that there had been great loss of life . . .'

As the disastrous day continued on the battlefield, behind the lines 'the wounded kept moving towards the dressing stations. Carts full of exhausted, bandaged men made their way slowly over the pot-holed Hamel–Albert road, each jolt an agony . . .'

The next time that Hamel was in the battle news was as part of the Ancre operations dated 3 September, and we have an eyewitness to the pre-battle conditions and also to the battle itself in the writings of Edmund Blunden, a lieutenant with 11th Royal Sussex (116th Brigade, 39th Division). His battalion moved south to Hamel and detached some parties on 26 and 27 August; on the latter day, they all moved to Mailly-Maillet Wood, which was viewed by German observation balloons and 'shelled unpleasantly'. The battalion shared the Wood and suffered the shelling. Blunden was in charge of work at Hamel and had his good friend Sgt Worley with him to help him with getting an ammunition store ready. In his book Blunden writes of places in Hamel that became familiar to them and the troops such as the Café du Centre,

which was all that was left of the level-crossing keeper's house. In the direction of THIEPVAL, the enormous British trench mortar, the 'flying pig', was discharging from a cellar in Hamel into the German lines.

On the evening of 2 September, 11th Royal Sussex moved from MAILLY-MAILLET by cross-country tracks through ENGLEBELMER over the downs of Mesnil and then assembled in the Hamel trenches to attack the following morning. They had used the long communication called JACOB'S LADDER, which emerged close to the Hamel bridge road, south of the village. They entered the assembly trenches at about midnight and Blunden stood at the junction of four advanced trenches, directing several companies into them as planned. Every man remembered the practice attacks carried out at Monchy Breton. When the rum and coffee was duly on the way to these men, he then went to his other duty. A carrying party from another battalion were to meet up with him in Hamel and for a time he and a fellow officer had nothing to do but wait. They walked along the river road and past a sandbagged dressing station that had been set up only 1 or 2 days earlier where the front line (Shanklin Terrace) crossed the road, which had already been battered in. They entered no man's land and saw some wounded troops of the Black Watch, who were trailing down the road; they had been wading the marshes of the River Ancre trying to take a machine-gun post called the Summer House (see THIEPVAL entry).

The Ancre operations had been postponed several times but this had not affected 39th Division, as they had only recently come into the sector. On 3 September, they were expected to capture three lines of hostile trenches on the spur south of BEAUMONT-HAMEL and, by an advance up the river valley, cover the flank of 49th Division to the right. In their positions to the north-west of the river, 116th and 117th Brigades (both 39th Division) began their advance at 0510hrs; 14th Hampshires (116th Brigade, 39th Division) and 11th Royal Sussex made progress, but the advance failed for a number of reasons, not least being the failure of 49th Division to their right, which allowed the enemy to enfilade their former trenches from the area of SAINT-PIERRE-DIVION. Having begun their attack at 0513hrs, 49th Division had been withdrawn by 1000hrs, by which time they were in no state to make a second attempt. The idea of a frontal attack against the Schwaben, however efficient the role of the artillery was, did not seem to have much chance of success.

Some parties of 11th Royal Sussex were not back in their lines until nightfall and Blunden mentions that his battalion were relieved by 'the Cheshires', probably 1/6th Cheshires (118th Brigade, 39th Division). After assembling in a trench along Hamel village street, 11th Royal Sussex arrived at ENGLEBELMER in the setting sun, 300 fewer in number than when they had passed through the village previously; Blunden described the battalion as being 'much impaired'. By 6 July, they had received 400 reinforcements and on 14 July they took over the extensive trenches in front of BEAUMONT-HAMEL.

In early October, the battalion headquarters of 1/1st Cambridgeshires (118th Brigade, 39th Division) was in dugouts burrowed out of the hillside. Below, 300yds away, they could see Hamel mill, with the Summer House (referred to above), the German strongpoint, in front of it. Further to the south was the SCHWABEN REDOUBT. They could observe the enemy lines and especially the German dressing station at MIRAUMONT. One of 1/1st Cambridgeshires' companies had sheltered in early October in Kentish Caves, alternating in and out of the line for 3 weeks. Mill Road, along which ammunition and stores had to travel each day, was always risky.

In October the lines were taken over by 63rd Division, whose sector Hamel now became. A renewed attack against BEAUMONT-HAMEL and BEAUCOURT-SUR-L'ANCRE was postponed several times, owing mainly to poor weather, before finally being arranged for 13 November. The Naval battalions (63rd Division) took turns to go in and out of the line; in preparation for the battle, the Hood Battalion went from Mesnil to Hamel in full battle order, and was in the firing line in the Hamel sector on 6 November. On 10 November, they were relieved by the Hawke Battalion and returned to Mesnil.

On 13 November, 63rd Division's front stretched for 1,200yds north of the river. On the right was 189th Brigade, adjacent to the river; the Hood and Hawke Battalions were in front, with the Drake and Nelson Battalions to the rear. Behind were 1/1st Honourable Artillery Company and 7th Royal Fusiliers (both 190th Brigade, 63rd Division). To the left were 188th Brigade (63rd Division), with the Howe Battalion and 1st Royal Marine Battalion in the van and the Anson Battalion and 2nd Royal Marine Battalion in the second line. In the rear were 4th Bedfords and 10th Royal Dublin Fusiliers (both 190th Brigade, 63rd Division). Lt Col F.J. Saunders, Commanding Officer Anson Battalion, was killed while waiting for the battle to begin. 63rd Division's left flank was in touch with 153rd Brigade (51st Division).

At 0545hrs, the Hood Battalion went forward, and the Hawke Battalion on the left were held up by heavy machine-gun fire from a redoubt midway between the German first and second lines. This redoubt had been missed by the British artillery and as a result two battalions of 63rd Division were virtually destroyed in 30 minutes. Nevertheless, Lt Col B.C. Freyberg led the 'remnants' of the Hood Battalion to the next objective, which was the trench in front of the sunken Station Road. There were many dugout entrances in Station Road and plenty of prisoners were taken.

On 11 November, 13th King's Royal Rifle Corps (111th Brigade, 37th Division) had marched to PUCHEVILLERS from GÉZAINCOURT and on 13 November arrived at ENGLEBELMER, the advanced headquarters of 63rd Division, to which they were attached. At about 1430hrs, they marched off to Mesnil and went up the Yellow Line; their orders were to prolong the line south of BEAUCOURT-SUR-L'ANCRE, which at that time was held by the remnants of the Hood and Drake Battalions, but they found the roads congested by the number of motorised ambulances. From Hamel, 13th King's Royal Rifle Corps moved off in file along Railway Road in the ANCRE VALLEY, and at 2130hrs halted at the junction of Beaucourt Trench and Railway Road. Freyberg and his troops from Hood Battalion were 150yds in front and 150yds from the edge of BEAUCOURT-SUR-L'ANCRE. 13th King's Royal Rifle Corps then went in on the left of Freyberg's men, and cleared part of the line. The next day they advanced through the village and flushed out the enemy from their many dugouts. On 15 November, they went to the shelter of Station Road valley. Three days later, the British advance reached the outskirts of GRANDCOURT, to the east of BEAUCOURT-SUR-L'ANCRE, on the same day that BEAUMONT-HAMEL also fell.

Hamel was lost to the enemy on 27 March 1918, but recovered later in the year.

Hamel Military Cemetery, designed by Sir Edwin Lutyens, is on the south side of the village, 20yds west of the road to ALBERT and 1 mile south-west of BEAUCOURT-HAMEL station. It was begun by fighting units and field ambulances in August 1915 and used until June 1917. It was known at times by the names of Brook Street Trench and WHITE CITY. It contains the graves of 486 soldiers (and sailors and Marines of 63rd Division). It is sheltered by rising ground on the south and west, but it looks to the east across the valley of the Ancre to the ULSTER TOWER and Thiepval Wood. Five members of the Royal Irish Rifles who died on 6 April 1916 are buried here side by side.

In *The Mind's Eye*, Edmund Blunden wrote: 'I find myself frequently living over again moments of experience on the Western Front . . . The mind suddenly yields to simple versions. Pale light striking through clouds in shafts like the sunrays of Rembrandt. Perhaps these moments occur according to the seasons, for it is now Autumn, and our share in the Somme fighting began towards the end of a splendid August.'

Blunden, in one of his later visits to the Ancre sector, 'may as well take another view of Hamel from above, and of the Schwaben from somewhere by Hamel Church, a touch of John Crome'.

HANGEST-SUR-SOMME is to the north-west of AMIENS, on the D3 road to ABBEVILLE, south of the River Somme. On 16 March 1916, 2nd Wiltshires (21st Brigade, 30th Division) came here from the CARNOY front to rest, although they left B Company at PONT-NOYELLES the day before to work on a new light railway, and stopping at AMIENS they left a platoon who were to be attached to the Lancashire Hussars for cutting brushwood at Fremont. The remaining members of 2nd Wiltshires marched to FLIXECOURT, north-west of AMIENS.

In Gilbert Frankau's novel *Peter Jackson, Cigar Merchant*, the main character is an artilleryman and also liaison officer who accompanies his battery when they march from AMIENS to Hangest-sur-Somme. It took 3 days to concentrate the four brigades of the 'Southdown' artillery; afterwards, they left the village one late summer morning and went up past 'the round fortress of the Citadel and on to the Bois des Tailles'.

Hangest-sur-Somme was part of 8th Division's resting and training area on 4 July, when the divisional headquarters was at Cavillon; other villages in the divisional area were Montagne and MOLLIENS. On 7 July, 110th Brigade (21st Division) came here after FRICOURT; elements of the brigade were also in OISSY and Riencourt. On 21 July, they were here a second time. 20th Division were here in early November.

HANNESCAMPS is a village on the D3 road northeast of FONCQUEVILLERS, between that village and Monchy-au-Bois. During the First World War, it was a 'behind the lines' village, and was often heavily bombarded. British troops took over from the French here in September 1915, when the village

was deserted, and found that trenches to the right in front of FONCQUEVILLERS needed to be improved, as did the sanitation.

On 17 December, a working party that set out for the front line met with disaster. Consisting of many men from several companies, they were assembled near Piccadilly Circus in the village when a salvo fell in their midst. Tragically, five men were killed and two died the following day.

On 13 February 1916, 1/7th Worcesters (144th Brigade, 48th Division) arrived here from COURCELLES-AU-BOIS and took over new trenches between the village and FONCQUE-VILLERS, which were found to be 'dangerous and uncomfortable'. In April, 1st Rifle Brigade (11th Brigade, 4th Division) were here. On 2 May, 11th Royal Warwicks (12th Brigade, 37th Division) took over the line here from 13th Rifle Brigade (111th Brigade, 37th Division); on 26 May, 11th Royal Warwicks relieved 8th Leicesters (110th Brigade, 37th Division).

Hannescamps later became home to 46th Division in their attempts to capture GOMMECOURT on 1 July, and battalion headquarters was set up in dugouts near the crossroads in front of the village. On 1 July, the village was about ½ mile inside the British lines; there was also an advanced dressing station in the village. Aubrey Smith of 1/5th Londons (169th Brigade, 56th Division) wrote that in the period around the first week of July, the village was more famous for bullets than for 'whizz bangs', as the enemy directed overhead machine-gun fire onto the road every minute or so.

Other battalions that were at Hannescamps included 2nd Royal Welsh Fusiliers (19th Brigade, 33rd Division), here on 18 September. At the end of September, when the village was deserted, the battalion headquarters of 1/4th Duke of Wellington's (147th Brigade, 49th Division) was in shelters along the road just south of the village.

The Hannescamps Churchyard is off the road to BIENVILLERS-AU-BOIS on the west side of the village; it was used for burials by French troops and later by the British between October 1915 and January 1916. Twenty-one soldiers are buried here from 13th Rifle Brigade, 13th Royal Fusiliers (111th Brigade, 37th Division) and 13th King's Royal Rifle Corps (also 111th Brigade, 37th Division). The church was rebuilt after the war.

Hannescamps New Military Cemetery is in fact an extension of the Churchyard to the south-west; begun in March 1916, it was used until February 1917 and again in March 1918. The majority of burials are from 1916, including seven men from 7th

East Lancashires (56th Brigade, 19th Division), who died from 29 June 1916. Of the 100-plus burials, 36 are of men who died prior to the battle.

Hannescamps was not reached by the German breakthrough of March 1918, but the village château was used as a battalion headquarters.

HAPPY VALLEY is a name given to several locations on the Somme battlefield in 1916. The main one is just north-west of BRAY-SUR-SOMME, towards MÉAULTE, but there is another one that ran close to MAMETZ WOOD, also known as DEATH VALLEY, which was a more accurate name for it. However, there were also many Death Valleys.

Today, the main Happy Valley is located close to the old road, which has provided a sort of lay-by. Ricourt Wood is on the site of Gibraltar, which was also the location of a military camp, and is adjacent to Happy Valley. Across the hill to the north-east, in the direction of FRICOURT, are the CITADEL and Points 71 South and 71 North. Formerly the Plateau railway line ran in a loop around the valley towards TRÔNES WOOD and GINCHY, having come from the direction of Pilla Junction and GROVE TOWN.

Happy Valley was the reserve area for battalions of Fourth Army's reserve, as were Sandpit Valley and TAILLES WOOD, which were close by. There are not many references to the Valley prior to 1 July 1916, but it is known that in August 1915 5th Division's artillery had their batteries here, which were rarely shelled owing to the lack of enemy observation.

Basil Liddell Hart of 9th King's Own Yorkshire Light Infantry (64th Brigade, 21st Division) wrote that his brigade, who had been in action at FRICOURT, had been part of 21st Division's night-time withdrawal on 3 July 1916. They reached Happy Valley, which he described as being a sheltered hollow behind the original British Front Line. Liddell Hart, who had been in reserve at the beginning of the battle, says that the men of his brigade were revived with panniers of tea laced with rum. Of his battalion, there were fewer than 70 men left from a previous 800.

In mid-July, there were serried ranks of artillery guns in the Valley; H.M. Tomlinson described the Valley at the time as being a monstrous fairground, with everybody going to the fair. The guns caused a continuous eruption, blasting down the exit from the Valley towards the north-east at MONTAUBAN-DE-PICARDIE, LONGUEVAL and other locations. By then the Valley had become a desert, its surface pulverised by a myriad feet, hooves and wheels. Restless brown lakes could be seen in it; they were congestions of horses. All the trees of the Valley were dead or dying because the horses had gnawed off their bark. Its slopes were covered with canvas dwellings, cattle and machinery. The land around was terraced with massed batteries and howitzers.

A few days later, the Dominions were represented amid the infantry, cavalry and artillery, in that the South Africans, after their mauling at DELVILLE WOOD, occupied a sadly small area near that of 2nd Highland Light Infantry (5th Brigade, 21st Division). Although the Valley was out of the battle area, the roar of the 13in guns that came up each night and were within a few hundred yards of the bivouacs made sleep impossible. These guns were mounted on railway platforms. In addition, there were no wells in the Valley nor any water supply, so the water had to be brought up from BRAY-SUR-SOMME by cart.

On 30 July, Brig Gen The Hon. C.J. Sackville-West, General Officer Commanding 21st Brigade (30th Division), was wounded as the result of a bomb dropped by an enemy aircraft; he was later wounded again at VARENNES.

In *A Passionate Prodigality*, Guy Chapman of 13th Royal Fusiliers (111th Brigade, 37th Division) noted that at the end of July, the brown banks of the Valley seemed to hold a million men and animals. All day long the dust, brown and golden in the sunlight, rose and choked the blackening trees as carts, wagons, men and horses, went by. All day long too, a band of the Royal Scots practised the 'Broken Doll'. The Valley was a meeting place, the market square of the Army. Broken divisions coming back paused here one night before being released to quiet sectors. Fresh divisions bivouacked on its stale earth before being sent up to their ordeal. Friends from other days strolled over as they waited, to ask the news, have a drink, and pass out into the 'rosy twilight dusk'.

At the beginning of August, German prisoners were being kept at Gibraltar Camp; at this time, the weather was very hot and the camp was plagued by flies. Troops bathed in the River Somme north of BRAY-SUR-SOMME in order to cool off.

On Minden Day, 1 August, the Lancashire Fusiliers held a parade in Happy Valley when the battalions wore red and white roses in their steel helmets. They paraded under their commander and were reviewed by their brigadier. In mid-August, 35th Division were in the area and left for TALUS BOISÉ on 18 August.

In *The Anatomy of Courage*, Lord Moran of 1st Royal Fusiliers (17th Brigade, 24th Division), who was later to become physician to Winston Churchill, wrote that one day in August, two officers of 20th Division came into his dugout to take over. They looked so fresh and sleek and young that they might have stepped out of a hot bath after hunting. They seemed to listen for shells, though it was peaceful enough at the time. The relief took place that afternoon when Moran and his colleagues left for a camp at Happy Valley. They assembled at CARNOY, where they met the cooks, who provided them with tea. The horses were also there for the use of the officers, and some buses for the use of the men. On the road they passed a Kitchener battalion going up. After tea the men clambered into the old buses with the novelty of being 'carriage folk', and the officers slowly mounted their chargers. On 23 August, there was a blue sky and peace, but all day the camp in Happy Valley appeared to be deserted and when you looked into tents you found that everybody in them was asleep. On the next day the men just sat about and enjoyed the sun. No one did anything.

In early September, the whole area was still stacked with troops on every side; in addition to the camps, there were also dumps and Nissen huts here. Every road was congested with guns and vehicles of all kinds.

On 3 September, 1/16th Londons (169th Brigade, 56th Division) moved by rail to CORBIE, and on 4 September marched to Happy Valley. The battalion reached it after dark on a cold and miserable night and the only shelter available consisted of a number of tents. Half of the battalion managed to pack into them and the remainder had to lie out in the open. Also on 4 September, 1st Scots Guards (2nd Guards Brigade, Guards Division) were here before moving to CARNOY; 1st Coldstream Guards and 2nd Irish Guards (both also 2nd Guards Brigade, Guards Division) were also here before going up the line. In *Have You Forgotten Yet?* C.P. Blacker of 4th Coldstream Guards (pioneers of the Guards Division) noted an aspect of community singing that went on in the Valley: 'At first there was a medley of voices but they fell into choruses and finally into unison so that the wide valley resounded with song, rising and falling as in response to an invisible conductor. The tempo was slow, the prevailing mood of nostalgic melancholy.'

In the period 4 to 9 September, Aubrey Smith reported on the experience of being with the transport of 1/5th Londons (169th Brigade, 56th Division). At the time, the eastern slopes of the Valley were dotted with hundreds of tents, into which 1/5th Londons were ushered. The first night that they spent there was stormy and tempestuous and the rain came down in torrents. The wind came up the Valley with a roar and the guns were going

incessantly like a continuous thunderclap. After 1800hrs, they set off for the water troughs and they could see more than on the night before. The Valley was as populated as before and half of the horses there belonged to French units. Over one hill came a long stream of cavalry; over another, an endless queue of artillery mules, in addition to a procession of animals to the water troughs. It seemed to Smith that the whole of the transports of the British and French armies were congregated here on the ridges above BRAY-SUR-SOMME. Soon Smith was to go up to CARNOY and DEATH VALLEY with the transport and then return to Happy Valley briefly on 8/9 September. He wrote that there was a disadvantage in that the Valley was some distance from the line, over 3 miles from CARNOY and 5 miles from DEATH VALLEY, as the crow flies.

The water problem was always difficult on the Somme, for hundreds of thousands of men and animals had to be supplied in the devastated wastes, and there were only a limited number of sources opened up by the Royal Engineers.

It would seem that September 1916 was the 'high point' for Happy Valley, as once HIGH WOOD and FLERS were taken in mid-September, the battle zone moved away. Even so, No. 4 Casualty Clearing Station was brought here from BEAUVAL in early October; No. 3 Australian Casualty Clearing Station replaced No. 11 Casualty Clearing Station.

Apart from those already mentioned, 3rd, 5th, 20th and 24th Divisions camped in Happy Valley.

HARBONNIÈRES is south of the old road from AMIENS to Vermand and SAINT-QUENTIN. Heath Cemetery, due north of the village, is predominantly a 1918 burial ground, but 1916 casualties were later concentrated here from Cerisy-Gailly Communal Cemetery French Extension, Etinehem French Military Cemetery and Méricourt-sur-Somme Communal Cemetery.

HARDECOURT-AU-BOIS is north-east of MARI-COURT and south of GUILLEMONT. In mid-August 1916, the Allied objective was the road between the two villages. The French were to take the northern edge of ANGLE WOOD. 1st Cheshires (15th Brigade, 5th Division) were detailed to cross the forward slopes of the hill north-west of Hardecourt-au-Bois; on 4 September, they were in full view of the enemy and came under heavy shell-fire. A barrage of 5.9in guns was 'playing' on the valley to the south of ANGLE WOOD. On 13 September, 1/16th Londons (169th Brigade, 56th Division) moved up from Citadel Camp to the former German trench system near to the Crucifix, where there was a dressing station, to the north of Hardecourt-au-Bois. During the morning, 1/16th Londons, who were in divisional reserve, were moved up from FAFFEMONT FARM to Angle Wood Valley to the north of the farm. They were not yet employed but it was the prelude to the fighting at LEUZE WOOD. The village had become so battered that even the cellars had disappeared.

HARPONVILLE is due east of TOUTENCOURT and south-west of ACHEUX-EN-AMIÉNOIS. On 8 March 1916, when 49th Division headquarters was at SENLIS-LE-SEC, 1/5th and 1/7th West York-shires (both 146th Brigade, 49th Division) were billeted in the village. On 3 April, 36th Division had their divisional headquarters here. In early June, 108th Brigade (36th Division) were here for training at CLAIRFAYE FARM, along with their colleagues in VARENNES and LÉALVILLERS. On 22 June, a field company of 49th Division were here; later, 75th and 77th Field Ambulances (both 25th Division) were here under canvas, when the village was full of troops. The field ambulances received orders to leave for CONTAY; the war diary noted: 'Arrange-ments and staff work very bad – stay in wood in Contay'. They supplied bearers to BOUZINCOURT as well as some to WARLOY-BAILLON.

On 4 July, 90th Field Ambulance (32nd Division) opened a divisional rest station here under canvas and took over three huts for sick officers. During the night of 9 July, 19th Northumberland Fusiliers (pioneers of 35th Division) were in the village and camped in an orchard; Nos. 203 and 205 Field Companies, Royal Engineers (both 35th Division), were also here at this time. In October and November, units of 32nd Division were in the village. 29th Division also had links with Harpon-ville.

There are two cemeteries on the north side of the village on the road to LÉALVILLERS, north-east of the village, the Harponville Communal Cemetery and Harponville Communal Cemetery Extension, which have burials of men who died in 1918, 34 in the first and 138 in the second.

HÉBUTERNE is a village on the D27 road between SAILLY-AU-BOIS and PUISIEUX and immediately south of GOMMECOURT. The area had already witnessed a 'severe action', fought by the French during the 'Second Battle of Artois' between 10 and 13 June 1915. The village was very close to the Allied lines and so was regularly subjected to enemy shell-fire prior to and during the battle. In addition,

the village was the boundary between Third and Fourth Armies. The Hébuterne–SAILLY-AU-BOIS road, the D27, was subjected to a great deal of hostile fire. It was exposed to the enemy position at Gommecourt Park for about 600yds, halfway between the two villages, and was accurately ranged by the Germans.

Surrounded by cider apple orchards, Hébuterne was to be turned into a fortress village, enclosed in a ring fence, by the British; it is particularly associated at this time with 56th Division, who were to launch themselves from here against the GOMMECOURT position on 1 July 1916. However, troops from 48th Division were here – 1/4th Royal Berkshires, for example – almost a year before, when they arrived in the area on 20 July 1915 and began to relieve the French, who were then in the line. The French had already turned the place into 'a formidable centre of resistance'. At this time there were still some civilians in the village, but they were soon evacuated. The dugouts had the appearance of luxury, as much of the furniture from the village was transported to them. These items included four-poster beds, but owing to the amount of 'livestock' in them, they were scrapped before they had been in use for more than a week. Initially the French artillery remained in the area, providing any assistance requested by the infantry.

At first the headquarters of 145th Brigade (48th Division), as well as the headquarters of 1/1st Buckinghamshires (145th Brigade, 48th Division) were both in Hébuterne, and even occupied buildings above ground; 1/1st Buckinghamshires had a company headquarters in the 'Keep' and a cemetery in an orchard. However, as shelling became more frequent, they were driven under-ground to dugouts and cellars. The 'Keep' was a popular billet and a 'charming spot' among trees and orchards. There seems little doubt that early on in their stay in the village, a tacit agreement existed between the two sides supposedly at war: 'If they would leave Hébuterne alone' then 'we would not entirely destroy Gommecourt . . .'

Units of 48th Division were often in occupation here, including 1/3rd (South Midland) and 1/2nd (South Midland) Field Ambulances, who ran the advanced dressing station here in October 1915 and often continued to do so during the coming months.

In January 1916, 1/7th and 1/8th Worcesters (both 144th Brigade, 48th Division) were billeted here for a time and also occupied the trenches. In early February, 144th Brigade were later pulled back into divisional reserve, when they moved to COUR-CELLES-AU-BOIS to the south-west.

In May 1916, 56th Division came to the area; at this time, the two lines were some 750yds apart and the British Front Line was roughly 100yds east of the orchards surrounding Hébuterne. Owing to the width and exposed nature of the land sloping up towards the German lines, it was decided to dig a new trench system pushing out into no man's land. 167th and 168th Brigades (both 55th Division) accomplished this task with very few casualties over the next few days, and took the lines to within 300yds from the enemy.

However, on 16 May the village was badly shelled, followed by an enemy attack in which 16 British were killed, 43 wounded and 27 missing. On 21 May, 1/13th Londons (168th Brigade, 56th Division) came here to relieve 1/8th Middlesex (167th Brigade, 56th Division), when they found that cellars under the ruined buildings had been fortified with sandbags and fitted with wire beds. Battalion headquarters was established in the cellars and ruins of Hébuterne mill.

Ammunition dumps appeared in the landscape, dotted around, and the Hébuterne plain became full of gun positions; one heavy battery was in the village itself, close to a thick hedge surrounding a copse. The Germans too had a strong artillery presence, with batteries at Quesnoy Farm, Biez Wood beyond ROSSIGNOL WOOD and PUISIEUX. In addition, they had more guns to the north, in the area of Adinfer Wood.

In *A Life of One's Own*, Gerald Brenan described his experiences in spring 1916, when he returned to Hébuterne and was put in charge of an observation post just outside it. Every day, new batteries would arrive and would then begin registering; new light railways sprang up, new shell dumps and notice-boards would appear. Through his telescope, Brenan could see mounds of white chalk appearing in the German support trenches; evidently they were building deep, shell-proof dugouts in preparation for the expected Allied attack. Brenan's observation post was immediately opposite SERRE, 1 mile to the south-east.

The advanced dressing station was in a spacious dugout built by the Royal Engineers underneath a house in the centre of the village and close to the cemetery. One of the billets in the village was a long, tunnel-like cellar that ran under farm buildings and was called 'The Grotto'. Dugouts were constructed in gardens and the church was in ruins. Carrying the date of 1866 or 1861, the church clock was on the ground instead of in the tower.

In *Battle of the Somme*, war correspondent Philip Gibbs wrote that beyond SAILLY-AU-BOIS village

was the road to Hebuterne. It led through open fields and past a belt of trees less than a thousand yards away, where the Germans lay watching behind their rifle-barrels. But the French had a friendly little arrangement. If an open car crawled down slowly the Germans did not snipe. If it was a covered car, presumably a General's, or went fast, they had the right to shoot. Queer, though it seemed to work. But I was always glad to get the length of that road and to find some cover in the fortress-village of Hebuterne, with its deep dug-outs, proof against the lighter kind of shells. The Germans had been here first and had dug in with their usual industry. Then the French had turned them out after ferocious fighting – there are many French graves there in the Orchard and in the trenches . . . In the Orchard young fruit of life fell before it had ripened, and I did not linger there among the apple-trees . . .

On 1 June, the trenches here were taken over by 1/7th Royal Warwicks (143rd Brigade, 48th Division) and 1/7th Worcesters (144th Brigade, 48th Division) returned to COUIN. In early June, 1/9th Londons (169th Brigade, 56th Division) also had men in the front line, when shelling caused them some casualties over 3 days. On 3 June, they were relieved by 1/2nd Londons (also 169th Brigade, 56th Division). From 3 to 8 June, the three companies of 1/12th Londons (168th Brigade, 56th Division) billeted in the 'Keep' had to march to trenches at SAILLY-AU-BOIS, where they worked on a new trench system.

On the night of 5 June, 1/9th Londons supplied working parties to work on the new front line, which was to be 300yds in front of the previous line, to the east of the village; they were also to clear sapheads in preparation for the digging of the new line further forward. On 9 June, 1/9th Londons moved back to Hébuterne, relieving 1/2nd Londons in Y Sector between Hébuterne and GOMMECOURT.

A.S. Dolden of 1/14th Londons (168th Brigade, 56th Division) noted that on 2 June, his battalion left SOUASTRE for Hébuterne; the cooks followed separately, and stopped at BAYENCOURT to pick up company rations. There was a very deep well in the village, which provided a plentiful water supply to the troops who were in occupation. Dolden's party arrived at Hébuterne after dark; by this time, part of the battalion were in the line, in front of the village, and the rest were in Hébuterne itself. On 8 June, 1/14th Londons were relieved by 1/12th Londons and moved up to the 'Keep' in the north-west part of the village. Here, they were relieved by

1/13th Londons (168th Brigade, 56th Division) on 13 June and marched back to SAINT-AMAND. By now, roads and byways had been further barricaded and were defended by machine guns.

On 16 June, 1/16th Londons (169th Brigade, 56th Division) were relieved by 1/5th Londons (also 169th Brigade, 56th Division) and moved back to BAYENCOURT. As always, Aubrey Smith with the transport of 1/5th Londons is a good source for detail; he notes that they had collected pit props from a dump at BAYENCOURT and taken them to Hébuterne with other vehicles, having previously journeyed from SAINT-AMAND. On 29 and 30 June they had to cross the plain from SAILLY-AU-BOIS to Hébuterne, where they were supposed to be under observation from the right. Smith describes the topography of the front in the following way. The ground fell away gently for a few hundred yards and then rose again in a long slope towards the German position. To the right the white tower of the church at Achiet-le-Petit was visible half hidden among the trees, while in the foreground the ruins of Nameless Farm stood up among the labyrinth of the enemy trenches. Further to the right, the ground dipped sharply to the valley overlooking SERRE; to the left, on slightly higher ground, stood GOMMECOURT. Keep at the rear of Hébuterne was a system of trenches protected by barbed wire and commanded the flanks, front and rear. It was a tactical reserve place. Along the main street at intervals of about 100yds were the entrances to communication trenches bearing such names as Yankee Street, Yellow Street, York Street and Yule Street.

On 30 June, 1/12th Londons went from BAYEN-COURT along the blue track, keeping to the right of the BAYENCOURT–SAILLY-AU-BOIS road, which dipped into the valley behind the SAILLY-AU-BOIS road, and on to the plain between SAILLY-AU-BOIS and Hébuterne. Men from 2/3rd (London) Field Ambulance (56th Division) left COUIN on the night of 30 June and camped in tents on a hill about 1 mile from Hébuterne. It was a lovely summer evening with a glorious sunset when they visited the advanced dressing station at Hébuterne; on their return to the camp, they witnessed columns of marching troops: 'the 12th London Rangers and the 14th London Scottish moving up to their positions for the attack next morning. It was a most moving and unforgettable sight – the comparatively quiet, almost peaceful evening and all these men – many were young boys singing as they marched, very many to witness for the last time a sunset and the fields in all their summer glory!'

In the morning, the field ambulance moved down into the village, took over some huts and prepared to make the dressing station ready for 1 July. It was not long before the wounded began to arrive and the field ambulance had to make journeys to the advanced dressing station and back. In *Unarmed Comrades*, Pte A.L. Ellis of 2/3rd (London) Field Ambulance (56th Division) remembered: 'My memory of that morning a few hours later is of the field of fully grown crops being rapidly flattened by stretcher cases of wounded lying all round the huts of the M.D.S. The long lines of motor ambulances and bearers loading them were stretching nose to tail along the road in front of and on the side of the road adjoining . . .' Cpl Challis, quoted in the same history, stated: 'We were soon flooded out with wounded cases everywhere lying around and crying for help. After all 20 Ambulance cars had gone I would go around selecting the worst cases, sending them in to the Dressing Hut for the M.O.'s to deal with. They too were soon overwhelmed and had to have help . . .'

During the last days of June, 1/7th Middlesex (167th Brigade, 56th Division) had been in the front line opposite GOMMECOURT during a period of incessant shelling and in trenches sometimes knee-deep in water. By 28 June, they had reached the last stages of exhaustion and were no longer fit for action. They were relieved that night by 1/2nd Londons and taken back in wagons to SOUASTRE.

There is a typescript in the Imperial War Museum archive by Gunner W.R. Price of C Battery, CCXL Brigade, Royal Field Artillery (48th Division). His battery used inefficient Boer War 15-pounders, which they looked forward to replacing with 18-pounders; the latter were light and easy to run forward and switch around. They had four positions at Hébuterne: one south-west of FONCQUEVILLERS, two on the Hébuterne–AUCHONVILLERS road and the fourth on the COLINCAMPS road. The first Hébuterne position was on the plain, close behind an escarpment. Between Hébuterne and COLINCAMPS was a former French position. Price became a layer for A Gun. On 20 July, they were replaced by a Welsh battery. On a lighter note, Price mentions three songs that were especially popular at the time and that they were always singing: 'Again, Again and Again', 'Fred Karno's Army' and 'Grooming'.

In *Johnny Get Your Gun*, J.F. Tucker of 1/13th Londons wrote of great activity in the fields behind Hébuterne at the end of June; great gun pits were being dug and the number of artillery guns increased. He described the transport, who at this time were living in the open, the horses tethered to a long rope line or lines in a large green field. They were ensconced in shacks made from oddments of timber, corrugated iron and pieces of tarpaulin. On 30 June they took most of the limbers, General Staff wagons and pack ponies to Hébuterne, loaded with supplies of hand grenades, picks, spades and axes, and food and water. These supplies were unloaded in the main road leading to the front line and dumped in a ruined brick shed.

During June, the advanced dressing station in the village was kept busy as there were often as many as 100 casualties each day. On 27 June, many casualties had to be dug out of collapsed dugouts in the village.

On the first day of the battle, 1 July, 1/5th Royal Warwicks (143rd Brigade, 48th Division), who were holding part of the line in front of Hébuterne, discharged a cloud of smoke and poison gas, so as to mask the fire of the concentrated artillery behind Gommecourt Wood. On the right, the main attack was to be delivered on 1 July by Fourth Army, while on the left a subsidiary attack was to be made by Third Army. The remainder were held in reserve to exploit the gains of the attacking troops. For a description as to what happened at GOMMECOURT on 1 July 1916, readers are referred to that entry.

The advanced dressing station in Hébuterne now had to deal with a sudden and vast increase in casualties as large numbers began to arrive at the sandbagged cottage with its two large dugouts, which were connected to the cellars of the cottage with leading trenches. As the village was always being targeted by enemy guns, every effort was made to keep it clear of wounded. It became necessary to send cases directly to the main dressing station. The best way, it was thought, to deal with 2,000 casualties in 24 hours, was to rush up ambulance cars to the village and clear them up at once. At the beginning of July, medical staff concentrated on the worst cases, which were then sent on by motor ambulance to COUIN, where the main dressing station was situated.

Hébuterne continued to be shelled on 2 July and there was a serious problem with bringing in the wounded still out in no man's land. On 2 and 3 July, a large number of wounded and dead were lying out between the lines, and were proving very difficult to recover. However, in the afternoon, the enemy themselves emerged from their trenches to dress the wounded from both sides. The British took full advantage of the opportunity and managed to get in 50 cases, but there were still others lying out waiting for help. A German medical

officer had gathered up identity discs of some of the British dead and handed them over to staff of 2/2nd (London) Field Ambulance (56th Division). On 5 July, 100 volunteers left Hébuterne to search for the dead, and on the next day, 17 bodies were recovered from between the lines. On 7 July, the advanced dressing station was taken over by a section of 2/3rd (London) Field Ambulance (56th Division); their quarters, in a deep shelter, were full of water that they had to pump out.

On 5 July, Graham Greenwell of 1/4th Oxfordshire & Buckinghamshire Light Infantry (145th Brigade, 48th Division) wrote home from G Sector at Hébuterne: 'Here we are again, back in the trenches, or rather canals, as the water is over our knees'. He was to be there until 8 July.

> Yesterday afternoon I had a good look at the battlefield of 1 July through the telescope at a splendid observation post. It was a very interesting sight; it lay just to the right of us; the whole plain sloping up to the village called Serre held by the Germans was visible. Our troops attacked it after 6 days' bombardment, and after getting into the village were driven back to their original trenches. Heaps of bodies are still lying out there unburied, but the Germans and ourselves have been sending out stretcher parties each night. The three lines of German trenches in front of the village are absolutely shattered and are almost levelled; their thick wire is absolutely wrecked, but their machine guns did appalling damage in spite of everything. The village is one mass of ruins with a few gaunt trees standing up, before the battle it was thickly wooded and almost invisible. Far to the right I could see our guns shelling a large German railway centre behind the line – good sight.

On 16 July, Greenwell wrote home and noted: 'This is tremendous news about Bazentin le Petit. If only we can hold these places against counter-attacks.'

From 4 to 18 July, 1/5th Glosters (also 145th Brigade, 48th Division) were in the Hébuterne sector. They found plenty of stores at Hébuterne when they arrived; biscuits, bully beef and pork and beans, left by the Scots. These two battalions took turns in and out of the line at this time.

Around 24 July, 11th King's Royal Rifle Corps (59th Brigade, 20th Division) were in the area for 3 weeks, and 10th and 11th King's Royal Rifle Corps (both 59th Brigade, 20th Division) and 12th King's Royal Rifle Corps (60th Brigade, 20th Division) were in trenches south-east of Hébuterne from the end of July until 16 August.

On 16 August, 1st Scots Guards (2nd Guards Brigade, Guards Division) left BERTRANCOURT and went into line at Hébuterne, when 1/14th Londons were on their left. Hugh Wansey Bayly, medical officer of 1st Scots Guards, established a new aid post on the side of a communication trench. They sapped as far as Sixteen Poplars and they were in the line here until 21 August, when they went into rest at BUS-LÈS-ARTOIS.

In *A Subaltern on the Somme*, Max Plowman of 10th West Yorkshires (50th Brigade, 17th Division) wrote that in August his company headquarters was in an imposing farmhouse, and that on the previous day, when on the march, they had halted at SOUASTRE, close to Hébuterne. The quickest way to the front line was under enemy observation from the rising ground at GOMMECOURT. They entered the village and came across the ruined church. The troops that they were relieving were 1/14th Londons, who told them that this had been a quiet sector since 1 July, when they buried half a battalion of men in an abandoned front-line trench.

Plowman's line was the second line; there were no bays, and so they posted men at various firing points at fairly wide intervals and put Lewis gunners out on both flanks. His dugout was not very deep, but he says that it was a 'wonderful place'. At the bottom of the steps on the left were two canvas bunks that were extremely comfortable. Their trenches were just a little to the right of the trenches that the battalion had held previously, with a battalion of the Royal Fusiliers on their right flank. The ground to the front sloped gently away for a few hundred yards, then rose again in a long sweep. To the left was GOMMECOURT, a sinister spot which was now a heap of ruins and contained the remains of a wood. The whole area suggested to him the sharpest contrast to the rough bayless chasm of St Georges Hill that they had occupied the previous week. Plowman was probably in a dugout in Welcome Street, a chalk dugout about 30ft deep.

On 25 August, 1st King's Royal Rifle Corps (99th Brigade, 2nd Division) relieved 23rd Royal Fusiliers. In mid-September, 16th King's Royal Rifle Corps (100th Brigade, 33rd Division) were in reserve billets for the line to the north of GOMMECOURT. J.F. Tucker of 1/13th Londons (168th Brigade, 56th Division) wrote that

at the end of August they were relieved by a York-shire Brigade who were fresh from the Somme battlefield further south, where they were now to

go. They marched via Corbie and Sailly le Sec to Bray where they spent the night before proceeding to Citadel Camp. The ground to the north of Hébuterne was in a dreadful state having been shelled since the end of June. The 56th Division with the help of the Guards Brigade helped to clear up the battlefield. It was altogether a dreary village and the trenches were in a poor state. It was also a daily target for the German artillery.

H.E. Harvey of 22nd Royal Fusiliers (99th Brigade, 2nd Division) mentions at the end of September or beginning of October that the 'Gas Experts' were in the area. He describes them as affixing taps and gas piping along the parapet with rows of gas jets, which were called 'pot hooks and hangers'. They had to wait for a favourable moment in the weather. With the appointed signal, a single white British rocket, the masked men standing by turned the small circular cylinder ends, and with a frightful hiss like compressed steam from a 100-ton locomotive, the deadly green-yellow cloud spouted outwards from the line of jets. The long drifting cloud of gas, withering white the first few yards of green grass before it, carried slowly and menacingly towards the post 50yds away. Inevitably some of the gas blew back over the British lines.

In mid-September, 17th Division's artillery were reinforced by bringing up several batteries of heavy artillery, which were concentrated on the high ground behind Hébuterne, and wire cutting by gun fire began. On 20 September, 17th King's Royal Rifle Corps (117th Brigade, 39th Division) moved into the line at Hébuterne from Y Camp at BERTRANCOURT, where they returned on 30 September.

The sector held by 18th West Yorkshires (93rd Brigade, 31st Division) was a busy area, known at the time as Suicide Corner; the code word 'Gasper' indicated that there was a wind here favourable to a gas discharge. This caused extra hardship as troops turned around in the village and retreated, another reason why the village had a sinister reputation.

Pte J. Cunningham of 12th East Yorkshires (92nd Brigade, 31st Division) was to be awarded the Victoria Cross for his action on 13 November opposite Hébuterne.

After the enemy's front line had been captured Private Cunningham proceeded with a bombing section up a communication trench. Much opposition was encountered, and the rest of the section became casualties. Collecting all the bombs from the casualties, this gallant soldier went on alone. Having expended all his bombs, he returned for a fresh supply, and again proceeded to the communication trench, where he met a party of ten of the enemy. These he killed, and cleared the trench up to the enemy line . . .

Hébuterne Communal Cemetery, on the south side of the village, contains graves of men in two plots. The 55 British casualties buried here include 3 men from the Royal Warwickshire Regiment who died in July 1915 and 7 men from the Royal Field Artillery who died in October 1916. The burials are of men who mostly belonged to 20th and 31st Divisions. An employee of the Commonwealth War Graves Commission is also buried here. The cemetery was badly damaged in the war.

Hébuterne Military Cemetery is in a secluded position on the north-west side of the village; begun by 48th Division in August 1915, it was used by fighting units and field ambulances, particularly those of 56th Division, until the spring of 1917. Of the 750 burials, approximately 320 are of men who died prior to the battle. It was reopened in 1918. There are a considerable number of group casualties among the graves here, which indicates how often and how heavily the village was shelled.

Owl Trench Cemetery is 1½ miles east of the village, on the south side of the GOMMECOURT–PUISIEUX road. Owl Trench was a German cross trench before ROSSIGNOL WOOD, and was raided by 4th New Zealand Rifle Brigade (New Zealand Division) on 15 July 1918 and cleared 5 days later. Hébuterne was in Allied hands from 1915 to March 1918, but the eastern part of the commune was in German hands until February 1917 and the cemetery mainly contains the graves of men who died on 27 February 1917 during an attack on German rearguards by 31st Division. There are 43 graves from 16th West Yorkshires (93rd Brigade, 31st Division) buried in Row A, which is one large grave. The cemetery register lists 53 graves.

Rossignol Wood Cemetery is on the south side of the GOMMECOURT–PUISIEUX road; the Wood 400yds to the east was captured by the Germans at the end of March 1918 and retaken in July. The first burials were made in March 1917 by 46th Division burial officer. At some point in the 1920s, a memorial cross to 1/9th Durham Light Infantry was moved here for safe keeping, from a point whose map reference was 57d.L.7a6.2. During the 1920s, a 21ft memorial to the Royal Scots Fusiliers in the village 'was left to nature'.

Hébuterne was completely rebuilt after the war, including its very large church. A plaque, unveiled in June 2002 to the memory of 16th West Yorkshires is to be found on the wall of the cemetery grounds, facing the road.

La Grande rue, Hébuterne.
(Peter F. Batchelor Collection)

HÉDAUVILLE is on the D938 road south-west of FORCEVILLE; there is a First World War sign on one of the buildings when approaching from the VARENNES (D47E) road.

On 25 November 1915, two enemy flyers killed the day before were given a full military funeral in the village. On 11 February 1916, two sections from a field ambulance of 49th Division opened a dressing station here. On 23 April, 1/4th Duke of Wellingtons (147th Brigade, 49th Division) arrived by bus in the village and provided working parties for 36th Division in the subsequent 2 months; they were bussed to BOUZINCOURT and from there conducted to their work. 'The ground was full of roots, which greatly hindered digging, and, a foot or two below the surface, much flint was encountered.'

The wood at Hédauville was often used for camping purposes and life in the woods was quite enjoyable, despite the odd spell of rain. 'Hédauville Wood was full of nightingales, and many men sat out at night to listen to their song.'

The area became closely linked with 36th Division; in mid-April, men from 108th Field Ambulance (36th Division) were collecting brushwood to be used for the walls of a second hut at AUT-HUILLE. At the end of the month the village was heavily shelled.

After their gallant efforts at Thiepval on 1 July, units of 36th Division returned to Hédauville the next day. On 3 June, the transport of 1/4th Duke of Wellingtons moved to the village. On 1 July, 1st East Lancashires (11th Brigade, 4th Division) were here; a post constructed close to a burnt house was named Lancashire Post. Huts in the village were used by troops for billeting purposes. There is a note that at one point, battalions of the Princess of Wales's Own (Yorkshire) Regiment used the village for rest billets.

From 1 July, divisions who had units here included 2nd, 11th, 12th, 18th, 25th, 37th, 39th, 48th, 49th and 51st Divisions; of these, 2nd, 18th, 25th and 39th Divisions had their headquarters in the village. At the end of October, the Hood Battalion (189th Brigade, 63rd Division) were billeted in barns in the village.

Hédauville Communal Cemetery Extension, designed by W.H. Cowlishaw, is on the south side of Hédauville Communal Cemetery, on the right of the D938 road to FORCEVILLE. It was used for burials from March 1918 and 95 graves were brought in after the war. A total of 176 identified casualties are buried here.

Vera Brittain, whose fiancé died in December 1915, has referred to a poem entitled 'Hédauville', written by Lt R.A. Leighton of 1/7th Worcesters (144th Brigade, 48th Division) and dated November 1915. It was partly reminiscent of a road the couple knew before the war. When visiting Roland's grave in LOUVENCOURT in 1921, Vera wrote of her travels 'through the still disfigured landscape'. Coming from the direction of AMIENS, she saw a white board with 'Hédauville' written on it. 'The place was then as it must have looked after a year or two's fighting, with only the stumpy ruins of farmhouses crumbling into the tortured field to show where a village had been.' In 1933, on another visit to the Somme battlefield, she recalled the name of the village being on a placard, whereas it was now painted in black on a wall of a barn (see above). The former bumpy, shattered road, full of shell-holes, was now a 'smooth & smiling' road.

HEILLY is on the River Ancre on the D52 road to ALBERT, 1¼ miles west of MÉRICOURT-L'ABBÉ and south-west of RIBEMONT-SUR-ANCRE. The village was to become one of the principal railheads used for supplies when the battle opened. In addition, a motor ambulance convoy was established here, but the village became most well known for its casualty clearing stations and its adjacent large military cemetery, to the south-west of the village.

Before these developments, 51st Division had their headquarters here, on 27 July 1915; 3 days later, 51st Division took over responsibility for a section of the front line from the French. On 20 September, 1/6th Seaforth Highlanders (152nd Brigade, 51st Division) marched here from BOUZINCOURT and marched past Gen Sir Charles Monro, General Officer Commanding Third Army, taking the salute at the château on the south-west side of the village. In August and September, elements of 18th Division were here. On 29 December, 1/6th Seaforth Highlanders left with the rest of 152nd Brigade and marched in a westerly direction to SAINT-GRATIEN for the night. In late June 1916, 17th Division had a brigade here; they had a rest camp on the banks of the Ancre.

On 1 March 1916, No. 36 Casualty Clearing Station arrived at Heilly, having travelled by road from CORBIE; according to their war diary (WO95/344), they 'proceeded to pitch a camp in a field close to Heilly Railway Station, south of the line . . . The ground of the camp is 180 × 75 yards. The ground is clay and very soft. It is bounded on the west by a cultivated patch (ryegrass) and on the East by ploughed land. North is the railway line and South the main Corbie–Merricourt [sic MÉRICOURT-L'ABBÉ] road . . .'

Eventually, the hospital camp spread over the whole area between the railway halt and the MÉRICOURT-L'ABBÉ–CORBIE road, with access at both ends. The marquees for the use of the patients were at the road end while the staff, stores, latrines and bathhouses were adjacent to the railway line and sidings. The ground that was later to be earmarked for the cemetery was marked 'field under construction'.

Apart of course from the cemetery and the railway halt, there is little left today of what was almost a 'medical town' in the summer of 1916. Amid the scrubland adjacent to the former railhead sidings, one can find what might be traces of lifting gear used in the war for the handling of supplies.

No water was laid on at the camp and the nearest supply of water suitable for drinking was 1½ miles away. In early March, a new road was begun running from west to east at the railway end of the camp, which would assist in evacuating patients to trains and in bringing in supplies of coal, hospital supplies and so on. 'Chalk was brought from a quarry by motor lorries; cinders were fetched from Amiens (15 miles each way). A layer of cinders was laid on first, then chalk, as dry as possible and then cinders on top of the chalk.'

At first, any burials were made in MÉRICOURT-L'ABBÉ, as the cemetery at Heilly was not begun until the end of May. On 18 April, seven nursing sisters arrived at the hospital to take up duties. On 12 May, the war diary of No. 36 Casualty Clearing Station notes that half a crate of oranges had been bought locally for 30 francs and 12 coffins for 180 francs. On 24 May, the casualty clearing station made another purchase locally, with two dozen fresh eggs for 4 francs 80 cents and 12 more coffins for 180 francs.

By the end of May, the water problem at the casualty clearing station was being attended to; the estimated requirements were of a minimum of 4,000 gallons per day, based on the needs of 1,000 patients and 100 personnel. In early June, further changes were carried out, with 'marquees in pairs being joined up to make large wards of 4 marquees'. On 6 June, it is noted in the war diary that barges were put to medical use: 'Cases evacuated by barge from Corbie, an unsuitable method as the barges are intended for the very severe cases who are not improved by the preliminary car run to Corbie . . .'

On 2 May, No. 36 Casualty Clearing Station was joined by No. 38, who opened their hospital on 19 June; the two casualty clearing stations proceeded to operate the hospitals in tandem. In July, they were joined by No. 2/2 (London) Casualty Clearing Station. The wounded and dying were brought here in large numbers, especially in early July, when by noon on 1 July itself, No. 38 Casualty Clearing Station was rapidly filled by the arrival of over 1,000 lightly wounded. 'The ambulance trains were not arriving at all regularly or punctually and being the first port of call from the front line trains from there reach the Hospitals speedily but conversely trains from the rear reached it last. It was not surprising that during the night 36th Casualty Clearing Station became "over taxed".' This resulted in the closure of the casualty clearing station at Heilly, when the cases went to CORBIE. Many of the casualties had come from the areas in the centre of the Somme battlefield, from LA BOISSELLE to MONTAUBAN-DE-PICARDIE.

On 2 July, 1,533 wounded were admitted. Sir Douglas Haig, together with the Adjutant General, Lt Gen G.H. Fowke, visited the camp; they also visited the casualty clearing station at MONTIGNY. At the end of the day, Fowke reported to Haig that casualties so far were estimated at being 40,000. Both the war diary and Haig in his diary report on the good spirits of the wounded. On 3 July, the number of casualties came down to 478, together with 24 Germans. As for the ambulance trains: 'they were running much better – the back pressure produced by their early failure is now practically relieved . . .' More than 10 per cent of the day's casualties were suffering from gas gangrene. During the next 6 days, over 3,170 patients were admitted to No. 36 Casualty Clearing Station, together with about 100 Germans.

No. 38 Casualty Clearing Station had similar problems; having been used to handling only small numbers of casualties, they were called upon to handle 1,757 cases on 1 July, 1,212 on 2 July, 945 on 3 July and about 500 a day for the next week.

Although the casualty figures for 1 July were very high, what perhaps is not so easy to explain is why they were so high on 7 July, when the two hospitals together handled over 1,800 patients, 6 days after the battle began.

Obviously, the high point of the casualty clearing stations at Heilly was in July 1916. Robert Graves of 2nd Royal Welsh Fusiliers (19th Brigade, 33rd Division) was one of the patients handled here, after being given up for dead at the former German dressing station on the north side of MAMETZ WOOD, following his severe wounding at BAZENTIN on 20 July. When seen to be still alive, Graves was sent down to a casualty clearing station at Heilly.

The pain of being jolted down the Happy Valley (or Death Valley), with a shell-hole at every three or four yards of the roads, woke me for a while. I remember screaming . . . Heilly was on the railway; close to the station was a hospital – marquee tents with the red cross painted prominently on the roof to discourage air-bombing. It was fine July weather and the tents were insufferably hot. I was semi-conscious now . . .

Graves asked the doctor if he could be moved to somewhere cooler, but was advised to lie still; Graves got his way, however, as on 24 July (his 21st birthday), cases were being quickly evacuated to make room for further casualties expected that night. Shortly afterwards, Graves was taken from the hot tent and lifted onto a train, which carried him and others to a base hospital at Rouen, before being returned to England.

The three casualty clearing stations were moved in early June 1917 and little remains of their presence today.

Maj R.G. Raper of 8th South Staffords (51st Brigade, 17th Division) was killed at FRICOURT on 2 July and is buried in Fricourt British Cemetery (B.24.A). He was first buried in a private grave outside the cemetery and is commemorated by a road named after him. In death, Raper became a famous figure in FRICOURT, but he also left his mark in the village of Heilly to the south-west. His battalion arrived in tents in a marshy valley on 27 June; after more rain, the place became a swamp. On 29 June, he left for MORLANCOURT, the battalion starting-point on 2 July for the front line at FRICOURT, where he was killed.

After returning to Heilly on 29 June, Raper visited a teashop in the village run by a superior French family, who had lost most of their wealth in the war but who were now making a small fortune. He drank Scottish beer brewed in Edinburgh and the place was crowded with officers. The teashop did not serve dinners as well and closed at 1930hrs. He later had a dip in a trout stream near his tent and the next day he and a brother officer called Coleridge gave a lunch party in the village restaurant to celebrate 'our last day in civilization'. They then left for MORLANCOURT at 2210hrs.

Before 1 July, 102nd Brigade (34th Division) trained here and in the FRANVILLERS area for their forthcoming role in the fighting for the village of LA BOISSELLE. There was a camp here and 9th Northumberland Fusiliers (52nd Brigade, 17th Division) were camped on the banks of the River Ancre.

Later, 1st Royal Welsh Fusiliers (22nd Brigade, 7th Division), Siegfried Sassoon's battalion, were camped at the village, and left at 1600hrs on 10 July on their way to the CITADEL via MORLANCOURT, which they reached by 2100hrs. During their march, they had been passed by Haig's party between the villages of MARICOURT and TREUX. Sassoon wrote in his diary they started back for Heilly, which was about 12 miles away; when they came through MAMETZ, they were heavily shelled. The total casualties of 1st Royal Welsh Fusiliers for the previous 7 days had been 132, but only 14 dead.

In mid-July, 16th Cheshires (105th Brigade, 35th Division) were camped in what was described as a 'wooden place in the marsh by the river'. In early August, there was a large area around the crossroads to the north of the village which had close to it ammunition dumps, refilling points, innumerable camps and also horse-lines. The roads were full of vehicles, horses and men.

There were seven casualty clearing stations in the village at different times, including No. 21 (XV Corps) and No. 27 (Fourth Army, attached to I Anzac Corps). As we have seen, No. 36 Casualty Clearing Station was here from 1 April 1916 to April 1917, was joined in May 1916 by No. 38 Casualty Clearing Station, and in July by No. 2/2 (London) Casualty Clearing Station. The last hospital left Heilly in June 1917, but No. 20 Casualty Clearing Station was still there in August and September 1918.

Heilly Station Cemetery, designed by Sir Edwin Lutyens, was begun in May 1916 and used by the above medical units until April 1917. In the first week of July 260 men were buried here, a very high figure. Some of the burials were carried out in the cemetery under great pressure and many of the graves are so close together that they cannot be marked individually, or they contain several burials. Where regimental badges cannot be included, 117 have been reproduced on the cloister wall of the north side of the cemetery instead. Some private memorials are still present here, which is now unusual.

Brig Gen A.S. Buckle (II.F.23) of the Royal Artillery (17th Division), who died on 18 August, is buried here. Lt Col A. F. Townsend (IV.F.8) of 11th Queen's (123rd Brigade, 41st Division) is also buried here, having died of wounds sustained in the fighting at FLERS on 16 September. A third senior officer buried here is Brig Gen D.J. Glasfurd (V.A.17), General Officer Commanding 12th Australian Brigade (4th Australian Division), who died of wounds on 12 November, having been mortally wounded by a shell in front of FLERS in a sunken lane known as Cheese Road. A senior officer brought here was Lt Col Walmisley-Dresser (IV.F.10), Commanding Officer 12th East Surreys (122nd Brigade, 41st Division); wounded in the FLERS attack in mid-September, he died at Heilly on 17 September and was buried in the cemetery.

The last burial was made in May 1919. The cemetery stands on high ground that rises sharply to the south, commanding a wide view of the wooded valley of the Ancre. It was occasionally named from Hareng Wood, which was behind it. The number of identified casualties buried here comes to 2,951.

HEM-HARDINVAL is north-west of DOULLENS and south of the River Authie. On 12 June 1916, 1/8th Worcesters (144th Brigade, 48th Division) were billeted here for one night, having come from training at SAINT-RIQUIER; they left for ACHEUX-EN-AMIÉNOIS via COIGNEUX, where they arrived on 14 June. Burials in Hem-Hardinval Communal Cemetery were begun by No. 2/1 (South Midland) Casualty Clearing Station in September 1916; the cemetery continued in use until February 1917.

HEM-MONACU lies on the north bank of the River Somme, to the south-east of CURLU. 137th Brigade (46th Division) were here at the end of February 1916. On 1 July, the French took CURLU from the Germans; it was taken over by British troops later in the year.

Hem Farm Military Cemetery is on the west side of a large farm and close to the river. Begun by the British in January 1917, it was used until March 1917 and then again in September 1918. It contains the graves of nearly 600 men, including 2 men who won the Victoria Cross. 2/Lt G.E. Cates (I.G.15) won his award posthumously east of Bouchavesnes on 8 March 1917 and Pte R. Mactier (II.J.3) gained his at Mont-Saint-Quentin, PÉRONNE on 1 September 1918.

HÉNENCOURT is 3½ miles west of ALBERT on the D91 road. The château buildings in the centre of the village and the large wood on its north-western side played very major military roles during the war and virtually *were* the village.

Although large shells fell on the village on 30 August 1915 and the staff of either XXX Corps or 51st Division were obliged to move back to QUERRIEU, Hénencourt was to be a comparatively safe billet, which explains the very considerable number of references to it in war diaries.

On 2 September 1915, 1/5th Seaforth Highlanders (152nd Brigade, 51st Division) arrived here, having already been on the Somme for several weeks on trench duty in the AUTHUILLE and LA BOISSELLE sectors. They were supposedly here for a rest, but on most nights had to supply fatigue parties for digging new trenches or repairing existing ones, or carrying up ammunition. There were compensations, however, as their billets were clean barns and stables; there were *estaminets* in the village too. On 11 September they left for LA BOISSELLE trenches, but were back again on 18 September. Three days later they were inspected by Field Marshal Lord Kitchener, prior to going up the line to Aveluy; they returned to Hénencourt on 26 September.

On 20 September, 1/6th Seaforth Highlanders (also 152nd Brigade, 51st Division) marched past Gen Sir Charles Monro, General Officer Commanding Third Army, who took the salute in front of the château. On at least one occasion, a battalion concert took place in a large hall in the château, where the battalion poet, Lt E.A. Mackintosh, 'cheered us with his own songs'.

Having spent Christmas at BOUZINCOURT, 1/5th Seaforth Highlanders returned to their previous lines at AUTHUILLE, and for a period, alternated between the AUTHUILLE and Aveluy sectors, while resting in between at Hénencourt or BOUZINCOURT. They left Hénencourt on 28 December, when they marched south to MOLLIENS-AU-BOIS.

On 23 December, 1/6th Seaforth Highlanders returned here 'covered in mud' from the AVELUY WOOD sector and 'found comfortable, dry billets in barns, and soon made ourselves comfortable'. They spent Christmas in the village, when the men were provided with excellent hot dinners – supplemented by Christmas puddings and other delicacies – which were provided by the Morayshire Comforts Committee. Company concerts also took place in the evening. On 29 December, 152nd Brigade (51st Division) began moving to a 'rest area' and halted at SAINT-GRATIEN for a night before moving on to PIERREGOT, about 10 miles north of AMIENS.

At the end of December, units of 32nd Division were here, as well as at MILLENCOURT and SENLIS-LE-SEC; they were also here again in mid-January and February. On 24 February, 17th Highland Light Infantry (97th Brigade, 32nd Division) changed their quarters 'from billets into huts in the wood. Most unpleasant, firstly on account of snow and frost, and then, following a thaw, on account of knee-deep mud.' They left for DERNANCOURT on 29 December.

On 12 April 1916, 2nd Royal Berkshires (25th Brigade, 8th Division) were in divisional reserve here and in MILLENCOURT, where sports took place. Elements of 70th Brigade (23rd Division) left the wood on 19 May, and a week later some of the personnel of No. 15 Field Company, Royal Engineers (8th Division), were in the wood for 5 days. Owing to the delay of the start of the battle, No. 15 Field Company had to arrange a sports day in the village on 29 June; officers contributed 75 francs for prizes, and activities included wheelbarrow races, a relay race and the 20yds dash. The field company returned to the village on 4 July. On 20 June, No. 94 Field Company, Royal Engineers (19th Division), were in bivouacs in the wood when carrying out road work for 8th Division.

On 27 June, 7th Loyal North Lancashires (56th Brigade, 19th Division), who had arrived from RAINNEVILLE, were here when 7th East Lancashires (also 56th Brigade, 19th Division) were given permission to light fires in the wood, which at the time was in full foliage and untouched by shell-fire. In the heart of the wood, as many as 20 great fires were lit, which almost reached the tops of the trees; up to 1,000 men were on the ground, attempting to get dry from the heavy rain that fell before the battle and delayed its start by 2 days. There were many groups of rival singers and wits, and much yelling, laughter and fooling.

7th Loyal North Lancashires marched off to the Intermediate Line, south-west of ALBERT; on 2 July, they were attached to 34th Division in the struggle for LA BOISSELLE, and on 6 July were involved in the fighting at HORSESHOE TRENCH. On 30 June, 1st Sherwood Foresters (24th Brigade, 8th Division) arrived at the wood, where they remained for 3 days. After leaving this area, 7th South Lancashires (56th Brigade, 19th Division) took part in the fighting for OVILLERS. At the end of June, during the bombardment, the effect of the barrage was watched by crowds of troops on the high ground between Hénencourt, BRESLE and MILLENCOURT.

Infantry units of 12th Division who had marched after dusk fell reached Hénencourt and MILLENCOURT by 1000hrs on 1 July, including 7th Norfolks (35th Brigade, 12th Division); at 1850hrs, they left to occupy the Intermediate Line, south-west of ALBERT, in preparation for an attack planned for 2 July, later cancelled. They were then in reserve behind the embankments of the ALBERT–Arras railway, and remained there until late at night, when they moved up into trenches for the attack against OVILLERS.

On 8 July, 25th Division moved to the village and 2nd King's Royal Rifle Corps (2nd Brigade, 1st Division) bivouacked in Hénencourt Wood. The village was described as a very pleasant camp, surrounded by woods; a few hundred yards away was the headquarters of Lt Gen Sir W. Pulteney, General Officer Commanding III Corps, in the Louis XIV château in the centre of the village.

After their heavy involvement in the HIGH WOOD fighting of 15 September, 1/15th Londons (140th Brigade, 47th Division) arrived in ALBERT, where they spent the night in billets. Next day, the march continued to the tented camp in the wood just outside Hénencourt; here, the process of reorganising took place close to MAMETZ WOOD before going to Eaucourt. Other battalions used the village in the autumn and by coincidence they were often on their way to or from the fighting at EAUCOURT L'ABBAYE. Between February and November 1916, other divisions who had units here included 1st, 8th, 12th, 15th, 19th, 23rd, 32nd, 37th, 34th and 50th Divisions; 12th and 15th Divisions had their headquarters here in the first 4 days of July.

Pte J. Jackson of 1st Cameron Highlanders (1st Brigade, 1st Division) noted in his journal that his unit were in wooden billets here; 'The whole camp was in a very bad state, being little more than a mud-hole'. Later, units from 5th and 17th Divisions were also here. Hénencourt was also the site of III Corps' main dressing station.

Outside the firing line, the village was used as a place of rest, and it even escaped extensive bombardment. However, the billeting conditions in the wood seem to have been appalling throughout 1916. The village did not have its own cemetery, but MILLENCOURT did.

The château is still a very substantial building, although at one point one of its wings was destroyed by fire. Its impressive gates came from Heilly Castle some time after 1848 and it often appears as a subject in picture books on the war. The four pillboxes at each corner of the village are from the Second World War.

HÉNU, north-west of ALBERT, is to the west of SOUASTRE on the D6 road; the château was in the north-west of the village.

On 30 August 1915, a satisfactory dressing station was chosen by 50th Field Ambulance (37th Division), and they moved here on 5 September. The staff began to get the château ready for the sick and wounded and the whole building was scrubbed out. The building was in the north-west of the village, between it and Hénu Wood. 50th Field

Ambulance left the château on 18 March 1916. An early casualty was a Pte Knowles, admitted with gunshot wounds on 20 March; Knowles died of his injuries the following day.

On 18 March, 4th Division opened a divisional rest station in the village and ran it until 3 May. On 23 April, a unit from 36th Division were based in the wood to the north-west of the village. On 6 May, 56th Division's headquarters was in the village, in preparation for the assault against GOMMECOURT; on 11 May, 1/4th Londons (168th Brigade, 56th Division) supplied a working party of 250 men to work in chalk quarries, where they dug out road material. On 1 July, 2/1st (London) Field Ambulance (56th Division) sent walking cases to Hénu, where casualties were fed and had their wounds dressed. On 2 July, 9 officers and 214 men were admitted and half of them were evacuated to a casualty clearing station.

Also on 1 July, 46th Division (involved at Gommecourt with 56th Division) arranged for all available motor ambulances and horse transport to rendezvous at the crossroads ½ mile to the west of the SOUASTRE–Hénu road; walking wounded cases reached the village, a journey of 4 miles, where they were fed and had their wounds dressed.

On 5 July, advance headquarters of 56th Division was here again; later in the year, 17th and 33rd Divisions also had units or headquarters here.

HÉRISSART, on the D114 road, is between TOUTENCOURT and RUBEMPRÉ and north-east of AMIENS. On 1 July 1916, elements of 113th Brigade (38th Division) were here and at PUCHE-VILLERS at Zero Hour, when other brigades were in nearby villages. On 17 October, elements of 19th Division were in the area, including TOUTEN-COURT and RUBEMPRÉ, and on 30 October, half of 97th Brigade (32nd Division) were here, as well as at RUBEMPRÉ.

During the mid-1920s, there were 13 British graves in Hérissart Communal Cemetery, from which plants and flowers were continually being stolen, as well as from the civilian graves.

HERLEVILLE is south-east of BRAY-SUR-SOMME on the D143E road. There were two graves here in the mid-1920s, when the churchyard, which can be found on the north side of the road to Raine-court, was in a very bad state, and the church itself in ruins.

HIGH WOOD (Bois de Fourcaux) is on the D107 road between MARTINPUICH and LONGUEVAL.

In July 1916, it was behind the German Second Line, which ran in front of the villages of BAZENTIN-LE-GRAND and BAZENTIN-LE-PETIT. The defences ran through the Flers Ridge to THIEPVAL, and although the ridge was scarcely more than 100ft in height, it nevertheless dominated the countryside for miles around. From High Wood the enemy could observe any Allied attempts to capture it; the summit ran from east to west through the northern section. At the time of the initial fighting, the trees in the Wood had not been damaged by shell-fire and the country beyond it was not pockmarked by shell-holes. From the high ground just west of the Wood, it would be possible to enfilade any attacker, and the enemy had turned it into a fortress. It had grassy rides and a lot of young saplings, which were later to make progress difficult for any attacker.

On 6 July, 16th King's Royal Rifle Corps (100th Brigade, 33rd Division) were involved in an attempt on the Wood and part of the Switch Line, which ran through the northern part of the Wood; it was unsuccessful, however, as was a similar attack on 13 July. On 14 July, after the enemy Second Line had been successfully breached by a combination of a dawn attack and a creeping barrage, there was an opportunity for 7th Division to make an advance on the Wood, but they were held back by Lt Gen Sir H. Horne, General Officer Commanding XV Corps, who wanted to give the chance of capturing the Wood to the cavalry. With hindsight, this seems to have been a fatal mistake, as at the time some patrols reported the Wood was not even occupied. This missed opportunity allowed for enemy reserves to be brought up, and led to the Wood remaining in German hands for a further 2 months. In turn, this affected the length of time that the enemy were able to retain possession of LONGUEVAL and DEL-VILLE WOOD.

Lt Col N.M. Hughes-Hellett (IWM 86/13/1) was another observer of the situation, when in command of 7th King's Shropshire Light Infantry (8th Brigade, 3rd Division); from Bazentin Ridge, he could see no sign of life in High Wood, and sought permission from 91st Brigade (7th Division) to occupy it, but the request was not granted until artillery penetrations had been carried out. He noted that next day the Indian cavalry went forward, only to be slaughtered.

On 14 July, the Indian cavalry were ordered to seize the Wood and the enemy's new line to the east and west of it, as a stepping-stone to a further advance. At 0740hrs, 20th Deccan Horse (Secund-erabad Brigade, 2nd (Indian) Cavalry Division) set off from MONTAUBAN-DE-PICARDIE, but owing to the slippery nature of the ground they did not arrive until early afternoon, after a journey that had taken 4 hours. They and 7th Dragoon Guards (also Secunderabad Brigade, 2nd (Indian) Cavalry Division) were to move forward to Sabot Copse (between MAMETZ WOOD and Bazentin-le-Grand Wood) and then attack towards the east side of the Wood, while 20th Deccan Horse on the right would operate at the front of the Wood and then move eastwards towards DELVILLE WOOD. Their advance was delayed because LONGUEVAL had not been taken, one of the conditions of the advance.

Finally, when on the flanks of 7th Division, two squadrons of 7th Dragoon Guards galloped up the slope towards the Wood with lances and pennants flying while other squadrons patrolled the high ground between DELVILLE WOOD and High Wood. Although presenting a good target for the enemy to fire down the slope on with their machine guns, the British cavalry did manage to enter the Wood at about 2000hrs, but were unable to hang on. It was an uneven contest and 7th Dragoon Guards lost 3 men killed and 21 wounded, and 40 of their horses became casualties; 20th Deccan Horse were to fare far worse, with 11 men killed, 39 wounded, and 72 casualties among their horses. The enemy had clearly been waiting for the attack and were well-protected by concrete positions.

The rest of the battle plan in this sector of the battlefield was for 7th Division to relieve 2nd (Indian) Cavalry Division and for 21st Division to move northwards and clear the communication trenches between BAZENTIN-LE-PETIT and the light railway at MARTINPUICH. At 1430hrs, 21st and 1st Divisions were to provide a combined operation, and at the same time 34th Division were to push forward strong patrols towards POZIÈRES on their left. However, 21st and 1st Divisions did not make progress, and the attack was postponed; 62nd Brigade (21st Division) had become severely depleted as a result of the fighting in the afternoon for the north-west corner of Bazentin-le-Petit Wood, which was not actually cleared until 1900hrs. False news of the fall of LONGUEVAL reached Corps headquarters and the plan was for 7th Division to advance at 1715hrs, but these instructions did not reach 7th Division until later. 91st Brigade, the reserve brigade of 7th Division, lay to the east of MAMETZ WOOD, and were to be supported on the left by the leading brigade of 33rd Division, which would pass through 21st Division.

Finally, the advance began at about 1900hrs, with the cavalry and 1st South Staffords and 2nd Queen's (both 91st Brigade, 7th Division), who went into the Wood but were unable to clear it as they were held up by the Switch Line and defences on the western side of the Wood. According to the *Official History of the War*, 33rd Division never received the order to support 7th Division. Isolated British troops were holding on in the Wood, but next day they were withdrawn to the general line of the LONGUEVAL–BAZENTIN road.

In his books *Warrior* and *Pilgrimage*, Lt Col G.S. Hutchison refers to the fighting at High Wood on 15 July; in addition, he wrote a *History of the 33rd Division in France and Flanders 1915–1919*. Although he tends to repeat himself, he does have a good story to tell, and was there at the time. It is because of this that the author has depended on his accounts, whereas the *Official History of the War* is almost dismissive of the role played by 33rd Division on 15 July. Hutchison wrote that on the eve of 15 July patrols went out to make contact with the enemy and were fired upon from the edge of the Wood and by the riflemen lying out in scrapes, and in narrow trenches south of the village. The British discovered that the enemy had laid out several strands of wire which were uncut by the artillery and hidden by the long grass. This formed a dangerous obstacle and requests for bombardment were not met.

At around the same time, 1/9th Highland Light Infantry and 1st Queen's (both 100th Brigade, 33rd Division) took up positions between High Wood and BAZENTIN-LE-PETIT to the south-west. At dawn, a thick ground mist obscured completely both High Wood and the village of MARTINPUICH to the north. The brigade concentrated in the valley about 800yds to the west of High Wood, and there was no cover to screen them across the area of no man's land. 1st Queen's were ordered to attack on the left and 1/9th Highland Light Infantry on the right, supported by 16th King's Royal Rifle Corps and with 2nd Worcesters (both 100th Brigade, 33rd Division) in reserve.

Each of the battalions in the forward wave was to be supported by one machine-gun section consisting of four guns. According to *The Machine Gunner*, the machine-gun section with 1st Queen's were under Lt Heseltine and that of 1/9th Highland Light Infantry under Lt Huxley. Under cover of the mist, the transport were even able to get forward to the area of concentration. At the same time, 98th Brigade (33rd Division), together with their machine-gun company, were in position at the south-west on the outskirts of BAZENTIN-LE-PETIT.

Hutchison's brigade were deployed behind 1/9th Highland Light Infantry and they lay down in the long grass awaiting the signal to assault. The mist was clearing and then rising rapidly, and suddenly High Wood seemed quite near and just up a slope. They could even see the village of MARTINPUICH with its jagged ruins and rafters askew, broken walls and shattered fruit trees apppearing to look down on them. However, the men who crouched in the grass were probably visible to German observers in High Wood.

Hutchison noted that he could see 'broad-kilted buttocks' and 'the bronzed thighs and knees' of 1/9th Highland Light Infantry lining the slope in front of him before the attackers rose and swept forward under the cover of a weak bombardment. It was the first of several attempts that day to take the Wood. There was an inferno of rifle and machine-gun fire, from the edge of the Wood and its trees all along the ridge to MARTINPUICH. To Hutchison's left, he could see men of 1st Queen's passing up the slope towards MARTINPUICH and stumbling on a low wire entanglement. They were cut down and there was no movement; 1/9th Highland Light Infantry, too, were virtually annihilated. At the same time, an enemy barrage of great intensity suddenly opened up.

Hutchison's orders were to move forward in close support of the advancing waves and as his company rose, they too were cut down, by machine-gun fire. Hutchison managed amid the hottest fire to get two machine-gun sections to within 150yds of the Wood, and engage the enemy who were posted in the trees. He could see them moving forward, silhouetted against the skyline. The attack of 16th King's Royal Rifle Corps had also failed and Hutchison rushed forward two companies of 16th King's Royal Rifle Corps, as they had no officer left, in support of the guns. They were able to inflict some damage on the enemy. Hutchison wrote a hurried note to Col Pardoe of 2nd Worcesters, who were in reserve in a sunken road 300yds to the rear.

Meanwhile, a field battery began to enfilade from the valley between POZIÈRES and MARTINPUICH and commenced shelling among the wounded. Hutchison turned his gun in the direction of the battery and claimed to have hit two of the gun loaders. By noon, 2nd Worcesters had obtained a footing in High Wood and 98th Brigade (33rd Division) began to come up on the left in order to fill the gap made by 1st Queen's. The brigade on the right were showing signs of weakness and began to dribble back, which exposed in turn the right flank of 100th Brigade on the south-east side of the Wood. Hutchison said that he saw a squadron of Indian cavalry, their faces dark under glistening helmets,

galloping across the valley towards the slope. A few disappeared over the slope but never came back.

During the advance, Hutchison had noticed a small quarry screened by a hedge and they dismantled their guns and began to retire to the safety of the quarry. He then found himself in charge of about 41 soldiers who were the remnants from three battalions that had been involved in attacking the Wood. They 'reversed' the former German trench and manned a German machine gun to ward off any counter-attacks. During this time, Hutchison could see men moving up to the Wood.

Hutchison's party rushed over the lip of the quarry where they had retreated, towards the Wood, and collected ammunition from the dead of earlier in the day. His group then secured a position in the Wood, and after dusk, signalled for help and sent a runner back to headquarters. After 2 hours, he could see men moving up the valley towards the Wood, and was soon among men from 2nd Royal Welsh Fusiliers (19th Brigade, 33rd Division); on the left were battalions of 98th Brigade and others from Manchester, men fresh from divisional reserve. Brigade by this time had sent orders to Hutchison to return with his men.

The six machine-gun teams of No. 100 Company, Machine Gun Corps had all become casualties; Hutchison gathered up the rest and got five into action as a battery that guarded the right of the brigade, while the remaining guns were disposed in groups covering the whole front. If Hutchison's company had not retired then, the company to a man would have perished, according to *The Machine Gunner*.

Commenting on the day's activities, the Official Historian notes that there seemed to have been little co-operation between 7th and 33rd Divisions.

In *The War in the Air* by H.A. Jones, it is noted that at 1700hrs an aeroplane of No. 3 Squadron was sent to find the exact situation in High Wood; the observer reported that the British were holding on to a trench to the west of the Wood, and were also collecting south of the BAZENTIN-LE PETIT road. From just inside the Wood on the west side, he could see flags being waved in reply to his signals, but on the east side the Germans were in strength and opened rapid fire on his aeroplane. The whole length of the troublesome Switch Line was seen to be full of German infantry. Until the Switch Line was taken the cost of hanging on to High Wood would be exceedingly heavy, and it was evacuated by 0800hrs on 16 July.

Although the above account has been mainly based on 100th Brigade's involvement, it would be churlish to neglect 98th Brigade (also 33rd Division), who had also been involved, having come up from BAZENTIN-LE-PETIT in the early part of the morning of 15 July. 1st Middlesex led the way, forming the left of 33rd Division's attack on a frontage of 1,000yds, but on leaving BAZENTIN-LE-PETIT they too came under machine-gun and shell-fire. By mid-afternoon, the attack had been abandoned.

By 0800hrs on 16 July, 91st Brigade (7th Division) were concentrated behind BAZENTIN-LE-GRAND, having withdrawn from High Wood at 2325hrs on 15 July. On succeeding days, the preparations for a renewal of the attack were hampered by the bombardment of CATERPILLAR VALLEY with gas and lachrymatory shells.

In *The Machine Gunner*, it is noted that 19th Brigade relieved 100th Brigade, and what was left of them returned to defensive positions on the north side of MAMETZ WOOD. Awards were presented, including a Military Cross to Hutchison.

Fighting of the bitterest kind ensued, in which both 19th and 98th Brigades (33rd Division) were involved; in particular, 1st and 1/5th Cameronians (both 19th Brigade, 33rd Division) suffered heavy losses. The attack was held up, and holding on to the ground gained became ever more costly, owing to the very heavy shell-fire; trenches dug by night by 18th Middlesex (pioneers of 33rd Division) were obliterated by day.

On the night of 17/18 July, 21st Division handed over their position in BAZENTIN-LE-PETIT to 33rd Division and withdrew to reserve; 7th Division relieved 3rd Division on 300yds of front eastward from Bazentin-le-Grand Wood. High Wood was to be included in the objectives of the main operation, now fixed for 18 July. It was to be a part of a main Anglo-French attack planned for 19 and 20 July.

On 19 July, 2nd King's Own Scottish Borderers (13th Brigade, 5th Division) marched up past FRICOURT and MAMETZ and across country that was freely shelled towards the Wood. After dark, they were guided to the former German Second Line between BAZENTIN-LE-PETIT and GUILLEMONT to take up positions; relief was completed by 0230hrs. The line extended from north of BAZENTIN-LE-PETIT to the south end of High Wood, whence it went in front of a track leading south-west and then to LONGUEVAL. About 400yds north-east of this latter position and roughly parallel to it was a sunken road, lying invisible some 50yds down the reverse slope of the crest.

The first task was the acquisition of the track as a jumping-off place, and this was given to 2nd King's

Own Scottish Borderers to accomplish. Divisional orders were for them to move immediately to reinforce 7th Division, holding the line between High Wood and LONGUEVAL; 13th Brigade were on the left of 95th Brigade, close to LONGUEVAL. From there, the line was continued by XIII Corps past the crossroads and church in the centre of the village, through the southern part of DELVILLE WOOD and then due south past WATERLÔT FARM, to the west of GUILLEMONT. The German Third or Switch Line was opposite them.

Robert Graves of 2nd Royal Welsh Fusiliers wrote that his battalion were relieved at BAZENTIN-LE-PETIT and were ordered to attack High Wood, which was 1,000yds away to the right at the top of the slope; at this time, 2nd Royal Welsh Fusiliers had been reduced by casualties to about 400. They waited at BAZENTIN-LE-PETIT cemetery on the reverse slope of a slight rise, about ½ mile from the Wood. Their role in the attack was to be part of the reserve. Graves reported that the 'Jocks' got into the Wood and that 2nd Royal Welsh Fusiliers were not called upon until 1100hrs. The enemy then put down a heavy barrage on Bazentin Ridge and a third of the battalion were lost before the 'show' had even begun. Graves himself was wounded in Bazentin Cemetery and was taken down to the former German dressing station at the north end of MAMETZ WOOD.

According to Capt C.H. Pigg of 2nd Worcesters, on the evening of 19 July, orders had come through for them to move forward. They passed again through the front line, to take up a covering position on the left flank of troops who were to make another attack on High Wood. Battalion headquarters was at Bazentin Cemetery with their A Company, who were to be in reserve; C Company were in support some 200yds further forward while B and D Companies were in front and to the left of C Company, facing north-westwards towards the Switch Line, from which trouble might be expected. They dug in in pairs in slits, using shell-holes and previously made excavations.

Heavy firing went on through most of the night and especially around 0300hrs, when 19th Brigade (33rd Division) attacked the Wood. After the night had passed, the hot sun rose in a cloudless sky; all that day they sat tight, and casualties were few as the German artillery had not 'found' them. At around midday, Pigg walked down the slope to report to headquarters, but there were no fresh orders or information to be had. Having spent a day in this exposed position, 2nd Worcesters finally received orders to withdraw, which they did at dusk, when they went to support trenches on Windmill Ridge. They returned in the darkness through German shelling, which included gas ammunition.

On 20 July, on the right of 5th and 7th Divisions, the first objective was to be BLACK ROAD, a track that ran north-north-west to the southern corner of High Wood. 95th Brigade (5th Division) had already taken over Pont Street, whence 3rd Division's attack began after a bombardment at 0325hrs against LONGUEVAL and DELVILLE WOOD, which was to coincide with this latest attempt to take High Wood. 13th Brigade (5th Division) were to advance in tandem with 7th Division, which then had to secure 800yds of BLACK ROAD up to High Wood. BLACK ROAD to Wood Lane ran south-easterly towards LONGUEVAL and parallel to the ridge connecting High Wood with LONGUEVAL and DELVILLE WOOD. SWITCH TRENCH was in turn behind them and full of enemy machine-gunners. The ground was also littered with the dead horses of the Secunderabad Brigade (2nd (Indian) Cavalry Division). The second objective, 300yds beyond BLACK ROAD, was Wood Lane, which reached High Wood at its eastern corner. The task of capturing the Wood itself was given again to 33rd Division, who were to advance from the south-west.

The planned advance began at 0325hrs; 8th Devons and 2nd Gordon Highlanders (both 20th Brigade, 7th Division) made progress and kept in touch with troops of 5th Division to their right. All the time under enemy shell-fire, 8th Devons and 2nd Gordon Highlanders went on over the crest to Wood Lane. The British artillery lifted at 0325hrs. However, despite the hour, the Germans were waiting for the attackers in full force and had concealed their machine guns in the standing corn. The attackers came under heavy fire, 2nd Gordon Highlanders in particular. The two battalions dug in 25yds short of Wood Lane, but the position quickly became untenable and they had to crawl back to BLACK WOOD and consolidate. As High Wood had not been taken, a further attack was thought to be pointless, and after dark 5th Division relieved the troops of 7th Division on the BLACK ROAD. Sadly, Lt Col B.G.R. Gordon DSO, Commanding Officer 2nd Gordon Highlanders, was killed during this relief; he was later buried at Dernancourt Communal Cemetery (K.4).

On 20 July, Pte T.W.H. Veale of 8th Devons (20th Brigade, 7th Division) gained his Victoria Cross at the east end of High Wood; in brief, his citation noted:

Hearing that a wounded officer was lying out in front, Private Veale went out in search, and found him lying amid the growing corn within fifty yards of the enemy. He dragged the officer to a shell-hole, returned for water, and took it out. Finding that he could not single-handed carry in the officer he returned for assistance, and took out two volunteers. One of the party was killed when carrying the officer, and heavy fire necessitated leaving the officer in a shell-hole. At dusk Private Veale went out again with volunteers to bring in the officer. Whilst doing this an enemy patrol was observed approaching. Private Veale at once went back and procured a Lewis gun, and with the fire of the gun he covered the party, and the officer was finally carried to safety . . .

Canon Crosse of 8th Devons (see MAMETZ entry) also played a role here, when he acted as one of the stretcher-bearers with Pte Veale.

Meanwhile, 33rd Division had been fighting hard in High Wood and indeed had made some progress, at least in the southern part. On 19 July, 20th Royal Fusiliers (19th Brigade, 33rd Division) had moved to battle positions in the valley about 1 mile from High Wood; one of their companies had dug in at the side of a small sunken road and moved forward over open ground that was badly shelled. They went to a support position at the edge of the Wood. On the previous evening, 2nd Worcesters had pushed out a line of posts from BAZENTIN-LE-PETIT in the direction of the western corner of the Wood to protect the flank of the assault of 1st and 1/5th Cameronians; these battalions had been in reserve at MAMETZ on 19 July and, after a march of 3 miles, formed up near the windmill east of BAZENTIN-LE-PETIT, facing the south-west side of the Wood. With the help of No. 11 Field Company, Royal Engineers (33rd Division), the Scottish battalions forced their way into the Wood, coming under fire from part of the Switch Line and also from a strongpoint on the western corner; 20th Royal Fusiliers, in support, followed close behind the attacking Scots, and there was fierce and muddled fighting. At 0900hrs, 2nd Royal Welsh Fusiliers were called up, and on their way were heavily shelled.

The very hard fighting in the Wood necessitated the help of a relief force; accordingly, 1st Queen's and 16th King's Royal Rifle Corps were then brought up. Before they arrived, however, the enemy began a gas and shell barrage after dusk; this, coupled with the British retreat to the southern half of the Wood, brought the day's fighting to an end and the two sides consolidated. Pte Frank Richards of 2nd Royal Welsh Fusiliers, author of *Old Soldiers Never Die*, noted that his brigade were hanging on to three parts of High Wood and were relieved at 2200hrs; three-quarters of them became casualties. According to Richards, half of the brigade had been 'knocked over' before they even entered the Wood.

In 1955, J.L. Hodson published a book called *Return to the Wood*; in it, he described the experiences of a 'William Hargreaves'. In real life, Hodson was with 20th Royal Fusiliers (19th Brigade, 33rd Division) and was later commissioned into 63rd Division. In this book, the protagonists' role in the attack on High Wood began at 1240hrs, 2 or 3 hours after 1st Cameronians. They advanced in open order, and on their way up via Mametz Valley, were exposed to a gas barrage. On the roadside, they saw dead soldiers with haversacks which were daubed with red paint to indicate their brigade or division. They could see the 'Scotties' streaming back from High Wood, resembling a ragged football crowd. On 21 July, Hodson noted that they crossed the same 100yds that the 'Scotties' had. When they reached the Wood, it was a mass of broken blazing trees; they were protected by a superb bombardment of French 75s. They got into the Wood without much loss, although it was 'taped' by either side's artillery, to the yard. However, in 24 hours, they lost two-thirds of their battalion, mainly from shelling.

Conditions in the Wood were hellish, and eventually they were relieved by 16th King's Royal Rifle Corps. Sgt A.G. Skelton of 20th Royal Fusiliers, a record of whose experiences is held at the Imperial War Museum, wrote that he escorted a machine-gun party to the strongpoint at the north-west corner of the Wood, which had been made by a field company.

On the night of 21 July, 33rd Division in and around High Wood were finally relieved by 51st Division. During this period, the poet Lt E.A. Mackintosh of 1/5th Seaforth Highlanders (152nd Brigade, 51st Division) was wounded. He recovered later, only to be killed by enemy fire from Cantaing Mill during the Battle of Cambrai when serving with 1/4th Seaforth Highlanders on 21 November 1917.

Before he became a brigadier, R.E. Fryer was with a field company of 38th Division when they moved up from MAMETZ WOOD, with High Wood as the prize. The brigade to which he was attached, mostly Scots, were ordered to attack High Wood. A British gun was firing short as they lay outside the Wood, but with no wireless and only runners, it was difficult to get a message through to the battery. The brigade did attack and capture the Wood, but the enemy counter-attacked.

When in the Wood, Fryer came across a concrete dugout. At about 2100hrs or 2200hrs, still in the Wood, he was wounded by a large shell; his orderly got him back to the rapid aid post in CATERPILLAR VALLEY, and then on to a casualty clearing station at BRAY-SUR-SOMME, where his wounds were dressed and he was given a good breakfast. He then travelled by hospital barge and on to hospital at Etaples, followed by a voyage to Southampton and hospital in Reading.

Back at High Wood, the barrage lifted at 2200hrs; 1st Royal West Kents and 14th Royal Warwicks (both 13th Brigade, 5th Division) advanced and made some progress, until beyond the crest and in the lights of German flares; they were enfiladed by enemy machine guns from the eastern corner of High Wood. The fire became intense and the attack turned into a disaster for the two battalions. The same strongpoint also defeated 1/9th Royal Scots and a platoon of 1/4th Gordon Highlanders (both 154th Brigade, 51st Division); 2nd King's Own Scottish Borderers and 15th Royal Warwicks (both 13th Brigade, 5th Division) were also ordered to advance towards the Switch Line, but without any positive gain.

In their time in the line, 33rd Division had not adequately dealt with the strong machine-gun positions in High Wood, and 2nd King's Own Scottish Borderers ended their part in the attack by being called upon as a support, instead of being able to develop a success. The whole of 5th Division found themselves back where they had started; 51st Division fared little better.

On 23 July, a trench was taped out in broad daylight from the windmill at BAZENTIN-LE-PETIT to High Wood; a communication trench known as High Alley, running from BAZENTIN-LE-GRAND to High Wood, was improved, and a new communication trench known as Thistle Alley was begun. A footing had been established in the Wood and proved sufficient to deprive the enemy of the wide observation that they had previously enjoyed. Nevertheless, the position taken over by 51st Division was very dangerous to traverse. The route by which troops went up the line, and by which all stores and rations were brought, was an indifferent path along the valley just south of MAMETZ WOOD, and the Germans knew this. The road was never empty of men or vehicles at any hour of the day or night, and although the Germans did not have direct observation, they could see what was going on in HAPPY VALLEY by means of observation balloons.

At 2100hrs on 23 July, 1st Norfolks (15th Brigade, 5th Division) relieved 2nd King's Own Scottish

Borderers, who retired to POMMIERS REDOUBT. On the night of 28 July, the headquarters of 1/5th Gordon Highlanders (153rd Brigade, 51st Division) was in the south-east corner of High Wood. On 1 August a new device, called a Bartlett forcing jack, was used to help with trench digging. It comprised an ammonal mixture and iron pipes that exploded in the ground; the resultant crater could then be used as trenches. On the night of 2 August, the line of 51st Division up to the western edge of High Wood was taken over by 34th Division, and in the Wood itself saps were pushed out as far as the German positions in advance of the Switch Line. Additionally, a new forward trench was dug, closer to the German position along Wood Lane, east of the Wood.

On the night of 6 August, 33rd Division relieved 51st Division. During the period 6–12 August there was patrol activity on both sides of High Wood. On 18 August, 98th Brigade (33rd Division) were ordered to take a portion of Wood Lane and some German positions in High Wood. Wood Lane itself was to be taken by 4th King's and 1/4th Suffolks (both 98th Brigade, 33rd Division), but they were not successful. Flame-throwers, burning oil drums and pipe-pushers were used on this occasion; the last-named blew a crater in the lines of 2nd Argyll & Sutherland Highlanders (98th Brigade, 33rd Division). Later, 19th Brigade (33rd Division) were brought up to relieve the whole front line until the morning of 19 August.

Pte Frank Richards wrote that in mid-August, 2nd Royal Welsh Fusiliers took over trenches in High Wood; the British trench ran just inside the Wood towards the centre of it. Richards, who was in signals, wrote that he dumped their telephone on the firestep and that they were in a bay by themselves. Anyone who left the centre of the Wood would have to pass them to make their way to the communication trenches. 2nd Royal Welsh Fusiliers were to provide working parties to dig a communication trench to High Wood and to fetch and carry from the Bazentin dumps. On 18 August, an unsuccessful attack on the Wood was made by 1st Brigade (1st Division).

Towards the end of August, 33rd Division were called upon once again to capture the Switch Line, although they had already lost 799 men in previous attempts. They worked in preparation in DEATH VALLEY and loaded ammunition at Green Dump. Hutchison placed 10 machine guns in Savoy Trench, from where they had a magnificent view of the German line at a range of about 2,000yds. For 2 days they carried ammunition to the battery positions, as well as great quantities of water for cooling purposes, that was stored in empty petrol cans. It was planned that No. 100 Company, Machine Gun Corps (33rd Division), were to stage a machine-gun barrage under Hutchison; the fire was to be maintained for 12 hours in order to cover attacks and consolidation. The Vickers guns proved their stamina; during the attack on 24 August, 250 rounds short of 1 million were fired by the 10 guns. The attack was successful and the operation ended with the capture of DELVILLE WOOD, but the north-east corner of High Wood still remained in German hands. However, 19th and 98th Brigades had gained certain tactical advantages at High Wood in the recapture of Orchard Trench, Black Watch Trench and the snipers east of Black Watch Trench. 2nd Argyll & Sutherland Highlanders were involved in a further attack through High Wood.

On 26 August, 2nd Royal Welsh Fusiliers returned to High Wood when 33rd Division were marking time before the next attempt to take it. On 3 September, 8th Buffs (17th Brigade, 24th Division) made some progress west of Wood Lane by a frontal attack, which was later checked. Also on 3 September, four pipes were fired by the Royal Engineers when the infantry attacked; a tube of 21 pipes was successfully fired to the south-east of the Wood, after great trouble and many casualties. The overall results of these and other mining experiments did not encourage further pipe-pushing in High Wood.

According to Pte J. Jackson, 1st Cameron Highlanders (1st Brigade, 1st Division) relieved a battalion of the Norfolk Regiment in front of the Wood on or around 3 September, when the whole area was little more than a sea of mud. By now, High Wood

had been reduced to a tangled mass of broken trees, and smashed wire fences, through which, in various directions, ran lines of trenches. Guides were to meet us, and lead us to the front lines, but we could find none of these, so we set off to locate the Norfolks ourselves . . . The trenches were full of bodies both British and German. They lay in grotesque shapes, some indeed stood propped against the parapet, and more than once in the inky darkness we spoke to men who were beyond the power of answering our questions . . . In passing, I might mention that a large wooded monument in the shape of St Andrew's Cross was erected to the memory of the Cameron Highlanders, who fell in defence of ground at High Wood. This bore a Gaelic inscription 'To the brave who are no more'.

This memorial was later destroyed in the German 1917 offensive.

It seems that around 7 September, the German hold on the Wood began to weaken, because on that day there was found to be no opposition at Wood Lane; it was subsequently consolidated. On 8 September, 2nd Welsh (3rd Brigade, 1st Division) made some progress in the western half of High Wood; 1st Glosters (3rd Brigade, 1st Division), too, were in action and also remarked on how few Germans were now in the Wood. Nevertheless, the enemy still kept up steady machine-gun fire from the north. The situation deteriorated; suddenly, the whole area was 'alive with bullets', and was quickly strewn with British dead and wounded. The shelling, too, became severe, and the artillery support was inadequate. In support were 1st South Wales Borderers (also 3rd Brigade, 1st Division); Col Pritchard was much grieved at their losses. Maj Gen E.P. Strickland, General Officer Commanding 1st Division, began an enquiry as to why 3rd Brigade were unable to take the Wood; one would have thought that the Wood being so strongly defended was reason enough.

On 9 September, a second mine was blown, which destroyed the enemy garrison holding the lip of the earlier mine crater; this time, an advance proceeded unchecked. The combined craters were 135ft across and 35ft deep. 1st Division tried to clear the Wood. 2nd King's Royal Rifle Corps and 2nd Royal Sussex (2nd Brigade, 1st Division) assembled at Wood Lane; this time, there was progress, and contact was maintained with 165th Brigade on the right. On 11 September, just under half the Wood was in British hands and it was full of charred tree stumps and bodies.

After 2 months of fighting and hundreds of casualties, 47th Division were now chosen to take High Wood. On 12 September, 1/15th Londons (140th Brigade, 47th Division) left FRANVILLERS; after their training, every man understood what he had to do and where he had to go in the battle plan. With two tanks allotted to them in the place of an artillery barrage, the battalion left FRANVILLERS and marched to Bécourt Wood, where they relieved 2nd Royal Sussex (2nd Brigade, 1st Division) in what appeared to be a 'big rubbish tip'. They were to remain there until 14 September.

A corporal attached to No. 140 Trench Mortar Battery (47th Division) wrote that his unit were camped in bivouacs on the crest of a ridge just behind the old front line, and to the left of Bécourt Wood. As far as the eye could see there were miles of tents, bivouacs, limbers and horse-lines; huge dumps of supplies and ammunition covered the ground, and between them, in any old corner, were the big guns. The sky was continuously patrolled by Allied aircraft. In the dip below them lay FRICOURT, and the Allied guns were firing non-stop.

Although 47th Division were to capture the Wood itself, they did not succeed on their own; two other divisions were involved in the battle, 50th and 15th. The objectives of 47th and 50th Divisions ran from east to west, along the reverse slope of the ridge linking the FLERS defences with the village of MARTINPUICH; 15th Division were to wait until the High Wood flank was progressing before pressing on to capture the whole of MARTIN-PUICH. 47th Division were also to cover the left of the New Zealand Division, who were to attack with two brigades.

1/15th Londons were to be allotted the first German line in the Wood itself, with 1/7th Londons (also 140th Brigade, 47th Division) on the right and 1/17th Londons (141st Brigade, 47th Division) on their left. Full 'dress rehearsals' at FRANVILLERS had been attended by the whole division and included units of artillery, trench mortars and contact aeroplanes attached to the division.

The second objective was to be the Starfish Line, down the forward slope, and the third, on the right, was the strong Flers Line, where 140th Brigade were to join up with the New Zealanders, falling back to 141st Brigade in a communication trench, Drop Alley, when the final objective was progressed westerly along Prue Trench in the valley.

After they had taken the first objective, 1/7th and 1/15th Londons were to be in the van, including the Switch Line and the northern point of High Wood; 1/8th Londons (140th Brigade, 47th Division) were to come through and secure the second line, while 1/6th Londons (also 140th Brigade, 47th Division) were to take the final objective. In the first stage of the advance, 1/15th Londons were to clear the enemy from High Wood in conjunction with 1/7th Londons and 1/18th Londons (141st Brigade, 47th Division). Four tanks were to pass through the Wood and four were to be involved in the attack against MARTINPUICH.

The attack was to begin at 0550hrs on 15 September. Troops of 1/15th Londons assembled in Black Watch Trench and were issued with rum. At that time the tanks had not been seen or even heard. The assembly trenches were irregular in formation and the men of B, C and D Companies were told to creep out before Zero Hour, so that when the attack began they would be on the extreme right. These companies began to creep up soon after 0330hrs.

The enemy soon retaliated, and even before Zero Hour these companies were under murderous rifle and machine-gun fire; at the same time, the German artillery barraged the Allied assembly trenches. Unsurprisingly, casualties were very high. Leaving their assembly trenches later, A Company fared better, as the enemy were occupied with the other companies, and carried the first and second German trenches outside High Wood with comparatively little loss.

One of the tanks showed up late and then got stuck in a communication trench; another got in front of D Company's objective and caught fire. By 1100hrs, No. 140 Trench Mortar Battery (47th Division) had come to the rescue; as a result, C and D Companies were able to go forward again. The tanks could make no headway over broken tree stumps and deeply pitted ground, however, and were stuck before they could give the help expected of them.

The infantry were short of artillery coverage, due to the planned assistance of the tanks. By 1140hrs, after No. 140 Trench Mortar Battery had fired 750 mortar shells into High Wood, the Germans began surrendering to bombing parties of the Londoners, who worked forward around the flanks; several hundred prisoners were taken, along with machine guns and howitzers. By noon, the whole of High Wood was in British possession, together with the Switch Line beyond. Only 150 men of the four companies of 1/15th Londons reached their objective; the remnants of the battalion advanced a little beyond the Switch Line and dug themselves in to a new trench. The Starfish Line was still to be carried.

During the day, 1/6th and 1/8th Londons (both 140th Brigade, 47th Division) had pushed through to take trenches some distance beyond, known as the Flers Line, connecting FLERS with EAUCOURT L'ABBAYE and the Starfish Line, which was the German Intermediate Line. These operations were only partly successful and in the early evening of 15 September, 1/21st Londons (142nd Brigade, 47th Division), who up to then had been in reserve, were sent up to attack the western part of the Starfish Line, known as the COUGH DROP; 1/15th Londons were to take over the Starfish Line once 1/21st Londons had vacated it. The latter battalion, however, were caught by intense artillery and machine-gun fire when they emerged from High Wood. The attack subsequently failed, but the Starfish Redoubt was taken.

In *The History of the 47th (London) Division*, it is noted that 1/17th and 1/18th Londons (both 141st Brigade, 47th Division) and half of 1/15th

Londons had a desperate struggle in High Wood for every foot of the advance. The Germans met them with bombs and rifle fire from their trenches, and machine guns from their concrete emplacements, still undamaged, mowed them down. No. 140 Trench Mortar Battery had a dramatic effect on the German garrison, however, and by 1300hrs, the Wood was reported clear.

On the flanks, the progress had been faster; essentially, the Wood was taken because the troops on either side went forward and left High Wood behind. On the right, the tanks had been a success, causing dismay to the German garrison at FLERS. They had gone forward with the New Zealanders, with 7th Battalion, Tank Corps, fighting their way to the Starfish Line and 6th Battalion, Tank Corps, beyond this again. The objective was to make good a ridge running north-east from High Wood to a point above the villages of FLERS and EAUCOURT L'ABBAYE; this involved the capture of the COUGH DROP, a group of trenches, lozenge in shape, that were just under this ridge, and a communication trench called Drop Alley that ran from it in a north-easterly direction to the Flers Line itself. It was thought to be imperative that a footing should be made where Drop Alley joined the Flers Line.

In 4 days of fighting, 47th Division lost 4,500 casualties, including Lt Col A.P. Hamilton of 1/19th Londons (141st Brigade) on 15 September; according to *The History of the 47th (London) Division*, 'he had called all available men to follow him, and went up into the wood to try to restore order in the confused fighting'. (See Flat Iron Copse Cemetery in entry for MAMETZ WOOD.) The battalions that suffered most were those which had been in the open and had been caught by German machine-gun and artillery fire, namely 1/6th Londons (140th Brigade) and 1/21st and 1/23rd Londons (both 142nd Brigade).

According to *The History of the 47th (London) Division*, these heavy losses – and also the subsequent delays in the prosecution of the attack – were primarily due to the conflicting views of the divisional and brigade commanders, who had made personal visits to the Wood. The tanks, which were unable to make progress under the conditions in the Wood, should have been placed outside it, as the infantry would then not have been starved of artillery assistance. Communications between division and brigade were very poor, chiefly because headquarters remained to the south-west of ALBERT, even though Fricourt Farm had been prepared as an advanced divisional headquarters.

Sgt D.F. Brown of 2nd Otagos (2nd New Zealand Brigade, New Zealand Division) gained the Victoria Cross

for most conspicuous bravery in determination and attack when the company to which he belonged suffered very heavy casualties in officers and men from machine-gun fire. At great personal risk the N.C.O. advanced with a comrade and succeeded in reaching a point within thirty yards of the enemy guns. Four of the gun crew were killed and the gun captured. The advance of the company was continued till it was again held up by machine-gun fire. Again Sergt. Brown and his comrade with great gallantry rushed the gun and killed the crew. After this second position had been won, the company came under very heavy shell-fire, and the utter contempt for danger and coolness under fire of this N.C.O. did much to keep up the spirit of his men . . .

Having taken the Switch Line with few casualties, the New Zealanders hurried on to the heavily protected Flers Line and endured 5 hours of fierce fighting. Brown's company was decimated and eventually emerged with one officer and 49 men, with Sgt Brown and his colleague Sgt Rogers in command. On another occasion, too, Brown captured a machine gun from the enemy. He was killed on 1 October during a second attack in the area close to EAUCOURT L'ABBAYE.

There is a considerable amount of literature on High Wood and many works are first-hand accounts. Obviously, there is a lot of overlap with many of these accounts, but the author would like to quote from W. Beach Thomas, a *Daily Mail* correspondent, who wrote a book called *With the British on the Somme*. Thomas notes that the Wood might have been planted for the purposes of defence; on the further side it sloped down, which offered a perfect artillery target from the north, altogether cutting off guns from the south, the northern end being protected by the southern trees.

The battlefield had to be imagined, he wrote, for he had seen nothing like it on earth: in desolation, in horror, in pitifulness, in grimness. At the west corner were mine craters which were lined with fragments of kit, with helmets and masks, and half-tunics and bones. Every tree was beheaded or maimed and at the door of the Wood lay a lop-sided tank in a shell-hole with its nose against the base of a tree. One walked through the roots and pits and ditches that had supplanted the undergrowth, but there were worse things in the Wood than the sights.

The Wood had been a target for any and every battery for over 2 months and the Germans had made no attempt during that time to bury their dead. It was also a difficult task for the British, as the Germans almost always held the upper hand in the Wood. Machine-gun emplacements had been built by the enemy, along with concrete blockhouses, and wiring had been attempted quite close to the British trench, all the while that artillery fire was kept chasing up and down the Wood and across it.

John Glubb of No. 7 Field Company, Royal Engineers (50th Division), took part in the High Wood battle; in his memoirs, *Into Battle*, he wrote that the sappers worked all day and night on 16 and 17 September, carting bricks from the ruins of BAZENTIN-LE-PETIT in order to fill the shell-holes in the road up to High Wood. They dug Boast Trench, connecting the right flank of 50th Division with the left flank of 47th Division, where there had been a gap for 3 days; his company also hastily built a *decauville* light tramline from the left of High Wood towards EAUCOURT L'ABBAYE, which was later extended to BAZENTIN-LE-PETIT. The other tramlines ran from behind CONTALMAISON to MARTINPUICH and beyond. These, together with the railway, reduced the need to use the ruins, which had been demolished by shell-fire and the weather. There were 8 miles of tramlines.

Glubb also commented that 'High Wood was quite the place for the tourist now with the following items of interest: Two derelict tanks dating from 15 September, two crosses commemorating the 1st Division, the 47th and his own North'd Fus., several very fine German dugouts and a concrete blockhouse and lastly one of the finest views, nearly all the Somme battlefield and the then German front line.'

Col Whitehead, who at the time was attached to 1/8th Londons, wrote home in a letter that there was nothing between the Wood and Starfish Redoubt, not a single square foot of original surface. In mid-September it was like a honeycomb. R. Derry, a bandsman and stretcher-bearer of a battalion of the London Regiment, said that on 15 September the objective had been a strongpoint. His company were at the edge of the Wood. As the tanks arrived at daybreak, one was destroyed by a direct hit; the second got mixed up with tree trunks, while the third fell into a trench and was burnt out. They were a complete disaster and the fact that there was no artillery support at the time contributed to the overall failure. The further ridge was cleared except for one strongpoint, a large dugout cut into the side of the hill that was laid out like a field hospital. Mud was ankle-deep. The next objective was to be the BUTTE

DE WARLENCOURT. 2nd Welsh were ordered up to take over the Starfish system of trenches on the slope beyond High Wood.

C.P. Clayton of 2nd Welsh found himself in command because of losses; his headquarters was in a deep dugout in an old German reserve line close to FLERS. They were later relieved by 2nd Royal Munster Fusiliers (3rd Brigade, 1st Division) and went back to a hut camp close to MAMETZ WOOD.

A shadow overhung the triumph of 47th Division at High Wood. In the words of *The History of the 47th (London) Division,*

> the heavy losses incurred in the capture of High Wood, and the delays occurred later in the prosecution of the attack by the 47th Division, as also by the Division on its left, were mainly due to the unfortunate decision regarding the disposition of the IIIrd Corps Tanks in the area of the 47th Division, a decision which was taken in opposition to the urgent representation, more than once expressed to higher authority by the Divisional Commander after personally visiting High Wood in conjunction with the Brigadier concerned, that the Tanks could not move through the wood, owing to the insurmountable nature of the obstacles inside it. Had the tanks been placed outside the wood, as urged by Sir C. Barter, they could have materially helped the attackers in the wood. As it was they were the cause of the infantry being obliged to attack the wood without artillery assistance.

The post at High Alley became the main dressing station and headquarters of the Field Ambulance. Here, the horse transport, of necessity, had their lines by the side of four batteries of heavy howitzers, with a battery of 9.2in pieces in the rear. Night and day, tea could be obtained for the asking at the Field Ambulance post established on the side of High Alley. On 13 and 21 September, 47th Division buried 47 of their dead in a large shell-hole opposite High Wood, on the west side of the road from MARTINPUICH to LONGUEVAL. Other burials were brought in later, bringing the number to 101, mainly of soldiers who fell on 15 September. The little burial ground was called London Cemetery.

On 18 September, 1/15th Londons were provided with some reinforcements, who arrived from a camp at BOTTOM WOOD. On 19 September, a few officers were relieved by 1st Black Watch (1st Brigade, 1st Division). 1/15th Londons had to undertake two more operations; the first, on 18 September, was to advance into the Flers Line. This

was achieved without loss because the enemy had evacuated this trench, but they still held the junction of Flers Line and Drop Alley, and that portion of the line west of the junction. On 20 September, 1/15th Londons were relieved and went down to BOTTOM WOOD; their losses amounted to 380 men.

On 28 September, Maj Gen C. St L. Barter was replaced as General Officer Commanding 47th Division by Maj Gen Sir G. Gorringe. Barter later appealed against his dismissal, but his plea for an investigation was ignored.

In *The Somme, 1916*, Norman Gladden of 1/7th Northumberland Fusiliers (149th Brigade, 50th Division) wrote that their resting place on 24 October was behind High Wood in bivouacs. The weather was poor but on 25 October the rain had stopped; even so, everywhere was a quagmire. He inspected High Wood, which was 'seared and torn', full of all kinds of rubbish. There was an abandoned tank amid the tree stumps. A little way from the edge of the Wood was a derelict German battery with guns of a light type. On rising ground behind the Wood were the stark walls of a high building whose shape had survived. The Germans made a last stand in this ex-factory.

In *Grandfather's Adventures in the Great War*, C.M. Slack of 1/4th East Yorkshires (150th Brigade, 50th Division) mentions a brief but miserable time at the Wood on 24 October. He had been told to go there to wait for the rest of 1/4th East Yorkshires; getting to the Wood after dark, he then dismissed his men and they had to make the best of it. Later, the rest of the battalion turned up and he was able to get some sleep. Then eight of their officers were wiped out by one shell.

Slack's party cleared out of the Wood after that and made themselves 'homes' in some old trenches a few hundred yards away. It was raining almost continuously at this time and the conditions grew worse and muddier. At one time Slack's company were standing in mud over their knees for 18 hours. The landscape became so bleak that it was difficult to find a feature that remained static in it. When he saw High Wood for the first time he thought that the trees were covered in black tar. This tar turned out to be masses of great fat bluebottle flies. On another occasion, one of his gumboots sank into something soft, which turned out to be a 'very dead' stomach.

In October and November, 2nd Welsh were bivouacked in huts at a new camp that was called the High Wood West Camp. It was a group of huts and tents on the open part of the country between High Wood and Bazentin Camp. It was the nearest to the front of reserve camp.

In 1917, when William Orpen was painting scenes from the battlefield, he visited the COUGH DROP, just beyond High Wood, which he described as a large mine crater, with a stench coming from its watery bottom. At the edge of the Wood, Orpen saw a German and a Highlander locked in a deadly embrace.

London Cemetery, a small burial ground, is a little way south-west of the MARTINPUICH–LONGUEVAL road, opposite High Wood. Containing 101 graves by the time of the Armistice, it was extended in 1934. The original London Cemetery (Plot 1A) began with the burial of 47 men 'in a large shell-hole' by 47th Division on 18 and 21 September; other graves were added later. It now contains the graves of 3,870 men, of whom 3,114 are unnamed.

The cemetery, one of five in LONGUEVAL that together contain the graves of more than 15,000 dead, is the third largest on the Somme. It stands on high ground, commanding extensive views over the countryside; at least five churches can be seen from it. One man buried here, Capt D. Henderson (1A.A.4), attached 1/19th Londons, was killed on 15 September; he was a son of the former Labour Party leader, Sir Arthur Henderson. Opposite London Cemetery and London Cemetery Extension is a memorial to 47th Division, unveiled on 13 September 1925, and a cairn to the memory of 1/9th Highland Light Infantry (100th Brigade, 33rd Division), unveiled in 1972.

Rather than simply erecting a monument to commemorate their time on the Somme, 47th Division were in favour of a useful form of memorial, such as a drinking fountain. In the end, they decided to have both, and raised funds for a memorial cross as well as a school playground to be constructed at MARTINPUICH, a village close by. According to *47th (London) Division Memorials – High Wood and Martinpuich*:

> Our London soldiers are remembered by the people of Northern France, to whose barns and estaminets they returned at intervals for a few weeks of rest, as being *tres gentils*; carrying madame's water for her, fond of the children, always playing games. It seemed, therefore, more fitting to their memory that the memorial should not be merely a piece of stone that served no purpose in a needy land, but should take the form of a gift to the French people, suggesting by its use those swiftly-passing figures whom they knew so well.

In 1924, 47th Division decided to bring home the two wooden crosses at EAUCOURT L'ABBAYE and High Wood and set them up in the Duke of York's Headquarters, Chelsea. The one at EAUCOURT L'ABBAYE had suffered from the weather and had been shored up; it was not expected to last another winter. The cross on the edge of High Wood, facing the road to LONGUEVAL, was in better condition, but would be replaced by a stone one in the same position. MARTINPUICH was one of the nearest villages to High Wood and it was decided 'to transform an expanse of broken ground in front of the school and Mairie then being built by the French Government, with the addition of a Memorial gateway'.

The memorial cross at High Wood was made from Euville stone from Verdun, with paving stones from the neighbourhood of Nîmes in Provence. Unveiled by Maj Gen W. Thwaites KCMG, CB on 13 September 1925, the handsome memorial began to show signs of subsidence as early as 1932, as it was too heavy for its foundations, which were in a former trench line at the front of the Wood.

On the peak of a nearby hill can be seen an isolated monument in memory of the New Zealand Division. It is on the crest of the rise between High Wood and DELVILLE WOOD.

On the eastern flank of High Wood is a St Andrew memorial to the Cameron Highlanders and the Black Watch, who fought here when a large mine was blown by the Royal Engineers. In 1924, the memorial replaced a wooden cross set up in November 1916. It is close to the spot where the right flank of the 1st Black Watch linked up with the left of the 1st Cameronians in the attack on the wood on 3 September 1916. Originally, a stone cross within a frame of stones from Verdun stood on the south-west edge of the Wood to replace the wooden memorial erected by 47th Division in 1916. Other temporary memorials were erected in the Wood by 1st and 51st Divisions, 1st Northumberland Fusiliers, the Cameron Highlanders, 1st South Wales Borderers, 10th Glosters and 20th Royal Fusiliers.

Thistle Dump Cemetery stands in a field south of the southern apex of the Wood. It was begun in August 1916 and used as a front-line cemetery until February 1917. Surrounded by cultivated fields in a valley running between LONGUEVAL and BAZENTIN, it was enlarged after the Armistice, and contains the graves of soldiers from the UK, New Zealand and Australia, as well as some German graves.

It appears that many of the regiments desired to set up memorials to the memory of their men who died in the vicinity; during the 1920s, there were still many individual memorials in the Wood itself. In 1935, the *Ypres Times* mentioned that bodies of men were still being found, and that they were then buried in London Cemetery; the writer saw many wooden crosses awaiting replacement with white headstones. Of the 887 bodies recovered in France in 1934–35, 603 were recovered on the Somme; in 1935–36, the proportion was even higher, 721 out of 821.

Needing to acquire more land, the Imperial War Graves Commission sought permission to go ahead and expand this cemetery close to High Wood, with space for 3,140 bodies. While waiting for permission, which was given on 27 January 1934, they used Combles Communal Cemetery Extension and Ovillers Military Cemetery. The expansion at London Road went ahead and the first reburial took place on 16 February 1934; by November 1935, another 980 men had been reburied. At the time, the French people received 10 francs for each body discovered. Today, the cemetery contains 3,872 burials, 80 per cent of which are unidentified.

It seems appropiate to finish this piece on High Wood by quoting once again from J.L. Hodson's novel *Return to the Wood*. Hodson returned to the High Wood area with some friends in 1954, and they traced some of the places where he had been in 1916. They went to the place where they came that summer night or early morning in July, the Wood that had been a mass of broken blazing trees under the superb bombardment of the French 75s. This was the place with the noise and thunder where they had lain down before the final rush into the Wood. In 1916 they had got into the Wood with little difficulty but they had lost two-thirds of the battalion, mostly to shell-fire.

The trees in the Wood were now youthful, like the men who had been killed there. They inspected the cemetery, which was full of nameless graves. After a storm they entered the Wood (in 1954) at the right-hand corner. At the far end was a pond, formerly a mine crater, from which cattle now drank. They found bits of weapons and the remains of German machine-gun posts of broken concrete, and broken slabs, which, legend has it, covered the remains of seven officers who had had their heads cut off. The party walked around the Wood and found the approximate place where their Lewis gun had fought a duel with a German machine gun.

At the rear of the Wood, commanding the left, was the strongpoint. They had sung 'In Summertime on Bredon' or 'My Old Shako' or 'Twelve are the Apostles'. Hodson said to his friends that if ghosts walk, then they must parade in companies or even in brigades around this place, for there, in 3 months, thousands of men were slain. Hodson mused as to whether the ghosts were friendly and whether the

two sides were friendly with one another. The party wrote their names in the cemetery book and drove away from that place of both hideous and hallowed memory, away from their youth.

On 3 May 1987, with the permission of the owner of High Wood, a young oak tree was planted by the late Don Price, a veteran from Nottinghamshire and former member of 20th (S) Battalion (19th Brigade, 33rd Division), who attacked the Wood on 20 July 1916. The tree was planted at the side of the MARTINPUICH–LONGUEVAL road, a few yards from the memorial to 47th Division.

In the 1990s, the 14ft high 47th Division memorial, which had been unveiled in 1925, was beginning to collapse as a result of subsidence caused by the remains of a trench underneath it and from the vibration of sugar beet lorries passing by over the years. A figure close to £11,000, including a generous donation from the Royal Mail to honour members of the Post Office who served with the division, was raised for its repair, and on 13 October 1996, after being totally rebuilt, the memorial was rededicated.

HORSESHOE TRENCH, south-west of CONTAL-MAISON, was part of the German line running from OVILLERS-LA-BOISSELLE through Round Wood and The Dingle to an area behind Fricourt Wood. In early July 1916, it was attacked simultaneously from two sides, from the southern end and the northern end, which was protected by a strongly fortified redoubt. Further to the east there was a hard and prolonged struggle for possession of BIRCH TREE and PEAKE WOODS. Horseshoe Trench and Lincoln Redoubt stood on high ground between MAMETZ WOOD and LA BOISSELLE, some 1,200yds south-west of CONTALMAISON.

On 5 July, the objective of 9th Yorkshires (69th Brigade, 23rd Division) was the section of Horseshoe Trench running from Lincoln Redoubt to SCOTTS REDOUBT; a gun to the left of the trench cut into the attackers' positions, however, and had to be put out of action. 2/Lt D. Bell of 9th Yorkshires won a posthumous Victoria Cross. Shouting for two men to follow him, Bell made his way down the communication trench. They reached as close to the enemy as possible before Bell threw a bomb over a distance of 20yds before racing towards the enemy with his two colleagues, firing his revolver. The group then went beyond Horseshoe Trench, killing over 50 of the enemy with their Mills bombs. The citation said:

During an attack a very heavy enfilade fire was opened on the attacking company by a hostile machine gun. Second Lieut. Bell immediately, and on his own initiative, crept up a communication trench, and then, followed by Corpl. Colwill and Private Batey, rushed across the open under very heavy fire and attacked the machine gun, shooting the firer with his revolver, and destroying gun and personnel with bombs. This very brave act saved many lives and ensured the success of the attack. Five days later this gallant officer lost his life performing a very similar act of bravery.

Lincoln Redoubt was taken on 5 July, and in the evening Horseshoe Trench was cleared. Bell was buried in what became known as Bell's Redoubt, but after the war his remains were reburied in Gordon Dump Cemetery, OVILLERS-LA-BOISSELLE (VI.A.8). The Green Howards, as Bell's regiment became known after the war, later erected a memorial to Bell on the site of Bell's Redoubt outside CONTALMAISON, which was dedicated on 9 July 2000.

HUMBERCAMPS

HUMBERCAMPS is north-east of SAINT-AMAND, on the D26 road; in 1916 it was 3 miles behind the lines. From present-day appearances, the village seems to have been left undamaged by the war and its historic barns would certainly have been used to house troops during the period 1915/16. In the autumn of 1915, elderly French civilians were still working in the fields in the absence of their sons, away at the war, and a few shops and *estaminets* were still carrying on business.

It appears that 37th Division were one of the earliest British formations to have links with the village, when 48th Field Ambulance (37th Division) came here from PAS-EN-ARTOIS on 6 November 1915. Seven weeks later, 13th Rifle Brigade (111th Brigade, 37th Division) spent 'a convivial Christmas Day in the village . . . The cooks did their best that day, providing a welcome "roast" . . . The village's reserves of beer, *vin rouge* and *vin blanc* were brought up in great force, and the decrepit beams of every barn echoed with singing and laughter as the hours passed.'

On 1 May 1916, 11th Royal Warwicks (112th Brigade, 37th Division) took over the line at HANNESCAMPS from 13th Rifle Brigade; three companies held the front line, with one in reserve. The HANNESCAMPS ravine, and the line for about 500yds to the south of it, was also part of their front system. On the same day, 48th Field Ambulance returned to the village and were accommodated in two marquees and two huts.

After being relieved by 1/4th Leicesters (138th Brigade, 46th Division) in the front at FONCQUE-VILLERS, 1/8th Sherwood Foresters (139th Brigade, 46th Division) came here on 5 May, leaving the next night for le Souich, near LUCHEUX. On 15 May, 1/8th Sherwood Foresters returned to the village from their work at LUCHEUX. At the same time, transport moved to LA BAZÈQUE FARM, a complex to the north-west, on the other side of the GAUDIEMPRÉ–BAILLEULMONT road. During the next 3 days they provided working parties for digging cable trenches and putting up screens to conceal approaches to trenches.

On 7 May, 1/7th Sherwood Foresters (139th Brigade, 46th Division) arrived in the village from Invergny; during their time here they moved forward to the trenches in the FONCQUEVILLERS area, where they repaired trenches and dug 6ft deep telephone trenches. Lt Col A.W. Brewill, Commanding Officer 1/7th Sherwood Foresters, became ill in mid-May and on 18 May was taken to hospital at LUCHEUX and then sent home; he was replaced by Lt Col L.A. Hind. On 19 May, the battalion marched out of the village in platoon order at intervals of 30 minutes, passing through POMMIER to Bienvillers, where they entered a long communication trench taking them to the north-west corner of FONCQUEVILLERS.

In early June, 1/6th North Staffords (137th Brigade, 46th Division) were billeted here while providing working parties in the FONCQUE-VILLERS sector; No. 1/1 (North Midland) Field Company, Royal Engineers (also 46th Division), were also based here.

On 18 June, 1/5th Lincolns (138th Brigade, 46th Division) were in rest billets here, described as 'a prettily situated and practically unshelled village'; at this time, 21st Division also had part of their divisional reserve here. On 27 June, local inhabitants came to their doors to watch 1/6th West Yorkshires (146th Brigade, 49th Division) march by; at this time, they did not know the battle had been delayed by 48 hours.

On 11 July, elements of 63rd Brigade (37th Division) were here; on 24 September, the divisional headquarters of 49th Division were in the village.

Humbercamps Communal Cemetery has two men from September 1915, buried in the north-west corner. Humbercamps Communal Cemetery Extension, part of an old orchard, has the graves of 79 men from 1915 and 1917, including a company sergeant-major, as well as six casualties from March 1918; 52 of the 79 burials are of men who died prior to the battle. The cemeteries were used by field ambulances from September 1915 until February 1917. The church and cemetery are in the north-east part of the village.

HUMBERCOURT is north-east of DOULLENS on the D127, east of Lucheux Wood. From 29 February to 2 March 1916, 13th Field Ambulance (5th Division) manned a dressing station here. On 24 September, 49th Division had their headquarters here and on 10 October, 1/6th Glosters (144th Brigade, 48th Division) were billeted here.

HUPPY is south of ABBEVILLE on the D13 road. On 17 February 1916, two sections of 1/3rd (West Riding) Field Ambulance (49th Division) established a field hospital in a farmhouse here with accommodation for 60 cases. Their billets were in the farm and in houses in the village.

J

JACOB'S LADDER was a communication trench running north-east from Mesnil to HAMEL village; it then bent south-eastwards and connected up with Hamel Bridge across the River Ancre. In mid-December 1915 it was very wet, and if anyone of below average height used it, it could be uncomfortable.

On 1 July 1916, Jacob's Ladder was in the sector of 36th Division. In mid-August, the miners of 1st East Lancashires (11th Brigade, 4th Division) were set to dig deep dugouts, which became known as Kentish Caves. In his memoir, Edmund Blunden of 11th Royal Sussex (116th Brigade, 39th Division) wrote that 'if ever there was to be a vile, unnerving and desperate place in the battle zone, it was the Mesnil end of Jacob's Ladder, among the heavy battery positions, and under perfect enemy observation'. This long communication trench was good in parts and, apart from being unusually long, also required a flight of stairs at one or two steep places. Leafy bushes and great green and yellow weeds looked into it as it dipped sharply into the green valley by HAMEL; hereabouts, according to Blunden, the aspect of peace and innocence was as yet prevailing. Further on was a small chalk cliff, facing the river, with a rambling but remarkable dugout called Kentish Caves. The front line was sculptured over this brow, and descended to the wooded marshes of the Ancre. Running across it towards the German line went the narrow BEAUCOURT-SUR-L'ANCRE road, and the railway to MIRAUMONT and BAPAUME; in the railway bank was a lookout post called Crow's Nest, with a large periscope, but none seemed very pleased to see the periscope. South of the Ancre was broad-backed high ground, and on that a black vapour of smoke and naked tree trunks or charcoal, an apparition which Blunden discovered was Thiepval Wood.

Men of the Royal Warwickshire Regiment resting at Jacob's Ladder, Beaumont-Hamel, in July 1916. *(IWM Q730)*

L

LA BAZÈQUE FARM is north-west of HUMBER-CAMPS, just south of the N25 DOULLENS–Arras road. In 1916 the substantial complex of farm buildings was capable of billeting a large number of troops at any one time; indeed, infantry units were using the farm as early as 31 December 1915. The buildings were also used by field ambulances; 1/3rd (North Midland) Field Ambulance (46th Division) arrived here on 10 May 1916, when the barns were inspected with a view to using them as a dressing station for 300 patients.

At the advanced dressing station at FONCQUE-VILLERS, 1,000yds of new trench was required for coping with any future evacuation of casualties. The transport section of 1/8th Sherwood Foresters (139th Brigade, 46th Division) were here the next day, and a fortnight later No. 1/1 (North Midland) Field Company, Royal Engineers (46th Division), were based here while they worked on dugouts and huts at FONCQUEVILLERS and huts at GAUDIEMPRÉ.

La grande rue, La Boisselle.
(Peter F. Batchelor Collection)

At the same time, 2/1st (North Midland) Field Ambulance (also 46th Division) were here, when they were inspected by Maj Gen The Hon. E. Montagu-Stuart-Wortley, General Officer Commanding 46th Division.

LA BOISSELLE is the first village one comes to after leaving ALBERT on the D929 BAPAUME road. In 1916, it had 35 houses and was the centre of a small but pronounced salient in the enemy lines, the apex of which was as little as 100yds from the British lines. On the eastern or right-hand side was Sausage Valley, and various German strongpoints such as Heligoland, Kipper and Bloater Trenches were connected up to it. To the north-west and across the main road was another valley called, appropriately, Mash Valley. The village therefore stood on a spur between the two valleys; at this point, the valley between the villages of La Boisselle and OVILLERS-LA-BOISSELLE resulted in no man's land being very wide.

After the British 5th Division had taken over the then quiet front from troops of the French Army in early August 1915, the enemy exploded two mines on 8/9 August 1915. French miners who had not yet left the area replied by exploding their own mines 4 days later. A few weeks later, on 29 August and again on 4 September, the British artillery

shelled the trenches opposite. Enemy miners were active again in December, when they blew more mines here on 9 and 19 December. The British 18th Division replied in kind on 31 December and 2 January 1916. As at BEAUMONT-HAMEL or the Tambour at FRICOURT, there was continuous mining and counter-mining activity here; this increased between February and the end of June, and could often prove extremely hazardous for both sides. For example, 2 officers and 16 other ranks from No. 185 Tunnelling Company, Royal Engineers, were killed on 4 February 1916 as a result of a German camouflet blowing at Inch-Saint-Mint at 1415hrs. The 16 men were later buried in Bécourt Military Cemetery and the 2 officers are side by side in Albert Communal Cemetery Extension, Capt T.C. Richardson (I.F.1) and 2/Lt A.J. Latham (I.F.2), Royal Engineers.

In the first week of April, there was hostile trench mortar fire; on 10 April, two more camouflets were exploded here and British trenches were bombarded. This was prior to 28 men from 1st Royal Irish Rifles (25th Brigade, 8th Division) being captured at the Glory Hole during an enemy raid; there were 48 other casualties. Eleven days later, 8th Division carried out a raid of their own opposite La Boisselle, killing two Germans on entering the enemy trenches. In early May, the enemy made another raid, and a further one in mid-May.

To set the scene for the events of 1 July, the writer has depended heavily on the *Official History of the War*, which states that the position was in the territory of III Corps, between the villages of BÉCOURT and AUTHUILLE. The elements of III Corps lay on the forward slopes of a long low ridge that went from ALBERT to La Boisselle, marked by Tara Valley on the right and Usna Valley on the left. They were a continuation of the spur of the main GINCHY–POZIÈRES ridge. Behind this ridge, the divisional artillery were deployed in rows and were dug in on open ground, on both sides of the AMIENS road, just west of ALBERT. The right of III Corps faced the western slope of the long FRICOURT spur and La Boisselle was at its centre. The distance between the opposing lines varied from 50yds to 1,000yds; any advance would have to pass over open land, which could be covered by crossfire from both sides of the position and also from the Thiepval Spur, which overlooked the position. The spurs themselves were covered with a network of trenches and machine-gun nests.

The German defences consisted of a front system with four main strongpoints in its southern half. Sausage Redoubt (Heligoland) had SCOTTS

REDOUBT behind it, while Schwaben Hohe was the ground that was being made ready for a huge mine explosion and La Boisselle village itself was heavily fortified. The fifth German defence was OVILLERS-LA-BOISSELLE to the northwest. Behind the German front defences were two intermediate lines, the first from Fricourt Farm to OVILLERS-LA-BOISSELLE and the second, which was unfinished, in front of CONTALMAISON and POZIÈRES. Behind these again was the second position from BAZENTIN-LE-PETIT to MOUQUET FARM, consisting of two lines. The front of the German line was not as completely exposed to fire as was the ground behind it.

Two brigades of 34th Division were to provide the attack on the very strongly held La Boisselle positions, 101st Brigade on the right and 102nd Brigade on the left. The positions to be captured included Sausage Redoubt, Heligoland, Bloater Trench, SCOTTS REDOUBT and Gordon Post. The objectives of 101st Brigade for the first day of the battle were in a north-easterly direction across Sausage Valley towards CONTALMAISON and going across the top of FRICOURT. A cluster of trees known as Round Wood, and beyond it PEAKE WOODS, mounted a spur to CONTALMAISON village. The starting position of 101st Brigade was to the north-east of Bécourt Wood and just beyond Chapes Spur to the south-east of La Boisselle. One of the Edinburgh battalions, 15th Royal Scots, were in the front line, with 16th Royal Scots behind them. They had assembled at the bottom of the valley. On their left were 10th Lincolns and behind them were 11th Suffolks.

No. 179 Tunnelling Company, Royal Engineers, had prepared two very large mines at Y Sap in the main area where mining and counter-mining had been going on for months. One of the mines was charged with 60,000lb of ammonal and the other with 40,000lb; in addition, three Russian saps had also been dug on III Corps' front in order to provide a covered approach after the assault. The use of Russian saps by the assaulting troops was limited and impractical, as only small numbers of men could emerge from them at one time; also, once the exit was spotted by the enemy, it would be no problem to cover it with machine guns and thus bottle up men underground. The real use of these saps was for messengers and reinforcements after the capture of an enemy front line.

At Y Sap, south of La Boisselle village, two charges were set at a depth of about 52ft. The charges were 60ft apart but a single crater was to result, to a depth lower than that of the original chambers and with remarkably wide rims. They were fired a couple of minutes before 0730hrs on 1 July; then, the plan was that the Allied infantry would be able to seize on the advantage from the 'dazed' defenders. The explosion created a huge hollow, 100yds across and 30yds deep. As hoped for, the mine threw up a high lip that cut off the north of La Boisselle and accorded the infantry a little protection for their advance. However, it appears that the Germans had had advance warning of the explosion time, probably as a result of 'listening in' to a British telephone line; as a consequence, they evacuated the position and had comparatively few casualties. However, one of the German strongholds, the Schwaben Hohe on the west of the crater, was destroyed in the explosion.

Although the explosion of these mines was indeed very effective, it was very local; on these occasions, it always seemed that the defenders were well able to take advantage of the subsequent chaotic situation rather than allow the advantage to remain with the attacker. On this occasion the Germans, because of underground protection and early warning, were able to come up and get themselves into a position from which they could take toll of any attacking waves. Once the mines had gone up, 15th Royal Scots, on the right of the divisional line, had climbed their parapets and advanced into no man's land. The explosion from which they had expected so much had failed to demoralise the German garrison, and the fighting for the village surpassed their worst expectations.

In the words of their regimental history, 15th Royal Scots were 'buffeted by the storms of shells and bullets'; then came 16th Royal Scots behind them. It was probably at the exposed zone just in front of the parapets that so many of their officers and men were killed. Nevertheless, 15th Royal Scots did secure some of their objectives, being the only unit in the division to do so. C Company, for example, 'plodded grimly on' and, crossing SCOTTS REDOUBT, reached Peake Trench.

To the left and behind the Edinburgh battalions, 10th Lincolns and 11th Suffolks were caught by the same flanking fire and suffered very heavy casualties indeed. Although they reached the lip of the crater, they had not only been caught by machine-gun fire but some were even burnt to death, as they were repelled by flame-throwers when reaching the German lines. According to John Keegan's *The Face of Battle*, an artillery officer was later to come upon line after line of dead men, lying where they had fallen with the various battalions, who had undergone a bizarre and pointless massacre.

To the left of 101st Brigade's attack was 102nd Brigade, which consisted of 20th, 21st, 22nd and 23rd Northumberland Fusiliers. A new dugout had been made for them prior to the battle, part of the trench line linking the Usna and Tara Redoubts. The dugout was about 50yds north of the ALBERT–BAPAUME road and contained underground chambers connected by tunnels. On the other side of the road, 101st Brigade were housed in a similar position. Both positions were connected to divisional headquarters by telephone. Next to Lt Col W.T. Lyle's 23rd Northumberland Fusiliers battalion headquarters was a deep dugout which contained his signallers. Picked men, six of them, were killed prior to the battle when a shell crashed through the deep dugout.

On the La Boisselle side of the road were 21st Northumberland Fusiliers, with 24th Northumberland Fusiliers (103rd Brigade, 34th Division) due to come through on their right and 26th Northumberland Fusiliers (also 103rd Brigade, 34th Division) due to attack on their left. Beyond them, to the left and across the road, were 23rd Northumberland Fusiliers and 25th Northumberland Fusiliers (103rd Brigade, 34th Division); their left flank bordered on the right flank of 8th Division, whose task was to capture OVILLERS-LA-BOISSELLE. 102nd Brigade could make no progress on the open landscape in the face of fire that swept them from OVILLERS-LA-BOISSELLE. This failure in turn affected 101st Brigade's attack. From the time that the first wave of infantry had sprung from their trenches they also came under heavy barrage, and many were killed before getting clear. The heaviest fire came not only from the concealed fortifications of La Boisselle, but also from high ground to the left of the battalion, and only men who knew that they risked almost certain death would have made any progress. It can be understood today how impossible was the task of the Tyneside battalions, when one sees that they had to come from the direction of the Tara-Usna Line and go down into an open slope and across Avoca Valley. They presented a perfect target to the German machine-gunners.

The plan had been that a heavy trench mortar barrage should be maintained on La Boisselle until such time as bombers from 102nd Brigade had reached points from which they could attack the village from both the north and the south. 34th Division had decided to move all their brigades forward simultaneously, including the reserve brigade, 103rd Brigade. This decision, made prior to the battle, assumed of course that the British

Site of La Boisselle, July 1916, with a small mine crater in the foreground. *(IWM Q3998)*

artillery would have destroyed the German defences; as they had not, the German machine-gunners were still very much in evidence. The simultaneous use of 3,000 troops could only lead to divisional suicide. It was truly remarkable that any progress was made at all under such adverse conditions, but small groups of men were somehow able to make their way through the very heavy shelling and the machine-gun fire from La Boisselle and the ground beyond it. However, the British did gain part of La Boisselle, and 34th Division penetrated as far as PEAKE WOODS. This proved to be the point of the wedge into the line north of FRICOURT.

All the commanding officers of 102nd Brigade were killed on 1 July south of La Boisselle. Lt Cols A.P.A. Elphinstone (Thiepval Memorial) of 22nd Northumberland Fusiliers, W.T. Lyle (I.G.1) of 23rd Northumberland Fusiliers and C.C.A. Sillery (I.G.2) of 20th Northumberland Fusiliers were all killed at Usna Hill. It was said that Maj Gen E.C. Ingouville-Williams, General Officer Commanding 34th Division, found the bodies of Lyle and Sillery at the head of their battalions. They were later buried at Bapaume Post Military Cemetery. The fourth senior officer to be killed was Lt Col F.C. Heneker of 21st Northumberland Fusiliers, whose grave is at Ovillers Military Cemetery (III.A.1). Ingouville-Williams, known as Inky Bill, was himself to be killed 3 weeks later, close to MAMETZ WOOD.

Other senior officer casualties of this tragic day were Lt Col B.L. Maddison, Commanding Officer 8th York & Lancasters (70th Brigade, 23rd Division), and Lt Col A.J.B. Addison of 9th York & Lancasters (also 70th Brigade, 23rd Division). Brig Gen N.J.G. Cameron, General Officer Commanding 103rd Brigade (34th Division), was hit by a machine-gun bullet at 0750hrs when observing the brigade moving down the slope from its assembly position on the Tara-Usna Line. Two battalion commanders of 103rd Brigade were wounded, namely Lt Col M.E. Richardson of 26th Northumberland Fusiliers and Lt Col J.H.M. Arden of 25th Northumberland Fusiliers; a third, Lt Col L.M. Howard of 24th Northumberland Fusiliers, was killed.

Bernard Charles de Boismaison White, who had published a book of verse called *Remembrance and other Verses*, was born in 1886. He had worked before the war with the Marconi Company and later was the Assistant Editor of *Wireless World* before joining the publishing firm of Hutchinsons. He was a member of 20th Northumberland Fusiliers and became a casualty in the advance over Tara Hill. Also, Capt J. Charlton of 21st Northumberland Fusiliers, a famous naturalist of the time, was killed when leading his company against the enemy third line.

On 2 July, 34th Division, who had been so tragically cut down on 1 July, were still in the line in front of La Boisselle. When they were supported by 19th Division, 101st and 102nd Brigades were in the area of SCOTTS REDOUBT.

The task of capturing SCOTTS REDOUBT fell to two companies of 7th East Lancashires (56th Brigade, 19th Division, attached to 34th Division) who took it during the afternoon of 2 July. To their right were the rest of their brigade and to their left and across the main road were 57th Brigade (19th Division). While still holding the right sector of III Corps, 34th Division had made unsuccessful attempts by bombing out from their forward position to link up with 19th Division, but had failed to do so. When night fell on 3 July, 23rd Division began to relieve 34th Division and 69th Brigade (23rd Division) took over the captured trenches.

At this time, 8th North Staffords (57th Brigade, 19th Division) were involved in the fighting in La Boisselle and their ground included the large mine crater that had been blown on 1 July. Maj C. Wedgwood (I.C.2), Commanding Officer 8th North Staffords, was killed on 3 July, aged 53, and buried at Bapaume Post Military Cemetery. The Commanding Officer of 10th Worcesters (also 57th Brigade, 19th Division) was forward of his battalion and had reached the mine crater with his adjutant when he, too, was killed.

The battalions of 57th Brigade, 10th Royal Warwicks, 8th Glosters, 10th Worcesters and 8th North Staffords, were fighting hard in La Boisselle on 3 July; at the end, the line that the enemy held ran through the church ruins. 57th Brigade were then reinforced by 56th Brigade. After dark, 12th Division dug a forward trench to connect their right with the flank of 19th Division.

Adrian Carton de Wiart, who was a temporary lieutenant-colonel attached to 8th Glosters, was in command of 57th Brigade during the period 2/3 July. He had been in the Army since 1899 and had lost an eye in Somaliland and a hand in Zonnebeke, in addition to being wounded several other times. He was awarded the Victoria Cross for his work at La Boisselle. The citation noted:

After three battalion commanders had become casualties, he controlled their commands, and ensured that the ground won was maintained at all costs. He frequently exposed himself in the organization of positions and of supplies, passing unflinchingly through fire barrage of the most intense nature . . .

The *Official History of the War* noted that he led the fight in person and pulled the pins from Mills grenades with his teeth.

The same award was also made to Pte T.G. Turrall of 10th Worcesters:

During a bombing attack by a small party against the enemy, the officer in charge was badly wounded, and the party having penetrated the portion to a great depth, was compelled eventually to retire. Private Turrall remained with the wounded officer for three hours under continuous and very heavy fire from machine guns and bombs, and notwithstanding that both himself and the officer were at one time completely cut off from our troops, he held to his ground with determination, and finally carried the officer into our lines after our counter-attack made this possible.

La Boisselle fell to 19th Division in the period 3/4 July, after a thunderstorm during the night had filled the trenches with water; 58th Brigade attacked from the south and 57th Brigade attacked from the north. At the same time, across the road, the adjoining 12th Division attacked towards OVILLERS-LA-BOISSELLE, but barbed wire and machine guns from Mash Valley checked them. In 57th Brigade, 8th North Staffords had moved forward with 10th Worcesters on their left and fought their way to the south end of La Boisselle salient in the small hours of 3 July. Losses were very heavy.

On 3 July, members of No. 81 Field Company, Royal Engineers (19th Division), inspected the German tunnels in the village and found that enemy dugouts were often 30ft deep, with electric light, beds, wallpaper and much comfort. On 4 July, the village was cleared and III Corps at last held the whole village.

A third, posthumous, Victoria Cross was awarded in this sector, to T/Lt T. Wilkinson of 7th Loyal North Lancashires (56th Brigade, 19th Division):

During an attack when a party from another unit was retiring without their machine gun, Lieut Wilkinson rushed forward, and, with two men, got the gun into action, and held up the enemy till they were relieved. Later, when the advance was checked during a bombing attack, he forced his way forward and found four or five men of different units stopped by a solid block of earth, over which the enemy was throwing bombs. With great pluck and promptness he mounted a machine gun on the top of the parapet and dispersed the enemy bombers. Subsequently he made two most gallant attempts to bring in a wounded man, but at the second attempt he was shot through the heart just before reaching the man.

Wilkinson's name is recorded on the Thiepval Memorial.

In early July, the official War Office photographer, Geoffrey Malins, visited the area, although he had been warned that it was not a 'healthy' sector to be in. He talked with the troops of one battery and was told that the place was 'strafed' every day; as soon as he arrived, there were crumps behind him, probably in the direction of BÉCOURT. After much dodging and twisting, he halted the car close to a forward dressing station, and was told of a German battery of 77mm guns on the left-hand side of the valley leading to POZIÈRES. He decided to make for it, and filmed from a position 800yds from POZIÈRES.

On 5 July, 74th Brigade were attached to 12th Division and took over a sector of the line in La Boisselle that had fallen on 4 July. On the morning of 7 July, the brigade participated in a further attack by 12th Division on OVILLERS-LA-BOISSELLE and the trenches across the POZIÈRES road.

On 7 July, 13th Rifle Brigade (111th Brigade, 37th Division) spent some time in the trenches and buried many of the dead from the start of the battle. There were scores of dead of the Northumberland Fusiliers and the great mine crater was virtually one vast tomb.

One observer described the scene at Tara-Usna Ridge on 7 July as being like a vast crowded fun fair with bivouacs, dumps, horse-lines, batteries, cookers, water carts, and French 75mm artillery pieces. John Masefield said of La Boisselle that after being battered and taken by the British, it was destroyed by German fire. It was then cleared by the British, who wished to use the roads just outside it. One commentator noted that the Germans, who were from a Guards battalion, held out in La Boisselle in the ruins for nearly a week, finally emerging as starving prisoners. The final number was 124 men and 2 officers, who surrendered on 17 July.

Between the old lines, there was a spur that was useful for observation purposes, and for which both sides had fought bitterly. For about 200yds, no man's land was a succession of pits in the chalk where the mines had been set off. The lines crossed this debated

Captured German trenches at La Boisselle, July 1916.
(IWM Q890)

area, and went across a small and ill-defined bulk of chalk which was known as Chapes Spur, on the top of which was a vast heap of dazzlingly white chalk, so bright that it was painful to look at. One man killed at La Boisselle that day was T/Capt A.O. Trefusis of 9th Loyal North Lancashires, a son of the Bishop of Crediton; he was buried at Pozières British Cemetery (III.D.43).

On 12 July, the poet Capt R.M. Dennys of A Company, 10th Loyal North Lancashires (112th Brigade, 37th Division), was wounded in the La Boisselle fighting and was taken to hospital in Rouen, where he arrived on 17 July. His file in The National Archives (WO339/13015) states that he died of wounds at No. 8 General Hospital at 0430hrs on 24 July. His father had been informed as to how dangerously wounded his son was, with a fractured skull, and asked the War Office if they could arrange to bring his son back to London where he could visit him. The War Office could not agree to this request, however. Dennys's file poses a slight query; he appears to have really died at 28 Route de Neufchâtel and not in No. 8 General Hospital. His effects were later returned to his father and included two pieces of shrapnel in a leather bag and two German helmet badges. Dennys was buried at Saint-Sever Communal Cemetery, Rouen (A.4.7).

In the following weeks, the fighting towards POZIÈRES became particularly associated with the Australians, who had a vast number of artillery batteries in the valley. On 18 July, a battalion of the Worcestershire Regiment were called upon to supply working parties to dig a communication trench along the ALBERT–POZIÈRES road in the neighbourhood of La Boisselle. The party were very severely hit by an unexpected bout of gas shelling. There were 500 casualties and they were brought back to BOUZIN-COURT. Later, the still very unfit battalion received a new draft of men while at CRUCIFIX CORNER, near Aveluy. It was two weeks before the medical authorities sent home at least some of the men to convalescent camps, and at the end of August they were still unfit.

In 1917, the painter William Orpen came across the great mine at La Boisselle when he was touring the battlefield making sketches and paintings. He described it as a wonderful sight and a great wilderness of white chalk without a tuft of grass, no flowers, nothing but blazing chalk dotted thickly all over with bits of shrapnel. He walked up to the edge of the crater and he felt himself to be in another world. He remarked on there being another large crater just by the BAPAUME road, which was later built over.

John Masefield was on a similar mission as Orpen, only he was a writer and poet rather than a painter. Both men probably obtained a unique intimacy and understanding of the 1916 Battle of the Somme, simply because they spent so much time in the study of the landscape, attempting to grasp the significance of the various lines, hills, woods, fortified villages and other features. Like Orpen, Masefield preferred to work on the spot; in the morning, he would get a lift out from AMIENS by lorry and work all day by himself, at some spot like La Boisselle, for example. Later, he would walk back to the bridge at ALBERT and thumb a lift back to AMIENS.

During the German spring offensive of 1918, the British lost La Boisselle in March but regained it in August.

After the war, on the other side of the road from the Grand Mine there was a well-known café called the Café de la Grand Mine, which at the time testified to the inhabitants' pride in the possession of the crater. In the 1930s many sunken roads and old trenches remained, with their communication trenches still visible.

In the village, is a granite cross which stands in front of the church and commemorates the 19th (Western) Division or Butterfly Division. The divisional sign was of a butterfly of the 'peacock' group with eyes on its four wings. The 34th Division Memorial unveiled by Maj Gen Nicholson on 23 May 1923 at the north-east end of the village is a white stone obelisk surmounted by a bronze figure and is on the site of the divisional headquarters of 1916. Also in the village, in the main street, is a memorial granite seat that commemorates the attack of the Tyneside 102nd and 103rd Brigades, who fought to win the road here. It was unveiled by Marshal Foch on 20 April 1922.

In *Thirteen Years After*, Will R. Bird of 42nd Canadian Battalion (7th Canadian Brigade, 3rd Canadian Division) wrote of a visit to the village in 1932: 'It is a tiny village. A few heroic ones have tried to reclaim that wilderness, but only the main street and another lane or so have resulted. All else are craters, shell-holes, gullies, rifts in the earth, barren in spots of anything that grows . . .'

During a visit to the Somme in August 1933, Vera Brittain visited the great crater, as she had 12 years before, when it was in the centre of a 'completely devastated region'. It had been used as a German headquarters in 1918.

> The craters are now becoming grown-over with coarse grass & all gradually (though very slowly) filling up as the earth silts down into them in rainy seasons. Homely hens now peck peacefully around them and placid cows crip the rough grass at the edge. The chauffeur pointed out the hump of earth ¾ mile back where the shaft was let down for the tunnel to the mine; it was started three months

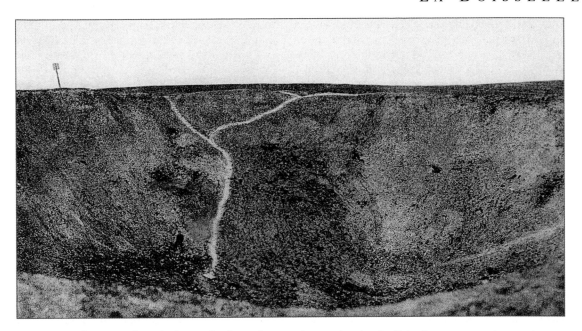

before July 1st and made by coal-miners from Northumberland and Durham . . .

La grande mine, La Boisselle.
(Peter F. Batchelor Collection)

Brittain was informed that the former German Front Line used to run through the village cemetery, now completely demolished.

In recent years, more and more of the numerous small craters have been filled in; since 1978 the Grand Mine Crater itself has been protected by Mr Richard Dunning, who wished to save it from the ravages of youthful French motorcyclists. He has erected a cross and memorial seats. A Breton cross also placed at this site has succumbed to the water and exposure, but in recent years has been lovingly replaced with a new one which uses wood from north-east England. Each year there is a service at the crater on 1 July; one feels that even when all the survivors of the First World War have finally faded away, there will always be people to come to this spot to commemorate the great sacrifice made by 34th Division on 1 July 1916. Visitors to the annual service include people from Germany as well as Britain and France, who share in a spirit of reconciliation.

In October 1998, the remains of Pte G.J. Nugent of 22nd Northumberland Fusiliers (102nd Brigade, 34th Division) were found here on the lip of the crater, close to the main circular path. After his identity was confirmed, his remains were reburied at Ovillers Military Cemetery (I.A.26A) on 1 July 2000. An oak cross was placed at the site of his first grave on the day of his funeral. There are other memorials at the crater, including a seat to the memory of L/Cpl H. Fellows of 12th Northumberland Fusiliers (62nd Brigade, 21st

Division), placed here by his son after his father's death in 1987, and three others, including one to the memory of the Grimsby Chums (10th Lincolns).

Gordon Dump Cemetery is about ½ mile due east of La Boisselle village and about 4 miles from ALBERT railway station. Plot 1 of Gordon Dump Cemetery was made by fighting units after 10 July 1916, and closed in September; it contained the graves of 95 soldiers, mainly Australians. It was called variously Gordon or Gordon's Dump Cemetery or Sausage Valley Cemetery. The remainder of the cemetery was formed after the Armistice. The great majority of the soldiers thus reburied fell in July 1916.

On 1 July 2016 it has been decided to limit access to 5,000 visitors to the annual service at Lochnagar Crater and admission will be by ticket only.

In 2010–11 the La Boisselle Study Group was formed and its initial brief was to carry out a close archaeological study of the ground below what was formerly known as the Glory Hole. The site is off the D20 road to CONTALMAISON. In 2010 it was rumoured that the site would be used for new housing, but the Lejeune family who owned the land invited the Study group to carry out their researches. Work was begun on 3 October 2010. The ground had been fought over by the German, French and British armies. The work revealed a massive underground network of tunnels and trenches, and on open days small groups of visitors have been given escorted tours of the site. At the time of writing the project has been suspended.

LA HERLIÈRE is north of HUMBERCAMPS on the D26, south of the N25 DOULLENS–Arras road. From 12 to 19 March 1916, a bearer division was opened here by 49th Field Ambulance (37th Division). On 2 May, 50th Field Ambulance (also 37th Division) took over from 10th Field Ambulance (4th Division). The village had a road which led direct to LA BAZÈQUE FARM via la Herlière Communal Cemetery to the south of the village. In the south-west corner are the graves of two men who died in May and June 1916 respectively. After the war a number of burials in a small military cemetery in the village were transferred to Warlincourt Halte British Cemetery, SAULTY, to the south-west.

LAHOUSSOYE is 8 miles to the north-east of AMIENS. During the First World War, it was much used for billeting purposes and working parties, especially those working on railway construction. 1st Norfolks (15th Brigade, 5th Division) arrived in the village as early as 2 August 1915 before relieving the French in trenches at FRICOURT. Three days later, 8th East Surreys (55th Brigade, 18th Division) marched here from BERTANGLES and stayed for 3 days with 7th Queen's (also 55th Brigade, 18th Division); both battalions then marched to DERNANCOURT. In mid-September, 12th Highland Light Infantry (46th Brigade, 15th Division) arrived here from FRANVILLERS. No. 21 Motor Ambulance Convoy of III Corps were based in Lahoussoye.

In January 1916, 7th Queen's were here again and also at QUERRIEU, where they provided working parties for railway construction and to serve as a demonstration party to the divisional school. Between 5 and 13 February, No. 59 Field Company, Royal Engineers (5th Division), worked on making bunks at Lahoussoye.

In March, No. 3 Squadron, Royal Flying Corps, commanded by Maj H.O. Harvey-Kelly, arrived in the village and remained until the following January.

On 29 April, 8th Suffolks (53rd Brigade, 18th Division) came to Lahoussoye, and 56th Field Ambulance (18th Division) were here for 24 hours. On 1 May, 6th Royal Berkshires (53rd Brigade, 18th Division) moved here from billets in CORBIE and then to VAUX-EN-AMIÉNOIS to the north-west of the city. On 5 May, 103rd Field Ambulance (34th Division) arrived in Lahoussoye, leaving for the hospital at BRESLE the next day. On 6 May, 102nd Field Ambulance (34th Division) opened a hospital for the sick; 4 days later, they struck tents and left for FRANVILLERS. On 10 May, 104th Field Ambulance (34th Division) took over and used tents for the dressing station; the men were billeted in barns in the village.

At the end of June, 1/9th Londons (169th Brigade, 56th Division) were briefly in billets here. On 1 July, No. 81 Field Company, Royal Engineers (19th Division), marched 20 miles to reach Lahoussoye. Three days later, 104th Field Ambulance marched here from ALBERT, where they opened a corps clearing station for lightly wounded. At the beginning of July, a motor ambulance convoy operated from here. In mid-July, 15th Brigade (5th Division) were in the village; on 30 July, 58th Brigade (19th Division) arrived in Lahoussoye, as well as in BÉHENCOURT to the north-west. On 24 October, 145th Brigade (48th Division) were here; on 9 November, 11th Argyll & Sutherland Highlanders (45th Brigade, 15th Division) were in the village.

LA NEUVILLE is north-west of CORBIE on the River Ancre, separated from the latter by the AMIENS–ALBERT railway line. On 30 July 1915, 13th Brigade (5th Division) were possibly the first British unit to arrive here, as well as RIBEMONT-SUR-ANCRE to the north-east. On 6 August, 55th Brigade (18th Division) were billeted here. On 29 August, No. 21 Casualty Clearing Station took over the Hubert-Brière factory here, and on 30 August spent the day cleaning and repairing the factory building. At the same time, troops were billeted in Fagot Farm by the marshes on the banks of the River Somme. The hospital was close to the broad-gauge lines so that trains could come right up to the casualty clearing station and evacuate the wounded without using the motor ambulances.

On 16 December, 10th Essex (53rd Brigade, 18th Division) were here; 6th Royal Berkshires (also 53rd Brigade, 18th Division) left for BUIRE-SUR-L'ANCRE on 31 December. At the end of December, a field company of 5th Division were billeted here and made bunks in barns. On 7 February 1916, No. 401 Field Company, Royal Engineers (51st Division), were here; on 26 February, men of No. 36 Casualty Clearing Station were billeted here while arranging their hospital at HEILLY.

Between the end of March and the end of June, 63rd and 64th Field Ambulances as well as 63rd and 64th Brigades (all 21st Division) were often here and were billeted at Fagot Farm. The war diary of 63rd Field Ambulance described the billets as being 'sheep pens and pig sties, in a farm on the banks of the river Somme'.

From the first arrival of No. 21 Casualty Clearing Station at the end of August 1915, burials had been carried out in Corbie Communal Cemetery. On 21 April, permission was sought and given for future burials to be carried out at La Neuville Communal

Cemetery. The first seven men buried in Row A died in the casualty clearing station in the period 20–21 April. As pressure for space built up, the Communal Cemetery had to be extended and encompassed a field adjoining the casualty clearing station. From the middle of June, casualties to and evacuations from the casualty clearing station increased dramatically; barges were in continuous use and ambulance trains ran from VECQUEMONT.

On the eve of the battle, the well-known toast made by officers of 9th King's Own Yorkshire Light Infantry occurred in their officers' mess in a farmhouse/château in La Neuville (see the entry for FRICOURT). One of the witnesses to the toast was Basil Liddell Hart, who had digs at Verité, No. 5 rue de la Republique, La Neuville, les Corbie; in a letter home, he mentions that his kit had been stolen (LH7/1916).

On 1 July, a large number of wounded arrived at the casualty clearing station and those casualties who died here were buried in the adjoining cemetery extension. A considerable number of casualties were handled throughout July. A harrowing description of the hospital conditions appeared in *People at War*, written by the Revd J.M.S. Walker, a member of the staff of No. 21 Casualty Clearing Station. Walker described the hospital as being converted from a partly burnt down car factory, its grounds dotted with huts, marquees and tents. Its function was to provide immediate treatment for casualties from the nearby front line, before they were moved by ambulance train or specially fitted barges down the River Somme to base hospitals at Rouen, le Havre, and elsewhere.

Prior to the start of battle, the staff of the casualty clearing station included six surgeons, three physicians, a dentist and eight sisters. There were two hospitals in the Somme area exclusively for the use of officers; one was at GÉZAINCOURT and the other at CORBIE. Casualty numbers remained high for several days and about 80 officers and men died at the hospital during this period, including 6 German casualties. No. 21 Casualty Clearing Station left La Neuville in March 1917.

La Neuville British Cemetery, designed by Sir Edwin Lutyens, is on the west side of La Neuville, on the south side of the road to DAOURS. It is square, on level ground on the edge of the Somme marshes, surrounded by poplars and willows. It was opened in early July 1916 and contains 888 identified graves. It was finished in 1922, apart from the replacement of the wooden crosses by headstones. T/Capt T.R. Crawley-Boevey of 14th Glosters (105th Brigade, 35th Division), a son of the 5th baronet, is buried here (II.B.11); he died of wounds in CORBIE on 30 August 1916.

La Neuville Communal Cemetery is on the north side of La Neuville, with military burials in one long row on the east side of the cemetery, with 186 graves; a row had to be added later to cover the men who died in 1918. In a file in the Commonwealth War Graves Commission archive is a note written in the mid-1920s, which states: 'The long neat row of British graves was in pleasant contrast to the rough and tumble condition of the rest of the Communal Cemetery.'

L'ARBRET is a hamlet to the north of the N25 Arras–DOULLENS road and south of BAVINCOURT. In the period prior to the start of the July 1916 battle, the railway station was severely bombarded; some shells fell in the village and wounded patients of 50th Field Ambulance (37th Division), who were sent to a casualty clearing station. Horses and mules stampeded and several were not recovered. For about 6 weeks prior to 1 July, No. 152 Field Company, Royal Engineers (37th Division), had their headquarters and two sections here. On 4 July, 49th Field Ambulance (37th Division) left l'Arbret.

LA SIGNY FARM is due west of SERRE, at the end of a track leading from the HÉBUTERNE–AUCHONVILLERS road, the D174. On 1 August 1915, a well was discovered here, but a pump would be required to make it work, manned by either horses or an engine. In what appear to have been the very first tasks for a British unit to carry out on the Somme, No. 9 Field Company, Royal Engineers (4th Division), worked on the farm's water supply and defences; by October 1915, a machine-gun emplacement had been set up. The Farm was also used as an advanced dressing station and casualties were collected from here.

On 22 May 1916, No. 211 Field Company, Royal Engineers (31st Division), provided working parties to connect the Farm with a new trench, making it a strongpoint. There is a dugout near the Farm associated with the poet Wilfred Owen, who was here in January 1917. The site was excavated in 2004.

LAVIÉVILLE, on the D119 road, is a small village to the north of the ALBERT–AMIENS road (D929), south-west of MILLENCOURT and south-east of HÉNENCOURT. During the struggle on the Somme, the village remained behind the battle lines; 51st Division trained other units here, including those from 18th Division. At the end of December 1915, units of 32nd Division were billeted here, including 2nd Royal Inniskilling Fusiliers (96th Brigade, 32nd Division); on 2 January 1916, they left for a section of the line opposite THIEPVAL. At the beginning of January, units of 55th Division were here.

On 3 April 1916, an advance party of 24th Field Ambulance (8th Division) arrived to prepare billets and a hospital; 5 days later, 205 patients could be catered for, including 30 in the church in the southeast of the village and 40 in the school next door. A hospital barn could take 50 and 'B' Section billets 65. A well in a cellar provided 6,000 gallons of water daily, which was pumped by the Royal Engineers, chlorinated and stored in tanks.

On 16 June, 24th Field Ambulance left Laviéville and were replaced by 57th Field Ambulance (19th Division), who took over the hospital and billets. On 1 July, 463 patients were admitted to the hospital from the battle raging just a few miles to the northeast; all had been evacuated by the evening. Many of the casualties had poured into MILLENCOURT, only to be redirected to Laviéville because 25th Field Ambulance (8th Division) had become overwhelmed. At the beginning of July, a main dressing station run by III Corps was here; a walking wounded post and a motor ambulance convoy were also established.

In August, No. 18 Squadron, Royal Flying Corps, commanded by Maj G.I. Carmichael, arrived here from Bruay and remained for 3 months. For much of September, 15th Division had men billeted here, as did 47th Division in October. At the end of November, the motor ambulance convoy still operated from here, as did a divisional rest station. During this period, the ALBERT–AMIENS road became impossible to use as it had been largely destroyed by enemy shelling.

Laviéville Communal Cemetery is just outside the village, on the east side of the road to Hénencourt; it has seven British graves. In the mid-1920s it was reportedly in a poor state. Another casualty was buried there during the Second World War.

LÉALVILLERS is north-west of ALBERT on the D114 road from ACHEUX-EN-AMIÉNOIS and the D31 to ARQUÈVES. During 1916, the village was used mainly for billeting and training purposes. In January 1916 a new large railway cutting was being constructed here to the north-east of the village. Léalvillers Halt was actually closer to ACHEUX-EN-AMIÉNOIS than to Léalvillers, and the same applied to Varennes Halt further eastwards. The nearest station was at LOUVENCOURT, to the north-west.

Prior to the battle, 24th, 25th, 36th and 37th Divisions had units billeted at Léalvillers; apart from work on the railway cutting, their tasks included the construction of hutting and trench bridges for the artillery. The village was also used as a divisional rest station. From 27 June until 1 July, 49th Division

had their divisional headquarters in the village; on 1 July, 49th Division were succeeded here by 25th Division and went into reserve at AVELUY WOOD.

During the battle period, 6th, 11th, 25th, 35th, 37th, 38th, 51st and 63rd Divisions had men here. From 5 October, the recently arrived 63rd Division had their headquarters in the village; a week later, the division's General Officer Commanding, Maj Gen A. Paris CB, was seriously wounded in the Redan Sector at BEAUMONT-HAMEL. A German shell had exploded in the trench called 6th Avenue and Maj E.F.P. Sketchley of the Royal Marine Light Infantry (GSO2) was killed. On 12 October, Paris was taken to No. 3 Casualty Clearing Station at PUCHEVILLERS, where his leg had to be amputated. He relinquished command of 63rd Division on 16 October, having been in command since its formation in 1914.

Travelling from ACHEUX-EN-AMIÉNOIS to Léalvillers on the D114, one can still see one of the increasingly rare military village signs used during the war.

LE HAMEL is a small village on the D71 road between CORBIE and Cerisy-Gailly. In the southwest of the village, le Hamel Communal Cemetery contains the grave of Driver J. Gilpin of No. 129 Field Company, Royal Engineers (24th Division) who died on 1 August 1916. Having been shelled during the war, the cemetery was in a very rough state afterwards.

LEIPZIG SALIENT is just north-east of the crossroads of the OVILLERS-LA-BOISSELLE–AUTHUILLE and the THIEPVAL–Aveluy roads. In 1916, the German Front Line bent round like a nose at this point on its way southwards in front of OVILLERS-LA-BOISSELLE. Behind the salient, which was then a quarry on high ground, was a series of further defensive lines, including Hindenburg Trench and WONDERWORK, another strongpoint a few hundred yards beyond. Nab Valley – or BLIGHTY VALLEY as it was to become – was further eastwards, with the remains of THIEPVAL and its château to the north. The strongly held MOUQUET FARM was in the north-easterly direction towards POZIÈRES.

On 1 July, 32nd and 36th Divisions were ordered to capture German-held territory from GRAND-COURT in the north to MIRAUMONT in the south; with hindsight, this seems to have been a hopelessly optimistic task.

In *The Old Front Line*, John Masefield described the Salient as a long sloping spur, wooded at one end, which was known as Thiepval Hill. He noted that this hill was of the greatest importance to the enemy and that it was a sort of eyrie for the SCHWABEN REDOUBT, which was on the higher ground to the north. It was the key to the covered way to the plateau from which all the spurs in this area thrust southwards. There were two large enemy works on the Leipzig Spur, one being WONDER-WORK, a six-angled, star-shaped redoubt, the other, still further southwards, being Leipzig Salient, which Masefield described as being a big, disused, and very evil-looking quarry. It had another name, Hohenzollern, from the trench of that name that ran straight across the spur about halfway down the Salient. The enemy could look down easily on the Allied line from these eyries; though, in the end, the British artillery blasted the Germans off the hill, it was to be a hugely costly place to hold on to in terms of casualties and suffering. Enemy fire could be directed from the rear above HAMEL, from the hill itself or from the left flank towards THIEPVAL.

On 1 July 1916, 97th and 14th Brigades (both 32nd Division) were given the task of capturing the Leipzig Salient; 17th Highland Light Infantry had made preparations, taking water up to the line in petrol cans that were then stacked in dugouts and along the Allied trench to form their reserve water supply. The battalion then moved via Aveluy and AUTHUILLE to the trenches. The day before the battle began, 17th Highland Light Infantry spent the night in huts at BOUZINCOURT, to the east of Aveluy. BOUZINCOURT stands on a hill and Lt B. Meadows, who was with the battalion, described the battlefield as being stretched out like a map below. Near the Crucifix on the Aveluy road, a long naval gun barked; just behind 17th Highland Light Infantry were 15in howitzers and around ALBERT there was a long line of observation balloons. The air was thick with aeroplanes and the German lines looked like long ribbons of white fur. The air was also full of shrapnel balls, especially over the woods and the villages that were burning. The Germans were putting shrapnel into the woods that lay in the triangle between HAMEL, BOUZINCOURT and Aveluy. Here the Allied guns were massed, and despite the troops putting cotton wool in their ears they were deaf for days after 1 July. Meadows also noted that prior to the battle they made a bonfire, using boxes from the company quartermaster's stores, on which they destroyed their letters, and had a sing-song – the last that the old 17th Highland Light Infantry were to have.

During their attack of 1 July against the Leipzig Salient, 32nd Division planned to use most of their battalions. On the right were 2nd Manchesters, 1st Dorsets and 19th Lancashire Fusiliers (all 14th Brigade, 32nd Division); in the centre were 11th Borders, elements of 2nd King's Own Yorkshire Light Infantry and 17th Highland Light Infantry (all 97th Brigade); on the left were 16th Highland Light Infantry (also 97th Brigade) and more companies of 2nd King's Own Yorkshire Light Infantry.

On the evening of Z-Day (1 July), 17th Highland Light Infantry marched off by platoons; Meadows described the very heavy concentration of 18-pounders on the way up. They entered Oban Avenue at the right end of the village of AUTHUILLE, which was the 'up' stretch for the advance; Campbell Avenue, the road towards OVILLERS-LA-BOISSELLE, was the 'down'. The line in which they spent the night had almost been blown out of existence, but they took up their battle positions. At 0625hrs on 1 July, the final bombardment began; at 0725hrs, they left their trench and walked over to within 60yds of the barrage. At 0730hrs, the barrage lifted and they rushed up the front-line defences, destroying the German garrison in and out of the dugouts. 17th Highland Light Infantry overran the Salient, gaining its summit, known to the British as Leipzig Redoubt, but this initial success was short-lived.

Meadows wrote that his battalion were working up between two communication trenches; after two or three rushes, further progress was impossible. They therefore waited for their own reserve waves as well as those of 11th Borders, who had also moved up the night before from dugouts built into a high bank at CRUCIFIX CORNER to their assembly trenches in the thickest part of Authuille Wood. The battalion subsequently moved out of the Wood and swung to the east. On leaving their trenches, they had come under terrific machine-gun fire and were cut down opposite the redoubt and massacred by enfilade fire from the Nord Werk and by machine-gun fire from the Ovillers Spur. Their Commanding Officer, Lt Col P.W. Machell, was one of their casualties; he was later buried at Warloy-Baillon Communal Cemetery Extension (A.17). He had virtually raised and trained the whole of 11th Borders himself, only to have them tragically cut down in one morning – 1 July.

Meadows noted that 17th Highland Light Infantry began to work towards the communication trench, but owing to the lie of the land they were badly exposed. At about noon, Meadows managed to leap the parapet; around this time, an order came up the trench that 17th Highland Light Infantry were to move to the left and support 1st Dorsets.

Lt Col J.V. Shute, Commanding Officer 1st Dorsets, was wounded in the fighting. The communication trench was chiefly manned at this time by 2nd King's Own Yorkshire Light Infantry, who should have given support to 16th Highland Light Infantry; the latter had been held up by the German wire and were cut down before being able to take the first line of defence. They had suffered heavy machine-gun fire from Thiepval Château. A few of 11th Borders who had not been casualties had come up through Blighty Wood together with a company of 2nd Manchesters, but were not able to give 17th Highland Light Infantry much support. The barbed wire was impossible to cut through.

At 1700hrs, the Germans counter-attacked; although they were repulsed, men of B Company, 17th Highland Light Infantry, were caught up in the wire and cut to pieces by machine-gun fire. By this time, Meadows's own A Company were very low in numbers. The battalions on the flanks of the attack were unsuccessful in storming the enemy's front-line defences and thus the flanks of 17th Highland Light Infantry became exposed; blockades had to be formed at the front lines forward to their advanced positions, which developed into a series of bombing posts.

The nature of the Leipzig defences, a maze of trenches and underground saps, made advancing into the Salient extremely difficult. Sgt J.Y. Turnbull of 17th Highland Light Infantry was awarded a posthumous Victoria Cross

> when, his party having captured a post apparently of great importance to the enemy, he was subjected to severe counter-attacks, which were continuous throughout the whole day. Although his party was wiped out and replaced several times during the day, Sergt. Turnbull never wavered in his determination to hold the post, the loss of which would have been very serious. Almost single-handed he maintained his position, and displayed the highest degree of valour and skill in the performance of his duties. Later in the day this very gallant soldier was killed whilst bombing a counter-attack from the parados of our trench . . .

Having reached Hindenburg Trench, 150yds beyond the Redoubt, 17th Highland Light Infantry were repulsed by machine guns at WONDERWORK and forced back to the Redoubt. With 1st Dorsets there were the remnants of five battalions in the Salient at the end of the day. The quarry was full of corpses.

The northern end of the Salient was the most northerly point permanently secured by the first day's fighting, and a small party of 32nd Division remained in the Redoubt. On the morning of 2 July, 17th Highland Light Infantry handed over their section of front line of attack to divisional reserve and went into support. At sunset they were relieved by a battalion of the Cheshire Regiment and moved back to dugouts at CRUCIFIX CORNER.

In *Sir Douglas Haig's Great Push*, the achievement of holding on in the Leipzig Salient is described as a brilliant success. Lt Gen Sir Hubert Gough, General Officer Commanding Reserve (later Fifth) Army, wrote that it was a wonder that the British managed to hang on to this small holding and the troops were set to work at once to dig good communication trenches back to their own lines.

On 2 July, the enemy made unsuccessful bombing attacks towards the Redoubt. The objective of 32nd Division was now a south–north line from the eastern end of the Redoubt to WONDERWORK on Thiepval Spur, a frontage of 800yds. On 3 July, an attack on the right was to be made by 14th Brigade (32nd Division), who had relieved 97th Brigade in the tip of the Salient, and on the left by 75th Brigade (attached to 25th Division), who had assembled in AVELUY and Martinsart Woods by 1530hrs on 2 July.

The attack of 14th Brigade firstly consisted of two companies of 15th Highland Light Infantry, moving from the tip of the Salient; they entered the enemy front trench at around 0615hrs, only to be driven out. Three hours later, 75th Brigade repeated the exercise, with the same negative result. On 5 July, 1st Wiltshires (7th Brigade, 25th Division) gained a foothold in Hindenburg Trench, the German Front Line position in the Salient. On 6 July, Capt H.L.G. Hughes of the Royal Army Medical Corps went out looking for seven men who had been wounded under heavy fire and brought them back at night through a barrage. On 7 July, two companies of 1st Wiltshires completed the capture of the German Front Line in the Salient and held it with the assistance of 3rd Worcesters (also 7th Brigade, 25th Division), under severe bombardment.

The Michelin battlefield guide describes the action on 7 July in the following way: 'The British carried the greater part of the Leipzig Redoubt (Hill 141), a powerful stronghold which protected Thiepval from the south, and consisting of a system of small blockhouses connected up by a network of trenches. A wide breach opened by the Artillery enabled the troops to gain a footing in the position and conquer it trench by trench.' 36th Brigade (12th Division) had been kept on the south side of the spur in order to avoid as much as possible the machine-gun fire from the Salient.

On 15 July, 49th Division repelled attacks on the Salient that were delivered with gas bombers and flame-throwers. At this time, 1/6th West Yorkshires (146th Brigade, 49th Division) held the Salient; the night of 14/15 July was much quieter than usual, as both sides were thoroughly tired. At about 0330hrs, they heard the terrifying shrieks of the sentries, who had been caught without any warning by the German liquid fire attack. However, 1/6th West Yorkshires beat off the counter-attacks, which lasted about 3 hours.

Cpl Robertson of 3rd Worcesters (7th Brigade, 25th Division) wrote that at 1100hrs on 19 July, he was having a look around when suddenly about two dozen gas shells arrived. They came quietly and burst quietly. Heavy gas bombardment followed and lasted for 3 hours. Everything was coated yellowish green, including their food.

On 17 August, 3rd Worcesters heard that they were due to go into the trenches in and around the Salient again on the following day. Charles Carrington of 1/5th Royal Warwicks wrote that 143rd Brigade (48th Division) carried the Redoubt by a sudden attack with a limited objective; with their flanks covered by 1/7th Royal Warwicks, 1/5th and 1/6th Royal Warwicks (all 143rd Brigade) went over the top in waves that followed close behind the barrage – the first creeping barrage that they had seen – created by the concentration of fire by 18 batteries on this small front.

Another attack had been planned for 21 August. Throughout the day, final arrangements were being made in the Redoubt, in which 25th and 48th Divisions were to be involved. At 1800hrs, there was a 3-minute barrage onto the German trench, under cover of which two companies of 1st Wiltshires entered the German positions very quickly. On the right, where the troops were close up to the German trench, in which the enemy had a block, a 'push pipe' was used for the first time with great success; it was a contrivance that bored a pipe at the rate of 18yds an hour underground under the German trench. The pipe was full of ammonal; as the boring was silent, the Germans were unaware of its presence. When 1st Wiltshires began their advance, the pipe was 'touched off'. In addition to blowing up the German block, it created a ready-made communication trench in their line, up which British bombing parties could rush. 1st Wiltshires attacked eastwards and captured important points in the German front and Support Line of the Redoubt.

Beginning their advance from the Nab Trenches to the south, 1/4th Glosters (144th Brigade, 48th Division) advanced behind an excellent barrage to attack the south-east face of the Salient; 1/6th Glosters (also 144th Brigade, 48th Division) entered Hindenburg Trench and virtually surrounded the Salient. 2/Lt L.A. Bessant of the Royal Engineers was awarded the Military Cross for work achieved on this day, when he laid out and superintended the work on 250yds of communication trench up to the captured trenches, under heavy shell-fire.

On 23 August, a further attack was postponed and the line was rearranged to take a bigger objective. On 24 August, 1st Wiltshires and 3rd Worcesters, with the aid of push pipes, again assaulted the German positions. There was furious hand-to-hand fighting and the British battalions inflicted frightful losses on the enemy. On 26 August, they were relieved by their own brigade, except for 8th Loyal North Lancashires, who were to carry out a small attack in the left-hand corner of the Salient. This they did at 1800hrs, but without success. At this time, 75th Brigade (25th Division) were in Authuille Wood.

On 2 September, the Germans shelled all the communication trenches, the bridges over the Ancre, BLIGHTY VALLEY and AUTHUILLE; 3rd Worcesters marched forward from BOUZINCOURT via BLACK HORSE BRIDGE near AUTHUILLE in order to have another crack at the Salient. This time they were to attack the western side of a small salient from the original line further down the slope, but the attack was destroyed by the German artillery; Lt Col W.B. Gibbs, Commanding Officer 3rd Worcesters, was mortally wounded and later buried at Blighty Valley Cemetery (I.D.36).

Later in September, Edmund Blunden described the Redoubt's underworld comforts, from bakehouse to boudoir. Companies of 11th Royal Sussex (116th Brigade, 39th Division) were accommodated there, while the battalion headquarters was in Authuille Wood, at a spot called Tithe Barn.

The Redoubt is now a disused chalk quarry; after the war, it was planted with poplars, which were cut down in 2001 leaving the site bare. However, the quarry remains and is now closer to its original condition. A visitor to the spot can very easily appreciate the tremendous advantage that the Germans had here, with the whole of the hill within their lines.

LE SARS is a small village that straddles the main ALBERT–BAPAUME road, the D929; to the south-west is COURCELETTE, to the north-west Pys and MIRAUMONT, to the south-east EAUCOURT L'ABBAYE. To the north-east is the BUTTE DE WARLENCOURT and just off the main ALBERT road south-west of le Sars is the site of DESTRE-MONT FARM.

In 1916 the German Flers Line ran to the south-west of the village from the direction of Pys, bending towards FLERS to the south-east. In *The War in the Air* by H.A. Jones, it is noted that on the afternoon of 6 July pilots of No. 21 Squadron had bombed enemy dumps at le Sars; on 21 July, No. 4 Squadron reported that new entrenchments could be seen around le Sars and COURCELETTE and No. 3 Squadron discovered a new line between LE TRANSLOY and Warlencourt and a doubling up of the third line between Eaucourt and FLERS.

On 1 October, a battalion of the Durham Light Infantry attacked le Sars, but were unable to consolidate. Norman Gladden of 1/7th Northumberland Fusiliers (149th Brigade, 50th Division) described the area as being of dirty brown slime and mud, criss-crossed with trenches; on the horizon beyond the German positions were trees and open country. In a recess just behind 1/7th Northumberland Fusiliers, a Vickers machine gun had been set up to assist in the barrage that would protect the attackers.

On 4 October, 2/Lt H.T. Kelly of 10th Duke of Wellington's (69th Brigade, 23rd Division) gained the Victoria Cross for his actions:

He showed the utmost valour in an attack on Flers Line, immediately to the south-west of le Sars, on the 4th October 1916. He twice rallied his company under the heaviest fire, and eventually led the only three available men left in his company into the enemy's trench, remaining there bombing until two of his men became casualties and enemy reinforcements arrived from the rear. He then carried his wounded Company Sergeant Major back to our trenches, a distance of 70 yards, and subsequently three others . . .

On 7 October, 47th Division to the right and 23rd Division to the front of le Sars were first to make an advance of 500yds, which would include the capture of the village. The remains of the village were to be secured when the attack was resumed again, on the Butte and Gird Lines, known as the Warlencourt Line.

On 5 November, Brig Gen J. Paton CB, General Officer Commanding 7th Australian Brigade (2nd Australian Division), was wounded by a German sniper when his brigade was about to attack a small salient in the German line known as the Maze, south-east of the village. He had been standing on the trench parapet, as the trenches were too muddy.

In *All Our Yesterdays*, H.M. Tomlinson described the area of le Sars. He wrote that the village was most foul and full of dreadful heaps that had once been a community. There was a track through it and the sound of machine-gun fire was not far off. Battalion headquarters was at le Coupe Queule. Beyond le Sars was Loupart Wood, a wooded ridge beyond the German lines. It had been full of machine guns because of its protection of BAPAUME. A famous sign nearby was Via Dolorosa. Cut Throat Corner, a deep cave in the district, was an aid post where surgeons did their work. There was also a deep German dugout in the village with two entrances.

It was the bad weather as much as anything that ended the advance in this area; continuous rain churned the landscape into a swamp. The crest of the rise that overlooked BAPAUME was to mark the limit of the British advance. On 25 November rations were brought by limber to DESTREMENT FARM, when 1/4th Oxfordshire & Buckinghamshire Light Infantry (145th Brigade, 48th Division) were at le Sars.

Hexham Road, which led from Warlencourt to Eaucourt, gave its name to the cemetery, which is on the west side of l'Abbaye grounds.

After the German retreat in early 1917, le Sars was lost again in March 1918, but retaken by infantry of the New Zealand Expeditionary Force in August. There is a German memorial in the village dedicated to Reserve-Infanterie-Regiment Nr. 111 (28. Reserve Division).

LESBŒUFS, south of BAPAUME, is on the D74 road between MORVAL and GUEUDECOURT. By 18 September 1916, the British line had reached a point about ½ mile to the south-west of the village, by now demolished, after the capture of GINCHY. A previous attempt to capture the village earlier in the month had been a failure and the plan now was to capture MORVAL and Lesbœufs on 25 September. 56th Division were to form the flank in front of COMBLES while 5th Division on their left were to take MORVAL and 6th Division were to occupy the southern part of Lesbœufs; the Guards Division were to finish off by taking the rest of Lesbœufs.

On this occasion, 1st and 3rd Guards Brigades (both Guards Division) were to be involved in the frontal advance, with 2nd and 3rd Coldstream Guards (both 1st Guards Brigade) on the right and 4th Grenadier Guards (3rd Guards Brigade) and 2nd

Scots Guards, supported by 1st Welsh Guards (all 3rd Guards Brigade), on the left. A creeping barrage came down at Zero Hour, 1235hrs, when it appears that the enemy were taken by surprise. The attackers made rapid progress and maintained close contact between the flanks.

A support battalion, 1st Grenadier Guards (3rd Guards Brigade), moved forward through the leading troops to try and enter the northern part of Lesbœufs, which they achieved by 1530hrs. Despite the narrowness of the trenches – men were hardly able to move when occupying them – as well as the presence of uncut wire, Lesbœufs and MORVAL were both captured and then kept clear of troops and bombarded. There had only been one real hitch in this day of success; on the left of the Guards' attack, 21st Division were held up, meaning that the Guards Division's left flank were left in the air. Accordingly, 4th Grenadier Guards threw out a defensive flank to the left.

In *The Irish Guards in the Great War*, Rudyard Kipling wrote that the plan for 25 September was much less ambitious than that of 15 September. The distance to the first objective was 300yds, to the second 700yds and to the last 1,300yds. In each case, Kipling says, the objective was clearly defined. Also the ground sloped down towards Lesbœufs, and the artillery did their work more accurately than on 15 September.

Nevertheless, casualties were very high, especially among the officers. Three officers buried in the Guards Cemetery, Lesbœufs, are Lt Col W.D. Drury-Lowe (VII.A.6) of 1st Grenadier Guards; Lt Col C. Anderson (V.A.1) of 1st North Staffords (72nd Brigade, 24th Division), killed on 18 September; and Lt W. Parnell MC (I.C.1.), attached 2nd Grenadier Guards (1st Guards Brigade), a son of Lord Congleton, killed on 25 September.

Capt E.P. Dark of 9th Field Ambulance (Guards Division) visited Lesbœufs soon after its capture. 'I found a big cellar in the middle of the village full of badly wounded men who needed to be roughly fixed up and then sent off on stretchers. The town was being fairly heavily shelled, and every minute or so the lantern, which was the only light one had for doing the dressings, was blown out by the blast of some shell falling near the entrance of the cellar . . .'

On 26 September, 3rd Grenadier Guards moved up to TRÔNES WOOD and 1st Scots Guards (both 2nd Guards Brigade) were sent up as relief at Lesbœufs. On 29 September, 3rd Grenadier Guards relieved 1st Scots Guards in front of Lesbœufs. H.L.N. Dundas, temporary adjutant as well as bombing officer of 1st Scots Guards at this time,

noted that his battalion were 'beside' Lesbœufs. On 29 September they were in Support Line, and on the following day went back to tents or billets. On 2 October, 1st Scots Guards moved to a training area south-west of AMIENS.

According to Oliver Lyttelton (later Viscount Chandos), after the Guards Division were relieved, they were allotted the task of building a railway in the Somme Valley. The division were close to the river and established in a comfortable camp on one of the islands. Lyttelton describes the valley as a place of great beauty and peace, bathed in autumn light.

On 30 September, 56th Division relieved the Guards Division and 6th Division in the area. On 7 October, the poet Pte H.N. Todd of 1/16th Londons (169th Brigade, 56th Division) was killed near DEWDROP and Spectrum Trenches during the fighting for the Transloy Ridges. Born in 1878, Todd had been a schoolmaster before the war; his verse had been published in a book called *Poems and Plays*. Another poet who was mortally wounded near the village was Sgt L. Coulson, a former journalist who had written a volume called *From an Outpost, and other Poems*, posthumously published in 1917. Coulson had seen action in Gallipoli and in April 1916 was attached to 1/12th Londons (168th Brigade, 56th Division). He had taken part in the Somme fighting on 1 July. He died of wounds on 8 October and was buried at Grove Town Cemetery (I.J.24), south-east of MÉAULTE.

On 14 October, 2nd Sherwood Foresters (71st Brigade, 6th Division) were ordered to attack a troublesome gun in the north of the village, and also some new German trenches. In supervising this operation their Commanding Officer, Lt Col C.J.W. Hobbs, was mortally wounded and died on 16 October; he too was buried in Grove Town Cemetery (I.B.6).

Between 12 and 18 October, further attacks were made to the east of the Lesbœufs–GUEUDECOURT line. By this time the trenches around Lesbœufs were in an increasingly poor state, and battalions reported that the men were up to their knees in mud. During the period 17–19 October, 1st Rifle Brigade (11th Brigade, 4th Division) were involved in a night attack to the left of Lesbœufs. On 19 October, 2nd Rifle Brigade (25th Brigade, 8th Division) were in trenches to the east. On 23 and 24 October, 1st and 2nd Rifle Brigade were involved in an attack, but made little progress. Lt T. Rouse-Boughton-Knight of the Rifle Brigade, a brother of Sir William, was killed in action at Frosty Trench and later buried in Péronne Road Cemetery (III.G.34).

Also around 23 October, Pte Frank Richards' battalion, 2nd Royal Welsh Fusiliers (19th Brigade, 33rd Division), were lent to 4th Division for a time and took over trenches in front of Lesbœufs; the German trenches were directly facing them in front of LE TRANSLOY, to the north-west. A small trench about 60yds behind the front line was used as an advance signal station; runners used the old German communication trenches to carry messages between this station and battalion headquarters, which was in a sunken road about 500yds behind. It had been raining again and the landscape was a sea of mud, the ground just a series of connected shell-holes. Later returning to a sunken road on the edge of TRÔNES WOOD, 2nd Royal Welsh Fusiliers were then billeted in huts.

On the same day, east of Lesbœufs, Sgt R. Downie of 2nd Royal Dublin Fusiliers (10th Brigade, 5th Division) gained the Victoria Cross:

When most of the officers had become casualties, this non-commissioned officer, utterly regardless of personal danger, moved about under heavy fire and reorganized the attack, which had been temporarily checked. At the critical moment he rushed forward alone, shouting: 'Come on, the Dubs!' This stirring appeal met with immediate response, and the line rushed forward at his call. Sergt. Downie accounted for several of the enemy, and in addition captured a machine gun, killing the team. Though wounded early in the fight, he remained with his company, and gave valuable assistance whilst the position was being consolidated. It was owing to Sergt Downie's courage and initiative that this important position, which had resisted four or five previous attacks, was won . . .

On 28 October, 1/4th Suffolks (98th Brigade, 33rd Division) occupied some poor front-line trenches of newly gained ground in front of Lesbœufs; on the same day, DEWDROP TRENCH fell to 98th Brigade. By early November, the mud in the area had become even worse. On 2 November, 2nd Royal Welsh Fusiliers returned here, with their head-quarters in a German chalk dugout in a bank facing the 'wrong way', in a sunken road about 800yds north-west of Lesbœufs church. On 4 October they knew that their objective was to be the cemetery at LE TRANSLOY, which was about 1 mile away, perched on the highest ridge in the area.

Also in early November, having taken over the front trenches from 2nd Lincolns (25th Brigade, 8th Division), 1st King's Own Scottish Borderers (8th Brigade, 29th Division) were in the line between Lesbœufs and LE TRANSLOY; the latter was still in German hands. At this location, the extreme right of the British sector, the line faced north-eastwards; units of the French 152nd Division were neighbours of 1st King's Own Scottish Borderers at this point.

On 6 November, Lt E.P. Bennett of 2nd Worcesters (100th Brigade, 33rd Division) was awarded the Victoria Cross for his involvement in the fighting towards LE TRANSLOY (see that entry). These attacks were still being pursued despite the very adverse conditions.

In the period 10–11 November, 2nd West Yorkshires relieved 2nd Devons (both 23rd Brigade, 8th Division) in the front line. The sector taken over was at the apex of the salient formed by the offensive, a little to the left of Lesbœufs. In *Twelve Days*, Sidney Rogerson of 2nd West Yorkshires (23rd Brigade, 8th Division) reported that Citadel Camp was only about 6 miles behind the LE TRANSLOY line, yet the distance took a very long time to cover in the conditions. Rogerson's battalion had to wind their way along crazy duckboard tracks, past holes in the ground, many of which were occupied by men, until, as dawn was breaking, they reached 2nd Devons' headquarters, in a sunken road to the left of Lesbœufs Wood. On 14 November, 1st King's Own Scottish Borderers bussed to BUIRE-SUR-L'ANCRE before marching to Lesbœufs.

In visiting the former battlefields in this area, it is as well to appreciate the tremendous importance of the sunken roads, many of which can still be easily traced; they virtually divide up the landscape. One such road linked up with LE TRANSLOY, and Thistle and High Alley were important communication trenches.

The Guards Cemetery, Lesbœufs, is ½ mile to the south-west of the village, on the north-west of the GINCHY road. The 1916 fighting is commemorated by the Guards Division Memorial, further along the road towards GINCHY. The cemetery itself was greatly enlarged by a concentration of graves from the battlefield and small cemeteries around Lesbœufs. At the time of the Armistice, it contained only about 40 graves of men of 2nd Grenadier Guards, who had fallen on 25 September. Many of the dead were brought in from places such as Flers Dressing Station Cemetery, GINCHY, between FLERS and DELVILLE WOOD; Flers Road Cemetery, on the FLERS–LONGUEVAL road; Ginchy Advanced Dressing Station Cemetery, on the north side of GINCHY; Ginchy Royal Field Artillery Cemetery, which contained the graves of 21 artillerymen; Guards' Burial Ground, on the east side of GINCHY, with 21 casualties from 15 September 1916; Needle Dump Cemetery, Lesbœufs, on the road to FLERS; Needle Dump South Cemetery, Lesbœufs; Switch Trench Cemetery, FLERS, where most of the graves were of Australian soldiers; and Windmill Trench Cemetery, on the road leading north from Lesbœufs.

The Guards Cemetery is an indication of the very great losses and sacrifice made by Britain's premier infantry division, underlined by the number of different memorial services to the various regiments which took place in London soon after the capture of Lesbœufs and MORVAL.

In *Goodbye to the Battlefields*, Capt H.A. Taylor of the Royal Fusiliers wrote that a visit to this cemetery completed the story, partly told by the Guillemont Road Cemetery, of how dearly the Guards brigades paid in the attack they launched against Lesbœufs; this is enhanced by the Guards Memorial on the GINCHY road. He notes that, standing near the cemetery, one can understand why the enemy clung so desperately to Lesbœufs, GUEUDECOURT and MORVAL, as from the ridge one could see the BAPAUME–PÉRONNE road, the best means of communication running parallel to the former German front.

At first, the Guards Division Memorial on the left-hand side of the road to Lesbœufs consisted of a large wooden cross, later replaced by a new memorial; this was unveiled on 21 October 1928 by Gen Sir Geoffrey Feilding, who had been in command of the Guards Division all through the Battle of the Somme. It stands on the summit of a ridge to the west of Lesbœufs. According to *The Times*, 'Detachments from each battalion of the five regiments of Foot Guards . . . were present at the unveiling in service dress and without arms . . .' A French guard of honour was mounted at the memorial, and various French organisations took part; the mayor of GINCHY took the memorial into his keeping. HM the King was represented by Lt Gen the Earl of Cavan, in 1916 General Officer Commanding XIV Corps, and HRH the Prince of Wales by Lt Col R.E.K. Leatham of the Welsh Guards. In a brief speech, Lord Cavan invited Sir Geoffrey to unveil the memorial. He outlined the particular difficulties of the battle that the Guards had been faced with, which led to the deaths of no fewer than 232 officers and 7,072 other ranks.

After the ceremonies 'the drummers sounded the Guards' call, the Last Post, and Reveille; then three pipers – one Irish and two Scots – played a Lament, marching and counter-marching in slow time on the road in front of the memorial. When the last notes of the pipes had died away wreaths were laid round the memorial by the representatives of the King, the Prince of Wales, and the Duke of Connaught . . .

Last of all, a line of school children from Ginchy laid flowers on the memorial . . .'

Later, the Divisional Memorial Committee had lunch at the Hôtel de la Paix in ALBERT. The director of the Imperial War Graves Commission, Fabian Ware, was invited, but he was attending an unveiling of a table in Saint-Omer cathedral.

In the following year, the memorial to the Grenadier Guards outside the Guards Cemetery was sent back to Wellington Barracks. This too was a wooden cross but was 'in a much damaged condition'. It was 7ft high and painted white with black lettering.

To the south-west of the Guards Cemetery is a memorial to Capt H.P. Meakin of 3rd Coldstream Guards' trench mortar battery, killed on 25 September 1916 during the fight for Lesbœufs. He was buried at a point 40yds north-west of the GINCHY–Lesbœufs road. He had joined the Army in October 1914 and is commemorated on the Thiepval Memorial. It is hoped to raise sufficient funds to renovate and move the obelisk memorial to a site nearer the road to allow for easier access. If this operation is successful a memorial service will be held at the site on 25 September 2016.

LE TRANSLOY is on the N17 main road, between BAPAUME to the north-west and SAILLY-SAILLISEL to the south-east. The name le Transloy was given to the Battle for the Transloy Ridges, the official dates of which were 7–20 October, rather than to the village itself.

To the south-west is the village of LESBŒUFS, from which the battle on the extreme right of the line was to be launched, although the French were to be involved even further to the right in cooperation with the British and in the direction of SAILLY-SAILLISEL. The trench names in the sector between LESBŒUFS and le Transloy, which appear again and again in the accounts of fighting on this front over these 2 weeks in October, include Rainy, Hazy, Cloudy, Spectrum, Misty and Rainbow.

The attack on the ridges was planned for 5 October but, owing to poor and wet weather, it was postponed until 7 October. At 1515hrs on 6 October, a bombardment began from the British side, and companies sheltered in the valley to the south of the GUEUDECOURT–LE TRANSLOY road. The first task of 56th Division, who were in the LESBŒUFS sector, included the capture of disconnected trenches known as Hazy, Spectrum and part of Rainbow. The second objective was to establish a line on the forward slope of the ridges from which the le Transloy system could be seen. The attack was to be made in conjunction with the French, on their right.

Le Transloy when occupied by German troops.
(Peter F. Batchelor Collection)

To the left of 56th Division's front were 20th Division; their role was to establish a position on the top of the ridge overlooking both le Transloy and the village of Beaulencourt to the north. This line could then serve as a point of departure for a further advance against these villages. The first objective for 20th Division was a section of Rainbow Trench on the near side of the crest; the next objective included Cloudy Trench and was about 1,200yds of the Brown Line, facing the original divisional front.

The assault itself finally began at 1345hrs on 7 October; 1/4th and 1/14th Londons (both 168th Brigade, 56th Division) were on the right and 1/1st Londons and 1/7th Middlesex (both 167th Brigade, 56th Division) were on the left. 1/14th Londons captured the southern group of gun pits and part of Hazy Trench beyond, but on their left, 1/12th Londons (168th Brigade, 56th Division) failed in front of DEWDROP TRENCH; the battalions withdrew that evening.

To the left of 56th Division, 60th and 61st Brigades (both 20th Division) made some progress, holding their trenches until the night of 8/9 October, when they were relieved by 6th Division. At 1530hrs on 8 October, 56th Division attacked again; 1/2nd Londons (169th Brigade, 56th Division) reached Hazy Trench, but were forced to withdraw

that night. Between 8 and 11 October, 4th Division relieved 56th Division.

On 12 October another attempt was made; this time Zero Hour was 1405hrs. 10th Brigade (4th Division) were to attack with the French on their right and 12th Brigade (also 4th Division) were to be involved. To their left 16th, 18th and 71st Brigades (all 6th Division) were to assist.

Lt Gen the Earl of Cavan, General Officer Commanding XIV Corps, protested to Haig as to whether these continuous attacks through the mud towards le Transloy were necessary; certainly, with hindsight, it does appear to have been a particularly futile battle. Unfortunately, but hardly surprisingly, no real progress in achieving the original 5 October objectives had been made by mid-October.

On 14 October, 2nd Seaforth Highlanders (10th Brigade, 4th Division) made a surprise attack, but a counter-attack drove them back; 2nd Royal Dublin Fusiliers (also 10th Brigade, 4th Division) also made no progress. There was more heavy rain and the conditions grew worse and worse, and all hopes of Allied progress had gone. The good news was that by mid-October the French had managed to reach and gain parts of SAILLY-SAILLISEL.

Capt E.R. Street, a poet and a company commander of 2nd Sherwood Foresters (71st Brigade, 6th Division), was mortally wounded when involved in the fighting for the gun pits close to Hazy and Cloudy Trenches east of the LESBŒUFS–

GUEUDECOURT road, and died on 15 October. He was later buried at Grove Town Cemetery, MÉAULTE (I.B.7).

Capt R. Johnstone of the Royal Flying Corps was awarded the Military Cross for turning Allied artillery on to columns of German infantry; on one occasion, he carried out counter-battery attack work in cloud and mist at 800ft under heavy fire from the ground.

According to his papers held at the Imperial War Museum (77/179/1), Brig Gen H.C. Rees DSO, General Officer Commanding 11th Brigade (4th Division), noted that there was a saucer-shaped depression between LESBŒUFS and le Transloy, in the centre of which were two sets of old German gun pits. The ground sloped gently upwards to a well-marked ridge. Several attacks were made on the position but all ended in failure and casualties. Rees himself was called upon to make another attempt on 18 October. Zero Hour was 0340hrs, and with the conditions as bad as they could be, with water and mud in the trenches and shell-holes, the attackers also had to begin their advance in the dark. It is not surprising that 4th Division made slow progress.

It was the conditions, as much as anything, that brought the battle to a close in this area, and the historian of 8th Division describes the whole great enterprise as coming to an end, drowned in a sea of mud and rain. On 19 October, another day of incessant rain, 24th and 25th Brigades (both 8th Division) went forward from reserve positions in and around TRÔNES and BERNAFAY WOODS, in order to relieve 6th Division in the line. The roads or tracks were deep in liquid mud and crowded with traffic. The changeover process was a lengthy one as a result, but was completed during the night of 19/20 October.

At 0900hrs on 20 October, Maj Gen H. Hudson, General Officer Commanding 8th Division, took command of the LESBŒUFS–GUEUDECOURT front, this being the left sector of XIV Corps. On the night of 21 October, 23rd Brigade (also 8th Division) took over part of 4th Division's front to the right of 25th Brigade, and the whole of 8th Division were once more in the line. With the arrival of 8th Division, the weather took a turn for the better; the days were bright and the nights frosty, which improved conditions.

Preparations for a fresh assault were made for 23 October. The operation was designed to prepare the way for a later attack on le Transloy from the south-west. The preliminary bombardment was in progress when 8th Division came into the line. 25th Brigade were meant to capture the remainder of Zenith Trench, midway between GUEUDECOURT and le Transloy, and then similarly establish a line beyond it with 23rd Brigade.

Gen J.L. Jack, a witness to these events, wrote in his diary that at around 0500hrs on 23 October, 2nd West Yorkshires (23rd Brigade, 8th Division) reached Windmill and Shine Trenches. The late arrival of the battalion was due to their having been required by the staff, after Jack had gone on ahead the previous day, to carry stores of ammunition, of which duty he had received no notice. As it turned out they were not required for 'major exertions' that day. The attack on le Transloy was to be carried out by the extreme right of 8th Division, with 4th Division to its right, 25th Brigade on the left and 24th Brigade further left. 2nd Cameronians and 2nd Middlesex (both 23rd Brigade) captured Zenith Trench and pushed on to Orion Trench, but neighbouring units were unable to keep abreast; this prevented further advances, and subsequent counter-attacks led to many gains being lost.

On 27 October, Jack was instructed to prepare for bombing attacks in order to clear parts of Zenith Trench still in enemy hands. The *Official History of the War* notes that it was captured by 17th Division, which had relieved 8th Division at the end of October. The part taken was the south-western face of the German salient, midway between the two villages.

In early November, H.L.N. Dundas of 1st Scots Guards (2nd Guards Brigade, Guards Division) was alternately close to le Transloy or in a dugout by the side of a hill beside the road to COMBLES. Throughout October and well into November, the French strove to take Saillisel, with the British cooperating with them. On 2 November, 17th Division captured the remaining section of Zenith Trench, and a new trench was dug to connect with Misty Trench.

On 4 November, 2nd Royal Welsh Fusiliers (19th Brigade, 33rd Division) were warned to be ready for a three- or four-division attack planned for the following day, with the cemetery in front of le Transloy as the objective. 2nd Royal Welsh Fusiliers were to dig in about 200yds beyond the crest of the ridge; little progress was made because of the openness of the ground.

On 5 November, some success was gained by 2nd Worcesters (100th Brigade, 33rd Division), who had concentrated in the French area and had struggled forward to their objective, which was to be called Bennett Trench after Lt E.P. Bennett of 2nd Worcesters. The position is described in *The Machine Gunner* as being opposite le Transloy, the infantry squatting like ducks in the mud; they were accompanied by two machine guns from No. 100 Company, Machine Gun Corps (33rd Division).

Bennett was awarded the Victoria Cross for his actions at this time, when in command of the second wave of the attack.

> Finding that the first wave had suffered heavy casualties, its commander killed and the line wavering, Lieut. Bennett advanced at the head of the second wave, and by his personal example of valour and resolution reached his objective with but 60 men. Isolated with his small party, he at once took steps to consolidate his position under heavy rifle and machine-gun fire from both flanks, and, although wounded, he remained in command directing and controlling . . .

After the failure to capture the Transloy ridges, the British lines remained to the south-west of the village of le Transloy, in front of LESBŒUFS and GUEUDECOURT.

LEUZE WOOD, or Lousy Wood as the British inevitably called it, is south of the D20 road between COMBLES and GUILLEMONT, with the narrow BOULEUX WOOD on the opposite side of the road. To the south-west is the site of the original FAFFE-MONT FARM, which is in Faffemont Wood. Leuze Wood is roughly square in shape and BOULEUX WOOD, its extension, is rectangular.

During the second phase of the Battle of the Somme, Leuze Wood occupied a very commanding position, northwards and eastwards, though the view was partially restricted by the Morval Spur. It over-looked the basin and both branches of COMBLES valley and the main valley, while south-westwards it commanded all the low ground between HARDECOURT-AU-BOIS and GUILLEMONT.

As it leaves the cover of the trees, the main road here drops rapidly down the hill into COMBLES. This sunken road was a very marked feature and a source of trouble to the British in their several attacks. Leuze Wood itself consisted of bare stumps and was thickly entangled with barbed wire. Its southern face was lined by a number of German gun emplacements; in recent years there was still a surviving German pillbox of the two-man variety in the south-west corner. Loop Trench was 300yds to the east of Leuze Wood and ran parallel to its edge, the sunken road from GINCHY to COMBLES and the northern edge of the Wood. The capture and holding of this position was a prerequisite to the capture of COMBLES, which was to fall to a combined 'pinching out' by the Allies.

On 4 September 1916 the enemy delivered a counter-attack on the newly won British position in the vicinity of MOUQUET FARM, which was easily repulsed by the Australians. To the right of the battlefield, WEDGE WOOD was captured; ground to the north of FAFFEMONT FARM was also gained. On 5 September the British advanced 1,500yds in this sector and were nearly 1 mile to the east of GUILLEMONT and had reached Leuze Wood; they were now 1,000yds from COMBLES. In addition, all the ground between Leuze Wood and FAFFEMONT FARM had been taken, as had the ground between Leuze Wood and GINCHY. These bald facts hide the stark horror of the fighting in and around Leuze Wood; one battalion alone, 7th Royal Irish Fusiliers (49th Brigade, attached 5th Division) were ruthlessly cut down by machine-gun fire when attacking Combles Trench. They had 251 casualties.

According to the *Official History of the War*, during the night of 5/6 September, 8th Royal Irish Fusiliers (49th Brigade, 16th Division) relieved 1st Devons (95th Brigade, 5th Division); they were to attack across the COMBLES–GINCHY road on 6 September. On the right, BOULEUX WOOD was entered, but all day a German barrage was maintained against the south-west corner of Leuze Wood and the German infantry were able to cut them off. Those men who survived reached as far as a cornfield in front of COMBLES, but had to withdraw to shell-holes in the area of FAFFEMONT FARM.

During the night, patrols of 56th Division were due to take over; meanwhile, patrols from the left of 16th Division tried to advance along the light railway track, but lost many men from fire at the QUADRILATERAL, an enemy strongpoint to the south of the GINCHY–MORVAL road. When they reached the higher ground, they could go no further. 49th Brigade of 16th Division advanced by swinging forward their left from the line GUILLEMONT–LEUZE WOOD to the north-east.

One of the best memoirs describing the fighting at Leuze Wood is *Johnny Get Your Gun* by J.F. Tucker, who served with 1/13th Londons (168th Brigade, 56th Division). Tucker's battalion were at MARI-COURT before moving about 7 miles to Angle Wood Valley. The top of the ridge on their left had shallow dugouts and strongpoints, which overlooked the valley that they had just crossed. On the right was a steep embankment facing the German lines; ½ mile along the ridge was WEDGE WOOD, south-east of GUILLEMONT, a small – and by now a shattered – copse. 1/13th Londons were on the extreme right of the British Army.

At WEDGE WOOD, Tucker's party entered a trench full of dead Prussian Guards clad in white vests and trousers. Apparently they had come from bathing at COMBLES and because of the heat of the day had been given permission to wear these clothes, in which they had paraded. Further on, Tucker was to come across bodies of the Royal Irish Fusiliers, some of whom had obviously been killed by concussion. Many unexploded bright steel shells lay about, which he thought were either 'whizz bangs' or even from French 75s. He later saw a battery of French 75s in action firing over Leuze Wood, and noted that half of the shells were prematures.

A few survivors of the Royal Irish Fusiliers came past 1/13th Londons and said that they had been stopped only by a wired trench which had been concealed in standing corn, probably Combles Trench. Moving forward, 1/13th Londons took up positions in shell-holes, which they connected by digging a trench line from the southern corner of Leuze Wood to beyond FAFFEMONT FARM. The battalion were in touch with the left flank of the French Army, south of the farm. Tucker also reported seeing the signs of a detachment of 20th Deccan Horse (Secunderabad Brigade, 2nd (Indian) Cavalry Division), a cavalry patrol that had obviously been ambushed. Tucker tells us that 1/13th Londons were relieved from time to time and went back into reserve trenches for a few hours or a day or so, but they were still under shell-fire in places such as MALTZ HORN FARM, Casement Trench, Chimpanzee Trench and WATERLÔT FARM. Frontal attacks were attempted by 56th Division, but without success.

In *The Machine Gunner*, Arthur Russell wrote that in early September he was detailed to join No. 13 Company, Machine Gun Corps (5th Division); he joined them in Leuze Wood on 8 September. The Wood had been a German stronghold and had only recently been wrested from the enemy by 16th Division. Russell saw tanks and also masses of Allied dead at Leuze Wood. Company headquarters and those of the infantry battalions were in a large quarry, half-circular in shape and with numerous German-constructed dugouts built into the high wall face. It was situated not 25yds behind the infantry front-line positions.

At 2330hrs on 8 September, 169th Brigade attempted to push south-east towards COMBLES, with 1/2nd Londons (169th Brigade, 56th Division) bombing down Combles Trench from Leuze Wood; a heavy counter-attack early next morning compelled withdrawal. On 9 September, 169th Brigade had the task of establishing a defence line

along the slopes of Combles Ravine; 1/2nd Londons advanced from the south-east edge of Leuze Wood against Loop Trench, but were forced to retire. Sent up in the evening, 1/16th Londons (169th Brigade, 56th Division) were to drive the Germans out of Leuze Wood if they gained a footing there. Moving in darkness over very difficult ground and through a severe barrage while passing over the FAFFEMONT FARM line, they reached Leuze Wood by 2300hrs. The Wood was full of barbed-wire entanglements and the Germans were shelling it heavily. The fighting here was very tough indeed and the Allied line was not to be straightened for 3 days.

Before 1/13th Londons were relieved, Tucker saw a tall tree trunk that had been used as a German lookout and would have given a wonderful view for miles, but had been abandoned once the British had got too close. Tucker's battalion themselves could see beyond Angle Wood Valley and towards GUILLEMONT, GINCHY and LESBŒUFS. After they were relieved and re-formed, they marched off past Citadel Camp and on to MORLANCOURT.

At 0700hrs on 10 September, in heavy mist, 1/16th Londons attacked south-eastwards from Leuze Wood under the cover of a weak barrage; no ground was covered while enemy machine guns in Loop Trench and along the sunken COMBLES road were still in action. Another attempt was made in mid-afternoon, but without success. That evening, 169th Brigade were relieved by a composite brigade from 5th Division. L/Cpl H.G.R. Williams of 1/5th Londons (169th Brigade, 56th Division) gives the following account.

At the time, the high ground in front of COMBLES was still in German hands. Leuze Wood was to the left and was shelled by both sides at the same time. Reserve were in a small valley called ANGLE WOOD. They lived in shelters out in the hillsides or else in a trench in DEATH VALLEY. 167th Brigade relieved 168th Brigade. On 12 September, 1/8th Middlesex (167th Brigade, 56th Division) formed up in the valley between the south end of Leuze Wood and WEDGE WOOD; on 15 September, 1/7th Middlesex (also 167th Brigade, 56th Division) were brought to a standstill by the German rifle and machine-gun fire from the road that led into COMBLES. By this time, a dressing station had been established in the Wood.

On 10 September, Maj C.C. Dickens of 1/13th Londons, a grandson of Charles Dickens, died. His body was never found; he is commemorated on the Thiepval Memorial, and is remembered by a special memorial taking the form of a wooden cross, signposted to the north of the GUILLEMONT–COMBLES road. The memorial was damaged and in September 1995 it was replaced and moved to its present site to allow for greater access. It was rededicated on 29 June 1996. The original Dickens cross is in Ginchy Church.

On 15 September, BOULEUX WOOD was finally cleared by a British assault. Their attack actually coincided with a German counter-attack and the result was a very hard fight between the two sides. Once the redoubt to the east of the wood was captured, the British were able gradually to outflank the Germans; pressing them on all sides, the British forced their opponents to retire about ½ mile northwards.

In *The War the Infantry Knew*, it is noted that Leuze Wood was less mutilated than woods further to the rear; it became a main feature in a wide and bare winter landscape of grey-green stubble, stripped here and there with chrome grey shell-holes and scarred with trenches. In October 1916, there were still 'heaps of unburied corpses where the fighting had been severe'.

Perhaps Tucker should be left to have the last word when commenting on the fighting here:

> From all this you can see how muddled the situation was from the start. I am afraid that my mind also is very muddled, these incidents and what followed for the next six weeks or so, together with the appalling conditions making it impossible to recall what really happened. Incidents become isolated and confused. We in the ranks have no knowledge of the battlefield as a whole and without access to maps of any kind, had very little idea of our whereabouts and only meagre snippets of information or rumours of what was going on in our own sector. Often one knew nothing of what was happening beyond a few yards away . . .

In an issue of the *Ypres Times* of 1935 it was reported that Leuze Wood was green and dense again, except for the shooting drive. They shoot rabbits and partridges there now.

LONGPRÉ-LES-CORPS-SAINTS was used
mainly as a railway junction for DOULLENS, north-west of AMIENS, close to the River Somme on the D3 road. On 9 February 1916, 1/7th Middlesex (167th Brigade, 56th Division) arrived here and remained until 27 February, when they moved to BERTEAUCOURT-LES-DAMES. In the third week of March, 10th East Yorkshires (92nd Brigade, 31st Division) were billeted here when French civilians were still in the village and the *estaminets* sold 'weak beer to thirsty troops'. Between March and

October, elements of 21st, 31st, 34th, 38th, 51st and 55th Divisions detrained or entrained here.

Longpré-les-Corps-Saints British Cemetery is ½ mile to the south of the village on the D70. It has graves of men who died in 1918. Two British soldiers who died in 1916 are buried in Longpré-les-Corps-Saints Communal Cemetery.

LONGUEAU, to the south-east of AMIENS, was
really a railway village during the two world wars; its sidings were in an angle 'formed by the junction of the Ancre with the Somme'. It was a loading station for troops and stores from 1915 and for casualties later on. It was much used and would have been the place where many troops set foot in the Somme region for the first time, often in the middle of the night.

On 4 October 1915, 108th Field Ambulance (36th Division), having arrived at Longueau, departed for RUBEMPRÉ. On 6 October, 110th Field Ambulance (also 36th Division) arrived here and marched to VIGNACOURT. When 1/3rd (West Riding) Field Ambulance (49th Division) arrived at the station on 2 February 1916, their horses were watered ½ mile from the station. They came with 146th Brigade (also 49th Division) who, after detraining, marched to AILLY-SUR-SOMME to the north-west of AMIENS. 1/3rd (West Riding) Field Ambulance then left for le Mesge, north-west of Amiens, where they took over a large house for use as a hospital for 60 patients.

On 21 February, 14th Division arrived in the Longueau area. On 29 February, 2nd West Yorkshires (23rd Brigade, 8th Division) detrained here and halted 1 mile from the station, where they had breakfast; they moved off later in the morning via AMIENS to SAINT-VAAST-EN-CHAUSSÉE, 10 miles distant. Battalion drums were a great help to the marching column. On 30 March, 21st Division detrained at Longueau and left for RIBEMONT-SUR-ANCRE and on 13/14 April, 9th Division entrained from here. On 11 June, 50th Brigade (17th Division) entrained here for Saint-Omer; on 13/14 June, 9th Division detrained here.

Following the 1916 battle, Longueau remained behind Allied lines, but was in serious danger of falling to the enemy in 1918, when German forces got within 7 miles of the village. In *Pageant of the Years*, war correspondent Philip Gibbs put it perfectly when he wrote of 1918: 'The Germans came as near to Amiens as Villers-Bretonneux on the low hills outside. Their guns had smashed the railway station of Longueau, which to Amiens is like Clapham Junction to Waterloo . . .'

In 1925, Longueau Communal Cemetery contained the graves of four British soldiers, crowded in by 'ostentatious civilian tombs'. The cemetery was almost surrounded by the Longueau railway works, and so the British casualties were later moved to Longueau British Cemetery, begun in April 1918. This latter cemetery has 202 British, Australian and Canadian graves. The two cemeteries are to be found south of the N29 main road and Longueau railway station.

During the Second World War, the marshalling yards became the target of first the Luftwaffe and then the Royal Air Force, who bombed them in 1944.

LONGUEVAL was built along three roads, and the crossroads or junction formed its centre. The road that extended to meet a track midway between HIGH WOOD and FLERS was called North Street. The second branch went in a south-westerly direction and skirted the west side of BERNAFAY WOOD and the third went in a south-easterly direction towards GUILLEMONT. From the main square itself the road branched westwards towards the BAZENTINs, and was known as Claridges Street. Parallel to it and to the north was Duke Street; these two roads were cut by a track called Piccadilly. Thus four roads formed a rectangle.

In 1916 Longueval was also gateway to DELVILLE WOOD, where so much fighting was to take place in July and August. In other words, any attack had to deal with capturing Longueval first, prior to taking on the adjacent Wood. The German trench line skirted the south of Longueval and then turned south-eastwards past WATERLÔT FARM in the direction of GUILLEMONT. As usual, the Germans had the advantage, as their positions could not be precisely located; in addition, they had a good view over the ground that any attacker would have to traverse. An important feature to the British was Longueval Alley, which was to the south of the village; the quarry there was often used as a battalion headquarters.

Longueval makes its first appearance in the Battle of the Somme as part of Lt Gen Sir Henry Rawlinson's plan to make a night attack against the Bazentin Ridge, which included the villages of BAZENTIN and Longueval. The proposal was to form up two divisions in the dark and to attack at dawn. Sir Douglas Haig was worried about the consequences of the possible confusion of troops forming up in the dark, but after the plan had been modified slightly, he did agree to it – which was just as well, as the battle turned out to be a brilliant success.

On 14 July, 1st Division captured CONTAL-MAISON and Lower Wood. At 0325hrs, after 5 minutes of intense bombardment, 3rd, 9th and 21st Divisions attacked the enemy's second line from the west of Bazentin-le-Petit Wood. The attackers reached their objectives without a hitch; by 0900hrs, the British held BAZENTIN-LE-GRAND village and also half of Longueval, but not the strongly fortified northern end, which encompassed some orchards. Also involved in the fighting were 12th Royal Scots (27th Brigade, 9th Division); their history describes the fortifications in the orchards as being 'of quite exceptional strength'. Nevertheless, 9th Division had a firm hold on the southern end of Longueval and had also made a lodgement in DELVILLE WOOD. Under a heavy bombardment, 22nd and 27th Brigades (both 9th Division) continued fighting in the village; machine-gun fire and also that of German snipers was very fierce. The men in Longueval Alley were in touch with elements of 18th Division.

The historian of 17th Division noted that Longueval and DELVILLE WOOD were persistently shelled by the enemy. The fire came from three directions: from the rising ground of the Bapaume Ridge to the west of FLERS; on the left, from the ground north of HIGH WOOD; and from the right, around GINCHY. For the German artillery, Longueval and DELVILLE WOOD were on the skyline, as they stood on the crest of the COMBLES–THIEPVAL ridge, the outlying high ground running parallel to BAPAUME ridge. During the day's fighting, Lt Col A. St H. Gibbons, Commanding Officer 13th King's (9th Brigade, 3rd Division), was mortally wounded; he died the next day and was buried in Daours Communal Cemetery Extension (I.B.2).

On 15 September, a company of 5th Cameron Highlanders (26th Brigade, 9th Division) and two companies of 4th South African Infantry (South African Brigade, 9th Division) made several attempts to capture WATERLÔT FARM on the GUILLEMONT road, which was part of the German Second Line. The Royal Scots made a further attempt to take the north of Longueval but were unsuccessful.

In *Sir Douglas Haig's Great Push*, it is noted that Longueval was garrisoned by Prussians and that although they fought fiercely, they had no chance against the Scots. Many Germans had taken refuge in the houses in the village and had to be winkled out.

W.D. Croft, the historian of 9th Division and formerly General Officer Commanding 27th Brigade (9th Division), mentioned the subterranean passages that went right through the village, which were

La Sucrerie, Longueval. *(Peter F. Batchelor Collection)*

difficult to penetrate. The enemy had entrances on their side of the village and could escape down the passages from the houses, which had bolt-hole entrances to the passages. A company headquarters of 7th Seaforth Highlanders and 8th Black Watch (both 26th Brigade, 9th Division) was nearly captured as a result of the enemy appearing unexpectedly.

On 16 July, Lt R.B. Talbot Kelly of LII Brigade, Royal Field Artillery (9th Division), described going up as brigade forward observation officer from MONTAUBAN-DE-PICARDIE to Longueval, which he entered by a sunken road between the shattered orchards. He observed the fire of the British 9.2in howitzers from the first floor of a house in the village square. Across the street were Germans who were crouched in houses, as indeed he was; the distance was 20yds or less. He was a witness to the fighting in the village, and in particular, the part played by 5th Cameron Highlanders.

On 18 July, 1st Gordon Highlanders and 8th King's Own (both 76th Brigade, 3rd Division) moved out from trenches near Bazentin windmill and, forming up to the right, attacked Longueval from the west. Again the orchards were not carried, but Longueval was occupied as far as Duke Street

and a line taken up on the north-west edge of DELVILLE WOOD. They were also in contact with the South African Brigade.

On 19 July, 95th Brigade (5th Division) went up to the Longueval positions; at this time the front line ran along the road leading from the southern corner of HIGH WOOD to Longueval. The German artillery again shelled Longueval heavily, and after close fighting 27th Brigade (9th Division) were forced back to the southern edge of the village; 26th Brigade saved the situation and the centre of Longueval. That night, 3rd Division began to relieve 9th Division.

The plan for 20 July was to make another attempt to clear the village and DELVILLE WOOD in the morning. B/Maj W. la Touche Congreve DSO, MC, of the Rifle Brigade was awarded the Victoria Cross for his bravery between 6 and 20 July. The citation stated:

This officer constantly performed acts of gallantry, and showed the greatest devotion to duty, and by his personal example inspired all those around him with confidence at critical periods of the operations. During preliminary preparations for the attack he carried out personal reconnaissances of the enemy lines, taking out parties of officers and non-commissioned officers for over 1,000 yards in front of our line, in order to acquaint them with the ground. All these preparations were made under fire. Later, by night, Major Congreve conducted a battalion to its position of employment, afterwards returning to it to ascertain the situation after assault. He established himself in an exposed forward position from whence he successfully observed the enemy, and gave orders necessary to drive them from their position. Two days later, when Brigade Headquarters was heavily shelled and many casualties resulted, he went out and assisted the medical officer to remove the wounded to places of safety, although he himself was suffering severely from gas and other shell effects. He again on a subsequent occasion showed supreme courage in tending wounded under heavy shell-fire. He finally returned to the front line to ascertain the situation after an unsuccessful attack, and whilst in the act of writing his report was shot and killed instantly . . .

Congreve served with 76th Brigade and one of its battalions were 2nd Suffolks, whose Commanding Officer, Maj Stubbs, had talked to Congreve; they went up the line together and entered a freshly dug trench along the side of Duke Street. Stubbs warned Congreve about the danger of snipers, but at 1055hrs on 20 September, Congreve was shot in the throat and died a few seconds later. A son of Lt Gen Sir Walter Congreve, who also had been awarded the Victoria Cross, Congreve was buried in Corbie Communal Cemetery Extension (I.F.35); there is a memorial to him in Corbie Abbey.

On 23 July the plan was for 2nd Royal Scots (8th Brigade, 3rd Division) to attack and bomb down the trenches from WATERLÔT FARM and capture GUILLEMONT station. The rest of 3rd Division were to attack the northern part of DELVILLE WOOD, as well as the northern part of the village: 9th Brigade (3rd Division) were to attack from the west side while 95th Brigade (5th Division) cleared the left flank and the rest of 5th Division dealt with the strongpoint in the orchards. However, the attacks were unsuccessful.

The fighting for the complete possession of Longueval now entered its last week and intensified between 24 and 31 July. On 25 July, the relief of 3rd Division began when the village became the objective of 5th Division. Until late at night on 26 July, 1st Norfolks (15th Brigade, 5th Division) had been at POMMIERS REDOUBT to the south; it was now their turn to attack Longueval village and part of the Wood. The capture of the north-west portion

of DELVILLE WOOD was made especially difficult by enemy machine guns firing from HIGH WOOD, SWITCH TRENCH and many strongpoints in the open outside it.

On 27 July, 15th Brigade were to advance against DELVILLE WOOD on the left of 99th Brigade (2nd Division), with 1st Norfolks in front and 1st Bedfords (15th Brigade, 5th Division) in support. The enemy still held on to the north of the village and fierce fighting continued in the orchards all day, in particular in the area of a German redoubt called the Machine Gun House by the British. On 28 July, Longueval was yet again heavily shelled and 2nd South Staffords and 17th Middlesex (both 6th Brigade, 2nd Division) were involved in a counterattack. On the night of 27 July, 15th Brigade had been relieved by 95th Brigade (5th Division). At 0330hrs on 29 July, the brigade made some progress; on 30 July, 13th Brigade (5th Division) were also successful.

By the end of July, the village was in Allied hands, but the fighting from DELVILLE WOOD was to continue for another month. On 31 July and 1 August, 1st Norfolks were again in Longueval before returning to le Quesnoy for training. One account mentions that the village was in flames on 1 August and continuously shelled on 2 August. On 14 August, 8th Rifle Brigade, 7th King's Royal Rifle Corps and 7th Rifle Brigade (all 41st Brigade, 14th Division) were to the north of Longueval, preparing for an attack on 18 August on trenches at Longueval that were still held by the enemy. The attack was only partially successful.

Talbot Kelly later wrote that his unit were relieved from Longueval in August and that their column of 1,000 or more horses, with guns and ammunition wagons, presented an extraordinary sight as they went through the valley below these chalk downs. Everyone except for the first few was shrouded in a great pall of white dust.

On 9 September, the sunken road between Longueval and HIGH WOOD was captured, and on 16/17 September, 1st Norfolks moved forward from BILLON FARM to WATERLÔT FARM. They saw many bodies that remained unburied from earlier battles. In early October, the Longueval road to FLERS was always busy with wheeled traffic and was frequently shelled. On 16 October, C.E. Montague went up to Longueval with John Masefield and they walked around DELVILLE WOOD. Most of the bodies had been removed by this time, but the Wood was still 'haggard and sinister'.

In *Field Guns in France*, Lt N. Fraser-Tytler of CL Brigade, Royal Field Artillery (30th Division), noted that up the road near Longueval one reached a 'big gun farmyard', full of vast guns that had seemingly been dumped anywhere close to the road, with the usual piles of shells half-buried in mud all around, and stacks of empty canisters and boxes holding charges.

On 5 November, C.E. Montague was again doing one of his battlefield tours, and on this occasion left his car and chauffeur Harris at the entrance to Longueval, with orders to go back a little and wait. When Montague had gone about 250yds, a German shell pitched roughly where the car had been. Harris had, in fact, already moved the car, but the shell destroyed a limber and its crew.

In *Notes on the Somme*, McLellan wrote of the village in July: 'It was simply a gigantic tumbled rubbish heap, with a few [?], dusty fragments of brick and wood in place of houses. So bashed about was it that it was difficult to follow the course of streets through the piled heaps of brick and rubble . . .' A year later John Masefield described the site of the village in 1917 as being simply a reddish patch, such was the destruction.

Longueval Road Cemetery is on the east side of the road from Longueval to BERNAFAY WOOD and MARICOURT, less than ½ mile south of the village. Designed by Arthur Hutton, it was begun in September 1916, near a dressing station known as Longueval Alley or Longueval Water Point, used until January 1917; a few more graves were added in August and September 1918 and 49 others from around Longueval in the period 1923–24. It stands on relatively high ground, and in addition to Longueval, other features can be seen from it, including GUILLEMONT, MONTAUBAN-DE-PICARDIE, BERNAFAY and TRÔNES WOODs.

In May 1986, a wooden cross was erected at the Longueval crossroads close to HIGH WOOD, replacing one that was lost in the Second World War. It is in memory of 12th Glosters (95th Brigade, 5th Division), known as 'Bristol's Own'. There appear to have been three crosses dedicated to 12th Glosters over the years, as one that was erected during the war was left to decay in the 1920s. This would mean that it was replaced by one broken up during the next war.

On 20 July 2002, a memorial commemorating the role of the pipers who served in the British and Commonwealth forces, was unveiled in the centre of the village. The figure is of a Scottish piper mounting the parapet of a trench. The wall behind it carried the badges of every British and Commonwealth unit that had a pipe band during the First World War. Several hundred pipers and bandsmen from the Black Watch, London Scottish and London Irish played at the unveiling ceremony.

On 21 October 2010, a Footballers' memorial to the members of the two Football Battalions from the Middlesex Regiment, the 17th (S) Battalion (1st Football) and 23rd (S) Battalion (2nd Football), who served during the Battle of the Somme, was unveiled. They were part of the 2nd and 41st Divisions respectively.

LOUVENCOURT, north-west of ALBERT on the D938 road, is a village on the main road between DOULLENS and ALBERT, about 13 miles from each. British troops took over from the French here in July 1915 and troops from 48th Division were here at the end of the month. For a year until August 1916, British field ambulances were established in the village, which at the beginning of July 1916 was 6 miles behind the front line.

A typical French farming village, Louvencourt suffered from the usual absence of men unless they were elderly; even so, the women and children who were left continued to carry out their usual farm work. The village housed a corps main dressing station, shared with three other villages. The progress of the battle meant that these medical units moved further eastwards, until in April 1917 enemy offensives pushed the British line back to its former position.

Maj Gen Sir B. de Lisle, General Officer Commanding 29th Division, took over the sector in early April 1916. On 4 April, 88th Brigade (29th Division) arrived in the Louvencourt area, having journeyed from BONNEVILLE, and until 11 April carried out training duties in connection with their involvement at BEAUMONT-HAMEL and the AUCHONVILLERS sector. Although the villagers had previously had an uneasy relationship with British troops, they were to strike up an excellent relationship with the 'colonial troops' of 1st Newfoundlanders (88th Brigade, 29th Division). On 11 April, 4th Worcesters (also 88th Brigade, 29th Division) left the village and marched through heavy rain to MAILLY-MAILLET.

From 8 April, 2nd South Wales Borderers (87th Brigade, 29th Division) spent 3 weeks in divisional reserve. They had recently been at the receiving end of British artillery, as a result of which 24 men had become casualties, with 8 men being killed. While billeted here, they carried out training and were in and out of the line with 1st Newfoundlanders. On 13 April, 87th Field Ambulance (29th Division), having just come from BEAUSSART, reported that accommodation was 'again filthy'.

On 25 April, Lt Gen Sir A.G. Hunter-Weston, General Officer Commanding VIII Corps, addressed 87th Brigade. As former commander of 29th Division in Gallipoli, he wished to address the veterans of that campaign who had taken part in the Allied landings at Helles and Anzac a year before on that very day.

On 8 May, 1st Newfoundlanders were here after a further spell in trench preparation; they returned on 23 June. By now Louvencourt had become home to 29th Division, but especially so to 1st Newfoundlanders, who were so far from home and had spent nearly 5 whole weeks here since early April; small groups of men had even been able to travel to England for short leave. The great rapport built up between 1st Newfoundlanders and the French was cemented in the evenings in the village *estaminets*, when the talk was often of back home in far distant Newfoundland. Friendships forged at this time lasted for many years after the war was over. On 25 and 27 June, the battalion took part in raids on the enemy lines at BEAUMONT-HAMEL; both failed, however, owing to the great strength of the German positions and wire. On the day between these two raids they were addressed by Maj Gen Sir B. de Lisle, General Officer Commanding 29th Division.

On 26 June, a party of 3 officers (Butler, Green and Strong) and 57 other ranks left their billets in the village in charabancs. The buses stopped 2 miles from the front line and at 2330hrs the men went out into no man's land. Their orders were to move towards Y Ravine. The wire was not only very dense but also had not been adequately cut by the British artillery. In addition, the group's Bangalore Torpedoes were almost useless. Capt Butler decided that progress was unlikely and called off the raid, and the party returned to Louvencourt without any prisoners.

However, they had to do it all over again the following night. Conditions were poor when they set off and the heavy rain made the going very muddy; as a consequence, the men were quickly soaked and covered in mud. This time they did find a gap in the wire, but unfortunately a flare lit them up at the wrong moment, when they were only 20 yards from the German Front Line, which was packed with men. Bombs soon rained down on the hapless party and again, no prisoners were taken. They lost 4 men killed, 21 wounded, 2 taken prisoner and 1 man missing.

On 30 June, the eve of the battle, with the villagers waiting to see them off, groups of men began to form up outside the village before forming up behind their commanding officer and marching off on the road to BEAUMONT-HAMEL. They by-passed certain villages owing to the risk of shelling, and eventually reached the dugouts at St John's Road support trench.

Although 1st Newfoundlanders and 1st Essex (both 88th Brigade, 29th Division) were destined to take part in the fighting at BEAUMONT-HAMEL (see that entry), on that day their pre-battle training area north of Louvencourt and subsequent familiarisation counted for nothing, as 88th Brigade's role had been changed.

In early July, a section of 1/2nd (South Midland) Field Ambulance (48th Division) took over the château here in the main street; during this period, they dealt with over 800 casualties. After their involvement at SERRE on 1 July, 18th Durham Light Infantry (93rd Brigade, 31st Division) were in the Louvencourt area.

In August, 9th Suffolks (71st Brigade, 6th Division), having been in the trenches in front of Mailly Wood, had a week's intermission at Louvencourt. While in the village, they were allotted the task of clearing the battlefield in the THIEPVAL sector, where men of 36th Division had fallen on 1 July. On 27 August, 9th Norfolks (also 71st Brigade, 6th Division) were here for a day before going on to BEAUVAL. In early October tanks were assembled in the village, and units from 37th and 51st Divisions were in the area in the October/November period.

Louvencourt Military Cemetery is on the narrow road to LÉALVILLERS, south of the village. The first burials, in Rows A and B, are those of French soldiers who died in June or July 1915, the end of their occupation here. The British graves here are from the period 30 July 1915 until 22 July 1918. Thirty-three of the graves are of men who died prior to the battle.

Several of the graves in the Louvencourt Military Cemetery were later brought in from the VAUCHELLES-LÈS-AUTHIE Communal Cemetery Extension, 1 mile away on the road to DOULLENS. This Extension had been opened in July 1916 for field ambulances at VAUCHELLES-LÈS-AUTHIE, but no more than eight burials took place in Row E. They include that of Brig Gen C.B. Prowse (I.E.9), General Officer Commanding 11th Brigade (4th Division), mortally wounded when crossing no man's land early in the action on 1 July 1916 while moving his brigade headquarters from the Old British Line trenches taken by 1/8th Royal Warwicks (143rd Brigade, 48th Division) and cheering them on. Prowse's grave used to have a unique brass plate dated 'Vauchelles 1919', but sadly it was stolen some time after 2003. Its inscription read: 'As a tribute to his memory from his Old Comrades of the 7th Bn. Somerset L.I.'; his grave inscription is 'Be thou faithful unto death and I will give thee a crown of life'.

In recent years, Louvencourt Military Cemetery has become a place of pilgrimage, owing to the presence of the grave of Lt R.A. Leighton (1.B.20) of 1/7th

Worcesters (144th Brigade, 48th Division), poet and fiancé of the writer Vera Brittain. He was mortally wounded near HÉBUTERNE on 23 December 1915 and taken 10 miles to Louvencourt, where he was operated on in the château, adjacent to the church, used as a hospital by field ambulances. He died later that evening. He received the Catholic Last Rites just after the operation, from the same padre who had received him into the Catholic Church earlier in the year. Leighton was buried in the cemetery after a ceremony at the village church, after which the cortège moved down the main road before turning right to the Military Cemetery off the narrow road to LÉALVILLERS.

Although it seems certain that Leighton did indeed die in the château, the facts are at odds with a sketch map of the route used of the procession of the funeral cortege. The map was probably drawn by Father Albert Purdie, Leighton's chaplain, and was given to Ronald Leighton, Roland's father.

Leighton's fiancée, Vera Brittain, also served in the war, working at the General Hospital, Etaples, in 1917–18; she visited Louvencourt at least twice, in 1921, when on her way back from a visit to Italy with the writer and great friend Winifred Holtby, and again on 4 August 1933. Her classic memoir of a generation, *Testament of Youth*, was to be published on 28 August 1933; on this trip she was again accompanied by Winifred Holtby, and by a journalist friend, Violet Scott-James. On 11 November 2015, the road adjacent to the cemetery was named l'Allée Roland Leighton when it was unveiled by the mayor in a ceremony arranged for by the village of Louvencourt.

Also in the cemetery are the graves of two men shot for desertion. Pte H. MacDonald (I.D.17) of 12th West Yorkshires (9th Brigade, 3rd Division) had served in the Boer War and was executed on 4 November 1916. Rfmn F.M. Barratt (I.D.20) of 7th King's Royal Rifle Corps (41st Brigade, 14th Light Division) was shot on 10 July 1917.

Louvencourt Military Cemetery was one of the first three designed by Sir Reginald Blomfield (Forceville and Le Treport were the other two) and was begun in 1919. It was described as a small cemetery on an exposed site on the Somme, and although work on it was slow it was virtually completed by spring 1920. As this cemetery design was a model for future designs, it was considered that the walls of future cemeteries should not be higher than 3ft, a decision that would depend on the individual site. The ground at Louvencourt, for example, suffered from subsidence and had to be underpinned.

LOZENGE WOOD is just to the north of FRICOURT, on the eastern side of the D147 road to CONTALMAISON. Lozenge Wood was part of the line that was reached and maintained on 1 July. It had been protected by several lines of strong German trenches.

In *Goodbye to the Battlefields*, Capt H.A. Taylor of the Royal Fusiliers described the area in the following way:

> Over to the left is Lozenge Wood, barely to be distinguished. At best it was nothing much of a wood, though a distinct trouble to our men when they sought to dislodge the enemy from it. And if Lozenge Wood can hardly be seen, what are we to expect of the Poodles. Two trees so proud and important that they were deemed worthy of special designation and a place on the trench map. But still, only two trees, and so much happened after they were put on the map.

In August 1916, 11th Sherwood Foresters (at this time 70th Brigade, 23rd Division) buried their dead here while out of the line; on 8 September, 1/5th Northumberland Fusiliers (149th Brigade, 50th Division) were in dugouts around the Wood.

LUCHEUX, north-east of DOULLENS on the D5 road, was used by many battalions to rest and train prior to the battle. On 17 March 1916 sections from a field company of 51st Division were here when engaged in special training. From 26 April to 2 May, 48th Field Ambulance (37th Division) ran a hospital here before leaving for HUMBERCAMPS.

From 2 to 5 May, a field company of 4th Division were here, working on water supplies, troughs and pontoons. Between 2 and 7 May, 12th Field Ambulance (also 4th Division) took over billets in the village before opening up the château for reception of the sick. Between 10 May and 20 May, 1/5th Leicesters (138th Brigade, 46th Division) were in this 'very old French village with its castle and gateway'; the 10 days here were 'as pleasant as any in the war'. The mounted officers were particularly fortunate, for the forest was full of tracks and rides, and each morning soon after dawn the more energetic could be seen cantering under the dripping trees in the early morning May mist, bare headed and in shirt sleeves. On 20 May, 1/5th Leicesters left for SOUASTRE. Meanwhile, 1/6th South Staffords (137th Brigade, 46th Division), who were billeted at SUS-SAINT-LÉGER, spent much of their time working in the forest cutting saplings for later use as revetments in the trenches.

In June, a large-scale model of the German lines was dug near the village and brigades that were to take part in the battle immediately began to use it for practice. The model took up many acres of arable land;

although the French farmers were well compensated, 46th Division were known as *les autres Boches* by the locals in Lucheux. On 6 June, 1/5th Sherwood Foresters (139th Brigade, 46th Division) came here for further battle practice and took over the line from 1/8th Sherwood Foresters (also 139th Brigade, 46th Division) on 27 June. On 7 June, 139th Brigade came to the area; when billeted in le Souich to the north-west, 1/8th Sherwood Foresters worked in the forest for a week, cutting wood and making wattle hurdles. It was very wet and their billets were uncomfortable.

While 1/7th Sherwood Foresters (also 139th Brigade, 46th Division) were billeted at SUS-SAINT-LÉGER between 6 and 18 June, men from the battalion sometimes spent time here felling trees as an alternative to battle training.

On 9 August, HM the King and HRH the Prince of Wales drove through the forest here on their way to inspect the Guards Division. On 17 August, 17th Division arrived in the area. On 30 September, 1st Scots Guards (2nd Guards Brigade, Guards Division) were also here, when they stayed for 18 days. Between June and the end of September, 12th and 17th Divisions also had units here.

The Lucheux Military Cemetery, made by French troops, stood at the south end of the village; it included 13 Commonwealth graves, later transferred to Rows A and G in Beauval Communal Cemetery, south of DOULLENS.

LUISENHOF FARM lies to the south of Ligny-Thilloy and to the north of Factory Corner. It was where Maj L.G. Hawker VC of No. 24 Squadron, Royal Flying Corps, crashed on 23 November 1916, having been brought down by von Richthofen in an 'epic duel'. There is no trace of Hawker's grave; his name is commemorated on the Arras Memorial. There is no trace of the farm either.

M

MAILLY-MAILLET is a village about 5½ miles north of ALBERT, south of COLINCAMPS, north-west of ENGLEBELMER and due west of AUCHONVILLERS on the D919 road. The British took over the village from the French Army in the summer of 1915; being 2 miles from the front lines, it was a very 'busy' village. Like its neighbours, it had many tunnels in the subterranean quarries from

which building stone had been extracted, which now provided safe cover for troops. The village also boasts a church with a splendid Gothic carving on its western façade; during the war, special measures were taken to preserve it, similar to those adopted for the protection of AMIENS cathedral, with the door being well sandbagged. Fortunately, despite heavy bombardments in 1917 and 1918, these precautions were successful.

The village used to have a railway station on the light railway between ALBERT and DOULLENS. During the war, the village provided a continuous home for British troops, both before and during the battle. From the end of July 1915 until the end of October 1915, 10th and 12th Brigades (both 4th Division) were here; battalions were often billeted here when not carrying out tours of duty in the AUCHONVILLERS sector. From early on, a collecting post for casualties, called Café Fly, was established at the railway station north of the village on the SERRE road; there was also an advanced dressing station in a large château in the village.

Prior to March 1916, the village had been little shelled and men lived in the unfurnished houses, where they did have fires. Troops regularly provided working parties for mining operations, especially to the north-west of BEAUMONT-HAMEL. On 15 February, 1/5th Sherwood Foresters (139th Brigade, 46th Division) came here from BERNAVILLE by lorry, when they carried out general training and provided working parties at the Redan for 36th Division, filling sandbags. They were relieved after 4 days by 1/5th Lincolns (138th Brigade, 46th Division), while attached to Third Army for a short time.

At the end of March or early in April, men from a battalion of the Prince of Wales's Own (West Yorkshire) Regiment billeted at SENLIS-LE-SEC walked the 4½ miles to Mailly-Maillet in order to welcome 16th West Yorkshires (93rd Brigade, 31st Division) to France.

On 11 April, 4th Worcesters (88th Brigade, 29th Division) arrived here from LOUVENCOURT and found their trenches to be in very poor condition; the poor weather had only made them worse. Until the end of June, the battalion was regularly in and out of the line at BEAUMONT-HAMEL or billeted in the area.

There was a large wood to the south of the village, which was divided by the main D919 road, and the two sections were very often used for troops to bivouac and to camp. On 28 April, 2nd South Wales Borderers (87th Brigade, 29th Division) arrived here from LOUVENCOURT. A raid was planned to take place at Hawthorn Redoubt the next evening; by some mischance it began too soon, and as a consequence suffered heavily from British shelling. The raid served no purpose at all and led to 24 casualties, including 8 killed or missing.

In early May, 2nd South Wales Borderers were back in the line in the AUCHONVILLERS sector for 10 days, when they worked on trenches until they were relieved on 13 May. At the end of May, they were back in their former trenches for 10 days, and again at the end of June. On 22 June, 1st Somerset Light Infantry (11th Brigade, 4th Division) arrived here from BERTRANCOURT and remained in the village until they moved up to assembly trenches at the end of the month. 2nd Royal Dublin Fusiliers (10th Brigade, 4th Division) took up positions in trenches in the neighbourhood, and on 25 June moved out of the line into fields west of the village, where German shells were falling in response to the British bombardment.

As well as the units of 4th, 29th, 39th and 48th Divisions mentioned above, 110th Field Ambulance (36th Division) were in this area in January and February 1916 and No. 150 Field Company, Royal Engineers (also 36th Division) spent much of February repairing trenches.

Mailly Wood Cemetery, on the eastern edge of the Wood, was begun on 24 June when 13 men from 2nd Seaforth Highlanders (10th Brigade, 4th Division) were buried, having been killed earlier in the day; 24 June was the first day of the Allied bombardment, at which time the battalion were in their tented billets in Mailly. At about 0130hrs, two enemy 5.9s fell among trees under which their bivouacs were sited; when the men moved quickly out into the open, they were caught by a third shell, which burst among the battalion scouts. In addition to those killed, 34 other men were wounded, of whom 6 later died. The name of the camp, located in gorse bushes behind the village, was Fox Covert. The dead were buried in what became Row A of Plot I of Mailly Wood Cemetery.

On 26 June, 1/6th Royal Warwicks (143rd Brigade, 48th Division) arrived in the village and two companies took over the SERRE road, to the north-east of the village. They were relieved after 3 days, by which time the front-line system in this sector had been flattened by the enemy guns. On 1 July the rest of 48th Division moved up to the village, which at the time was 2 miles behind the front.

One observer mentions that on 1 July there was a 15in gun in a plantation to the south-west of the village that fired every half-hour. Graham Greenwell's battalion, 1/4th Oxfordshire & Buckinghamshire Light Infantry (145th Brigade, 48th Division),

were camped 400yds from this gun. Greenwell reported that on 1 July they moved to their allotted positions, a large field behind Mailly-Maillet. He was able to ride with the battalion and was never so thankful for the use of a horse, as the march was very hot and dusty. Part of VIII Corps' reserve were camped in the Wood during the afternoon of 1 July.

On 8 July, after their tragic involvement in the 1 July fighting at BEAUMONT-HAMEL, 1st Newfoundlanders (88th Brigade, 29th Division) withdrew from ENGLEBELMER, which was being shelled by the enemy, and occupied tents in Mailly Wood. On 10 July, Brig Gen H.C. Rees, General Officer Commanding 11th Brigade (4th Division), was billeted in a house in the village for 10 days. The day before he arrived a shell had penetrated the house, but as the building was empty there were no casualties. His staff slept in the cellars of the building and Rees sensibly slept in the wine cellar. His brigade left for BEAUVAL near DOULLENS on 21 July, when Rees dined with Lt Gen Sir A.G. Hunter-Weston, General Officer Commanding VIII Corps.

At the end of July, 7th Somerset Light Infantry (61st Brigade, 20th Division) had their headquarters in a large house on the corner of the village square; their signallers occupied outbuildings to the rear of the building. Headquarters of 113th Brigade (38th Division) was in a château, and 1/7th Durham Light Infantry (pioneers of 50th Division) occupied cellars in the village. In early August, 7th Somerset Light Infantry made use of the church tower as an observation post. Mailly, with its former delightful orchards and gardens, was also especially associated with the artillery, and there were many batteries in the area during the battle.

Between 4 and 28 August, 9th Suffolks (71st Brigade, 6th Division) were in the area and took over the trench in front of Mailly Wood, with the intermission of a week in LOUVENCOURT. On 14 August, a battalion of the Coldstream Guards arrived here.

Edmund Blunden was also billeted in the village, and mentioned it in his *Undertones of War*. In August his battalion, 11th Royal Sussex (116th Brigade, 39th Division) had moved forward to Mailly Wood, which he described as a straggling wood, called P18 from its map reference. They were 3 miles from the German guns, and camped in tents. According to Blunden, Mailly had until recently been a delightful and flourishing place, but now it was in the 'sere and yellow'. Its long château wall had been broken down by trees that had fallen as a result of shell-fire. Its church was protected by straw mats. Blunden continued: 'Another postponement took me dustily back to the battalion in the wood watched by so many German observation balloons in the morning sun, the wood shelled deliberately because of its camps and accidentally because of some conspicuous horse-lines, and silhouetted movements on the hill to the west, had frayed the men's keenness'; there had been casualties.

On the evening of 2 September, 11th Royal Sussex moved from Mailly-Maillet through ENGLEBELMER and on to Mesnil, and assembled in the HAMEL trenches to attack the Beaucourt Ridge the next morning. At one time Blunden mentioned being in the cellars of a house in Mailly; these were concealed by an ingenious contrivance that opened into a subterranean passage running underground for several miles.

From 24 September to 7 October, Brig Gen H.C. Rees, General Officer Commanding 11th Brigade (4th Division), was back again at his brigade headquarters in a 'fine building in the main square'. On 30 September, he visited the battlefield, and was able to take his car as close as the outskirts of LONGEUVAL. A week later, he mentions that the mud was very deep; 11th Brigade left for Arraignes.

Frederic Manning, author of *The Middle Parts of Fortune* and a member of the 7th King's Shropshire Light Infantry (8th Brigade, 3rd Division) described his battalion's stay at Mailly. The wood in which they were encamped was just behind Mailly-Maillet, in an angle formed by two roads, one rising over the slope to Mailly-Maillet and the other skirting the foot of the hill to HÉDAUVILLE. It was on a rather steep reverse slope, which gave some protection from shell-fire; there were a few shelter trenches, which had been hastily and rather inefficiently dug, as a further protection. It was well screened from observation. A road running from COLINCAMPS converged towards the road they had just left, to meet it at a point known as the Sugar Refinery. Just before striking the road, they came to a large dump called Euston, and halted there. It can be seen by glancing at a map of the area that Manning was very accurate in his description of these topographical features. This was probably around 8 October, when they were preparing for the Ancre battle, which finally took place in mid-November.

On 9 October, 20th King's Royal Rifle Corps (pioneers of 3rd Division) were involved in duties here; on 29 October, they moved to COURCELLES-AU BOIS, where they worked for the rest of the year.

A member of a trench mortar battery of 32nd Division mentioned the batteries situated at ENGLEBELMER and at Mailly around 21 October; on 22 October, he reported seeing about 30 tanks in a field close to the village. Everywhere was muddy after the continuous rain.

Mailly Wood Cemetery, designed by Sir Reginald Blomfield, is about 400yds south of the centre of the village, on the further edge of the wood bordering the road to HÉDAUVILLE. It is close to the château with its walled garden, beyond which is the famous church. Begun in June 1916, the cemetery was heavily used in July 1916; here 51st Division buried many of their dead from the battle for BEAUMONT-HAMEL, which took place in November 1916. Twenty per cent of the casualties are men who served in the Seaforth Highlanders. The cemetery was also used for burials in 1918, and after the Armistice 101 graves from the battlefield immediately north-east of the village were brought in. Included here are the graves of Maj H.G. Lush-Wilson (II.Q.Sp) of Y Battery, Royal Horse Artillery (29th Division), a former fencing champion who was killed on 21 July; Lt The Hon. F.S. Trench (I.D.28) of 1st King's Royal Rifle Corps (99th Brigade, 2nd Division), son of Baron Ashtown, who was wounded in Munich Trench at BEAUMONT-HAMEL on 14 November and died 2 days later; and Sgt Harold Colley VC, MM (II.Q.4), of 10th Lancashire Fusiliers (52nd Brigade, 17th Division), who died of wounds at MARTINPUICH on 25 August 1918.

Mailly-Maillet Communal Cemetery is about ½ mile north-west of the village, a little west of the road to COURCELLES-AU-BOIS; Mailly-Maillet Communal Cemetery Extension, designed by W.C. von Berg and begun by French units in June 1915, is on the east side of it. It was taken over by British troops in August of that year and used by field ambulances and fighting units until December 1916. Some of the men buried here were among the very first British troops who arrived in the Somme area in July 1915. Many passed through the hands of 11th Field Ambulance (4th Division). The surrounding countryside is under cultivation.

Although Mailly-Maillet was much shelled in 1916, it was later a comparatively quiet place until the German breakthrough in March 1918. Although it was to remain in Allied hands, the village was severely shelled and the British troops once more had to use the catacombs as shelter.

After the war the village was 'adopted' by the city of Winchester. In August 1933, Vera Brittain came to the village while on a visit to the Somme, when she found many of the houses to be new.

MALTZ HORN FARM was south-east of TRÔNES WOOD, off the road that led to HARDECOURT-AU-BOIS. Today the position can be found by visiting the crucifix close to the site of the original farm. Before the Farm was captured by the Allies, it was a protruding point in the German defence line; the Farm was close to where the British and French lines flanked one another. The enemy defence line or trenches moved in a south-easterly direction towards MAUREPAS and northwards towards ARROW HEAD COPSE and GUILLEMONT village. Beyond Maltz Horn lay FAFFEMONT FARM and the village of COMBLES; this was the direction in which the battle was to move.

According to the *Official History of the War*, the Farm fell on 30 July 1916 to an Allied attack that began at 0445hrs, when the objective was in fact FAFFEMONT FARM to the east; 89th and 90th Brigades (both 30th Division) were involved in its capture. When 89th Brigade advanced, they kept in touch with the French on their right. Simultaneously, 5th Brigade (2nd Division) were to try and capture GUILLEMONT station, as well as the trenches to the north-west of it. Advancing from TRÔNES WOOD, 89th Brigade were heavily shelled with high explosive and gas shells; 90th Brigade were also affected. After a dawn fog, which cleared later, the Farm fell to an assault by 2nd Bedfords (89th Brigade, 30th Division) after they had attacked it from the west, alongside a company of the French Army from the south. The advance then continued eastwards down the hill.

After capturing the German front trenches, 20th King's (89th Brigade, 30th Division) got as far as the HARDECOURT-AU-BOIS–GUILLEMONT road. Advancing across the TRÔNES WOOD–GUILLEMONT road, 2nd Royal Scots Fusiliers (90th Brigade, 30th Divison) entered GUILLE-MONT from the south-west and repulsed a counter-attack from the direction of the cemetery. 18th Manchesters (also 90th Brigade, 30th Divison) advanced, leaving their left on the TRÔNES WOOD–GUILLEMONT railway, but were caught by crossfire from machine guns in the station and quarry at GUILLEMONT. After they had been forced to withdraw, another attack was planned, but was checked by uncut wire in the area of GUILLE-MONT station.

In early August, the valley to the east of the Farm, known as Maltz Horn Valley, was also called the Valley of Death, as it was continuously shelled. In mid-August, while the enemy still held ANGLE WOOD in strength, 1st Gordons (76th Brigade, 3rd Division) were in positions in front of the Farm.

Their objective was the road from ANGLE WOOD to GUILLEMONT; the French were again involved in this advance. However, the enemy had organised a powerful resistance at the junctions between the British and French Armies.

On 26 August, 35th Division were relieved on Maltz Horn Ridge; their position covered the whole of the eastern slope on which the Farm stood. Their advanced posts on the right were in the valley running from MAUREPAS to COMBLES. Opposite the right brigade front rose the spur on which LEUZE WOOD and BOULEUX WOOD were situated, and which ran diagonally across the divisional front. It was to the south-west of this spur that FAFFEMONT FARM was located.

On 1 September, the battalion headquarters of 1/8th Middlesex (167th Brigade, 56th Division) was in a quarry on the east side of Maltz Horn Ridge. On 3 September there were plans to blow up the Farm road, but the mine failed to explode. The fighting continued in the direction of COMBLES. Until FAFFEMONT FARM was taken, the French Army would be unable to advance along the valley. The French artillery undertook the bombardment and barrage in early September and finally the Farm was captured, followed by LEUZE WOOD. GUILLEMONT was also taken after several weeks of continuous British attacks.

MAMETZ is 4 miles east of ALBERT on the D64 FRICOURT–GUILLEMONT road and was formerly a railway halt on the line from ALBERT to PÉRONNE. MAMETZ WOOD is 1,000yds to the north-west, and is in fact closer to CONTAL-MAISON, with which it was to be more closely associated during 1916.

Prior to the war, Mametz was the fifth largest village in the area, with about 120 houses. During August and September 1915 the village was mainly associated with the British 18th Division, units of which were often here when in and out of the lines. During the last few weeks of 1915, 1st Norfolks (15th Brigade, 5th Division) were often in front-line trenches here, and when out of them they supplied working parties.

On 1 July, the village was the objective of 7th Division, with 18th Division on their right. Between the CARNOY–Mametz track and the quarry to the south of Hidden Wood, 91st Brigade on the right and 20th Brigade in the centre were to attack from the south-east on a front of 1,800yds. On the left of 91st Brigade's attack were 22nd Manchesters, with 2nd Queen's (both 91st Brigade, 7th Division) behind them; on the right were 1st South Staffords, with 21st Manchesters (also both 91st Brigade, 7th Division) in support. Meanwhile, 20th Brigade deployed 2nd Gordon Highlanders, 9th Devons – which consisted of Devon men, Londoners and Midlanders – and 2nd Borders; 8th Devons (also 20th Brigade, 7th Divison) were to the rear in Lucknow Redoubt, with 2nd Royal Warwicks (22nd Brigade, 7th Division) on their left. Behind 2nd Royal Warwicks, 2nd Royal Irish (also 22nd Brigade, 7th Division) were to come up to the front via MINDEN POST in order to support the attacking battalions of 91st Brigade.

Prior to 22nd Manchesters' and 1st South Staffords' attack, three large mines were exploded in FRICOURT, to the west of the Tambour, as well as a series of smaller mines in front of Mametz village; the largest of these was at Bulgar Point in front of Bulgar Trench, the enemy front line. Despite heavy casualties from machine guns, 22nd Manchesters captured Bucket Trench and actually reached DANTZIG ALLEY, but once there were unable to hold on.

Alongside 22nd Manchesters, 1st South Staffords were to advance towards Mametz between two mined positions in Bulgar Trench and would still have at least 1,000yds to cover. Maj Gen H.E. Watts, General Officer Commanding 7th Division, had kept the front and Support Lines empty, and instead, a new special assembly trench had been dug about 250yds to the rear; it was from this new line that 1st South Staffords advanced, while the Allied artillery were still shelling the German defensive positions in front of them. At 0730hrs they moved forward, only to be met by a good deal of shrapnel and machine-gun fire. They took many prisoners who had been sheltering in their dugouts and in half an hour the forward companies had reached the outskirts of the village, which meant that they had covered 1,200yds in 30 minutes.

When 1st South Staffords tried to enter the village, they came under more severe machine-gun fire from points on their right that 22nd Manchesters had not yet reached. By about 1000hrs, these guns had been dealt with, and together with a company of 21st Manchesters, 1st South Staffords penetrated the village, pushing right through DANTZIG ALLEY and establishing themselves to the north of the village; there, the rest of the battalion, which had been clearing DANTZIG ALLEY, were able to join them. Although at midday the position was still not secure and the enemy were on either flank in DANTZIG ALLEY, the attacking troops were slowly clearing the cellars and strongpoints. At around 1300hrs, the leading companies moved on in order to secure Bunny Alley, to the north-west of

the village, but their flanks were 'in the air' and they were forced to withdraw to the village to consolidate DANTZIG ALLEY.

The reserve battalion of 91st Brigade, 2nd Queen's, were committed in the afternoon and secured both ends of DANTZIG ALLEY, while 1st South Staffords continued to 'mop up' in the village and consolidate. At about 1700hrs, battalion headquarters moved up to the village and a fresh attempt on Bunny Alley was successful; 1st South Staffords had reached their 1 July objective.

On the night of 30 June, 21st Manchesters had taken up positions opposite Mametz, when their battalion headquarters was in a deep dugout in Queen's Road Trench close to the Rat Hole. On 1 July, 2nd Queen's and 22nd Manchesters were to push through the lines of 21st Manchesters, who were in reserve, although two of their companies helped 1st South Staffords in capturing the village. The historian R.H. Tawney, who was with 22nd Manchesters as a sergeant on 1 July, was wounded in the fight for Mametz. He was shot in the chest and abdomen and was not rescued for 24 hours.

On 2 July, 1st South Staffords were brought back into the village, when they were able to turn light machine-gun and rifle fire on parties of retiring Germans; together with 21st Manchesters, they put the village into a state of defence. On 3 July, they moved up to BOTTOM WOOD, north-west of Bunny Alley and about 500yds to the south-west of MAMETZ WOOD. Here, before being relieved, they found themselves alongside a sister battalion, 8th South Staffords (51st Brigade, 17th Division), which had been involved in capturing Fricourt Farm. They were relieved on 5 July. On the previous day, 21st Manchesters had been relieved; their battalion headquarters had been at Mametz church, which by then was a heap of white stone, and patrols had pushed out to BOTTOM WOOD without meeting any resistance. During their relief, they occupied billets in the village of Mametz – except for C Company, who were at MINDEN POST.

In contrast to the success of 91st Brigade, 20th Brigade experienced very mixed fortunes. The brigade's right-hand attacking battalion were 2nd Gordon Highlanders, who were to attack down in the valley close to the railway line; in doing so, they were cut down by machine-gun fire from the direction of the Shrine, to the south-west of Mametz. Their right company got as far as Cemetery Trench, the German intermediate trench in front of the village, but could go no further. Capt B. Brooke of 2nd Gordon Highlanders, in charge of B Company's right wing, was wounded on 1 July and died of wounds on 25 July. Brooke was a member of a military family; a book of his poems was published in 1917.

Six officers and 93 other ranks of 2nd Gordon Highlanders were later buried in Gordon Cemetery, close to Mansell Copse; three artillerymen who fell on 19 July are buried beside them. The cemetery stands on the level of the road and was formerly separated from it by a light railway. The headstones are ranged in two semicircles.

On the left of 2nd Gordon Highlanders were 9th Devons; their sister battalion, 8th Devons, were to join up with them from reserve. By the end of June it was very well known that the enemy had protected Mametz with a network of trenches that were studded with strongpoints and redoubts shielding many machine guns. A particularly well-placed machine gun was in Shrine Alley, to the south-west of the village, with a clear field of vision that included Mansell Copse. A few weeks before, on 9 April, the enemy had made a successful raid on British trenches here, when they took eight prisoners; 10 days later, the copse was destroyed by fire. On 5 May, the enemy exploded two mines to the south of the copse, but caused no casualties.

It is sometimes stated that Mansell Copse – spelled sometimes with one 'l' and sometimes with two – was named after 2/Lt S.L.M. Mansel-Carey of 9th Devons, who died of wounds on 24 February 1916 and was buried in Corbie Communal Cemetery (I.D.9). This may well have been so, but the feature must have been named when he was still alive, as the name appears on 1915 trench maps; in any event, the Official Historian uses two 'l's. Another pre-battle officer casualty was 2/Lt P.F. Gethin (B.4), attached 8th Devons, who was killed here on 28 June during the Allied bombardment.

On 1 July, 9th Devons were to penetrate Mansell Copse. Accordingly, the battalion assembled 250yds behind the front trench and went forward on what was the steep side of a valley, with dugouts among the undergrowth. From the moment the first lines of men entered no man's land, they were caught by devastating machine-gun fire, not only from trenches south of Mametz village but also from Fricourt Wood. As forecast, the machine-gun post that inflicted the most damage to 9th Devons was at Shrine Alley, about 800yds away, and caught them as they filed through and around Mansell Copse. A gap also opened up between them and 2nd Gordon Highlanders on their right flank.

As the ground protected them from the destructive machine gun at the Shrine, 8th Devons fared better; they managed to cross as far as Danube Trench and actually reached Shrine Alley. They then pushed along Dantzig Trench to the west of the village, and were able to clear the high dugouts along it.

8th and 9th Devons had attacked from a point to the south-west of the ALBERT–MARICOURT road, close to Mansell Copse. Disaster had been predicted by Capt D.L. Martin of A Company, 9th Devons, who had forecast that his battalion would be caught by machine-gun fire from Shrine Alley sweeping Mansell Copse track; that was exactly what happened, and Martin was one of the first to fall. While on leave Martin, working from a large-scale map, had made a contoured model in plasticine of the whole area to be attacked by 20th Brigade. His commander gave instructions for as many officers in the brigade as possible to visit the model in brigade headquarters at GROVE TOWN after 0900hrs on 22 June. When explaining the model to his colleagues, Martin pointed out the position of the machine-gun post in Shrine Alley that could sweep Mansell Copse. He even pointed out where he would fall.

A witness to Martin's death is quoted in his file at The National Archives (WO 339/13105): 'Having gone fifteen yards forward he was shot above the right temple. He turned his head to the left, flung out his right arm and fell dead on his back. He was a secret service man.' Another source stated that he was killed between the first and second lines by a machine-gun bullet. After the war, Martin's model was held at the United Services Museum.

The casualties of 9th Devons, and of men from A Company in particular, were appallingly high; many of these men were buried in a portion of their front-line trench, a burial ground immediately called Devonshire Cemetery. It stands on the top of a high, steep bank containing dugouts, and is bounded on the north-eastern side by Mansell Copse. It contains the graves of 2/Lt P.F. Gethin (B.4), attached 8th Devons and killed during the preliminary bombardment, 7 of the 10 officers and 121 of the 141 other ranks of 9th Devons killed on 1 July.

Among the 1 July graves are those of three officer friends. The poet Lt W.N. Hodgson of 9th Devons, son of the Bishop of St Edmundsbury and Ipswich, had taken a first-class degree in Classical Mods at Oxford in 1913 and was a contemporary of Rupert Brooke and E.A. Mackintosh. During the war he served as a lance-sergeant before being awarded a temporary commission. On 31 December 1915 he was Mentioned in Despatches, having already earned the Military Cross during the Battle of Loos in October 1915. His poem 'Before Action' tells of the period before the Battle of the Somme began and was first published under the name of 'Edward

Melbourne' in *New Witness* on 29 June 1916. He was battalion bombing officer, and his book *Verse and Prose in Peace and War* was published posthumously later in the year 1916. The other two of the friends were the battlefield modeller, Capt D.L. Martin (A.1), and 2/Lt H.L. Rayner (A.5). Hodgson's Military Cross was sent to his father after his death.

2/Lt C.H. Shepard of 9th Devons, elder brother of the illustrator Ernest Shepard of the Royal Artillery, was also buried here. Ernest was informed of his brother's death by his family and went up to the Copse in early July.

Also buried here are 3 officers and 29 of the 47 other ranks of 8th Devons who fell on 1 July; a sergeant and a driver of B Battery, XCII (Howitzer) Brigade, Royal Field Artillery (20th Division), killed later in the Somme battle; and 10 unidentified men of 9th Devons. On the evening of 4 July, a special service was held at the Copse by Canon E.C. Crosse DSO, MC, chaplain to the two battalions, and a wooden noticeboard was erected with the inscription:

The Devonshires held this trench
The Devonshires hold it still

On the night prior to the attack Canon Crosse had formed up with 9th Devons when they were wished good luck by their colonel. After a long wait at Vauxhall, he conducted stretcher-bearers to the junction of Lord and 70 Streets. He later wrote in his memoir (IWM 80/22/1) of confusion in the trenches as 9th Devons' assembly positions had been moved back a row, owing to the damaged state of the front line. After reporting to the medical officer at Wellington Redoubt 'he snatched an hour's sleep'.

On 9th Devons' left, 2nd Borders suffered their first casualties north of Wellington Redoubt. By 0630hrs on 30 June, the British artillery fire had become very intense. The Revd Crosse noted that the wounded soon came back, but the stretcher-bearers seemed to be moving very slowly. After assisting with the wounded, Crosse and the medical officer walked down the road towards Mansell Copse, when the road was already strewn with dead. Almost the first casualty he came across was that of Capt D.L. Martin of 9th Devons.

Crosse continued to organise the tending of the wounded in the heavily cratered ground, including German casualties, while the medical officer did what he could and was very unhappy about the inefficiency of the stretcher-bearers. Finally, when 'dead beat', Crosse returned to Wellington Redoubt

where he 'lay down till dawn'. On the morning of 1 July he went out again; organising a search of every crater, he rescued more wounded, including more Germans. The only landmark left was Shrine Alley, running from Mametz village to the former railway halt.

On 2 July, Crosse organised the recovery of more of the dead, assisted by men of both 8th and 9th Devons. He had been given permission to bury the dead in Mansell Copse; prior to that, he took them to a collecting station at the foot of the Copse, where identity discs and personal effects were removed from the bodies. At 2100hrs, 9th Devons received orders to return to Citadel Camp.

On 4 July, Crosse continued the work of recovering the dead, but this time was only assisted by about 30 men from 8th Devons. In all, they collected 163 men from the two battalions and covered them up in the Copse. By this time the working party was exhausted and the task of filling in the trench was very slow; at 1400hrs the searchers were held up in their work by a colossal thunderstorm. Later in the afternoon, Crosse 'read the funeral service and the Thanksgiving for Victory' over the graves. Later, he returned to the headquarters of 8th Devons and had a 'splendid dinner'.

Crosse's work at the Copse was still not quite finished. On 5 July, he asked a pioneer sergeant 'to paint a board with red lead borrowed from the R.E.'s and then went up to Mansell Copse to mark the cemetery. I put up the board.' It read:

Cemetery
Of
163 Devons
Killed July 1st 1916

Crosse then 'placed twelve crosses in two rows, and after wiring in the area I rode back to Ribemont where the 9th Devons had just arrived . . .' On 5 July he spent some time making out burial returns and drawing up plans for the cemetery. Over the next 2 days he requested a salvage company to put the cemetery in order and arranged for a special service of Holy Communion for Sunday 8 July in the school room at TREUX. On 9 July, he was preparing for a memorial service in the evening, but 2 days later the battalion were given orders to take over a 'front line trench' at FRICOURT.

In 1967 John Anthony Crosse, son of Canon Crosse, visited Mansell Copse and noted: 'In my father's day Mansell Copse must have been but a battered mass of shell blasted tree stumps . . . Today Mansell Copse is a neat spinney of young birches, as neat as the little cemetery where my father buried those 163 Devons that memorable day long ago . . .'

Because of its very tragic story, Devonshire Cemetery has become a particularly poignant place for visitors. In July 1986, HRH the Duke of Kent visited the spot and unveiled a new memorial to the memory of 8th and 9th Devons.

The other attacking battalion of 20th Brigade (7th Division), 2nd Borders, were involved in the frontal assault close to Mametz on 1 July; their particular objective was Apple Alley in the direction of FRICOURT. At 0727hrs, they moved forward and reached Danube Support Trench; on coming under indirect machine-gun fire both from Mametz and FRICOURT, they began to wheel further to the left. The advance continued to Hidden Lane, where it was held up by machine-gun fire from Hidden Wood on the right flank, and from the junction of Kiel Support and Bois Français Support.

By late afternoon 2nd Borders had reached their final objective, when two companies reached Apple Alley. A party of 8th Devons were to their right, two other companies of 2nd Borders were in support in Hidden Lane Trench, and battalion headquarters was established in a dugout in Support Trench. As for the other battalions attacking Mametz, the cost was very high, with 334 casualties of officers and men. Later in the battle, 2nd Borders were in deployment to the rear of Caterpillar Wood, and on 13 July they were in the area of Flat Iron Copse before being withdrawn to POMMIERS REDOUBT from 15 to 19 July.

Although there had been a great number of casualties in the capture of Mametz, it was a considerable success, as indeed was the taking of MONTAUBAN-DE-PICARDIE and the land in between the two on the same day. Most of the original objectives in this sector had been taken on a day when there had been little or no British progress elsewhere on the battlefield.

On 2 July the Germans conceded defeat at FRICOURT, the neighbouring village to the west, and the Allied line was pushed forward onto rising ground facing the south-west of CONTALMAISON, north-west of MAMETZ WOOD. At the same period, a position on the right was established along the Mametz Valley, which included Caterpillar Wood and BERNAFAY WOOD. Haig was going to push on where there had been some success with the Allied advance, as opposed to his original plan, which had been to attack across the THIEPVAL plateau.

On 24 July Maurice Baring, who was on the staff of Maj Gen H.M. Trenchard, General Officer Commanding First Wing, Royal Flying Corps, described Mametz as having nothing left in it but crumbling stones. The village had been annihilated. On the next day a divisional ammunition dump near the village, containing some 100,000 rounds of trench-mortar and artillery ammunition and a large quantity of bombs and rifle ammunition, was set on fire by a shell and the whole dump exploded.

Max Plowman of 10th West Yorkshires (50th Brigade, 17th Division) described Mametz in early August: 'now as we near Mametz, we come upon guns hidden under the banks of the roadside and camouflaged above by netting. The road through Mametz is still under enemy observation; so we turn sharply to the right to go round the back of the rising ground that faces us.' Plowman's unit went on to FRICOURT but were back here, camped in tents in the Copse with 11th West Yorkshires (69th Brigade, 23rd Division), in September, at which time they looked down on the no man's land of 1 July. On his first visit to Mametz, John Masefield described it as 'eight feet of brick'.

Dantzig Alley British Cemetery's name was taken from the German trench of that name. It is a little to the east of the village on the north side of the road to MONTAUBAN-DE-PICARDIE. Following hard fighting at DANTZIG ALLEY and at other points in the village, 7th Division erected a memorial to their dead in Mametz village. Later, a plaque to the Royal Welsh Fusiliers was erected here, and also a memorial seat to 38th Division.

In the 1930s, a memorial to the members of 38th Division was erected in Mametz church; it took the form of three panels, side by side, made of light grey marble.

In an article on the Manchester 'Pals' in the *Manchester Guardian*, dated 14 August 1926, it is noted: 'At the cross-roads in Mametz to-day . . . you will find nothing but a rough wooden cross to commemorate one of the historic struggles of the war in which it can be truly said, Manchester took the largest share.' This wooden cross had 'R.I.P.' in big letters at the top and was erected during the war to honour 7th Division. It was destroyed on 20 May 1940 by German panzer tanks as they swept through the village. In the 1990s it was replaced by a new memorial on the other side of the road, commemorating the Manchester 'Pals' battalions of the division (20th, 21st and 22nd Manchesters) that helped to capture the village on 1 July 1916. Dedicated on 1 July 1994, it is near the crossroads and was arranged for by members of the Western Front Association.

After the war, the village was 'adopted' by Llandudno.

A captured German machine-gun post near Mametz, August 1916. *(IWM Q870)*

MAMETZ WOOD has probably been written about more than any other wood, feature or village in the Somme area, perhaps because it was a very hard position to capture, along with TRÔNES and HIGH WOODS. Also, battalions were continuously 'fed into the position' under conditions that were very unfavourable to any attacker. Maybe it is also because of its literary associations that it has become so well known; the associations are mostly connected with the Royal Welsh Fusiliers and include Siegfried Sassoon, David Jones, Wyn Griffith and Robert Graves. In David Jones's long poem 'In Parenthesis', the poet's involvement in the Wood is the central theme.

The Wood was the next objective after MAMETZ village, but was only captured 12 days after the village fell. It is due north of MAMETZ, east of CONTALMAISON and south-west of the two BAZENTIN villages. The German Second Line ran in a south-easterly direction from POZIÈRES, through the gap between the top of Mametz Wood and the front of Bazentin-le-Petit Wood. Its capture was essential in order to avoid a salient in the Allied lines, and to enable the Allied artillery to be brought in for an attempt to take the German Second Line.

In *The Battle of the Somme*, John Masefield noted that the spur was covered with the bogwood of

MAMETZ, which was divided into three prongs of woodland in a gradual north-facing ascent. The highest part of the Wood was at its northern limit, and then the land broke into a natural scarp or disused quarry, which is where the Second Line ran, with a redoubt of machine guns and trench mortars. The trees in the Wood included hornbeams, limes, oaks and a few beeches. Having been neglected for 2½ years, the undergrowth was very wild and thick, especially to the north, where there was bramble as well as hazel. Allied shelling had brought down many of the trees; they added to the hazards for the attackers in the forthcoming battle, as they had fallen in full growth.

The enemy had built machine-gun posts, which they camouflaged with the use of green paint in some of the trees. There were also heavy guns in the Wood, as well as field-gun batteries to its rear in the Second Line. Barbed wire was strung from tree to tree in the southern section and machine-gun pits were also dotted here, giving command of some of the clearings. After the Poodles and SHELTER WOOD, to the north-east of FRICOURT, had been taken, along with the villages of MAMETZ and FRICOURT, the way was clear for attacks towards Mametz Wood.

The German 3. Garde Infanterie Division relieved the remnants of 28. Reserve Division that had their right on the ALBERT–BAPAUME road and their left on Flat Iron Copse – which, along with Sabot Copse, was to the north-west of Mametz Wood. After the advance on 1 July, the Germans continued to hold various positions across the spur of the ridge reaching out into the MAMETZ–MONTAUBAN-DE-PICARDIE valley. The main point taken up by 3.Garde Infanterie Division was Kaiser Trench, which protected CONTALMAISON on the south-west. Made a few months prior to the battle, this trench was well wired and had dugouts in the chalk that were 20ft deep. On its right, it was connected with OVILLERS using Fourth Street, which ran in front of BAILIFF WOOD, its left end connected to Mametz Wood by Wood Trench, which ran into the southern section.

Haig required the capture of Mametz Wood and CONTALMAISON in order to secure the British left flank, while on the right TRÔNES WOOD also needed to be captured. One gets the impression that Haig became impatient with the slow progress in the attempts to capture the Wood, and feels that he would not have been so impatient if he had seen for himself the conditions confronting the attackers. If only the Allies had known at the time that the Wood was virtually undefended on 3 July.

On the night of 4/5 July, 17th Division managed to capture part of Kaiser Trench between the CONTALMAISON–FRICOURT road and Wood Trench, named Quadrangle Trench; they also captured part of Wood Trench. On 5 July, 91st Brigade (7th Division) were in front of Mametz Wood; on the right flank were 18th Division, following their progress in the area between MONTAUBAN-DE-PICARDIE and MAMETZ, and on the left, 17th Division were still in the front line.

Over the following week, 38th Division became the division most associated with the fight for the Wood and with its eventual capture. 113th Brigade (38th Division) marched through the old front line up to MAMETZ village and then entered the former German communication trench. This led to what some accounts name HAPPY VALLEY, while others call it DEATH VALLEY; it ran along the front of the Wood and the QUADRANGLE, which was a small copse to the south-west of the Wood. The communication trench was DANTZIG ALLEY and there were no duckboards. On the night of 4 July, 113th Brigade occupied positions to the south-west of the Wood.

According to Sassoon, 1st Royal Welsh Fusiliers (22nd Brigade, 7th Division) had started out at 2115hrs on 4 July; they went up a communication trench and came down across the open hillside looking towards the Wood. They found that 2nd Royal Irish (also 22nd Brigade, 7th Division) had been bombed and machine-gunned by the Germans in the Wood itself. It was a still and grey morning. At 1230hrs, Sassoon saw 30 dead from 1st Royal Welsh Fusiliers laid out in two rows by the MAMETZ–CARNOY road. Both 1st Royal Welsh Fusiliers and 2nd Royal Irish had been sent up to consolidate trenches close by and were meant to clear the outskirts of the Wood.

First on the scene, 2nd Royal Irish found German machine-gunners, bombers and snipers in the Wood. A Company, 1st Royal Welsh Fusiliers, went to help out but were caught by snipers and took shelter in a quarry; 2nd Royal Irish had tried to bomb the Wood but had suffered casualties. After that, the Allied artillery assisted with a barrage that enabled 2nd Royal Irish to escape. It had been assumed by the staff that the nearside of the Wood was unoccupied. It was during an attack against Wood Trench in the south corner of the Wood that Lt Moore-Brabazon of B Company, 2nd Royal Irish, was wounded in the foot. The battalion were out for 11 hours before returning to their 'field' at 0830hrs on 5 July.

Later, 1st Royal Welsh Fusiliers moved off again for an attack on the QUADRANGLE position, close to the Wood. Rather undermanned, they attacked on a front of 600yds from BOTTOM WOOD. After a short bombardment, they struggled up to MAMETZ and BOTTOM WOOD in awful mud and had to cross 500yds of open ground. Quadrangle Trench had some wire in front, but was also quite shallow and roughly dug. The Germans were bombing up a communication trench from the Wood; 2nd Royal Irish were to attack on the right, but failed to get into the enemy trench called Strip Trench.

1st Royal Welsh Fusiliers established a bombing point on the right where Quadrangle Trench came to a sudden end. The Germans continued to snipe from the Wood. At 0230hrs on 4 July, Sassoon was with C Company, 1st Royal Welsh Fusiliers, at BOTTOM WOOD, their attack having been cancelled. Sassoon went to a bombing post and frightened 50 or 60 Germans into running back into the Wood. According to Graves, Sassoon captured a trench by himself without signalling for reinforcements and sat down and read a book of poetry in the German trench instead. A Lewis gun followed the enemy and Quadrangle Trench had fallen.

Sassoon was not popular with his colonel, who told him that he had held up the attack on Mametz Wood for 2 hours. On 5 July, Sassoon had been heavily involved in the fighting against the QUAD-RANGLE; although Quadrangle Trench was secure, the Support Trench did not fall until several days later. Sassoon was recommended for a decoration, but it was not awarded because the attack had not been 'official'.

On 6 July, 114th Brigade (38th Division) were to the right and 113th Brigade (also 38th Division) to the left of the position in front of the Wood. On 7 July, 115th Brigade (also 38th Division) were to replace 114th Brigade; the day before, 11th South Wales Borderers (115th Brigade, 38th Division) halted with 10th South Wales Borderers (also 115th Brigade, 38th Division) behind MAMETZ village; they were both to attack the Wood as part of 115th Brigade's attack. At 2000hrs, loaded with bombs, sandbags and steel stakes, they moved to a position in HAPPY/DEATH VALLEY from which to make their advance. The communication trench ran through Caterpillar Wood, and they came across timber-line dugouts and even some German allotments.

On the night of 6/7 July, a section of 10th Lancashire Fusiliers (52nd Brigade, 17th Division) pushed out from Quadrangle Trench and reached the southern end of CONTALMAISON village, but were unable to hold it. The section of the Kaiser Graben in front of the western end of CONTALMAISON, north of the CONTALMAISON–FRICOURT road, was still in enemy hands.

According to *The War in the Air* by H.A. Jones, No. 3 Squadron, Royal Flying Corps, was ordered to reconnoitre Mametz Wood and the German positions to the west of it, especially Quadrangle Support Trench, which connected the Wood with Acid Drop Copse to the north-east of the trench. The Copse had been levelled with shell-fire, but the majority of trees in the Wood were seen to be still standing; one observer reported that not enough of them had been blown over to form a barrier. Quadrangle Support Trench was strongly manned on 7 July, when the next attacks on the Wood were due to take place.

7 July began with heavy showers, as well as a variable wind. It was planned to attack the two German trenches, Quadrangle Support Trench, about 500yds north of Quadrangle Trench, and the point of Pearl Alley running forward from it. At this point the ground was quite open. 17th Division were to take these trenches, although it was thought that the attack might well be enfiladed from the Wood,

which turned out to be the case. Furthermore, the enemy made a counter-attack; this was followed by another attack by 52nd Brigade (17th Division), which again failed. There was a heavy bombardment, as well as fire from the Wood; in addition, the attacking troops were slightly late in arriving, which did not help with artillery cooperation. There was little or no hope of reaching Quadrangle Support over the open ground. On the right, bombers of 50th Brigade (17th Division) were sent to work up Quadrangle Alley, but were driven back; a company of 6th Dorsets (50th Brigade, 17th Divison) were decimated by machine-gun fire from Strip Trench.

At 0830hrs, 38th Division attacked the Wood again, when 115th Brigade advanced across the valley; 16th Welsh and 11th South Wales Borderers were held up by machine-gun fire, and the latter's commanding officer was killed. Two more attempts were made during the day, but the Welshmen could get no closer than 250yds to the Wood. They were particularly affected by machine-gun fire, which came not only from the Wood itself but also from the valley higher up to the north-east, from Flat Iron and Sabot Copses. The operation was abandoned with the loss of 400 men; 115th Brigade withdrew and two companies of 17th Royal Welsh Fusiliers (115th Brigade, 38th Division) were left behind to hold the MARLBOROUGH WOOD–Caterpillar Wood position. To the left of 38th and 17th Divisions, the advance of 23rd Division was held up by the lack of support on their right flank and they were forced back from CONTALMAISON.

During the night of 7/8 July, in the German positions, Reserve-Infanterie-Regiment Nr. 122 took over from Infanterie-Regiment (Schleswig-Holstein-ischen) Nr. 163 between the south-west corner of Mametz Wood and the village of CONTAL-MAISON; Lehr-Infanterie-Regiment (3. Garde Infanterie Division), which had been holding the southern edge of the Wood and the area around Flat Iron Copse, were not relieved. The headquarters of Reserve-Infanterie-Regiment Nr. 122 was in Contalmaison Château and that of Lehr-Infanterie-Regiment was in Mametz Wood.

On 8 July, the British battle situation was as follows: 38th Division were still south of the Wood, with 3rd Division on their right and 17th Division on their left. Facing the Wood were 114th Brigade to the right and 113th Brigade on their left (both 38th Division). At around 1730hrs, Quadrangle Support Trench was again attacked and the enemy had been quickly alerted; rockets were seen going up behind CONTALMAISON, which was the signal for a heavy German barrage to be brought down on the attackers. The German artillery was in a position of BAILIFF WOOD to the west of CONTALMAISON. Not surprisingly, the British attack once more failed. The fighting for the Wood over the next few days was ceaseless.

On 9 July, 38th Division were closely supported by 7th Division in front of the Wood, with 3rd Division still to the right. On the left of 38th Division, however, 17th Division were now supported by 21st Division. On the morning of 9 July no attack towards the Wood took place; 17th Division attacked towards CONTALMAISON from a starting point at Quadrangle Trench. 8th South Staffords and 7th Lincolns (both 51st Brigade, 17th Division) advanced to the village from the western end of Quadrangle Support and parties did reach as far as Acid Drop Copse and Pearl Alley, but they were unsupported and had to return to Quadrangle Trench, leaving behind them a machine-gun crew at the Copse.

Also on 9 July, a large artillery telescope was found in the cliff between White Trench and Mametz Wood. It had clearly been used by the enemy for observation purposes earlier in the battle. On the same day, the German 28. Reserve Division were relieved by units of 10. Bayerische Infanterie Division, who were the only reserve of XIV Reserve Korps.

An account of how the Germans had been faring during this time of intense Allied pressure on the Wood has been left by Lt Köstlin, a member of II Bataillon, Reserve-Infanterie-Regiment Nr. 122. His unit were ordered to reinforce III Bataillon, who occupied the Wood. He had taken his company to an ammunition depot at MARTINPUICH to collect hand grenades and other ammunition and also to have a square meal, when they were interrupted by a shell that hit the field kitchen cart and frightened the horse away. Köstlin then took his company across the open land between CONTALMAISON and Mametz Wood; they were harassed by the darkness of the night and also by British shelling. On reaching the German front positions in the small hours, Köstlin was told that the British had broken through the western end of a trench close to the Wood. The Germans were ordered to act on their own initiative and Köstlin took charge, being the most senior officer present. The Wood was difficult to defend with only a few machine guns in shelter pits; Köstlin concentrated his men on the trench along the southern edge, with Support Lines in the open ground on both sides halfway up to it, Wood Trench and Wood Support on the west and a line of trench around Flat Iron Copse on the east.

At 1530hrs on 10 July, the British bombardment began. 38th Division were to make a direct assault against the southern edge of the Wood and units assembled at both corners of the southern narrow strip of the Wood, which reached out some 200yds towards the bed of Mametz Valley. The accuracy of the artillery bombardment allowed the attack on the right and left to make progress, but the centre part was held up because of the distance of open ground that companies had to cover.

There are several accounts of the fighting both towards and within Mametz Wood, which are so well-written and seemingly historically accurate that it is very difficult not to draw considerably upon them. In particular, there is Wyn Griffith's *Up to Mametz*, David Jones' *In Parenthesis* and Guy Chapman's anthology *Vain Glory*. Griffith and Jones were both members of 15th Royal Welsh Fusiliers (113th Brigade, 38th Division), although Jones was a private and Griffith was a lieutenant on the staff. They did not meet during this period, and in fact it was unusual for men from the 'other ranks' to have much of a relationship with anyone who was commissioned.

Griffith vividly described 38th Division's attempts to take the Wood during the period 9/10 July, as well as the build-up and delays of the days before the main battle. He was with Lt Taylor, the brigade signalling officer, and they were on their way to POMMIERS REDOUBT, east of MAMETZ village, which looked towards the Wood. The two men saw the preparations for the big attack, including lines of batteries, ammunition dumps, wagons and stores; he slept in what was previously a German dugout. At this time, it was CONTALMAISON, to the west of Mametz Wood, that was due to be barraged and captured, as a prelude to the taking of the Wood. From POMMIERS REDOUBT they scanned the Wood with their field glasses, and Griffith wrote that it seemed 'as thick as a virgin forest'; there was seemingly no sign of life in it, though there could have been 10 machine guns concealed in it or 10,000 men. The Wood's edges were clean-cut, much as they are 90-odd years later, and the ground between POMMIERS REDOUBT and the Wood was completely bare of cover.

The men of 38th Division were assembled in trenches above a dip in the ground; the plan was to advance, and then descend into the hollow before crossing the bare slope, which was bound to be covered by machine guns. As they advanced, they would be exposed on their right to enfilade fire from the direction of Flat Iron Copse. Brig. Gen. H.J. Evans, commander of 115th Brigade of the 38th

Division the arrived with Griffiths his staff captain, establishing headquarters in the signaller's dugout. The shelling of CONTALMAISON continued, and after a while the artillery bombarded the edge of the Wood. The infantry were to go forward in three stages before entering the Wood.

A few minutes after 0800hrs, the enemy artillery cut the wires to the battalions, and there was no smokescreen to give the advance protection. After the advance began, runners brought bad news, in particular that the artillery had made no real difference to the German defences. However, the attack continued towards the Wood and the artillery were to begin another bombardment. For some reason the operation was carried out in isolation, without support from either flank. The second attack began, but under such conditions a frontal attack towards the Wood was always going to be doomed to failure.

Griffith and Evans set off to Caterpillar Wood to make contact with the battalions; on their way, Griffith came across a disused trench after passing through Caterpillar Wood and asked an artillery officer in it whether his telephone line was still working, which it was. He was in touch with the heavy artillery beyond POMMIERS REDOUBT. Griffith joined Evans when they dropped down into the Nullah between Caterpillar Wood and Mametz Wood. In a bank close to the Nullah there were scores of stretchers on the ground because it was an advanced dressing station. In addition, the Nullah was used as a dump for materials; there was a similar dump in Caterpillar Wood.

On the bare ridge beyond, the Welsh battalions were burrowing into the open ground with their entrenching tools; the Nullah was out of sight of the enemy. The time for the third attack towards the Wood drew near, and Evans and Griffith planned to cancel it, as to go on was a senseless waste of men's lives. The General had thought that the best approach had been to creep up to the edge of the wood at night and to rush it in the morning. Griffith remembered the artillery officer's telephone and Evans used it to call off the attack and to save the total annihilation of the attacking brigade. Six weeks later, Evans was sent home 'under a cloud'.

On 9 July the two remaining brigades of 38th Division were to attack Mametz Wood once more and Griffith's brigade were to take over the defence of the Wood if the attack were successful. This time the front was to be narrower and there was to be greater artillery support, but at the last moment the attack was postponed for 12 hours. Griffith wrote that it was not until dawn of 10 July that the 'flower

of young Wales stood up to machine guns with a success that astonished all those who knew the ground'. On 10 July, Griffith had assumed the duties of a staff captain.

From 9 July, Maj Gen H.E. Watts was in temporary command of 38th Division for 3 days, the very period during which the Wood was finally to fall into Allied hands. At 0415hrs on 10 July, 38th Division planned to attack; 114th Brigade were to take the eastern portion of the Wood while 113th Brigade were allocated the western section. The central ride running through the Wood was the dividing line. As with DELVILLE WOOD, Mametz Wood was divided into sections by various rides. 115th Brigade was in reserve near MINDEN POST and MAMETZ. Three-quarters of an hour before the attack was due to start, a heavy barrage was concentrated on the southern edge of the Wood; smoke cover was provided at the eastern end, as well as to the south-west of the Wood. The latter activity was planned to draw German fire while the main thrust was carried out to the east of these positions.

At 0415hrs, 113th Brigade (38th Division) began to advance, with 13th Royal Welsh Fusiliers to the right, 14th Royal Welsh Fusiliers in the centre and 16th Royal Welsh Fusiliers on the left; the latter suffered very heavy casualties, including their commanding officer, when they were repulsed by German machine-gun fire. Although 14th Royal Welsh Fusiliers speedily cleared their portion in the centre of the line, 13th Royal Welsh Fusiliers had to be reinforced by 15th Royal Welsh Fusiliers. David Jones was a member of No. 6 Platoon, B Company, 15th Royal Welsh Fusiliers. Eventually, 13th, 14th and 15th Royal Welsh Fusiliers were able to form a line just south of the most southern cross-ride eastwards, from its junction with the main ride.

However, on the south-west side of the Wood the Germans still held Wood Support, and their enfilading fire held up the advance in the Wood itself. There was a gap between the battalions of 113th Brigade that was filled by 10th Welsh (114th Brigade, 38th Division). 19th Welsh (pioneers of 38th Division) were ordered up to dig a trench all along the southern side and also to wire it. By early afternoon, Wood Support was taken by 13th Royal Welsh Fusiliers under Lt Col O.S. Flower, who was later killed by a shell and buried at Morlancourt British Cemetery No. 1 (B.21).

On 10 July, the officer who had signed the entry for No. 123 Field Company, Royal Engineers (38th Division) went up from MAMETZ village and got as far as Mametz Wood. Owing to the number of officer casualties, 13th Royal Welsh Fusiliers found themselves leaderless, and the diarist was obliged to take command until relieved by Maj Bell 2 hours later. By now, the Wood was partly in Allied hands, and troops from 115th Brigade (38th Division) were sent up from MINDEN POST to reinforce 114th Brigade.

At 1600hrs on 11 July a further advance took 38th Division to the northern end of the Wood. The eastern side of the Wood was captured and the Germans fled to Sabot Copse, in the direction of Bazentin-le-Grand Wood. Allied machine-gun fire from both Caterpillar Wood and MARLBOROUGH WOOD resulted in many casualties among the German defenders. 15th Welsh, east of the central ride in the Wood, and 17th and 15th Royal Welsh Fusiliers to the west of it, fought to within 40yds of the northern edge of the Wood. In due course, the remainder of 115th Brigade were brought up and 113th and 114th Brigades were relieved.

During the fighting Jones was wounded in the southern part of the Wood. In his book *In Parenthesis*, he describes in poetic form what happened to him and his colleagues. He describes the Wood, which is one of the largest on the Somme, as the 'Queen of the Woods'. The whole experience of his fighting with 15th Royal Welsh Fusiliers is brilliantly portrayed, and it was an experience that was to become an obsession with him for the rest of his life, as did Mametz Wood for Wyn Griffith. Jones found that with his wound he could neither walk nor stand, and so he crawled towards the British line and hoped that he would meet up with a member of the Royal Army Medical Corps.

Jones still had his rifle with its bayonet in the fixed position and somehow it fouled his helmet. It was with feelings of guilt that he abandoned his rifle, although he kept hold of his gas mask. A corporal came across him and carried him to safety on his back until a major told the corporal to set him down. Jones recalled being in a large marquee with other casualties; it was very hot. He had what was called a 'beautiful blighty'. Some of the men in Jones's poem, if not all, were based on real persons. Thus there was a major referred to as 'that shit Major Lillywhite', who was killed in the Wood, and 'Aunty Bebbridge' was based on Brig Gen L.A.E. Price-Davies VC. Maj Bell is 'Well Dell', and Reg Allen, in the dedication, was a Lewis gunner.

To find out what happened to Wyn Griffith, we turn once more to his book *Up To Mametz*. Just before dawn on 10 July, Maj Gen H.E. Watts and the brigade major went up towards the Wood, leaving Griffith to follow at noon. The major was wounded, however, which meant that Griffith had to be up at the Wood at 0700hrs, having passed through two barrages. He saw dead from his old battalion, 15th Royal Welsh Fusiliers, with the distinctive yellow band on their sleeves. Before the division actually attacked the Wood it was known that it was full of dense undergrowth and had a labyrinth of trenches and dugouts, as well as wire stretched across from tree to tree. The central ride joined a communication trench leading to the German Second Line to the north of the Wood. This was useful for enemy reinforcements and it also meant that the Wood could at any time be quickly evacuated and subsequently bombarded.

Griffith found that while he was on a ride he could make progress, but it was very difficult to struggle through the undergrowth to the left and right. There were other horrors, not just dead soldiers but bits of soldiers, mutilated trunks, detached heads and splashes of blood on the green leaves. It was these sorts of horrible sights that were to give the Wood its sinister reputation for troops who passed this way once it had been taken by the British. Griffith recalled vividly the smell of 'green' timber; in later life, when he smelt this smell again it recalled the horrors that he had witnessed in 1916. He reached a cross-ride in the Wood where four lanes broadened, and near this ring was a group of officers. The brigadier-general was talking to one of his battalion commanders and to Lt Taylor, the signals officer, and to the intelligence officer.

At that time, the line held was about 300yds south of the northern edge of the Wood. The units were very mixed up and Griffith was responsible for deciding their boundaries. They were attempting to dig themselves in amid the undergrowth. The battalions in the Wood were relieved at dawn. 162nd Brigade (21st Division) completed the job of reaching the northern edge of the Wood, and consolidated it; their line was linked up with 7th Division on the right and 1st Division on the left.

The German officer, Lt Köstlin, had been defending Quadrangle Support Trench to the west of the Wood; according to the British plan, this should have been captured the night before, thus making the German position untenable. He shot down many bombers at the Sap Head, including those of 7th East Yorkshires (50th Brigade, 17th Division), but at the time was not aware that 38th Division had reached the centre of the Wood, although he could see khaki figures behind him who were probably from 6th Dorsets (50th Brigade, 17th Division). The Germans were able to shoot down many of the British troops who had appeared in the large clearing south of the Wood, across which was Wood Support.

Basil Liddell Hart of 9th King's Own Yorkshire Light Infantry (64th Brigade, 21st Division) wrote in his *Memoirs* that his division moved up on 10 July. He said that it was astonishing to see how 'trench warfare had vanished for the moment, with lines of guns standing out in the open almost wheel to wheel'. On 10 July the Allied attack had reached within 40yds of the northern edge of the Wood; on the same day CONTALMAISON had been taken for the third time, by 23rd Division, and this time it was held. The remaining strip of Mametz Wood was taken by 21st Division, who had relieved 38th Division; the latter eventually moved to COIGNEUX, where they relieved 48th Division, taking over the line to the south of HÉBUTERNE and GOMME-COURT.

Griffith was to write about his experiences in Mametz Wood not only in his book *Up to Mametz*, but also in his piece *The Pattern of One Man's Remembering*.

I can only call it a kind of emotional explosion inside me, and under its impetus I wrote on and on until I came towards a kind of climax, the Battle of Mametz Wood in July 1916, where so many of my countrymen, including my own brother, were killed. There I stopped, because I was afraid of my own memories and dreaded their coming to life . . . But the challenge was still there, in Mametz Wood, and I found that there was no peace within me until I had faced and recorded this high point of the war where for me and so many other Welshmen the tragedy reached its culmination. The words had to be torn out of me, hurt as it must. The events are mere history, to be found in many books, but my own reactions, as I recorded them, turned remembering into a surgical operation. And, as happens with the body, there came afterward a kind of peace within. I had spent my emotional capital, in this detailed recovery of what I thought to have been buried beneath years of happiness, and I was left in what I can only call a neutral state. This kind of remembering had done its work, and I was purged of the pain of war, untroubled, confident that I had nothing more to fear from its recurrence in the years ahead.

Returning to the battle, the immediate objective of 7th Division was the trench that ran south of Bazentin-le-Grand Wood, known here as Flat Iron Trench, which 2nd Queen's (91st Brigade, 7th Division) reached and overran on 13 and 14 July. The division's final objective was the establishment of a line from the north-east corner of that wood to the northern edge of BAZENTIN-LE-PETIT. As stated, the main task of taking the Wood had been carried out on 10 July, when 38th Division were virtually brought to a standstill by the conditions in the Wood. Apart from all the horrors of wood fighting and the continuous German shelling, there was also an acute shortage of water. It was not until the early morning of 12 July, however, that the Wood was completely in British hands. When it was finally cleared, hundreds of dead Germans were found, and also 13 heavy guns just beyond it, including two batteries of old French fortress guns from Mauberge on high overback carriages.

On 13 July, 62nd Brigade (21st Division) had their headquarters on the western edge of the Wood, which was the headquarters of one of the battalions of the Leicestershire Regiment, as well as of 21st Division. They found the Wood littered with dead and the rides blocked by fallen trees. Before dawn, 62nd Brigade exchanged with 63rd Brigade (21st Division) and the 6th and 7th Leicesters (110th Brigade, 21st Division) carried the German Second Line trench to the north of Mametz Wood; seven enemy machine guns alone were captured in this trench. Col Haigh of 9th Leicesters (110th Brigade, 37th Division) was in Forest Trench; he gave instructions for the troops to go forward to occupy the north side of the Wood. The attack had been very costly, partly because cooperation between the artillery and infantry was still in its infancy and it was hard for the infantry always to keep up with their own barrage.

Although 7th Leicesters lost 14 officers in the attack, they had the satisfaction of seeing the enemy routed, as from an orchard near BAZENTIN village they could see the Germans running back. During this time, though, the Germans were still shelling the north-west part of the Wood, which cost a lot of casualties. On 14 July they were ordered to withdraw, although, as it happened, there was no one on hand to relieve them. One company of 1st East Yorkshires (64th Brigade, 21st Division), who had come up to reinforce the line, were left behind. Brigade casualties were about 2,000 out of 3,000, with high officer casualties. Communication had been very poor, which had contributed to the carnage.

The scheme to capture the rest of the German Second Line had been worked out by Lt Gen Sir Henry Rawlinson, General Officer Commanding Fourth Army, in cooperation with his corps and divisional commanders. The commander-in-chief was at first reluctant to grant permission to carry it out, as he thought that there would be greater risk in the attack as planned, which was to be a night attack. However, it finally began at 0325hrs on 14 July. The task of XV Corps was to give cover for XIII Corps, under which assaulting lines could form. At this time flies had settled thickly in the Wood. There was sticky sediment at the bottom of the shell-holes; another horror in the Wood was the wreckage of an Allied aeroplane.

In a letter dated 10 July 1941 to Robert Graves (King's College LH 1/327/35), Liddell Hart mentions that his battalion (9th King's Own Yorkshire Light Infantry) had moved up from FRICOURT in order to take up position in support in BOTTOM WOOD, just by the QUADRANGLE, which 1st Royal Welsh Fusiliers had taken. In the early hours of 14 July they had moved slightly forward and flankwise up to the fringe of Mametz Wood, where they found themselves among the dead of the Welsh battalions who had attacked it earlier.

In Liddell Hart's *Memoirs*, he describes members of 64th Brigade lying on the edge of Mametz Wood under a hot sun, amid rows of decaying and strongly smelling corpses. Pushing on into the Wood, the dead were even thicker; often, German and Briton were locked in a death grapple. In Liddell Hart's letter referred to above, he also told Graves that he marched up the MÉAULTE–FRICOURT road in the early hours of 15 July and that 9th King's Own Yorkshire Light Infantry had gone up the same road on the afternoon of 12 or 13 July, having been out of the line since 1 July in order to recuperate.

Indeed, in *Goodbye to All That*, Graves wrote that on 15 July they struck the MÉAULTE–FRICOURT–BAZENTIN road, which ran through HAPPY VALLEY. Just beyond FRICOURT a German barrage made progress on the road impossible, and so they left it; they arrived at Mametz Wood at 0800hrs. Although he himself was still with the transport, Sassoon's battalion, 1st Royal Welsh Fusiliers, were involved in the Mametz Wood fighting from 14 to 17 July. On 14 July, he met up with his friend Graves, who, before going up to Mametz Wood, had been bivouacked by the Bécordel road, and they managed to have a long talk.

In his autobiography Graves mentions that on 16 July his unit, 2nd Royal Welsh Fusiliers, were among the dead of their own New Army Battalion who had helped to capture Mametz Wood. They had halted in thick mist, which had been caused by the Germans using lachrymatory shells. They spent 2 days in bivouac outside the Wood; like Richards,

Graves went into the Wood and took greatcoats from the bodies of the dead Prussians who lay there. There were also the dead of the South Wales Borderers, whom Graves describes as small New Army men.

Graves wrote at least three poems as a result of this experience. One is called 'Letter to S.S. from Mametz Wood', in which he describes what he and his friends will do after the war. He talks of them living in North Wales in a country seat, a sort of 'Morlancourtish Billet'; the final line is 'And God, what poetry we'll write'.

Another dialogue poem between him and Sassoon begins:

Back from the Somme two Fusiliers
Limped painfully home; the elder said,
S. 'Robert, I've lived three thousand years
This summer, and I'm nine parts dead'.

In 1917 Graves published a collection of poems dedicated to his regiment, called *Fairies and Fusiliers*. One of the poems is called 'A Dead Boche' and part of it is as follows:

Today I found in Mametz Wood
A certain cure for lust of blood:
where, propped against a sheltered trunk,
In a great mess of things unclean,
Sat a dead Boche; he scowled and stunk
with clothes and face a sodden green,
Big-bellied, spectacled, crop-haired,
Dribbling black blood from nose to beard.

Pte Frank Richards of 2nd Royal Welsh Fusiliers wrote a book called *Old Soldiers Never Die*; he was also a contributor to *The War the Infantry Knew*, which was a book on the history of the same battalion. In his own book, Richards noted that his unit had arrived from a railhead, and that on 15 July they had passed through FRICOURT, where 1st Royal Welsh Fusiliers had broken through on 1 July. He had been transferred to A Company; after FRICOURT they reached Mametz Wood. He described the valley as being thick with guns, and wrote that there were small howitzers on the ridge behind them. The enemy had been sending over tear gas, and the valley was thick with it, and the ground all around was covered with the bodies of the men who had been killed during the taking of the Wood. The battle was going on about ¾ mile ahead.

A few hours later, his battalion moved round the corner of Mametz Wood, and Richards's company occupied a shallow trench. The majority of the company then went 'on the scrounge' in the Wood for food and German greatcoats. It was at this time that the German artillery were firing with pinpoint accuracy; this had been made possible by a German officer who had volunteered to stay behind when, with the use of a communications cable stretching from BAZENTIN-LE-PETIT as far back as HIGH WOOD, he had directed the German artillery. He was later discovered and captured by the patrol of a battalion of the Middlesex Regiment on 17 July.

On 15 July, Liddell Hart wrote home to his parents (LH7/1916/15) and told them that he was on his way up from the rest position to take up residence in a line of rough shelter trenches that had been dug on the north side of Mametz Wood. The artillery grouped around his position, he told them, was from three divisions, and was subsequently very noisy. This artillery also attracted enemy retaliation. Liddell Hart's battalion, 9th King's Own Yorkshire Light Infantry, moved up towards the front line via the east side of Mametz Wood and were relieved 3 days later, when Liddell Hart was wounded.

In *The Machine Gunner*, Arthur Russell of No. 98 Company, Machine Gun Corps (33rd Division), noted that in mid-July he was within 4 miles of the forward infantry positions. He and his colleagues spent a night on the slopes of a ridge beyond MAMETZ village, prior to going up the line the next morning. He reported 15in, 12in, 9.2in howitzers and 6in naval guns as being situated all around the area where they were bivouacked. The next day, the machine-gun teams moved off with the infantry platoons. As A Section of No. 98 Company, Machine Gun Corps (33rd Division), together with 4th King's (98th Brigade, 33rd Division), reached a point some 300yds behind the Allied line, they were ordered to dig in along a ridge of high ground at the end of Mametz Valley, close to Bazentin-le-Petit Wood. Their job was to sit tight and await orders; they were to support 33rd Division, who were involved in the fighting beyond the BAZENTIN villages, in the vicinity of HIGH WOOD.

Gerald Brenan served with 48th Division, who in mid-July were involved in the battle for Bazentin Ridge. In *A Life of One's Own*, Brenan described the scene in Mametz Wood at this time:

Its trees were torn and shattered, its leaves had turned brown, and there was a shell-hole every three yards. This was a place where something almost unheard of had taken place – fierce hand-to-hand fighting in the open with bombs and bayonets. What seemed extraordinary was that all the dead bodies there lay just as they had fallen in their original places as though they were being kept as an exhibit for a war museum. German in their field-grey uniforms, British in their khaki, lying side by side, their faces and their hands a pale waxy green, the colour of rare marble. Heads covered with flat mushroom helmets next to heads in domed steel helmets that came down behind the ears. Some of these figures still sat with their bare backs against a tree and two of them – this had to be seen to be believed – stood locked together by their bayonets, which had pierced one another's bodies and sustained in that position by the tree trunk against which they had fallen.

On 16 July, 19th Brigade's transport, which had followed the infantry of 2nd Royal Welsh Fusiliers, were dismissed. Battery after battery were rolling into Mametz Valley and onto the slight rise of Caterpillar Wood, until the site was crowded not just with guns but with batteries. Whole brigades sat down en masse in a field, and they bivouacked there for several nights. The 'whole show' was in the open, guns and all.

Capt C.H. Pigg of 2nd Worcesters (100th Brigade, 33rd Division) has left a diary, in which he wrote:

Early on 16 July we reached the Bazentins, reformed and marched back a short distance to the south-eastern side of Mametz Wood, where the remnants of the Brigade reassembled and rested. Water was scarce we couldn't shave ourselves. As the day wore on the shell-fire became incessant, and presently we saw coming up the valley beside Mametz Wood a long and curious caravan containing guns. Nothing less war like could have been imagined; but the word to halt was given, the caravan deployed and, in less time than it takes to write, a battery of French 75s was in action. Their precision and speed was beautiful to watch, and equally was the skill with which they went to ground. It was the only time I saw these superb gunners in action. We sat down to tea on ammunition boxes by the track in the open. There were about a dozen officers surviving, and we had reached that last stage when bullets and shell-fire became meaningless; some part of the creature was numb, and we seemed immune to fear. On our left lay Mametz Wood, torn by shell-fire and strewn with dead of both armies; in the open there still lay some of the men who had fallen in the assault; on our right lay the main track leading up to the front, crowded with traffic of all kinds, and lined by dead mules and horses.

The brigade was busy beside us going to ground (they began to be shelled) . . . Soon after dark we had orders to move into Mametz Wood to occupy the old front line trenches on its northern face. We moved into and up the wood in single file with a bright moon filtering through the shattered trees; a few shells broke the eerie stillness. Along our path lay many Boches frightfully bloated and distorted by death . . . We reached our position along its northern edge and fixed company headquarters in a deep German dugout near a howitzer gun which they had been unable to remove. Here the enemy must have lived for many months, and, though the dugout was fairly clean, its typical Boche-stench was nauseating. But we had no greatcoats or blankets and were glad of some cover.

It was on about 17 July that Liddell Hart, moving back with 9th King's Own Yorkshire Light Infantry after relief, was passing through Mametz Wood and heard a lot of shells falling around them; these didn't explode, but then there was a strong smell of gas. Liddell Hart began to cough violently; he stayed on

Troops digging in or resting at Mametz Wood, July 1916. *(IWM Q3979)*

to warn platoons of the danger before leading his company back to battalion bivouac. On 18 July, he reported to the nearest field ambulance to get his earlier wound seen to, and on examining his chest, the doctor immediately put him on a stretcher. Liddell Hart was on his way to the King Edward VII Hospital for Officers in London.

In his book, Richards wrote that during the period 19/20 July, after being shelled at BAZENTIN-LE-PETIT, his battalion were relieved and returned to Mametz Wood. Eight of them and the brigade signalling corporal were detailed off to form a transmitting station for visual signallers between HIGH WOOD and brigade headquarters – presumably 19th Brigade – which was situated on the fringe of Mametz Wood. No telephones could be carried, so their station would receive messages by flag from the signallers with the attacking force, which they would transmit by heliograph or flag.

The position that they had to take was by a large mill on the BAZENTIN-LE-PETIT side of HIGH WOOD. It was built on rising ground, which made it a very important landmark. They fixed up the heliograph and the telescope and at 0800hrs were in communication with brigade. The enemy then started a terrific barrage and the mill seemed to be in the middle of it. One message said that the Wood

A brigadier-general and staff officers study a map in Mametz Wood, July 1916. *(IWM Q868)*

would be taken and another gave news of a counter-attack. As the signallers in the Wood were knocked out, messages later came by runners. The enemy then turned a machine gun on the mill, as the flag-waving had attracted the Germans' attention.

On 20 July, 2nd Royal Welsh Fusiliers were relieved in confusion, and held in reserve in shell-holes between the LONGUEVAL–CONTALMAISON road and Flat Iron Copse. Any exit point from Mametz Valley was a busy traffic route, and subsequently a favourite target of the German gunners. Artillery was formed up behind the Welsh battalion, and headquarters and details were under the muzzles of two batteries. Brigade was in poor quarters, a thinly roofed trench in the south-east of Mametz Wood. On 21 July, some of the battalion, even the most hard-bitten, were beginning to show signs of the strain through which they had been passing.

On 22 July, Maj Gen E.C. Ingouville-Williams, General Officer Commanding 34th Division, who had been reconnoitring the ground in the vicinity of Mametz Wood, was killed on the bank at Queen's Nullah after having walked back from CONTAL-MAISON round the south side of the Wood to meet his car. He was later buried at Warloy-Baillon Communal Cemetery and Extension (III.D.13).

Dumps stored at the south-east corner of the Wood were used to get material forward to HIGH WOOD; the Wood at this time had two shallow trenches and very insecure dugouts. All around, the guns continued almost incessantly, and along the road was an almost endless stream of transport of all kinds: water wagons, motors and horse ambulances, cyclists, and officers on horseback. Many gunners slept beside their guns during this period of the battle.

On 5 August, C.S. Collison of 11th Royal Warwicks (112th Brigade, 37th Division) went forward with a brother officer via Quadrangle Trench on the south-west side of the Wood, and into the Wood itself, to arrange for the relief of 11th Suffolks (101st Brigade, 34th Division), who were entrenched in the southern outskirts of Bazentin-le-Petit Wood, and also in the north-western section of Mametz Wood. The battalion left BÉCOURT by half platoons on the afternoon of 6 August, and established itself in its new positions, two companies being in Mametz Wood. 10th Loyal North Lancashires occupied the north-eastern border of the

Wood, while 6th Bedfords and 8th East Lancashires (all 112th Brigade, 37th Division) held the trenches to the north of BAZENTIN-LE-PETIT.

The space that divided Bazentin and MAMETZ WOODs was ploughed and furrowed by shell-fire, and in many places arms and legs were to be seen protruding from the ground. At 1930hrs on 10 July, 11th Royal Warwicks relieved 6th Bedfords in the line to the north of the village, and 10th Loyal North Lancashires took over the ground to the right, in relief of 8th East Lancashires. The British troops were now approaching the summit of the great ridge, whose southern slopes were marked by the villages of BAZENTIN-LE-PETIT, POZIÈRES and THIEPVAL.

In the evening of 14 August, 11th Royal Warwicks were relieved by 10th Lincolns (101st Brigade, 34th Division) and moved to the northern and north-western border of Mametz Wood. On relief they proceeded through the desolation, past Fricourt Farm to Bécourt Wood, where the battalion bivouacked. Collison was fortunate to get a small room to himself in Bécourt Château.

Also on 14 August, 2nd King's Royal Rifle Corps (2nd Brigade, 1st Division) were positioned in Mametz Wood as part of divisional reserve; they were frequently shelled and supplied working parties.

The southern road in Mametz Wood. *(IWM Q3978)*

Five days later, they moved off to positions north-west of HIGH WOOD. Towards the end of the month, and also briefly in early September, they were back in Mametz Wood for a short time.

W.V. Tilsley of 1/4th Loyal North Lancashires (164th Brigade, 55th Division), author of the novel *Other Ranks*, noted that on 6 September, on the way to the front line in the dusk, C Company turned into a saturated cornfield near MAMETZ. On the crest behind them there was an amazingly long naval gun, on stupendous mountings. Still further behind, in a deep basin between the ridges, a diminutive battalion of the Guards paraded. Along the road to HAPPY VALLEY wormed a toylike procession of transports.

On 10 September, 149th Brigade (50th Division) were involved in fighting here. At 0725hrs on 11 September, Brig Gen H.F.H. Clifford DSO, General Officer Commanding 149th Brigade (50th Division), who had only been in command of 149th Brigade for a few hours, was killed by a sniper when checking the new assembly trenches, accompanied by a staff captain; Lt Col C. Turner, Commanding Officer 1/5th Northumberland Fusiliers (149th Brigade, 50th Division), took over command of 149th Brigade. Clifford was buried in Albert Communal Cemetery Extension (I.L.1) 2 days later.

In *Into Battle*, John Glubb of No. 7 Field Company, Royal Engineers (50th Division), wrote that he

marched with the sappers to some dugouts behind Mametz Wood for the attack on HIGH WOOD, which was to begin at 0620hrs on 15 September. The cavalry were stationed at BÉCOURT and long streams of troops and wagons poured up the MAMETZ road. He first saw tanks at this time, having had no prior knowledge of them. Also on 15 September, the sappers left with their forage carts at 0600hrs to mend the road from BAZENTIN-LE-PETIT to HIGH WOOD, as soon as the latter was taken. Glubb had to spend the day in Mametz Wood in case messages came in for company headquarters. The sappers were not disturbed for the first few hours, as the German guns were concentrated on the infantry instead.

Just before the 15 September attack, 47th Division were up near the line by Flat Iron Copse, and the ground was 'alive' with field guns, many of them hidden by the roadside and startling the unwary. 5th (London) Field Ambulance (47th Division) were set up at the Copse alongside the New Zealand and 2/3rd (Northumberland) Field Ambulances (50th Division).

On 15 September, 142nd Brigade (47th Division) lay in reserve around Mametz Wood, ready to move forward to BAZENTIN-LE-GRAND, where they would be in support to the attacking brigade.

On 2 October, 18th King's Royal Rifle Corps (122nd Brigade, 41st Division) were in the Wood for one night, and on 12 October were at Mametz Wood Camp. Around 7 October, 11th Royal West Kents (also 122nd Brigade, 41st Division) left bivouacs near the Wood and entrained at the local siding, which the Royal Engineers had built.

In mid-October, the enemy began to night-bomb, which was another disturbing element to add to the artillery shelling. The Allied guns were still very much in evidence in the area of the Wood and in Mametz Valley. Towards the end of October, 151st Brigade (50th Division) were in the Wood as divisional reserve. At the end of November, after the battle had 'officially finished', the work of repairs and consolidation was still to be done, as well as that necessary for a winter stay for the infantry. In addition, plank roads were built in Mametz Wood.

Originally, 7th Division erected a memorial in MAMETZ village and 14th and 16th Royal Welsh Fusiliers erected memorials in the Wood to commemorate their involvement. 38th Division, with whose name the Wood will be always most associated, captured the Wood again after the German breakthrough in the spring of 1918.

Flat Iron Copse Cemetery, designed by Sir Herbert Baker, is at the southern end of the Copse, north-east of Mametz Wood. On 14 July, elements of 3rd and 7th Divisions cleared the ground and an advanced dressing station was established; begun on about 20 July, it remained in use until April 1917. One Victoria Cross-winner, and two lieutenant-colonels who died on the same day are among those buried here. Cpl E. Dwyer (III.J.3) of 1st East Surreys (95th Brigade, 5th Division) won his medal at Hill 60 in Belgium on 20 April 1915. Lt Col A.P. Hamilton MC (VII.I.2), attached 1/19th Londons (141st Brigade, 47th Division) was killed on 15 September 1916; finding 'congestion in communication trenches . . . he climbed out of the trench to lead the attack and was killed almost at once . . .' Lt Col J. Mortimer (IV.J.5) of 1/5th Yorkshires, attached Machine Gun Corps, was also killed on 15 September.

Two sets of brothers are also buried here: Lt A. Tregaskis (VI.G.1) and Lt L. Tregaskis (VI.G.2), both of 16th Welsh (115th Brigade, 38th Division) as well as L/Cpl H. Hardwidge (VIII.F.5) and Cpl T. Hardwidge (VIII.F.6), both of 15th Welsh (114th Brigade, 38th Division). Also buried here is Maj G. Parnell (VII.H.2) of 1st Queen's (100th Brigade, 33rd Division), a son of the 3rd Baron Congleton, killed in action near MARTINPUICH on 15 July 1916. Only one named man is buried here who died prior to the battle, a private of 1/4th Suffolks (98th Brigade, 33rd Division)who died on 19 January 1916.

After the Armistice, 1,149 graves were brought in from smaller cemeteries in the neighbouring battle-field. These former cemeteries included Caterpillar Cemetery, MONTAUBAN-DE-PICARDIE; Cross Roads Cemetery, BAZENTIN; Mametz Wood Cemetery, which had been on the western outskirts of the Wood; Quadrangle Cemetery, between BOTTOM WOOD and Mametz Wood; Valley Cemetery between the MONTAUBAN-DE-PICARDIE brickworks and MALTZ HORN FARM; and Villa Wood Cemeteries, close to a small copse north of Mametz Wood.

Today, the Wood has very much the same outward shape of 1915; the only signs of life at the southern edge over the open ground that the Welshmen had to attack are the quietly chewing cows. The Wood is pretty dense, although one can easily retrace the rides that were such a feature of the fighting and discover equipment and former elephant-hutting shelters.

After several years of fundraising and preparation, a new memorial to the memory of troops of 38th Division was sited opposite the Hammerhead, in front of the Wood. It was dedicated during the afternoon of 11 July 1987 in the presence of several veterans of the action and men from the Royal Regiment of Wales, together with 500 people from Wales, England and France. Welsh hymns were sung and prayers were said in all three languages. The band of 1st Royal Regiment of Wales also took part, together with the regimental goat. BBC Wales filmed the whole proceedings. The memorial is in the form of a large red dragon and stands on a high bluff overlooking DEATH VALLEY, pointing in the direction of the Hammerhead. In recent years the memorial has needed considerable maintenance. The dragon has been repainted and replacement steps have been installed from the roadway to the memorial; the road to the memorial has also been resurfaced. It is intended to hold a major centenary ceremony here on 7 July 2016.

Although L/Cpl H. Fellows of 12th Northumberland Fusiliers (62nd Brigade, 21st Division) was never involved in the fighting in the Wood, he was involved in the clearing up later. Permission was granted by the owner of the Wood for his ashes to be placed there after his death in September 1987, together with a memorial stone inscribed with one of his poems. During the 1980s, Fellows had been a regular visitor to the annual service at Lochnagar Crater, when he was often invited to read from his own poetry.

MAPLE REDOUBT was behind the British lines, due south of BOIS FRANÇAIS trenches at FRICOURT and adjacent to the track that led to the rear of Point 71 South. The Redoubt was a strongpoint and aid post which had been built in case the enemy attacked the British Front Line and pierced it. In such an eventuality, the Redoubt was to be held at all costs and to the last man, even if the Germans were to get right past and down the hill towards BRAY-SUR-SOMME. There was a dugout there, provisioned with enough bully beef and water in petrol cans for such an emergency. There was also a certain amount of barbed wire, which was erected to the east and north-west of the position, supported by two Lewis guns. There was another store of provisions at Point 71 North.

The main source of information on life behind the British lines south of FRICOURT in the late winter and spring of 1916 is Bernard Adams of 1st Royal Welsh Fusiliers (22nd Brigade, 7th Division) in his book *Nothing of Importance*. In February, he wrote: 'We are in support in a place called Maple Redoubt, on the reverse slope of a big ridge. Good dug-outs, and a view behind, over a big expanse of chalk downs, which is most exhilarating. A day of blue sky and a tingle of frost. Being on the reverse slope, you can walk about anywhere, and so can see everything.' On another occasion in early February

he wrote that 'I sat up in "the fort" most of the day, watching the bombardment'. Adams wrote that there was a small quarry on the 100-metre contour line and 'there was a disused support trench running west from the Quarry . . . It ran just along the crest of the hill, and commanded even a better view of Fricourt than the Quarry itself.'

Another writer who was in the same area was Siegfried Sassoon of 1st Royal Welsh Fusiliers (19th Brigade, 33rd Division), who often refers to these same redoubts and trenches in his autobiography and diary. In his *Memoirs of an Infantry Officer*, he mentions going up the line and using Canterbury Trench, and passing the dugouts of the support company of 1st Royal Welsh Fusiliers at Maple Redoubt on his way to the company headquarters dugouts.

On 1 July, the battalions in the area were 20th Manchesters (22nd Brigade, 7th Division) and 1st Royal Welsh Fusiliers; FRICOURT village, which had been overlooked for so long by the British, was evacuated by the Germans during the night of 1/2 July. Sassoon mentions that he talked to men of 7th Division on 12 July and also saw the French 75s at Maple Redoubt. On 13 July, he noted that he was reading novels of Thomas Hardy such as *Tess of the d'Urbervilles* and *The Return of the Native*.

MARICOURT is situated on the D938 ALBERT–PÉRONNE road, south of MONTAUBAN-DE-PICARDIE and east of CARNOY. The village was just behind the Allied front line and marked the junction of the British and French forces. On 2 August 1915, units from 5th Division arrived in the area and during much of August the village was regularly shelled by the German artillery. In the third week of October, 6th Royal Berkshires (53rd Brigade, 18th Division) were billeted at BUIRE-SUR-L'ANCRE, when their men enjoyed the film shows in the 'cinema' at Maricourt, which was visited daily by 150 men from 18th Division.

By the end of November, Maricourt was already a 'ruined village' and had a collecting post in the village high street, run by a field ambulance that could hold 16 stretcher cases. When 2nd Royal Inniskilling Fusiliers (14th Brigade, 5th Division) were in trenches near here in early December, their company headquarters, together with a supporting company, was stationed in Maricourt. Much work had to be carried out on the front trenches during the month, as they were in a very bad state owing to the weather; everywhere, trenches were collapsing and needed revetting.

At one point, 12th Glosters (95th Brigade, 5th Division), who had just arrived in France, were attached to 2nd Royal Inniskilling Fusiliers for trench instruction. On 8 December, 2nd Royal Inniskilling Fusiliers withdrew from the front trenches to billets in Maricourt for 4 days; during this time, the batttalion supplied a working party of 300 men to No. 184 Tunnelling Company, Royal Engineers, for 'conducting operations in the vicinity of Maricourt'. After another spell in the line, the battalion were back in support in Maricourt and again supplied working parties for mining operations. Towards the end of December, 2nd Royal Inniskilling Fusiliers were one of the battalions transferred to 96th Brigade (32nd Division).

When still part of 14th Brigade (5th Division), 15th Royal Warwicks moved up to Maricourt from SUZANNE; 5th Division were holding the right of the line adjacent to the French. There was no fighting during this period, but the crossroads was sometimes targeted by 'whizz bangs', often when a relief was in progress or when transport was using it. When not in trenches here, 15th Royal Warwicks spent time in billets in SUZANNE.

In 1916, there were three aid posts in the village, including two on the PÉRONNE road in the cellars of the brewery, which was heavily sandbagged. A third was ¼ mile distant.

Throughout the first half of 1916, Maricourt was the centre of an important salient on the right of the British line and was home to 16th and 17th Manchesters, with 18th Manchesters sometimes in the area (all 90th Brigade, 30th Division). When 30th Division relieved 5th Division on 10 January, 15th Royal Warwicks were relieved by 16th Manchesters, whose battalion history noted that they had arrived here on 5 January 1916, at the beginning of what was to become a long period of association. Three days were spent in the line and two in the village itself, before they were relieved by 17th Manchesters on 12 January, when they left for SUZANNE.

In early 1916 the village was described as follows:

The straggling village of Maricourt, with its château, its brewery, its battered cottages, and orchards and farm courtyards was sheltered by Maricourt Wood, and had a defence system of its own, making it a 'point d'appui' in case the front line should go. It was the centre of an important salient that formed the extreme right of the British front. On the right the 18th Manchesters held posts on the Somme Marshes and at Fargny Mill, facing the Chapeau de Gendarme . . . The wood resounded with the crash of trees and the incessant shriek and whistle overhead . . . The Sixteenth's Headquarters took up battle positions in the wood.

16th Manchesters were in the Maricourt–SUZANNE area off and on until 17 March, when they were relieved by 7th Buffs (55th Brigade, 18th Division) and marched to BRAY-SUR-SOMME. By now the trenches were again in a wretched condition and the weather was very cold.

The historian of 17th Manchesters wrote that two communication trenches ran from the village to the front line, 'one from the north end of the main street through Maricourt Wood, past Headquarters' dug-out and dressing station to "Piccadilly Circus", where it divided, the left branch leading to one company front along the edge of the Wood, the right branch to another company just outside the Wood. The second communication trench roughly followed the Péronne road to a third company.'

Battalion headquarters were in dugouts in the SUZANNE–Maricourt valley, where a long communication trench, known as Fargny Wood Avenue, led up to the right of the position. 'Battalion snipers using telescopic sights were successful in targeting any movement in Curlu'; a steep, ladder-like cut 'led down to the level of the Somme and from thence a track ran to Fargny Mill'. It was in full view of a German bombing post at le Chapeau de Gendarme (see entry for FARGNY MILL).

On 1 June, 17th Manchesters were relieved by 1st Battalion, the French 37th Infantry Regiment, and the line between the two armies then became 'a line running approximately north and south through the centre of Maricourt village'; in other words, the French had the eastern section.

Southwards of the British and the French lines were several copses, which gave shelter to batteries. A XIII Corps advanced dressing station was established here at the beginning of the battle on the road between the village and BRAY-SUR-SOMME. At the end of June, assembly trenches were in front of Oxford Copse in a hollow. Both Oxford and CAMBRIDGE COPSEs were south of the Maricourt–CARNOY road, to the west of the last-named village.

The objective for 30th Division was to be MONTAUBAN-DE-PICARDIE. Machine Gun Wood was to the north-west of the village, just behind the 1 July front line. At Zero Hour on 1 July, 27th Brigade and the South African Brigade (both 9th Division) were at BRAY-SUR-SOMME and 26th Brigade at CHIPILLY. The French 39th Infantry Regiment were based at the Old Brewery and the château was home to an 89th Brigade reserve dump. The château also received rations and a water supply. Water tanks were kept in the château redoubt, and the village church was used as a dump for heavy trench mortar ammunition.

One observer of the situation in this area before the battle began was Lt R.B. Talbot Kelly of LII Brigade, Royal Field Artillery (9th Division), who was busy taking up supplies of ammunition to the spur behind Maricourt, where battle positions were being prepared. Because of the closeness of the British and French lines, the two armies shared many tracks and roads, and the French used some of the 1870 mortar guns. Talbot Kelly was busy for 2 or 3 days, helping to prepare a more advanced position in the British second-line trenches and helping to register the guns from an observation post in the hedge in front of the village.

On 23 June, the British artillery had begun to cut the wire in front of Glatz Redoubt, which was south-west of the Brickworks outside MONTAUBAN-DE-PICARDIE. The British guns fell steeply away on the right into Suzanne Valley; across the valley, there were four lines of French batteries, firing at right angles to the British line. At 0500hrs on 1 July, Talbot Kelly set out through a white mist for the observation post in Maricourt. In front of him on the left stretched a little valley by a small, battered coppice, on the edge of which he could just pick out the uneasy twistings of the British front-line trench.

Maricourt Ridge contained masses of artillery, heavy and field, partly because it was a reverse slope towards the enemy. There was also excellent observation from the Ridge towards the MONTAUBAN-DE-PICARDIE–MAMETZ road. 30th Division set off towards MONTAUBAN-DE-PICARDIE and readers are referred to that entry for further details of the action; 19th King's (89th Brigade, 30th Division) were in reserve in the north-west corner of the village. The battle went well, and after lunch Talbot Kelly, together with his major and two signallers, walked across the battlefield towards MONTAUBAN-DE-PICARDIE, the divisional objective.

During the attack towards MONTAUBAN-DE-PICARDIE, G.D. Fairley, medical officer of 2nd Royal Scots Fusiliers (90th Brigade, 30th Division), was wounded in the right arm. Although he fainted and was far from well, he carried on attending both British and German casualties before being evacuated to hospital himself. In his account of the battle, held in the Peter Liddle collection at Leeds, Fairley described the German prisoners as being either young or towards middle age.

John Masefield noted that in modern war, wet weather favours defence, as so much depends on the roads being hard enough to bear the advancing cannon in order to secure a conquered strip. The success between OVILLERS and Maricourt had made it necessary to advance the British guns along a front of 6 miles, which meant that the British had to put on little country roads a great traffic of horse, gun, caissons and mechanical transport. When the weather broke, as it broke on 4 July, the holes and trenches that had been filled in became canals and pools, and the surface of the earth 'a rottenness'.

The *Official History of the War* describes the situation at Maricourt Salient as being 'embarrassingly congested' with both French and British troops. In *We Band of Brothers*, G.W. Warwick of 4th South African Infantry (South African Brigade, 9th Division) noted that on 5 July his unit marched to the old German trenches opposite Maricourt. He was involved in digging new trenches under machine-gun fire at Glatz Redoubt. They camped at MONTAUBAN-DE-PICARDIE. During this time, Warwick was wounded and was taken by a small motor ambulance to the Maricourt dressing station.

On 8 July, the much-loved Lt Col E.H. Trotter, Commanding Officer 18th King's (21st Brigade, 30th Division) was killed at 21st Brigade headquarters at Train Alley to the west of Glatz Redoubt, south-west of MONTAUBAN-DE-PICARDIE, as was Lt Col W.A. Smith, Commanding Officer 18th Manchesters (90th Brigade, 30th Division). A shell had hit 21st Brigade headquarters. Trotter was buried at Péronne Road Cemetery, Maricourt (IV.H.28); Smith, who died the following day, was buried in Corbie Communal Cemetery Extension (I.C.59).

In the *Official History of the War*, it is noted that on 18 July the French were allotted a larger area behind the battlefront, which resulted in moving some of the British headquarters and reserve communications positions. The new boundary line gave the whole of Maricourt to the French; it passed to the north of the BRONFAY FARM–Maricourt road but did not include the BRAY-SUR-SOMME–FRICOURT road at a point 1¼ miles north of BRAY-SUR-SOMME. At that time, Fourth Army had a right of passage for up to 150 lorries per day from Maricourt to BRAY-SUR-SOMME via BRONFAY FARM.

On 19 July there was a constant stream of casualties coming into the village from the direction of LONGUEVAL and DELVILLE WOOD. They were later entrained for ABBEVILLE at MÉAULTE.

Brigade HQ was often situated at Stanley's Hole, described by one observer as an evil-smelling dugout, about 400yds south-west of Maricourt. In *Memoirs of the Great War*, H.M. Davson, who was with the artillery of 35th Division, described how he had moved his artillery brigade into action between Maricourt and TRÔNES WOOD. He had his headquarters in an old French trench close to Oxford Copse, with one battery in the château grounds and another further in advance. On 30 July, he was forced to move his brigade position, owing to communication problems; the enemy had simply become too accurate with their shelling.

In *Johnny Get Your Gun*, J.F. Tucker of 1/13th Londons (168th Brigade, 56th Division) noted that on 10 August he marched a short distance to a camp of Nissen huts at either FRICOURT or Maricourt siding. This camp was at the edge of a plateau, with a main road that ran past at the bottom of a cliff-like bank. Tucker's unit spent some time in the huts, and on the next afternoon moved off and crossed a road; they entered what appeared to be a valley or large quarry, where they dumped their packs and overcoats and changed into 'battle order'. They were to relieve 7th Royal Irish Fusiliers (49th Brigade, 16th Division) in trenches close to FAFFEMONT FARM and LEUZE WOOD. Tucker described the landscape from there onwards for about 7 miles as being entirely bare and devasted, with no greenery, and covered with shell-holes that merged one with another.

On 11 August, 1st King's Royal Rifle Corps (99th Brigade, 2nd Division) were here, having journeyed from BRONFAY FARM. On 12 August, Capt Gilmore of No. 32 Squadron, Royal Flying Corps, flying a DH2 fighter, was forced down at Oxford Copse, on the same day as another pilot from the same squadron fell to earth at CONTALMAISON.

At the beginning of September Maricourt was bristling with French batteries of all sizes. On 15 September, the journalist C.E. Montague made one of his front-line visits, visiting a point between Maricourt and HARDECOURT-AU-BOIS to the north-east, close to Nameless Copse. Setting out in moonlight at 0500hrs, he mentioned seeing the cavalry with their lances against the dawn twilight in fields beside the road. They were waiting to be used in the 'breakthrough' planned for that day.

On 24 September, 1/16th Londons (169th Brigade, 56th Division) went into divisional reserve in Casement Trench, just north of Maricourt. Aubrey Smith of 1/5th Londons (169th Brigade, 56th Division) was involved in the attack when elements of 56th Division stormed BOULEUX WOOD; they had to wait for a couple of minutes while the 15in railway gun at Maricourt prepared to fire.

Péronne Road Cemetery, which at one time was called Maricourt Military Cemetery No. 3, is on the north side of the road to ALBERT, on the western outskirts of the village. Begun by fighting units and field ambulances in 1916, it was used until August 1917 and was completed after the Armistice by the concentration of 1,146 graves from the battlefields in the neighbourhood. It stands above the level of the road, looking over the valley towards the River Somme. Burial grounds that were concentrated here include Authuille Communal Cemetery Extension; Briqueterie East Cemetery, MONTAUBAN-DE-PICARDIE; Carnoy Communal Cemetery Extension; Casement Trench Cemetery, Maricourt; Fargny Mill French Military Cemetery, CURLU; la Cote Military Cemetery, Maricourt; Maricourt French Military Cemetery; Montauban Road French Military Cemetery; and Talus Boisé British Cemetery, CARNOY.

Lt Col E.H. Trotter DSO (IV.H.28), attached 18th King's (21st Brigade, 30th Division), was killed in action on 8 July. Also buried here is Lt Col W. Anderson (II.G.36), who won his Victoria Cross at FAVIÈRE WOOD on 25 March 1918. Lt T. Rouse-Boughton-Knight, a brother of Sir William, is also buried here (III.G.34). He was killed in action at Frosty Trench, LESBŒUFS, on 18 October 1916.

After the war, Blackburn helped Maricourt and PÉRONNE with their reconstruction and presented them with a threshing and baling machine named Blackburn.

MARIEUX, which boasts a very grand château and which has a large wood to the north-east, is on the D11 road between PUCHEVILLERS and THIÈVRES. In July 1915, VII Corps had its headquarters here; Lt Gen Sir Thomas d'Oyly Snow, previously of 27th Division (IWM 76/79/1) arrived here on 22 July and in time found it 'very snug'. He observed that farming in the area was still being carried on, with women, children and a few old men succeeding well in doing the job. Of the postal service, he noted that if mail left the village before 0830hrs, it would reach London by first post the following day. He also mentioned the Royal Flying Corps as being close by.

At around the same time, 1/4th Royal Berkshires (14th Brigade, 48th Division) were billeted in a great wood here and 'the ground was littered with empty petrol tins, the legacy of the French aerodrome, below in the orchard two batteries of long French 155s were packing up; an enormous house close by, called Mon Plaisir', was used by VII Corps as a headquarters. 1/1st Buckinghamshires (also 14th Brigade, 48th Division) were also in bivouacs in July. It would appear that the château at Marieux was not called Mon Plaisir, as Montplaiser was further south-west, close to a track that went towards BEAUQUESNE. The château, built in 1777, is just off the main road; behind it are the church and school.

Lt Gen Sir A.G. Hunter-Weston, General Officer Commanding VIII Corps, and staff officers at Marieux, 24 June 1916. *(IWM Q736)*

On one of his several visits to the Western Front, HM the King came to VII Corps headquarters on 25 October 1915 and gave a lunch party.

In April 1916, VIII Corps, commanded by Lt Gen Sir A.G. Hunter-Weston, replaced VII Corps; it, too, had its headquarters in the château. On 9 August, HM the King and his equerry, Lord Stamfordham, visited the château a second time, when it was XIV Corps headquarters. Lt Gen the Earl of Cavan, General Officer Commanding XIV Corps, came from Vauchelles to lunch, and the King presented him with the Star of St Patrick.

From 27 March, No. 15 Squadron, Royal Flying Corps, commanded by Maj H. le M. Brock, were based in the village and flew Bristol Scouts; on 1 April, they were attached to VIII Corps. On 18 July, the Canadian, and future ace, William George Barker joined the squadron here, having already scored the first of what were to become 57 victories. On 12 August, No. 15 Squadron, together with No. 4 Squadron, were inspected by HM the King and HRH the Prince of Wales. The latter was a frequent visitor to the squadron while they were based at Marieux.

In early October, 19th Division were in the area and 37th Division had its divisional headquarters here at the end of November.

MARLBOROUGH WOOD is a small copse to the north-west of MONTAUBAN-DE-PICARDIE, due south of Bazentin-le-Grand Wood. During the period 4/5 July 1916 it was in the line of 18th Division, who were attacking between MONTAUBAN-DE-PICARDIE on the right and MAMETZ village on the left. Parties of 18th Division occupied the Wood unopposed, and it was used as an advanced post in the attacks towards MAMETZ WOOD. On 9 July two machine guns were placed here, and two more in Caterpillar Wood; together, they were able to sweep the ground to the north-west between the Wood and the German Second Line.

MARTINPUICH, a strongly fortified village in the German defences, lies south-west of LE SARS, west of FLERS and north-west of HIGH WOOD. According to H.P. Robinson, war correspondent of *The Times*, in his book *The Turning Point*, Martinpuich was the hinge and key of the whole German front. Trenches in front or south of the village included Hook Trench to the right, the Tangles trenches and Bottom Trench.

In early September 1916, the new British line was just beyond the crest of the rising ground south of Martinpuich, which was the next objective. The jumping-off trenches included such names as Bacon, Ham, Egg and Liver. Martinpuich was the centre of the German line beyond which the ground sloped; 15 September was the date chosen for the attack, the same date that HIGH WOOD and FLERS were to be taken.

To the south-east of the village, 50th Brigade (17th Division) had 45th and 46th Brigades (both 15th Division) on their right. The attacking force was to be assisted by the presence of four tanks, two for each division. The outskirts of the village were quickly taken in the morning of 15 September, and the following trenches rapidly fell into British hands: Cutting, Tangle South, Tangle and Gun Pit. A line of posts was quickly established to the north of Gun Pit Trench, west of the Martinpuich–EAUCOURT L'ABBAYE road, and a further chain of posts was established eastwards of Gun Pit Trench.

The capture of Martinpuich had, nevertheless, been more difficult than this swift progress makes it appear, as the village was full of dugouts manned by Bavarian troops. The four tanks diverged right and left in pairs. The pair to the right reached as far as a dump near Starfish Line, to the north-east of the village, towards Prue Trench. The Michelin battlefield guide notes that the tanks crashed down the walls of the village, which had still been standing and behind which were hidden machine guns. Geoffrey Malins, the official War Office photographer, filmed the advancing tanks from a position opposite Martinpuich. He was a witness to 13th Royal Scots' (45th Brigade, 15th Division) progress through the village towards Prue Trench.

In *And All for What?* D.W.J. Cuddeford of 12th Highland Light Infantry (46th Brigade, 15th Division) noted that on 14 September he was in charge of making a bomb base at the head of a communication trench called Highland Alley; brigade headquarters dugout was at CONTAL-MAISON. The communication trenches used from there to Martinpuich were Gordon Alley and Highland Alley. Cuddeford said that 7th/8th King's Own Scottish Borderers were to the right and 10th Cameronians were to the left, with 10th/11th Highland Light Infantry in support (all 46th Brigade, 15th Division).

Cuddeford also mentioned that he heard two tanks clanking up in the small hours of 15 September. Once the front German positions had been carried, it was possible to establish a forward ammunition dump in an enemy position in Bacon Trench while the attack was pushed on, into and through the village. Cuddeford saw many dead Germans in the part of Factory Lane where it crossed the sunken road leading to the village. They had presumably been 'caught' by the British artillery. Cuddeford later joined C Company, 12th Highland Light Infantry (46th Brigade, 15th Division) after his task had been completed.

At 1350hrs, according to the *Official History of the War*, 150th Brigade (50th Division) had been ordered to push patrols into the northern end of Martinpuich so as to link up with 15th Division, who were already in possession. At 1500hrs, 6th Cameron Highlanders (45th Brigade, 15th Division) had advanced, driving the enemy from the north-east sector of the village. Forward troops of 46th Brigade took over the remaining ruins of the village, which had been virtually flattened before the battle began. German prisoners, a field battery and a 5.9in howitzer were captured.

Cuddeford noted that at about 0200hrs on 16 September, while the village was under continuous German shelling, he started off with half a company to take over a section of Gun Pit Trench. A little to the right, just where the road cleared Martinpuich, was a temporary causeway that had been constructed by the enemy for their artillery and wheeled traffic crossing the road from bank to bank; the German artillery shelled and destroyed it. Relieved by 8th/10th Gordon Highlanders (44th Brigade, 15th Division), 12th Highland Light Infantry went back to old German dugouts near to Villa Wood on Old German Trench One.

In *Memoirs of a Camp Follower*, Philip Gosse of 69th Field Ambulance (23rd Division) wrote of the news of the discovery of 'an excellent German dug-out for an advanced dressing station'. On 24 September, Gosse and his colonel were standing outside the dugout 'while a party of men were clearing a space for our motor ambulances to turn in. Suddenly a salvo of shrapnel burst just over our heads and we all rushed to take cover. When I turned round I found the Colonel lying on the ground dead, killed by a bullet which had passed through his steel helmet into his brain . . .' (See entry for CONTAL-MAISON.)

At around this time, C.E. Montague, the writer and journalist, visited Martinpuich. He reported that there were many dead on the ridge, and more Germans in the sunken lane under trees. As a result, there were millions of flies swarming around; the bodies had blackened faces with open, staring eyes.

Later in the year, a 16lb Decauville tramway was put into working order from the village to PEAKE WOODS. Sidings were built and a regular service operated, and the petrol locomotive was able to run right up to Gun Pit Road. The rail track was also chalk-ballasted, and provision was made for pedestrian troops.

Martinpuich was lost to the Germans in April 1918 and retaken in August by troops from V Corps.

Martinpuich Communal Cemetery is on the south side of the village and contains the graves of five men from the United Kingdom who fell during September–November 1916. Martinpuich British Cemetery, also on the south side, was begun in November and was used by fighting units and field ambulances until June 1917, and again at the end of August 1918.

The school playground in the village was designed and presented as a living memorial by 47th Division, who took HIGH WOOD on 15 September. The playground, which had a memorial gateway, was handed over to the village on 13 September 1925 after being unveiled by Lt Gen Sir George Gorringe. During excavations for the gate, the foundations revealed old cellars that needed to be filled in, as well as an unexploded bomb and other wartime detritus. After the official ceremonies, the officers and other ranks were invited to the *mairie* for light refreshments before returning home via AMIENS. In 2008 it was realised that the substantial memorial was in need of restoration and an appeal fund was launched, but contributions were slow in coming in. In the end the CWGC stepped in and carried out restoration work on the wall and at the same time replaced the roof of the loggia. The work was scheduled to be carried out in time for a service of rededication held on 22 September 2013.

When the memorial to 47th Division at HIGH WOOD was rebuilt in 1996, the sum of £5,271 was also raised to restore the division's memorial at Martinpuich school.

In 1935 the *Ypres Times* mentioned that the village still had rows of filled-in dugouts, clearly visible in the bank of the sunken road as one dropped down from the direction of COURCELETTE.

MARTINSART is a village on the D129 road between Aveluy to the south-east and ENGLE-BELMER to the north-west; AVELUY WOOD is between the village and the valley of the Ancre. The first British unit to arrive in the village were 12th Field Ambulance (4th Division), who arrived on 21 July 1915. Nine days later troops from 1/5th Seaforth Highlanders (152nd Brigade, 51st Division) arrived in Martinsart, already a battered village, from PONT-NOYELLES; they were the first Scottish troops to

be seen here, when they took over part of the lines at AUTHUILLE from the French 116th Infantry Regiment, who had been here for some time. The château in the village was commandeered from very early on and VII Corps had its headquarters there on 1 August.

On 11 December, 1/6th Seaforth Highlanders (also 152nd Brigade, 51st Division) arrived in the village, although some platoons had camped here earlier when involved in training 16th Highland Light Infantry (97th Brigade, 32nd Division) in trench warfare techniques in front of THIEPVAL. Although they were in billets, enemy shelling caused the deaths of one man and the wounding of 13 others while they were asleep. They spent the next 5 days in fatigues before moving up to the AVELUY WOOD sector, where they relieved part of 154th Brigade (51st Division).

On 12 December, 15th Highland Light Infantry (97th Brigade, 32nd Division) arrived here and camped in 'bell tents planted in a sea of mud'; the tents had probably been pitched in the summer, but successive battalions had made use of them and had churned the ground into a quagmire. Fifteen muddy men slept in a muddy tent. The men never won the battle against the poor conditions at this time, but sometimes they were able to visit 'the excellent bathhouses' in SENLIS-LE-SEC, to the south-west.

On 12 February, when the village still had plenty of civilians living in it, 1/6th and 1/8th West Yorkshires (both 146th Brigade, 49th Division) arrived here from AILLY-SUR-SOMME and took over the front trenches from units of 32nd Division; 1/5 and 1/7th West Yorkshires (both 146th Brigade, 49th Division) were in reserve. Their lines ran east of Thiepval Wood.

During the spring of 1916, as battle preparations grew, the village became increasingly crowded, and sometimes there were thousands of troops milling about the streets. Strangely, the village was rarely shelled at this time. Early in March, 36th Division extended their front, with their 109th Brigade taking over responsibility of the area to the south of the River Ancre known by the name of Thiepval Wood. They were also responsible for a field ambulance here. The advanced dressing station was based in a small house at the junction of the Martinsart–ENGLEBELMER road in the centre of the village. Martinsart's own wood is on the south-western and western side of the village.

In his history of 36th Division, Cyril Falls tells us of Martinsart: 'It was possible to call on Brigade Headquarters at their château as one returned from the trenches, and drink a cup of tea poured out by the daughter of the house, who rang for a British orderly to bring hot water . . .' At the beginning of June the divisional front was held by 107th Brigade, with 108th Brigade at Martinsart in support while 109th Brigade were engaged in training at CLAIRFAYE FARM. The border with 32nd Division ran through the lower portion of AVELUY WOOD to the northeast of Thiepval Wood, towards MOUQUET FARM. Behind 36th Division were 49th Division.

A light railway ran from ALBERT to the east of the village, along the side of AVELUY WOOD, which linked up with Mesnil and AUCHONVILLERS. The track known as Northumberland Avenue linked the railway to BOUZINCOURT to the south-west.

On 27 June, due to the postponement of the battle, troops of 36th Division were billeted in huts in Martinsart Wood. According to one witness, the huts at that time trembled and creaked as a result of the terrific roar of siege howitzers that fired close by, day and night. The Wood was to be used by troops for the remainder of the Battle of the Somme.

Prior to the battle, an advanced dressing station had been set up close to the main ALBERT–Arras road in AVELUY WOOD. The motors for the field ambulance were lined up to the south of the village on the Martinsart–ALBERT road. The walking wounded were to be catered for by a 'collecting station west of Martinsart, whence horsed wagons carried them by cross-country track through Hédauville to Clairfaye'.

On 30 June, 1/6th West Yorkshires left VARENNES for Martinsart, when special tracks had been marked out from HÉDAUVILLE; these had been allotted to each unit moving into battle. Every 500yds there was a lamp with a different colour, and 1/6th West Yorkshires' colour was green. This way, parallel columns of marching men moved up towards THIEPVAL, as the roads were reserved for motor traffic and artillery, and crammed with limbers and wagons. Reaching the village, the green lights led the battalion into AVELUY WOOD and white tapes on trees indicated the route to their assembly trenches.

After 36th Division's heroic attempts to capture and hold on to ground at THIEPVAL, the remaining exhausted troops returned to Martinsart on 2 July and 'they flung themselves down to sleep'. In 2 days, 5,500 officers and men had become casualties and the Ulster region was thrown into mourning.

After the failed attempts to capture THIEPVAL, 1/6th West Yorkshires were billeted in empty houses in the village. On 11 July, 1/4th York & Lancasters (148th Brigade, 49th Division) were in huts in the Wood; they too remarked on the howitzers that were in their midst, which were called 'Lucky Jims'. The guns kept them awake and blew out their candles.

In early October, when a battalion of the Sherwood Foresters were in the Wood, they had to put up with a plague of rats, which at the time were becoming more and more numerous. In mid-October, at least, there was a camp on the reverse slope of the spur which runs north from the village. A week earlier, Edmund Blunden of 11th Royal Sussex (116th Brigade, 39th Division) mentions in his book *Undertones of War* that his unit made a circuit through Englebelmer Wood and Martinsart Wood on their way up to the HAMEL trenches; he too remarked on the howitzers, the mud and the 'confusion' of hutments, and added a poetical touch when he wrote 'and yet its sylvan genius lingering in one or two steep thorny thickets'. 11th Royal Sussex crossed the NAB sunken road on their way to positions. Blunden was very aware of the changing seasons, and after the war he was continually reminded of the Somme battle as the period between August and November came around each year. His division had their headquarters here after the November Ancre battles.

Martinsart British Cemetery is on the south of the village, beside the road to Aveluy. It was begun with Row A at the end of June 1916, when 14 men of 13th Royal Irish Rifles (108th Brigade, 36th Division) were killed by a shell close to the church on 28 June, including a company sergeant-major and a sergeant-major. Cyril Falls tells the tragic story:

On the evening of the 28th, 'Y' day, the battalion was relieving the 11th Rifles in Thiepval wood, and marching out of Martinsart by platoons at two hundred yards' interval. As number 11 Platoon and battalion headquarters were about to march out together a shell fell right in the midst of the party. Fourteen were killed on the spot, and ten more died later. Almost all the rest were wounded, including second-in-command Major R.P. Maxwell . . .

On the wall of the mairie opposite the chapel is a plaque (July 2007) commemorating this tragedy.

Five days later two officers, also from the Royal Irish Rifles, were killed and later buried here, 2/Lt C.F. Craig (I.A.2) of 10th Royal Irish Rifles and 2/Lt D.B. Corbett (I.A.2) of 17th Royal Irish Rifles.

In *The Road to the Somme*, Philip Orr wrote:

With a total of almost sixty casualties, the confusion in the darkness was grim. A group of the South Antrim men took charge of the clearing-up operations. As dawn broke, Tommy Russell could see the ghastly debris of the tragedy, a huge crater in the road, bloodstains everywhere, and most horrifically of all, men's internal organs blown up and scattered over the statues on the walls of Martinsart's damaged chapel . . .

The cemetery was used as a front-line cemetery until October 1916, and then again in 1918. After the war it was enlarged by the concentration of 346 graves from the areas north, east and south of the village. Those buried in the cemetery include Lt Col H.C. Bernard (I.A.16), Commanding Officer 10th Royal Irish Rifles (107th Brigade, 36th Division), killed in Thiepval Wood on 1 July when he should, according to orders, have remained at battle headquarters. Also here is Lt Cdr F.S. Kelly (I.H.25) of the Hood Battalion (189th Brigade, 63rd Division), a contemporary of Rupert Brooke, who was killed on 13 November. A Balliol College scholar known as 'Cleg', he was better known as a sculler than a musician and had won the Diamond Sculls many times. If he had been spared, though, he might well have become better known as a composer.

During a recent visit, it was sad to discover that vandals had torched many of the red sandstone graves, including that of 'Cleg' Kelly. The original stones came from quarries in the Border region of England and are of a type also used at AUCHON-VILLERS and MÉAULTE.

MAUREPAS is due east of HARDECOURT-AU-BOIS and south-west of COMBLES, on the D146 road. At the beginning of the battle the Germans had strongly fortified the village, as it protected the ground towards the village of COMBLES, where there was a junction of roads that came from several directions. The main German defence line bent round the western side of the village.

According to the Michelin battlefield guide, Maurepas was made up of a group of large farms, each of which possessed a meadow surrounded by trees. The farms had to be captured one at a time and the subsequent advance proved to be slow. As a prelude to the complete capture of the village, the French had taken ANGLE WOOD to the north-east the day before, with the assistance of 17th Lancashire Fusiliers (104th Brigade, 35th Division).

As Maurepas was in French Army territory, they led the first attack against it on 12 August 1916; troops advanced eastwards from HARDECOURT-AU-BOIS and captured the third line of enemy trenches. This meant that only the southern and western parts of the village were carried, but these included the fortified cemetery and church. The northern part of the village was captured a few days later, and on 24 August the last centre of resistance fell, the houses along the side of the road leading towards COMBLES.

MÉAULTE is south of ALBERT between the two main roads that converge on ALBERT from the south-east, the D329 from BRAY-SUR-SOMME and the D42 from MORLANCOURT. The village was occupied by British troops from 1915; one of the first units to take up positions here was LXXXIV Brigade, Royal Field Artillery (18th Division).

On 3 August 1915, Lt (later Col) F.J. Rice rode to the village from HEILLY (IWM 78/29/1) in order to meet up with Lt Col W.B.R. Sandys, Commanding Officer XXVIII Brigade, Royal Field Artillery (5th Division), to which his battery was to be attached. During this time, Gen Sir Edmund Allenby's Third Army was in the process of taking over the line south of Arras; LXXXIV Brigade's task was to take over French artillery positions about 1 mile east of Méaulte, close to a factory. In his papers Rice noted his visits to an observation post, known as the GRANDSTAND, which was to become a popular place for viewing the battlefield during the following months. According to Rice, 'we were astonished to find people walking about more or less openly. There was no hostile fire, and the French fired a few rounds of HE for our own benefit, to show us various points.' The group then returned to Méaulte, where they were entertained to an excellent lunch by the French artillery officers before returning to HEILLY. A section of the brigade's guns went into action; later, Rice made regular visits to the GRANDSTAND.

Also on 3 August, No. 59 Field Company, Royal Engineers (5th Division), took over billets from the French, which were opposite the church. They found the communication trenches excellent, being 6ft deep in hard chalk soil and with limestone in places at the bottom.

Initially, units of the British Army at Méaulte shared the village with three-quarters of its peace-time population. The mixture of the two nationalities did not always gel and it certainly seems strange that the French civilian population was allowed to get so close to the front line. An advanced dressing station was here from very early on. As well as 5th Division, 18th, 32nd and 51st Divisions used the village during the rest of 1915.

During the spring and early summer of 1916, infantry brigades were regularly billeted in BRAY-SUR-SOMME and Méaulte; the enemy regularly shelled both villages and carried out a gas bombardment on 20 April. On 9 April, 8th Somerset Light Infantry (63rd Brigade, 21st Division) arrived here from VILLE-SUR-ANCRE and 5 days later went up to a section of the front line north-west of FRICOURT.

On 26 May, 64th Field Ambulance (21st Division) inspected the château here, which in reality was a ruined file factory turned into a divisional rest station. The staff spent the next few days clearing out large quantities of refuse, work that was finished in early June. At the end of June, there were a main dressing station and two walking wounded collecting points in Méaulte, as well as a ration dump on the north side of the village.

At the beginning of the battle, the boundary between III Corps and XV Corps ran just outside the north-west side of Méaulte. On 1 July, 13th Northumberland Fusiliers and 1st Lincolns (both 62nd Brigade, 21st Division) moved off to the front line, as well as 6th Dorsets (50th Brigade, 17th Division); the latter battalion went past Carcaillot Farm on the BRAY-SUR-SOMME road on their way up to FRICOURT.

In *Twelve Days*, Sidney Rogerson of 2nd West Yorkshires (23rd Brigade, 8th Division), noted that the village was one of the bottlenecks through which was fed the flood of men and munitions for the offensive. Here hundreds of battalions and batteries had spent a last night's rest before moving on nearer the line. Beyond the village was a forward slope, over which German balloons observed.

Siegfried Sassoon of 1st Royal Welsh Fusiliers (19th Brigade, 33rd Division) noted in his diary that on 12 July his battalion were in reserve lines close to Méaulte and that in the morning he rode up to Citadel Camp; on 13 and 14 July he saw the Indian cavalry on their way up to HIGH WOOD. At 1100hrs on 14 July, 1st Royal Welsh Fusiliers moved to Méaulte, which he described as a squalid and only slightly damaged village, where they had a haversack lunch. Then the whole brigade bivouacked on a forward slope nearby.

In mid-July, 20th Royal Fusiliers (19th Brigade, 33rd Division) were bivouacked on the high ground above the village, when they were under groundsheets. The whole village was swarming with troops. From 16 July, 21st Manchesters (21st Brigade, 7th Division) were bivouacked in the village; on 18 July they entrained at MÉRICOURT-L'ABBÉ for HANGEST-SUR-SOMME. Heavily involved in the DELVILLE WOOD fighting towards the end of July, 22nd Royal Fusiliers (99th Brigade, 2nd Division) were also in Méaulte after their ordeal. Here Maj Gen W. Walker VC, General Officer Commanding 2nd Division, told the battalion, which was 'diminished and badly battered', of his great pride in their achievement.

Rogerson noted that night after night, unit had succeeded unit since the battle had begun. Morning

after morning they had been pitchforked towards the battle. He also noted that a bakery had become the office of the French mission and that some farm buildings round a midden sheltered the mobile workshops of a brigade of heavy artillery, and 8in howitzers stood to have their recoil buffers repaired, where previously a *percheron* plough had waited to be unharnessed.

On 10 August, HM the King arrived in Méaulte, during his August visit to the Somme front; here he met Lt Gen Sir Walter Congreve VC, General Officer Commanding XIII Corps, who escorted him to the original 1 July line. Congreve took the party to an observation point just south and between the villages of FRICOURT and MAMETZ at BOIS FRANÇAIS, where the King was shown the 1 July front-line trenches on both sides; the party were about 3½ miles from the British Front Line. Visibility was poor and the King could not see as much as he would have wished. However, he did venture into a former German dugout and saw the grave of a French officer, one of an unknown British soldier with his steel helmet lying on the grave with a hole right through it, and also a grave of a German with his boots sticking out of the ground. He then motored back to QUERRIEU, where Lt Gen Sir Henry Rawlinson, General Officer Commanding Fourth Army, gave him lunch.

Harold Macmillan of 4th Grenadier Guards (3rd Guards Brigade, Guards Division) wrote in his memoirs, *The Winds of Change*, that his battalion came to Méaulte from COURCELLES-AU-BOIS around 25 August. The village was to be the base for their September involvement in the battle. In A.D. Gristwood's fictionalised account of the battle, *The Somme*, he wrote that in September, 'from Death Valley the Loamshires marched over the hills to Méaulte . . . Méaulte lies on the edge of "the old front line" and, to normal eyes, was hideous enough.'

In *Other Ranks*, W.V. Tilsley of 1/4th Loyal North Lancashires (164th Brigade, 55th Division) wrote that on 14 September his unit arrived at Méaulte, which was a well-worn many times second-hand village known to most infantrymen. The tanks also passed through at this time.

After 1/16th Londons (169th Brigade, 56th Division) had been involved in the clearing of COMBLES, their brigade were withdrawn from the line during the day and evening to billets at Méaulte; on the night of 30 September they relieved 9th Suffolks (71st Brigade, 6th Division). On 8 October, 1st Royal Welsh Fusiliers were back at Méaulte.

In *The Middle Parts of Fortune*, Frederic Manning of 7th King's Shropshire Light Infantry (8th Brigade, 3rd Division) wrote that his battalion moved back about 2 miles to another camp at Sandpits, which was a camp close to the village. The next day they moved to the 'sordid squalor' of Méaulte, where they spent 2 nights in stables, and the draft ceased to have a separate existence, being absorbed by the various companies.

During October, Max Plowman of 10th West Yorkshires (50th Brigade, 17th Division) was billeted in Méaulte and wrote:

> I hate this place. It lies low, near the Ancre, and has the dejected utilitarian air of a poor industrial town. It is one of those waste places that are neither in or out of the line. Méaulte has a hang-dog look. Almost every house is used by troops for one purpose or another, and all the country round is strewn with dumps and the refuse of an army scrapheap. On its churned-up roads, over which the stream of traffic never ceases to pass, pitifully miserable-looking German prisoners work, scraping and sweeping.

Later, 11th West Yorkshires made another move forward and bivouacked in Mansell Copse.

Aubrey Smith of 1/5th Londons (169th Brigade, 56th Division) described the civilians as extraordinarily hostile; they would not lift a finger to help the men and profiteered most shamefully. His battalion were at BERNAFAY WOOD at the time. Rogerson noted that at the end of the village there was a Foden Disinfector, or to use the vernacular a 'delousing machine', the function of which was to receive the highly populated undergarments of men coming out of the line and fumigate them so that, it was hoped, all livestock, whether actual or in embryo, should perish, and the garments be fit for reissue.

On 8 October, 10th King's Royal Rifle Corps (59th Brigade, 20th Division) arrived here from BERNAFAY WOOD. On 5 November, 1/4th Suffolks (98th Brigade, 33rd Division) were in a canvas camp at the village.

Between July and November the Guards, 3rd, 4th and 17th Divisions, also had units billeted in the area. At some time during the battle, a light railway was built that ran from DERNANCOURT on the original line to Méaulte towards GROVE TOWN and the Loop line, and also towards Bel Air to the south-west.

Méaulte Churchyard, to the north of the church, has the graves of two British soldiers. Méaulte Military Cemetery, on the west side of the road to ETINEHEM, was designed by Sir Edwin Lutyens; like Martinsart British Cemetery, it has red,

Corsehill stone graves, which are also to be found in the cemeteries at AUCHONVILLERS. It was begun at the end of 1915 and used until February 1917. More graves were made after the village's recapture in 1918, and after the Armistice 154 graves were brought in, mainly from the 1918 fighting. The cemetery register lists 300 war graves, but many of them have faded badly.

Two cemeteries were concentrated here. Made by units of 12th Division, Sandpit Cemetery was on the ALBERT–BRAY-SUR-SOMME road, a little east of the village. As already mentioned, the Sandpit had been the site of a camp; in early August, 'an amazing panorama of flashes, flares and explosions could be seen from dawn to dusk from the hillside there'. It was retaken by 7th Royal Sussex in August 1918. Méaulte Triangle Cemetery, which was between a road junction and a light railway crossing on the MORLANCOURT road, was made by 12th Division and heavy artillery units of III Corps and contained the graves of 36 soldiers from the United Kingdom who fell during the 23–25 August 1918 period.

MÉRICOURT-L'ABBÉ is south-west of ALBERT on the D120 road from TREUX, due south of the River Ancre and the main AMIENS–ALBERT railway. In the early summer of 1915, when the Somme front was taken over from the French, Méricourt-l'Abbé became a main railhead and terminus for the Somme battlefield.

In *A Medico's Luck in the War*, Maj D. Rorie of the Royal Army Medical Corps, serving with 1/2nd (Highland) Field Ambulance (51st Division), mentions that the Highland troops were the very first Scottish troops who had ever been seen in the district. He lived in a billet in the local policeman's house and was in the village for a week before moving to WARLOY-BAILLON. A hospital was set up as a main dressing station in a school and very large barn in the main square of the village, and two casualty clearing stations were set up in the south-west of the village. The barn still exists.

As well as 51st Division's field ambulances, medical units of 5th, 18th and 32nd Divisions also looked after the main dressing station during the rest of the year. From early October, patients were sometimes accommodated in a small château and in specially built wooden huts. During much of December, 91st Field Ambulance (32nd Division) ran the hospital here.

In January 1916, when billeted in VAUX-SUR-SOMME to the south, troops from 14th Royal Warwicks (13th Brigade, 5th Division) visited Méricourt-l'Abbé to listen to 'Gilbert the Filbert'

(Lt B.H. Radford of the Royal Flying Corps), who regularly took part in concerts.

On 24 June, 64th Field Ambulance (21st Division) arrived here and took over the main dressing station from 23rd Field Ambulance (7th Division), who left for MORLANCOURT, in the barn that at one time had been used as a cinema. It required a considerable amount of work on it and was half-finished 5 days later. Few wounded came in, with 65 casualties on 26 June, but everything changed on 1 July, when the wounded began to arrive in large numbers from 1130hrs; on 2 July, the casualties were even higher.

As well as being a regular village for billeting purposes, Méricourt-l'Abbé was to become a centre of vast traffic, both men and materials, especially after the battle began in July; there were immense stores and endless pits of ammunition stacked up ready for use in the trenches. On 18 July, 21st Manchesters (91st Brigade, 7th Division) went from MÉAULTE to Méricourt-l'Abbé station, and on 19 July travelled on to HANGEST-SUR-SOMME. On 22 July, Siegfried Sassoon's battalion, 1st Royal Welsh Fusiliers (22nd Brigade, 7th Division), took the train from here and also went to HANGEST-SUR-SOMME.

A few days later, 8th King's Own (76th Brigade, 3rd Division) attended a church service here in a wooded glade with three other battalions present. Pte J. Miller of that battalion gained a posthumous Victoria Cross at BAZENTIN-LE-PETIT when in action alongside 10th Royal Warwicks (57th Brigade, 19th Division) on 30/31 July; he is buried at Dartmoor Cemetery in BÉCORDEL-BÉCOURT (I.C.64). At 0030hrs on 8 August, 9th King's Royal Rifle Corps (42nd Brigade, 14th Division) arrived in Méricourt-l'Abbé and marched to billets, leaving for FRICOURT on 12 August. In early August, 9th Suffolks (71st Brigade, 6th Division) moved to the village; 2nd Suffolks (76th Brigade, 3rd Division) were here for a fortnight before moving up the line to the south-west of TRÔNES WOOD.

Later in the month, around 25 August, the Guards Division were in the vicinity; they were billeted in a large farm in the centre of the village, with the exception of some officers and one platoon of 1st Welsh Guards (3rd Guards Brigade, Guards Division). While here, they bathed in the River Ancre. Around 11 September, 14th Royal Warwicks (13th Brigade, 5th Division) were in the area, and were accustomed to seeing HRH the Prince of Wales, who was on the staff of the Guards Division, going past their camp on a bicycle.

In *The Middle Parts of Fortune*, Frederic Manning of 7th King's Shropshire Light Infantry (8th Brigade, 3rd Division) mentioned that his battalion marched from MÉAULTE to Méricourt-l'Abbé and that Bourne, the main character in the book, had been set to pull a Lewis gun cart – a task that he liked because it enabled him to rid himself of his pack, which he stowed in the cart. The next day they moved on to MAILLY-MAILLET. Lastly, 1st Essex (88th Brigade, 29th Division) were billeted in the village for 2 weeks during November. Throughout 1916, 5th, 6th, 20th and 51st Divisions also had units here.

Méricourt-l'Abbé Communal Cemetery is a little way east of the village; Méricourt-l'Abbé Communal Cemetery Extension is to the south, between it and the road to TREUX. Begun in August 1915, it lies on the north side of the hills separating the River Ancre and the River Somme, in pleasant and well-wooded country; it was used mainly by field ambulances until July 1916 and again between March and August 1918. Méricourt-l'Abbé Communal Cemetery Extension has the graves of about 48 men who died prior to the battle. After the Armistice, 74 isolated graves from north-east of Méricourt l'Abbé were brought in and reburied in Rows G to K in Plot III; only one of these men could be identified. Méricourt-l'Abbé Communal Cemetery Extension was designed by Sir Edwin Lutyens and there are 347 identified graves. It was finished in 1924–1925.

MESNIL-MARTINSART is on the west bank of the River Ancre, between ALBERT and BEAUMONT-HAMEL; it comprises two villages, Mesnil to the north of AVELUY WOOD, and MARTINSART (see that entry), to the south-west of Mesnil and divided from the River Ancre by AVELUY WOOD. The Wood, virtually a forest of oak and birch prior to hostilities, was shattered during the war. It is bounded on the east by the main railway line from ALBERT to AMIENS, and the road from ALBERT to HAMEL runs through it; a dump was established there called Lancashire Dump, which later became a cemetery. On some maps it is known as East Lancashire Dump.

According to the history of 18th Manchesters (90th Brigade, 30th Division), in mid-December 1915 Mesnil Château, adjacent to the northern edge of AVELUY WOOD (now the D174), was in a far better state than Thiepval Château, which was already virtually destroyed. Mesnil Château 'provided accommodation for the whole of the Company which was not undergoing instruction actually in the trenches. It was hardly luxurious and the officers' billet was called, with good reason, "Rat Cottage" . . .'

At some point during the war, the hands were removed from the village church clock. In July 1927 a party of about 60 members of the Young Citizen Volunteers returned on a battlefields tour which included a visit to key sites on the Somme battlefield such as Mesnil, NEWFOUNDLAND PARK, DELVILLE WOOD and ALBERT. They returned the hands of the clock in a special open-air ceremony with the mayor of the village, which was followed by a reception. It appears that the hands of the church clock had been removed in order to stop them from being used by German sympathisers for the signalling of information useful to the enemy.

There were three particularly well-known features in Mesnil. One was JACOB'S LADDER, a long communication trench that began here, which in December 1915 was reported to be very wet; another was Brock's Benefit, an artillery observation trench named after Brig Gen J.H. Brock of 36th Division; and a third, Mesnil Ridge, commanded an excellent view.

As with MARTINSART, the area was very much 36th Division country at the beginning of the battle. There were a number of observation posts in the sector, as it was such a good position for observing the progress of the battle, and for the artillery. An advanced dressing station or collection post was here prior to the battle and from time to time the village was shelled. On 31 May 1916, 14 men were wounded by shelling here.

On 5 July, 1/3rd Monmouths (pioneers of 49th Division) arrived at Lancashire Dump and immediately set about working on the 'business' end of the trench railway; this was quite an elaborate affair and connected Mesnil with Knightsbridge Barracks (where there was an advanced dressing station) and Thurles Dump, before meeting up with another track running between MAILLY-MAILLET and Auction Lodge via AUCHONVILLERS. In addition, a light railway from ALBERT connected Mesnil with AUCHONVILLERS; Mesnil station was on the west side of the village and on 30 June, 88th Field Ambulance (29th Division) were in charge of a collecting post here, formed in the dugouts in a bank by the station building. Stretcher-bearers used what was called Catacomb Dugouts, just to the north of the village, and on 1 July they were to move up to Knightsbridge to cope with the expected casualties. A third aid post was at Vitermont church and also in the cellars of an adjacent house.

The plan for handling 29th Division's wounded at BEAUMONT-HAMEL on 1 July was for walking wounded to walk across the open to the divisional collecting station at Vitermont via a communication trench called Gabion Avenue. Sitting cases were to use trolleys on the trench tramway and light railway to Mesnil and stretcher cases would be taken to the corps collecting station at ACHEUX-EN-AMIÉNOIS. On 1 July over 1,700 casualties were dealt with, but the number was very much reduced by the next day. The wounded arrived faster than the ambulance cars could evacuate them and extra General Service wagons were acquired to help clear the backlog. Shelled by both sides, the roads were impassable for ambulance traffic.

In early July, the wounded who arrived at Lancashire Dump came from HAMEL and RAMC Trench, an aid post called Cookers on the HAMEL–ALBERT road; they were then taken by cars to ACHEUX-EN-AMIÉNOIS via Northumberland Avenue, HÉDAUVILLE and FORCEVILLE.

In *The Press and the General Staff*, Neville Lytton mentions without quoting a date that he 'observed' from a hill immediately to the east of Mesnil and had a magnificent view of the ANCRE VALLEY. A friend of Edward Blunden, with whom he served in 11th Royal Sussex, Lytton was based at ENGLE-BELMER and his brigade headquarters was in the village of Vitermont close by, in French-built dugouts.

On 3 September, Lytton and Blunden were in the area on their way to HAMEL using the communication trench JACOB'S LADDER. On the same day, Capt W.B. Allen of the Royal Army Medical Corps, attached CCXLVI Brigade, Royal Field Artillery (49th Division), gained the Victoria Cross close to Mesnil.

When gun detachments were unloading high-explosive ammunition from wagons which had just come up, the enemy suddenly began to shell the battery. The first shell fell on one of the limbers, exploded the ammunition and caused several casualties. Capt. Allen saw the occurrence and at once, with utter disregard of danger, ran straight across the open, under heavy shell-fire, commenced dressing the wounded, and undoubtedly by his promptness saved many of them from bleeding to death. He was himself hit four times during the first hour by pieces of shells, one of which fractured two of his ribs, but he never even mentioned this at the time, and coolly went on with his work till the last man was dressed and safely removed. He then went over to another battery and tended a wounded officer. It was only when this was done that he returned to his dug-out and reported his own injury . . .

In a manuscript held at the Imperial War Museum called *Gunner on the Somme*, the author, a Gunner W.R. Price of CCXL Brigade, Royal Field Artillery (48th Division), mentioned being at Mesnil high up under a ridge just to the west of the village and directly opposite the village of THIEPVAL, which was in enemy hands. His brigade stayed in this position until mid-September.

In *A Call to Arms*, J. Murray of the Hood Battalion (189th Brigade, 63rd Division) mentioned that on 23 October his unit left ENGLEBELMER for Mesnil, where there were no houses or barns left standing. A week later they moved back to HÉDAU-VILLE. On 10 November they were relieved by the Hawke Battalion (also 189th Brigade, 63rd Division) and moved to shelters in the railway embankment at Mesnil, taking refuge in cubbyholes covered with corrugated iron sheeting. On 12 November they moved to HAMEL. The history of the Hawke Battalion notes that Mesnil and ENGLEBELMER will always be associated with the weary period of waiting for the 13 November attack against BEAUMONT-HAMEL. By then both villages had been deserted by their civilian inhabitants and Mesnil was only a heap of ruins that insecurely covered a handful of cellars, where the troops or marines sat and shivered by day and night alike.

Mesnil Ridge Cemetery, with its four chestnut trees, lies midway between Mesnil and AUCHON-VILLERS to the north-west, on the eastern slope of the valley running north from Mesnil; it was made by field ambulances and fighting units, mainly of 29th and 36th Divisions, between August 1915 and August 1916. No fewer than 25 members of 2nd South Wales Borderers (87th Brigade, 29th Division) are buried here; they were killed or died of wounds as a result of a German raid on 29th Division's positions opposite BEAUMONT-HAMEL on 6 April 1916. There had been over 100 casualties in total. Four men from the Royal Inniskilling Fusiliers who died on 25 June are also buried here.

As Knightsbridge Cemetery, designed by Reginald Blomfield, lies in a valley in the middle of cultivated fields, it is best to take a right turn onto a rough track north of the village; this is also the best route to Mesnil Ridge Cemetery. Knightsbridge Cemetery was named after a communication trench and was begun at the outset of the battle; it was used until February 1917 and again between March and July 1918. Perhaps in view of its position, close to the modern-day NEWFOUNDLAND PARK, there are many graves from 1st Newfoundlanders and 1st Essex (88th Brigade, 29th Division). Fifteen men of 13th Cheshires (74th Brigade, 25th Division),

killed by German shells at the end of July 1916, are buried here. Casualties from 39th Division's attack on 3 September can be traced in the long rows on the left of the main part of the cemetery. 4th Bedfords (190th Brigade, 63rd Division) erected a memorial in the cemetery to eight of their number killed on 13/14 November during the capture of BEAUMONT-HAMEL and two others killed in February 1917; the 1916 men included Capt F.G.C. Ashmead-Bartlett (B.33). After the war, 112 graves, now in Rows G, H and J, were brought in from the battlefields around Mesnil.

Mesnil Communal Cemetery is off the road between Mesnil and MARTINSART, near the north-west corner of AVELUY WOOD, and Mesnil Communal Cemetery Extension is on the south side of it. The Extension was begun in July 1916, and used again as a front-line cemetery in 1918. It was gradually enlarged after the Armistice by the concentration of 244 graves from Mesnil dressing station and from the battlefields of 1916 and 1918, north-east of Mesnil. It lies in a valley among cultivated fields. The dressing station was to the west of the village across a light railway; it was used from June 1916 until February 1917, especially by 63rd Division, who were in the area in November 1916.

Lancashire Dump Cemetery (see Aveluy Wood Cemetery) was begun in June 1916 and was used by fighting units and field ambulances until the German withdrawal in February 1917. Around 100 graves here are of casualties found in the wood after the Armistice. The cemetery stands in AVELUY WOOD, and four of the original trees still remain there, covered with climbing roses. The view from it to the south is open and includes Thiepval Wood and AUTHUILLE village.

In 1931, 13 years after the war, one visitor to the area saw several funk-holes and dugouts as well as many battered positions, and in the wood old craters and torn earth. In the wood also could be seen former gun positions, with posts and saps. Two posts on the road between Mensil and AUCHONVILLERS have concrete design with the imprint of sandbags still clearly marked.

Even after 100 years, it is easy to trace the former trench lines and shell-holes to the rear of AVELUY WOOD. Mills bombs, still live, are hidden among the moss on the ground in the wood, and further down the road, artillery saps can still be seen quite clearly.

In recent years, a small cross has been placed in Mesnil valley in a coppice close to the track leading from the village to Knightsbridge Cemetery. It commemorates the memory of 2/Lt H.V. Sewell, who was killed in the area on 13 November 1916; his name is listed on the Thiepval Memorial. His brother, Lt C. Sewell, gained a posthumous Victoria Cross when serving with the Tank Corps in August 1918.

MILLENCOURT is due west of ALBERT on the D91 road to HÉNENCOURT. The French Army had already been using some of the buildings in the village during the summer of 1915 before 1/3rd (Highland) Field Ambulance (51st Division) took them over on 28 July as a main dressing station. During the following year, Millencourt was to become very much a hospital. The chief wards and offices and dressing stations were grouped near the church, which was used as a dispensary and pack store as well as reserve accommodation for patients. Some buildings lent themselves well to hospital purposes while others needed improvisation. Patients leaving here were often evacuated to No. 5 Casualty Clearing Station at VILLERS-BOCAGE and 51st Division's casualty clearing station. On 3 August, units from 18th Division began to move into the village and were involved in trench work. On 8 August, 1/3rd (Highland) Field Ambulance were here again, returning on 22 August and 6 September.

On 30 December, two companies of 2nd Royal Inniskilling Fusiliers (96th Brigade, 32nd Division) arrived here, but left with two companies from LAVIÉVILLE on 2 January for the front lines opposite THIEPVAL. On 1 January 1916, 90th Field Ambulance (32nd Division) were here, returning in February and March.

On 17 February, 17th Highland Light Infantry (97th Brigade, 32nd Division) were in billets here for a week, when many of their fatigues consisted of the laying of cables and the improvement of roads. They left for HÉNENCOURT a week later.

In early April, when a field ambulance of 8th Division took over from 90th Field Ambulance (32nd Division), they noted that the accommodation was defective and the water supply scanty; only 140 patients could be dealt with and a special ward near the church had been set up to provide an operating room. A small house nearby was used by the hospital sisters. Also in early April, 2nd Royal Berkshires (25th Brigade, 8th Division) were in divisional reserve here for 4 days. Their tours were to alternate with being in the village or at Hénencourt Wood.

On 26 June casualties were brought into the church from the south side; about a third of the church was divided off by a canvas screen, where everything else went on, including four operating

tables. At least six other buildings in the village were used for patients, billeting purposes and stores.

Despite the hospital having been established for more than a year, conditions seem to have been far from ideal. On 1 July, the first casualties arrived at 0800hrs; by 1000hrs, there was a steady stream of walking wounded. Soon the numbers greatly increased, and with the arrival of a very great number of casualties from the front the whole system became overwhelmed and broke down.

In the afternoon, owing to congestion, a number of patients had to be redirected to LAVIÉVILLE to the south-west, using the field ambulance's own wagons for transport to the casualty clearing station at VECQUEMONT. The sitting or lying cases were taken to Nos. 36 and 38 Casualty Clearing Stations at HEILLY; these were closed at 2030hrs, and all casualties were then sent to PUCHEVILLERS, a hospital to the north-west, which involved a road journey of 4 hours. Despite this, by midnight the hospital facilities at Millencourt were still choked with cases, and more barns had to be opened up to cope with the influx. At 1500hrs the following day the two casualty clearing stations at HEILLY were reopened.

Later in the battle the hospital was mainly used for the sick, but in mid-September was still having to cope with the wounded from the HIGH WOOD fighting.

In his published diary, Brig Gen J.L. Jack described the involvement of 2nd Cameronians (23rd Brigade, 8th Division) at the beginning of the battle. On 1 July, if all went according to plan, 8th Division were to capture the village of OVILLERS-LA-BOISSELLE. They left Millencourt after sunset on 30 June. The headquarters and four companies of 2nd Cameronians, with some 20 officers and 650 other ranks, filed along the way to ALBERT; here they turned northwards, crossed the River Ancre via a temporary wooden bridge and made their way along the marshy valley to Aveluy. They then climbed the slopes eastwards until they reached Preston Communication Trench for the last part of their 5-mile walk to their assembly positions in Ribble Street, with battalion headquarters at Ovillers Post close by.

At 0700hrs on 1 July, Jack led two companies up Hodder Street to the rear of 2nd West Yorkshires (also 23rd Brigade, 8th Division) in Houghton Street; the last-named, together with the assembly trenches, had been blasted by the enemy howitzers. On 2 July, after 8th Division's failure to gain ground at OVILLERS, 23rd Brigade returned to Millencourt.

During July, other brigades came and went. C.S. Collison of 11th Royal Warwicks (112th Brigade, 37th Division) recorded that one evening at the end of July his unit moved forward via Millencourt and ALBERT to a position in reserve close to Bécourt Wood.

Having failed in one of the many attempts to capture HIGH WOOD, 2nd Welsh (3rd Brigade, 1st Division) returned to Millencourt, having been in dugouts at the northern end of MAMETZ WOOD; they had lost 193 men in the attack.

On 24 August, 6th (London) Field Ambulance (47th Division) arrived here and bivouacked in a field outside the village; they moved into the village the next day. Their headquarters and hospital were established in the village and their advanced dressing station was at Flat Iron Copse near MAMETZ WOOD. By the end of August, the surrounding countryside had become like one huge camp.

At the beginning of September, 1/4th Yorkshires (150th Brigade, 50th Division) were in the area. On 5 October, 149th Brigade (also 50th Division) marched here after being in the line at Eaucourt. In the period 5 to 18 September, 1/5th Yorkshires (150th Brigade, 50th Division) were involved in active operations. During this time, four of their officers were killed, including Lt Col J. Mortimer, who was later buried in Flat Iron Copse Cemetery, MAMETZ (IV.J.5).

After 47th Division captured HIGH WOOD, bearers of 6th (London) Field Ambulance had great difficulty in recovering casualties from a regimental aid post at the COUGH DROP, a former enemy dugout about 200yds behind the front line. After several attempts, the post was finally cleared by 22 September; a few days later it was destroyed by fire. On 23 September fire broke out close to the Millencourt headquarters, but was quickly dealt with.

One night, probably after their success at MARTINPUICH in mid-September, 12th Highland Light Infantry arrived in Scotts Wood before going on to Millencourt. Between 30 September and 3 October, 2nd King's Royal Rifle Corps (2nd Brigade, 1st Division) were here, then out of the area. It seems that 7th/8th King's Own Scottish Borderers (46th Brigade, 15th Division) were in tents at Millencourt Camp; the wood had been turned into a camp and consisted of gaunt tree stumps. At the end of October there is mention of troops arriving in the village from the front-line direction, in a London bus.

Many divisions had units who trained here and who were billeted or camped in the area from July 1915 to the end of October 1916. As well as elements of 18th Division who came here for instruction with 51st Division, at various times 1st, 8th, 9th, 15th, 17th, 19th, 23rd, 32nd, 34th, 46th, 47th, 48th, 50th and 51st Divisions spent time at Millencourt; 9th, 19th, 48th and 50th Divisions had their headquarters in the village during their stay.

Millencourt Communal Cemetery, north-west of the village, was used by field ambulances from August 1915 to May 1916 and again in March and April 1918. These 64 graves were later taken into the Millencourt Communal Cemetery Extension, which was used by field ambulances and III Corps' main dressing station in 1916 and 4th Australian Division and other units in March and April 1918. Designed by Sir Reginald Blomfield, the Extension has 338 identified graves of British and Dominion troops.

MINDEN POST, a famous dressing station, was close to CARNOY; its headquarters was on the southern side of the D929 FRICOURT–MARICOURT road, in a deep hollow close to the turning to CARNOY opposite CAFTET WOOD.

On 21 August 1915, No. 79 Field Company, Royal Engineers (18th Division), were involved in digging and construction work here. From 1 October to 15 December, No. 527 Field Company, Royal Engineers (5th Division), were here. On 2 March 1916, No. 528 Field Company, Royal Engineers (7th Division), were working on an advanced dressing station that was being set up underneath the road, and on a new communication trench stretching 1,000yds to Francis Avenue. Apart from being a dressing station and military camp, Minden Post was a regular jumping-off place for troops going up to the front line.

In the spring of 1916, the battalion headquarters of 21st Manchesters (91st Brigade, 7th Division) was here. At the beginning of the battle, the headquarters of 1st South Staffords (also 91st Brigade, 7th Division) was also here; on 1 July, this battalion attacked the village of MAMETZ from a position to the north-east. The boundary between XIII and XV Corps ran along the eastern boundary of the position.

Geoffrey Malins, the official War Office photographer, if we are to rely on his account, left 29th Division's positions on the morning of 1 July and then drove to Minden Post for filming. He was joined by Macdowell, a colleague, who was filming the wounded of both sides as they came out of the line after the first attacks.

On 4 July, 2nd Queen's (91st Brigade, 7th Division) were bivouacked at Minden Post.

On 10 July, 115th Brigade (38th Division) were in reserve both here and at MAMETZ. By this time, a trolley line had been built, running from Minden Post to the CITADEL and a divisional rest station; it was shortly to be used by casualties of 38th Division. On the following day, 8th Devons were camped in the vicinity. From 6 to 12 July, Minden Post handled 3,059 casualties, most of them resulting from the MAMETZ WOOD fighting. On 23 July, 30th Division returned here after their capture of MONTAUBAN-DE-PICARDIE.

Later in the battle, elements of the Guards Division were in the area before being involved in the September attacks against GINCHY and LESBŒUFS. The traffic congestion at the time was very great and lorries could scarcely make one trip a day from the railhead to the main dump at Minden Post. Between 21 July and 10 September, the Guards, 2nd, 16th, 20th, 24th and 35th Divisions had elements camped here, of whom the Guards, 16th, 20th and 35th Divisions had their headquarters in Minden Post.

MIRAUMONT lies south-east of PUISIEUX and north-east of GRANDCOURT. The village is split into two sections by the River Ancre and the main railway line.

Miraumont remained in German hands throughout 1916, and from the British perspective there is not a great deal to say about what happened there. Possibly the main event was that on 5 August 1916 the British artillery destroyed a German supply base and reserve ammunition store near an old watermill, causing an explosion so violent that it virtually destroyed the village.

In early October, 1/1st Cambridgeshires (118th Brigade, 39th Division) reported seeing from HAMEL the activity of a German dressing station, with ambulances going to and fro. Indeed, there exists a German postcard showing what is probably this very dressing station. Apart from the openness of the site, another surprise is the apparent lack of damage to the surrounding landscape.

The Allied line was halted before Miraumont for many months, and the village was not in British hands until February 1917, when the enemy withdrew. On 25 March 1918 it was reoccupied by the German Army, only to be retaken by 42nd Division on 24 August.

Philip Gibbs, the writer and journalist, visited the area in March 1917. In a despatch dated 12 March he mentioned that the enemy had suffered very considerably in the area of Miraumont, Pys and below Loupart Wood. The land had been destroyed by continuous shell-fire and there were many German dead in evidence, many of whom were half-buried by their colleagues or by high explosives. He visited Boom Ravine, into which REGINA TRENCH leads between Miraumont and Pys and described it as a 'shambles of German troops'. The Germans had had machine-gun emplacements there and also deep dugouts under cover of earth banks, but the Allied artillery had 'found them out'; all the garrison had been killed and shelled to pieces. Their bodies or fragments lay in every shape and shapelessness of death, in puddles of broken trenches or on the edge of deep ponds in shell-craters. Gibbs counted about 850 dead in this small area, the majority of them German. Boom Ravine was not directly associated with the 1916 battles although troops in REGINA TRENCH would have been aware of the closeness of the enemy positions, which can be easily traced south-east of Miraumont.

Miraumont Communal Cemetery was mainly used by German troops, but 27 British casualties are buried there, including 2 men from a RAF bomber crew killed in 1940 and Maj V.A. Barrington-Kennett (A.1), Commanding Officer No. 4 Squadron, Royal Flying Corps, who was killed in action on 13 March 1916; he was shot down by the German ace, Max Immelmann. Barrington-Kennett was one of four sons, three of whom were killed during the war. Three members of 1st Dorsets (14th Brigade, 32nd Division) who died on 17 May 1916 are also buried here, including Lt H.G.M. Mansel-Pleydell MC and another officer awarded the Military Cross.

Another cemetery associated with Miraumont and Pys – although actually nearer to COURCELETTE – is Adanac Military Cemetery, which can be found on the east side of the D107 road from Miraumont to COURCELETTE. The concentration cemetery was made after the Armistice, in particular from the Canadian battlefields; it contains more than 3,000 graves and over half of the headstones are of 'unknowns'. The main cemeteries brought into it were Pys British Cemetery; Pys New British Cemetery; Aqueduct Road Cemetery, Pys; New Zealand Cemetery, GRÉVILLERS; and Shrine Cemetery, GRÉVILLERS.

Two holders of the Victoria Cross are buried here. Piper J.C. Richardson (III.F.36) of 16th Canadian Battalion (3rd Canadian Brigade, 1st Canadian Division) gained a posthumous Victoria Cross at REGINA TRENCH on 8 October 1916. Sgt S. Forsyth (I.1.39) attached 2nd Aucklands (2nd New Zealand Brigade, New Zealand Division) won his award at GRÉVILLERS on 24 August 1918 and died on the same day. Only one man was buried here prior to the Armistice, Pte A. Edwards of the Machine Gun Corps (IV.D), who died in August 1918.

In November 1998 the remains of Pte J. McArthur of 31st Canadian Battalion (6th Canadian Brigade, 2nd Canadian Division) were buried in the cemetery. During the battle he had been 'reported missing, believed killed, in September 1916'. Members of his family attended the burial service.

Miraumont was later 'adopted', together with COLINCAMPS and COURCELLES-AU-BOIS, by the town of Burnley.

MIRVAUX is off the D11 north-easterly road from AMIENS to RUBEMPRÉ. In the autumn of 1915, 30th and 32nd Divisions sent field ambulance units here. At the end of December, 1/2nd (Highland) Field Ambulance (51st Division) arrived here from WARLOY-BAILLON. At the end of January 1916, the village contained 45 officers and 1,200 men, together with 180 horses, and its hospital could cope with 40 patients. Maj D. Rorie of the Royal Army Medical Corps, serving with 1/2nd (Highland) Field Ambulance (51st Division), described the village as being 'a rather dirty and poverty stricken place of about 170 inhabitants . . .' The chief work carried out by the Highland field ambulances was usually connected with sanitation. On 4 April, No. 458 Field Company, Royal Engineers (49th Division) were in the village, when their work consisted of putting up extra huts.

MOLLIENS-AU-BOIS is north-east of AMIENS off the D11 road to RUBEMPRÉ, on the D30. During the war it was mainly used as a billeting village. During the afternoon of August Bank Holiday, 1915, 10th Essex (53rd Brigade, 18th Division) took part in an inspection of the whole brigade by Gen Sir Charles Monro, General Officer Commanding Third Army, which took place in a field close to the château. Unfortunately, as they waited to be inspected, a heavy storm broke over the troops and thoroughly soaked those taking part. After a hurried tea the battalion left 20 minutes later for a 12-mile march to BOUZINCOURT, together with 6th Royal Berkshires (also 53rd Brigade, 18th Division).

On 28 November, 17th Highland Light Infantry (97th Brigade, 32nd Division) arrived here and stayed in the village for 2 days before leaving for the front, where they found in their first tour that the trenches were in a dilapidated condition. They were back in the village on 12 December, when

they spent 11 days resting and training and began to take timber from a nearby wood south of the village in order to make duckboards – until the practice was stopped by the forester.

On 28 December, 1/5th Seaforth Highlanders (152nd Brigade, 51st Division) marched to rest billets here, which their unit history described 'as a cheerful little place'; they got on well with the inhabitants. They spent several happy weeks here during which time they were carrying out training. The Scots made an occasion of the New Year and 'each barn had its own little sing-song, each Sergeants' Mess was also very much alive, the whole of the officers of the battalion, on the Colonel's invitation, were present at a dinner at headquarters, which in the present instance is part of the village school. Twenty-two officers sat down to dinner at 7.30 . . .'

After dinner there was a concert consisting of songs and recitations, and many toasts were proposed. 'On the return of the pipe-band to headquarters about 12.30 a.m. after their march through the village, a crowd of two or three hundred men of the battalion followed them and the Colonel went out and wished them a happy New Year. On the call of one of the men three hearty cheers were given for the Colonel . . .' Later in the morning, the officers of 1/6th Seaforth Highlanders (also 152nd Brigade, 51st Division) beat the officers of 1/5th Seaforth Highlanders by two goals to one in a friendly football match. After training here for a month, 1/5th Seaforth Highlanders left for ACHEUX-EN-AMIÉNOIS on 29 December.

The poet E. Alan Mackintosh, who was a lieutenant in 1/5th Seaforth Highlanders, was here from 15 January 1916, although his battalion had arrived at the end of December. While here, he may have attended an officers' course at VILLERS-BOCAGE.

On 12 February, 91st Field Ambulance (32nd Division) had men billeted in barns on either side of Badenoch road; an empty house in the same road was cleaned out and turned into a small hospital that could take 12 patients. A convalescent camp was set up in a barn at Café Commerce that was very unsanitary, with 'dung heaps and ponds of dirty water all over the yards. All wells were contaminated . . .'

On 1 March, 152nd Brigade (51st Division) were based here. On 3/4 April, 1/6th West Yorkshires (146th Brigade, 49th Division) arrived here and then marched the 9 miles to VIGNACOURT, where they were to remain for 2 months. On 12 June, 8th North Staffords (57th Brigade, 19th Division) were here for one night before marching to DERNANCOURT;

57th Brigade had their headquarters here when it was their training area.

Together with RAINNEVILLE to the south-west, the village held a brigade of 23rd Division at Zero Hour on 1 July; two other brigades of the same division were here in the second week of July.

In 1914 the château, due north of the village, was occupied by an English Army Major; it was used by American troops in 1917. On 12 August 1918, Gen John Pershing, General Officer Commander-in-Chief of the American Expeditionary Force, entertained HM the King here, during which time the English monarch awarded various decorations.

South-west of the village, Molliens-au-Bois Communal Cemetery has six Allied graves of men who died in 1917 or 1918.

MOLLIENS-DREUIL, known as Molliens-Vidame in 1916, is on the D211 road, due east of the D901 road to ABBEVILLE. On 4 January 1916, 22nd Field Ambulance (7th Division) were in the village. On 3 February 1916, 1/2nd (West Riding) Field Ambulance (49th Division) bussed here from a station at AMIENS; their billets consisted of some rooms in the first floor of a château due west of the village and previously occupied by another field ambulance. Owing to the large number of troops billeted in the village, it was found necessary to billet personnel in the château as well and provide for an officers' mess. Although this limited the accommodation for patients, 22nd Field Ambulance were only here a few days before leaving on 11 February; their place was taken by 15th Field Ambulance (5th Division) until they in turn left, on 23 February.

After their 1 July experiences at FRICOURT, 10th Yorkshires (62nd Brigade, 21st Division) came here and stayed for 4 days before leaving for MÉAULTE. On 11 and 12 July respectively, 53rd and 52nd Field Ambulances (both 17th Division) came to the village.

MONDICOURT lies south of the N25 DOULLENS–Arras road, to the west of WARLIN-COURT-LÈS-PAS. On 18 July 1915, 1/5th Royal Warwicks (143rd Brigade, 48th Division) detrained here from Lillers and for a few days were bivouacked in the neighbouring villages. On 29 August, 110th Brigade (37th Division) were based here; 2 days later, six men of 8th Leicesters (110th Brigade, 37th Division) were accidentally killed.

On 4 February 1916, No. 1/1 (Durham) Field Company, Royal Engineers (4th Division), were working here, improving billets and building latrines; they also carried out work in DOULLENS. On the same day, 11th Field Ambulance (also 4th Division) took over White House as a hospital and Red House as an officers' mess and billets; the men were billeted in the village, in North Road.

It is unclear which buildings in present-day Mondicourt might have been the original White and Red Houses, but a couple of candidates may be the two large houses in the north of the village. The grander of the two, which boasts a *pigionnaire* with a clockface, has a very imposing entrance; the second is on the right-hand side of the D6, close by. Also in the village is a factory; the 1916 billets just might have been here, being adjacent to the two possible châteaux candidates.

On 19 March, part of 49th Field Ambulance (37th Division) came to the village and for the next few weeks alternated with 50th and 48th Field Ambulances (both also 37th Division) in running the divisional rest station. On 4 May, 10th Field Ambulance (4th Division) were based at 'the château'; 2 days later, one of their motor lorries damaged the château's gateway.

From now on, the village was much used by troops of 56th Division before they took part in the fighting opposite GOMMECOURT on 1 July. On 22 May, 2/3rd (London) Field Ambulance (56th Division) set up a divisional rest station in the village. From 19 May to 2 June, 1/16th Londons (169th Brigade, 56th Division) felled trees here for use as gun emplacements and also unloaded trains at Mondicourt station; there was a large Royal Engineers dump in the village. On 29 June, 2/3rd (London) Field Ambulance returned to the divisional rest station here; prior to 1 July, a brigade sports day was organised.

A motor ambulance convoy depot was here, at least at the beginning of July, and units from 37th Division were here in the first 2 weeks of July; 144th Brigade (48th Division) were here on 1 October.

Mondicourt Communal Cemetery, south-east of the village, contains the graves of 12 British troops in the north-west corner, in addition to a member of the Chinese Labour Corps. It appears that none of these died anywhere near the front line, and six (members of 8th Leicestershire Regiment) died accidentally on 31 August 1915 during a grenade practice demonstration, while others died of sickness or heart failure.

MONTAUBAN-DE-PICARDIE, or Monty-Bong as the British Army used to call it, is on the D64 road between GUILLEMONT in the west and MAMETZ to the east; to the north-west are the

BAZENTIN villages and to the south is the village of MARICOURT. BERNAFAY and TRÔNES WOODs are both east of the village and north of the GUILLEMONT road.

The village was close to the ridge on which lay the German Second Line Position. A very long communication trench called Montauban Alley ran from POMMIERS REDOUBT, east of MAMETZ, north of Montauban-de-Picardie and on to the margin of BERNAFAY WOOD. The Franco-British Army boundary ran from a point south of BERNAFAY WOOD down through MARICOURT, cutting the village in half, and then southwards towards CAPPY and the River Somme.

On 1 July, Lt Gen Sir Walter Congreve's XIII Corps were given the task of capturing the ruined village of Montauban-de-Picardie. The French 39th Division were to the right of the British 30th Division; on the left was 18th Division, who were to advance to the west of Montauban-de-Picardie. Behind these three divisions, from right to left, were 11th, 9th and 7th Divisions.

The *Official History of the War* sets the scene in the following way: The front line of XIII Corps, which was on the right of the British line next to the French, extended from MARICOURT to beyond CARNOY. It lay near the bottom of the northern slope of the valley between MARICOURT and Montauban ridges, in which the village of CARNOY is situated. The German Front Line was higher up the same slope. Between the Montauban ridge – on whose crest the red roofs of the village were a conspicuous landmark before the bombardment – and the GINCHY–POZIÈRES ridge is a long valley, known from the shape of a wood it contains as CATERPILLAR VALLEY. In the Carnoy Valley, known as Railway Valley, ran a pre-war light railway line, and on its steep eastern slope stretched a long plantation called TALUS BOISÉ. The level of the attack was, in the main, a gentle upwards slope. There was splendid observation from the Maricourt Ridge.

The German defences were strengthened by a recently dug reserve line, Dublin Trench–Train Valley–Pommiers Trench, behind them. The communication trench called Montauban Alley ran from Montauban-de-Picardie to MAMETZ on the reverse slope of CATERPILLAR VALLEY. Redoubts in the front line included Glatz Redoubt, POMMIERS REDOUBT and the Castle. Montauban-de-Picardie had been placed in a strong state of defence.

On 30th Division's right were Brig Gen The Hon. F.C. Stanley's 89th Brigade. In his history of 89th Brigade, Stanley mentions his position prior to the battle. It was a pit 400yds south-west of MARI-COURT, into the side of which the British had tunnelled and made accommodation for about 10 officers and 70 men. It served as a brigade head-quarters as well as that of the gunners. Stanley described it as a really foul place. The French, to the right, had been doing good work, but three long communication trenches from MARICOURT to SUZANNE, being chalk, showed up terribly. Stanley's Hole, as the pit had been christened, was stacked with guns and ammunition and was surrounded by artillery.

On 1 July 1916, 89th Brigade (30th Division) began to move forward from four lines of assembly trenches; at 0730hrs, 17th and 20th King's, the two leading battalions, made rapid progress through mist and smoke. Lt Col B.C. Fairfax, Commanding Officer 17th King's, went forward himself in the second wave of attacking troops. Casement Trench, Alt Trench and German's Wood were all reached and passed. The wire, for a change, was well cut; as the advancing Allies were to find out, the artillery had done a good job on this particular front, and the dugouts were very often found to be blown in. Also, many prisoners were captured on the way. Dublin Trench, the first objective, south-west of the Brick-works, was taken at 0830hrs. It was empty. Three batteries of CXLIX Brigade, Royal Field Artillery (30th Division), were brought up to the north-west of MARICOURT; one was knocked out but the other two remained unscathed. 89th Brigade had advanced in tandem with the French 39th Division.

To the left of 89th Brigade, 21st Brigade (also 30th Division) had similar success; their leading battalions were 19th Manchesters and 18th King's. However, the enemy held them up in their advance towards Glatz Redoubt, their first objective, and 2nd Yorkshires (21st Brigade, 30th Division), in support, also suffered from machine-gun fire. Despite this, Glatz Redoubt was reached by 0835hrs; the capture of the Dublin Trench–Glatz Redoubt–Train Alley line paved the way for 90th Brigade's (also 30th Division) advance through 21st Brigade's lines.

Having assembled with the rest of 90th Brigade in and around CAMBRIDGE COPSE, west of MARICOURT, the leading battalions, 16th and 17th Manchesters, moved off at 0830hrs, supported by 2nd Royal Scots Fusiliers (also 90th Brigade, 30th Division). The collecting post was at TALUS BOISÉ and a second one was at Maricourt Avenue. The advance through TALUS BOISÉ was sheltered, but Lt Col H.A. Johnson, Commanding Officer 17th Manchesters, was wounded during it; this left the commanding officer of 2nd Royal Scots Fusiliers virtually in command of the whole 90th Brigade. Train Valley was reached ahead of timetable and a previously troublesome German machine gun was destroyed. There was a delay while the flanking division caught up; during this time, the commanding officers of both 16th and 17th Manchester battalions became casualties. In effect, without demoting the efforts of the Manchester battalions, it is really 2nd Royal Scots Fusiliers who should take much of the credit for the capture of Montauban-de-Picardie.

By 1100hrs, part of Montauban Alley had been reached and many Germans had surrendered; others could be seen in CATERPILLAR VALLEY, streaming towards BAZENTIN-LE-GRAND. With Montauban-de-Picardie in Allied hands, the way was now clear to capture the Brickworks, with its chimney stack, a very important German observation post. Situated to the north-east of the village, it had been converted into a place of exceptional strength by the enemy. It was beside the MARICOURT–LONGUEVAL road, about ½ mile to the south-east of Montauban-de-Picardie, and consisted of two large blocks of buildings. The buildings were on either side of the road, with outlying offices and furnaces. The Germans had excavated under them and had made an underground fort, over which the ruins made excellent cover. The fort had been strengthened with concrete and reinforced by iron girders. There was living accommodation for troops, and emplacements for machine guns. As the works were on the top of a plateau and well back from the contour line, there was a good field of fire in all directions.

The journalist Philip Gibbs noted that there had been anxiety about this German strongpoint and that it had been suggested that the British should just bypass it and not attempt to take it directly. However, when the position was approached it was found to have been already utterly destroyed by Allied artillery. In the event, 20th King's captured the Brickworks. Due north were BERNAFAY and TRÔNES WOODs, for which the Brickworks acted as an advance redoubt. Today's chimney is postwar and is within what was previously a circle of trench works.

In *The War in the Air* by H.A. Jones it is mentioned that an observer of No. 9 Squadron, Royal Flying Corps, watched the fight for Montauban-de-Picardie. He observed men of 30th Division move forward, with little opposition, towards the line Dublin Trench–Glatz Redoubt, which had been taken at 0830hrs. He also saw 18th Division take Pommiers Trench and advance quickly to capture

POMMIERS REDOUBT. Another observer could see a line of flashes reflected from the mirrors that men of 30th Division carried on their backs as they left Glatz Redoubt and moved along the trench known as Train Alley in the direction of Montauban-de-Picardie. Suddenly he saw a battery come into action at BERNAFAY WOOD. His pilot flew across at once and attacked the crew with machine-gun fire from 700ft. After the aeroplane left, a company of 20th King's captured the Brickworks south-east of Montauban-de-Picardie; this completed the advance of XIII Corps on the first day of the battle.

Following Montauban-de-Picardie's fall, at about midday, Lt R.B. Talbot Kelly of LII Brigade, Royal Field Artillery (9th Division), went across the battlefield with his major and two signallers towards the village to reconnoitre for a new observation post. Glatz Redoubt was a turmoil of brown earth and splintered wood. In Montauban-de-Picardie itself, there remained no recognisable ruins, although there had been 274 houses there prior to the war, which made the village the largest in the Somme area. Almost immediately, Talbot Kelly's battery moved from its second-line position into action in the open behind the ruins of the Brickworks, and he experienced wood fighting for the first time. As Forward Observation Officer in BERNAFAY WOOD and later in TRÔNES WOOD, he was to endure days of intense terror.

Montauban-de-Picardie was the first German-held village to fall into British hands and was one of the few British successes on an otherwise totally disastrous day for the British Army. XIII Corps were fortunate; not only were they good at making skilful plans, but the lines in this sector were much narrower than those in front of LA BOISSELLE, for example.

The fact that the great dugouts had been smashed by the Allied artillery, along with much of the wire, helped the advance enormously. Unfortunately no all-out attempt was made to capture BERNAFAY WOOD to the north-east, which would have saved a lot of fighting and hundreds of casualties over the next 2 weeks. Attempts to take the Wood were made a couple of days later; when patrols had been sent out to the Wood, it was found to be empty except for a few of the enemy. Although the troops could have gone on, the time was spent in consolidating the important road from MARICOURT to Montauban-de-Picardie, which was repaired to a point close to the old German Front Line. The village cellars were found to be full of German soldiers who had been killed during the Allied shelling. Maj L.P. Walsh of 2nd Royal Dublin Fusiliers (10th Brigade, 4th Division) died of wounds sustained at Montauban-de-Picardie on 1 July. Walsh is buried in Beauval Communal Cemetery (A.12).

In *Three Years with the 9th Division*, W.D. Croft, who had been General Officer Commanding 27th Brigade (9th Division) and then a divisional commander, reports that on the morning of 2 July, 'they got it where the chicken got the axe'. The enemy simply blew BERNAFAY WOOD, which they were occupying, to pieces. And shelling in a wood, 'as everyone knows who has tried it, is far worse than anywhere, not excepting a village'.

Being the first German-held village to fall to the Allies, Montauban-de-Picardie became an object of considerable interest to the brass-hats, who came in swarms, according to Croft. After a week in the area, 27th Brigade were relieved by 8th Black Watch (26th Brigade, 9th Division) and returned to BILLON WOOD, where they had been on the eve of the battle, to recuperate.

In his diary entry of 2 July, Lt Gen Sir Henry Rawlinson, General Officer Commanding Fourth Army, wrote that as FRICOURT had fallen and the British were getting forward, with opposition weakening, it was decided to make a strong line from LA BOISSELLE to Montauban-de-Picardie as a firm basis from which to carry out further attacks.

On 3 July, the positions held by 11th Royal Scots (27th Brigade, 9th Division) lay along the eastern side of the village, the western edge being guarded by 9th Cameronians with 12th Royal Scots (both also 27th Brigade, 9th Division) in reserve. From the Montauban-de-Picardie defences, Montauban Alley led towards BERNAFAY WOOD; to prevent the enemy from closing in on the village, bombing sections from 11th Royal Scots and 9th Cameronians worked this trench to a strongpoint known as Triangle Post, which they garrisoned easily on the morning of 3 July.

John Masefield wrote of this day that on the right the British at the top of the ridge, though often sharply attacked and continuously being shelled, were preparing to go down the hill to attack the enemy in the valley below. This was a long valley between chalk cliffs, the eastern end of which ran into the valley dividing MAMETZ from FRICOURT. In *The Turning Point*, H.P. Robinson, war correspondent of *The Times*, notes that by 5 July, the Allies had forced their way about 1,000yds beyond Montauban-de-Picardie in the direction of MARLBOROUGH WOOD. This brought them almost abreast of the centre of MAMETZ WOOD.

In *We Band of Brothers*, G.W. Warwick of 4th South African Infantry (South African Brigade, 9th Division) described setting off from MARICOURT on 5 July with the night fatigue party to dig new trenches under machine-gun fire at Glatz Redoubt, to the south of Montauban-de-Picardie. They then camped at Montauban-de-Picardie. Warwick said that they had trouble with a water cart in the heavy mud and finished up carrying the water in cans by hand; the quota was two cans of water per platoon, which worked out at about half a bottle per man. While carrying out these tasks, he saw BERNAFAY WOOD coming under very heavy German shell-fire.

During the period 8/9 July, the headquarters of 89th Brigade was in dugouts at the Brickworks. On 9 July, 16th Manchesters were ordered to the sunken road to attack TRÔNES WOOD from there. Three days after Lt Col E.H. Trotter, Commanding Officer 18th King's (21st Brigade, 30th Division), had visited Stanley for what was to be the last time he was killed at 21st Brigade headquarters, west of Glatz Redoubt at Train Alley. He was with Lt Col W.A. Smith, Commanding Officer 18th Manchesters, when a shell hit brigade headquarters. Smith died the next week (see MARICOURT entry).

Talbot Kelly wrote that behind the Brickworks he slept in a slit trench in the side of a large shell-hole. On 13 July, he went up with his major to establish an observation post for the next day. They returned slowly along Montauban Alley and checked their communication wire. The Highlanders were assembling for the battle planned for 15 July and at dusk these men filed out, to lie all night in quiet lines in no man's land, as close to the German wire as possible. On 16 July, Talbot Kelly, as Brigade Forward Observation Officer, moved off towards LONGUEVAL.

In *A Doctor's War*, Geoffrey Keynes of the Royal Army Medical Corps wrote that

gradually our artillery moved forward, and on the 17th July they were in Montauban Alley, a trench just in front of Montauban with a view from Mametz to Delville Wood, of evil memory. At nine thirty that evening we had just finished our supper of bully beef, when suddenly small shells began whistling over our heads at the rate of thirty or forty a minute, making no detonation as they hit the ground . . . We were in a shallow trench, and while the other officers were putting on their gas masks, I thought it better to climb up into the open air, where the concentration of gas was much lighter, and so escaped with only a mouthful of gas.

On the same date, Brig Gen Sir A. Home noted that all that was left of the village was a 'small side chapel of the Church and the figure of the Virgin was then practically untouched . . .'

On 19 July, the headquarters of 76th Brigade (3rd Division) were in the quarry, to the north of Montauban-de-Picardie, when they were heavily shelled. The headquarters was too far forward and had to be evacuated to the sunken road leading down from Montauban-de-Picardie. This location was also shelled, however, and they retreated to a dugout in the village itself.

B/Maj W. Congreve of 76th Brigade (3rd Division) thought that too little time was being given to the preparation of an attack on LONGUEVAL and DELVILLE WOOD and went with Maj Stubbs, Commanding Officer 2nd Suffolks (also 76th Brigade, 3rd Division) to see the situation for himself, when he was shot dead by a German sniper.

Around 24 July, most of the artillery batteries were still behind Montauban-de-Picardie. H.E. Harvey of 22nd Royal Fusiliers (99th Brigade, 2nd Division) noted towards the end of July that 'up the long rising slope to the orchard was the great wreckage of Montauban'. They went on, despite the 5.9s that crashed down on the rubbish heap ahead, past the overturned water wagon and its slain horses, rotting in the bloodstained pond. On, across the road that led down to the quarry and to CATERPILLAR VALLEY; when he was on his way back, delivering bombs and water, roads were taboo, and his party struck off across the hard-fought fields, directly towards Montauban-de-Picardie, hurrying empty handed through its evil-smelling ruins and on to the corner of BERNAFAY WOOD.

In the dusk, Harvey's battalion moved up to the brigade reserve position, the dugouts and cellars of mutilated Montauban-de-Picardie. They watched a panorama – a long curling wall of smoke, 1¼ miles distant across the sweeping valley on the high ridge of CONTALMAISON and the Bazentin Woods to the left; and the smoke-palled LONGUEVAL, DELVILLE and TRÔNES WOODs on the right, 8 to 10 miles of bristling, terrifying battle. Away below the valley was the stripped and stunted line of trees once called Caterpillar Wood. To the right of it, the old quarry with its ruined railtrack, and the field guns belching death; away to the left, the heavy-foliaged MAMETZ WOOD on the furthest slope; speckled and dotted with white chalk torn up by the 'tornado'. Next morning, on 26 July, they had to dig again under hostile fire beyond the quarry and were told to draw extra rounds of bombs. By way

of the battered trench between BERNAFAY and TRÔNES WOODs, 22nd Royal Fusiliers advanced into action in sections, and as brigade supports found themselves amid odious destruction.

On 30/31 July, 106th Brigade (35th Division) were in the quarry, north of Montauban-de-Picardie, at a time when an attack was being carried out against GUILLEMONT. On 11 August, the village was surrounded by British batteries and on 19 August, 5th Oxfordshire & Buckinghamshire Light Infantry (42nd Brigade, 14th Division) were in the village, with their headquarters in a former German blockhouse.

At this time, 9th King's Royal Rifle Corps (42nd Brigade, 15th Division) were occupying Montauban Alley and were involved in part of the fighting for DELVILLE WOOD. On 25 August, 1/4th Suffolks (98th Brigade, 33rd Division) were to attack 2 hours after the bombardment; in the afternoon, 1/4th Suffolks first occupied Montauban Alley and then Carlton Trench. At 0600hrs on 29 August, 2nd Royal Welsh Fusiliers (19th Brigade, 33rd Division, but attached 99th Brigade, 2nd Division) moved into a trench in front of Montauban-de-Picardie, which was virtually a ditch.

In *The Anatomy of Courage*, Lord Moran, medical officer, 1st Royal Fusiliers (5th Brigade, 2nd Division), wrote:

We hurried on through the silence and desolation of Montauban. On that road which was usually so crowded with troops and transport we seemed that night to be the only living things. It was like being left out in no man's land, wounded, forgotten. Now that I had not the support of numbers, I was full of apprehension. I had a feeling that something was about to happen. I wondered vaguely if it was the cold night air rising up out of the valley that made my teeth chatter . . . For some time we had noticed a strange smell and there was something that made our eyes prick; presently tears began to run down our cheeks. The road turned sharply to the left and dipped into a valley and all at once we appeared to be wading through a ground mist. Shells were coming over in great numbers. They detonated almost silently and without the burst of an ordinary shell. We had run into a gas shell barrage. I wanted to ask my servant if his chest felt as if it was being pressed in by an iron band that was gradually getting smaller. I wondered what gas they were using. I remembered we were told that many of the men had heart failure after the last attack.

A gunner came by spitting and rubbing his eyes. He said that there was a sunken road a little further on which led to the quarry. He thought that there was an aid post there; this was a landmark we had been told to look out for . . . Apparently our batteries were everywhere, it was impossible in the darkness and in the fog to steer through them except by the flash of a gun as it fired . . . Just there the rising ground was fairly clear of gas, it was past three o'clock and we decided to wait for the light. The night lifted reluctantly as if it were loath to let us escape and the cold dawn had passed slowly into the promise of a summer day before we found Carlton Trench. The last companies had just arrived after eight hours pilgrimage in the gas to find that no one expected them or knew why they had come. The Colonels of five battalions were collected in one dug-out and the men were packed in the trench like herrings.

The road between Montauban-de-Picardie and CARNOY was severely cratered. In *Other Ranks*, W.V. Tilsley of 1/4th Loyal North Lancashires (164th Brigade, 55th Division) wrote that on 7 September, after MAMETZ, they wheeled past Montauban-de-Picardie. The village resembled little more than a series of brickwork heaps and twisted ironwork. Guns lurked around corners and were under camouflage netting and futuristic paintwork. Darkness touched the stark tree tops of BERNAFAY WOOD as they dropped down the slope before LONGUEVAL. Later they marched back through Montauban-de-Picardie.

On 14 September, 12th East Surreys (122nd Brigade, 41st Division) arrived at night near the quarry, where they saw tanks for the very first time. Three days later, 9th King's Royal Rifle Corps were relieved in Montauban Alley by 6th Somerset Light Infantry (43rd Brigade, 14th Division) and returned to their former camp at BÉCORDEL. They had been close to elements of the Guards Division.

On 19 September, D.V. Kelly of the Leicestershire Regiment noted that when his unit arrived in Montauban-de-Picardie, which was then packed with heavy artillery, they occupied trenches that they had reconnoitred in the afternoon. On 5 October, the village was the battle headquarters of 29th Division.

In *A Soldier's Diary*, Capt G.A. Prideaux of 1st Somerset Light Infantry (11th Brigade, 4th Division) notes that on 9 October his battalion moved from Citadel Camp by cross-country tracks, up to the knees in mud, via CAFTET WOOD and TALUS BOISÉ valley to the Brickworks, south-east of Montauban-de-Picardie, where they took over from 169th Brigade (56th Division). At this time, at least eight horses were needed to move one limber wagon through the mud. Most of the field-gun ammunition was carried up by pack mules. On 15 October they were fired on by the enemy, who were using a long-range gun.

On 19 October, 16th King's Royal Rifle Corps (100th Brigade, 33rd Division) were at the Brickworks Camp when in support. On 24 October, 1/4th Suffolks moved to TRÔNES WOOD in very wet weather; on 4 November, they moved back to hutments on the Montauban-de-Picardie–CARNOY road for a couple of days.

In *Twelve Days*, Sidney Rogerson of 2nd West Yorkshires (23rd Brigade, 8th Division) wrote of marching back to GINCHY and arriving at the Brickworks Camp, where they were once again under canvas, in bell-tents where originally stood the brick yards which had featured so prominently in the despatches describing the September battles around Montauban-de-Picardie.

In November, only heavy traffic used the Montauban-de-Picardie–CARNOY roads until the weather broke. 1st Welsh Guards (3rd Guards Brigade, Guards Division) moved for one night to Camp H near Montauban-de-Picardie, and from there they took over the line. Montauban-de-Picardie was to remain in British hands until the end of March 1918.

Having been an advanced dressing station, Quarry Cemetery was begun in July 1916 and used until February 1917; it was enclosed by a flint wall, irregular in outline where it borders the quarry. Nearly 600 graves were brought in after the war, mainly of those who died in July–December 1916. Four cemeteries were concentrated in Quarry Cemetery. Quarry Cemetery Briqueterie No. 3 contained soldiers, mainly from 1/5th King's Own (166th Brigade, 55th Division) who fell in July and August. Caterpillar Wood Cemetery No. 2 was at the east end of Caterpillar Wood and had been begun by 2nd Suffolks. Green Dump Cemetery, LONGUEVAL, and Quarry Scottish Cemetery, Montauban-de-Picardie, which were between the quarry and the north end of BERNAFAY WOOD, contained mainly men from 11th and 12th Royal Scots (both 27th Brigade, 9th Division). Not surprisingly, owing to the exposed nature of the position, a great many of the graves belong to members of the artillery.

In 1930, a 7ft high wooden regimental cross to the memory of the Royal Scots, which had been leaning on the cemetery wall, was returned to the regimental

Ration wagons on the muddy road, Montauban-de-Picardie, November 1916. *(IWM Q4600)*

headquarters at Ayr. It was a memorial to the men from the battalion who died on 14 July 1916 during the fighting at Longueval Ridge.

After the war, the village was 'adopted' by Maidstone, Kent, and rebuilt, together with its railway. In the early 1990s the Merseyside branch of the Western Front Association decided on a project commemorating the role of the Liverpool and Manchester 'Pals' (17th, 18th, 19th and 20th King's and 16th, 17th, 18th and 19th Manchesters) of 30th Division who captured the village on 1 July 1916. It was dedicated on 1 July 1994, the same day as the memorial to the Manchester 'Pals' (20th, 21st and 22nd Manchesters of 7th Division) at MAMETZ, and about 500 people came to the service, including most of the population of Montauban-de-Picardie. It had been hoped that Lord Derby, whose grandfather, the 17th Earl, originated the idea of the 'Pals' battalions, would be present but he was too unwell to attend and indeed died later in the year.

MONTIGNY-SUR-L'HALLUE is south of the D919 AMIENS–CONTAY road. On 9 August

1915, 18th Division had its headquarters here. On 10 September there were plans for a divisional rest station to be set up by 13th Field Ambulance (5th Division) at the château, but in early October the idea was abandoned as the château owner wanted too much money. Clearly some compromise was reached, as the château was later used for medical purposes and in January 1916 it was also being prepared for use as a grenade school.

On 10 February 1916, 91st Field Ambulance (32nd Division) noted there was no place in the village suitable for a small hospital when neither the château nor another large house – being used as a brigade headquarters – was available. From 10 to 20 March, the headquarters of 18th Division was back here again. On 23 March, part of X Corps headquarters had to leave Querrieu Château, as Fourth Army required the building; many X Corps staff were at BAIZIEUX and later moved to TOUTENCOURT. In mid-March, 30th Division headquarters was here.

From Sir Douglas Haig's diary, we know that on 2 July he made a visit to the casualty clearing station here, which was under the control of Maj Thomas and Col Macpherson. 'They were very pleased at my visit. The wounded were in wonderful spirits. I saw Sir Wilmot Herringham with his coat off, setting a fine example, by washing and attending to slightly wounded cases. I thanked him. I believe he is consulting physician to Bart's Hospital, London. Everything seemed to be going on well.'

At the end of July, 1st Division had their headquarters here. In mid-August, 50th Division's headquarters was in the château, and 1st Division were back in mid-September.

Montigny-sur-l'Hallue Communal Cemetery, south-west of the village, contains the graves of men of 47th and 58th Divisions who died between May and August 1918. The main château with its imposing gates, occupied by the German Army in 1940–44, is surrounded by a low wall, and grounds within which housing has recently been built.

MONTONVILLERS is west of the N25 AMIENS road. On 28 November 1915, 91st Field Ambulance (32nd Division) stayed here for 3 days and used a schoolhouse as a hospital; men were billeted in the yard of the château and had accommodation in various lofts, while horses were picketed in a field. In December, 1/2nd (Highland) Field Ambulance (51st Division) opened a dressing station here for the care of 153rd Brigade (also 51st Division). When No. 201 Field Company, Royal Engineers (30th Division), were in the village, 30 civilians lived there. The château was not available, so the men used mud huts, while the officers found an empty vicarage to stay in; the water was undrinkable. A brigadier-general and his staff occupied the château. On 11 July 1916, 1st Division's headquarters was here. Though not lived in since the German occupation of the 1940s, the château remains in good order.

MORLANCOURT is on the D42 road between ALBERT and SAILLY-LAURETTE, which runs along the north bank of the River Somme on the slope of the ridge separating the Rivers Somme and Ancre close to their junction. It was behind the Allied lines in 1915 and 1916.

In August 1915, 1st Norfolks (15th Brigade, 5th Division) were billeted here and supplied parties to work in local support trenches. The pattern of work continued in September during reliefs of 1st East Surreys (95th Brigade, 5th Division) at MARICOURT. 18th Division also had units here during the September–November period.

In mid-January 1916, 15th Royal Warwicks were transferred from 14th Brigade (32nd Division) to 13th Brigade (5th Division); arriving here from SUZANNE on 11 January, they were billeted in canvas huts for 3 days before moving southwards to SAILLY-LAURETTE.

In the early part of 1916, Morlancourt was closely associated with 7th Division, and in particular with 1st Royal Welsh Fusiliers (22nd Brigade, 7th Division); both Siegfried Sassoon and Bernard Adams mention it in their books as a rather idyllic place. In his fictional memoirs, Sassoon wrote that in January 1916, 'Sherston', his main character, rode with the transport and arrived at Morlancourt, which was 4 or 5 miles from the trenches. It was 'tucked away among the fold of long slopes and bare rides of ploughland'.

In *Nothing of Importance*, Bernard Adams wrote of 1 February: 'To-day we marched to Morlancourt and are spending the night in huts. It is very cold, and we have a brazier made out of a biscuit tin, but it smokes abominably. We are busy getting trench-kit ready for the next day. From outside the hut I can see starlights and hear the machine guns tapping. It thrills like the turning up of the footlights.' Between February and June they were often to be billeted in the village. Several roads ran down into the village and Adams described it as a 'cosy spot, and a very jolly thing' after that long, long weary grind up from MÉAULTE at the end of 6 weary days, to look down on the snug little village waiting below. It was just too far off for shelling.

Sassoon was in the village around 16 March and he too mentions in his diary the friendly convergence of roads. There was a church with a giant vane, over which birds wheeled and cackled. In the hollow ground, where the five roads met, there was a congregation of farm buildings round an open space with a pond on one side. The long lines of high ground hid the rest of the world. Sassoon slept in canvas huts close to the transport, as he was transport officer at the time.

In the spring, 21st Manchesters (91st Brigade, 7th Division) were in the village and were involved in railway construction between here, MÉAULTE and Waterloo Junction. Robert Graves mentioned that his battalion, 2nd Royal Welsh Fusiliers (19th Brigade, 33rd Division), were in the village while being in and out trenches opposite FRICOURT and MAMETZ. He wrote in his memoirs, *Goodbye to All That*, that the village was untouched by shell-fire and that A Company headquarters was a farmhouse kitchen where they slept on the brick floor.

In *Memoirs of an Infantry Officer*, Sassoon mentioned that after Easter he proceeded to the Fourth Army School for a month's refresher course. He left the centre of Morlancourt and returned there on 22 May at the end of a hot day. The bus turned off the bumpy road from CORBIE and began to crawl down the steep winding lane.

When close to the front in June, Sassoon noted that TAILLES WOOD was full of men from 2nd Borders and 8th and 9th Devons (all 20th Brigade, 7th Division); and while walking home to Morlancourt, Sassoon saw the village in the basin with smoke rising and looking very peaceful. On 9 June, he rode down to the village with the quartermaster in a perfect sunset; the muddy road as they moved away from the CITADEL was red before their feet.

On 13 June, 50th Brigade (17th Division) moved here from BUSSY-LÈS-DAOURS; the village was full of troops and supply columns and a main dressing station was set up, as well as an advanced dressing station in a churchyard. It is important to note that, unusually, the village boasted two churches, which were to the west and east (Villers church) of the village respectively. Today, only the western one survives.

Morlancourt became very well known for its two hospitals over the coming weeks, rather than for its role as a billeting village. On 27 April, 21st Field Ambulance (7th Division) came here from CORBIE for 4 days but did not open a hospital; 22nd Field Ambulance (also 7th Division) came here on 4 May, and as there was still no place for a hospital their unit also remained closed. They left for DAOURS on 11 May.

Beginning in early May 1916, field ambulances of 7th Division ran the medical arrangements here very efficiently. On 7 May, 21st Field Ambulance returned, but still didn't open a hospital until 15 May, when it opened a 20-bed hospital under canvas. On 10 June a field was pegged out for a new hospital and on 23 June, 21st Field Ambulance received instructions that during active operations it was to take in both sick and wounded.

On 26 June, 22nd Field Ambulance arrived; they took over a large church hut and recreation room for the lightly wounded for use as a hospital accommodating about 150 cases. On the eve of the battle their bearers left for MINDEN POST.

On 24 June, 23rd Field Ambulance (7th Division) arrived in Morlancourt and established a main dressing station in Villers church (known in war diaries as the Old Church) for up to 300 sitting up and walking cases, who would be evacuated to No. 36 Casualty Clearing Station at HEILLY. The ordinary lightly wounded were to be sent to 22nd Field Ambulance at the church hut.

It would appear that prior to and during the early part of the battle, all three field ambulances of 7th Division were actively involved in hospital work in the village, but at separate locations. On 1 July, the first wounded arrived at 21st Field Ambulance at 0900hrs; by noon, 30 cases had been admitted. The wounded then arrived steadily all day and the total number admitted over a 12-hour period came to 529, including 26 Germans. Lying cases came to 480 and all cases were evacuated to Nos. 38 and 5 Casualty Clearing Stations.

At 0200hrs on 2 July, the medical chain was beginning to break down, as 21st Field Ambulance received instructions that no more casualties were to be evacuated until further orders. However, from 0600hrs patients could be evacuated again, either to South Midland Casualty Clearing Station at AMIENS or No. 36 Casualty Clearing Station; No. 38 Casualty Clearing Station was now also open again. By 1630hrs the crisis had passed and most cases had been evacuated.

On 3 July casualties fell to 13. On 6 July, 21st Field Ambulance were still in the village, temporarily attached to 30th Division and helping out with lying cases. On 19 July their bearer division were ordered up to Flat Iron Copse to relieve the bearers of 22nd Field Ambulance.

On 1 July, 22nd Field Ambulance, as well as expecting casualties, were also placed in medical charge of XV Corps' prisoners cage. Beginning at 1900hrs on 1 July, the hut was 'in full swing', coping with walking cases. The patients were first assessed outside and then brought into the hut before being evacuated by lorry. The rush of casualties eased by 0600hrs on 2 July. By the following day, MINDEN POST had been almost cleared of wounded, but hundreds of German prisoners were arriving.

On 5 July, 22nd Field Ambulance were relieved when 129th and 131st Field Ambulances (both 38th Division) arrived in the village. However, a week later, 22nd Field Ambulance returned to take over the hut and other buildings at Morlancourt. On 14 July several hundred wounded arrived; on 21 July, 22nd Field Ambulance left for DERNANCOURT.

On 1 July casualties were brought down from aid posts at Crawley Ridge, MAPLE REDOUBT and Wellington Redoubt and the advanced dressing station at the CITADEL to the divisional collecting station at BRONFAY FARM, under the control of 21st Field Ambulance, where they were taken by horse or motor ambulances along the BRAY-SUR-SOMME–CORBIE road (now the D1) before taking the turning up to Morlancourt after passing TAILLES WOOD. Horse ambulances usually transported walking or sitting cases and the motor ambulances or lorries took the stretcher cases.

At 1020hrs on 1 July, the first cases to arrive at the main dressing station came in; they were men hit near MAMETZ. During the afternoon the cases came in at about a rate of 100 per hour. By now, the three medical officers and dressers were becoming overwhelmed and could not keep up with the flow. Some men had been treated at the CITADEL already and these men were not touched. By 2000hrs, 23rd Field Ambulance could not cope and permission was given to send further wounded to 22nd Field Ambulance at the church hut. Lorries steadily evacuated casualties to No. 5 Casualty Clearing Station at CORBIE.

At 0100hrs on 2 July, 23rd Field Ambulance were informed that all casualty clearing stations were full and that no men were to be evacuated for the time being. 22nd Field Ambulance had become full as well and 23rd Field Ambulance were forced to receive more wounded before they were ready to cope with them efficiently. Helped by a fall in casualty numbers, however, 23rd Field Ambulance were again up to date by 0500hrs. German troops regularly featured among the incoming casualties.

In the early afternoon of 2 July, orders were received that casualties could be evacuated to Nos. 36 and 38 Casualty Clearing Stations, work that was carried out by a dozen lorries. Between 600 and 700 men passed through the advanced dressing station at the CITADEL in the first 36 hours of the battle. Back at Morlancourt, the main dressing station was completely cleared by 1715hrs on 2 July, but Nos. 36 and 38 Casualty Clearing Stations were closed once again. Evacuations were now to be sent to VECQUEMONT.

After 1300hrs on 4 July, a violent thunderstorm burst at Morlancourt and heavy rain brought down so much mud that the entrance to the church was blocked. A working party spent 2 hours clearing the mud, and by 1530hrs the station was again cleared.

On 6 July, 23rd Field Ambulance left for MÉRICOURT-L'ABBÉ and 130th Field Ambulance (38th Division) took over; 2,400 casualties were dealt with over the next few days, and great problems occurred when trying to evacuate casualties in the open. The war diary of 130th Field Ambulance (WO95/2549) noted that the main dressing station was located in a derelict church, which carried the date of 1741; it appeared 'to have been allowed to get into a neglected and dilapidated condition'. Much of the roof had fallen and there were two entrances on either side of the tower on the west side. The door to the north became an entrance door for casualties, where a cookhouse and packstore were erected. The patients, who were sitting cases, were checked in and occupied the pews in the aisle while waiting to have their wounds dressed. The chancel was sectioned off and used as an operating and dispensary room. The vestry was used as a dispensary store. After having their wounds dressed, the patients moved to the south aisle, where further details of their condition were taken down. These ranged from gun-shot wounds to shell shock.

On 12 July, 23rd Field Ambulance returned to the main dressing station; 130th Field Ambulance left the next day. Hundreds of wounded again came in on 14 July, when rain added to their difficulties. On 5 July, 131st Field Ambulance moved to Morlancourt, and left on 13 July for WARLOY-BAILLON.

At Zero Hour on 1 July, 51st Brigade (17th Division) were at Morlancourt. Maj R.G. Raper, Second in Command 8th South Staffords, noted in his papers that he had visited the village on 29 June, having come from HEILLY, where he had been camped. After returning to HEILLY for a brief time, 8th South Staffords marched out at 2210hrs on 30 June and arrived at Morlancourt at 0030hrs on 1 July. Raper noted the many German prisoners who kept arriving and were then put into an enclosure in a farm. At least 400 passed through and were fed with bully-beef and biscuits. Sadly, Raper was killed 2 days later at FRICOURT.

On 21 July, 1st King's Royal Rifle Corps (99th Brigade, 2nd Division) arrived in Morlancourt, at a time when there were five battalions bivouacked in the village. In July, the headquarters of XIII Corps was in the village, and throughout July the village hutments and billets accommodated troops. In early August, 35th Division were here for a few days, and while in the village bathed in the river at VILLE-SUR-ANCRE, to the north-west.

On 25 August, 1st Scots Guards (2nd Guards Brigade, Guards Division) arrived here from BUS-LÈS-ARTOIS, where they had been training for 2 weeks. In early September, the rest of 2nd Guards Brigade were billeted in the village while training for the battles that they were to take part in later in the month.

Aubrey Smith, who served with the transport of 1/5th Londons (169th Brigade, 56th Division), wrote that the Guards looked very smart and soldierly when he passed them on his way to HAPPY VALLEY, north-west of BRAY-SUR-SOMME. In *Johnny Get Your Gun*, J.F. Tucker of 1/13th Londons (168th Brigade, 56th Division) described how, after being at LEUZE WOOD, his battalion were reinforced and marched off past Citadel Camp and on to Morlancourt. There they were billeted in some 'nice dry barns', but not for long, as they had to move back to Citadel Camp.

In September, No. 9 Squadron, Royal Flying Corps, commanded by Maj A.B. Burdett, arrived here from CHIPILLY, remaining in the village until April 1917.

Apart from 7th and 38th Divisions, which were particularly associated with Morlancourt, 6th, 20th, 24th, 30th, 33rd and 35th Divisions occasionally had units in the area.

There are two military cemeteries in the village. Morlancourt British Cemetery No. 1 is on the west side of the village. Formerly known as Morlancourt Military Cemetery, it was made by field ambulances in June and July 1916, and stands on the western slope of a long and narrow valley. It has 71 identified graves; 1, who had died in September 1915, was brought in from Morlancourt Communal Cemetery in 1926, 4 were buried prior to the battle, and 66 died during the battle, mainly in July. These include 12 men from the Manchester Regiment, 12 from the Royal Welsh Fusiliers, 7 from the Welsh Regiment, 5 from the Border Regiment, 5 from the Royal Field Artillery and 30 from other battalions.

Lt Col O.S. Flower, Commanding Officer 13th Royal Welsh Fusiliers (113th Brigade, 38th Division), mortally wounded at Wood Support Trench, died of wounds on 12 July and was buried here (B.21). The following account of the attempts to capture MAMETZ WOOD is based on the regimental history:

> To clear up the situation the Brigadier ordered Lieutenant-Colonel Flower to take the two re-maining companies of his battalion forward (13th) and reorganise the 113th Brigade. About the same time he went forward with Colonel Gosset, attached from the Fourth Army. In Strip Trench 'a party of men were found running back in panic'. Flower and his two companies had arrived at the edge of the wood, the leading line to carry the troops in front forward, the second line to dig in. Actually these companies joined the mass of troops assembled south of the first ride . . .

Later, 38th Division were relieved by 21st Division and returned to billets round TREUX. The brigadier-general commanding 113th Brigade said: 'In particular the names of Lieutenant-Colonel Flower, Lieutenant-Colonel Carden, and Major R.H. Mills should ever be remembered by us as officers who have set a glorious example, an example we should all endeavour to copy . . .'

Morlancourt British Cemetery No. 2 is on the north-west side of the village, near the road to VILLE-SUR-ANCRE; it was made in August 1918 and contains the graves of 54 identified men.

Morlancourt was captured by the enemy in March 1918 and became a front-line village. It was retaken by Australian troops in May, lost at the end of July, and recaptured on 9 August by 1/1st Cambridge-shires (118th Brigade, 39th Division), together with tanks. The damage caused in 1918 was far worse than that of 1916.

The village was 'adopted' by Folkestone after the war, and the rebuilding was extensive.

MORVAL is on the D74 road between LESBŒUFS to the north-west and COMBLES to the south. On high ground, in 1916 it was in effect the key to COMBLES. It had an underground labyrinth and a maze of fortifications above ground, and was a fortress of similar type to THIEPVAL. Prior to the start of the battle, the enemy continuously used the byroad on which the village stands to take supplies to COMBLES.

With its commanding position and a well-fortified line of trenches in front of it facing the Allies, it was always going to be a very difficult village to capture. In addition, there were numerous sunken roads in the area, together with timbered ravines, all carefully fortified for defence, which made it even more formidable. Twin trench lines came down from the north-westerly direction in front of GUEUDE-COURT, known as Gird Trench and Gird Support; their names altered as they came closer to LES-BŒUFS and Morval and they became known as Cow and Ox, with their supports the Bovril, Meat and Mutton Trenches. The comparable German trenches in the Morval area were known as Rainbow, Cloudy, Misty, Zenith and so on.

On 15 September 1916 the first objective of 20th Division was the Blue Line facing Morval and LESBŒUFS, about 1,200yds west of the two villages. The second objective skirted Morval on the west and LESBŒUFS on the east and ended at the crossroads halfway between LESBŒUFS and GUEUDECOURT. On this day, 61st Brigade were delayed in their attacks because 6th Division were held up by the QUADRILATERAL, a German strongpoint about ¾ mile to the east of GINCHY. Another attack was planned for 25 September.

This time, 5th Division were chosen; the attacking brigades were 95th Brigade on the right and 15th Brigade on the left. Further to the left were 18th and 16th Brigades (both 6th Division). LESBŒUFS was successfully captured. The attack was part of an offensive along the whole front between COMBLES and MARTINPUICH. In fact, it was 15th Brigade, the left brigade of 5th Division's attack, which managed to take Morval after mopping up the dugouts and cellars in the village; the troops then moved out into the open country to the east. By nightfall, the final objective that ran southwards from Morval windmill was consolidated.

Once Morval had fallen, the capture of COMBLES to the south-west was assured. Meanwhile, the French Army, on the right of the British, had captured Fregicourt and 5th Division's 95th Brigade made their way southwards to join up with them. The whole Morval operation had been very successful and was the biggest Allied success in the Somme battle since mid-July. In addition, many prisoners and machine guns were captured. Much of the spotting and observation for the artillery had been done from observation balloons. The one group that did not help were the tanks. Of the three allocated to 5th Division, one failed to start, the second proceeded some distance and then grounded in the mud in the vicinity of the jumping-off line by a sunken road, and the third, after various adventures, arrived after the infantry on the southern side of Morval and assisted 95th Brigade.

Pte T.A. ('Todger') Jones of 1st Cheshires (15th Brigade, 5th Division) gained the Victoria Cross during the capture of Morval on 25 September. According to his citation, when

> he was with his company consolidating the defences in front of the village, and noticing an enemy sniper at 200 yards' distance, he went out, and though one bullet went through his helmet and another through his coat, he returned the sniper's fire and killed him. He then saw two of the enemy firing at him, although displaying a white flag. Both of these he also shot. On reaching the enemy trench he found several occupied dug-outs, and, single-handed, disarmed 102 of the enemy, including three of four officers, and marched them back to our lines through a very heavy barrage. He had been warned of the misuse of the white flag by the enemy, but insisted on going after them . . .

Between 25 and 28 September, Morval, LESBŒUFS and GUEUDECOURT were the Allied objectives, as well as a belt of countryside about 1,000yds deep, curving around the north of FLERS; all this was in preparation for the attack against LE TRANSLOY to the north-east. In the period 26–27 September, 12th King's Royal Rifle Corps (60th Brigade, 20th Division) gained ground to the right of Morval and joined hands with the French Army.

Further progress was delayed by poor weather. On 23 October, 2nd Royal Welsh Fusiliers (19th Brigade, 33rd Division) were settled astride a road between GINCHY to the south-west and Morval. Conditions were wintry and cold, and the ground was very soggy; the field guns were in what little shelter there was about 60yds behind them. The officers' headquarters was a sort of shack made out of shell-boxes.

2nd Royal Welsh Fusiliers had been lent to 4th Division, who were in action on the Morval–LESBŒUFS front. The idea was to improve the line in readiness for a full-scale attack against LE TRANSLOY. However, this attack failed and 33rd Division relieved 4th Division. 2nd Royal Welsh Fusiliers moved closer to Morval, and on 25 October they were in what was known as Hazy Trench, a sunken road between Morval and LESBŒUFS. On 28 October they moved back to GUILLEMONT, still very cold. On 30 October they withdrew to trenches between BERNAFAY and TRÔNES WOODs.

Morval remained in Allied hands until 24 March 1918; after fierce fighting by 38th Division, it was regained on 1 September 1918.

Morval British Cemetery is on the western outskirts of the village. The graves are of men from 38th Division who fell in August and September 1918.

MOUFLERS, north-west of AMIENS on the N1 road, was an early billeting stop for 17th Highland Light Infantry (97th Brigade, 32nd Division) on 25 November 1915. Although the weather was fine, the actual billets were very poor, except for those used by the headquarters staff who were in the château. This may have been the château to the north-east of the village, which in fact is closer to Vauchelles. On 27 November, 17th Highland Light Infantry set out to march nearer to AMIENS, arriving at la Chaussée-Tirancourt on a frosty and bright day, headed by their band; 17th Northumberland Fusiliers (pioneers of 32nd Division) followed, together with two Army Service Corps companies.

MOUQUET FARM (Mucky Farm) can be found off the D73 road between POZIÈRES and THIEPVAL. The right wing of the Farm was burnt down in September 1914 and the present farm complex was built close to the ruins of the former buildings 10 years after the war.

At the beginning of the Battle of the Somme, the Farm was a forward advance headquarters for the German Army in their second-line positions. There were two supply dumps there, and also an artillery dump in the vicinty. A water pipeline ran from the Farm to THIEPVAL; it also contained several wells and a telephone exchange. Under the two barns were four large cellars with windows about 3ft above the ground. Men could fire or use machine guns from these windows and each cellar could hold 40 men.

On 1 July 1916 the Mouquet Switch, which included the Farm, was the objective of 1st Dorsets (14th Brigade, 32nd Division). However, 1st Dorsets were unable to make much progress as many of them were cut down at the LEIPZIG SALIENT to the south-west by machine-gun fire from the Nord Werk; the machine guns were concentrated in the Ovillers Spur. On 1 July, 2/Lt E.H. Brittain, attached 11th Sherwood Foresters (70th Brigade, 8th Division), won a Military Cross here for his leadership, but was also badly wounded. Brittain, brother of the writer and pacifist Vera Brittain, was back in England a few days later and ended up in the same London hospital where Vera was a nurse.

The LEIPZIG SALIENT was virtually a bastion that defended Mouquet Farm to the south-east; as long as POZIÈRES was in German hands, the Farm was protected from this direction as well. On the night of 10 August, patrols of 4th Australian Division pushed out and established posts in the valley south of the Farm, which had already been reduced to what appeared to be just a mound of rubble. They also established posts to the east. An attack was made, however, from a captured section of the German Fabeck Trench, which was to the north-east. There was an attempt to make the Salient deeper in the attacks that were to follow.

By 22 August, 2nd Australian Division had tried with the use of increased forces to capture the Farm; by now, it may have appeared to be just a pile of rubble, but in effect it was a very superior German strongpoint, with the emphasis on the subterranean nature of the position, as Mouquet Farm contained very large dugouts and passages. On 3 September, 13th Australian Brigade (4th Australian Division) attacked and captured much of the Farm and the neighbouring trenches. There was fierce fighting both above ground and in the underground passages. 13th Australian Brigade were then forced to withdraw, but did manage to cling to part of Fabeck Trench. During this time, 4th Australian Division had 2,049 casualties.

It was now the turn of the Canadian divisions; they managed to capture Mouquet Farm on 16 September but without totally clearing it, and they were subsequently driven out. By 25 September the Farm was shared by the two opposing sides, but the tunnels under it were still in German hands. On 26 September the Farm was attacked and taken by 11th Division, 34th Brigade completing its capture with 33rd Brigade to their left. Meanwhile, 18th Division were busy capturing the stronghold of THIEPVAL to the west.

Heavily involved in the fighting in the ruins of the Farm, 9th Lancashire Fusiliers (34th Brigade, 11th Division) tried to bomb the exit points and managed to reach their second objective, the west end of Zollern Trench to the north-west of the Farm; German machine guns had been very active here. This confused fighting ended with the surrender of 56 Germans, including 1 officer, after smoke bombs had been flung down into the cellars. Two tanks had been allocated to assist, but they had to be ditched before reaching the objective. In the event, Mouquet Farm, ZOLLERN REDOUBT and THIEPVAL were all to fall on the same day.

The official War Office photographer, Geoffrey Malins, saw the Farm shortly after its capture and described it in his book as the 'most wonderful defensive point that could possibly be conceived, and chosen by men who made a special study of such positions'. He said that the whole place had been thickly planted with machine guns that were cunningly concealed and able to cover the ground that attackers would have to cross, which had no vestige of cover. Although the Farm and the surrounding area had been shelled continuously, this made little impact on the German garrison, which had been in dugouts some 40ft or 50ft underground. According to Malins, many of the Allied field gun batteries took up their positions in former shell-holes near the Farm, turning them into gun pits. Malins actually entered the underground defences with a guide and found some of it blown in. It was a veritable 'rabbit warren' and his party emerged at a point about 100yds from their entrance point.

Apart from being a strongpoint with deep dugouts, the Farm had also served as a main dressing station. It wasn't until 1924 that the area was finally cleared of the remains of Australian, British and German casualties. In 1928 the Farm was rebuilt on a new site.

On 1 September 1997, a monument and plaque were unveiled close to the road here by the deputy prime minister of Australia to commemorate the role of Australian troops between August and September 1916. In the form of a vertical stone slab bearing a bronze relief, the memorial is at the junction of the track to the present site of the Farm. The ground was given freely by the mayor of COURCELETTE who owns the Farm, and whose grandfather owned it in 1914.

Mouquet Farm. *(IWM E (Aus) 4043)*

MUNSTER ALLEY, off the main D929 ALBERT–BAPAUME road, was a continuation of Pozières Trench, going in a north-easterly direction and running parallel to it. It was also parallel to the Pozières Mill beyond POZIÈRES. The Old German trenches linked up with the German Switch Line beyond and it was an important point in the enemy's communications with MARTINPUICH.

On 3 July 1916, 68th Brigade (23rd Division) spent one night in trenches at ALBERT before going to Bécourt Wood the next day. From 7 to 10 July they took part in a series of operations, including an attack on CONTALMAISON to the south-east, when 12th and 13th Durham Light Infantry (both 68th Brigade, 23rd Division) succeeded in capturing BAILIFF WOOD, one of the brigade's main objectives, to the west of CONTALMAISON. For his part in the fighting, the British musician and composer George Butterworth, an officer with 13th Durham Light Infantry, was recommended for the award of the Military Cross. Butterworth was left in charge after his company commander was wounded. On 11 July, 68th Brigade were relieved and returned to ALBERT.

On the night of 17 July, 68th Brigade took part in fighting at POZIÈRES, making an unsuccessful frontal attack. After consolidating their trenches during the next 2 days they were relieved by 3rd Australian Brigade (1st Australian Division) on 20 July and returned to ALBERT. They re-formed with 23rd Division near FRANVILLERS and Butterworth was once again recommended for the Military Cross.

On 26 July, 13th Durham Light Infantry relieved 2nd Royal Munster Fusiliers (3rd Brigade, 1st Division) in support trenches at CONTALMAISON; on the following day, they relieved 10th Northumberland Fusiliers (68th Brigade, 23rd Division). Munster Alley was the dividing line between the two divisions; the trench ran at right angles to the British front, straight through the enemy's line. On 27 July, 70yds of the trench were secured and consolidated, and on the same day Butterworth was wounded but remained at duty. 68th Brigade then withdrew to Sausage Valley and ALBERT; during a short rest period, Butterworth wrote what turned out to be his last letter home, dated 29 July. The day before, his company had succeeded in advancing the line some 200yds on the right of Munster Alley before it was relieved. They had been assisted by a company of 12th Durham Light Infantry and had gained the ground on the right by digging a trench, which was henceforth given the name of Butterworth Trench. It was almost parallel to the German Switch Trench.

On 1 August, 68th Brigade went up the line again. On 4 August, it appears that two attacks were made on Munster Alley simultaneously, with a bombing party under Butterworth moving up the trench while another group attacked over the top from the loop in Butterworth Trench. Possibly owing to the British artillery, the latter attempt failed, but Butterworth's party succeeded in gaining some 100yds of Munster Alley and in then making a block. Tragically, on 5 August, Butterworth was killed by a shot through the head, falling close to the section of the line where 68th Brigade's line joined that of the Australians at the southern end of the Alley, behind the modern radio station. In addition, Lt N.A. Target was killed, two other officers wounded, and 30 other ranks became casualties. 13th Durham Light Infantry were relieved by 8th Yorkshires (69th Brigade, 23rd Division); one member of this battalion, Pte W. Short, was awarded a posthumous Victoria Cross for his actions at Munster Alley on 6 August.

Butterworth may have been killed by 'friendly fire', rather than by a sniper. This might have been brought about because the Allied and enemy lines were extremely close in this section, and shelling short was inevitable. Born in 1885, son of Sir A. Kaye-Butterworth, general manager of the North East Railway, George Butterworth applied for a temporary commission on 2 October 1914, when he gave his occupation as a musician. He is most remembered as a collector of folk-songs, as an excellent folk-dancer and as an arranger of A.E. Housman's verse, for which he produced several fine settings. Quintessentially English at the time of its composition, his orchestral idyll *The Banks of Green Willow* (1913) was a musical statement that today still somehow summons up an innocence of the pre-war period.

Butterworth's name is commemorated on the Thiepval Memorial. The composer Ralph Vaughan Williams dedicated the 1918 revision of *A London Symphony* to his memory. It appears that it was Butterworth who, one evening in 1910, had suggested to the composer that he should try writing a second symphony. Vaughan Williams took up the idea and worked on the score for the next 3 years; the work was first performed in May 1914. However, the score was lost during the early part of the war and Butterworth helped Vaughan Williams to reconstruct a full score from the orchestral parts. Although it was this symphony that brought Vaughan Williams into the public eye, he continued to tinker with it for the rest of his life. How the two

men found the time to work on it during the war is difficult to explain, with one working with the Royal Army Medical Corps and the other a battalion officer on the Western Front.

N

THE NAB was a sharp salient at the head of Nab Valley, later better known as BLIGHTY VALLEY, in the north-east corner of Authuille Wood. At the end of June 1916, the head of the Valley was almost on the front line, while the rest of it was virtually a maze of battered trenches. The reserve line ran to the south of the Nab; at one point, it ran along what became known as Dead Man's Bank, the scene of many deaths on 1 July. Although it was only a few feet high, Dead Man's Bank was halfway across no man's land.

On 1 July, 32nd Division were to the left and 11th Sherwood Foresters (70th Brigade, 8th Division) to the right. Two battalions who suffered many casualties when they tried in vain to break out towards MOUQUET FARM and POZIÈRES were 8th King's Own Yorkshire Light Infantry and 8th York & Lancasters (both also 70th Brigade, 23rd Division); 9th York & Lancasters (also 70th Brigade, 23rd Division) also had many casualties here, as did 11th Sherwood Foresters.

In early September, Nab Valley contained many guns of differing calibres and seemed to be safe from counter-shelling. By the middle of the month the advance had at last made some progress; later in the month, the fortress of THIEPVAL to the north was finally captured.

Blighty Valley Cemetery is signposted from the D50 ALBERT–HAMEL road and can be reached after a short walk. It is a predominantly 1916 concentration cemetery and the earliest burials from the beginning of the battle can be found in Plot I. After the Armistice, 789 more men were brought in, mainly of 8th Division, which had suffered so much early in the battle.

NAOURS is a village due north of AMIENS, to the west of the N25 road to DOULLENS. In September 1915, 30th Division had units in training here. Men from 49th Division were billeted in the village in mid-March 1916. On 31 March, 49th Division's headquarters was here, with 1/8th West Yorkshires

(146th Brigade, 49th Division) at BÉHENCOURT, north-east of AMIENS, and companies of 1/6th West Yorkshires (also 146th Brigade, 49th Division) at SENLIS-LE-SEC and BOUZINCOURT; 1/7th West Yorkshires were at FRÉCHENCOURT and 1/5th West Yorkshires (both also 146th Brigade, 49th Division) at BAVELINCOURT. The office of 49th Division's Assistant Director of Medical Services was in the *mairie* in North Street. On 29 September, 21st Brigade (30th Division) came here for training.

NEWFOUNDLAND PARK or the Parc de Terre-Neuvien is on the D73 road between THIEPVAL and AUCHONVILLERS. It was named after the Newfoundland Regiment, which had been formed at the outbreak of the First World War as a result of 'popular feeling in the Dominion'. Reaching France via Egypt, 1st Newfoundlanders were sent to the Somme region in March 1916 and developed a very close relationship with the village of LOUVEN-COURT and its inhabitants. On 1 July they took part in the attack on BEAUMONT-HAMEL, a total disaster which cost the battalion 715 casualties.

After the war, a memorial in Newfoundland Park to the memory of 51st Division, victors of Y RAVINE in November 1916, was commissioned, and was scheduled to be ready by the summer of 1924. The original site for the memorial, donated by the *Maire* of BEAUMONT-HAMEL on behalf of the commune, was on the BEAUCOURT-SUR-L'ANCRE road overlooking the village. While the foundations were being dug, however, it was found that subterranean caves and quarries ran beneath it, and the site was abandoned. Fortunately, during their occupation of the village the enemy had no idea of the existence of these features, which would have been of great assistance to them.

An alternative site was offered by the Newfoundland government in the 84-acre site which they had recently purchased and which was being laid out as a park to commemorate the Newfoundland Regiment. The site chosen for the 51st Division memorial was at the top of Y RAVINE, close to the German Front Line. The sculptor for the memorial, in the form of a bronze figure of a Highlander, was Mr George H. Paulin, who was already working on the 1/8th Argyll & Sutherland Highlanders memorial to be set up near the Sunken Road at BEAUMONT-HAMEL. The figure would be set up on a cairn made from Aberdeen granite. The date of unveiling was to be 28 September 1924 and a committee was set up to provide financial assistance for relatives of men who had lost their lives in BEAUMONT-HAMEL. In addition, a lunch for 500 people was planned, which

would take place in the Park. Accommodation was prepared in the Log Cabin and in a large marquee set up for the purpose. Apart from veterans and relatives, other guests included young French girls dressed in white, soldiers in resplendent uniforms, generals in full dress, British ladies and French peasants dressed in their Sunday best. The 51st Division memorial was draped with a Union Jack on one side and the French *tricolore* on the other.

On 28 September an early morning mist began to lift and at 1100hrs the British guard of honour took up positions to the right of the memorial, followed by pipers from 2nd Argyll & Sutherland Highlanders and members of the French 51st Infantry Regiment. Then the civilian procession appeared, representing many of the villages from round about. Marshal Foch, who was to unveil the memorial, attended a church service in the small wooden church in the village; afterwards, he and his staff walked down the road to a 'small eminence' overlooking the AUCHONVILLERS road known as Windy Corner. Here at BEAUMONT-HAMEL, in the presence of 2,000 people, on enclosed ground a 45ft flagpole had been erected with a bronze plate in French and English: 'Presented to the Inhabitants of Beaumont-Hamel (Somme), by the Officers, Non-Commissioned Officers and Men of the 51st (Highland) Division, in commemoration of the recapture of the village by the Division on 13th November, 1916.' The pole flying the French *tricolore* was duly handed over to the *Maire*, together with a Scottish standard, which was to be flown every anniversary of 13 November. Soon afterwards the party returned to the Park, where Foch unveiled the memorial soon after 1130hrs and the sound of bugles playing the Last Post was soon heard, coming from Y RAVINE. The dedication, addresses and official handing over of the memorial to the care of the commune then followed and visitors began to lay wreaths and other floral tributes at the foot of the memorial. In recent years the flagpole was destroyed during a storm and it was replaced and unveiled on 13 November 2006.

It would appear that the American writer F. Scott Fitzgerald visited the Park in 1924 and subsequently published the following description in his novel *Tender is the Night*.

Dick turned the corner of the traverse and continued along the trench walking on the duck-board. He came to a periscope, looked through it a moment, then he got up on the step and peered over the parapet. In front of him beneath a dingy sky was Beaumont-Hamel; to his left the tragic hill of Thiepval. Dick stared through his field-glasses, his throat straining with sadness. He went along the trench, and found the others waiting for him . . . 'This land here cost twenty lives a foot that summer', he said to Rosemary. She looked out obediently at the rather green plain with its low trees of six years' growth . . . 'See that little stream – we could walk to it in two minutes. It took the British a month to walk it – a whole Empire walking very slowly, dying in front and pushing forward behind. And another Empire walked very slowly backward a few inches a day, leaving the dead like a million bloody rugs. No Europeans will ever do that again in this generation' . . . 'this western-front business couldn't be done again, not for a long time, the young men think they could do it but they couldn't. They could fight the first Marne, but not this. This took religion and years of plenty and tremendous sureties and exact relation that existed between the classes . . . You had to have a whole souled sentimental equipment going back further than you could remember. You had to remember Christmas, and postcards of the Crown Prince and his fiancée, and little cafés in Valence and beer gardens in Unter den Linden' . . . They came out of a restored trench, and faced a memorial to the Newfoundland dead . . . After that they got in their car and started back towards Amiens. A thin warm rain was falling on the new scrubby woods and underbush and they passed great funeral pyres of sorted duds, shells, bombs, grenades and equipment, helmets, bayonets, gun stocks and rotten leather abandoned six years in the ground . . .

On 7 June 1925, the 29th Division memorial at the entrance to the Park was unveiled by Lt Gen Sir Beaumont de Lisle, General Officer Commanding 29th Division in 1916.

In 1930, Capt H.A. Taylor of the Royal Fusiliers published his book *Goodbye to the Battlefields*; he noted that a little west of the railway was a strange building which had not been there before the war, or during it. It was built of logs, on a slight eminence and 'came as a great relief from the monotony of new red brick'. This was the lodge of the Park and was a replica of the log cabin of the oldest settlers of Britain's oldest colony. The modern house of the park superintendent can be seen towards THIEPVAL and below, over the same ridge where the skeletons of the 'Tree of Death' rises in front of the former German trenches, is the ridge where the 51st Division memorial stands. Tall

fir trees, the sweep of which is interrupted in the hollow by Y Ravine Cemetery, grow around the statue.

Between Hawthorn Ridge Cemetery No. 2, hidden over to the left, and the 51st Division memorial, is the smallest of the Park cemeteries, Hunter's Cemetery, made from a large shell-hole with the Cross of Sacrifice in the middle, around the base of which are the headstones of 46 men, mostly of the Black Watch and the Gordon Highlanders, who died there when the area was captured by 51st Division in November 1916. It stands at the upper end of Y RAVINE.

Hawthorn Ridge Cemetery No. 2 is 500 yards south of Hawthorn Ridge Cemetery No. 1, a little west of the top of Y RAVINE. It was made by V Corps in spring 1917, as V Corps Cemetery No. 12, and seven isolated graves were brought in after the Armistice. It contains the graves of 190 soldiers from the United Kingdom, mainly of 29th Division, of whom the great majority fell on 1 July 1916. Some 40 acres of the Park's 80 acres are in the original sector of 1st Newfoundlanders on 1 July.

The 29th Division memorial stands at the entrance to the Park, and all around are the grass-covered trenches of the battlefields as left in 1918. At the base of the great bronze caribou is the Memorial to the Newfoundland Missing, on land and sea; the names of over 800 men are listed on the bronze panels. The site of the caribou marks the place where 1st Newfoundlanders left for the attack on 1 July.

The ground of which the Park was originally part fell into German hands in March 1918 and was retaken later the same year, on the same day as Thiepval Ridge. The grass-covered trenches, which are preserved in their approximate state in 1918 are, if anything, much shallower than originally because the ground levels have altered.

In March 1932 a spark from a farmer's brushwood fire blew across on to the grass in the Park and a fire broke out, but it only did slight damage to 7.5 acres of the site, destroying a number of spruce trees. The Newfoundland authorities asked the Imperial War Graves Commission whether the latter would clear up the damage if the former met the cost. In addition, the base of the caribou on the 29th Division memorial, designed by Basil Gotto, needed repairing. The ownership of the land in the Park was always a complex issue and there is much correspondence in the Commonwealth War Graves Commission archives concerning the administration and care of this large memorial area at such long distance. The land on which the cemeteries within the Park stood was owned by the French government, which was normal practice, but the Park as a whole was not. In reading the correspondence in the file (WG 857/4/3 Box 1962), one gets the distinct impression that the Newfoundland government was forever asking favours from both the French and British governments without giving much in the way of return. Indeed, even the original unveiling of the Park was carried out in an unusual manner and without the usual consultations and formalities.

In August 1933, Vera Brittain visited Newfoundland Park and was 'struck by the extent by which the Dominions had taken possession of Somme region, as though they had fought in all the battles. No large British memorial except that to the Missing at Thiepval Ridge.'

In 1935, at a time when much of the Park had become overgrown, it was decided that there was simply too much land in the Park to superintend. It was the 12 acres of Plot One which contained the main memorials and cemeteries, and there seemed no reason why the rest of the land should not be used for farming.

After the First World War, BEAUMONT-HAMEL was considerably helped in its recovery by the town of Winchester in Hampshire, which 'adopted' it; a new road was built flanked with poplars. During the 1930s a decayed pillbox could still be seen in the village, and while the village was being rebuilt, the inhabitants lived in former Army Nissen huts.

On 30 June 1956 a special Canadian 40th anniversary service was held in the Park, and services of commemoration have been held here for the last 50 years, in particular on the major anniversaries every 10 years. From 1 June 1969, when acting as agent for the Canadian government, the Commonwealth War Graves Commission agreed to maintain the Park.

In the late 1990s the Canadian government decided to invest funds in the Canadian Memorial site at Vimy Ridge near Arras, as well as Newfoundland Park at BEAUMONT-HAMEL. The need to educate or inform visitors, particularly about the experiences of 1st Newfoundlanders, seemed to be the main aim, together with making visitors more welcome by providing a visitors' centre and lavatories. In addition, free guided tours are provided, with Canadian students acting as guides, as they always had been at Vimy Ridge. The car park was greatly expanded to accommodate more cars and coaches.

O

OISSY is west of AMIENS on the D156 road to Cavillon. In the third week of June 1916, 16th Manchesters (90th Brigade, 30th Division) were billeted here. On 24 June, a memorable concert took place in the château grounds: 'In peaceful setting of trees the men lay at their ease on the grass, with little groups of officers on the terrace, and listened to the old familiar songs of Grantham and Lark Hill.'

Nearly 2 weeks later, 62nd Brigade (21st Division) were here on 7 July for a couple of days; on 21 July, the brigade returned to Oissy for 3 more days.

In the 1920s there was one British war grave in the churchyard, which is north of the village.

OVILLERS-LA-BOISSELLE is to the north-east of ALBERT, to the left of the D929 ALBERT–BAPAUME road. It is north-east of Aveluy, south-west of POZIÈRES and is twinned with LA BOISSELLE, which is across the main road and slightly to the south-east.

During 1915 the village was in enemy hands, one of several left untouched by British artillery until it was shelled on 14 October and 25 November. In 1916 the village lay along a road at right angles to the Allied front line, protected by rising ground and parapets that hid it from British eyes. To the east was Mash Valley, also in enemy hands, which complemented Sausage Valley on the LA BOISSELLE side of the road. Mash Valley was very broad and the lines went across as they bent south-eastwards, having come down northwards in a relatively north-to-south fashion.

Behind Mash Valley was Usna Hill and beyond that Usna Valley. Usna Hill was full of reserve and support trenches at the beginning of the battle, and from it Allied observers could obtain a view of the extremely powerful-looking enemy positions at Ovillers. There had been mining activity on this front opposite Ovillers; two saps, known as Rivington and Clay, were made within 30ft of the German line and were connected to it.

On 1 July, the three brigades of 8th Division were allocated Ovillers as their objective. Right from the start, it was known that there would be no chance of success if the flanking divisions did not make simultaneous progress with 8th Division's advance. On the right, 23rd Brigade (8th Division) were to attack up Mash Valley and gain the ALBERT–POZIÈRES road due south of POZIÈRES. In the

centre, 25th Brigade (8th Division) were to carry the German defences in and around Ovillers village; they were thought to have the easiest task, as they would be out of sight of the German defenders at Ovillers for the first 300 or 400yds. On the left, in front of Authuille Wood, 70th Brigade (8th Division) were to attack up the slopes of Nab Valley, on to the northern part of Ovillers Spur, and to then continue on into POZIÈRES. If they got this far, their left would then rest on MOUQUET FARM.

During the final bombardment, just before 0730hrs on 1 July, the attacking waves began to move forward into no man's land; in many cases it was exceptionally wide, as wide as 800yds and as narrow as 300yds. When the barrage lifted at 0730hrs, the first waves advanced; despite the appalling machine-gun and rifle fire and the completely exposed territory that they had to cross, they somehow made enough progress not only to reach the German first line, but also parties actually reached the second line as well. When the attackers got up close to the German line, the German artillery fire intensified, leading to the advancing waves becoming mixed up.

On the right, 23rd Brigade had had an appalling stretch of no man's land to traverse, with the German garrison at LA BOISSELLE to the right, and the fortified village of Ovillers in higher ground to the left. Despite the deadly flanking fire, parties of 2nd Middlesex and 2nd Devons (both 23rd Brigade, 8th Division) passed through the German defences. They were caught by crossfire and after a time were forced to withdraw. Before the battle began, Lt Col E.F.T. Sandys DSO, Commanding Officer 2nd Middlesex, had been concerned about uncut German wire and the enemy trenches that were still occupied despite the heavy Allied barrage in the area of Mash Valley. With 750yds of no man's land to cross, Sandys' battalion were cut down as predicted, with 623 casualties.

The disaster so preyed on Sandys' mind that he shot himself in the Cavendish Hotel in September and died in St George's Hospital on the 13th; he was awarded the Distinguished Service Order 9 days after he died. Sandys was buried in Brompton Cemetery, Kensington. During the war, he had been wounded five times and had been admitted to hospital in HÉNENCOURT on 17 June, returning to the trenches 4 days later. He had been right to be extremely worried about the attack on 1 July, for of the 23 officers of 2nd Middlesex who took part, only

Ovillers-la-Boisselle church before the Allied bombardment. *(Peter F. Batchelor Collection)*

one got back to the lines unwounded. Of the 650 other ranks, only 50 answered the roll call. Involved in the same attack, 2nd Devons had 450 casualties. 2nd West Yorkshires and 2nd Cameronians (both also 23rd Brigade, 8th Division) suffered in similar fashion to 2nd Middlesex. The brigade orders did not press a further attempt that day to take the village.

On the left of 23rd Brigade, 25th Brigade had a similar story, with 2nd Royal Berkshires and 2nd Lincolns (both 25th Brigade, 8th Division) advancing under similar heavy fire; the latter, under Lt Col R. Bastard, lost 471 officers and men. Though the lines were close together, the village was a terrible obstacle. During the attack, Lt Col A.M. Holdsworth, Commanding Officer 2nd Royal Berkshires, was mortally wounded; he died on 7 July and was buried at Etaples. In support, 1st Royal Irish Rifles (also 25th Brigade, 8th Division) also lost heavily, including their Commanding Officer, Lt Col C.C. Macnamara, who was wounded and died in mid-July; he was buried in Chorley Wood Churchyard, Hertfordshire. Many casualties from 23rd and 25th Brigades were taken down to CRUCIFIX CORNER.

To the left of 25th Brigade, 70th Brigade were in front of Authuille Wood; they lost even more heavily than their two sister brigades, although 8th King's Own Yorkshire Light Infantry and 8th York & Lancasters did make some progress. In support, 9th York & Lancasters were cut down by gunfire at Thiepval Spur.

It is not surprising that, in view of 8th Division's disaster, the attack was not renewed that day. There had been little progress on the right flank and what there had been was held up by the enemy wire; on the left, only a small lodgement was made in the LEIPZIG SALIENT. The following morning, 12th Division relieved 8th Division by 0540hrs; there was no further attack on Ovillers, but the village was bombarded in order to confuse the enemy when 58th Brigade (19th Division) attacked LA BOISSELLE. Preparation included the clearing of the heaps of bodies blocking the communication trenches.

At 0215hrs on 3 July, the bombardment was renewed; against the same targets as those of 1 July, 12th Division were to repeat the experience of 8th Division and were to be no more successful. Rough assembly trenches had been dug in no man's land in order to make it much narrower. To the right was 35th Brigade, with 5th Royal Berkshires and 7th Suffolks in front; 37th Brigade was on the left, with 6th Queen's and 6th Royal West Kents. The extreme left of 12th Division's line was held by 36th Brigade, who were to cover the flank with the help of a smoke discharge.

At 0315hrs the advance began in the dark, but the enemy soon became aware of the attack. The leading waves did make progress, but on reaching the second line they were met by the defenders, who had swarmed out of their dugouts and trenches, with bomb and bayonet. The whole of 6th Royal West Kents (37th Brigade, 12th Division) had gone forward, with two companies of 6th Buffs (also 37th Brigade, 12th Division) acting in support. Three other battalions were held back pending progress, but at 0900hrs, 12th Division had to report that the attack had failed except for a small footing in the German line, which was soon lost. The Official Historian considered inadequate flank protection and lack of surprise to be the main reasons for the lack of progress.

On 7 July, 12th Division were still trying; 8th and 9th Royal Fusiliers and 7th Royal Sussex (all 36th Brigade, 12th Division) were still fighting, in a further attempt to capture Ovillers. With 8th Royal Fusiliers on the right, the plan was to take the village from the south-west flank. The bombardment began at 0430hrs, when two leading companies crawled over the parapet into no man's land; 8th Royal Fusiliers made progress into the German first and second trenches, but at a considerable cost in casualties. 9th Royal Fusiliers fared in similar fashion and Capt R. Philipps MC, a son of Viscount St Davids, was killed. One of seven officers of 9th Royal Fusiliers killed that day, he was later buried in Aveluy Communal Cemetery Extension (H.32).

Also on 7 July, 13th Royal Fusiliers (111th Brigade, attached 34th Division) moved to the right of 9th Royal Fusiliers and delivered an attack. Both the composer Arthur Bliss and the writer and historian Guy Chapman were members of 13th Royal Fusiliers. The attack began at 0830hrs; Bliss was almost immediately wounded and was picked up by stretcher-bearers and soon returned to England. At one point he recalled being transported by barge; this was a recognised and gentle way of transporting the wounded. Arthur had a brother named Kennard with the Royal Garrison Artillery, who was to be killed on 28 September. His guns were being used in support of the fighting for the SCHWABEN REDOUBT. Arthur Bliss returned to France in 1918 and revisited his former trenches at Monchy-au-Bois and Adinfer Wood.

Together with 25th Division, 12th Division had managed to gain part of Ovillers, and on 8 July decided to bomb forward at 0345hrs, when their troops were held up by deep and clinging mud. At the edge of Ovillers, 36th Brigade were relieved by 7th East Surreys (37th Brigade, 12th Division) and

9th Essex (35th Brigade, 12th Division) and made some progress in the ruins of Ovillers. Maj C.I. Ryan of 9th Essex was killed and 74th and 75th Brigades (both 25th Division) bombed forwards from the valley. At 2000hrs, 74th Brigade renewed their attacks. Before morning, 14th Brigade (32nd Division) relieved 12th Division. On 10 July, 13th Rifle Brigade (111th Brigade, 37th Division) attacked the village to the south-east, when they captured 200 prisoners.

On 12 July Bernard Montgomery (104th Brigade, 35th Division) wrote to his mother; never one to censor his own letters, he told her that his unit were at Ovillers, being heavily shelled, and were expected to advance at any moment. He had been over the whole ground and had seen all the recent battlefields including BEAUMONT-HAMEL, HAMEL, THIEPVAL, Ovillers, LA BOISSELLE, CONTALMAISON and MAMETZ WOOD. He was living in a very damp dugout at the time and described his experiences as 'all most interesting'.

On 12 July, 19th Lancashire Fusiliers (14th Brigade, 32nd Division) were ordered to capture as much of Ovillers as possible and a strongpoint known as Point 18. At 0200hrs on 15 July, 25th Division attacked the village from the north-east and the south while 32nd Division attacked from the south-west, but little progress was made. On 14 July, the poet Lt D.F.G. Johnson of 2nd Manchesters (14th Brigade, 32nd Division) moved into trenches here and a large bombing party was organised for 15 July to move from Point 52 to Point 53. The bombing attack came under a heavy bomb barrage and there were 25 casualties, including Johnson, who died of wounds. He was taken back to Bouzincourt where he had been billeted and buried in Bouzincourt Communal Cemetery Extension (I.B.8).

The men of 32nd Division were relieved by 144th Brigade (48th Division). Attacking without a preliminary bombardment, 143rd Brigade (also 48th Division) crossed 1,000yds of open ground and occupied a knot of trenches in the rear of the Ovillers defenders; it fell to Charles Carrington of 1/5th Royal Warwicks (143rd Brigade, 48th Division) to lead the assault. By such tactics 48th Division contained the garrison and compelled its occupants to surrender. 143rd Brigade (attached to 25th Division) closed in from the north-west while 74th Brigade (25th Division) and 144th Brigade pressed in from the south and east. That night the enemy surrendered and 25th Division handed over to 145th Brigade (48th Division).

On 16 July, 48th Division attempted to cut off the remainder of the German garrison, and with the village virtually surrounded, the German survivors, 2 officers and 124 men, surrendered.

In *A Life of One's Own*, Gerald Brenan noted that around 21 July he went back after crossing again the old front line, the ground torn up by shells and littered with dead bodies from the attack of 1 July. The wounded who could not be brought in had crawled into shell-holes, wrapped their waterproof sheets around them, taken out their Bibles, and died like that. Between 20 and 23 July, when visiting the area, Brenan had turned off towards Ovillers, which he described as above. He was in search of his friend Ralph Partridge, who was in charge of a company. The further end of the trench was occupied by Germans: 'What was needed . . . was a bomb up it so as to reach a machine gun that was holding up our advance', but Brenan's men were 'tired and not out for taking risks'.

After the capture of Ovillers, Brenan wrote that 'A thing that had happened again and again was that our troops pushed their way up a trench and took a strongpoint without loss and were told to retire in order to consolidate. Two hours later, there having been no change in the meantime, they would be ordered to retake the strongpoint, which was now full of Germans, by a frontal attack. This might be impossible, but it had to be tried and perhaps fifty men would be killed in the attempt.'

On 7 August, 7th Norfolks (35th Brigade, 12th Division) took over the line at Ovillers; the line was now facing north-west in and behind Ration Trench, which ran south-west from Pozières Trench. During the night of 12/13 August, the Germans were in Sixth Avenue and Ridge Trench, on the right. On 13 August, 12th Division were relieved.

Graham Greenwell of 1/4th Oxfordshire & Buckinghamshire Light Infantry (145th Brigade, 48th Division) wrote home and noted: 'I have just taken over some trenches, such as they are, full of equipment, filth and bodies and am being heavily shelled.' On 17 August he was sitting in Skyline Trench at Ovillers, in the bottom of an old German dugout about 10ft or 12ft under the earth. The floor was covered with German clothing and filth. The remains of the trench outside were blown to pieces and full of corpses from the different regiments which had been there lately, German and English. The ground was ploughed up by enormous shell-holes; there wasn't a single landmark to be seen for miles, except a few giant sticks where the trees once were.

Probably on 27 August, the poet Lt C.W. Winterbotham of 1/5th Glosters (145th Brigade, 48th Division), a solicitor commissioned in September 1914, was buried by the battalion chaplain to the

north of Ovillers at map reference 57D R32 C4 1. As his grave was later lost, his name is listed on the Thiepval Memorial.

On 11 November, 11th Essex (18th Brigade, 6th Division) rested here under tarpaulin bivouac sheets on the hillside. The poet Ivor Gurney of 2/5th Glosters (184th Brigade, 61st Division) probably passed the ruins of Ovillers when on his way to GRANDCOURT on 21 November; a poem that he wrote called 'Ballad of the Three Spectres' follows:

> As I went up by Ovillers
> In mud and water cold to the knee,
> There went three jeering, fleering spectres,
> They walked abreast and talked to me.

Ovillers-la-Boisselle was recaptured by the enemy in March 1918 and retaken on 24 August by 38th Division.

Ovillers Military Cemetery is a little way southwest of Ovillers village, on the right-hand side of the road to Aveluy. It was begun before the capture of Ovillers, as a battle cemetery behind a dressing station, and was used until March 1917. It was greatly enlarged after the Armistice, mainly from the battlefields at POZIÈRES, LA BOISSELLE, Ovillers and CONTALMAISON. The great majority of the graves belong to men who fell in July 1916. It was in this valley that so many of 8th Division, who had to cross 750yds to reach the German trenches, were killed. Sir Harry Lauder's son, Capt J. Lauder of 1/8th Argyll & Sutherland Highlanders (152nd Brigade, 51st Division), was killed on 28 December and was buried in the cemetery (I.A.6). Other officers here include Lt Col F.C. Heneker (III.A.1), Commanding Officer 21st Northumberland Fusiliers (102nd Brigade, 34th Division), killed on 1 July and T/Lt Col L.M. Howard (II.D.4), Commanding Officer 24th Northumberland Fusiliers (103rd Brigade, 34th Division), who died of wounds on 2 July. Lt Col G. A. Royston-Pigott (XIII.H.1), attached 10th Worcesters (57th Brigade, 19th Division) was killed in action on 3 July during the fighting for LA BOISSELLE, close to a mine crater.

22nd Royal Fusiliers (99th Brigade, 2nd Division) erected a wooden memorial in Ovillers Military Cemetery to 78 officers and men of the battalion who fell in 1917. 12th Division also had a wooden memorial, which was abandoned to nature in the mid-1920s. The cemetery contains the graves of more than 3,000 soldiers, of whom about two-thirds have not been identified.

By 1933, the Somme cemeteries were becoming full; while awaiting permission to expand London

Road Cemetery, the Imperial War Graves Commission used Ovillers Military Cemetery, as well as Combles Communal Cemetery Extension, where in 1933 there was still room for 300 graves.

In November 1982, a grave containing the remains of 51 men was found 20yds from the Ovillers Military Cemetery. Forty-nine of the skeletons were of men of British units from Sussex, Berkshire, Essex and West Yorkshire; the other two sets of remains were German. All of the remains were taken for reburial in Terlincthun British Cemetery, Wimille, near Boulogne.

In 2000, the remains of several more soldiers were found close to Ovillers and were reburied in the same row as those of Capt J. Lauder in the Military Cemetery. All were unidentified, but they included a company sergeant-major of the Prince of Wales's Volunteers (South Lancashire Regiment).

Even more recently, on 1 July 2000, the remains of Pte G.J. Nugent of 22nd Northumberland Fusiliers (102nd Brigade, 34th Division) were buried here (I.A.26A) after they had been found close to the rim of the Lochnagar Crater, found on 31 October 1998; it would appear that he died on 1 July 1916. After a nationwide appeal for contact from his relatives, some were tracked down and attended the burial ceremony, alongside 1,500 other visitors. The inscription on Nugent's grave is:

> Lost Found
> But Never Forgotten
> May He Rest
> In Eternal Peace

P

PAS-EN-ARTOIS is on the D6 road south of WARLINCOURT-LÈS-PAS. During the autumn of 1915 the village provided bathing facilities for soldiers, when great vats in a local brewery were filled with soapy water and naked Tommies. There was a Royal Engineers dump in the village and on 12 May 1916, 1/4th Londons (168th Brigade, 56th Division) supplied a working party of 200 men to help with felling and sawing trees for dugouts and gun pits; they returned 3 weeks later for similar work. The village was the headquarters of both V Corps and 46th Division.

On 21 June, 1/12th Londons (168th Brigade, 56th Division) marched here via SOUASTRE and HÉNU on their way to HALLOY; they had marched 'through Hénu, down the long tree-bordered hill into Pas and up again to Halloy . . .' On 22 June, 1/14th Londons (also 168th Brigade, 56th Division) arrived here and went into a hut camp; they were still in the village on 25 June when a German squadron carried out a bombing raid.

PEAKE WOODS lay on the south side of the road to FRICOURT, just outside CONTALMAISON. It was the site of an advanced dressing station where the road crossed a high ridge. In *Memoirs of a Camp Follower*, Philip Gosse of 69th Field Ambulance (23rd Division) wrote of the wounded who were to be treated at FRICOURT pouring down from BAILIFF WOOD and Peake Woods. The advanced dressing station was in full view of the enemy, and the wounded were taken down to FRICOURT for treatment during the night.

PEPPERBOX HILL, south of TOUTENCOURT, was the site of several batteries on the uplands in a disorderly camp of shelters, according to Donald Boyd, who noted that towards the end of August 1916 he was here with the artillery. Having reconnoitred and climbed Pepperbox Hill, Boyd's unit made contact with the battery officer and returned to BAVELINCOURT; here they had tents under a crescent of ilex trees planted about a crucifix that looked towards the village.

The next day, Boyd's unit went off along the ALBERT road; two or three sections of 9.2in howitzers shot up over their heads. They halted behind Beaucourt Wood, close to the D919 road from AMIENS towards ACHEUX-EN-AMIÉNOIS, and put up their own lines, close to some Australians. Boyd noted that some of the British disliked the Australians in the encampment; this was because, despite a system of allotted times for watering at the canvas tanks, the Australians galloped down when other horses were in possession. This broke down the troughs so that the precious water was wasted and the horses were thrown into disorder.

Boyd said that they went into action on the hill on 25 August, just when light was breaking between Bazentin Wood and MAMETZ WOOD. They used tracks that followed the firm ground among shell-holes and refuse of the battle. The reserve of the Scottish infantry sat among the low mounds marking the entrance to Welsh Alley, which was about 4ft deep; its walls were irregular and collapsed, having been blown in. It was full of telephone wire that looped across and under the long walls. There were two observation posts, one in 70 Avenue, the front line on the left of Welsh Alley, the other in a forward sap that ended in a barricade.

The 4.2s had been falling sporadically as Boyd's unit came to these places. They fired their guns and received replies from the enemy. They continued their registration of the front at intervals as the 8in guns played continually about 70 Avenue and Welsh Alley. Boyd describes the routine in the trench, and how he managed to sleep for 12 hours. Ammunition wagons came up and everyone helped with the unloading, passing the shells to the pits. The deep German dugout faced the wrong way. His battery's guns were sheltered at the side by walls made of brass 18-pounder cartridge cases that were filled with earth. These costly ramparts supported eight wooden rafters, a roof of corrugated iron and a row of sandbags that were filled with chalk.

PERNOIS is north-west of AMIENS on the D57 road. From 19 June 1916, 3rd Worcesters (7th Brigade, 25th Division) were here for 5 days, before moving to BERNEUIL. In the north-west part of the village, an artilleryman was buried in Pernois Communal Cemetery in April 1916 by artillerymen of 49th Division. Pernois British Cemetery, to the south of the village, was used for burials by No. 4 Casualty Clearing Station in 1918. Casualties would have been brought by train to the nearby halt to the north.

PÉRONNE, although surrounded by protective marshland and water, still managed to fall to the Germans both in 1870 and in 1914. Though not directly linked with the 1916 Somme battlefields, the town was a difficult place for the Allies to recapture.

The town, adopted by Blackburn after the First World War, had a new bridge over the Somme Canal, named after the Lancashire town. By 1933, 15 years after the war, it had been rebuilt and boasted a new hospital. On seeing the town, Vera Brittain noted that the use of many original bricks had lessened the impact of 'newness' and some buildings showed signs of damage from 1870 as well as from 1917. One building, a milliner's premises, was built in 1792, destroyed in 1870 and 1916, and rebuilt in 1873 and 1924.

In 1986, an idea was mooted that a new war museum should be built in the Château de Péronne; it would commemorate the roles of France, Britain and the Dominions – as well as Germany – during the First World War. The town was an ideal choice, as it is easily accessible by the A1 and A29 autoroutes, as well as by the TGV railway system.

The museum, the Historial de la Grande Guerre, was grafted onto the remains of the medieval castle and opened in 1992. Exhibits in four main galleries explore the everyday life of soldiers and civilians of the three countries; in addition, the museum arranges educational programmes and lectures and has an extensive archive, a cinema and a bookshop. It has become a centre for academic research. Outside Péronne, the Historial has also been very active, and is responsible for the erection of various direction signs, for example, indicating the position of the 1916 front line.

PICQUIGNY is north-west of AMIENS, in the valley of the River Somme on the D3 main road to ABBEVILLE. During the Somme battle it was a 'lines of communication' village.

On 11 December 1915, 15th Highland Light Infantry (97th Brigade, 2nd Division), predominantly made up from volunteers from the Glasgow tramways, arrived in the quaint village in frosty weather: 'The men went to their barns and relaxed pleasurably and the officers dined with the large family of a café proprietor . . .' Next day, the battalion left the village, when the main street was 'flooded with lorries, wagons, and what not going to and coming from the Front'.

On 18 December, 7th Division had their headquarters here. On 12 February 1916, 1/9th Londons (169th Brigade, 56th Division) were here for a night on their way to Fresnes for 12 days; it was on this day that they transferred from 5th Division to 56th Division. On 13 February, 1/2nd (West Riding) Field Ambulance (49th Division) moved to WARLOY-BAILLON and took over the hospital and billets. For a brief period they were responsible for a party of 120 'unfits' who had been billeted in Picquigny for a short time. These were men who were no longer able to take an active part in the war. Between 13 and 24 February, 13th Field Ambulance (5th Division) were billeted to the east of the town in a large house prepared as a rest station.

On 29 March, when the weather was good, 2nd Wiltshires (21st Brigade, 30th Division) moved to open country here from FLIXECOURT and remained in the village for a fortnight before two companies left for QUERRIEU and one for AILLY-SUR-SOMME, in both cases to assist the Royal Engineers.

On 11 April, 18th Manchesters (90th Brigade, 30th Division) arrived here for training before leaving for CORBIE on 30 April. Elements of 7th Queen's (55th Brigade, 18th Division) trained here from the beginning of May and were here until mid-June, when they left for CARNOY. 54th Field Ambulance (18th Division) took over the hospital here from 96th Field Ambulance (30th Division). On 11 June, 2nd Wiltshires detrained here from HEILLY after a spell on the CARNOY front and then proceeded to march southwards to billets at SAISSEVAL.

On 2 July, after their drubbing opposite OVILLERS-LA-BOISSELLE, elements of 8th Division arrived in the area for 4 days; 2 days later, 64th Brigade (21st Division) were here.

Between December 1915 and July 1917, 10 soldiers, including 6 from 1916 who had died in or near Picquigny, were buried in Picquigny Communal Cemetery opposite the church; Pte H. Broadbent of the Army Service Corps had a special memorial. At the end of March 1918, casualty clearing stations were brought here to deal with casualties due to the enemy advance towards AMIENS, and Picquigny British Cemetery was opened a little west of the town on the road to SOUASTRE.

There is a vast amphitheatre near the village, where the military occasionally held horse shows; the village also has the ruins of a huge château.

PIERREGOT

PIERREGOT is on the D11 road between RUBEMPRÉ and RAINNEVILLE, west of MIRVAUX. The German Army had passed through the village in the early part of the war, during their advance towards Paris. In mid-December 1915, 15th Highland Light Infantry (97th Brigade, 32nd Division) arrived here; they had the village to themselves and were billeted in barns. Later, 16th Highland Light Infantry (also 97th Brigade, 32nd Division) rested in the village for 10 days, having been in the line opposite THIEPVAL. Pipes and drums sounded the retreat in the main street. While the battalion were in the village, bombing classes were carried out. Towards the end of the month they left for MARTINSART and SENLIS-LE-SEC, villages well behind the front, where they camped in bell tents.

On 30 December, 152nd Brigade (51st Division) arrived here; one of their battalions, 1/6th Seaforth Highlanders, found the country not only pleasant, but untouched by war. Their billets were good, too. Apart from a week in ACHEUX-EN-AMIÉNOIS, 15–22 January, they were here until 8 February and celebrated Hogmanay, when officers danced reels in the village street at midnight to the strains of the battalion band.

The troops spent time training and route marching, but also played football and rugby, and attended regular concerts. The battalion were back in their 'favourite village' on 29 December for one night before moving further down the road to RAINNE-VILLE, where they remained until 6 March 1916, when the whole brigade marched to BEAUVAL, south-west of DOULLENS. On 4 April, No. 458 Field Company, Royal Engineers (49th Division), put up extra huts in the village.

POMMIER

POMMIER is north-west of HANNESCAMPS on the D30 road. On 4 September 1915, No. 152 Field Company, Royal Engineers (37th Division), had their headquarters here for several months. In mid-March 1916, Royal Engineers of 37th Division were working on six redoubts on the Pommier–BERLES-AU-BOIS line and were billeted in the village. At the same time, Pommier was home to several infantry battalions, including 1/8th Sherwood Foresters (139th Brigade, 46th Division), who were here on 27 June 1916 after 9 days holding the line. On 30 June, the enemy began to shell the church and shell-bursts damaged some of the billets close to the building; on the eve of the battle 1/8th Sherwood Foresters left the village for FONCQUEVILLERS.

In mid-July, 1/5th Lincolns (138th Brigade, 46th Division) marched to Pommier from SAULTY, a village to the north-west. On 16 and 17 July company training was carried out and the officers visited the new trench sector to the north of Monchy, which was to be taken over the next day by 1/4th Lincolns (also 138th Brigade, 46th Division).

In 1925 Pommier Communal Cemetery contained the graves of 26 British servicemen.

POMMIERS REDOUBT

POMMIERS REDOUBT is on the south side of the D64 road between MONTAUBAN-DE-PICARDIE and MAMETZ; it is just after DANTZIG ALLEY, as one travels from MAMETZ. The Redoubt was well protected by Pommiers Trench, which was about 400yds away on the south side. Montauban Alley entered the Redoubt from the north-east. Beyond the Redoubt to the north was Beetle Alley, beyond that White Trench, which was east of Queen's Nullah, and beyond that MAMETZ WOOD.

On 1 July 1916 Pommiers Redoubt was one of the objectives of 18th Division; the assaulting brigades in this sector were 53rd Brigade on the right and 54th Brigade on the left. It was the latter that were to be most closely involved in the Redoubt's eventual capture, with 7th Bedfords on the right and 11th Royal Fusiliers on the left, supported by 6th Northamptons and with 12th Middlesex in reserve. Two machine guns went forward with each assaulting battalion, and trench mortars were in position for a hurricane bombardment.

The attack pressed forward from the north of CARNOY and the advancing troops suffered casualties when they reached Emden Trench, a defence line in front of Pommiers Trench; flanking fire from Austrian Trench and uncut wire between Bund Trench and Pommiers Trench held up the advance for a time. However, Pommiers Trench was captured 20 minutes after the attack had begun at 0730hrs, when the enemy in their dugouts were 'little disposed to surrender'; Beetle Alley to the north of the redoubt was also seized by 11th Royal Fusiliers and 7th Bedfords and consolidated by 6th Northamptons.

Parties even managed to get as far as White Trench, nearly 1,000yds beyond the Redoubt to the right of Queen's Nullah and within easy distance of MAMETZ WOOD. By 1020hrs, 6th Royal Berkshires (53rd Brigade, 18th Division) had captured the Loop, a trench system running eastwards from Pommiers Trench, and by 1100hrs other parties of 53rd Brigade were in touch with 54th Brigade at the north-east corner of the Redoubt.

Before midday, 6th Royal Berkshires found themselves held up within 75yds of Montauban Alley; 8th Norfolks (53rd Brigade, 18th Division) also had to fight hard at the junction of Loop Trench and the MONTAUBAN-DE-PICARDIE–MAMETZ road. 10th Essex (53rd Brigade, 18th Division) went up to support 6th Royal Berkshires. By 1330hrs, elements of 55th Brigade (18th Division), on the right of 53rd Brigade and assisted by three companies of 8th Suffolks (53rd Brigade, 12th Division), were working west along Montauban Alley towards Loop Trench. Later in the afternoon, British patrols reached and probed the German Support Lines towards Caterpillar Wood Valley.

The capture of Pommiers Redoubt and the village of MONTAUBAN-DE-PICARDIE to the east were two of the successes of the day.

On 3 July, Lt Col F.A. Maxwell, Commanding Officer 12th Middlesex (54th Brigade, 12th Division) reconnoitred nearly 2 miles of the new line, taking with him a Vickers gun team for emergencies. By 8 July, 3rd Division had taken over the front from 18th Division; 53rd Brigade settled at GROVE TOWN, 54th Brigade rested at TAILLES WOOD and 55th Brigade rested at BRONFAY FARM.

On 19 July, 15th Brigade (5th Division) moved into position as divisional reserve in the trenches on Pommiers Ridge. After the HIGH WOOD battles, 2nd King's Own Scottish Borderers (13th Brigade, 5th Division) retired and bivouacked at Pommiers Redoubt and absorbed a new draft. On the evening of 29 July they left the Redoubt and relieved 95th Brigade (5th Division) in LONGUEVAL on the west side of DELVILLE WOOD. After a long and difficult relief in the small hours of 31 July, 2nd King's Own Scottish Borderers 'crawled back' in small parties to Pommiers Redoubt.

On 4 August an attempt was made to capture Orchard Trench; this failed and 12th Manchesters (52nd Brigade, 17th Division) suffered 171 casu-alties. The attack, which began at 0050hrs, was checked by a very heavy enemy bombardment, including gas shells. Many of the casualties were too close to the enemy line to be brought in safely.

In addition to his book *A Subaltern on the Somme*, Max Plowman published a volume of letters called *Over the Bridge*; in this book, he 'fills out' some of the material in the first book. During July and August 1916, Plowman was in C Company, 10th West Yorkshires (50th Brigade, 17th Division); in a letter home at the beginning of August, he wrote:

> Here we are for instance in what is known as divisional reserve, about 3 or 4 miles back and we are entertaining ourselves in what rather more than a month ago was a German Redoubt. As far as my company is concerned it consists of about 150 holes in the ground none more than 3 or 4 feet deep – in fact they are glorified shell-holes with a light roof of wood and sandbags over them without any covering and in one of them I slept very comfortably last night with another officer and I am now sitting in the step of it as I write. Here we are just dotted about anywhere while we wait to go farther up, which may be tonight and may be in two or three days time – or we might even go back unwanted. There are some heavy guns behind us and every minute we hear the shell from them travelling over our heads but the nearest I've seen a German shell burst to this place is a good 300 yards away . . .

After 4 days opposite HIGH WOOD, Plowman and his colleagues returned to Pommiers Redoubt; he was wounded in the neck during this time. He quotes from an order: 'Two half companies under the command of two subalterns per half-company will report to the officer of the Royal Engineers for digging on the communication trench at St Georges Hill this evening.'

The history of 5th Division gives some informa-tion on the origin of the name of Pommiers Redoubt:

> owing to the prominence of a group of apple trees midway along this ridge (Montauban to Mametz)

it was known as Pommiers Ridge. For weeks they were used by the British Artillery for registration purposes, until it became a daily habit; one night the Germans felled and removed the trees, and the ensuing consternation of the FOOs the following morning was most entertaining to those not directly concerned.

From 11 August, 8th King's Royal Rifle Corps (41st Brigade, 14th Division) were at the Redoubt and on 12 August they were in the line opposite Orchard Trench, their objective; on 17 August, they were back in POMMIER. The POMMIER area at the time was covered with horses, mules and boxes of shells, with big guns firing in the midst of it all. On 12 September, 8th King's Royal Rifle Corps were again in the Redoubt when taking part in the DELVILLE WOOD fighting. On 14 September, 9th King's Royal Rifle Corps (42nd Brigade, 14th Division) were moved up to the Redoubt from a camp south of BÉCORDEL.

On 19 September, 55th Division had their headquarters here and 10 days later their 164th Brigade were here. Later on, 73rd Brigade (25th Division) were here; according to Lord Moran, in mid-September, the Redoubt was being used as a bivouac camp. At the end of September, 7th Royal Sussex (36th Brigade, 24th Division) bivouacked here, by which time the ground had become a quagmire. The FLERS road was the worst track, the trenches there being littered with dead men, mules and horses; sometimes it took teams of six mules to haul a limber to deliver rations. At the beginning of October, the Redoubt housed a brigade headquarters of 12th Division. Towards the end of October, 26th Royal Fusiliers (124th Brigade, 41st Division) bivouacked there.

PONT-NOYELLES is a hamlet on the main D929 road; it is close to QUERRIEU, where Fourth Army headquarters arrived in February 1916. On 27 July 1915, 1/5th and 1/6th Seaforth Highlanders (both 152nd Brigade, 51st Division) arrived here before moving up to MARTINSART 3 days later. They were the first British troops to be billeted in the village. 1/6th Seaforth Highlanders bathed in a splendid lake in the village, whose inhabitants welcomed 'les Ecossais' to their village. The Scottish troops were inspected the following day by Gen Sir Charles Monro, General Officer Commanding Third Army.

On 29 July the two battalions took to the road again, moving up towards ALBERT. 'As we passed through villages with our pipers playing, all the inhabitants and the French troops turned out to cheer us on our way.' The destination of 1/6th Seaforth Highlanders was BOUZINCOURT, where they spent the night.

For the most part, Pont-Noyelles was used for short stays by field companies and field ambulances of 5th, 18th and 30th Divisions. In January 1916, the girls' school was taken over for use as accommodation by men from British field ambulances. On 16 March, when 2nd Wiltshires (21st Brigade, 30th Division) were on their way from the CARNOY front to rest billets at FLIXECOURT, they left a company here who were to carry out some work on a new light railway. On 12 April, 19th Manchesters (21st Brigade, 30th Division), then billeted at FRÉCHENCOURT, supplied fatigue parties for work in the village.

North of the FRÉCHENCOURT road, in Parmont Wood, Lt Gen Sir Henry Rawlinson, General Officer Commanding Fourth Army, had his 'observation fort' built among the trees. It was from here, and not the GRANDSTAND at DERNANCOURT, that Rawlinson observed the opening of the Battle of the Somme on 1 July 1916, having arrived in the early morning mist at 0630hrs; he stayed for an hour until he witnessed the attack going in.

There are three British graves in Pont-Noyelles Communal Cemetery, all buried by 1st Cavalry Brigade (1st Cavalry Division); two of these men died in July 1916, including a private who drowned. The cemetery is north of the main ALBERT road.

PONT-RÉMY is on the D901 road, north west of AMIENS, on the north bank of the River Somme. Its role in the First World War was mainly linked to its importance as a rail and billeting centre, many troops having their first sight of the Somme area as they detrained here.

In early November 1915, 20th King's (89th Brigade, 30th Division) were here when 89th Brigade suffered their first casualty of the war; a man was wounded during bomb practice. No. 201 Field Company, Royal Engineers (30th Division) carried out work here when billeted at LONGPRÉ-LES-CORPS-SAINTS to the south-east of the village.

A couple of weeks later, No. 121 Field Company, Royal Engineers, and 109th Field Ambulance (both 36th Division) were here when a divisional rest station was opened at the co-op stores, which could accommodate up to 200 patients; the dining room was in the rear of the building. In early December, bathing and laundry facilities were opened on the Route d'Abbeville for the use of all troops billeted in the town. On 9 December a regimental band beat the retreat through the town and attracted a large crowd of inhabitants.

On Christmas Day the hospital was decorated by some of its patients, and turkey, plum puddings, a barrel of beer, together with other luxuries were provided. On 1 January 1916, 36th Division had their headquarters in Pont-Rémy for 2 days. On 19 January, 109th Field Ambulance left for BERTEAUCOURT-LES-DAMES. On 27 January, 1/5th Sherwood Foresters (139th Brigade, 46th Division) detrained at Pont-Rémy and marched to GORENFLOS, east of ABBEVILLE.

On 9 February, 1/7th Middlesex (167th Brigade, 56th Division) detrained here. Having just joined 56th Division, 1/16th Londons detrained here the next day and marched south-westwards to HUPPY, where they reported to 169th Brigade (56th Division) for the first time. After improving the barns and stables for use as ther billets, 1/16th Londons soon began to carry out their training. On 27 February, 169th Brigade left for AILLY-SUR-SOMME, 12 miles away. In the third week of July, 17th Division were here and 95th Brigade (5th Division) were here at the end of September.

Pont-Rémy Communal Cemetery lies to the east, beside the road to FLIXECOURT, and has the grave of one man who died in October 1916. Pont-Rémy British Cemetery to the north of the village has the graves of three men who died in 1916, including a private who drowned in June, and 47 other casualties who were brought from casualty clearing stations from May 1918 to May 1919.

POULAINVILLE, due north of AMIENS, is just to the east of the N25 road. On 21 November 1915, 96th Field Ambulance (30th Division) moved here, occupying billets and establishing a hospital. The next day they moved to another, which was in a poorer state, and left for BERTEAUCOURT-LES-DAMES on 28 November.

On 3 January 1916, 1/3rd (Highland) Field Ambulance (51st Division) came here and occupied billets in a large granary at the end of the village on the AMIENS road; the hospital was in a large barn. On 7 February, 15th Field Ambulance (5th Division) arrived here from BERTANGLES and took over from 1/3rd (Highland) Field Ambulance, using the same large barn. They left 3 days later, in the snow. On 31 March, 63rd Field Ambulance arrived here after detraining at LONGUEAU, erecting a tent hospital and motor ambulance area. Apart from providing billcting and medical facilities, Poulainville was mainly used as a training area. Between May and September, 4th, 18th, 23rd, 30th, 33rd and 51st Divisions came here.

POZIÈRES is a village on the main ALBERT–BAPAUME road, the D929; it is south-east of MOUQUET FARM and THIEPVAL and south-west of COURCELETTE. In 1916 it was another of the villages that the enemy had fortified extremely strongly; being on a ridge, it overlooked the positions of any attackers who might advance from the south-west. At the end of June 1916, the German Second Line ran behind the village from the direction of BAZENTIN-LE-GRAND in the south-east to the direction of MOUQUET FARM. There was a windmill on the north-east side of the village, which during the battle was to become very well known to the troops who fought for its possession.

John Masefield acquired a deep understanding of the Somme battlefield in the several months during which he was stationed in the area carrying out research for a book on the battle. In the end he wrote two books, one called *The Old Front Line* and the other *The Battle of the Somme*. In the latter book, he noted that routes that could be used by attackers were overlooked by the Germans, who had arranged their trenches and machine guns so that any advance would be virtually impossible, especially in daylight. The approach from Sausage and Mash Valleys was commanded by Pozières plateau, the one from Mouquet Valley was flanked and enfiladed by points that had not yet been captured and the route by the main road over the central spur was strongly wired, trenched and flanked.

There was, however, some dead ground to the south-east of the main road, though much of it could be seen from Pozières. It was sometimes called Quarry Gully and in it were two chalk quarries on the eastern bank. The small spur to the east of Quarry Gully hid the next valley – which Masefield says may have been called Hospital Valley because a dressing station was once there – from the village.

Again, though most of the valley was visible to the enemy trenches at its head, Masefield wrote that troops who advanced from Bazentin-le-Petit Wood had a better chance of success than from any other direction. Quarry Road began from the ALBERT–CONTALMAISON road at the top of the rise. Just at the junction, it was sunken between two deep banks; here there was a field dressing station, known as Dressing Station Corner. Quarry Road was forked and close to the fork was a second quarry which was twice the size of the previous one and about half as deep again; it gave better shelter and was better screened.

In the village itself, on the extreme south-west of the main road, was a position called Gibraltar. Masefield described it as a 'grey concrete fragment'. It stood well up on the bank above the road and overlooked Mash Valley. It was an observation post and could also be used as a machine-gun emplacement. A concrete stairway led down to a cellar some 12ft to 15ft below, barely large enough to contain two men; beside it were two gun emplacements that were covered or camouflaged with banks of timber. The cellars had been fitted with machine guns, as had the windmill, the school and Gibraltar, and these defences were especially strong.

The German Second Line, also known as Old German (OG)1 and OG2, had been dug to enfilade any attack on the village from the east. At the time of the first attack, the Allies held lines to within 600yds of the village. Centre Way was a German trench line that ran from close to Pozières church in a north-westerly direction towards the OG lines, which it reached about ¾ mile to the west of the windmill. There were also two orchards to the west of the village.

In *Anzac to Amiens*, the Australian historian C.E.W. Bean wrote that the breach in the line was only 2 miles wide and that attempts by the British III Corps to widen it had been prevented by the stubborn German defences. Pozières protected the German THIEPVAL flank to the north and also hemmed in Fourth Army's flank. It was Sir Douglas Haig's idea that Fourth Army should still thrust further forward where they had already been successful and so, went the thinking, the villages of Pozières and THIEPVAL would automatically fall. Thus strikes towards GINCHY and GUILLEMONT were continued and the left flank moved slowly forward towards the Pozières position.

In mid-July the British made four attacks against Pozières. In the early hours of the morning of 15 July, 11th Royal Warwicks (112th Brigade, 37th Division) were informed of an attack on Pozières, scheduled to take place at 0920hrs. The plan was for 8th East Lancashires, followed by 6th Bedfords (both also 112th Brigade, 37th Division) to clear part of the village south and north of the main road; 11th Royal Warwicks were to act as a back-up battalion and assist in consolidating the ground gained, while 10th Loyal North Lancashires (also 112th Brigade, 37th Division) were to carry bombs and stores.

The advance was unopposed at first, but as the troops went over the crest, above the Chalk Pit, they were met by heavy and continuous machine-gun fire. The fire was extremely accurate; this, coupled with 112th Brigade's narrow frontage, immobilised the three battalions, who then became intermixed.

C.S. Collison of 11th Royal Warwicks (112th Brigade, 37th Division) and a fellow officer named Hart walked to the Chalk Pit and found there a 'great gathering'. The majority of 10th Loyal North Lancashires were there, ready to move forward. Well into the small hours of 16 July, the stretcher-bearers were still busy evacuating the wounded and moving them to the shelter of the crossroads, north of BAILIFF WOOD and to the west of CONTAL-MAISON.

On 15 July, 10th Royal Fusiliers (111th Brigade, 37th Division) advanced to Sausage Valley in support of the main attack; about 300yds from the village, they were held up by machine-gun fire. The battalion reached the orchards on the south-west side of Pozières, when it became obvious to them that the attack had failed, as they found that the hollow road was blocked with troops in the same way as the Chalk Pit.

In *The War in the Air* by H.A. Jones, it is noted that an observer reported that the artillery bombardment had wrecked many buildings in Pozières, but had done little damage to the trenches that commanded it. Once the bombardment lifted, the German infantry and machine-gunners came down from their dugouts and cellars, ran to their trenches to the fire-steps and opened immediate fire. It appeared to the observer that the attacking troops got as close to the bombardment as possible, but that the enemy had sufficient time to man their positions.

Collison reported that 11th Royal Warwicks suffered 275 casualties and that the casualties of 6th Bedfords, 8th East Lancashires and 10th Royal Fusiliers were probably much greater, as they had opened the attack; the losses of 10th Loyal North Lancashires were rather lighter, as they had not been heavily engaged. However, Collison went on: 'the fighting around the Chalk Pit was but an incident in the far-flung battle that raged long on the Franco-British front'.

In *Anzac to Amiens*, C.E.W. Bean wrote that

> the loop trench around the village was twice entered, there was little show for the effort except the crumpled bodies of British soldiers left hanging in the German wire entanglements . . . the second German defence line, an immensely strong system comprising two parallel trenches (and many long approaches) which ran along the actual crest 500 yards behind the village. South-east of Pozières this line lay on ground seized by the Fourth Army on 14 July, and from that foothold the bombing squads attacked north-westwards.

In the period 18 to 19 July the Pozières front was transferred from Lt Gen Sir Henry Rawlinson's Fourth Army to Lt Gen Sir Hubert Gough's Reserve Army, later Fifth Army. On 18 July, 24th Division made a direct attack on Pozières that failed. In *The Fifth Army*, Gough said that in order to relieve Rawlinson of the necessity of attending to his left flank, and to allow him to concentrate his efforts on pushing his right forward, where he had made some progress, Haig had asked Gough to undertake the attacks on Pozières as well as on OVILLERS-LA-BOISSELLE. This meant that Gough had more territory to look after, and he was allocated 1st Australian Division in order to help out.

The next attack was launched soon after midnight on 23 July, at the same time as the left-hand formations of Third Army made their advance. The village had been heavily bombarded for the 4 previous days, especially on the western side between the BAPAUME road and the cemetery, as well as on the Old German trenches and Pozières Trench. Also, the barrage had been put down on the German line to the west of the village, in order to simulate preparation for an attack from the south-west.

3rd and 1st Australian Brigades (both 1st Australian Division) attacked and achieved their objectives, but did not completely capture the OG lines on the right; the Germans were thus able to fire into the exposed flank of the Australians attacking the eastern end of the village. Very anxious to maintain their hold on the village, the Germans bombarded it methodically, as they did the approach roads to it.

During this fighting two Australians gained the Victoria Cross. 2/Lt A.S. Blackburn of 10th Australian Battalion (3rd Australian Brigade, 1st Australian Division)

> was directed, with fifty men, to drive the enemy from a strongpoint. By dogged determination, he eventually captured their trench, after personally leading four separate parties of bombers against it, many of whom became casualties. In the face of fierce opposition he captured 250 yards of trench. Then, after crawling forward with a sergeant to reconnoitre, he returned, attacked and seized another 120 yards of trench, establishing communication with the battalion on the left.

The other VC winner was Pte J. Leak of 9th Australian Battalion (also 3rd Australian Brigade, 1st Australian Division):

He was one of a party which finally captured an enemy strongpoint. At one assault, when the enemy's bombs were outranging ours, Private Leak rushed out of the trench, ran forward under heavy machine-gun fire at close range, and threw bombs into the enemy's bombing post. He then jumped into the post and bayoneted three unwounded enemy bombers. Later, when the enemy in overwhelming numbers was driving his party back, he was always the last to withdraw at each stage, and kept on throwing bombs. His courage and energy had such an effect on the enemy, that, on arrival of reinforcement, the whole trench was captured.

One of the first points to be captured was the strongpoint called Gibraltar, on the south-west of the village and just off the main road. The village was by no means completely captured on 23 July, and though a foothold was made in it by the Australians, it was to be several weeks before the whole village and the second line beyond it were to fall into Allied hands. Even so, some high ground had been captured, which allowed the British to overlook the valleys of MARTINPUICH and Pys and the German artillery positions on the high ground to the east. In addition, the ground gained threatened the flank of the German main fortifications around THIEPVAL.

On the left flank of the Australians, 145th Brigade (48th Division) gained some ground in the direction of the cemetery, having attacked up Mash Valley. On 24 July, 1st Australian Division consolidated their positions; the plan for 25 July was to secure OG1 Trench and to capture OG2 Trench. The attacking troops had to file out of Pozières Trench in the early hours of 25 July and then turn to the right. By 0200hrs, OG1 had been taken, but attempts to take OG2 failed.

During the fighting, Pte T. Cooke of 8th Australian Battalion (2nd Australian Brigade, 1st Australian Division) was to earn the Victoria Cross:

> After a Lewis gun had been disabled, he was ordered to take his gun and gun-team to a dangerous part of the line. Here he did fine work, but came under very heavy fire, with the result that finally he was the only man left. He still stuck to his post, and continued to fire his gun. When assistance came he was found dead beside his gun . . .

Cooke's name is commemorated on the VILLERS-BRETONNEUX memorial.

At night, 2nd Australian Division began to relieve 1st Australian Division and moved up Sausage Valley, which was full of incoming and outgoing troops, artillery supply wagons, ammunition limbers and ambulances, all under enemy bombardment. While the Germans were fighting to keep a hold on the ridge, however slight, 5th Australian Brigade (2nd Australian Division) were carrying on a mammoth bomb fight at MUNSTER ALLEY, to the north-east of the village. On the right of the Australians, 23rd Division assisted by bombing along this communication trench and the enemy counter-attacked.

By the end of 26 July, the enemy had definitely been driven from Pozières, or at least the northern parts, as well as from the fortified cemetery to the north-east in the direction of MOUQUET FARM. The windmill on Hill 160, being beyond the village to the north, had yet to be captured.

Sgt C.C. Castleton of No. 5 Company, Australian Machine Gun Corps (2nd Australian Division), gained the Victoria Cross when stationed in a sandbag block in OG1.

During an attack on enemy's trenches the infantry was temporarily driven back by the intense machine-gun fire opened by the enemy. Many wounded were left in 'No Man's Land' lying in shell-holes. Sergt. Castleton went out twice in the face of this intense fire and each time brought in a wounded man on his back. He went out a third time, and was bringing in another wounded man when he was himself hit in the back and killed instantly . . .

Castleton is buried in Pozières British Cemetery (IV.L.43).

The next attempt to take the rest of the Pozières Heights was to be made the following day; the attack was to begin at 0015hrs. The plan was for the part of OG1 between the railway and the ALBERT road to be captured. Once this was done, the whole of OG2 could be bombed from the direction of MUNSTER ALLEY. North of the main road, the objectives were the continuation of the OG Trenches. Just before midnight the attacking battalions assembled along the line of the railway to the east of the cemetery. Under very heavy enemy shell-fire, the attack failed, although 23rd Australian Battalion (6th Australian Brigade, 2nd Australian Division) made some progress despite being unsupported on their right flank. The Australians took some time to recuperate and to plan their next attack, which they made on 3 August.

At 2300hrs on 2 August, units of 12th Division attacked and made progress; 8th Royal Fusiliers (36th Brigade, 12th Division) captured the south-west part of Fourth Avenue with 6th Buffs (37th Brigade, 12th Division) assisting. Later they were to take a section of Ration Trench on the right, with 7th Royal Sussex (36th Brigade, 12th Division) and 9th Royal Fusiliers (36th Brigade, 12th Division) attacking frontally and 8th Royal Fusiliers bombing from the left. Although 7th Suffolks (35th Brigade, 12th Division) were attacked twice in a section of Ration Trench, by sundown on 8 August it had been regained.

The Australians had dug new assembly trenches, which the enemy were aware of and subsequently bombarded very heavily, but south-east of BAPAUME road OG1 and OG2 were captured. On the right, 20th Australian Battalion (5th Australian Brigade, 2nd Australian Division) blocked the entrance to Torr Trench. Between the BAPAUME road and the track that led to COURCELETTE, 7th Australian Brigade (2nd Australian Division) fought a very savage battle resulting in many dead on both sides. The left flank was checked by machine-gun fire, but the windmill was captured, along with many prisoners.

This fighting resulted in more Australians being killed in this sector than in any other part of the Somme battlefield, and the consolidation process was very grim because the Germans knew the ground so well. Nevertheless, the crest and the German Second Line had been finally taken, and the Australians were at last able to look over the wide valley beyond the second line. They could see COURCELETTE in the foreground and the woods close to BAPAUME, about 5½ miles away; German guns could also be identified.

Naturally, the German commanders were very anxious to retake their lost positions. The Allied plan was not to push on further eastwards, but to go northwards, towards MOUQUET FARM and THIEPVAL. Having been in the line for 11 days, 2nd Australian Division were replaced by 4th Australian Division.

There were times during the fighting when liquid fire was used, and Sgt C.R. Quinnell, in one of the interviews kept in the sound archives at the Imperial War Museum, described an incident on 5 August: 'a German came over the barricade on the right flank with a canister of liquid fire on his back, squirting the liquid out of the hose, burning twenty-three of our chaps to death – but somebody threw a bomb – a Mills bomb – and it burst behind him – he went down.'

Heavily bombarded in their defensive positions, 4th Australian Division managed to keep the heights and push northwards towards MOUQUET FARM as planned. The farm was camouflaged and was a very well-fortified strongpoint; the defences went as much as 30ft down. As the Australians had made what was virtually a big bulge in the German lines, they were vulnerable to shelling from German artillery in the rear, from the direction of THIEPVAL and from both flanks. The enemy even overran the village briefly before being driven off by the Australians.

Pte M. O'Meara of 16th Australian Battalion (4th Australian Brigade, 4th Australian Division) was awarded the Victoria Cross for conspicuous bravery, 9–12 August.

> During four days of heavy fighting he repeatedly went out and brought in wounded officers and men from 'No Man's Land' under intense artillery and machine-gun fire. He also volunteered and carried up ammunition and bombs through a heavy barrage to a portion of the trenches which was being heavily shelled at the time . . .

From having been a very strongly fortified village in the German line, Pozières had by now been gradually reduced to just a shapeless mass of rubble and dust and had virtually ceased to exist. One source said that no fewer than 200 enemy machine guns had been used in its defence.

In his despatches of 9 August war correspondent Philip Gibbs discussed the handling of the German dead:

> Search parties are sent out under shell-fire to collect them, even though many of the searchers may join the dead, and the bodies are put into mortuary chambers like the one found by us the other day at Pozières. It was filled with dead bodies waiting to be taken away on a light railway which runs up to the place, but the enemy's artillery fired upon this mortuary and set it on fire, as though they were more jealous of their dead than of the living who were our prisoners . . .

On 13 August, the Allies made further progress, advancing their line 400yds on a front of nearly 1 mile; casualties were light, despite a heavy German gun barrage.

On 27 August, Lt C.W. Winterbotham of 1/5th Glosters (145th Brigade, 48th Division) was killed at Skyline Trench, south-west of Pozières, aged 29.

Called to the bar in 1911 and prospective candidate for the Liberal Party for East Gloucestershire in 1913, Winterbotham had published poetry, including a volume called *The Muse in Arms*. His name is commemorated on the Thiepval Memorial.

Later in August, 4th Australian Division were relieved, first by 1st Australian Division and then by 2nd Australian Division, after which it was 4th Australian Division's turn again. Little progress was made during this period and the Australians, whose 'holy ground' the village had become, were finally relieved by units of the Canadian Army on 9 September.

Sgt L. Clarke of 2nd Canadian Battalion (1st Canadian Brigade, 1st Canadian Division) gained the Victoria Cross on 9 September near Pozières.

> He was detailed with his section of bombers to clear the continuation of a newly captured trench and cover the building of a 'block'. After most of his party had become casualties, he was building a 'block' when about 20 of the enemy with two officers counter-attacked. He boldly advanced against them, emptied his revolver into them, and afterwards two enemy rifles which he picked up in the trench. One of the officers then attacked him with the bayonet, wounding him in the leg, but he shot him dead. The enemy then ran away, pursued by Acting Corporal Clarke, who shot four more and captured a fifth. Later he was ordered to the dressing station, but returned next day to duty.

All this activity took place in the vicinity of Walker Avenue, a salient that lay between the Canadian positions and COURCELETTE. On 19 October, Clarke died of wounds at No. 1 General Hospital, Etretat, and was buried in Etretat Churchyard (II.C.3A).

On 15 September, the stump of the windmill at Pozières was a starting point for some of the tanks that were about to make history; it was the first time that the machines had been used in a battle. They assisted the Canadian infantry to drive the enemy almost to the bottom of the valley that the Australians had previously only looked over.

The whole of the fighting for Pozières had been very slow, stretching over nearly 2 months, and extremely costly in terms of casualties. According to the Australian historian C.E.W. Bean, 1st, 2nd and 4th Australian Divisions suffered some 22,826 casualties; in their attack on Fromelles to the north, 5th Australian Division suffered 5,533 casualties.

John Masefield described the site of Pozières after the battle, as seen from OVILLERS-LA-BOISSELLE, in the following way: 'A clump of small fir and cypress trees stood up dark on the hill at the western end of this row, and behind the trees was a line of green hills topped with the ruins of a windmill. The ruins, now gone, were the end of Pozières village, the dark trees grew in Pozières Cemetery and the mill was the famous mill of Pozières, which marked the crest that was one of the prizes of the battle.'

The painter William Orpen described the village at the same time in the following way: 'On up the hill past the mines to Pozières. An Army railway was then running through, and the station was marked by a big wooden sign, painted black and white, like you see at any country station in England, with POZIÈRES in large Roman letters, but that's all there was of Pozières except a little red in the mud.'

Pozières was lost to the Germans in the period 24/25 March 1918.

In October 1923, Boyd Cable revisited the village and wrote about it in *The Times*: 'I doubt, for instance, if any man who ever fought there would know Pozières as it is to-day. At the end of 1916 all that I can recall of a village there was a waste of broken bricks and overlapping shell-holes for acres round.' Although 'a fragment of mill is left, with an Australian memorial beside it, and another monument to the Tank Corps just across the road', he could no longer see the miles of trenches there once had been, and a new road went 'straight through the new village, littered no longer with the wreckage of war, but with stacks of new bricks and heaps of sand, where children play at building castles . . .'

After his visit to Pozières in 1932, Will R. Bird of 42nd Canadian Infantry Battalion (7th Canadian Brigade, 3rd Canadian Division) described it in *Thirteen Years After* as 'a straggling village with many wooden huts, small houses, and a few big farm homes. Villa Victoria is the name of the only expansive front we saw . . . Pozières British Cemetery is beside the road, and is a beautiful square of double columns, a splendid structure . . .'

During her visit to the cemetery in August 1933, Vera Brittain wrote of the missing: 'What has become of all these bodily remnants? Are they collected together in huge common graves, or have they been exploded, ploughed & steam-rollered into the soil, & are we driving over them all the time?' As for the village, Brittain noted that 'the new red-roofed mayor's house and school [were] built out of penny subscriptions from the children of Melbourne . . .'

Eighteen years later, in an article of 1 July 1935 in an issue of *Reveille*, C.E.W. Bean wrote:

Members of the A.I.F. who at any time revisit the battlefields in France, may be glad to know, that the small plot of land on which stood or lay the famous Windmill at Pozières has been purchased by Australia. It is now fenced in, and the following inscription has been put in place:
'The ruin of Pozières windmill, which lies here, was the centre of the struggle in this part of the Somme battlefields in July and August, 1916. It was captured on August 4 by Australian troops, who fell more thickly on this ridge than on any other battlefield of the war.'

Bean also wrote:

The old wooden memorial cross of the 2nd Australian Division used to stand upon this ground, between the stump of the windmill and the Bapaume Road; and when the cross was taken down there occurred the opportunity of securing the land for a small price. As the site – with the stump of the windmill reinforced with German concrete – lay beside the Albert–Bapaume road on the sumit of the Somme battlefield, passed by all visitors the chance was gladly seized . . . and the site is now open for visitors.

Although more Australians gave their lives in the Pozières area than at any other place in the First World War, it was decided that VILLERS-BRETONNEUX would be a more suitable place in which to commemorate their role in the war.

Designed by W.H. Cowlishaw, Pozières British Cemetery is on the west side of the main road, on the site of the place which in 1916 was known as Tramway Crossing or Red Cross Corner, close to the former railway station. It would have been a place for field ambulances to bring their dead from the battlefield. Pozières British Cemetery contains more than 2,400 graves, of which about half are unidentified. Many isolated graves were brought in after the war. The earlier plots of the cemetery contain the original burials of 1916–1918 by fighting units and field ambulances. The remaining plots were made after the Armistice, by the concentration of graves from the surrounding battlefields. The great majority were of men who had been killed in the autumn of 1916.

As mentioned earlier, the cemetery contains the grave of a Lowestoft-born VC-winner, Sgt C.C. Castleton (IV.L.43); also that of a son of the

Bishop of Crediton, T/Capt A.O. Trefusis (III.D.43) of 9th Loyal North Lancashires (74th Brigade, 24th Division), killed at LA BOISSELLE on 7 July 1916. Two recent graves are those of Pte D.J. Carlson of 49th Canadian Battalion (7th Canadian Brigade, 3rd Canadian Division), killed aged 19 on 8 September 1916; in May 2000 he was reburied with full military honours (III.E.48). Carlson's remains had been found by members of the public close to Pozières on the site of an attack against MOUQUET FARM and his ID was still with them. The other reburial was that of an Australian who could not be identified.

Pozières British Cemetery includes a Memorial to the Missing from the battle period of March and April 1918 and the German breakthrough against Fifth Army, designed by W.H. Cowlishaw. The men who were missing from the Somme battlefield from June 1915 up to March 1918 are commemorated at THIEPVAL, while those who were missing from the Advance to Victory in 1918 are remembered at Vis-en-Artois. The Memorial was finished by November 1928 but was not inaugurated until 4 August 1930, by Gen Sir Horace Smith-Dorrien. The panels list the names of the 14,644 officers and men who have no known grave. Names on the panels include those of Pte H. Columbine VC, 2/Lt E. De Wind VC and Lt Col W. Elstob VC, as well as the poet R.B. Marriott-Watson, a lieutenant in the Royal Irish Rifles who was killed on 24 March 1918.

Another literary connection is with the imagist poet Lt T.E. Hulme of the Royal Marine Artillery, who had been involved in the Pozières fighting with 1st Division; Hulme was killed later in the war and buried at Coxde, near Dunkirk.

C.E.W. Bean collected many mementoes and artefacts from the battlefield and these have been deposited in the Canberra Museum. They include a bag of debris from the site of the village, which was placed in the Cenotaph in the Australian capital.

As already stated, on 15 September 1916 tanks went into action opposite the site of Pozières windmill, which had been fortified as a German bunker. The mill, which was reduced to a pile of bricks and was the highest point on Pozières Ridge, is now a grassy mound with a memorial slab that gives details of the Australian stand in the months of July and August in their attempts to capture the feature, also known as Hill 160. Across the road is the 30ft-high Tank Corps Memorial, which is made up of scale model tanks of the 1916–1918 period and was unveiled by Lt-Gen. Sir Thomas Morland ADC to the King (Colonel-in-Chief) on 22 July 1922. the encircling chains came from tanks. Pozières also has a memorial to the King's Royal Rifle Corps. The Regiment wasn't too keen on having a

The King's Royal Rifle Corps Memorial at Pozières after the war. *(Peter F. Batchelor Collection)*

shared memorial and wanted one to themselves. At the beginning, the original site chosen was found to be far too close to the Tank Memorial and was altered to a position near the 1st Australian Division Memorial. There was no inauguration ceremony. The owner of the land was Monsieur L. Magnier Marceau. In 1938, at the site of the 2nd Australian Division memorial, a new oak gate facing the road was put in place with a set of regimental badges. In 1993 the Australian government tidied up the site at the windmill and erected a plaque to honour the members of the Australian Imperial Force who had died in the fighting for the village in 1916.

The water tower on the Bapaume side of the village has an image of a Digger painted on it and below are the names of seven men who won a VC during the Allied struggle to capture the village in July–August 1916.

The Commonwealth War Graves Commission noted in its annual report of 2001–2002:

> A significant structural challenge currently facing the Commission is the condition of the Pozières Memorial in France. Water penetration to the heart of the structure has caused staining of name panels, in some instances, the failure of

the panels themselves. Action had to be taken and a major project to cover the roof with lead was one aspect of a programme intended to make the memorial as water resistant as possible before replacement name panels, which have already been manufactured at the workshops in France, are secured in place . . .

Although a recent visit to the Memorial confirmed that the roof leading operation had been carried out successfully, it appeared that some of the panels had been replaced before sufficient time had been given for drying out; as a consquence, damp has seeped through once more.

In the mid-1980s Gibraltar, the former blockhouse and site of a German command headquarters, was opened up and the area around the blockhouse was later purchased by the Conseil Général de la Somme. Sadly, at this time many items found during excavations were unofficially removed. In 1996 a second excavation was carried out, which did not lead to the recovery of many more artefacts. The site was then fenced off while a decision was taken as to what to do next. By 2000 the site had been completely renovated and it now features a flight of concrete steps leading into the former cellar of the house on which the bunker was built. An information plaque was put in place, and a large wooden orientation platform built to the height of

Captured German pillbox, Gibraltar, Pozières, 20 September 1916. *(IWM Q1089)*

the original bunker allows visitors to appreciate the importance of the position during 1916.

PROUVILLE is north-west of AMIENS off the D925 road. At the end of November 1915, 19th Manchesters (21st Brigade, 30th Division) were billeted here; at this time, Prouville was a poor and overcrowded little village. On 1 February 1916, 1/1st (North Midland) Field Ambulance (46th Division) established a hospital here in an empty house, where there was good accommodation for 30 patients. On 12 February work began on a bathhouse and drying room. Until 21 February, when they left the village, the field ambulance's daily pattern was to collect casualties from their immediate area. The 12th Brigade of 4th Division were billeted in the area on 23 May.

Prouville Churchyard has the graves of two British soldiers from 1/5th South Staffords (137th Brigade, 46th Division) who died as a result of a training accident on 28 February, when the battalion was billeted in the village. Pte W. Hough was killed instantly and Sgt S.C. Rooker died later of his wounds; the additional number of wounded came to 13, and 3 others were slightly wounded. At the inquiry into the accident no blame was attached to anyone. During live grenade throwing practice in the morning the instructor, Sgt G. Pritchard (one of the wounded), had drawn the pin from a Mills grenade prior to throwing it, when it exploded in his hand.

PROYART is due south of BRAY-SUR-SOMME on the D329 road and housed No. 61 Casualty Clearing Station in early September 1916. Proyart Communal Cemetery had one British soldier buried in it.

Here, according to Vera Brittain, was a 'Valley of Death', where British gun positions were very often shelled and slow-moving lorries constantly hit. Apparently the Germans set up a 'Big Bertha' gun with which they began to shell AMIENS in 1918. To the north-east of the village is a German military cemetery; Proyart also includes a magnificent French war memorial.

PUCHEVILLERS, situated 12 miles north-east of AMIENS, is on the D11 road between AMIENS and THIÈVRES. On 6 December 1915, 18th Manchesters (90th Brigade, 30th Division) spent a night here on their way to ENGLEBELMER, and they were here again when on their way from CANAPLES.

On 4 February 1916 a new broad-gauge railway line was being built from CANDAS via Puchevillers and LÉALVILLERS to ACHEUX-EN-AMIÉNOIS, and another from DAOURS through QUERRIEU and CONTAY. On 1 March, 48th Division provided working parties and at the end of March, a 49th Division field company worked on ammunition huts at the railway station. In early March, No. 458 Field Company, Royal Engineers (49th Division), were in the village and carried out work on water trough lines serving 500 animals; cavalry units that might have made use of this water supply could have included 6th Dragoons (Mhow Brigade, 1st (Indian) Cavalry Division), who were in the village at the end of April. In the third week of April, 36th Division had units here.

Arriving here from SAINT-OUEN on 1 May, No. 3 Casualty Clearing Station took over school buildings and a camping ground at Puchevillers. The present school is in rue des Prieurs, but is not the original building. No. 3 Casualty Clearing Station remained here until 6 March 1917.

In May and June, a 49th Division field company were working on ammunition huts again and there was a big camp in the village used for railway workers. By that time the railway line had reached Puchevillers from CONTAY and HÉRISSART.

Puchevillers will be remembered more for its hospitals and cemetery in 1916 than for its billeting and training role. After No. 44 Casualty Clearing Station arrived on 17 May, they were allotted an area of farmland 80yds × 200yds, 1 mile from the village, on which they were to set up a hospital handling 800 patients. The next week was spent in constructing the camp, with marquees being pitched on what was partly a wheat field and partly ploughed land, neither of which would hold the front 10 pegs. The first patients were admitted on 18 June.

On 16 June, 1/6th West Yorkshires (146th Brigade, 49th Division) were camped in Puchevillers orchard, on the outskirts of the village; they were rejoined by working parties who had left the battalion 5 weeks earlier. By now the village showed considerable signs of the approaching battle and a huge casualty clearing station (No. 44) had been built within a short distance of the camp. The casualty clearing station was busy accumulating stretchers and other medical stores. During their 10-day stay 1/6th West Yorkshires watched the casualty clearing station orderlies 'working overtime digging graves'. There were also enormous railway sidings in the village with hundreds of shells of all calibres.

Puchevillers was described as 'a very lively place': champagne, games and horseplay were available to tempt the soldiers into spending their pay. On 25 June a church parade was held in the orchard; it was attended by almost everyone and was probably the most impressive held by the battalion. At 2030hrs on 27 June, 1/6th West Yorkshires marched out of the village towards VARENNES. Villagers came to their windows and doors in TOUTENCOURT and HARPONVILLE as the men marched by.

On 27 June, 3rd Worcesters (7th Brigade, 25th Division) arrived here after a long march from BERNEUIL.

At the beginning of the battle, Puchevillers was not only one of the principal railheads for ammunition but was also a place where trains were to take away the wounded expected from the first days of the battle. Both No. 3 and No. 44 Casualty Clearing Stations were intended for the seriously wounded.

The first burials in Puchevillers British Cemetery, towards the end of June, were made by No. 3 Casualty Clearing Station; the cemetery was intended for use by both hospitals and it would appear that the tented No. 44 Casualty Clearing Station was next to the present site of the cemetery.

On the eve of the battle, the village, together with HÉRISSART, was home to 113th Brigade (38th Division); 114th Brigade was at RUBEMPRÉ and 115th Brigade at TOUTENCOURT (both also 38th Division). On 1 July, 129th Field Ambulance (38th Division) helped No. 3 Casualty Clearing Station near the railhead handle some 449 casualties. On 2 July, after a casualty clearing station at HEILLY was closed for a time, Puchevillers was used instead, meaning that many of the wounded faced a long, rough journey; 2 July was the casualty clearing station's busiest day. In all, No. 3 Casualty Clearing Station was to treat 7,959 patients in July, of whom 974 were operated on.

A similar sequence of events occurred at No. 44 Casualty Clearing Station; the wounded came in very rapidly in great numbers all night, and by 1900hrs on 1 July the station had received 96 officer casualties and 1,042 other ranks. On 2 July, after having evacuated 59 casualties, the station was instructed to cease evacuating casualties for the time being; as a result, casualties began to overflow from the station, as they had No. 3. Even the dining tent and living quarters were commandeered for use.

At noon there were 96 officers and 983 other ranks in the camp, when a telegram arrived stating that more casualties were being sent on to Nos. 3 and 44 Casualty Clearing Stations. Fourth Army's Deputy Director of Medical Services was informed of the chaotic situation and the instruction was subsequently cancelled. Evacuation was slowly resumed, but casualties from No. 44 had to be taken to the siding by hand, as No. 3 Casualty Clearing Station had already taken the wheeled stretcher-carriers.

By 5 July, the handling situation of casualties had returned to normal. The very high number of casualties had not been sufficiently anticipated by the military railway authorities, who tragically had

made a great blunder by their inadequate planning.

On 5 July a brigade of 36th Division were here again, and two other brigades were at RUBEMPRÉ and HÉRISSART. On 8 September, 74th Brigade (25th Division) were in the area. On 12 October, Maj Gen A. Paris CB, General Officer Commanding 63rd Division, was brought to No. 3 Casualty Clearing Station after being wounded at BEAUMONT-HAMEL; his leg had to be amputated. Between the end of June and the end of November, 6th, 11th, 25th, 37th, 49th, 51st and 63rd Divisions had units at Puchevillers.

Puchevillers British Cemetery, designed by Sir Edwin Lutyens and finished in 1924, is on high ground to the west of the village. Plots I to V and most of Plot VI were made by Nos. 3 and 44 Casualty Clearing Stations. In Row A.1 of the cemetery are the graves of some of the first men to be buried here, including eight who died as a result of a gas raid that blew back on men of the Royal Irish Rifles; all told, there had been 23 casualties. The very first man buried here was Pte J. Erwin (I.A.1) of No. 96 Company, Machine Gun Corps (32nd Division), who died on 19 June. In Plot VI, the dead were buried in the date order of death, some having survived a few days before succumbing. Plot VII mostly contains the graves of men caught up in the German advance of 1918; these casualties would have been buried by No. 49 Casualty Clearing Station or by 49th Labour Group. All told, there are 1,763 men buried here.

The conductor Eugene Goosens had several extremely talented children who became musicians, including the harpist Sidonie, who died in December 2004, more than 88 years after her brother Eugene (I.C.60), who was also a conductor, a 20-year-old officer with 7th Norfolks (35th Brigade, 12th Division), and died of wounds on 17 August 1916.

Lt H.W. Crowle of 10th Australian Battalion (3rd Australian Brigade, 1st Australian Division) has a special memorial which notes that he was wounded at MOUQUET FARM in August 1916 and died 5 days later at Puchevillers.

PUISIEUX, on the D919, D6 and D27 roads, is a village between HÉBUTERNE and Achiet-le-Petit and north-east of SERRE. Puisieux was part of the operations to take GOMMECOURT, le Barque, Ligny-Thilloy, SERRE and several other villages in the same area. In June 1916 the road from MAILLY-MAILLET to SERRE and Puisieux entered no man's land about 1,400yds south-west of SERRE. On 1 July, 31st and 4th Divisions attacked north and south of this road. Small parties of 31st Division did manage to reach SERRE, but the attack failed; in November, 3rd and 31st Divisions attacked again, still without success.

On 24 February 1917 the Germans left Puisieux, and the next day 22nd Manchesters (91st Brigade, 7th Division) entered it. Although the village, which is in undulating country, had been destroyed by artillery fire, the ground yielded was of significance and importance, as the position had been a strong one. The church was the last stronghold that the Germans had held on to. In March 1918 the enemy retook the village, only to lose it again in August 1918.

Q

THE QUADRANGLE was the name given to a strongpoint 500yds to the south-west of MAMETZ WOOD, adjacent to the road to CONTALMAISON. Part of a German defensive line running down from OVILLERS-LA-BOISSELLE to a position in front of MAMETZ WOOD, it consisted of Quadrangle Trench and, some distance behind it, the Quadrangle Support. In addition, Quadrangle Alley ran into it from the outskirts of MAMETZ WOOD, just behind Wood Support. As the trench reached towards the Wood, it became known as Wood Trench, which in turn came out at a right angle, named Strip Trench.

John Masefield noted that the Quadrangle was sited so that men approaching it from the south could be seen and fired on from both flanks, as well as from the rear. Well-hidden supports linked it with the village of CONTALMAISON and MAMETZ WOOD. The work defended the spur on the eastern side. On the west it was defended by the work in SHELTER WOOD, just beyond the Poodles on the FRICOURT–CONTALMAISON road; by two fortified copses to the north of SHELTER WOOD; and by a field work to the north of these copses known as the Horseshoe. In *The Turning Point*, H.P. Robinson, war correspondent of *The Times*, noted that the position was a formidable one; Quadrangle Trench was the longest side and Quadrangle Support was the shortest, but both had extremely strong positions at their two ends. It was, in fact, commanded on the one hand by CONTALMAISON and on the other by MAMETZ WOOD, whence it could be easily reinforced. Quadrangle Support looked down on a bare natural glacis, which was without a scrap of cover, except for a few shell-holes.

THE QUADRILATERAL was a fortified German strongpoint of machine-gun posts, rectangular in shape and about 750yds to the east of GINCHY, where the road to MORVAL bent northwards. It was sheltered by a clump of trees and protected in front by trenches that ran east and west as defence against the Allied direction from the south, and also by lines of more trenches on the west side, that ran north and south. Just beyond the bend in the road, the road ran through a deep ravine with wooded sides. This had been strongly fortified with deep dugouts. The whole position consisted of a veritable redoubt forming the southern angle of a 'V', the two lines of which ran eastwards in the fortified ravine. This comprehensive description of the position comes from *The Turning Point* by H.P. Robinson, war correspondent of *The Times*.

On 15 September 1916 the Quadrilateral strongpoint held up the attack of the Guards Division and 6th Division, whose objectives were LESBŒUFS and MORVAL, but after continuous and heavy fighting the position was taken on 18 September, followed by the two villages a week later.

QUERRIEU is on the AMIENS–ALBERT road, the D929, a few miles north-east of AMIENS. At the beginning of August 1915, units of 5th Division were concentrated in the area between Querrieu and BRAY-SUR-SOMME to the east. On 30 August, 51st Division arrived in the area at the same time as units of 18th Division who had been shelled out of their previous billets.

Between 17 January and 23 February 1916, No. 59 Field Company, Royal Engineers (5th Division), made bunks for billeting purposes in barns here. On 1 February, 13th Field Ambulance (5th Division) arrived here. On 6 February, 7th Royal West Kents (55th Brigade, 18th Division) played drum and bugle to 1st Royal West Kents (13th Brigade, 5th Division) when they marched through the village. On about 23 February, X Corps headquarters left Querrieu Château, as the building was required by Fourth Army headquarters, which set up here on the following day.

Although February was relatively quiet, between March and June considerable mining activity was carried out. On 1 March, Fourth Army took over the line to the south of Third Army (the SERRE–MAILLY-MAILLET road) as far as the River Somme, where they linked hands with the French Army.

On 18 March, No. 200 Field Company, Royal Engineers (30th Division), were here when working on hutments for Fourth Army headquarters. On

3 April, 2nd Middlesex (23rd Brigade, 8th Division) passed through the village on their way to billets in ALBERT. They were welcomed by the drums of 4th Middlesex (63rd Brigade, 21st Division), 'who played them through the village, to the great delight and unbounded enthusiasm of all ranks . . .' In mid-April, two companies of 2nd Wiltshires (21st Brigade, 30th Division) arrived here to assist the Royal Engineers.

As the months of preparation for the Battle of the Somme progressed, Lt Gen Sir Henry Rawlinson, General Officer Commanding Fourth Army, used what he called his 'Operation Fort', a specially constructed platform from where he observed the lines and later followed the progress of the bombardment and the battle itself. The spot is a few hundred yards off the main road and closer to PONT-NOYELLES (see that entry) than to Querrieu. On 27 June, Rawlinson took Sir Douglas Haig there to enable him to observe the barrage. This viewing platform among the trees was really Rawlinson's personal observation post, but he also frequently visited another and much more public position known as the GRANDSTAND, just outside DERNANCOURT (see that entry).

The British High Command considered that the enemy would not survive a relentless bombardment. During the final week before the attack, 150,000 rounds were being fired each day and 50,000 each

HM King George V, Haig and Rawlinson, Querrieu Château, August 1916. *(IWM 3922)*

night. Fifteen hundred guns were being used, 450 of them of a large calibre.

Although Rawlinson, supported by Lord Kitchener, advocated a 'bite and hold' strategy, Haig disagreed; he was convinced that the enemy positions would be so damaged that the British infantryman, together with his 66lb of equipment, would be able simply to walk over no man's land, in places 4,000yds wide, and into empty German lines. In addition, Haig was not convinced of the ability of the men serving in the many divisions of the New Army.

Before the battle began on 1 July, Lt Gen Sir Hubert Gough's Reserve (later Fifth) Army were billeted behind Rawlinson's headquarters and Gough and his troops had been placed at Rawlinson's disposal. At the time, three cavalry divisions were under Gough, as well as 19th and 49th Divisions; the cavalry were to be used when the expected breakthrough of the enemy lines occurred. This situation did not happen; the two infantry divisions were thrown in with Fourth Army's struggle in early July, while the cavalry, bivouacked among the poplar groves at one hour's notice, were later withdrawn.

On 1 July, Rawlinson was up at his fort at 0630hrs and remained there an hour, before seeing the attack go in at 0730hrs; at 0800hrs, he rode back to the château and spent the rest of the day awaiting reports from his corps commanders.

After attending church service at his château in BEAUQUESNE, Sir Douglas Haig and Lt Gen

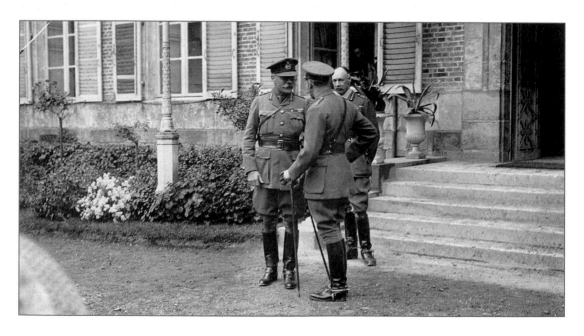

Sir Launcelot Kiggell, Haig's Chief of General Staff, drove to Querrieu after lunch to confer with Rawlinson; at 2100hrs, Marshal Foch came over to report on the successes of the French Army.

The war correspondent Philip Gibbs was a regular visitor to Fourth Army headquarters and described Rawlinson in his book *Pageant of the Years*: 'He was always genial, amusing, and quick in judgement. Generally in riding breeches, he would slap his gaiters with his crop, and seemed to be enjoying the war in spite of its appalling casualties and daily routine of death for masses of men . . .'

During his visit to the troops in August, HM the King recorded in his diary that he visited Rawlinson's château on 10 August, after he had been to BOIS FRANÇAIS – which was about as close to the front line as he was allowed to go – in the morning. Accompanied by his eldest son, HRH the Prince of Wales, the King was given lunch there and met the French Generals Fayolle and Balfourier, presenting them with the Grand Cross of the Order of St Michael and St George; Lt Gen Sir William Pulteney, General Officer Commanding III Corps, and Lt Gen Sir H. Horne, General Officer Commanding XV Corps, also attended the luncheon.

Haig arrived soon afterwards and the King decorated some 20 French artillery officers and decorated Pte A. Procter of 1/5th King's (165th Brigade, 55th Division) with his Victoria Cross, won near Ficheux on 4 June. At 1425hrs, the King left for CONTAY to continue his tour, meeting up with Lt Gen Sir Hubert Gough, General Officer Commanding Reserve (later Fifth) Army, and Lt Gen Sir William Birdwood, General Officer Commanding I Anzac Corps. As the King motored with Birdwood through the Australian lines, the two men were greeted by 'tremendous cheering'.

Querrieu British Cemetery, designed by G.H. Goldsmith, is south of the village, 110 yards after the church and on the left-hand side of the road leading to BUSSY-LÈS-DAOURS. It was begun in March 1918 by Australian divisions and closed the following August. Lt Col C. Bushell (E.6) of 7th Queen's, who won a Victoria Cross west of the Saint-Quentin Canal on 23 March 1918, is one of the 194 men buried here.

In 1954, the former Prince of Wales, since 1936 the Duke of Windsor, revisited the château. The building is occasionally open for visitors by appointment and the original family still owns the property, which houses a small photographic exhibition of its links with the Battle of the Somme.

R

RAINCHEVAL, north-east of AMIENS, lies to the east of the D11 road, on the D31 road between BEAUQUESNE and ARQUÈVES. During the First World War the village was used as an advance depot for medical stores. The church bears the date 1865 and has a fine French memorial in front of it; the imposing château, which has clearly seen better days, bears the date 1719. The château, dovecot and farm would have been used for military purposes during the war.

In mid-October 1915, 16th Royal Irish Rifles (pioneers of 36th Division) were here and carried out work on the Third Army lines. Between August and October 1916, 3rd, 6th, 11th, 25th, 37th, 49th and 51st Divisions had units in the area. Raincheval Communal Cemetery is to the south-east of the village.

RAINNEVILLE is north-east of AMIENS on the D11 road. During the war, the village was often linked with MOLLIENS-AU-BOIS, to the north-east, in providing billets. Between 6 and 13 February 1916, 1st Royal West Kents (13th Brigade, 5th Division) were here.

From mid-June, a number of units were in the village. These included 7th Loyal North Lancashires (56th Brigade, 19th Division), who were here for a few days before moving to Hénencourt Wood. On 1 July, 24th Brigade (23rd Division) were here prior to joining 8th Division on 15 July, while 23rd Division's other two brigades, 69th and 68th Brigades, were at BERTANGLES and COISY respectively. On 9 July, units of 98th Brigade (33rd Division) billeted here, while 19th Brigade (also 33rd Division) were at POULAINVILLE and 100th Brigade (also 33rd Division) at SAINT-SAUVEUR. In September, 10th Brigade (4th Division) were here.

RANCOURT is a village on the D944 main road between PÉRONNE to the south and BAPAUME to the north, and was in the area of responsibility of the French, who captured it on 24 September 1916. Rancourt remained in Allied hands until 24 March 1918, when it fell to the Germans once again; it was recaptured by 47th Division on 1 September.

Rancourt Military Cemetery is about ½ mile south of the village, on the west side of the main road; the cemetery register records the names of 89 men. The cemetery was begun by units of the Guards Division in the winter of 1916–17. It stands on fairly high ground among cultivated fields. A church is adjacent to it.

The Rancourt French National German Cemetery, with nearly 4,000 burials, is to the west. A museum which tells the story of the fighting in this area is now located inside the chapel in the French National Cemetery, but is not permanently open; the cemetery warden, who lives in the nearby cottage, will open it on request. The chapel has several memorials to British soldiers, as well as many French ones.

REDAN RIDGE, a group of British front-line trenches in 1916, was north of the village of BEAUMONT-HAMEL. In *The Old Front Line* John Masefield described the situation there during the period prior to the battle. He wrote that

it was a question here, which side should hold the highest point of the spur. Right on top of the spur there is one patch of ground, measuring, it may be, two hundred yards each way, from which one can see a long way in every direction. From this path, the ground drops a little towards the English side and stretches away fairly flat towards the enemy side, but one can see far either way and to have this power of seeing, both sides fought desperately.

Redan Ridge was an active mining area, like the Tambour, FRICOURT and LA BOISSELLE. It was the most northerly point in the British sector where mining was still in progress in June 1916. Two mines, one 57ft deep and the other 62ft deep, were in active use close to their German counterparts.

On 1 July, Redan Ridge was one of the objectives of 4th Division; 11th Brigade (4th Division) were the formation most directly involved in the attempt to take it. The brigade's battalions had formed up on either side of Watling Street, which was the track leading from BEAUMONT-HAMEL village in a north-westerly direction to the SERRE road; 1st East Lancashires were on the right with 1st Hampshires while 1st Rifle Brigade and 1st Somerset Light Infantry were on the left. Further to the north, to the left of 1st Rifle Brigade, was the Quadrilateral, a German strongpoint.

The story of 4th Division's failure to capture Redan Ridge is told in the entry for BEAUMONT-HAMEL; in fact it was not captured until the November battles, and even then only partly taken, by 2nd Division. At the end of the battle, the Allied line was consolidated across Waggon Road, which was roughly parallel to the still German-held Munich Trench and beyond that, Frankfurt Trench.

John Masefield noted that

the whole of the summit for all its two hundred yards, is blown into pits and craters from twenty to fifty feet deep, and sometimes fifty yards long . . . For many weeks, the armies fought for this patch of hill. It was all mined, counter-mined, and re-mined, and at each explosion the crater was fought for and lost and won. It cannot be said that either side won that summit till the enemy was beaten from all that field, for both sides conquered enough to see from. On the enemy side, a fortification of heaped earth was made; on our side, castles were built of sandbags filled with flint. These strongholds gave both sides enough observation. The works face each other across the ponds.

Redan Ridge is the site of a group of cemeteries made in the spring of 1917 by V Corps. Redan Ridge Cemetery No. 1, on the top of the ridge and midway between the former front lines, contains the graves of 154 soldiers who, with few exceptions, belonged to 4th Division, which attacked the area on 1 July 1916, or to 2nd Division, which gained ground here on 13 November. It commands a wide view of the neighbouring villages and memorials. Redan Ridge Cemetery No. 2 is on lower ground, about 100yds to the west of the former German Front Line. It contains the graves of 279 soldiers of 2nd, 4th and 29th Divisions who fell, with one exception, in July and November 1916. The 'unknowns' total 124 men. Redan Ridge Cemetery No. 3 is located amid the former German front-line trenches and contains the graves of 67 soldiers. Most of the graves are those of 2nd Division men who fell in November 1916; 13 graves were replaced by special memorials.

REGINA TRENCH was part of the German line which ran from the north of COURCELETTE to SAINT-PIERRE-DIVION. It connected up with STUFF TRENCH, which in turn joined SCHWABEN REDOUBT. On the easterly side, it ran in a north-easterly direction across the GRAND-COURT road, West Miraumont Road, Courcelette Trench and Pys Road towards LE SARS.

The fighting for this position is particularly associated with Canadian battalions who were involved in very hard fighting in the period 8 to 10 October 1916. It was during this time that one of their number, Piper J.C. Richardson of 16th Canadian Battalion (3rd Canadian Brigade, 1st Canadian Division), gained the Victoria Cross. Richardson had been born in Lanarkshire; prior to the start of the attack, he had obtained permission to play his company 'over the top'. As his company approached the objective, they found that it was protected by very strong wire, and they subsequently came under intense fire, which caused casualties and demoralised the formation.

Piper Richardson strode up and down outside the wire, playing his pipes with the greatest coolness. The company were inspired and rushed the wire and overcame the objective. Later, Richardson was detailed to take back a wounded man and some prisoners. After proceeding for about 200yds, he remembered that he had left his pipes behind, and insisted on returning to fetch them. He was never seen alive again, and his grave is at Adanac Cemetery (III.F.36) just north of COURCELETTE on the COURCELETTE–MIRAUMONT road.

On 21 October, Regina Trench was reached after an effective artillery barrage; 18th, 25th and 4th Canadian Divisions were directly involved in the attack. On the right, 87th Canadian Battalion (11th Canadian Brigade, 4th Canadian Division) formed a defensive flank east of the Pys road, and posts were established well forward of Regina Trench. On the left were 10th Essex and 8th Norfolks (both 53rd Brigade, 18th Division), who overcame resistance; 250 Germans were killed and there were over 300 prisoners taken. The conditions here were appalling, and as it rained a great deal in October and November, most parts of Regina Trench were to become knee deep in clinging mud. A commentator who visited the area of the trench in 1931 could find no trace of it.

RIBEAUCOURT is east of ABBEVILLE on the D185 road. During the build-up to the Somme battle, the village was mainly used for billeting purposes; 1st Norfolks (15th Brigade, 5th Division) were one of two battalions representing X Corps for HM the King's inspection here on 25 October 1915.

In early January 1916, 89th Brigade (30th Division) had their headquarters in the château here, north-west of the village and close to a very large wood. In early February, 164th Brigade (55th Division) had their headquarters here when 1/4th Loyal North Lancashires (164th Brigade, 55th Division) were at PROUVILLE to the north.

RIBEMONT-SUR-ANCRE is on the north-west bank of the River Ancre, south of the main AMIENS–ALBERT road, the D929, between HEILLY and BUIRE-SUR-L'ANCRE. This sector of the front was taken over from the French in the early summer of 1915 and the station at MÉRICOURT-

L'ABBÉ–Ribemont-sur-Ancre became the railhead. On 27 July, 1/4th Loyal North Lancashires (at this time 154th Brigade, 51st Division) arrived here and stayed for 4 days before moving up into divisional reserve in MARTINSART.

At the end of July, 1st Royal West Kents (13th Brigade, 5th Division) marched here when they took over from the French Army, leaving for north-east of BRAY-SUR-SOMME on 3 August. On 3 August, 1/9th Londons (also 13th Brigade, 5th Division) arrived here before departing to BRAY-SUR-SOMME the next day. On 23 August, 54th Brigade (18th Division) came here from SUZANNE; in early September, 8th East Surreys (55th Brigade, 18th Division) carried out training here for a fortnight before leaving for VILLE-SUR-ANCRE on the south bank of the river to the east on 18 September.

From February to October 1916, 5th, 7th, 17th, 18th, 21st, 29th, 30th, 33rd, 38th, 41st, 51st and 55th Divisions used the village during the battle and often had their headquarters here.

Ribemont-sur-Ancre Communal Cemetery, no longer a separate cemetery, is a little to the north of the village. Burials here did not begin until the end of March 1918, when 14 Australian soldiers were buried among civilian graves in the south corner; they were later moved into the Ribemont-sur-Ancre Communal Cemetery Extension, designed by Sir Edwin Lutyens, which was used in the summer of 1918 and greatly enlarged after the Armistice with the interment of casualties from the 1918 battles.

At least four cemeteries were concentrated in the cemetery extension, including Heilly British Cemetery No. 2, from the grounds of Heilly Château; Hénencourt Wood Cemetery, about ½ mile to the west of HÉNENCOURT village; Hénencourt Communal Cemetery; and Point 106 British Cemetery, north-west of BRESLE. In the cemetery extension are the graves of four men who were court-martialled and executed. Tpr A. Butler (IV.M.5) of the Royal Canadian Dragoons (Canadian Cavalry Brigade, 2nd (Indian) Cavalry Division), who was executed on 2 July 1916 for murder. Dvr T.G. Hamilton (III.K.5) No. 72 Battery, XXXVIII Brigade, Royal Field Artillery (6th Division), who 'struck a senior officer' and was shot on 3 October 1916 is buried next to Dvr J. Mullany (III.K.4), who committed the same offence and received the same sentence. The fourth man was Pte J. Cameron (II.A.7) of 1/5th Northumberland Fusiliers (149th Brigade, 50th Division), who deserted and was executed on 4 December 1916. The cemetery originally had 468 burials, later increased to 482.

ROSSIGNOL FARM, north of COIGNEUX, is a substantial farm off the road to SOUASTRE. Prior to the battle, the Farm was to become a base for field companies of 48th Division. On 9 September 1915, No. 2/1 (South Midland) Field Company, Royal Engineers (48th Division), moved into billets here until mid-February 1916, having travelled from WARNIMONT WOOD; during this period they worked on stables at the Farm.

At 1800hrs on 26 December 1915, after a church service in the morning, they had a Christmas dinner consisting of goose, plum pudding and so on. This was followed by a concert and 2 days later by entertainment given by the Vivacious Varlets. On 17 February 1916 the headquarters of No. 1/2 (South Midland) Field Company, Royal Engineers (48th Division), came here after No. 2/1 (South Midland) Field Company had left for Bienvillers.

Due east, north of BAYENCOURT, was an old mill, which was converted by sappers into an observation post; it faced the villages of HÉBUTERNE, GOMMECOURT and FONCQUE-VILLERS and was 25ft deep with a 23ft gallery and an 8ft × 6ft shelter.

In early May, No. 2/1 (South Midland) Field Company were back here when involved in new trench work and communication trenches east of the PUISIEUX road. On 28 May, No. 1/2 (South Midland) Field Company were here again; on 13 June they left their horses and drivers at the farm and moved to bivouacs 1,000yds west of SAILLY-AU-BOIS.

On 11 June, two sections of No. 2/1 (South Midland) Field Company were here, and a third section, engaged in road work at LOUVENCOURT, joined their colleagues on 21 June. On 8 July, No. 204 Field Company, Royal Engineers (35th Division) worked here and north-east of LOUVENCOURT.

ROSSIGNOL WOOD

ROSSIGNOL WOOD is between GOMMECOURT and PUISIEUX, off the D6 road. It is more remembered for the later fighting than for that of 1916, although it did play a part in the Battle of GOMMECOURT on 1 July 1916, when it was opposite the right of 56th Division's front. During the afternoon, howitzers fired heavily on the positions of 1/14th Londons (168th Brigade, 56th Division); in addition, German batteries boldly galloped up and opened fire from the slope close to Rossignol Wood. Having been exposed both to enfilade fire from the high ground on the right, and to fire from their immediate front, 1/14th Londons were compelled to withdraw. The impossible position and the lack of counter-battery work rendered it untenable.

Prior to the battle, the enemy had a good point of observation from Rossignol Wood and were able to bring a very oblique artillery fire from their position between the Wood and GOMMECOURT on any troops attacking from the Allied line. The machine-gun site close to Moa Trench was a communication trench that ran from the Wood to PUISIEUX; later in the battle, it was used by Ernst Jünger to get up to the Wood against the New Zealanders. Close by is the site where Sgt R.C. Travis of 2nd Otagos gained his Victoria Cross in July 1918. The Wood also has links with the Victoria Cross won by the Revd T.B. Hardy in April 1918.

Rossignol Wood Cemetery, on the other side of the road, contains the graves of 41 Commonwealth troops and 70 Germans; it was begun in March 1917 by 46th Division's burial officer.

RUBEMPRÉ

RUBEMPRÉ is north-east of AMIENS on the D11 road and north-east of SEPTENVILLE. At the end of July and beginning of August 1915, it was home to 10th Essex (53rd Brigade, 18th Division), whose battalion history described it 'as a fair-sized village' north of AMIENS. They lived in barn-billets, close to a dung-heap courtyard. There was an *estaminet* in the village that was very dirty but had a good cellar of red and white wines. Their sister battalion, 6th Royal Berkshires, were also here with them, as well as other troops of 53rd Brigade. On August Bank Holiday, 53rd Brigade were inspected in the soaking wet by Gen Sir Charles Monro, General Officer Commanding Third Army, in a field near to the Château de Péronne at MOLLIENS-AU-BOIS to the south-east of Rubempré, and then marched to BOUZINCOURT. From 5 to 8 October, 36th Division were in the area.

In June 1916, 17th Highland Light Infantry (97th Brigade, 32nd Division) had a fairly easy time resting here, apart from divisional exercises at BAIZIEUX. There were sports and games in the afternoons and concerts and sing-songs in the evenings. Villagers attended the concerts together with the troops.

On 25 June, 1/3rd (West Riding) Field Ambulance (49th Division) set up a divisional rest station here; 38th Division's headquarters and 114th Brigade (38th Division) were here at the end of June, when other brigades were at HÉRISSART, PUCHE-VILLERS and TOUTENCOURT.

Up to October 1916, 3rd, 5th, 19th, 25th and 49th Divisions also had links with the village. Rubempré Communal Cemetery has graves of three British soldiers who died during the First World War.

SAILLY-AU-BOIS, west of HÉBUTERNE on the D27 road, was very much a 'behind the lines' village, although it was occasionally shelled. Like most French villages on the Somme, Sailly-au-Bois was initially a mass of flies, owing to the general filth everywhere and also because the weather was extremely hot.

Troops were billeted not only in the village but also in the valley between it and COIGNEUX to the west, where there was a pretty dell. The village was to become an important concentration point for troops proceeding up the line, especially to HÉBUTERNE.

In early July 1915, Sailly-au-Bois was first associated with 48th Division, who regularly sent units here over the next 2 months. On 22 July, 1/3rd (South Midland) Field Ambulance (48th Division) established an advanced dressing station in the village. On 8 September, two sections and the headquarters of No. 1/2 (South Midland) Field Company, Royal Engineers (48th Division), came here and worked on brigade headquarters dugouts at the CHÂTEAU DE LA HAIE, due north of the village. On 14 September, a section of No. 2/1 (South Midland) Field Company, Royal Engineers (48th Division), came here, while two other sections went to HÉBUTERNE for trench work. From 15 to 19 September, the three sections were all working at HÉBUTERNE on the inner defences of the front line, and the pattern for the rest of the month was to alternate between HÉBUTERNE and Sailly-au-Bois.

On 22 September the German artillery sent 12 5.9in shells into the village; shelling was now often severe. On 17 October no fewer than 189 shells were fired onto Sailly-au-Bois, resulting in a lot of damage. On 1 November, two large bomb-proof shelters for the wounded were built at a dressing station in the village. In the same month, 3,400yds of trench boarding was laid from the junction at Sailly-au-Bois–SOUASTRE to FONCQUEVILLERS. Work continued at the last-named and at CHÂTEAU DE LA HAIE.

From 5 December to 8 January 1916, Sailly-au-Bois was again regularly shelled. A field company from 48th Division completed bathing facilities for the troops, 500yds west of the village, and work was also carried out on constructing gun emplacements. On 3 January, 1/3rd (South Midland) Field Ambulance took over the advanced dressing station from

1/2nd (South Midland) Field Ambulance (48th Division).

On 23 March, 1/1st (South Midland) Field Ambulance's (48th Division) advanced dressing station here was taken over by 1/2nd (South Midland) Field Ambulance.

56th Division also had strong links with Sailly-au-Bois and the surrounding area. On 5 May, 1/7th Middlesex (167th Brigade, 56th Division) arrived here for 3 days while in brigade reserve, until relieved by the 1/3rd Londons (also 167th Brigade, 56th Division) on the HÉBUTERNE front to the east. At the beginning of May, 56th Division's field ambulances ran a divisional rest station here. When the village was shelled on 26 May, it was crowded with troops and transport; 1/7th Middlesex suffered about 60 casualties in the space of a few minutes when their barn was hit by a large shell after the enemy had begun to target the crossroads. They later moved to a series of newly constructed dugouts, a few hundred yards from the village. Outside the village, where a road crossed the open plain, it was safer for troops to break into groups of two or three when moving forward.

In the same month, 1/13th Londons (168th Brigade, 56th Division) noted that after leaving Sailly-au-Bois: 'the road passed over a crest of a low hill, when the Very lights and the dark silhouette of Gommecourt Wood against the night sky could be seen . . .'. They were back in the village on 8 June when relieving 1/12th Londons (also 168th Brigade, 56th Division) in the trenches. During this time of battle preparation, the village attracted much shelling and consisted of poor 'ruins', but was still full of camps and dumps; west of Sailly-au-Bois were range after range of guns.

On 1 June, 1/6th Royal Warwicks (143rd Brigade, 48th Division) moved here from Couin Wood, when they were part of brigade reserve for a week. Part of this time was spent in trench-digging; after briefly relieving 1/5th Royal Warwicks (also 143rd Brigade, 48th Division), they left for BEAUVAL for further training.

On or around 8 June, 1/5th Royal Warwicks (143rd Brigade, 48th Division) were relieved at HÉBUTERNE and returned here, where they bivouacked in the Dell, mentioned above. The writer Charles Carrington was one of their officers. Hidden batteries were in every copse or farm, and on the bare slopes towards HÉBUTERNE and GOMMECOURT Allied guns were ranged tier upon tier. On 10 June, 1/4th Royal Berkshires (145th Brigade, 48th Division) arrived in the village after a 2-day long, dusty march and took up 'filthy billets'; they left for COUIN on 24 June. In mid-June, 1/4th Oxfordshire & Buckinghamshire Light Infantry (also 145th Brigade, 48th Division) were camped in the Dell.

On 21 June, 1/12th Londons (168th Brigade, 56th Division) left the trenches and marched along the screened road in a north-westerly direction back to 'Sailly over duck-boards along the "screened" road to Bayencourt then to Souastre . . .'. On 30 June, the eve of the battle, the village was heavily shelled, and again on 13 and 23 July.

In *The Battle of the Somme*, war correspondent Philip Gibbs wrote of the village: 'a charming place it must have been once, with quaint old cottages and a market square. When I went there first the Germans disliked it, plugged shells into most of the houses and into one where a number of Sussex gentlemen were sitting down to lunch. It spoilt their meal and made a new entrance through the dining-room wall. Beyond the village was the road to Hebuterne . . .'

At Zero Hour on 1 July, 144th Brigade (48th Division) were here in reserve to 143rd Brigade (also 48th Division), who were at HÉBUTERNE; 145th Brigade (also 48th Division) were at COUIN and COIGNEUX. Soon hundreds of wounded from the GOMMECOURT sector to the north-east were walking down to Sailly-au-Bois or even to COUIN before having their wounds dressed.

After the failure at GOMMECOURT, 1/5th Cheshires (pioneers of 56th Division) were building a new headquarters for 168th Brigade in dugouts at Sailly-au-Bois. Elephant trenches were sunk deep into the ground and then covered with earth, trees and bricks.

In mid-August, 7th Somerset Light Infantry (61st Brigade, 20th Division) were bivouacked in the Dell. In September, 17th Division were in the area and a brigade from 48th Division were here at the end of the month. In October, a battalion of the East Yorkshire Regiment were in the village. A few days later, 18th Durham Light Infantry (93rd Brigade, 31st Division) took over support trenches in the 'shattered' village.

The road that led westwards from Sailly-au-Bois and ran up the Authie Valley through AUTHIE and COIGNEUX was fairly sheltered from enemy shelling, but, being situated in the bottom of a valley, it was almost impossible to keep in a good state of repair during the winter. The road between Sailly-au-Bois and COURCELLES-AU-BOIS was very often under enemy fire, especially the 500yds of it south of Sailly-au-Bois where, before turning up the long road to HÉBUTERNE, 'men often said

their prayers'. It was also an area where balloons were often seen.

In mid-November, in connection with the Ancre battles, 18th Durham Light Infantry and the 18th West Yorkshires (both 93rd Brigade, 31st Division) were billeted in huts and sandbag shelters in the Dell.

Sailly-au-Bois Military Cemetery, designed by W.C. von Berg, is at the western end of the village, on the south side of the D23 road between BAYENCOURT and SOUASTRE. It was begun in May 1916 'in a field opposite the Town Major's Dugout' and used by field ambulances and fighting units, and at the end of May and June several artillerymen were buried here. The cemetery was in use until March 1917, and again from April to August in 1918. Fifty-five of the graves are of men from battalions of the West Yorkshire Regiment who died in October and November 1916. All told, about 40 per cent of the graves are from the Battle of the Somme itself and the cemetery register lists 239 British and Dominion casualties, of whom 7 died prior to the battle.

Sailly-au-Bois was 'adopted' by Hastings after the war.

SAILLY-LAURETTE is north of the River Somme, on the road between SAILLY-LE-SEC and CHIPILLY. In October 1915 arrangements were made for taking over the boys' school as a hospital; set up on 21 October, it was to be run by 15th Field Ambulance (5th Division), who had been in the village before in early September.

On 4 December, 95th Brigade (32nd Division) had their headquarters here. At the end of November or beginning of December, 14th Royal Warwicks, who came under the orders of 13th Brigade (5th Division), arrived here when they were about to go up to the front for the first time. On 3 December two companies moved to ETINEHEM, and on 5 December went on to trenches in front of CARNOY; the other two companies reached ETINEHEM on 6 December and went up the line 2 days later. On 8 December the first two companies were relieved and left for CHIPILLY. At the end of December, 2nd Royal Inniskilling Fusiliers (96th Brigade, 32nd Division) were in the village; after a church parade, they spent Christmas Day in their billets here. On 30 December two companies left for MILLENCOURT and two for LAVIÉVILLE.

On 5 January 1916, 19th Manchesters (21st Brigade 30th Division) were in Sailly-Laurette for 1 day before moving to BRAY-SUR-SOMME. On 11 January, 1/9th Londons (169th Brigade, 56th

Division) arrived here from BRAY-SUR-SOMME to rest until the end of the month, spending time in cleaning up, instruction, drill and sports; during their stay the weather was 'amazingly mild'. They left on 30 January and arrived at TALMAS the following day.

On 14 January, 15th Royal Warwicks (13th Brigade, 5th Division) arrived in Sailly-Laurette and were billeted in barns, remaining here for a fortnight and carrying out general training. They left for TALMAS, when their division moved to a new sector at the end of the month. On 26 February, 21st Field Ambulance (7th Division) were here and 13th Field Ambulance (also 5th Division) were in the village between 4 January and 7 February.

On 1 May, 96th Field Ambulance (30th Division) arrived here from ALLONVILLE, leaving for ALBERT a fortnight later; they were back in the village on 21 June. In mid-June motor ambulances parked in the village and the horse transport and men were billeted in the village.

On a recent visit to Sailly-Laurette, there was still a small school adjacent to the *mairie* and the post office; it may well have been the original boys' school and is now a school for young children of both sexes.

The village has a cemetery, Beacon Cemetery, south of the BRAY-SUR-SOMME–CORBIE road; it was used in the heavy 1918 fighting, in particular at the end of March.

SAILLY-LE-SEC, a village on the north bank of the River Somme, is on the D42 road between VAUX-SUR-SOMME and SAILLY-LAURETTE. On 28 August 1915, 14th Field Ambulance (5th Division) arrived here and stayed until 23 September; they camped in a wood south of the village. On 13 January 1916, 55th Field Ambulance (18th Division) camped in WELCOME WOODS, a spot on high ground between Sailly-le-Sec and VAUX. From 1 to 15 March, 98th Field Ambulance (30th Division) were in Sailly-le-Sec before leaving for FRANVILLERS and on 10 March, 96th Field Ambulance (also 30th Division) were here. On 17 June, 56th Field Ambulance (18th Division) spent time in the village.

Dive Copse British Cemetery, designed by Sir Edwin Lutyens, is about 1 mile to the north-east, south of the D1 BRAY-SUR-SOMME–CORBIE road. A small wood close by, just south of this road, was known as DIVE COPSE, after the officer commanding the main dressing station, and the cemetery was made by the medical units of the station. In June 1916 the cemetery was laid out for 150 burials on the east side of the road leading to Sailly-le-Sec, 200yds from the main dressing station at DIVE COPSE. On 1 July there was a church service at DIVE COPSE; soon, stretcher cases began to arrive, followed by an increased rush of casualties. On 3 July, walking wounded began to be evacuated.

Plots I and II of the cemetery were taken up by casualties from the period July–September 1916; Plot III contains the graves of men who fell in 1918, when the area was retaken by the enemy. Later, 115 scattered graves were brought in from across the area. Essex Cemetery, 1,000yds to the north, was concentrated here with the remains of men who died in 1918. Of the 589 burials there, the cemetery register records the names of 559 identified British and Dominion burials.

The ground to the north of Dive Copse British Cemetery was chosen for a concentration of tent subdivisions of several field ambulances, which in turn became XIV Corps' main dressing station. Tents were also used for the storage of equipment and for men serving with the field ambulances. A dump was also established at SAILLY-LAURETTE for surplus medical stores and horse transport was billeted there as well.

The main dressing station was an unsanitary place; according to A.H. Habgood of 9th Field Ambulance (Guards Division), 'the flies so numerous that the insides of the tents were black with them . . .' Large sheets of gummed paper were used to try and deal with them. Habgood and another medical officer, Maurice Buckley, ran a marquee for officers; some of their friends came through their hands, including Brig Gen Potter and Lt Col W.D. Oswald, Commanding Officer 12th West Yorkshires (9th Brigade, 3rd Division), who died on admission.

On 14 July 1916, Lt Col D.G. Blois DSO (II.A.22), Commanding Officer LXXXIV Brigade, Royal Field Artillery (18th Division), died of wounds and was buried in the row nearest the entrance gates. Lt Col W.D. Oswald, who died of wounds the next day, is also buried here (II.B.25). Not wishing to miss out on the fighting, he had joined the Dragoon Guards in 1914 and then transferred to the artillery; he was later posted to the infantry and mortally wounded when in command of 12th West Yorkshires (9th Brigade, 3rd Division).

Having fallen to the Germans in spring 1918, the village of Sailly-le-Sec was recaptured by 58th Division on 8 August 1918.

On the main BRAY-SUR-SOMME–CORBIE road is a memorial to the memory of 3rd Australian Division, which was erected not far from von

Richthofen's crash site of 21 April 1918. After the Second World War it was found that the top of the memorial had been damaged by a bomb-blast at some point; the edge of the actual crater was only 3yds away. In a report in the Commonwealth War Graves Commission Archives it was noted that a bronze plaque needed to be replaced, as many of the letters were missing; the Australian government would pay the bill. In 1954 the door of an oak box made from the timbers of HMAS *Sidney* and housing the visitors' book was found to be missing.

SAILLY-SAILLISEL is a village on the N17 road between PÉRONNE and BAPAUME and east of MORVAL; Saint-Pierre-Vaast Wood is to the south-east. In *Goodbye to the Battlefields*, Capt H.A. Taylor of the Royal Fusiliers asserted that the village was 'shaved' to the ground during the war. During the battle for the Transloy Ridges in 1916, the headquarters of 1st Somerset Light Infantry (11th Brigade, 4th Division) was in an old German mine-shaft.

There are two continuous villages, the western one is called Sailly-Saillisel and the eastern one Saillisel. Sailly-Saillisel British Cemetery is south of the former, on the west side of the road to RANCOURT. The cemetery register records that the village standing at the north end of the ridge was the object of French attacks in September and October 1916, and was captured on 18/19 October. It was retaken by the enemy on 24 March 1918 and recaptured on 1 September by 18th and 38th Divisions.

Sailly-Saillisel British Cemetery was made after the Armistice by the concentration of graves from four small graveyards; these were Charing Cross Cemetery to the south-west, Hebule Military Cemetery on the south side of the road to MORVAL, Aldershot Cemetery to the north of Bouchavesnes and Morval New Cemetery on the north side of the MORVAL–Sailly-Saillisel road. The cemetery register records the details of 763 British and Dominion casualties; the dates of death are almost exclusively from the period September 1916 to March 1917, and August and September 1918.

SAINT-AMAND is on the D23 road, to the north of SOUASTRE and due east of DOULLENS. A brigade from 48th Division arrived here in early September 1915 and from then on the village was mainly used for billeting or hospital purposes. On the southern side of the village a system of trenches ran behind a farm building which was used as a hospital, and part of a reserve line, 4 miles from the FONCQUEVILLERS-GOMMECOURT front.

In March 1916, 2nd Royal Dublin Fusiliers (10th Brigade, 4th Division) arrived here from Orville; they left for the front line before Bienvillers on 17 March, when 12th Field Ambulance (also 4th Division) arrived here from COUIN. During the following weeks, when the village was regularly shelled, the village was used mainly by 4th, 46th and 56th Divisions.

On 2 May, 49th Field Ambulance (37th Division) arrived from MONDICOURT and took over the hospital and billets previously occupied by 12th Field Ambulance. Leaving after a few days, they were replaced by 2/2nd (London) Field Ambulance (56th Division), who regularly stationed field ambulance sections here and left on 18 June. The building used as the hospital still exists and is a substantial farm with an imposing gateway and entrance. It is on the left of the road to SOUASTRE on emerging from Saint-Amand.

On 7 May, when 56th Division moved up to look after the lines opposite GOMMECOURT, 1/14th Londons (168th Brigade, 56th Division) were in reserve in the village; on 20 May they left for intensive training in HALLOY, where they were billeted in huts. On 20 May, 1/5th Londons (169th Brigade, 56th Division) marched to Saint-Amand from HALLOY and left for trenches at HÉBUTERNE the following day. On 21 June, they were relieved at HÉBUTERNE and returned to Saint-Amand, but left again for HALLOY the next day for battle training.

On 25 May, No. 1/1 (North Midland) Field Company, Royal Engineers (46th Division), built an advance dugout for divisional headquarters. On 16 June, 1/7th Middlesex (167th Brigade, 56th Division) were in Saint-Amand until moving up the line on 26 June. On 27 June, 1/16th Londons (169th Brigade, 56th Division) moved from HALLOY to Saint-Amand, prior to taking up positions in the assembly trenches opposite the Gommecourt Salient. During this time there was a 'highly successful concert' on 29 June. On 30 June, at a time when 46th Division's headquarters was in the village, Saint-Amand suffered an intense bombardment.

Aubrey Smith of 1/5th Londons wrote that his unit were at HALLOY for a period until 27 June, when the companies went into huts at SOUASTRE while the transport, of which Smith was a member, made for Saint-Amand. There was a narrow valley or gully about 1 mile long in the neighbourhood of the village where every division took up its quarters. The bottom of the valley may have been 20 to 30yds across, and this space was available for horses. On either side were big slopes rising to normal ground level, the easy one being somewhat steep and perhaps 100ft high.

Towards the end of June, Smith's unit put up tarpaulin tents near the horses at the bottom of the valley. Smith was still involved in taking up stores by limber to HÉBUTERNE, which at this stage of the battle preparations had become a vast dump. At the end of June, there were a number of heavy guns here, including a battery of 9.2in howitzers and there was also one very large gun, of either 12in or 15in calibre. On his way to and from HÉBUTERNE, Smith saw vast gun pits, earthworks and ramifications stretching from north to south.

The transport units made an important contribution, having taken up tons of Royal Engineer stores, ammunition and reserve rations to the line in the previous few weeks. If all went well, this was to continue during the night of 1/2 July as the transport sections took water, rations and ammunition over the captured German territory. However, it was not to be, and the first stragglers on 1 July got back to their lines at about 1000hrs. 'A failure, back again where we started,' Smith wrote. He believed that the British had advertised their intention to attack too much. That afternoon more survivors of the defeated battalion came down to Saint-Amand, with the grim look of men who had been through a furnace.

On 5 July, 2/2nd (London) Field Ambulance (56th Division) took over the hospital to the south of the village and 100 volunteers were sent out to HÉBUTERNE in search of the dead. On 6 July, the hospital was opened as a main dressing station, but casualties were sent elsewhere.

On 7 October, 143rd Brigade (48th Division) were in the area.

Saint-Amand British Cemetery is on the northern edge of the village and was begun in April 1916; it was used by fighting units and field ambulances, particularly of 37th and 56th Divisions, until August 1918. Twenty of the men buried here died prior to the battle and 15 during the battle. The 1916 men appear to be mainly in the centre of the cemetery; 186 out of 221 casualties are from 1918.

SAINT-GRATIEN is north-east of AMIENS, off the D919 road to CONTAY. The headquarters of 54th, 55th and 56th Field Ambulances (all 18th Division) were here for about a fortnight in August 1915, when they were quartered in the eighteenth-century château to the south of the village. A dressing station was opened as a temporary hospital in the school, opposite the church. However, on 10 August an order from the Assistant Director of Medical Services requested the removal of this

hospital; it was to be re-established in a stable barn attached to the château, as this was 'the least insanitary place in the village'. This directive was later countermanded and the medical units were told to stay in the school until 25 August, when cases were evacuated to a casualty clearing station at VILLERS-BOCAGE.

On 12 October, 13th Royal Irish Rifles (108th Brigade, 36th Division) were in billets here. At the end of December, units of 152nd and 153rd Brigades (both 51st Division) spent time here; 154th Brigade (also 51st Division) were here a few days later.

On 16 June 1916, 19th Division had their headquarters in the village when they were carrying out training east of the DOULLENS–AMIENS road.

On 26 June, 1st Division had their headquarters in Saint-Gratien; 12th Division's headquarters was here from 28 to 30 June and 23rd Division had their headquarters here on 12 July, when 24th Brigade (23rd Division) were also in the village. At the end of July, 1st Division were here and units of 15th Division were here on 4 August and 20 September. At the end of August, 100th Brigade (33rd Division) moved here from RIBEMONT-SUR-ANCRE.

The château was later used as an Australian headquarters. Today, it still shows signs of having been used as a German Army headquarters in May 1940, during the Second World War.

SAINT-LÉGER-LÈS-AUTHIE is on the AUTHIE–COUIN road, the D152. On 27 July 1915, 1/3rd (South Midland) Field Ambulance (48th Division) arrived here and occupied barns and outbuildings of Cardon Farm. On 12 September, No. 2/1 (South Midland) Field Company, Royal Engineers (48th Division), worked on the preparation of water troughs for horses on the River Authie, as well as in Saint-Léger-lès-Authie. On 17 July, 97th Brigade (32nd Division) were billeted here at the same time as No. 400 Field Company, Royal Engineers (51st Division). From 26 October, 90th Brigade (30th Division) were here.

SAINT-OUEN is north-west of AMIENS and VIGNACOURT close to the D159 road, and was once on a branch railway line from LONGPRÉ-LES-CORPS-SAINTS to DOULLENS. On 17 December 1915, No. 30 Casualty Clearing Station came here and replaced Lucknow Cavalry Field Ambulance (1st (Indian) Cavalry Division).

On 21 March 1916, having detrained at PONT-RÉMY the day before, No. 3 Casualty Clearing Station opened at the Catholic school and camp located on the road leading to the cemetery on the east side of the village. On 2 May, No. 3 Casualty

Clearing Station left for PUCHEVILLERS; No. 39 Casualty Clearing Station were here from 18 May to 30 July, having previously been at ETAPLES.

Saint-Ouen Communal Cemetery is east of the village. Twenty-nine Allied soldiers are buried in the east corner, around half of them men who died in 1916.

SAINT-PIERRE-DIVION is north-west of THIEPVAL between the villages of GRANDCOURT and AUTHUILLE, to the south of the River Ancre. On 1 July 1916 the village was one of the objectives of 36th Division, but the Allied troops do not seem to have reached it that day, let alone to have been able to capture it, and German troops from Saint-Pierre-Divion were sent to repel the British attack to the south-east at the SCHWABEN REDOUBT.

In *Sir Douglas Haig's Great Push*, it is noted that, by the nature of its fortifications and its situation, it was an important position in itself; between it and the Allied line lay a maze of new and old trenches. But the position's chief feature was its subterranean

A working party about to start off in the rain, wearing waterproof sheets and trench waders, near Saint-Pierre-Divion, November 1916. *(IWM Q4602)*

defence network, which lay on the south side of the Ancre and was the site of an underground labyrinth known by British intelligence officers as the Tunnel. There was a perpendicular bank of clay about 20ft high, which showed towards the water-meadows side. German trenches were on the lip of the bank, and under them a vast refuge. The labyrinth was connected to the ground above by a broad flight of stairs and was proof against even the largest shell. The underground shelter had its entrances in the hills of Saint-Pierre-Divion, stretching back to THIEPVAL.

Apart from these considerably strong defences, capture was also made difficult by the marshy ground of the ANCRE VALLEY. In addition, the enemy had excellent observation from the THIEPVAL heights over ground across which attackers would have to move. On 3 September, 16th Rifle Brigade (117th Brigade, 39th Division) were involved in an unsuccessful attack north-west of the village. After the fall of THIEPVAL in late September, it became possible to take the village of Saint-Pierre-Divion from the rear. From 21 to 23 October, 16th Rifle Brigade were near the River Ancre, south of Saint-Pierre-Divion, and took part in another unsuccessful attack on 21 October.

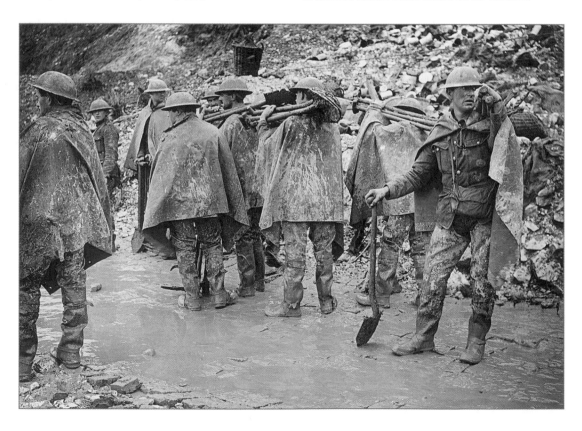

Saint-Quentin when occupied by German troops.
(Peter F. Batchelor Collection)

On 13 November, elements of 39th Division captured Saint-Pierre-Divion, together with the Hansa Line, a system of dugouts and tunnels; 4th/5th Black Watch (118th Brigade, 39th Division) captured many prisoners in the numerous tunnels. Five members of one British tank crew were recommended for the Military Medal for deeds carried out in the battle; theirs was the only tank to start. They reached the Germans' second Support Line and were able to maintain their position without assistance from the infantry, who had got lost in the mist. When the officer in charge was killed, Cpl Taffs took his place; the tank drove on for 200yds and reached a German dugout before becoming bogged down. After spending 2 hours trying to extricate it, the crew abandoned the tank and joined 4th/5th Black Watch in the fighting.

An advanced dressing station or collection post was located at Saint-Pierre-Divion in November 1916. Lost to the Germans in March 1918, Saint-Pierre-Divion was regained by the British in August.

SAINT-QUENTIN is south-east of PÉRONNE. Although it was well away from the 1916 Somme battle area, in the 1920s an idea was mooted to commemorate the Missing from the Advance to Victory of 1918 with a memorial at Saint-Quentin, which would list 30,000 names. Hand in hand with this scheme was one to commemorate the

Missing from the 1916 battle, which would be set up at either CONTALMAISON or the BUTTE DE WARLENCOURT. Both of these sites were close to the area of the 1916 fighting as well as to the well-known ALBERT–BAPAUME road. Another idea was to commemorate the names of 50,000 Missing from the Somme at a site in AMIENS.

As these various schemes and suggestions were considered by the interested parties, priorities seem to have changed considerably. For example, although the Saint-Quentin site was to include the names of the Missing from the Advance to Victory in 1918, at some point POZIÈRES was brought into the picture in order to record the names of the Missing from the retreat of Fifth Army in the spring of 1918. This latter scheme was to be designed by Sir Herbert Baker.

Sir Edwin Lutyens signed an agreement on 17 March 1925, 2 years after he had first visited the area, for a design for the Memorial at Saint-Quentin. Indeed, by June 1923 he had already produced a design that would include the names of 60,000 of the Missing from the Advance to Victory who had no known graves. When the local commune was first approached about the choice of a suitable site it was suggested that it should be placed in a new square in the town created to accommodate its own war memorial. The Mayor did not want an obelisk or statue and expressed a wish for a commemorative building, a pantheon or hall of memory which would accommodate the names of the Fallen. In July 1923 the site was considered to be unsuitable as the British memorial would dominate the French one. Instead, Lutyens suggested a position on the Cambrai road to the north of the town, but this idea was no good as the site was in Fayet, a neighbouring commune. The next choice was further southwards nearer the town on an intermediate ridge 2 km north of the town, but a proposed arch design across the road didn't receive French support and gradually the whole scheme petered out only to be resurrected for building at Thiepval. This was how the idea of a large memorial to the Missing of the Somme at THIEPVAL evolved. The site chosen would present no problems so far as height or transport were concerned. It was known that THIEPVAL was not a site in the centre of the Somme battlefield but in all other respects it fitted the bill. By the autumn of 1926 all was going well with the design, which was partly adapted from the Saint-Quentin scheme; the Imperial War Graves Commission had full cooperation from the French authorities and the ground for the memorial was being cleared. The names of the

The German Cemetery at Saint-Quentin.
(Peter F. Batchelor Collection)

Missing on this new memorial would include those who fell in the Somme area from 1915 up to March 1918. The Imperial War Graves Commission considered that the contract with Lutyens for the Saint-Quentin design would not need to be amended, as the designs to be used at THIEPVAL were so similar; only the site was different.

The schemes at CONTALMAISON, the BUTTE DE WARLENCOURT and AMIENS were all subsequently dropped.

SAINT-RIQUIER is north-east of ABBEVILLE, on the D925 road. On 4 October 1915, 10th Brigade (4th Division) were carrying out training in the area. On 23 November, 90th Field Ambulance (30th Division) billeted in barns and farms for 4 days.

On 31 May 1916, 145th Brigade (48th Division) came to the training area here from BEAUVAL. On 3 June, 144th Brigade (also 48th Division) arrived here for training, having previously been at GÉZAINCOURT; they stayed here for some 10 days. The village was filled 'with troops of every arm busily rehearsing the Somme battles'. 1/4th Royal Berkshires (145th Brigade, 48th Division), who spent 10 days training here, were billeted in Maison Road and Gapennes successively. They left on 10 June.

At the end of May, 57th and 58th Brigade (both 19th Division) came to the Fourth Army training area here for a fortnight and were taught how to deal with

attacking and fighting in villages. While here, half of 10th Worcesters (57th Brigade, 19th Division) were billeted in a farm used by Joan of Arc before her trial at Rouen.

On 5 August, 47th Division came to the training area; on 16 August their headquarters was 2 miles south-west of Saint-Riquier. Although there are no 1916 battle casualties in the British cemetery here, there are graves of men who died either before or after the battle. Indian and French casualties are also buried here. Although there are no 1916 battle casualties in the British Cemetery here, there are graves of men who died either before or after the battle. Indian and French casualties are also buried here.

SAINT-SAUVEUR

SAINT-SAUVEUR is on the D191, north-west of AMIENS. From 14 to 23 February 1916, No. 491 Field Company, Royal Engineers (5th Division), were at ARGŒUVRES and Saint-Sauveur while making bunks and horse troughs from timber from Montières sawmill. In early July, field ambulances of 21st Division were in the village. On 9 July, 100th Brigade (33rd Division) arrived here; at the same time, 19th Brigade (also 33rd Division) were at POULAINVILLE and 98th Brigade (also 33rd Division) were at RAINNEVILLE.

SAINT-VAAST-EN-CHAUSSÉE

SAINT-VAAST-EN-CHAUSSÉE is on the D12 road, 7 miles north-west of AMIENS. On 29 March 1916, 2nd West Yorkshires (23rd Brigade, 8th Division) arrived here from LONGUEAU; during their march they had moved through undulating, intensively cultivated country, with villages every 3 miles. Cottages were on the small side, and there were no large farms. The French people were charming and the weather perfect. Their division had their headquarters at FLESSELLES together with 25th Brigade (also 8th Division), while 70th Brigade (also 8th Division) were at VIGNACOURT.

On 25 June and again on 1 July, 69th Field Ambulance (23rd Division) were in Saint-Vaast-en-Chaussée.

SAISSEMONT

SAISSEMONT is to the north-east of Saisseval, west of AMIENS. On 30 April 1916, 56th Field Ambulance (18th Division) left LAHOUSSOYE for Saissemont and spent the following day tidying up their new camp. From 4 May, NCOs and men of the field ambulance carried out plenty of route marching with full packs and also squad drill. Other training was carried out as well, and men were also being dispatched to GROVE TOWN for labouring duties. The field ambulance left Saissemont for Montières, near AMIENS, on 12 June.

SAISSEVAL

SAISSEVAL is on the D211 road, due west of AMIENS. Late in the evening of 11 June 1916, 2nd Wiltshires (21st Brigade, 30th Division) arrived here after a long journey that had begun on the CARNOY front in the early morning. Saisseval was close to a large training theatre set up to aid 30th Division in their preparation for the planned offensive. The training was intensive and continued until 20 June; soon after, 21st Brigade left for the line via BRAY-SUR-SOMME. 2nd Wiltshires halted for the night in tents at VAUX, on the banks of the Somme, before moving back to the CARNOY sector.

On 18 June, three companies of 18th Manchesters (90th Brigade, 30th Division) arrived here by train from HEILLY and AILLY-SUR-SOMME, having come from ETINEHEM, and returned there after special training on 26 June.

SARTON

SARTON is on the River Authie, south-east of DOULLENS on the D938 road. During the build-up to the 1916 Somme battle it was used as a divisional rest station and a rest camp, which was first established behind Sarton and Orville on 3 August 1915. After men of 1/6th Royal Warwicks (143rd Brigade, 48th Division) were soaked by the rain in WARNIMONT WOOD to the east, they were allowed to dry out in barns at Sarton.

On 20 February 1916, 1/2nd (South Midland) Field Ambulance (48th Division) arrived at Sarton. On 11 June, 93rd Field Ambulance (31st Division) moved here to run a medical stores depot. Stores could be kept in the *estaminet*, in the cinema-cum-theatre, or in a paddock to the north-east of the building that was later converted into a rest camp. In June 1916, medical units used the cinema, where 50 patients could be accommodated, the Café de la Place, which could take 20 patients in an emergency, and the *curé*'s presbytery, which was used as an operating theatre. The field ambulance staff were billeted in the village. On 22 June, orders were received that a tent subdivision was to be set up here.

Heavy fire was heard during the night of 30 June and early morning of 1 July; it was rumoured that 31st Division had captured SERRE, but 2 days later this news proved to be unfounded. Three days later, 93rd Field Ambulance left for BEAUVAL; 38th Field Ambulance (12th Division) arrived in Sarton 5 days after that.

On 12 August, HM the King visited Sarton and was received by Lt Gen Sir Hubert Gough, General Officer Commanding Reserve (later Fifth) Army, and his staff, together with Maj Gen E.G.T. Bainbridge, General Officer Commanding 25th Division. While here, the King inspected four battalions of 7th Brigade (25th Division) drawn up at the side of the road; Royal Flying Corps personnel from 15th Wing were also present. The King later left for BEAUQUESNE, Sir Douglas Haig's headquarters.

On 28 August, the Guards Division were billeted in the area. A brigade from 48th Division were here in early September, and a month later one from 51st Division. Units from 37th Division were in Sarton at the end of November.

SAULTY is a small village north-west of HUMBERCAMPS on the D23E road, just north of the DOULLENS–Arras road. As they travelled from SUS-SAINT-LÉGER to BIENVILLERS-AU-BOIS on 18 June 1916, 1/7th Sherwood Foresters (139th Brigade, 46th Division) marched past the railway station to the south-east of the village, close to the main road; here they saw a temporary field hospital that had been set up to accommodate casualties expected in the forthcoming battle.

At the beginning of the battle, the headquarters of 139th Brigade (46th Division) was at the château, a building to the east of the village. After their involvement in the Gommecourt fighting, 1/5th and 1/6th Sherwood Foresters (both 139th Brigade, 46th Division) returned to the village via WARLIN-COURT-LÈS-PAS; their cadre had been at LA BAZÈQUE FARM.

SCHWABEN REDOUBT, an oval-shaped German fortification, was sited close to the present D75 road to HAMEL. It overlooked the German-held village of THIEPVAL and Thiepval Wood, which was in Allied hands, as well as the ANCRE VALLEY where the two opposing lines crossed the river and the marshy area around it. The Redoubt had a 'face' that stretched about 500yds to 600yds and it was about 200yds in depth; it was virtually a parallelogram of trenches. To the north and west, the ground fell away steeply; to the east, Schwaben Redoubt overlooked German lines and battery positions.

According to the history of 18th Division, the THIEPVAL position was without doubt one of the main pivots of the whole of the northern section of the German defences on the Western Front; included with it was the Schwaben Redoubt, which lay on a ridge about 1,000yds to the north and rear of THIEPVAL.

On 1 July 1916, the Redoubt was one of the objectives of 36th Division; three brigades were involved in the attempt to capture it and at least four battalions who had advanced from Thiepval Wood across the THIEPVAL road and up the hill

to the summit had managed to gain a foothold in the position. Five hundred Germans were taken prisoner and then the attackers began to advance on the second position, the GRANDCOURT line.

In their enthusiasm, the attackers were in front of the Allied barrage, which prevented them from capturing the line. As the day went on, they found themselves without support, despite their progress; this allowed the enemy time to recoup and to push the British out of the Redoubt. According to *The War in the Air* by H.A. Jones, No. 4 Squadron, Royal Flying Corps, reported that at 1630hrs the British hold on the Schwaben Redoubt looked insecure. An hour later, an observer reported that British troops were still in possession of the Redoubt and the point known as the Crucifix to the south-east. The Crucifix was at the point where the roads from AUTHUILLE and THIEPVAL met at a fork.

Having failed to hold the Redoubt, despite the tremendous courage of 36th Division, the Allies found themselves unable to make any more serious attempts on it until several weeks later, and then not until the end of September after THIEPVAL had fallen. It was to this village that the Redoubt gave great protection, as it allowed the enemy to fend off attacks; the position could also be enfiladed by machine-gun crossfire from Beaucourt Redoubt and SAINT-PIERRE-DIVION and from Nord Werk, a machine-gun stronghold on the Ovillers Spur. The Pope's Nose was a strongpoint close to the Redoubt.

In early September, deadly German crossfire could always be brought to bear on any British attack, unless it was well protected by artillery; an attack made by a battalion of the West Yorkshire Regiment was broken up this way. But during the battle, 11th Lancashire Fusiliers (74th Brigade, 25th Division) established a block close to the Pope's Nose.

The battle of Thiepval Ridge lasted for 4 days, between 26 and 30 September. THIEPVAL itself was captured on 26 September and most of the THIEPVAL plateau and the Schwaben Redoubt were in Allied hands by 30 September; 18th Division had played a major role in these operations. The division had the use of four tanks, one of which was to do sterling service in the attack on Thiepval Château.

On 27 September, 53rd and 54th Brigades (both 18th Division) lay in a continuous line running north of THIEPVAL and along Zollern Trench to the point where 53rd Brigade were in touch with 11th Division on the right. In 53rd Brigade, 8th Norfolks and 10th Essex were exhausted but 8th Suffolks and 6th Royal Berkshires were still strong and available for an attack; 55th Brigade (also 18th Division) were in support.

Zero Hour was fixed for 1300hrs on 28 September, and there was difficulty in forming up in daylight. The assaulting battalions were 8th Suffolks and 7th Queen's (55th Brigade, 18th Division); 10th Essex were detailed to garrison Zollern Trench and 8th Norfolks were to provide 'mopping up' companies to attend the assaulting battalions. Almost entirely composed of recent recruits, 6th Royal Berkshires were in reserve in Authuille Wood.

After very hard fighting, a footing was gained in the Redoubt. By 5 October only a small strip of the Redoubt along the north-west corner was still in enemy hands, but it was not until 14 October that 39th Division finally cleared the Germans completely out of the position. It was not so much the capturing of the Redoubt that was the problem; it was the retaining of it that was the greater challenge.

During the fighting, T/2/Lt T.E. Adlam of 7th Bedfords (54th Brigade, 18th Division) won a Victoria Cross for conspicuous gallantry on 27/28 September:

A portion of a village [Thiepval] which had defied capture had to be taken at all costs, to permit subsequent operations to develop. The minor operation came under very heavy machine-gun and rifle fire. Second Lieut Adlam, realizing that time was all-important, rushed from shell-hole to shell-hole under heavy fire, collecting men for a sudden rush, and for this purpose also collected many enemy grenades. At this stage he was wounded in the leg, but nevertheless he was able to out-throw the enemy, and then, seizing his opportunity, and in spite of his wound, he led a rush, captured the position, and killed the occupants. Throughout the day he continued to lead his men in bombing attacks. On the following day he again displayed courage of the highest order, and although again wounded and unable to throw bombs, he continued to lead his men. His magnificent example of valour, coupled with the skilful handling of the situation, produced far-reaching results . . .

Adlam's experience before the war as a schoolmaster had stood him in good stead, as he had learnt to throw a cricket ball very long distances; this was the skill he applied to throwing grenades at the Germans, who were subjected to a whirlwind attack. He was able to lead his platoon forward and either capture or kill any German who was in their way;

reaching the objective by 0830hrs, Adlam's party went on to gain a further 300yds. He continued to lead his men all day and was wounded a second time. He had materially assisted in the capture of Schwaben Redoubt (see the THIEPVAL entry).

In *Undertones of War*, Edmund Blunden of 11th Royal Sussex (116th Brigade, 39th Division) wrote that

it was now approaching the beginning of November, and the days were melancholy and the colour of clay. We took over that deathtrap known as the Schwaben Redoubt, the way to which lay through the fallen fortress of Thiepval. One had heard the worst accounts of the place and they were true. Crossing the Ancre again, one went up through the scanty skeleton houses of Authuille, and climbing the dirty little road over the steep bank, one immediately entered the land of despair.

At the Schwaben Redoubt, there was always some shelling; on 31 October, Blunden's party were systematically bombarded, and suffered 32 casualties before being relieved the next day. The relief was expensive, particularly to 1/6th Cheshires (118th Brigade, 39th Division), whom the Germans saw coming.

Blunden was back here on 11 November, when his battalion took a subsidiary part in the final battle of GRANDCOURT and BEAUMONT-HAMEL. Shortly after the Schwaben Redoubt was taken, the *Illustrated London News* featured a two-page panoramic spread of the capture of the Redoubt by an artist called S. Begg. On 13 November, when Blunden was at the Redoubt with 11th Royal Sussex amid a few deep dugouts and a maze of choked and crushed trenches, the other units of 39th Division passed through the battalion positions and overran, or over-waded the German fort beyond. Their task should have been to carry and dump wire for the division in front of its extreme advance, but there was so much shelling that they were allowed off, and only had to take the materials as far as the old front line.

In the 1920s, Henry Williamson wrote a book about a return visit to the battlefields, called *The Wet Flanders Plain*. He wrote that one could still see many of the former trenches in the hillside near the Schwaben Redoubt. On the high ground above Thiepval Wood, where thousands of men perished on 1 July, stood the Ulster Memorial Tower. The trenches where, for a few hours that hot summer afternoon, the men of 36th Division rested and watched eastwards, until the enfilade from the north drove them back to their old trenches like mole-runs, were half-hidden by long grass. These former trenches, with names such as Wretched Way, Lucky Way, Tea Trench, Coffee Trench and Rum Trench, were now half-hidden seams in the hillside and filled Williamson with an indescribable emotion – the haunting of ancient sunlight.

It would be very interesting to know just how much of the Schwaben Redoubt is still intact under the hillside; possibly all of it has by now vanished. One can see though the odd entrance or two, but they are in fields under cultivation.

The cemeteries in this area are mentioned in the entry for Thiepval. Mill Road Cemetery shows the most obvious postwar association with the Redoubt, in that some of the headstones have had to be laid flat to avoid subsidence.

SCOTTS REDOUBT was a strongpoint to the east of the village of LA BOISSELLE, north-east of BÉCOURT and south-west of PEAKE WOODS and the village of CONTALMAISON. It was reached by a trench that ran westwards from Round Wood and was one of several redoubts in the German First Line, made up from a cluster of trenches that contained many shelters grouped around one 'palatial' dugout. To the west, between it and LA BOISSELLE, were Sausage Redoubt and Heligoland, two more strongpoints in the German line.

On 1 July 1916, Scotts Redoubt was one of 34th Division's objectives, which included PEAKE WOODS and CONTALMAISON to the north-east. However, 1 July was a disastrous day for 34th Division, as they progressed for only about a third of the way towards their objectives. Parties of men had in fact reached as far as CONTALMAISON but then had to withdraw. Advancing from the direction of BÉCOURT, the attacking battalions in the Scotts Redoubt area were 15th and 16th Royal Scots (both 101st Brigade, 34th Division) and 24th and 27th Northumberland Fusiliers (both 103rd Brigade, 34th Division).

In the history of the Royal Scots it is noted that C Company, 15th Royal Scots, plodded on, crossed Scotts Redoubt and reached as far as Peake Trench. At Wood Alley, a strip of trench adjoining Scotts Redoubt, they met up with a company of 16th Royal Scots. Wood Alley had to be retained as security for 21st Division, which was on 34th Division's right flank. It was still held that night but the enemy had regained their hold on their front trench, with Heligoland the key strongpoint; this in turn led to Wood Alley being cut off from the British Front Line. The situation was precarious for the attacking troops, but for some reason the enemy did not press home a counter-attack.

Having gone past to the north of Scotts Redoubt, 24th and 27th Northumberland Fusiliers then had to withdraw. On the following day, 15th Royal Scots attacked and carried the Redoubt, taking 50 prisoners; 16th Royal Scots attacked HORSESHOE TRENCH, a long trench running down from the direction of OVILLERS-LA-BOISSELLE, and managed to take 150yds of it. Later, communication was established between Scotts Redoubt and the old Allied front line, which facilitated the supplies of reinforcements and equipment. On 3 July, having held their positions at great cost in casualties, 15th and 16th Royal Scots were relieved by troops of 33rd Division and moved back to Scotts Redoubt.

In *Somme Harvest*, Giles Eyre of 2nd King's Royal Rifle Corps (2nd Brigade, 1st Division) wrote that in mid-July, after a few instructions, his battalion went off to meet up with 1st Loyal North Lancashires (also 2nd Brigade, 1st Division), who were lying in Scotts Redoubt. They scrambled down a deep, sandbagged trench, arrived at the head-quarters of 1st Loyal North Lancashires and settled down in their dugouts. Eyre wrote that the Redoubt trenches were deep and well sandbagged and had stood the past fortnight of fighting well. 2nd King's Royal Rifle Corps were in support and liable to go forward at short notice.

After the battles of the first half of July, there is little mention of Scotts Redoubt, although it is documented that the Royal Army Medical Corps made full use of the deep dugouts there as accom-modation for stretcher-bearers.

In the period 4/5 September, 7th/8th King's Own Scottish Borderers (46th Brigade, 15th Division), who had been in the front line, were relieved and withdrawn to divisional reserve at Scotts Redoubt in the former German line. On 9 October they went forward to the Redoubt and occupied dugouts there, training and working on roads until in mid-October they relieved the 6th/7th Royal Scots Fusiliers (45th Brigade, 15th Division) in recently captured trenches north-west of LE SARS.

At some point during the autumn of 1916, Scotts Redoubt became a camp and there is mention of the place being used in early September. Towards the end of November, 1/5th Glosters and the 1/4th Oxfordshire & Buckinghamshire Light Infantry (both 145th Brigade, 48th Division) were both camped there, the latter in Nissen huts.

SENLIS-LE-SEC is north-west of ALBERT, between HÉNENCOURT and BOUZINCOURT on the D119 road. On 5 August 1915, 51st Division had their headquarters here as they took over front-line positions. The division also had units here in December, including 1/6th Seaforth Highlanders (152nd Brigade, 51st Division), who arrived in various stages on 8 December from a spell at the THIEPVAL front and were billeted in unboarded tents in a camp that 'was one large sea of mud'. Divisional headquarters was again in the village at the time and troops could get a good hot bath and also enjoy the delights of 51st Division's concert party, known as the Balmorals, who used to perform nightly to crowded houses. Three days later, 1/6th Seaforth Highlanders left for divisional reserve in MARTINSART.

On 28 December, 19th Lancashire Fusiliers (14th Brigade, 32nd Division) were here. In early January 1916, when 32nd Division had their headquarters here alongside that of 51st Division, troops from 15th Highland Light Infantry (14th Brigade, 32nd Division) were camped in bell tents in MARTINS-ART to the north-east; they too made use of 'the excellent bathhouses' at Senlis-le-Sec, and visited a theatre known as the Empire. In reality, this theatre consisted of 'an old barn with a clay floor and *frateuils* [sic] of wood in which troops sat with their hats on and saw performances in which women's parts were gaily played by soldiers of the line so successfully, indeed that the French interpreter ecstatically blew them kisses under the impression they were genuinely girls . . .' 91st Field Ambulance (32nd Division) were also in Senlis-le-Sec at the time.

On 10 January, 2nd Royal Inniskilling Fusiliers (96th Brigade, 32nd Division) were billeted here and much training was carried out. In addition, two companies were employed in constructing reserve trenches. After a spell in the front or in reserve, they were back in the village on 26 January. All available troops were engaged in making a new road to BOUZINCOURT.

On 8 March, 49th Division had their headquarters at Senlis-le-Sec, while 1/5th and 1/7th West Yorkshires (both 146th Brigade, 49th Division) were billeted at HARPONVILLE and 1/6th and 1/8th West Yorkshires (both also 146th Brigade, 49th Division) at VARENNES. The battalions changed their billeting arrangements in the middle of the month, when large working parties needed to be closer to their work until 2 April. On 31 March, two companies of 1/6th West Yorkshires were in Senlis-le-Sec. The men of 146th Brigade were working on a new 2-mile road leading from BOUZINCOURT to MARTINSART called Northumberland Avenue; the stone used for the road came from BOUZINCOURT.

In addition, an advanced observation post was established on Bouzincourt Hill.

In early April and again in early June, 32nd Division had their headquarters here again; some of its Highland units were here on 9 June. A field company of 49th Division were working on erecting Armstrong huts as part of a divisional headquarters, together with four tents; the huts were camouflaged with rabbit netting. Field companies from 25th Division were in Senlis-le-Sec at the end of June and the beginning of July. At the end of June, two brigades of 49th Division bivouacked to the west of the village; one of their battalions left on 30 June for assembly trenches in AVELUY WOOD, where they arrived at about 0200hrs on 1 July.

Sgt E. Shephard of 1st Dorsets (14th Brigade, 32nd Division) noted in his diary that his battalion was camped between Senlis-le-Sec and WARLOY-BAILLON on 23 June before moving later to Black Horse dugouts. He mentions walking across the high ground to Senlis Mill, to the south-east of the village, from where he got a good view of the bombardment. On 26 June, Maj Gen W.H. Rycroft, General Officer Commanding 32nd Division, addressed 1st Dorsets and the three other battalions of 14th Brigade and told them how they were to capture THIEPVAL. In retaliation for the earlier loss of Capt W.B. Algeo and Lt H.G.M. Mansel-Pleydell, who, Rycroft said, had been murdered, 1st Dorsets were told to take no prisoners.

At around 2020hrs on 30 June, 1st Dorsets left Senlis-le-Sec for the front line and were cheered by hundreds of troops. They went via BOUZINCOURT and halted close to a 12in gun at Northumberland Avenue after a circuitous journey via the AUTHUILLE road; turning down Black Horse Road and over BLACK HORSE BRIDGE, they took the track behind the batteries near Brookers Pass and into AUTHUILLE (Blighty Wood) and followed Dumbarton Track.

At the end of June, Senlis-le-Sec gave shelter to members of 49th Division; on 1 July, they were to support 36th Division, whose objective was the ground between the north-west of THIEPVAL and the village of SAINT-PIERRE-DIVION above the River Ancre. On 29 June, men of 1/4th Duke of Wellington's (147th Brigade, 49th Division) visited the observation post at Senlis Mill, where they had a very good view of the Allied bombardment. 15th Highland Light Infantry (14th Brigade, 32nd Division) were in billets in the village in the same period. On 30 June, 1/5th York & Lancasters (148th Brigade, 49th Division) left the village for assembly trenches in AVELUY WOOD.

On 1 July, 32nd Division were on the right flank of 36th Division; 32nd Division's wagon lines were close to Senlis-le-Sec. On 3 July and again in mid-July, 14th Brigade (32nd Division) were relieved by 7th Brigade (25th Division). On 9 July, the headquarters of 36th Brigade (12th Division) moved to the village; on the afternoon of 10 August, 36th Brigade were formed up on either side of the road just to the north of Senlis-le-Sec and about 1 mile to the west of BOUZINCOURT. They were then inspected by HM King George V; HRH the Prince of Wales; Lt Gen Sir Hubert Gough, General Officer Commanding Reserve (later Fifth) Army; Lt Gen C.W. Jacob, General Officer Commanding II Corps; and Maj Gen A.B. Scott, General Officer Commanding 12th Division. The King, who had travelled from WARLOY-BAILLON, walked down the road between the troops, accompanied by this party of high-ranking officers.

On 5 August, 51st Division had their headquarters at Senlis-le-Sec. In early August, 7th Royal Sussex (36th Brigade, 12th Division) were in the village before going east to BOUZINCOURT for 2 days; their Division were involved in the battle for Pozières Ridge at this time. 1/4th Oxfordshire & Buckinghamshire Light Infantry were in huts in the orchards to the west of BOUZINCOURT with trenches in Senlis-le-Sec. On 27 August, 25th Division had their headquarters in the village, as did 51st Division on 30 September.

As well as providing accommodation for infantry battalions, Senlis-le-Sec housed the field artillery wagon lines. In *Undertones of War*, Edmund Blunden of 11th Royal Sussex (116th Brigade, 39th Division) remarks that in early November his battalion rested at Authuille Bluffs after their experiences at the SCHWABEN REDOUBT, before going further back to Senlis-le-Sec. Two days later, they were back in Thiepval Wood, but soon returned to the barns and *estaminets* of Senlis-le-Sec. On 7 November, they were carrying our fatigues in the Aveluy region.

From the end of August to November, 11th and 25th Divisions had units in the area. From 29 October to 2 November, a battalion of the King's Royal Rifle Corps were in reserve at the divisional rest station in Senlis-le-Sec.

Senlis-le-Sec Communal Cemetery Extension, designed by W.H. Cowlishaw, is on the north-west side of the village, on the south-east side of Senlis-le-Sec Communal Cemetery; begun in April 1918, it has 104 graves, including a number of Australians who died mainly in the period from April to August 1918 during the German advance and subsequent retreat. The cemetery register records details of 97 casualties.

SEPTENVILLE, north of AMIENS, is on the north side of the D113 road between RUBEMPRÉ and VILLERS-BOCAGE. On 28 July 1915, 56th Field Ambulance (18th Division) arrived here. On 5 March 1916, 1/1st (West Riding) Field Ambulance (49th Division) arrived here from BOUZINCOURT, where they had handed over to 36th Division; they remained in Septenville until 28 March, when they took over the divisional rest station and hospital at EBART FARM from 1/3rd (West Riding) Field Ambulance (also 49th Division).

In mid-June, 1/1st (West Riding) Field Ambulance returned here from billets in VIGNACOURT and took over billets and hospital accommodation from 91st Field Ambulance (32nd Division), who had been here since 4 April, before moving to LÉALVILLERS on 27 June and HÉDAUVILLE on 1 July. The billets, divisional rest station and hospital at Septenville were housed in a large complex behind the hedge-lined VILLERS-BOCAGE–RUBEMPRÉ road going northwards to TALMAS.

SERRE is on the D919 road between PUISIEUX and MAILLY-MAILLET. In 1916 the lines of the two armies bent south-eastwards from the direction of HÉBUTERNE and GOMMECOURT, and then headed in a south-westerly direction in front of Serre and BEAUMONT-HAMEL. GOMMECOURT, Serre and BEAUMONT-HAMEL to the south had been turned into German 'fortress' villages and all three were to hold up the Allied advance on the first day of the battle, and subsequently. In June 1915 the German and French armies had fought a major battle here.

British divisions began to arrive in the Somme area from July 1915, and increasingly in the spring of 1916 units of 48th and 31st Divisions were spending time in preparations for the planned attack on the German positions. One chronicler from 144th Brigade (48th Division) spoke of the line opposite Serre as having 'deep gloomy trenches infested with rats'. Having been formerly in French hands, the trench system here bore such names as Vercingetorix, du Guesclin and Jean Bart.

In *A Life of One's Own*, Gerald Brenan noted that every day in the period prior to the battle, new batteries would arrive and begin registering, new light railways would spring up, new shell-dumps were laid along the roads and new noticeboards made their appearance, while the woods and villages a little way behind filled up with khaki figures.

The Serre position, mainly in the area of 4th Division, was to advance towards REDAN RIDGE and the section of Munich Trench due south of Serre village. On their left, opposite Serre and beyond the village of PUISIEUX was 31st Division, who feature most prominently in this entry. The plan was for units of 31st Division to reach beyond Serre and take in Pendant Copse to the south-east of the village, reaching as far as Pendant Trench and Flank Trench. The focal parts of the Allied line in this area were the four copses – from south to north, Matthew, Mark, Luke and John – which were to be the points of assembly on 1 July.

In a document in the Peter Liddle collection, 2/ Lt F.P. Roe of 1/6th Glosters (114th Brigade, 48th Division) noted that at the end of June he had the job of escorting a group of war correspondents on a tour of the VIII Corps trench system. During this time, Roe met Brenan, who at this time was an observer for VIII Corps headquarters; Roe also mentioned meeting Lt Gen Sir Henry Rawlinson, General Officer Commanding Fourth Army, and said that the latter was not as keen as Sir Douglas Haig was on the prospect of the Somme battle.

Roe also described 31st Division's front at this period. His own trenches were at the bottom of a slope and close to them were 10th and 11th East Yorkshires (92nd Brigade, 31st Division). He was 200yds west and a little to the north of Matthew Copse. The front line ran roughly along the bottom of a small valley or depression, the ground sloping upwards on the east side towards the German positions and westwards to the British support and reserve trenches. 31st Division were to form a defensive flank facing the north-east.

After a 48-hour delay owing to wet weather, the battle was due to commence in the morning of 1 July. Opposite Serre, 93rd Brigade (31st Division) assembled on the right of the line and 94th Brigade (31st Division) on the left, while 92nd Brigade were to be in reserve all day.

On 1 July, 93rd Brigade (31st Division) deployed 15th West Yorkshires in front, with 16th West Yorkshires immediately behind them. On the right of 16th West Yorkshires were a company of 18th Durham Light Infantry and behind were 18th West Yorkshires; the remaining companies of 18th Durham Light Infantry brought up the rear. Meanwhile, 94th Brigade (31st Division) deployed 11th East Lancashires with 13th York & Lancasters behind them. On the left of 11th East Lancashires were 12th York & Lancasters, who were to feature in John Harris's novel *Covenant of Death.* Immediately behind them were a half-company of

14th York & Lancasters; further back, beyond the track between LA SIGNY FARM and la Louvière Farm, were the rest of 14th York & Lancasters.

The assaulting battalions attacked from lines over which the enemy had observation; the strength of any Allied bombardment was equalled by that of the German guns, which systematically destroyed the advance. Unknown to the British attackers, the enemy had a great mass of guns behind Serre and PUISIEUX, which of course were not visible.

At 0720hrs, 15th West Yorkshires began to climb out of their trenches and to lie down in front of them; they were subsequently annihilated by the German machine guns, which the British artillery were supposed to have dealt with over the previous few days. Maj R.B. Neill, Commanding Officer 15th West Yorkshires, was killed within the first few minutes. Ordered to advance through the line of 15th West Yorkshires and make their way towards the northern section of Munich Trench, 16th West Yorkshires lost a great number, killed during the first few minutes of the battle, including their Commanding Officer, Maj C.S. Guyon, who was later to be commemorated on the Thiepval Memorial.

Their assault cut down before it had even begun, 18th Durham Light Infantry suffered in the same fashion as 15th and 16th West Yorkshires. Heavy casualties, of course, only made matters worse as the communication trenches became very congested; one observer reported that he had never seen a queue like there was on this morning at the regimental aid post. The dead were spread out in thick clumps behind their own wire.

On the right flank of 93rd Brigade were 1/8th Royal Warwicks (143rd Brigade, 48th Division), and behind them, 1/6th Royal Warwicks (also 143rd Brigade, 48th Division), with 1st King's Own (12th Brigade, 4th Division) in support. They managed to make some progress but had the German strongpoint called the Quadrilateral on their right. The latter was very important to the enemy as it gave flanking fire along the whole position and positively bristled with machine guns. The frontage of the Quadrilateral was 400yds and there was no cover between the German and British trenches. There was, however, a slight rise in the direction of the German positions. The objective was Pendant Copse, to the south-east of Serre village. The survivors of 143rd Brigade were helped by the presence of three large craters on the Serre–Mailly road.

Brig Gen C.B. Prowse, General Officer Commanding 11th Brigade (4th Division), was wounded mortally as he moved his headquarters forward from the old British line to the German trenches, which had been taken by 1/8th Royal Warwicks. Prowse was buried later at Vauchelles Communal Cemetery (I.E.9).

On the left of 93rd Brigade, 94th Brigade fared no better. The brigade frontage was about 700yds from John Copse to the southern part of Matthew Copse; 12th York & Lancasters were to the left and 11th East Lancashires to the right. Having reached assembly trenches behind John and Mark Copses in the front line at 0720hrs, A and C Companies, 12th York & Lancasters lay down about 100yds in front; shallow assault trenches had been dug to hold the second, third and fourth waves.

In *A Life of One's Own*, Gerard Brenan, an observer of VIII Corps' Cyclist Battalion, noted that he had heard that the assault trenches were manned in the incorrect order; this led to confusion when the moment for advance arrived. Indeed, two of the waves never started at all. In addition, a terrible artillery barrage fell on the attackers, which churned up the earth all around them. Brenan moved back to his observation post, which was probably in front of Observation Wood facing Matthew Copse and in direct line with Serre village, only to be hit by gas shells.

The headquarters of 12th York & Lancasters had to be moved from John Copse to Mark Copse because the former was so full of wounded. The battalions had been told to make for Serre church steeple, but they were cut down by machine-gun and shell-fire; many of the enemy simply ignored any potential danger from British artillery fire and stood on their parapets, firing. The dead and wounded lay in clumps and mounted up. Lt Col A.W. Rickman, Commanding Officer 11th East Lancashires, was 'knocked out' by a shell at around 0940hrs but survived, only to die in a tragic accident after the war had ended.

In *Covenant of Death*, John Harris painted a very authentic picture of one of the 'Pals' battalions from the north of England. His novel is based upon the experiences of 12th York & Lancasters, although it could probably have been applied to many other of the Northern New Army battalions. In Harris's novel, before the battle began the trenches were divided into 'up' trenches and 'down' routes for the offensive; engineers erected divisional signs and constructed bridges to be placed across trenches for reserves to pass over, many of them wide enough to carry cavalry. The narrator comments at the beginning of the battle that he thinks that he can see Serre just among the smoke which is rolling in the hollow in front. Where there had been trees and

hedges, they were now bare and leafless. Someone said 12th York & Lancasters had reached Serre village, but were then destroyed from behind by Germans coming up out of deep shelters. All was to end in the most tragic of failures.

According to *The War in the Air* by H.A. Jones, VIII and X Corps met with a similar fate on 1 July. Nos. 15 and 4 Squadrons, Royal Flying Corps, were able to see what the infantry were unaware of. There was an isolated, deep penetration into the German defences which air observers alone could report, notably at Pendant Copse, where a few of the men of 18th Durham Light Infantry had succeeded in reaching the Copse.

Gerard Brenan ran an observation post in front of LA SIGNY FARM and was ideally placed to see the tragedy unfold. The left of the advance against Serre was opposite his observation post and about ¾ mile distant from their front trenches; Brenan's task was to send back reports of how the fighting was going. Corps headquarters was at MARIEUX, 10 miles behind the line, in a beautiful château. Each of the troops carried a triangle on his back that assisted the artillery in their identification, and in the early morning the sun shone on those triangles and made them glitter. (These triangles are usually associated with troops from 29th Division at BEAUMONT-HAMEL.)

But as the hours passed, Brenan could not see any of them reach the German Front Line; later, he found out that the bombardment had never penetrated the deep dugouts the Germans had excavated in the chalk, and that their machine-gunners had emerged and were mowing down the attackers. The failure of the assault on Serre became obvious; 300yds or 400yds of rough ground that lay in front of the Allied lines were thickly sprinkled with silver triangles, only a few of which moved, while the German parapet was bare. And still the pounding of the front-line trenches went on. The young men were dead on the Corps front line and not a yard of ground had been gained.

In *A Victorian Son*, Stuart Cloete of 9th King's Own Yorkshire Light Infantry (64th Brigade, 21st Division) wrote:

The only previous experience I had had of rotting bodies had been at Serre, where, as a battalion, we dealt with the best part of a thousand dead who came to pieces in our hands. As you lifted a body by its arms and legs they detached themselves from the torso, and this was not the worst thing. Each body was covered inches deep with a black fur of flies which flew up into your face, into your mouth, eyes and nostrils, as you approached. The bodies crawled with maggots. There had been a disaster here . . .

In summary, the British attempt to take Serre, where the ground sloped upwards to the German trenches – which in turn had not been adequately bombarded by the artillery in the previous few days – was an absolutely disastrous plan; the infantry never had a chance of making any progress in these circumstances. As it was, each of the five front-line battalions – 12th York & Lancasters, 11th East Lancashires, 15th West Yorkshires, 16th West Yorkshires and 1/8th Royal Warwicks – suffered well over 500 casualties, leaving about 550 men unwounded out of 3,000.

Brig Gen H.C. Rees DSO, newly appointed temporary commander of 94th Brigade (31st Division), left for the Somme by car at the end of June and was first briefed by Lt Gen A.G. Hunter-Weston, General Officer Commanding VIII Corps. The battle instructions alone ran to 76 pages. On 1 July, Rees's advance brigade headquarters opposite Serre was in front of Observation Wood, 500yds behind the front trench. Ten feet deep, it took the form of a steel shelter with two exits and could accommodate 15 men; the brigade signallers had a similar shelter.

On 2 July, before handing back command to Brig Gen Carter, who was now fit again, Rees issued a special order of the day: 'I have been through many battles in this war, and nothing more magnificent has come to my notice. The Waves went forward as if on a drill parade and I saw no man turn back or falter.' On 4 July, Rees took over from Brig Gen C.B. Prowse, General Officer Commanding 11th Brigade (4th Division), who had died of wounds the previous day; his brigade headquarters on 10 July was MAILLY-MAILLET.

Three men who had previously published poetry became casualties on 1 July during the planned attack towards Serre. Cpl A. Robertson of 12th York & Lancasters was hit and lost in no man's land coming from the Copses towards Serre; his name is commemorated on the Thiepval Memorial. Born in 1882, Robertson had been a lecturer at Sheffield University and had published *Comrades: Last Poems* (Erskine Macdonald). 2/Lt H.L. Field of 1/6th Royal Warwicks was also killed on 1 July, by shell-fire near the QUADRILATERAL; his grave is in Serre Road Cemetery No. 2 (II.C.10). An art student, Field had published *Poems and Drawings* (Cornish Bros.). Sgt J.W. Streets of 13th York & Lancasters, wounded and missing on 1 July,

had published *The Undying Splendour* (Erskine Macdonald); he was a Derbyshire miner.

Later in the year, a revised plan to capture Serre was fixed for 25 October, only to be postponed. Some tunnels that had been bored for the July attempt to take the hamlet were to be reopened for the fresh attempt; the two in the area of 76th Brigade (3rd Division) were named Mark and John after two of the four copses. They were dug to within 100yds of no man's land and were large enough to take not only men, but also guns and gun teams.

3rd Division were chosen for the attack, which was finally to take place on 13 November; 8th and 76th Brigades (both 3rd Division) were in the centre, 6th and 5th Brigades (both 2nd Division) were on the right flank and 92nd and 93rd Brigades (both 31st Division) were on the left flank. The ground was very muddy and heavy and the weather was cold and inclined to be misty.

8th Brigade, 3rd Division deployed 2nd Royal Scots and 1st Royal Scots Fusiliers in front, with instructions to advance as far as Serre, the second objective; 8th East Yorkshires and 7th King's Shropshire Light Infantry (both also 8th Brigade, 3rd Division) were in the second line. Parties of 8th Brigade did manage to reach the German Support Line, but no further.

It was 76th Brigade on the left that really bore the brunt of the attack; Lt Duffield of 2nd Suffolks (76th Brigade, 3rd Division), in charge of machine guns with the battalion, left a first-hand account. On 12 November, Duffield's party had to 'plod' 9 miles to the line to use Mark and John Tunnels, which were to be opened up for his gun teams at about 0100hrs on 13 November, the day of the attack; small bombing parties accompanied a machine-gun team. Headquarters had moved up to Rob Royal Trench and occupied Dugout No. 213. The attacking infantry formed up in what was virtually a series of swamps and soupy mudholes. By 0200hrs, they had been issued with a rum ration, which made some of the men intoxicated; some walked about on top, smoking, with the enemy only 200yds away.

As Duffield went up with his team to Mark Tunnel, four British shells from the direction of HÉBUTERNE dropped short among his party. Luke Copse, to the left of Mark Copse, was virtually a huge crater and was used as a large magazine dump. Due to join the team going out of the left hand of John Tunnel at Zero Hour, which had been set for 0545hrs, Duffield settled down for a short rest in Dugout 214. At 0540hrs, he entered the tunnel with his men and with great caution went down 80yds of it, taking care not to alert the enemy.

All of a sudden there was a terrific rumble and roar. The orders had been changed and the tunnel opened at 0540hrs; consequently, Duffield's men could only go out with the infantry. Through a gaping hole they could see a dense mist, smoke from 1,000 shells and all manner of coloured lights. Duffield saw a ladder, which his party used to climb up, and they discovered waterlogged holes everywhere. Once 2nd Suffolks had taken the enemy's first line, Duffield was to go and establish dumps of ammunition for his guns. However, the attack miscarried and by 0615hrs, most of the battalion had been withdrawn. He saw many casualties, some of whom were floundering in an absolute sea of mud and water.

Duffield remained with a small party of eight or nine, as to return immediately would be too dangerous, and besides, the commanding officer would need all the information that he could get. For lunch, the small party had two mess sandwiches between them and a small round of whisky from Duffield's flask. They then spent their time reading the *Continental Daily Mail*, in which the sandwiches had been wrapped. After 1400hrs, the German artillery began to 'search' no man's land in every direction with high explosives and trench mortars. Duffield himself was hit several times and at 1645hrs his party began to return in twos and threes through the mud and water to the front line, about 150yds away. He discovered that headquarters had gone to Monk Trench, which he found after he had had his wounds dressed. By early evening the casualties of the battalions were 273, including 11 officers, and Duffield himself was one of only three officers left who had not been seriously hurt.

According to the Suffolk Regiment's history, the Battle of Serre on 13 November was ruefully remembered by those who took part in it as the least successful and most dispiriting engagement of 2nd Suffolks in France. In fact, the whole period in the Serre sector was one of unhappy memory. In *Goodbye to the Battlefields*, Capt H.A. Taylor of the Royal Fusiliers described 2nd Suffolks' attack in a sea of mud as a futile attempt.

F.H. Vinden, then a battalion adjutant with 2nd Suffolks, also wrote of this tragic period. It had been raining incessantly and the trenches were water-logged up to the knee. In addition, the ground was churned up by the artillery of both sides. Men were sometimes drowned in shell-holes; the glutinous mud drew boots off the feet and made a sucking noise. Maj Stubbs urged 76th Brigade headquarters to inform Maj-Gen C. Deverell, General Officer Commanding 3rd Division,

of the certain failure of any attack in these impossible conditions. These representations went unheeded and 'the attacking troops dragging their feet out of the mud moved at a snail's pace and were slaughtered'. Deverell appeared at Stubbs' headquarters the next day and told him: 'The next time your battalion attacks, I shall put machine guns behind it and the men won't come back.' A witness to this encounter, Vinden noted: 'I wished that I had had the courage to shoot him.'

During mid-November, the Somme battle had gone better further south, where 63rd Division had reached BEAUCOURT-SUR-L'ANCRE and 51st Division had captured BEAUMONT-HAMEL. On 14 November, a small group of men from 1st Gordon Highlanders (76th Brigade, 3rd Division) came back to the lines of 2nd Suffolks and told them that when they were lying exhausted close to the German lines, a German doctor had tended to their wounds and thus enabled them to return to safety in the early morning.

The war diary of 2nd Suffolks cited mist, early officer casualties, muddy conditions, concertina wire, rifles caked with mud, invisibility of the barrage and the strength of the enemy in their second line, as well as machine-gun fire, as the reasons for their lack of success. Duffield, together with another officer and the adjutant, tried to sort out the remains of the battalion and in Rolland Trench found members of his former gun team. He himself returned to COLINCAMPS for medical attention.

On 15 November, Duffield was caught by a German gas attack that seriously affected his eyes, which continued to water badly. On his way back to the front line, he mentions Euston Dump, a huge Royal Engineers supply dump; he also mentions LA SIGNY FARM, which was in ruins, a few hundred yards back from the front line. Duffield visited Legend Trench, where 13th King's (9th Brigade, 3rd Division) were in occupation. Eight or nine snipers who had made themselves comfortable under an elephant shelter had recently been killed by a 5.9in shell.

Duffield returned with messages to the second-in-command and to the transport lines at BUS-LÈS-ARTOIS. His next duty was to prepare billets at Vauchelles for the battalion, who were to return from the line in lorries from COLINCAMPS. Around 23 November, a new draft joined 2nd Suffolks when lorries took them to COURCELLES-AU-BOIS; the battalion then had a 6-mile march to Euston Dump, where they collected loads of wire and stakes in the area of Rolland and Nairn Trenches. They used the light railway over the top past LA SIGNY FARM, behind Serre, which housed troops in its cellars. The going was awful; they were obliged to use trenches and were up to their knees in water.

On 26 November, a working party was organised, which necessitated wire and other supplies being taken to Waterloo Bridge, which was close to the Euston batteries. On 27 November, Duffield's unit moved to the château at COURCELLES-AU-BOIS. He mentions at this time a huge crater at Staff Copse, which had previously been a dump; it had blown up, with thousands of trench mortar 'puddings' and Mills bombs all going off together. On 2 December they rode back on trolleys to Euston Dump; as his eyes were no better, Duffield reported sick and went into hospital at LOUVENCOURT.

Serre was never in Allied hands in 1916 and was only occupied after the enemy had evacuated it on 24 February 1917, when 22nd Manchesters (91st Brigade, 7th Division) entered the hamlet the following morning.

It is not surprising that in this area, where there had been two such disastrous attempts to capture Serre, there should be several cemeteries very close together. Serre Road Cemetery No. 1 is about 1,000yds west of the village on the north side of the road. It is in two departments and in three communes, being divided equally between PUISIEUX and HÉBUTERNE in the Pas de Calais and BEAUMONT-HAMEL in the Somme. The cemetery was made by V Corps in 1917 and after the Armistice was greatly enlarged by the concentration of 2,054 graves, which for the most part were from the 1916 Ancre and Somme battlefields. It has a large number of 'unknowns'. Concentrations were brought in from Acheux Communal Cemetery French Extension, Albert German Cemetery, Beaucourt-sur-l'Ancre British Cemetery, Cerisy-Buleux Churchyard, Puisieux Churchyard and Ten Tree Alley Cemetery No. 1.

The land above the cemetery is part of the former no man's land ground over which 15th and 16th West Yorkshires attacked in July 1916. Above the ridge are the sites of the contested features named after the four evangelists, Matthew, Mark, Luke and John. The cart track leading up the slope opposite the cemetery was used in the actual battle. The cemetery has over 3,300 graves and the cemetery register lists the names of 2,424 casualties. During the war a wooden cross memorial was set up, 500yds behind the cemetery, to men of the Royal Scots Fusiliers who fell in the fighting here. A hundred yards to the west of Serre Road Cemetery No. 1 is the Hébuterne-Serre French National Cemetery. Close by on the road is a French memorial chapel; a German plaque dated 1964 is displayed outside.

Close to the chapel is where the poet Wilfred Owen briefly occupied a dugout in no man's land during part of January 1917. The spot was excavated in October 2004 by Channel 4's *Time Team* and the site later covered up. During the research the remains of an unknown soldier but member of 1st King's Own (Royal Lancaster Regiment) were discovered and later reburied in Serre Road No. 2. His position when found suggested that he fell on 1 July 1916 during an attack on the Heidenkopf, a German defensive position.

Serre Road Cemetery No. 2, designed by Sir Edwin Lutyens, is on the south side of the road, about 1 mile from Serre. About two-thirds of it is in BEAUMONT-HAMEL (Somme Department) and one-third in HÉBUTERNE (Pas de Calais). It is on the site of the former German Quadrilateral position. There are 7,133 graves of officers and men here, which makes it the largest of this group of cemeteries; Plots I and II were made in May 1917. Sixteen cemeteries were concentrated here, of which four contained casualties from 1916. Lt Col C. Marten, Commanding Officer 18th King's Royal Rifle Corps (122nd Brigade, 41st Division), killed in action during the capture of FLERS on 15 September, is buried here (XXXIV.J.1).

The greater proportion of the burials is from concentration of graves in 1922 and between 1926 and 1934. In 1928 the parents of a Pte Butler were able to visit their son's grave during the British Legion great pilgrimage; their son's remains had only recently been found in an old shell-hole and before that, of course, he had only been listed as Missing. Also in 1928, the Leeds 'Pals' of 15th West Yorkshires came to Serre on a pilgrimage and also visited BUS-LÈS-ARTOIS. They had hoped that a memorial to commemorate their battalion would be set up in the road to MAILLY-MAILLET, but the idea was rejected by the French authorities.

Serre Road led from MAILLY-MAILLET and entered no man's land about 1,400yds south-west of Serre. On 1 July, 31st and 4th Divisions had attacked north and south of this road. Outside the cemetery is a memorial to Lt V.A. Braithwaite MC of 1st Somerset Light Infantry (11th Brigade, 4th Division), who was killed on 2 July near this spot and is commemorated on the Thiepval Memorial. He was a friend of Compton MacKenzie; they had met in the Turkish peninsula. After the war, Braithwaite's father, Lt Gen Sir W. Braithwaite, commissioned a memorial cross made of wood, to be set up about 100yds to the east of Serre Road Cemetery No. 2. After he bought the land, the wooden memorial was replaced by a stone one in 1922.

Serre Road Cemetery No. 2 is still used; on 21 April 2004, the remains of an unknown soldier of 1st King's Own (12th Brigade, 4th Division) were reburied here, one of 112 casualties of the battalion on 1 July 1916. During the military funeral, the coffin was carried by six soldiers from Somme Company, the King's Own Royal Border Regiment.

Made by V Corps in the spring of 1917, Serre Road Cemetery No. 3 is in the fields about 300yds to the north-east of Serre Road Cemetery No. 1; a new road now leads to it. East of PUISIEUX and commanding extensive views on all sides except for the east, it contains the graves of 81 soldiers from the United Kingdom who fell in July and November 1916, mainly from 31st Division.

Railway Hollow Cemetery, 1,300yds west of Serre and 200yds west of the former Mark Copse, is on the site of the British Support Line of July 1916; it too was made by V Corps in 1917. It contains the graves of 107 soldiers of 3rd, 19th and 31st Divisions who fell on 1 July or 13 November. It stands in a low-lying field, through which a military light railway once ran. Adjacent to the cemetery is Sheffield Park, a memorial park, and a portion of the old front-line trench can still be traced near the edge of the park by the gate; 11th East Lancashires attacked from this trench, and there is a separate commemorative plaque dedicated to them on a beech tree. A more substantial memorial to the battalion, a 7ft wall of two panels made from bricks from Accrington, was dedicated in the early 1990s. Another memorial in the park, this time to the memory of 13th and 14th York & Lancasters, was unveiled in 1998.

A short walk across the field facing the old lines, no man's land in 1916, will bring one to the site of the former German Front Line and one can still see the roof of a former concrete machine-gun post. Pte A.E. Bull of 12th York & Lancasters is commem-orated near the entrance to the park where he fell; he was reburied in Serre Road Cemetery No. 2 (XIX.E.16).

Sheffield Park has never been forgotten by the people of Sheffield, and over the years there have been many pilgrimages to this tragic reminder of the slaughter of many of the 'Pals' battalions. Even in August 1939, with a new war less than a month away, the annual Sheffield pilgrimage was still made to the Ypres Salient and the Somme.

Luke Copse British Cemetery, on the site of the former British Front Line of July 1916, was named from one of four plantations and made in February 1917 when the Ancre battlefields were cleared. The graves are those of members of 31st and 3rd Divisions who attacked the German lines on 1 July and 13 November 1916. It is a small cemetery with 72 graves

and a memorial to 2nd Suffolks. Queen's Cemetery, also on the line of the old British Front Line, is south of Mark Copse; it was made by V Corps as 'The Queen's' in 1917 and the cemetery register lists the details of 312 soldiers who were members of 31st, 3rd and 19th Divisions who fell either in July and November 1916 or in February 1917.

Ten Tree Alley Cemetery, 1,200yds south of Serre, was made by V Corps as Ten Tree Alley Cemetery No. 2 in 1917. It stood beside a former German trench, captured by 32nd Division on the night of 10/11 February 1917. It contains the graves of 67 soldiers from the United Kingdom who fell on 18 November 1916 and 10–18 February 1917.

After the war, the city of Sheffield was keen to commemorate the role played by its local battalions during the war and to remember them in some unique way. At the same time, it wished to establish strong ties with the town of BAPAUME, which in some way it adopted. The relationship was to become a sort of miniature *Entente Cordiale*. A memorial to the men of 12th York & Lancasters who fell here on 1 July 1916 was unveiled on 21 May 1923, when 150 officers and men who had taken part in the battle were present. The chief Sheffield members of the party were invited to lunch at BAPAUME by the mayor, and the French architect of the monument was presented with a silver casket.

However, it seems that a more substantial commemoration was envisaged, and in 1927 the Sheffield branch of the British War Graves Association purchased 7 acres of land close to the original front line, which it hoped to turn into a memorial park that would also include a shelter for visitors. There were no shelters in the other cemeteries in the area. On 25 May 1931 the park and shelter were duly dedicated and Fabian Ware was presented with a ceremonial key by the architect of the memorial. The dedication was a big affair and former Old Comrades and their families were invited, together with other interested parties. Mayors of nearby French villages, including a group from BAPAUME, were also invited.

In the years that followed, the park became a place of pilgrimage but the memorial shelter seems to have regularly needed attention; in the winter of 1933/34 it was badly damaged by the weather. Eventually, it was agreed that the Imperial War Graves Commission should take on the maintenance of the park and that the city of Sheffield would recompense them.

The Commonwealth War Graves Commission has several large files of correspondence devoted to the upkeep of the park (WG 1879, Pt 1, Box 1116). In the cash-strapped 1930s, the Commission was rightly only too anxious not to be drawn into an open-ended situation, not of its own making, for which it might have to pick up the bill. As with NEWFOUNDLAND PARK, there seems to have been just too much land within Sheffield Park for it to be responsible for. Within the files, the subject of rabbit-proof fencing comes up time and time again, as do the adverse effects of poorly managed land on the adjacent farms. However, the Commission continued to look after the grounds and the memorial, but was still not responsible for repairs or renovations.

During the Second World War the Park did not suffer as badly as it might have, as for some reason the Germans allowed a Commission gardener, Mr B.M. Leach, to carry on with his usual duties; Leach hid a memorial casket and a roll of honour in his toolshed. As the enemy were always on the lookout for Allied airmen who might be hiding in the area, toolsheds were often searched. Somehow Leach got away with it, and during the hostilities managed to shelter no fewer than 17 airmen, hiding in sheds in the various cemeteries in the area. As for the casket, Leach kept moving it around, but at the end of hostilities in 1945 it was kept in the nearby Chapel of Notre Dame de la Treile, Serre; found to be in a damp condition, it was moved to the Albert Branch Office of the Commission.

After the Second World War, when finances were again very tight, the memorial was again restored; the cost – £550 in 1946 – was, as usual, paid by the City of Sheffield. In May 1946 a service of rededication took place, to which the mayors of BAPAUME and PUISIEUX will have been invited.

It seems only appropriate to finish this short account of Serre by drawing once again on the novelist John Harris, whose father had served on the Somme. In his novel *Covenant With Death*, launched in Sheffield in 1961, one of Harris's characters says

we never did get Serre, and by Christmas the mud was so deep we couldn't have advanced if we'd wanted to . . . I never fancied going back . . . in spite of the Tours of the Battlefields that they organised in the twenties. I felt I'd left a bit of me behind, there in front of Serre. Everything that seemed to belong to my youth was there.

However, he finally did return and drove up the Serre road and found the Sheffield city battalion memorial.

You can see from the position of the little cemeteries the route we took . . . Down in that little hollow just behind the crest where the machine guns caught us, I found a small cemetery and saw all their names again . . . Seven hundred and seventeen we lost in those three or four hours between seven thirty and midday when the field finally emptied of human life, and of these most vanished from the earth in the first ten minutes of the battle – Two years in the making. Ten minutes in the destroying. That was our history.

SHELL VALLEY was another name for DEATH VALLEY, to the south of MAMETZ WOOD. After being involved in the fighting for Bazentin Ridge on 15 July 1916, 1/4th Suffolks (9th Brigade, 33rd Division) went on relief in Shell Valley and dug themselves into road trenches for the night. After a day they returned to front-line duty. On 20 July they were relieved, and returned to Shell Valley, but they were shortly afterwards moved up to a position near the cemetery in support of 19th Brigade (also 33rd Division) in an attack on HIGH WOOD.

SHELTER WOOD was north-west of Fricourt Wood on the west side of the road to CONTAL-MAISON. It is mostly associated with the fighting in early July 1916 in the FRICOURT area, but was also used later on in the battle; it contained brigade headquarters and was a very congested camp during September 1916.

SNAG TRENCH, located between EAUCOURT L'ABBAYE and the BUTTE DE WARLENCOURT to the north-west of it, was a front-line trench that zigzagged in an irregular line between the MARTINPUICH–WARLENCOURT–EAUCOURT–le Barque roads. It was the scene of fighting in mid-October 1916, as the British struggled to take the Transloy Ridges in a battle that lasted from 7 to 20 October.

In mid-October, 9th Division attacked, with 26th Brigade on the right, the South African Brigade on the left and 68th Brigade (23rd Division) in reserve. The men of 26th Brigade reached their objective but the South Africans were held up at a position called the Pimple; they were therefore unable to reach Snag Trench, their objective. According to the history of 9th Division, one of the South African companies went 'into the blue' and was neither seen nor heard of again.

Brig Gen W.D. Croft, General Officer Commanding 27th Brigade (9th Division), was under the impression that 9th Division were the third division to try to take the Pimple, although the South Africans had done most of the spade-work.

The Pimple commanded the Snag absolutely, so once 6th King's Own Scottish Borderers (27th Brigade, 9th Division) had captured this natural fort they simply shot the Germans out of it. They were assisted by a heavy concentration of artillery fire, the results of which became evident once the Snag was taken. 11th Royal Scots (also 27th Brigade, 9th Division) took the position in a brilliant night attack, and at dawn the next morning there were 300 dead Germans at the junction of Snag Trench and the communication trench, which ran back from it at right angles. The battalion then pushed on to higher ground and were confronted by the BUTTE DE WARLENCOURT. At the end of October and in early November, Snag Trench was in 2ft of mud and lacked duckboards.

SOUASTRE is on the D6 road, between FONCQUEVILLERS to the east and HÉNU to the west. In 1915 it was 3 or 4 miles behind the Allied lines and lay due west of the northern part of the Somme battlefield. Indeed, the high ground at Souastre overlooked GOMMECOURT. Like several other villages in the area, Souastre, in the build-up to the battle, was to become most associated with 30th, 37th, 46th, 48th and 56th Divisions; on the first day of the battle, 46th and 56th Divisions were involved in the failed attempt to capture the German stronghold of GOMMECOURT.

In the autumn of 1915, elements of 111th Brigade (37th Division) occupied billets in the area. On 12 December, elements of 89th Brigade (30th Division) were billeted in buildings that had been damaged by shell-fire. During April 1916, field ambulances of 48th Division ran a hospital for the sick and wounded, consisting of hut shelters and tents. The hospital huts in Souastre were ready by the beginning of April. Prior to the battle, there were many tents in the open country between Souastre and COUIN to the south-west.

To the north of the village are the remains of an old mill, which would have been used as an important observation post during 1916 and which has graffiti links with battalions from 56th Division.

To move to a lighter note, 46th Division's concert party began in a large barn in the village but were not so popular as 56th Division's troupe, The Bow Bells, who used to perform nightly to packed houses. Many troops found the time to go more than once and hugely enjoyed the songs, dances and sketches.

On 26 April, 1/5th Royal Warwicks (143rd Brigade, 48th Division) moved into billets in Souastre; 143rd Brigade had held this sector without relief for 8 months. On 11 May, 143rd Brigade marched the 12 miles to GÉZAINCOURT south-west of DOULLENS.

On 4 May, 168th Brigade (56th Division) were in reserve at Souastre. On 6 May, 1/4th Londons (168th Brigade, 56th Division) arrived, and remained here for a fortnight, during which time they drew 1–1 in a football match with 1/13th Londons (also 168th Brigade) on 12 May. After a spell in the front line, 1/4th Londons were back in Souastre on 1 June, when they were billeted in huts for 24 hours before moving on to HALLOY. On 4 May, 1/7th Middlesex (167th Brigade, 56th Division) were here for the night before moving on to SAILLY-AU-BOIS.

Units from 46th Division were in the village in May and June, during which time they carried out training and provided working parties. For much of May, 1/5th Leicesters (138th Brigade, 46th Division) were billeted here and mainly worked down the road at FONCQUEVILLERS, where numerous battery positions were being built. During this period, a gunner died on 18 May and was buried in the churchyard in the rue de Bienvillers. On 11 May, 1/5th Sherwood Foresters (139th Brigade, 46th Division) arrived here after a spell with Third Army and carried out attack training, as well as supplying working parties. On 19 May, they relieved 1/5th South Staffords (137th Brigade, 46th Division) in front of FONCQUEVILLERS; when relieved by 1/5th Leicesters in June, they returned to Souastre.

From 19 May, 1/2nd Londons (169th Brigade, 56th Division) were in huts in the village; at this time they supplied working parties for roads, light railways, dumps and for burying cables. Here from the end of May until the middle of June, 1/7th Middlesex were called upon to provide troops for a raid on Gommecourt Park on 28 May.

From early June the area suffered a considerable amount of rainfall and there are references in battalion histories to having to spend time removing mud from both equipment and uniforms. On 1 June, 1/14th Londons (68th Brigade, 56th Division) moved from HALLOY to Souastre, where they stayed in huts made of corrugated iron and canvas; on the next day they left for the trenches at HÉBUTERNE. On 13 June, 1/12th Londons (143rd Brigade, 48th Division) were relieved by 1/13th Londons and arrived at Souastre from HÉBUTERNE 'covered with mud, and exhausted, but singing cheerily . . .' They were here for a week while working on digging a divisional cable line, which had reached SAILLY-AU-BOIS but needed to connect with HÉBUTERNE.

In mid-June, The Bow Bells entertained troops in an old barn in Souastre. They were back in the village again from HÉBUTERNE on 21 June, having marched via SAILLY-AU-BOIS and BAYENCOURT and seen 'ripening corn and red poppies on either side of them making them forget, for the time being, the dark days left behind . . .' They then rested in a green field outside the village before marching to PAS-EN-ARTOIS via HÉNU and HALLOY. Also in June, two 15in howitzers were installed in the village.

On 23 June, 1/6th North Staffords (137th Brigade, 46th Division) arrived here and received orders telling the troops that Z Day was to be 29 June. It was during these last days of June that an advance assault trench was accomplished by 1/6th North Staffords, accompanied by 1/5th North Staffords (also 137th Brigade, 46th Division). When, on the eve of 29 June, 1/6th North Staffords paraded in Souastre, they were informed of the 2-day postponement; they moved up 2 days later to take part in the attack against the enemy-held Gommecourt Wood.

In *Four Years on the Western Front*, Aubrey Smith of 1/5th Londons (169th Brigade, 56th Division) says that his transport section had made their quarters at Souastre. He also says that the road to FONCQUEVILLERS, where they dumped the rations, could not be used by day, and so there was a congestion of traffic after dusk. Artillery convoys were very numerous, as every gun needed reserve supplies of ammunition. Large quantities of stores of all kinds had to be taken up behind the trenches by infantry transports, Royal Engineers and motor lorries. Smith wrote that tracks seemed to branch both to the right and the left, to one battery or another. The absence of woods meant that the guns were in gun pits in open fields. In addition, the heavy guns were hauled up by tractors and in the process frequently held up all the horse traffic until they branched off either right or left.

At the end of June, Smith wrote that he heard the big howitzers at Souastre firing, some heavy guns firing in the vicinity of SAINT-AMAND and also guns at BAYENCOURT. All these guns, he wrote, were firing their hardest; in addition, batteries on the Hébuterne Plain, and around SAILLY-AU-BOIS and FONCQUEVILLERS, were contributing their share to the indescribable uproar that was going on. Some reports, such as those from Souastre, were distinct in themselves; these guns were firing on more distant objectives, while the 'heavies' were firing 9.2in ammunition in the direction of the German trenches.

On 27 June, 1/5th Londons marched to Souastre, where they dumped surplus kits and stores; on 30 June they moved up towards the front. On 28 June, 1/7th Middlesex arrived back at Souastre, totally exhausted after several days in the front line; after a day's rest, they moved forward again at midnight on 30 June.

At the end of June, the assembly point of 1/4th Lincolns (138th Brigade, 46th Division) was to be the Corps Line Trench, which ran north and south 500yds to the east of Souastre, between the Souastre–Bienvillers road and the Souastre–FONCQUEVILLERS road. Midland Trench was the assembly line for 46th Division on 1 July against Gommecourt Wood. At daybreak on 1 July, 1/5th Lincolns (also 138th Brigade, 46th Division) were resting in the corps line; they were to be involved in the fighting against Gommecourt Wood later on that day.

At 0715hrs on 1 July, when the hospital here was being run by 1/3rd (North Midland) Field Ambulance (46th Division), all available motors and horse transport were sent to rendezvous at the crossroads about ½ mile west of Souastre on the Souastre–HÉNU road. Casualties were brought in from 0900hrs onwards. Walking cases went back to the dip in the FONCQUEVILLERS road, where they were picked up and loaded onto horse ambulances and General Staff wagons.

After the failure at GOMMECOURT on 1 July, 1/5th Cheshires (pioneers of 56th Division) returned to Souastre. On 9 September, 16th King's Royal Rifle Corps (100th Brigade, 33rd Division) were in reserve billets here for the HÉBUTERNE sector.

During the October/November period, the barns in Souastre were used by 1/4th Duke of Wellington's (147th Brigade, 49th Division).

STUFF TRENCH and **STUFF REDOUBT** were German strongholds that lay north of THIEPVAL, north-west of ZOLLERN REDOUBT and due east of its more famous neighbour, the SCHWABEN REDOUBT. Stuff Redoubt lay about midway between POZIÈRES to the east and GRANDCOURT to the west, and was reached but not completely taken in the Battle of Thiepval Ridge, 26–30 September 1916. Beyond Stuff Redoubt was Stuff Trench, which on the right became REGINA TRENCH to the north of COURCELETTE; it met the SCHWABEN REDOUBT at the junction of an enemy communication trench called Grandcourt Road.

By 27 September, 24 hours after the SCHWABEN REDOUBT's southern face had been captured, a footing had in fact been made in Stuff Redoubt. Capt A.C.T. White of 6th Yorkshires (32nd Brigade, 11th Division) gained the Victoria Cross between 27 September and 1 October:

He was in command of troops that held the southern and western faces of a redoubt. For four days and nights by his indomitable spirit, great personal courage, and skilful dispositions, he held his position under heavy fire of all kinds and against several counter-attacks. Though short of supplies and ammunition, his determination never wavered. When the enemy attacked in greatly superior numbers and had almost ejected our troops from the redoubt, he personally led a counter-attack, which finally cleared the enemy out of the southern and western faces. He risked his life continually, and was the life and soul of the defence . . .

On the morning of 28 September, Lt Col C.E. Fishbourne of 8th Northumberland Fusiliers (34th Brigade, 11th Division) was wounded by a shell here and died in Rouen 8 days later. He was buried in Saint-Sever Cemetery (A.12.3).

During the evening of 12 October, the north-western corner of Stuff Redoubt was the scene of another German counter-attack, which was driven off by 8th Loyal North Lancashires (7th Brigade, 25th Division). Two days later, the same battalion attacked north-westwards from Stuff Redoubt and secured a position called the Mounds, which gave observation over GRANDCOURT. The enemy showed little fight, and on the same day 39th Division drove the Germans from their last hold on the SCHWABEN REDOUBT.

On 21 and 22 October, Edmund Blunden of 11th Royal Sussex (116th Brigade, 39th Division) was involved in an assault planned to begin soon after noon; the attacking force would have to move forward over a long approach. Stuff Trench was taken and Blunden established 'bombing blocks'. However, they were being steadily blown out of Stuff Trench and on the next day the troops in Stuff Trench were compelled to eat their 'iron rations'. By the time the position was in Allied possession, the Canadian troops to the south were also holding REGINA TRENCH, the continuation of Stuff Trench.

SUS-SAINT-LÉGER is north-east of DOULLENS and close to Lucheux Forest on the D59 road. In the latter half of May 1916, 1/6th South Staffords (137th Brigade, 46th Division) were in comfortable billets here; their days were spent in cutting saplings for making hurdles that could then be used as revetments in the line. They were back again from the line between 18 and 23 June, when the plan of the coming attack was fully explained to them

and when they carried out training and battlefield organisation. They left for SOUASTRE on 23 June.

After being relieved in the line at FONCQUE-VILLERS by 1/8th Sherwood Foresters (139th Brigade, 46th Division), 1/7th Sherwood Foresters (also 139th Brigade, 46th Division) arrived here from Bienvillers in pouring rain on 6 June. They were allocated excellent billets in a beautiful area. A large tract of land had been allocated in order to make a full-scale model of the enemy lines at GOMMECOURT. The battalion returned to Bienvillers after 12 hard days of battle training, with some light relief when they felled trees in Lucheux Forest.

There is a grave of one British casualty buried in Sus-Saint-Léger churchyard.

SUZANNE, on the north bank of the River Somme, is on the D197 road, south of MARICOURT. In the summer of 1915 the village was close to where the British and French lines joined after the British took over part of the sector; in particular, 5th and 30th Divisions were to become associated with the area. On 13 August, 54th Brigade (5th Division) arrived here for instruction and on 21 August an advanced dressing station was established in the village. Infantry battalions and other units from 5th Division were here, off and on, over the next few weeks.

On 1 September, Lt S.E. Gordon of 1/6th King's (15th Brigade, 5th Division) noted that after leaving MORLANCOURT his unit arrived in Suzanne, a quiet village still occupied by civilians. Within the dining room of the imposing château, which was still occupied by its French owners, was an ornament depicting a full-sized man mounted on a horse; a picture gallery set apart from the château had been slightly damaged, but the château itself was hardly touched. The château owners shared their home with a brigade headquarters. 1/6th King's took over from 1/5th Cheshires, then of 14th Brigade (5th Division).

On 8 October, 1st East Surreys (95th Brigade, 5th Division) noted that their billets in Suzanne 'were commodious and good, all being situated in one street. The Headquarters offices and those of three companies were in the "Petit Château". Three training grounds were available, and, as the weather was fine, full use was made of them . . .' Towards the end of December, the battalion were back here, but this time they were in a camp: 'This camp had its drawbacks, though tents were appreciated, as it stood in a swamp by the River Somme . . . The officers are in billets of sorts, one being a hen-house the fowls of which are absent, but the smell remains . . .'

On 16 November, 2nd Royal Inniskilling Fusiliers marched here from BRAY-SUR-SOMME and joined 14th Brigade (5th Division); they relieved 1st Duke of Cornwall's Light Infantry (also 14th Brigade, 5th Division) in the trenches on 19 November. Soon after 2nd Royal Inniskilling Fusiliers arrived here, one of their men picked up an unexploded German shell close to a company billet; this caused it to explode, killing seven men and injuring four others. Later the battalion were in and out of the line for the next few weeks, when they were usually billeted in MARICOURT or Suzanne.

In December, 5th Division's first line of transport were bivouacked in a wood close to Suzanne, but it was such a thin wood that it afforded little shelter for either man or horse. The transport had a long way to travel in order to fetch rations, as it was only possible to send supplies up to Maricourt by night.

Lt S.E. Gordon returned to Suzanne on 17 December; by now, most of the château's windows had been broken. Towards the end of December, 15th Royal Warwicks (also 14th Brigade, 5th Division) first arrived here; they moved up to the line at MARICOURT for their first spell in the line there on 22 December. For the next few days they were in and out of the line, alternating with billets in Suzanne. After being relieved by 16th Manchesters (90th Brigade, 30th Division), 15th Royal Warwicks left for MORLANCOURT via BRAY-SUR-SOMME.

On 9 January 1916, 17th Manchesters (also 90th Brigade, 30th Division) reached Suzanne for the first time, just as the village was being shelled; they suffered six casualties. On the following day, they relieved 16th Manchesters to the west of Maricourt Wood.

According to the battalion history, 16th Manchesters (90th Brigade, 30th Division) arrived in Suzanne for the first time on 12 January after being in the line west of Maricourt Wood. Although the village was only 2 miles from the front, there were still a few civilians living in Suzanne; the marquess shared his château with 90th Brigade's headquarters. The great building of brick and stone, the nucleus of the village, stood among trees at the foot of a hill up which the village ran, with great gates and spacious forecourt, and a formal water-garden linked up with the Somme itself. By this time, the gardens had fallen into a state of neglect. State coaches were still in the stable block, but now the place echoed to the bustle of a brigade headquarters with horses, cars and orderlies. Deep in the stable block was a dressing station that could cater for 30 patients in the cellar; stretcher-bearers at VAUX collected casualties at FARGNY MILL during the night and brought them here.

Suzanne was laid out in the grand manner of the period; Centre Street, with the church on its left, ran up the hill towards MARICOURT,

with West Street and East Street looping to left and right whilst Cannon Street lay under the brow of the hill leading to Eclusier. Along these roads lay the barns and cottages that housed troops during their periods of 'rest'; flimsily constructed of half timber and mud, with solidly built cellars. North Street crowned the valley, in the chalk side of which Manchester fatigues burrowed tunnelled dug-outs under the direction of the 11th South Lancashires (Pioneers), and below the crucifix lay the cemetery that proved the last resting-place for many a Manchester man.

For a long time Suzanne had been relatively left alone by enemy guns, but the village began to receive more attention from German artillery when British artillery began to shell GUILLEMONT and MAUREPAS. In January 1916, the enemy were planning to attack the French outlying post at FRISE; on 13 January they shelled the village and there was a great rush of casualties at No. 5 Casualty Clearing Station at CORBIE on 14 January. The main supply road from BRAY-SUR-SOMME to Suzanne was under observation and a company from 89th Brigade (30th Division) were left to guard the bridge at Eclusier to the south-east, for which the French were supposedly meant to be responsible. If the enemy crossed the canal and marshes, they would be able to get behind the British line at Royal Dragon's Wood on the VAUX road.

At about midnight on 27/28 January the enemy began to shell MARICOURT very heavily, as well as the trenches in front of it. They then bombarded the batteries in the valley between MARICOURT and Suzanne, a battery outside Suzanne and then Suzanne itself, mostly with 5.9s. The German artillery 'systematically registered down the streets' and houses 'fell like packs of cards – brick-dust filled the air . . .' Civilians had to be evacuated and a 'mournful procession of old men and women, girls and children began. The French cling to their homesteads, and the pathos of their exodus, carrying such of their worldly goods as they could from their crumbling homes, emphasized the devastating effect of the war.' British troops were not in the village at the time, but shelling caused the horses to stampede; in addition, the tram railway running from Suzanne to BRONFAY FARM was targeted. The enemy did manage to capture FRISE and its crossing, and 89th Brigade headquarters were ordered to leave Suzanne for ETINEHEM.

As previously noted, the distance from the front line was 2 miles; the front-line trenches were 'along the road that skirted Maricourt valley, dotted with its battery positions. Across the near horizon stretched the great Péronne road, with its dwindling avenue of trench.' Rations, post and stores came up from Suzanne during the night. The village was shelled again on 12 and 14 February, close to where the mules were tethered.

On 17 March, 16th Manchesters were relieved by 7th Buffs (55th Brigade, 18th Division) and marched to BRAY-SUR-SOMME, where they dug deep shelters in chalk. They then spent much of early April in training at BREILLY, west of AMIENS, but were back in Suzanne in early May, as were 18th Manchesters, who supplied working parties both day and night. In March and April, 7th Queen's (55th Brigade, 18th Division) were near Suzanne for several weeks when they were protecting the Somme marshes. On 1 June, 90th Brigade (30th Division) were replaced by units from the French Army.

Suzanne was captured by the enemy during the German offensives of spring 1918 and recaptured on 26 August 1918 by 3rd Australian Division.

Suzanne has two Commonwealth war cemeteries, Suzanne Communal Cemetery Extension and Suzanne Military Cemetery No. 3. The latter is on the left of the long valley dropping down from MARICOURT, just off the road, and was originally a French cemetery. The graves cover the dates from 1915 to 1918 and include a German who died in February 1916. More than half of the graves are of unknowns. Suzanne Communal Cemetery Extension is about about 385 yards north-west of the village, on the south-east side of Suzanne Communal Cemetery. It was also begun by French troops, and was used by the British from August 1915 to January 1917, before being taken over by the Germans in March 1918 and then reused by British units in August and September.

The main feature in this attractive Somme Valley village is still the great château at the bottom of the hill. Now a protected monument, it was much used by the military in the war; it is now privately owned and not open to the public.

SWITCH TRENCH was a trench hastily dug by the Germans once HIGH WOOD became threatened. It ran from the direction of MARTINPUICH to the north-west of HIGH WOOD and went towards the north of DELVILLE WOOD. Most important, however, was the section of Switch Trench that ran through the northern part of HIGH WOOD; this

sector considerably helped the Germans to maintain their hold on the Wood for 2 months.

In mid-July 1916, Allied cavalry rode through Switch Trench but were badly cut down and quickly withdrawn; their headquarters, formerly used by the Germans, was heavily shelled. Although they were only engaged in a secondary role at Switch Trench, 7th/8th King's Own Scottish Borderers (46th Brigade, 15th Division) nevertheless suffered heavy casualties and were relieved on 18/19 August by 10th Cameronians (also 46th Brigade, 15th Division). On 19 August, 6th Cameron Highlanders (45th Brigade, 15th Division) were in support as 7th/8th King's Own Scottish Borderers withdrew to a camp on the ALBERT side of the AMIENS road to rest and clean up. It was probably Hénencourt Camp, which at that time had the reputation of being one of the worst camps to be billeted in.

In mid-September, the portion of the Switch Trench in front of 50th Division consisted of three lines of trenches known as Hook Trench, with MARTINPUICH behind it. Switch Trench met the LONGUEVAL–FLERS road just to the south-west of FLERS; it was the first objective of 2nd New Zealand Brigade (New Zealand Division) on 15 September, when HIGH WOOD finally fell into the hands of the Allies. Alexander Aitken of 1st Otagos (1st New Zealand Brigade, New Zealand Division) was involved in the attack and later wrote of his experiences in his book *Gallipoli to the Somme*.

In *Field Guns in France*, Lt Col N. Fraser-Tytler of CL Brigade, Royal Field Artillery (30th Division), noted that Switch Trench was captured towards mid-October and that 'just before zero hour everybody comes up to Switch Trench. It makes a splendid grandstand, and as the batteries have already all their lifts and alterations in range, we at the observation post, are simply spectators.'

T

TAILLES WOOD runs along the side of the valley and stretches across the D1 MORLANCOURT–BRAY-SUR-SOMME road south of MÉAULTE. On 20 February 1916, 1/5th Seaforth Highlanders (152nd Brigade, 51st Division) arrived here from CORBIE, and worked for a week on repairing roads. Unfortunately, frost and snow came at the same time and enemy aircraft had a habit of dropping bombs on their tents. On 7 March, 19th Manchesters (21st Brigade, 30th Division) marched here from BRAY-SUR-SOMME and stayed a week before moving to CORBIE and then to FRÉCHEN-COURT. On 19 March, troops from 18th Manchesters (90th Brigade, 30th Division) arrived here from the MARICOURT sector and were engaged for 10 days in general training, drill and route marching. They left for FRÉCHENCOURT on 29 March when relieved by 19th King's (89th Brigade, 30th Division).

On 1 June, 8th Lincolns (63rd Brigade, 21st Division) arrived here and worked on the railway at BRAY-SUR-SOMME as well as carrying out their training. At the end of May, Siegfried Sassoon (1st Royal Welsh Fusiliers, 22nd Brigade, 7th Division) described the Wood as being full of men from 8th and 9th Devons and 2nd Borders (all 20th Brigade, 7th Division). A water point was established between here and MONTAUBAN-DE-PICARDIE as well as at CARNOY.

On 28 June, 21st Manchesters (91st Brigade, 7th Division) were here, and on the night of 30 June took up positions opposite MAMETZ village. At Zero Hour on 1 July, the north of the Wood was home to 52nd Brigade (17th Division); 50th Brigade (21st Division) were to the west of the Wood. Before and during the battle the Wood was much used by artillery batteries and at one time also housed a corps kite balloon unit, which could receive messages at night by lamp from a battalion or brigade headquarters as well as from the artillery. Few messages would get through during the day, however.

On 14 July, H.M. Davson, an artilleryman of 35th Division, reported that his unit marched to the Wood in inclement weather and the camp, which had been used previously by the French reserves, had been left in a dirty state. On 18 July, 54th Brigade (18th Division) were camped in the Wood.

On 19 July, the whole of 54th Brigade (18th Division) were still in the Wood; on 2 August, 15th and 16th Cheshires (both 105th Brigade, 35th Division) arrived at the edge of the Wood, but had no tents. On 22 July, units from LXXX Brigade, Royal Field Artillery (17th Division), marched back here after having breakfast at BILLON WOOD, at a time when enemy 15cm shells were 'searching for' a 6in howitzer battery in the Wood.

When 24th Manchesters (pioneers of 7th Division) were in the Wood they listened to a concert. In *Peter Jackson, Cigar Merchant*, Gilbert Frankau wrote that his battery had arrived at the Wood from HANGEST-SUR-SOMME, where they bivouacked. Their horses were tethered between the limbers on the red sandy floor of the valley below. They were later in action for 18 days and lost some of the battery around Arrowhead Copse.

On 6 September, 10th King's Royal Rifle Corps (59th Brigade, 20th Division) moved into the Wood from the GUILLEMONT area, and were here again on 11 and 16 September before going up to relieve 2nd Grenadier Guards (1st Guards Brigade, Guards Division) in the Support Line before LESBŒUFS.

TALMAS is on the N25 AMIENS–DOULLENS road to the north of VILLERS-BOCAGE. On 1 August 1915, 54th Field Ambulance (18th Division) arrived here. At the end of January 1916, 5th Division left the MARICOURT sector to the right of the line and moved to the north of AMIENS. 15th Royal Warwicks (13th Brigade, 5th Division) were here for a week before moving southwards to COISY.

From 1 February 1916, Talmas was home for a week to 1/9th Londons (169th Brigade, 56th Division), who were involved in training here, including wood and village fighting. The latter was carried on in the village streets; live bombs were replaced by mouldy or rotten cider apples. On 8 February, they left for CARDONNETTE to the south-east.

In early April, 49th Division had units in the area, including No. 458 Field Company, Royal Engineers, who carried out work on horse standings and water troughs close to wells and pipes. The village also had a Royal Engineers yard. On 28 October, 9th Division opened their headquarters here.

Talmas Communal Cemetery has the graves of two soldiers in the south-east corner, a private of the Army Service Corps who died in February 1916 and a Canadian soldier who died in September 1916. In the 1920s the cemetery was much neglected and covered in weeds.

TALUS BOISÉ was a long strip of woodland in low ground east of CARNOY and north-west of MARICOURT. On 6 January 1916, 2nd Wiltshires (21st Brigade, 30th Division) arrived in this section of the front. A single-track railway line ran through the wood, crossing both the British and the German lines and continuing towards MONTAUBAN-DE-PICARDIE and BERNAFAY WOOD.

On 30 June, 90th Brigade were in the wood as part of 30th Division's line; the railway track there formed the line between it and the next formation. On 1 July, 18th King's (21st Brigade, 30th Division) arrived in Talus Boisé; 104th Brigade (35th Division) came here on 19 July and 18 August, when they marched from HAPPY VALLEY. Shells rained down on the wood frequently.

Along the track leading north to MONTAUBAN-DE-PICARDIE was Machine Gun Wood, running through the west end of Glatz Redoubt to MONTAUBAN-DE-PICARDIE. Silesia Trench and Silesia Support to the north-east of Talus Boisé were formerly part of the German Front Line.

TERRAMESNIL is on the D23, north-west of BEAUQUESNE. On 24 July 1915, 11th Field Ambulance (4th Division) arrived here, marching to BERTRANCOURT 2 days later. On the same day, Gunner R.E. Read of 4th Division died; he was buried in Terramesnil Communal Cemetery to the south-east of the village. At the end of January 1916, a section of No. 122 Field Company, Royal Engineers (36th Division) were in the village.

THIEPVAL is on the crossroads of the POZIÈRES–AUCHONVILLERS road, the D73, and the AUTHUILLE–GRANDCOURT road, the D151. As early as 1914 the Germans chose the site as a place of very strong – if not impregnable – defence on the heights of the Ancre Valley, from which they could not be budged. Although the buildings were systematically destroyed by Allied artillery, and eventually no brick remained on top of another, as always with French villages, there was an extensive cellarage, which provided safe billets for German troops, in turn protected by the rubble above them. A group of these cellars on the west side of the village were interconnected and formed a position known as Thiepval Fort. The machine guns of the fort, as well as those set up in a post in the ruins of the château, were excellently sited for defence purposes; 'as they commanded the British trenches to the north in front of Thiepval Wood, they could sweep the entire western face of the spur and, to the south, they could bring a withering enfilade fire upon any forward move from Authuille'. In the Battle of the Somme, the Germans were to hold on to this fortress for nearly 13 weeks.

Prior to the battle Thiepval had 93 houses and was thus the sixth largest village on the Somme at that time. A document with the papers (WO 95/2383) of No. 218 Field Company, Royal Engineers (32nd Division), contains further details of some of these buildings when the village was already in ruins. Much of this 'inside' information probably came from refugees. The buildings included the west-facing château – obviously an important building with very large cellars that were always full of lodging German soldiers, although most of the building had been destroyed by the end of 1915 – a church and a presbytery or *curé*'s house. The latter

was described as 'a substantial building of brick with cellars in which 62 people lived for 40 days'. Other buildings, which were farmhouses, houses or barns, generally had spacious cellars that could accommodate troops; in addition, the village had a good water supply. There were wells 30 metres in depth within the village and most farmhouses had a good supply or well of their own. The water supply at the château, for example, was described as 'abundant'. MOUQUET FARM, to the east, had a good water supply too, and provided a water pipeline to the village. Other information mentioned in this document was that the 'well in the square North of the church was mined and had a gallery running towards the Church'. A café, which had burnt down in 1915, also had cellars, which could take 30 to 40 men.

On 30 July 1915, 1/6th Seaforth Highlanders (152nd Brigade, 51st Division) took over a section of Thiepval Wood from French troops; the day before, two officers had gone ahead and were shown around the trench system. The officers were later entertained to an 'excellent dinner' by the ever-hospitable French in their headquarters dugout, when they were even persuaded to sing some Scottish songs. All the French officers were very agreeable and could not do enough to make the changeover to British occupation as smooth as possible. Neither side really understood the other's language but this did not hinder their friendship. The French left their artillery behind for a week, when they continued to use their very businesslike 75s.

The French line ran along the east side of Thiepval Wood, which was still in its summer foliage; the trenches were dug out of chalk to a depth of about 5ft and were excellent. A shell had almost to land right in the trench if it was to do much damage. Opposite the right of the battalion sector was the ruined Thiepval Château, which was surrounded by trees, and on its left was the small village of Thiepval itself. The French battalion headquarters was in the centre of Thiepval Wood and boasted a rustic table and benches set out as if for afternoon tea. Another touch of normality was the exchange of French and German newspapers. Each side left a paper at an agreed pole in no man's land.

Not normally slow off the mark as to what the other side was up to, the Germans were slow to recognise that the occupants of Thiepval Wood were no longer French; this conclusion was possibly reached when their newspaper delivery abruptly ceased. However, before the French finally left the Wood, their interpreter went forward and met up with a couple of Germans while waving an English newspaper. Sadly, the Scots did not continue with the practice.

A communication trench named Elgin Avenue ran from here to the centre of the front line. Stores and ammunition could be brought up by road and the padre ran a canteen for the men at battalion headquarters. 1/6th Seaforth Highlanders were here for 15 days until relieved by the Indian cavalry; during this time, the weather was perfect, apart from one violent thunderstorm. Mosquitoes were the worst problem. The battalion returned to BOUZINCOURT for a week and were back in the Wood in October for another 10-day spell when not billeted at BOUZINCOURT, and again at the end of November and beginning of December.

During August, 10th Essex (53rd Brigade, 18th Division) were in front of the village, receiving instruction in the line from elements of 51st Division. They had witnessed French heavy artillery trying to destroy that part of Thiepval Château which was still standing. Apart from the official training, they were able to have a daily swim in the Ancre backwaters in the valley below, when their 'pool' was within 500yds of the German Front Line.

During December, having relieved 2/5th Lancashire Fusiliers (154th Brigade, 51st Division) again, 1/6th Seaforth Highlanders also gave instruction to battalions from 32nd Division. Platoons from 16th Highland Light Infantry (97th Brigade, 32nd Division) replaced platoons from 1/6th Seaforth Highlanders, who then went back to MARTINSART for 2 days, but the latter battalion deemed this practice inefficient and wasteful of time. The Thiepval trenches were now 'much more lively' than earlier in the summer; enemy trench mortars had become a particular nuisance and the battalion cow, kept close to battalion headquarters, had a narrow escape. On 8 December, 16th Highland Light Infantry took over the line completely from 1/6th Seaforth Highlanders, who then returned to tents in SENLIS-LE-SEC.

The *Official History of the War* described the Thiepval Plâteau as standing out like a great buttress at the western edge of the Pozières Ridge. It overlooked the River Ancre towards which the ridge sloped down on the west and north. The three spurs called Ovillers, Thiepval and Thiepval Wood stood out from its southern face. Nab or BLIGHTY VALLEY lay between Ovillers and Thiepval and led up towards MOUQUET FARM. The front line of X Corps at Authuille Wood ran for about 2,500yds on the lower slopes of the west face of the Thiepval Spur with the River Ancre behind it; it

then passed over the Thiepval Wood Spur along the front edge of the Wood and crossed in front of the village of HAMEL on the western bank of the river and continued for 1,000yds across the AUCHON-VILLERS spur to the right flank of VII Corps.

The enemy defences came down from the Ovillers Spur and fell back a little up Nab Valley and then went forward into a sharp salient in order to include the upper slopes of the western edge of both the Thiepval Plâteau and Spur, towards SAINT-PIERRE-DIVION, a village in the river valley. Thus the German position as a whole overlooked the British position, but Thiepval Wood could be used to conceal Allied troops, as indeed it was.

Thiepval itself had been transformed into a fortress and much work had been done by the Germans in order to make it impregnable. Redoubts, blockhouses and concrete vaulted shelters had been built on the surrounding ground and a continuous line of trenches went around the village. Behind the front line was the strongest German position of all, to the north of the fortified village, and that was the famous SCHWABEN REDOUBT. STUFF and Goat REDOUBTs were to the east and south-eastwards was MOUQUET FARM. There were subforts and the entire complex was linked by trenches, which were very deep and studded with machine-gun pillboxes. Some of the dugouts were 30ft deep and some of them had trap doors that led to lower chambers. Many of these shelters were shell-proof.

There were several collecting posts in the Wood; one in the south-east corner, called the Colonnade, consisted of three large dugouts backed by a tunnel. A tunnel also joined it to a large double company dugout.

After they were transferred to Fourth Army on 2 March 1916, 36th Division were to become indelibly associated with Thiepval in the following weeks. The division became acquainted with the area and took over part of the extended front line from opposite the Thiepval–SERRE road, including both sides of the River Ancre, on 4 March. On 9 March, Thiepval Wood was shelled and 36th Division were made responsible for the Thiepval Wood–HAMEL sector only. In April, the Wood was again shelled and on 22 April, 32nd Division carried out a raid in which they took 13 prisoners and accounted for 30 more Germans.

The Wood was again shelled from 4 to 6 May. On 7/8 May, 1st Dorsets (14th Brigade, 32nd Division) were involved in a raid north of Thiepval Wood that went terribly wrong, partly due to the enemy planning a raid of their own to take place at the same time. The cost was very high and 13 men, including 1 officer, were killed, 30 other ranks wounded and 24 other ranks declared missing. The casualties were taken to 108th Field Ambulance (36th Division).

On 7 May, 108th Brigade (36th Division) went to Thiepval Wood subsector, with 107th Brigade (also 36th Division) in support at MARTINSART and 109th Brigade (also 36th Division) in reserve. On 17 May, 1st Dorsets lost two officers, Capt W.B. Algeo and Lt H.G.M. Mansel-Pleydell, when they went off to try and locate an enemy machine-gun emplacement and failed to return.

On 1 June, 108th Brigade were relieved by 147th Brigade (49th Division) and went back into training with 109th Brigade. On 10/11 June, 30 casualties from HAMEL and Thiepval Wood were taken to 108th Field Ambulance. On 16 June, Paisley Dump in Thiepval Wood was bombarded and on 23 June, 109th Brigade headquarters was heavily shelled. The Ulster troops of 36th Division had named the German strongpoints Lurgan, Strabane, Duncannon, Lisnakith; 1 July was also the anniversary of the Battle of the Boyne.

The Allied bombardment started 7 days before the battle actually began, and although it targeted many of the buildings in Thiepval village this still left the cellars intact. A group of these on the west side of the village were organised for a machine-gun defence known as Thiepval Fort, as were the ruins of Thiepval Château, which was to the south-west of the village. These machine guns were to combine and sweep the entire upper part of the western slope of the Thiepval Spur and could also enfilade to the south from the river valley down as far as AUTHUILLE village, and to the north could cover the open ground in front of the Allied trenches along the east side of Thiepval Wood.

Lancashire Dump was the meeting place for a mass of transport after dark on 30 June, when munitions, rations and stores were brought up for the offensive. Large stores of rations were placed in specially built dugouts on the bank of the river. The work of 36th Division's train was organised by Col H.C. Bernard, Commanding Officer 10th Royal Irish Rifles (107th Brigade, 36th Division); wheels were bound with straw and old motor tyres, steel chains were replaced by leather straps, and boots, like those used in rolling a cricket pitch, were placed over the horses' hooves.

According to the history of 36th Division, the most difficult task for the division before the battle began was the construction of two causeways over the River Ancre and the marshes. The only communication with the Allied line on the left bank was

provided by some footbridges that had been put up by the French troops who had previously occupied the sector. The causeways were built of sandbags filled with chalk. At night the river was constantly swept by machine-gun fire. 16th Royal Irish Rifles (pioneers of 36th Division) had made their name in building the CANDAS–Acheux railway.

The plan for the battle was that 36th Division, who had been formed from the Ulster Volunteer Force, should take the SCHWABEN REDOUBT and advance towards GRANDCOURT; 32nd Division, who were also part of X Corps, were on their right and 29th Division, who had recently arrived from Gallipoli, were on their left, while 49th Division were in X Corps Reserve. The headquarters of 36th Division was at Gordon Castle and their closest transport connection was Doncaster Camp.

Thiepval village was the objective of 32nd Division; when addressing his troops, the divisional commander, Maj Gen W.H. Rycroft, told them: 'When we go over to-morrow or the next day, all we'll find in Thiepval will be the caretaker and his dog.' Following a football kicked off by a well-known player, 16th Northumberland Fusiliers and 15th Lancashire Fusiliers (both 96th Brigade, 32nd Division) were hit by machine-gun fire from the village as soon as they scrambled out of their trenches at 0730hrs. During 1 July, 32nd Division were unable to make any progress at all.

To their left, however, 36th Division did make real progress after attacking the enemy's lines on both sides of the River Ancre; casualties were very heavy, though, and on 2 July they were relieved. Since that day they have become the division most associated with Thiepval, having penetrated deep into the German lines but later having to withdraw through lack of support.

At the beginning of the battle on 1 July, 36th Division's movements were concealed by a smoke screen, put down by 4in Stokes mortars; the smoke screen drifted along the northern edge of Thiepval village and then flooded the ANCRE VALLEY. The other thing that concealed their movements was the intensity of the Allied fire.

Comprised of 9th, 10th and 11th Royal Inniskilling Fusiliers and 14th Royal Irish Rifles, 109th Brigade were to emerge from the right of Thiepval Wood while 108th Brigade, made up of 11th, 12th and 13th Royal Irish Rifles and 9th Royal Irish Fusiliers, attacked on their left. The four battalions of 107th Brigade – 8th, 9th, 10th and 15th Royal Irish Rifles – began from their points of assembly in the north side of AVELUY WOOD and were to proceed across the Ancre soon after 0500hrs on 1 July. The troops formed up in no man's land, facing their objective; for the most part, their line followed the line of the sunken Thiepval–HAMEL road.

The leading waves of the British attack reached the German front-line trench and were able to move straight across it. They did not suffer heavily, but hardly were they across when the German barrage fell on no man's land and on the rear companies of the first-line battalions, and also on the second British line. As their barrage lifted, flanking machine-gun fire began from the dominant position of Thiepval Cemetery and 11th Royal Inniskilling Fusiliers and 14th Royal Irish Rifles were literally mown down as they emerged from Thiepval Wood. The enemy were able to come up from the cellars in the village and to pour bullets into the backs of the men of 109th and 108th Brigades. On the left of 109th Brigade, 13th Royal Irish Rifles suffered most of all at this stage of the attack, as they were under direct long-range fire from the direction of Beaucourt Redoubt, across the river. The immediate breakdown of 32nd Division, the flanking division on the right, resulted in the gravest losses in the ranks of 36th Division.

Moving from AVELUY WOOD and across the River Ancre, 107th Brigade reached the western outskirts of Thiepval Wood, almost at the bottom of the valley. At 0630hrs they assembled at the track known at Speyside, parallel to Elgin Avenue. They had an hour to wait and shells passed over their heads and fell into the marshes beyond. At Zero Hour, led by 10th Royal Irish Rifles under Bernard, they moved to the right for a short distance in order to reach the rides, which were to be the paths for their route to the front line. Here the men could see troops of 32nd Division on the right emerging from their trenches and being gunned down in no man's land by enemy machine-gun fire. The ride or track used by 10th Royal Irish Rifles had been denuded of its foliage by artillery fire and was subsequently in full view. The battalion came under machine-gun fire from three directions, including the rear. Casualties were high and included Bernard himself. Lewis guns were brought forward to engage the German machine-gunners but their teams were destroyed. Other attacking battalions were not so handicapped, as they were screened in their rides and were further away from the Thiepval guns.

It was quite clear to Maj Gen Sir O.S.W. Nugent, General Officer Commanding 36th Division, that if the attack went forward in a sort of wedge shape into the enemy lines without support on either flank, the Ulstermen would simply be destroyed. He therefore asked X Corps whether 107th Brigade could be stopped from advancing to their final line. X Corps wanted the attack to continue and then changed their mind. Unfortunately it was too late for the message to get through.

The German bombers poured up from the trenches at SAINT-PIERRE-DIVION to the north of 36th Division's attack, but were beaten off by 8th and 15th Royal Irish Rifles and the handful of 13th Royal Irish Rifles on the flank of 109th Brigade. In the afternoon, 11th Royal Inniskilling Fusiliers reached the Crucifix, to the north-east of Thiepval Cemetery, and 9th Royal Inniskilling Fusiliers reached the SCHWABEN REDOUBT. The troops at the Crucifix found that holding the ground there was impossible unless Thiepval was taken.

F.P. Crozier, Commanding Officer 9th Royal Irish Rifles, and Col H.C. Bernard, Commanding Officer 10th Royal Irish Rifles, had agreed before the battle to meet up in no man's land, if they were still alive. There they were to supervise the deployment and make any necessary changes to the battle plan. If either of the senior officers became a casualty, then the other was to deploy both battalions. If both of them were to become casualties, then their seconds-in-command should carry on. We know that Bernard was killed at the head of his battalion by trench-mortar fire from Thiepval village; this fire also destroyed his two leading companies, who were behind him in columns of four. Crozier had doubled to the sunken road, where he rallied the remnants of 10th Royal Irish Rifles and told his batman at the same time to go to the battalion headquarters in order to help with bringing up ammunition. Most of the stretcher-bearers who reached Doncaster Dump were wounded in carrying casualties. Crozier found the remaining 10th Royal Irish Rifles had gone to ground in desperation and that his own 9th Royal Irish Rifles could not go forward without their right being guarded, as the ground beyond Thiepval was still held. The two battalions were then given the task of leap-frogging the rest of 36th Division and of carrying on to the final objective, which they actually reached but were unable to hold on to without support from behind.

At noon, 1/7th West Yorkshires (146th Brigade, 49th Division) were sent up to assembly trenches in the Wood but during the afternoon there had been a misunderstanding about the use that 146th Brigade (49th Division) were to be put to, and their attack at 1500hrs failed under terrific machine-gun fire. There was a deep valley or re-entrant from the River Ancre halfway up to Johnstone Post and the enemy had full view of 1/6th West Yorkshires (also 146th Brigade, 49th Division) as they doubled across it. There had been a good many casualties, especially among the Lewis gun teams.

Cpl G. Sanders of 1/7th West Yorkshires gained the Victoria Cross for most conspicuous bravery:

> After an advance into the enemy's trenches he found himself isolated with a party of thirty men. He organised his defences, detailed a bombing party, and impressed on his men that his and their duty was to hold the position at all costs. Next morning he drove off an attack by the enemy and rescued some prisoners who had fallen into their hands. Later, two strong bombing attacks were driven off. On the following day he was relieved, after showing the greatest courage, determination and good leadership during thirty-six hours under very trying conditions. All the time his party was without food and water, having given all their water to the wounded during the first night. After the relieving force was firmly established, he brought in his party, nineteen strong, back to our trenches.

The headquarters of 1/7th and 1/8th West Yorkshires (also 146th Brigade, 49th Division) were at Belfast City in AVELUY WOOD and after the disastrous attack the survivors were concealed in trenches near Gordon Castle, a battalion headquarters to the south-west of Thiepval Wood.

It is impossible to imagine the conditions, as the day wore on, in the woods from which the Ulstermen had launched themselves only a few hours before. Conditions were indescribably terrible. At Johnstone Post 'the dead lay around in heaps. Casualties were so appalling that the medical staffs were inadequate to deal with them. Hour after hour they worked at the aid posts, yet fresh cases arrived before earlier ones could be attended to and evacuated. And all the time, into the midst of the deadly valley, the 5.9's screamed.'

At Paisley Dump, all the trenches in Thiepval Wood and the tracks to AUTHUILLE and across the River Ancre met. The wounded lay there in hundreds and the noise was inhuman. The road back to MARTINSART behind Aveluy Wood became choked with walking wounded and with ambulances. One sunken road that went in the direction of HAMEL became known as 'Bloody Road' because of the massive heaps of dead there at the end of the day on 1 July.

No. 121 Field Company, Royal Engineers (36th Division), sent a section to the Wood from MARTINSART to assist in evacuating the wounded to Lancashire Dump. There were two main dressing stations for stretcher cases and walking wounded, one at FORCEVILLE, to the west of Thiepval, which was manned by 108th Field Ambulance (36th Division) and a second at CLAIRFAYE FARM, further west, manned by 110th Field Ambulance (also 36th Division). The advanced dressing station was situated near the ALBERT–Arras road to AVELUY WOOD.

Evacuation of wounded from regimental aid posts in Thiepval Wood and AUTHUILLE took place over Authuille Bridge, which connected the village of that name with AVELUY WOOD. The alternative was for the trench tramway, which crossed the River Ancre to the north, to be used. The motor vehicles of the field ambulance were parked on the MARTINSART–ALBERT road, south of MARTINSART itself. For walking wounded, there was a collection station to the west of MARTINSART, whence horse-drawn wagons carried the wounded by cross-country track through HÉDAUVILLE to CLAIRFAYE FARM. From HAMEL, evacuation was simpler, though it had to follow a specially dug trench from HAMEL village to a point on the ALBERT–HAMEL road that was screened from enemy observation. The tramway running to Thiepval Wood from the south followed Paisley Avenue to just beyond Johnstone Post. On 1 July it was being repaired.

To sum up the deeds of 36th Division on this day, the author would like to draw on Capt H.A. Taylor's *Goodbye to the Battlefields*. Taylor stated that 36th Division wrote no more glorious chapter of history than it did here at Thiepval. The Ulster battalions hurled themselves upon Thiepval's underground fortress with such determination that all its wire and all its machine guns, manned by the German regiment that had held the point for 2 years and had boasted that it was impregnable, could not check the onward rush. On they went, 2 miles into the enemy system, and although, ultimately, in danger of being cut off, they retired and brought back with them over 500 prisoners.

On 1 July, 36th Division gained two Victoria Crosses at Thiepval for outstanding bravery. The first was awarded posthumously to Pte W.F. McFadzean of 14th Royal Irish Rifles for action near Thiepval Wood prior to the attack:

> While in a concentration trench and opening a box of bombs for distribution prior to an attack, when the box slid down into the trench, which was crowded with men, and two of the safety pins fell out. Private McFadzean instantly realised the danger to his comrades, and with heroic courage threw himself on top of the bombs. The bombs

exploded, blowing him to pieces, but only one other man was injured. He knew well the danger, being himself a bomber, but without a moment's hesitation gave his life for his comrades . . .

McFadzean's name is commemorated on the Thiepval Memorial.

T/Capt E.N.F. Bell of 9th Royal Inniskilling Fusiliers (attached No. 109 Trench Mortar Battery, 36th Division) also won the Victoria Cross, in his case also posthumously:

> He was in command of a Trench Mortar Battery, and advanced with the infantry in the attack. When our front line was hung up by enfilading machine-gun fire, Capt. Bell crept forward and shot the machine gunner. Later, on no less than three occasions, when our bombing parties, which were clearing the enemy's trenches, were unable to advance, he went forward alone and threw trench-mortar bombs among the enemy. When he had no more bombs available, he stood on the parapet, under intense fire, and used a rifle with great coolness and effect on the enemy advancing to counter-attack. Finally, he was killed rallying and reorganizing infantry parties which had lost their officers. All this was outside the scope of his normal duties with his battery. He gave his life in supreme devotion to duty . . .

Bell's name is commemorated on the Thiepval Memorial.

On 2 July, 109th Field Ambulance at Paisley Avenue sent a wire to CLAIRFAYE FARM requesting 100 stretchers and blankets, which were sent immediately. Paisley Avenue had shell-proof shelters and was also used as a brigade headquarters.

With over 5,500 casualties, 36th Division were taken out of the battle, relieved by 49th Division. These very high figures promptly threw the Ulster Province into a state of mourning. During 2 July a force of about 400 men was collected in order to support a small number of British troops who could be seen from Mesnil Ridge to be in the first two lines of enemy trenches.

F. Starrett, who was Crozier's batsman at the time of the Somme battle and who had helped on 1 July with bringing up ammunition, described 9th Royal Irish Rifles as holding out before their relief. He also mentions in his unpublished memoirs that there were three women workers as close to the battlefield as Doncaster Dump. They would have been nurses or drivers. At the time of 36th Division's relief, Starrett's master, Crozier, was promoted to general.

Although most of the fighting associated with Thiepval occurred on 1 July and again nearly 3 months later, there was still some action during the next few days of July. Capt Stevenson-Jones MC of 2nd South Lancashires (75th Brigade, 25th Division) has left a detailed account of the situation on 2 July in 2nd South Lancashires' regimental journal. At about 1100hrs, they received orders to go up to the advance headquarters of Maj Gen Sir E.G.T. Bainbridge, General Officer Commanding 25th Division, which was close to two 4.7in Naval guns. At about 0200hrs, they had piled arms in Martinsart Wood, a small wood immediately behind AVELUY WOOD. They watched the howitzers performing and then had a meal. Just before dusk they fell in and the plan was to move through the Wood and then take over trenches in front of Thiepval. The attack was to be at dawn on 3 July.

Singing 'Keep the Home Fires Burning', 2nd South Lancashires went through the Wood, along the road at the top of the hill and then down into the ANCRE VALLEY. They had trouble in getting over BLACK HORSE BRIDGE owing to a stream of side-car ambulances that were crossing the opposite way. They were also shelled at this time. They then went past Ration Dump and the dressing station, which was very crowded, with rank upon rank of stretchers in front of it. They reached the communication and then the assembly trench. The attack was postponed until 0600hrs.

Although 75th Brigade attacked on a three-battalion front, they were blown to pieces and only 8th South Lancashires (75th Brigade, 25th Division), who were in reserve, were left to prevent a counter-attack from getting through to BLACK HORSE BRIDGE. Stevenson-Jones noted that advance companies were less in danger than those who followed, because of the time that it took the Germans to emerge from their dugouts; 8th Borders were on his right flank and 11th Cheshires (both 75th Brigade, 25th Division) on his left. 11th Cheshires in particular had been 'mauled' by the enemy and their commander, Lt Col R.L. Aspinall, had been killed. 75th Brigade headquarters had been hit by a shell, which prevented communication from running properly.

Many men got back during the night from no man's land, when they rested in Campbell Trench. That night they moved back to bivouac at Martinsart Wood. On their return, they were passed by 1st Wiltshires (7th Brigade, 25th Division), who were on their way to have 'another go' for Thiepval. However, their attack was called off. Stevenson-Jones informed Maj Gen E.G.T Bainbridge, General

Officer Commanding 25th Division, that their attack had failed because the trenches and no man's land were under direct observation and enfiladed from the high ground on the left, and swept by machine-gun fire from high ground well back. He said that Thiepval could never be taken by frontal attack unless SERRE and GOMMECOURT were taken first. On 2 July, the headquarters of 1/4th York & Lancasters (148th Brigade, 49th Division) was at Speyside, on the edge of the marsh. However, despite this advice, another attack was arranged for 1st Wiltshires (7th Brigade, 25th Division) for 4 July and they attacked, incurring great losses, including their commanding officer, Lt Col W.S. Brown.

Five bombing squads, together with a party of snipers, were organised by Maj G.T. Shaw, Second-in-Command 1/5th York & Lancasters (148th Brigade, 49th Division) and set off from Gordon Castle. The commanding officer, Lt Col F.H. Shuttleworth Rendall DSO, accompanied them to the front line. Although all the bombs were duly used, the enemy were not budged and soon what was left of the party returned across the open. Rendall had been wounded early on in the operation and taken to a German dugout. It proved impossible to bring him in. He died on 9 July and was buried in Lebucquière Communal Cemetery Extension (II.B.21). Maj G.T. Shaw of 2nd Northamptons (24th Brigade, 23rd Division) and later second in command of the 1/5th York & Lancasters (148th Brigade 49th Division) was killed two days before Rendall and was commemorated on the Thiepval Memorial.

Around 8 July, the conditions were ghastly in the sunken road at Thiepval Wood, with many bodies of 36th Division still awaiting burial. The Allied trenches had received a fearful hammering and some of them had been obliterated. Some of the dugouts were, in fact, quite deep, but others not nearly deep enough, and some of the communication trenches that led back to headquarters at Gordon Castle and the crossings over the River Ancre had been badly sited and constructed. For example, the main ones lay along or just beside the chief rides in the Wood and they could thus be easily enfiladed by enemy gunners.

By the end of July, Thiepval village, the objective of 32nd Division on 1 July, had been totally destroyed. Communication trenches close to battalion headquarters at Gordon Castle were Elgin and Inniskilling Avenue. Because of the accuracy of enemy shelling, headquarters was moved 200yds back from Gordon Castle to Belfast City, which was a very well-camouflaged position.

On 3 September another attempt was made against the SCHWABEN REDOUBT using 147th and 146th Brigades (both 49th Division). By 0513hrs the infantry had assembled in trenches along the HAMEL–Thiepval road. The Allied artillery bombarded the enemy lines accurately and gas bombs were used to good effect. However, 1/4th and 1/5th Duke of Wellington's (both 147th Brigade, 49th Division) to the right lost direction in part and failed to find and capture the German strongpoint known as the Pope's Nose. Machine-gun fire from the SCHWABEN REDOUBT added to their problems.

On their left, 146th Brigade did a bit better and 1/6th West Yorkshires, who were next to cross the river, even reached the enemy Support Line. But this was an isolated case and troops from 146th Brigade drifted back to their assembly trenches and 147th Brigade did likewise. Once again, the impossibility of making a frontal attack against a position such as the SCHWABEN REDOUBT was underlined. On 3 September, 49th Division could not get 20yds forward from Thiepval Wood.

In *Undertones of War*, Edmund Blunden of 11th Royal Sussex (116th Brigade, 39th Division) noted that the wounded of 4th/5th Black Watch (118th Brigade, 39th Division) were trailing down the road. 4th/5th Black Watch had been wading in the marshes of the Ancre, trying to knock out a machine-gun post called the Summer House. A few yards ahead, on the rising ground, the enemy front line could not be clearly seen, the water mist and smoke veiling it. 1/6th Cheshires (also 118th Brigade, 39th Division) took over the front line, the huge throat of the howitzer still being elevated to hurl horror at Thiepval Crucifix.

The British came up with another plan to capture the Thiepval stronghold and the redoubts to the north and north-east of it. On the right flank, 11th Division were given the objective of MOUQUET FARM while 18th Division were on the left flank. Opposite them the German defence was in the hands of 7. Infanterie, 8. Infanterie and 26. Reserve Divisions; at this point, the line went around the northern face of COURCELETTE and then westwards past MOUQUET FARM and into no man's land. It then continued to the southern side of the ruins of Thiepval village, which was about 300yds behind the line. The line then bent northwards towards SAINT-PIERRE-DIVION. Behind the line was STUFF REDOUBT, and behind it was the Grandcourt Redoubt. These were three lines of defensive systems, which included the forts, and the SCHWABEN, ZOLLERN and STUFF REDOUBTS. The nose around Thiepval and the village itself was defended by Infanterie-Regiment *Großherzog Friedrich von Baden* (8. Württembergisches) Nr. 180

(26. Reserve Division) and part of Reserve-Infanterie-Regiment Nr. 77 (2. Garde Reserve Division). The SCHWABEN REDOUBT and the front defences to the north-west of SAINT-PIERRE-DIVION were held by Infanterie-Regiment (3. Magdeburgische) Nr. 66 (52. Infanterie Division).

Having observed the activity of the British in the construction of new assembly trenches, the enemy were ready for a fresh attack several days before 26 September and were well prepared. However, for once it was not to be their day, which was to belong to 18th Division. On the right flank were 53rd Brigade, whose battalions were 8th Suffolks, 8th Norfolks, 10th Essex and 6th Royal Berkshires. On their left were 54th Brigade, whose battalions were 12th Middlesex, 11th Royal Fusiliers, 7th Bedfords and 6th Northamptons.

MOUQUET FARM to the south-east of Thiepval village, which had held up the Australians for some weeks, had held out until 26 September, owing to its deep cellars. It was 6th East Yorkshires (pioneers of 11th Division) who finally captured the Germans remaining at the Farm; one officer and 55 men were left of a brave garrison. For the viewpoint of the Allies, the author has drawn heavily upon the history of 18th Division and the views and letters of Lt Col F.A. Maxwell VC, Commanding Officer 12th Middlesex.

On 25 September the headquarters of 18th Division was moved to HÉDAUVILLE, where it remained until 6 October. The attack was to be launched from the south instead of from the west as before, and four tanks were allotted to 18th Division. Dumps had been laid down and trenches had been deepened and improved. Grids had also been put down. One brilliant idea was to clear the road from AUTHUILLE to Thiepval and then to erect a brush-wood screen along its whole length. The road thus became invaluable for bringing up stores and rations and later for taking back wounded troops. The screen had the effect of reducing German shelling. In addition to the enormous range of underground tunnels under the German position, from the centre of Thiepval village there ran a sunken road, up as far as the cemetery, which was lined with dugouts. Around the château itself, the dugouts were immensely strong and deep. According to the history of 18th Division, there were as many as 144 deep dugouts, marked on a German map that had fallen into British hands.

The Allied bombardment began 3 days before the battle was due to commence and Zero Hour was fixed for 1235hrs on 26 September. The distance to the trenches was about 250yds and on the extreme right 8th Suffolks pushed forward steadily, keeping close to the Allied barrage. However, they found stiffening resistance in Schwaben and Bulgar Trenches. On the left of the Suffolks, 10th Essex had also reached their objective, which was just beyond Thiepval village. A heavy fire was poured into the assaulting companies from the direction of Martin and Bulgar Trenches and they were also enfiladed by machine guns.

On the left flank in 54th Brigade's attack, 12th Middlesex under Maxwell had the task of capturing Thiepval village itself. 11th Royal Fusiliers under Lt Col C.C. Carr had the task of clearing the enemy network of trenches and dugouts on the left flank of 12th Middlesex as well as the dugouts behind the latter battalion, for which C Company was detailed. 6th Northamptons under Lt Col G.E. Ripley were to move up in close support of 12th Middlesex and 11th Royal Fusiliers, while 7th Bedfords under Lt Col G.D. Price were in dugouts in Thiepval Wood and its neighbourhood, so as to be close up when called upon.

The first waves of 54th Brigade's attack came under very heavy fire but 12th Middlesex managed to carry line after line of trenches until they reached the château, where they were checked by deadly machine-gun fire. At a critical moment in the battle, a tank lumbered up from Thiepval Wood, supported by a third wave of British infantry. The tank dealt with the enemy machine guns and the leading company of 12th Middlesex were then able to pass around the two flanks of the château. 54th Brigade had been allotted two tanks; the successful one, having led the infantry into Thiepval, then got bogged down on its way to SCHWABEN REDOUBT. The second tank suffered the same fate. That was the end for the time being of the two tanks, which were named *Crème de Menthe* and *Cordon Bleu*. In addition to the above success of 12th Middlesex, two of their members were to gain the Victoria Cross on this day.

On 26 September the local German telephone headquarters, which had been identified on a captured map, was also captured; it turned out to be a palatial dugout in direct communication with the enemy artillery, and contained 20 operators as well as other staff, who were all taken prisoner. Although the enemy had been pushed back, they were by no means beaten; they still possessed the advantage of the high ground and were able to direct accurate machine-gun fire on the British positions. Maxwell sent a message via carrier pigeon from Thiepval Château saying that although they had been successful, they were exhausted and in need of assistance. Meanwhile, 6th Northamptons, who had moved up in support, had been having a tough time but reached the château at 1715hrs, when they were sent forward in support of 12th Middlesex and 11th Royal Fusiliers. Ripley, 6th Northamptons' senior officer, joined Maxwell but at some point was mortally wounded, dying in England on 16 October.

In the evening, 53rd Brigade (Brig Gen H.W. Higginson) were in position to the right of 54th Brigade; 8th Suffolks and 10th Essex were consolidating the Zollern Line, while 8th Norfolks were in support in Schwaben Trench and 6th Royal Berkshires were being used for carrying parties. Maxwell, by now the only surviving battalion commander, assessed the situation and took over command of all the attacking battalions, gathering the scattered units into two defence lines with about 50yds between them. They then provided a defence of the château, which became a keep, and a strongpoint was made around one of the stranded tanks. 7th Bedfords were to relieve the attacking battalions and 7th Royal West Kents (55th Brigade, 18th Division) were to take their place in reserve.

The German account of the day's battle noted that the British had broken against COURCELETTE on the north-east of the battlefield. They broke through to the east of the village and three front companies of Reserve-Infanterie-Regiment Nr. 77 were captured almost to a man, while Infanterie-Regiment Nr. 180 found themselves being attacked by bombers from the rear. The advance at COURCELETTE had enabled the British to advance simultaneously on Thiepval and on the ground beyond from the south and west. The enemy were forced to evacuate Thiepval and to make a new line astride the Thiepval–GRANDCOURT road.

Summing up, 26 September was a great day for the British and Canadian advance; four divisions had been involved in an attack on a front of about 5,000yds, and the great fortress of Thiepval fell at last.

Pte F.J. Edwards of 12th Middlesex gained the Victoria Cross:

> His part of the line was held up by machine-gun fire, and all officers had become casualties. There was confusion and indication of retirement. Private Edwards, grasping the situation, on his own initiative dashed towards the gun, which he knocked out with bombs. This very gallant act, coupled with great presence of mind and a total disregard of personal danger, made further advance possible and cleared up a dangerous situation . . .

Edwards's actions made further advance possible and Maxwell recommended the award. Pte R. Ryder, also of 12th Middlesex, was awarded the Victoria Cross as well:

> His company was held up by rifle fire, and all of his officers had become casualties. For want of leadership the attack was flagging. Private Ryder, realizing the situation, without a moment's thought for his own safety, dashed absolutely alone at the enemy trench, and by skilful manipulation of his Lewis gun, succeeded in clearing the trench. This very gallant act not only made possible but also inspired the subsequent advance, and turned possible failure into success.

Finally, for the last comment on the day's events, the author would like to quote from a letter written by Maxwell and dated 27 September, which is kept in the National Army Museum. He wrote of the attack: 'I hadn't personally any hopes of accomplishing it.' The attackers were required to move forward for 1 mile, an enormous distance, over the parapet at an unknown hour. The Prussians and the Württembergers had held the line for a year and were supposed to have left, but were still there. It was a very difficult battle, as every landmark shown on maps had been obliterated. He described the trenches at Thiepval as 'white' and the enemy uniforms as being absolutely 'black'. After Maxwell's success, he was given the command of 27th Brigade (9th Division), but sadly was killed nearly a year later, on 21 September 1917, while reconnoitring no man's land.

The battle was to be continued the following day. The plan was that on the morning of 27 September the German rectangle position was to be stormed by two companies; it was then to be cleared in a rush with the use of the bayonet. Maxwell remained at the château in his headquarters, which was one of the arches with a few steps that led below ground, until 7th Bedfords attacked at about 0545hrs; this they did, moving successfully to the north-west corner of Thiepval village. Although the village had been cleared, there were still pockets of the enemy holding out with fortified nests of machine guns, and they also used the underground passages to good effect. In the evening, Thiepval Cemetery was completely cleared, as well as ZOLLERN REDOUBT.

After that, the SCHWABEN REDOUBT was the next objective of 18th Division. D Company, 11th Lancashire Fusiliers (74th Brigade, 25th Division), were involved in an attack against the enemy line known as the Pope's Nose, and were successful; J.R.R. Tolkien was a member of this battalion.

During the fighting, T/Lt T. Adlam of 7th Bedfords earned the Victoria Cross:

A portion of a village which had defied capture had to be taken at all costs, to permit subsequent operations to develop. This minor operation came under very heavy machine-gun and rifle fire. Second Lieut Adlam, realizing that time was all-important, rushed from shell-hole to shell-hole under heavy fire, collecting men for a sudden rush, and for this purpose also collected many enemy grenades. At this stage he was wounded in the leg, but nevertheless he was able to out-throw the enemy, and then, seizing his opportunity, and in spite of his wound, he led a rush, captured the position, and killed the occupants. Throughout the day he continued to lead his men in bombing attacks. On the following day he again displayed courage of the highest order, and although again wounded and unable to throw bombs, he continued to lead his men. His magnificent example of valour, coupled with the skilful handling of the situation, produced far-reaching results . . .

Finally, Adlam was sent down the line to get his wounds attended to, but not before clearing the enemy from a dangerous trench. (See entry for SCHWABEN REDOUBT.)

The fighting over the next few days resulted in the British pushing slowly forward, mainly by using continuous hand-grenade fighting; they managed to reach the SCHWABEN REDOUBT and STUFF REDOUBT to the north-east of Schwaben. The fighting had been bitter and some positions changed hands several times.

In early October, 16th Sherwood Foresters (117th Brigade, 39th Division) had their headquarters in deep dugouts in Thiepval Château; their support company were to the south, in Leipzig Redoubt. At the time, the most serviceable communication trench that they used was St Martin's Lane. To reach the line, after leaving AVELUY WOOD, to the south-west, they passed brigade headquarters, crossed the River Ancre by a narrow bridge called Passerelle de Magenta and made their way to Paisley Dump. The communication trench then ran along the south side of Thiepval Wood and could absorb the main body of a battalion. The area was combed with dugouts. At the time, the front line went underground in parts

The remains of Thiepval Château during the Battle of Thiepval Ridge, 26–28 September 1916. *(IWM Q1328)*

for 30yds or 40yds at a time. The companies lived in them and had periscopes set up at the end of each tunnel. The land on their left flank dropped down to the River Ancre.

For the October attack towards the SCHWABEN REDOUBT, the points of assembly for troops were Wood Post, which was on the main AUTHUILLE road, and also BLIGHTY VALLEY. North Bluff was just behind Thiepval Wood. Around 21 October, 8th South Lancashires (75th Brigade, 25th Division) were in the centre of an attack against REGINA TRENCH and STUFF REDOUBT. Edmund Blunden of 11th Royal Sussex wrote: 'Then we went into trenches round about Thiepval Wood (23rd October) which not long before had been so horrible and mad; but now they had assumed a tenderer aspect, were voted a rest-cure sector . . .' Occasionally heavy shells blocked parts of Inniskilling Avenue, one of the communication trenches, or the waterside path to Mill Post, opposite the old mill at HAMEL. According to Blunden, 'In Paisley Valley, alongside the wood, some tanks were lying veiled with brown nets . . .'

During the next few weeks, the Ancre battle was continually postponed and a week or two passed without much happening except for rain and fog. Blunden reports that they sheltered in what he called 'a bedroom of corridored chalk bank'. Beyond, the area he called St Martin's Lane led forward; 'the Schwaben Redoubt ahead was an almost obliterated cocoon . . . and there were deep dugouts, which faced the German guns . . . The whole zone was a corpse.' Here the British were to hold the line 'for an uncertain sentence of days'.

11th Royal Sussex used tunnels with the names of KOYLI West and Mill Post, which were so small that the men couldn't stand up in them. Between 25 and 27 October, they were back in billets in Pioneer Road. In early November, Col Harrison, Commanding Officer 11th Royal Sussex, had his headquarters at the Thiepval end of St Martin's Lane. The place was deep down and decorated with German drawings that belonged to its former occupants. The old German Front Line on its west slope retained its outline, despite the number of explosions that it had swallowed up, month after month. The Germans had fortified the position with logic and imagination, in that they used steel rails and concrete to the best effect. In front of the head-quarters there were concealed concrete emplace-ments, which had formerly lurked in the weeds and flowers of no man's land. Beneath, their reserve company lived in the prodigious dugouts, which were arranged in two storeys; in the lower storey,

there was a little door in the wall. If one opened it, it led to steadily descending dark galleries and stacked in them were box after box of explosives. In another great dugout there were elaborate surgical appliances and medical supplies. Another was a quartermaster's stores. Blunden mentioned the smell of the dugouts as being peculiar to the German soldier, heavy and clothy.

Blunden also records that on 13 November there was a feat of arms worth recording, in which the enemy were surprised and beaten. From Thiepval Wood, 39th Division sprang forth, passed their old dead, mud-craters and wire and captured the tiny village of SAINT-PIERRE-DIVION with its enormous labyrinth and also 2,000 Germans sheltering in the galleries there.

In *The Old Front Line*, written in 1917, John Masefield noted that but for the stricken Thiepval Wood, the eastern bank of the Ancre was 'a gentle sloping hill, bare of trees . . . It is worthwhile', he added, to 'clamber up to Thiepval from the Allied lines'. The road ran through a deep cutting, which, Masefield says, might once have been lovely. There was nothing left of the trench, a big reddish mound of brick, the château garden or the village pond.

In *The Weary Road*, Charles Douie of 1st Dorsets (14th Brigade, 32nd Division) wrote that the garden of Thiepval Château was a shell trap of the worst description, and in particular in the days that pre-ceded the opening of the battle. Although the right sector of the division facing the Leipzig Redoubt was comparatively quiet, the château trenches, such as the Broomielaw, Trongate, Sauchiehall Street and the Hammerhead and Maison Grise saps were of evil omen. One of these saps ran into no man's land and soldiers who ventured to its far end could hear the conversation of the enemy in an outlying post. Behind the château lay Douie's battalion headquarters at Johnstone Post. It was a position in the narrow, deep valley that lay along the eastern side of Thiepval Wood and was a point at which many trenches met, but apart from these and a few shelters in the bluff along the edge of the Wood was Paisley Avenue, which was a constant mark for the German artillery, and which led to a high bank above the River Ancre. On the Allied side of the Wood, a safer trench called Hamilton Avenue also led to the bank.

According to his biographer Michael Hurd, Ivor Gurney of 2/5th Glosters (184th Brigade, 61st Division) arranged a setting of a poem by F.W. Harvey, a great friend from pre-war days in Gloucestershire, while at CRUCIFIX CORNER in January 1917. It was a 'tender cry of longing for Gloucestershire's fields and rivers'. Harvey himself later became a prisoner of war when captured at Douai in August 1917. His first volume of poetry had been called *A Gloucestershire Lad*. CRUCIFIX CORNER was to the east of Aveluy.

In *An Onlooker in France*, the painter William Orpen asserted that Thiepval Château, previously one of the largest in northern France, was practically flattened, and all that was left of it was a mound with flowers on top. In August 1917, a burial party worked in the Thiepval area; Lt Clark, 'a sturdy little Scot', was in charge of it. During the month or so that they worked there, they dug up, identified and reburied some thousands of bodies. Some of them could not be identified, and what was found on them in the way of money and other valuables was divided up among the burial party. Orpen also mentioned a great colony of Indians being down in the valley of the Ancre, close to Thiepval Mill Road. They were all Catholics, and were headed by an old padre who had worked in India for 45 years. Orpen described him as a 'fine old fellow'. Wonderful open-air services were held each Sunday afternoon on the side of Thiepval Mill. The padre had put up an altar about 30ft high with wonderful draperies behind it. The Indians cleaned up the face of Thiepval in no time at all.

After Thiepval was captured at the end of September 1916, it remained in British hands until 25 March 1918 and was retaken on 24 August by 38th and 17th Divisions. After the Armistice, the village was 'adopted' by Tonbridge.

In *The Wet Flanders Plain*, Henry Williamson mentions that, after the war, the wooden military bridge remained over Mill Causeway. The memorial just outside the Thiepval Memorial grounds, between it and the site of Thiepval Château and Thiepval Wood, was erected to the memory of 18th Division, who captured the village at the end of September 1916. Owing to their flexible ideas on training and their excellent senior officers, they have gained the deserved reputation of being one of the best British divisions who served in the First World War. 18th Division also have another memorial in front of TRÔNES WOOD. 11th Division, whose role to the right of 18th Division on 26 September was vital, had their application for their own memorial rejected. When offered the chance of sharing 18th Division's memorial, 11th Divison's Divisional Association turned the proposal down, as they had no wish to share a memorial with other claimants.

Apart from the Thiepval Memorial, which was not unveiled until 1932, several cemeteries were finished in the area during the 1920s. Mill Road Cemetery is to the east of ULSTER TOWER and was made in 1917 when the battlefield was cleared; most of the casualties are to be found in Plot 1.

Thiepval in ruins. *(Peter F. Batchelor Collection)*

Mill Road itself runs south-east from the rail line at HAMEL village until it joins the more southerly road from SAINT-PIERRE-DIVION to Thiepval village. The cemetery was at one time called Mill Road Cemetery No. 2 and is a little east of the junction of the two roads, midway between Thiepval village and SAINT-PIERRE-DIVION. After the Armistice, it was enlarged by the concentration of 1,038 graves from smaller cemeteries and from the battlefields of BEAUMONT-HAMEL and Thiepval. The register records details of 1,301 war graves. After 1951 some of the graves here had to be laid flat because of the subsidence of the SCHWABEN REDOUBT tunnels, which are directly underneath. The cemetery stands on high ground and has commanding views of the Ancre battlefield.

Connaught Cemetery, standing on high ground overlooking the ANCRE VALLEY, is roughly between ULSTER TOWER and Mill Road; it was begun in the early autumn of 1916. At the Armistice, it contained 228 graves, which were mainly in Plot I. It was then very greatly increased by the concentration of graves from at least 10 named smaller cemeteries and the battlefield that surrounded it, the great majority being of men of 36th Division and also of those who fought in the summer and autumn of 1916. The cemetery contains the graves of 1,278 soldiers and Marines of 63rd Division. A memorial erected in the cemetery to the men of 1/5th West Yorkshires who fell on 28 September at the SCHWABEN REDOUBT was later moved to the battalion's drill hall at York. A new white Cross was installed here in May 2006 to the Memory of the Men of Derry by the City Project and Somme Association.

Three important cemeteries were incorporated in Connaught Cemetery. Thiepval Village Cemetery had been on the ridge summit to the west of the GRAND-COURT road and contained 215 British graves; Thiepval Valley Cemetery, on the south-east side of Thiepval Wood, contained 11 British graves; and Quarry Palace Cemetery, close to the river and a little north-east of the hamlet of SAINT-PIERRE-DIVION, contained 23 British graves. Others that were 'gathered in' included Saint-Pierre-Divion Cemetery No. 1, a little south-east of the hamlet, which contained 10 British graves from November 1916; Divion Road Cemetery No. 2, which almost adjoined SAINT-PIERRE-DIVION and contained 60 graves from July to September 1916; Small Connaught Cemetery, opposite Connaught Cemetery, which contained 41 graves, mainly from 1 July 1916; Battery Valley Cemetery, ½ mile south-west of GRANDCOURT, with 56 British graves; Paisley Hillside Cemetery, on the south side of Thiepval Wood alongside Paisley Avenue Cemetery and named from the same trench, which contained 32 British graves, mainly of 49th Division, from July and August 1916; Gordon Castle Cemetery, just inside the south border of Thiepval Wood, with 33 British graves; and Bluff Cemetery, ½ mile north of AUTHUILLE village, with 43 British graves from July and September 1916. The remains of Sgt D.H. Blakey of the Royal Inniskilling Fusiliers were reburied in Connaught Cemetery on 8 October 2015. He died on 1 July 1916 and his bones were found during a road-widening scheme close to the Ulster Tower on 21 November 2013.

To add a postscript to Thiepval, Douie was for a time in trenches at the south-east corner of the Wood and used to look up the slope towards the village and the former gardens of Thiepval Château. That same slope is now bare farmland. A circular drive went from the château down the slope, but the drive and the paths around the garden disappeared, either during or after the First World War. The entrance to the château was where the entrance to the memorial is today. The car park is on the ground where the carriages used to turn.

In *We'll Shift Our Ground*, published in 1933, Blunden's character Duncan has the following conversation with a Frenchman:

But I am really more interested in the ground than in these new buildings of yours – I suppose there's not a dugout or anything left now? How about Koyli tunnels, or Mills Post, or St Martins Lane up there? . . . meanwhile he was looking down from the old enemy position into the margins of Thiepval Wood, a vast coppice now, and could not detect through the verdant tangle the cliff banks in which he had once slept through midnight's thunderings over his table loaded with telegram forms and typed orders and mugs and maps, grenades and steel hats . . . He turned north leaving St Martins Lane alone . . . the road ran past the edge of the wood, whence the old Armies . . . had come forward to be mauled and murdered by the machine guns. A cemetery in all its simplicity . . . now lay near their places of assembly.

Probably because of the almost total devastation of the Thiepval area, work on the clearing and rebuilding of the village did not begin until at least a decade after the war was over. During the Great Pilgrimage of 1928, when the mayor of Thiepval was asked when the village would be rebuilt, he simply replied 'pouf'. The area was still as it had been at the end of the war, whereas much of the ground around POZIÈRES and the high ground around MARTINPUICH had already been redeemed. One of the reasons for concentrating on restoring the POZIÈRES landscape may have been because there were quite a lot of French farmers who were joint owners of the land.

The story of how the design and building of the Thiepval Memorial came about is quite a complex one, and begins with the French Beaux-Arts Commission, which rejected Lutyens' original SAINT-QUENTIN design in July 1926. It was to be a memorial to the Missing of the Somme and one of the Beaux-Arts Commission's reasons was that the intended height of the structure, 55 metres, was considered 'unreasonably obtrusive'. After this rejection, Fabian Ware of the Imperial War Graves Commission sent Lutyens to France in August 1926 and arranged for the British architect to have a meeting with the French director of works at Thiepval. The hope was that the basic principles of the arch memorial designed for SAINT-QUENTIN could still be used, but at a site where the height of the finished building would not be a problem. The site in mind was the bare ridge at Thiepval. There was some urgency, as the option to buy the necessary land would soon lapse.

The two men duly had a site meeting on 11 October, and, despite language difficulties, seemed to have reached an agreement; they agreed to meet again at the site in November, and soon after the project was given the go-ahead, although not rubber-stamped until 14 April 1929. It was not felt by the Imperial War Graves Commission that Lutyens needed a new contract, as the designs for SAINT-QUENTIN and Thiepval were similar; only the site was different. The purpose of the memorial was now to commemorate the Missing in the Somme area from June 1915, when it was in the hands of Third Army, through 1916 and 1917 to March 1918. The Missing from the Fifth Army Retreat of spring 1918 were to be commemorated at POZIÈRES in a design by Sir Herbert Baker, while those who fell in the Advance to Victory in 1918 were to be remembered on the memorial at Vis-en-Artois.

The unveiling of the Thiepval Memorial had been set for 16 May 1932, but, owing to the assassination of the French president, the unveiling was put back to 1 August. The ceremony was performed by HRH the Prince of Wales, president of the Imperial War Graves Commission, and the new French President, M. Lebrun, was the chief guest, alongside many other dignitaries. The Prince arrived at 1500hrs and was received by Sir Fabian Ware of the Imperial War Graves Commission and the British representatives. In turn, the Prince welcomed the President, together with some of his ministers. The two men then inspected the French guard of honour and took up their positions with the chief guests on a tribune set up on the lawn at the foot of the Memorial.

After a short service of prayers and hymns, the Prince stepped to the rostrum and spoke not only to the official guests and families of the fallen but also to wireless. After he had spoken, he pressed a button on the rostrum and the French and British flags fell from the tablets. The French President then replied on behalf of the French nation to the welcome and remarks of the Prince. The dedication of the memorial and its benediction were then pronounced, followed by the wail of pipes. Then three buglers from the Durham Light Infantry appeared before the Stone of Remembrance and sounded the Reveille. As they did so, the Union Jack and French Tricolor broke from the two flagstaffs on the summit of the memorial.

After that, ashes from wooden crosses planted at Westminster Abbey on Armistice Day were scattered over the graves in the new Anglo-French cemetery nearby. After inspecting the graves, the Prince and the President laid wreaths at the Stone of Remembrance. The cemetery, also designed by Sir Edwin Lutyens, symbolically contains the graves of 300 men each from France and the Commonwealth. The bodies, a vast number of unknowns, were found between December 1931 and March 1932 and came from as far as Loos to the north and le Quesnel to the south. However, the majority came from the Somme battlefield of July–November 1916. The ceremony ended with the Last Post ringing out from among the pillars, and the Prince left for Arras, from where he flew back to his private landing-ground at Sunningdale.

The Somme Memorial to the Missing, near the south boundary of the former park of Thiepval Château, is certainly the most important memorial in France designed by Lutyens; geometrically, it was a brilliant exercise, being designed in a stepped pyramidal form and made up of a series of intersecting arches. On the walls of the 16 piers are the names of 73,357 men who fell in the original Third Army area from 1915 to March 1918, whose graves at that time were unknown. Since 1932, many more sets of remains have been found and many of these have in turn been identified before reburial. Lutyens himself hoped that his design would convey a sense of 'the eternally tragic'.

According to Capt H.A. Taylor of the Royal Fusiliers in his book *Goodbye to the Battlefields*, when the foundations for the memorial were being excavated – which, as it was to stand 140ft, had to be substantial – the workmen struck tunnels and dugouts which were once part of the former German Second Line. After the tunnels had been found, digging was continued to a depth of 10ft and then a 'raft' of 12,000 tons of concrete was laid, 9ft 7in thick.

It would appear that the original intention was for visitors to be able to use a viewing platform, which could be reached from within the memorial itself. During clearance of the site carried out prior to the building of the Thiepval Memorial, the remains of six Germans were found, as well as a 15in shell.

There are, of course, many famous Somme names commemorated on the panels of the memorial. These include seven Victoria Cross holders: Capt E.N.F. Bell of 9th Royal Inniskilling Fusiliers; Pte W. Buckingham of 2nd Leicesters; Lt G.S. Cather of 9th Royal Irish Rifles; Pte W. McFadzean of 14th Royal Irish Rifles; Rfmn W. Mariner of 2nd King's Royal Rifle Corps; Lt T.O. Wilkinson of 7th Loyal North Lancashires; and Sgt Maj A. Young, who won his VC in the Boer War. Other names include George Butterworth of 13th Durham Light Infantry, a promising composer who died in MUNSTER ALLEY; T.S. Kettle, the poet; Lt D.W.A. Hankey of 1st Royal Warwicks, who wrote *A Student in Arms*; H.H. Munro of 22nd Royal Fusiliers, better known as the writer Saki, killed in the fighting for BEAUMONT-HAMEL in November 1916; Wyn Griffith's brother Pte W.E.O. Griffith of 17th Royal Welsh Fusiliers, killed in the attacks against MAMETZ WOOD; and 2/Lt C. Rowley, a son of the 3rd Baronet Rowley, attached to 1st Lancashire Fusiliers (86th Brigade, 39th Division), who was killed in action on 10 July 1916. Also remembered are the 539 men who died prior to 1 July 1916 in the previous 11 months.

At least 11 lieutenant-colonels who died during the Somme battle are also commemorated on the panels. Lt Col E. Benson of 9th King's Royal Rifle Corps (42nd Brigade, 14th Division) was killed in action at battalion headquarters on 15 September 1916. Lt Col H.T. Cotton of 2nd South Lancashires (75th Brigade, 25th Division) was killed in action when taking part in an attack against Thiepval on 3 September 1916. His battalion were involved in the struggle for WONDERWORK, Leipzig Redoubt and Hindenburg Trench. 2nd South Lancashires were in front with 1st Wiltshires and 3rd Worcesters (both 7th Brigade, 25th Division), while 8th South Lancashires were in support of 1st Wiltshires (75th Brigade, 25th Division). The machine-gun fire was deadly and Cotton was found to be missing; his body was never recovered. Lt Col A.P.A. Elphinstone, Commanding Officer 22nd Northumberland Fusiliers (102nd Brigade, 34th Division), was killed in action on 1 July 1916 (see LA BOISSELLE entry).

Lt Col C. Goff, Commanding Officer 1st King's (6th Brigade, 2nd Division), was killed in action on 8 August 1916. According to *The Story of the King's Regiment*,

On the left of the 55th Division the 2nd Division attacked with the 1st King's on the right. This battalion of the regiment was therefore advancing in line with the 8th. The objective given to the 1st Bn just north of Guillemont, and the road from the village of Longeuval, which lay some little way beyond the station. To reach these objectives, the German front line trenches had first to be captured.

The 1st Bn advanced on a three company front and quickly over-ran the enemy forward positions. The three companies then moved onto their final objectives . . . The fourth company of the battalion moved forward in rear of the advance for the purpose of mopping up the enemy front line. But that company was surprised to meet with resistance as it advanced. It soon found that the trenches, over-run by the leading companies, were being rapidly re-occupied by the enemy. Lieut-Colonel Goff, the commanding officer, went forward to clear up the situation, but was himself killed. The fourth company was not able to make any further progress. As for the three leading companies, they were not seen again. Guillemont had claimed another victim.

Lt Col G.S. Guyon of 2nd Royal Fusiliers (86th Brigade, 29th Division) was killed in action on 1 July 1916. According to the main history of the Royal Fusiliers, Guyon was in command of 16th West Yorkshires (93rd Brigade, 31st Division) when killed: 'The total casualties for the day amounted to 490, including 20 officers, three of them killed. This was in addition to the eight officers who became casualties during the preliminary bombardment. Lieut-Col G.S. Guyon was killed while gallantly leading the 16th Bn West Yorkshires.'

Lt Col L.A. Hind of 1/7th Sherwood Foresters (139th Brigade, 46th Division) was killed in action on 1 July 1916. According to *The Robin Hoods*, the battalion history, at 0727hrs,

there was a smoke screen discharged and at 7.30am the first wave moved out of the newly advance trench, and the second wave out of the original front line. Immediately the German artillery and machine gun barrage opened up and practically annihilated the 3rd and 4th waves. A few men reached the German front line. In the early stage of the battle the C/O was killed, Lt Col L.A. Hind, as well as the adjutant, Capt. R.M. Gotch. When the smoke barrage cleared the men were exposed to full view of the German machine guns.

Lt Col E. Innes of 1/8th Royal Warwicks (143rd Brigade, 48th Division) was killed in action on 1 July 1916. His battalion took part in an attack on the German trench system north of BEAUMONT-HAMEL known as the Quadrilateral on 1 July.

Lt Col M. Kennard of 18th West Yorkshires (93rd Brigade, 31st Division) was killed in action on 1 July 1916. According to Ralph N. Hudson's *The Bradford Pals*, 'Standing calm and erect amid the crack and whine of bullets and carrying only a walking stick he called out "come on boys, up you get", turned and began to walk at an easy gait towards the enemy. The Battalion rose to their feet and followed him.' Kennard was then killed by a shell that exploded close to him.

Lt Col J. Mignon of 8th Leicesters (110th Brigade, 37th Division) was killed in action on 15 July 1916 during an enemy counter-attack up Aston and Villa Trenches.

Lt Col S.J. Wilkinson, Commanding Officer 10th South Wales Borderers (115th Brigade, 38th Division), was killed in action on 7 July 1916. The battalion history notes: 'Not until the Division moved to the Somme were the 10th or 11th Bns called upon to go over the top.' The 7 July attack on MAMETZ WOOD, which developed into a 5-day struggle in the confusing intricacies of a thick wood, was their first severe trial. It was a task that might have taxed more experienced troops and it was no small feat to have accomplished what they did, despite stubborn opposition, and difficulties with communications and obtaining artillery support.

Lt Col D. Wood, Commanding Officer 1st Rifle Brigade (11th Brigade, 4th Division), was killed in action on 1 July 1916 to the north of BEAUMONT-HAMEL. On 1 July, 1st Rifle Brigade suffered 23 officer casualties and over 400 casualties of other ranks.

Apart from at least 11 lieutenant-colonels being commemorated here, there are several men who were 'shot at dawn' during the second half of 1916. Pte P. Cairnie of 1st Royal Scots Fusiliers (8th Brigade, 3rd Division) was executed for desertion on 28 December 1916. Pte H. Farr of 1st West Yorkshires (18th Brigade, 6th Division) was executed for cowardice at CARNOY at 0645hrs on 18 October 1916. Pte C.W. Skilton of 22nd Royal Fusiliers (99th Brigade, 2nd Division) was executed for desertion on 26 December 1916.

In August 1933, Vera Brittain visited Thiepval and noted that it was the only village in France not yet rebuilt, although work on the restoration of the church had just begun. Of the Thiepval Memorial itself, Brittain wrote: 'And I thought what a cheating and a camouflage it all is, this combined effort of man and nature to give once more the impression that war is noble and glorious, just because its aftermath can be given an appearance of dignity and beauty after fifteen years. I never had before so clear an impression of the scene of Edward's Battle on July 1st . . .' 2/Lt E.H. Brittain of 11th Sherwood Foresters (70th Brigade, 8th Division), Vera's brother, was badly wounded in the fighting before MOUQUET FARM and was awarded the Military Cross. Vera Brittain also wrote: 'The caretakers of these memorials must live a very strange, isolated life, in dug outs, shelters and log-cabins . . .'

A special 40th anniversary ceremony was held here on 1 July 1956; with each decade, the attendance at this annual ceremony has increased. It appears that problems first identified in the mid-1950s with the Thiepval Memorial were becoming increasingly serious. It has to be remembered that for 5 years, during the Second World War, it was not possible to supervise the structure adequately. Damp, water penetration and deterioration were getting worse, and by 1962 it was felt that a new approach to the problems was required. Whatever the expense, it was felt that it would be justified, if only because of the symbolic significance of the memorial. However, in the 1960s it was not known just how long it would take to solve the problems and one suggestion would take 12 years to carry out. The main problem was that the type of bricks chosen by Lutyens, being brittle and liable to erosion, did not take kindly to the exposed nature of the site, open to all weathers on its hilltop position. The Pozières Memorial was suffering some of the same problems of damp penetration. The problems were not only with the structure, but also with the name panels. In recent years, with the help of computer engraving, many of the names have been successfully replaced.

In 1968 the French authorities decided to commemorate the 1918 Armistice; on 10 November torches were lit at the Arc de Triomphe in Paris by the Ministre des Anciens Combattants et Victimes de Guerre and were transported with armoured car escort to certain symbolic places, including the memorial at Thiepval.

On 1 July 1976, the 60th anniversary of the start of the Battle of the Somme, the ceremonies were attended by members of the Argyll & Sutherland Highlanders, as well as a band of the Royal Irish Rangers and the French 51st Infantry Regiment, who were in the forecourt. Veterans were present, as well as many young soldiers. In 1979, the 12-year project commissioned by the Commonwealth War Graves Commission was finally completed.

In July 2003, Thiepval Wood was purchased by the Somme Association, with the help of a £400,000 grant from the British government, and it was felt that Thiepval Wood, which meant so much to the people of Ulster, would now have a secure future. The aim of the Somme Association is to keep the Wood as a memorial to the fallen.

It is possible that the remains of Pte W. McFadzean VC are still in the Wood to this day, although his nephew, another Billy, thought they might well be in Connaught Cemetery. There is no proof either way.

In the late 1990s, Thiepval was being visited by more than 200,000 people a year; as noted by pilgrims to the area between the wars, there was not even a lavatory to cater for their needs. In addition, it was thought that there was a lack of information about what happened here during the war. To remedy this situation, a charity called the Thiepval Project was set up by Sir Frank Sanderson, a former insurance broker, which sought to remedy these problems by creating a visitors' centre. Enthusiastically taken up by fundraisers, the scheme became a joint project between the French and the Royal British Legion.

The problem of lavatories and lack of information was not a new one; in 1937 Mr L. Fraser Miller, an ex-soldier, had written to the Imperial War Graves Commission about his recent visit to Thiepval. Apart from stating that the site was in a poor state and that the gardens were neglected, he mentioned the lack of lavatories or guidebooks. To cap it all, he complained about another ex-soldier who lived in a wooden bungalow nearby and served bad beer.

It has to be said that not everyone was happy with the idea of a visitors' centre and that it could be argued that there were enough museums in the area already. Possibly the building would not blend in with the landscape and would detract from Lutyens' design and, most importantly, from the feeling of repose that visitors to the memorial should surely feel.

In early October 2004, Sir Frank Sanderson's vision became a reality with the opening of the visitors' centre. Although it is sited very close to the Thiepval Memorial, it does not intrude, as it is sunk into the ground, thus preserving the sight lines of the memorial. The doors of the centre were opened for the first time by two children whose great uncles had died on the Somme during the war. The building, avowedly educational in intent, provides facilities, including lavatories and information, for visitors to Thiepval and the Somme area. A service of dedication was held at Thiepval Memorial; 1,000 visitors attended, including HRH the Duke of Kent. A memorial plaque, paid for by the Belgian Government, to the memory of Lt. Gen. Sir Adrian Carton de Wiart was unveiled on 2 July 2006 on the outside of Thiepval Church. In 2014 BBC's *Antiques Roadshow* broadcast two programmes from the Thiepval memorial.

The Thiepval memorial is being restored in the period 2015–16 and on 20 June 2015 the first stone for an extension to Thiepval visitors' centre was laid.

THIÈVRES is on the D1 road, south-west of PAS-EN-ARTOIS. The village was one of the first in the Somme to receive British troops, when 4th Division's artillery were bivouacked in the Thièvres–SARTON area on 20 July 1915. On 24 July, No. 9 Field Company, Royal Engineers (4th Division) camped here, in 'a marshy field amongst trees at the bottom of a hill'; they were later shown around the French first and second lines. In early October 1916, a battalion from 51st Division were billeted in the village.

TOUTENCOURT is on the D23 road, west of HARPONVILLE and north of CONTAY. Its chief association is as the headquarters of Lt Gen Sir Hubert Gough, General Officer Commanding Reserve (later Fifth) Army. In early October 1915, units from 36th Division were billeted here, returning a month later and again in early February 1916. On 4 March, X Corps had their headquarters here, and a few days later men from 36th Division were back here again. Lt Gen Sir Henry Rawlinson, General Officer Commanding Fourth Army, visited the village on 7 April.

At the end of June, troops of 49th and 25th Divisions were billeted in barns at Toutencourt; 17th Division had their headquarters here on 30 June. From 29 June to 1 July, 115th Brigade (38th Division) were here when 38th Division were in the area. On 30 July, 20th King's Royal Rifle Corps (pioneers of 3rd Division) arrived here and camped under canvas under 'great trees close to a small stream'. On 11 August, 52nd Division were in the area, and 19th Division likewise in the third week of October.

During November, Gough had his headquarters at a farm at one end of the village and wrote: 'I gazed out of the poky little window looking on the dull and dirty courtyard and considered what my decision should be, i.e. the November battle.' A possible candidate for the building he described is in the rue de Contay.

Toutencourt Communal Cemetery, to the north of the village on the PUCHEVILLERS road, has the graves of 23 British casualties; these include 2 from the period before the battle, one of whom was Driver W. Baker (I.B.3), Royal Field Artillery, who served with 4th Division and died on 27 October 1915. His grave has a special memorial, which was paid for by his comrades.

TREUX is south of BUIRE-SUR-L'ANCRE on the D120 road; the AMIENS–ALBERT railway passes through it. From April to November 1916, it was continuously used as divisional headquarters by the Guards, 2nd, 3rd, 5th, 6th, 7th, 8th, 17th, 20th, 29th, 38th and 55th Divisions. The village remained in Allied hands until the last stages of the German offensive in April 1918.

TRÔNES WOOD, which is best described as having the shape of a pear, is adjacent to BERNAFAY WOOD, north of the D64 road to GUILLEMONT. In the period early to mid-July 1916, the Wood was desperately fought for by both sides in the Somme battle.

In *Sir Douglas Haig's Great Push*, there is a good description of the Wood on 8 July, when the Somme fighting was mainly taking place on the Allies' extreme right flank, where Trônes Wood, some 1,400yds long from north to south with a southern frontage of 400yds, was the objective. The Wood was in a position of considerable strategic importance, since it was only 2 miles from the German station at COMBLES, one of the enemy's most important nerve centres in the region, with roads that branched from it, whereby PÉRONNE could be threatened from the north. The enemy recognised this only too well and protected the Wood by very strong trenches, a perfect network of wire entanglements and a small arsenal of machine guns.

The problem for any attackers was not so much to capture Trônes Wood, but to hold on to it when they had. As it was commanded by artillery from both armies, it was to become a death trap for the infantry of both sides. The centre of Trônes Wood was cut by the MONTAUBAN-DE-PICARDIE–GUILLEMONT railway and lay in a dip across the head of CATERPILLAR VALLEY. The Wood itself was a dense thicket and it had not been cut for 2 years, making it very difficult to force a way through. Trônes Alley, a German communication trench, ran roughly along the top edge of the Montauban Ridge between Trônes and BERNAFAY WOODS.

An Allied attack was planned for 7 July, when French troops on the right flank were to assist; however, it was subsequently postponed to 0800hrs on 8 July. The Allies were to take the southern end of Trônes Wood and Maltz Horn Trench as far as MALTZ HORN FARM, while on the right flank the French were to take the remainder of the Maltz Horn Trench and the general line from the Farm to HARDECOURT-AU-BOIS village. In *Field Guns in France*, Lt Col N. Fraser-Tytler of CL Brigade, Royal Field Artillery (30th Division), noted that his guns began at 0720hrs on 8 July and went on firing until 1530hrs the following day.

Moving through BERNAFAY WOOD, 2nd Yorkshires (21st Brigade, 30th Division) deployed on the

Railway in Trônes Wood, 1916. *(IWM Q17490)*

eastern edge facing Trônes Wood, although a machine gun from the south-west corner caused heavy loss. The French, however, had taken HARDECOURT-AU-BOIS knoll and a section of Maltz Horn Trench, leaving their left flank exposed. At 1300hrs, 2nd Wiltshires (also 21st Brigade, 30th Division) were detailed to attack; thanks to an accurate bombardment, the enemy were driven out of the trench and the Wood was entered with only a few casualties. A counter-attack from the north was repelled.

Maltz Horn Trench was on the forward slope of the HARDECOURT-AU-BOIS knoll and the enemy spent some time digging a fresh line about 300yds beyond, in the hard chalk on the reverse slope. In the small hours, 2nd Royal Scots Fusiliers (90th Brigade, 30th Division) occupied MALTZ HORN FARM, which lay between the two lines; 18th Manchesters (also 90th Brigade, 30th Division) reinforced 2nd Wiltshires on the southern edge of Trônes Wood and 17th Manchesters (also 90th Brigade, 30th Division) were able to enter the Wood without loss. When captured, the central trench in the Wood was found to be connected up to three battery positions.

However, the Wood remained in Allied hands for only a few hours. On the eastern edge of the Wood, 17th Manchesters were being badly shelled and signalled for help, but the range was too great for the British artillery to be effective. They therefore had no alternative but to withdraw, which they did along Trônes Alley westwards to BERNAFAY WOOD. This left 18th Manchesters in a vulnerable position and they withdrew to the Brickworks at MONTAUBAN-DE-PICARDIE; 2nd Royal Scots Fusiliers did, however, manage to hang on to Maltz Horn Trench. 16th Manchesters (90th Brigade, 30th Division) had sent in parties to assist their sister battalion, 17th Manchesters, but they too had to retire.

At 1430hrs on 9 July, 90th Brigade ordered 16th Manchesters to attack – and to hold on to – the southern edge of Trônes Wood. They formed up on the sunken part of the MONTAUBAN-DE-PICARDIE Brickworks–HARDECOURT-AU-BOIS road, south of the Wood. This time, the enemy were caught out, expecting an attack on the western side of the Wood, and 17th Manchesters were able to reach the southern edge of the Wood. However, with the presence of German snipers in the trees and of German bombers, 17th Manchesters found that they had to dig a fresh line, about 60yds from the south-west edge and parallel to the Wood, and were ordered to prepare for an advance through the Wood on 10 July, assisted by 4th South African Infantry (South African Brigade, 9th Division). When it was practicable, small parties attempted to go through

the Wood, but the thick undergrowth prevented the patrols from seeing very far either to left or right.

At around 0300hrs on 19 July, the British began a bombardment; the infantry managed to enter the Wood from both ends and this made the centre untenable for the enemy, who were forced to withdraw to large shell craters about 200yds to the east of Trônes Wood, north of the GUILLEMONT road. However, the Wood was not really in British hands at all and small parties of Germans had hung on at various parts of the Wood to the south and especially to the centre. Replacing 90th Brigade, 89th Brigade (also 30th Division) endeavoured to secure the Wood; a company of 17th King's (89th Brigade, 39th Division) made an unsuccessful attack from BERNAFAY WOOD, which was repulsed.

On the night of 10/11 July, there were no British troops in the Wood at all; small German posts held the edge but the main body of enemy troops was along Central Trench, in the centre. At 0100hrs on 11 July, 20th King's and 2nd Bedfords (both also 89th Brigade, 30th Division) formed up along the sunken road immediately east of the Brickworks. After a heavy bombardment at 0327hrs, the advance began. While 20th King's were to attack the part of the Wood to the south of Trônes Alley and then relieve 2nd Royal Scots Fusiliers in Maltz Horn Trench, 2nd Bedfords on their left were to attack between Trônes Alley and the railway and push on to the eastern edge of the Wood.

Machine-gun fire from the Trônes Alley block forced the attackers southwards, but the Wood was entered. The fighting continued for some time during the day, until 2nd Bedfords were pushed back to BERNAFAY WOOD. The Wood was once again in German hands, except for a wedge on the western side, which was occupied by a small party of 2nd Bedfords.

Orders for a fresh German attack were found on a captured German officer; this led to the British bringing down a barrage between the Wood and GUILLEMONT, and the ground to the east of GUILLEMONT was also kept under artillery fire. At 2230hrs on 11 July, 17th King's set off for a renewed attempt on the Wood, advancing from the sunken road to the east of MONTAUBAN-DE-PICARDIE Brickworks. They were fortunate, as the enemy had been carrying out a relief in the Wood, that had been held up; this delay coincided with 17th King's attack and they were able to enter the Wood unopposed. At 0100hrs, the relieving Germans were surprised to find 17th King's in the Wood and were forced back.

On 12 July, a new line was dug to connect 17th King's line with 2nd Bedfords' in the western side of the Wood. A fresh attempt by the enemy to advance on Maltz Horn Trench and Trônes Wood from an easterly direction was discovered early enough for it to be checked by the combined fire of the British and French artillery. The Germans were forced to return to their second-line trench.

After nearly 4 days, 90th and 89th Brigades were finally relieved by 18th Division, and 90th Brigade were withdrawn to Celestins Wood, while their German counterparts, Infanterie-Regiment (16. Sächsische) Nr. 182, returned to a sheltered valley between MORVAL and GINCHY. In the period from 8 to 12 July, 30th Division sustained casualties which totalled 1,934, including 250 killed, 1,272 wounded and 412 missing.

It was now planned that Fourth Army's offensive against the German second position would be carried out at 0320hrs on 14 July; the capture of Trônes Wood was vital to the success of this advance. If successful, it would secure the right flank of the attack against LONGUEVAL, and allow British guns to move forward on the northern slope of CATERPILLAR VALLEY and support the main thrust against the German defences. Lt Gen Sir Henry Rawlinson, General Officer Commanding Fourth Army, thus wanted the Wood taken at all costs by midnight on 13/14 July.

In the evening of 12 July, 18th Division arrived and 55th Brigade (18th Division) took over the front-line trenches; 7th Buffs went to Maltz Horn Trench and 7th Royal West Kents deployed to the south of Trônes Wood, while 7th Queen's and 8th East Surreys were in support. 7th Buffs were not only to hold on to Maltz Horn Trench, but also to capture the German strongpoint on the GUILLE-MONT road; 7th Royal West Kents were to push on through the Wood or that part of it south of the railway; and 7th Queen's were to attack the north part of the Wood from the direction of Longueval Alley. The plan then was for the eastern side of the Wood, facing GUILLEMONT, to be consolidated.

The attack began at 1900hrs on 13 July; 7th Royal West Kents suffered heavily, even in going across the sunken road to Trônes Wood, mainly from artillery fire. Nevertheless, those men left managed to enter the Wood and move past the recently dug King's Liverpool–Bedford Trench line, but were soon checked by Germans positioned in the centre of the Wood around the southern part of Central Trench. Two companies did manage to get as far as the railway line but lost contact with their colleagues. The headquarters of 7th Royal West Kents at this time was the Brickworks at MONTAUBAN-DE-PICARDIE.

The Germans continued to hold on to their strongpoint on the GUILLEMONT road and 7th Buffs were unable to capture it. 7th Queen's attack was met by machine-gun and rifle fire from the north-west side of Trônes Wood and most of the attack was checked before it even reached the Wood. From the British point of view, the situation was very unsatisfactory and the attack on the Second Line was in jeopardy. It was therefore decided that 54th Brigade should replace 55th Brigade immediately; it was hoped that they would have greater success and gain the Wood, allowing the main attack to be carried out. The plan was now to approach from the south and sweep straight through to the north, and to then establish a defensive flank along the eastern edge of the Wood, facing GUILLEMONT.

After 6th Northamptons and 12th Middlesex (both 54th Brigade, 18th Division) gathered in the sunken road to the south of Trônes Wood, 6th Northamptons reached the edge of the Wood, despite suffering from shell and rifle fire. They then rushed the end of Central Trench and overcame the Germans in that position. Lt Col F.A. Maxwell, Commanding Officer 12th Middlesex, then took command and formed defensive lines drawn from the various units, as well as from the parties of 7th Royal West Kents, who had been in the Wood all night. This line was then advanced; in its path, it drove the remaining Germans out of the Wood to the east and north of the railway. They then made for GUILLEMONT. By 0900hrs, the northern part of the Wood was reached and the remainder was at last clear of the enemy.

During this successful attack, Sgt W.E. Boulter of 6th Northamptons gained the Victoria Cross, the first member of his unit to do so:

When one company and part of another were held up in the attack on a wood by a hostile machine gun, which was causing heavy casualties, Sergt. Boulter, with utter contempt of danger, and in spite of being severely wounded in the shoulder, advanced alone over the open in front of the gun, and bombed the gun team from their position. This very gallant act not only saved many casualties, but was of great military value, as it materially expedited the operation of clearing the enemy out of the wood, and thus covering the flank of the whole attacking force . . .

The enemy made no attempt to retake Trônes Wood, but instead subjected it to incessant shelling by heavy guns. 53rd Brigade (18th Division) moved up to support 54th Brigade until the troops of 18th

Division were relieved at 0330hrs on 17 July. It would be interesting to know whether Maxwell succeeded where others failed by the force of his command, or whether it was simply a case of the enemy being finally worn down by the whole terrible business of the continuous taking of the Wood and then losing it. One wonders whether, by now, they had prepared to withdraw anyway.

Maxwell's action in arranging the attack from the various units is well-documented. In his own view of the action, Maxwell described the organising of the scattered bodies in order to make a drive through Trônes Wood. He had about five officers all told, as the others were out of action. He said that the advance through the Wood began very slowly and that the men were very shaken and jumpy because of the clamour and continuous shell-fire and the problems of going forward through the debris of the previous fighting and the fallen trees. Instead of organising the attack and controlling it with the use of runners, he found that it would only succeed if he led from the front and steadied the men. There was a tendency to go forward in a single file behind him, but he made the line spread out; the men had fixed bayonets, and he encouraged them by ordering them to also fire ahead, which gave them confidence. After dealing with the Germans in the centre of the Wood, the extended line continued on, slowly driving out the Germans like beaters in a pheasant shoot. When they had got to the north of the Wood they did not show themselves, for fear of reprisals from the German artillery.

Between 8 and 14 July, Trônes Wood had changed hands several times and the terribleness of the conditions in the Wood cannot be over-emphasised. They were to remain unspeakable for several weeks. In an interview recorded with the Imperial War Museum, L.J. Ounsworth, a corporal signaller in the Somme battle, said that on or around 17 July his unit visited Trônes Wood. At that time there were no trees intact at all, just stumps of a low height, with tree tops all mixed up with them, as was barbed wire. There were dead bodies from both sides all over the place. He saw a concrete emplacement, from which the Germans would have observed. The ground was completely open, and even sticking up a flag brought immediate retaliation from the German artillery, 'so we got out of that', as Ounsworth says in his interview.

It was during this period that Bernard Montgomery (104th Brigade, 35th Division) of Second World War fame wrote home, reporting on 20 July that they were ordered to take part in a suicidal attack, and that on 23 July, they were holding the front line to the east

of Trônes Wood. Facing them was Guillemont Farm, with WATERLÔT FARM to their left. MALTZ HORN FARM, he wrote, was in no man's land. On 27 July, he wrote home again, saying that they had had a hellish time and that on the morning of 26 July he had gone up to Trônes Wood to extricate one of their battalions, who had had a particularly bad time. On 31 July, 104th Brigade were withdrawn, decimated and exhausted, to HAPPY VALLEY. In early August a concrete pillbox just south of the empty sunken road from Trônes Wood to GUILLEMONT caused many casualties.

In mid-August, Capt F.C. Hitchcock's 2nd Leinsters (73rd Brigade, 24th Division) were still employed in digging a communication trench, called Leinster Avenue, that ran through Trônes Wood. His battalion were situated in the ruins of the northern side of CARNOY, where they managed to get cover in the cellars. On 28 August, 21st Manchesters (91st Brigade, 7th Division) were established in a line between Trônes Wood and DELVILLE WOOD, when battalion headquarters was in the quarry at the north end of BERNAFAY WOOD. On 31 August they moved to Pommiers Trench and battalion headquarters was then in a position to the north of Trônes Wood.

In the evening of 15 September, 9th Norfolks (71st Brigade, 6th Division) moved back to trenches close to Trônes Wood after being involved in 'an unfortunate action', according to the regimental history. In the latter half of September, Max Plowman of 10th West Yorkshires (50th Brigade, 17th Division) noted that his unit were halted one day at midday on sloping ground above Trônes Wood, waiting while the cooks at their field kitchens did their best in the drizzling rain to make a hot stew. On this slope a number of tarpaulins had been stretched over the ground tentwise in order to provide low shelters, and into these the men scrambled to get out of the wet. Others went off to explore the dugouts in Trônes Wood below them. They later returned and recounted the horrors that they had seen in the Wood. At dusk they marched away from the gruesome place through GUILLEMONT and GINCHY.

Geoffrey Malins, the official War Office photographer, wrote that around 25 September he made his way towards Trônes Wood, on the outskirts of which the Guards Division had a dressing station. Many casualties were there, lying about on stretchers in all directions, waiting to be taken to casualty clearing stations. On 26 September, H.L.N. Dundas of 1st Scots Guards (2nd Guards Brigade, Guards Division) reported that he was still in Trônes Wood and that his line was behind the front on the forward slope of the FLERS road. Capt E.P. Dark, a medical officer with 9th Field Ambulance (Guards Division), worked at the same Guards dressing station just in front of the Wood, which he described as being 'full of shattered trees and rotting men, when the wind was in the wrong direction it brought the horrible sickly sweet stink of rotting flesh . . .'

On 2 October, Sgt A.G. Skelton of 20th Royal Fusiliers (19th Brigade, 33rd Division) reported that they had moved into Nissen huts in the area of Trônes Wood, which was constantly shelled, and that during this period they were visited by HRH the Prince of Wales. In *Old Soldiers Never Die*, Pte Frank Richards of 2nd Royal Welsh Fusiliers (19th Brigade, 33rd Division) noted that in October, his unit returned to the sunken road on the edge of Trônes Wood, where they too were in huts, perhaps the same as those mentioned by Skelton.

Aubrey Smith of 1/5th Londons (169th Brigade, 56th Division) wrote that in early October he had been taking his water cart beyond Trônes Wood. Despite the efforts of clearance parties, there were still traces of the severe fighting that had gone on in the Wood. The Wood was really one vast cemetery, and by no means had all the bodies been buried. Just inside the hedge on the far side were the remains of what had once been the British Front Line trench. Beyond lay the land from where many fruitless attempts to take GUILLEMONT had been launched. Smith came across the grave of Lt Raymond Asquith of 3rd Grenadier Guards (2nd Guards Brigade, Guards Division), which was marked by a wooden cross, among a handful of other graves by the roadside.

At a meeting on 3 October, the DCF (*Directeur des Chemins de Fer*) suggested that for the sake of uniformity of material and therefore convenience of maintenance, the second railway line to Trônes Wood should be laid with British material beyond Trônes Wood station. The main line and any points and crossings on it should be laid with French materials.

At noon on 7 October, during the battle for the Transloy Ridges, 1/16th Londons (169th Brigade, 56th Division) moved across country tracks to a position to the east of Trônes Wood, where they remained until the evening. 1/16th Londons were then placed at the disposal of 167th Brigade (also 56th Division) after going forward to a point south of GINCHY.

On 22 October, 2nd Royal Welsh Fusiliers (19th Brigade, 33rd Division) resumed a march across country tracks that had thawed, which made the going very heavy for the men; the transport skidded

on the muddy slopes and strung out as wagons got stuck. They left it to collect in its allotted part in a vast expanse of mud at CARNOY and marched across to Trônes Wood, which was a ruin of branches, riven trunks, standing or fallen, amid shell-holes and crumbling trenches. With only little overhead shelter, they huddled for warmth for a few hours around green wood fires, blinking and choking. On 24 October, 1/4th Suffolks (98th Brigade, 33rd Division) moved in very wet weather into Trônes Wood and 4 days later occupied some poor front-line trenches on newly gained ground in front of LESBŒUFS.

In early November, 6th Dorsets (50th Brigade, 17th Division) were in a rest camp in Trônes Wood, which consisted of shelters made of tarpaulins over pits. A few braziers of smoke were the only method of getting dry. There was a covered approach to the Wood from the west, called Trench Alley, while the southern part was commanded by the Maltz Horn Ridge.

On 2 November, 33rd Division bivouacked close to Trônes Wood; by then the weather had broken and the roads were a morass of treacly mud, through which stuck out tree stumps that were supposed to form foundations. Cover of every description had been swept away by shell-fire and every yard of ground was pitted by shell-holes. Repeated attacks were carried out on 3 and 4 November in the area of Hazy, Antelope, German and Brimstones Trenches. The enemy had put out a lot of wire and the thick mists at the time prevented accurate observation; in any event, the ground was a quagmire covered with shell-holes, making an attack impossible.

In his diary, Gen J.L. Jack noted that on 7 November his battalion, 2nd West Yorkshires (23rd Brigade, 8th Division), moved forward 5 miles to bivouacks in Trônes Wood, relieving 19th Brigade (33rd Division): 'At Trônes Wood we found the nearly officerless remnant of the 5th Cameronians, who had just suffered heavily, still in possession of our bivouac.' 1/5th Cameronians (19th Brigade, 33rd Division) refused to vacate this 'wretched spot' before the appointed time and so 2nd West Yorkshires were forced to sit in the rain for an hour before the Scotsmen vacated their scraps of shelter and several bell-tents. Battalion headquarters was housed in an old German trench, blocked at one end by a door and roofed with some sheets of corrugated iron, with sandbags filling the cracks. There was a stove also, to Jack's joy, which had been 'purloined' from Sidney Rogerson's batman.

In *Twelve Days*, Sidney Rogerson of 2nd West Yorkshires wrote that the camp was situated in an open space of what had once been grassland between the mangled remains of Trônes Wood and BERNAFAY WOOD. The distance was shrouded by rain and mist, from out of which the boom of gunfire came distant and muffled. 'Camp 34' itself was camp only in name and a few forlorn groups of rude tarpaulin-sheet shelters huddled together, as though they shrank from the surrounding desolation.

On 15 November, Jack was again at the Brique-terie Camp. It had been a very wet morning and 2nd West Yorkshires had marched 4 miles to Citadel Camp, near FRICOURT. At Bernafay crossroads a young officer was directing the traffic duties in a most businesslike manner. On 18 November, Citadel Camp was dry but 'perishing cold'. Although officially described as resting, at 0600hrs on 16 November, 2nd West Yorkshires found 6 officers and 300 other ranks, who proceeded in motor lorries to the Trônes Wood area and were engaged after 1500hrs in levelling a track for a light railway. It was high time that these lines were laid, as the waste of time and the exhaustion of men and animals was very great.

In 1917, Lt Col The Hon. R.G.A. Hamilton, better known as the 'Master of Belhaven', revisited the Somme battlefield. His party left their horses and went to ARROW HEAD COPSE, where he noticed that there was a large railway junction at the corner of Trônes Wood.

Up to the mid-1920s, a memorial to 53rd Brigade stood alongside the edge of the Wood but, being made of timber, it did not survive. In 1925, a memorial obelisk was dedicated to 18th Division on the southern side of Trônes Wood, close to the road, and unveiled by Lt Gen Sir I. Maxse, formerly General Officer Commanding 18th Division; survivors from 10th Essex took part in the ceremonies. Towards the end of the Second World War, the Commonwealth War Graves Commission received a report that it was still in good condition.

U

ULSTER TOWER is on a hilltop site just off the D73 road. The idea of a memorial to the memory of former members of 36th Division was first mooted in April 1919, possibly by Sir James Craig MP. An area of land measuring 112yds by 65yds was the proposal offered to the French government, which gave its permission. It was quickly agreed in Belfast that such a monument should be in the form of a prominent Ulster landmark, and the one chosen was William Burn's nineteenth-century Helen's Tower at Clandeboye in Northern Ireland. It was close to where the volunteers of the newly founded 36th Division had first drilled and trained during 1914–15.

The replica stone tower house, standing about 70ft high, was built remarkably quickly; it was the first official memorial to be erected on the Western Front, when the land all around was still very battle-scarred. On behalf of Sir Edward Carson, Craig wrote to the commanding officer of the 36th (Ulster) Division informing him that by the spring of 1919, more than £5,000 had been subscribed to a memorial fund and that Thiepval was the chosen site. The architects were J.A. Bowden M.S.A. and Major A.L. Abbot and the builders were Messers. Fenning & Co. Ltd of Palace Wharf, Middlesex. It was up to the first stage by 5 August 1921 and the Thiepval Memorial, as it was then known, was dedicated and unveiled on Saturday 19 November 1921 by Field Marshal Sir Henry Wilson; Wilson took the place of Sir Edward Carson, who was unwell, as was Sir James Craig, the first Prime Minister of Northern Ireland. Always the life and soul of any party, Wilson, speaking first in perfect French, welcomed Gen Weygand, who was representing Marshal Foch. Wilson was then presented with a key by Maj J.C. Boyle, who had dreamt up the original Thiepval Memorial scheme, and unlocked the door to the little chapel of the inner sanctuary. Weygand then unveiled the chapel itself; at this point, the room only contained a marble tablet, which recorded HM King George V's tribute to the Ulster troops who fought and fell at THIEPVAL. Beneath the oaken beams of the ceiling were shields bearing the names of the battalions from 36th Division who took part in the fighting during the war. A service of dedication was then performed by Union church leaders, including Archbishop D'Arcy, Archbishop of Armagh and Primate of All Ireland. As the service concluded, the Duchess of Abercorn launched two flags at the top of the Tower to the British and French nations.

Sir Henry Wilson also planted a tree, to the memory of 'the Men of Ulster who served in the forces other than the Ulster Division' and Gen Weygand planted one in the memory of 'our Allies'. Others who planted trees at the ceremony included Brig Gen A. Ricardo, who planted one in memory of 9th Royal Inniskilling Fusiliers (109th Brigade, 36th Division) and Maj Gen Sir O.S.W. Nugent, on behalf of 36th Division. Other guests included the Marquess of Londonderry and the Marquess of Dufferin and Ava, each of whom planted two trees, as did the Duchess of Abercorn when she came down from the top of the Tower.

In total, 47 plaques were sited at the base of the trees lining the avenue from the memorial gates to Ulster Tower. All of these plaques represented groups or organisations that had connections with 36th Division. At some time when the original trees had gone and the plaques were considered a bit of a nuisance, they were discarded. Other trees and shrubs planted in the early 1920s did not survive very long, and by 1934 many of them had been replaced by smaller trees or bushes.

Later, after the Second World War, a list, in the form of a scroll, of the people who had taken part in the ceremonies, was framed and placed inside the Memorial Room. This main room within the Tower is a square chamber and the walls include an adapta-tion of lines written by Lord Tennyson in 1861 and which are inscribed in the Tower at Clandeboye as a symbol of love. A memorial to 2/Lt M.J. Wright of 14th Royal Irish Rifles (109th Brigade, 36th Division), who was killed on 1 July 1916 and buried in Thiepval Wood, is at present in the Tower; his name is also commemorated on the Thiepval Memorial. The upper portion of the Tower provided accommodation for a caretaker.

On her visit in August 1933, Vera Brittain wrote of Ulster Tower: 'It looked rather too much of a pleasure park for souvenir hunters to suit my taste in memorials.' She suggested that the building itself 'is more like an enormous water tower. The trees which line the path were planted by famous men & generals – one being Sir Henry Wilson . . .'

The original caretaker of the Tower, Sgt Savage, later gave way to a Mr William McMaster, a former corporal in 10th Royal Irish Rifles (107th Brigade, 36th Division), who arrived in March 1922. McMaster was the caretaker at the time of the British Legion Pilgrimage in August 1928, when he and his wife greeted the party. To quote one of the pilgrims, McMaster was 'a veritable encyclopaedia concerning the battlefield and the doings of the individual battalions, aye, and individuals too. When we asked him as to the number of visitors, he said that for the first two years of his stay at the Tower the number of summer visitors averaged about three hundred, and now about one hundred and fifty per week.'

It appears that McMaster was still in the Tower in 1934, as a document in the Commonwealth War Graves Commission Archive dated 27 June 1934 (868 Pt.1) refers to a visit and survey made by Maj J.C. Boyle on 16 June 1934, when the Commission was perhaps considering whether or not to get involved in the running and management of the Tower. Boyle noted that the bronze plate on the flagpole which flew the Union Jack was in a very dirty state and the inscription difficult to read and in need of attention. The wooden gate at the roadside needed repainting, and at present

it was an unsuitable green colour; he suggested dark brown. The Memorial Room bore little resemblance to a chapel as it was so bare, containing simply a table and visitors' book and a well-thumbed copy of the *History of the 36th (Ulster) Division* by Cyril Falls. At the junction of the ceiling and walls there were some painted shields, but they had been obliterated. The caretaker did not know what they were and was advised to remove them.

Boyle also recommended that the room should perhaps have a list of battles in which 36th Division fought during the war and the names of the units involved at THIEPVAL, together with a roll of honour. This way, relatives would feel more welcome. If an Ulster flag were available, then this, too, could be placed on display. Postcards and small booklets could be offered for sale and a proper pen tray for visitors to use, together with a change of blotting paper.

To sum up, the memorial at first sight was impres-sive, but after a visit to British cemeteries, with their flowers and shrubs, a visitor might well find the Tower making a rather lonely impression, not helped by the dark stone of which it was built. Outside in the grounds the situation was not much better; the trees had not done well and the lack of soil did not help. Only a few laburnums, some Austrian pines and one or two yew trees had survived. Although the enamel nameplates were still there from 1921, Boyle did not deem it necessary to advertise the names of the people who had planted the trees; anyway, many of the trees were no longer there, and some of those that were, were not even the originals. His own tree was a laurel bush, which he knew he had never planted in the first place. He suggested that the enamel plates should be removed. As for the perimeter, Boyle suggested the planting of an evergreen or golden privet hedge around the wire boundary fence; this would also hide McMaster's vegetable patch, which ran right up to the back of the memorial. The lawn 'was not too bad and had just been mown'.

It seems that, by 1934, only French people visited Ulster Tower, which was now totally overshadowed by the new Thiepval Memorial, dedicated in 1932. Boyle suggested that the Imperial War Graves Com-mission should be asked to take over the grounds, as McMaster was no gardener, nor even interested. He also added that the Tower was not an attractive place for a man and wife to live. The Commission agreed to take over the maintenance of Ulster Tower, as well as the grounds, and the custodian was paid £3 a week.

Ulster Tower was closed in 1939, when a gardener from Connaught Cemetery would keep an eye on it. During the Second World War it was occupied by the German Army, who used it as an observation point. After the war it seems to have been occupied by squatters for a period. A reminder of the German occupation is a swastika scratched in the stone. In 1956, an important 40th anniversary ceremony took place here, as well as at the Thiepval Memorial, when a pilgrimage from the Royal Ulster Rifles, led by Gen Sir James Steele, visited the former battlefields.

In 1963/4, the caretaker's quarters in the Tower were improved and important structural work was also carried out, at the request of the government of Northern Ireland. In July 1966, the 50th anniversary of the battle was marked. In 1972 further structural work was carried out. In 1975, when the French authorities were keen for the 60th anniversary to be commemorated, support from the United Kingdom was muted, except from Ulster. The official policy of the Ministry of Defence was not to get involved beyond any 50th anniversary, but the Ministry was encouraged to change its mind and a 3-day commemoration was organised, in which the French and British played equal roles. The British contingent was led by Gen Sir John Anderson and Field Marshal Sir Gerald Templar. The services began with one at Ulster Tower, when British and French troops took part, together with about 400 people, including a contingent of Somme veterans from South Africa. Those in attendance then moved to the Thiepval Memorial for the next service. Other commemorations were held at BEAUMONT-HAMEL, LONGUEVAL, VILLERS-BOCAGE, RANCOURT, ALBERT and PÉRONNE. Each of these services reflected its own national character.

For much of the year, a caretaker still lived in the Tower, but after direct rule from Westminster took over Northern Ireland affairs in the early 1970s, Ulster Tower seems to have fallen into limbo; the building showed signs of wear and public access was limited. The grounds, too, were in need of care and attention, and many trees and shrubs needed replacing. In 1988 a body called the Farset Association, based in Belfast, began to raise public awareness of the situation and sought funding from the Government. Legally, the building belongs to the people of Northern Ireland, who paid for it in the first place, but as with the nearby Thiepval Memorial, it had always presented unique problems of upkeep, maintenance and, of course, expense. After a long drawn-out correspondence, the Commonwealth War Graves Commission agreed to take care of the grounds; in addition, it would also deal with any necessary running repairs to Ulster Tower.

On 1 July 1989, the Tower was rededicated in the presence of the late HRH Princess Alice, Duchess of Gloucester. The Somme Association, which seems to have grown out of the Farset Association, was now to continue to manage it. Sometimes the Association

gives the impression of being the real owner of Ulster Tower and its grounds, but this is not so. The continued presence of the Tower, with its symbolic links with the memory of 36th Division, the Orange Order and the Union Movement, makes the question of ownership a highly politically charged issue.

On 1 July 1991, amid tight security and during pouring rain, the Duke of Kent unveiled a new memorial to nine holders of the Victoria Cross from 36th Division and other divisions. Outside the gates of Ulster Tower, another memorial was put up on 12 September 1993, this time to the memory of all Orangemen who served in the First World War. It appears that permission for the erection of this memorial was given, but not for this particular site. As the original site was not ready, the contractors erected it in the wrong place; it was later moved to a new site inside the grounds of Ulster Tower itself. Nearby is a memorial bench dedicated to five Victoria Cross holders of the Orange Brethren.

In 1994, a new shop and visitors' centre was opened. Originally, permission to climb the steps to the top of the Tower would be granted on request, and here the views over the ANCRE VALLEY were well worth the climb. Sadly, the top of Ulster Tower is no longer open to visitors. It has been mooted that parts of the nearby SCHWABEN REDOUBT may one day be opened for visitors and that student guides from Northern Ireland would help out during the summer months.

The bleak hilltop site is obviously not really suitable for trees, and at present two lines of Irish yews (by no means 47) line the path between the gate and the Tower. After a period in the cellar of the Tower, the tree plaques were thrown out a few years ago, and were found buried on the site of an old scrapyard near ALBERT that was being redeveloped for housing. Twenty-two of the original plaques were recovered and are on display in the Musée des Abris in ALBERT, while another 24 are in private hands, or perhaps lost, and one more is on display in the Somme Heritage Centre, which is close to the Clandeboyne Estate in County Down.

During the spring of 2005, excavations in Thiepval Wood, opposite Ulster Tower, were carried out by a group from Northern Ireland under the direction of the Curator of the Royal Irish Fusiliers Regimental Museum, Armagh. Several sections of the original trench system used by 109th Brigade (36th Division) were unearthed and a large underground bunker was discovered at the rear of Connaught Cemetery. Walking tours of the trench system can be organised from the visitors' centre at Ulster Tower. Important services to commemorate the men of 36th Division take place at THIEPVAL every 1 July. On 26 June 2006, a Battle of the Somme commemorative stamp was issued in Ireland.

V

VACQUERIE is north-west of AMIENS and south of BERNAVILLE and the D925 road between ABBEVILLE and DOULLENS. On 24 October 1915, 108th Field Ambulance (36th Division) went into billets 2 miles from the village, which had been used by the Indian Cavalry and had been left in an 'indescribably filthy state'. In early December, 98th Field Ambulance (30th Division) were here and at BERNAVILLE; after cleaning the premises from top to bottom, they opened a hospital here on 5 December. The hospital was handed over to 108th Field Ambulance on 7 January 1916.

VADENCOURT is east of CONTAY on the D919 road. During the Battle of the Somme it was mostly known as a collecting point for walking wounded cases, who were often taken there by rail. On 14 June 1916, 91st Field Ambulance (32nd Division) came to a camp here; there were 120 bell-tents and 5 marquees. On 23 June, 147th Brigade (49th Division) were billeted in the large wood to the north of the village, as well as in CONTAY to the west; 148th Brigade (also 49th Division) arrived on 29 June.

During early July, 32nd Division still had a field ambulance at Vadencourt. During the early morning of 1 July, some 53 casualties were here, but the number then proceeded to increase greatly; by 2030hrs, the field ambulance staff were struggling to accommodate 14 officers and 684 other ranks of the Allied forces, together with 2 German officers and 24 German other ranks. Casualties lessened during the night, but during this time three dressing tents were occupied continuously. On 3 July, 97th Brigade (32nd Division) rested in the wood.

On 23 October, a brigade of 25th Division were at Vadencourt. On 19 November, 53rd Brigade (18th Division) were in the area.

VAIRE-SOUS-CORBIE, east of CORBIE, is on the south bank of the River Somme close to the D71 road. When they arrived back in the Somme area on 22 July 1916, 1/5th South Lancashires (166th Brigade, 5th Division) came to the village. Vaire-sous-Corbie Communal Cemetery has the graves of four Australian artillerymen, killed on 8 August 1918, who would have been part of the 'thin line' protecting CORBIE and the Somme crossings in August of that year.

VAL DES MAISONS is a farm north-east of AMIENS, between TALMAS and PUCHEVILLERS on the D125 road. From 26 to 29 February 1916, No. 1/1 (North Midland) Field Company, Royal Engineers (46th Division), were here. Billets here were not satisfactory, as they were too crowded with men from other units. On 2 April, 1/3rd (West Riding) Field Ambulance (49th Division) arrived here and took up an unoccupied farm building, which was considered very suitable for use as a hospital, although the buildings were filthy. The plan was to accommodate 150 patients in the farm, which had plenty of outhouses, as well as three Armstrong huts to be used for officers. The field ambulance left the farm on 27 June 1916 for FORCEVILLE, where they billeted in barns in the village. They collected the sick of 49th Division from LÉALVILLERS, CONTAY and VADENCOURT. On 1 July, 130th Field Ambulance (38th Division) arrived at the farm.

VARENNES is a village south of ACHEUX-EN-AMIÉNOIS on the D74 road. In early March 1916, 1/6th and 1/8th West Yorkshires (both 146th Brigade, 49th Division) were billeted here; the writer of 1/6th West Yorkshires' history described Varennes as 'one of the dirtiest villages in which the Battalion was billeted. The civilians seemed to have no sanitary arrangements in their farms.'

During 1916, Varennes developed a close relationship with 36th Division. Towards the end of March, a field ambulance of 36th Division arrived at Varennes; units of 36th Division were still here in mid-April and in early June. Elements of 36th Division were also billeted in HARPONVILLE to the north-west and LÉALVILLERS to the south-west.

On 27 June, 1/6th West Yorkshires left PUCHE-VILLERS and marched via TOUTENCOURT and HARPONVILLE; the civilians came out to watch them march by and each village had a lighted direction sign to guide them. 'The men were in great spirits, singing and shouting, till the hill between Harponville and Varennes was reached, when the column quietened down . . .' The battalion, who never seemed to be very comfortable in Varennes, were back again, in both heavy rain and darkness, when the men filed into 'their crowded and dirty billets to get as much sleep as possible before morning'. Because the start of the battle was delayed for 48 hours, 1/6th West Yorkshires had to stay in the village for two additional days before leaving for AVELUY WOOD. They found that special tracks had been marked out across country from HÉDAU-VILLE to MARTINSART.

At Zero Hour on 1 July, 7th Brigade (25th Division) were in Varennes, as well as at LÉALVILLERS, while 25th Division's 75th Brigade were at FORCEVILLE and HÉDAUVILLE and 74th Brigade were at HARPONVILLE and WARLOY-BAILLON. On 3 July, 12th Division arrived in the area.

On 12 November, 111th Brigade (37th Division) were billeted in Varennes and 37th Division had their headquarters here. Later in the month, 51st Division had a brigade and 1/3rd (Highland) Field Ambulance in the village.

Varennes Military Cemetery, designed by Sir Reginald Blomfield and previously known as the Varennes British Cemetery, is just outside the village on the north side of the road to LÉALVILLERS. It was laid out by No. 39 Casualty Clearing Station in August 1916, but the first burials made here were by mobile units of field ambulances of three divisions; the burials were made in trenches. From 9 October 1916 to 17 June 1917, No. 4 Casualty Clearing Station used Varennes Military Cemetery for burials, as did No. 11 Casualty Clearing Station from 10 October to 14 May 1917; No. 47 Casualty Clearing Station used it from December 1916 to May 1917. There was then a break of a year before further Allied formations used it between April and August 1918, particularly 17th and 38th Divisions. In early September 1918, No. 3 Canadian and No. 59 Casualty Clearing Stations came to Varennes.

Several senior officers are buried in Plot I of Varennes Military Cemetery, including Brig Gen P. Howell CMG (I.B.37) of 4th Hussars (attached General Staff), who died on 7 October 1916 after being struck by a shell in AUTHUILLE; the inscription on his grave is: 'Fellowship is heaven and the lack of fellowship is hell.' Also buried here is Lt Col A.S. Tetley RNVR (I.C.37), Commanding Officer Drake Battalion (189th Brigade, 63rd Division), who died on 15 November 1916; his grave inscription is the same as that of Brig Gen C.B. Prowse, General Officer Commanding 11th Brigade (4th Division), at LOUVENCOURT: 'Be thou faithful unto death and I will give thee a crown of life.'

Brig Gen G. Bull DSO (I.C.31) of the Royal Irish Fusiliers, General Officer Commanding 8th Brigade (3rd Division), was wounded by a sniper on 7 December 1916 and died on 11 December. He was a son of Robert George Bull, Registrar Magistrate at Newry, County Down, Northern Ireland. The cemetery also contains an unusual memorial which is a sort of bird-bath or animal watering trough about the size of a car wheel, given in memory of Pte E.A.F. Allen (I.G.36) of 10th Royal Fusiliers (111th Brigade, 37th Division) by his parents.

Varennes Communal Cemetery used to have the graves of two men from November 1915 and July 1916 in the south-west corner, but they were brought into Varennes Military Cemetery in 1934. The register records the details of 1,219 British and Dominion casualties.

VAUCHELLES-LÈS-AUTHIE is to the north-west of LOUVENCOURT, on the D938 road. It was used as a divisional rest station both at the beginning and at the end of the 1916 battle. On 28 July 1915, 1/3rd (South Midland) Field Ambulance (48th Division) marched to the village and occupied the château and school rooms, opening a divisional rest station at the former on 6 August. On 17 October, No. 121 Field Company, Royal Engineers (36th Division), came here from ARQUÈVES, to the south, and stayed for nearly a fortnight.

At the end of February 1916, 109th Field Ambulance (36th Division) were at Vauchelles-lès-Authie for just over a week before leaving for BERTRANCOURT on 4 March. On the same day, 1/2nd (West Riding) Field Ambulance (49th Division) arrived here from WARLOY-BAILLON and used the small village school, with two canvas huts behind the building providing accommodation; they could take 50 patients at the most. The château included accommodation for an officers' mess and its outbuildings were used for billeting purposes for the other ranks.

Several buildings, including the school, a barn and outbuildings were used for medical purposes and 16 bell-tents were erected, including operating marquees, in a large orchard. One barn was set apart to be used for cases of scabies. At first, the village was full of manure heaps; the inhabitants were required to spread them on their fields. The village had some very deep wells, which provided a good water supply.

On 23 March, 1/2nd (West Riding) Field Ambulance were still in the village, as were 93rd and 94th Field Ambulances (both 31st Division); 93rd Field Ambulance were still here on 8 April, but were out of bounds. On 21 May, huts were being built in the village by No. 1/1 (Durham) Field Company, Royal Engineers (4th Division). On 20 June, 11th Field Ambulance (4th Division) arrived here and opened a divisional rest station, taking over the château and school. At the end of the month, they left for MAILLY-MAILLET and BERTRANCOURT.

On 24 July, a brigade of 12th Division were at Vauchelles-lès-Authie and on 30 July, 75th Field Ambulance (25th Division) were here. On 9 August, HM the King and HRH the Prince of Wales arrived here from WARNIMONT WOOD to visit the headquarters of 1st Guards Brigade (Guards Division),

1st Irish Guards and 3rd Coldstream Guards (both 1st Guards Brigade, Guards Division). The royal party then moved to MARIEUX, headquarters of XIV Corps. In early October, 153rd Brigade (51st Division) were in the village, as were elements of 112th Brigade (37th Division) on 12 November.

Eight casualties were buried by British field ambulances in Vauchelles-lès-Authie Communal Cemetery Extension, including Brig Gen C.B. Prowse, General Officer Commanding 11th Brigade (4th Division), mortally wounded when crossing no man's land early in the action on 1 July 1916. In early July 1916, Lt Gen Sir A.G. Hunter-Weston, General Officer Commanding VIII Corps, attended Prowse's funeral and arranged for an oak cross and iron railings to be placed around the grave. All eight casualties were later transferred after the war to Louvencourt Military Cemetery to the south-east.

VAUCHELLES-LES-QUESNOY is north-east of ABBEVILLE on the D925. Towards the end of November 1915, 14th Royal Warwicks (at this time 95th Brigade, 32nd Division) arrived here after enduring 'a gruelling twelve-mile march in full marching order', which came on top of another route march the previous afternoon. The roads were coated with ice, which gave no surface grip to the marching troops. They remained in the village for 5 days before leaving for VIGNACOURT, where they stayed for a few days.

VAUX is little more than a small collection of houses, north-east of BRAY-SUR-SOMME and between SUZANNE and CURLU. The other main features close to the village were FARGNY MILL to the north, Vaux Wood, and to the south, Royal Dragon's Wood. Although Vaux was small, it presented the right flank sector of the British front. As early as 14 August 1915, the role of 1/5th Cheshires was to patrol the river salient in front of Vaux. Vaux, on the right bank, faced the German-held village of CURLU, 800yds distant. From the high ground, observers of 5th Division could see German company headquarters in CURLU 'with the sentry walking up and down outside, and a cow tethered in the field behind'; no doubt the enemy could also see them. The space between was marsh, and punts armed with rifles and a machine gun patrolled there. Special observation points included one mined out close to a French battery position, one in a tree and one in a boiler close to Vaux Ecole, which lay on the edge of a hill.

On 17 August, 15th Field Ambulance (5th Division) ran an advance collection post in Vaux; a few days later, 14th Field Ambulance (also 5th Division)

were here. The church could be used for casualties, who were brought down by motor ambulances at night, as in daytime they could only go to the corner of Royal Dragon's Wood.

6th King's (15th Brigade, 5th Division) relieved 1/5th Cheshires and they were accommodated in houses and barns in Vaux itself. No civilians remained in the village at the time. The houses, close to the marshes, connected with Vaux Wood by a communication trench running up the side of the hill.

Vaux has been much written about and the following is based on an account in a history of 18th Manchesters (90th Brigade, 30th Division). The battalion arrived in the area on 6 January 1916, when A Company were sent to Royal Dragon's Wood, due south of Vaux, where they sheltered in the willows close to the Somme Canal. During their time here they traded with French troops, exchanging tins of bully beef for wine. B Company went to Vaux village: 'Their outposts were placed in the marshes of the Somme. The chief post was situated on the end of the causeway which led across the marshes . . .' B Company's task was to guard the small village of Vaux

by occupying a series of posts on the edge of a maze of tributaries of the river Somme, which separated Vaux village from a large piece of land shaped like the tongue of a boot. The land was afterwards named by the Battalion Trafford Park. The foremost post was called Duck Post, in front of which was a swampy piece of land of some 60 yards in width, dividing the causeway on which the post stood from the dryland known as Trafford Park. It was decided after the Battalion had taken over this area to place an outpost on the edge of a small wood to protect Duck Post from surprise, and further to form a base for the scouts, whose duty it was to patrol the whole of Trafford Park, which was covered at the northern edge by thick woods and was some 800 yards in length, and in the widest part some 400 yards across . . .

C Company moved to Vaux Wood, 'where they lived in rustic simplicity' and D Company took up positions in battle dugouts. Each company also had to send a platoon to trenches at FARGNY MILL, which was on the extreme left.

The work of patrolling the innumerable tributaries of the river which surrounded Trafford Park was both hazardous and interesting, for which purpose the scouts used several of the duck-shooting punts to paddle quietly up the various streams to examine the duck-shooting huts which would have made an excellent place for the enemy from which to observe the movements of our troops. It was the duty of the scouts to patrol as far south as Frise, which was held by the French, who kept a battalion of infantry there.

If danger threatened at Duck Post, the sentry would press an alarm bell to alert troops in the village. It was not always a 'cushy' front, as on 4 February, B Company, 18th Manchesters, had 6 men killed and 15 wounded by shell-fire.

Lt Col N. Fraser-Tytler of CL Brigade, Royal Field Artillery (30th Division), often mentioned Vaux in his book *Field Guns in France*. He noted that in November he rode back to his former position in Vaux Valley, only to find that his former 'beautiful gunpits' were now being used as stables by French officers' chargers. His former observation post had been blown out, but the lower chamber was still intact.

VAUX-EN-AMIÉNOIS is north-west of Amiens, north of the D97 road between BERTANGLES and SAINT-SAUVEUR. In mid-November 1915, 89th Brigade (30th Division) had their headquarters in a 'château' here that 'was just like an ice-house and filthy dirty'. About 10 days later, 90th Field Ambulance (32nd Division) were billeted in Vaux-en-Amiénois.

In mid-June 1916, 9th Division had their headquarters here; 63rd Brigade (21st Division) arrived here on 4 July. In mid-August, elements of 2nd Division were 'resting' in the village for a couple of days. Throughout part of 1916, Fourth Army ran a Trench Mortar School in the village, which seems to have resulted in at least 14 and maybe 15 fatal accidents, mostly in November and December 1916; six men were killed on 8 December alone. The men were buried in Vaux-en-Amiénois Communal Cemetery; one, Sgt H.S. Meehan (A.11) of 13th Australian Battalion (4th Brigade, 4th Division), used to have a special memorial.

VAUX-SUR-SOMME is to the east of CORBIE on the north bank of the River Somme, on the D233 road to SAILLY-LE-SEC. On 10 January 1916, 14th Royal Warwicks (13th Brigade, 5th Division) arrived here from the line opposite CARNOY via BRAY-SUR-SOMME for one night and were to spend several happy days here. They were right down in the valley, close to the river and canal.

The troops spent a great deal of time in cleaning themselves up and were given passes to visit nearby CORBIE in the afternoons. Route marches became

part of their daily training, when they were accompanied by an increasingly competent band; 'Lily of Laguna' was a particular favourite. Furthermore, there were many concert parties in the district and at MÉRICOURT-L'ABBÉ they were able to listen to Lt B. Hallam Radford of the Royal Flying Corps, better known as Basil Hallam of 'Gilbert the Filbert' fame, before his death later in the year. 14th Royal Warwicks' stay here was extended, owing to an outbreak of German measles, and they remained in the area when other units left. Contact cases were isolated in the village château, while the rest of the battalion continued with their training.

A small detachment of French gunners billeted at Vaire, across the river, used to fraternise with the British troops; they sampled both English rations and rum in Vaux-sur-Somme, while 14th Royal Warwicks tried 'astounding dishes' of bully beef and vegetables cooked by a pre-war Parisian chef. Concerts were put on in the schoolroom and inter-company rugby and football matches were played; the rugby was played on a field where the road to Vaux-sur-Somme leaves the main BRAY-SUR-SOMME–CORBIE road. French people watching the game were often at a loss as to what was going on in the games. On 10 March, 14th Royal Warwicks left for the Arras front after a very pleasant stay of 2 months.

Many other units spent time here, including 2nd Highland Light Infantry (5th Brigade, 21st Division), who camped on the river bank before going up the line, and No. 63 Field Company, Royal Engineers (9th Division), in mid-June. In early July, the village suffered considerably from enemy bombardments. On 9 July the village was the home of 6th Cavalry Brigade (3rd Cavalry Division); on 13 July, Vaux-sur-Somme was described as being 'full of cavalry'. This is a reference to their intended use for the HIGH WOOD battles in mid-July. On 21 July, a battalion of the Durham Light Infantry were camped in the village.

VECQUEMONT is due east of AMIENS, south of the D1 road and DAOURS and adjacent to the AMIENS–ALBERT main railway line. On 4 May 1916, No. 34 Casualty Clearing Station took over the rest station at DAOURS from 22nd Field Ambulance (7th Division), who then reopened it on 10 May when No. 34 Casualty Clearing Station left for Vecquemont, where an area of grassland was to be turned into a casualty clearing station under canvas. No. 45 Casualty Clearing Station was in the village between 19 May and 16 July. By 16 June, the casualty clearing station was ready to admit patients, which it began to do the following day. The hospital could take 800 patients and was 'capable of expansion'. A large red cross was painted on the roof of one of the sheds while another, made from broken brick and chalkstone, was placed in front of the hospital. A paddock beside the cemetery, to the east of the hospital, was selected as a site for a new burial ground. From October 1916 to February 1917, it was used by No. 8 (RNAS) Squadron, commanded by Cdr G.R. Bromet.

Prior to the start of the battle, the nearby loading station was equipped with five trains ready to transport the wounded. This was by no means enough, however, and 14 more trains had to be brought up on 2 July in order to cope with the enormous number of casualties, many of whom had been sent from DIVE COPSE.

Planned to take 800 casualties, the casualty clearing station had to cope with 7,000, destined for ambulance trains, passing through its hands during the first 5 days of the battle,. This figure included 3,000 men transferred from Nos. 5 and 21 Casualty Clearing Stations at CORBIE, who arrived in empty trucks. Dealing with so many casualties led to a chaotic situation, but somehow, the medical staff, who included 10 nursing sisters, restored the situation to normality. By 6 July, the hospital was empty. A barge at Daours Lock transported a small number of casualties.

Discussing the chaotic handling of casualties, the war diary of No. 45 Casualty Clearing Station (WO 95/416) pulls no punches:

The great outstanding feature is the totally inadequate staff of a casualty clearing station. This had been well realised by so noted an organizer as DMS 4th Army and three MO's, 3 NCO's and 20 men from Field Ambulances were sent to help me. Later on a further addition of 3 officers by Sir A. Bowlby and four by Colonel MacNab IMS and the staffing of a large shed turned into a temporary hospital saved the situation. It would appear that besides the additional medical personnel at least 5 NCO's and 50 men for bearer work by day & and the same for night work is absolutely essential. The use of 45 Casualty Clearing Station as an evacuation and transfer point for two other casualty clearing stations entailed the most arduous stretcher carrying, which could not have been done, had not the Cavalry Signals & DSAP voluntarily come to our aid. Even then, these on their own would have broken down had not 30 Dooli bearers & 20 Canadian Medical Corps men from neighbouring units helped us. I must emphasize this point as lack of bearers means blocking of roads & railways by delays which cannot be helped.

On 7 July, Lucknow B Section from an Indian casualty clearing station arrived here and used the large shed and triangle of ground near the railway for a hospital and transfers. They were able to take up to 600 cases for transfer to trains from Nos. 5 and 21 Casualty Clearing Stations.

After the original chaotic rush, 2,000 more cases came through the casualty clearing station in the period 9 to 11 July, by which time the ambulance trains had belatedly become much better organised. On 14 July, 1,000 cases were evacuated by three trains; on the following day, another 957 cases were admitted, including 51 Germans.

Although the village was mostly used as a casualty clearing station, it was also used for billeting purposes, and in particular by 19th Brigade (33rd Division) in mid-July and 16th Division at the end of August.

VERT GALAND is close to the N25 road beyween AMIENS and DOULLENS, to the north of the village of la Vicogne. During 1916 the village was a major base for the Royal Flying Corps. Set up on the land belonging to Vert Galand Farm, the aerodrome consisted of seven sheds on the right-hand side of the road; it was used by Cdr G.R. Bromet's No. 8 (RNAS) Squadron, flying Sopwith Pups, and No. 23 Squadron, Royal Flying Corps, on the other side of the road, using FE2bs. The huts and billets were clustered around the crossroads to the north of the field and included the farm buildings. No. 8 Squadron messed and slept there. Even a cinema was established here, to which army personnel often came. Twenty-second Wing were accommodated in the buildings of Rosel Farm, ½ mile away on the east side of the DOULLENS road.

On 3 November, No. 8 Squadron carried out their first line patrol, and around this time were called upon by numerous visitors, including Maj Gen H.M. Trenchard, General Officer Commanding First Wing, Royal Flying Corps; Lt Gen Sir Hubert Gough, General Officer Commanding Reserve (later Fifth) Army; Maurice Baring, aide-de-camp to Maj Gen Trenchard; J.T.C. Moore-Brabazon the aviation pioneer; and Sir Douglas Haig, General Officer Commander-in-Chief British Expeditionary Force.

Prior to No. 8 Squadron's arrival, No. 22 Squadron, equipped with FE2bs, were here for a few days in March before moving to nearby BERTANGLES. From 16 June, No. 60 Squadron, flying Morane Bullets, were here; No. 70 Squadron were present in June and on 1 July. On 3 July, Maj F.F. Waldron, Commanding Officer No. 60 Squadron, was forced down in the enemy lines near Epinoy and died of wounds the same day. Although now buried in Honourable Artillery Company Cemetery, Ecoust-Saint-Mein (VIII.A.26), he may well have been one of three airmen first buried in Epinoy churchyard. He was No. 60 Squadron's first casualty. When news that Waldron was missing reached Vert Galand, his place was taken by Maj R.R. Smith-Barry. In September, No. 23 Squadron, commanded by Maj A. Ross-Hume, came here from FIENVILLERS, remaining until February 1917.

VIGNACOURT is north-west of AMIENS on the D113 road from FLESSELLES and was well behind the lines in 1915 and 1916; the village was mainly used for training, medical and billeting purposes. In early October 1915, 110th Field Ambulance (36th Division) were accommodated in a farm, and 80th Field Ambulance (26th Division) were here on 22 October.

On 17 November, 17th Manchesters (90th Brigade, 30th Division) were here briefly before moving on to BERTANGLES and No. 200 Field Company, Royal Engineers (also 30th Division) were here for bomb-throwing training. On 18 November, 98th Field Ambulance (also 30th Division) established a hospital in a small house here; later, the field ambulance reception hospital moved to a building nearer to the *mairie*. At the end of November, 14th Royal Warwicks (at this time 95th Brigade, 32nd Division) were billeted here for a few days before moving to ALLONVILLE. At the end of December, XIII Corps had their headquarters here.

The 70th Brigade of 8th Division arrived here at the end of March 1916, when their division headquarters was at FLESSELLES, with the 25th Brigade and the 23rd Brigade at Bourdon. Two battalions from 31st Division were here before leaving on 27 March.

On 4 April 1916, a field ambulance of 49th Division arrived here, and opened a hospital in the rue d'Amour the next day. On the same day, 1/6th West Yorkshires (146th Brigade, 49th Division) arrived at Vignacourt – they were to remain for 8 weeks – and 1/5th and 1/7th West Yorkshires (also 146th Brigade, 49th Division) were inspected by Field Marshal Lord Kitchener on the BÉHEN-COURT–FRÉCHENCOURT road. The other battalions of the brigade were concentrated together with brigade headquarters in Vignacourt. The troops enjoyed their stay here, which was one of the longest in one place during their whole service in France. During their stay, they carried out training and supplied men for work on the new railway sidings in the village.

The main street in Vignacourt was 2 miles long and very wide. In the centre of the street were half a dozen pools with willow trees surounding them. Several great lime trees towered over the houses, which gave shade during hot summer afternoons. Battalion headquarters was in the doctor's house, opposite the church. The Tykes, a concert party, performed every night in the Salle des Concerts to audiences drawn from the village itself, as well as from those billeted at NAOURS, FLESSELLES, FLIXECOURT and Havernas. 1/6th West Yorkshires trained close to the local forest, to the south-west of the village, where brigade field days were organised. On a clear day, AMIENS cathedral could be seen, and in Vignacourt itself the church was a prominent landmark. The units of 146th Brigade got on exceedingly well with the villagers, who made their stay very comfortable. On 15 April, the first anniversary of the battalion's arrival in France, the occasion was duly celebrated by special concerts and anniversary dinners.

On 9 May, 430 officers and men left the village for FORCEVILLE as working parties to work on cable trenches and assembly positions; on 9 June, the rest of 1/6th West Yorkshires finally left the village and marched to PUCHEVILLERS. On 11 June, news of the drowning at sea of Field Marshal Lord Kitchener came through and a battalion memorial service was held, at which the battalion buglers played the Last Post. Officers wore crêpe armbands for several days in Kitchener's memory.

On 7 May, 8th North Staffords (57th Brigade, 19th Division) arrived here from AMIENS, remaining for 3 weeks while training; 10th Worcesters (also 57th Brigade, 19th Division) arrived here via LONG-UEAU station on the next day, having marched in windy weather. The battalion carried out strenuous training until the end of May, but life was enlivened by the presence of 49th Division's concert party. On 29 May, 8th North Staffords and 10th Worcesters left the village for SAINT-RIQUIER; on 8 June, 8th North Staffords returned to Vignacourt for 4 days before leaving for DERNANCOURT, and on 10 June, 10th Worcesters returned for a day.

On 10 July, the Australian historian C.E.W. Bean came south and stayed in the village for a short time. Apart from those formations already mentioned, the Guards, 1st, 2nd, 3rd, 19th, 20th, 30th 47th and 49th Divisions had units in the area, of which 2nd, 20th and 30th Divisions had their headquarters in Vignacourt, up to the third week of October.

In 1918 the village was under siege during the fight for AMIENS, but Australian troops held on in the hard fighting of August.

Six burials, five British and one Australian, made in Vignacourt Communal Cemetery between October 1915 and March 1918 were transferred to Vignacourt British Cemetery after the war. Designed by Sir Reginald Blomfield, it contains the graves of 585 identified British and Commonwealth casualties from the First World War and two men from the Second World War. Sited on the south-east side of the village and close to a railway line, Vignacourt British Cemetery was begun in April 1918 when Nos. 20 and 61 Casualty Clearing Stations, as well as a Royal Air Force headquarters, were in the village; it was then closed in August. Inside the cemetery is a monument to the memory of the Allied dead, in the form of a statue of a French soldier. Unveiled in August 1921, it carries the following moving inscription at its base: 'Brothers in arms of the British Army, fallen on the field of honour, sleep in peace; we are watching over you.'

VILLERS-BOCAGE is north of AMIENS on the N25 road. On 25 July 1915, No. 51 Casualty Clearing Station arrived in the village. On 12 December, 15th Highland Light Infantry (at this time 97th Brigade, 32nd Division) arrived here. As their billets were not yet ready, they were forced to wait by the roadside while an icy wind blew across the treeless plain. As the village was on the direct route from the front line, 'Ambulances came and went all day long: some stayed. There was a motor ambulance depot in the village. Besides, the Mairie was used as a hospital. Villers-Bocage was more dilapidated than any village yet encountered.' During the time that 15th Highland Light Infantry were in the village, a 'decrepit barn' burnt down after bacon being fried in a company cooker caught fire. The owner of the farm put in for a massive compensation claim, but, after talks, a compromise was reached. On 16 December 15th Highland Light Infantry left the village and moved 3 miles eastwards to PIERREGOT.

On 17 January 1916, No. 404 Field Company, Royal Engineers (51st Division), carried out work in Villers-Bocage, as well as in several other villages, when they were making beds and horse standings.

No. 51 Casualty Clearing Station were posted to the village in April and May 1916 and 3rd Division had units here in early July. A note in the war diary of 1/3rd (Highland) Field Ambulance (51st Division) mentions that patients at MILLENCOURT were sometimes evacuated to Nos. 5 and 51 Casualty Clearing Stations in the Villers-Bocage area in April and May. In mid-August, 50th Division had a brigade here and at the end of August, 33rd Division had their headquarters here. In mid-September, 4th Division

had their headquarters in Villers-Bocage. Between September 1915 and August 1916, 22nd, 26th, 30th and 32nd Divisions also sent field ambulances here.

Villers-Bocage Communal Cemetery, adjacent to an older cemetery and north-east of the village, off a road to TALMAS, was used by British troops between August 1915 and April 1916; there are 13 British burials on its eastern side. In 1921, there were still four special memorials in the cemetery, including a 6ft cross behind the grave of Pte Lawson, Army Service Corps, which had been erected by his comrades. Other men commemorated by individual memorials included Pte Ferguson, L/Cpl Marshall and Sgt Pike. On the south side of the cemetery is Villers-Bocage Communal Cemetery Extension, which was begun in October 1915 and remained in use until February 1917; it contains the graves of 60 soldiers, including 13 members of the Royal Field Artillery and 2 soldiers from the Second World War. Many of the 80 First World War graves reflect links with 51st Division, which ran an infantry school here from 21 January 1916, with many of the casualties having died of illness or as a result of an accident. About a third of the casualties died in 1915.

VILLERS-BRETONNEUX, on the AMIENS–SAINT-QUENTIN road, is more associated with the 1918 Somme battle than with that of 1916, but Pte T. Cooke of 8th Australian Battalion (2nd Australian Brigade, 1st Australian Division), who won a posthumous Victoria Cross during the struggle for Pozières Ridge on 24/25 July 1916, is commemorated on the panels of the Australian Memorial. The memorial, inaugurated on 22 July 1938, honours the memory of 11,000 Australians who died in France and who had no known grave. Lt J. Brillant of 22nd Canadian Battalion (5th Canadian Brigade, 2nd Canadian Division), who won his Victoria Cross on 8/9 August 1918, is also buried here (VIA.B.20).

The people of the city of Melbourne, Australia, adopted Villers-Bretonneux after the war and contributed substantially to the cost of its reconstruction. Victoria School in the village houses a museum that illustrates the role the Australian Army played in the war. A plaque on the wall of the mairie refers to Australia's role in the Great War After the war, the Australian government presented a set of silver bugles to the village; in the 1930s, at least, the Last Post was still being sounded on four nights a year, including the day of the Gallipoli landings, 25 April.

At one point it was thought that the area around the former windmill at POZIÈRES would be a sensible place to commemorate the role of Australian troops in the war, simply because more of them were killed in that area than anywhere else, but the site at Villers-Bretonneux was deemed to be more suitable. First mooted in 1919, designed by Edwin Lutyens, it was unveiled on 22 July 1938 by King George VI. It is adjacent to the Military Cemetery, also designed by Lutyens. On 2 November 1993 an unknown Australian soldier was exhumed from Adelaide Cemetery for reburial in the chapel of the Australian War Memorial in Canberra. Before being flown home, the coffin was taken through the Menin Gate for a short service.

Vera Brittain had visited this same cemetery in August 1933, one where all the dead were from 1918.

No original trees – only undergrowth – in wood. Marvellous straight road – in front the gradually looming view of Amiens impressed me more than anything throughout the journey except the view from Thiepval Ridge, for it made me realise what the Germans must have felt as they came in sight of what must have been the largest town in France that they had the chance to take during the war. It must have seemed so near, so accessible, yet they never took it . . .

Brittain was wrong here, as the enemy did occupy the town, albeit briefly, in August 1914.

In June 2005, the Australian cricket team, who had just arrived in Europe at the start of their tour of England, spent time at Villers-Bretonneux memorial and cemetery, visiting their compatriots killed on the Somme during the First World War. In 2001, the Ashes squad had also visited the former battlefields at Gallipoli.

In 2014 the road parking at Villers-Bretonneux MC and Memorial was upgraded and the local road layout was changed, as well as a dedicated car park laid out. An Australian Interpretation Centre at Villers-Bretonneux is due to be ready by Anzac Day, 25 April 2018.

VILLE-SUR-ANCRE is 4 miles south of ALBERT, on the left bank of the River Ancre on the D120 road between MÉAULTE and TREUX. During the First World War, it was occasionally used by field ambulances, including 56th Field Ambulance (18th Division) in early September 1915.

On 7 April 1916, 8th Somerset Light Infantry (63rd Brigade, 21st Division) moved to Ville-sur-Ancre from ALLONVILLE, and to MÉAULTE 2 days later. On 2 June, 8th Somerset Light Infantry returned here from the line and billeted for 9 days before returning to the trenches; they were back here again on 20 June before moving up to the trenches on 25 June, taking over assembly trenches. From April to October 1916, 3rd, 5th, 6th, 21st, 29th and 56th Divisions had brigades staying in the village. In August, an officer serving with 5th Division described the village as 'a dirty place with millions of flies'.

At the end of April 1918, Ville-sur-Ancre was captured by the Germans, only to be recaptured by 2nd Australian Division, who 'mopped up' the village on 19 May, having first taken a roll-call against a battered wall near the church, a building that was rebuilt in 1924.

Ville-sur-Ancre Communal Cemetery is south-west of the village on the road to TREUX; it has a British plot at the southern end containing the graves of 20 soldiers from the United Kingdom, including 11 members of the Royal Engineers, and 4 Australians killed in 1918, as well as 1 French grave. Three men who died in the Second World War are also buried here.

The Royal Engineer casualties included 1 man from No. 94 Field Company, Royal Engineers (19th Division), and 10 men from No. 97 Field Company, Royal Engineers (21st Division), who all died on 26 June 1916 and who were buried the same day. On 3 May, No. 1 Section, No. 97 Field Company, were shelled out of their billets here and moved to a spot close to the MORLANCOURT–MÉAULTE road, the D42. Just over 7 weeks later, they left BÉCOURT valley, where they had been working on a forward hospital or dressing station, for a 3-day 'holiday' at Ville-sur-Ancre.

According to records compiled by Sgt F.H. Aincham, Royal Engineers, and kept in the Imperial War Museum (85/51/1), Maj, later Lt Col, B.S. Phillpotts, Officer Commanding No. 97 Field Company, ran a very efficient company to which he brought continuous flair and innovation, combined with a very real concern for the welfare of the men under his command. One example of his interest was when he allowed his men special passes to visit AMIENS towards the end of June. When visiting the city himself, Phillpotts came across a group there and asked them whether they had any money; receiving a negative reply, he gave them some with which to enjoy themselves.

Having already been bombed out of their billets once, No. 97 Field Company experienced disaster on 26 June when their billets, consisting of a large barn, were hit by a German 13cm shell.

At 1.30pm whilst a lot of men were still talking after the mid-day meal, an enemy shell blast at the door of the mess-room, killing 11 men and wounding 15, including two officers and a sergeant. Among the killed were the Major's servant, Picker, a splendid fellow to whom the Major was greatly attached. One of the officers wounded was the present commanding officer of the 126th Field Coy. of our division, Major Marsden. Funeral same afternoon.

After the billets were struck, Phillpotts immediately had the area cleared, in case another shell landed in the same place. After the dead, dying and wounded had been attended to, he sat alone and, according to an eyewitness, berated the enemy for the terrible consequences of what they had done. After that, he returned to his office and took up a newspaper.

Phillpotts, born in 1875 and a younger son of a former headmaster of Bedford School, was appointed Commander, Royal Engineers 38th Division, in the autumn and won a Distinguished Service Order in mid-July at BAZENTIN-LE-PETIT. He was then out of the Somme for a few weeks, but in September had a headquarters at LONGUEVAL, which consisted of sheet thrown over a wagon. He died of wounds on 2 September 1917, having already been slightly wounded in the Battle of the Somme.

Ville-sur-Ancre Communal Cemetery Extension adjoins the southern end of the Communal Cemetery and was made in August 1918, although six of the graves are from the 1916 Battle of the Somme.

VIVIER MILL was south of ALBERT on the D42 road to MORLANCOURT and north-west of MÉAULTE. 70th Brigade (23rd Division) had their headquarters here; on 9 May the main building of the mill was allocated to 103rd Field Ambulance (34th Division) to run as a main dressing station from 10 May. Between 21 May and 26 May at least, 34th Division had their headquarters dugouts here.

The mill had its own railway siding, part of a short line that linked up with the railway line at DERNAN-COURT, which would have been used for transporting casualties and for bringing up supplies. On 1 July, 34th Division had their headquarters here while their troops were involved in attacks against LA BOISSELLE; they left for Baizeux on 20 July. On 4 July, 23rd Division also had their headquarters here when their troops were in the line between 17th and 19th Divisions.

WARGNIES, north-west of AMIENS, lies on the D60 road west of TALMAS. On 16 January 1916, 96th Field Ambulance (30th Division) were billeted at the château, with the personnel in the yard and officers in the château. Other field ambulances that were based here later included 1/2nd (West Riding) Field Ambulance (49th Division) in mid-April, 7th Field Ambulance (3rd Division) on 3 July and 1st Field Ambulance (1st Division) on 7 July.

WARLENCOURT-EAUCOURT, a commune, contains the village of Warlencourt on the north-west side of the ALBERT–BAPAUME D929 road, and just excludes EAUCOURT L'ABBAYE, on the south-east side of it.

Warlencourt British Cemetery is on the south-east side of the main road and was a concentration cemetery made in 1919 from the nearby battlefields; the register records particulars of 3,450 graves. The only considerable cemetery brought in was Hexham Road Cemetery in LE SARS, named after the road leading from Warlencourt to Eaucourt. Sgt D.F. Brown VC (III.F.11) of 2nd Otagos (2nd New Zealand Brigade, New Zealand Division), who won his Victoria Cross south-east of HIGH WOOD on 15 September 1916 and died on 1 October, is buried here.

WARLINCOURT-LÈS-PAS is south of the DOULLENS–Arras road, the D925. Before the 1916 Somme battle began, the village was in a sector used by 46th Division; it was particularly associated with 1/4th and 1/5th Lincolns and 1/5th Leicesters (all 138th Brigade, 46th Division), when 46th Division's headquarters was at SAINT-AMAND, to the south-east.

In May 1916, 1/5th Leicesters, while working in the local quarries, found that 'the work was very hard, for digging a deep narrow trench, or loading flints at Warlincourt quarries are no light task'; it was often very hot as well. The battalion were also here a few weeks later on, when their camp was uncomfortable and there was no officers' mess. An improvised marquee made up of wagon sheets and spare tarpaulins was used, and although the rain got in, it was possible to carry on cooking almost in the open and some excellent evenings were spent there.

On 23 June, when 138th Brigade's headquarters was again in the Warlincourt-lès-Pas, the plans of the attack against the enemy positions at GOMME-COURT were explained at a commanding officers' conference at brigade headquarters; the preliminary artillery bombardment began on the following day. On 26 June, 1/4th and 1/5th Lincolns came here from HUMBERCAMPS and moved into huts, and on 28 June they received their final orders for the attack on GOMMECOURT, now planned for 1 July. During this period, they only had 2 hours of light training and enjoyed the remainder of the time as a break.

The assembly point for the front line was the Corps Line Trench, which ran north and south 500yds east of SOUASTRE, between the Bienvillers–SOUASTRE and FONCQUEVILLERS–SOUASTRE roads. After the postponement, the troops were to be ready to go at 1800hrs on 30 June; the advance party proceeded to their stations, and at 2100hrs 1/5th Lincolns marched off from their huts at Warlincourt-lès-Pas to the strains of 'The Lincolnshire Poacher' played by the band. They took up their assembly positions in the Corps Line Trench in front of SOUASTRE.

Units from 48th Division were in the village during the first half of October; 145th Brigade (48th Division) arrived on 1 October, when 144th Brigade (also 48th Division) were at MONDICOURT and 143rd Brigade (also 48th Division) in the line opposite the south of GOMMECOURT.

Warlincourt Halte British Cemetery, SAULTY, designed by Charles Holden, is 500yds from the former railway halt and on the north side of the main road. It was chosen in May 1916 and begun in June, and was used by Nos. 20 and 43 Casualty Clearing Stations. Of the 1,266 burials in this cemetery about 30 are from the pre-battle period. After the Armistice, graves were brought in from small cemeteries at GAUDIEMPRÉ, LA HERLIÈRE and Couturelle. Lt Col W. Burnett DSO (I.F.5) of 1/5th North Staffords (137th Brigade, 46th Division), who died of wounds on 3 July 1916, is buried here in the third line. The regimental history tells the story of how he died:

> I went forward to my Battalion Headquarters, and found Colonel Burnett at the telephone, speaking to the Brigadier, who told him that he must reorganise the attack and push on . . . Colonel Burnett then announced that he was going out to see what was going on, and told me to remain where I was. I believe that he met Captain Fletcher, and sent him forward to the advanced trench.
>
> After the Colonel had been gone a short time the Brigadier asked for him on the telephone, and several runners were sent out to find him, but failed to do so. It afterwards transpired that he had been mortally wounded. The Brigadier then told me to get into touch with the Colonel of the 5th South Staffs, reorganise, and attack again at 3.30 in the afternoon . . .

This plan was later cancelled at the last minute.

Three men who were executed are also buried here. L/Cpl F. Hawthorne (XII.C.8) of 1/5th South Staffords was executed for cowardice on 11 August 1916; after taking part in the disaster at GOMMECOURT on 1 July, he was tried on 31 July and sentenced to death. His grave, which carried no inscription, is in the back row. Pte W.J. Earl (XII.B.10) of 1/7th Lancashire Fusiliers (125th Brigade, 42nd Division) was executed for desertion on 27 May 1918. Pte T. Brigham (XI.C.15) of 1/10th Manchesters (126th Brigade, 42nd Division) was executed for desertion on 4 June 1918.

The site of the halt on the south side of the road is quite recognisable and the former track has been turned into a public footpath. The railway house still exists, as do a number of reused railway sleepers.

WARLOY-BAILLON is a village to the west of ALBERT on the D91 road to the south of VARENNES and 2 miles to the north of the main AMIENS–ALBERT road. During the 11 months prior to the 1916 Somme battle, the village had become an important medical centre. On 31 July 1915, Maj D. Rorie of the Royal Army Medical Corps, serving with 1/2nd (Highland) Field Ambulance (51st Division), arrived in the village from MÉRICOURT-L'ABBÉ; his unit took over the civilian hospital from the French field ambulance personnel who had been in the village for 9 months. Rorie described the village as a combination of two communes, which prior to the war had a population of 800 people; its main centre of manufacture was a small weaving factory.

The French medical staff left the buildings the following day after a convivial evening and sang their version of 'Tipperary' as they marched down the village street. That evening, men of 1/2nd (Highland) Field Ambulance attended a concert arranged by French troops, which took place in a building next to the Hôtel des Voyageurs in the main street; they were to attend many similar cheerful functions over the next 5 months. On 2 August, the field ambulance staff were invited to a lunch in a garden in the next door village of VADENCOURT, which was again provided by their French Allies. This round of hospitality could not go on for ever and on 3 August, 1/2nd (Highland) Field Ambulance soon settled down to work, running a divisional rest station for 51st Division which was opened on 6 August. 1/3rd (Highland) Field Ambulance (also 51st Division) functioned as a main dressing station in MILLENCOURT and sent stretcher cases here, while 2/1st (Highland) Field Ambulance (also 51st Division) were at Ebart near AMIENS.

According to *A Medico's Luck in the War*, the memoirs of Maj D. Rorie of the Royal Army Medical Corps, serving with 1/2nd (Highland) Field Ambulance (51st Division), the hospital at Warloy-Baillon was a modern two-storey building, used before the war as a cottage hospital and as a hospice for the aged poor of the district . . . In the orchard behind, we ran up some canvas where the ground sloped down to the old church and to the village school; and the school rooms there and a small farm building beside the hospital were also used for divisional sick and the inevitable scabies ward. The men were billeted in the Rue D'Harponville; while further up the street the officers' mess was established in a disused and somewhat dilapidated villa . . .

On 1 December, 1/2nd (Highland) Field Ambulance was out of action, owing to a failure in the water supply. On 29 December, 92nd Field Ambulance (32nd Division) arrived in Warloy-Baillon and took over the divisional rest station from 1/2nd (Highland) Field Ambulance. At this time, there were 120 to 140 patients in the hospital.

At the turn of the year 1915, 15th Highland Light Infantry (14th Brigade, 51st Division) attended a church service at a 'drab little Protestant chapel at Warloy on the Somme. The pastor was serving with the French forces and his wife was a nurse. The key was handed over by the Maire. A colour of the Royal Scots and two probationers of the Scottish Church helped in the holy rite.'

In early 1916, sappers of No. 527 Field Company, Royal Engineers (5th Division), sank wells and organised an additional water supply and pump line linking Warloy-Baillon with HÉNENCOURT to the south-east.

Over the following months, 32nd, 49th and 51st Divisions were the main users of the hospital buildings. As the hospital had been stripped, 92nd Field Ambulance and 1/2nd (West Riding) Field Ambulance (49th Division) were forced to start from scratch when they arrived on 13 February 1916, yet 200 patients arrived within 24 hours. The hospital was set up with the hospice as the main building in the Grande Rue, with five Sisters of Mercy, four wards of 12 beds and several private wards. In addition, there was a small block for infectious cases; two schools, about 200yds away, also provided accommodation. The officers' hospital was a well-built house that housed 8, later 11, patients. A large yard in the complex was surrounded by outbuildings and barns.

On 4 March, a day of heavy snow, 1/2nd (West Riding) Field Ambulance left for VAUCHELLES-LÈS-AUTHIE; they were replaced by 92nd Field Ambulance (32nd Division), which was back in the village at a time when its divisional headquarters was at HÉNENCOURT.

By the spring of 1916, Warloy-Baillon had become a popular billeting area. The hospital specialised in handling abdominal and chest cases and ran an operating centre from 24 April 1916 to 7 January 1917. In mid-May, 90th Field Ambulance (32nd Division) began building a combined receiving and dressing room hut at the end of the officers' hospital garden; by the end of June, there was an operating centre in the small civilian hospital, together with 75 beds, supplemented by accommodation for 375 patients in tents, huts and other buildings. On 29 June, 90th Field Ambulance received 20 dead, brought down from the front area for burial.

At the end of June, units of 25th Division were in the village; at this time, there seems to have been bad blood between some of the field ambulances who ran the hospital. One comment recorded in the war diary of 76th Field Ambulance (25th Division) (WO95/2239) suggests that the hospital 'should have been run as a base hospital and not by Field Ambulances'.

On 2 July, the situation at the hospital was said to be chaotic, with 'too many wounded unable to be evacuated', lying outside the tents. Once it became generally known that 76th Field Ambulance were to take over from 92nd Field Ambulance, the medical officers of the latter field ambulance 'slackened off'; their commanding officer was preoccupied with paperwork, whereas the writer of 76th Field Ambulance's war diary rolled up his sleeves and got 'stuck in'. At 0530hrs on 5 July, 92nd Field Ambulance marched out, leaving everything dirty.

In the months following 1 July, 12th and 32nd Divisions continued to use Warloy-Baillon and units from 25th Division were here at the beginning of the battle and at the end of October. On 10 August, HM the King visited the hospital for abdominal cases, having come from CONTAY through the Australian lines.

In *Private 12768*, Pte J. Jackson of 1st Cameron Highlanders (1st Brigade, 1st Division) recalls being billeted in wooden huts in Hénencourt Wood at the beginning of November; he and a friend visited Warloy-Baillon; 'noticing a church lit up, we entered and found ourselves in the midst of a Catholic service, but no one took any exception to us as we joined the congregation'. He returned to the village at the end of January 1917: 'Our billets at Warloy were cold, draughty, outbuildings belonging to farms, and there were no fires allowed. So severe was the frost that even our bread was as hard as stones . . .'

When last visited, Warloy-Baillon appeared to be pretty run down, and has seen better days. The hospice in the main road still exists and is called Maison de

Retraite F. Carnoy. The village has two cemeteries on the east side where Dominion casualties are buried, Warloy-Baillon Communal Cemetery and Warloy-Baillon Communal Cemetery Extension.

The first burial by field ambulances in Warloy-Baillon Communal Cemetery was made in July 1915 and the last on 1 July 1916. The cemetery contains the graves of 46 men from the Commonwealth and 158 Frenchmen. One of the men buried here, and possibly the last to be so, is Lt Col P.W. Machell (A.17), Commanding Officer 11th Borders (97th Brigade, 32nd Division), who was killed on 1 July in the area of LEIPZIG SALIENT; 54 years old at the time of his death, Machell had virtually raised 11th Borders single-handed between 1914 and 1916. There was once a bronze wreath at the foot of his grave, but it has been stolen. A second senior officer buried here is Lt Col T.M.M. Berkeley (A.2) of the Black Watch (Royal Highlanders), who was killed in action near ALBERT on 20 May while serving as Camp Commandant, VIII Corps, Staff Deputy Adjutant Quartermaster General. He had been a member of the 'Gentlemen at Arms'.

Warloy-Baillon Communal Cemetery Extension, designed by Sir Reginald Blomfield, has 1,348 identified Commonwealth casualties, as well as 18 German war graves of prisoners of war. The graves in the main reflect the fighting during July to November 1916 and from the spring of 1918. Lt Col A. Annesley (III.B.1) of 8th Royal Fusiliers, who died of wounds on 8 July 1916, is buried here; his battalion had been involved in the fighting for OVILLERS. Another 'notable' senior officer buried here is Maj Gen E.C. Ingouville-Williams CB, DSO (III.D.13), General Officer Commanding 34th Division, who was killed by shell-fire on 22 July 1916 after reconnoitring in the vicinity of MAMETZ WOOD when walking back from CONTALMAISON to reach his car at MONTAUBAN-DE-PICARDIE; some accounts say he was 'souvenir hunting' and others that he was 'out for a walk'. Known as 'Inky Bill', he was formerly with the Worcestershire Regiment and was 54 years old. One of the officers who attended the funeral, which was a spectacular affair, was the author C.S. Collison of 11th Royal Warwicks (112th Brigade, 34th Division). The hearse was drawn by black horses with black plumes supplied by 34th Division's artillery.

The grave of L/Cpl F.H. Murphy (V.E.5) of 24th Australian Battalion (6th Australian Brigade, 2nd Australian Division) has a special memorial consisting of a heavy stone cross about 5½ft high. Also buried here is L/Cpl G.E. Hughes (VI.D.18) of 7th King's Own (56th Brigade, 19th Division), who was executed on 23 November 1916 on a charge of desertion.

WARNIMONT WOOD (Bois de Warnimont) is on the D176 road in a valley between BUS-LÈS-ARTOIS and AUTHIE. On 22 July 1915, No. 2/1 (South Midland) Field Company, Royal Engineers (48th Division), were already felling trees and cutting timber here, having taken over from the French, and later supplied logs to the artillery for emplacements. A few days later, elements of 48th Division were in reserve in the Wood, during which time there was thunder and terrible rain over two nights; they were forced to use barns as billets in SARTON, a village to the west, before they returned to the line.

In the second part of April 1916, 11th East Lancashires (94th Brigade, 31st Division) were in Warnimont Wood when in divisional reserve. On 10 May, 12th York & Lancasters (also 94th Brigade, 31st Division) were inspected here by Sir Douglas Haig during their training. He had come through the Wood with a brilliant cavalcade of staff officers, Lancers and Guards. 12th York & Lancasters were camped here between 6 and 15 May and again between 19 and 30 June.

On 14 May, 10th East Yorkshires (92nd Brigade, 31st Division) moved back here after spending a night in BUS-LÈS-ARTOIS. The Wood 'lay in the valley between Bus and Authie and here we occupied huts and tents pitched out of sight under the tall trees. The distance of this camp, about seven miles, from the line.' They spent 9 days of complete rest from trench life in 'this delightful spot'. They used to have a bath in BUS-LÈS-ARTOIS from time to time.

The band brought out its instruments once again and made the woods sing with all the brightest tunes of the day, whilst we lay around in the thick undergrowth. When it became too cold to remain in the open any longer we retired into our huts and our vocal efforts replaced the more tuneful music of the band. How great it was to hear the boom of the guns and yet to feel for a short time at least one was out of it all and free to sleep. Concerts arose in the evening without much arrangement – almost spontaneously. Those men who were later on to form the 'Tonics', as good a concert party as any brigade possessed, used to make the wood re-echo with songs like 'Nirvana'. Their voices have been heard many a time since, to the delight of their pals fresh from the trenches, and in fact at frequent intervals during these long years after the War, but never so sweetly as in those happy days in Warnimont Wood . . .

Later in May, 10th East Yorkshires provided a massive working party for the trenches. On 24 May they handed over their quarters in Warnimont Wood to 16th West Yorkshires (93rd Brigade, 31st Division). On 12 May, 95th Field Ambulance (31st Division) arrived here, followed by the rest of the field ambulances. On 24 May, 18th Durham Light Infantry (93rd Brigade, 31st Division) moved back into camp here and spent their time digging assembly trenches, burying cables, building mined dugouts and aid posts and many other tasks. They moved forward on 30 June.

Warnimont Wood was used regularly as a hutment camp behind the lines by several battalions, including those of 7th Brigade (25th Division) in mid-July; 10th King's Royal Rifle Corps (59th Brigade, 20th Division) spent time here on 26 July, before going on to bivouac at SAILLY-AU-BOIS on 27 July and trenches at HÉBUTERNE on 1 August. At the beginning of August, 1st Scots Guards (2nd Guards Brigade, Guards Division) were in the Wood, then described as a wooded plateau, whose steep sides rose from the eastern side of the BUS-LÈS-ARTOIS–AUTHIE road. On 6 August, 2nd Irish Guards rejoined 2nd Guards Brigade here; on 9 August, HM the King and HRH the Prince of Wales visited 2nd Irish Guards and 1st Coldstream Guards (both also 2nd Guards Brigade, Guards Division). They left for Vauchelles, where they saw 1st Irish Guard and 3rd Coldstream Guards (both 1st Guards Brigade, Guards Division).

In early September, 1st Buckinghamshires (145th Brigade, 48th Division) were in Warnimont Wood. In October, the battalions of 92nd Brigade, 31st Division) played each other at football and rugby; by this time, the camp had become extremely muddy.

Between 5 June and early October, 4th, 12th, 20th, 25th, 31st, 39th, 48th and 51st Divisions had units camped here.

WATERLÔT FARM was a German strongpoint in the second line between LONGUEVAL and GUILLEMONT. It was called a farm to distinguish it from buildings on the D20 LONGUEVAL–GUILLEMONT road, but it was really a sugar refinery. The road from the refinery to GUILLE-MONT as far as the level railway station and just south, then south-east to the crossroads east of the station, was a divisional boundary. The real farm was in the south-west quarter of GINCHY, which in mid-July 1916 was still in German hands.

In mid-July, the right-hand elements of XIII Corps had yet to capture the ruins of the sugar refinery. Although Allied troops entered it on 15 July, they were forced to withdraw owing to heavy shelling; the refinery was captured and consolidated on 17 July. Later it was used, among other things, as a base for pigeons for communication between BERNAFAY WOOD and CORBIE.

Although once the Allies had taken the sugar refinery they used it continuously as a base, there is little mention of it in accounts of the later stages of the battle. It was constantly bombarded by the Germans and by September the reserve trenches were in a very bad state. In September, 60th Brigade (20th Division) were here during the FLERS and COURCELETTE fighting, soon after 15th Brigade (5th Division). There were no dugouts and, as the year went on, conditions grew worse because relentless rain made the position very muddy.

WEDGE WOOD is between GINCHY and MAUREPAS and is north-west of FAFFEMONT FARM; it derives its name from its shape. On 3 September 1916, 1st Bedfords (15th Brigade, 5th Division) captured the Wood, and part of the battalion reached the GINCHY road in the area of 95th Brigade (5th Division). Having taken GUILLE-MONT, 20th Division also reached the Wedge Wood–GINCHY road, but were in no condition to attack any further. Gun pits ran south of the Wood, which was under fire from FAFFEMONT FARM. On 4 September, the German line ran north-east of the valley close to the Wood; by this time, Wedge Wood Farm had ceased to exist. Battalion headquarters therefore moved to shell-holes in the low ground to the south-west of LEUZE WOOD.

WELCOME WOODS were in the CORBIE–BRAY-SUR-SOMME area. Towards the end of June 1916, the South African Brigade (9th Division) slept in huts here; after breakfast they marched 1 mile downhill to the Somme Canal, where they washed and filled their dixies. Later, they left the Woods and marched to SAILLY-LE-SEC, further along the Somme Valley towards BRAY-SUR-SOMME.

WHITE CITY quarries were behind the British line at BEAUMONT-HAMEL in 1916 and were excavated before the battle began. The position was so-named because the excavated chalk appeared to observers as a 'white streak across the countryside'. The position was on the reverse side of a chalk cliff about 40ft high and could not be ranged accurately by the German artillery; shells tended to skim over the cliff edge and burst some 60yds or 70yds back from the cliff. White City was very important to the British as it provided a relatively secure head-quarters close to the line, and in the caves there were a battle headquarters, dressing stations and dumps for the Royal Engineers.

On 1 July, Lt Col C. Howkins of 1/6th Royal Warwicks (143rd Brigade, 48th Division) was severely wounded here. There are many accounts of battalions spending time in the White City trenches and these include 13th Royal Welsh Fusiliers (113th Brigade, 38th Division) in mid-July. During the November battles, when much of BEAUMONT-HAMEL was finally captured, 22nd Royal Fusiliers (99th Brigade, 2nd Division), 17th Royal Fusiliers (5th Brigade, 2nd Division) and 16th Highland Light Infantry (97th Brigade, 32nd Division) had their headquarters here.

WONDERWORK, a German strongpoint guarding the southern side of the THIEPVAL defences, was behind the Hindenburg Trench, which in turn was in front of the LEIPZIG SALIENT; there was much fighting in order to secure it. On 3 September 1916, Lt Col H.T. Cotton DSO of 2nd South Lancashires (75th Brigade, 25th Division) was killed here when leading an attack against THIEPVAL. The enemy line was entered but the attackers were forced to withdraw. Cotton's name is commemorated on the Thiepval Memorial.

Eleven days later, Wonderwork was finally captured, together with the German Front Line and 250yds of Hohenzollern Trench to the right; the two battalions involved were 8th Duke of Wellington's and 9th West Yorkshires (both 32nd Brigade, 11th Division). 6th Yorkshires (also 32nd Brigade, 11th Division) relieved the latter battalion when the enemy were still retaliating, at last making three violent bombing attacks. Officer casualties during the night operations included four officers, one of whom was Lt Col C.G. Forsyth DSO, Commanding Officer 6th Yorkshires (32nd Brigade, 11th Division) who was later buried at Blighty Valley Cemetery (I.F.13).

Y

Y RAVINE is on the south side of BEAUMONT-HAMEL and can easily be reached from either NEWFOUNDLAND PARK or from the D163 road. The Ravine ran about ½ mile south of the village and has two arms that extend outwards at the western end, giving it a Y shape.

On 1 July 1916, Station Road, leading south-eastwards from BEAUMONT-HAMEL village, was an objective of 29th Division. Y Ravine had steep banks in which numerous deep dugouts could safely stand the heaviest bombardments. In addition to being honeycombed with dugouts, it was crossed with numerous trenches. This meant that the garrison there could be relieved or supported from either Station Road or the neighbouring trenches.

In *The Old Front Line*, John Masefield explained that Y Ravine gave the British a great deal of trouble; the German defenders had sunk shafts into the banks of the Ravine, tunnelled living rooms, both above and below the gulley bottom, linked the rooms with galleries, and cut hatchways and bolting holes that led to the surface as well as to the gully. In this gully barracks, and in similar shelters cut in the chalk of the steeper banks near BEAUMONT-HAMEL, the enemy could hold ready large numbers of men to repel an assault or make a counter-attack.

On 1 July, apart from the attack of 1st Newfound-landers (88th Brigade, 29th Division), Y Ravine was also assaulted by 2nd South Wales Borderers, 1st Borders and 1st King's Own Scottish Borderers (all 87th Brigade, 29th Division), but with little success. Starting out from St John's Road, between AUCHONVILLERS and HAMEL, 1st Borders, followed by 2nd South Wales Borderers, made towards the western end of the Ravine and reached the area just to the north of 1st Newfoundlanders' attack. 2nd South Wales Borderers were wiped out by machine-gun fire; despite this disaster, 1st Borders were ordered to follow up, and also suffered very heavy losses at the hands of the German machine-gunners.

Y Ravine also came to prominence during the mid-November attempts to capture BEAUMONT-HAMEL. One witness at this time was Paul Maze, a French liaison officer who worked with the British and who was also a painter. In *A Frenchman in Khaki*, Maze wrote that he made his way in appalling visibility towards Y Ravine, through destroyed barbed wire and over caved-in trenches. Reaching a steep bank that rose before him and ascending to the top, he could barely see the bottom or opposite sides and heard bombs exploding all along this blurred crevasse; the rest of the escort had gone below to inspect a tunnel that communicated with another dugout.

Maze stepped down into darkness, stretched out his map and located his position in front of Station Road. The fighting continually came from there, as well as from BEAUCOURT-SUR-L'ANCRE, lying lost in the fog about 1,000yds away. It was evident

Z

to him that enemy troops and the Allies had got mixed up in the fog. Yet 'surprisingly', from all accounts, the day had been a great success: over 5,000 prisoners had been taken. On 13 November, 153rd Brigade (51st Division) reached Y Ravine and consolidated in Beaucourt Trench, north-west of BEAUCOURT-SUR-L'ANCRE.

Made in the spring of 1917, Y Ravine Cemetery was then redesignated Y Ravine Cemetery No. 1; Y Ravine Cemetery No. 2 was concentrated into Ancre British Cemetery after the Armistice. The cemetery register records the details of 366 graves, including 328 soldiers (or sailors or Marines of 63rd Division) from the United Kingdom and 38 from Newfoundland. Most of these men fell on 1 July when serving with 29th Division.

In *The Wet Flanders Plain*, Henry Williamson described a visit to Y Ravine in 1925. 'The dugouts of the ravine had subsided, the dry-rotted timbers broke with a touch; the pistons and mainshaft and cylinders of an aeroplane rusted in the grasses.' Williamson wrote that he remembered the 'charred framework on the ridge above Station Road, with rifle barrels and holed helmets and burst minewerfer cases. Those dreaded oil drums of the minnies.'

In recent years, the Durand Group, who have been actively involved in subterranean work on Vimy Ridge, have also turned their attentions to Y Ravine. They began their survey by trying to access a German mining tunnel at the head of the Ravine. Using German archive material, they wanted to establish that this particular tunnel might have been used for intercepting the British First Avenue tunnel. The whole project of assessing the underground workings of Y Ravine is ongoing and also, in places, highly dangerous.

ZOLLERN REDOUBT and Zollern Trench were part of the German redoubt system to the north of THIEPVAL village; STUFF REDOUBT was to the immediate north-west. Zollern Trench ran from THIEPVAL village to Zollern Redoubt and then towards COURCELETTE; the most easterly part was the first Allied objective in the Battle for Thiepval Ridge on 26 September 1916, while the section of Zollern Trench between THIEPVAL and Zollern Redoubt was part of the second objective and was reached on that day.

The *Official History of the War* notes that the Allies were aware that the Germans had withdrawn from Zollern Redoubt by 0630hrs on 27 September. In *Sir Douglas Haig's Great Push* the action is described in this way: 'on the right, our troops, advancing in three waves, carried the outer defences of Mouquet Farm, and pushing on, penetrated into Zollern Redoubt, which they stormed and proceeded to consolidate'.

There is a link here with the poet Ivor Gurney of 2/5th Glosters (184th Brigade, 61st Division); he appears to have been a signaller at the end of the Somme battle. In November, 2/5th Glosters' headquarters office was in Zollern Trench; they had come to the Somme from the Laventie Line at the end of October. Gurney wrote songs in the trenches and his 'By a Bierside' is the first that he was known to have composed in these circumstances. The song deals with a longing for peace and security, left behind at home, and a troubled concern with the nature of death. The words were written by John Masefield. Later Gurney was to write 'In Flanders' at CRUCIFIX CORNER near THIEPVAL in January 1917. In *Severn To Somme*, Gurney wrote 'that those who buy or read the book with the idea of obtaining information about the doings of the 2/5th Glosters would be disappointed'.

APPENDIX I

A NOTE ON CASUALTIES INCURRED IN THE SOMME BATTLE

I have no wish to enter the controversy over the casualties incurred in the Battle of the Somme in 1916, as the subject has been written about on many occasions. If readers wish to look deeply into the controversy then they should consult the following books or sources: the Official History volumes, the Liddell Hart Archive at King's College, London, the writings of Winston Churchill, Lloyd George, Sir Charles Oman, G. Wynne and M. Williams. All these writers are in the main concerned with the British viewpoint and the continuing re-assessment of the casualty figures.

The main reason for the continuing debate, I suppose, is to try and agree on figures that are the most accurate but secondly with some commentators to show that the Germans suffered more losses than the Allies. However, comparisons are not easy, as the two sides treated their casualties statistically differently. The British took their figures from the daily roll calls recorded at casualty clearing stations. This figure was therefore always too high, as it included those men missing or taken prisoner, who subsequently returned. Thus this figure had always to be adjusted downward. The British casualty figure is now accepted by the majority to be in the region of 419,000 and the number of these who were killed or mortally wounded was probably in the region of 125,000.

Although agreement on the French casualty figures as having been 204,000 has been reached, it is the German figure which appears to be the most difficult one for historians to agree upon and there are at least twelve differing sets of their casualty figures and this is without going into the subject very deeply. The number which this author prefers is the figure of 419,989, which has been taken from the *German Medical History*, Volume III,

which covers the period of the Allied bombardment from 21 June until the end of November. General Edmonds, the British Official Historian, wrote in the preface to the *Official History of the War: Military Operations France and Belgium 1916, Volume Two*: 'The German Historians seem to be torn between the two conflicting sentiments: first a desire to show how heavily their troops suffered before they gave up, and secondly, a determination to assert that they did not suffer as heavily as their opponents.'

However, it was Edmonds himself who had the obsession about the comparative casualty figures, which is what the controversy is really about, and he does appear to be clearly guilty of trying to make the figures tell the story in the best light for the Allies, yet at the same time to show how the Germans lost more men than they owned up to. I am afraid that the reason for this can only be a political one and that at the time of writing he was trying to protect reputations. If one needs evidence to support this theory, then one only has to look at some of the correspondence between Edmonds and C.E.W. Bean, the Official Australian Historian.

Bean sent Edmonds the drafts of the volumes of the *Official History of Australia in the War* as they became available and, as the letter below demonstrates, he took note of what Edmonds' comments on his text and made suitable adjustments to his manuscript. However, it is in the second paragraph that the Edmonds' case is severely damaged, in that Bean quotes John Buchan as saying that the British authorities could maintain the Somme offensive until a loss of 500,000 men was reached. This sentence damages Edmonds' thesis, in that unknown to him, the British were allowing for another 80,000 casualties if one accepts that 419,000 is the nearest accurate figure.

CONFIDENTIAL

Dear Edmonds,

Many thanks for your final comments upon my Volume III. I have again modified the judgements contained in it by bringing out more clearly the undoubted damage inflicted on the German morale by the Somme offensive, damage which was obvious at the time and which we all recognised.

You ask who was the official who informed me that the authorities recognised that the offensive of 1916 could be maintained until the British had lost 500,000 men. I can of course only give you the name in the strictest confidence. It was John Buchan, then working in the Foreign Office, who told me this on the opening day of the Somme offensive, while we were watching the artillery bombardment. I made a full note in my diary (which is now one of the most important of the Australian records). Buchan was in touch with G.H.Q. and with the British Cabinet and, to some extent, in the confidence both of Ministers and of the staff – which we war correspondents were not. I don't know from which source the information came, but there can be no possible question of its truth, for he was speaking of a conversation of which he had recent personal knowledge, and he was a most reliable man. I don't know if he would remember the matter now, but you have my leave to mention it to him if you care to do so.

Yours sincerely,

C.E.W. BEAN.

Sir James Edmonds, C.B., C.M.G.,
Historical Section (Military Branch),
Committee of Imperial Defence,
Audit House,
Victoria Embankment,
London EC4, England.
Ref. LH/Edmonds VI/2

For the wounded on the Somme, the British figures were approximately 300,000 and of these the great majority were evacuated by ambulance train; 8,739 were transported by barge and 6,183 by road. In addition to this figure, the figure for the sick was 13,766.

To sum up then, it is obvious that although the British and Germans might be around the 419,000 figure, it is the French figure of 204,000 casualties that tips the scale in favour of the Germans. It can hardly be surprising that for the first part of the Somme battle at least, that the Allies lost more men than the enemy did. Although initially nearly 30 per cent of our shells were defective, the Germans were often well protected by their deep dugouts and their superior positions in defending what was often high ground or the best position on the battlefield.

The officer casualties were approximately 4.8 per cent of the total British casualties, which was three or four times the corresponding German figure. However, the Germans might have 'economised' on officers but they did not 'economise' on their NCOs, who had been very highly trained, and at the beginning of the battle there were still many left in the German Army who had been in at the beginning of the war, but their ranks were savagely depleted by the end of the Somme battle.

HIGHER COMMAND, BRITISH EXPEDITIONARY FORCE

GENERAL HEADQUARTERS

General Officer Commander-in-Chief: Gen Sir Douglas Haig

Chief of the General Staff: Lt Gen Sir L.E. Kiggell

Major-General Royal Artillery: Maj Gen J.F.N. Birch

FOURTH ARMY

General Officer Commanding: Lt Gen Sir Henry Rawlinson

Major-General General Staff: Maj Gen A.A. Montgomery

Deputy-Adjutant & Quartermaster-General: Maj Gen H.C. Holman

Major-General Royal Artillery: Maj Gen C.E.D. Budworth

Chief Engineer: Maj Gen R.U.H. Buckland

Deputy-Director Signals: Col R.G. Earle

RESERVE (LATER FIFTH) ARMY

General Officer Commanding: Lt Gen Sir Hubert Gough

Major-General General Staff: Maj Gen N. Malcolm

Deputy-Adjutant & Quartermaster-General: Maj Gen H.N. Sargent

Major-General Royal Artillery: Maj Gen H.C.C. Uniacke

Chief Engineer: Maj Gen R.P. Lee

Deputy-Director Signals: Col E.G. Godfrey-Faussett

CAVALRY CORPS

General Officer Commanding: Lt Gen C.T. McM. Kavanagh

Brigadier-General General Staff: Brig Gen A.F. Home

Brigadier-General Royal Artillery: Brig Gen H.H Tudor

II CORPS

General Officer Commanding: Lt Gen C.W. Jacob

Brigadier-General General Staff: Brig Gen P. Howell

Brigadier-General Royal Artillery: Brig Gen C.E. Lawrie

III CORPS

General Officer Commanding: Lt Gen Sir W.P. Pulteney

Brigadier-General General Staff: Brig Gen C.F. Romer

Brigadier-General Royal Artillery: Brig Gen T.A. Tancred

V CORPS

General Officer Commanding: Lt Gen E.A. Fanshawe

Brigadier-General General Staff: Brig Gen G.F. Boyd

Brigadier-General Royal Artillery: Brig Gen A. Stokes

VII CORPS

General Officer Commanding: Lt Gen Sir T. d'O. Snow

Brigadier-General General Staff: Brig Gen F. Lyon

Brigadier-General Royal Artillery: Brig Gen C.M. Ross-Johnson

VIII CORPS

General Officer Commanding: Lt Gen Sir A.G. Hunter-Weston

Brigadier-General General Staff: Brig Gen The Hon. W.P. Hore-Ruthven

Brigadier-General Royal Artillery: Brig Gen W. Strong

X CORPS
General Officer Commanding: Lt Gen Sir T.L.N. Morland
Brigadier-General General Staff: Brig Gen A.R. Cameron
Brigadier-General Royal Artillery: Brig Gen C.C. Van Straubenzee

XIII CORPS
General Officer Commanding: Lt Gen Sir W.N. Congreve VC
Brigadier-General General Staff: Brig Gen W.H. Greenly
Brigadier-General Royal Artillery: Brig Gen R. St C. Lecky

XIV CORPS
General Officer Commanding: Lt Gen the Earl of Cavan
Brigadier-General General Staff: Brig Gen The Hon. J.F. Gathorne-Hardy
Brigadier-General Royal Artillery: Brig Gen A.E. Wardrop

XV CORPS
General Officer Commanding: Lt Gen H.S. Horne
Brigadier-General General Staff: Brig Gen L.R. Vaughan
Brigadier-General Royal Artillery: Brig Gen E.W. Alexander VC

I ANZAC CORPS
General Officer Commanding: Lt Gen Sir W.R. Birdwood
Brigadier-General General Staff: Brig Gen C.B.B. White
Brigadier-General Royal Artillery: Brig Gen W.J. Napier

CANADIAN CORPS
General Officer Commanding: Lt Gen The Hon. Sir J. Byng
Brigadier-General General Staff: Brig Gen P.P. de B. Radcliffe
Brigadier-General Royal Artillery: Brig Gen H.E. Burstall

MACHINE GUN CORPS (HEAVY SECTION)
Commander: Col E.D. Swinton
Commander in France: Lt Col R.W. Bradley
Brigade-Major: Capt G. LeQ. Martel

APPENDIX III

Battles and Engagements

FOURTH ARMY

Fourth Army Headquarters began to form at Tilques on 5 February 1916, and 19 days later Army Headquarters moved to Querrieu. A week later, Fourth Army took over the right sector of the BEF front, a 15-mile stretch from Curlu on the Somme to Hébuterne. Fourth Army was in touch on the south with the French Sixth Army and to the north with the right of the British Third Army. Fourth Army took over this front with XIII Corps (7th, 18th and 30th Divisions) and X Corps (32nd, 36th, 48th and 49th Divisions) in the line and VIII Corps (31st Division) in Army Reserve.

Battles of the Somme, 1916: III, VIII, X, XIII, XIV, XV and Cavalry Corps, plus C and D Companies, Heavy Machine Gun Corps.

1–13 July	Battle of Albert: III Corps, VIII Corps (until 4 July), X Corps (until 4 July), XIII Corps and XV Corps.
1 July	Capture of Montauban: 30th Division (XIII Corps).
1 July	Capture of Mametz: 7th Division (XV Corps).
2 July	Capture of Fricourt: 17th Division (XV Corps).
2–4 July	Capture of La Boisselle: 19th Division (III Corps).
3 July	Capture of Bernafay Wood: 9th Division (XIII Corps).
7–11 July	Mametz Wood: 38th Division (XV Corps).
10 July	Capture of Contalmaison: 23rd Division (III Corps).
7–13 July	Fighting in Trônes Wood: 30th Division (XIII Corps).
14–17 July	Battle of Bazentin Ridge: III, XIII and XV Corps.
14 July	Capture of Trônes Wood: 54th Brigade (18th Division, XIII Corps).
14–18 and 29 July	Capture of Longueval: 3rd and 9th Divisions (XIII Corps), 14–18 July; 5th Division (XV Corps), 29 July.
15 July–3 September	Battle of Delville Wood: XIII Corps, 15 July–16 August; XIV Corps, 17 August–3 September; XV Corps, 31 August–3 September.
20–30 July	Attacks on High Wood: 19th Division (III Corps) and 5th, 7th, 33rd and 51st Divisions (XV Corps).
27 and 28 July	Capture and consolidation of Delville Wood: 2nd Division (XIII Corps).
8 and 9 August	Attack of Waterlôt Farm–Guillemont: 2nd Division (XIII Corps).
23 July–3 September	Battle of Pozières Ridge: III Corps.
3–6 September	Battle of Guillemont: XIV and XV Corps.
9 September	Battle of Ginchy: XIV and XV Corps (part).
15–22 September	Battle of Flers-Courcelette: III Corps plus 8 tanks of D Company, XIV Corps plus 17 tanks of C Company, XV Corps plus 17 tanks of D Company, 1st Cavalry and 2nd (Indian) Cavalry Divisions (Cavalry Corps).
15 September	Capture of Flers: 41st and NZ Divisions (XV Corps) plus 1 tank.
15 September	Capture of Martinpuich: 15th Division (III Corps) plus 4 tanks.
25–28 September	Battle of Morval: III Corps (plus 2 tanks of D Company, 25 September), XIV Corps

(plus 2 tanks of C Company, 26 September), XV Corps (plus 1 tank of D Company, 26 September), Cavalry Corps.

25 September	Capture of Lesbœufs: Guards and 6th Divisions (XIV Corps).
26 September	Capture of Combles: 56th Division (XIV Corps) plus 2 tanks of C Company.
26 September	Capture of Gird Trench and Gueudecourt: 21st Division (XV Corps) plus 1 tank of D Company.
1–18 October	Battle of the Transloy Ridges: III Corps, XIV Corps plus 3 tanks, XV Corps plus 2 tanks.
1–3 October	Capture of Eaucourt l'Abbaye: 47th Division (III Corps).
7 October	Capture of le Sars: 23rd Division (III Corps).
7 October– 5 November	Attacks on the Butte de Warlencourt: 9th, 23rd, 47th, 48th and 50th Divisions (III Corps).
3–11 November	Battle of the Ancre Heights: III Corps (part).
13–18 November	Battle of the Ancre: III Corps (part).

RESERVE, LATER FIFTH ARMY

Headquarters of the Reserve Corps (then at Regnière Écluse – 5 miles west-north-west of Crécy-en-Ponthieu) became the Headquarters of the Reserve Army on 22 May 1916. Three weeks later, Reserve Army HQ moved to Daours (6 miles east of Amiens); and on 2 July 1916, preparatory to taking over the northern part of the Somme battle-front, Reserve Army HQ was installed at Toutencourt (10 miles south-east of Doullens).

Two days later, the Reserve Army took over (from Fourth Army) the left of the Somme battle-front from La Boisselle to Hébuterne (8 miles), and with it X Corps (25th, 32nd, 36th and 49th Divisions) and VIII Corps (4th, 29th, 31st and 48th Divisions). At the outset of this change of command, the immediate attack of this sector of the German position was postponed and on this part of the front trench-warfare tactics were adopted; though X Corps fought on to extend the two footings it had already gained to the north and south of Thiepval. The Reserve Army was renamed Fifth Army on 30 October.

Battles of the Somme, 1916: II, V, VIII, X, XIII, Canadian and I Anzac Corps, plus A, C, and D Companies, Heavy Machine Gun Corps.

4–13 July	Battle of Albert: VIII and X Corps.
14–17 July	Battle of Bazentin Ridge: X Corps.
17 July	Capture of Ovillers: 58th Division (X Corps).
23 July–3 September	Battle of Pozières Ridge: X Corps (23–4 July), II Corps (24 July–3 September), I Anzac Corps (28 July–3 September).
6 August– 3 September	Fighting for Mouquet Farm: 12th, 25th and 48th Divisions (II Corps) and 1st Australian, 2nd Australian and 4th Australian Divisions (I Anzac Corps).
14 September	Capture of the Wonder Work: 11th Division (II Corps).
15–22 September	Battle of Flers-Courcelette: II Corps, Canadian Corps plus 6 tanks of C Company.
26–28 September	Battle of Thiepval Ridge: II Corps (plus 6 tanks of C Company, 26 September), V Corps (part), Canadian Corps (plus 2 tanks of C Company, 26 September).
26 September	Capture of Mouquet Farm: 11th Division (II Corps) plus 2 tanks of C Company.
1–18 October	Battle of Transloy Ridges: Canadian Corps.
1 October– 11 November	Battle of the Ancre Heights: II Corps plus 4 tanks of A Company, V Corps (part), Canadian Corps.
9 October	Capture of Stuff Redoubt: 25th Division (II Corps).
14 October	Capture of Schwaben Redoubt: 39th Division (II Corps).
21 October	Capture of Regina Trench and Redoubt: 18th Division plus 4 tanks of A Company and 25th Division (both II Corps).
21 October	Capture of Stuff Trench: 39th Division (II Corps).
13–18 November	Battle of the Ancre: II Corps (plus 3 tanks of A Company, 13 and 18 November), V Corps (plus 2 tanks of D Company, 13 November; 3 tanks of D Company, 14 November; 2 tanks of D Company, 16 November; 5 tanks of D Company, 18 November), XIII Corps.
13 November	Capture of Beaumont-Hamel: 51st Division (V Corps) plus 2 tanks of D Company.
14 November	Capture of Beaucourt: 190th Brigade (63rd Division, V Corps) plus 2 tanks of D Company.

ARMY DIVISIONS

At the beginning of the First World War in 1914 a British infantry division contained over 18,000 men. In each typically there were three infantry brigades, which had four battalions each; four artillery brigades with their batteries, including a heavy battery; and a cavalry squadron. Later, field companies of the Royal Engineers were added, along with a cyclist company, a signals company, also of the Royal Engineers, and medical and supply units. In the months before the opening of the Battle of the Somme, independent trench-mortar batteries and machine-gun companies were added to each infantry brigade.

The British infantry divisions that took part in the Battle of the Somme were drawn from three groups, the Regular Army, the Territorial Army and the New Army. The latter had been raised since the outbreak of war in 1914. In the first group were the following: the Guards Division, followed by 1st, 2nd, 3rd, 4th, 5th, 6th, 7th, 8th and 29th Divisions. The Territorial Army divisions that took part in the first Somme battle were 46th (North Midland), 47th (1/2nd London), 48th (South Midland), 49th (West Midland), 50th (Northumbrian), 51st (Highland), 55th (West Lancashire) and 56th (1/1st London) Divisions. The New Army divisions which took part were as follows: 9th (Scottish), 11th (Northern), 12th (Eastern), 14th (Light), 15th (Scottish), 16th (Irish), 17th (Northern), 18th (Eastern), 19th (Western), 20th (Light), 21st, 23rd, 24th, 25th, 30th, 32nd, 33rd, 34th, 35th (Bantam), 36th (Ulster), 37th, 38th (Welsh), 39th, 41st and 63rd (Royal Naval) Divisions.

It was Third, Fourth and Reserve Armies that were associated with the Battle of the Somme, during which Reserve Army became Fifth Army (on 30 October 1916). In turn these were broken down into corps that were made up of divisions, each made up of brigades, which broke down into battalions. It is the last-named that I have used in the main as the most useful for my purposes. I have attempted to include brigade and divisional numbers in the text itself on most occasions.

GUARDS DIVISION

16 AUGUST 1916

GENERAL OFFICER COMMANDING:

MAJ GEN G.P.T. FEILDING

1ST GUARDS BRIGADE
2nd Battalion, The Grenadier Guards
2nd Battalion, The Coldstream Guards
3rd Battalion, The Coldstream Guards
1st Battalion, The Irish Guards
No. 1 Guards Company, Machine Gun Corps
No. 1 Guards Trench Mortar Battery

2ND GUARDS BRIGADE
3rd Battalion, The Grenadier Guards
1st Battalion, The Coldstream Guards
1st Battalion, The Scots Guards
2nd Battalion, The Irish Guards
No. 2 Guards Company, Machine Gun Corps
No. 2 Guards Trench Mortar Battery

3RD GUARDS BRIGADE
1st Battalion, The Grenadier Guards
4th Battalion, The Grenadier Guards
2nd Battalion, The Scots Guards
1st Battalion, The Welsh Guards
No. 3 Guards Company, Machine Gun Corps
No. 3 Guards Trench Mortar Battery

DIVISIONAL ARTILLERY
LXI (Howitzer), LXXIV, LXXV and LXXVI
    Brigades, Royal Field Artillery
V Guards Heavy Trench Mortar Battery, Royal
    Field Artillery
X, Y and Z Guards Medium Mortar Batteries, Royal
    Field Artillery
Guards Divisional Ammunition Column

DIVISIONAL TROOPS
4th Battalion (Pioneers), The Coldstream Guards
Nos. 55, 75 and 76 Field Companies, Royal
    Engineers
Guards Divisional Signal Company, Royal
    Engineers
3rd, 4th and 9th Field Ambulances, Royal Army
    Medical Corps
Guards Divisional Train (Nos. 11, 124, 168 and 436
    Companies, Army Service Corps)
No. 46 Mobile Veterinary Section, Army Veterinary
    Corps
No. 45 Sanitary Section

1ST DIVISION

11 JULY 1916

GENERAL OFFICER COMMANDING:

MAJ GEN E.P. STRICKLAND

1ST BRIGADE

10th (Service) Battalion, The Gloucestershire
Regiment
1st Battalion, The Black Watch (Royal Highlanders)
8th (Service) Battalion, Prince Charlotte of Wales's
Royal Berkshire Regiment
1st Battalion, The Queen's Own Cameron
Highlanders
No. 1 Company, Machine Gun Corps
No. 1 Trench Mortar Battery

2ND BRIGADE

2nd Battalion, The Royal Sussex Regiment
1st Battalion, The Loyal North Lancashire Regiment
1st Battalion, The Northamptonshire Regiment
2nd Battalion, The King's Royal Rifle Corps
No. 2 Company, Machine Gun Corps
No. 2 Trench Mortar Battery

3RD BRIGADE

1st Battalion, The South Wales Borderers
1st Battalion, The Gloucestershire Regiment
2nd Battalion, The Welsh Regiment
2nd Battalion, The Royal Munster Fusiliers
No. 3 Company, Machine Gun Corps
No. 3 Trench Mortar Battery

DIVISIONAL ARTILLERY

LXI (Howitzer), XXV, XXVI and XXXIX Brigades,
Royal Field Artillery
X.1, Y.1 and Z.1 Medium Mortar Batteries, Royal
Field Artillery
1st Divisional Ammunition Column

DIVISIONAL TROOPS

1/6th (Glamorgan) Battalion TF (Pioneer),
The Welsh Regiment
Nos. 23, 26 and 1 (Lowland) Field Companies,
Royal Engineers
No. 1 Divisional Signal Company, Royal Engineers
1st, 2nd and 141st Field Ambulances, Royal Army
Medical Corps
1st Divisional Train (Nos. 6, 13, 16 and 36
Companies, Army Service Corps)
No. 2 Mobile Veterinary Section, Army Veterinary
Corps

2ND DIVISION

25 JULY 1916

GENERAL OFFICER COMMANDING:

MAJ GEN W.G. WALKER, VC

5TH BRIGADE

17th (Service) Battalion (Empire), The Royal
  Fusiliers (City of London Regiment)
24th (Service) Battalion (2nd Sportsman's), The
  Royal Fusiliers (City of London Regiment)
2nd Battalion, The Oxfordshire & Buckinghamshire
  Light Infantry
2nd Battalion, The Highland Light Infantry
No. 5 Company, Machine Gun Corps
No. 5 Trench Mortar Battery

6TH BRIGADE

1st Battalion, The King's (Liverpool Regiment)
2nd Battalion, The South Staffordshire Regiment
13th (Service) Battalion (West Ham), The Essex
  Regiment
17th (Service) Battalion (1st Football), The
  Middlesex Regiment (Duke of Cambridge's
  Own)
No. 6 Company, Machine Gun Corps
No. 6 Trench Mortar Battery

99TH BRIGADE

22nd (Service) Battalion (Kensington), The Royal
  Fusiliers (City of London Regiment)
23rd (Service) Battalion (1st Sportsman's), The
  Royal Fusiliers (City of London Regiment)
1st Battalion, Princess Charlotte of Wales's Royal
  Berkshire Regiment
1st Battalion, The King's Royal Rifle Corps
No. 99 Company, Machine Gun Corps
No. 99 Trench Mortar Battery

DIVISIONAL ARTILLERY

XXXIV, XXXVI and XLI Brigades, Royal Field
  Artillery
X.2, Y.2 and Z.2 Medium Mortar Batteries, Royal
  Field Artillery
2nd Divisional Ammunition Column

DIVISIONAL TROOPS

10th (Service) Battalion (Cornwall Pioneers),
  The Duke of Cornwall's Light Infantry
Nos. 5, 226 (Tottenham) and 1 (East Anglian) Field
  Companies, Royal Engineers
No. 2 Divisional Signal Company, Royal Engineers
5th, 6th and 100th Field Ambulances, Royal Army
  Medical Corps
2nd Divisional Train (Nos. 8, 28, 31 and 35
  Companies, Army Service Corps)
No. 3 Mobile Veterinary Section, Army Veterinary
  Corps
No. 11 Sanitary Section

3RD DIVISION

9 JULY 1916

GENERAL OFFICER COMMANDING:

MAJ GEN J.A.L. HALDANE

8TH BRIGADE

2nd Battalion, The Royal Scots (Lothian Regiment)
8th (Service) Battalion, The East Yorkshire
    Regiment (The Duke of York's Own)
1st Battalion, The Royal Scots Fusiliers
7th (Service) Battalion, The King's Shropshire
    Light Infantry
No. 8 Company, Machine Gun Corps
No. 8 Trench Mortar Battery

9TH BRIGADE

1st Battalion, The Northumberland Fusiliers
4th Battalion, The Royal Fusiliers (City of London
    Regiment)
13th (Service) Battalion, The King's (Liverpool
    Regiment)
12th (Service) Battalion, The Prince of Wales's
    Own (West Yorkshire) Regiment
No. 9 Company, Machine Gun Corps
No. 9 Trench Mortar Battery

76TH BRIGADE

8th (Service) Battalion, The King's Own (Royal
    Lancaster Regiment)
2nd Battalion, The Suffolk Regiment
10th (Service) Battalion, The Royal Welsh Fusiliers
1st Battalion, The Gordon Highlanders
No. 76 Company, Machine Gun Corps
No. 76 Trench Mortar Battery

DIVISIONAL ARTILLERY

XXIII, XL and XLII Brigades, Royal Field Artillery
V.3 Heavy Trench Mortar Battery, Royal Field
    Artillery
X.3, Y.3 and Z.3 Medium Mortar Batteries, Royal
    Field Artillery
3rd Divisional Ammunition Column

DIVISIONAL TROOPS

20th (Service) Battalion (British Empire League
    Pioneers), The King's Royal Rifle Corps
Nos. 56, 1 (Cheshire) and 1 (East Riding) Field
    Companies, Royal Engineers
No. 3 Divisional Signal Company, Royal Engineers
7th, 8th and 142nd Field Ambulances, Royal Army
    Medical Corps
3rd Divisional Train (Nos. 15, 21, 22 and 29
    Companies, Army Service Corps)
No. 11 Mobile Veterinary Section, Army Veterinary
    Corps
No. 5 Sanitary Section

4TH DIVISION

1 JULY 1916

GENERAL OFFICER COMMANDING:

MAJ GEN THE HON. W. LAMBTON

10TH BRIGADE

1st Battalion, The Royal Warwickshire Regiment
2nd Battalion, The Seaforth Highlanders (Ross-shire
Buffs, The Duke of Albany's)
1st Battalion, The Royal Irish Fusiliers (Princess
Victoria's)
2nd Battalion, The Royal Dublin Fusiliers
No. 10 Company, Machine Gun Corps
No. 10 Trench Mortar Battery

11TH BRIGADE

1st Battalion, Prince Albert's (Somerset Light
Infantry)
1st Battalion, The East Lancashire Regiment
1st Battalion, The Hampshire Regiment
1st Battalion, The Rifle Brigade (Prince Consort's
Own)
No. 11 Company, Machine Gun Corps
No. 11 Trench Mortar Battery

12TH BRIGADE

1st Battalion, The King's Own (Royal Lancaster
Regiment)
2nd Battalion, The Lancashire Fusiliers
2nd Battalion, The Essex Regiment
2nd Battalion, The Duke of Wellington's Regiment
(West Riding)
No. 12 Company, Machine Gun Corps
No. 12 Trench Mortar Battery

DIVISIONAL ARTILLERY

XIV, XXIX and XXXII Brigades, Royal Field
Artillery
V.4 Heavy Trench Mortar Battery, Royal Field
Artillery
X.4, Y.4 and Z.4 Medium Mortar Batteries, Royal
Field Artillery
4th Divisional Ammunition Column

DIVISIONAL TROOPS

21st (Service) Battalion (Wool Textile Pioneers),
The Prince of Wales's Own (West Yorkshire)
Regiment
Nos. 9, 1 (Renfrew) and 1 (Durham) Field
Company, Royal Engineers
No. 4 Divisional Signal Company, Royal Engineers
10th, 11th and 12th Field Ambulances, Royal Army
Medical Corps
4th Divisional Train (Nos. 18, 25, 32 and 38
Companies, Army Service Corps)
No. 4 Mobile Veterinary Section, Army Veterinary
Corps
No. 3A Sanitary Section

5TH DIVISION

20 JULY 1916

GENERAL OFFICER COMMANDING:

MAJ GEN R. STEPHENS

13TH BRIGADE

14th (Service) Battalion (1st Birmingham),
The Royal Warwickshire Regiment
15th (Service) Battalion (2nd Birmingham),
The Royal Warwickshire Regiment
2nd Battalion, The King's Own Scottish Borderers
1st Battalion, The Queen's Own Royal West Kent
Regiment
No. 13 Company, Machine Gun Corps
No. 13 Trench Mortar Battery

15TH BRIGADE

16th (Service) Battalion (3rd Birmingham),
The Royal Warwickshire Regiment
1st Battalion, The Norfolk Regiment
1st Battalion, The Bedfordshire Regiment
1st Battalion, The Cheshire Regiment
No. 15 Company, Machine Gun Corps
No. 15 Trench Mortar Battery

95TH BRIGADE

1st Battalion, The Devonshire Regiment
12th (Service) Battalion (Bristol),
The Gloucestershire Regiment
1st Battalion, The East Surrey Regiment
1st Battalion, The Duke of Cornwall's Light
Infantry
No. 95 Company, Machine Gun Corps
No. 95 Trench Mortar Battery

DIVISIONAL ARTILLERY

XV, XXVII and XXVIII Brigades, Royal Field
Artillery
X.5, Y.5 and Z.5 Medium Mortar Batteries, Royal
Field Artillery
5th Divisional Ammunition Column

DIVISIONAL TROOPS

1/6th (Renfrewshire) Battalion TF (Pioneers),
Princess Louise's Argyll & Sutherland
Highlanders
Nos. 59, 1/2 (Home Counties) and 2 (Durham) Field
Companies, Royal Engineers
No. 5 Divisional Signal Company, Royal Engineers
13th, 14th and 15th Field Ambulance, Royal Army
Medical Corps
5th Divisional Train (Nos. 4, 6, 33 and 37
Companies, Royal Army Service Corps)
No. 5 Mobile Veterinary Section, Army Veterinary
Corps
No. 6 Sanitary Section

6TH DIVISION

16 AUGUST 1916

GENERAL OFFICER COMMANDING:

MAJ GEN C. ROSS

16TH BRIGADE
1st Battalion, The Buffs (East Kent Regiment)
8th (Service) Battalion, The Bedfordshire Regiment
1st Battalion, The King's Shropshire Light Infantry
2nd Battalion, The York and Lancaster Regiment
No. 16 Company, Machine Gun Corps
No. 16 Trench Mortar Battery

18TH BRIGADE
1st Battalion, The Prince of Wales's Own (West
    Yorkshire) Regiment
11th (Service) Battalion, The Essex Regiment
2nd Battalion, The Durham Light Infantry
14th (Service) Battalion, The Durham Light Infantry
No. 18 Company, Machine Gun Corps
No. 18 Trench Mortar Battery

71ST BRIGADE
9th (Service) Battalion, The Norfolk Regiment
9th (Service) Battalion, The Suffolk Regiment
1st Battalion, The Leicestershire Regiment
2nd Battalion, The Sherwood Foresters
    (Nottinghamshire and Derbyshire Regiment)
No. 71 Company, Machine Gun Corps
No. 71 Trench Mortar Battery

DIVISIONAL ARTILLERY
II, XXIV and XXXVIII Brigades, Royal Field
    Artillery
W.6 Heavy Trench Mortar Battery, Royal Field
    Artillery
X.6, Y.6 and Z.6 Medium Mortar Batteries, Royal
    Field Artillery
6th Divisional Ammunition Column

DIVISIONAL TROOPS
11th (Service) Battalion (Midland Pioneers),
    The Leicestershire Regiment
Nos. 12, 2/2 (West Riding) and 1 (London) Field
    Companies, Royal Engineers
No. 6 Divisional Signal Company, Royal Engineers
16th, 17th and 18th Field Ambulances, Royal Army
    Medical Corps
6th Divisional Train (Nos. 17, 19, 23 and 24
    Companies, Army Service Corps)
No. 6 Mobile Veterinary Section, Army Veterinary
    Corps
No. 8 Sanitary Section

7TH DIVISION

1 JULY 1916

GENERAL OFFICER COMMANDING:
MAJ GEN H.E. WATTS

20TH BRIGADE
8th (Service) Battalion, The Devonshire Regiment
9th (Service) Battalion, The Devonshire Regiment
2nd Battalion, The Border Regiment
2nd Battalion, The Gordon Highlanders
No. 20 Company, Machine Gun Corps
No. 20 Trench Mortar Battery

22ND BRIGADE
2nd Battalion, The Royal Warwickshire Regiment
2nd Battalion, The Royal Irish Regiment
1st Battalion, The Royal Welsh Fusiliers
20th (Service) Battalion (5th City), The Manchester Regiment
No. 22 Company, Machine Gun Corps
No. 22 Trench Mortar Battery

91ST BRIGADE
2nd Battalion, The Queen's Royal (West Surrey)
1st Battalion, The South Staffordshire Regiment
21st (Service) Battalion (6th City), The Manchester Regiment
22nd (Service) Battalion (7th City), The Manchester Regiment
No. 91 Company, Machine Gun Corps
No. 91 Trench Mortar Battery

DIVISIONAL ARTILLERY
XIV Brigade, Royal Horse Artillery
XXII and XXXV Brigades, Royal Field Artillery
V.7 Heavy Trench Mortar Battery, Royal Field Artillery
X.7, Y.7 and Z.7 Medium Mortar Batteries, Royal Field Artillery
7th Divisional Ammunition Column

DIVISIONAL TROOPS
24th (Service) Battalion (Oldham Pioneers), The Manchester Regiment
Nos. 54 and 3 (Durham) Field Companies, Royal Engineers
No. 7 Divisional Signal Company, Royal Engineers
21st, 22nd and 23rd Field Ambulances, Royal Army Medical Corps
7th Divisional Train (Nos. 39, 40, 42 and 86 Companies, Army Service Corps)
No. 12 Mobile Veterinary Section, Army Veterinary Corps
No. 10 Sanitary Section

8TH DIVISION

1 JULY 1916

GENERAL OFFICER COMMANDING:
MAJ GEN H. HUDSON

23RD BRIGADE
2nd Battalion, The Devonshire Regiment
2nd Battalion, The Prince of Wales's Own (West Yorkshire) Regiment
2nd Battalion, The Middlesex Regiment (Duke of Cambridge's Own)
2nd Battalion, The Cameronians (Scottish Rifles)

25TH BRIGADE
2nd Battalion, The Lincolnshire Regiment
2nd Battalion, Prince Charlotte of Wales's Royal Berkshire Regiment
1st Battalion, The Royal Irish Rifles
2nd Battalion, The Rifle Brigade (Prince Consort's Own)

70TH BRIGADE
11th (Service) Battalion, The Sherwood Foresters (Nottinghamshire and Derbyshire Regiment)
8th (Service) Battalion, The King's Own Yorkshire Light Infantry
8th (Service) Battalion, The York and Lancaster Regiment
9th (Service) Battalion, The York and Lancaster Regiment

DIVISIONAL ARTILLERY
V Brigade, Royal Horse Artillery
XXXIII and XLV Brigades, Royal Field Artillery

DIVISIONAL UNITS
22nd (Service) Battalion (3rd County Pioneers), The Durham Light Infantry
Nos. 2, 15 and 1/1 (Home Counties) Field Companies, Royal Engineers
24th (1/1st Wessex), 25th (1/2nd Wessex) and 26th (1/3rd Wessex) Field Ambulances, Royal Army Medical Corps
8th Divisional Train (Nos. 42, 84, 85 and 87 Companies, Army Service Corps)

9TH (SCOTTISH) DIVISION

3 JULY 1916

GENERAL OFFICER COMMANDING:
MAJ GEN W.T. FURSE

26TH BRIGADE
8th (Service) Battalion, The Black Watch (Royal Highlanders)
7th (Service) Battalion, The Seaforth Highlanders (Ross-shire Buffs, The Duke of Albany's)
5th (Service) Battalion, The Queen's Own Cameron Highlanders
10th (Service) Battalion, Princess Louise's Argyll & Sutherland Highlanders
No. 26 Company, Machine Gun Corps
No. 26 Trench Mortar Battery

27TH BRIGADE
11th (Service) Battalion, The Royal Scots (Lothian Regiment)
12th (Service) Battalion, The Royal Scots (Lothian Regiment)
6th (Service) Battalion, The King's Own Scottish Borderers
9th (Service) Battalion, The Cameronians (Scottish Rifles)
No. 27 Company, Machine Gun Corps
No. 27 Trench Mortar Battery

SOUTH AFRICAN BRIGADE
1st South African Infantry (Cape Province)
2nd South African Infantry (Natal & Orange Free State)
3rd South African Infantry (Transvaal & Rhodesia)
4th South African Infantry (Scottish)
No. 28 Company, Machine Gun Corps
South African Trench Mortar Battery

DIVISIONAL ARTILLERY
L, LI, LII and LIII (Howitzer) Brigades, Royal Field Artillery
V.9 Heavy Trench Mortar Battery, Royal Field Artillery
X.9, Y.9 and Z.9 Medium Mortar Batteries, Royal Field Artillery
9th Divisional Ammunition Column

DIVISIONAL TROOPS
9th (Service) Battalion (Pioneers), The Seaforth Highlanders (Ross-shire Buffs, The Duke of Albany's)
Nos. 63, 64 and 90 Field Companies, Royal Engineers
No. 9 Divisional Signal Company, Royal Engineers
27th, 28th and South African Field Ambulances, Royal Army Medical Corps
9th Divisional Train (Nos. 104, 105, 106 and 107 Companies, Army Service Corps)
No. 21 Mobile Veterinary Section, Army Veterinary Corps
No. 20 Sanitary Section

11TH (NORTHERN) DIVISION

7 SEPTEMBER 1916

GENERAL OFFICER COMMANDING:
LT GEN SIR C.L. WOOLLCOMBE

32ND BRIGADE
9th (Service) Battalion, The Prince of Wales's Own (West Yorkshire) Regiment
6th (Service) Battalion, The Princess of Wales's Own (Yorkshire) Regiment
8th (Service) Battalion, The Duke of Wellington's Regiment (West Riding)
6th (Service) Battalion, The York and Lancaster Regiment
No. 32 Company, Machine Gun Corps
No. 32 Trench Mortar Battery

33RD BRIGADE
6th (Service) Battalion, The Lincolnshire Regiment
6th (Service) Battalion, The Border Regiment
7th (Service) Battalion, The South Staffordshire Regiment
9th (Service) Battalion, The Sherwood Foresters (Nottinghamshire and Derbyshire Regiment)
No. 33 Company, Machine Gun Corps

34TH BRIGADE
8th (Service) Battalion, The Northumberland Fusiliers
9th (Service) Battalion, The Lancashire Fusiliers
5th (Service) Battalion, The Dorsetshire Regiment
11th (Service) Battalion, The Manchester Regiment
No. 34 Company, Machine Gun Corps

DIVISIONAL ARTILLERY
LVIII, LIX, LX and CXXXII (Howitzer) Brigades, Royal Field Artillery
V.11 Heavy Trench Mortar Battery, Royal Field Artillery
X.11, Y.11 and Z.11 Medium Mortar Batteries, Royal Field Artillery
11th Divisional Ammunition Column

DIVISIONAL TROOPS
6th (Service) Battalion (Pioneers), The East Yorkshire Regiment (The Duke of York's Own)
Nos. 67, 68 and 86 Field Companies, Royal Engineers
No. 11 Divisional Signal Company, Royal Engineers
33rd, 34th and 35th Field Ambulances, Royal Army Medical Corps
53rd Divisional Train (Nos. 479, 480, 481 and 482 Companies, Army Service Corps)
No. 22 Mobile Veterinary Section, Army Veterinary Corps
No. 21 Sanitary Section

12TH (EASTERN) DIVISION

2 JULY 1916

GENERAL OFFICER COMMANDING:

MAJ GEN A.B. SCOTT

35TH BRIGADE

7th (Service) Battalion, The Norfolk Regiment
7th (Service) Battalion, The Suffolk Regiment
9th (Service) Battalion, The Essex Regiment
5th (Service) Battalion, Prince Charlotte of Wales's
   Royal Berkshire Regiment
No. 35 Company, Machine Gun Corps
No. 35 Trench Mortar Battery

36TH BRIGADE

8th (Service) Battalion, The Royal Fusiliers (City of
   London Regiment)
9th (Service) Battalion, The Royal Fusiliers (City of
   London Regiment)
7th (Service) Battalion, The Royal Sussex Regiment
11th (Service) Battalion, The Middlesex Regiment
   (Duke of Cambridge's Own)
No. 36 Company, Machine Gun Corps
No. 36 Trench Mortar Battery

37TH BRIGADE

6th (Service) Battalion, The Queen's Royal (West
   Surrey)
6th (Service) Battalion, The Buffs (East Kent
   Regiment)
7th (Service) Battalion, The East Surrey Regiment
6th (Service) Battalion, The Queen's Own Royal
   West Kent Regiment
No. 37 Company, Machine Gun Corps
No. 37 Trench Mortar Battery

DIVISIONAL ARTILLERY

LXII, LXIII, LXIV and LXV (Howitzer) Brigades,
   Royal Field Artillery
X.12, Y.12 and Z.12 Medium Mortar Batteries,
   Royal Field Artillery
12th Divisional Ammunition Column

DIVISIONAL TROOPS

5th (Service) Battalion (Pioneers),
   The Northamptonshire Regiment
Nos. 69, 70 and 87 Field Companies, Royal
   Engineers
No. 12 Divisional Signal Company, Royal
   Engineers
36th, 37th and 38th Field Ambulances, Royal Army
   Medical Corps
12th Divisional Train (Nos. 116, 117, 118 and 119
   Companies, Army Service Corps)
No. 23 Mobile Veterinary Section, Army Veterinary
   Corps
No. 23 Sanitary Section

14TH (LIGHT) DIVISION

12 AUGUST 1916

GENERAL OFFICER COMMANDING:

MAJ GEN V.A. COUPER

41ST BRIGADE
7th (Service) Battalion, The King's Royal Rifle
  Corps
8th (Service) Battalion, The King's Royal Rifle
  Corps
7th (Service) Battalion, The Rifle Brigade (Prince
  Consort's Own)
8th (Service) Battalion, The Rifle Brigade (Prince
  Consort's Own)
No. 41 Company, Machine Gun Corps
No. 41 Trench Mortar Battery

42ND BRIGADE
5th (Service) Battalion, The Oxfordshire &
  Buckinghamshire Light Infantry
5th (Service) Battalion, The King's Shropshire
  Light Infantry
9th (Service) Battalion, The King's Royal Rifle
  Corps
9th (Service) Battalion, The Rifle Brigade (Prince
  Consort's Own)
No. 42 Company, Machine Gun Corps
No. 42 Trench Mortar Battery

43RD BRIGADE
6th (Service) Battalion, Prince Albert's (Somerset
  Light Infantry)
6th (Service) Battalion, The Duke of Cornwall's
  Light Infantry
6th (Service) Battalion, The King's Own Yorkshire
  Light Infantry
10th (Service) Battalion, The Durham Light
  Infantry
No. 43 Company, Machine Gun Corps
No. 43 Trench Mortar Battery

DIVISIONAL ARTILLERY
XLVI, XLVII, XLVIII and XLIX (Howitzer)
  Brigades, Royal Field Artillery
V.14 Heavy Trench Mortar Battery, Royal Field
  Artillery
X.14, Y.14 and Z.14 Medium Mortar Batteries,
  Royal Field Artillery
14th Divisional Ammunition Column

DIVISIONAL TROOPS
11th (Service) Battalion (Pioneers), The King's
  (Liverpool Regiment)
No. 8 Motor Machine Gun Battery, Machine Gun
  Corps
Nos. 61, 62 and 89 Field Companies, Royal
  Engineers
No. 14 Divisional Signal Company, Royal
  Engineers
42nd, 43rd and 44th Field Ambulances, Royal Army
  Medical Corps
14th Divisional Train (Nos. 100, 101, 102 and 103
  Companies, Army Service Corps)
No. 26 Mobile Veterinary Section, Army Veterinary
  Corps
No. 25 Sanitary Section

15TH (SCOTTISH) DIVISION

8 AUGUST 1916

GENERAL OFFICER COMMANDING:
MAJ GEN F.W.N. MCCRACKEN

44TH BRIGADE

9th (Service) Battalion, The Black Watch (Royal Highlanders)

8th (Service) Battalion, The Seaforth Highlanders (Ross-shire Buffs, The Duke of Albany's)

8th/10th (Service) Battalion, The Gordon Highlanders

7th (Service) Battalion, The Queen's Own Cameron Highlanders

No. 44 Company, Machine Gun Corps

No. 44 Trench Mortar Battery

45TH BRIGADE

13th (Service) Battalion, The Royal Scots (Lothian Regiment)

6th/7th (Service) Battalion, The Royal Scots Fusiliers

6th (Service) Battalion, The Queen's Own Cameron Highlanders

11th (Service) Battalion, Princess Louise's Argyll & Sutherland Highlanders

No. 45 Company, Machine Gun Corps

No. 45 Trench Mortar Battery

46TH BRIGADE

7th/8th (Service) Battalion, The King's Own Scottish Borderers

10th (Service) Battalion, The Cameronians (Scottish Rifles)

10th/11th (Service) Battalion, The Highland Light Infantry

12th (Service) Battalion, The Highland Light Infantry

No. 46 Company, Machine Gun Corps

No. 46 Trench Mortar Battery

DIVISIONAL ARTILLERY

LXX, LXXI, LXXII and LXXIII (Howitzer) Brigades, Royal Field Artillery

X.15, Y15 and Z.15 Medium Mortar Batteries, Royal Field Artillery

15th Divisional Ammunition Column

DIVISIONAL TROOPS

9th (Service) Battalion (Pioneers), The Gordon Highlanders

Nos. 73, 74 and 91 Field Companies, Royal Engineers

No. 15 Divisional Signal Company, Royal Engineers

45th, 46th and 47th Field Ambulances, Royal Army Medical Corps

15th Divisional Train (Nos. 138, 139, 140 and 141 Companies, Army Service Corps)

No. 27 Mobile Veterinary Section, Army Veterinary Corps

No. 32 Sanitary Section

16TH (IRISH) DIVISION

3 SEPTEMBER 1916

GENERAL OFFICER COMMANDING:
MAJ GEN W.B. HICKIE

47TH BRIGADE

6th (Service) Battalion, The Royal Irish Regiment
6th (Service) Battalion, The Connaught Rangers
7th (Service) Battalion, The Prince of Wales's
    Leinster Regiment (Royal Canadians)
8th (Service) Battalion, The Royal Munster Fusiliers
No. 47 Company, Machine Gun Corps
No. 47 Trench Mortar Battery

48TH BRIGADE

7th (Service) Battalion, The Royal Irish Rifles
1st Battalion, The Royal Munster Fusiliers
8th (Service) Battalion, The Royal Dublin Fusiliers
9th (Service) Battalion, The Royal Dublin Fusiliers
No. 48 Company, Machine Gun Corps
No. 48 Trench Mortar Battery

49TH BRIGADE

7th (Service) Battalion, The Royal Inniskilling
    Fusiliers
8th (Service) Battalion, The Royal Inniskilling
    Fusiliers
7th (Service) Battalion, The Royal Irish Fusiliers
    (Princess Victoria's)
8th (Service) Battalion, The Royal Irish Fusiliers
    (Princess Victoria's)
No. 49 Company, Machine Gun Corps
No. 49 Trench Mortar Battery

DIVISIONAL ARTILLERY

LXXVII (Howitzer), CLXXXVII and CLXXX
    Brigades, Royal Field Artillery
X.16, Y.16 and Z.16 Medium Trench Mortar
    Batteries, Royal Field Artillery
16th Divisional Ammunition Column

DIVISIONAL TROOPS

11th (Service) Battalion (Pioneers), The Hampshire
    Regiment
Nos. 155, 156 and 157 Field Companies, Royal
    Engineers
No. 16 Divisional Signal Company, Royal
    Engineers
111th, 112th and 113th Field Ambulances, Royal
    Army Medical Corps
16th Divisional Train (Nos. 142, 143, 144 and 145
    Companies, Army Service Corps)
No. 47 Mobile Veterinary Section, Army Veterinary
    Corps
No. 81 Sanitary Section

17TH (NORTHERN) DIVISION

2 JULY 1916

GENERAL OFFICER COMMANDING:

MAJ GEN T.D. PILCHER

50TH BRIGADE
10th (Service) Battalion, The Prince of Wales's
  Own (West Yorkshire) Regiment
7th (Service) Battalion, The East Yorkshire
  Regiment (The Duke of York's Own)
7th (Service) Battalion, The Princess of Wales's
  Own (Yorkshire) Regiment
6th (Service) Battalion, The Dorsetshire Regiment
No. 50 Company, Machine Gun Corps
No. 50 Trench Mortar Battery

51ST BRIGADE
7th (Service) Battalion, The Lincolnshire Regiment
7th (Service) Battalion, The Border Regiment
8th (Service) Battalion, The South Staffordshire
  Regiment
10th (Service) Battalion, The Sherwood Foresters
  (Nottinghamshire and Derbyshire Regiment)
No. 51 Company, Machine Gun Corps

52ND BRIGADE
9th (Service) Battalion, The Northumberland
  Fusiliers
10th (Service) Battalion, The Lancashire Fusiliers
9th (Service) Battalion, The Duke of Wellington's
  Regiment (West Riding)
12th (Service) Battalion, The Manchester Regiment
No. 52 Company, Machine Gun Corps
No. 52 Trench Mortar Battery

DIVISIONAL ARTILLERY
LXXVIII, LXXIX, LXXX and LXXXI (Howitzer)
  Brigades, Royal Field Artillery
17th Divisional Ammunition Column

DIVISIONAL TROOPS
7th (Service) Battalion (Pioneers), The York and
  Lancaster Regiment
Nos. 77, 78 and 93 Field Companies, Royal
  Engineers
No. 17 Divisional Signal Company, Royal
  Engineers
51st, 52nd and 53rd Field Ambulances, Royal Army
  Medical Corps
17th Divisional Train (Nos. 146, 147, 148 and 149
  Companies, Army Service Corps)
No. 29 Mobile Veterinary Section, Army Veterinary
  Corps
No. 34 Sanitary Section

18TH (EASTERN) DIVISION

1 JULY 1916

GENERAL OFFICER COMMANDING:

MAJ GEN F.I. MAXSE

53RD BRIGADE
8th (Service) Battalion, The Norfolk Regiment
8th (Service) Battalion, The Suffolk Regiment
10th (Service) Battalion, The Essex Regiment
6th (Service) Battalion, Prince Charlotte of Wales's
 Royal Berkshire Regiment
No. 53 Company, Machine Gun Corps
No. 53 Trench Mortar Battery

54TH BRIGADE
11th (Service) Battalion, The Royal Fusiliers (City
 of London Regiment)
7th (Service) Battalion, The Bedfordshire Regiment
6th (Service) Battalion, The Northamptonshire
 Regiment
12th (Service) Battalion, The Middlesex Regiment
 (Duke of Cambridge's Own)
No. 54 Company, Machine Gun Corps
No. 54 Trench Mortar Battery

55TH BRIGADE
7th (Service) Battalion, The Queen's Royal (West
 Surrey)
7th (Service) Battalion, The Buffs (East Kent
 Regiment)
8th (Service) Battalion, The East Surrey Regiment
7th (Service) Battalion, The Queen's Own Royal
 West Kent Regiment
No. 55 Company, Machine Gun Corps
No. 55 Trench Mortar Battery

DIVISIONAL ARTILLERY
LXXXII, LXXXIII, LXXXIV and LXXXV
 (Howitzer) Brigades, Royal Field Artillery
V.18 and W.18 Heavy Trench Mortar Batteries,
 Royal Field Artillery
X.18, Y.18 and Z.18 Medium Mortar Batteries,
 Royal Field Artillery
18th Divisional Ammunition Column

DIVISIONAL TROOPS
8th (Service) Battalion (Pioneers), The Royal
 Sussex Regiment
Nos. 79, 80 and 92 Field Companies, Royal
 Engineers
54th, 55th and 56th Field Ambulances, Royal Army
 Medical Corps
18th Divisional Train (Nos. 150, 151, 152 and 153
 Companies, Army Service Corps)
No. 30 Mobile Veterinary Section, Army Veterinary
 Corps
No. 35 Sanitary Section

19TH (WESTERN) DIVISION

2 JULY 1916

GENERAL OFFICER COMMANDING:

MAJ GEN G.T.M. BRIDGES

56TH BRIGADE

7th (Service) Battalion, The King's Own (Royal Lancaster Regiment)

7th (Service) Battalion, The East Lancashire Regiment

7th (Service) Battalion, Prince of Wales's Volunteers (South Lancashire Regiment)

7th (Service) Battalion, The Loyal North Lancashire Regiment

No. 56 Company, Machine Gun Corps

No. 56 Trench Mortar Battery

57TH BRIGADE

10th (Service) Battalion, The Royal Warwickshire Regiment

8th (Service) Battalion, The Gloucestershire Regiment

10th (Service) Battalion, The Worcestershire Regiment

8th (Service) Battalion, The Prince of Wales's (North Staffordshire Regiment)

No. 57 Company, Machine Gun Corps

No. 57 Trench Mortar Battery

58TH BRIGADE

9th (Service) Battalion, The Cheshire Regiment

9th (Service) Battalion, The Royal Welsh Fusiliers

9th (Service) Battalion, The Welsh Regiment

6th (Service) Battalion, The Wiltshire Regiment (Duke of Edinburgh's)

No. 58 Company, Machine Gun Corps

No. 58 Trench Mortar Battery

DIVISIONAL ARTILLERY

LXXXVI, LXXXVII, LXXXVIII and LXXXIX (Howitzer) Brigades, Royal Field Artillery

W.19 Heavy Trench Mortar Battery, Royal Field Artillery

X.19, Y.19 and Z.19 Medium Mortar Batteries, Royal Field Artillery

19th Divisional Ammunition Column

DIVISIONAL TROOPS

5th (Service) Battalion (Pioneers), The South Wales Borderers

Nos. 81, 82 and 94 Field Companies, Royal Engineers

No. 19 Divisional Signal Company, Royal Engineers

57th, 58th and 59th Field Ambulances, Royal Army Medical Corps

19th Divisional Train (Nos. 154, 155, 156 and 157 Companies, Army Service Corps)

No. 31 Mobile Veterinary Section, Army Veterinary Corps

No. 36 Sanitary Section

20TH (LIGHT) DIVISION

22 AUGUST 1916

GENERAL OFFICER COMMANDING:

MAJ GEN W. DOUGLAS-SMITH

59TH BRIGADE

10th (Service) Battalion, The King's Royal Rifle Corps

11th (Service) Battalion, The King's Royal Rifle Corps

10th (Service) Battalion, The Rifle Brigade (Prince Consort's Own)

11th (Service) Battalion, The Rifle Brigade (Prince Consort's Own)

No. 59 Company, Machine Gun Corps

No. 59 Trench Mortar Battery

60TH BRIGADE

6th (Service) Battalion, The Oxfordshire & Buckinghamshire Light Infantry

6th (Service) Battalion, The King's Shropshire Light Infantry

12th (Service) Battalion, The King's Royal Rifle Corps

12th (Service) Battalion, The Rifle Brigade (Prince Consort's Own)

No. 60 Company, Machine Gun Corps

No. 60 Trench Mortar Battery

61ST BRIGADE

7th (Service) Battalion, Prince Albert's (Somerset Light Infantry)

7th (Service) Battalion, The Duke of Cornwall's Light Infantry

7th (Service) Battalion, The King's Own Yorkshire Light Infantry

12th (Service) Battalion, The King's (Liverpool Regiment)

No. 61 Company, Machine Gun Corps

No. 61 Trench Mortar Battery

DIVISIONAL ARTILLERY

XC, XCI, XCII (Howitzer) and XCIII Brigades, Royal Field Artillery

V.20 Heavy Trench Mortar Battery, Royal Field Artillery

X.20, Y.20 and Z.20 Medium Mortar Batteries, Royal Field Artillery

20th Divisional Ammunition Column

DIVISIONAL TROOPS

11th (Service) Battalion (Pioneers), The Durham Light Infantry

Nos. 83, 84 and 96 Field Companies, Royal Engineers

No. 20 Divisional Signal Company, Royal Engineers

60th, 61st and 62nd Field Ambulances, Royal Army Medical Corps

20th Divisional Train (Nos. 158, 159, 160, 161 Companies, Army Service Corps)

No. 32 Mobile Veterinary Section, Army Veterinary Corps

No. 33 Sanitary Section

21ST DIVISION

1 JULY 1916

GENERAL OFFICER COMMANDING:

MAJ GEN D.G.M. CAMPBELL

62ND BRIGADE

12th (Service) Battalion, The Northumberland
 Fusiliers
13th (Service) Battalion, The Northumberland
 Fusiliers
1st Battalion, The Lincolnshire Regiment
10th (Service) Battalion, The Princess of Wales's
 Own (Yorkshire) Regiment
No. 62 Company, Machine Gun Corps
No. 62 Trench Mortar Battery

63RD BRIGADE

8th (Service) Battalion, The Lincolnshire Regiment
8th (Service) Battalion, Prince Albert's (Somerset
 Light Infantry)
4th Battalion, The Middlesex Regiment (Duke of
 Cambridge's Own)
10th (Service) Battalion, The York and Lancaster
 Regiment
No. 63 Company, Machine Gun Corps
No. 63 Trench Mortar Battery

64TH BRIGADE

1st Battalion, The East Yorkshire Regiment
 (The Duke of York's Own)
9th (Service) Battalion, The King's Own Yorkshire
 Light Infantry
10th (Service) Battalion, The King's Own Yorkshire
 Light Infantry
15th (Service) Battalion, The Durham Light Infantry
No. 64 Company, Machine Gun Corps
No. 64 Trench Mortar Battery

DIVISIONAL ARTILLERY

XCIV, XCV, XCVI and XCVII (Howitzer)
 Brigades, Royal Field Artillery
V.21 Heavy Trench Mortar Battery, Royal Field
 Artillery
X.21, Y.21 and Z.21 Medium Mortar Batteries,
 Royal Field Artillery
21st Divisional Ammunition Column

DIVISIONAL TROOPS

14th (Service) Battalion (Pioneers),
 The Northumberland Fusiliers
Nos. 94, 97, 98 and 126 Field Companies, Royal
 Engineers
No. 21 Divisional Signal Company, Royal
 Engineers
63rd, 64th and 65th Field Ambulances, Royal Army
 Medical Corps
21st Divisional Train (Nos. 182, 183, 184 and 185
 Companies, Army Service Corps)
No. 33 Mobile Veterinary Section, Army Veterinary
 Corps
No. 38 Sanitary Section

23RD DIVISION

3 JULY 1916

GENERAL OFFICER COMMANDING:

MAJ GEN J.M. BABINGTON

24TH BRIGADE

1st Battalion, The Worcestershire Regiment
2nd Battalion, The East Lancashire Regiment
1st Battalion, The Sherwood Foresters
(Nottinghamshire and Derbyshire Regiment)
2nd Battalion, The Northamptonshire Regiment
No. 24 Company, Machine Gun Corps
No. 24 Trench Mortar Battery

68TH BRIGADE

10th (Service) Battalion, The Northumberland
Fusiliers
11th (Service) Battalion, The Northumberland
Fusiliers
12th (Service) Battalion, The Durham Light Infantry
13th (Service) Battalion, The Durham Light Infantry
No. 68 Company, Machine Gun Corps
No. 68 Trench Mortar Battery

69TH BRIGADE

11th (Service) Battalion, The Prince of Wales's
Own (West Yorkshire) Regiment
8th (Service) Battalion, The Princess of Wales's
Own (Yorkshire) Regiment
9th (Service) Battalion, The Princess of Wales's
Own (Yorkshire) Regiment
10th (Service) Battalion, The Duke of Wellington's
Regiment (West Riding)
No. 69 Company, Machine Gun Corps
No. 69 Trench Mortar Battery

DIVISIONAL ARTILLERY

CII, CIII, CIV and CV Brigades, Royal Field
Artillery
V.23 Heavy Trench Mortar Battery, Royal Field
Artillery
X.23, Y.23 and Z.23 Medium Mortar Batteries,
Royal Field Artillery
23rd Divisional Ammunition Column

DIVISIONAL TROOPS

9th (Service) Battalion (Pioneers), The South
Staffordshire Regiment
Nos. 101, 102 and 128 Field Companies, Royal
Engineers
No. 23 Divisional Signal Company, Royal
Engineers
69th, 70th and 71st Field Ambulances, Royal Army
Medical Corps
23rd Divisional Motor Ambulance Workshop
23rd Divisional Train (Nos. 190, 191, 192 and 193
Companies, Army Service Corps)
No. 35 Mobile Veterinary Section, Army Veterinary
Corps
No. 40 Sanitary Section

24TH DIVISION

9 AUGUST 1916

GENERAL OFFICER COMMANDING:

MAJ GEN J.E. CAPPER

17TH BRIGADE

1st Battalion, The Royal Fusiliers (City of London Regiment)

12th (Service) Battalion, The Royal Fusiliers (City of London Regiment)

8th (Service) Battalion, The Buffs (East Kent Regiment)

3rd Battalion, The Rifle Brigade (Prince Consort's Own)

No. 17 Company, Machine Gun Corps

No. 17 Trench Mortar Battery

72ND BRIGADE

8th (Service) Battalion, The Queen's Royal (West Surrey)

9th (Service) Battalion, The East Surrey Regiment

8th (Service) Battalion, The Queen's Own Royal West Kent Regiment

1st Battalion, The Prince of Wales's (North Staffordshire Regiment)

No. 72 Company, Machine Gun Corps

No. 72 Trench Mortar Battery

73RD BRIGADE

9th (Service) Battalion, The Royal Sussex Regiment

7th (Service) Battalion, The Northamptonshire Regiment

13th (Service) Battalion, The Middlesex Regiment (Duke of Cambridge's Own)

2nd Battalion, The Prince of Wales's Leinster Regiment (Royal Canadians)

No. 73 Company, Machine Gun Corps

No. 73 Trench Mortar Battery

DIVISIONAL ARTILLERY

CVI, CVII, CVIII and CIX (Howitzer) Brigades, Royal Field Artillery

V.24 Heavy Trench Mortar Battery, Royal Field Artillery

X.24, Y.24 and Z.24 Medium Mortar Batteries, Royal Field Artillery

24th Divisional Ammunition Column

DIVISIONAL TROOPS

12th (Service) Battalion (Pioneers), The Sherwood Foresters (Nottinghamshire and Derbyshire Regiment)

Nos. 103, 104 and 129 Field Companies, Royal Engineers

No. 24 Divisional Signal Company, Royal Engineers

72nd, 73rd and 74th Field Ambulances, Royal Army Medical Corps

24th Divisional Train (Nos. 194, 195, 196 and 197 Companies, Army Service Corps)

No. 36 Mobile Veterinary Section, Army Veterinary Corps

No. 41 Sanitary Section

25TH DIVISION

4 JULY 1916

GENERAL OFFICER COMMANDING:

MAJ GEN E.G.T. BAINBRIDGE

7TH BRIGADE

10th (Service) Battalion, The Cheshire Regiment
3rd Battalion, The Worcestershire Regiment
8th (Service) Battalion, The Loyal North Lancashire Regiment
1st Battalion, The Wiltshire Regiment (Duke of Edinburgh's)
No. 7 Company, Machine Gun Corps

74TH BRIGADE

11th (Service) Battalion, The Lancashire Fusiliers
13th (Service) Battalion, The Cheshire Regiment
9th (Service) Battalion, The Loyal North Lancashire Regiment
2nd Battalion, The Royal Irish Rifles
No. 74 Company, Machine Gun Corps
No. 74 Trench Mortar Battery

75TH BRIGADE

11th (Service) Battalion, The Cheshire Regiment
8th (Service) Battalion, The Border Regiment
2nd Battalion, Prince of Wales's Volunteers (South Lancashire Regiment)
8th (Service) Battalion, Prince of Wales's Volunteers (South Lancashire Regiment)
No. 75 Company, Machine Gun Corps
No. 75 Trench Mortar Battery

DIVISIONAL ARTILLERY

CX, CXI, CXII and CXIII (Howitzer) Brigades, Royal Field Artillery
X.25, Y.25 and Z.25 Medium Mortar Batteries, Royal Field Artillery
25th Divisional Ammunition Column

DIVISIONAL TROOPS

6th (Service) Battalion (Pioneers), The South Wales Borderers
Nos. 105, 106 and 130 Field Companies, Royal Engineers
No. 25 Divisional Signal Company, Royal Engineers
75th, 76th and 77th Field Ambulances, Royal Army Medical Corps
25th Divisional Train (Nos. 198, 199, 200 and 201 Companies, Army Service Corps)
No. 37 Mobile Veterinary Section, Army Veterinary Corps
No. 42 Sanitary Section

29TH DIVISION

1 JULY 1916

GENERAL OFFICER COMMANDING:
MAJ GEN H. DEB. DE LISLE

86TH BRIGADE

2nd Battalion, The Royal Fusiliers (City of London Regiment)
1st Battalion, The Lancashire Fusiliers
16th (Service) Battalion (Public Schools), The Middlesex Regiment (Duke of Cambridge's Own)
1st Battalion, The Royal Dublin Fusiliers
No. 86 Company, Machine Gun Corps
No. 86 Trench Mortar Battery

87TH BRIGADE

2nd Battalion, The South Wales Borderers
1st Battalion, The King's Own Scottish Borderers
1st Battalion, The Royal Inniskilling Fusiliers
1st Battalion, The Border Regiment
No. 87 Company, Machine Gun Corps
No. 87 Trench Mortar Battery

88TH BRIGADE

4th Battalion, The Worcestershire Regiment
2nd Battalion, The Hampshire Regiment
1st Battalion, The Essex Regiment
1st Battalion, The Newfoundland Regiment
No. 88 Company, Machine Gun Corps
No. 88 Trench Mortar Battery

DIVISIONAL ARTILLERY

XVI Brigade, Royal Horse Artillery
XVII, CXLVII and CXXXII Brigades, Royal Field Artillery
V.29 Heavy Trench Mortar Battery, Royal Field Artillery
X.29, Y.29 and Z.29 Medium Mortar Batteries, Royal Field Artillery
29th Divisional Ammunition Column

DIVISIONAL TROOPS

1/2nd Battalion TF (Pioneers), The Monmouthshire Regiment
Nos. 1 (West Riding), 3 (Kent) and 2 (London) Field Companies, Royal Engineers
No. 29 Divisional Signal Company, Royal Engineers
87th (1/1st West Lancashire), 88th (1/1st East Anglian) and 89th (1/1st Highland) Field Ambulances, Royal Army Medical Corps
No. 18 Mobile Veterinary Section, Army Veterinary Corps
No. 16 Sanitary Section

30TH DIVISION

1 JULY 1916

GENERAL OFFICER COMMANDING:

MAJ GEN J.S.M. SHEA

21ST BRIGADE

18th (Service) Battalion (2nd City), The King's (Liverpool Regiment)

2nd Battalion, The Princess of Wales's Own (Yorkshire) Regiment

2nd Battalion, The Wiltshire Regiment (Duke of Edinburgh's)

19th (Service) Battalion (4th City), The Manchester Regiment

No. 21 Company, Machine Gun Corps

No. 21 Trench Mortar Battery

89TH BRIGADE

17th (Service) Battalion (1st City), The King's (Liverpool Regiment)

19th (Service) Battalion (3rd City), The King's (Liverpool Regiment)

20th (Service) Battalion (4th City), The King's (Liverpool Regiment)

2nd Battalion, The Bedfordshire Regiment

No. 89 Company, Machine Gun Corps

No. 89 Trench Mortar Battery

90TH BRIGADE

2nd Battalion, The Royal Scots Fusiliers

16th (Service) Battalion (1st City), The Manchester Regiment

17th (Service) Battalion (2nd City), The Manchester Regiment

18th (Service) Battalion (3rd City), The Manchester Regiment

No. 90 Company, Machine Gun Corps

No. 90 Trench Mortar Battery

DIVISIONAL ARTILLERY

CXLVIII, CXLIX, CL and CLI (Howitzer) Brigades (County Palatine), Royal Field Artillery

X.30, Y.30 and Z.30 Medium Mortar Batteries, Royal Field Artillery

30th (County Palatine) Divisional Ammunition Column

DIVISIONAL TROOPS

11th (Service) Battalion (St Helens Pioneers), Prince of Wales's Volunteers (South Lancashire Regiment)

Nos. 201, 202 and 203 Field Companies (County Palatine), Royal Engineers

30th Divisional Signal Company, Royal Engineers

96th (County Palatine), 97th (County Palatine) and 98th (1/2nd West Lancashire) Field Ambulances, Royal Army Medical Corps

30th Divisional Train (Nos. 186, 187, 188 and 189 Companies, Army Service Corps)

No. 40 Mobile Veterinary Section, Army Veterinary Corps

No. 70 Sanitary Section

31ST DIVISION

1 JULY 1916

GENERAL OFFICER COMMANDING:
MAJ GEN R. WANLESS O'GOWAN

92ND BRIGADE

10th (Service) Battalion (1st Hull), The East
  Yorkshire Regiment (The Duke of York's Own)
11th (Service) Battalion (2nd Hull), The East
  Yorkshire Regiment (The Duke of York's Own)
12th (Service) Battalion (3rd Hull), The East
  Yorkshire Regiment (The Duke of York's Own)
13th (Service) Battalion (4th Hull), The East
  Yorkshire Regiment (The Duke of York's Own)
No. 92 Company, Machine Gun Corps
No. 92 Trench Mortar Battery

93RD BRIGADE

15th (Service) Battalion (1st Leeds), The Prince of
  Wales's Own (West Yorkshire) Regiment
16th (Service) Battalion (1st Bradford), The Prince
  of Wales's Own (West Yorkshire) Regiment
18th (Service) Battalion (2nd Bradford), The Prince
  of Wales's Own (West Yorkshire) Regiment
18th (Service) Battalion (1st County), The Durham
  Light Infantry
No. 93 Company, Machine Gun Corps
No. 93 Trench Mortar Battery

94TH BRIGADE

11th (Service) Battalion (Accrington), The East
  Lancashire Regiment
12th (Service) Battalion (Sheffield), The York and
  Lancaster Regiment
13th (Service) Battalion (1st Barnsley), The York
  and Lancaster Regiment
14th (Service) Battalion (2nd Barnsley), The York
  and Lancaster Regiment
No. 94 Company, Machine Gun Corps
No. 94 Trench Mortar Battery

DIVISIONAL ARTILLERY

CLXV, CLXIX, CLXX and CLXXI (Howitzer)
  Brigades (2nd County Palatine), Royal Field
  Artillery
V.31 Heavy Trench Mortar Battery, Royal Field
  Artillery
X.31, Y.31 and Z.31 Medium Mortar Batteries,
  Royal Field Artillery
31st Divisional Ammunition Column

DIVISIONAL TROOPS

12th (Service) Battalion (Miners) (Pioneers),
  The King's Own Yorkshire Light Infantry
Nos. 210, 211 and 223 Field Companies (Leeds),
  Royal Engineers
No. 31 Divisional Signal Company, Royal
  Engineers
93rd, 94th and 95th Field Ambulances, Royal Army
  Medical Corps
31st Divisional Train (Nos. 221, 222, 223 and 279
  Companies, Army Service Corps)
No. 41 Mobile Veterinary Section, Army Veterinary
  Corps
No. 71 Sanitary Section

32ND DIVISION

1 JULY 1916

GENERAL OFFICER COMMANDING:

MAJ GEN W.H. RYCROFT

14TH BRIGADE
19th (Service) Battalion (3rd Salford),
    The Lancashire Fusiliers
1st Battalion, The Dorsetshire Regiment
2nd Battalion, The Manchester Regiment
15th (Service) Battalion (1st Glasgow),
    The Highland Light Infantry
No. 14 Company, Machine Gun Corps
No. 14 Trench Mortar Battery

96TH BRIGADE
16th (Service) Battalion (Newcastle),
    The Northumberland Fusiliers
15th (Service) Battalion (1st Salford),
    The Lancashire Fusiliers
16th (Service) Battalion (2nd Salford),
    The Lancashire Fusiliers
2nd Battalion, The Royal Inniskilling Fusiliers
No. 96 Company, Machine Gun Corps
No. 96 Trench Mortar Battery

97TH BRIGADE
11th (Service) Battalion (Lonsdale), The Border
    Regiment
2nd Battalion, The King's Own Yorkshire Light
    Infantry
16th (Service) Battalion (2nd Glasgow),
    The Highland Light Infantry
17th (Service) Battalion (3rd Glasgow),
    The Highland Light Infantry
No. 97 Company, Machine Gun Corps
No. 97 Trench Mortar Battery

DIVISIONAL ARTILLERY
CLV, CLXI, CLXIV (Howitzer) and CLXVIII
    (Rotherham) Brigades, Royal Field Artillery
V.32 and W.32 Heavy Trench Mortar Batteries,
    Royal Field Artillery
X.32, Y.32 and Z.32 Medium Mortar Batteries,
    Royal Field Artillery
32nd Divisional Ammunition Column

DIVISIONAL TROOPS
17th (Service) Battalion (North Eastern Railway
    Pioneers), The Northumberland Fusiliers
Nos. 206, 218 and 219 Field Companies (Glasgow),
    Royal Engineers
No. 32 Divisional Signal Company, Royal
    Engineers
90th, 91st and 92nd Field Ambulances, Royal Army
    Medical Corps
32nd Divisional Train (Nos. 202, 203, 204 and 205
    Companies, Army Service Corps)
No. 42 Mobile Veterinary Section, Army Veterinary
    Corps
No. 72 Sanitary Section

33RD DIVISION

15 JULY 1916

GENERAL OFFICER COMMANDING:
MAJ GEN H.J.S. LANDON

19TH BRIGADE
20th (Service) Battalion (3rd Public Schools), The
  Royal Fusiliers (City of London Regiment)
2nd Battalion, The Royal Welsh Fusiliers
1st Battalion, The Cameronians (Scottish Rifles)
1/5th Battalion TF, The Cameronians (Scottish
  Rifles)
No. 19 Company, Machine Gun Corps
No. 19 Trench Mortar Battery

98TH BRIGADE
4th Battalion, The King's (Liverpool Regiment)
1/4th Battalion TF, The Suffolk Regiment
1st Battalion, The Middlesex Regiment (Duke of
  Cambridge's Own)
2nd Battalion, Princess Louise's Argyll &
  Sutherland Highlanders
No. 98 Company, Machine Gun Corps
No. 98 Trench Mortar Battery

100TH BRIGADE
1st Battalion, The Queen's Royal (West Surrey)
2nd Battalion, The Worcestershire Regiment
16th (Service) Battalion (Church Lads Brigade),
  The King's Royal Rifle Corps
1/9th Battalion TF (Glasgow Highland),
  The Highland Light Infantry
No. 100 Company, Machine Gun Corps
No. 100 Trench Mortar Battery

DIVISIONAL ARTILLERY
CLVI, CLXII, CLXVI and CLXVII (Howitzer)
  Brigades, Royal Field Artillery
V.33 Heavy Trench Mortar Battery, Royal Field
  Artillery
X.33, Y.33 and Z.33 Medium Mortar Batteries,
  Royal Field Artillery
33rd Divisional Ammunition Column

DIVISIONAL TROOPS
18th (Service) Battalion (1st Public Works
  Pioneers), The Middlesex Regiment (Duke of
  Cambridge's Own)
Nos. 11, 212 (Tottenham) and 222 (Tottenham)
  Field Companies, Royal Engineers
No. 33 Divisional Signal Company (Tottenham),
  Royal Engineers
19th, 99th and 101st Field Ambulances, Royal
  Army Medical Corps
33rd Divisional Train (Nos. 8, 170, 171 and 173
  Companies, Army Service Corps)
No. 43 Mobile Veterinary Section, Army Veterinary
  Corps
No. 73 Sanitary Section

34TH DIVISION

1 JULY 1916

GENERAL OFFICER COMMANDING:
MAJ GEN E.C. INGOUVILLE-WILLIAMS

101ST BRIGADE

15th (Service) Battalion (1st Edinburgh), The Royal
  Scots (Lothian Regiment)
16th (Service) Battalion (2nd Edinburgh), The
  Royal Scots (Lothian Regiment)
10th (Service) Battalion (Grimsby Chums),
  The Lincolnshire Regiment
11th (Service) Battalion (Cambridgeshire),
  The Suffolk Regiment
No. 101 Company, Machine Gun Corps
No. 101 Trench Mortar Battery

102ND (TYNESIDE SCOTTISH) BRIGADE

20th (Service) Battalion (1st Tyneside Scottish),
  The Northumberland Fusiliers
21st (Service) Battalion (2nd Tyneside Scottish),
  The Northumberland Fusiliers
22nd (Service) Battalion (3rd Tyneside Scottish),
  The Northumberland Fusiliers
23rd (Service) Battalion (4th Tyneside Scottish),
  The Northumberland Fusiliers
No. 102 Company, Machine Gun Corps
No. 102 Trench Mortar Battery

103RD (TYNESIDE IRISH) BRIGADE

24th (Service) Battalion (1st Tyneside Irish),
  The Northumberland Fusiliers
25th (Service) Battalion (2nd Tyneside Irish),
  The Northumberland Fusiliers
26th (Service) Battalion (3rd Tyneside Irish),
  The Northumberland Fusiliers
27th (Service) Battalion (4th Tyneside Irish),
  The Northumberland Fusiliers
No. 103 Company, Machine Gun Corps
No. 103 Trench Mortar Battery

DIVISIONAL ARTILLERY

CLII (Nottingham), CLX (Wearside),
  CLXXV(Staffordshire), CLXXVI (Howitzer)
  Brigades, Royal Field Artillery
X.34, Y.34 and Z.34 Medium Mortar Batteries,
  Royal Field Artillery
34th Divisional Ammunition Column (Nottingham)

DIVISIONAL TROOPS

18th (Service) Battalion (1st Tyneside Pioneers),
  The Northumberland Fusiliers
Nos. 207, 208 and 209 Field Companies (Norfolk),
  Royal Engineers
No. 34 Divisional Signal Company, Royal
  Engineers
102nd, 103rd and 104th Field Ambulances, Royal
  Army Medical Corps
34th Divisional Train (Nos. 229, 230, 231, 232
  Companies, Army Service Corps)
No. 44 Mobile Veterinary Section, Army Veterinary
  Corps
No. 74 Sanitary Section

35TH (BANTAM) DIVISION

18 JULY 1916

GENERAL OFFICER COMMANDING:
MAJ GEN R.J. PINNEY

104TH BRIGADE

17th (Service) Battalion (1st South-East Lancashire), The Lancashire Fusiliers

18th (Service) Battalion (2nd South-East Lancashire), The Lancashire Fusiliers

20th (Service) Battalion (4th Salford), The Lancashire Fusiliers

23rd (Service) Battalion (8th City), The Manchester Regiment

No. 104 Company, Machine Gun Corps

No. 104 Trench Mortar Battery

105TH BRIGADE

15th (Service) Battalion (1st Birkenhead), The Cheshire Regiment

16th (Service) Battalion (2nd Birkenhead), The Cheshire Regiment

14th (Service) Battalion (West of England), The Gloucestershire Regiment

15th (Service) Battalion (Nottingham), The Sherwood Foresters (Nottinghamshire and Derbyshire Regiment)

No. 105 Company, Machine Gun Corps

No. 105 Trench Mortar Battery

106TH BRIGADE

17th (Service) Battalion (Rosebery), The Royal Scots (Lothian Regiment)

17th (Service) Battalion (2nd Leeds), The Prince of Wales's Own (West Yorkshire) Regiment

19th (Service) Battalion (2nd County), The Durham Light Infantry

18th (Service) Battalion (4th Glasgow), The Highland Light Infantry

No. 106 Company, Machine Gun Corps

No. 106 Trench Mortar Battery

DIVISIONAL ARTILLERY

CLVII (Aberdeen), CLVIII (Accrington and Burnley), CLVIX (Glasgow) and CLXIII (Howitzer) Brigades, Royal Field Artillery

X.35, Y.35 and Z.35 Medium Mortar Batteries, Royal Field Artillery

35th Divisional Ammunition Column (British Empire League)

DIVISIONAL TROOPS

19th (Service) Battalion (2nd Tyneside Pioneers), The Northumberland Fusiliers

Nos. 203 (Cambridge), 204 (Empire) and 205 (Dundee) Field Companies, Royal Engineers

No. 35 Divisional Signal Company (Reading), Royal Engineers

105th, 106th and 107th Field Ambulances, Royal Army Medical Corps

35th Divisional Train (Nos. 233, 234, 235 and 236 Companies, Army Service Corps)

No. 45 Mobile Veterinary Section, Army Veterinary Corps

No. 29 Sanitary Section

36TH (ULSTER) DIVISION

JULY 1916

GENERAL OFFICER COMMANDING:

MAJ GEN O.S.W. NUGENT

107TH BRIGADE

8th (Service) Battalion (East Belfast), The Royal
Irish Rifles
9th (Service) Battalion (West Belfast), The Royal
Irish Rifles
10th (Service) Battalion (South Belfast), The Royal
Irish Rifles
15th (Service) Battalion (North Belfast), The Royal
Irish Rifles
No. 107 Company, Machine Gun Corps
No. 107 Trench Mortar Battery

108TH BRIGADE

11th (Service) Battalion (South Antrim), The Royal
Irish Rifles
12th (Service) Battalion (Central Antrim),
The Royal Irish Rifles
13th (Service) Battalion (County Down), The Royal
Irish Rifles
9th (Service) Battalion, The Royal Irish Fusiliers
(Princess Victoria's)
No. 108 Company, Machine Gun Corps
No. 108 Trench Mortar Battery

109TH BRIGADE

9th (Service) Battalion (County Tyrone), The Royal
Inniskilling Fusiliers
10th (Service) Battalion (Derry), The Royal
Inniskilling Fusiliers
11th (Service) Battalion (Donegal and Fermanagh),
The Royal Inniskilling Fusiliers
14th (Service) Battalion (Young Citizens),
The Royal Irish Rifles
No. 109 Company, Machine Gun Corps
No. 109 Trench Mortar Battery

DIVISIONAL ARTILLERY

CLIII (Empire), CLIV (Howitzer), CLXXII (East
Ham) and CLXXIII (West Ham) Batteries, Royal
Field Artillery
V.36 Heavy Trench Mortar Battery, Royal Field
Artillery
X.36, Y.36 and Z.36 Medium Mortar Batteries,
Royal Field Artillery
36th Divisional Ammunition Column

DIVISIONAL TROOPS

16th (Service) Battalion (2nd County Down)
(Pioneers), The Royal Irish Rifles
Nos. 121, 122 and 150 Field Companies, Royal
Engineers
No. 36 Divisional Signal Company, Royal
Engineers
108th, 109th and 110th Field Ambulances, Royal
Army Medical Corps
36th Divisional Train (Nos. 251, 252, 253 and 254
Companies, Army Service Corps)
No. 76 Sanitary Section

37TH DIVISION

15 NOVEMBER 1916

GENERAL OFFICER COMMANDING:

MAJ GEN H. BRUCE-WILLIAMS

63RD BRIGADE
8th (Service) Battalion, The Lincolnshire Regiment
8th (Service) Battalion, Prince Albert's (Somerset Light Infantry)
4th Battalion, The Middlesex Regiment (Duke of Cambridge's Own)
10th (Service) Battalion, The York and Lancaster Regiment
63rd Brigade Machine Gun Company
No. 63 Trench Mortar Battery

111TH BRIGADE
10th (Service) Battalion, The Royal Fusiliers (City of London Regiment)
13th (Service) Battalion, The Royal Fusiliers (City of London Regiment)
13th (Service) Battalion, The King's Royal Rifle Corps
13th (Service) Battalion, The Rifle Brigade (Prince Consort's Own)
No. 111 Company, Machine Gun Corps
No. 111 Trench Mortar Battery

112TH BRIGADE
11th (Service) Battalion, The Royal Warwickshire Regiment
6th (Service) Battalion, The Bedfordshire Regiment
8th (Service) Battalion, The East Lancashire Regiment
10th (Service) Battalion, The Loyal North Lancashire Regiment
No. 112 Company, Machine Gun Corps
No. 112 Trench Mortar Battery

DIVISIONAL ARTILLERY
CXXIII, CXXIV, CXXV and CXXVI (Howitzer) Brigades, Royal Field Artillery
37th Divisional Ammunition Column

DIVISIONAL TROOPS
9th (Service) Battalion (Pioneers), The Prince of Wales's (North Staffordshire Regiment)
Nos. 152, 153 and 154 Field Companies, Royal Engineers
No. 37 Divisional Signal Company, Royal Engineers
48th, 49th and 50th Field Ambulances, Royal Army Medical Corps
37th Divisional Train (Nos. 288, 289, 290 and 291 Companies, Army Service Corps)
No. 28 Mobile Veterinary Section, Army Veterinary Corps
No. 37 Sanitary Section

38TH (WELSH) DIVISION

5 JULY 1916

GENERAL OFFICER COMMANDING:

MAJ GEN I. PHILIPPS

113TH BRIGADE

13th (Service) Battalion (1st North Wales),
  The Royal Welsh Fusiliers
14th (Service) Battalion, The Royal Welsh Fusiliers
15th (Service) Battalion (1st London Welsh),
  The Royal Welsh Fusiliers
16th (Service) Battalion, The Royal Welsh Fusiliers
No. 113 Company, Machine Gun Corps
No. 113 Trench Mortar Battery

114TH BRIGADE

10th (Service) Battalion (1st Rhondda), The Welsh
  Regiment
13th (Service) Battalion (2nd Rhondda), The Welsh
  Regiment
14th (Service) Battalion (Swansea), The Welsh
  Regiment
15th (Service) Battalion (Carmarthenshire),
  The Welsh Regiment
No. 114 Company, Machine Gun Corps
No. 114 Trench Mortar Battery

115TH BRIGADE

17th (Service) Battalion (2nd North Wales),
  The Royal Welsh Fusiliers
10th (Service) Battalion (1st Gwent), The South
  Wales Borderers
11th (Service) Battalion (2nd Gwent), The South
  Wales Borderers
16th (Service) Battalion (Cardiff City), The Welsh
  Regiment
No. 115 Company, Machine Gun Corps
No. 115 Trench Mortar Battery

DIVISIONAL ARTILLERY

CXIX, CXX, CXXI and CXXII (Howitzer)
  Brigades, Royal Field Artillery
X.38, Y.38 and Z.38 Medium Mortar Batteries,
  Royal Field Artillery
38th Divisional Ammunition Column

DIVISIONAL TROOPS

19th (Service) Battalion (Glamorgan Pioneers),
  The Welsh Regiment
Nos. 123, 124 and 151 Field Companies, Royal
  Engineers
No. 38 Divisional Signal Company, Royal
  Engineers
129th, 130th (St John) and 131st Field Ambulances,
  Royal Army Medical Corps
38th Divisional Train (Nos. 330, 331, 332 and 333
  Companies, Army Service Corps)
No. 49 Mobile Veterinary Section, Army Veterinary
  Corps
No. 77 Sanitary Section

39TH DIVISION

3 SEPTEMBER 1916

GENERAL OFFICER COMMANDING:

MAJ GEN G.J. CUTHBERT

116TH BRIGADE
11th (Service) Battalion (1st South Down),
  The Royal Sussex Regiment
12th (Service) Battalion (2nd South Down),
  The Royal Sussex Regiment
13th (Service) Battalion (3rd South Down),
  The Royal Sussex Regiment
14th (Service) Battalion (1st Portsmouth),
  The Hampshire Regiment
No. 116 Company, Machine Gun Corps
No. 116 Trench Mortar Battery

117TH BRIGADE
16th (Service) Battalion (Chatsworth Rifles),
  The Sherwood Foresters (Nottinghamshire and
  Derbyshire Regiment)
17th (Service) Battalion (Welbeck Rangers),
  The Sherwood Foresters (Nottinghamshire and
  Derbyshire Regiment)
17th (Service) Battalion (British Empire League),
  The King's Royal Rifle Corps
16th (Service) Battalion (St Pancras), The Rifle
  Brigade (Prince Consort's Own)
No. 117 Company, Machine Gun Corps
No. 117 Trench Mortar Battery

118TH BRIGADE
1/6th Battalion TF, The Cheshire Regiment
4th/5th Battalion TF, The Black Watch (Royal
  Highlanders)
1/1st Battalion TF, The Cambridgeshire Regiment
1/1st Battalion TF, The Hertfordshire Regiment
No. 118 Company, Machine Gun Corps
No. 118 Trench Mortar Battery

DIVISIONAL ARTILLERY
CLXXIV, CLXXIX, CLXXXIV and CLXXXVI
  (Howitzer) Brigades, Royal Field Artillery
V.39 Heavy Trench Mortar Battery, Royal Field
  Artillery
X.39, Y.39 and Z.39 Medium Mortar Batteries,
  Royal Field Artillery
39th Divisional Ammunition Column

DIVISIONAL TROOPS
13th (Service) Battalion (Forest of Dean) (Pioneers),
  The Gloucestershire Regiment
132nd, 133rd and 134th Field Ambulances, Royal
  Army Medical Corps
Nos. 225, 227 and 234 Field Companies (Stockton-
  on-Tees), Royal Engineers
No. 39 Divisional Signal Company (Empire), Royal
  Engineers
39th Divisional Train (Nos. 284, 285, 286, 287
  Companies, Army Service Corps)
No. 50 Mobile Veterinary Section, Army Veterinary
  Corps
No. 82 Sanitary Section

41ST DIVISION

15 SEPTEMBER 1916

GENERAL OFFICER COMMANDING:

MAJ GEN S.T.B. LAWFORD

122ND BRIGADE

12th (Service) Battalion (Bermondsey), The East
Surrey Regiment
15th (Service) Battalion (2nd Portsmouth),
The Hampshire Regiment
11th (Service) Battalion (Lewisham), The Queen's
Own Royal West Kent Regiment
18th (Service) Battalion (Arts and Crafts),
The King's Royal Rifle Corps
No. 122 Company, Machine Gun Corps
No. 122 Trench Mortar Battery

123RD BRIGADE

11th (Service) Battalion (Lambeth), The Queen's
Royal (West Surrey)
10th (Service) Battalion (Kent County), The
Queen's Own Royal West Kent Regiment
23rd (Service) Battalion (2nd Football),
The Middlesex Regiment (Duke of Cambridge's
Own)
20th (Service) Battalion (Wearside), The Durham
Light Infantry
No. 123 Company, Machine Gun Corps
No. 123 Trench Mortar Battery

124TH BRIGADE

10th (Service) Battalion (Battersea), The Queen's
Royal (West Surrey)
26th (Service) Battalion (Bankers), The Royal
Fusiliers (City of London Regiment)
32nd (Service) Battalion (East Ham), The Royal
Fusiliers (City of London Regiment)
21st (Service) Battalion (Yeomen Rifles),
The King's Royal Rifle Corps
No. 124 Company, Machine Gun Corps
No. 124 Trench Mortar Battery

DIVISIONAL ARTILLERY

CLXXXIII (Howitzer), CLXXXVII, CLXXXIX and
CXC Brigades, Royal Field Artillery
V.41 Heavy Trench Mortar Battery, Royal Field
Artillery
X.41, Y.41 and Z.41 Medium Mortar Batteries,
Royal Field Artillery
41st Divisional Ammunition Column (West Ham)

DIVISIONAL TROOPS

19th (Service) Battalion (2nd Public Works
Pioneers), The Middlesex Regiment (Duke of
Cambridge's Own)
Nos. 228 (Barnsley), 233 (Ripon) and 237
(Reading) Field Companies, Royal Engineers
No. 41 Divisional Signal Company, Royal
Engineers
138th, 139th and 140th Field Ambulances, Royal
Army Medical Corps
41st Divisional Train (Nos. 296, 297, 298 and 299
Companies, Army Service Corps)
No. 52 Mobile Veterinary Section, Army Veterinary
Corps
No. 84 Sanitary Section

46TH (NORTH MIDLAND) DIVISION (TF)

1 JULY 1916

GENERAL OFFICER COMMANDING:

MAJ GEN THE HON. E. MONTAGU-STUART-WORTLEY

137TH (STAFFORDSHIRE) BRIGADE

1/5th Battalion TF, The South Staffordshire Regiment

1/6th Battalion TF, The South Staffordshire Regiment

1/5th Battalion TF, The Prince of Wales's (North Staffordshire Regiment)

1/6th Battalion TF, The Prince of Wales's (North Staffordshire Regiment)

No. 137 Company, Machine Gun Corps

No. 137 Trench Mortar Battery

138TH (LINCOLN AND LEICESTER) BRIGADE

1/4th Battalion TF, The Lincolnshire Regiment

1/5th Battalion TF, The Lincolnshire Regiment

1/4th Battalion TF, The Leicestershire Regiment

1/5th Battalion TF, The Leicestershire Regiment

No. 138 Company, Machine Gun Corps

No. 138 Trench Mortar Battery

139TH (NOTTS AND DERBY) BRIGADE

1/5th Battalion TF, The Sherwood Foresters (Nottinghamshire and Derbyshire Regiment)

1/6th Battalion TF, The Sherwood Foresters (Nottinghamshire and Derbyshire Regiment)

1/7th (Robin Hood) Battalion TF, The Sherwood Foresters (Nottinghamshire and Derbyshire Regiment)

1/8th Battalion TF, The Sherwood Foresters (Nottinghamshire and Derbyshire Regiment)

No. 139 Company, Machine Gun Corps

No. 139 Trench Mortar Battery

DIVISIONAL ARTILLERY

CCXXX, CCXXXI, CCXXXII and CCXXXIII (Howitzer) Brigades, Royal Field Artillery

V.46 Heavy Trench Mortar Battery, Royal Field Artillery

X.46, Y.46 and Z.46 Medium Mortar Batteries, Royal Field Artillery

46th (North Midland) Divisional Ammunition Column

DIVISIONAL TROOPS

1/1st Battalion TF (Pioneers), The Monmouthshire Regiment

Nos. 1/1 (North Midland), 1/2 (North Midland) and 1/3 (North Midland) Field Companies, Royal Engineers

No. 46 Divisional Signal Company, Royal Engineers

1/1st (North Midland), 1/2nd (North Midland) and 1/3rd (North Midland) Field Ambulances, Royal Army Medical Corps

46th Divisional Train (Nos. 451, 452, 453 and 454 Companies, Army Service Corps)

No. 1 (North Midland) Mobile Veterinary Section, Army Veterinary Corps

No. 17 Sanitary Section

47TH (1/2ND LONDON) DIVISION (TF)

15 SEPTEMBER 1916

GENERAL OFFICER COMMANDING:
MAJ GEN C. ST L. BARTER

140TH (4TH LONDON) BRIGADE
1/6th (City of London) Battalion TF (Rifles),
  The London Regiment
1/7th (City of London) Battalion TF, The London
  Regiment
1/8th (City of London) Battalion TF (Post Office
  Rifles), The London Regiment
1/15th (County of London) Battalion TF (Prince of
  Wales's Own Civil Service Rifles), The London
  Regiment
No. 140 Company, Machine Gun Corps
No. 140 Trench Mortar Battery

141ST (5TH LONDON) BRIGADE
1/17th (County of London) Battalion TF (Poplar
  and Stepney Rifles), The London Regiment
1/18th (County of London) Battalion TF (London
  Irish Rifles), The London Regiment
1/19th (County of London) Battalion TF
  (St Pancras), The London Regiment
1/20th (County of London) Battalion TF
  (Blackheath and Woolwich), The London
  Regiment
No. 141 Company, Machine Gun Corps
No. 141 Trench Mortar Battery

142ND (6TH LONDON) BRIGADE
1/21st (County of London) Battalion TF
  (First Surrey Rifles), The London Regiment
1/22nd (County of London) Battalion TF
  (The Queen's), The London Regiment
1/23rd (County of London) Battalion TF,
  The London Regiment

1/24th (County of London) Battalion TF
  (The Queen's), The London Regiment
No. 142 Company, Machine Gun Corps
No. 142 Trench Mortar Battery

DIVISIONAL ARTILLERY
CCXXXV, CCXXXVI, CCXXXVII and
  CCXXXVIII (Howitzer) Brigades, Royal Field
  Artillery
X.47, Y.47 and Z.47 Medium Mortar Batteries,
  Royal Field Artillery
47th (2nd London) Divisional Ammunition Column

DIVISIONAL TROOPS
1/4th (Denbighshire) Battalion TF (Pioneers),
  The Royal Welsh Fusiliers
Nos. 1/3 (London), 1/4 (London) and 2/3 (London)
  Field Companies, Royal Engineers
No. 47 Divisional Signal Company, Royal
  Engineers
1/4th (London), 1/5th (London) and 1/6th (London)
  Field Ambulances, Royal Army Medical Corps
47th Divisional Train (Nos. 455, 456, 457 and 458
  Companies, Army Service Corps)
No. 2 (London) Mobile Veterinary Section, Army
  Veterinary Corps
No. 47 Sanitary Section

48th (South Midland) Division (TF)

16 JULY 1916

GENERAL OFFICER COMMANDING:

MAJ GEN R. FANSHAWE

143RD (WARWICKSHIRE) BRIGADE

1/5th Battalion TF, The Royal Warwickshire
Regiment
1/6th Battalion TF, The Royal Warwickshire
Regiment
1/7th Battalion TF, The Royal Warwickshire
Regiment
1/8th Battalion TF, The Royal Warwickshire
Regiment
No. 143 Company, Machine Gun Corps
No. 143 Trench Mortar Battery

**144TH (GLOUCESTER AND WORCESTER)
BRIGADE**

1/4th (City of Bristol) Battalion TF,
The Gloucestershire Regiment
1/6th Battalion TF, The Gloucestershire Regiment
1/7th Battalion TF, The Worcestershire Regiment
1/8th Battalion TF, The Worcestershire Regiment
No. 144 Company, Machine Gun Corps
No. 144 Trench Mortar Battery

145TH (SOUTH MIDLAND) BRIGADE

1/5th Battalion TF, The Gloucestershire Regiment
1/4th Battalion TF, The Oxfordshire &
Buckinghamshire Light Infantry
1/1st Buckinghamshire Battalion TF,
The Oxfordshire & Buckinghamshire Light
Infantry
1/4th Battalion TF, Princess Charlotte of Wales's
Royal Berkshire Regiment
No. 145 Company, Machine Gun Corps
No. 145 Trench Mortar Battery

DIVISIONAL ARTILLERY

CCXL, CCXLI, CCXLII and CCXLIII (Howitzer)
Brigades, Royal Field Artillery
V.48 Heavy Trench Mortar Battery, Royal Field
Artillery
X.48, Y.48 and Z.48 Medium Mortar Batteries,
Royal Field Artillery
48th (South Midland) Divisional Ammunition
Column

DIVISIONAL TROOPS

1/5th (Cinque Ports) Battalion TF (Pioneers),
The Royal Sussex Regiment
Nos. 1/1 (South Midland), 1/2 (South Midland) and
2/1 (South Midland) Field Companies, Royal
Engineers
No. 48 Divisional Signal Company, Royal
Engineers
1/1st (South Midland), 1/2nd (South Midland) and
1/3rd (South Midland) Field Ambulances, Royal
Army Medical Corps
48th Divisional Train (Nos. 459, 460, 461 and 462
Companies, Army Service Corps)
No. 1 (South Midland) Mobile Veterinary Section,
Army Veterinary Corps
No. 48 Sanitary Section

49TH (WEST RIDING) DIVISION (TF)

2 JULY 1916

GENERAL OFFICER COMMANDING:
MAJ GEN E.M. PERCEVAL

146TH (WEST RIDING) BRIGADE
1/5th Battalion TF, The Prince of Wales's Own (West Yorkshire) Regiment
1/6th Battalion TF, The Prince of Wales's Own (West Yorkshire) Regiment
1/7th Battalion TF, The Prince of Wales's Own (West Yorkshire) Regiment
1/8th Battalion TF, The Prince of Wales's Own (West Yorkshire) Regiment
No. 146 Company, Machine Gun Corps
No. 146 Trench Mortar Battery

147TH (2ND WEST RIDING) BRIGADE
1/4th Battalion TF, The Duke of Wellington's Regiment (West Riding)
1/5th Battalion TF, The Duke of Wellington's Regiment (West Riding)
1/6th Battalion TF, The Duke of Wellington's Regiment (West Riding)
1/7th Battalion TF, The Duke of Wellington's Regiment (West Riding)
No. 147 Company, Machine Gun Corps
No. 147 Trench Mortar Battery

148TH (3RD WEST RIDING) BRIGADE
1/4th Battalion TF, The King's Own Yorkshire Light Infantry
1/5th Battalion TF, The King's Own Yorkshire Light Infantry
1/4th (Hallamshire) Battalion TF, The York and Lancaster Regiment
1/5th Battalion TF, The York and Lancaster Regiment

No. 148 Company, Machine Gun Corps
No. 148 Trench Mortar Battery

DIVISIONAL ARTILLERY
CCXLV, CCXLVI, CCXLVII and CCXLVIII (Howitzer) Brigades, Royal Field Artillery
W.49 and V.49 Heavy Trench Mortar Batteries, Royal Field Artillery
X.49, Y.49 and Z.49 Medium Mortar Batteries, Royal Field Artillery
49th (West Riding) Divisional Ammunition Column

DIVISIONAL TROOPS
1/3rd Battalion TF, The Monmouthshire Regiment
Nos. 57, 1/2 (West Riding) and 2/1 (West Riding) Field Companies, Royal Engineers
No. 49 Divisional Signal Company, Royal Engineers
1/1st (West Riding), 1/2nd (West Riding) and 1/3rd (West Riding) Field Ambulances, Royal Army Medical Corps
49th Divisional Train (Nos. 463, 464, 465 and 466 Companies, Army Service Corps)
No. 1 (West Riding) Mobile Veterinary Section, Army Veterinary Corps
No. 49 Sanitary Section

50TH (NORTHUMBRIAN) DIVISION (TF)

15 SEPTEMBER 1916

GENERAL OFFICER COMMANDING:

MAJ GEN P.S. WILKINSON

149TH (NORTHUMBERLAND) BRIGADE
1/4th Battalion TF, The Northumberland Fusiliers
1/5th Battalion TF, The Northumberland Fusiliers
1/6th Battalion TF, The Northumberland Fusiliers
1/7th Battalion TF, The Northumberland Fusiliers
No. 149 Company, Machine Gun Corps
No. 149 Trench Mortar Battery

150TH (YORK AND DURHAM) BRIGADE
1/4th Battalion TF, The East Yorkshire Regiment
(The Duke of York's Own)
1/4th Battalion TF, The Princess of Wales's Own
(Yorkshire) Regiment
1/5th Battalion TF, The Princess of Wales's Own
(Yorkshire) Regiment
1/5th Battalion TF, The Durham Light Infantry
No. 150 Company, Machine Gun Corps
No. 150 Trench Mortar Battery

151ST BRIGADE
1/5th (Cumberland) Battalion TF, The Border
Regiment
1/6th Battalion TF, The Durham Light Infantry
1/8th Battalion TF, The Durham Light Infantry
1/9th Battalion TF, The Durham Light Infantry
No. 151 Company, Machine Gun Corps
No. 151 Trench Mortar Battery

DIVISIONAL ARTILLERY
CCL, CCLI, CCLII and CCLIII (Howitzer)
Brigades, Royal Field Artillery
V.50 Heavy Trench Mortar Battery, Royal Field
Artillery
X.50, Y.50 and Z.50 Medium Mortar Batteries,
Royal Field Artillery
50th (Northumbrian) Divisional Ammunition
Column

DIVISIONAL TROOPS
1/7th Battalion TF (Pioneers), The Durham Light
Infantry
Nos. 7, 1/1 (Northumbrian) and 1/2 (Northumbrian)
Field Companies, Royal Engineers
No. 50 Divisional Signal Company, Royal
Engineers
1/1st (Northumbrian), 1/3rd (Northumbrian) and
2/2nd (Northumbrian) Field Ambulances, Royal
Army Medical Corps
50th Divisional Train (Nos. 467, 468, 469 and 470
Companies, Army Service Corps)
No. 1 (Northumbrian) Mobile Veterinary Section,
Army Veterinary Corps
No. 50 Sanitary Section

51ST (HIGHLAND) DIVISION (TF)

21 JULY 1916

GENERAL OFFICER COMMANDING:

MAJ GEN G.M. HARPER

152ND (1ST HIGHLAND) BRIGADE

1/5th (The Sutherland and Caithness) Battalion TF, The Seaforth Highlanders (Ross-shire Buffs, The Duke of Albany's)

1/6th (Morayshire) Battalion TF, The Seaforth Highlanders (Ross-shire Buffs, The Duke of Albany's)

1/6th (Banff and Donside) Battalion TF, The Gordon Highlanders

1/8th (The Argyllshire) Battalion TF, Princess Louise's Argyll & Sutherland Highlanders

No. 152 Company, Machine Gun Corps

No. 152 Trench Mortar Battery

153RD (2ND HIGHLAND) BRIGADE

1/6th (Perthshire) Battalion TF, The Black Watch (Royal Highlanders)

1/7th (Fife) Battalion TF, The Black Watch (Royal Highlanders)

1/5th (Buchan and Formartin) Battalion TF, The Gordon Highlanders

1/7th (Deeside Highland) Battalion TF, The Gordon Highlanders

No. 153 Company, Machine Gun Corps

No. 153 Trench Mortar Battery

154TH (3RD HIGHLAND) BRIGADE

1/9th (Highlanders) Battalion TF, The Royal Scots (Lothian Regiment)

1/4th (Ross Highland) Battalion TF, The Seaforth Highlanders (Ross-shire Buffs, The Duke of Albany's)

1/4th Battalion TF, The Gordon Highlanders

1/7th Battalion TF, Princess Louise's Argyll & Sutherland Highlanders

No. 154 Company, Machine Gun Corps

No. 154 Trench Mortar Battery

DIVISIONAL ARTILLERY

CCLV, CCLVI, CCLVIII (Howitzer) and CCLX Brigades, Royal Field Artillery

X.51, Y.51 and Z.51 Medium Mortar Batteries, Royal Field Artillery

51st (Highland) Divisional Ammunition Column

DIVISIONAL TROOPS

1/8th Battalion TF (Pioneers), The Royal Scots (Lothian Regiment)

Nos. 1/1 (Highland), 1/2 (Highland) and 2/2 (Highland) Field Companies, Royal Engineers

No. 51 Divisional Signal Company, Royal Engineers

1/1st (Highland), 1/2nd (Highland), 1/3rd (Highland) and 2/1st (Highland) Field Ambulances, Royal Army Medical Corps

51st Divisional Train (Nos. 471, 472, 473 and 474 Companies, Army Service Corps)

No. 1 (Highland) Mobile Veterinary Section, Army Veterinary Corps

No. 51 Sanitary Section

55TH (WEST LANCASHIRE) DIVISION (TF)

30 JULY 1916

GENERAL OFFICER COMMANDING:

MAJ GEN H.S. JEUDWINE

164TH (NORTH LANCASHIRE) BRIGADE

1/4th Battalion TF, The King's Own (Royal Lancaster Regiment)

1/8th (Irish) Battalion TF, The King's (Liverpool Regiment)

2/5th Battalion TF, The Lancashire Fusiliers

1/4th Battalion TF, The Loyal North Lancashire Regiment

No. 164 Company, Machine Gun Corps

No. 164 Trench Mortar Battery

165TH (LIVERPOOL) BRIGADE

1/5th Battalion TF, The King's (Liverpool Regiment)

1/6th (Rifle) Battalion TF, The King's (Liverpool Regiment)

1/7th Battalion TF, The King's (Liverpool Regiment)

1/9th Battalion TF, The King's (Liverpool Regiment)

No. 165 Company, Machine Gun Corps

No. 165 Trench Mortar Battery

166TH (SOUTH LANCASHIRE) BRIGADE

1/5th Battalion TF, The King's Own (Royal Lancaster Regiment)

1/10th (Scottish) Battalion TF, The King's (Liverpool Regiment)

1/5th Battalion TF, Prince of Wales's Volunteers (South Lancashire Regiment)

1/5th Battalion TF, The Loyal North Lancashire Regiment

No. 166 Company, Machine Gun Corps

No. 166 Trench Mortar Battery

DIVISIONAL ARTILLERY

CCLXXV, CCLXXVI, CCLXXVII and CCLXXVIII (Howitzer) Brigades, Royal Field Artillery

V.55 Heavy Trench Mortar Battery, Royal Field Artillery

X.55, Y.55 and Z.55 Medium Mortar Batteries, Royal Field Artillery

55th Divisional Ammunition Column

DIVISIONAL TROOPS

1/4th Battalion TF (Pioneers), Prince of Wales's Volunteers (South Lancashire Regiment)

Nos. 1/1 (West Lancashire), 2/1 (West Lancashire) and 2/2 (West Lancashire) Field Companies, Royal Engineers

No. 55 Divisional Signal Company, Royal Engineers

1/3rd (West Lancashire), 2/1st (West Lancashire) and 2/1st (Wessex) Field Ambulances, Royal Army Medical Corps

55th Divisional Train (Nos. 95, 96, 97 and 98 Companies, Army Service Corps)

No. 1 (West Lancashire) Mobile Veterinary Section, Army Veterinary Corps

No. 55 Sanitary Section

56TH (1/1ST LONDON) DIVISION (TF)

1 JULY 1916

GENERAL OFFICER COMMANDING:

MAJ GEN C.P.A. HULL

167TH (1ST LONDON) BRIGADE

1/7th Battalion TF, The Middlesex Regiment (Duke of Cambridge's Own)

1/8th Battalion TF, The Middlesex Regiment (Duke of Cambridge's Own)

1/1st (City of London) Battalion TF (Royal Fusiliers), The London Regiment

1/3rd (City of London) Battalion TF (Royal Fusiliers), The London Regiment

No. 167 Company, Machine Gun Corps

No. 167 Trench Mortar Battery

168TH (2ND LONDON) BRIGADE

1/4th (City of London) Battalion TF (Royal Fusiliers), The London Regiment

1/12th (County of London) Battalion TF (The Rangers), The London Regiment

1/13th (County of London) Battalion TF (Kensington), The London Regiment

1/14th (County of London) Battalion TF (London Scottish), The London Regiment

No. 168 Company, Machine Gun Corps

No. 168 Trench Mortar Battery

169TH (3RD LONDON) BRIGADE

1/2nd (City of London) Battalion TF (Royal Fusiliers), The London Regiment

1/5th (City of London) Battalion TF (London Rifle Brigade), The London Regiment

1/9th (City of London) Battalion TF (Queen Victoria's Rifles), The London Regiment

1/16th (County of London) Battalion TF (Queen's Westminster Rifles), The London Regiment

No. 169 Company, Machine Gun Corps

No. 169 Trench Mortar Battery

DIVISIONAL ARTILLERY

CCLXXX, CCLXXXI, CCLXXXII and CCLXXXIII (Howitzer) Brigades, Royal Field Artillery

V.56 Heavy Trench Mortar Battery, Royal Field Artillery

X.56, Y.56 and Z.56 Medium Mortar Batteries, Royal Field Artillery

56th Divisional Ammunition Column

DIVISIONAL TROOPS

1/5th Battalion TF (Pioneers), The Cheshire Regiment

Nos. 1/1 (Edinburgh), 2/1 (London) and 2/2 (London) Field Companies, Royal Engineers

No. 58 Divisional Signal Company, Royal Engineers

2/1st (London), 2/2nd (London) and 2/3rd (London) Field Ambulances, Royal Army Medical Corps

56th Divisional Train (Nos. 213, 214, 215 and 216 Companies, Army Service Corps)

No. 1 (London) Mobile Veterinary Section, Army Veterinary Corps

No. 56 Sanitary Section

63RD (ROYAL NAVAL) DIVISION

6 OCTOBER 1916

GENERAL OFFICER COMMANDING:

MAJ GEN A. PARIS

188TH BRIGADE
Howe Battalion
Anson Battalion
1st Royal Marine Battalion
2nd Royal Marine Battalion
No. 188 Company, Machine Gun Corps
No. 188 Trench Mortar Battery

189TH BRIGADE
Drake Battalion
Hawke Battalion
Nelson Battalion
Hood Battalion
No. 189 Trench Mortar Battery

190TH BRIGADE
7th (Extra Reserve) Battalion, The Royal Fusiliers
   (City of London Regiment)
4th (Extra Reserve) Battalion, The Bedfordshire
   Regiment
10th (Service) Battalion, The Royal Dublin Fusiliers
1/1st Battalion TF, The Honourable Artillery
   Company
No. 190 Company, Machine Gun Corps
No. 190 Trench Mortar Battery

DIVISIONAL ARTILLERY
CCCXV, CCCXVII and CCCXVIII Brigades, Royal
   Field Artillery
V.63 Heavy Trench Mortar Battery, Royal Field
   Artillery
X.63, Y.63 and Z.63 Medium Mortar Batteries,
   Royal Field Artillery
63rd Divisional Ammunition Column

DIVISIONAL TROOPS
14th (Service) Battalion (Severn Valley Pioneers),
   The Worcestershire Regiment
Nos. 1 (RND), 2 (RND) and 3 (RND) Field
   Company, Royal Engineers
No. 63 Divisional Signal Company, Royal
   Engineers
Nos. 1 (Royal Naval), 2 (Royal Naval) and 3 (Royal
   Naval) Field Ambulances, Royal Army Medical
   Corps
Royal Naval Divisional Train (Nos. 761, 762, 763
   and 764 Companies, Army Service Corps)
No. 53 Mobile Veterinary Section, Army Veterinary
   Corps
No. 63 Sanitary Section

1ST CAVALRY DIVISION

14 JULY 1916

GENERAL OFFICER COMMANDING:
MAJ GEN R. MULLENS

1ST CAVALRY BRIGADE
2nd Dragoon Guards (Queen's Bays)
5th (Princess of Wales's) Dragoon Guards
11th Prince Albert's Own Hussars
No. 1 Signal Troop, Royal Engineers
No. 1 Squadron, Machine Gun Corps

2ND CAVALRY BRIGADE
4th (Royal Irish) Dragoon Guards
9th (Queen's Royal) Lancers
18th (Queen Mary's Own) Hussars
No. 2 Signal Troop, Royal Engineers
No. 2 Squadron, Machine Gun Corps

9TH CAVALRY BRIGADE
15th (The King's) Hussars
19th (Queen Alexandra's Own Royal) Hussars
1/1st Bedfordshire Yeomanry
No. 9 Signal Troop, Royal Engineers
No. 9 Squadron, Machine Gun Corps

DIVISIONAL ARTILLERY
H, I and No. 1 (Warwickshire) Batteries, Royal
  Horse Artillery
1st Cavalry Divisional Ammunition Park (No. 45
  Motor Transport Company, Army Service
  Corps)

DIVISIONAL TROOPS
No. 1 Field Squadron, Royal Engineers
No. 1 Signal Squadron, Royal Engineers
No. 8 Motor Machine Gun Battery, Machine Gun
  Corps
1st Cavalry Divisional Train (No. 27 Horse
  Transport Company, Army Service Corps)
1st Cavalry Divisional Auxiliary (Horse) Company
  (No. 574 Horse Transport Company, Army
  Service Corps)
1st Cavalry Divisional Supply Column (Nos. 57 and
  58 Motor Transport Companies, Army Service
  Corps)
1st, 3rd and 9th Cavalry Field Ambulances, Royal
  Army Medical Corps
Nos. 1, 10 and 39 Mobile Veterinary Sections,
  Army Veterinary Corps
No. 9 Sanitary Section

2ND CAVALRY DIVISION

14 JULY 1916

GENERAL OFFICER COMMANDING:
MAJ GEN C. KAVANAGH

3RD CAVALRY BRIGADE
4th (Queen's Own) Hussars
5th (Royal Irish) Lancers
16th (The Queen's) Lancers
No. 3 Signal Troop, Royal Engineers
No. 3 Squadron, Machine Gun Corps

4TH CAVALRY BRIGADE
6th Dragoon Guards (Carabiniers)
3rd (King's Own) Hussars
1/1st Oxfordshire Yeomanry
No. 4 Signal Troop, Royal Engineers
No. 4 Squadron, Machine Gun Corps

5TH CAVALRY BRIGADE
2nd Dragoons (Royal Scots Greys)
20th Hussars
12th (Prince of Wales's) Lancers
No. 5 Signal Troop, Royal Engineers
No. 5 Squadron, Machine Gun Corps

DIVISIONAL ARTILLERY
III and IV Brigades and J Battery, Royal Horse
    Artillery
2nd Cavalry Divisional Ammunition Park (No. 56
    Motor Transport Company, Army Service Corps)

DIVISIONAL TROOPS
No. 2 Field Squadron, Royal Engineers
No. 2 Signal Squadron, Royal Engineers
2nd Cavalry Divisional Train (No. 424 Horse
    Transport Company, Army Service Corps)
2nd Cavalry Divisional Auxiliary (Horse) Company
    (No. 575 Horse Transport Company, Army
    Service Corps)
2nd Cavalry Divisional Supply Column (Nos. 46
    and 413 Motor Transport Companies, Army
    Service Corps)
7th, 8th and 9th Mobile Veterinary Sections, Army
    Veterinary Corps
No. 4A Sanitary Section

3RD CAVALRY DIVISION

14 JULY 1916

GENERAL OFFICER COMMANDING:

MAJ GEN J. VAUGHAN

6TH CAVALRY BRIGADE
3rd (Prince of Wales's) Dragoon Guards
1st (Royal) Dragoons
1/1st North Somerset Yeomanry
No. 6 Signal Troop, Royal Engineers
No. 6 Squadron, Machine Gun Corps

7TH CAVALRY BRIGADE
1st Life Guards
2nd Life Guards
1/1st Leicestershire Yeomanry
No. 7 Signal Troop, Royal Engineers
No. 7 Squadron, Machine Gun Corps

8TH CAVALRY BRIGADE
Royal Horse Guards
10th (Prince of Wales's Own Royal) Hussars
1/1st Essex Yeomanry
No. 8 Signal Troop, Royal Engineers
No. 8 Squadron, Machine Gun Corps

DIVISIONAL ARTILLERY
IV Brigade and G Battery, Royal Horse Artillery
3rd Cavalry Divisional Ammunition Park
 (No. 76 Motor Transport Company, Army
 Service Corps)

DIVISIONAL TROOPS
No. 3 Field Squadron, Royal Engineers
No. 3 Signal Squadron, Royal Engineers
3rd Cavalry Divisional Train (No. 81 Horse
 Transport Company, Army Service Corps)
3rd Cavalry Divisional Auxiliary (Horse) Company
 (No. 576 Horse Transport Company, Army
 Service Corps)
3rd Cavalry Divisional Supply Column (Nos. 73
 and 414 Motor Transport Companies, Army
 Service Corps)
6th, 7th and 8th Cavalry Field Ambulances, Royal
 Army Medical Corps
Nos. 13, 14 and 20 Mobile Veterinary Sections,
 Army Veterinary Corps
No. 7 Motor Machine Gun Battery, Machine Gun
 Corps
No. 12 Sanitary Section

1ST (INDIAN) CAVALRY DIVISION

14 JULY 1916

GENERAL OFFICER COMMANDING:
MAJ GEN H.P. LEADER

SIALKOT BRIGADE
17th (Duke of Cambridge's Own) Lancers
6th King Edward's Own Cavalry
19th Bengal Lancers (Fane's Horse)
No. 10 Squadron, Machine Gun Corps

MHOW BRIGADE
6th (Inniskilling) Dragoons
2nd Lancers (Gardner's Horse)
38th King George's Own Central India Horse
No. 11 Squadron, Machine Gun Corps

LUCKNOW BRIGADE
1st (King's) Dragoon Guards
29th Lancers
36th Jacob's Horse
No. 12 Squadron, Machine Gun Corps

DIVISIONAL ARTILLERY
I (Indian) Brigade and A, Q and U Batteries, Royal
   Horse Artillery
1st (Indian) Cavalry Divisional Ammunition Park
   (No. 79 Company, Army Service Corps)

DIVISIONAL TROOPS
No. 1 Indian Field Squadron, Royal Engineers
No. 1 Indian Signal Squadron, Royal Engineers
1st (Indian) Cavalry Divisional Train (No. 426
   Company, Army Service Corps)
1st (Indian) Cavalry Divisional Supply Column
   (No. 89 Company, Army Service Corps)
1st (Indian) Cavalry Divisional Auxiliary Horse
   Transport Company (No. 577 Company, Army
   Service Corps)
Sialkot, Mhow, Lucknow and Jodhpur Cavalry
   Field Ambulances, Royal Army Medical
   Corps
Sialkot, Mhow and Lucknow Mobile Veterinary
   Sections, Army Veterinary Corps

2ND (INDIAN) CAVALRY DIVISION

14 JULY 1916

GENERAL OFFICER COMMANDING:

MAJ GEN H.J.M. MACANDREW

AMBALA BRIGADE
8th (King's Royal Irish) Hussars
9th Hodson's Horse
18th King George's Own Tiwana Lancers
No. 14 Squadron, Machine Gun Corps

SECUNDERABAD BRIGADE
7th (Princess Royal's) Dragoon Guards
20th Deccan Horse
34th Poona Horse
No. 13 Squadron, Machine Gun Corps

CANADIAN CAVALRY BRIGADE
The Royal Canadian Dragoons
Lord Strathcona's Horse
The Fort Garry Horse
Canadian Squadron, Machine Gun Corps

DIVISIONAL ARTILLERY
II (Indian) Brigade and N and X Batteries, Royal
    Horse Artillery
Royal Canadian Horse Artillery Brigade
2nd (Indian) Cavalry Divisional Ammunition Park
    (No. 72 Company, Army Service Corps)

DIVISIONAL TROOPS
No. 2 (Indian) Field Squadron, Royal Engineers
No. 2 (Indian) Signal Squadron, Royal Engineers
2nd (Indian) Cavalry Divisional Train (No. 427
    Company, Army Service Corps)
2nd (Indian) Cavalry Divisional Supply Column
    (No. 83 Company, Army Service Corps)
2nd (Indian) Cavalry Divisional Auxiliary Horse
    Transport Company (No. 578 Company, Army
    Service Corps)
Ambala, Secunderabad and 7th Canadian Cavalry
    Field Ambulances, Royal Army Medical Corps
Ambala, Secunderabad and A Canadian Mobile
    Veterinary Sections, Army Veterinary Corps

1ST AUSTRALIAN DIVISION

21 JULY 1916

GENERAL OFFICER COMMANDING:
MAJ GEN H.B. WALKER

1ST AUSTRALIAN BRIGADE
1st (New South Wales) Australian Infantry Battalion
2nd (New South Wales) Australian Infantry Battalion
3rd (New South Wales) Australian Infantry Battalion
4th (New South Wales) Australian Infantry Battalion
No. 1 Company, Australian Machine Gun Corps
No. 1 Australian Trench Mortar Battery

2ND AUSTRALIAN BRIGADE
5th (Victoria) Australian Infantry Battalion
6th (Victoria) Australian Infantry Battalion
7th (Victoria) Australian Infantry Battalion
8th (Victoria) Australian Infantry Battalion
No. 2 Company, Australian Machine Gun Corps
No. 2 Australian Trench Mortar Battery

3RD AUSTRALIAN BRIGADE
9th (Queensland) Australian Infantry Battalion
10th (South Australia) Australian Infantry Battalion
11th (Western Australia) Australian Infantry Battalion
12th (Tasmania, South Australia, West Australia) Australian Infantry Battalion
No. 3 Company, Australian Machine Gun Corps
No. 3 Australian Trench Mortar Battery

DIVISIONAL ARTILLERY
I, II, III and XXI (Howitzer) Brigades, Royal Australian Field Artillery
V.1A Heavy Trench Mortar Battery, Royal Australian Field Artillery
X.1A, Y.1A and Z.1A Medium Trench Mortar Batteries, Royal Australian Field Artillery
1st Australian Divisional Ammunition Column

DIVISIONAL TROOPS
1st (New South Wales) Australian Pioneer Battalion
Nos. 1 (New South Wales), 2 (Victoria) and 3 (Outer States) Field Companies, Australian Engineers
No. 1 Divisional Signal Company, Australian Engineers
1st (New South Wales), 2nd (Victoria) and 3rd (Outer States) Field Ambulances, Australian Army Medical Corps
1st Australian Divisional Train (Nos. 1, 2, 3, 4 Companies, Australian Army Service Corps)
No. 1 Mobile Veterinary Section, Australian Army Veterinary Corps
No. 1 Sanitary Section

2ND AUSTRALIAN DIVISION

25 JULY 1916

GENERAL OFFICER COMMANDING:

MAJ GEN J.G. LEGGE

5TH AUSTRALIAN BRIGADE
17th (New South Wales) Australian Infantry
  Battalion
18th (New South Wales) Australian Infantry
  Battalion
19th (New South Wales) Australian Infantry
  Battalion
20th (New South Wales) Australian Infantry
  Battalion
No. 5 Company, Australian Machine Gun Corps
No. 5 Australian Trench Mortar Battery

6TH AUSTRALIAN BRIGADE
21st (Victoria) Australian Infantry Battalion
22nd (Victoria) Australian Infantry Battalion
23rd (Victoria) Australian Infantry Battalion
24th (Victoria) Australian Infantry Battalion
No. 6 Company, Australian Machine Gun Corps
No. 6 Australian Trench Mortar Battery

7TH AUSTRALIAN BRIGADE
25th (Queensland) Australian Infantry Battalion
26th (Queensland and Tasmania) Australian Infantry
  Battalion
27th (South Australia) Australian Infantry Battalion
28th (West Australia) Australian Infantry Battalion
No. 7 Company, Australian Machine Gun Corps
No. 7 Australian Trench Mortar Battery

DIVISIONAL ARTILLERY
IV, V, VI, XXII Brigade, Royal Australian Field
  Artillery
V.2A Heavy Trench Mortar Battery, Royal
  Australian Field Artillery
X.2A, Y.2A and Z.2A Medium Trench Mortar
  Battery, Royal Australian Field Artillery
2nd Australian Divisional Ammunition Column

DIVISIONAL TROOPS
2nd (Western Australia) Australian Pioneer
  Battalion
Nos. 5 (Victoria), 6 (Outer States) and 7 (New
  South Wales) Field Companies, Australian
  Engineers
No. 2 Divisional Signal Company, Australian
  Engineers
5th (New South Wales), 6th (Victoria) and 7th
  (Outer States) Field Ambulances, Australian
  Army Medical Corps
2nd Australian Divisional Train (Nos. 15, 16, 17, 20
  Companies, Australian Army Service Corps)
No. 2 Mobile Veterinary Section, Australian Army
  Veterinary Corps
No. 2 Sanitary Section

4TH AUSTRALIAN DIVISION

6 AUGUST 1916

GENERAL OFFICER COMMANDING:

MAJ GEN H.V. COX

4TH AUSTRALIAN BRIGADE
13th (New South Wales) Australian Infantry
  Battalion
14th (Victoria) Australian Infantry Battalion
15th (Queensland and Tasmania) Australian Infantry
  Battalion
16th (Western Australia and Southern Australia)
  Australian Infantry Battalion
No. 4 Company, Australian Machine Gun Corps
No. 4 Australian Trench Mortar Battery

12TH AUSTRALIAN BRIGADE
45th (New South Wales) Australian Infantry
  Battalion
46th (Victoria) Australian Infantry Battalion
47th (Queensland and Tasmania) Australian Infantry
  Battalion
48th (Western Australia and Southern Australia)
  Australian Infantry Battalion
No. 12 Company, Australian Machine Gun Corps
No. 12 Australian Trench Mortar Battery

13TH AUSTRALIAN BRIGADE
49th (Queensland) Australian Infantry Battalion
50th (Southern Australia) Australian Infantry
  Battalion
51st (Western Australia) Australian Infantry
  Battalion
52nd (Southern Australia, Western Australia,
  Tasmania) Australian Infantry Battalion
No. 13 Company, Australian Machine Gun Corps
No. 13 Australian Trench Mortar Battery

DIVISIONAL ARTILLERY
X, XI, XII and XXIV Brigades, Royal Australian
  Field Artillery
V.4A Heavy Trench Mortar Battery, Royal
  Australian Field Artillery
X.4A, Y.4A and Z.4A Medium Trench Mortar
  Batteries, Royal Australian Field Artillery
4th Australian Divisional Ammunition Column

DIVISIONAL TROOPS
4th (Queensland) Australian Pioneer Battalion
Nos. 4, 12 and 13 Field Companies, Australian
  Engineers
No. 4 Divisional Signal Company, Australian
  Engineers
4th, 12th and 13th Field Ambulances, Australian
  Army Medical Corps
4th Australian Divisional Train (Nos. 7, 14, 26, 27
  Companies, Australian Army Service Corps)
No. 4 Mobile Veterinary Section, Australian Army
  Veterinary Corps
No. 4 Sanitary Section

5TH AUSTRALIAN DIVISION

7 AUGUST 1916

GENERAL OFFICER COMMANDING:
MAJ GEN J.W. MCCAY

8TH AUSTRALIAN BRIGADE
29th (Victoria) Australian Infantry Battalion
30th (New South Wales) Australian Infantry
    Battalion
31st (Queensland and Victoria) Australian Infantry
    Battalion
32nd (Southern Australia and Western Australia)
    Australian Infantry Battalion
No. 8 Company, Australian Machine Gun Corps
No. 8 Australian Trench Mortar Battery

14TH AUSTRALIAN BRIGADE
53rd (New South Wales) Australian Infantry
    Battalion
54th (New South Wales) Australian Infantry
    Battalion
55th (New South Wales) Australian Infantry
    Battalion
56th (New South Wales) Australian Infantry
    Battalion
No. 14 Company, Australian Machine Gun Corps
No. 14 Australian Trench Mortar Battery

15TH AUSTRALIAN BRIGADE
57th (Victoria) Australian Infantry Battalion
58th (Victoria) Australian Infantry Battalion
59th (Victoria) Australian Infantry Battalion
60th (Victoria) Australian Infantry Battalion
No. 15 Company, Australian Machine Gun Corps
No. 15 Australian Trench Mortar Battery

DIVISIONAL ARTILLERY
XIII, XIV, XV and XXV (Howitzer) Brigades,
    Royal Australian Field Artillery
V.5A Heavy Trench Mortar Battery, Royal
    Australian Field Artillery
X.5A, Y.5A and Z.5A Medium Trench Mortar
    Batteries, Royal Australian Field Artillery
5th Australian Divisional Ammunition Column

DIVISIONAL TROOPS
5th (Southern Australia) Australian Pioneer
    Battalion
12th Light Horse Regiment (New South Wales)
No. 5 Cyclist Company
No. 8, 14 and 15 Field Companies, Australian
    Engineers
No. 5 Divisional Signal Company, Australian
    Engineers
8th, 14th and 15th Field Ambulances, Australian
    Army Medical Corps
5th Australian Divisional Train (Nos. 10, 18, 28, 29
    Companies, Australian Army Service Corps)
No. 5 Mobile Veterinary Section, Australian Army
    Veterinary Corps
No. 5 Sanitary Section

1ST CANADIAN DIVISION

31 AUGUST 1916

GENERAL OFFICER COMMANDING:

MAJ GEN A.W. CURRIE

1ST CANADIAN BRIGADE
1st (Ontario) Canadian Infantry Battalion
2nd (East Ontario) Canadian Infantry Battalion
3rd Canadian Infantry Battalion (Toronto Regiment)
4th Canadian Infantry Battalion
No. 1 Company, Canadian Machine Gun Corps
No. 1 Canadian Trench Mortar Battery

2ND CANADIAN BRIGADE
5th (Western Cavalry) Canadian Infantry Battalion
7th Canadian Infantry Battalion (1st British Columbia)
8th Canadian Infantry Battalion (90th Infantry)
10th Canadian Infantry Battalion
No. 2 Company, Canadian Machine Gun Corps
No. 2 Canadian Trench Mortar Battery

3RD CANADIAN BRIGADE
13th Canadian Infantry Battalion (Royal Highlanders)
14th Canadian Infantry Battalion (Royal Montreal Regiment)
15th Canadian Infantry Battalion (48th Highlanders)
16th Canadian Infantry Battalion (Canadian Scottish)
No. 3 Company, Canadian Machine Gun Corps
No. 3 Canadian Trench Mortar Battery

DIVISIONAL ARTILLERY
I and II Brigades, Canadian Field Artillery
1st Canadian Divisional Ammunition Column

DIVISIONAL TROOPS
1st Canadian Pioneer Battalion
1st, 2nd and 3rd Battalions, Canadian Engineers
No. 1 Divisional Signal Company, Canadian Engineers

2ND CANADIAN DIVISION

15 SEPTEMBER 1916

GENERAL OFFICER COMMANDING:

MAJ GEN R.E.W. TURNER

4TH CANADIAN BRIGADE
18th (Western Ontario) Canadian Infantry Battalion
19th (Central Ontario) Canadian Infantry Battalion
20th (Central Ontario) Canadian Infantry Battalion
21st (Eastern Ontario) Canadian Infantry Battalion
No. 4 Company, Canadian Machine Gun Corps
No. 4 Canadian Trench Mortar Battery

5TH CANADIAN BRIGADE
22nd (Canadien Français) Canadian Infantry
   Battalion
24th Canadian Infantry Battalion (Victoria Rifles)
25th Canadian Infantry Battalion (Nova Scotia
   Rifles)
26th (New Brunswick) Canadian Infantry Battalion
No. 5 Company, Canadian Machine Gun Corps
No. 5 Canadian Trench Mortar Battery

6TH CANADIAN BRIGADE
27th (City of Winnipeg) Canadian Infantry
   Battalion
28th (North-West) Canadian Infantry Battalion
29th (Vancouver) Canadian Infantry Battalion
31st (Alberta) Canadian Infantry Battalion
No. 6 Company, Canadian Machine Gun Corps
No. 6 Canadian Trench Mortar Battery

DIVISIONAL ARTILLERY
V and VI Brigades, Canadian Field Artillery
2nd Canadian Divisional Ammunition Column

DIVISIONAL TROOPS
2nd Canadian Pioneer Battalion
4th, 5th and 6th Battalions, Canadian Engineers
No. 2 Divisional Signal Company, Canadian
   Engineers

3RD CANADIAN DIVISION

15 SEPTEMBER 1916

GENERAL OFFICER COMMANDING:

MAJ GEN L.J. LIPSETT

7TH CANADIAN BRIGADE
Princess Patricia's Canadian Light Infantry
The Royal Canadian Regiment
42nd Canadian Infantry Battalion (Royal
   Highlanders)
49th (Edmonton) Canadian Infantry Battalion
No. 7 Company, Canadian Machine Gun Corps
No. 7 Trench Mortar Battery

8TH CANADIAN BRIGADE
1st Canadian Mounted Rifles
2nd Canadian Mounted Rifles
4th Canadian Mounted Rifles
5th Canadian Mounted Rifles
No. 8 Company, Canadian Machine Gun Corps
No. 8 Trench Mortar Battery

9TH CANADIAN BRIGADE
43rd Canadian Infantry Battalion (Cameron
   Highlanders)
52nd (New Ontario) Canadian Infantry Battalion
58th Canadian Infantry Battalion
60th Canadian Infantry Battalion (Victoria Rifles)
No. 9 Company, Canadian Machine Gun Corps
No. 9 Trench Mortar Battery

DIVISIONAL ARTILLERY
IX and X Brigades, Canadian Field Artillery
3rd Canadian Divisional Ammunition Column

DIVISIONAL TROOPS
3rd Canadian Pioneer Battalion
7th, 8th and 9th Battalions, Canadian Engineers
No. 3 Divisional Signal Company, Canadian
   Engineers

4TH CANADIAN DIVISION

10 OCTOBER 1916

GENERAL OFFICER COMMANDING:

MAJ GEN D. WATSON

10TH CANADIAN BRIGADE
44th Canadian Infantry Battalion
46th (South Saskatchewan) Canadian Infantry
  Battalion
47th (British Columbia) Canadian Infantry Battalion
50th (Calgary) Canadian Infantry Battalion
No. 10 Company, Canadian Machine Gun Corps
No. 10 Canadian Trench Mortar Battery

11TH CANADIAN BRIGADE
54th (Kootenay) Canadian Infantry Battalion
75th (Mississauga) Canadian Infantry Battalion
87th Canadian Infantry Battalion (Canadian
  Grenadier Guards)
102nd Canadian Infantry Battalion
No. 11 Company, Canadian Machine Gun Corps
No. 11 Canadian Trench Mortar Battery

12TH CANADIAN BRIGADE
38th (Ottawa) Canadian Infantry Battalion
72nd Canadian Infantry Battalion (Seaforth
  Highlanders)
73rd Canadian Infantry Battalion (Royal
  Highlanders)
78th Canadian Infantry Battalion (Winnipeg
  Grenadiers)
No. 12 Company, Canadian Machine Gun Corps
No. 12 Canadian Trench Mortar Battery

DIVISIONAL ARTILLERY
III and IV Brigades, Canadian Field Artillery
4th Canadian Divisional Ammunition Column

DIVISIONAL TROOPS
67th Canadian Pioneer Battalion
10th, 11th and 12th Battalions, Canadian Engineers
No. 4 Divisional Signal Company, Canadian
  Engineers

NEW ZEALAND DIVISION

15 SEPTEMBER 1916

GENERAL OFFICER COMMANDING:
MAJ GEN SIR A.H. RUSSELL

1ST NEW ZEALAND BRIGADE
1st Battalion, The Auckland Regiment
1st Battalion, The Canterbury Regiment
1st Battalion, The Otago Regiment
1st Battalion, The Wellington Regiment
No. 1 Company, New Zealand Machine Gun Corps
No. 1 New Zealand Trench Mortar Battery

2ND NEW ZEALAND BRIGADE
2nd Battalion, The Auckland Regiment
2nd Battalion, The Canterbury Regiment
2nd Battalion, The Otago Regiment
2nd Battalion, The Wellington Regiment
No. 2 Company, New Zealand Machine Gun Corps
No. 2 New Zealand Trench Mortar Battery

3RD NEW ZEALAND RIFLE BRIGADE
1st Battalion, New Zealand Rifle Brigade
2nd Battalion, New Zealand Rifle Brigade
3rd Battalion, New Zealand Rifle Brigade
4th Battalion, New Zealand Rifle Brigade
No. 3 Company, New Zealand Machine Gun Corps
No. 3 New Zealand Trench Mortar Battery

DIVISIONAL ARTILLERY
I, II, III and IV Brigades, New Zealand Field
    Artillery
New Zealand Divisional Ammunition Column

DIVISIONAL TROOPS
New Zealand Pioneer Battalion

German Divisions Facing the British on the Somme

JULY–NOVEMBER 1916

3 GARDE-INFANTERIE DIVISION
GenMaj von Lindequist (Bazentin, 2–16 July)
Garde-Füsilier-Regiment
Lehr-Infanterie-Regiment
Colberg-Grenadier-Regiment (2. Pommeranisches)
  Nr. 9

4. GARDE-INFANTERIE DIVISION
GenMaj Graf von Schweinitz (Mouquet Farm,
  23 August–11 September; Ligny-Thilloy, from
  4 November)
Garde-Regiment zu Fuß Nr. 5
Garde-Grenadier-Regiment Nr. 5
Reserve-Infanterie-Regiment (Anhalt) Nr. 93

5. INFANTERIE DIVISION
GenLt Wichura (Delville Wood, 20 July–4 August)
Leib-Grenadier-Regiment (1. Brandenburgisches)
  Nr. 8
Grenadier-Regiment (2. Brandenburgisches) Nr. 12
Infanterie-Regiment (5. Brandenburgisches) Nr. 52

6. INFANTERIE DIVISION
GenLt Herhudt von Rohden (Gueudecourt,
  9–26 October)
Infanterie-Regiment (3. Brandenburgisches) Nr. 20
Infanterie-Regiment (4. Brandenburgisches) Nr. 24
Infanterie-Regiment (8. Brandenburgisches) Nr. 64

7. INFANTERIE DIVISION
GenLt Riedel (Martinpuich, 12–25 July; Pys,
  18 September–2 October)
Infanterie-Regiment (1. Magdeburgische) Nr. 26
Infanterie-Regiment (2. Magdeburgische) Nr. 27
  (later, Infanterie-Regiment Nr. 393)
Infanterie-Regiment (5. Hannoverschen) Nr. 165
Infanterie-Regiment Nr. 393

8. INFANTERIE DIVISION
Gen der Inf Ernst II, Herzog von Sächsen-Altenburg
  (Flers, 15–25 July; Thiepval, 18 September–
  2 October)
Infanterie-Regiment (4. Thüringisches) Nr. 72
Infanterie-Regiment (Anhalt) Nr. 93
Infanterie-Regiment (8. Thüringisches) Nr. 153

12. INFANTERIE DIVISION
GenLt Châles de Beaulieu (Moislains, 1 July;
  Hardecourt-aux-Bois, 2–4 July; Beaumont-
  Hamel, 22 October–18 November)
Infanterie-Regiment (2. Oberschlesisches) Nr. 23
Infanterie-Regiment (3. Oberschlesisches) Nr. 62
Infanterie-Regiment (4. Oberschlesisches) Nr. 63

16. INFANTERIE DIVISION
GenLt Fuchs (Mouquet Farm, 9–25 August; Sailly,
  8–27 October)
Infanterie-Regiment (2. Rheinischen) Nr. 28
Infanterie-Regiment (3. Rheinischen) Nr. 29
Infanterie-Regiment (6. Rheinischen) Nr. 68
Infanterie-Regiment (7. Rheinischen) Nr. 69

24. INFANTERIE DIVISION
GenMaj Hammer (Martinpuich, 9–27 August;
  Warlencourt, 11 October–7 November)
Infanterie-Regiment (9. Sächsische) Nr. 133
Infanterie-Regiment (11. Sächsische) Nr. 139
Infanterie-Regiment (14. Sächsische) Nr. 179

26. INFANTERIE DIVISION
GenLt Herzog Wilhelm von Urach (Ginchy,
  4–26 August)
Grenadier-Regiment (1. Württembergisches) Nr. 119
Infanterie-Regiment (3. Alt-Württemberg) Nr. 121
Infanterie-Regiment (7. Württembergisches) Nr. 125

27. INFANTERIE DIVISION

GenLt von Moser (Guillemont, 31 July–25 August;
  Sailly, from 17 November)
Infanterie-Regiment (2. Württembergisches) Nr. 120
Grenadier-Regiment (5. Württembergisches) Nr. 123
Infanterie-Regiment (6. Württembergisches) Nr. 124
Infanterie-Regiment (9. Württembergisches) Nr. 127

38. INFANTERIE DIVISION

GenMaj von Schultheis (Grandcourt, 21 October–
  16 November)
Infanterie-Regiment (5. Thüringisches) Nr. 94
Infanterie-Regiment (6. Thüringisches) Nr. 95
Infanterie-Regiment (7. Thüringisches) Nr. 96

40. INFANTERIE DIVISION

GenLt Götz von Olenhusen (Flers, 9–28 August;
  Ligny-Thilloy, 11 October–6 November)
Infanterie-Regiment (5. Sächsische) Nr. 104
Infanterie-Regiment (10. Sächsische) Nr. 134
Infanterie-Regiment (15. Sächsische) Nr. 181

52. INFANTERIE DIVISION

GenLt von Borries (Serre, from July)
Infanterie-Regiment (3. Magdeburgische) Nr. 66
Infanterie-Regiment (8. Badische) Nr. 169
Infanterie-Regiment (9. Badische) Nr. 170

56. INFANTERIE DIVISION

GenMaj von Wichmann (Ginchy, 25 August–
  9 September; Pys, from 16 November)
Füsilier-Regiment (Brandenburgisches) Nr. 35
Infanterie-Regiment (2. Nassauische) Nr. 88
Infanterie-Regiment (4. Hessen-Großherzog) Nr.
  118

58. INFANTERIE DIVISION

GenLt von Gersdorff (Pys, 26 October–
  21 November)
Infanterie-Regiment (7. Sächsische) Nr. 106
Infanterie-Regiment (8. Sächsische) Nr. 107
Reserve-Infanterie-Regiment
  (2. Württembergisches) Nr. 120

111. INFANTERIE DIVISION

GenMaj Sontag (Guillemont, 23 August–
  9 September; Moislains, from 7 November)
Füsilier-Regiment (Hannoverschen) Nr. 73
Infanterie-Regiment (2. Hansa) Nr. 76
Infanterie-Regiment (4. Hannoverschen) Nr. 164

117. INFANTERIE DIVISION

Gen der Inf Kuntze (Courcelette, 20 July–
  10 August)
Infanterie-Regiment (8. Lothringische) Nr. 157

Reserve-Infanterie-Regiment (2. Schlesisches)
  Nr. 11
Reserve-Infanterie-Regiment (1. Oberschlesisches)
  Nr. 22

183. INFANTERIE DIVISION

GenMaj von Schüßler (Contalmaison, 6–18 July)
Infanterie-Regiment (16. Sächsische) Nr. 183
Infanterie-Regiment Nr. 184
Reserve-Infanterie-Regiment (4. Württembergisches)
  Nr. 122

185. INFANTERIE DIVISION

GenMaj von Uthmann (Pozières 1–14 July;
  Combles, 6–19 September; Saillisel,
  9 November–5 December)
Infanterie-Regiment Nr. 185 (later Infanterie-
  Regiment (5. Rheinischen) Nr. 65)
Infanterie-Regiment Nr. 186 (later Infanterie-
  Regiment (10. Rheinischen) Nr. 161)
Infanterie-Regiment Nr. 190 (later Reserve-
  Infanterie-Regiment (2. Rheinischen) Nr. 28)

208. INFANTERIE DIVISION

GenMaj Heße (east of Beaumont-Hamel, from
  14 November)
Infanterie-Regiment (1. Rheinischen) Nr. 25
Infanterie-Regiment Nr. 185
Reserve-Infanterie-Regiment (5. Rheinischen) Nr.
  65

222. INFANTERIE DIVISION

GenMaj Küster (east of Lesbœufs, from
  1 November)
Infanterie-Regiment Nr. 193
Infanterie-Regiment Nr. 397
Reserve-Infanterie-Regiment (1. Hessen) Nr. 81

223. INFANTERIE DIVISION

GenMaj Mühry (Grandcourt, from 10 November)
Infanterie-Regiment (5. Lothringische) Nr. 144
Infanterie-Regiment (9. Lothringische) Nr. 173
Ersatz-Infanterie-Regiment Nr. 29

1. GARDE RESERVE INFANTERIE DIVISION

GenLt Albrecht (Courcelette, 23 August–
  9 September; Warlencourt, from 5 November)
Garde-Reserve-Regiment Nr. 1
Garde-Reserve-Regiment Nr. 2
Reserve-Infanterie-Regiment (8. Brandenburgisches)
  Nr. 64

2 GARDE RESERVE INFANTERIE DIVISION

Gen der Inf Freiherr von Sußkind (Gommecourt,
  July–November)

Reserve-Infanterie-Regiment (2. Westfalische) Nr. 15
Reserve-Infanterie-Regiment (7. Westfalische) Nr. 55
Reserve-Infanterie-Regiment (2. Hannoverschen) Nr. 77
Reserve-Infanterie-Regiment (Oldenburg) Nr. 91

7. RESERVE INFANTERIE DIVISION
Gen der Inf Graf Schwerin (Gueudecourt, 25 September–12 October)
Reserve-Füsilier-Regiment (Magdeburgische) Nr. 36
Reserve-Infanterie-Regiment (3. Magdeburgische) Nr. 66
Reserve-Infanterie-Regiment (4. Thüringisches) Nr. 72

12. RESERVE INFANTERIE DIVISION
GenMaj von Kehler (Guillemont, 1–18 July)
Reserve-Infanterie-Regiment (2 Oberschlesisches) Nr. 23
Reserve-Füsilier-Regiment (Schlesisches) Nr. 38
Reserve-Infanterie-Regiment (4 Niederschlesischen) Nr. 51

17. RESERVE INFANTERIE DIVISION
GenMaj von Zieten (Flers, 24 July–10 August; Saillisel, 29 September–14 October)
Infanterie-Regiment (3. Lübeck, Hansa) Nr. 162
Infanterie-Regiment (Schleswig-Holsteinischen) Nr. 163
Reserve-Infanterie-Regiment (Bremen) Nr. 75
Reserve-Infanterie-Regiment (2. Hansa) Nr. 76

18. RESERVE INFANTERIE DIVISION
GenMaj Wellmann (Martinpuich, 24 July–10 August; Rocquigny, 29 September–16 October)
Reserve-Infanterie-Regiment (1. Thüringisches) Nr. 31
Reserve-Infanterie-Regiment (Schleswig) Nr. 84
Reserve-Infanterie-Regiment (Schleswig-Holsteinischen) Nr. 86

19. RESERVE INFANTERIE DIVISION
Gen der Inf von Wartenburg (le Transloy, 10–29 October)
Reserve-Füsilier-Regiment (Hannoverschen) Nr. 73
Reserve-Infanterie-Regiment (Ost-Frisien) Nr. 78
Reserve-Infanterie-Regiment (3. Hannoverschen) Nr. 79
Reserve-Infanterie-Regiment (Braunschweig) Nr. 92

23. RESERVE INFANTERIE DIVISION
GenLt von Watzdorf (Beaulencourt, from 24 October)
Infanterie-Regiment (19. Sächsische) Nr. 392

Reserve-Infanterie-Regiment (3. Sächsische) Nr. 102

24. RESERVE INFANTERIE DIVISION
GenMaj Morgenstern-Döring (Guillemont, 14 July–1 August; Rancourt, 4–16 September; le Transloy, from 10 November)
Reserve-Grenadier-Regiment (2. Sächsische) Nr. 101
Reserve-Infanterie-Regiment (8. Sächsische) Nr. 107
Reserve-Infanterie-Regiment (9. Sächsische) Nr. 133

26. RESERVE INFANTERIE DIVISION
GenLt Freiherr von Soden (Beaumont-Hamel, to 10 October)
Infanterie-Regiment (8 Württembergisches) Nr. 180
Reserve-Infanterie-Regiment (2. Oberrhein) Nr. 99
Reserve-Infanterie-Regiment (1. Württembergisches) Nr. 119
Reserve-Infanterie-Regiment (3. Alt-Württemberg) Nr. 121

28. RESERVE INFANTERIE DIVISION
GenLt von Hahn (Fricourt, to 7 July; Grandcourt, 6–24 October)
Reserve-Infanterie-Regiment (1. Badische) Nr. 109
Reserve-Infanterie-Regiment (2. Badische) Nr. 110
Reserve-Infanterie-Regiment (3. Badische) Nr. 111

45. RESERVE INFANTERIE DIVISION
Gen der Inf Schöpflin (Courcelette, 5–19 September)
Reserve-Infanterie-Regiment Nr. 210
Reserve-Infanterie-Regiment Nr. 211
Reserve-Infanterie-Regiment Nr. 212

50. RESERVE INFANTERIE DIVISION
GenMaj von Petersdorf (Martinpuich, 15–29 September; Grandcourt, 19 November–23 December)
Reserve-Infanterie-Regiment Nr. 229
Reserve-Infanterie-Regiment Nr. 230
Reserve-Infanterie-Regiment Nr. 231

51. RESERVE INFANTERIE DIVISION
GenLt Balck (Combles, 18–30 September)
Reserve-Infanterie-Regiment Nr. 233
Reserve-Infanterie-Regiment Nr. 234
Reserve-Infanterie-Regiment Nr. 235
Reserve-Infanterie-Regiment Nr. 236

52. RESERVE INFANTERIE DIVISION
GenLt Waldorf (Lesbœufs, 18–30 September)
Reserve-Infanterie-Regiment Nr. 238
Reserve-Infanterie-Regiment Nr. 239
Reserve-Infanterie-Regiment Nr. 240

4. ERSATZ DIVISION
Gen der Kav von Werder (Warlencourt,
  1–15 October)
Infanterie-Regiment Nr. 359
Infanterie-Regiment Nr. 360
Infanterie-Regiment Nr. 361
Infanterie-Regiment Nr. 362

5. ERSATZ DIVISION
GenLt von Basedow (Pys, 11–30 October)
Ersatz-Reserve-Infanterie-Regiment Nr. 3
Landwehr-Infanterie-Regiment Nr. 73
Landwehr-Infanterie-Regiment Nr. 74

2. BAYERISCHE INFANTERIE DIVISION
GenLt von Hartz (east of Lesbœufs, 13 October–
  4 November)
Bayerische Infanterie-Regiment Nr. 12
Bayerische Infanterie-Regiment Nr. 15
Bayerische Infanterie-Regiment Nr. 20

3. BAYERISCHE INFANTERIE DIVISION
GenLt Ritter von Wenninger (Martinpuich,
  26 August–17 September)
Bayerische Infanterie-Regiment Nr. 17
Bayerische Infanterie-Regiment Nr. 18
Bayerische Infanterie-Regiment Nr. 23

4. BAYERISCHE INFANTERIE DIVISION
GenLt Ritter von Schrott (Flers, 26 August–
  17 September)
Bayerische Infanterie-Regiment Nr. 5
Bayerische Infanterie-Regiment Nr. 9
Bayerische Reserve-Infanterie-Regiment Nr. 5

5. BAYERISCHE INFANTERIE DIVISION
GenLt Endres (Ginchy, 6–18 September)
Bayerische Infanterie-Regiment Nr. 7
Bayerische Infanterie-Regiment Nr. 14

Bayerische Infanterie-Regiment Nr. 19
Bayerische Infanterie-Regiment Nr. 21

6. BAYERISCHE INFANTERIE DIVISION
GenLt Ritter von Höhn (Gueudecourt,
  6–28 September)
Bayerische Infanterie-Regiment Nr. 6
Bayerische Infanterie-Regiment Nr. 10
Bayerische Infanterie-Regiment Nr. 11
Bayerische Infanterie-Regiment Nr. 13

10. BAYERISCHE INFANTERIE DIVISION
GenMaj Burkhardt (Thiepval, 1–23 July)
Bayerische Infanterie-Regiment Nr. 16
Bayerische Reserve-Infanterie-Regiment Nr. 6
Bayerische Reserve-Infanterie-Regiment Nr. 8

**6. BAYERISCHE RESERVE INFANTERIE
DIVISION**
GenLt Scanzoni von Lichtenfels (Eaucourt
  l'Abbaye, 28 September–13 October)
Bayerische Reserve-Infanterie-Regiment Nr. 16
Bayerische Reserve-Infanterie-Regiment Nr. 17
Bayerische Reserve-Infanterie-Regiment Nr. 20
Bayerische Reserve-Infanterie-Regiment Nr. 21

BAYERISCHE ERSATZ DIVISION
GenLt Kiefhaber (le Transloy, 25 October–
  16 November)
Bayerische Reserve-Infanterie-Regiment Nr. 14
Bayerische Reserve-Infanterie-Regiment Nr. 15
Bayerische Ersatz-Infanterie-Regiment Nr. 28

89. RESERVE INFANTERIE BRIGADE
GenLt Schumann (Mouquet Farm,
  10–20 September)
Reserve-Infanterie-Regiment Nr. 209
Reserve-Infanterie-Regiment Nr. 213

MARINE BRIGADE
GenMaj Graf von Moltke (Courcelette,
  30 September–17 October)
Marine-Infanterie-Regiment Nr. 1
Marine-Infanterie-Regiment Nr. 2
Marine-Infanterie-Regiment Nr. 3

APPENDIX VI

'LOST' SOMME CEMETERIES

Although the text includes the names of approximately 40 British Commonwealth War Cemeteries that were concentrated into larger ones after the war, there were about a further hundred cemeteries from which casualties were also taken in from and concentrated into larger burial grounds. In many cases the names on the following list are of particular significance as they will often be the first burial position of a casualty close to where he died.

AUCHONVILLERS
White City Cemetery

AUTHUILLE
French Military Cemetery
Lonsdale Cemetery No. 2, Authuille Wood

BAYONVILLERS
British Cemetery
German Cemetery

BAZENTIN
Cross Roads Cemetery
Martinpuich Road Cemetery
Quadrangle Cemetery
Snowdon British Cemetery

BEAUCOURT-SUR-L'ANCRE
Baillescourt Farm Cemetery
Ten Tree Alley British Cemetery No. 1

BEAUMONT-HAMEL
Ancre British Cemetery No. 2
Beaucourt British Cemetery
Beaucourt Station Cemetery
Beaumont-Hamel Ravine Cemetery
Green Dump British Cemetery
RND Cemetery
Sherwood Cemetery
Station Road Cemetery
Y Ravine British Cemetery No. 2
Y Ravine German Cemetery No. 2

BOUCHAVESNES
Albert Military Cemetery

BOVES
Military Cemetery

BUIRE-SUR-L'ANCRE
Albert Road British Cemetery

CARNOY
Briqueterie Graves Cemetery
Montauban Road Cemetery
Talus Boisé British Cemetery
Vernon Street Cemetery (Squeak Forward Position)

COLINCAMPS
British Cemetery
Lonely British Cemetery No. 2

COMBLES
Bouleaux Wood Cemetery
Priez Farm Cemetery

CONTALMAISON
Casualty Corner Cemetery
Villa Wood Cemetery

CORBIE
Bonnay British Cemetery
Vaire Wood British Cemetery

COURCELETTE
Red Château Cemetery

CURLU
Battery Copse Military Cemetery
French Military Cemetery

DERNANCOURT
Moor British Cemetery, Edgehill

ETINEHEM
Taille Wood British Cemetery

FLERS
Switch Trench Cemetery

FONCQUEVILLERS
Gommecourt Wood No. 1 Cemetery
Gommecourt Wood No. 2 Cemetery
Gommecourt Wood No. 4 Cemetery

Gommecourt Wood No. 5 Cemetery
Gommecourt Wood No. 8 Cemetery
Little Z British Cemetery
Military Cemetery Extension

FREMICOURT
Communal Cemetery Extension

FRICOURT
Bottom Wood Cemetery
Bray Road Cemetery
Fricourt Wood Cemetery
Hare Lane Cemetery

GOMMECOURT
Gommecourt No. 1 Cemetery
Gommecourt No. 3 Cemetery
Gommecourt No. 4 Cemetery
Gommecourt Château Cemetery
Gommecourt Wood No. 6 Cemetery
Point 75 British Cemetery

GOUZEAUCOURT
British Cemetery

HAMEL
Bouzincourt Trench Cemetery

HANNESCAMPS
Gommecourt Wood British Cemetery No. 3

HÉBUTERNE
Cat Lodge Cemetery
John Copse British Cemetery No. 1
John Copse British Cemetery No. 2
32nd Divisional Cemetery

HIGH WOOD
Black Watch Cemetery
Clark's Dump Cemetery
Highland Cemetery

LESBŒUFS
Needle Dump South Cemetery
Rose Trench Cemetery
Sunken Road Cemetery No. 2

LONGUEVAL
Lone Ridge British Cemetery
Welsh Cemetery

MARICOURT
Military Cemetery

MARTINPUICH
Seven Elms Dressing Station Cemetery

MESNIL
Dressing Station Cemetery

MILLENCOURT
Communal Cemetery

MOLLIENS-AU-BOIS
Communal Cemetery

MONTAUBAN-AU-BOIS
Bernafay Wood North Cemetery
Briqueterie Cemetery
Talus Boisé German Cemetery Extension

OVILLERS-LA BOISSELLE
Mash Valley Cemetery
Nab Junction Cemetery
Quarry Post Cemetery, Authuille Wood
Red Dragon British Cemetery

PETIT MIRAUMONT
Triangle Cemetery

POZIÈRES
Cemetery Post Station

SAILLY-AU-BOIS
Jeanbart British Cemetery
Lonely British Cemetery

SAILLY-LE-SEC
High British Cemetery
Kangaroo British Cemetery

SAINT-AMAND
Communal Cemetery
Communal Cemetery Extension

SENLIS
Communal Cemetery

SUZANNE
French Military Cemetery No. 2

THIEPVAL
Danube Post Military Cemetery
Mill Road Cemetery No. 1
Mill Road Cemetery No. 3
Quarry Palace Cemetery
Saint-Pierre-Divion Cemetery No. 1
Saint-Pierre-Divion Cemetery No. 2
Saint-Pierre-Divion Cemetery No. 3
Village Cemetery

VAUX-SUR-SOMME
Communal Cemetery Extension
Vaux Wood British Cemetery

VILLE-SUR-ANCRE
New British Cemetery

BIBLIOGRAPHY

I would like to acknowledge the help derived from the Battalion, Regimental and Divisional Histories which I have consulted over the years, which are unfortunately too numerous to list here.

Adams, Bernard. *Nothing of Importance: A Record of Eight Months at the Front with a Welsh Battalion, October 1915 to June 1916*, London, Methuen, 1917

Adcock, A. St. John. *For Remembrance: Soldier Poets Who Have Fallen in the War*, London, Hodder & Stoughton, 1920

Aiken, Alex. *Courage Past: A Duty Done*, Glasgow, Aiken, 1971

Aitken, Alexander. *Gallipoli to the Somme: Recollection of a New Zealand Infantryman*, Oxford, Oxford University Press, 1963

Anon, *Officers Died in the Great War, 1914–1919*, HMSO, 1919

Anon, 'Report on the Defence of Gommecourt on July 1st 1916', *Royal United Service Institution*, Volume LXII, 1917

Anon, *Sir Douglas Haig's Great Push: The Battle of the Somme*, London, Hutchinson, 1917

Anon, *The Western Front Then and Now*, C. Arthur Pearson, 1938

Army Quarterly, various issues

Ashurst, G. *My Bit: A Lancashire Fusilier at War 1914–18*, Marlborough, Crowood Press, 1987

Ashworth, T. *Trench Warfare, 1914–1918: Live and Let Live System*, London, Macmillan, 1980

Baker-Carr, C.D. *From Chauffeur to Brigadier*, Benn, 1930

Baring, M. *Flying Corps Headquarters 1914–1918*, Blackwood, 1968

Barrie, A. *War Underground: The Tunnellers of the Great War*, Muller, 1962

Beach Thomas, W. *With the British on the Somme*, London, Methuen, 1917

Bean, C.E.W. *Anzacs to Amiens: a Shorter History of the Australian Fighting Services in the First World War*, Canberra, Australian War Memorial, 1946

—— *Official History of Australia in the War of 1914–1918: Volume III*, Sydney, Angus & Robertson, 1929

Becke, Maj A.F. *The History of the Great War, Based on Official Documents: The Order of Battle of Divisions, I–IV*, HMSO, 1935–1945

Bidwell, S. and Graham, D. *Fire Power: British Army Weapons and Theories of War, 1904–1945*, London, Allen & Unwin, 1982

Blacker, C.P. *Have You Forgotten Yet? The First World War Memoirs of C.P. Blacker*, London, Leo Cooper Pen & Sword, 2000

Blake, R. (ed.). *The Private Papers of Douglas Haig 1914–1919*, London, Eyre & Spottiswoode, 1952

Blunden, E. *The Mind's Eye: Essays*, London, Cape, 1934

—— *Undertones of War*, Cobden Sanderson, 1928

Blunden, E. and Norman, S. *We'll Shift Our Ground or Two on a Tour*, Cobden Sanderson, 1933

Boraston, J.H. (ed.). *Sir Douglas Haig: Despatches (December 1915–April 1919)*, London, Dent, 1920

Bott, A.J. *An Airman's Outing*, Toronto, McClelland, Goodchild & Stewart, 1917

Bowyer, C. *The Flying Elephants: a History of No. 27 Squadron Royal Flying Corps. Royal Air Force, 1915–1969*, London, Macdonald, 1977

Boyd, D. *Salute of Guns*, London, Cape, 1930

Bray, A.T.E. *The Battle of the Somme 1916: A Bibliography*, University Microfilms International, 1967

Brenan, G. *A Life of One's Own: Childhood and Youth*, London, Cape, 1975

Brittain, V. *Testament of Youth*, London, Arrow/Hutchinson, 1960

Brophy, J. and Partridge, E. *The Long Trail: What the British Soldier Sang and Said in 1914–1918*, London, Deutsch, 1965

Buchan, J. *The Battle of the Somme: First Phase*, London, Nelson, 1916

—— *The Battle of the Somme: Second Phase*, London, Nelson, 1917

Cameron, J. *1916: Year of Decision*, Oldbourne, 1962

Carrington, C. *Soldier from the Wars Returning*, London, Hutchinson, 1965

Cemeteries & Memorials in Belgium & Northern France, Maidenhead, Commonwealth War Graves Commission, 2004

Channing-Renton, E.M. *The Somme Battlefields and War Cemeteries, Summer 1926*

Chapman, G. *A Kind of Survivor*, London, Gollanz, 1975

—— *A Passionate Prodigality: Fragments of Autobiography* (second edition), MacGibbon & Kee, 1965

—— (ed.). *Vain Glory: A Miscellany of the Great War, 1914–1918, Written by Those who Fought in it on Each Side and all Fronts*, London, Cassell, 1937

Charteris, Brig Gen J. *At GHQ*, London, Cassell, 1931

Christie, N.M. *For King & Empire: The Canadians on the Somme September-November 1916: A Social History and Battlefield Tour*, Ontario, CEF Books, 1999

BIBLIOGRAPHY

Churchill, W.S. *The World Crisis, 1911–1918*, Thornton Butterworth, 1931

Clayton, C.P. *The Hungry One*, Llandysul, Gomer Press, 1978

Cloete, S. *A Victorian Son: An Autobiography*, London, Collins, 1971

Clout, H. *After the Ruins: Restoring the countryside of Northern France after the Great War*, Exeter, University of Exeter Press, 1996

Collier, B. *Brasshat: A Biography of Field Marshal Sir Henry Wilson*, London, Secker & Warburg, 1961

Collison, B/Col C.S. *The 11th Royal Warwicks in France 1915–16: From the Personal Diary of its Commanding Officer*, Birmingham, Cornish Brothers, 1928

Cook, A.H. *A Soldier's War*, edited by Lt Gen G.N. Molesworth, Taunton, E. Goodman, 1957

Coombs, R.E.B. *Before Endeavours Fade: A Guide to the Battlefields of the First World War*, After the Battle, 1976

Cooper, A.D. *Haig*, two volumes, London, Faber & Faber, 1935

Coppard, G. *With a Machine Gun to Cambrai: The Tale of a Young Tommy in Kitchener's Army 1914–1918*, Imperial War Museum, 1969

Corns, C. 'So Ended the Golden Age: 9th York and Lancaster Regiment on 1st July 1916', *Battlefields Review* No. 27, 2003

Corrigan, G. *Mud, Blood and Poppycock*, London, Orion, 2003

Creagh, Sir O'M. and Humpris, E.M. *The VC and DSO*, three volumes, Standard Art Book Company, no date

Croft, Lt Col W.D. *Three Years with the Ninth (Scottish) Division 1914–1919*, London, John Murray, 1921

Croney, P. *Soldier's Luck: Memoirs of a Soldier of the Great War*, Stockwell, 1965

Crozier, Brig Gen F.P. *A Brass-hat in No Man's Land*, London, Cape, 1930

— — *The Men I Killed*, London, Cape, 1937

Crutchley, C.E. *Machine Gunner, 1914–1918: Personal Experiences of the Machine Gun Corps*, Folkestone, Bailey Brothers & Swinfen, 1975

Cruttwell, C.R.M.F. *A History of the Great War 1914–1918* (2nd Edition), Oxford, Oxford University Press, 1936

Cuddeford, D.W.J. *And All for What? Some Wartime Experiences*, Heath Cranton, 1933

Davies, F. and Maddocks, G. *Bloody Red Tabs: General Officer Casualties of the Great War, 1914–1918*, Barnsley, Leo Cooper Pen & Sword, 1995

Davson, Lt Col H.M. *Memoirs of the Great War*, Gale & Polden, 1964

Delattre, D. *La Somme les 783 Communes*, Grandvilliers, Daniel Delattre, 1999

De Sousa, D. *La Reconstruction Et Sa Memoire Dans Les Villages De La Somme (1918–1932)*, Editions la Vague verte, 2001

Dewar, G.A.B. and Boraston, J.H. *Sir Douglas Haig's Command December 19th 1915 to November 11th 1918: Volume I*, London, Constable, 1922

Dolden, A.S. *Cannon Fodder: An Infantryman's Life on the Western Front, 1914–1918*, Poole, Blandford Press, 1980

Douie, C, *The Weary Road: Recollections of a Subaltern of Infantry*, London, Murray, 1929

Doyle, Sir A.C. *The British Campaign in France and Flanders 1916*, London, Hodder & Stoughton, 1918

Dundas, H.L.N. *Henry Dundas, Scots Guards: A Memoir*, Blackwood, 1921

Dunn, Capt J.C., DCM, DSO, MC and Bar (ed.). *The War the Infantry Knew, 1914–1919: A Chronicle of Service in France and Belgium with the Second Battalion His Majesty's Twenty-Third Foot, the Royal Welch Fusiliers, Founded on Personal Records, Recollections and Reflections Assembled, Edited and Partly Written by One of Their Medical Officers*, P.S. King, 1938

Eden, A. (Earl of Avon) KG, PC, MC, *Another World, 1897–1917*, London, Allen Lane, 1976

Edmonds, Brig Gen Sir J.E. (ed.). *The History of the Great War, Based On Official Documents: Military Operations, France and Belgium 1916, Sir Douglas Haig's command to the 1st July: Battle of the Somme*, Macmillan and HMSO, 1922–1949

Enser, A.G.S. *A Subject Bibliography of the First World War: Books in English 1914–1978*, London, Deutsch, 1979

Eyre, G.E.M. *Somme Harvest: Memories of a PBI in the Summer of 1916*, Jarrold, 1936

Falls, C. *The History of the 36th (Ulster) Division*, Belfast, Stevenson & Orr, 1922

Farrar-Hockley, A.H. *The Somme*, London, Batsford, 1964

Feilding, R. *War Letters to a Wife: France and Flanders, 1915–1919*, Medici Society, 1929

Fitzgerald, F.S. *Tender is the Night*, London, Bodley Head, 1959

Foley, J. *The Boilerplate War*, Muller, 1963

Foulkes, Maj-Gen C.H. *'Gas!': The Story of the Special Brigade*, William Blackwood, 1934

Frankau, G. *Peter Jackson, Cigar Merchant: A Romance of Married Life* (a novel), London, Hutchinson, 1920

Fraser-Tytler, Lt Col N. *Field Guns in France*, edited by Maj F.N. Baker RGA, London, Hutchinson, 1922

Fry, W. *Air of Battle*, London, Kimber, 1974

Fussell, P. *The Great War and Modern Memory*, Oxford, Oxford University Press, 1975

Gardner, B. *The Big Push: The Somme 1916*, London, Cassell, 1961

Germains, V.W. *The Kitchener Armies: The Story of a National Achievement*, Peter Davies, 1930

Gibbs, P. *The Battles of the Somme*, London, Heinemann, 1917

— — *Now It Can Be Told*, New York, Harper & Brothers, 1920

— — *Realities of War*, London, Heinemann, 1920

Gibson, C. *The British Army, French Farmers and the War on the Western Front 1914–1918*, Past & Present, August 2003

Giles, J. *The Somme Then and Now*, Folkestone, Bailey Brothers & Swinfen, 1977

Gladden, N. *The Somme 1916: A Personal Account*, London, Kimber, 1974

Gliddon, G. *The Aristocracy and the Great War*, Norwich, Gliddon Books, 2002

—— *Legacy of the Somme 1916: The Battle in Fact, Film and Fiction*, Stroud, Sutton Publishing, 1996

—— *VCs of the Somme*, VCs of the First World War Series, Stroud, Alan Sutton, 1994

—— (ed.). *VCs Handbook: The Western Front 1914–1918*, Stroud, Sutton Publishing, 2005

—— *When The Barrage Lifts: A Topographical History of the Battle of the Somme 1916*, Stroud, Alan Sutton, 1994

Glubb, Sir J.B. *Into Battle: A Soldier's Diary of the Great War*, London, Cassell, 1978

Gosse, P. *Memoirs of a Camp Follower: Adventures and Impressions of a Doctor in the Great War*, London, Longmans Green, 1934

Gough, Gen Sir H. *The Fifth Army*, London, Hodder & Stoughton, 1931

Graham, S. *The Challenge of the Dead*, London, Cassell, 1921

Graves, R. *Fairies and Fusiliers* (poems), London, Heinemann, 1917

—— *Goliath and David* (poems), Chiswick Press, 1916

—— *Good-Bye to All That: An Autobiography*, London, Cassell, 1957 and Oxford, Berghahn Books, 1995

Green, A. *Writing the Great War: Sir James Edmonds and the Official Histories 1915–1948*, London, Cass, 2003

Greenwell, G.H. *An Infant in Arms: War Letters of a Company Officer 1914–1918*, London, Allen Lane, 1972

Grieve, Capt W.G. and Newman, B. *Tunnellers*, Jenkins, 1936

Griffith, Ll.W. *Up to Mametz*, London, Faber & Faber, 1931

Gristwood, A.D. *The Somme* (novel), London, Cape, 1927

Gurney, I. *Severn and Somme* (poems), London, Sidgwick & Jackson, 1917

Hamilton, N. *Monty: The Making of a General 1887–1942*, London, Hamish Hamilton, 1981

Hammerton, Sir J.A. (ed.). *The Great War: I Was There, Volume II: The Somme*, The Amalgamated Press, 1938–39

Harris, J. *Covenant with Death* (novel), London, Hutchinson, 1961

—— *The Somme: Death of a Generation*, London, Hodder & Stoughton, 1966

Hart-Davis, R. (ed.). *Diaries of Siegfried Sassoon 1915–1918*, London, Faber & Faber, 1983

Harvey, H.E. *Battle-Line Narratives, 1915–1918*, Brentano, 1928

Hawker, T.M. *Hawker VC: The Biography of the Late Major Lanoe George Hawker*, Mitre Press, 1965

Hawkins, F. *From Ypres to Cambrai: The 1914–1919 Diary of an Infantryman*, edited by Arthur Taylor, Morley, Elmfield Press, 1974

Herbert, A.P. *Secret Battle*, London, Methuen, 1919

Hill, Capt A.W. 'Our Soldiers' Graves', *Journal of the Royal Horticultural Society*, Volume XLV, Part 1, 1919

Hitchcock, Capt F.C. *'Stand To': A Diary of the Trenches 1915–1918*, Hurst & Blackett, 1937

Hodson, J.L. *Return to the Wood: A Novel*, London, Gollanz, 1955

Holt, Maj and Mrs. *Battlefield Guide to the Somme*, 4th Edition, Barnsley, Leo Cooper Pen & Sword, 2004

Hughes, C. *Mametz: Lloyd George's 'Welsh Army' at the Battle of the Somme*, Gerrards Cross, Orion Press, 1982

Hurd, M. *The Ordeal of Ivor Gurney*, Oxford, Oxford University Press, 1978

Hurst, S.C. *The Silent Cities: An Illustrated Guide to the War Cemeteries and Memorials to the 'Missing' in France and Flanders: 1914–1918*, Reprinted, London, The Naval & Military Press, 1993

Hutchison, Lt Col G.S. *Footslogger: An Autobiography*, London, Hutchinson, 1931

—— *Pilgrimage*, Rich & Cowan, 1935

—— *Warrior*, London, Hutchinson, 1932

Jackson, J. *Private 12768: Memoirs of a Tommy*, Stroud, Tempus Publishing, 2004

James, Brig Gen E.A. *British Regiments 1914–18*, Samson Books, 1978

Jerrold, D. *The Hawke Battalion: Some Personal Records of Four Years, 1914–1918*, London, Ernest Benn, 1925

—— *The Royal Naval Division*, London, Hutchinson, 1923

Johnstone, E.G. *Naval Eight: A History of No. 8 Squadron RNAS*, Signal, 1931

Jolliffe, J. (ed.). *Raymond Asquith: Life and Letters*, London, Collins, 1980

Jones, D. *In Parenthesis*, London, Faber & Faber, 1937

Jünger, E. *The Storm of Steel: From the Diary of a German Storm-Troop Officer on the Western Front*, London, Chatto & Windus, 1929

Keegan, J. *The Face of Battle: A study of Waterloo, Agincourt and the Somme*, London, Cape, 1976

Kelly, D.V. *39 Months With the 'Tigers', 1915–1918*, Benn, 1930

Keynes, G. *The Gates of Memory*, Oxford, Oxford University Press, 1981

King, A. *Commonwealth War Graves Commission Archive Catalogue*, Maidenhead, Commonwealth War Graves Commission, 1997

Leed, E.J. *No Man's Land*, Cambridge, Cambridge University Press, 1979

Lewis, C. *Sagittarius Rising*, Davies, 1936

Lewis, G.H. *Wings Over the Somme*, London, Kimber, 1976

Liddell Hart, Sir B.H. unpublished manuscript (LH7/1916/23)

BIBLIOGRAPHY

— — *A History of the First World War*, London, Cassell, 1934

Liddell Hart, Sir B.H. *Memoirs*, Volume I, London, Cassell, 1965

— — *The Tanks: History of the Royal Tank Regiment and Its Predecessors; Heavy Branch Machine Gun Corps, Tank Corps and Royal Tank Corps, 1914–1945*, Volume I, London, Cassell, 1959

Liveing, E.G.D. *Attack: An Infantry Subaltern's Impressions of July 1st 1916*, Stevenage, Spa Books/Tom Donovan, 1986

Lloyd, D.W. *Battlefield Tourism: A Study of the Rise of the Tourist Industry*, Oxford, Berg, 1998

Lloyd George, D. *War Memoirs of David Lloyd George*, two volumes, Odhams Press, 1938

Lyttelton, O. (Viscount Chandos) PC, DSO, MC, LLD, *The Memoirs of Lord Chandos*, London, Bodley Head, 1964

Lytton, N. *The Press and the General Staff*, London, Collins, 1921

Macdonald, L. *Somme*, London, Michael Joseph, 1983

Macmillan, H. *Winds of Change 1914–1939*, London, Macmillan, 1966

Macmillan, N. *Into the Blue*, Jarrold, 1969

Malins, G.H. *How I Filmed The War*, Herbert Jenkins, 1920

Manning, F. *The Middle Parts of Fortune*, Peter Davies, 1977

Masefield, J. *Battle of the Somme*, London, Heinemann, 1919

— — *The Old Front Line: Or the Beginning of the Battle of the Somme*, London, Heinemann, 1917

Mason, T. *History of the Nine Squadron*, Beaumont, no date

Maurice, Maj Gen Sir F., KCMG, CB (ed.). *The Life of General Lord Rawlinson of Trent GCB: Journals and Letters*, London, Cassell, 1928

Maze, P. *A Frenchman in Khaki*, London, Heinemann, 1934

Michelin Guides, *The Somme, Volume I: The First Battle of the Somme 1916–1917*, Clermont-Ferrand, Michelin, 1919

Middlebrook, M. *The First Day on the Somme 1 July 1916*, London, Allen Lane, 1971

Middlebrook, M. and M. *The Somme Battlefields: A Comprehensive Guide from Crecy to the Two World Wars*, London, Viking, 1991

Montague, C.E. *Disenchantment*, London, Chatto & Windus, 1922

Moore, W. *The Thin Yellow Line*, Barnsley, Leo Cooper, 1974

Moran, Lord. *The Anatomy of Courage*, London, Constable, 1945

Murray, J. *Call to Arms*, London, Kimber, 1980

Neville, J.E.H. *The War Letters of a Light Infantryman*, Sifton Praed, 1930

Nicholson, Col G.W.L. *The Fighting Newfoundlanders: A History of the Royal Newfoundland Regiment*, Government of Newfoundland, 1964

Norman, T. *The Hell They Called High Wood: Somme 1916*, London, Kimber, 1984

— — (ed.). *Armageddon Road: A VC's Diary, 1914–1916*, Kimber, 1982 (B/Maj William La Touche Congreve VC)

Oman, Sir C. 'The German Losses on the Somme, July–December 1916' in Lord Sydenham of Combe and others, *A Criticism of 'The World Crisis' by Winston Churchill*, London, Hutchinson, no date

O'Prey, P. (ed.). *In Broken Images: Selected Letters of Robert Graves 1914–1946*, London, Hutchinson, 1982

Orpen, Sir W. *An Onlooker in France, 1917–1919*, Williams & Norgate, 1921

Orr, P. *The Road to the Somme: Men of the Ulster Division Tell Their Story*, Belfast, Blackstaff Press, 1987

Pagan, A.W. *Infantry: An account of the 1st Bn Gloucestershire Regiment during the war 1914-1918*, Aldershot, Gale & Polden, 1951

Palmer, F. *With the New Army on the Somme: My Second Year of the War*, London, Murray, 1917

Panichas, G.A. (ed.). *Promise of Greatness: The War of 1914–1918*, London, Cassell, 1968

Pidgeon, T. *The Tanks at Flers: An Account Of The First Use Of Tanks in War At The Battle Of Flers-Courcelette, The Somme, 15th September 1916*, Esher, Fairmile Books, 1995

Plowman, M. *Bridge Into Future: Letters of Max Plowman*, Andrew Dakers, 1944

— — *A Subaltern on the Somme in 1916*, London, Dent, 1927

Pound, R. *The Lost Generation*, London, Constable, 1964

Prideaux, G.A. *A Soldier's Diary of the Great War 1914–1917*, London, Chiswick Press, 1918

Prior, R. and Wilson, T. *Command on the Western Front: The Military Career of Sir Henry Rawlinson 1914–18*, Oxford, Blackwell, 1992

Putkowski, J. and Sykes, J. *Shot at Dawn: Executions in World War One by authority of the British Army Act*, Barnsley, Wharncliffe Publishing, 1989

Raleigh, Sir W. and Jones, H.A. *The War in the Air*, six volumes, Oxford, Oxford University Press, 1922–1937

Reed, P. *Walking the Somme: A Walker's Guide to the 1916 Somme Battlefields*, Battleground Europe, Barnsley, Leo Cooper Pen & Sword, 1997

Repington, C. à C. *The First World War, 1914–1918: Volume 1: Personal Experiences of Lt-Col C. à Court Repington*, London, Constable, 1921

Richards, F. *Old Soldiers Never Die*, London, Faber & Faber, 1933

Robertson, Field-Marshal Sir W. *Soldiers and Statesmen 1914–1918, Volume I*, London, Cassell, 1926

Robinson, H.P. *The Turning Point: The Battle of the Somme*, London, Heinemann, 1917

Rogerson, S. *Twelve Days*, Arthur Barker, 1930

Rorie, Col D.A. *A Medico's Luck in the War: Being Reminiscences of RAMC Work with the 51st Highland Division*, Aberdeen, Milne & Hutchinson, 1929

Russell, A. *The Machine Gunner*, Roundwood, 1977

Sassoon, S. *Memoirs of an Infantry Officer*, London, Faber & Faber, 1930

— — *Siegfried's Journey*, London, Faber & Faber, 1945

Saunders, T. *West Country Regiments on the Somme*, London, Leo Cooper Pen & Sword, 2004

Scott, F.G. *The Great War as I Saw It*, Toronto, Goodchild, 1922

Scott, S.J.L. *Sixty Squadron RAF: A History*, London, Heinemann, 1920

Sellars, L. *The Hood Battalion, Royal Naval Division: Antwerp, Gallipoli, France 1914–1918*, Barnsley, Leo Cooper Pen & Sword, 1995

Seydoux, P. *Gentilhommieres en Picardie: Amiens et Santerre*, Paris, Editions de la Morande, 2003

Seymour-Smith, M. *Robert Graves: His Life and Work*, London, Hutchinson, 1982

Sheffield, G. *The Somme*, London, Cassell, 2003

Sheffield, G. and Bourne, J. *Douglas Haig: War Diaries and Letters 1914-1918*, London, Weidenfeld & Nicolson, 2005

Sheldon, J. *The German Army on the Somme, 1914–1916*, Barnsley, Pen & Sword, 2004

Shephard, E. *A Sergeant-Major's War From Hill 60 to the Somme*, Marlborough, Crowood Press, 1987

Skelton, T. and Gliddon, G. *Lutyens and the Great War*, London, F. Lincoln, 2008

Slack, C.M. *Grandfather's Adventures in the Great War 1914–1918*, Ilfracombe, Arthur H. Stockwell, 1977

Smith, A. *Four Years on the Western Front by a Rifleman: Being the Experiences of a Ranker in the London Rifle Brigade, 4th, 3rd and 56th Divisions*, Odhams Press, 1922

Smithers, A.J. *Wonder Aces of the Air: The Flying Heroes of the Great War*, Gordon & Cremonesi, 1980

Sparrow, A.A.H. *The Land-locked Lake*, Barker, 1932

Spears, E.L. *Liaison, 1914*, London, Heinemann, 1930

Spicer, Capt L.D. *Letters from France 1915–1918*, Robert York, 1979

Stansky, P. *The World of Philip and Sybil Sassoon*, London, Yale University Press, 2003

Statistics of the Military Effort of the British Empire, 1914–1920, HMSO, 1921

Tawney, Sgt R.H. *The Attack and Other Papers*, London, Allen & Unwin, 1953

Taylor, A.J.P. *The First World War: An Illustrated History*, London, Hamish Hamilton, 1963

Taylor, A.R. *Spring on the Somme: A River Journey*, London, Constable, 1995

Taylor, H.A. *Good-bye to the Battlefields: To-day and Yesterday on the Western Front*, Stanley Paul, 1928

Terraine, J. *Douglas Haig: The Educated Soldier*, London, Hutchinson, 1963

— — (ed.). *General Jack's Diary 1914–1918: The Trench Diary of Brigadier-General J.L. Jack, DSO*, London, Eyre & Spottiswoode, 1964

— — *The Smoke and the Fire: Myths and Anti-myths of War 1861–1945*, London, Sidgwick & Jackson, 1980

Thorpe, B. *Private Memorials of the Great War on the Western Front*, London, The Western Front Association, 1999

Tilsley, W.V. *Other Ranks* (a novel), Cobden-Sanderson, 1931

The Times Digital Archive

Tomlinson, H.M. *All Our Yesterdays*, London, Heinemann, 1930

Tredrey, F.D. *Pioneer Pilot: The Great Smith Barry Who Taught the World How to Fly*, P. Davies, 1976

Tucker, J.F. *Johnny Get Your Gun: A Personal Narrative of the Somme, Ypres and Arras*, London, Kimber, 1978

Turner P.W. and Haigh, R.H. *Not for Glory*, Maxwell, 1969

Uys, I. *The Delville Wood Story*, Rensbury, South Africa, Uys Publishers, 1983

Wade, A. *The War of the Guns: Western Front 1917 and 1918*, London, Batsford, 1936

Warwick, G.G. *We Band of Brothers*, Cape Town, South Africa, Timmins, 1962

Westlake, R. *British Battalions on The Somme*, Barnsley, Leo Cooper Pen & Sword, 1994

Whinyates, R. *Artillery and Trench Mortar Memories: 32nd Division*, Whinyates, 1932

White, A.S. *A Bibliography of Regimental Histories of the British Army*, The Society for Army Historical Research in conjunction with The Army Museums Ogilby Trust, 1965

Whithorn, D.P. *Bringing Uncle Albert Home: A Soldier's Tale*, Stroud, Sutton, 2003

Williams, M.J. 'The Treatment of German Losses on the Somme in the British Official History: "Military Operations France and Belgium, 1916"', Volume 2, *Royal United Service Institution Journal*, February 1966

Williamson, H. *The Golden Virgin* (a novel), London, Macdonald, 1957

— — *The Wet Flanders Plain*, London, Faber & Faber, 1929

Winter, D. *Death's Men: Soldiers of the Great War*, London, Allen Lane, 1978

Woods, E.S., MA, CF, (ed.). *Andrew R. Buxton, The Rifle Brigade: A Memoir*, Robert Scott, 1918

Wortley, R.S. *Letters from a Flying Officer*, Stroud, Alan Sutton, 1982

Wynne, C.W. *If Germany Attacks: The Battle in Depth in the West: Lessons From the Western Front, 1915–17*, London, Faber & Faber, 1940

Ypres Times, Volume 3, 1927

INDEX OF PERSONS

INDEX OF PLACES

Main references in bold type. Those cemeteries marked with an asterisk* are those later concentrated into larger ones.

INDEX OF MILITARY UNITS